The Gettysburg Companion

General Robert E. Lee, C.S.A.

Major-General George G. Meade, U.S.A.

THE GETTYSBURG COMPANION

The Complete Guide to America's Most Famous Battle

MARK ADKIN

STACKPOLE
BOOKS

Also by Mark Adkin

The Trafalgar Companion
The Waterloo Companion
Urgent Fury (the American Invasion of Grenada in 1983)
The Last Eleven?
Goose Green
The Quiet Operator (with John Simpson)
Prisoner of the Turnip Heads (with George Wright-Nooth)
The Charge
The Sharpe Companion
The Sharpe Companion – The Early Years
The Battle for Afghanistan (with Mohammad Yousaf)
The Daily Telegraph Guide to Britain's Military Heritage

Published by
STACKPOLE BOOKS
5067 Ritter Road
Mechanicsburg, PA 17055 USA
www.stackpolebooks.com

Produced by
Aurum Press Ltd, 7 Greenland Street, London NW1 0ND, U.K.

ISBN 978-0-8117-0439-7

1 3 5 7 6 4 2

2008 2010 2012 2014 2013 2011 2009

Book design by Robert Updegraff

Printed in China

Portraits of army officers reproduced courtesy of the Gettysburg National Military Park, U.S. Library of Congress and the Tipton Archive

All other monochrome photographs reproduced by courtesy of the U.S. Library of Congress except those on pages 321 and 492 by courtesy of the Tipton Archive and those on pages 235, 245, 328, 332 and 454 by courtesy of the Virginia Center for Digital History: The Valley of the Shadow

A note on the cover painting

This detail from *The High Water Mark* by Don Troiani shows Brigadier-General Lewis A. Armistead leading a handful of Rebels over the wall at the Angle a few moments before he fell mortally wounded. Pickett's charge, indeed the Confederacy itself, had reached its high water mark.

A plate section illustrating Union and Confederate uniforms appears between pages 256 and 257.

ACKNOWLEDGMENTS

I owe a considerable debt of gratitude to a number of individuals without whose help this enormous project could not have been completed in the time available. They not only made my visit to Gettysburg in September 2005 enjoyable and rewarding, but also assisted in assembling the huge diversity of information needed to complete this book. Foremost among them is Scott Hartwig, Supervisory Historian at the Gettysburg National Military Park, who has been on the staff there, except for one year, since 1979. Not only did he facilitate my visit to the Park, but also in the years since has promptly answered dozens of email queries; without his expertise I am certain to have made many fundamental errors. Other staff at the Park have also been of great assistance and I would like to record my thanks to them. Among them is Greg Goodell, Supervisor of Museums and Archivist, who spent considerable time locating photographs and transferring them to a CD for potential use in the book.

I would also mention the Friends of the National Parks at Gettysburg for agreeing to my using as the base map for virtually all the maps in this book the *Battlefield of Gettysburg* map developed and produced by Thomas A. Desjardin. Tom Desjardin, a Historic Site Specialist at the Maine Bureau of Parks and Lands, and a cartographer, supplied the electronic masters of the maps used, which has greatly enhanced the quality of the information provided here.

I am also grateful on several counts to Mike Russert, a former guide at the Park, who is a member of the Company of Military Historians, and a coordinator of the New York State Veterans Oral History Project. He was the first to encourage me to take on the formidable task of writing this *Companion*, and his suggestions and advice have been most welcome and helpful. He also went out of his way to assist me in finding my feet during my visit, and gave me a complete and comprehensive tour of the battlefield. Also of great help was Jim McLean, owner of the well-known Butternut and Blue Civil War bookstore in Baltimore, whose expertise on July 1 operations was most useful. He also kindly took more photographs of the battlefield that I had been unable, or had forgotten, to take during my visit.

Finally I would say how much I appreciate the helpful and friendly advice and assistance I have had from Robert and Brenda Updegraff. Robert was the book designer and to him must also go the credit for producing the splendid maps and diagrams from my rather scruffy originals, while Brenda as the editor labored painstakingly to polish and correct the text. As usual, Clive Farmer has produced numerous beautifully drawn plates and illustrations that are an essential part of the *Companion*.

INTRODUCTION

At least 618,000 men died during the Civil War – divided approximately as 360,00 Union and 258,000 Confederates – of whom some two-thirds succumbed to disease. Thomas Livermore, a renowned statistical researcher, while admitting the handicap of poor records in many cases (particularly for the Confederates), concluded that of every 1,000 Union soldiers in battle 112 were hit, while for the Confederates the number was 150. Over 46,000 men became casualties during the three-day battle at Gettysburg, representing some 28 percent of those that took part. Of these, over 7,800 died on the field and well over 27,000 were wounded (the balance being missing and captured).

Gettysburg has, probably rightly, been called the turning point of the Civil War. As far as the Confederacy was concerned, it was seen by many as the high water mark of their efforts to remain independent of the Union. This high water mark is actually commemorated by a memorial on Cemetery Ridge marking the limit of the advance of Southern soldiers during the so-called Pickett's charge (other formations also participated). This charge was General Robert E. Lee's final fling for victory on the final day of the battle. It failed, and just as the Confederate troops receded like an ebbing tide, so did Southern hopes of a decisive victory and consequential recognition of their independence. This defeat in the East was followed the next day by the fall of Vicksburg in the West. It was a double blow from which the Confederacy never really recovered and led almost inevitably to Lee's surrender at Appomattox in April 1865.

Hundreds, if not thousands, of books have been written about the Battle of Gettysburg. Controversies abounded among the surviving participants, and countless authors and historians have disputed the reasons for Lee's defeat and debated innumerable "what ifs" ever since. Re-enactment societies are to be found all over the United States, and even across the Atlantic in England. The battle is the most celebrated event in American military history, with almost 2 million people each year visiting the splendid Gettysburg National Military Park, where huge efforts are made to preserve the battlefield as near as possible to the way it looked in July 1863 by the Friends of the National Parks at Gettysburg – an organization devoted to this purpose. So, with some justification, the reader might ask, "Why another book on Gettysburg?"

Well, as anyone who picks up this publication will quickly discover, it is not another rehash of the battle. It is a "companion" to the battle. A companion is a friend, a helper, an associate – someone who accompanies you, who shares your interest, explains, guides and comments. *The Gettysburg Companion* is such a book. It does not provide a blow-by-blow account of the action, but rather looks at a series of differing aspects of the campaign, the commanders, the troops, their weapons and administration, and the battlefield itself, while a number of highlights in the fighting are dealt with in considerable detail. All this is done with the help of an extensive number of maps, diagrams, uniform plates, photographs and panoramic views – virtually all in color. The *Companion* is a unique, comprehensive gathering together of information on Gettysburg and the events leading to it, which can be dipped into for facts, comments or accounts of the experiences of soldiers from both armies.

The twelve sections include orders of battle, the infantry, the artillery, the cavalry, other arms and services, command and control, the campaign, the battlefield, a separate section on each of the three days of the battle, and a final look at Lee's retreat. In each section I have included discussion and comment on a selection of controversies. The comments and opinions are of course mine, but I have attempted to be impartial throughout the book – something perhaps an English author finds easier than an American. Every section contains numerous "boxes" giving additional interesting facts, figures or anecdotal information to enhance and enliven the main text.

Some further comment on the way the *Companion* has been compiled and on the content of some sections may be useful.

Text and "boxes"

The text is not always primarily descriptive. A deliberate emphasis has been placed on assessing and commenting on decisions, plans, actions and events. These comments are mine, but they are made after careful study of the evidence, by trying to view the situation without using the benefit of hindsight, using my own experience as a soldier and by a close examination of the actual ground. I spent three weeks at Gettysburg, during which I passed almost every day on the battlefield, so I gained a reasonable understanding of how the ground affected both sides during the struggle. Only three of the twelve sections are devoted to the battle itself, but all the others are closely related to it and I believe are crucial to understanding what happened during the fighting and why. Incidents that occurred during the battle are frequently used to illustrate the text of these sections. The reader will find that on occasion merely the outline of events is given, sometimes using only maps to show what happened – this is deliberate, as the *Companion* is not a chronological account.

Maps

No battle can be properly understood without the help of detailed maps. The *Companion* has seventy – all in full color with the troop information superimposed on them, depicting the ground as near as possible to what it was like at the time. The base map was developed and produced by Thomas A. Desjardin as a project of the Friends of the National Parks of Gettysburg in 1998, using what is known as the "Warren Map," which was surveyed and drawn under the direction of Major-General G. K. Warren (Meade's chief engineer at the battle) during 1868 and 1869. The only major alteration has been the substitution of the latest geographical survey for the heights above sea level. Each map has comprehensive notes, which in many cases take the place of long textual descriptions. While it is impossible to position every unit or show all movements with complete certainty, considerable effort has been made to depict events as accurately as possible, any errors being down to me.

Photographs

The text is accompanied by a considerable number of color photographs, many panoramic, almost all of them taken by me during my visit; they include views of where most of the important events took place. The panoramic views have troop dispositions and movements marked on them and hopefully, in conjunction with the relevant map, will help readers and visitors understand and visualize what happened and where. In addition, a number of archive photographs illustrate the text. These photographs were taken at or around the time of the battle, and cracks in the original glass negatives and other signs of aging have not been removed or retouched.

Orders of Battle

As usual, strengths and losses in any battle, certainly of this size, defy definitive accuracy. However, the most recent, superbly detailed compilation and analysis of the figures is contained in the fourth edition of *Regimental Strengths and Losses at Gettysburg* by John W. Busey and David G. Martin, published in 2005. This work is the result of years of research and is probably the nearest we will ever get to the engaged strengths of both sides. This has been my main source both for the orders of battle figures and unit losses noted in the text or on maps.

Command and Control

As the title implies, this section sets out to explain how each army was commanded at both the political and military level, how they were staffed and how they obtained their intelligence. There are also biographical notes on all army and corps commanders, together with information on senior officer casualties.

The Battlefield

I felt that a close look at the battlefield itself, the ground, hills, woods and buildings, as well as the town of Gettysburg, merited a separate section. An understanding of the ground over which men fought usually reveals why certain movements were made, or why positions were difficult to attack or defend. This is certainly true of Gettysburg, and I have commented on how the terrain features affected both sides in terms of advantages and disadvantages. There are also notes on a number of the farms and buildings in Gettysburg around which fighting developed.

The Battle

Sections Nine, Ten and Eleven are devoted to the battle itself – one section for each day. Each section looks at the problems facing the army commanders at the start of that particular day and examines the options open to them. The events of the day are largely explained by maps and their accompanying notes, while the text gives an outline of what happened, and a number of highlights in the fighting have been selected for a more detailed look and discussion.

Finally, I hope the reader will find the *Companion* an enjoyable and rewarding read, and I apologize sincerely for any errors that may have crept in – they are entirely mine.

Mark Adkin
January 2008

ABBREVIATIONS AND SYMBOLS

States

Alabama	Ala
Arkansas	Ark
Connecticut	Conn
Delaware	Del
Florida	Fla
Illinois	Ill
Indiana	Ind
Louisiana	La
Maine	Me
Maryland	Md
Massachusetts	Mass
Michigan	Mich
Minnesota	Minn
Mississippi	Miss
New Hampshire	NH
New Jersey	NJ
New York	NY
North Carolina	NC
Ohio	Oh
Pennsylvania	Pa
Rhode Island	RI
South Carolina	SC
Tennessee	Tenn
Texas	Tx
Virginia	Va
Vermont	Vt
West Virginia	WVa
Wisconsin	Wis

Military

(–)	under-strength formation/unit
(k)	killed
(w)	wounded
(mw)	mortally wounded
(c)	captured
A.D.C.	Aide-de-camp
Amb.	Ambulance
Art.	Artillery
BR	10-pounder Blakely Rifle
H (12)	12-pounder howitzer
H (24)	24-pounder howitzer
JR	3-inch 12-pounder James rifle
N	12-pounder Napoleon (smoothbore)
Ny	12-pounder Navy rifle
OR	3-inch ordnance rifle
P(10)	10-pounder Parrott (rifled)
P(20)	20-pounder Parrott (rifled)
W	12-pounder Whitworth (rifled)
Asst.	Assistant
Bat.	Battalion or Battery
Bde.	Brigade
Brig.-Gen.	Brigadier-General
Capt.	Captain
Cav.	Cavalry
Col.	Colonel
Co.	Company
Comm.	Commissariat
Cpl.	Corporal
Det.	Detachment
Div.	Division
Fd.	Field
F.A.	Field Artillery
Gen.	General
Hvy.	Heavy
H.A.	Horse Artillery
Inf.	Infantry
Lgt.	Light
Lt.	Lieutenant
2nd Lt.	Second Lieutenant
Lt.-Col.	Lieutenant-Colonel
Lt.-Gen.	Lieutenant-General
Maj.	Major
Maj.-Gen.	Major-General
Med.	Medical
M.I.	Mounted Infantry
Ord.	Ordnance
P.o.W.	Prisoner of War
Pte.	Private
Q.M.	Quartermaster
Res.	Reserve
S.S.	Sharpshooter
Sgt.	Sergeant
Sqn.	Squadron
Surg.	Surgeon
U.S. Army	United States Army (Regular)
Vol.	Volunteer

MAP KEY

ARMY COMMANDER

CORPS COMMANDER

Division Commander

Brigade Commander

Regiment Commander
Battery Commander

post and rail fence   worm fence   stone wall

corn   oats

wheat   wood

grass/hay   orchard

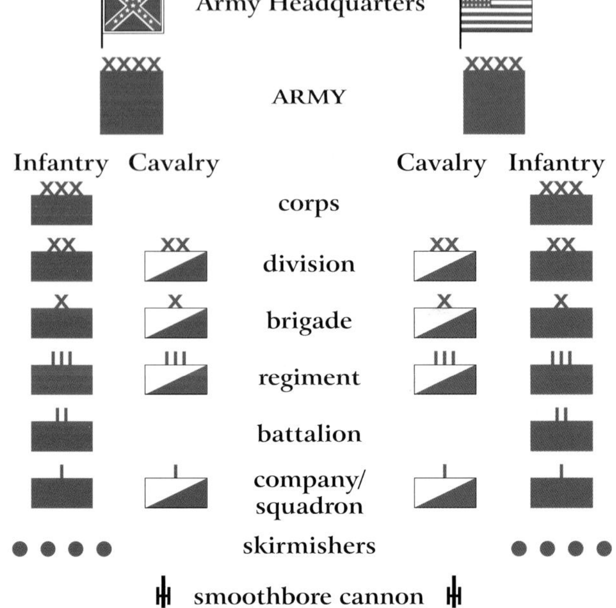

To my son
Lieutenant Robert M. Adkin
The King's Royal Hussars

The muffled drum's sad roll has beat
The soldier's last tattoo;
No more on Life's parade shall meet
The brave and fallen few.

On Fame's eternal camping-ground
Their silent tents are spread,
And Glory guards, with solemn round,
The bivouac of the dead.

Theodore O'Hara
"The Bivouac of the Dead"

Theodore O'Hara was born in 1820 in Danville, Kentucky. He fought in the Mexican and Cuban Wars, achieving the brevet rank of major. In the Civil War he was a Confederate colonel commanding the 12th Alabama Infantry (it fought in O'Neal's Brigade at Gettysburg) and on the staff of Generals J. C. Breckinridge and A. S. Johnson. He was also in action at the Battles of Shiloh and Stones River. He died in 1867. Extracts of his famous poem feature on numerous U.S. national memorials.

Prologue

CHANCELLORSVILLE – THE REBELS LOSE A GENERAL, THE YANKEES A BATTLE

"Mystify, mislead and surprise" – *Jackson's abiding military maxim*

Saturday, May 2

Next to Robert E. Lee, "Stonewall" Jackson remains the most revered of all Confederate commanders. At around 9:30 p.m. on Saturday, May 2, 1863, exactly two months before the Battle of Gettysburg, Jackson was riding along a wooded lane less than a mile west of the tiny hamlet of Chancellorsville, Virginia, located in an area of tangled scrub, brambles, fields and woodland appropriately named the Wilderness. With him was a group of aides, couriers and signalmen, numbering eight individuals: Captain Richard E. Wilbourn (Jackson's signal officer), Lieutenant Joseph G. Morrison (Jackson's A.D.C. and brother-in-law), Captain William F. Randolph, 39th Virginia Cavalry Battalion (the unit supplying the couriers), and five enlisted soldiers. One of the soldiers, Private David J. Kyle, 9th Virginia Cavalry, had lived within a few hundred yards of where they were now riding.

Earlier that day Jackson had led well over half (some 25,000 men) of the force readily available to Lee in a 14-mile outflanking march in searing heat to arrive on the exposed right flank of the Union Army, double the Rebel strength, under General Joseph "Fighting Joe" Hooker. Jackson had successfully achieved arguably the most fundamental principle of war – surprise. Surprise is nine-tenths of any battle. Never mind numbers, never mind the terrain; an enemy surprised and attacked immediately is invariably an enemy defeated, often crushed. And so it was that evening for the men of the Federal XI Corps under Major-General Oliver O. Howard. At the end of his long march Jackson had sat on his horse on a hill not far from Old Wilderness Tavern (see Map 1) with an uninterrupted view east as far as Dowdall's Tavern. Lieutenant-Colonel G. F. R. Henderson, in his book *Stonewall Jackson*, describes what he saw:

> Below, and but a few hundred yards distant, ran the Federal breastworks, with abattis in front and long lines of stacked arms in rear: but untenanted by a single company. Two cannon were seen on the highroad, the horses grazing quietly near at hand. The soldiers were scattered in small groups, laughing, cooking, smoking, sleeping and playing cards, while others were butchering cattle and drawing rations.

Shortly after 5:00 p.m. the Confederates surged forward through the trees and underbrush, the wild shriek of the Rebel yell rolling up and down the line. Ahead of them dashed scores of terrified deer and rabbits. Beyond the fleeing animals frantic Federal troops grabbed muskets and rushed to man their defenses. It was far too late. A hesitant, stuttering volley, a smattering of single shots, a few shells had no chance of stopping the Rebel rush. XI Corps quickly collapsed. Some Confederate regiments advanced and fired at the same time, reloading at the walk. "The front line fired and loaded while walking on, and the rear gaining the front, fired and continued to march, loading as they proceeded" was the way one soldier described what was an almost unique occurrence

General Jackson's Party at Chancellorsville

In addition to the general, the following made up his party:

Captain Richard E. Wilbourn: signal officer; horse and rider untouched.

Captain William F. Randolph: 39th Virginia Cavalry Battalion, which supplied couriers (as it did at Gettysburg, where Captain Randolph was with Lieutenant-General Ewell's corps headquarters); neither he nor his horse hit.

Lieutenant Joseph G. Morrison: A.D.C. and Jackson's brother-in-law; his horse was killed.

W. T. Wynn: Signal Corps enlisted man; neither he nor his horse injured.

William E. Cuncliffe: Signal Corps enlisted man; killed.

Private David J. Kyle: 9th Virginia Cavalry (part of William H. F. Lee's brigade in the Gettysburg campaign); co-opted as guide as he had lived in the area; horse and man unscathed.

Private Joshua O. Johns: 39th Virginia Cavalry; courier; wounded and his horse carried him into Federal lines and into captivity.

Private Lloyd T. Smith: 39th Virginia Cavalry; courier; horse killed.

Jackson was incredibly unfortunate to be struck by three of the five bullets that hit men in the party.

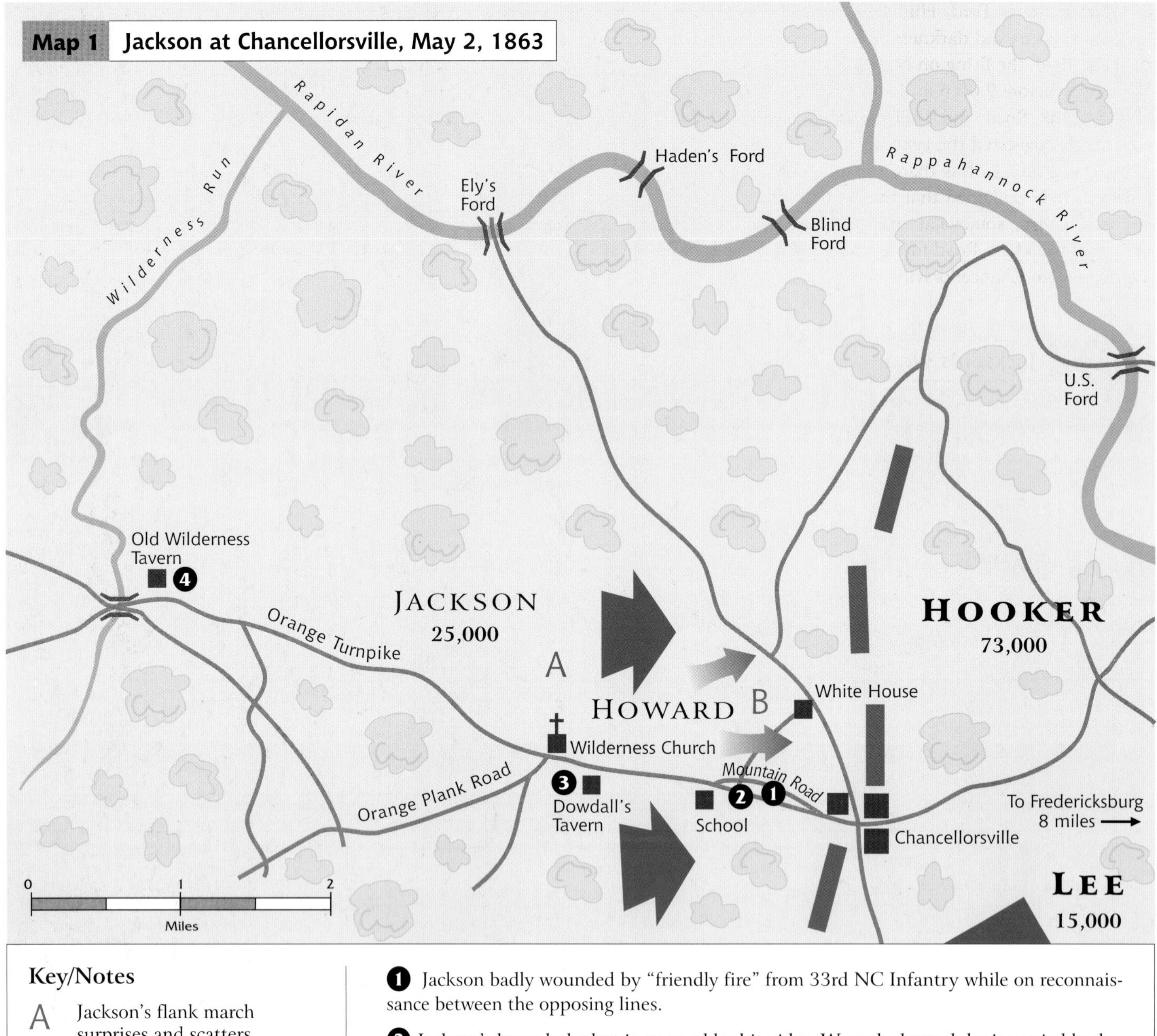

Key/Notes

A Jackson's flank march surprises and scatters Hooker's XI Corps under Howard

B Howard's retreat endangers the Union position

❶ Jackson badly wounded by "friendly fire" from 33rd NC Infantry while on reconnaissance between the opposing lines.

❷ Jackson's horse bolts but is stopped by his aides. Wounds dressed, he is carried back under artillery fire.

❸ Jackson transferred to an ambulance. His physician, Dr. McGuire, joins him and adjusts his dressings before the wagon takes him to 2nd Corps field hospital at Old Wilderness Tavern.

❹ Around 11 p.m. the ambulance arrives at the field hospital. At about 2 a.m. Jackson's left arm is amputated at the shoulder

during the Civil War. Lieutenant Oliver E. Mercer summed up the attack briefly but accurately: "We poured it into them and they to us for a short while, but soon we charged them and they fled like dogs leaving everything behind – knapsacks, trunks, arms, fat beeves already skinned." Howard's command would lose over 2,200 men at Chancellorsville and the Army of the Potomac ever afterward blamed the "Germans" (although only thirteen of the Corps' twenty-seven regiments were composed mainly of German immigrants) for the embarrassing debacle.

By dusk, however, the Union line had been reinforced and rallied. A counterattack was mounted and the erstwhile Rebel reserve regiments of Brigadier-General James H. Lane's North Carolina Brigade had taken over the lead and were quick-timing up the Orange Plank Road immediately east of the schoolhouse (see Map 2). However, by this time a furious cannonade of guns and muskets was sweeping the road, so the men from North Carolina were ordered into the underbrush and told to lie down. As Jackson and his staff approached the front along the Plank Road, intent on reconnoitering the ground and enemy toward the United States Ford, they were overtaken by one of his divisional commanders, Major-General Ambrose P. Hill. Jackson's order to Hill was brief but unmistakable: "Press them! Cut them off from the United States Ford, Hill! Press them!" Slowly, as the moon replaced the sun and darkness enveloped the woods that covered the battlefield, the firing on both sides died away.

Shortly before 9:00 p.m. Jackson's party came to the junction of the Plank Road and Bullock Road. Private Kyle was summoned. He suggested the general follow the Bullock Road, so the party swung left. In less than 200 yards they arrived at another junction. Kyle explained that the track to the right (east) was an old road called, somewhat inappropriately, Mountain Road. It paralleled the Plank Road for several hundred yards before rejoining it closer to Chancellorsville. With Kyle as guide, Jackson took the track east toward the enemy lines. He was now beyond his own front line of the 18th North Carolina Infantry, but not beyond the skirmishers of the 33rd North Carolina. The enemy skirmishers were only a few hundred yards ahead. Before long the noise of axes on timber and the voices of Hooker's men could be heard as they worked on their defenses. Jackson had soon heard enough. The attack must be followed up and every effort made to secure the United States Ford, thus cutting off the bulk of the enemy south of the Rappahannock River. Jackson turned his horse back the way he had come. At about the same time General Hill and his staff, who had followed some 60 yards behind

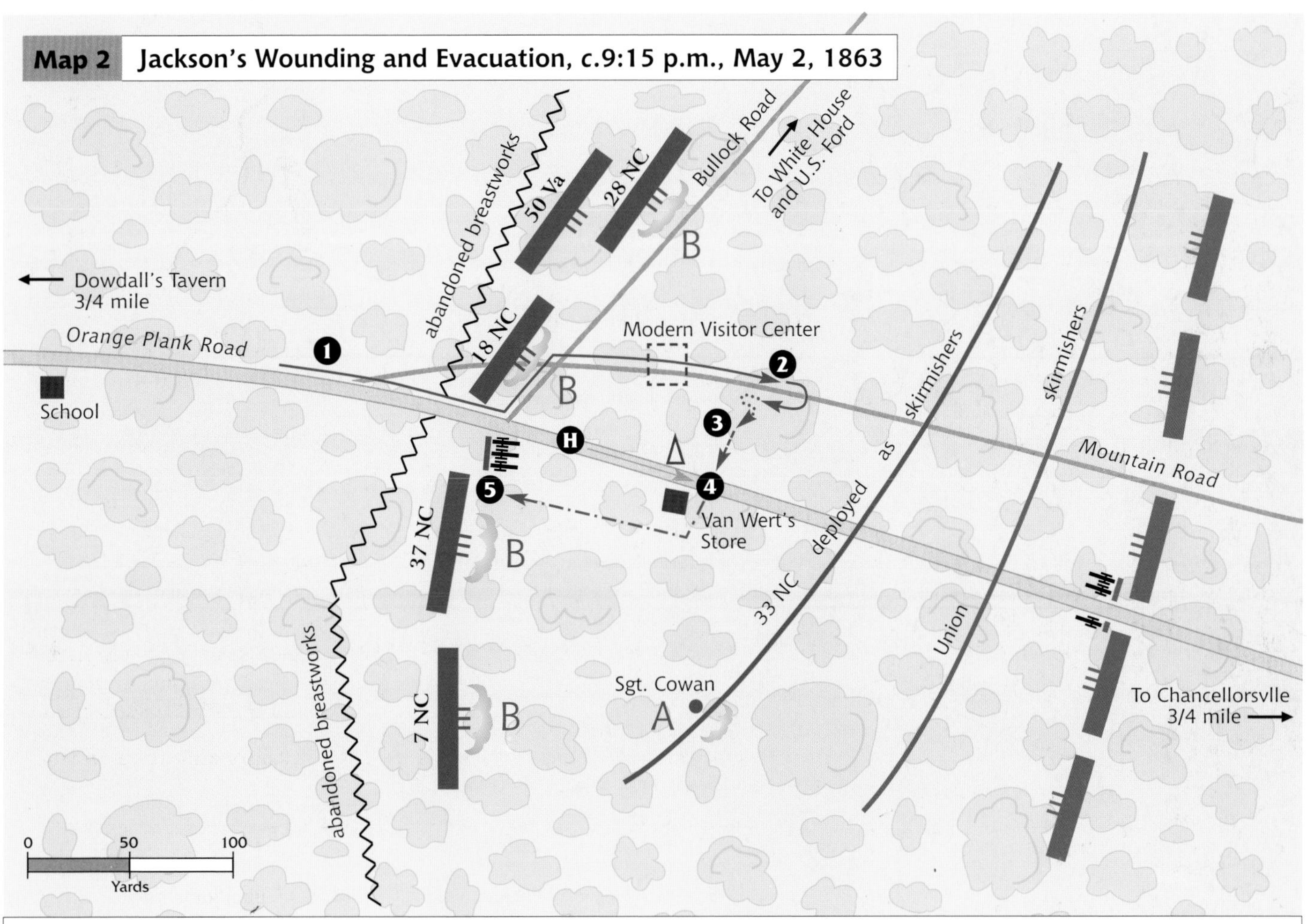

Key/Notes

- Jackson's route forward
- wounded Jackson on runaway horse
- Jackson supported by staff through the wood to the Plank Road
- Jackson taken into the trees south of the road and carried toward the rear by stretcher
- Δ 1888 Monument

1 Jackson moves forward to reconnoiter, accompanied by eight men.

2 Jackson does not venture beyond his skirmishers. After listening to the enemy ahead he turns back. At this moment a Sgt. Thomas A. Cowan A with the skirmishers of the 33rd NC challenges persons in the darkness ahead. On hearing they are Yankees he yells to the 33rd NC to fire at the noise. Firing spreads north BBBB and Gen. Hill's party **H** is hit. Moments later Jackson's party is hit and Jackson struck by three balls.

3 Jackson's runaway horse is halted. Jackson is lowered to the ground and his wounds bound up by Gen. Hill, who has joined the group, and others.

4 Jackson and the party that have supported him through the trees come under artillery fire from down the road to the east. He is then carried across the Plank Road and taken on a stretcher to the rear. During this time he is dropped twice.

5 From about here Jackson is taken by stretcher and ambulance to a field dressing station at Dowdall's Tavern where he is joined by the corps medical director, Dr. Hunter H. McGuire.

Jackson but along the edge of the Plank Road, also decided to return to their own lines.

The North Carolina troops, by now deployed on either side of the Plank Road, were jumpy. They had been brought up from a supporting role to take over the front line, and the noise of battle, the darkness and the undergrowth caused confusion and uncertainty. A number of disoriented Yankees had been taken prisoner near the right flank of the brigade to the south of the road. Lane's men knew the enemy was close but his precise location was unclear. Just after nine o'clock Sergeant Thomas A. Cowan found himself the senior rank in his company of the 33rd North Carolina, deployed as skirmishers on the brigade's right flank. Just ahead there was the noise of voices and of men forcing their way through the underbrush. Cowan yelled a challenge. "Friends," was the response. "To which side?" shouted Cowan. "The Union," came the reply. The young sergeant immediately ordered his men to fire in the direction of the voice. At first a few hesitant shots. Then a more sustained crackle of musketry as nervous soldiers with itchy fingers in the 7th North Carolina to the rear shot at shadows. The urge to fire was contagious and the ripple of flashes quickly spread northward as each regiment of North Carolinians opened up. According to Captain Leigh of his staff, General Hill's party was "within fifteen or twenty paces of our line" when they were hit "by a blaze of fire." They had become the recipients of what is today called "friendly fire." Hill himself was not hit, though he was later badly bruised in both calves by a near miss that prevented him from riding and he was thus later unable to take command from Jackson, the corps passing to Major-General J. E. B. "Jeb" Stuart, the cavalry commander. However, seven of the nine men accompanying Hill were killed, wounded or carried away to captivity on terrified horses. Leigh described how "General Hill's staff disappeared as if stricken by lightning." Hill yelled, "You have shot your friends! You have destroyed my staff!" His shouts failed to prevent another ragged volley. An officer of the 18th North Carolina yelled back, "It's a lie! Pour it into them boys!" This time Jackson and his group were on the receiving end.

Five shots found a mark, with the unlucky Jackson taking three of them. He had just turned his horse, Old Sorrel, off the lane to enter the trees when the heavy bullets slammed into him. One struck his left arm just below the shoulder. His humerus was fractured and the brachial artery injured, causing heavy bleeding. The second hit his upper left forearm on the inside, just below the elbow, and tore through the flesh before exiting on the opposite side just above the wrist. The third struck his right hand in the palm, breaking bones before lodging beneath the skin on the back of his hand. His horse bolted through the trees and he was nearly knocked from the saddle when his head struck a low-hanging branch as he struggled to control his mount with a useless left arm and a shattered right hand. Within a few moments several staff members caught up with and restrained the terrified horse, while Jackson was lifted from the saddle and laid on the ground in considerable pain.

Within moments General Hill appeared on the scene and, with the aid of a soldier, immediately set about cutting away Jackson's sleeve, removing his blood-soaked gauntlets and tying handkerchiefs tightly above and below the worst wound in his upper arm, from which he was losing a great deal of blood. The first surgeon to arrive, Dr. Benjamin P. Wright, decided the dressing applied was sufficient and that a proper tourniquet was not required at this stage. The general was lifted up and, supported on both sides, began to stagger slowly through the wood toward the Plank Road. Within a short distance it was obvious he was on the point of collapse. A stretcher was produced and four of the group began to carry him on their shoulders up the Plank Road toward the rear. However, they immediately came under bursts of artillery fire from Federal guns across the road a short distance to the east and were forced to place the litter on the road while the whole party crouched around it. Jackson struggled to rise but Captain Smith held him down, telling him to lie still. During a brief lull in the firing he was carried over the road into the woods to the south. Miraculously, at this stage no further casualties had occurred. Several more soldiers were found to help carry the stretcher. As they moved slowly through the darkness, one of the bearers (Private John J. Johnson) was hit in both arms and dropped the stretcher, depositing Jackson on his injured side. They had hardly restarted when another man stumbled and Jackson was again thrown to the ground. This rough handling reopened his wounds and blood poured from his damaged artery.

After a few hundred yards Jackson was placed on an ambulance wagon and taken to a field dressing station at Dowdall's Tavern. Here he was seen by Dr. Hunter H. McGuire, medical director of Jackson's Corps. By now Jackson's clothes were saturated with blood, his skin was pale and clammy with shock, his face rigid and lips tightly compressed. At last a proper tourniquet was applied and some whiskey and morphia given to alleviate the pain. Jackson, along with his wounded chief of artillery, Major Crutchfield, was again placed in the ambulance for the 3-mile

Chancellorsville – a Battle of Flank Marches

Hooker commanded some 135,000 men in his positions north of the Rappahannock River opposite Fredericksburg. To the south was Lee with about 60,000 (he had sent Hood's and Pickett's divisions of Longstreet's Corps to the south) – a huge discrepancy in the Union's favor. Hooker felt confident enough to split his army in two. Five of its seven corps would undertake an ambitious move to outflank Lee's left. No fewer than three right hooks of varying length were planned and carried out. By May 1 Hooker was established around Chancellorsville. He then sat on his hands and awaited attack – a bad blunder. Lee marched to meet 73,000 men with some 43,000. It then became the Confederates' turn to be bold, far bolder. Lee sent Jackson on his outflanking march round Hooker's right with most of his army. In the face of vastly superior numbers, Lee had split his force, putting the enemy between the two parts of his army. He did it because he trusted his troops and, above all, he trusted Jackson. Over 25,000 men, marching four abreast with more than 110 guns plus hundreds of wagons, advanced throughout May 2. At some points the column stretched for 10 miles. The result – a spectacular success for Lee and Jackson and a classic example of an inferior force surprising, attacking and defeating a much superior force by boldness and maneuverability.

The implications for Gettysburg are discussed on pages 20–21.

journey back to the corps field hospital at Old Wilderness Tavern. Dr. McGuire, who accompanied Jackson, later wrote:

> The General expressed, very feelingly, his sympathy for Crutchfield, and once, when the latter groaned aloud, he directed the ambulance to stop, and requested me to see if something could be done for his relief . . . I sat in the front part of the ambulance, with my finger resting upon the artery above the wound, to arrest bleeding if it should occur . . . At one time he put his right hand upon my head, and pulling me down to him, asked if Crutchfield was dangerously injured. When answered, "No, only painfully hurt," he replied, "I am glad it is no worse." In a few moments after Crutchfield did the same thing [cry out], and when he [Crutchfield] was told that the General was very seriously wounded, he groaned and cried out, "Oh my God!" It was then that the General directed the ambulance be halted and requested that something be done for Crutchfield's relief.

At the tavern Jackson was put to bed in a tent by the surgeon in charge, Dr. Henry Black but proper examination of his wounds was prevented by the pain and shock. He was given a sedative, some whiskey and water, and allowed to rest.

General Hill's Party at Chancellorsville

Apart from the general, the following composed his party:

Major William H. Palmer: horse killed and Palmer's shoulder broken.

Captain James K. Boswell: Jackson's topographic engineer sent to Hill to familiarize him with the terrain; killed with two bullets through his heart.

Captain Conway R. Howard: engineer officer; his horse was hit, bolted and carried him through the Federal lines almost to Chancellorsville, where he was taken prisoner.

Captain Benjamin W. Leigh: A.D.C.; horse killed but he was unhurt.

Lieutenant Murray F. Taylor: A.D.C.; horse killed but Taylor unscathed.

James F. Forbes: temporary volunteer aide; mortally wounded.

Sergeant George W. Tucker: N.C.O. in charge of the couriers; like Howard's, his horse panicked and carried him into enemy lines where he was captured.

Private Richard J. Muse: courier; badly wounded in the face but survived.

Private Eugene L. Saunders: courier; horse killed but Saunders untouched.

Hill was incredibly fortunate that he was untouched.

Sunday, May 3

At 2:00 a.m., with three surgeons present, Jackson's arm was examined again. When he was told an amputation was probably necessary he responded, "Yes, certainly. Dr. McGuire, do for me whatever you think best." An anesthetist, Dr. Coleman, administered chloroform. As Jackson felt the pain easing he murmured, "What an infinite blessing." He continued to repeat the word "blessing" until he slipped into unconsciousness. The ball lodged under the skin in the back of his right hand was removed first. Dr. McGuire then amputated the left arm about 2 inches below the shoulder, using the usual circular technique. It was quick and there was little further loss of blood. McGuire cut the flesh above the wound, sliced the tendons, and sawed through the bone, while Dr. Black monitored Jackson's heart and Dr. Walls tied up the severed arteries. Finally the stump was sutured shut. Several deep scratches on his face, received from tree branches as his horse careered through the woods, were dressed with plasters.

At 3:00 a.m. Captain Wilbourn of Jackson's staff arrived at General Robert E. Lee's army headquarters with the news of Jackson's wounding. According to Wilbourn, Lee "moaned and wept." About half an hour later Major S. "Sandie" Pendleton (the son of Lee's artillery commander at Gettysburg), who was serving as assistant adjutant general, arrived at the field hospital urgently seeking to speak with Jackson. The battle was still raging and General Stuart, now the corps commander, wanted Jackson's advice. Reluctantly, Dr. McGuire allowed Pendleton in. According to McGuire, Jackson was briefed on the situation, responded with several questions and appeared to be considering issuing instructions. However, the effort was too much, "his face relaxed again, and presently he answered very feebly and sadly, 'I don't know, I can't tell; say to General Stuart he must do what he thinks best.'" Pendleton departed and Jackson fell asleep.

At 9:00 a.m. Jackson awoke and felt strong enough to eat some breakfast, his first meal in two days. However, an hour later the pain in his side became intense and he asked McGuire to examine it. No evidence of injury could be found. Jackson then sent Lieutenant Morrison to Richmond to inform his wife of his injuries and to bring her to see him. With the noise of fierce fighting not far off, Jackson's mind was alerted to matters of the battlefield. He directed that all his aides except Captain Smith return to their duties in the field.

At 11:30 a.m. Captain Smith read out a message received from General Lee:

> Headquarters
> May 3, 1863
> General Thomas J. Jackson, Commanding Corps
>
> General: I have just received your note, informing me that you were wounded – I cannot express my regret at the occurrence. Could I have directed events, I should have chosen for the good of the country to be disabled in your stead. I congratulate you upon the victory, which is due to your skill and energy.
> Very respectfully, your obedient servant
> R. E. Lee, General.

Jackson's response was, "General Lee is very kind, but he should give the praise to God."

At about this time he had a visit from the 2nd Corps chaplain, the Reverend Tucker Lacy, during which Jackson insisted he had already made his peace with God and could face death without fear. In his words, "It [his wounding] has been a precious experience for me that I was brought face to face with death and found all well." Later a Captain Kyd Douglas came to the hospital with a message on how well Jackson's old "Stonewall Brigade" had done. This was relayed to him by Captain Smith and elicited the reply, "Good, good. The men of that brigade will

Lieutenant-General Thomas Jonathan Jackson C.S.A. (1824–1863)

Jackson was born at Clarksburg, [now West] Virginia, on January 21, 1824, the third child of Jonathan Jackson, an attorney, and Julia Beckwith Neale; he had one brother and two sisters. In 1926, when Thomas was only two, his father died of typhoid fever. The following day his mother gave birth to his sister Laura. Julia Jackson married a second time but her husband, Blake Woodson, disliked his stepchildren and the family also suffered acute financial difficulties. These two factors led to Thomas and Laura, the two youngest, being sent to live with relatives. When Thomas was seven his mother died of childbirth complications.

In July 1842 Jackson attended the United States Military Academy at West Point for the four-year course. Shy and silent, clad in Virginia homespun and with all his personal possessions in a pair of scruffy saddlebags, he did not impress. He made no particular mark at the Academy and was remembered, if at all, for his gravity, his silence, his kind heart (he saved his cadet's pay to buy his sister Laura a silk dress) and his awkward movements – he was often laughed at for his large hands and feet. He seemed to lack ambition and there was no trace of any outstanding leadership qualities, although his scrupulous honesty and unbending views on right and wrong were clear to staff and cadets alike. His early months at West Point were a struggle, but gradually his performance improved and in June 1846 he graduated 17th out of 59 – not outstanding but above average. He was commissioned into the 1st Artillery Regiment as a second lieutenant.

In the war with Mexico, 1846–48, Lieutenant Jackson had command of three guns in Captain John B. Magruder's Battery at the Battle of Churubusco. Magruder wrote of Jackson's conduct, "I cannot too highly commend him to the Major-General's favorable consideration." His courage and leadership as his guns traded shot for shot at the Battle of Chapultepec were outstanding. When his men hesitated to man their pieces Jackson walked calmly up and down under intense fire exclaiming, "There is no danger. See, I am not hit." It was not enough and most of his men retreated. Their young lieutenant remained loading and firing his solitary gun single-handed. He received the brevet (temporary) rank of captain and then major (an almost unheard of promotion for a twenty-four-year-old lieutenant) and featured in the commander-in-chief's dispatches.

In 1851 Jackson resigned from the army to take up a professorship at the Virginia Military Institute (V.M.I.). During his ten years there he gained a reputation as a severe, exceedingly dull lecturer in physics, astronomy, acoustics, optics and other science subjects. He never drank, smoked or swore, and appeared to lack a sense of humor. His deep, unswerving religious conviction and scrupulous morality gained him the reputation as something of an oddball among the cadets, who nicknamed him "Tom Fool Jackson" and "Old Blue Light." While at the Academy he married Elinor Junkin (August 1853) but to his immense sorrow she died giving birth to a stillborn son in the fall of the following year. He was remarried four years later (July 1857) to Mary Anna Morrison. Nine months later tragedy struck again. Anna gave birth to a daughter, but the baby died within a month. In 1859 Jackson accompanied a contingent of cadets to Harper's Ferry to stand guard at the execution of the abolitionist John Brown.

In April 1861 the V.M.I. Corps of cadets was sent to Richmond to serve as drill instructors for recruits to the new Confederate States Army (C.S.A.). Jackson, promoted colonel at the outbreak of the Civil War, was in command. A week later he was ordered to take command at Harper's Ferry, where he formed what would become the renowned "Stonewall Brigade," comprising the 2nd, 4th, 5th, 27th and 33rd Virginia Infantry regiments. In July that year he was promoted brigadier-general and commanded a brigade at the First Battle of Manassas (Bull Run). There he acquired his legendary nickname when Brigadier-General Barnard E. Bee rallied his men by shouting, "Look, there stands Jackson like a stone wall." In October 1861, aged thirty-seven, he was promoted major-general. The following year Jackson was given an independent command in the Shenandoah Valley, where his brilliant campaign (still studied in military establishments as an outstanding example of conducting operations) included victories at Front Royal, Winchester, Cross Keys and Port Republic. This was immediately followed by the Seven Days Battles, during which Jackson inexplicably displayed hesitant and ineffective leadership – an extraordinary lapse that is still debated today. However, in 1862 Jackson redeemed himself at the Battles of Cedar Mountain, Clark's Mountain, Second Manassas (Second Bull Run) and Antietam. In October of that year General Lee reorganized his army into two corps with Jackson, promoted to lieutenant-general, in command of the 2nd Corps – half of Lee's Army of Northern Virginia (A.N.V.). In November Jackson, after losing a wife and two children to the trauma of childbirth, was delighted when his wife gave birth to Julia Laura. Jackson's corps played a vital role in the defeat of Hooker's Army of the Potomac at Fredericksburg in December 1862. On May 2,1863 he was struck down at Chancellorsville.

Jackson's wife never remarried and became known as the "Widow of the Confederacy." She died, aged eighty-four, in 1915 and is buried alongside her husband in Lexington, Virginia. Their daughter Julia died of typhoid in 1889, aged twenty-six.

some day [be] favored to say to their children, I was one of the Stonewall Brigade."

That evening a message was delivered from General Lee that Jackson should be moved if at all possible as the Federals were threatening to cross the Rapidan at Ely's Ford (see Map 1), although troops had been sent to block them. According to Dr. McGuire, Jackson preferred to remain where he was in the tent but requested that when his wife arrived she should be found accommodation in a nearby house. The prospect of being taken prisoner did not concern him unduly: "I am not afraid of them; I have always been kind to their wounded, and I am sure they will be kind to me." Nevertheless, another message urging that Jackson be moved prompted preparations for an early start the next day. Dr. McGuire would accompany him in the ambulance after handing over his duties as medical director to the next senior surgeon.

Monday, May 4

Jackson began the 27-mile journey south to the railhead at Guinea Station by way of Spotsylvania Court House. The ambulance was preceded by Major Jedediah Hotchkiss (who became the foremost mapmaker of the Civil War), at that time Jackson's topographical engineer, with a party of pioneers clearing obstructions. It soon became common knowledge that the ambulance carried the gravely wounded Jackson. Men and women, many of the latter weeping openly, rushed up with food and drinks, all blessing him and praying for his recovery. Some teamsters driving loaded wagons along the route at first refused to clear the road to allow the ambulance to pass; however, on hearing that General Jackson was inside they gave way and stood with hats off as he passed. The general bore the journey well. He was talkative and coherent, and although he suffered from slight nausea, a wet towel over his stomach brought some relief. At around 8:00 p.m. he arrived at the Fairfield Plantation home of Thomas and Mary Chandler, which was serving as a hospital. Despite the rough ride, Jackson was feeling sufficiently good humored to apologize to Mr. Chandler for not being able to shake his hand. Later he ate bread and drank tea before sleeping well throughout the night.

Tuesday, May 5

Jackson awoke in good spirits and Dr. McGuire thought his wounds were healing. He ate well and met with Chaplain Lacy.

Wednesday, May 6

Despite a slight loss of appetite, Jackson continued to show a general improvement. His wounds revealed no sign of septicemia or gangrene. He spent the morning discussing the military situation and theological matters, then dozed for much of the afternoon. That evening Dr. McGuire, who had had virtually no sleep for four days, felt able to lie down for some rest, leaving Jackson in the care of a servant, James Lewis.

Thursday, May 7

At around 1:00 a.m. Jackson woke with acute pain in his right side, along with nausea, and asked for a wet towel on his stomach. At the general's insistence, Lewis did not disturb Dr. McGuire. Through the night the pain became worse and at dawn Jackson complained of a severe stabbing pain with each breath and asked for Dr. McGuire, who was distressed not to have been called earlier. He considered that Jackson had developed "pleuro pneumonia" (the current term for various types of pulmonary illness) and Dr. Samuel B. Morrison, chief surgeon of General Early's Division, was now summoned. Their treatment consisted of drawing blood, applying mustard plasters and administering laudanum (a mixture of opium and whiskey). The drug relieved his pain but dulled his thinking, and Jackson drifted in and out of consciousness. His wife, Anna, arrived with their baby daughter, Julia; their presence was a great joy to the general.

Friday, May 8

Two more surgeons arrived, Drs. Robert J. Breckinridge and Philip Smith, and Jackson's wounds were examined again. All agreed they seemed to be healing while the laudanum appeared to be easing the pain. Nevertheless, his breathing was labored and he was often delirious.

Saturday, May 9

Dr. David Tucker, an expert on pneumonia, arrived from Richmond and confirmed McGuire's diagnosis. When Jackson awoke from a fitful sleep and saw himself surrounded by doctors he murmured, "I see from the number of physicians that you think my condition dangerous. But I thank God, if it is His will, that I am ready to go. I am not afraid to die." He suffered little pain that day and his breathing improved, although he was getting visibly weaker. However, he managed to play with Julia, stroking her head and calling her "his little comforter." That night his breathing became more difficult and he was very restless.

Sunday, May 10

The events of the day Jackson died are best described in the words of Dr. McGuire:

> About daylight on Sunday morning Mrs. Jackson informed him that his recovery was very doubtful, and that it was better that he be prepared for the worst. He was silent for a moment and then said, "It will be infinite gain to be translated to Heaven." He advised his wife, in the event of his death, to return to her father's house, and added, "You have a kind and good father, but there is no one so kind and good as your Heavenly Father." He still expressed a hope of his recovery, but requested her, if he should die, to have him buried in Lexington, in the Valley of Virginia. His exhaustion increased so rapidly that at 11 o'clock Mrs. Jackson knelt by his bed and told him that before the sun went down he would be with his Savior. He replied: "Oh no; you are frightened, my child, death is not so near; I may get well." She fell over the bed, weeping bitterly, and told him again that the physicians said there was no hope. After a moment's pause he asked her to call me. "Doctor, Anna informs me that you have told her that I am to die today; is that so?" When I answered he turned his eyes toward the ceiling and gazed for a moment or two as in intense thought, then replied, "Very good, very good, it is all right." He then tried to comfort his almost heart-broken wife, and told her he had a great deal to say to her, but he was too weak.
>
> Colonel [then Major] Pendleton came into the room about 1 o'clock, and he asked him, "Who was praying for him at headquarters today?" When told the whole army was praying for him, he replied, "Thank God, they are very kind." He said, "It is the Lord's Day; my wish is fulfilled. I have always desired to die on Sunday."
>
> His mind now began to wander, and he frequently talked as if in command upon the field, giving orders in his old way; then the scene shifted and he was at the mess-table, in conversation with members of his staff; now with his wife and child; now at prayers with his military family. Occasional intervals of return of his mind would appear, and during one of them I offered him some brandy and water, but he declined it saying, "It will only delay my departure, and do no good; I want to preserve my mind if possible to the last." At about half-past one he was told that he had but two hours to live, and he answered again, feebly, but firmly, "Very good, it is alright."
>
> A few moments before he died he cried out in his

delirium, "Order A. P. Hill to prepare for action! Pass the infantry to the front rapidly! Tell Major Hawks," then stopped, leaving the sentence unfinished. Presently a smile of ineffable sweetness spread itself over his pale face, and he cried quietly as if of relief, "Let us cross over the river and rest under the shade of the trees," and then, without pain or the least struggle, his spirit passed from earth to the God who gave it.

Jackson's Funeral and Burial

Jackson had two burials. The first, on May 3, was of his amputated arm, which the Reverend Tucker Lacy arranged to have interred in a field near Old Wilderness Tavern that was used by his brother as a family cemetery. A memorial stone was placed over the spot, engraved with the words,

"ARM OF STONEWALL JACKSON MAY 3, 1863."

The second funeral, of Jackson's body, took place at Lexington on May 15. Events leading up to it are best described in a letter written by V.M.I. Cadet Samuel B. Hannah, a copy of which is held in the V.M.I. Archives. Hannah had the difficult duty of security over the coffin while it awaited burial.

> V.M.I. Institute
> May 17, 1863
>
> I was Officer of the Day when the body of Gen. Jackson was brought in Barracks; no military escort accompanied him from Richmond only a few citizens, among them the Gov. His body was said to be embalmed, but of no avail. Decomposition had already taken place, in consequence of which his face was not exposed to view as the features were said not to be natural. The coffin was a perfect flower bed and under, that which was presented to his wife by the President, the first new Confederate flag ever made [this was the first time the public had seen the "Stainless Banner;" see page 256]. His body was placed in his old Section room which will remain draped for six months.
>
> Gen. Smith [Major-General Edmund Kirby Smith] then requested that none of the flowers should be removed from the coffin, which was an impossibility although I had a sentinel posted over the remains. Still the sentinels would remove things for themselves and of course they were afraid to inform on others for fear of being caught at it themselves. I did not think it right to take what others had placed there as a memorial of their love and esteem for our beloved Jackson, although I would prize a trophy like that the highest imaginable. Still as it had been entrusted to me that all was kept right, so long as his body was under my charge I couldn't conscientiously take any of the flowers when I knew that every cadet was afraid to let me see him take or touch the body.
>
> He only remained in barracks one day and night. He was buried on Friday the 15th May.
>
> Dr. White preached his funeral, the old gentleman seemed and I know he was deeply afflicted, from all accounts the Gen. [Jackson] took quite an active part in the church and was the founder of the Colored Sunday School and the main stay of it as long as he was in Lexington.

In 1891 the casket containing Jackson's body was moved to a new vault nearby, over which a bronze monument was to be placed. The casket was opened in the presence of several witnesses. Only his skeleton and the blue coat (strangely, not gray) in which he was buried remained.

JACKSON'S DEATH AND HOOKER'S DEFEAT – THE CONSEQUENCES FOR GETTYSBURG

Confederate

"God's will be done.
I trust He will raise up someone in his place."
General Robert E. Lee,
commander of the Army of Northern Virginia, on Jackson's death

"You will have heard of the death of General Jackson. It is a terrible loss. I do not know how to replace him. Any victory would be dear at such a cost."
Letter from Lee to his son, Custis

Swift marching, calculated risks and surprise attacks had been the hallmark of the Lee–Jackson military partnership for many months. Jackson's death destroyed all that. He fell at the summit of his career and thus his legend was never sullied by the later collapse of the Confederacy. Many A.N.V. veterans were wont to exclaim with every Confederate reverse after Chancellorsville, and especially with regard to Gettysburg, "If only Jackson had been there things would have been different." They forgot, of course, that even with Jackson the South would almost surely, barring a crushingly spectacular victory in the field, eventually have been ground down by the enormous advantages in economic, industrial and manpower resources of the North.

The loss of "Stonewall" compelled Lee to make fundamental structural changes to the A.N.V. and its command setup. Pressure of events brooked little delay. On May 20 he made his recommendations to President Jefferson Davis (see box opposite). These changes would be tested within six weeks at the costliest battle of the Civil War – Gettysburg.

Structural Reorganization

Until Chancellorsville the A.N.V. had two large corps, each commanded by a lieutenant-general. A corps of upwards of 30,000 was a cumbersome command for one man. It could be extremely difficult to control as it was so often spread over large distances, making communication, the essence of control, uncertain. Its ordnance and supply trains could stretch for 12–15 miles or more on a single road. Coordination of its various parts into a concerted effort was always going to be problematic. As Lee explained to President Davis, a corps of 30,000 was "more than one man can properly handle & keep under his eye in battle." With the experienced and trusted Jackson gone, Lee was compelled to seize that moment for restructuring.

The only practical option was to have three smaller corps. Having three maneuver units, of any size, is what the military call using a "triangular" organization. It has distinct operational and tactical advantages over maneuvering with two. With three a commander has greater flexibility. He can advance with one unit ahead and two in reserve, or two ahead and one in reserve, the essential point being that he can normally expect to have a readily available and uncommitted reserve to reinforce success, meet an unexpected threat, threaten an enemy flank or cover a withdrawal (see diagram, page 22). With only two formations/units this flexibility is substantially reduced. The A.N.V. would become a more manageable army when reorganized into three smaller corps, and with the need to promote two new generals to corps command this easing of the command problems for his senior generals was very necessary. The question was, how best to do it?

The figures used below are those of the painstakingly researched June 30 "present for duty" estimated strengths in the fourth edition of John W. Busey and David G. Martin's *Regimental Strengths and Losses at Gettysburg*. Lee created three corps of approximately equal strength – 1st Corps, 22,353; 2nd Corps, 21,806; and the new 3rd Corps, 23,376. (These are not the same as the number actually engaged during the battle, which is discussed below, page 29.) This gives a total for the army (infantry and artillery) of 67,535. This triangular organization was also established at divisional level. Each corps would consist of three divisions, although the number of brigades in a division varied from four to five. This was necessary in order to maintain a similar strength within divisions while avoiding the break-up of brigades.

The diagram on pages 24–25 illustrates how Lee reorganized the infantry element of his army. He took one division from each of the existing two corps, totaling eleven brigades, and to these added two more brigades from outside the A.N.V. to create his third corps. The three divisions in the new 3rd Corps were composed of regiments from eight states. The newly promoted corps commander, Lieutenant-General Ambrose P. Hill, had two veteran divisions. The first, which was until now unknown to Hill, consisted of Major-General Richard H. Anderson's five brigades from the 1st Corps. The second, from the 2nd Corps and well known to Hill, was his old Light Division, reduced to four brigades instead of six, now commanded by Major-General William D. Pender. Hill's third division, under the newly promoted Major-General Harry Heth, was formed from the other two brigades from Hill's old division along with two brigades from outside the A.N.V. These last were not Lee's first choice but were forced on him by Jefferson Davis; one of them was commanded by the inexperienced nephew of the President, Brigadier-General Joseph R. Davis. Apart from several command changes in one division of the 2nd Corps, both it and the 1st Corps, although reduced by a brigade each, had virtually the same men in July as they had had two months earlier. The only exception was that a new brigade under Brigadier-General Junius Daniel replaced Colquitt's Brigade in Rodes' Division of the 2nd Corps.

If there was a question mark over this reorganization it was over Heth's Division. He was new to divisional command (as was Hill to corps command) and his division had been cobbled together by mixing regiments from five different states. The two weakest brigades from Hill's former division, one under the dubious leadership of a colonel (Brockenbrough), had been amalgamated with two new brigades. A possible alternative would have been to keep the two veteran divisions, merely adding a new brigade to each. But that would have meant Hill's Corps being the only one without a triangular organization – and Heth, a close friend of his new corps commander and something of a protégé of Lee's, would not have got his promotion

The "Stonewall" Jackson Shrine

The Jackson Shrine is the plantation office building where he died. It was intended as a temporary stop where he could regain his strength before being transferred by train from Guinea Station to Richmond. When Jackson arrived in the ambulance he was offered the facilities of Thomas and Mary Chandler's house, but his staff felt the quiet, private office building better suited. Today the office is the only remaining plantation building, as the original house was burned down shortly after the Civil War and its shell later dismantled. Once the office was recognized as a historic building, restoration work was instituted and it was furnished with artifacts of Jackson's stay and other items of the time. Visitors can view the entrance hall, waiting room (used by his doctors and staff), the small room (probably used for storage) and the "death" room furnished as a bedroom.

Lee's Recommendations for Restructuring His Army

Chancellorsville and the loss of Jackson led Lee to overhaul the structure and command of the Army of Northern Virginia. On May 20 he wrote to Preseident Davis outlining his proposals:

> I have for the last year felt that the corps of this army were too large for one commander. Nothing prevented my proposing to you to reduce their size and increase their number but my inability to recommend commanders. Each corps contains, when in fighting condition, about 30,000 men. These are more than one man can properly handle & keep under his eye in battle in country that we have to operate in. They are always beyond the range of his vision, and frequently beyond his reach. The loss of Jackson from command of one half of the army seems to me a good opportunity to remedy this evil. If, therefore, you think Ewell is able to do field duty [had recovered from his wound], I submit it to your better judgment whether the most advantageous arrangement would not be to put him in command of three divisions of Jackson's corps, to take one of Longstreet's divisions, A. P. Hill's division and form a division of Ransom's, Cooke's [he got neither] and Pettigrew's brigades, and give the corps thus formed to A. P. Hill. In this event I also submit to you whether it would not be well to promote Ewell and A. P. Hill. The former is an honest, brave soldier, who has always done his duty well. The latter, I think upon the whole, the best soldier of his grade with me.

The Flexibility Inherent in a Force Adopting a Triangular Organization

Advancing "one up"

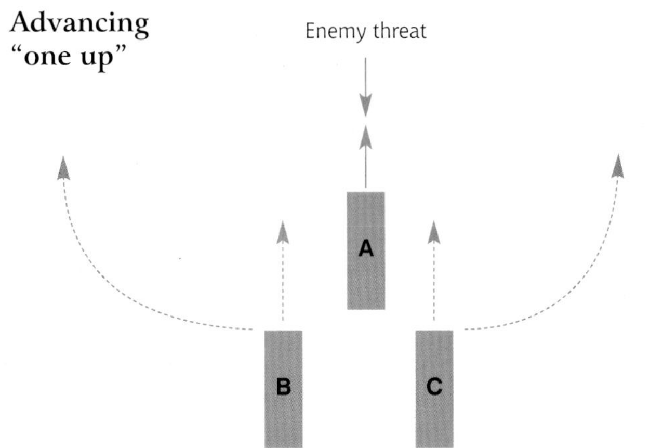

Notes

- **A** can meet – "fix" – the enemy.
- The commander then has several options with **B** and **C**.

Advancing "two up"

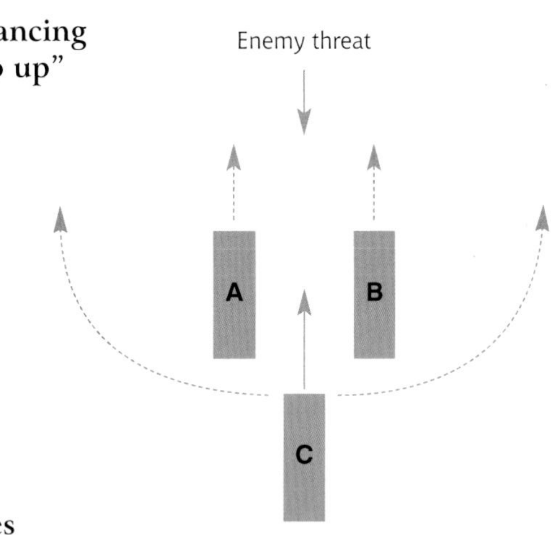

Notes

- **A** and **B** meet – "fix" – the enemy in greater strength on a wider front.
- The commander still has a third of his force as reserve with several options for **C**.

Additional threat from a flank

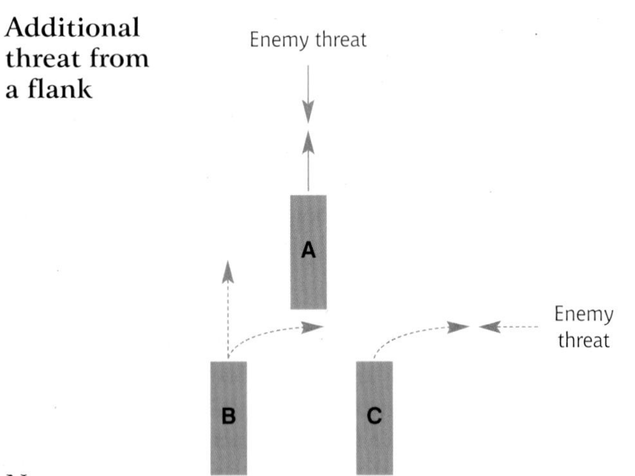

Notes

- A second enemy threat has appeared on the right.
- The commander still has the flexibility to meet it with **C** and to use **B** to reinforce either **A** or **C** as circumstances require.

Commander forced to withdraw

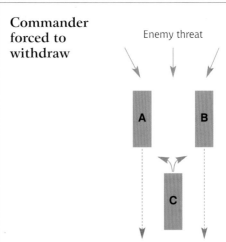

Notes

- Here there are several threats too strong for the force to deal with.
- **A** and **B** withdraw, leaving the commander to use his reserve **C** in a blocking position to delay the enemy while he regroups in the rear.

An unexpected threat from a flank

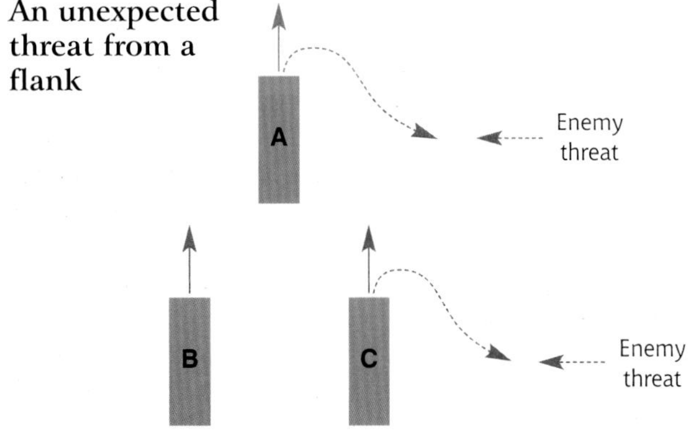

Notes

- In this instance the force is advancing north and a serious threat develops from the east.
- The commander has the flexibility to turn **A** and **C** to meet the threat, with **B** becoming his reserve. The formation has become a "two up" facing east.

A threat from a flank while in "two-up" formation

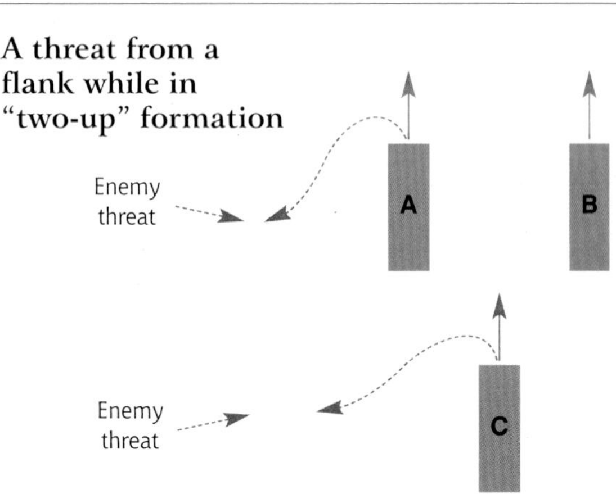

Notes

- Here the force is advancing north in a "two-up" formation when a threat develops from the west.
- The commander has the option of meeting the enemy with **A** and **C** and retaining **B** as his reserve.

Lee took the opportunity of further fine-tuning of the artillery organization, the basic restructuring of which had been put in place before Chancellorsville. Guns had then been taken from infantry brigades and an artillery battalion given to each division, which had noticeably facilitated the concentration of artillery fire at that battle. Major-General J. E. B. Stuart, who ended the battle as an infantry corps (Jackson's) commander, stated, "The effect of this [battalion] fire on the enemy was superb." Of equal significance, the Army Reserve was broken up and each corps allocated a reserve of two battalions, each of four to six batteries under a corps chief of artillery. Lee left the cavalry division under Jeb Stuart unchanged other than increasing its strength from four to six brigades – over 12,000 horsemen.

Command Changes

There was a command crisis. Chancellorsville had cost the A.N.V. its best corps commander mortally wounded (Jackson), one brigade commander killed (Paxton) and three wounded (McGowan, Warren and Nicholls). Additionally, a divisional commander had not been up to his job (Colston); nor had a brigade commander (J. R. Jones, who would later be charged with cowardice for leaving the field because of an ulcer on his leg). Taking into account these losses and the formation of a new corps, the A.N.V. needed to find, through promotions or transfers, two corps, three division and seven brigade commanders for the campaign north of the Potomac then being planned. Finding twelve suitable senior officers quickly was far more problematic than shuffling brigades around.

The two most critical posts whose occupants Lee had to recommend to his President were the corps commanders. Along with Lieutenant-General James Longstreet, commanding 1st Corps, they would be Lee's immediate subordinates in what was expected to be the most crucial campaign of the war, certainly for the Confederacy. They would be lieutenant-generals carrying the huge responsibilities of that rank for the first time. With Jackson's death, speculation within the A.N.V. as to his likely successor was rife. Names often mentioned included, in order of seniority (although all promotion dates were within six months of each other), Major-Generals Richard S. Ewell, Daniel H. Hill, Lafayette McLaws, Ambrose P. Hill and J. E. B. Stuart. What the gossipers around the mess tables did not appreciate to begin with was that there would be a third corps and so two men with three stars on their collars.

If Lee gave consideration to Stuart, McLaws or D. H. Hill it was probably only brief. Stuart was the most junior of the five but was Lee's senior and most trusted cavalry general. Although he had successfully commanded Jackson's Corps after A. P. Hill was slightly wounded at Chancellorsville, Lee was going to need him at the head of his greatly enlarged cavalry division in the forthcoming campaign. Stuart therefore remained a major-general, as did McLaws. McLaws, although an experienced and courageous divisional commander, had ruled himself out by his hesitation to attack at Salem Church. He therefore failed to receive a commendation in Lee's after-battle report on Chancellorsville – a sure sign of disapproval. The second most senior general was D. H. Hill who was commanding in North Carolina where he became involved in an unhelpful exchange of letters with Lee over the provision of reinforcements to the A.N.V. (see page 291). During the Gettysburg campaign he was sidelined and put in charge of the defense of Richmond. That left Ewell and A. P. Hill.

Ewell got the plum command – Jackson's old 2nd Corps. This was slightly strange, in that he had served directly under Lee for less than a month so was not well known on a personal level to the commanding general. All Lee could think of saying to the President in recommending Ewell was that he "is an honest, brave soldier, who has always done his duty well" – a commendation perhaps more enlightening about a private than a major-general. Ewell had been out of action for many months after losing a leg at Groveton – he could now walk only with a stick and had only just re-learned to sit a horse. However, his operational experience was first rate. In the Shenandoah Valley he had commanded his division under Jackson at Winchester and Cross Keys, and went with him to the Peninsula where he fought in the Seven Days Battles. He was also at Cedar Mountain and Second Manassas before losing his leg. Jackson had always considered him his right-hand man, and it was this familiarity with the corps, and with the headquarters staff that the new commander would take over, that made him the obvious choice for 2nd Corps – a promotion that was widely welcomed within the corps. The only slight uncertainty was how would he react to Lee's discretionary method of high command after being so used to Jackson's close control and supervision.

The new 3rd Corps went to A. P. Hill. His relationships with his immediate superiors had often been strained in the past: he had been involved in a long-running feud with Jackson, and he had only been transferred to Jackson's Corps in the first place because of "difficulties" with Longstreet. Although Hill had briefly taken over this corps at Chancellorsville, he would have found it hard to get more than grudging support from Jackson's staff on a permanent basis as all these officers were well aware of the deep-seated animosity between him and Stonewall. Undoubtedly this was a prominent factor in Lee's mind when choosing Ewell rather than Hill for the 2nd Corps. Nevertheless, Lee considered A. P. Hill "the best soldier of his grade [divisional commander] with me." In May 1863 Hill had been a major-general for a year, during which time he had successfully commanded what became known as "Hill's Light Division" for its speed of marching at Mechanicsville, Gaines' Mill and Frayser's Farm. After his quarrel with Longstreet he served under Jackson at Cedar Mountain, Second Manassas, Harper's Ferry, Antietam and Fredericksburg.

Brigadier-General Raleigh E. Colston C.S.A.

Although his mediocre performance at Chancellorsville precluded his presence at Gettysburg, Colston's extraordinary adventures after the war deserve a mention. Initially he established a military school in North Carolina, before serving as a colonel in the Egyptian Army. While on an exploration trip in the Sudan he fell from a camel and was paralyzed from the waist down. In this condition he continued his exploration until, months later, his party met with another that had come down from the source of the Nile. He was sent back on a litter to Alexandria, discharged from the army and returned home in 1879. Impoverished and a cripple, he got a job as a clerk in the War Department. He died in 1896 after two years in the C.S.A. Soldiers' Home in Richmond.

Lee Restructures the A.N.V. for the Gettysburg Campaign

XXXX A.N.V. Gen. Lee

XXX 1st Corps Lee (*de facto*)

XX McLaws
X Wofford
X Semmes
X Kershaw
X Barksdale

XX R. H. Anderson
X Wilcox
X Wright
X Mahone
X Posey
X Perry

XX Pickett
X Garnett
X Kemper
X Armistead

XX Hood
X Law
X Robertson
X G. T. Anderson
X Benning

These two divisions were not present at Chancellorsville, having been sent south under Lt.-Gen. Longstreet

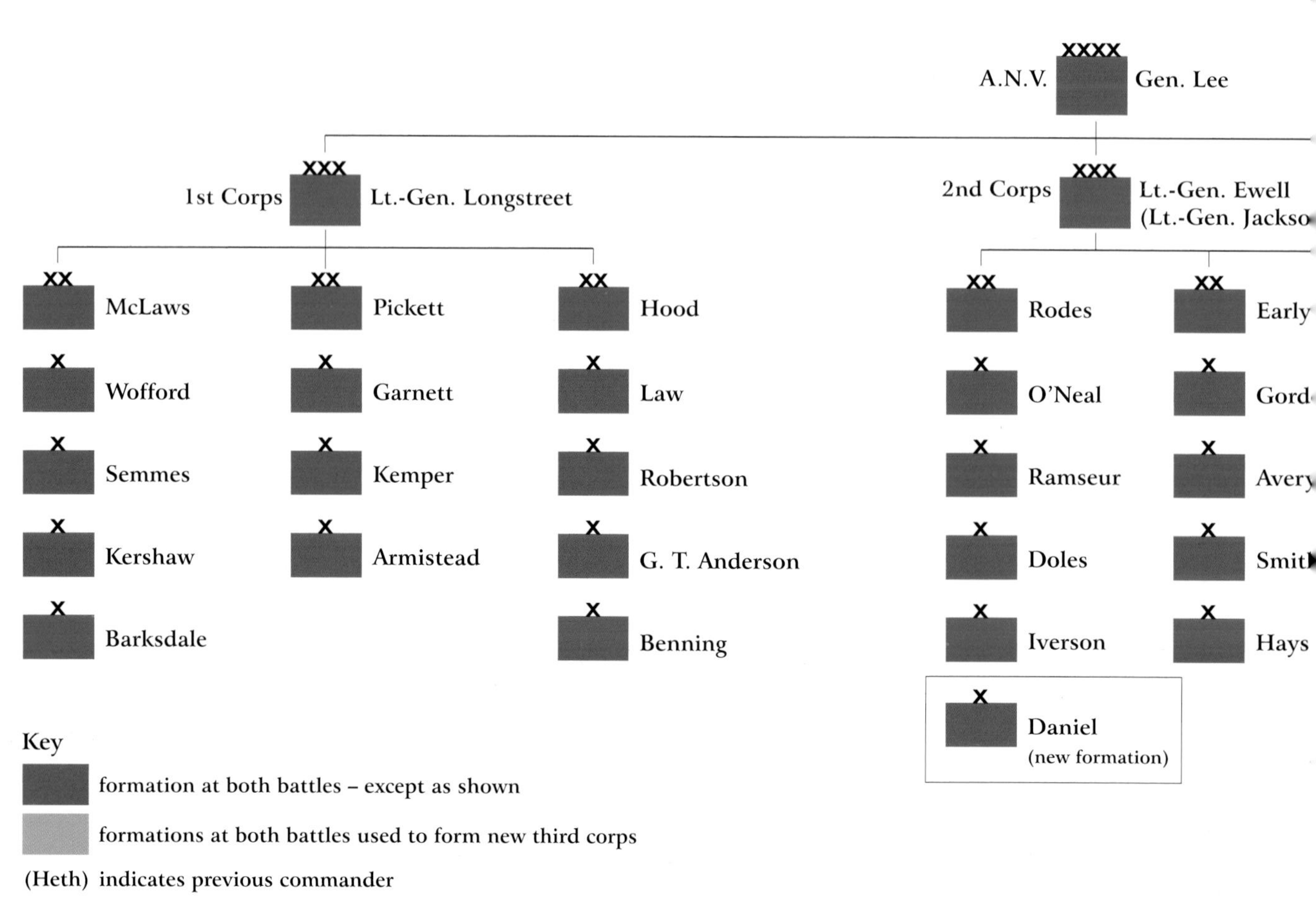

The A.N.V. at Chancellorsville, May 1–4, 1863

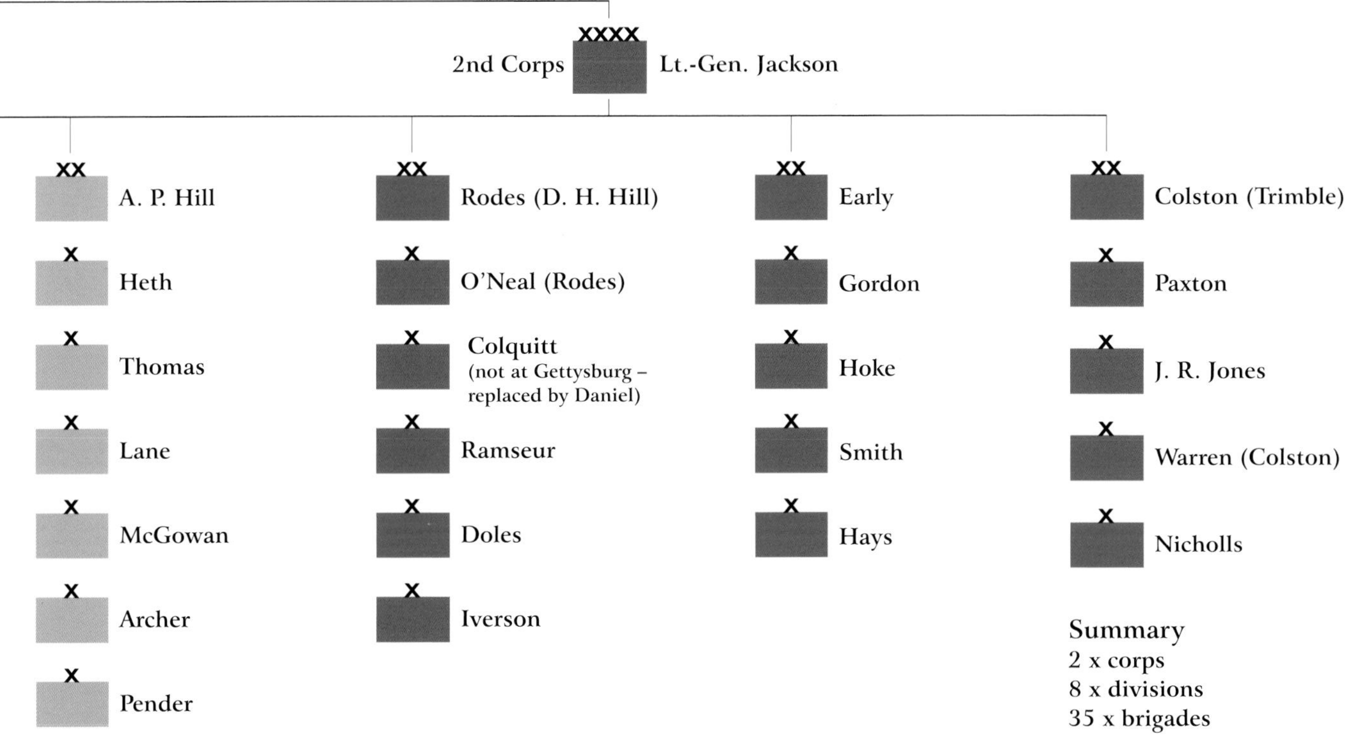
2nd Corps
XXXX
Lt.-Gen. Jackson
XX
A. P. Hill
X
Heth
X
Thomas
X
Lane
X
McGowan
X
Archer
X
Pender
XX
Rodes (D. H. Hill)
X
O'Neal (Rodes)
X
Colquitt
(not at Gettysburg – replaced by Daniel)
X
Ramseur
X
Doles
X
Iverson
XX
Early
X
Gordon
X
Hoke
X
Smith
X
Hays
XX
Colston (Trimble)
X
Paxton
X
J. R. Jones
X
Warren (Colston)
X
Nicholls
Summary
2 x corps
8 x divisions
35 x brigades

The A.N.V. at Gettysburg, July 1–3, 1863

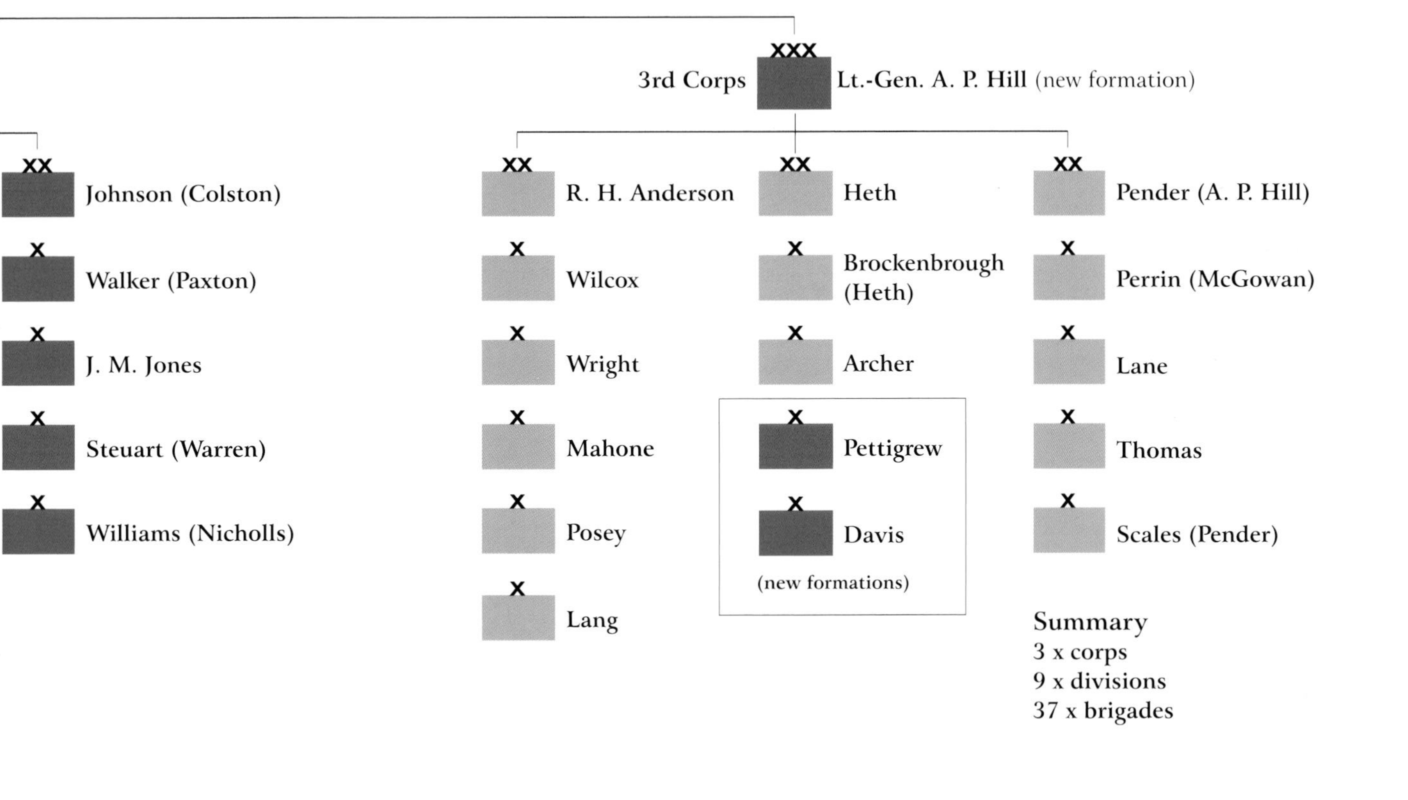
3rd Corps
XXX
Lt.-Gen. A. P. Hill (new formation)
XX
Johnson (Colston)
X
Walker (Paxton)
X
J. M. Jones
X
Steuart (Warren)
X
Williams (Nicholls)
XX
R. H. Anderson
X
Wilcox
X
Wright
X
Mahone
X
Posey
X
Lang
XX
Heth
X
Brockenbrough (Heth)
X
Archer
X
Pettigrew
X
Davis
(new formations)
XX
Pender (A. P. Hill)
X
Perrin (McGowan)
X
Lane
X
Thomas
X
Scales (Pender)
Summary
3 x corps
9 x divisions
37 x brigades

Formation	Commander at Chancellorsville	Reason for change	Commander at Gettysburg
Division	Brig.-Gen. Colston	unsuitable	Maj.-Gen E. Johnson
Division	Maj.-Gen. A. P. Hill	promotion	Maj-Gen H. Heth
Division	–	new formation	Maj.-Gen. W. D. Pender
Brigade	Brig.-Gen. H. Heth	promotion	Col. Brockenbrough
Brigade	Brig.-Gen. McGowan	wounded	Col. A.M. Perrin
Brigade	Col. E. T. H. Warren	wounded	Brig.-Gen. G. H. Steuart
Brigade	Brig.-Gen. Pender	promotion	Brig.-Gen. A. M. Scales
Brigade	Brig.-Gen. F. R. T. Nicholls	wounded	Col. J. M. Williams
Brigade	Brig.-Gen. E. F. Paxton	killed	Brig.-Gen. J. A. Walker
Brigade	Brig.-Gen. J. R. Jones	unsuitable	Brig.-Gen. J. M. Jones

With the corps commanders decided, that still left places on the promotion ladder for three divisional and seven brigade commanders. Finding a further ten senior commanders, all of whom would be new to their higher responsibilities, from a dwindling pool of suitable or available officers was something of a hit-and-miss undertaking. The results are summarized above.

In addition, Brigadier-General Alfred H. Colquitt, along with his brigade, was sent to North Carolina, probably because Lee felt his performance at Chancellorsville had been pedestrian. A new brigade under Brigadier-General Junius Daniel took his place.

Thus the Confederates' victory at Chancellorsville had necessitated a complete restructuring of their army. But perhaps more importantly, it compelled the A.N.V. to march into Maryland and Pennsylvania with a worryingly high proportion of its top commanders untested in their new responsibilities. Although an oversimplification, it has been said that the price of the Confederate victory at Chancellorsville was defeat at Gettysburg two months later.

Union

Defeat for the Army of the Potomac at Chancellorsville was yet another bruising blow to the Northern home front. When the news was broken to President Lincoln he exclaimed, "My God! My God! What will the country say?" Lee's reputation had been hugely enhanced; under him the Rebels seemed unbeatable. These sentiments had unwelcome repercussions within the North's high command. There was an almost mutinous undermining of Major-General Joseph Hooker's authority by a cabal of disloyal corps commanders. The plotters against Hooker took their case for his removal to President Lincoln. Lincoln, for reasons discussed below, reluctantly kept Hooker; however, he was well aware that at the start of the Gettysburg campaign his army, pitted against invaders under the seemingly invincible Lee, was under a general that lacked the loyalty of most of its senior commanders.

The sacking of army commanders was becoming a habit. The twelve months to May 1863 had witnessed a series of five successive operational failures by the Union Army in the East. The failure of Major-General George B. McClellan in the Peninsula in May 1862 resulted in his replacement as commander of the field army by Major-General John Pope. Pope then lost badly at Second Manassas so was replaced by McClellan again. His hesitation at Antietam cost him his job for the second time, his place now being taken by Major-General Ambrose E. Burnside. He was dismissed for leading the army to disaster at Fredericksburg and command went to Hooker, who did only marginally better at Chancellorsville. Each lost battle was followed by a different general, none of whom seemed able to do better than his predecessor.

The Union defeat in early May 1863 by an army half its size resulted in the Army of the Potomac starting the Gettysburg campaign a month later with six of the seven infantry corps commanders openly disloyal, lacking confidence in and critical of their commanding general – Hooker. It was a situation without precedent and potentially disastrous. In the preceding few weeks most of Hooker's senior generals had sought to have him removed and replaced by V Corps commander Major-General George G. Meade. This group of disgruntled generals had attempted a corps commanders' coup. It was in flagrant breach of military law (the Articles of War) and an offense meriting a court martial. The coup failed, there was no court martial and Hooker continued in command of the army for twenty-four of the twenty-seven-day first phase of the campaign that ended at Gettysburg on July 1. How had this poisonous situation arisen?

It began on May 7, just one day after Hooker had been forced to withdraw back across the Rappahannock River nursing some 17,000 casualties, with the visit to his army on a "fact-finding mission" of no lesser personages than President Lincoln accompanied by General-in-Chief Henry W. Halleck. Halleck, who had no time for Hooker, called all the corps commanders to what was, as far as Hooker was concerned, a private conference to which he was not invited. The senior generals were openly critical of Hooker's performance at Chancellorsville, opinions fully in accord with Halleck's views. Particularly vocal were the commanders of II and XII Corps, Major-Generals Darius N. Couch and Henry W. Slocum respectively. They went around canvassing their fellow corps commanders to petition the President there and then to sack Hooker and put Meade in his place. Meade, however, was not ready to fall into line with this dramatic scheme. He wrote to his wife, "I told these gentlemen I would not join in any movement against Hooker." Without Meade's consent there could be no immediate approach to Lincoln. However, it was the beginning, not the end, of the plotters' offensive.

Part of Hooker's problem was that he had few friends among his senior subordinates. His overblown order congratulating the army on their achievements at Chancellorsville contained the sentence, "In withdrawing from the south bank of the Rappahannock before delivering a general battle to our adversaries, the army has given renewed evidence of its confidence in itself and its fidelity to the principles it represents." He went on to contradict himself by adding, "If it has not accomplished all that was expected, the reasons are well known to the army." Hooker then let it be known where he thought the responsibility for this failure lay. He blamed his corps commanders. In particular he pointed at Major-General George Stoneman, his cavalry commander, who had failed to cut Lee's railroad supply line; Major-General John Sedgwick, commanding VI Corps, for his slowness on the left wing; and Major-General Oliver O. Howard for the collapse of XI Corps under Jackson's surprise attack. Much of Hooker's criticism was justified, but the effect of his voicing his opinions publicly was to ensure his corps commanders closed ranks against him. Out of the eight corps commanders, only Major-General Daniel E. Sickles of III Corps, who owed his appointment to Hooker, remained loyal.

Visits to Falmouth, where the army was encamped, by newspaper correspondents and politicians confirmed the lack of confidence felt by many in Hooker's ability. During a visit by Governor Andrew G. Curtin of Pennsylvania both Meade and Major-General John F. Reynolds, commanding I Corps, made clear their belief that Hooker was not up to his job. Curtin immediately reported this to Lincoln. On May 13 Hooker informed the President that he planned to resume the offensive. A telegraph message from the White House summoned him to Washington. There he was informed that any offensive must await the regrouping of the army. Lincoln's written instructions to this effect the next day ended with a bombshell: "I must tell you that I have some painful intimations that some of your corps and division commanders are not giving you their entire confidence. This would be ruinous if true . . . " Hooker was shocked and angry. Having heard of Meade's meeting with Governor Curtin, Hooker confronted him. A blazing row developed, during which Meade was said to have "damned Hooker very freely." He later wrote to his wife, "I am sorry to tell you I am at open war with Hooker." Hooker's reply to Lincoln's bombshell was that he claimed to be in ignorance of any disloyalty among his generals and that he would welcome the President making his own investigations as to its accuracy.

Several corps commanders visited Washington to see the President over the next two weeks. Couch, the most senior major-

Major-General Joseph "Fighting Joe" Hooker (1814–1879)

Like Jackson, Hooker was a West Pointer, originally an artillery officer who was brevetted (three times) for gallantry during the Mexican War. He particularly distinguished himself at the Battles of Monterey and Vera Cruz. Unfortunately for his later career, he made the mistake of testifying before a court of inquiry on the war against his commander-in-chief (General Winfield Scott). Banishment for five years as adjutant general of the Pacific Division persuaded a bored Hooker to resign and take up ranching, although he accepted an appointment as a colonel in the California Militia. It was at this time that he became notorious for his eye for "ladies of easy virtue" and the name "hookers" was coined for the type of woman he liked so well – a term still commonly used today.

After the outbreak of the Civil War Hooker's offers to serve were repeatedly snubbed by the War Department, who recalled his anti-Scott testimony. However, after the Union's resounding defeat at First Manassas, which Hooker observed as a civilian, he was appointed a brigadier-general of volunteers. He was thereafter continuously and actively involved in fighting up to three days before Gettysburg. He saw action as a senior commander during the siege of Yorktown and the engagements at Williamsburg, Seven Pines, throughout the Seven Days, Malvern Hill, Second Manassas, South Mountain, Antietam (where he was wounded in the foot) and Fredericksburg. Hooker had been given his nickname during the Seven Days Battles after a newspaper headed several articles with the words "Fighting-Joe Hooker" (perhaps surprisingly, given that it was complimentary, he disliked it). After Fredericksburg, President Lincoln, with considerable misgivings, replaced Major-General Ambrose E. Burnside with Hooker as commander of the Army of the Potomac. Although there was some severe fighting after Jackson's dramatic attack at Chancellorsville, by May 6 Hooker had retired north of the Rappahannock to lick his wounds (almost 17,000 Union casualties compared with 13,000 Confederates). Chancellorsville has been considered by many historians to be Lee's most spectacular victory.

Hooker was known throughout the army as a hard drinker. His army headquarters was referred to by some as a combination of brothel and bar. After his retreat at Chancellorsville there was persistent talk that Hooker had been drunk for most, if not all, of the battle and that this had affected his performance as commander and therefore the result. A few senior officers, including his chief of staff, Major-General Daniel Butterfield, asserted vehemently they had never seen Hooker drunk – a blatant lie. More junior ranks claimed the reverse. Colonel Clark S. Edwards, 5th Maine Infantry, wrote that Hooker was "beastly drunk and not fit to command a corporal's guard, much less an army." In a letter dated May 9, Captain Francis A. Donaldson, 118th Pennsylvania Infantry, stated he saw Hooker "guzzling (I can call it by no other name) wine and I saw him incapacitated for command by reason of strong drink." Perhaps one of his corps commanders, Major-General Darius N. Couch, who attributed Hooker's lack of success at Chancellorsville to the fact that he been unusually abstemious on that occasion, got it right: "I have always stated that he probably abstained from the use of ardent spirits when it would have been far better for him to have continued in his usual habit in that respect." However, although there is no denying Hooker's usual alcohol dependency, it is seldom mentioned that at the height of the battle a shell struck a pillar against which he was leaning. The shock and blast of such a narrow escape can hardly have sharpened his senses at a critical time.

Hooker resigned command of the Army of the Potomac three days before the Battle of Gettysburg but continued to serve as a corps commander in the Western theater, leading XX Corps at Lookout Mountain (the "Battle above the Clouds"), Missionary Ridge, Ringgold, Mill Creek Gap, Resaca, Cassville, New Hope Church, Pine Mountain, Chattahoochee, Peach Tree Creek and the siege of Atlanta. There seem more than sufficient grounds for thinking he was appropriately nicknamed – although after his performance at Chancellorsville the Confederates referred to him as "Fighting-fainting-fleeing" Joe Hooker. He retired in 1868 after a paralytic stroke, dying twenty-one years later, aged sixty-five.

general, was asked by Lincoln if he would take over command if necessary. Couch claimed his health was not up to it, requested a transfer and stated Meade was the man for the job. Other generals received more indirect approaches. Sedgwick could not be persuaded, telling his sister that "nothing would induce me to take it." Similarly Hancock refused to drink from what he considered a poisoned chalice, writing to his wife, "I should be sacrificed." Meanwhile, widespread rumors about Hooker's future circulated throughout the army, Washington and beyond. On May 17 newspaper boys ensured a brisk trade by shouting "General Hooker removed." It was not true.

Lincoln was in a quandary. Although Sickles had spoken up for Hooker, it was becoming increasingly difficult to ignore the obvious turmoil in the high command of the Army of the Potomac. Personally the President liked Hooker, and felt instinctively that the business of changing generals after every battle was not perhaps the most effective way of running a war. He had tried McClellan twice, so why not give Hooker another chance; after all, of those corps commanders who were so vocal in their criticisms all had excuses for why they could not do the job themselves.

Matters came to a head on May 25. News broke that Lee's army seemed to be stirring. A decision on any command change could not be further delayed. Reynolds was summoned to the White House. Lincoln had resolved, not without continuing misgivings, for a last attempt at making a change. However, to the President's dismay, Reynolds' response to the offer of command was so dependent on impossible conditions that there was realistically no possibility of his being appointed. Reynolds was demanding the army be freed from civilian control, together with an end to interference from the President and the Secretary of War, and even from his commanding general, Halleck. The failure of this final attempt of Lincoln's to lance the boil forced him to keep Hooker. Reynolds quoted him as saying he "was not disposed to throw away a gun because it missed fire once; that he would pick the lock and try again."

At the start of what became the Gettysburg campaign, the battle at Chancellorsville had been potentially wounding for both armies. Among the officers and soldiers of the Army of Northern Virginia there was a hint of overconfidence in their own ability and that of their commanding general – this despite the realization that Jackson had gone and that his successors and many of their subordinates were untested in their positions. The Yankees, meanwhile, marched with a high command that almost unanimously considered their commander unfit for his post.

The Presidential Letter Appointing Hooker to Command the Army of the Potomac

Because Hooker commanded the Army of the Potomac for all but three days of the Gettysburg campaign, and because it is an extraordinary military letter of appointment, Lincoln's words are worth quoting in full.

> EXECUTIVE MANSION
> Washington, D.C.
> January 26, 1863
>
> Major-General Hooker.
>
> GENERAL: I have placed you at the head of the Army of the Potomac. Of course I have done this upon what appears to me to be sufficient reasons, and yet I think it best for you to know that there are some things in regard to which I am not quite satisfied with you. I believe you to be a brave and skillful soldier, which, of course, I like. I also believe you do not mix politics with your profession, in which you are right. You have confidence in yourself, which is a valuable, if not indispensable, quality. You are ambitious, which, within reasonable bounds, does good rather than harm; but I think that during General Burnside's command of the army, you have taken counsel of your ambition, and thwarted him as much as you could, in which you did a great wrong to the country and to a most meritorious and honorable brother officer. I have heard, in such a way as to believe it, of your recently saying that both the army and the government need a dictator. Of course it was not for this, but in spite of it, that I have given you the command. Only those generals who gain success can set up dictators. What I now ask of you is military success, and I will risk the dictatorship. The Government will support you to the utmost of its ability, which is neither more nor less than it has done or will do for all commanders. I much fear that the spirit, which you have aided to infuse into the army, of criticizing their commander and withholding confidence from him, will now turn upon you. I shall assist you as far as I can to put it down. Neither you, nor Napoleon, if he were alive again, could get any good out of an army while such a spirit prevails in it. And now beware of rashness, but with energy and sleepless vigilance go forward and give us victories.
>
> Yours, very truly,
> A. LINCOLN

SECTION ONE

Orders of Battle

Napoleon once said that "God is on the side of the big battalions," by which he meant the secret of success on the battlefield usually lay in concentrating superior numbers at the decisive point. Of course there is much more to generalship than outnumbering your enemy but, other things being equal, if you have the stronger army your chances of victory are decidedly enhanced. However, history is full of examples of how small armies have defeated bigger ones – therein lies the art of war, be the battle between a handful of men or armies of hundreds of thousands. The two major clashes prior to Gettysburg are striking examples of the ability of smaller forces to beat bigger ones. First, on December 13, 1862 at Fredericksburg, 75,000 Confederates under Lee roundly defeated the Union General Burnside, with 120,000. In this case the Rebel victory was largely due to the incompetence of Burnside in issuing confusing orders and frittering away his numerical advantage by repeatedly hurling division after division in frontal attacks up the slope of Marye's Heights against heavily defended entrenchments. The second example was at Chancellorsville five months later. On this occasion the Union had, under Hooker, what he called "the finest army on the planet," numbering over 130,000 of all arms. Opposing him was Lee with a mere 60,000. The battle resulted in a stunning Confederate victory, due to bold maneuvering by Lee and a surprise flank attack by Jackson's command. Interestingly, although Lee had an army less than half the size of his enemy, he managed to have the "big battalions" in the right place at the right time. In war numbers and weaponry are important, but generalship far more so.

A look at the orders of battle of both armies at Gettysburg is a convenient starting point, as a comparison in terms of manpower and guns between the protagonists will give the reader a better understanding of why and how the campaign and battle were fought. An order of battle sets out how a military formation or unit is organized, how strong it is and its composition in terms of the troop types within it. Those in this section are set out in diagrammatic form along with a picture of all the army, corps and divisional commanders. They show the formations that actually fired a shot or came under fire during the period July 1–3: in other words, the overall "engaged" strength. This includes the cavalry actions fought away from the main battlefield between those dates, but not units detached guarding supply bases or trains that saw no action. As the battle was fought over three days and was initially a meeting engagement, the numbers on both sides varied from day to day, with some Union forces arriving late on July 2. Also, as the fighting was prolonged and casualties mounted, so many formations shrank in size. As explained in the Introduction, this book uses the numbers researched by John Busey and David Martin. These figures are very exact and to use them when describing the detailed fighting would be pedantic and almost certainly unrealistic, so they have been rounded up or down to the nearest fifty for brigades and above, and the nearest ten for regiments in all sections after this one.

Muster Rolls – Doubtful Documents

While the latest estimates by Busey and Martin of the relative strengths of both armies engaged at Gettysburg are undoubtedly the best-researched available and have been used in this book, they do not claim total accuracy for all units, particularly the Army of Northern Virginia where informed guesswork has sometimes been necessary. One of the reasons for the impossibility of complete accuracy was that once units left camp and went on campaign many routine administrative checks, such as parade states, were neglected, delayed or skimped. Exhausting marches, extra duties that required men to be detached, fighting and straggling became problems that interfered with normal procedures. In these circumstances the usual regimental morning reports were sometimes missed or in some way falsified by, for example, counting stragglers as present on the assumption they would turn up later. All of this meant the number on the muster roll as present and fit for duty was seldom the same as the number of men with rifles or muskets on the firing line. Edwin B. Coddington, in his book *The Gettysburg Campaign – A Study in Command*, gives a telling example of how, although a company of the 12th Massachusetts had thirty-four men present for duty on July 1, only seventeen men with rifles formed up on Seminary Ridge. The remainder had been "lost" on the following assignments: two as drummers, two as provost guards and one each as color guard, bugler, wagonmaster, teamster, ambulance driver, headquarters aide, hospital cook, brigade butcher, brigade engineering worker and brigade cattle guard. In addition, three stragglers had yet to rejoin.

FORMATION AND UNIT DEFINITIONS

The formations and units of both armies are explained below in descending order.

Army

An army is the sum total of all the formations/units of all arms (infantry, cavalry, artillery and supporting services) in a given area (geographical department) under one commanding general. In the Civil War at least sixteen Union and twenty-three Confederate "operational organizations" were known officially or unofficially as an army. The Union armies generally took their name from their department, usually the river near which they operated, whereas the Confederates named theirs from the area in which they were active. At times this could be confusing. The North had an Army of the Tennessee and the South an Army of Tennessee – just the word "the" making the distinction. At Gettysburg Lee's Army of Northern Virginia (a state) attacked Meade's Army of the Potomac (a river). In round figures, the former with 71,700 engaged an opponent with 93,900, giving a theoretical numerical advantage to Meade of over 22,000. Hindsight and research tell us this now, but the generals did not have such detailed information at the time; indeed Meade was half convinced he was outnumbered throughout the battle. Lee, lacking information from his cavalry, had no clear idea of how many Yankee men and guns had arrived on the battlefield during the first two days of the action.

An army was under a general officer, usually of full general's rank like Lee. Meade, however, was only a major-general – officers of this rank in the Union Army could command an army, a corps and often a division, the appointment often resting on seniority, influence and ability, in that order.

Corps

The armies at Gettysburg were composed of a number of corps – the Confederates had three large ones, the Union Army eight much smaller ones. The term "corps" comes from the French *corps d'armée*, popularized by Napoleon and now commonly used among the military worldwide. They were established in the Union Army in March 1862 and adopted by the Confederates in November of the same year. An infantry corps was effectively a small army, in that it was usually an all arms and services formation with its own staff, which could operate independently from army command if necessary.

At Gettysburg all was not so simple. First, designation. In Lee's army, although corps were given numbers, they were invariably referred to by their general's name – thus Longstreet's, or Hill's or Ewell's Corps – whereas Meade's command was divided into seven infantry corps (numbered I, II, III, V, VI, XI and XII) and a cavalry corps. Second, with all formations (corps, divisions or brigades) and units (regiments) at the battle, size varied enormously. The largest of the three Confederate corps was Hill's with almost 22,000 men, the smallest Ewell's with 20,500 – a negligible difference. Each of the

Conscription – the Military Draft

Although the armies that met at Gettysburg were almost wholly volunteer forces, both the North and South had by then resorted to conscription. The Confederacy passed the first of three Conscription Acts on April 16, 1862 and scarcely a year later the Union followed suit. Both governments, plagued by manpower shortages, regarded the draft as the only way of sustaining effective armies in the field. However, compulsory service embittered the public, who considered it a gross infringement of freedom of choice and personal liberty. Many believed, with some justification, that unwilling conscripts made poor soldiers.

The first conscription laws applied to men aged between eighteen and thirty-five (later raised to forty-five), with the actual selection (drafting) being the responsibility of the states; this meant their being given a quota based on population, which was filled by a lottery system. The numerous exemption clauses and loopholes ensured that the great majority of those selected could avoid service if they wished. Many occupations were exempt, such as telegraph operators, railroad engineers, river workers, miners, civil officials, teachers and druggists. Not until the Union Enrolment Act of March 3, 1863 did a branch of the War Department take effective control of the draft from state governors. In the South, until December 1863 anyone owning more than twenty slaves was also exempt. The wealthy could hire substitutes or pay up to $300 to avoid service, leading to the cry of "a rich man's war, a poor man's fight." A bar to conscription included various medical conditions, such as imperfect vision in the right eye, lack of front teeth and molars, and the loss of more than one finger of the right hand or two of the left. Unscrupulous doctors could be bribed to sign bogus medical certificates giving exemption. Several states in the Confederacy, notably Georgia and North Carolina (which together provided very large volunteer contingents at Gettysburg), were actively opposed to the draft and exempted thousands by the sham addition of their names to civil servant rolls or by enlisting them in state militias. One general described such a regiment as having "3 field officers, 4 staff captains, 10 captains, 30 lieutenants, and 1 private with misery in his bowels." Figures for the Union Army give the number of men drafted and held to service as only 52,068, while 86,724 avoided conscription by paying their $300 and another 42,581 men enlisted as substitutes. Many "volunteered" in order to qualify for the bounty paid to those who enlisted (see box opposite). To encourage this, the 150th New York (Lockwood's Brigade) recruited in late 1862 under the slogan "Come in out of the draft."

Shortly after Gettysburg some serious anti-draft rioting took place in New York. A report of Colonel Nugent, Acting Assistant Provost Marshal General, dated New York, July 15, reads, in part:

> SIR: Mob last evening attacked the quarters of provost-marshal first district, at Jamaica, destroying clothing, &. Records had been removed to a place of safety. Rioters still at work in the city. Mob assembled at Thirty-second Street this morning; were fired upon by the military. Quite a number killed. Object seems to be plunder, rather than any real objection to the draft . . .
>
> ROBERT NUGENT
> Colonel, and A.A.P.M.G.

Desertion

The daily hardships of war, low morale due to defeats, lengthy delays (sometimes up to fourteen months) in receiving pay, and solicitude for family were all reasons for the very high levels of desertion on both sides. Abuse of sick leave or furlough were among the chief means of deserting. The Union Provost Marshal General estimated that over 268,000 instances were reported during the war, of which some 25 percent were unintentionally or unavoidably absent – genuine deserters were thought to be around 200,000. Of these, 76,500 were arrested, punished and returned to their units.

In addition to the deserters, there were many thousands of other absentees. Just three months before Gettysburg, Hooker's returns for the Army of the Potomac showed 2,922 officers and 81,896 enlisted men absent, the great majority with no known reason. A number of deserters lived rough in the wild, turned outlaw, fled to Canada or, as happened in western Pennsylvania, formed bandit gangs. Desertion in the South was only slightly less of a problem than in the North. Many men who disappeared did so because they genuinely felt their services would be more use at home than in the army, spurred on by appeals such as that received by an Alabamian whose wife wrote, "We haven't got nothing in the house but a little bit o meal . . . I don't want you to stop fighting them Yankees . . . but try and get off and come home and fix us all up some and then you can go back." Private Edward Cooper from North Carolina, not surprisingly, deserted after reading the following letter:

> My dear Edward – I have always been proud of you, and since your connection with the Confederate Army, I have been prouder of you than ever before. I would not have you do anything wrong for the world, but before God, Edward, unless you come home we must die. Last night I was aroused by little Eddie crying. I called and said, "What is the matter Eddie?" and he said, "O Mamma, I am so hungry." And Lucy, Edward, your darling Lucy, she never complains but, she is getting thinner and thinner every day. And before God, Edward, unless you come home, we must die.

Cooper was later arrested and convicted but was saved from execution by the heartrending cry of despair in this letter, which he produced at his court martial

Lesser penalties than execution included fines, flogging, imprisonment or service increased to a longer period. Nevertheless, the death penalty was at times applied, especially after 1863, although this meant the selection of a few men as public examples out of the many thousands equally guilty (see box, page 33). After watching fourteen deserters executed at one time, a Tennessee chaplain wrote, "I think they were objects of pity, they were ignorant, poor, and had families dependent upon them. War is a cruel thing, it heeds not the widow's tears, the orphan's moan, or the lover's anguish."

three had a lieutenant-general commanding. The Army of the Potomac's seven infantry corps varied in strength from 14,000 (VI Corps) to 9,250 (XI Corps), the latter being less than half the size of a Confederate corps. There was a feeling among some that the Union corps and divisions were too many, too small and too weak, and that as they all required staffs, escorts, provosts and couriers they were wasteful of manpower. Additionally, as seven corps were inevitably spread over large areas, it was necessary for the army commander to divide the army into "wings" – as Hooker and then Meade did prior to Gettysburg – in order to maintain control.

A major-general commanded a Union corps. At Gettysburg the corps commanders in each army had an artillery reserve under their control. There was no cavalry, other than small units doing escort or courier duties, under the command of infantry corps commanders. A Confederate corps was a particularly unwieldy organization because of its size. Large supply, ambulance and ordnance trains, as well as up to eighty or more guns with their horse teams and wagons, often had to share road space with the marching infantry columns and thus the whole took considerable time and a lot of competent staff work to move from A to B. A thousand infantry in column of fours took up about 350 yards of road, and a battery of six guns with its wagons about 500 yards. Thus Hill's Corps on a single road would stretch for at least 6 or 7 miles – much longer if the supply train was involved. The tail would not start to march until the leading unit had been on the road for about three hours.

Bounty Jumpers and Brokers

The payment of a bounty of up to $300 on enlistment encouraged "bounty jumping," which entailed enlisting, collecting the bounty, deserting, and then repeating the cycle until apprehended. One man succeeded thirty-two times before being caught and sentenced to four years' imprisonment. Bounty brokers were dishonest agents who recruited men and robbed them of most of their bounty. They also enlisted men unfit for service who would have to be discharged after their bounties had been paid.

Divisions

In field armies on both sides the division was, discounting the army itself, the second largest formation. In modern armies a division is a semi-independent formation in that, like a corps, it is composed of all arms and services; however, at Gettysburg a division would be composed of either infantry or cavalry. In neither army did an infantry divisional commander have cavalry formations or units under command, but although Confederate divisions had artillery units under direct control, Union divisions did not. Horse artillery units supported a cavalry division and, while no infantry accompanied the horsemen, all could operate as infantry in a dismounted role if required. The South had 10 divisions at Gettysburg (9 infantry and one cavalry), all commanded by a major-general and varying in size from 7,981 (Rodes) to 5,475 (Pickett) but with an average strength of 6,900. The North mustered 22 divisions (19 infantry and 3 cavalry), four of which were commanded by major-generals, the remainder by brigadier-generals. The 1st Division (Williams) of XII Corps was the largest with 5,256 all ranks, and 3rd Division (Crawford), V Corps the smallest with 2,862. The average divisional strength

The Irish Brigade – the "Fearless Sons of Erin"

More than 144,000 Irish-born soldiers served in the Union Army during the Civil War, although only the 2nd Brigade, 1st Division, II Corps, which fought at Gettysburg under Colonel Patrick Kelly, was known as "the Irish Brigade." It was made up primarily of Irish immigrants from Boston, Philadelphia and New York who had a reputation as fearless fighters. The brigade was engaged in nearly all the major battles fought by the Army of the Potomac and took part in many of the most famous infantry charges of the war. In early 1862, in training camp, it mustered some 3,000 men. A year later there were barely 300 at roll call. During those twelve months the brigade had made a bloody bayonet charge at Fair Oaks, lost 700 men during the Seven Days Battles, lost 540 charging "Bloody Lane" at Antietam, and another 545 storming Marye's Heights at Fredericksburg. During all this time its commander had been Brigadier-General Thomas F. Meagher, who, after Chancellorsville, wrote to his divisional headquarters, "I beg most respectfully to tender you . . . my resignation as brigadier-general commanding what was once known as the Irish Brigade. That Brigade no longer exists."

However, the brigade was not disbanded but went into action at Gettysburg with five regiments totaling 532 all ranks – the smallest of the fifty-eight Union brigades that took the field with an average regimental strength of 106! It lost 37 percent at the battle, but by early 1864 new drafts had brought it back up to strength. In the Wilderness and at Cold Harbor it lost heavily again, but survived to march proudly in the victory parade in Washington at the end of the war.

was 3,800, only slightly over half that of a Rebel division. The scale of the difference in size between divisions in opposing armies is strikingly evident, as not even the largest Union division was equal to the smallest Confederate. This huge discrepancy means care must be taken in assessing the wisdom (strength) of divisional attacks in particular.

Brigades

The tactical unit on the Napoleonic battlefield was the battalion. Generals counted infantry battalions when assessing relative strengths, whereas in the Civil War it was usually the number of brigades available that counted. At Gettysburg Lee had 42 brigades (37 infantry and 5 cavalry); of these the strongest was Pettigrew's (Heth's Division) with 2,580 men, while the smallest, with a mere 742 (the size of one good-sized regiment), was Lang's Brigade (Anderson's Division). Their average strength was 1,518. The Confederate brigades were mostly commanded by brigadier-generals with a smattering of colonels (six infantry and one cavalry) and consisted of between three and six regiments, but with the great majority having four or five. Several had acquired unofficial titles or nicknames by which they were commonly known, such as the Stonewall Brigade (Johnson's Division) or Hood's Texas Brigade.

Brigade commanders on both sides were expected to lead from the front in battle and at Gettysburg, with only a few exceptions, they did so. Among the Confederate brigade commanders, including those who took temporary command during the battle, 22 became casualties (6 killed or mortally wounded, 12 wounded and 4 captured), the corresponding losses in the Army of the Potomac being 20 (7–11–2).

Meade counted 58 brigades (49 infantry and 9 cavalry) in his engaged army, 16 more that the Rebels, but then he had more divisions, each substantially smaller than that of his adversary. His strongest was the 2nd Brigade (Ward), 1st Division, III Corps with 2,186; the smallest, with a paltry 532, was the 2nd Brigade (Kelly's Irish Brigade), 1st Division, II Corps. However, an average of 1,433 meant there was little practical difference in the average brigade of both sides on the battlefield. Union brigade command was split fairly evenly between brigadier-generals (28) and colonels (30). As with the Army of Northern Virginia, several brigades had assumed nicknames, such as the Iron Brigade (1st Brigade, 1st Division, I Corps) and the Excelsior Brigade (2nd Brigade, 2nd Division, III Corps).

Because the average brigade strength was nearly equal for both sides, the reader who wishes to do a rough assessment of opposing strengths at the start of an attack is advised to count brigades deployed or available rather than regiments or divisions.

Regiments

Theoretically a regiment at full established strength and commanded by a colonel would be slightly over 1,000 strong, divided into ten companies with a small headquarters, but deaths, desertions, diseases and discharges all had the effect of reducing the average Confederate infantry regiment at Gettysburg by two-thirds to 334; similarly with a Union regiment to 298. This meant a company of thirty men instead of 100 was the average size for both armies. Of the 172 Confederate infantry regiments engaged between July 1 and 3, the strongest at the start of the battle was the 26th North Carolina with 839, the smallest the 27th Virginia with 148.

A Confederate cavalry regiment at full strength would have between 600 and 1,000 men divided into 10 squadrons but, like the infantry, the ravages of war had caught up with them. Thus the 6th Virginia Cavalry (Jones's Brigade) with 552 was the strongest of the 26 regiments and battalions, and the 2nd North Carolina Cavalry (Chambliss's Brigade) with 145 the weakest. The weakest of all was one of the five cavalry battalions, the 39th Virginia Cavalry Battalion (providing escorts), with 122. A Confederate cavalry regiment averaged 290.

The average strength Meade's 247 infantry regiments was 298, about 36 men (a company's worth) fewer than Lee's. The strongest Union regiment was the 1st Maryland (2nd Brigade, 1st Division, XII Corps) with 674; the smallest regiment represented on the battlefield was the 29th New York, which provided a company of 33 men as provost guard at the headquarters of the 2nd Division, XI Corps. To understand why a regiment "present ready for duty" was not able to put all its men in the front line, one need go no further than the 17th Maine (De Trobriand's Brigade). Its engaged strength was 350, but this was after 131 men (four companies at an average of 33 men per company) had been detached for duties other than that of rifleman. Those lost to the firing line included an officer, a sergeant and four corporals. Various supply or ammunition trains at brigade, division and corps headquarters had taken 60 men as wagoners and teamsters. Another 40 where involved in a range of medical duties, such as nurses at the divisional hospital, stretcher-bearers (mostly former musicians), assisting the regimental surgeon or working with the brigade ambulance corps. Provost guard duties at corps and divisional level absorbed 14, while 13 more were divided between four artillery batteries. The remainder had non-combat duties such as cattle guard, blacksmith, cook, orderly, saddler, clerk and even a corporal acting as corps postmaster. This regiment thus lost 27 percent of its rifle manpower to extraneous duties, with Company H detaching 21 men and Companies A, B, D, F and G all 12 or more.

Of the 33 Union cavalry regiments in the field the largest, with 645, was the 5th Michigan Cavalry and the smallest the squadron of 42 men of the Oneida New York Cavalry providing escorts and couriers at army headquarters. However, their average strength was 352, well above their rebel counterpart, as 18 Union cavalry regiments had 11 or 12 squadrons (companies).

Number of Regiments Raised During the War

According to Thomas Livermore in his study *Numbers and Losses in the American Civil War*, the North raised the equivalent of 2,047 regiments during the war, of which 1,696 were infantry, 272 were cavalry and 78 were artillery. These figures do not include the Veteran Reserve Corps.

By comparison, the South is estimated to have raised 1,009.

Battalions

The Rebels had a handful of smaller units – five independent infantry and five cavalry battalions that formed part of some brigades. The largest, with 400 (well above the strength of an average regiment), was the 3rd Maryland Battalion in Steuart's Brigade, and the smallest, providing the provost guard at Hill's Corps headquarters, was the 1st North Carolina Sharpshooters with 94 men. In theory each regiment of both armies consisted of two battalions (wings) commanded by the lieutenant-colonel and the major, but by the time of Gettysburg regiments had shrunk to such an extent that in practice a regiment seldom split into two on the battlefield.

Artillery

The Confederate artillery in action between July 1 and 3 was organized into three artillery brigades, one with each corps as its reserve, with each brigade consisting of two battalions of between three and six batteries. In addition, each of Lee's infantry divisions had its own artillery battalion of four batteries under command. With an average of fractionally over four pieces (guns or howitzers) in each of these 62 batteries, the infantry had the potential support of 250 pieces. The horse artillery (or artillery designated as such), in six batteries totaling 21 pieces, accompanied Stuart's cavalry at the outset of the campaign (see box, page 85, for how these guns were later deployed).

The Union artillery was organized into brigades of four to eight batteries, one brigade with each infantry corps plus an army reserve of a further five brigades, in all totaling nineteen batteries. Most Union batteries had six pieces (as against four with the Confederates), giving the Union infantry 56 batteries in support on the battlefield – a maximum of 312 pieces available. The Union horse artillery had 44 pieces in two brigades (eight batteries) plus a section of two guns (counted as a battery) permanently attached to Gregg's Brigade.

For a detailed breakdown of the types of ordnance in both armies, see Section Three: Artillery.

An Execution

Death by firing squad was supposedly the penalty for desertion. Countless thousands of men deserted during the Civil War, but only a minute fraction ever suffered the ultimate punishment. On June 25 a Private John Riley, a deserter three times over, of Garnett's Virginia Brigade was executed at the end of the day's march. We have a detailed description of another case that occurred three months after Gettysburg in the 1st Division of Sickles' III Corps. Again the man had deserted more than once and had given information to the enemy that resulted in the capture of some wagons (regarded as a more heinous crime than desertion). The execution was witnessed by the whole division formed up round three sides of a rectangle in two double ranks. The procession with the prisoner had to walk slowly between these ranks. First came the mounted provost marshal; then a band playing the Dead March from *Saul*; then twelve soldiers who would be deployed diagonally across the open end of the rectangle to prevent the condemned from making a break. Next came four men carrying the coffin, followed by the prisoner and chaplain with a single guard on either side; then the firing party of another twelve soldiers. Eleven of them had loaded muskets, one had a blank cartridge, all of which had been previously loaded by an officer and mixed up before being handed out. (This business of loading a blank cartridge to prevent the firer knowing if he was the one who fired the fatal shot is nonsense – if a musket has a ball loaded it kicks back into the shoulder, if loaded with a blank it does not, so the firer knows perfectly well the instant he pulls the trigger how his weapon was loaded.) Finally came another six soldiers acting as a reserve firing party.

The slow march completed, the prisoner sat on the end of his coffin, which was placed directly in front of a freshly dug grave in the center of the open end of the rectangle. The chaplain said a prayer, spoke to the prisoner, then said another prayer before the provost marshal stepped forward to blindfold the condemned man and to read out the General Order authorizing the execution. After moving to one side he gave the signal for the firing party to do their duty. A surgeon then examined the body to ensure death had occurred – if not he would be given the *coup de grâce* by the reserve firing party – and the division then marched past the corpse.

United States Regular Army

Both armies at Gettysburg were composed primarily of volunteer units raised by individual states – in the Confederacy law required that regiments from the same state must be brigaded together and did not allow soldiers enlisted in one state to serve in units of another. At the outbreak of war the U.S. Army was tiny, only around 16,000 strong, and its officer corps was seriously depleted when over 300 officers departed for the South. At Gettysburg professional soldiers provided less than 8 percent of Meade's army (see table below and box, page 69). The regular infantry regiments were largely grouped in the 1st and 2nd Brigades, 2nd Division, V Corps. They participated in the fighting on the evening of July 2 in the Wheatfield/Devil's Den area, while their artillery batteries and cavalry regiments served interspersed with their volunteer comrades on all parts of the battlefield.

STATE CONTRIBUTIONS

Of the twelve states that contributed to the Army of Northern Virginia at Gettysburg, three supplied a total of 48,143 men of all ranks. This represents nearly 68 percent of the army. These states were:

Virginia	20,776	(29%)
North Carolina	14,182	(20%)
Georgia	13,185	(19%)

From this 20,776, Virginia provided 41 infantry regiments (24 percent), 18 cavalry regiments (69 percent) and 40 artillery batteries (59 percent). The smallest state contribution came from Florida with just 739 (1 percent), with Tennessee a close second with 750 (1 percent). Full details are in the box on page 69.

The Army of the Potomac had troops from 18 states plus the U.S. Regular Army. The three largest contributors from these 19 provided a total 54,617, or 58.6 percent of the army. They were:

Pennsylvania	24,067	(26%)
New York	23,374	(25%)
U.S. Army	7,176	(8%)

Pennsylvania supplied 67 infantry regiments (27 percent), eight cavalry regiments (24 percent) and five artillery batteries (8 percent). New York, with slightly fewer men, fielded 70 infantry regiments (28 percent), six cavalry regiments (18 percent) and 15 artillery batteries (23 percent). These two states provided 51 percent of the Union troops at Gettysburg. The main U.S. Army contribution lay in the provision of artillery batteries – 22 out of 65, or 35 percent. Full details are in the box on page 69.

SUMMARY OF ENGAGED FORMATIONS AND UNITS

Formation	A.N.V.	A.P.	Remarks
Corps	3	8	In general terms an average A.N.V. corps was twice the size of a Union corps.
Divisions	10	22	Most Confederate divisions were almost twice as large as Union divisions at the start.
Brigades	42	58	The average strength of brigades was about the same in both armies.
Regiments/ battalions	172	247	Average strength: A.N.V. 334; A.P. 298.
Cavalry regiments/ battalions	26	33	Average strength: A.N.V. 290; A.P. 352.
Artillery batteries	68	65	Most A.N.V. batteries had 4 pieces, most A.P. had 6.
Artillery pieces	271	358	Most A.N.V. batteries had mixed types of ordnance, whereas most A.P. batteries had the same type.
Men	71,699	93,901	The overall ratio was approximately 7:9 in favor of the A.P.

Key to Order of Battle Diagrams

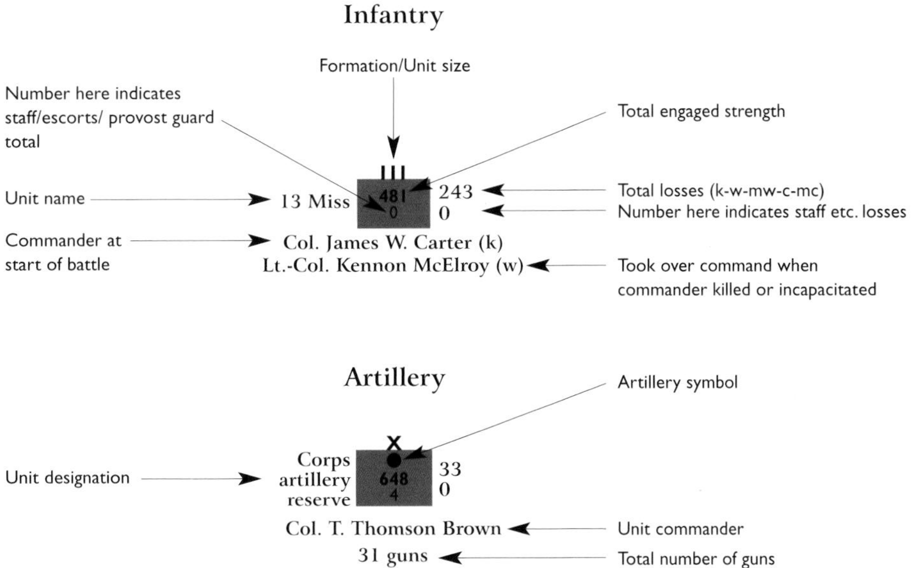

In the diagrams that follow the officer who commanded the formation or unit is placed immediately under the symbol. If he became a casualty the officer who assumed command is named below. In many cases several officers are listed, indicating several changes in command. In some instances where an officer has no casualty symbol after his name but was replaced as commander it indicates he was given other duties away from his regiment or assumed a higher command for some reason but later in the battle resumed his original position. In such cases his name will appear twice under his unit.

Key

k = killed
w = wounded
mw = mortally wounded
c = captured
mc = missing and captured

THE ARMY OF THE POTOMAC

Overall engaged strength July 1–3, 1863

XXXX 93386 / 1529 — 23054 / 4 *
Maj.-Gen. George G. Meade

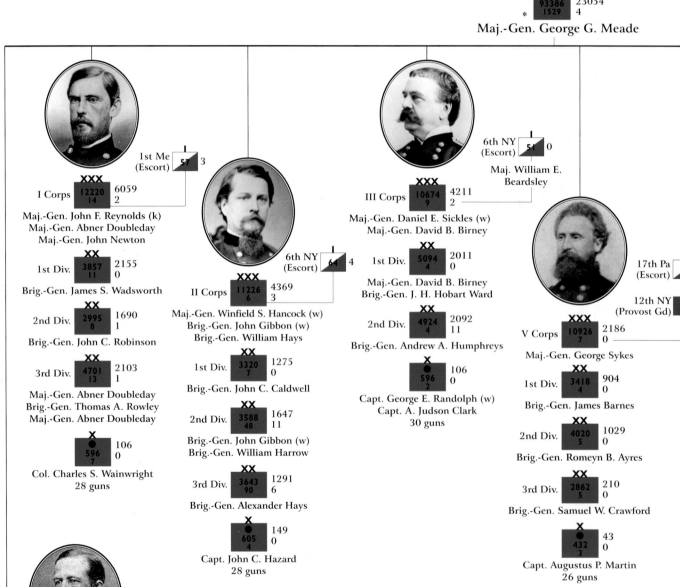

I Corps XXX 12220 / 14 — 6059 / 2
Maj.-Gen. John F. Reynolds (k)
Maj.-Gen. Abner Doubleday
Maj.-Gen. John Newton

1st Me (Escort) I 57 — 3

- 1st Div. XX 3857 / 11 — 2155 / 0 — Brig.-Gen. James S. Wadsworth
- 2nd Div. XX 2995 / 8 — 1690 / 1 — Brig.-Gen. John C. Robinson
- 3rd Div. XX 4701 / 13 — 2103 / 1 — Maj.-Gen. Abner Doubleday; Brig.-Gen. Thomas A. Rowley; Maj.-Gen. Abner Doubleday
- X 596 / 7 — 106 / 0 — Col. Charles S. Wainwright, 28 guns

II Corps XXX 11226 / 6 — 4369 / 3
Maj.-Gen. Winfield S. Hancock (w)
Brig.-Gen. John Gibbon (w)
Brig.-Gen. William Hays

6th NY (Escort) I 64 — 4

- 1st Div. XX 3320 / 7 — 1275 / 0 — Brig.-Gen. John C. Caldwell
- 2nd Div. XX 3588 / 48 — 1647 / 11 — Brig.-Gen. John Gibbon (w); Brig.-Gen. William Harrow
- 3rd Div. XX 3643 / 90 — 1291 / 6 — Brig.-Gen. Alexander Hays
- X 605 / 4 — 149 / 0 — Capt. John C. Hazard, 28 guns

III Corps XXX 10674 / 9 — 4211 / 2
Maj.-Gen. Daniel E. Sickles (w)
Maj.-Gen. David B. Birney

6th NY (Escort) I 51 — 0 — Maj. William E. Beardsley

- 1st Div. XX 5094 / 4 — 2011 / 0 — Maj.-Gen. David B. Birney; Brig.-Gen. J. H. Hobart Ward
- 2nd Div. XX 4924 / 4 — 2092 / 11 — Brig.-Gen. Andrew A. Humphreys
- X 596 / 2 — 106 / 0 — Capt. George E. Randolph (w); Capt. A. Judson Clark, 30 guns

V Corps XXX 10926 / 7 — 2186 / 0
Maj.-Gen. George Sykes

17th Pa (Escort) I 76
12th NY (Provost Gd) I 10

- 1st Div. XX 3418 / 4 — 904 / 0 — Brig.-Gen. James Barnes
- 2nd Div. XX 4020 / 5 — 1029 / 0 — Brig.-Gen. Romeyn B. Ayres
- 3rd Div. XX 2862 / 5 — 210 / 0 — Brig.-Gen. Samuel W. Crawford
- X 432 / 3 — 43 / 0 — Capt. Augustus P. Martin, 26 guns

Cavalry Corps XXX 11331 / 27 — 852 / 0
Maj.-Gen. Alfred Pleasonton

- 1st Div. XX 4069 / 4 — 418 / 0 — Brig.-Gen. John Buford
- 2nd Div. XX 2614 / 3 — 56 / 0 — Brig.-Gen. David McM. Gregg, 2 guns
- 3rd Div. XX 3852 / 3 — 355 / 0 — Brig.-Gen. Judson Kilpatrick
- 1st Horse Artillery XX 493 / 2 — 8 / 0 — Capt. James M. Robertson, 28 guns

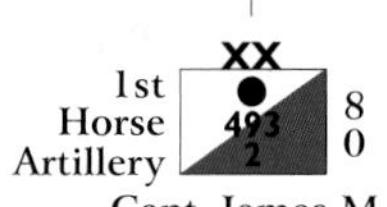

- 2nd Horse Artillery XX 276 / 2 — 1 / 0 — Capt. John C. Tidball, 16 guns

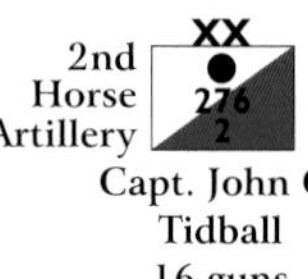

Statistics summary

Formation	*H.Q.*	*Infantry*	*Cavalry*	*Artillery*	*Total*	*Guns*	*Losses*	*Losses %*
Army HQ	1,529*	–	–	–	1,529	–	4 (staff)	–
I Reynolds	71	11,553	–	596	12,220	28	6,059	49.6
II Hancock	70	10,551	–	605	11,226	28	4,369	38.9
III Sickles	60	10,018	–	596	10,674	30	4,211	39.5
V Sykes	194	10,300	–	432	10,926	26	2,186	20.0
VI Sedgwick	99	13,038	–	937	14,074	48	242	1.7
XI Howard	137	8,501	–	604	9,242	26	3,807	41.2
XII Slocum	177	9,220	–	391	9,788	20	1,082	11.1
Pleasonton (Cav Corps)	27	–	10,535	769	11,331	46	852	7.5
Tyler (Art. Res.)	375	–	–	2,001	2,376	106	242	10.2
Totals	2,739	73,181	10,535	6,931	93,386	358	23,054	24.7

* This includes the army provost guard (1,142), escorts, couriers, signals and the 4th Massachusetts Cavalry (294) attached for various duties.

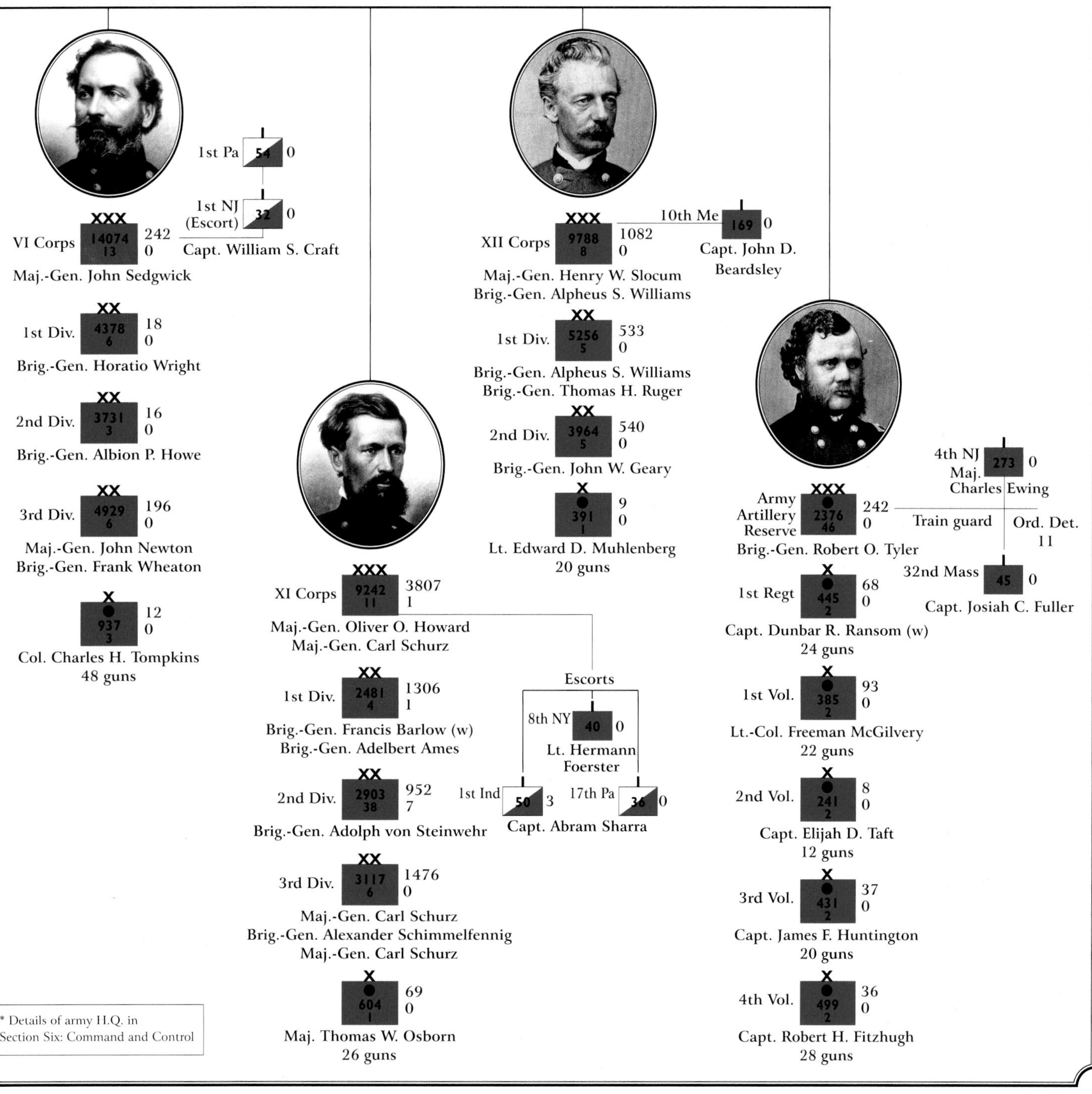

I CORPS 1ST DIVISION

Brig.-Gen. James S. Wadsworth U.S.V.

Divisional statistics summary

Senior commander casualties
1 x brigade commander w
2 x regimental commanders k
5 x regimental commanders w

Overall losses – percentage

Division	55.9
Meredith	63.0
Cutler	49.7

Some regimental statistics

Regiment	*Losses*	*Ranking (out of 247)*	*Percentage loss*
24th Michigan	363	1st	73.2
147th New York	296	5th	77.9
76th New York	234	12th	62.4
2nd Wisconsin	233	13th	77.2
84th New York	217	18th=	68.2

Action prior to Gettysburg

This division considered itself an elite veteran formation. It was the 1st Division of the I Corps and contained the famous Iron Brigade in their distinctive tall, black Hardee hats, which had been given its nickname by Maj.-Gen. Hooker after the battle at South Mountain. The division was renowned for its hard fighting and ability to sustain heavy losses without breaking. This had been well demonstrated at Groveton in August 1862 and at Antietam. However, both brigades were only lightly engaged at Fredericksburg and Chancellorsville.

Action at Gettysburg

By 10.00 a.m. on July 1 the division had marched up to within a mile of Gettysburg when it was ordered to double-quick across country to support Buford's cavalry in blocking the Confederate advance down the Chambersburg Pike. The leading brigade (Cutler's) was the first Union infantry formation onto the battlefield. The morning was spent in repelling heavy Rebel attacks north and south of the Pike and along McPherson's Ridge. The afternoon saw the division pull back first to Seminary Ridge and then through Gettysburg town to Cemetery Hill. It had lived up to its hard-fighting reputation and had gained time for reinforcements to arrive to consolidate the Union defensive position on Cemetery Hill. On July 2 it was sent to assist in the defense of Culp's Hill against Johnson's attacks that evening and early the following day. It paid a dreadful price for its efforts. Of the 247 Union regiments/battalions at Gettysburg five from this division were in the top eighteen with the highest numerical losses – see statistics above. This gave the division the highest total loss of any division in the army and the second highest percentage loss.

I CORPS 2ND DIVISION

Brig.-Gen. John C. Robinson U.S.A.

Divisional Badge

Divisional statistics summary

Senior commander casualties
1 x brigade commander w/c
3 x brigade commanders w
6 x regimental commanders w
2 x regimental commander c

Overall losses – percentage

Division	56.4 – the highest in the army
Paul	66.8
Baxter	45.7

Some regimental statistics

Regiment	*Losses*	*Ranking (out of 247)*	*Percentage loss*
94th New York	245	10th	59.6
16th Maine	232	14th	77.9

I Corps 2nd Div. XX 2995 8 1690 1
Brig.-Gen. John C. Robinson

1st Bde X 1536 3 1026 5
Brig.-Gen. Gabriel R. Paul (w)
Col. Samuel H. Leonard (w)
Col. Adrian R. Root (w/c)
Col. Richard Coulter (w)
Col. Peter Lyle

16th Me III 298 232
Col. Charles W. Tilden (c)
Maj. Archibald D. Leavitt

13th Mass III 284 185
Col. Samuel H. Leonard (w)
Lt.-Col. Walter Batchelder

94th NY III 411 245
Col. Adrian R. Root (w/c)
Maj. Samuel A. Moffett

104th NY III 285 194
Col. Gilbert G. Prey

107th Pa III 255 165
Lt.-Col. James MacThompson (w)
Capt. Emanuel D. Roath

2nd Bde X 1451 4 663 1
Brig.-Gen. Henry Baxter

12th Mass III 261 119
Col. James L. Bates (w)
Lt.-Col. David Allen

83rd NY III 199 82
Lt.-Col. Joseph A. Moesch

97th NY III 236 126
Col. Charles Wheelock (c)
Maj. Charles Northrup

Transferred to Paul's brigade, p.m. July 1 — 11th Pa III 270 132
Col. Richard Coulter (w)
Capt. Benjamin F. Haynes (w)
Capt. John B. Overmeyer

88th Pa III 273 110
Maj. Benezet F. Foust (w)
Capt. Henry Whiteside

90th Pa III 208 93
Col. Peter Lyle
Maj. Alfred S. Sellers

Action prior to Gettysburg

This was a division composed of veteran regiments but going into action under a divisional commander untested at this level. It had fought 2nd Manassas and lost heavily in covering the subsequent retreat. Again it was involved in fierce fighting at South Mountain, but it was at Antietam when it attacked piecemeal through a cornfield that it was heavily defeated, with crippling losses. Its assault on the Rebel line at Fredericksburg against the brigades of Pender and Thomas, whom it would face again at Gettysburg, was initially more successful but was eventually driven back. The division was only lightly engaged at Chancellorsville, its actions in no way testing the ability of the new divisional commander.

Action at Gettysburg

This division went into the battle well below the army's average divisional strength. Of the 22 divisions (including the cavalry), Robinson's ranked 18th in numerical strength. On July 1 it was in reserve but on the appearance of Confederates on Oak Hill Baxter's brigade was sent forward to extend the Union right. Paul's remained building breastworks then went forward as Rebel pressure increased. During the bitter fighting Baxter's men virtually destroyed Iverson's Brigade when they caught it in an ambush. The division was then forced to fight on two fronts and when the order to withdraw through Gettysburg arrived late the disordered retreat cost it over 1,000 casualties, many captured. It regrouped on Cemetery Hill then moved to the Zeigler's Grove area on Cemetery Ridge. On July 2 it initially returned to Cemetery Hill before being rushed that evening to reinforce the Union left, although it was not engaged. On July 3 it returned to Cemetery Hill before once more being sent to reinforce the Union line at Zeigler Grove. However, it arrived too late to participate in the repulse of Pickett's charge. The division started the battle with just under 3,000 and lost 56.4% (1,690), almost all on July 1. Two regiments were in the top 14 out of 247 in numerical losses – see above.

I Corps 3rd Division

Maj.-Gen. Abner Doubleday U.S.V.

Divisional Badge

Divisional statistics summary

Senior commander casualties
4 x brigade commanders w
1 x regimental commander k
6 x regimental commanders w

Overall losses – percentage

Division	44.7
Rowley	66.0
Stone	64.8
Stannard	18.0

Some regimental statistics

Regiment	*Losses*	*Ranking (out of 247)*	*Percentage loss*
151st Pennsylvania	337	2nd	72.2
149th Pennsylvania	336	3rd	74.7
150th Pennsylvania	264	6th	66.0
143rd Pennsylvania	253	7th	54.4

I Corps 3rd Div. XX 4701 13 — 2103 / 1
Maj.-Gen. Abner Doubleday
Brig.-Gen. Thomas A. Rowley
Maj.-Gen. Abner Doubleday

149th Pa Co. D — 60

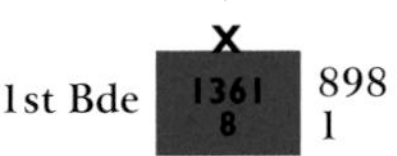

1st Bde X 1361 8 — 898 / 1
Brig.-Gen. Thomas A. Rowley
Col. Chapman Biddle (w)
Brig.-Gen. Thomas A. Rowley

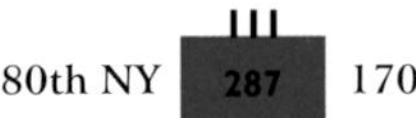

80th NY III 287 — 170
Col. Theodore R. Gates

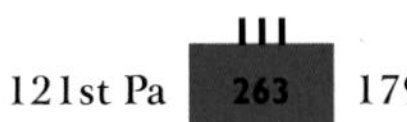

121st Pa III 263 — 179
Maj. Alexander Biddle
Col. Chapman Biddle (w)
Maj. Alexander Biddle

142nd Pa III 336 — 211
Col. Robert P. Cummins (k)
Lt.-Col. Alfred B. McCalmont

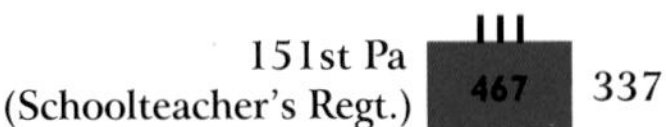

151st Pa (Schoolteacher's Regt.) III 467 — 337
Lt.-Col. George I. McFarland (w)
Capt. Walter I. Owens
Col. Harrison Allen

2nd Bde (Bucktails) X 1317 2 — 853 / 0
Col. Roy Stone (w)
Col. Langhorne Wister (w)
Col. Edmund L. Dana

143rd Pa III 465 — 253
Col. Edmund L. Dana
Lt.-Col. John D. Musser

149th Pa III 450 — 336
Lt.-Col. Walton Dwight (w)
Capt. James Glenn

150th Pa III 400 — 264
Col. Langhorne Wister (w)
Lt.-Col. Henry S. Huidekoper (w)
Capt. Cornelius C. Widdis

3rd Bde (Paper Collar Brigade*) X 1950 6 — 351 / 2
Brig.-Gen. George J. Stannard (w)
Col. Francis V. Randall

13th Vt III 636 — 123
Col. Francis V. Randall
Lt.-Col. William D. Munson (w)
Maj. Joseph J. Boynton

14th Vt III 647 — 107
Col. William T. Nicholls

16th Vt III 661 — 119
Col. Wheelock G. Veazey

* Nicknamed the "Paper Collar" Brigade because they were enlisted for only 9 months and their uniforms looked new and clean.

Action prior to Gettysburg

The old 3rd Division had a good fighting reputation, primarily won on the battlefields of Antietam and Fredericksburg. At the latter it had attacked up the slope with commendable courage and determination but had been beaten back with appalling losses. The damage was so severe that the division was removed from the Army of the Potomac and sent to recover in the Washington defenses. The division that marched to Gettysburg had been completely reorganized in February 1863 with the addition of two green brigades. The only regiment with experience was the 80th New York, many of the rest being recently joined 9-month men.

Action at Gettysburg

At the start of July 1 Brig.-Gen. Rowley led the division as Reynolds was commanding the army's entire left wing and so Doubleday was acting as I Corps commander. Initially Stannard's Brigade was left south of the battlefield guarding the corps trains while the other two hurried to Gettysburg to deploy on either side of the Iron Brigade. Arriving at around 11:30 a.m. they missed the first assaults by Heth's Division on the Union line along McPherson's Ridge. However, the two brigades were heavily engaged during the afternoon as Confederate pressure increased and were eventually forced back to a new line on Seminary Ridge. There, along with the Iron Brigade and artillery deployed wheel-to-wheel, they beat off assaults by Pender's Division until Perrin's Brigade joined in and outflanked them. There followed a disorganized retreat through the town to Cemetery Hill, where the remnants regrouped and were reinforced by Stannard's Brigade. On July 2 the division rested until early evening when they were rushed to the Union left to support Sickles' Corps, although only the 13th Vermont was engaged in driving some Rebels of Wright's Brigade from a toehold on Cemetery Ridge. The next day the division was involved in defeating Pickett's and Pettigrew's charge, in which Stannard's flank attack played a decisive part. The division went into action the sixth strongest of the 22 in the army but came out having lost some 45%, Rowley losing 66% and Stone almost 65%. Four Pennsylvania regiments were in the top seven in terms of losses out of 247 regiments deployed – see statistics above. This division had the second highest total loss of the army.

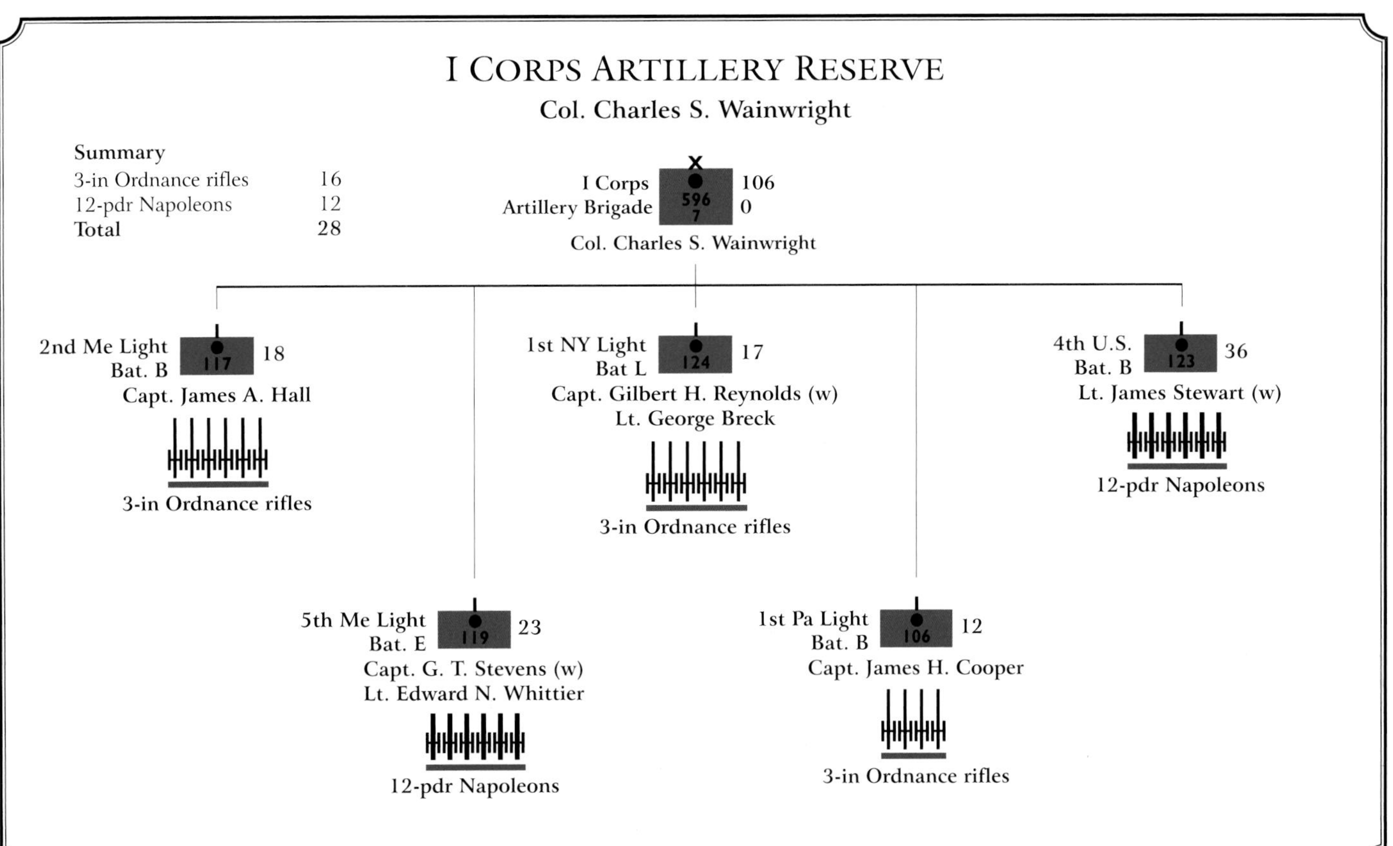
I CORPS ARTILLERY RESERVE
Col. Charles S. Wainwright
Summary
3-in Ordnance rifles 16
12-pdr Napoleons 12
Total 28
I Corps
Artillery Brigade
596
7
106
0
Col. Charles S. Wainwright
2nd Me Light
Bat. B
117
18
Capt. James A. Hall
3-in Ordnance rifles
1st NY Light
Bat L
124
17
Capt. Gilbert H. Reynolds (w)
Lt. George Breck
3-in Ordnance rifles
4th U.S.
Bat. B
123
36
Lt. James Stewart (w)
12-pdr Napoleons
5th Me Light
Bat. E
119
23
Capt. G. T. Stevens (w)
Lt. Edward N. Whittier
12-pdr Napoleons
1st Pa Light
Bat. B
106
12
Capt. James H. Cooper
3-in Ordnance rifles

II Corps 1st Division

Brig.-Gen. John C. Caldwell U.S.V.

Divisional Badge

Divisional statistics summary

Senior commander casualties
1 x brigade commander k
1 x brigade commander mw
1 x brigade commander w
2 x regimental commanders k
8 x regimental commanders w

Overall losses – percentage

Division	38.4
Cross	38.7
Kelly	37.2
Zook	36.7
Brook	45.7

Note: Out of 58 brigades in the Army of the Potomac at the start of the battle, the weakest numerically (at 58th) was the Irish Brigade, then Brooke's (55th), Cross's (54th) and Zook's (51st).

II Corps 1st Div. XX 3320 7 — 1275 0
Brig.-Gen. John C. Caldwell

116th Pa Co. B — 32
53rd Pa Cos. A, B & K — 70

1st Bde X 853 3 — 330 1
Col. Edward E. Cross (mw)
Col. H. Boyd McKeen

5th NH — 179 — 80
Lt.-Col. Charles E. Hapgood

61st NY — 104 — 62
Lt.-Col. K. Oscar Broady

81st Pa — 175 — 62
Col. H. Boyd McKeen
Lt.-Col. Amos Stroh

148th Pa — 392 — 125
Lt.-Col. Robert McFarlane

2nd Bde (Irish Brigade) X 532 2 — 198 0
Col. Patrick Kelly

28th Mass — 224 — 100
Col. R. Byrnes

63rd NY Cos. A & B — 75 — 23
Lt.-Col. Richard C. Bentley (w)
Capt. Thomas Touhy

69th NY Cos. A & B — 75 — 25
Capt. Richard Moroney (w)
Lt. James J. Smith

88th NY Cos. A & B — 90 — 28
Capt. Dennis F. Burke

116th Pa Cos. A, C & D — 66 — 22
Maj. St. Clair A. Mulholland

3rd Bde X 975 4 — 358 1
Brig.-Gen. Samuel K. Zook (k)
Lt.-Col. John Fraser

52nd NY — 134 — 38
Lt.-Col. G. C. Freudenberg (w)
Capt. William M. Scherrer

57th NY — 175 — 34
Lt.-Col. Alfred B. Chapman

66th NY — 147 — 44
Col. Orlando H. Morris (w)
Lt.-Col. John S. Hammell (w)
Maj. Peter Nelson

140th Pa — 515 — 241
Col. Richard P. Roberts (k)
Lt.-Col. John Fraser

4th Bde X 851 1 — 389 0
Col. John R. Brooke (w)

27th Conn Cos. A & B — 75 — 37
Lt.-Col. Henry Merwin (k)
Maj. James H. Coburn

2nd Del — 234 — 84
Col. William P. Baily
Capt. Charles H. Christman

64th NY — 204 — 98
Col. Daniel G. Bingham (w)
Maj. Leman W. Bradley

53rd Pa — 135 — 80
Lt.-Col. Richard McMichael

145th Pa — 202 — 90
Col. Hiram L. Brown (w)
Capt. John W. Reynolds (w)
Capt. Moses Oliver

Action prior to Gettysburg

By July 1863 this division had accumulated more casualties than any other division in the army. It had fought hard during the Peninsular campaign and at the bloodbath that was Antietam. It had charged the Marye Heights at Fredericksburg only to be thrown back with over 2,000 losses – about half the total casualties of II Corps. Over 1,000 more were lost at Chancellorsville. These appalling losses had not been made good by Gettysburg, which accounts for the fact that although it was the only division in the army with four brigades, all were less than 1,000 strong.

Action at Gettysburg

Not only was this division one of the weakest in Meade's army (the Irish Brigade being the weakest of all) but also its regiments came from six different states, four of them mustering fewer than 100 men – the established size of a company. The division arrived behind the main Union position in the early hours of July 2 and camped across the Taneytown Road. It was later moved forward to relieve Robinson's Division (I Corps) on Cemetery Ridge and there spent a quiet morning and afternoon. In late afternoon there was confusion and frustration as the division was rushed toward the Union left as reinforcements, only to be ordered back after half a mile. However, within a short time it was again summoned to the left. This time the last half mile was at the double-quick because the situation around the Wheatfield and Stony Hill was desperate as the thin Union line sought to hold back Hood's divisional assault. The leading brigade arrived at around 5:30 p.m. and was thrown straight into the action with other brigades joining as they arrived. The division was sucked into the fearful, close-quarter struggle for the Wheatfield and at one stage succeeded in driving the Rebels off Stony Hill. However, increasing pressure and more losses eventually forced the Union line back and the division re-formed again on Cemetery Ridge. On July 3 many men were kept busy building breastworks but the division was by now so small that it played little part in the repulse of Pickett's charge.

II CORPS 2ND DIVISION

Brig.-Gen. John F. Gibbon U.S.V.

Divisional Badge

Divisional statistics summary

Senior commander casualties

1 x divisional commander w
1 x brigade commander w
4 x regimental commanders k
3 x regimental commanders mw
3 x regimental commanders w

Overall losses – percentage

Division	45.9
Harrow	57.1
Webb	40.1
Hall	40.9

II Corps 2nd Div. XX 3588 6 1647 3
Brig.-Gen. John F. Gibbon (w)
Brig.-Gen. William Harrow

1st Co. Mass S.S. 42 8

Provost Guard
1st Minn Co. C 48

Capt. William Plumer

1st Bde X 1346 3 768 1
Brig.-Gen. William Harrow
Col. Francis Heath

19th Me III 439 203
Col. Francis Heath
Lt.-Col. Henry W. Cunningham

15th Mass III 239 148
Col. George H. Ward (mw)
Lt.-Col. George C. Joslin

1st Minn III 330 224
Col. William Colvill (w)
Capt. Nathan S. Messick (k)
Capt. Henry C. Coates

82nd NY III 335 192
Lt.-Col. James Huston (k)
Capt. John Darrow

2nd Bde (Philadelphia Brigade) X 1224 3+16 *491 0
Brig.-Gen. Alexander Webb (w)

69th Pa III 284 137
Col. Dennis O'Kane (k)
Capt. William Davis

71st Pa III 261 98
Col. Richard P. Smith

72nd Pa III 380 192
Col. DeWitt C. Baxter (w)
Lt.-Col. Theodor Hesser

106th Pa III 280 64
Lt.-Col. William L. Curry

* 16 in the Band

3rd Bde X 922 2 377 0
Col. Norman Hall

19th Mass III 163 77
Col. Arthur F. Devereux

20th Mass III 243 127
Col. Paul J. Revere (mw)
Lt.-Col. George M. Macy (w)
Capt. Henry L. Abbott

7th Mich III 165 65
Lt.-Col. Amos E. Steele (k)
Maj. Silvanus W. Curtis

42nd NY III 197 74
Col. James J. Mallon

59th NY III 152 34
Lt.-Col. Max A. Thoman (mw)
Capt. William McFadden

Action prior to Gettysburg

Very much a veteran division, having fought in most battles from the Peninsula to Chancellorsville. It lost heavily at Antietam when, during the advance on Dunker Church, it was attacked on three sides and overwhelmed, with the loss of some 2,200 men. A futile assault on Marye Heights at Fredericksburg cost the division another 900 casualties. Perhaps fortunately, it was only lightly engaged at Chancellorsville. On June 29 the division had a crippling march of 33 miles that ended at Uniontown, Maryland, 20 miles short of Gettysburg.

Action at Gettysburg

The division marched to the battlefield on July 1, arriving near Little Round Top around 9:00 p.m. It had moved into position on Cemetery Hill by 10:00 a.m. the next day. In the late afternoon on July 2 the 15th Massachusetts and 82nd New York were sent forward to line the Emmitsburg Road. There they faced the brunt of Wright's Rebel assault and were overwhelmed. The division was further split when another four regiments (19th Massachusetts, 42nd New York, 19th Maine and 1st Minnesota) were rushed to bolster III Corps' line on the left. The 2nd Brigade (Webb's Pennsylvanians) played a major role in repulsing Wright's attack, after which they too were broken up, the 106th Pennsylvania going to Cemetery Hill and the 71st Pennsylvania to Culp's Hill to assist Greene's Brigade. Regrettably, Col. Smith declined to join the action and retired back to Cemetery Ridge without orders. On July 3 the division was positioned in the center of the Union line on Cemetery Ridge and therefore bore the brunt of Pickett's charge in the afternoon.

II Corps 3rd Division

Brig.-Gen. Alexander Hays U.S.V.

Divisional Badge

Divisional statistics summary

Senior commander casualties
2 x brigade commanders k
1 x brigade commander w
1 x regimental commander k
5 x regimental commanders w

Overall losses – percentage

Division	35.4
Carroll	21.6
Smyth	33.7
Willard	47.3

Some regimental statistics

Regiment	*Losses*	*Ranking (out of 247)*	*Percentage loss*
11th New York	249	9th	63.8
126th New York	231	15th	50.8

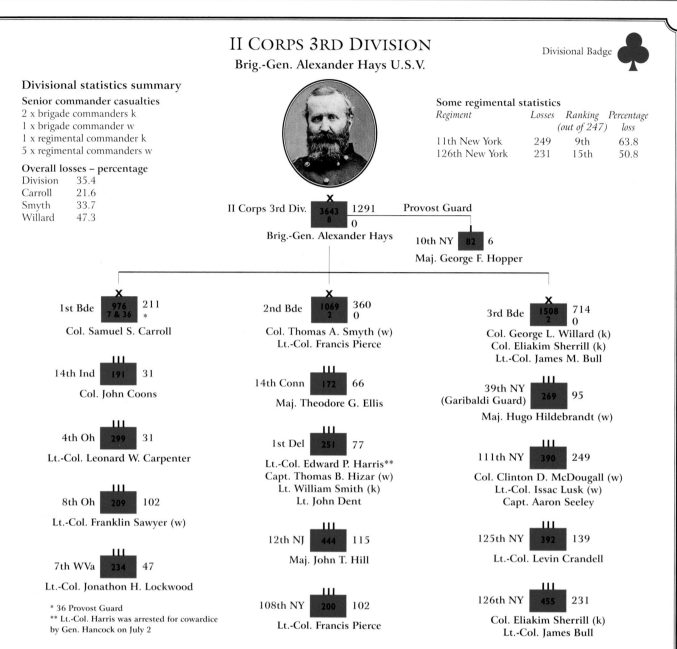

II Corps 3rd Div. 3643 / 8 — 1291 / 0
Brig.-Gen. Alexander Hays

Provost Guard
10th NY 82 — 6
Maj. George F. Hopper

1st Bde 976 / 7 & 36 — 211 / *
Col. Samuel S. Carroll

14th Ind 191 — 31
Col. John Coons

4th Oh 299 — 31
Lt.-Col. Leonard W. Carpenter

8th Oh 209 — 102
Lt.-Col. Franklin Sawyer (w)

7th WVa 234 — 47
Lt.-Col. Jonathon H. Lockwood

2nd Bde 1069 / 2 — 360 / 0
Col. Thomas A. Smyth (w)
Lt.-Col. Francis Pierce

14th Conn 172 — 66
Maj. Theodore G. Ellis

1st Del 251 — 77
Lt.-Col. Edward P. Harris**
Capt. Thomas B. Hizar (w)
Lt. William Smith (k)
Lt. John Dent

12th NJ 444 — 115
Maj. John T. Hill

108th NY 200 — 102
Lt.-Col. Francis Pierce

3rd Bde 1508 / 2 — 714 / 0
Col. George L. Willard (k)
Col. Eliakim Sherrill (k)
Lt.-Col. James M. Bull

39th NY (Garibaldi Guard) 269 — 95
Maj. Hugo Hildebrandt (w)

111th NY 390 — 249
Col. Clinton D. McDougall (w)
Lt.-Col. Issac Lusk (w)
Capt. Aaron Seeley

125th NY 392 — 139
Lt.-Col. Levin Crandell

126th NY 455 — 231
Col. Eliakim Sherrill (k)
Lt.-Col. James Bull

* 36 Provost Guard
** Lt.-Col. Harris was arrested for cowardice by Gen. Hancock on July 2

Action prior to Gettysburg

The division had fought hard at Antietam but at a cost of some 1,750 casualties. It led the II Corps assault up the slope of Marye's Heights at Fredericksburg with disastrous results, as it was thrown back with the loss of another 1,150. Although fighting defensively at Chancellorsville, 700 more fell. When it marched to Gettysburg, while two brigades (1st and 2nd) were veteran formations, the same could not be said for the 3rd Brigade of New Yorkers. It held two derogatory nicknames – the "Harper's Ferry Brigade" and the "Bandbox Soldiers". The former recalled its ignominious surrender at Harper's Ferry during the Antietam campaign in September 1862, and the latter the fact that its operational duties ever since had been pottering around in the Washington defenses. Like most formations, the division had much hard marching en route to Gettysburg, including a 30-miler in 24 hours (June 29–30). Its commander, Brig.-Gen. Hays, was inexperienced at this level, having been appointed only three days before the battle. A serious clash would be very much a test of all the commanders, as not only was the divisional commander new to the job but all three brigades were commanded by colonels.

Action at Gettysburg

The division arrived near Little Round Top between 8:00 and 9:00 p.m. on July 1. On the 2nd it deployed onto Cemetery Ridge between Zeigler's Grove and the Copse of Trees. That afternoon the 2nd Brigade sent several units forward to contest the occupation of Bliss Farm – an action that continued on the morning of July 3 until Hays ordered the buildings burned. On July 2 Willard's Brigade was sent as reinforcements on the left of the Union line, arriving just in time to counterattack successfully Barksdale's assault on Cemetery Ridge. That evening it was Carroll's turn to be rushed in the opposite direction to Cemetery Hill to drive back a dangerous Rebel attack by Avery's Brigade. On July 3 the division played a major part in stopping and hurling back Pettigrew's and Trimble's six-brigade assault made in conjunction with Pickett's charge. The 8th Ohio's attack on the Confederate left flank was crucial in this success. The division performed exceptionally well at Gettysburg, with the New Yorkers wiping out the stigma of Harper's Ferry – see "Action prior to Gettysburg."

II CORPS ARTILLERY RESERVE

Capt. John C. Hazard

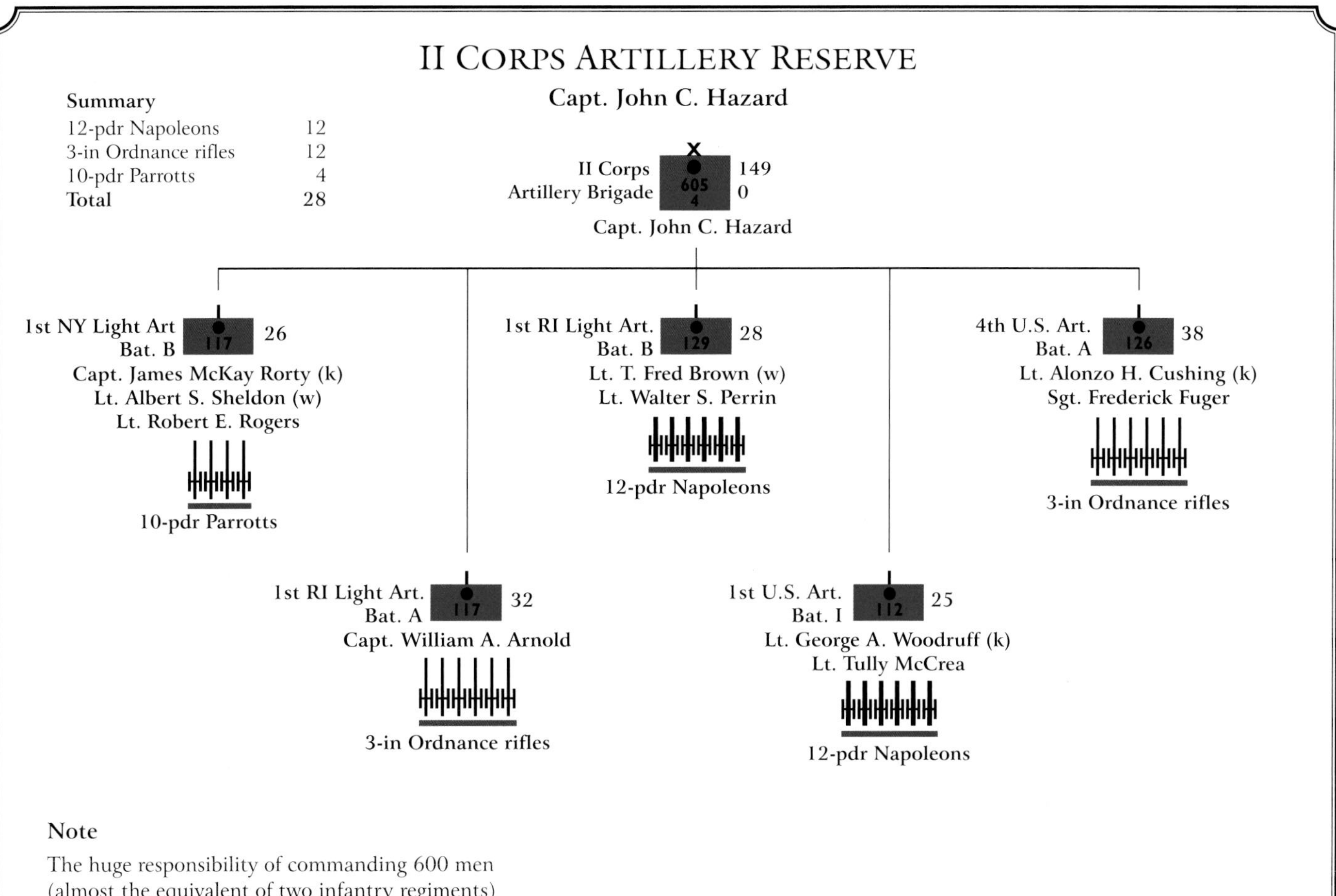

Note

The huge responsibility of commanding 600 men (almost the equivalent of two infantry regiments) and 28 guns was held by a junior officer – a captain.

III CORPS 1ST DIVISION

Maj.-Gen. David B. Birney U.S.V.

Divisional Badge

Divisional statistics summary

Senior commander casualties
1 x brigade commander w/c
2 x regimental commanders k
7 x regimental commanders w
1 x regimental commander c

Overall losses – percentage

Division	39.5
Graham	48.8
Ward	35.7
De Trobriand	35.3

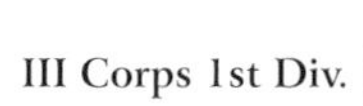

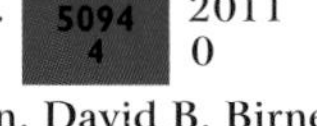

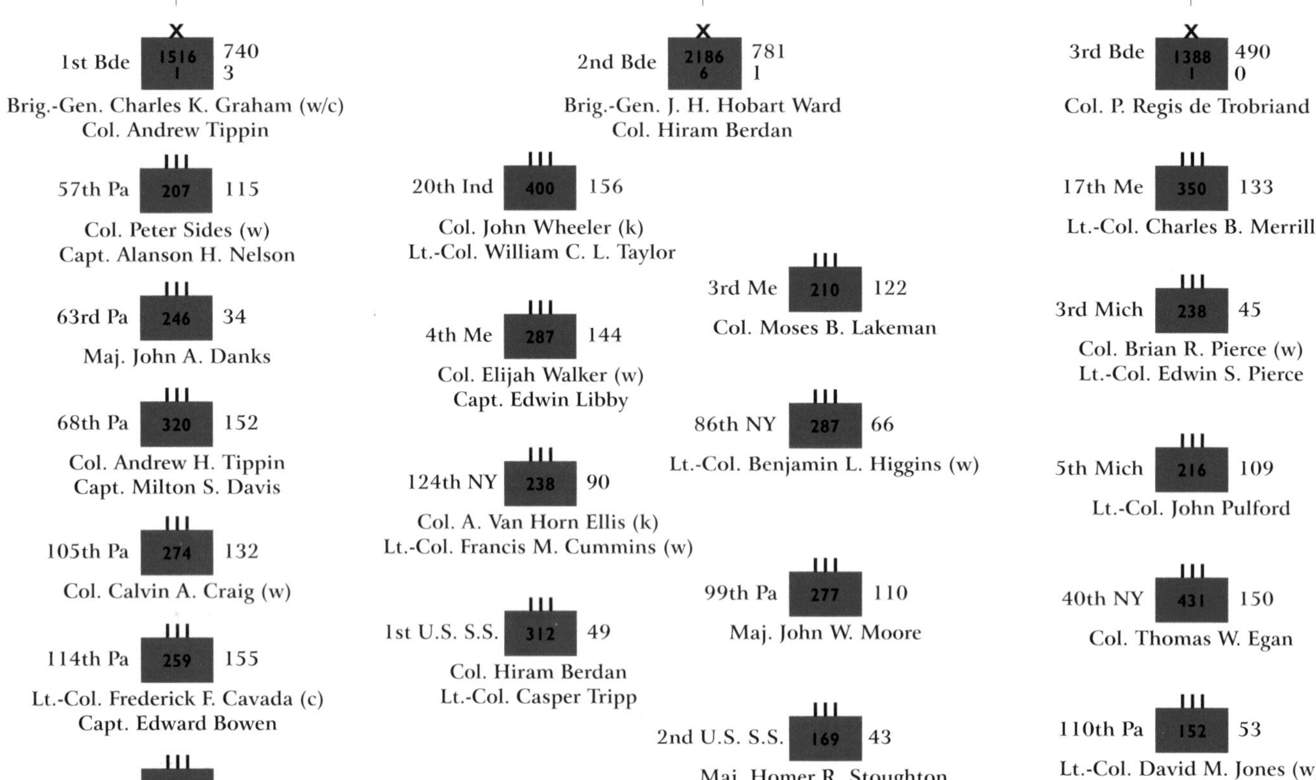

Action prior to Gettysburg

The division fought hard to earn its veteran status in the Peninsular campaign (Williamsburg and Fair Oaks) and then during the Seven Days Battles in June/July 1862 (Oak Grove, Glendale and Malvern Hill). As a reinforcement formation to Pope's Army of Virginia it was engaged on the Union right flank at 2nd Manassas. On September 1, 1862, at the Battle of Chantilly, it was so battered that it had to be sent to the Washington defenses to recover. Birney assumed command just prior to the Antietam campaign but the division did not participate. Although it lost over 900 men at Fredericksburg, Birney was charged with dereliction of duty for not properly supporting Meade's attack – he was later exonerated. Heavy losses (more than any other division) at Chancellorsville had been made good by Gettysburg so it went into action numerically the second strongest division in the Army of the Potomac.

Action at Gettysburg

On July 2 the division took up its position on the left center of the Union line on Cemetery Ridge with its left connected to Little Round Top. Its only action in that position that day was the sending of Berdan's Sharpshooters and the 3rd Maine forward to probe Seminary Ridge, where they discovered the build-up of Rebels in Pitzer's Wood. Later Sickles, against specific orders, pushed the division, along with the remainder of III Corps, forward to form what became the Sickles' salient threequarters of a mile in front of the main line. At around 4:00 p.m. Hood's Division attacked and Birney's command was embroiled in the confused and bitter fighting that stretched from the Devil's Den, the Rose Woods, Stony Hill and the bloodbath that was the Wheatfield to the Peach Orchard. Eventually III Corps was forced back to Cemetery Ridge. On July 3 it remained in reserve near the Taneytown Road. This was the fourth division to receive over 2,000 casualties at the battle.

III CORPS 2ND DIVISION

Brig.-Gen. Andrew A. Humphreys U.S.A.

Divisional Badge 

Divisional statistics summary

Senior commander casualties
1 x regimental commander k
1 x regimental commander mw
11 x regimental commanders w

Overall losses – percentage

Division	42.5
Carr	46.0
Brewster	42.4
Burling	37.6

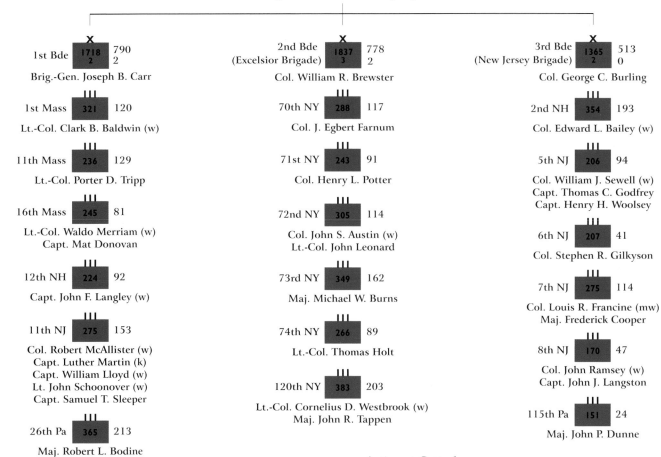

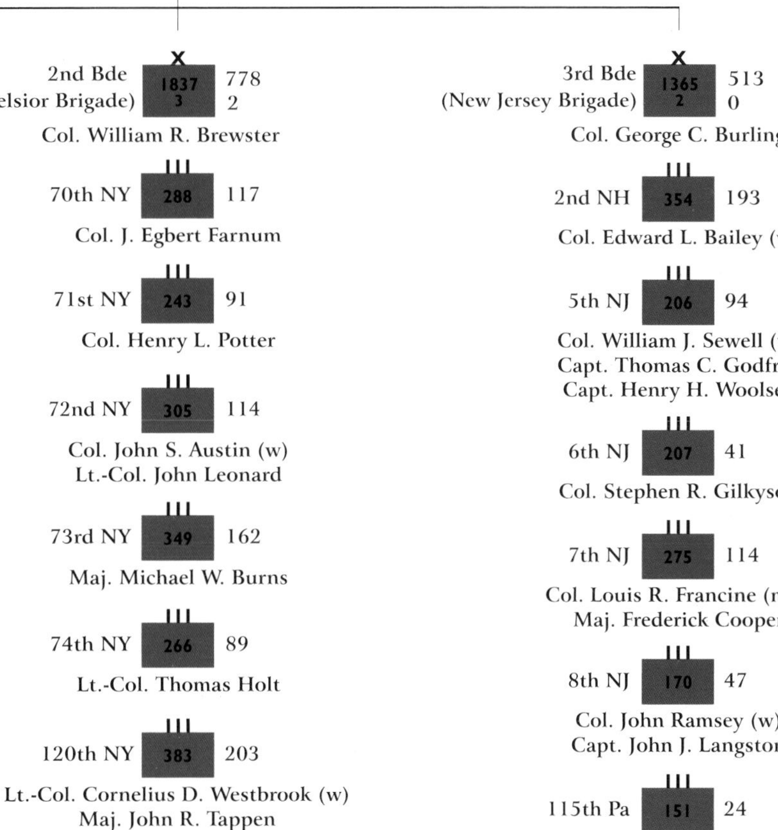

III Corps 2nd Div. XX 4924 / 4 — 2092 / 11
Brig.-Gen. Andrew A. Humphreys

1st Bde X 1718 / 2 — 790 / 2
Brig.-Gen. Joseph B. Carr

- 1st Mass III 321 — 120
  Lt.-Col. Clark B. Baldwin (w)
- 11th Mass III 236 — 129
  Lt.-Col. Porter D. Tripp
- 16th Mass III 245 — 81
  Lt.-Col. Waldo Merriam (w)
  Capt. Mat Donovan
- 12th NH III 224 — 92
  Capt. John F. Langley (w)
- 11th NJ III 275 — 153
  Col. Robert McAllister (w)
  Capt. Luther Martin (k)
  Capt. William Lloyd (w)
  Lt. John Schoonover (w)
  Capt. Samuel T. Sleeper
- 26th Pa III 365 — 213
  Maj. Robert L. Bodine
- 84th Pa III 240 — Not engaged (guarding trains)
  Lt.-Col. Milton Opp

2nd Bde (Excelsior Brigade) X 1837 / 3 — 778 / 2
Col. William R. Brewster

- 70th NY III 288 — 117
  Col. J. Egbert Farnum
- 71st NY III 243 — 91
  Col. Henry L. Potter
- 72nd NY III 305 — 114
  Col. John S. Austin (w)
  Lt.-Col. John Leonard
- 73rd NY III 349 — 162
  Maj. Michael W. Burns
- 74th NY III 266 — 89
  Lt.-Col. Thomas Holt
- 120th NY III 383 — 203
  Lt.-Col. Cornelius D. Westbrook (w)
  Maj. John R. Tappen

3rd Bde (New Jersey Brigade) X 1365 / 2 — 513 / 0
Col. George C. Burling

- 2nd NH III 354 — 193
  Col. Edward L. Bailey (w)
- 5th NJ III 206 — 94
  Col. William J. Sewell (w)
  Capt. Thomas C. Godfrey
  Capt. Henry H. Woolsey
- 6th NJ III 207 — 41
  Col. Stephen R. Gilkyson
- 7th NJ III 275 — 114
  Col. Louis R. Francine (mw)
  Maj. Frederick Cooper
- 8th NJ III 170 — 47
  Col. John Ramsey (w)
  Capt. John J. Langston
- 115th Pa III 151 — 24
  Maj. John P. Dunne

Action prior to Gettysburg

This division included two of the army's best-known brigades, the Excelsior and the New Jersey. The Peninsular campaign took a fearful toll of the division, including threequarters of III Corps casualties at Williamsburg in May 1862. It was heavily engaged in the battles outside Richmond before being withdrawn from the Peninsula in August, only to be involved at Bristoe Station and 2nd Manassas, where it attacked Stonewall Jackson's line along the railway embankment, which involved heavy hand-to-hand fighting. At the start of that campaign the division had mustered 10,000 men and had received 3,000 reinforcements during it, but after 2nd Manassas only 2,400 were drawing rations. Desperately in need of rest and refitting, it did not participate at Antietam and remained in reserve at Fredericksburg, but lost heavily again at Chancellorsville.

Action at Gettysburg

The division arrived in the vicinity of Gettysburg around 2:00 a.m. on July 2 but was not complete until rejoined by the 3rd Brigade at 9:00 a.m. Initially deployed on the left of Cemetery Ridge, it was later pushed forward to defend the line of the Emmitsburg Road on the orders of the corps commander, Sickles. The brigades of Carr and Brewster formed the apex of Sickles' controversial salient, so bearing the brunt of the Rebel attack that afternoon. Humphreys' front along the road was hit by the Confederate division of Anderson and his left flank at the Peach Orchard and at Wheatfield Road by Barksdale's Brigade (McLaws' Division). The steadily increasing Confederate pressure eventually forced the division, along with the rest of III Corps, back to Cemetery Ridge – the order to retire infuriating Humphreys, who maintained to his dying day that if his division had not been messed about and split up the position could have been held. On July 3 it was in reserve and so did not participate in Pickett's repulse. It ranked third among the four Union divisions to receive over 2,000 casualties at Gettysburg.

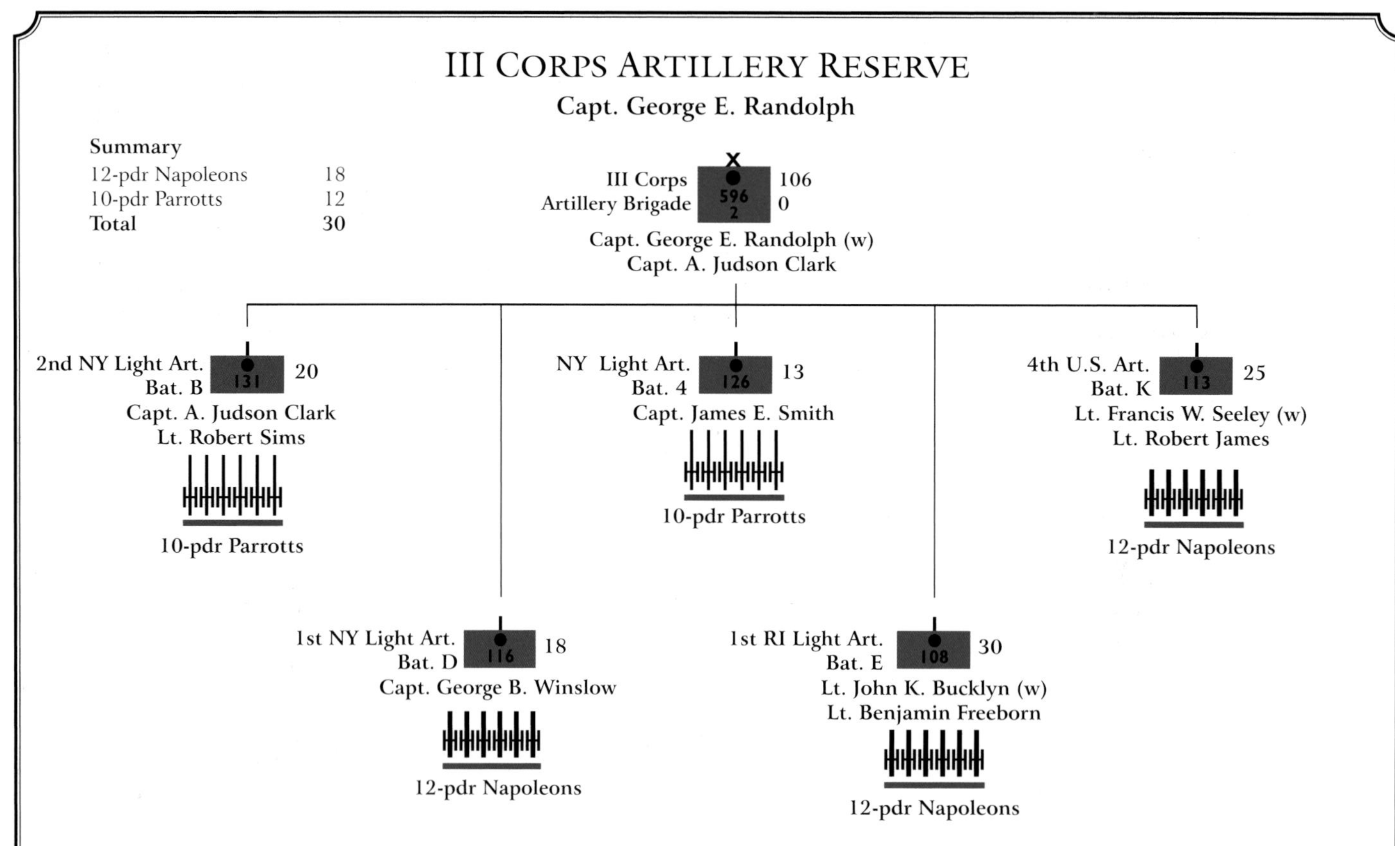
III CORPS ARTILLERY RESERVE
Capt. George E. Randolph
Summary
12-pdr Napoleons 18
10-pdr Parrotts 12
Total 30
III Corps Artillery Brigade 596 2 106 0
Capt. George E. Randolph (w)
Capt. A. Judson Clark
2nd NY Light Art. Bat. B 131 20
Capt. A. Judson Clark
Lt. Robert Sims
10-pdr Parrotts
NY Light Art. Bat. 4 126 13
Capt. James E. Smith
10-pdr Parrotts
4th U.S. Art. Bat. K 113 25
Lt. Francis W. Seeley (w)
Lt. Robert James
12-pdr Napoleons
1st NY Light Art. Bat. D 116 18
Capt. George B. Winslow
12-pdr Napoleons
1st RI Light Art. Bat. E 108 30
Lt. John K. Bucklyn (w)
Lt. Benjamin Freeborn
12-pdr Napoleons

V CORPS 1ST DIVISION

Brig.-Gen. James Barnes U.S.V.

Divisional Badge

Divisional statistics summary

Senior commander casualties
1 x divisional commander w
1 x brigade commander mw
1 x regimental commander mw
4 x regimental commanders w

Overall losses – percentage

Division	26.4
Tilton	19.1
Sweitzer	30.0
Vincent	26.3

Brigade/regimental statistics
Col. Tilton's Brigade was the smallest bar one of the 58 brigades in the Army of the Potomac, as the 18th and 22nd Massachusetts and 1st Michigan had an average strength of a mere 140 – hardly enough for two companies. Of the 247 Union regiments engaged at Gettysburg, only 17 were smaller.

V Corps 1st Div. XX 3418 4 904 0
Brig.-Gen. James Barnes
(w, but continued in command)

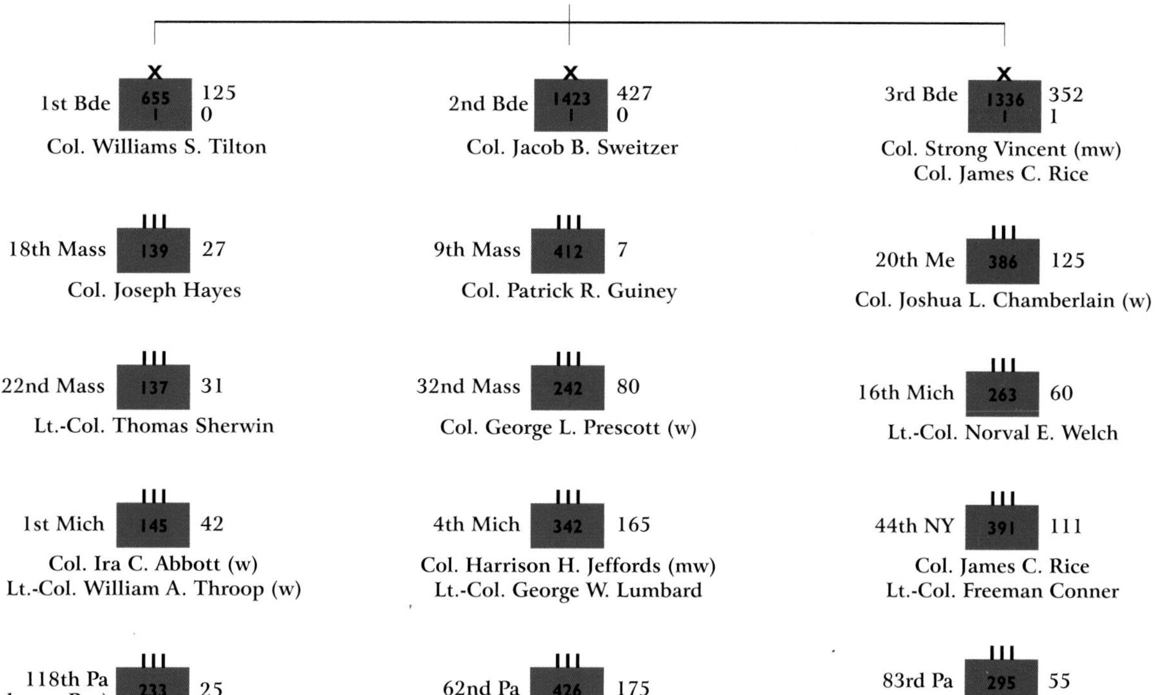

Action prior to Gettysburg

The division had participated in the battles around Richmond and had sustained over 3,000 casualties during the Seven Days Battles in June 1862. Two brigades had fought at 2nd Manassas, losing some 600 men apiece. The pointless slaughter attempting to storm Marye's Heights at Fredericksburg cost the division another 900. Perhaps fortunately, it was only lightly engaged at Chancellorsville.

Action at Gettysburg

Brig.-Gen. Barnes's only experience of serious combat had been the disastrous assault at Fredericksburg, so when he arrived with his division near Wolf Hill on the morning of July 2 there was perhaps a little apprehension as to how he would make out. The men had just marched for 36 hours and many were reeling with fatigue. That afternoon they were ordered to support III Corps, whose forward deployment had caused serious difficulties. As the division moved forward Brig.-Gen. Warren's observations of the absence of Union troops on Little Round Top caused Vincent's Brigade to peel off from the line of march and double-quick to occupy the hill. The remaining brigades moved on toward the desperate struggle going on around the Wheatfield. However, Barnes became anxious about a threat to his right flank and withdrew the brigades. Only the frantic pleading of Caldwell persuaded Barnes to release his 2nd Brigade to enter the cauldron of the Wheatfield again. Eventually, like all other formations caught up in Sickles' salient, these two brigades were driven back. Meanwhile, on Little Round Top Vincent had arrived just in time to throw back the attacking Rebels and hang on to the hill in a highly successful action. The division was not engaged on July 3.

V CORPS 2ND DIVISION

Brig.-Gen. Romeyn B. Ayres U.S.V.

Divisional Badge

Division known as the 13th Pennsylvania Reserves or "Bucktails"

Divisional statistics summary

Senior commander casualties
1 x brigade commander k
1 x regimental commander k
2 x regimental commanders w

Overall losses – percentage

Division	25.6
Day	24.5
Burbank	46.9
Weed	13.3

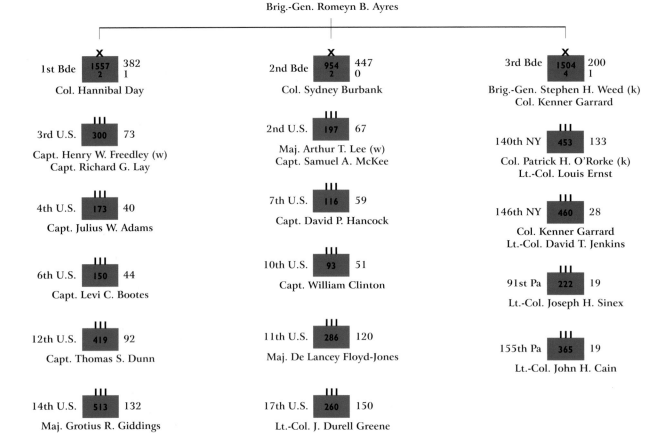

V Corps 2nd Div. XX 4020 5 1029 0
Brig.-Gen. Romeyn B. Ayres

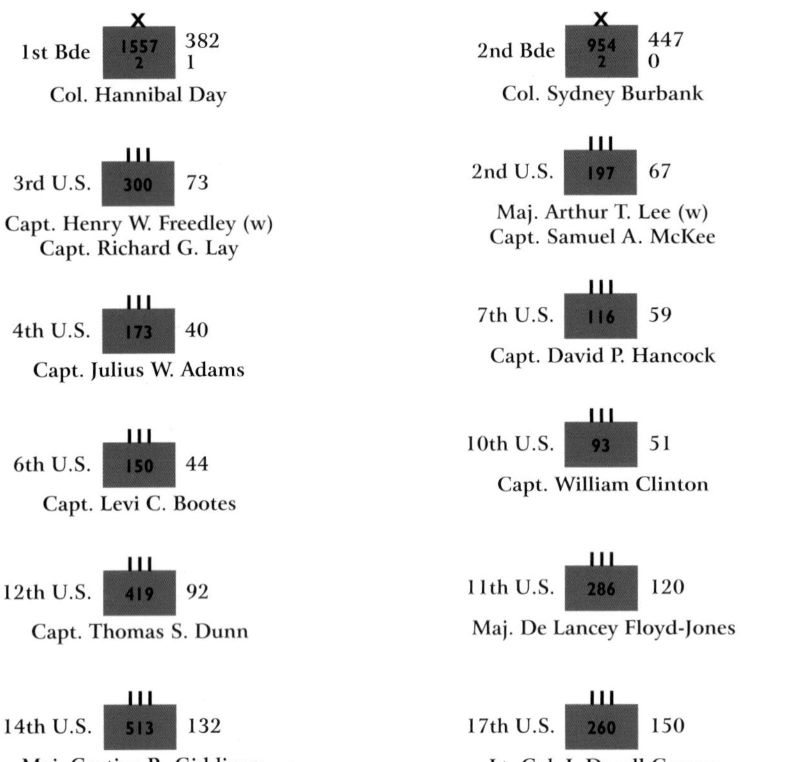

1st Bde X 1557 2 382 1
Col. Hannibal Day

3rd U.S. III 300 73
Capt. Henry W. Freedley (w)
Capt. Richard G. Lay

4th U.S. III 173 40
Capt. Julius W. Adams

6th U.S. III 150 44
Capt. Levi C. Bootes

12th U.S. III 419 92
Capt. Thomas S. Dunn

14th U.S. III 513 132
Maj. Grotius R. Giddings

2nd Bde X 954 2 447 0
Col. Sydney Burbank

2nd U.S. III 197 67
Maj. Arthur T. Lee (w)
Capt. Samuel A. McKee

7th U.S. III 116 59
Capt. David P. Hancock

10th U.S. III 93 51
Capt. William Clinton

11th U.S. III 286 120
Maj. De Lancey Floyd-Jones

17th U.S. III 260 150
Lt.-Col. J. Durell Greene

3rd Bde X 1504 4 200 1
Brig.-Gen. Stephen H. Weed (k)
Col. Kenner Garrard

140th NY III 453 133
Col. Patrick H. O'Rorke (k)
Lt.-Col. Louis Ernst

146th NY III 460 28
Col. Kenner Garrard
Lt.-Col. David T. Jenkins

91st Pa III 222 19
Lt.-Col. Joseph H. Sinex

155th Pa III 365 19
Lt.-Col. John H. Cain

Action prior to Gettysburg

This division had two brigades of regulars (3-year men) and they were one of the best-officered brigades in any Union army as they were all either West Point graduates or had risen through the ranks. It was difficult to recruit regular soldiers, so the ranks had a high proportion of foreigners and desertion was a problem. It had fought with distinction at the Seven Days Battles, 2nd Manassas, Fredericksburg and Chancellorsville.

Action at Gettysburg

Despite being boosted with four new strong regiments (11th, 12th, 14th and 17th U.S.), these two regular brigades of "Bucktails" (originally recruits had to bring a bucktail with them to prove their shooting ability and it was worn pinned to their caps) went into action at Gettysburg with five out of 10 regiments mustering fewer than 200 men. The 10th U.S. started the action with a mere 93, scarcely the strength of a company (it ranked 237th out of 247 regiments in terms of strength) and ended with 42, having lost over half. Six of these regular regiments started the battle commanded by captains. Neither Day nor Weed had commanded a brigade before, while Burbank was sick, although he stayed in command.

The division approached Gettysburg around 6:00 a.m. on July 2 and subsequently massed behind the center of the Union line along the Baltimore Pike. At about 4:30 p.m. it followed Gen. Barnes's 1st Division south to support III Corps fighting desperately to hold the Sickles' salient. Weed's Brigade was diverted to climb Little Round Top to help hold it against furious Rebel assaults, while the remaining two continued into the woods south of the Wheatfield to support Caldwell's Division of II Corps. However, Caldwell's men were overwhelmed and Ayres was forced to order his brigades to withdraw, which they accomplished at a heavy cost. On July 3 Weed's men remained on Little Round Top while the rest of the division stayed in reserve behind the hill.

V CORPS 3RD DIVISION

Brig.-Gen. Samuel W. Crawford U.S.V.

Divisional Badge

Divisional statistics summary

Senior commander casualties

1 x regimental commander k

Overall losses – percentage

Division	7.3
McCandless	12.3
Fisher	3.4

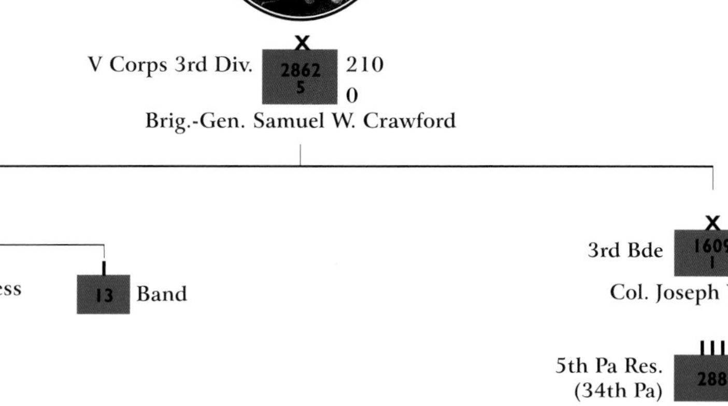

V Corps 3rd Div. 2862 / 5 — 210 / 0
Brig.-Gen. Samuel W. Crawford

1st Bde 1248 / 1 — 155 / 0
Col. William McCandless

13 Band

1st Pa Res. (30th Pa) 379 — 46
Col. William C. Tulley

2nd Pa Res. (31st Pa) 233 — 37
Lt.-Col. George A. Woodward

6th Pa Res. (35th Pa) 324 — 24
Lt.-Col. Wellington H. Ent

13th Pa Res. (42nd Pa) 298 — 48
Col. Charles F. Taylor (k)
Maj. William R. Hartshorne

3rd Bde 1609 / 1 — 55 / 0
Col. Joseph W. Fisher

5th Pa Res. (34th Pa) 288 — 2
Lt.-Col. George Dare

9th Pa Res. (38th Pa) 316 — 5
Lt.-Col. James McK. Snodgrass

10th Pa Res. (39th Pa) 401 — 5
Col. Adoniram J. Warner

11th Pa Res. (40th Pa) 327 — 41
Col. Samuel M. Jackson

12th Pa Res. (41st Pa) 276 — 2
Col. Martin D. Harden

Action prior to Gettysburg

Not only did this division consist of 3-year men but it was the only division in the Union armies to be composed entirely of men from one state. The 13th Reserve was formed from the old 1st Pennsylvania Rifles – the original "Bucktails" first in action in December 1861 at Dranesville, Virginia. The division fought with V Corps at Mechanicsburg, Gaines' Mill and White Oak Swamp. During this campaign it lost the staggering total of almost 3,000 men. It served under I Corps at 2nd Manassas, Antietam and Fredericksburg, where it was the only division to break through the Confederate line. However, more heavy losses ensured its being sent to recover in the Washington defenses. When Lee advanced over the Potomac and into Pennsylvania the soldiers clamored to be allowed to join the Army of the Potomac. Their wish was granted, although they were furious that their 2nd Brigade remained in Washington. On June 28 the division joined V Corps at Frederick. There followed the most frustrating and exhausting series of marches. Delays behind wagon trains resulted in criticism for slowness, but when they finally arrived on the battlefield in the late morning of July 2 they had covered 70 miles in about three and a half days – an incredible achievement.

Action at Gettysburg

The exhausted brigades had little time to recover. At around 4:30 p.m. the division was rushed south toward Little Round Top just in time for McCandless's Brigade and the 40th Pennsylvania from Fisher's Brigade to charge the advancing McLaws' Division as it swept forward across the Plum Run. This assault forced the Rebels back through the Wheatfield. The rest of Fisher's Brigade was sent to occupy Round Top, but due to confusion they did not reach it until midnight. On July 3 McCandless clashed with the 15th Georgia in the Wheatfield, but Fisher was not engaged. Apart from the 40th Pennsylvania, Fisher's men were not seriously involved at Gettysburg – a fact borne out by their negligible losses.

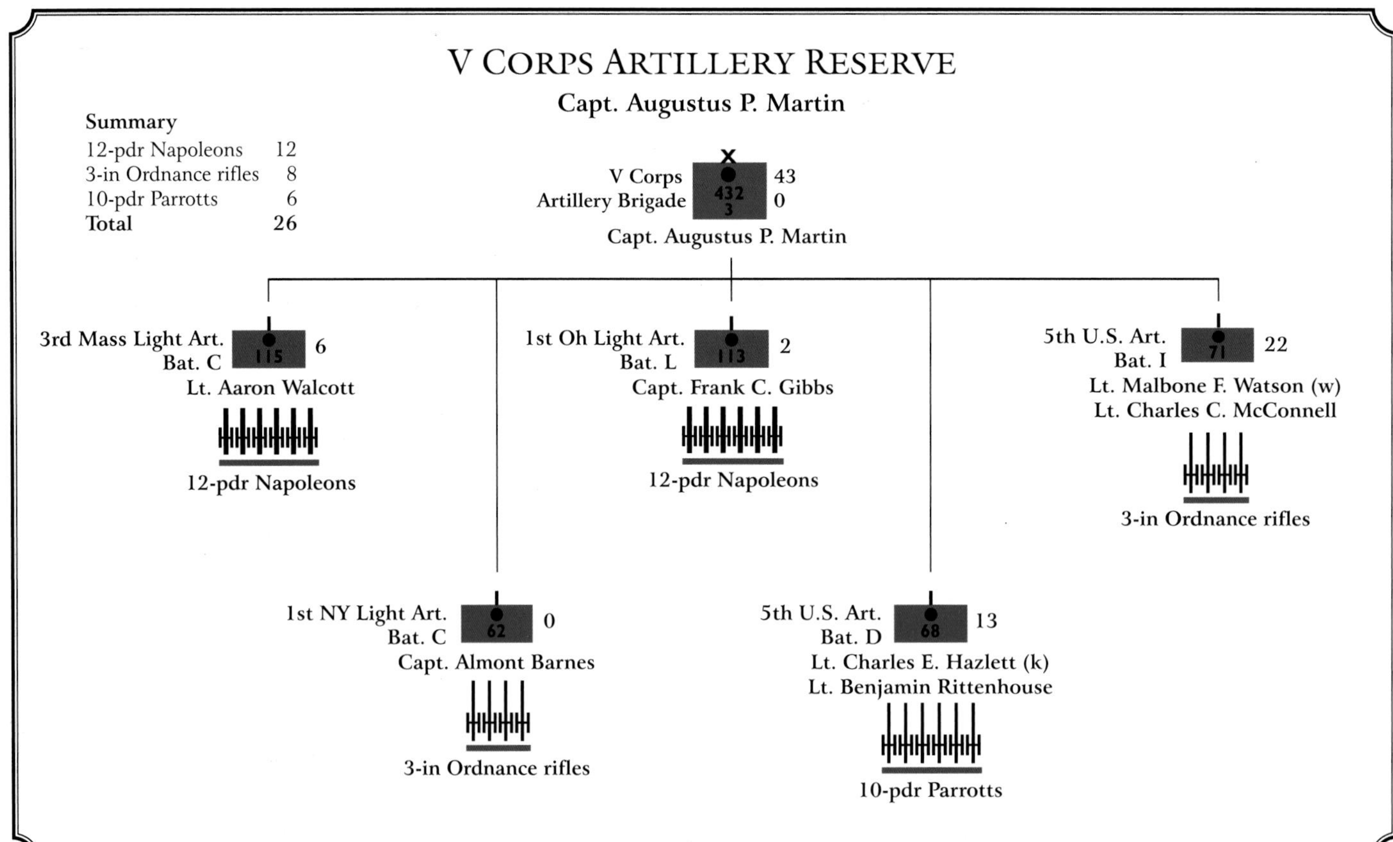
V CORPS ARTILLERY RESERVE
Capt. Augustus P. Martin
Summary
12-pdr Napoleons 12
3-in Ordnance rifles 8
10-pdr Parrotts 6
Total 26
V Corps Artillery Brigade
432
3
43
0
Capt. Augustus P. Martin
3rd Mass Light Art. Bat. C
115
6
Lt. Aaron Walcott
12-pdr Napoleons
1st Oh Light Art. Bat. L
113
2
Capt. Frank C. Gibbs
12-pdr Napoleons
5th U.S. Art. Bat. I
71
22
Lt. Malbone F. Watson (w)
Lt. Charles C. McConnell
3-in Ordnance rifles
1st NY Light Art. Bat. C
62
0
Capt. Almont Barnes
3-in Ordnance rifles
5th U.S. Art. Bat. D
68
13
Lt. Charles E. Hazlett (k)
Lt. Benjamin Rittenhouse
10-pdr Parrotts

VI CORPS 1ST DIVISION

Brig.-Gen. Horatio G. Wright U.S.V.

Divisional Badge

Divisional statistics summary

Senior commander casualties
None

Overall losses – percentage

Division	0.4
Torbert	0.8
Bartlett	0.4
Russell	0.1

Some regimental statistics
The minuscule number of casualties in the division (five regiments had none) was due to its late arrival on July 2 and the fact that it was broken up and deployed as reserves who were not required on July 3. The breakdown of the 18 losses is as follows: Torbert 11 x w; Bartlett 1 x k, 4 x w; Russell 2 x w (the second lowest casualties of any brigade in the battle).

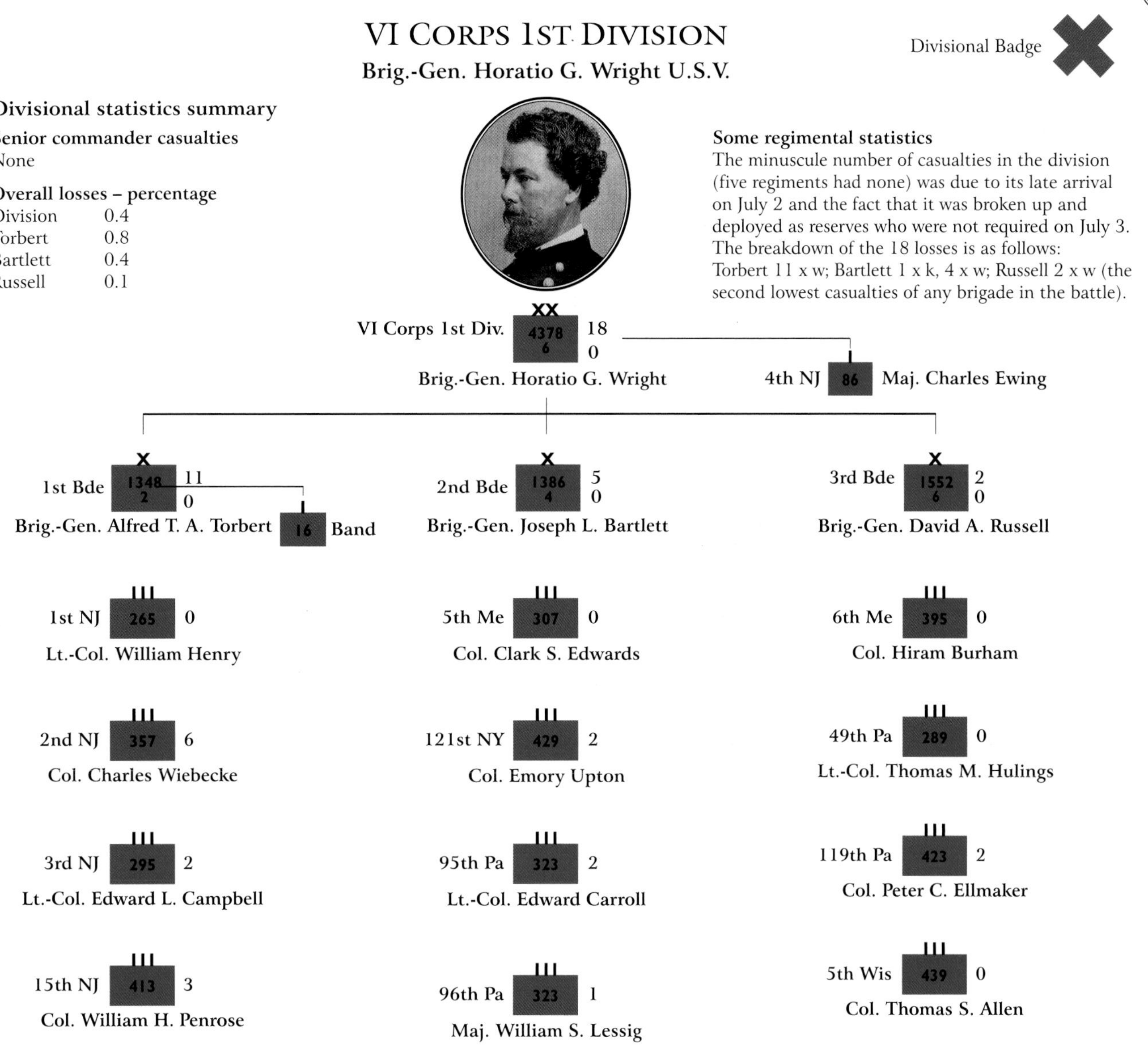

Action prior to Gettysburg

The division was involved in extensive operations during the Peninsular campaign, including the loss of over 2,000 at Gaines' Mill. It fought hard at 2nd Manassas and charged up the mountain at Crampton Gap in the Antietam campaign. It was only lightly engaged at Fredericksburg but lost many men to sickness during the 1862/63 winter at Falmouth. During the Chancellorsville campaign losses were again severe, topping 1,500. On May 23 the division got a new, unknown and untested commander, Brig.-Gen. Horatio Wright. The approach to Gettysburg is remembered for the crippling march rather than the fighting once they arrived. Both July 1 and most of the next day were spent on the road, with the marching men described as "haggard and distorted by fatigue, their feet swollen and their shoes in consequence thrown away." During a brief one-hour rest most men collapsed asleep within seconds.

Action at Gettysburg

The battle was something of an anticlimax for the division. Arriving late on July 2 it was initially placed in reserve behind and to the north of Little Round Top, but was soon split up as Bartlett's Brigade was sent to assist Wheaton's Brigade in repulsing a threatening Rebel attack by Wofford's men. However, its involvement was not required. On July 3 the division was further broken up when Torbert was sent north as a reinforcement and was placed under I Corps control, while Russell was dispatched in the opposite direction to the extreme left of the Union line. The overall result was that the division hardly fired a shot and suffered negligible casualties – one killed and 17 wounded out of 4,378 engaged.

VI Corps 2nd Division

Brig.-Gen. Albion P. Howe U.S.V.

Divisional Badge

Divisional statistics summary

Senior commander casualties

None

Overall losses – percentage

Division	0.4
Grant	0.05
Neill	0.8

Some regimental statistics

Four out of the five regiments in Grant's Brigade had no losses; the 4th Vermont had one wounded. Confederate artillery fire inflicted most, if not all, of the following on Neill's men:
7th Maine 6 x w
43rd New York 2 x k, 2 x w, 1 x mc
49th New York 2 x w
61st Pennsylvania 1 x w, 1 x mc

VI Corps 2nd Div. XX 3731 3 16 0
Brig.-Gen. Albion P. Howe

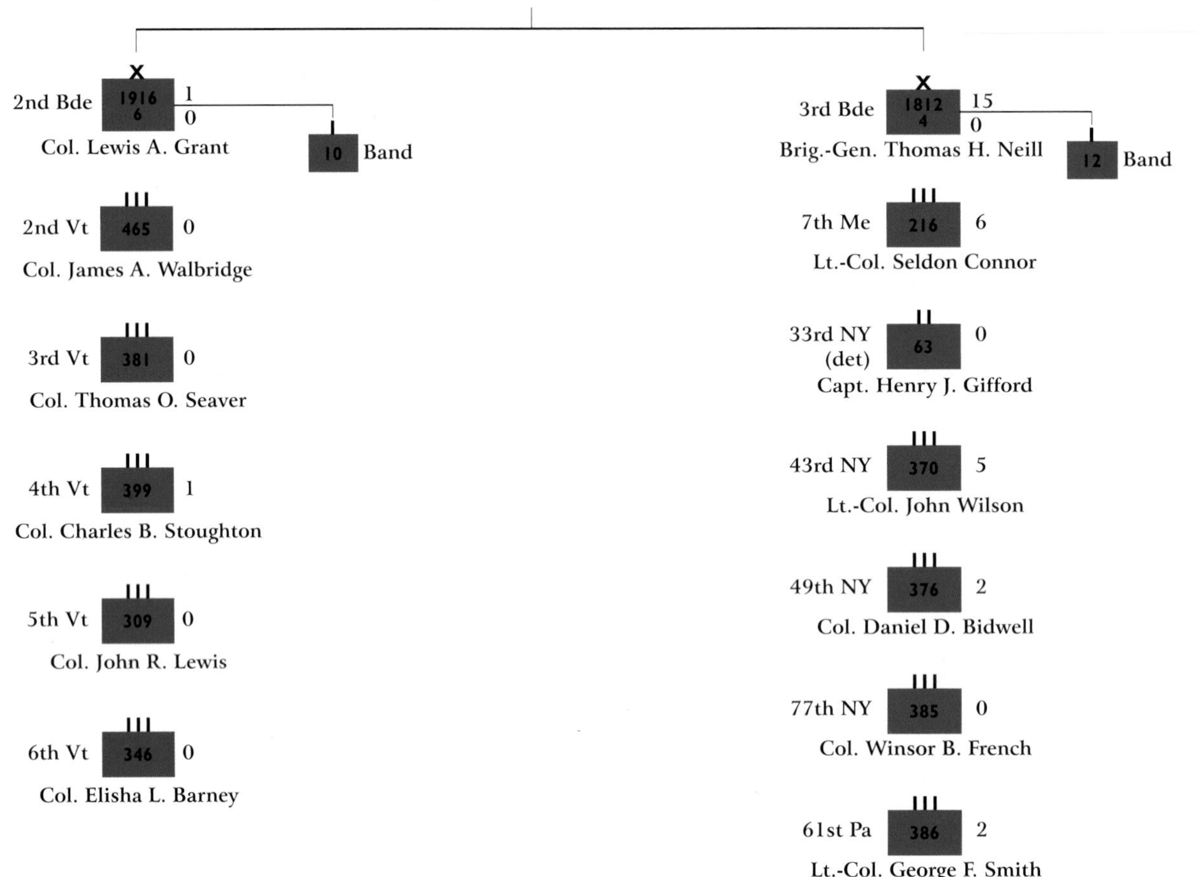

Action prior to Gettysburg

This division, which contained the famous Vermont Brigade, first saw action in the clash at Savage's Station on June 29, 1862 in the Seven Days campaign where it lost some 770 men. Although engaged at Antietam and Fredericksburg, the division escaped with slight losses. It shared the misery of Burnside's infamous "Mud March" in January 1863 when two days of torrential rain ruined his attempt to outflank Lee. The abandonment of this operation when "every road became a deep quagmire, and even small streams were impassable," coming on top of the disastrous defeat at Fredericksburg the previous month, led to Burnside's removal and replacement by Maj.-Gen. "Fighting Joe" Hooker. The division was successful in attacking the Rebel position on the right of Marye's Heights during the Chancellorsville operations, although it suffered some 1,300 casualties.

Action at Gettysburg

Like most other Union formations, this division suffered the crippling reality of continuous hard marching, often in intense heat, to join the action at Gettysburg. It arrived behind the center of the Union line around 5:00 p.m. on July 2, trailed behind the 1st Division up the Baltimore Pike. Hardly had it halted before the division was broken up as part of Meade's need to rush reinforcements to counter developing or likely threats. Neill's Brigade went to the right flank, to Power's Hill, where it came under XII Corps, Slocum's command. He sent it to support Wadsworth (I Corps) on Culp's Hill. Then around midnight it was back again to its original position near the center – it is not hard to imagine the soldiers' comments at these orders and counter-orders. Meanwhile Grant had been dispatched to the Union left to guard against that flank being turned. On July 3 Slocum sent Neill behind the right where it lay or crouched under the Confederate firestorm that preceded the Pickett–Pettigrew–Trimble attack – it was not required to assist in repulsing it. It was during this time that the brigade suffered its 15 casualties – the divisional total of 16 was the lowest of any division in the Union Army at the battle. Grant's Brigade remained on the periphery of the field and thus came away from the battle with only one man wounded – the lowest of any brigade.

VI Corps 3rd Division

Maj.-Gen. John Newton U.S.V.

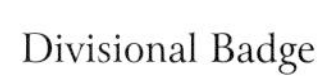

Divisional statistics summary

Senior commander casualties

1 x regimental commander w

Overall losses – percentage

Division	4.0
Shaler	4.0
Eutis	4.1
Wheaton	3.7

Some regimental statistics

The 102nd Pennsylvania's small detachment escorted a supply train to the battlefield, arriving on July 3. The remainder of the regiment was guarding trains at Westminster. The 37th Massachusetts, with 591 men, was the sixth largest out of 247 regiments in the army.

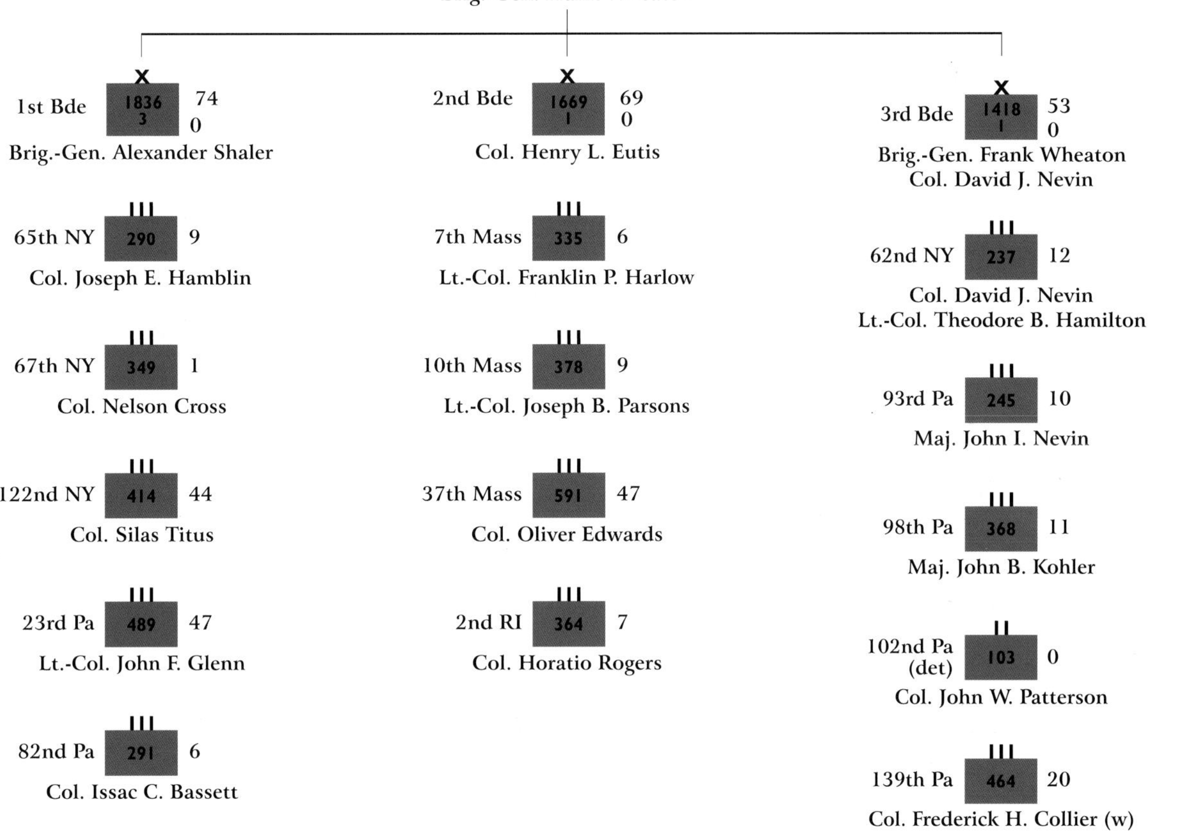

Action prior to Gettysburg

The division's first serious action was at the Battle of Seven Pines, where it lost 1,150 men. For much of the remainder of the campaign outside Richmond it was guarding army trains. It played a key role at Malvern Hill, the last of the Seven Days Battles (July 1, 1862) in the Peninsular campaign. It was only lightly engaged during the Antietam campaign and also at Fredericksburg, where it did not participate in the futile charges against entrenched positions up steep slopes. The division fought well at Chancellorsville, both in the attack on Marye's Heights and in the defensive line near Salem Church.

Action at Gettysburg

On July 1 the division halted at Manchester after a testing five-day march, only to be ordered on again that night. The grueling conditions, the heat, the lack of food and drink on the last leg caused many to straggle or collapse. The last mile or so was at the double-quick, with men fixing bayonets on the march. Wheaton's Brigade led the column and arrived exhausted at around 4:30 p.m., when it was rushed to Little Round Top to help repulse the threatening attack of McLaws' Rebels. The brigade, now under Col. Nevin, charged the Confederates and pushed them back. The remaining two brigades bivouacked that evening behind the Round Tops. At around 3:30 a.m. on July 3 Shaler's Brigade was sent to reinforce the defenders of Culp's Hill and came under command of Brig.-Gen. Geary (2nd Division, XII Corps), who sent each regiment forward as it arrived to man a section of the breastworks against the continuous Rebel attacks. Eutis's men were sent dashing from place to place as supports wherever the enemy threat seemed greatest and as a result never fired a shot, although they suffered some loss from the Rebel artillery fire during the afternoon. On July 3 Nevin's Brigade remained behind a stone wall near the base of Little Round Top, although later two regiments went forward toward the Wheatfield and fighting took place in which they recaptured a cannon lost the previous day.

VI Corps Artillery Reserve

Col. Charles H. Tompkins U.S.A.

Summary	
12-pdr Napoleons	18
10-pdr Parrotts	18
3-in Ordnance rifles	12
Total	**48**

VI Corps Artillery Brigade — 937 — 3 — 12 — 0

Col. Charles H. Tompkins

Mass Light Art. 1st Bat. — 135 — 0

Capt. William H. McCartney

12-pdr Napoleons

NY Light Art. 1st Bat. — 103 — 12

Capt. Andrew Cowan

3-in Ordnance rifles

NY Light Art. 3rd Bat. — 111 — 0

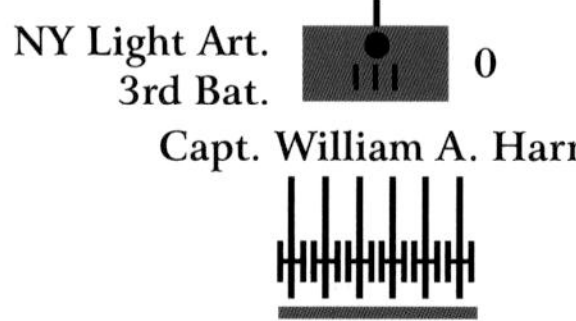

Capt. William A. Harn

10-pdr Parrotts

1st RI Light Art. Bat. C — 116 — 0

Capt. Richard Waterman

3-in Ordnance rifles

1st RI Light Art. Bat. G — 126 — 0

Capt. George W. Adams

10-pdr Parrotts

2nd U.S. Art. Bat. D — 126 — 0

Lt. Edward B. Williston

12-pdr Napoleons

2nd U.S. Art. Bat. G — 101 — 0

Lt. John H. Butler

12-pdr Napoleons

5th U.S. Art. Bat. F — 116 — 0

Lt. Leonard Martin

10-pdr Parrotts

XI CORPS 1ST DIVISION

Brig.-Gen. Francis Barlow U.S.V.

Divisional Badge

Divisional statistics summary

Senior commander casualties

1 x divisional commander w/c
1 x regimental commander k
3 x regimental commanders w
1 x regimental commander c

Overall losses – percentage

Division 52.6
Von Gilsa 46.2
Ames 58.2

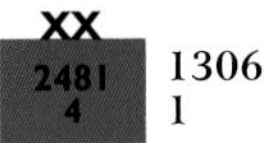

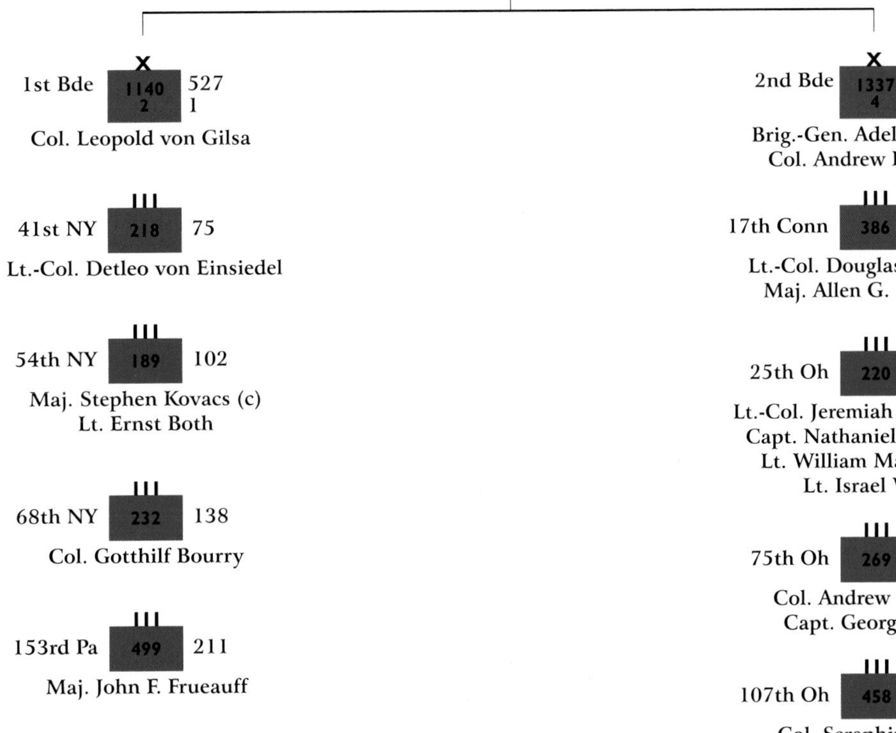

Some regimental statistics

The 25th Ohio ended the battle commanded by a lieutenant. It went into action with only 220 men and came out having suffered losses of 86.3 percent, the highest percentage loss of any of the 247 Union regiments at Gettysburg. The 75th Ohio suffered only marginally less. Casualties amounted to 69.1%, making it eleventh in terms of percentage loss. A high proportion of men were captured during the chaotic retreat, as is evidenced by the divisional statistics. Of the 1,306 casualties only 122 (9.3%) were killed, while 677 (51.8%) were wounded and 507 (38.8%) taken prisoner.

Action prior to Gettysburg

Most of the infantry regiments in this division were originally in West Virginia in Maj.-Gen. Fremont's Mountain Department and thus took part in the campaigning in the Virginia mountains and Shenandoah Valley. The division served at 2nd Manassas and then in the forward Washington defenses around Centerville during Lee's first invasion of Maryland. At Chancellorsville the division was unfortunate to be on Hooker's extreme right flank and thus bore the full weight of Stonewall Jackson's surprise flank attack. They were quickly overwhelmed and lost almost 1,000 men, about half as prisoners. Somewhat unjustly, the rest of the army tended to condemn the troops of XI Corps for the Union defeat at Chancellorsville. In particular the large number of officers and men of German descent came in for some vocal abuse. The "Dutchmen" were not popular, and their undignified retreat reinforced the misconception that they made unreliable soldiers. Consequently, confidence in, and of, this division – indeed all three divisions of XI Corps – had been severely shaken at Chancellorsville. On May 24, 1863 the young Brig.-Gen. Barlow, very much the disciplinarian, was appointed to command to knock the division, the smallest in the army, into shape.

Action at Gettysburg

After some hard marching the division moved through Gettysburg town during the early afternoon of July 1 while fierce fighting raged to the east as the Confederates built up the pressure down the Chambersburg Pike. Barlow was deployed north of the town but soon decided to advance further north to occupy Blocher's Knoll in order to secure a better shoot for his guns and prevent its seizure by the enemy. Unfortunately, it was too far forward and the attack by the strong Rebel division under Early, assisted by Doles's Brigade from Rodes' Division, soon had Barlow's men in difficulties. Attacks from the front and on the flanks could not be held and resistance collapsed. Barlow was badly wounded and the retreat rapidly became a shambles as disorganized units scrambled to get back through the town. Eventually the survivors regrouped on Cemetery Hill. It had the hallmarks of another Chancellorsville. On July 2 the reorganized remnants of the division were called on to fight again. Deployed at the base of Cemetery Hill, they bore the brunt of Early's determined attack that evening. Their line broke but timely assistance from other units drove the Rebels back and the men of 1st Division, XI Corps reoccupied their position. Its services were not required on July 3.

XI CORPS 2ND DIVISION

Brig.-Gen. Adolph W. A. F. von Steinwehr U.S.V.

Divisional Badge 

Divisional statistics summary

Senior commander casualties

None

Overall losses – percentage

Division	32.8
Coster	48.9
Smith	21.2

Some regimental statistics

The 154th New York lost 83.3%, the third highest of the 247 Union regiments at the battle. The 134th New York, with total losses of 252, had the eighth highest loss of any regiment.

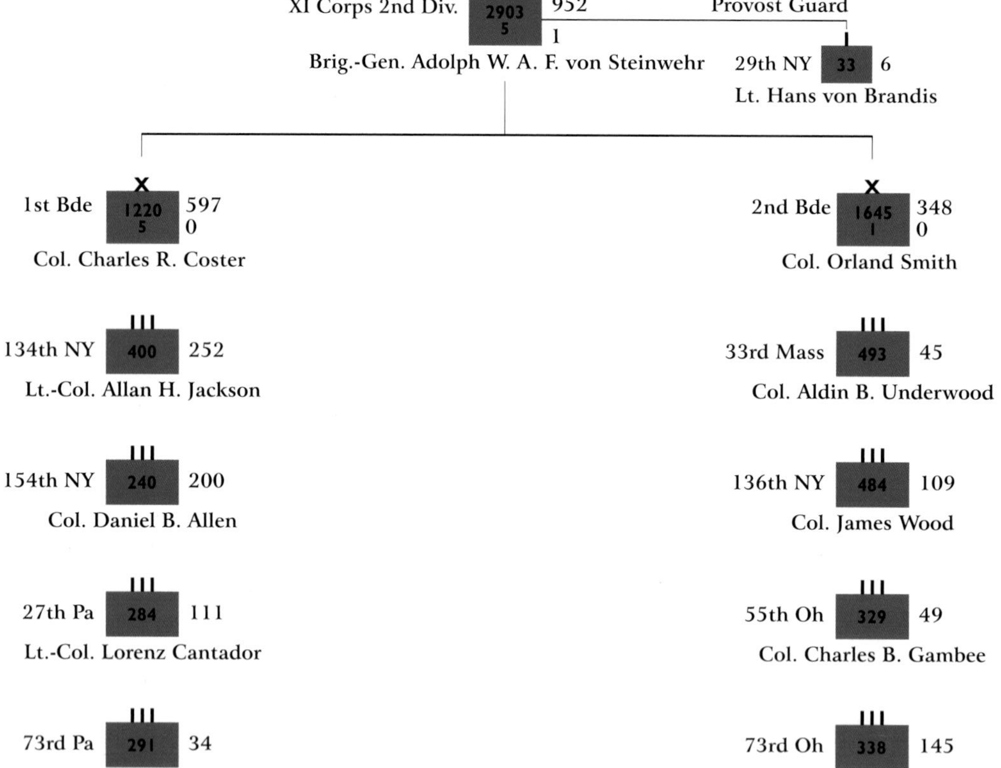

Action prior to Gettysburg

This division had seen little action apart from Chancellorsville in the year prior to Gettysburg. It had participated in the 1862 Shenandoah Valley campaign and a few regiments were at 2nd Manassas, but the division missed both Antietam and Fredericksburg. At Chancellorsville it was outflanked on its right as the whole Union right wing unraveled under the weight of Jackson's attack. Its losses exceeded 500, many of them prisoners. As with the 1st Division, the blame for this seemingly ignominious performance was laid on the large German element.

Action at Gettysburg

This division brought up the rear as XI Corps marched through Gettysburg on July 1. At around 2:00 p.m. it was halted on Cemetery Hill as the corps reserve. However, as the Rebel attacks to the north and east got stronger and the Union defenses began to give way, Coster's Brigade was sent to try to stem the tide that threatened to flood through Gettysburg from several directions. It deployed in a brickyard on the northern outskirts of the town but was quickly overwhelmed by hugely superior numbers and, despite desperate and gallant efforts, was swept away with almost 50% losses – many captured. On July 2 both brigades were positioned on Cemetery Hill where Smith's Brigade engaged in some skirmishing along the Taneytown Road, while the much-depleted Coster's Brigade assisted in driving off Early's evening attack. The division had a quiet day on July 3.

XI CORPS 3RD DIVISION

Maj.-Gen. Carl Schurz U.S.V.

Divisional Badge

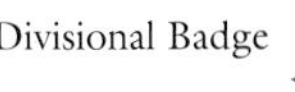

Divisional statistics summary

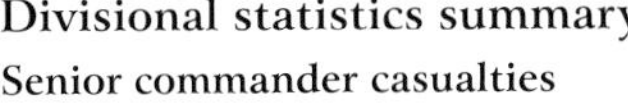

Senior commander casualties

6 x regimental commanders w
1 x regimental commander c

Overall losses – percentage

Division	47.4
Schimmelfennig	47.9
Kryzanowski	46.9

Some regimental statistics

Three regiments suffered particularly severely at Gettysburg. In the 1st Brigade the 157th New York, with 307 casualties (75.1%), suffered the fourth highest numerical loss and sixth highest percentage loss out of the 247 Union regiments engaged. The 45th New York, with 224 losses (59.7%), made it the 16th highest numerically. In the 2nd Brigade the 26th Wisconsin's 217 (48.7%) losses ranked 18th in terms of numerical losses.

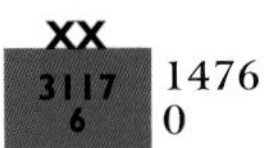

XI Corps 3rd Div. XX 3117 6 1476 0

Maj.-Gen. Carl Schurz
Brig.-Gen. Alexander Schimmelfennig
Maj.-Gen. Carl Schurz

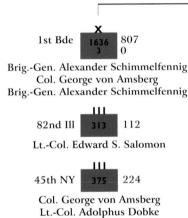

1st Bde X 1636 3 807 0

Brig.-Gen. Alexander Schimmelfennig
Col. George von Amsberg
Brig.-Gen. Alexander Schimmelfennig

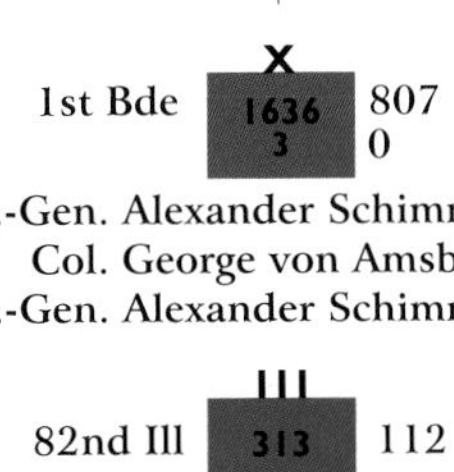

82nd Ill III 313 112

Lt.-Col. Edward S. Salomon

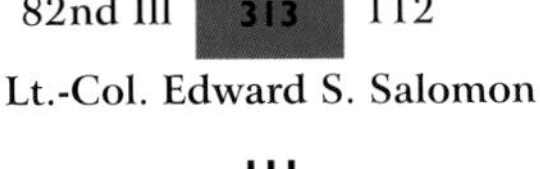

45th NY III 375 224

Col. George von Amsberg
Lt.-Col. Adolphus Dobke

157th NY III 409 307

Col. Phillip P. Brown

61st Oh III 247 54

Col. Stephen J. McGroarty

74th Pa III 334 110

Col. Adolph von Hartung (w)
Lt.-Col. Alexander von Mitzel (c)
Capt. Gustav Schleiter
Capt. Henry Krauseneck

2nd Bde X 1425 1 669 0

Col. Wladimir Kryzanowski

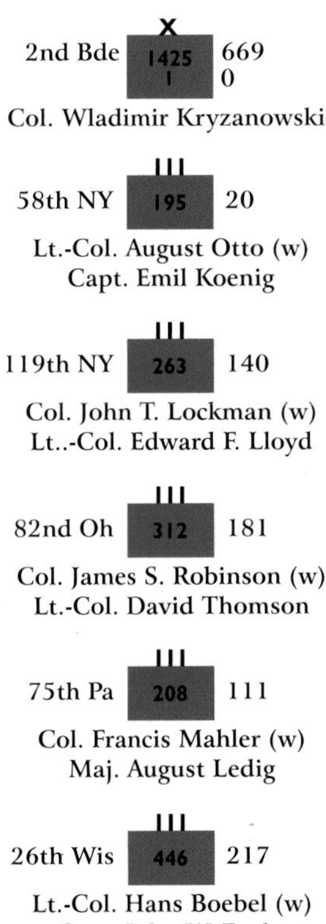

58th NY III 195 20

Lt.-Col. August Otto (w)
Capt. Emil Koenig

119th NY III 263 140

Col. John T. Lockman (w)
Lt..-Col. Edward F. Lloyd

82nd Oh III 312 181

Col. James S. Robinson (w)
Lt.-Col. David Thomson

75th Pa III 208 111

Col. Francis Mahler (w)
Maj. August Ledig

26th Wis III 446 217

Lt.-Col. Hans Boebel (w)
Capt. John W. Fuchs

Action prior to Gettysburg

Elements of this division under Maj.-Gen. Fremont took part in the West Virginia and Shenandoah Valley campaign in 1862. It was engaged at 2nd Manassas and, along with the rest of XI Corps, manned the forward defenses of Washington during the Antietam campaign. It did not participate at Fredericksburg and performed poorly at Chancellorsville, where it joined the rush to the rear following Jackson's surprise flank attack. This episode cost the division some 900 casualties, many captured, and reinforced the contempt with which the "Dutchmen" of XI Corps were regarded by many in the army before Gettysburg.

Action at Gettysburg

After a hard march, much of it through driving rain, the division, led by the 45th New York, moved through Gettysburg town in the late morning of July 1. The 1st Brigade was ordered to occupy the dominating Oak Hill, but was beaten to it by Rodes' Confederates. It then deployed on the right of Robinson's Division of I Corps with the 45th New York on the extreme left. There this regiment played a key role in repulsing O'Neal's attack, although the entire brigade was under continuous artillery fire from Oak Hill. The 2nd Brigade was initially held back in reserve, but when Barlow's Division showed signs of wavering it was rushed forward to assist. It was too late: Barlow's men retreated in disorder and the 2nd Brigade was fiercely attacked by two advancing Rebel brigades and driven back with heavy loss. The 157th New York (1st Brigade) was almost destroyed in attempting to halt the enemy advance. The division retired through the town and regrouped on Cemetery Hill. On July 2 the 1st Brigade was sent to Culp's Hill to help drive off Johnson's night attacks, while the 2nd Brigade did the same on the east side of Cemetery Hill when Early attacked that evening. On July 3 the division was lightly engaged, mostly trying to deal with snipers firing from the town.

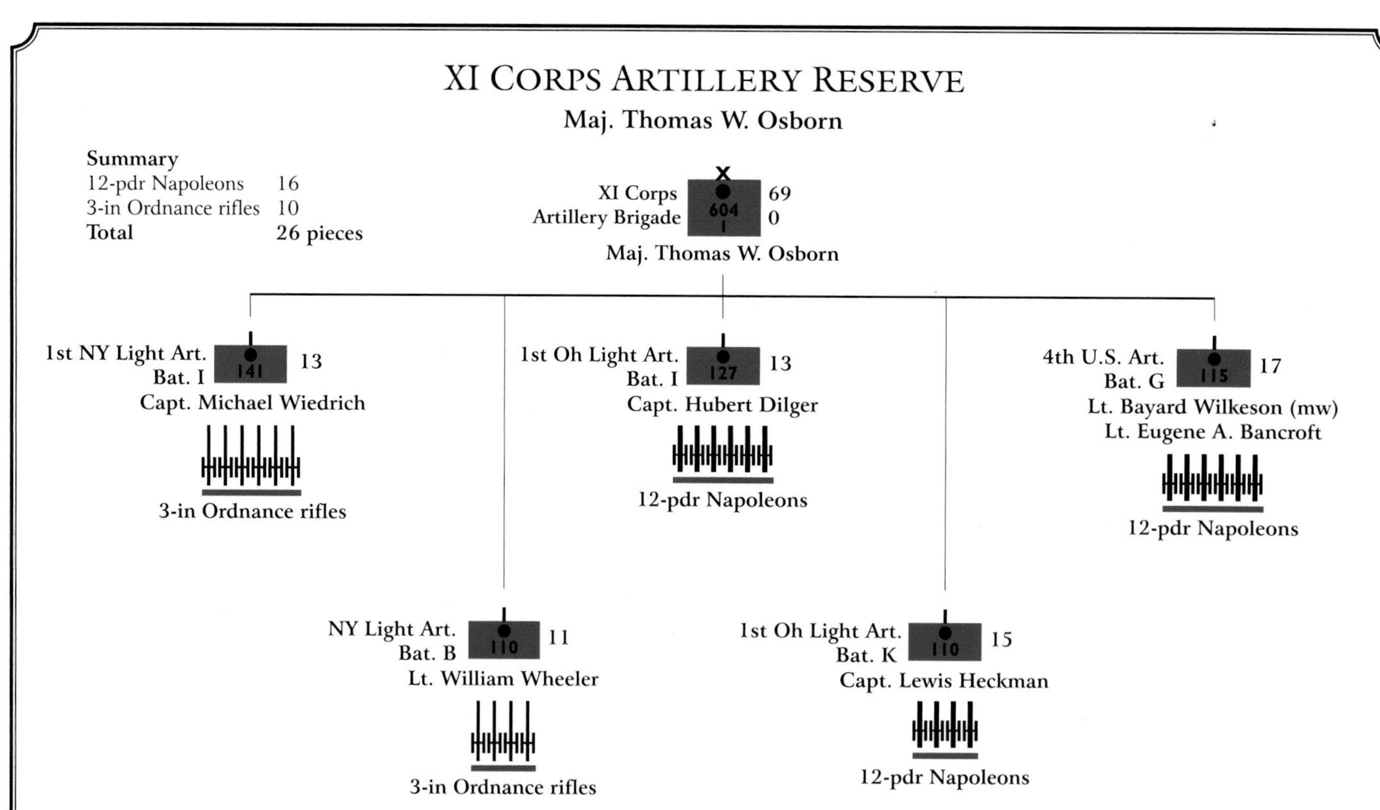
XI CORPS ARTILLERY RESERVE
Maj. Thomas W. Osborn
Summary
12-pdr Napoleons 16
3-in Ordnance rifles 10
Total 26 pieces
XI Corps
Artillery Brigade
604
I
69
0
Maj. Thomas W. Osborn
1st NY Light Art.
Bat. I
141
13
Capt. Michael Wiedrich
3-in Ordnance rifles
1st Oh Light Art.
Bat. I
127
13
Capt. Hubert Dilger
12-pdr Napoleons
4th U.S. Art.
Bat. G
115
17
Lt. Bayard Wilkeson (mw)
Lt. Eugene A. Bancroft
12-pdr Napoleons
NY Light Art.
Bat. B
110
11
Lt. William Wheeler
3-in Ordnance rifles
1st Oh Light Art.
Bat. K
110
15
Capt. Lewis Heckman
12-pdr Napoleons

XII CORPS 1ST DIVISION

Brig.-Gen. Alpheus S. Williams U.S.V.

Divisional Badge 

Divisional statistics summary

Senior commander casualties

1 x regimental commander k

Overall losses – percentage

Division	10.1
McDougall	4.4
Lockwood	9.6
Ruger	17.5

Brigade/regimental statistics

Although the two brigades were about equal in numbers, the 2nd Brigade had three very strong regiments to the 1st's six – a result of the reorganization noted below. The 1st Maryland (Potomac Home Brigade) was the largest in the army with 674 all ranks. The 150th New York was fifth with 609 and the 1st Maryland (Eastern Shore) eighth with 582.

XII Corps 1st Div. XX 5256 5 533 0

Brig.-Gen. Alpheus S. Williams
Brig.-Gen. Thomas H. Ruger

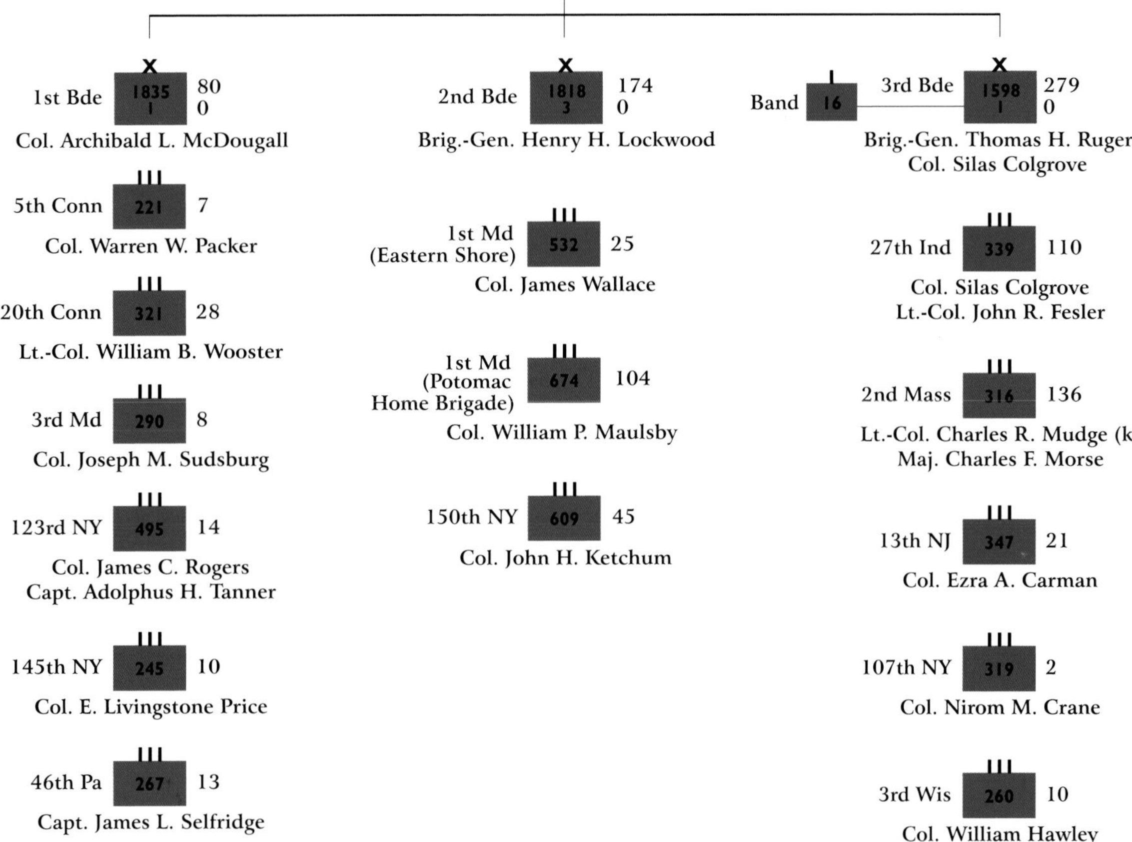

Action prior to Gettysburg

This division was exceptional in that it had been under the same divisional commander for 15 months prior to the battle. However, it had suffered badly in several actions during that time. While covering the Union retreat from Winchester in May 1862 it lost 1,460 men, of whom 1,242 were missing, mostly captured. At Cedar Mountain it fought hard against Jackson's veterans, but lost over 50%, a high proportion captured. It was held in reserve during the 2nd Manassas campaign, but when in action again at Antietam its attack on Dunker's Church was driven back with casualties numbering over 1,000. It missed Fredericksburg. At Chancellorsville it was able to halt Jackson's further advance after he had defeated XI Corps but in so doing lost another 1,565 men, 666 missing. Crippling losses, combined with the expiring of many enlistments, led to the 1st and 2nd Brigades merging to form a strengthened 1st Brigade, while three new, green but very large regiments joined to form the 2nd Brigade – although the 150th New York did not arrive until the evening of July 2.

Action at Gettysburg

The division, the strongest numerically in the Army of the Potomac, led XII Corps' march to Gettysburg on July 1. It approached Wolf's Hill during the afternoon, but as XI Corps was by then retreating it was pulled back for the night. On July 2 command passed to Brig. Ruger as Williams took over the corps. At about 9:00 a.m. the division moved to Culp's Hill, where the men spent their time constructing breastworks. However, Longstreet's assault on the Union left and center caused Ruger to be sent south in support, although by the time he arrived there was little to do. That evening the division marched back to Culp's Hill only to find their breastworks had been captured. As it was dark, it decided against attacking. On July 3 the division was engaged in helping to see off several Rebel attacks.

XII CORPS 2ND DIVISION

Brig.-Gen. John W. Geary U.S.V.

Divisional Badge 

Divisional statistics summary

Senior commander casualties

3 x regimental commanders w

Overall losses – percentage

Division	13.6
Candy	7.7
Cobham	14.0
Greene	21.3

Some regimental statistics

The division appeared unbalanced, as the 2nd Brigade with only 700 men was virtually half the size of the other two numerically and in numbers of regiments – it ranked 56th out of 58 in terms of Union brigade strengths. Two of its regiments mustered fewer than 200 men, with the tiny 109th Pennsylvania ranking 225th out of 247 in the regimental strength list.

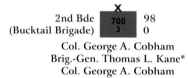

XII Corps 2nd Div. XX 3964 5 540 0
Brig.-Gen. John W. Geary

28th Pa Co. B 27 — Provost Guard

Band 10

1st Bde X 1798 2 139 0 
Col. Charles Candy

5th Oh 299 18
Col. John H. Patrick

7th Oh 282 18
Col. William R. Creighton

29th Oh 315 38
Col. Wilbur F. Stevens (w)
Capt. Edward Hayes

66th Oh 299 17
Col. Eugene Powell

28th Pa 303 28
Capt. John Flynn (w)

147th Pa 298 20
Lt.-Col. Ario Pardee

2nd Bde (Bucktail Brigade) X 700 3 98 0
Col. George A. Cobham
Brig.-Gen. Thomas L. Kane*
Col. George A. Cobham

29th Pa 357 66
Col. William Rickards

109th Pa 149 10
Capt. Frederick L. Gimber

111th Pa 191 22
Col. George A. Cobham
Lt.-Col. Thomas Walker

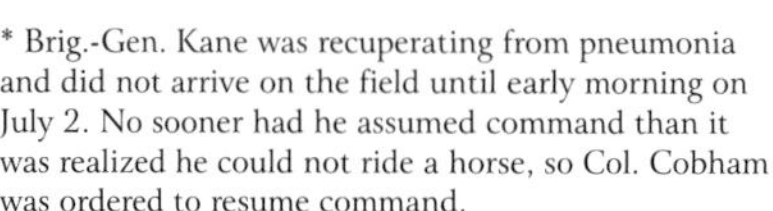
* Brig.-Gen. Kane was recuperating from pneumonia and did not arrive on the field until early morning on July 2. No sooner had he assumed command than it was realized he could not ride a horse, so Col. Cobham was ordered to resume command.

3rd Bde X 1424 3 303 0 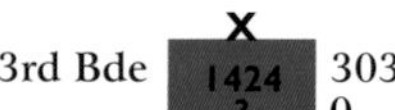
Brig.-Gen. George S. Greene

60th NY 273 52
Col. Abel Godard

78th NY 193 30
Lt.-Col. Herbert von Hammerstein

102nd NY 230 29
Col. James C. Lane (w)
Capt. Lewis R. Stegman

137th NY 423 137
Col. David Ireland

149th NY 297 55
Col. Henry A. Barnum (ill July 2)
Lt.-Col. Charles B. Randall (w)

Action prior to Gettysburg

Like the 2nd Division, the 3rd had its introduction to active duty in the Shenandoah Valley. At Kernstown in March 1862 it had the rare honor of inflicting a reverse on Stonewall Jackson. The division met Jackson again at Cedar Mountain, but this time suffered almost 950 casualties. Included among the wounded was Brig.-Gen. Geary, who would lead the division at Gettysburg. More heavy losses were incurred at Antietam under Brig.-Gen. Greene, and yet again with Geary back in command at Chancellorsville, where the casualty bill reached almost 1,200. Shortly after this battle the division lost two regiments whose terms of enlistment had expired, which explains the smallness of the 2nd Brigade; it had had 11 regiments pass through it in the preceding year. Nevertheless, the division that marched to Gettysburg had the same organization and the same divisional and brigade commanders as at Chancellorsville – exceptional continuity.

Action at Gettysburg

The division approached the battlefield at around 5:00 p.m. on July 1 and was initially assigned to the Union left at the base of Little Round Top. However, at 5:00 next morning it was marched to Culp's Hill to rejoin Williams' Division. There, on the heights of the hill, they spent the day building breastworks. At 7:00 p.m. on July 2 Geary was ordered to take his division, less Greene's Brigade, to bolster the Union left. Inadequate orders and poor staff work led the division to march south well beyond its objective before being halted. At around 9:00 p.m. Geary was ordered back to Culp's Hill. Meanwhile Greene's Brigade had been under sustained attacks that eventually captured some entrenchments on his right. When Geary arrived he decided to await daylight before throwing the Rebels from this position. On July 3 the division bore the brunt of Johnson's assaults, all of which were repulsed.

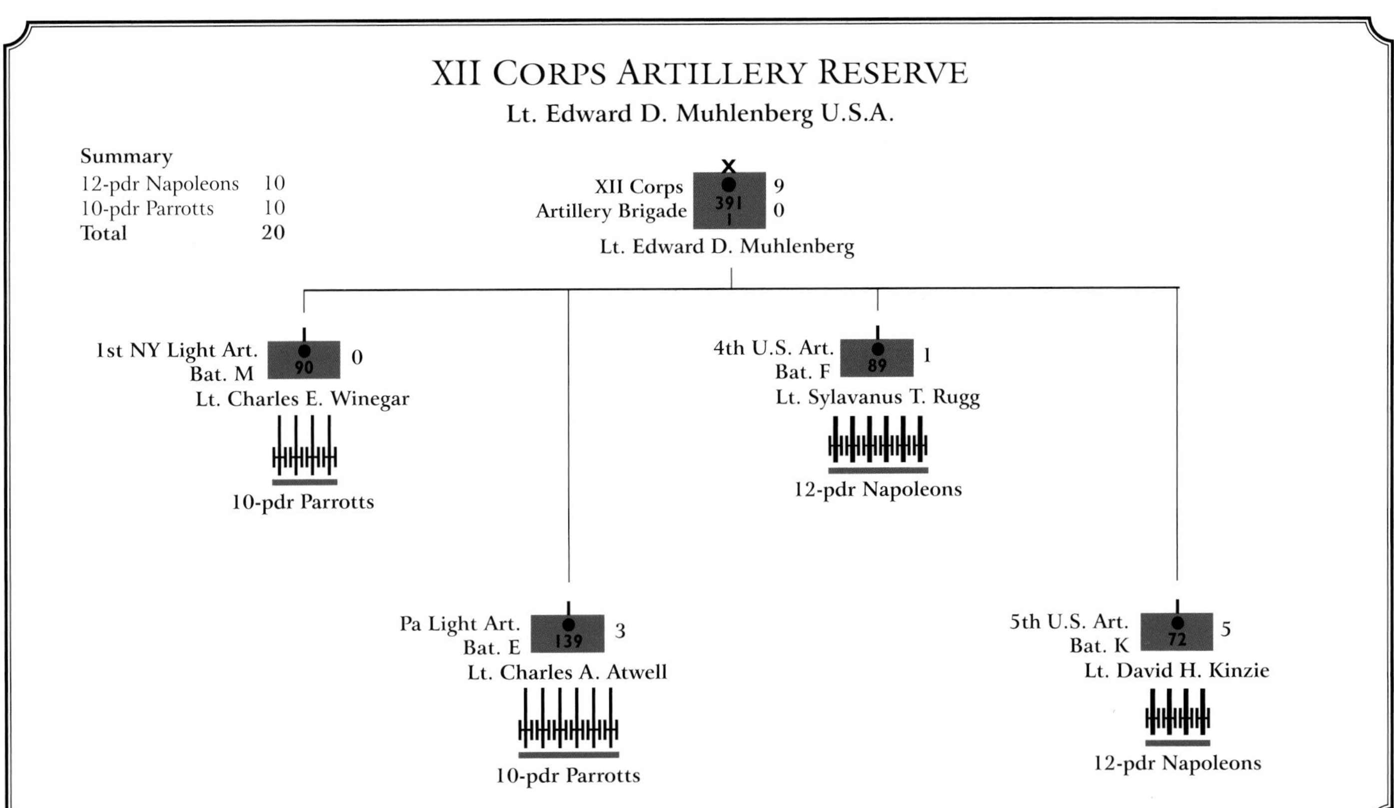
XII CORPS ARTILLERY RESERVE
Lt. Edward D. Muhlenberg U.S.A.
Summary
12-pdr Napoleons 10
10-pdr Parrotts 10
Total 20
XII Corps
Artillery Brigade
391
9
0
Lt. Edward D. Muhlenberg
1st NY Light Art.
Bat. M
90
0
Lt. Charles E. Winegar
10-pdr Parrotts
4th U.S. Art.
Bat. F
89
1
Lt. Sylavanus T. Rugg
12-pdr Napoleons
Pa Light Art.
Bat. E
139
3
Lt. Charles A. Atwell
10-pdr Parrotts
5th U.S. Art.
Bat. K
72
5
Lt. David H. Kinzie
12-pdr Napoleons

CAVALRY CORPS 1ST DIVISION

Maj.-Gen. John Buford U.S.V.

Divisional statistics summary

Senior commander casualties

1 x regimental commander w/c
(Maj. Starr attached Corps H.Q.)

Overall losses – percentage

Division	4.3
Gamble	6.2
Devin	2.4
Merritt	3.7

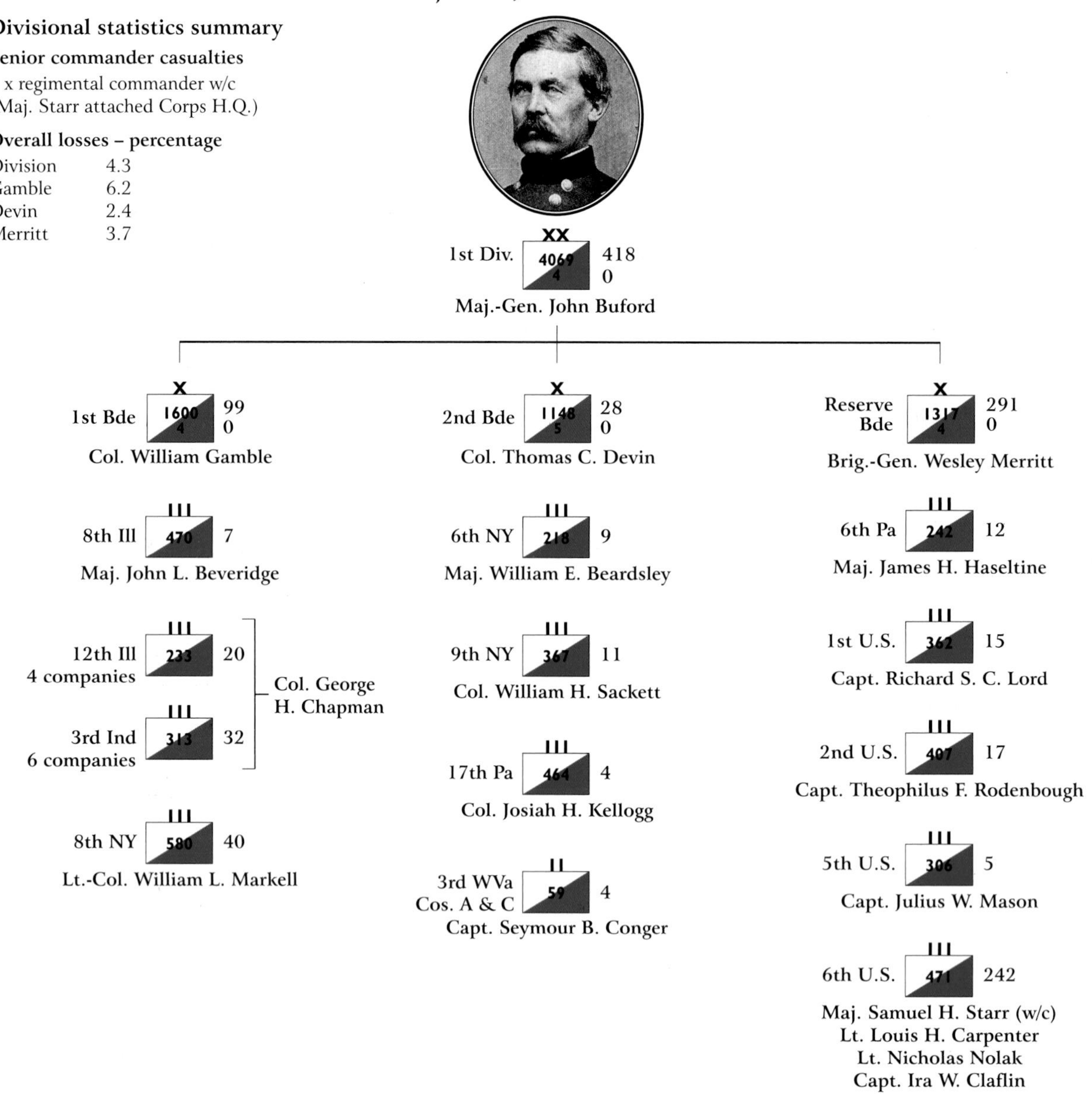

Action prior to Gettysburg

Following Maj.-Gen. Hooker's reorganization of the cavalry, the 1st Division initially operated as a cohesive formation at the start of the Gettysburg campaign. Although it remained inactive during the major cavalry battle of the Civil War at Brandy Station on June 9, 1863, it was fully engaged in the cavalry clashes at the Blue Ridge Mountain passes as it tried to discover Lee's line of march. Full details of its activities are discussed in Section Seven: The Road to Gettysburg. In the latter part of June this division covered the left flank of the Army of the Potomac as it force-marched north to block what was seen as the Confederate threat to Washington. On June 30 the division, less the Reserve Brigade which was escorting the divisional trains, entered Gettysburg township and Buford deployed his two brigades on picket duty on the approaches from the west and northwest, particularly the Chambersburg Pike and Mummasburg Road along which a Rebel advance was anticipated.

Action at Gettysburg

The 1st and 2nd Brigades, mostly fighting dismounted, delayed the Confederate advance down the Chambersburg Pike. It was a classic cavalry withdrawing action against superior numbers, carried out with considerable skill until relieved by Wadsworth's Division (I Corps) at around 10:30 a.m. The division then returned to the traditional cavalry role, that of protecting the flanks of the infantry – Gamble the left (south), Devin the right (north) – until the Union infantry forces engaged were forced back in disorder to regroup on Cemetery Hill. On July 2, after some skirmishing on the army's left flank, Buford requested, and was granted by his corps commander Pleasonton, permission to withdraw to reorganize. The problem was that Buford continued withdrawing all the way to Westminster and the hole he left was not plugged. On July 3 the Reserve Brigade moved up to join with Brig.-Gen. Kilpatrick in his attempt to attack the Confederate right flank. The brigade's initial advance was successful but was later halted by concentrated artillery and rifle fire. See also Section Eleven: July 3.

CAVALRY CORPS 2ND DIVISION

Brig.-Gen. David McM. Gregg U.S.V.

Divisional statistics summary

Senior commander casualties

None

Overall losses – percentage

Division	2.1
McIntosh	2.7
I. Gregg	1.7

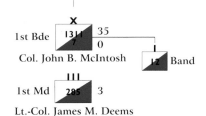

2nd Div. XX 2614 / 3 — 56 / 0
Brig.-Gen. David McM. Gregg

1st Oh Co. A — 37
Capt. Noah Jones

1st Bde X 1311 / 7 — 35 / 0
Col. John B. McIntosh

Band — 12

1st Md — 285 — 3
Lt.-Col. James M. Deems

Purnell Legion Co. A — 66 — 0
Capt. Robert E. Duvall

1st NJ — 199 — 9
Maj. Myron H. Beaumont

1st Pa — 355 — 2
Col. John P. Taylor

3rd Pa — 335 — 21
Lt.-Col. Edward S. Jones

*3rd Pa Hvy Art. Bat. H — 52 — 0
Capt. William D. Rank

3-in Ordnance rifles

1st Mass (attached Army H.Q.)
Lt.-Col. Greely S. Curtis

* Section of Bat. H serving as Horse Artillery

2nd Bde X 1436 — 0
Col. Pennock Huey

3rd U.S. Bat. C — 142
Lt. William D. Fuller

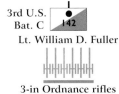

3-in Ordnance rifles

This brigade and the battery were at Westminster and took no part in the battle.

3rd Bde X 1263 / 8 — 21 / 0
Col. J. Irvin Gregg
(cousin of divisional commander)

1st Me — 315 — 5
Lt.-Col. Charles H. Smith

10th NY — 333 — 9
Maj. Matthew H. Avery

4th Pa — 258 — 1
Lt.-Col. William E. Doster

16th Pa — 349 — 6
Lt.-Col. John K. Robison

Action prior to Gettysburg

Following Hooker's reorganization of the cavalry the division took part in the fruitless "Stoneman Raid" during the Chancellorsville campaign. The division was heavily engaged in the great cavalry battle at Brandy Station on June 9, 1863, making repeated charges over a period of 90 minutes. After further reorganizing, it participated in the actions fought along the passes of the Blue Ridge Mountains, notably at Aldie (June 17) and Upperville (June 21).

Action at Gettysburg

On July 1 this division spent the day in somewhat aimless and exhausting marching some 25 miles east of Gettysburg. This continued into July 2, when Gregg received a series of confusing and conflicting orders. Eventually the division, marching to the sound of the guns, arrived a few miles east of Gettysburg from Hanover and were ordered to halt and rest. Only the 4th Pennsylvania Cavalry was sent to the battlefield, supposedly to replace the long-departed Buford on the left flank. This regiment was lightly engaged. The remainder of the division was involved in the clash with some of Ewell's infantry (2nd Virginia) for possession of the Brinkerhoff Ridge 2 miles east of Gettysburg on the Hanover Road. On July 3 most of the day was taken up with a major cavalry clash with Jeb Stuart's command around Rummel Farm – an action later known as East Cavalry Field.

CAVALRY CORPS 3RD DIVISION

Brig.-Gen. Judson Kilpatrick U.S.V.

Divisional statistics summary

Senior commander casualties

1 x brigade commander k

Overall losses – percentage

Division	9.1
Farnsworth	5.1
Custer	13.4

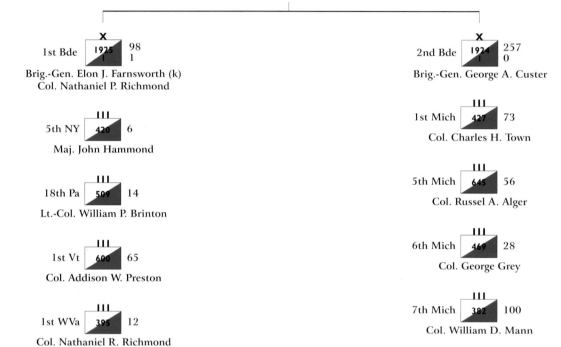

3rd Div. XX 3852 3 355 0
Brig.-Gen. Judson Kilpatrick

1st Bde X 1925 1 98 1
Brig.-Gen. Elon J. Farnsworth (k)
Col. Nathaniel P. Richmond

5th NY III 420 6
Maj. John Hammond

18th Pa III 509 14
Lt.-Col. William P. Brinton

1st Vt III 600 65
Col. Addison W. Preston

1st WVa III 395 12
Col. Nathaniel R. Richmond
Maj. Charles E. Capehart

2nd Bde X 1924 1 257 0
Brig.-Gen. George A. Custer

1st Mich III 427 73
Col. Charles H. Town

5th Mich III 645 56
Col. Russel A. Alger

6th Mich III 469 28
Col. George Grey

7th Mich III 382 100
Col. William D. Mann

Action prior to Gettysburg

On June 28, 1863 the Cavalry Corps was reinforced by the 3rd Division under the newly promoted Brig.-Gen. Kilpatrick (nicknamed "Killcavalry" for his propensity for launching ill-judged charges). Nevertheless, his command did well in the clashes with the Rebel horsemen along the passes of the Blue Ridge Mountains in the early part of the campaign. On June 30 it was in action against Jeb Stuart at Hanover, where it succeeded in forcing the Rebels out of town.

Action at Gettysburg

Not involved on July 1. On July 2 it had reached Hunterstown en route to Gettysburg where it skirmished with Hampton's Brigade – an encounter that involved the 6th Michigan in a charge and Custer having his horse shot under him. The 1st Brigade was not involved on July 2 but was later moved to the Union left to join with Merritt's Brigade (1st Division). July 3 was mostly taken up by Custer's Brigade participating in a furious fight with Stuart's men around Rummel Farm (East Cavalry Field) which involved more charges and resultant hand-to-hand fighting. On July 3 Farnsworth and Merritt launched a futile attack on Law's Rebel infantry, the highlight being the disastrous charge of Farnsworth's Brigade in which he was killed and his men scattered. This division had the highest numerical and percentage loss (mostly in Custer's Brigade) of the three divisions in the Cavalry Corps.

Cavalry Corps H.Q. and Union Horse Artillery

Maj.-Gen. Alfred Pleasonton U.S.V.

Summary		
Robertson	3-in Ordnance rifles	28
Tidball	3-in Ordnance rifles	16
Total		44

XXX
Cavalry Corps H.Q. 27
Maj.-Gen. Alfred Pleasonton

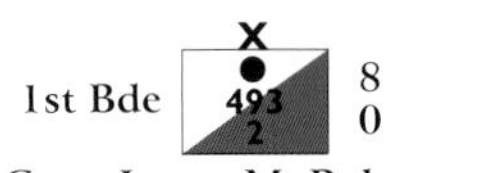

1st Bde 493 2 — 8 / 0
Capt. James M. Robertson

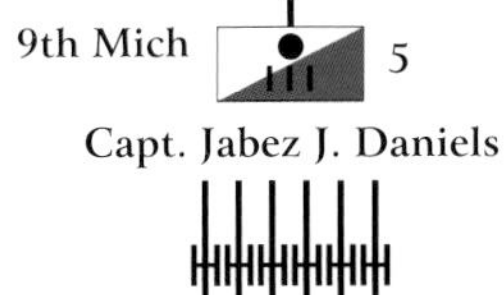

9th Mich 111 — 5
Capt. Jabez J. Daniels
3-in Ordnance rifles

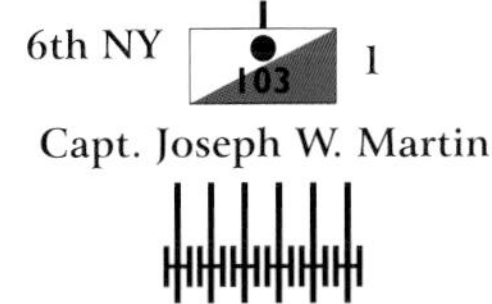

6th NY 103 — 1
Capt. Joseph W. Martin
3-in Ordnance rifles

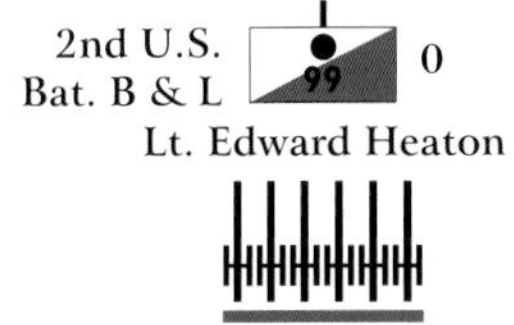

2nd U.S. Bat. B & L 99 — 0
Lt. Edward Heaton
3-in Ordnance rifles

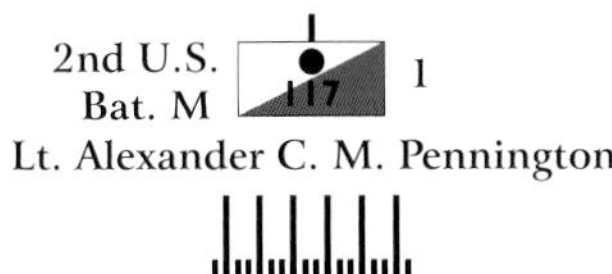

2nd U.S. Bat. M 117 — 1
Lt. Alexander C. M. Pennington

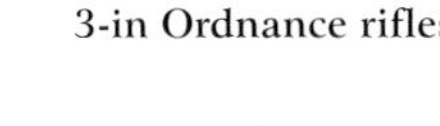

3-in Ordnance rifles

4th U.S. Bat. E 61 — 1
Lt. Samuel S. Elder

3-in Ordnance rifles

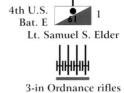

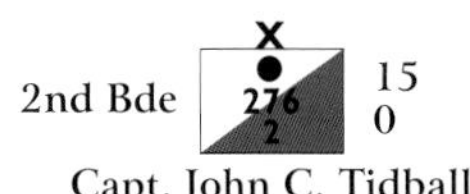

2nd Bde 276 2 — 15 / 0
Capt. John C. Tidball

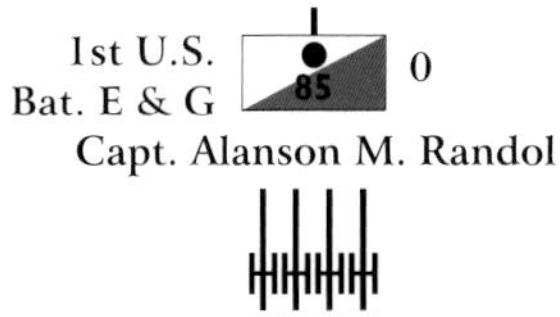

1st U.S. Bat. E & G 85 — 0
Capt. Alanson M. Randol
3-in Ordnance rifles

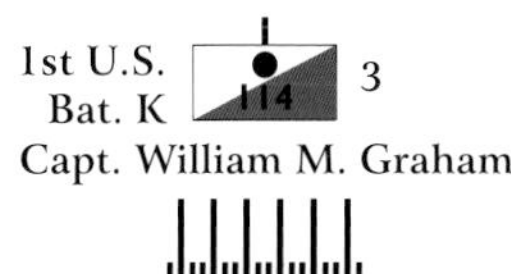

1st U.S. Bat. K 114 — 3
Capt. William M. Graham

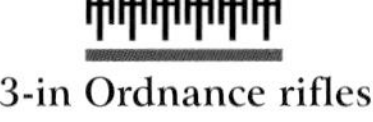

3-in Ordnance rifles

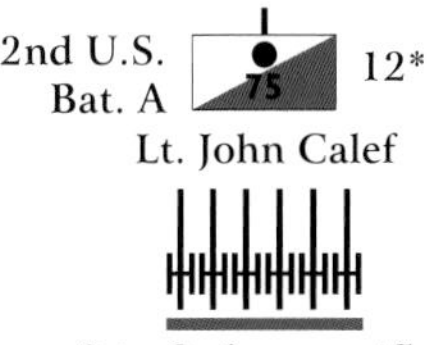

2nd U.S. Bat. A 75 — 12*
Lt. John Calef
3-in Ordnance rifles

* Attached to Buford's 1st Cavalry Division on July 1 and the first Union battery to open fire during the battle.

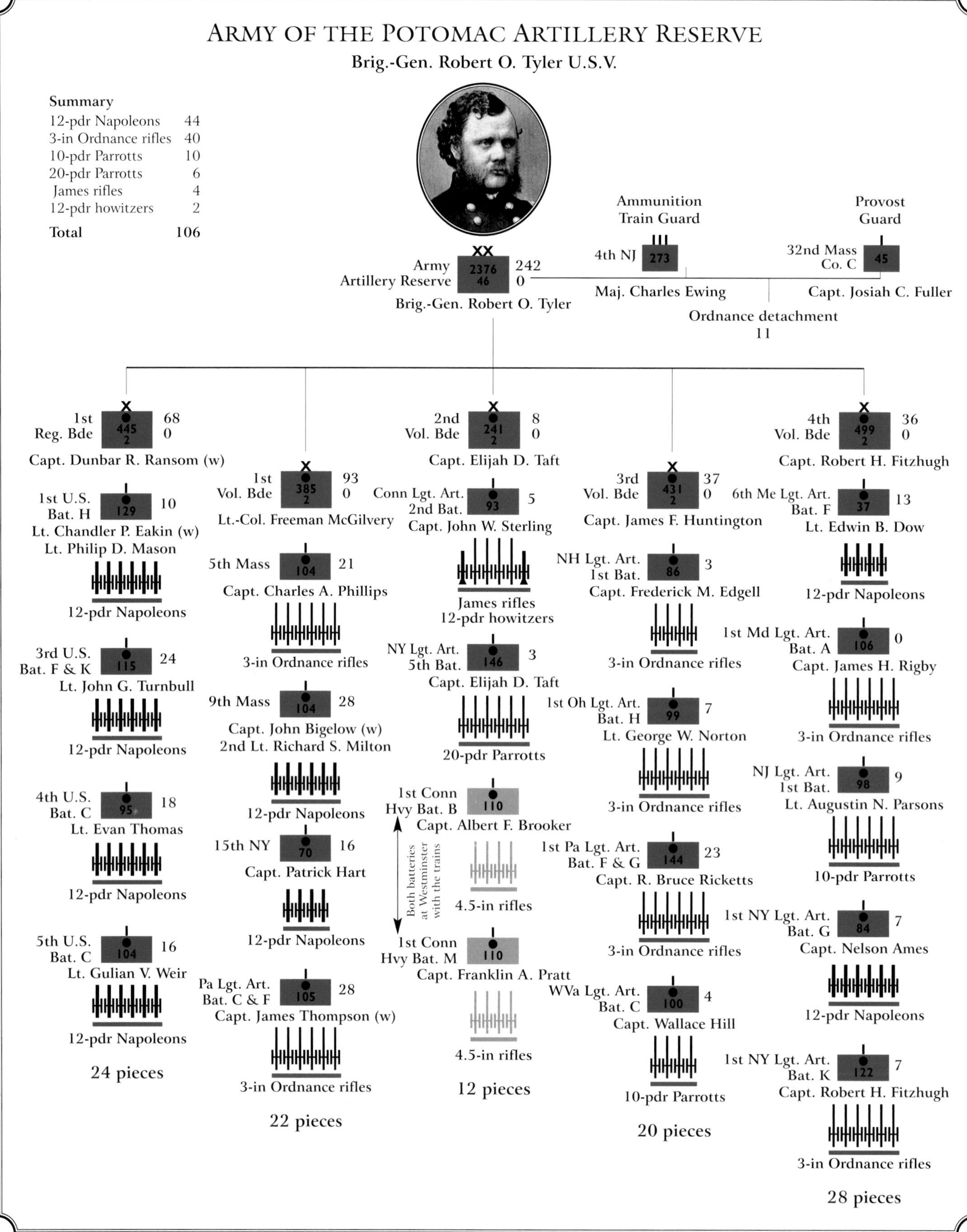
ARMY OF THE POTOMAC ARTILLERY RESERVE
Brig.-Gen. Robert O. Tyler U.S.V.
Summary
12-pdr Napoleons 44
3-in Ordnance rifles 40
10-pdr Parrotts 10
20-pdr Parrotts 6
James rifles 4
12-pdr howitzers 2
Total 106
Army Artillery Reserve 2376 46 242 0
Brig.-Gen. Robert O. Tyler
Ammunition Train Guard
4th NJ 273
Maj. Charles Ewing
Provost Guard
32nd Mass Co. C 45
Capt. Josiah C. Fuller
Ordnance detachment 11
1st Reg. Bde 445 2 68 0
Capt. Dunbar R. Ransom (w)
1st U.S. Bat. H 129 10
Lt. Chandler P. Eakin (w)
Lt. Philip D. Mason
12-pdr Napoleons
3rd U.S. Bat. F & K 115 24
Lt. John G. Turnbull
12-pdr Napoleons
4th U.S. Bat. C 95 18
Lt. Evan Thomas
12-pdr Napoleons
5th U.S. Bat. C 104 16
Lt. Gulian V. Weir
12-pdr Napoleons
24 pieces
1st Vol. Bde 385 2 93 0
Lt.-Col. Freeman McGilvery
5th Mass 104 21
Capt. Charles A. Phillips
3-in Ordnance rifles
9th Mass 104 28
Capt. John Bigelow (w)
2nd Lt. Richard S. Milton
12-pdr Napoleons
15th NY 70 16
Capt. Patrick Hart
12-pdr Napoleons
Pa Lgt. Art. Bat. C & F 105 28
Capt. James Thompson (w)
3-in Ordnance rifles
22 pieces
2nd Vol. Bde 241 2 8 0
Capt. Elijah D. Taft
Conn Lgt. Art. 2nd Bat. 93 5
Capt. John W. Sterling
James rifles
12-pdr howitzers
NY Lgt. Art. 5th Bat. 146 3
Capt. Elijah D. Taft
20-pdr Parrotts
1st Conn Hvy Bat. B 110
Capt. Albert F. Brooker
4.5-in rifles
Both batteries at Westminster with the trains
1st Conn Hvy Bat. M 110
Capt. Franklin A. Pratt
4.5-in rifles
12 pieces
3rd Vol. Bde 431 2 37 0
Capt. James F. Huntington
NH Lgt. Art. 1st Bat. 86 3
Capt. Frederick M. Edgell
3-in Ordnance rifles
1st Oh Lgt. Art. Bat. H 99 7
Lt. George W. Norton
3-in Ordnance rifles
1st Pa Lgt. Art. Bat. F & G 144 23
Capt. R. Bruce Ricketts
3-in Ordnance rifles
WVa Lgt. Art. Bat. C 100 4
Capt. Wallace Hill
10-pdr Parrotts
20 pieces
4th Vol. Bde 499 2 36 0
Capt. Robert H. Fitzhugh
6th Me Lgt. Art. Bat. F 37 13
Lt. Edwin B. Dow
12-pdr Napoleons
1st Md Lgt. Art. Bat. A 106 0
Capt. James H. Rigby
3-in Ordnance rifles
NJ Lgt. Art. 1st Bat. 98 9
Lt. Augustin N. Parsons
10-pdr Parrotts
1st NY Lgt. Art. Bat. G 84 7
Capt. Nelson Ames
12-pdr Napoleons
1st NY Lgt. Art. Bat. K 122 7
Capt. Robert H. Fitzhugh
3-in Ordnance rifles
28 pieces

Union States' Contribution to the Army of the Potomac at Gettysburg

(excluding field and staff units)

State	Engaged Strength	Infantry Regiments	Cavalry Regiments	Artillery Battalions
Connecticut	1,268	5	–	1
Delaware	485	2	–	–
Illinois	1,021	1	2	–
Indiana	2,035	5	1	–
Maine	3,752	10	1	3
Maryland	1,953	3	2	1
Massachusetts	6,104	19	1	4
Michigan	3,899	7	4	1
Minnesota	378	1	–	–
New Hampshire	843	3	–	1
New Jersey	4,073	12	1	2
New York	23,374	70	6	15
Ohio	4,402	13	–	4
Pennsylvania	24,067	67	8	5
Rhode Island	960	1	–	5
U.S. Regulars	7,176	13	4	22
Vermont	4,444	8	1	–
West Virginia	788	1	2	1
Wisconsin	2,155	6	–	–
Totals	**93,177**	**247**	**33**	**65**

Confederate States' Contribution to the Army of Northern Virginia at Gettysburg

(excluding field and staff units)

State	Engaged Strength	Infantry Regiments	Cavalry Regiments	Artillery Battalions
Alabama	5,928	17	–	2
Arkansas	429	1	–	–
Florida	739	3	–	–
Georgia	13,185	37	2	6
Louisiana	3,031	10	–	7
Maryland	981	1	1	3
Mississippi	4,929	11	1	1
North Carolina	14,182	34	2	4
South Carolina	4,959	11	2	5
Tennessee	750	3	–	–
Texas	1,250	3	–	–
Virginia	20,776	41	19	40
Totals	**71,139**	**172**	**27**	**68**

THE ARMY OF NORTHERN VIRGINIA

Overall engaged strength July 1–3, 1863

XXXX 71699 108 — 23231 5

General Robert E. Lee

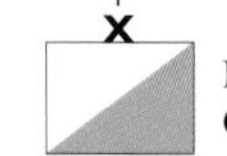

X — Not at Gettysburg

Brig.-Gen. Beverly H. Robertson

1st Corps XXX 20941 16 — 7665 0

Lt.-Gen. James Longstreet

XX 7373 11 — 2407 1

Maj.-Gen. John B. Hood (w)
Brig.-Gen. Evander M. Law
19 guns

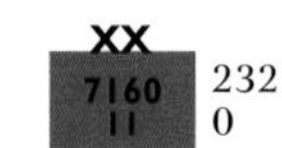

XX 7160 11 — 2327 0

Maj.-Gen. Lafayette McLaws
16 guns

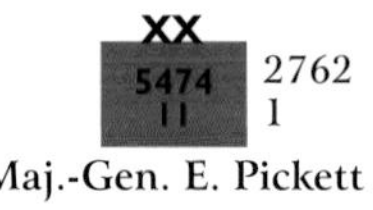

XX 5474 11 — 2762 1

Maj.-Gen. E. Pickett
18 guns

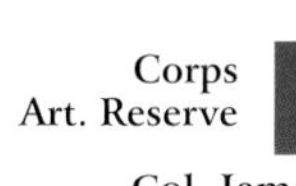

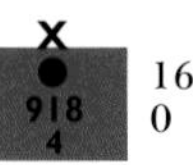

Corps Art. Reserve X 918 4 — 169 0

Col. James B. Walton
34 guns

2nd Corps XXX 20597 142 — 6686 7

Lt.-Gen. Richard S. Ewell

XX 6366 9 — 2005 2

Maj.-Gen. Edward Johnson
16 guns

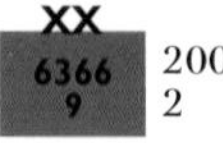

XX 5460 12 — 1530 0

Maj.-Gen. Jubal A. Early
16 guns

XX 7981 14 — 3111 0

Maj.-Gen. Robert E. Rodes
16 guns

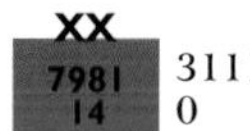

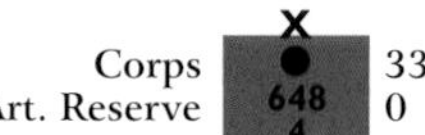

Corps Art. Reserve X 648 4 — 33 0

Col. T. Thompson Brown
31 guns

Statistics summary

Formation	*H.Q.*	*Infantry*	*Cavalry*	*Artillery*	*Total*	*Guns*	*Losses*	*Losses %*
Army H.Q.	108	–	–	–	108	–	5	4.6
Longstreet	16	18,806	–	2,119	20,941	87	7,665	36.6
Ewell	142	18,776	–	1,679	20,597	79	6,686	32.5
Hill	15	20,040	–	1,893	21,948	84	8,495	38.7
Stuart	20	–	7,451	634	8,105	23	380	4.7
Totals	301	57,622	7,451	6,325	71,699	273	23,231	32.4

XXX
3rd Corps 21948 / 15 — 8495 / 0
Lt.-Gen. Ambrose P. Hill

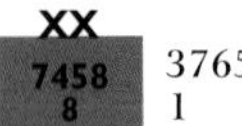

3765
1
Maj.-Gen. Henry Heth (w)
Brig.-Gen. J. Johnston Pettigrew (w)
15 guns

2446
5
Maj.-Gen. William D. Pender (mw)
Brig.-Gen. James H. Lane
Maj.-Gen. Issac R. Trimble (w/c)
Brig.-Gen. James H. Lane
16 guns

XX
7136 / 7 — 2185 / 0
Maj.-Gen. Richard H. Anderson
17 guns

Corps Art. Reserve — 99 / 0
Col. R. Lindsay Walker
36 guns

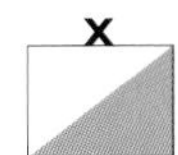

Train guard — not at Gettysburg
Brig.-Gen. John D. Imboden
(independent command)
6 guns

XX
8105 / 20 — 380 / 0
Maj.-Gen. J. E. B. Stuart
23 guns (Horse Artillery)

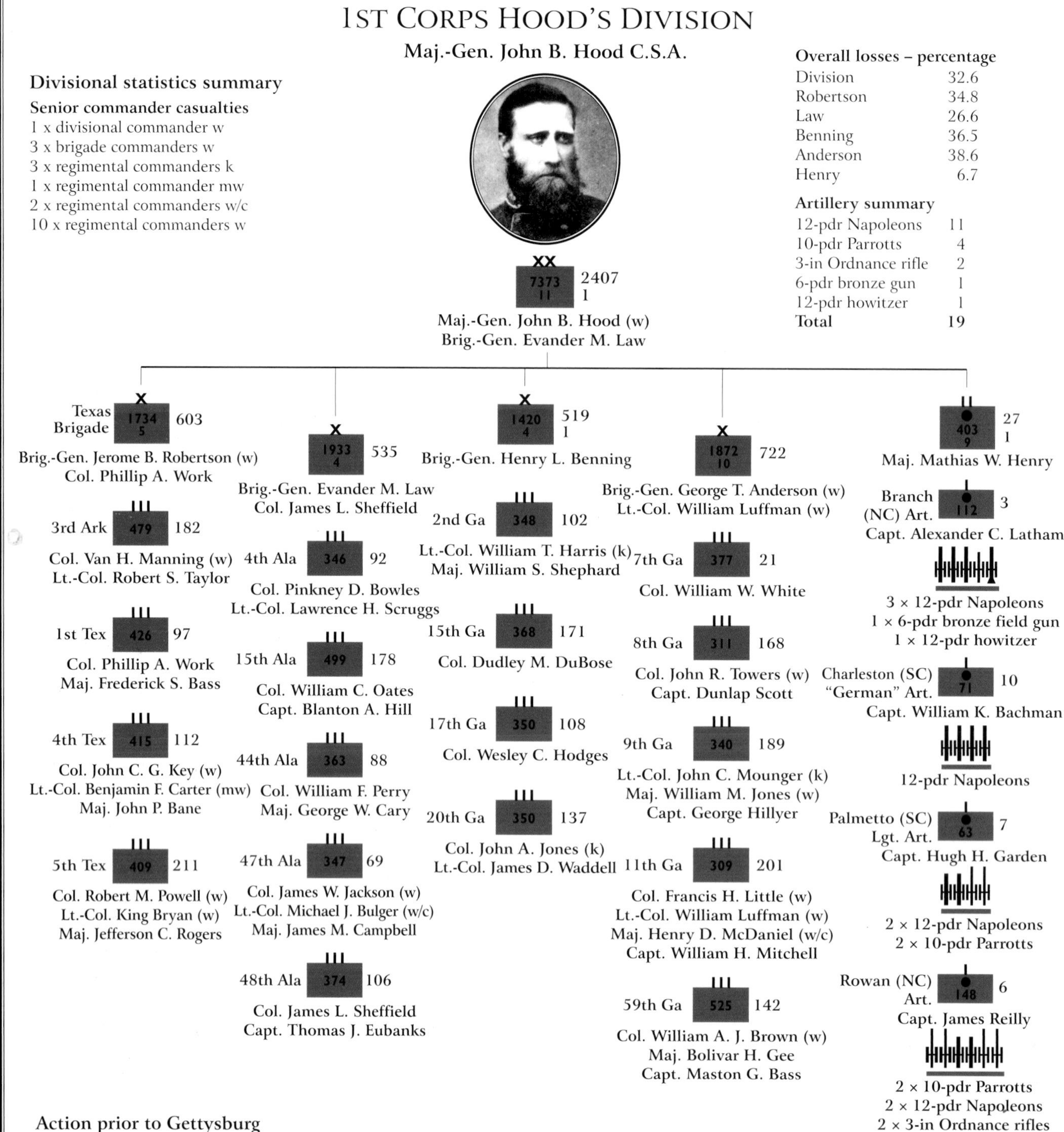

Action prior to Gettysburg

Under a fine divisional commander, this formation was rightly considered to possess some of the best assault troops in the A.N.V. The Texas Brigade in particular had a reputation rivaling that of the Iron Brigade in the A.P. for toughness and hard fighting. The division began its association with Hood during the Peninsular campaign when Hood led a brigade charge that broke the enemy line at Gaines' Mill. At 2nd Manassas it spearheaded Longstreet's attack which almost destroyed Pope's Union Army. Prior to the Battle of South Mountain in the Maryland campaign of 1862 Hood got himself put under arrest, but as his division marched up to the battle the troops started yelling, "Give us Hood! Give us Hood!" To which Lee responded, "You shall have him, gentlemen!" The division was heavily involved at Sharpsburg but was in a quiet part of the line at Fredericksburg and missed Chancellorsville altogether. Thus in June 1863 the division had not seen action for over eight months and was eager for a fight. It arrived at Chambersburg on June 27 but did not leave until June 30. Delays on the line of march caused by supply trains and Johnson's Division cutting in ahead of them meant they did not arrive on Seminary Ridge until around 9:00 a.m. on July 2.

Action at Gettysburg

The division's serious fighting was on July 2 when, as part of Longstreet's assault on the Union salient at the Peach Orchard and left flank, it was committed to the desperate struggle for Devil's Den and Little Round Top. Eventually, with the loss of almost a third of its strength, it took the former but not the latter. Anderson's Brigade suffered severely, with the brigade commander and every original regimental commander except one becoming casualties.

1ST CORPS MCLAWS' DIVISION

Maj.-Gen. Lafayette McLaws C.S.A.

Divisional statistics summary

Senior commander casualties

2 x brigade commanders mw
2 x regimental commanders k
7 x regimental commanders w
1 x regimental commander c

Overall losses – %	
Division	32.5
Barksdale	49.7
Semmes	32.4
Kershaw	30.6
Wofford	22.7
Cabell	13.8

Artillery summary	
12-pdr howitzer	4
10-pdr Parrotts	6
3-in Ordnance rifle	4
12-pdr Napoleons	2
Total	**16**

With 50% losses Barksdale's Brigade suffered the most severely. The 17th Mississippi, with 270 casualties (57.7 per cent), had the eighth highest regimental loss out of 172 in the A.N.V.

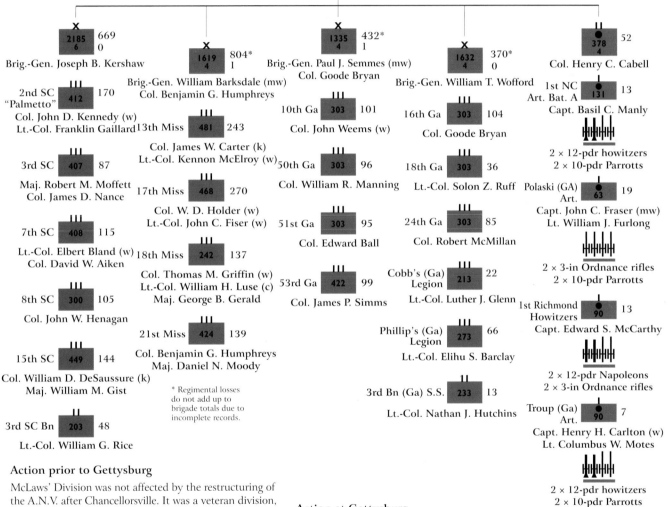

XX 7160 / 11 — 2327 / 0
Maj.-Gen. Lafayette McLaws

Kershaw's Brigade

X 2185 / 6 — 669 / 0
Brig.-Gen. Joseph B. Kershaw

2nd SC "Palmetto" — III 412 — 170
Col. John D. Kennedy (w)
Lt.-Col. Franklin Gaillard

3rd SC — III 407 — 87
Maj. Robert M. Moffett
Col. James D. Nance

7th SC — III 408 — 115
Lt.-Col. Elbert Bland (w)
Col. David W. Aiken

8th SC — III 300 — 105
Col. John W. Henagan

15th SC — III 449 — 144
Col. William D. DeSaussure (k)
Maj. William M. Gist

3rd SC Bn — II 203 — 48
Lt.-Col. William G. Rice

Barksdale's Brigade

X 1619 / 4 — 804* / 1
Brig.-Gen. William Barksdale (mw)
Col. Benjamin G. Humphreys

13th Miss — III 481 — 243
Col. James W. Carter (k)
Lt.-Col. Kennon McElroy (w)

17th Miss — III 468 — 270
Col. W. D. Holder (w)
Lt.-Col. John C. Fiser (w)

18th Miss — III 242 — 137
Col. Thomas M. Griffin (w)
Lt.-Col. William H. Luse (c)
Maj. George B. Gerald

21st Miss — III 424 — 139
Col. Benjamin G. Humphreys
Maj. Daniel N. Moody

* Regimental losses do not add up to brigade totals due to incomplete records.

Semmes' Brigade

X 1335 / 4 — 432* / 1
Brig.-Gen. Paul J. Semmes (mw)
Col. Goode Bryan

10th Ga — III 303 — 101
Col. John Weems (w)

50th Ga — III 303 — 96
Col. William R. Manning

51st Ga — III 303 — 95
Col. Edward Ball

53rd Ga — III 422 — 99
Col. James P. Simms

Wofford's Brigade

X 1632 / 4 — 370* / 0
Brig.-Gen. William T. Wofford

16th Ga — III 303 — 104
Col. Goode Bryan

18th Ga — III 303 — 36
Lt.-Col. Solon Z. Ruff

24th Ga — III 303 — 85
Col. Robert McMillan

Cobb's (Ga) Legion — III 213 — 22
Lt.-Col. Luther J. Glenn

Phillip's (Ga) Legion — III 273 — 66
Lt.-Col. Elihu S. Barclay

3rd Bn (Ga) S.S. — II 233 — 13
Lt.-Col. Nathan J. Hutchins

Cabell's Artillery

II 378 / 4 — 52
Col. Henry C. Cabell

1st NC Art. Bat. A — 131 — 13
Capt. Basil C. Manly
2 × 12-pdr howitzers
2 × 10-pdr Parrotts

Polaski (GA) Art. — 63 — 19
Capt. John C. Fraser (mw)
Lt. William J. Furlong
2 × 3-in Ordnance rifles
2 × 10-pdr Parrotts

1st Richmond Howitzers — 90 — 13
Capt. Edward S. McCarthy
2 × 12-pdr Napoleons
2 × 3-in Ordnance rifles

Troup (Ga) Art. — 90 — 7
Capt. Henry H. Carlton (w)
Lt. Columbus W. Motes
2 × 12-pdr howitzers
2 × 10-pdr Parrotts

Action prior to Gettysburg

McLaws' Division was not affected by the restructuring of the A.N.V. after Chancellorsville. It was a veteran division, described by some as the finest in the army, under a commander who had been associated with it since November 1861. McLaws had led his division during the Seven Days Battles at Savage's Station and Malvern Hill. It missed 2nd Manassas as it was manning the Richmond defenses, but participated in the Maryland campaign in September 1862, although it was criticized for taking 41 hours to march from Harper's Ferry to Sharpsburg (15 miles) to reinforce a hard-pressed Lee. At Fredericksburg it occupied rifle pits at the base of Marye's Hill and sent successive attacks reeling back with huge losses. At Chancellorsville McLaws was hesitant to attack at a critical moment when there was a chance of destroying a Federal corps – it ruled him out of promotion to corps command.

Action at Gettysburg

This division did not approach the battlefield until the morning of July 2. It was committed to playing a main part in the bitter and prolonged struggle for the area around the Peach Orchard, Wheatfield, Stony Hill and Rose Woods that afternoon. Kershaw's Brigade led the initial assault on Stony Hill supported by Semmes Brigade. Barksdale's somewhat delayed attack on the Peach Orchard and the Federal line immediately to the north along the Emmitsburg Road was one of the most outstanding of the battle, resulting in the defeat of two enemy brigades and the temporary capture of nine cannon. This attack penetrated as far east as Plum Run. Wofford's Brigade was heavily involved in the fight for the Wheatfield and into Trostle Wood. Wofford was furious at Longstreet's eventual order to withdraw, claiming he could have taken Little Round Top. The division was barely involved in the action on July 3; virtually all its losses arose from its struggle with Sickles' salient the day before.

1ST CORPS PICKETT'S DIVISION

Maj.-Gen. George E. Pickett C.S.A.

Divisional statistics summary

Senior commander casualties

1 x brigade commander k
1 x brigade commander mw/c
1 x brigade commander w/c
3 x brigade commanders w
5 x regimental commanders k
4 x regimental commanders mw
2 x regimental commanders mw/c
4 x regimental commanders w/c
13 x regimental commanders w

Overall losses – percentage

Division	50.5
Kemper	43
Armistead	55.6
Garnett	65
Dearing	6

Artillery summary

12-pdr Napoleons	12
10-pdr Parrotts	3
20-pdr Parrotts	2
3-in Ordnance rifle	1
Total	18

XX 5474 / 11 — 2762 / 1
Maj.-Gen. George E. Pickett

X 1634 / 4 — 703 / 4
Brig.-Gen. James L. Kemper (w/c)
Col. Joseph C. Mayo Jr (w)
Col. William R. Terry (w)

1st Va III 209 — 113
Col. Lewis B. Williams (k)
Lt.-Col. Francis G. Skinner
Maj. Francis H. Langley (w)
Capt. George R. Norton (w)
Capt. Thomas Davis (w)
Capt. Benjamin F. Howard

3rd Va III 332 — 128
Col. Joseph C. Mayo Jr. (w)
Lt.-Col. Alexander D. Callcote (k)

7th Va III 335 — 149
Col. Waller T. Patton (mw/c)
Lt.-Col. C. C. Floweree
Capt. Alfonso N. Jones

11th Va III 359 — 146
Maj. Kirkwood Otey (w)
Capt. James R. Hutter (w/c)

24th Va III 395 — 163
Col. William R. Terry (w)
Capt. William N. Bentley (w)

X 1950 / 4 — 1085 / 2
Brig.-Gen. Lewis A. Armistead (mw/c)
Col. William R. Aylett (w)

9th Va III 257 — 177
Maj. John C. Owens (mw)
Capt. James J. Phillips

14th Va III 422 — 250
Col. James G. Hodges (k)
Lt.-Col. William White (w)

38th Va III 356 — 194
Col. Edward C. Edmonds (k)
Lt.-Col. Powhatan B. Whittle (w/c)

53rd Va III 435 — 213
Col. William R. Aylett (w)
Lt.-Col. Rowley W. Martin (w/c)

57th Va III 476 — 249
Col. John B. Magruder (mw/c)
Lt.-Col. B. H. Wade (mw)
Maj. Clement R. Fontaine

X 1459 / 4 — 948 / 3
Brig.-Gen. Robert B. Garnett (k)
Maj. Charles S. Peyton

8th Va III 193 — 178
Col. Eppa Hunton (w)
Lt.-Col. Norborne (w/c)
Maj. Edward Berkeley (w)
Lt. John Gray

18th Va III 312 — 245
Lt.-Col. Henry A. Carrington (w)
Col. Robert E. Withers

19th Va III 328 — 151
Col. Henry Gantt (w)
Lt.-Col. John T. Ellis (mw)
Maj. Charles S. Peyton

28th Va III 333 — 182
Col. Robert C. Allen (k)
Lt.-Col. William Watts

56th Va III 289 — 189
Col. William D. Stuart (mw)
Lt.-Col. P. P. Slaughter

II 420 / 9 — 25 / 1
Maj. James Dearing

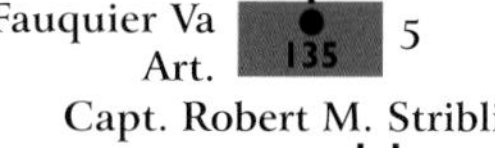
Fauquier Va Art. I 135 — 5
Capt. Robert M. Stribling
4 × 12-pdr Napoleons
2 × 20-pdr Parrotts

Lynchburg Va Art. I 96 — 10
Capt. Joseph G. Blount

12-pdr Napoleons

Richmond Fayette Va Lgt. Art. I 90 — 5
Capt. Miles C. Macon
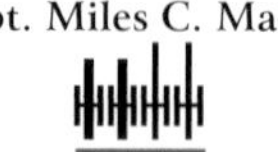
2 × 12-pdr Napoleons
2 × 10-pdr Parrotts

Richmond Hampton Va Art. I 90 — 4
Capt. William H. Caskie
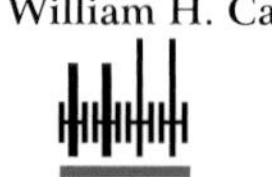
2 × 12-pdr Napoleons
1 × 3-in Ordnance rifle
1 × 10-pdr Parrott

Action prior to Gettysburg

At Gettysburg this division was composed entirely of Virginian troops. Unfortunately it had been compelled to leave Corse's and Jenkins' Brigades guarding the approaches to Richmond so went into battle with only two-fifths of its normal strength. It was a very young division, the average age of the troops being 19. It was only marginally engaged at Fredericksburg and was not present at Chancellorsville. When Longstreet's Corps set out for Gettysburg on June 30 this division was left at Chambersburg guarding the trains. Only when Imboden's cavalry brigade arrived in the early hours of July 2 was it able to start out for the battlefield. After a hard march of 25 miles they halted some 3 miles from Gettysburg and were rested. To the surprise and disappointment of many, as the sound of fighting was so loud and continuous, these Virginians were not called upon that day.

Action at Gettysburg

The division's march to join the battle began at 2:00 a.m. on July 3. There at around 3:00 p.m. the divisional commander gave his name to the most famous action of the Civil War – Pickett's charge. Of the seven officers who at some stage commanded the three brigades, six were casualties. Of the officers who commanded the 15 regiments in the attack, 28 were hit. The only senior officer to come away unscathed was Pickett himself. In the 19th Virginia Maj. Charles Peyton took command after the loss of the colonel and lieutenant-colonel. When Brig.-Gen. Garnett was killed Peyton found himself brigade commander. This brigade suffered 65% casualties, the 8th Virginia losing 178 men out of 193 – 92.2 percent, the highest percentage loss for any regiment in either army in the battle.

1ST CORPS ARTILLERY RESERVE A.N.V.

Col. James B. Walton

918
4
169
0
Col. James B. Walton

(34 pieces)

* 576 9 139 0
Col. E. Porter Alexander
Maj. Frank Huger

Madison (La) Bat. 135 33
Capt. George V. Moody

4 × 24-pdr howitzers

Brocks (SC) Light Bat. 71 36
Capt. William W. Fickling
Lt. S. Capers Gilbert (w)

4 × 12-pdr howitzers

Ashland (Va) Bat. 103 28
Capt. Pichegru Woolfolk (w)
Lt. James Woolfolk

2 × 20-pdr Parrotts
2 × 12-pdr Napoleons

Bedford (Va) Bat. 78 9
Capt. Tyler C. Jordon

4 × 3-in Ordnance rifles

Richmond (Va) Bat. 90 18
Capt. William Parker

3 × 3-in Ordnance rifles
1 × 10-pdr Parrott

Bath (Va) Bat. 90 13
Capt. Osmond B. Taylor

4 × 12-pdr Napoleons

24 pieces

The losses of individual batteries do not add up to the battalion total due to missing records.

Washington (La) Bat. 338 9 30 0
Maj. Benjamin F. Eshleman

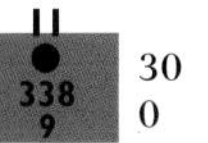

1st Co. 77 4
Lt. Charles H. C. Brown (w/c)
Capt. Charles W. Squires

1 × 12-pdr Napoleon

2nd Co. 80 6
Capt. John B. Richardson

2 × 12-pdr Napoleons
1 × 12-pdr howitzer

3rd Co. 92 10
Capt. Merritt B. Miller

3 × 12-pdr Napoleons

4th Co. 80 10
Capt. Joseph Norcom (w)
Lt. Henry A. Battles

2 × 12-pdr Napoleons
1 × 12-pdr howitzer

10 pieces

Overall losses – percentage

Brigade	18.4	
Alexander	24.1	
• Moody	24.4	3rd highest % loss of any A.N.V. battery
• Gilbert	50.7	highest % loss of any A.N.V. battery
• Woolfolk	27.2	2nd highest % loss of any A.N.V. battery
• Jordon	11.5	
• Parker	20.0	
• Taylor	14.4	
Eshlemen	8.9	
• Squires	5.2	
• Richardson	7.5	
• Miller	10.9	
• Norcom	12.5	

Statistics summary

Commander	*24-pdr howitzer*	*12-pdr howitzer*	*Napoleons*	*3-in Ordnance rifles*	*Parrotts*	***Total***
Alexander	4	4	6	7	3	24
Eshleman	–	2	8	–	–	10
Totals	4	6	14	7	3	34

* the strongest artillery battalion in the A.N.V.

2ND CORPS JOHNSON'S DIVISION

Maj.-Gen. Edward Johnson C.S.A.

Divisional statistics summary

Senior commander casualties
1 x brigade commander w
1 x regimental commander k
2 x regimental commanders w/c
5 x regimental commanders w

Overall losses – %	
Division	31.5
Williams	35.2
Steuart	36.3
Walker	25.5
Jones	31.4
Latimer	14.3

Artillery summary	
12-pdr Napoleons	6
10-pdr Parrotts	5
20-pdr Parrotts	2
3-in Ordnance rifle	3
Total	**16**

XX 6366 / 9 — 2005 / 0
Maj.-Gen. Edward Johnson

Nicholls' Brigade (Louisiana Tigers) X 1104 / 3 — 389* / 0
Col. Jesse M. Williams

- 1st La 172 — 39: Lt.-Col. Michael Nolan (k), Capt. Edward D. Willett
- 2nd La 236 — 62: Lt.-Col. Ross E. Burke (w/c)
- 10th La 226 — 110: Lt.-Col. Henry Monier
- 14th La 281 — 65: Lt.-Col. David Zable
- 15th La 186 — 38: Maj. Andrew Brady

* Unit losses do not add up to brigade totals due to incomplete records.

Steuart's Brigade X 2121 / 5 — 769 / 0
Brig.-Gen. George H. Steuart

- 1st NC 377 — 151: Lt.-Col. Hamilton A. Brown
- 3rd NC 548 — 218: Maj. William A. Parsley
- 10th Va 276 — 77: Col. Edward T. H. Warren
- 23rd Va 251 — 36: Lt.-Col. Simeon T. Walton
- 37th Va 264 — 98: Maj. Henry C. Wood
- 1st Md (II) 400 — 189: Lt.-Col. James R. Herbert (w), Maj. William C. Goldsborough (w/c), Capt. James P. Crane

Stonewall Brigade X 1323 / 4 — 338 / 0
Brig.-Gen. James A. Walker

- 2nd Va 333 — 25: Col. John Q. A. Nadenbousch
- 4th Va 257 — 137: Maj. William Terry
- 5th Va 345 — 58: Col. John H. S. Funk
- 27th Va 148 — 48: Lt.-Col. Daniel M. Shriver
- 33rd Va 236 — 70: Capt. Jacob B. Golladay

Jones' Brigade X 1453 / 7 — 456 / 2
Brig.-Gen. John M. Jones (w), Lt.-Col. Robert H. Dungan

- 21st Va 183 — 50: Col. William P. Moseley
- 25th Va 280 — 70: Col. John C. Higginbotham (w), Lt.-Col. John A. Robinson
- 42nd Va 252 — 89: Lt.-Col. Robert W. Withers (w), Capt. Jesse M. Richardson (w), Capt. Samuel H. Saunders
- 44th Va 227 — 59: Maj. Norvell Cobb (w), Capt. Thomas R. Buckner
- 48th Va 252 — 87: Lt.-Col. Robert H. Dungan, Maj. Oscar White
- 50th Va 252 — 99: Lt.-Col. Logan H. N. Salyer

Artillery II 356 / 9 — 51 / 2
Maj. James W. Latimer (mw), Capt. Charles I. Raine

- 1st Md Bat. 90 — 5: Capt. William F. Dement — 4 x 12-pdr Napoleons
- Allegheny (Va) Bat. 91 — 24: Capt. John C. Carpenter — 2 x 12-pdr Napoleons, 2 x 3-in Ordnance rifles
- 4th Md Bat (Chesapeake) 76 — 17: Capt. William D. Brown (k), Lt. Charles S. Contee (w) — 4 x 10-pdr Parrotts
- Lee (Va) Bat. 90 — 4: Capt. Charles I. Raine, Lt. William W. Hardwicke — 2 x 20-pdr Parrotts, 1 x 10-pdr Parrott, 1 x 3-in Ordnance rifle

Action prior to Gettysburg

The heart of this division was formerly the Stonewall Brigade – Jackson's old command of Shenandoah Valley fame – with two-thirds of its regiments Virginian. After Jackson left it the division had no fewer than five commanders through the heavy fighting at Cedar Mountain, 2nd Manassas and Sharpsburg. It was only lightly engaged at Fredericksburg, but formed the second wave of Jackson's famous flank attack at Chancellorsville. However, Lee was dissatisfied with the commander, Brig.-Gen. Raleigh Colston's, performance and sacked him with "uncharacteristic speed and finality." He summoned Maj.-Gen. Edward Johnson as a replacement. Early in the Gettysburg campaign the division cut off the retreating Winchester garrison, capturing some 2,300 men and 11 regimental colors. The division arrived northeast of Gettysburg at around 7:30 p.m. on July 1 after a 25-mile march, slowed by competing for road space with supply trains. After being told the enemy occupied Culp's Hill, Johnson put off an attack until next day.

Action at Gettysburg

Not until after 4:00 p.m. on July 2 did the division assault Culp's Hill. The struggle continued until around 10:30 p.m. with some desperate fighting in the darkness, up a steep slope through woods against defenders who had prepared substantial breastworks. The division was partially successful and secured some of the defenses. Late in the afternoon of July 3 further severe and bloody fighting took place for Culp's Hill, but the division made no real progress and had to withdraw.

2ND CORPS EARLY'S DIVISION

Maj.-Gen. Jubal A. Early C.S.A.

Divisional statistics summary

Senior commander casualties
1 x brigade commander mw
2 x regimental commanders k
4 x regimental commanders w

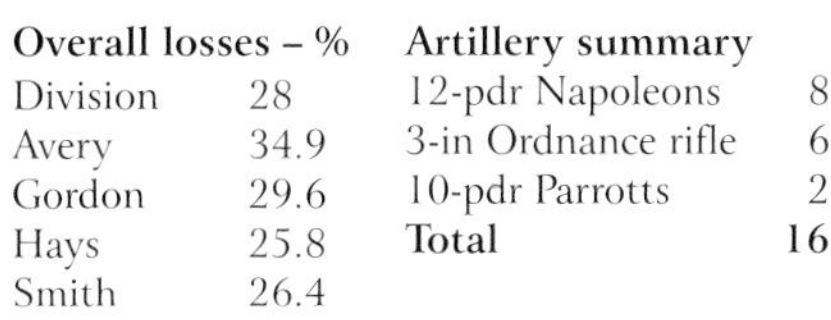

Overall losses – %	
Division	28
Avery	34.9
Gordon	29.6
Hays	25.8
Smith	26.4
Jones	4.1

Artillery summary	
12-pdr Napoleons	8
3-in Ordnance rifle	6
10-pdr Parrotts	2
Total	**16**

XX 5460 / 12 — 1530 / 0
Maj.-Gen. Jubal A. Early

X 1244 / 2 — 434 / 1
Col. Issac. E. Avery (mw)
Col. Archibald C. Godwin

- 6th NC — 509 — 208 — Maj. Samuel McD. Tate
- 21st NC — 436 — 139 — Col. William W. Kirkland
- 57th NC — 297 — 86 — Col. Archibald C. Godwin

X 1813 / 6 — 537 / 0
Brig.-Gen. John B. Gordon

- 13th Ga — 312 — 137 — Col. James M. Smith
- 26th Ga — 315 — 32 — Col. Edmund D. Atkinson
- 31st Ga — 252 — 65 — Col. Clement A. Evans (w)
- 38th Ga — 341 — 133 — Capt. William L. McLeod (k)
- 60th Ga — 299 — 59 — Capt. Walter B. Jones
- 61st Ga — 288 — 111 — Col. John H. Lamar

X 1295 / 3 — 334 / 0
Brig.-Gen. Harry T. Hays

- 5th La — 196 — 67 — Col. Henry Forno; Maj. Alexander Hart (w); Capt. Thomas H. Biscoe
- 6th La — 218 — 61 — Col. William Monaghan; Lt.-Col. Joseph Hanlon
- 7th La — 235 — 58 — Col. Davidson B. Penn
- 8th La — 296 — 75 — Col. Travanion D. Lewis (k); L.t-Col. Alcibiades de Blanc (w); Maj. German A. Lester
- 9th La — 347 — 73 — Col. Leroy A. Stafford

X 806 / 4 — 213 / 0
Brig.-Gen. William Smith

- 31st Va — 267 — 59 — Col. John S. Hoffman
- 49th Va — 281 — 100 — Lt.-Col. Johnathan C. Gibson
- 52nd Va — 254 — 54 — Col. James H. Skinner (w); Lt.-Col. John D. Ross

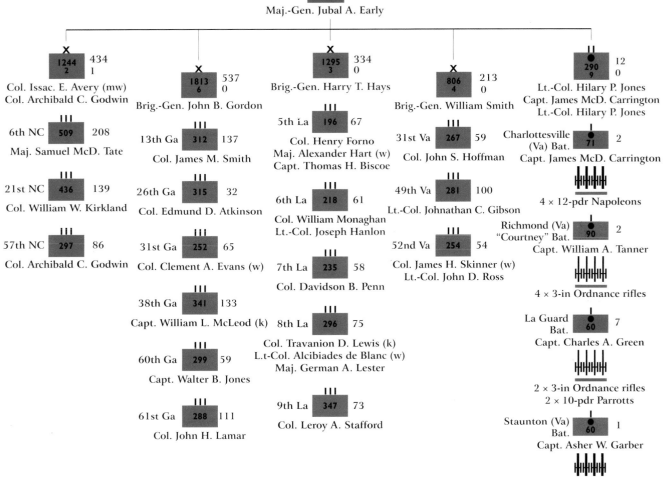

II 290 / 9 — 12 / 0
Lt.-Col. Hilary P. Jones
Capt. James McD. Carrington
Lt.-Col. Hilary P. Jones

- Charlottesville (Va) Bat. — 71 — 2 — Capt. James McD. Carrington — 4 x 12-pdr Napoleons
- Richmond (Va) "Courtney" Bat. — 90 — 2 — Capt. William A. Tanner — 4 x 3-in Ordnance rifles
- La Guard Bat. — 60 — 7 — Capt. Charles A. Green — 2 x 3-in Ordnance rifles; 2 x 10-pdr Parrotts
- Staunton (Va) Bat. — 60 — 1 — Capt. Asher W. Garber — 4 x 12-pdr Napoleons

Action prior to Gettysburg

A tough, hard-fighting division under a competent if crusty commander. Hays's Louisiana Brigade in particular had a reputation for drunkenness, desertion and pillaging as well as fighting. The division had done well at Sharpsburg and successfully counterattacked the Union penetration of the Confederate line at Fredericksburg. In the Chancellorsville campaign it was given the difficult task of holding the defenses at Fredericksburg against greatly superior numbers, while Lee took the rest of the army to meet and defeat Hooker. When the Union VI Corps attacked, the division was forced back after a prolonged struggle, losing over 800 men in the progress. However, it participated in the counterattack that pushed the enemy across the river. A fine success was its defeat of the Union forces in and around Winchester (June 14, 1863) on the march that ended at Gettysburg.

Action at Gettysburg

Of the 10 divisions (including Stuart's cavalry) in the A.N.V., Early's was the smallest. The average divisional strength was 6,912 – this division could muster only 79% of that.
Brig.-Gen. Smith's Brigade was very weak, and in Hays's Brigade the 5th Louisiana, with only 196 men, was one of only 11 regiments/battalions that fell below 200. Its best day at Gettysburg was July 1 when it marched to the sound of the guns and drove Barlow's Union Division off Blocher's Knoll, then scattered Coster's hastily deployed reserve brigade on the northern outskirts of the town. Late on July 2 it was engaged in a supposedly diversionary attack on Cemetery Hill that developed into a major assault which failed primarily through lack of support. It saw little action on July 3.

2ND CORPS RODES' DIVISION

Maj.-Gen. Robert E. Rodes C.S.A.

Divisional statistics summary

Senior commander casualties

1 x regimental commander k
1 x battalion commander k
2 x regimental commanders mw
8 x regimental commanders w
1 x regimental commander c
5 x regimental commanders w/c

Overall losses – %	
Division	39.0
Iverson	65.2
Daniel	46.2
O'Neal	40.2
Ramseur	26.8
Carter	9.6

Artillery summary	
12-pdr Napoleons	6
3-in Ordnance rifles	6
10-pdr Parrotts	4
Total	**16**

Note: The 23rd NC losses at 89% were the second highest losses in percentage terms of any regiment at Gettysburg.

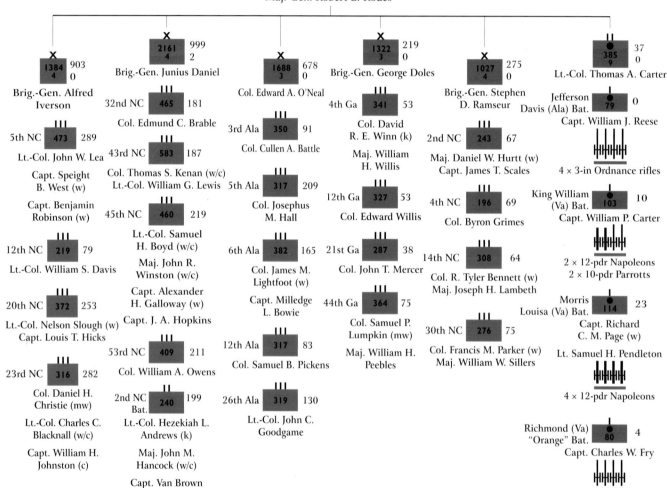

XX 7981 14 — 3111 0
Maj.-Gen. Robert E. Rodes

X 1384 4 — 903 0
Brig.-Gen. Alfred Iverson

- 5th NC — III 473 — 289 — Lt.-Col. John W. Lea; Capt. Speight B. West (w); Capt. Benjamin Robinson (w)
- 12th NC — III 219 — 79 — Lt.-Col. William S. Davis
- 20th NC — III 372 — 253 — Lt.-Col. Nelson Slough (w); Capt. Louis T. Hicks
- 23rd NC — III 316 — 282 — Col. Daniel H. Christie (mw); Lt.-Col. Charles C. Blacknall (w/c); Capt. William H. Johnston (c)

X 2161 4 — 999 2
Brig.-Gen. Junius Daniel

- 32nd NC — III 465 — 181 — Col. Edmund C. Brable
- 43rd NC — III 583 — 187 — Col. Thomas S. Kenan (w/c); Lt.-Col. William G. Lewis
- 45th NC — III 460 — 219 — Lt.-Col. Samuel H. Boyd (w/c); Maj. John R. Winston (w/c); Capt. Alexander H. Galloway (w); Capt. J. A. Hopkins
- 53rd NC — III 409 — 211 — Col. William A. Owens
- 2nd NC Bat. — II 240 — 199 — Lt.-Col. Hezekiah L. Andrews (k); Maj. John M. Hancock (w/c); Capt. Van Brown

X 1688 3 — 678 0
Col. Edward A. O'Neal

- 3rd Ala — III 350 — 91 — Col. Cullen A. Battle
- 5th Ala — III 317 — 209 — Col. Josephus M. Hall
- 6th Ala — III 382 — 165 — Col. James M. Lightfoot (w); Capt. Milledge L. Bowie
- 12th Ala — III 317 — 83 — Col. Samuel B. Pickens
- 26th Ala — III 319 — 130 — Lt.-Col. John C. Goodgame

X 1322 3 — 219 0
Brig.-Gen. George Doles

- 4th Ga — III 341 — 53 — Col. David R. E. Winn (k); Maj. William H. Willis
- 12th Ga — III 327 — 53 — Col. Edward Willis
- 21st Ga — III 287 — 38 — Col. John T. Mercer
- 44th Ga — III 364 — 75 — Col. Samuel P. Lumpkin (mw); Maj. William H. Peebles

X 1027 4 — 275 0
Brig.-Gen. Stephen D. Ramseur

- 2nd NC — III 243 — 67 — Maj. Daniel W. Hurtt (w); Capt. James T. Scales
- 4th NC — III 196 — 69 — Col. Byron Grimes
- 14th NC — III 308 — 64 — Col. R. Tyler Bennett (w); Maj. Joseph H. Lambeth
- 30th NC — III 276 — 75 — Col. Francis M. Parker (w); Maj. William W. Sillers

II 385 9 — 37 0
Lt.-Col. Thomas A. Carter

- Jefferson Davis (Ala) Bat. — 79 — 0 — Capt. William J. Reese — 4 x 3-in Ordnance rifles
- King William (Va) Bat. — 103 — 10 — Capt. William P. Carter — 2 x 12-pdr Napoleons; 2 x 10-pdr Parrotts
- Morris Louisa (Va) Bat. — 114 — 23 — Capt. Richard C. M. Page (w); Lt. Samuel H. Pendleton — 4 x 12-pdr Napoleons
- Richmond (Va) "Orange" Bat. — 80 — 4 — Capt. Charles W. Fry — 2 x 3-in Ordnance rifles; 2 x 10-pdr Parrotts

Action prior to Gettysburg

This was D. H. Hill's division before he was sent to North Carolina in January 1863. It had an impressive battlefield record, fighting well at Williamsburg, Seven Pines, Mechanicsville, Gaines' Mill and Malvern Hill. It held the center of the line at Fredericksburg, and at Chancellorsville was in the forefront of Jackson's flank attack, although it lost over 3,000 at that battle. In the Gettysburg campaign it was the first infantry division to cross the Potomac into Northern territory on June 15, reaching Carlisle on the 27th. On June 30 it had hoped to occupy Harrisburg but was ordered to turn back and march first for Cashtown and then to Gettysburg. It was a hard march until the 4th Georgia's band struck up, the effect of which, according to a soldier in Doles's Brigade, was "magical in its effect." On July 1 they double-quicked the last few miles to the north of Gettysburg, encouraged by the continuous roar of battle to the south.

Action at Gettysburg

The division arrived on Oak Hill around 1:00 p.m. and was quickly launched into a series of attacks on what was thought initially to be an exposed Union flank. The first attacks were unsuccessful and at one stage Iverson's Brigade in particular suffered appalling losses when it was in effect ambushed at close range. Not until later that afternoon did the division take Oak Ridge and help drive the Union defenders back through the town. The division spent July 2 in and around Gettysburg with little significant activity. On July 3 O'Neal's and Daniel's Brigades were sent to support Johnson's Division in its renewed attacks on Culp's Hill, the remainder being spectators of Pettigrew's attack on, and recoil from, Cemetery Ridge.

2ND CORPS ARTILLERY RESERVE A.N.V.

Col. T. Thompson Brown

XX
648 / 4 — 33 / 0
Col. T. Thompson Brown

(31 pieces)

1st Virginia Artillery — 367 / 9 — 32 / 0
Capt. Willis J. Dance

2nd Richmond (Va) Howitzer Bat. — 64 — 3
Capt. David Watson

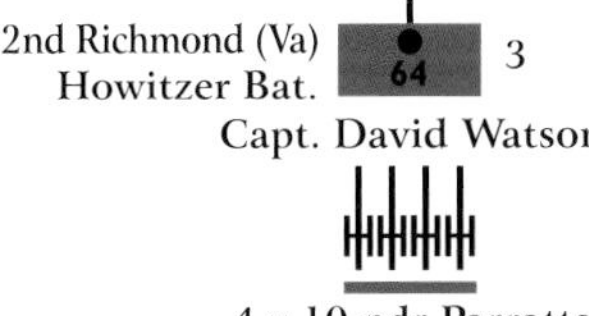

4 × 10-pdr Parrotts

3rd Richmond (Va) Howitzer Bat. — 62 — 4
Capt. Benjamin H. Smith

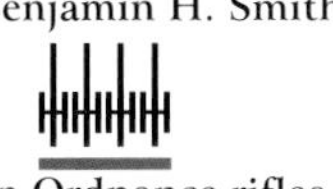

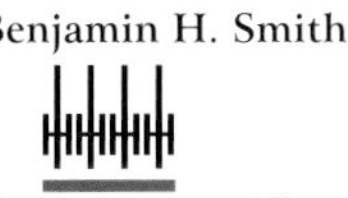

4 × 3-in Ordnance rifles

No longer equipped with howitzers.

1st Rockbridge (Va) Bat. — 85 — 20
Capt. Archibald Graham

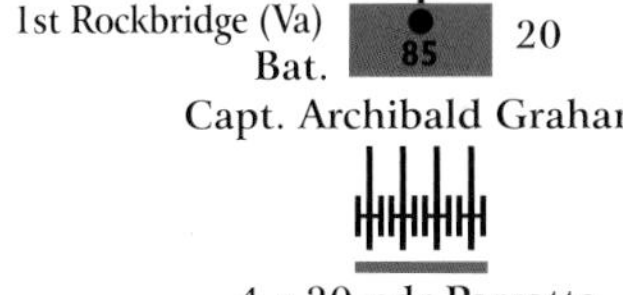

4 × 20-pdr Parrotts

Powhatan (Va) Bat. — 78 — 0
Lt. John Cunningham

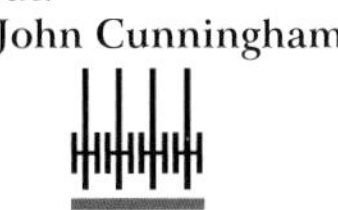

4 × 3-in Ordnance rifles

Salem (Va) "Flying" Bat. — 69 — 5
Lt. Charles B. Griffin

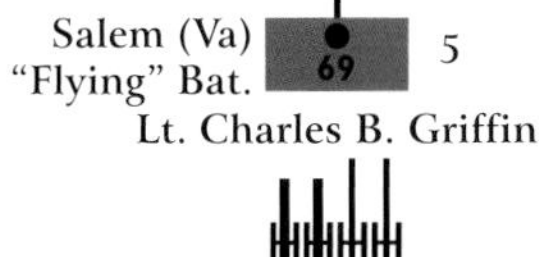

2 × 12-pdr Napoleons
2 × 3-in Ordnance rifles

20 pieces

277 / 9 — 1 / 0
Lt.-Col. William Nelson

Amherst (Va) Bat. — 105 — 0
Capt. Thomas J. Kirkpatrick

3 × 12-pdr Napoleons
1 × 3-in Ordnance rifle

Fluvanna (Va) "Consolidated" Bat. — 90 — 1
Capt. John L. Massie

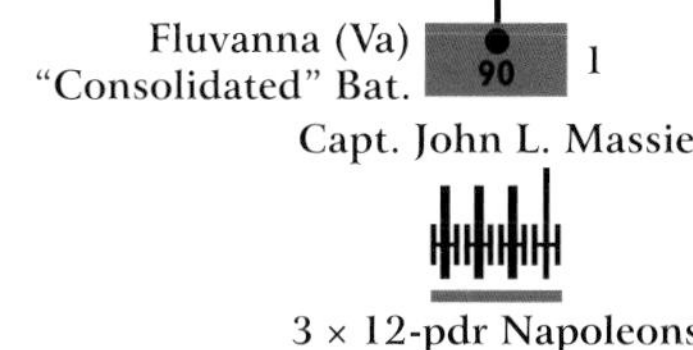

3 × 12-pdr Napoleons
1 × 3-in Ordnance rifle

Georgia Regular Bat. — 73 — 0
Capt. John Milledge

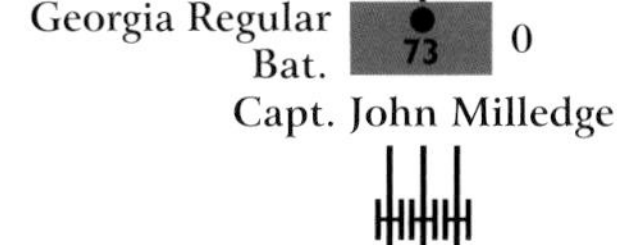

2 × 3-in Ordnance rifles
1 × 10-pdr Parrott

11 pieces

Overall losses – percentage

Brigade	5.1	
Dance	8.7	
• Watson	4.7	
• Smith	6.5	
• Graham	23.5	the seventh highest percentage loss of any A.N.V. battery
• Cunningham	0.0	one of nine batteries out of 68 with no casualties
• Griffin	7.2	
Nelson	0.4	
• Kirkpatrick	0.0	one of nine batteries out of 68 with no casualties
• Massie	1.1	
• Milledge	0.0	one of nine batteries out of 68 with no casualties

Statistics summary

Commander	*Napoleons*	*3-in Ordnance rifles*	*10-pdr Parrotts*	*20-pdr Parrotts*	***Total***
Dance	2	10	4	4	**20**
Nelson	6	4	1	–	**11**
Totals	**8**	**14**	**5**	**4**	**31**

3RD CORPS HETH'S DIVISION

Maj.-Gen. Henry Heth C.S.A.

Divisional statistics summary

Senior commander casualties

2 x divisional commanders w
1 x brigade commander k
3 x brigade commanders w, c or w/c
6 x regimental commanders k
1 x regimental commander mw
16 x regimental commanders w, c or w/c

Overall losses – %	
Division	50.5
Brockenbrough	22.0
Pettigrew	62.8
Davis	53.1
Archer	57.1
Garnett	5.6

Artillery summary	
3-in Ordnance rifle	7
12-pdr Napoleons	4
10-pdr Parrotts	2
12-pdr howitzers	2
Total	**15**

XX 7458 / 8 — 3765 / 1
Maj.-Gen. Henry Heth (w)
Brig.-Gen. James J. Pettigrew (w)

1st Bde X 2580 / 4 — 1619 / 3
Brig.-Gen. James J. Pettigrew (w)
Col. James K. Marshall (k)
Maj. John T. Jones

11th NC III 617 — 366
Col. Collett Leventhorpe (w/c)
Maj. Egbert A. Ross (k)

26th NC III 839 — 687
Col. Henry K. Burgwin (k)
Lt.-Col. John R. Lane (w)
Maj. John T. Jones
Capt. S. W. Brewer (w/c)
Capt. H. C. Albright

47th NC III 567 — 217
Col. George H. Faribault (w)
Lt.-Col. John A. Graves (w/c)
Maj. John T. Jones

52nd NC III 553 — 346
Col. James K. Marshall (k)
Lt.-Col. Marcus A. Parks (w/c)
Maj. John Q. A. Richardson (k)
Capt. Nathaniel A. Foster

2nd Bde X 972 / 4 — 214 / 0
Col. John M. Brockenbrough
Col. Robert M. Mayo

40th Va III 254 — 65
Capt. T. Edwin Betts (w/c)
Capt. Robert B. Davis

47th Va III 209 — 54
Col. Robert M. Mayo
Lt.-Col. John W. Lyell

55th Va III 268 — 64
Col. William S. Christian (c)
Capt. Charles N. Lawson

22nd Va Bat. II 237 — 31
Lt.-Col. Edward P. Taylor
Maj. John S. Bowles

3rd Bde X 1197 / 4 — 684 / 1
Brig.-Gen. James J. Archer (c)
Col. Birkett D. Fry (w/c)
Lt.-Col. Samuel G. Shepard

13th Ala III 308 — 214
Col. Birkett D. Fry

5th Ala Bat. II 135 — 48
Maj. A. S. Van De Graff

1st Tenn III 281 — 178
Lt.-Col. Newton L. George (w/c)
Maj. Felix G. Buchanan (w)

7th Tenn III 249 — 116
Col. John A. Fite (c)
Lt.-Col. Samuel G. Shepard

14th Tenn III 220 — 127
Lt.-Col. James Lockert (w/c)
Capt. B. L. Phillips

4th Bde X 2305 / 6 — 1225 / 1
Brig.-Gen. Joseph R. Davis

2nd Miss III 492 — 232
Col. John M. Stone (k)
Lt.-Col. David W. Humphreys (k)
Maj. John A. Blair (c)

11th Miss III 592 — 312
Col. Francis M. Green (w)
Lt. Stephen Moore

42nd Miss III 575 — 265
Col. Hugh R. Miller (mw)
Capt. Andrew McNelson

55th NC III 640 — 415
Col. John K. Connally (w/c)
Lt.-Col. Maurice T. Smith (k)
Maj. Alfred H. Belo (w)
Lt. George A. Gilreath
Lt. M. C. Stevens

Artillery II 396 / 9 — 22 / 0
Lt.-Col. John J. Garnett

Donaldsville (La) Bat. I 114 — 6
Capt. Victor Maurin
2 × 3-in Ordnance rifles
1 × 10-pdr Parrott

Norfolk (Va) "Huger's" Bat. I 77 — NR
Capt. Joseph D. Moore
2 × 12-pdr Napoleons
1 × 3-in Ordnance rifle
1 × 10-pdr Parrott

Pittsylvania (Va) Bat. I 90 — NR
Capt. John W. Lewis
2 × 12-pdr Napoleons
2 × 3-in Ordnance rifles

Norfolk (Va) "Light Artillery Blues" Bat. I 106 — 2
Capt. Charles R. Grandy
2 × 12-pdr howitzers
2 × 3-in Ordnance rifles

NR = not recorded

Action prior to Gettysburg

This division, under a commander with little battle experience at this level, was the second strongest in the A.N.V. However, not only was the strength unequally divided among the brigades but Pettigrew's and Davis's were new to the army, while a third, hardly mustering the establishment of a full-strength regiment, was under a commander of dubious ability (Brockenbrough). The two newest and biggest brigades had little experience, having joined the restructured A.N.V. from the backwater of North Carolina. Brockenbrough's tiny brigade had seen serious action as part of A. P. Hill's Light Division at Mechanicsville, Gaines' Mill, Glendale and 2nd Manassas. It sustained heavy losses at Chancellorsville and was woefully under strength at Gettysburg. Archer's men had similar battle experience and in addition had done well at Fredericksburg and Chancellorsville.

Action at Gettysburg

Heth's Division was the first into action on July 1, spending most of the day attacking on McPherson's Ridge. The ridge was taken, but with disproportionate losses. The next day the division rested. On July 3 further crippling losses were sustained when it was committed to the last-chance assault of the Pickett–Pettigrew (he replaced the wounded Heth)–Trimble combination. The battle ended with the division suffering 50% casualties, with Pettigrew's Brigade (under Maj. John Jones) losing 1,619 men – the highest in the A.N.V. Pettigrew's 26th North Carolina lost 687 men, the longest casualty list of any regiment in either army. The second and third highest losses occurred in NC regiments – the 55th NC losing 415 and the 11th NC 366. Of the 16 regiments, two ended the fighting commanded by lieutenants and six by captains.

3RD CORPS PENDER'S DIVISION

Maj.-Gen. William D. Pender C.S.A.

Divisional statistics summary

Senior commander casualties
1 x divisional commander mw
1 x divisional commander w/c
1 x regimental commander k
1 x regimental commander w/c
13 x regimental commanders w

Overall losses – %	
Division	37.0
Thomas	21.2
Perrin	34.4
Lane	45.7
Scales	52.1

Artillery summary	
12-pdr Napoleons	7
12-pdr howitzers	6
3-in Ordnance rifle	2
10-pdr Parrotts	1
Total	**16**

XX 6603 11 — 2446 5
Maj.-Gen. William D. Pender (mw)
Brig.-Gen. James H. Lane
Maj.-Gen. Issac R. Trimble (w/c)
Brig.-Gen. James H. Lane

1st Bde X 1882 4 — 647 0
Col. Abner M. Perrin

1st SC (Provn'l Army) III 328 — 115
Maj. Cornelius W. McCreary

1st SC Rifles III 366 — 7
Capt. William M. Hadden

12th SC III 366 — 129
Col. John L. Miller

13th SC III 390 — 144
Lt.-Col. Benjamin T. Brockman

14th SC III 428 — 252
Lt.-Col. Joseph N. Brown (w)
Maj. Edward Croft (w)

2nd Bde X 1734 4 — 792 0
Brig.-Gen. James H. Lane
Col. Clarke M. Avery
Brig.-Gen. James H. Lane
Col. Clarke M. Avery

7th NC III 291 — 159
Capt. John McL. Turner (w/c)
Capt. James G. Harris

18th NC III 346 — 88
Col. John D. Barry

28th NC III 346 — 237
Col. Samuel D. Lowe (w)
Lt.-Col. William H. A. Speer (w)
Maj. Samuel M. Stowe (w)
Lt. James M. Crowell

33rd NC III 368 — 132
Col. Clarke M. Avery

37th NC III 379 — 176
Col. William M. Barbour

3rd Bde X 1248 4 — 264 0
Brig.-Gen. Edward Thomas

14th Ga III 305 — 44
Col. Robert W. Folsom

35th Ga III 305 — 90
Col. Bolling H. Holt
Lt.-Col. William H. McCollohs

45th Ga III 305 — 45
Col. Thomas J. Simmons

49th Ga III 329 — 85
Col. S. T. Player
Capt. Charles Mc. Jones (k)
Capt. Oliver H. Cooke

4th Bde X 1351 4 — 704 2
Brig.-Gen. Alfred M. Scales (w)
Lt.-Col. George T. Gordon (w)
Col. William L. E. Lowrance

13th NC III 232 — 179
Col. Joseph H. Hyman (w)
Lt.-Col. Henry A. Rogers (w)
Lt. Robert L. Moir (w)
Lt. N. S. Smith (Adjt)

16th NC III 321 — 123
Capt. Leroy W. Stowe

22nd NC III 267 — 166
Col. James Conner

34th NC III 311 — 104
Col. William L. E. Lowrance
Lt.-Col. George T. Gordon (w)

38th NC III 216 — 130
Col. William J. Hoke (w)
Lt.-Col. John Ashford (w)
Lt. John M. Robinson
Capt. William L. Thornburg (w)
Lt. John M. Robinson
Capt. George W. Flowers

II 377 9 — 34 0
Maj. William T. Poague

Albermarle (Va) "Everett Artillery" 94 — 13
Capt. James W. Wyatt
2 x 3-in Ordnance rifles
1 x 10-pdr Parrott
1 x 12-pdr howitzer

1st NC Art. Bat. C 125 — 5
Capt. Joseph Graham
2 x 12-pdr Napoleons
2 x 12-pdr howitzers

Madison (Miss) Bat. 91 — NR
Capt. George Ward
3 x 12-pdr Napoleons
1 x 12-pdr howitzer

Warrenton (Va) Bat. 58 — 5
Capt. James V. Brooke
2 x 12-pdr Napoleons
2 x 12-pdr howitzers

NR = not recorded

Action prior to Gettysburg

This division consisted of the four best brigades of A. P. Hill's old Light Division. As such it was a veteran formation with extensive battle experience. In the summer of 1862 it had been in the forefront of Lee's Seven Days offensive, doing well at Mechanicsville, Gaines' Mill and Frayser's Farm. At Cedar Mountain its rapid marching and deployment saved the day for Stonewall Jackson. It fought hard at 2nd Manassas, assisted in the capture of Harper's Ferry and another epic march brought it to Sharpsburg in time to drive back the Federal left. It played a leading role in Jackson's famous flank march at Chancellorsville, although it was Lane's Brigade, and almost certainly the 18th NC in particular, that was responsible for the mortal wounding of Jackson.

Action at Gettysburg

On July 1 the division moved up in support of Heth's Division when it attacked McPherson's Ridge. In the afternoon Scales' and Perrin's Brigades assaulted the heavily defended Seminary Ridge. Scales' frontal advance in the face of massed artillery fire ended in an extremely bloody repulse. Perrin, however, managed to turn the Federal's left flank and the ridge fell. July 2 was mostly spent recovering on Seminary Ridge, although it was called on to protect Rodes' right flank in his unsuccessful assault on Cemetery Hill later in the afternoon. On July 3 the division formed the supporting line behind Pettigrew's (Heth's) in Pickett's ill-fated charge. The division's heavy losses are exemplified by the fact that it had three different commanders and three regiments (13th, 22nd and 38th NC) lost over 60%. The 13th NC lost 77.2% – a horrendous figure and the sixth highest in the Rebel Army.

3RD CORPS ANDERSON'S DIVISION

Maj.-Gen. Richard H. Anderson C.S.A.

Divisional statistics summary

Senior commander casualties

1 x brigade commander w/c
1 x regimental commander k
1 x battalion commander mw
5 x regimental commanders w/c
5 x regimental/battalion commanders w

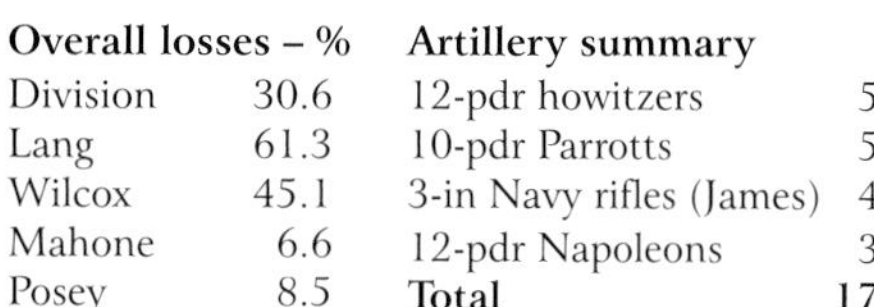

Overall losses – %	
Division	30.6
Lang	61.3
Wilcox	45.1
Mahone	6.6
Posey	8.5
Wright	49.3

Artillery summary	
12-pdr howitzers	5
10-pdr Parrotts	5
3-in Navy rifles (James)	4
12-pdr Napoleons	3
Total	**17**

XX 7136 / 7 — 2185 / 0
Maj.-Gen. Richard H. Anderson

Perry's (Florida) Brigade X 742 / 3 — 455*
Col. David Lang

- 2nd Fla III 242 — 106
  Col. William D. Blantine (w/c)
  Maj. Walter R. Moore (w/c)
  Capt. C. Seton Fleming
- 5th Fla III 321 — 129
  Col. Richard N. Gardner (w)
  Capt. Council A. Bryan
  Capt. John W. Holleyman
- 8th Fla III 176 — 108
  Lt.-Col. William Baya

* The number of missing listed by regiments does not add up to the brigade total due to incomplete records.

X 1726 / 5 — 778* / 1
Brig.-Gen. Cadmus M. Wilcox

- 8th Ala III 477 — 266
  Lt.-Col. Hilary A. Herbert
- 9th Ala III 306 — 116
  Capt. J. Horace King (w)
- 10th Ala III 311 — 104
  Col. William H. Forney (w/c)
  Lt.-Col. James E. Shelley
- 11th Ala III 311 — 75
  Lt.-Col. John C. C. Sanders (w)
  Lt.-Col. George E. Taylor
- 14th Ala III 316 — 48
  Col. Lucius Pinckard (w/c)
  Lt.-Col. James A. Broome

X 1542 / 4 — 102 / 0
Brig.-Gen. William Mahone

- 6th Va III 288 — 11
  Col. George T. Rogers
- 12th Va III 348 — 22
  Col. David A. Weisiger
- 16th Va III 270 — 22
  Col. Joseph H. Ham
- 41st Va III 276 — 22
  Col. William A. Parham
- 61st Va III 356 — 25
  Col. Virginius D. Groner

X 1322 / 4 — 112 / 0
Brig.-Gen. Carnot Posey

- 12th Miss III 305 — 13
  Col. William H. Taylor
- 16th Miss III 385 — 26
  Col. Samuel E. Baker
- 19th Miss III 372 — 34
  Col. Nathaniel H. Harris
- 48th Miss III 256 — 39
  Col. Joseph Mc. Jayne (w)

X 1413 / 4 — 696 / 0
Brig.-Gen. Ambrose R. Wright
Col. William Gibson (w/c)
Brig.-Gen. Ambrose R. Wright

- 3rd Ga III 441 — 219
  Col. Edward J. Walker
- 22nd Ga III 400 — 171
  Col. Joseph Wasden (k)
  Capt. Benjamin C. McMurray
- 48th Ga III 395 — 224
  Col. William Gibson (w/c)
  Capt. Matthew R. Hall
- 2nd Ga Bat. II 173 — 82
  Maj. George W. Ross (mw)
  Capt. Charles J. Moffett (w)

II 384 / 9 — 42 / 0
Maj. John Lane

- Co. A Sumter (Ga) Art. Bat. I 130 — 13
  Capt. Hugh M. Ross
  3 x 10-pdr Parrotts
  1 x 12-pdr Napoleon
  1 x 3-in Navy rifle
  1 x 12-pdr howitzer
- Co. B Sumter (Ga) Art. Bat. I 124 — 9
  Capt. George M. Patterson
  4 x 12-pdr howitzers
  2 x 12-pdr Napoleons
- Co. C Sumter (Ga) Art. Bat. I 121 — 20
  Capt. John T. Wingfield (w)
  3 x 3-in Navy rifles
  2 x 10-pdr Parrotts

Action prior to Gettysburg

The newly promoted Anderson had taken over Maj.-Gen. Benjamin Huger's division after the Seven Days Battles. He had been wounded at Sharpsburg and his division had then been driven from its position along Bloody Lane. However, it fought well on the Confederate right at Chancellorsville, although suffering heavily in the attack on the Federal VI Corps. It marched into Maryland and Pennsylvania in June 1863 with five small brigades, each from five different states, making it one of the most diverse in the army. Lang's Brigade, with 742 men, was the smallest in the army.

Action at Gettysburg

The division had an easy day on July 1, arriving via the Cashtown road in the late afternoon and deploying on Herr's Ridge. There it remained in reserve overnight. On July 2 it deployed on Seminary Ridge but was not committed until the end of Lee's attack on the Union salient and left. In the evening the division attacked the enemy center and elements of Wright's Brigade succeeded, at considerable cost, in reaching the crest of Cemetery Ridge, only to be forced back through lack of support. Neither Mahone's nor Posey's Brigades was fully committed – they ended the battle with the lowest percentage losses for any infantry brigade in the army. On July 3 it was intended to use the division to follow up Pickett's charge, but in the event this did not happen as Longstreet cancelled its advance when Pickett was repulsed.

3RD CORPS ARTILLERY RESERVE A.N.V.

Col. R. Lindsay Walker

X
736 / 4 — 99 / 0
Col. R. Lindsay Walker

(36 pieces)

Maj. David G. McIntosh

II
357 / 9 — 48* / 0
Maj. David G. McIntosh

Hardaway (Ala) Bat. — 71 — 8
Capt. William B. Hurt (w)

2 × 3-in Ordnance rifles
2 × 12-pdr Whitworth rifles

Danville (Va) Bat. — 114 — 2
Capt. R. Stanley Rice

4 × 12-pdr Napoleons

2nd Rockbridge (Va) Bat. — 67 — 10
Capt. Samuel Wallace

2 × 12-pdr Napoleons
2 × 3-in Ordnance rifles

Richmond (Va) Bat. — 96 — 10
Capt. Marmaduke Johnson

4 × 3-in Ordnance rifles

16 pieces

* Individual battery losses do not add up to the battalion total due to incomplete records.

Maj. William J. Pegram

II

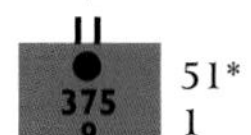

375 / 9 — 51* / 1
Maj. William J. Pegram
Capt. Ervin B. Brunson (w)

Pee Dee (SC) Bat. — 65 — 1
Capt. Ervin B. Brunson
Lt. William E. Zimmerman (w)

4 × 3-in Ordnance rifles

Richmond (Va) "Crenshaw" Bat. — 76 — 15
Capt. J. Hampden Chamberlayne (c)**
Lt. Andrew Johnston (w)

2 × 12-pdr Napoleons
2 × 12-pdr howitzers

Fredericksburg (Va) Bat. — 71 — 2
Capt. Edward A. Marye

2 × 12-pdr Napoleons
2 × 3-in Ordnance rifles

Richmond (Va) "Letcher" Bat. — 65 — 17
Capt. Thomas A. Brander

2 × 12-pdr Napoleons
2 × 10-pdr Parrotts

Richmond (Va) "Percell" Bat. — 89 — 6
Capt. Joseph McGraw

4 × 12-pdr Napoleons

20 pieces

** Captured before the battle.

Overall losses – percentage

Brigade	13.5	
McIntosh	13.4	
• Hurt	11.3	
• Rice	1.8	
• Wallace	14.9	
• Johnson	10.4	
Pegram	13.6	
• Zimmerman	1.5	
• Johnston	19.7	
• Marye	2.8	
• Brander	26.2	the fifth highest % loss of any A.N.V. battery
• McGraw	6.7	

Statistics summary

Commander	*Napoleons*	*3-in Ordnance rifles*	*10-pdr Parrotts*	*12-pdr Whitworth rifles*	*12-pdr howitzers*	*Total*
McIntosh	6	8	–	2	–	16
Pegram	10	6	2	–	2	20
Totals	16	14	2	2	2	36

CAVALRY DIVISION A.N.V.

Maj.-Gen. James Ewell Brown Stuart C.S.A.

Divisional statistics summary

Senior commander casualties
2 x brigade commanders w
5 x regimental commanders w

Overall losses – %	
Division	4.7
Chambliss	4.8
Hampton	6.4
F. Lee	5.3
Jenkins	2.0
Jones	3.9
Beckham	5.1

Artillery summary	
3-in Ordnance rifle	11
12-pdr howitzers	3
10-pdr Parrotts	4
12-pdr Napoleons	2
Blakely rifles	3
Total	**23**

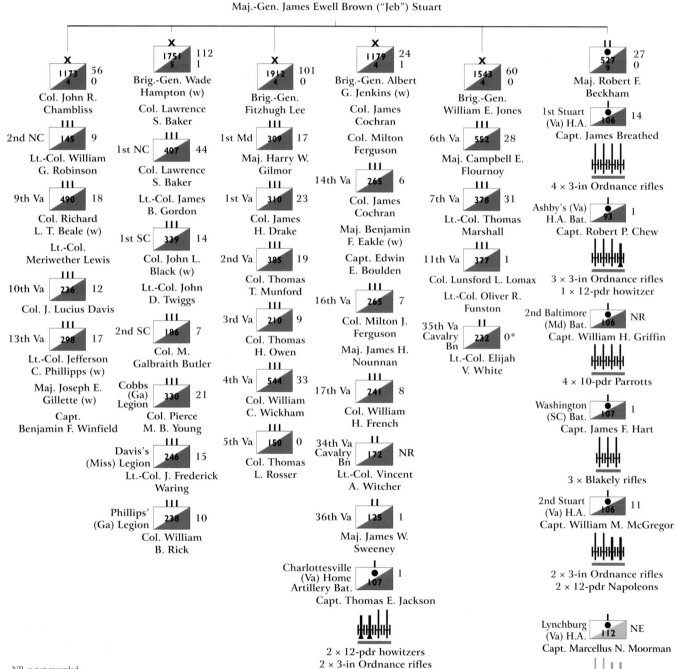

XX 8105 / 20 — 380 / 0
Maj.-Gen. James Ewell Brown ("Jeb") Stuart

X 1173 / 4 — 56 / 0
Col. John R. Chambliss
- 2nd NC III 145 — 9: Lt.-Col. William G. Robinson
- 9th Va III 490 — 18: Col. Richard L. T. Beale (w); Lt.-Col. Meriwether Lewis
- 10th Va III 236 — 12: Col. J. Lucius Davis
- 13th Va III 298 — 17: Lt.-Col. Jefferson C. Phillipps (w); Maj. Joseph E. Gillette (w); Capt. Benjamin F. Winfield

X 1751 / 5 — 112 / 1
Brig.-Gen. Wade Hampton (w); Col. Lawrence S. Baker
- 1st NC III 407 — 44: Col. Lawrence S. Baker; Lt.-Col. James B. Gordon
- 1st SC III 339 — 14: Col. John L. Black (w); Lt.-Col. John D. Twiggs
- 2nd SC III 186 — 7: Col. M. Galbraith Butler
- Cobbs (Ga) Legion III 330 — 21: Col. Pierce M. B. Young
- Davis's (Miss) Legion III 246 — 15: Lt.-Col. J. Frederick Waring
- Phillips' (Ga) Legion III 238 — 10: Col. William B. Rick

X 1912 / 4 — 101 / 0
Brig.-Gen. Fitzhugh Lee
- 1st Md III 309 — 17: Maj. Harry W. Gilmor
- 1st Va III 310 — 23: Col. James H. Drake
- 2nd Va III 385 — 19: Col. Thomas T. Munford
- 3rd Va III 210 — 9: Col. Thomas H. Owen
- 4th Va III 544 — 33: Col. William C. Wickham
- 5th Va III 150 — 0: Col. Thomas L. Rosser

X 1179 / 4 — 24 / 1
Brig.-Gen. Albert G. Jenkins (w); Col. James Cochran; Col. Milton Ferguson
- 14th Va III 265 — 6: Col. James Cochran; Maj. Benjamin F. Eakle (w); Capt. Edwin E. Boulden
- 16th Va III 265 — 7: Col. Milton J. Ferguson; Maj. James H. Nounnan
- 17th Va III 241 — 8: Col. William H. French
- 34th Va Cavalry Bn II 172 — NR: Lt.-Col. Vincent A. Witcher
- 36th Va II 125 — 1: Maj. James W. Sweeney
- Charlottesville (Va) Home Artillery Bat. I 107 — 1: Capt. Thomas E. Jackson; 2 × 12-pdr howitzers, 2 × 3-in Ordnance rifles

X 1543 / 4 — 60 / 0
Brig.-Gen. William E. Jones
- 6th Va III 552 — 28: Maj. Campbell E. Flournoy
- 7th Va III 378 — 31: Lt.-Col. Thomas Marshall
- 11th Va III 377 — 1: Col. Lunsford L. Lomax; Lt.-Col. Oliver R. Funston
- 35th Va Cavalry Bn II 232 — 0*: Lt.-Col. Elijah V. White

II 527 / 9 — 27 / 0
Maj. Robert F. Beckham
- 1st Stuart (Va) H.A. I 106 — 14: Capt. James Breathed; 4 × 3-in Ordnance rifles
- Ashby's (Va) H.A. Bat. I 93 — 1: Capt. Robert P. Chew; 3 × 3-in Ordnance rifles, 1 × 12-pdr howitzer
- 2nd Baltimore (Md) Bat. I 106 — NR: Capt. William H. Griffin; 4 × 10-pdr Parrotts
- Washington (SC) Bat. I 107 — 1: Capt. James F. Hart; 3 × Blakely rifles
- 2nd Stuart (Va) H.A. I 106 — 11: Capt. William M. McGregor; 2 × 3-in Ordnance rifles, 2 × 12-pdr Napoleons
- Lynchburg (Va) H.A. I 112 — NE: Capt. Marcellus N. Moorman; 2 × 3-in Ordnance rifles, 1 × 12-pdr Napoleon, 1 × 12-pdr howitzer

NR = not recorded
NE = not engaged

* The 35th Virginia Cavalry battalion ("White's Comanches") operated detached from Stuart's Division at Gettysburg under the direct command of Lt-Gen. Richard Ewell.

Action prior to Gettysburg

Stuart commanded a large veteran cavalry division, mostly of Virginians, that had acquired a fearsome reputation not only in battle but more especially as a wide-ranging raiding force capable of causing havoc behind enemy lines – successful examples being the raids in 1862 at Catlett's Station (August), Chambersburg (October) and Dumfries (December). These were in addition to his daring ride around McClellan's army during the Peninsular campaign in June 1862. In the Gettysburg campaign his cavalry battle at Brandy Station, his skirmishing in Loudoun County and the cavalry's actions at Aldie, Middleburg, Upperville and Hanover are discussed in Section Seven: The Road to Gettysburg.

Action at Gettysburg

The Confederate Cavalry Division did not participate in the main clash of armies at Gettysburg. Nevertheless, on July 3 the division took part in two peripheral actions, the main one at East Cavalry Field (Rummel Farm) and another minor clash near Fairfield. The former involved four brigades under Stuart (Chambliss, Hampton, Fitzhugh Lee and Jenkins), the latter action the detached brigade of Brig.-Gen. William "Grumble" E. Jones.

Jeb Stuart's Artillery

The Confederate horse artillery deployment can be confusing to general readers, so it is summarized here to assist in understanding its deployment as the campaign and battle unfolded.

- Stuart's artillery command consisted of six batteries in Major Robert F. Beckham's battalion. Of these, two (Captain Griffin's 2nd Maryland (Baltimore) Light Artillery Battery and Captain Hart's Washington (South Carolina) Battery) were not officially designated as horse artillery but were initially attached to Stuart. However, from the outset Griffin's Battery was attached to Ewell's Corps and Hart's to Longstreet's Corps. Hart was at first deployed with the army train but was engaged on July 3.
- When Stuart took three of his brigades on his march around Meade (see Section Seven: The Road to Gettysburg), the Confederate horse artillery was deployed as follows:

  With Stuart: 1st Stuart (Va) Horse Artillery Battery under Captain Breathed (4 guns) and one section 2nd Stuart (Va) Horse Artillery Battery under Captain McGregor (2 guns). McGregor's remaining two guns did not go on the campaign.

  With Jenkins' Brigade: the Charlottesville (Va) Horse Battery under Captain Jackson (4 guns).

  With Jones's Brigade: the Ashby (Va) Horse Artillery Battery under Captain Chew (4 guns).

  With Imboden's Brigade: the Staunton (Va) Horse Battery under Captain McClanahan (6 guns) – this brigade operated independently of Stuart from the outset.

Cavalry Brigades not in action at Gettysburg

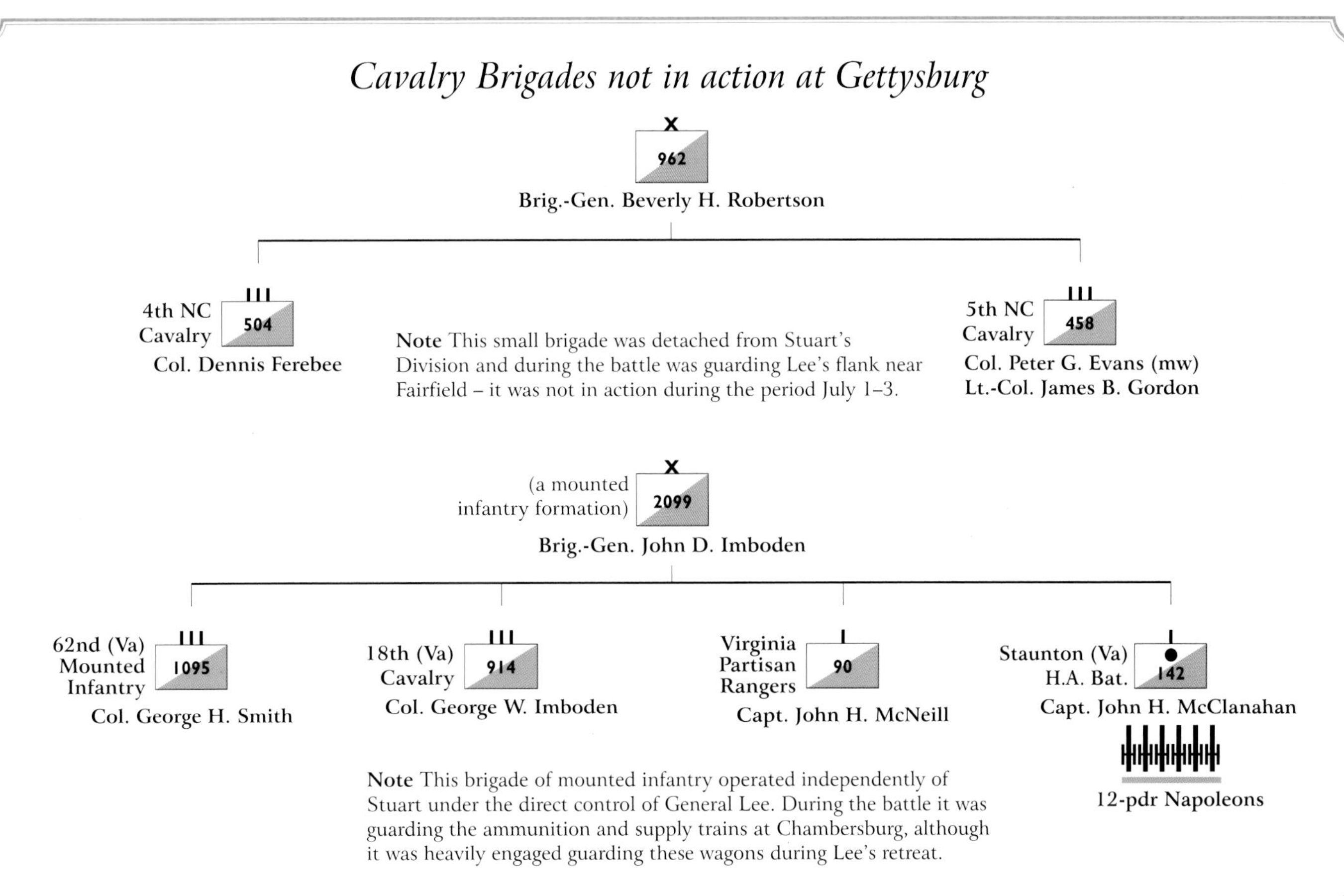

Note This small brigade was detached from Stuart's Division and during the battle was guarding Lee's flank near Fairfield – it was not in action during the period July 1–3.

Note This brigade of mounted infantry operated independently of Stuart under the direct control of General Lee. During the battle it was guarding the ammunition and supply trains at Chambersburg, although it was heavily engaged guarding these wagons during Lee's retreat.

Infantry Rank Insignia

Rank	Union: Shoulder Strap	Union: Upper Sleeve	Confederate[2]: Collar[3]	Confederate[2]: Cuff	Confederate[2]: Upper Sleeve
General or General-in-Chief[1]				General (all ranks)	
Lieutenant-General	none at Gettysburg			General (all ranks)	
Major-General				General (all ranks)	
Brigadier-General				General (all ranks)	
Colonel				Colonel and Lieutenant-Colonel	
Lieutenant-Colonel				Colonel and Lieutenant-Colonel	
Major				Captain and Major	
Captain				Captain and Major	
1st Lieutenant				Lieutenant (1st and 2nd)	
2nd Lieutenant				Lieutenant (1st and 2nd)	
Sergeant-Major					
Quartermaster Sergeant (regimental)					
Ordnance Sergeant					
1st Sergeant					
Sergeant					
Corporal					

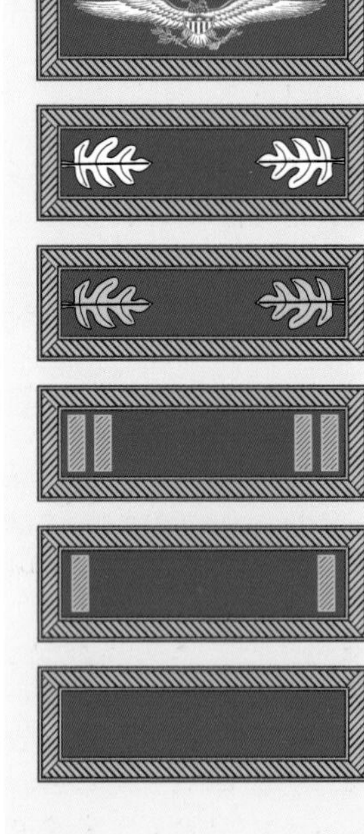

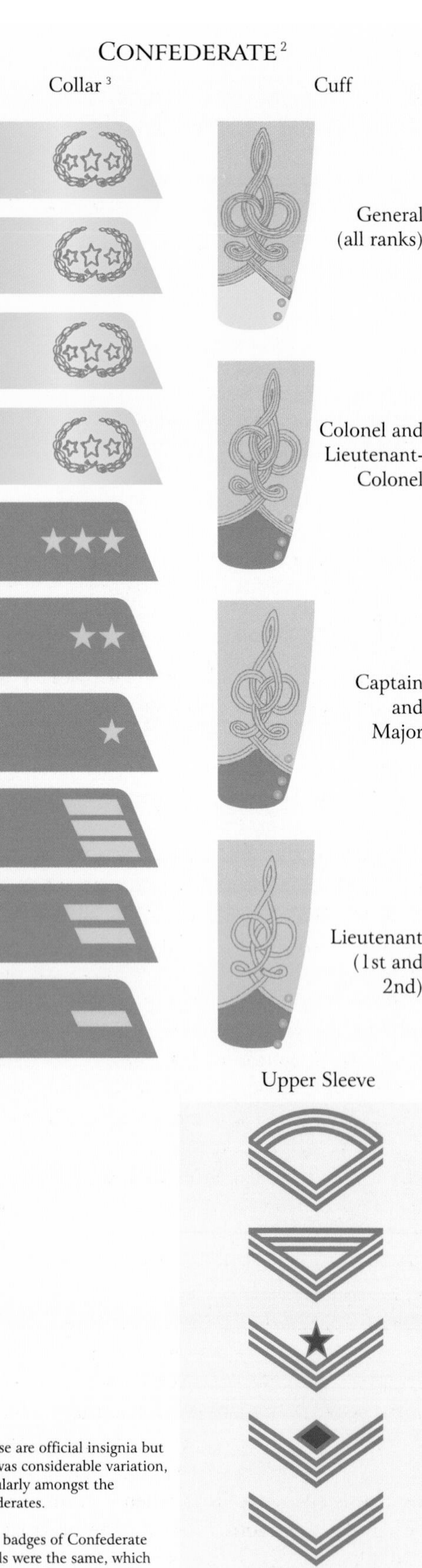

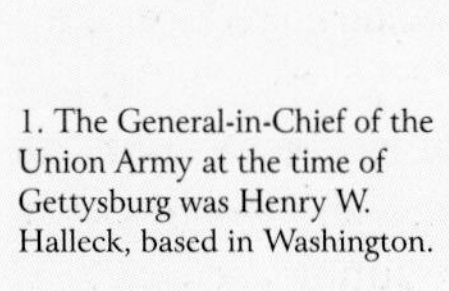

1. The General-in-Chief of the Union Army at the time of Gettysburg was Henry W. Halleck, based in Washington.

2. These are official insignia but there was considerable variation, particularly amongst the Confederates.

3. The badges of Confederate generals were the same, which was most confusing. Lee often wore three stars on his collar without a wreath – the badge of a colonel!

Section Two

The Infantry

Gettysburg was an infantry battle. Artillery played its part on the main battlefield on all three days, but Union cavalry was in action only on July 1 (mostly dismounted) – the cavalry clashes, and there were plenty, mostly occurring during the Confederate advance north and the subsequent withdrawal south. There were three significant mounted actions during the battle on July 3, but they were either peripheral or several miles from the decisive field of action. Only infantry can take and hold ground for any length of time. This is still true today, in some ways more so. NATO "boots on the ground" at the start would probably have prevented the ethnic cleansing in Kosovo, and certainly the aftermath of the 2003 Iraq war has seen many armored (cavalry) units dismounted doing an infantryman's job. As they were by far the most numerous component of both armies at Gettysburg (see pages 30–33) it was the infantry that inflicted and received the great majority of casualties. Despite the huge amounts of artillery ammunition expended, it was the rifle-musket bullet that inflicted 90 percent of all losses on the Gettysburg battlefield. Artillery fire was responsible for some 9 percent and bayonets, clubbed rifles and swords the remaining one percent. The struggle at Gettysburg saw three days of Confederate infantry attacks on defending Union infantry, albeit with considerable artillery support for both armies, but the object of the fighting was for infantry to close with the enemy, drive him from his position (in this case Cemetery Ridge) and, hopefully, destroy him as a fighting force.

Details of how the infantry was organized into corps, divisions, brigades and regiments have been discussed in Section One: Orders of Battle. This section will look more closely at the infantry in terms of its regiments, their internal organization, arms, equipment, formations, tactics and the life of the average soldier on the march to the battle. The regiment was a soldier's home: it was where he lived when in camp or on operations, it was where his comrades were and the organization to which he gave his first loyalty. There is no better example of this loyalty than that there was seldom, if ever, a shortage of men seeking the honor of carrying the regiment's battle flag or color, despite the knowledge that in battle such a duty meant almost certain wounding or death.

Regimental Strength and Organization

On operations the hemorrhaging of men through disease, sickness, desertion, wounds and death, or the end of their enlistment, could see entire regiments disappear. It was a critical problem for both sides. Neither the North nor South fully succeeded in developing a wholly satisfactory system of replacing individuals in volunteer units. The Confederacy, although hamstrung by its insistence that Texans be commanded by Texans and Georgians by Georgians, and by governors insisting on the retention of home guards, did at least try to maintain veteran status for depleted units by reinforcing them with individuals so that new arrivals learned their soldiering alongside some seasoned comrades.

A good example of how the strength of a veteran Rebel regiment – which fought from initial formation in May 1861 to Appomattox in April 1865 – fluctuated but was nevertheless kept in being, was the 55th Virginia Infantry, which served in A. P. Hill's famous Light Division, seeing action in the Seven Days Battles, Second Manassas, Fredericksburg, Chancellorsville, Gettysburg (where it fought in Brockenbrough's Brigade) and the defense of Petersburg and Richmond. Raised in Tidewater County, the first two companies were formed in 1860 in response to John Brown's raid on Harper's Ferry; six more volunteered within weeks of the fall of Fort Sumter in early summer 1861. Three further companies of ex-militiamen and men "volunteering" to avoid conscription were added in the spring of 1862, and a fourth joined in June of that year. However, despite having twelve companies rather than the usual ten, the regiment never exceeded 900 men. In August 1861 it was 600 strong, before jumping to 900 with the enlistment of the extra three companies. However, it quickly shrank to just over 400 as a result of a company. being transferred out, absence and sickness. Although another company was added, the latter part of 1862 saw the battles of Seven Days, Second Manassas and Sharpsburg, combined with normal wastage, reduce the 55th Virginia to around 150 men. Several months of rest, recuperation and recruiting brought it back to just under 500 by May 1863. Then came Chancellorsville, Gettysburg (initial engaged strength 268), and Falling Waters (during the retreat from Gettysburg), bringing the regiment back down to 150. From then until the end of the war its strength never rose above 250 before it was virtually destroyed at the Battle of Sayler's Creek on April 6, 1865, leaving only twenty-one men to surrender with General Lee at Appomattox three days later.

The North's replacement of losses usually followed a different path. It allowed many states to recruit regiments for limited periods, usually ranging from nine months (totally impractical) to two or three years, instead of for the duration of the war – an extreme example of this being the 26th Emergency Pennsylvania Infantry, who were called up for thirty days! This system was compounded by too often allowing battle-tested regiments to decline dramatically, sometimes to below company strength, before sending them to their home states to recruit – or face disbandment. Although the Union did attempt to rotate men through regiments, it was not done to the same extent as in the Confederacy. Not infrequently preference was given to forming recruits into new, green units with little or no leavening of veterans – the best examples at Gettysburg being the three large, newly recruited regiments in Stannard's ("Paper Collar") Brigade, formed of nine-month volunteers, and the three inexperienced regiments in Lockwood's Brigade. Another dubious system, applicable to both sides, was that of permitting the men to elect many of their junior officers and some senior N.C.O.s. In the Union an Act of July 22, 1861 wrote this unmilitary method into law. According to Colonel (later Major-General) Emory Upton, who commanded the 121st New York at Gettysburg, it was the "worst vice known in the military system of any of the States," for it "tempted every ambitious officer and soldier to play the demagogue." The Confederates did the same, prompting the British Lieutenant-Colonel Garnet (later Field Marshal Lord) Wolesley, who visited Lee's headquarters in 1862, to write:

As is usual in impromptu armies the chief deficiency lies with the officers, who, though possessed of high zeal and courage, seldom know more of their duty than the men under their command. The system of election from the first had worked badly . . . I never spoke with an officer on the subject who did not condemn it.

Nevertheless, with hugely expanding armies, use of such a system was probably unavoidable for the first two years, by which time proven individuals would have replaced many of the weak and useless. As happens in every war, a small proportion of officers failed to meet requirements but the majority of these citizen soldiers, however appointed, rose to the challenge of leadership in battle.

Infantry Pay Rates in July 1863

At the start of the war Union soldiers received the prewar rates of pay and the Confederates modeled their rates on this. However, by Gettysburg the Yankees had had a raise but the Rebels had to wait until 1864 for their increase. Black soldiers in the Union Army initially received a dollar a month less than their white comrades, which led to some black units refusing pay entirely until they received equal rates. In the South the way to make money from the military was to hire out your slaves to the government to work on fortifications as the going rate was $30 per month per slave – well over double that paid to a private. Union soldiers were supposed to be paid every two months in the field, but were fortunate to get paid at four-month intervals and it was not unknown for units to go without pay for up to eight months. Payment in the Confederate Army was often even less regular, with units sometimes waiting a year for their money. A comparison of monthly rates is shown below in dollars.

	Union	Confederate
Private	13	11
Corporal	15	13
Sergeant	17	17
1st Sergeant	20	20
Sergeant-Major	21	21
2nd Lieutenant	105.50	80
Lieutenant	105.50	90
Captain	115.50	130
Major	169	150
Lieutenant-Colonel	181	170
Colonel	212	195
Brigadier-General	315	301
Major-General	457	350
Lieutenant-General	none at Gettysburg	450
General	none at Gettysburg	500

The Confederates paid army commanders an additional $100 a month and other generals in the field $50. Engineers, artillery and cavalry were paid at higher rates than infantrymen.

Confederate

With occasional minor variation, a Confederate regiment had the same internal structure as a Union one. Commanded by a colonel, a regiment supposedly consisted of headquarters personnel and ten companies of 100, each company under a captain being divided into two platoons commanded by lieutenants, four sections commanded by sergeants and eight squads under corporals. Such a regiment never took the field. Gettysburg is a good example of the reality of regimental strengths at the start of a battle where units varied from 15–60 percent of established size, with 30 percent being about the average in both armies. Nevertheless, although numbers might have shrunk as low as 200, the internal structure of ten companies was usually maintained. They were designated by letters A–K, omitting J as it could be mistaken for I.

Taking the Adjutant General's Office instructions, dated Washington, May 4, 1861, as the initial hoped-for establishment and organization, a volunteer infantry regiment would have a maximum strength of 1,046 made up as follows:

Confederate Company Nicknames

Many, but not all, Rebel companies within regiments gave themselves nicknames on formation. They frequently referred to the town in which they were raised or reflected their original commander; others had no obvious origin. The company names of the 19th Virginia provide a good example:

Company A: "Monticello Guard"
Company B: "Albemarle Rifles"
Company C: "Scottsville Guard"
Company D: "Howardsville Grays"
Company E: "Piedmont Guards"
Company F: "Montgomery Guard"
Company G: "Nelson Grays"
Company H: "Southern Rights Guard"
Company I: "Amherst Rifle Grays"
Company K: "Blue Ridge Rifles"

Regimental H.Q. (Field and Staff)	Duties
1 x colonel	Commanding officer.
1 x lieutenant-colonel	2nd-in-command – commanded right wing (4 or 5 companies) if necessary.
1 x major	Third-in-command – commanded left wing (4 or 5 companies) if necessary.
1 x lieutenant (adjutant)	Drill, discipline, personnel matters.
1 x lieutenant (regimental quartermaster)	Responsible for arms, clothing, equipment.
1 x assistant surgeon	Care of sick and wounded.
1 x sergeant-major	Assisted the adjutant, supervised guards, fatigues, N.C.O. duty rosters, and record-keeping.
1 x regimental quartermaster sergeant	Took charge of all regimental property and equipment. Kept records, made issues, supervised fatigue parties.
1 x regimental commissary sergeant	Storing, transport, issuing and accounting for rations. Supervision of butchering, cooking, and cattle on the hoof.
1 x hospital steward	In the field supervised the care and transportation of sick, wounded, medicines and hospital equipment.
2 x principal musicians	Band instruments, daily calls, and training of regimental band.

Experience led to the addition to a regiment's headquarters of some or all of: assistant commissary of subsistence (captain or lieutenant) responsible for supply, distribution of, and accounting for, food through requisitioning and foraging; chaplain, surgeon, color sergeant, ordnance sergeant (responsible under the quartermaster for arms and ammunition), and a wagonmaster in charge of the regimental train. At Gettysburg few regiments had a complete staff.

Regimental Band	Duties
24 x bandsmen	Music on parade or march; daily regimental calls. In battle collecting wounded.

Total for the headquarters including the band: 36. By July 1863 manpower shortages had forced the replacement of many regimental bands by brigade bands.

Companies x 10 – each of 2 platoons, 4 sections and 8 squads	
1 x captain	Commander.
1 x 1st lieutenant	Platoon commander.
1 x 2nd lieutenant	Platoon commander.
1 x 1st sergeant	General supervision of all aspects of company routine, drill and discipline.
4 x sergeants (incl. a 1st sergeant)	Section commanders.
8 x corporals	Squad commanders.
2 x musicians	Bugle calls.
1 x wagoner	Responsibility for/driving company wagon.
82 x privates	

This gives a total of 101 per company and 1,046 for the regiment, made up of 36 officers, 56 sergeants (or equivalent), 80 corporals and 874 privates, giving an overall ratio of 1:28 for officers and enlisted men but 1:32.6 within the companies.

The reality was very different. The diagram on page 90 shows the 19th Virginia Volunteer Infantry Regiment in line of battle just prior to its advance as part of Pickett's Division in its attempt to take Cemetery Ridge on July 3. Lieutenant William Wood, the second lieutenant in Company A, described the moment his regiment got to its feet after lying in the open on the reverse slope behind their gun line under the sizzling sun for several hours:

> "Attention!" was heard along the infantry line, and every man sprang to his feet . . . All along the line men were falling from seeming sunstroke with dreadful contortions of the body, foaming at the mouth and almost lifeless . . . they were taken back to the shade [of Spangler Woods] and order in the ranks restored. "Forward, guide center [on the colors], march!" and we moved forward to the top of the hill [slope] – just in front of our artillery [Major Dearing's Battalion], and halted. There we formed a beautiful line of battle and were in full view of the enemy.

Bands

When volunteer regiments were recruited a regimental band was usually included in the establishment. In the Union Army each infantry and artillery regiment was authorized a 24-man band, but the cavalry was restricted to 16 men. In 1862 the Union War Department ordered the dismissal of regimental bands, which were to be replaced by brigade bands. Despite this some regiments managed to retain theirs. There were fewer Confederate bands because musicians were not as numerous in the South and quality brass instruments scarce. As in the North, Southern regimental bands were disbanded after a year but a few regiments, such as the 26th North Carolina, kept them. The quality of Confederate bands was decidedly mixed, one soldier describing his as "comparable to the braying of a pack of mules." Each infantry company was supposed to have a musician, who was normally a drummer (sometimes accompanied by a fifer). Drums got soldiers up in the morning, beat morning roll call, sick call or guard duty, and on the battlefield signaled orders from the commander. These musicians or bandsmen were often detailed to assist the surgeons in battle or were used to carry the badly wounded to the field dressing station.

Bands invariably proved their worth on the march. They played both armies to Gettysburg, the familiar tunes enlivening aching and exhausted bodies. They were to be heard at the crossings of the Potomac and the Shenandoah, and in the streets of towns such as Harper's Ferry, Sharpsburg, Williamsport, Hagerstown and Chambersburg, or Frederick, Westminster, Union Mills and Taneytown as endless columns of bone-weary troops tramped through. The Rebels' favorite tunes included "The Bonnie Blue Flag," "Maryland, My Maryland," "Lorena," "Goober Peas," "The Yellow Rose of Texas" and a Southern version of "The Battle Cry of Freedom." For the Yankees it was "The Battle Cry of Freedom," "The Battle Hymn of the Republic," "John Brown's Body," or "Tenting Tonight on the Old Camp Ground" that kept painful feet moving.

The Infantry Regiment in Line of Battle

The 19th Virginia Infantry Regiment formed up at the start of Pickett's charge (engaged strength 328)

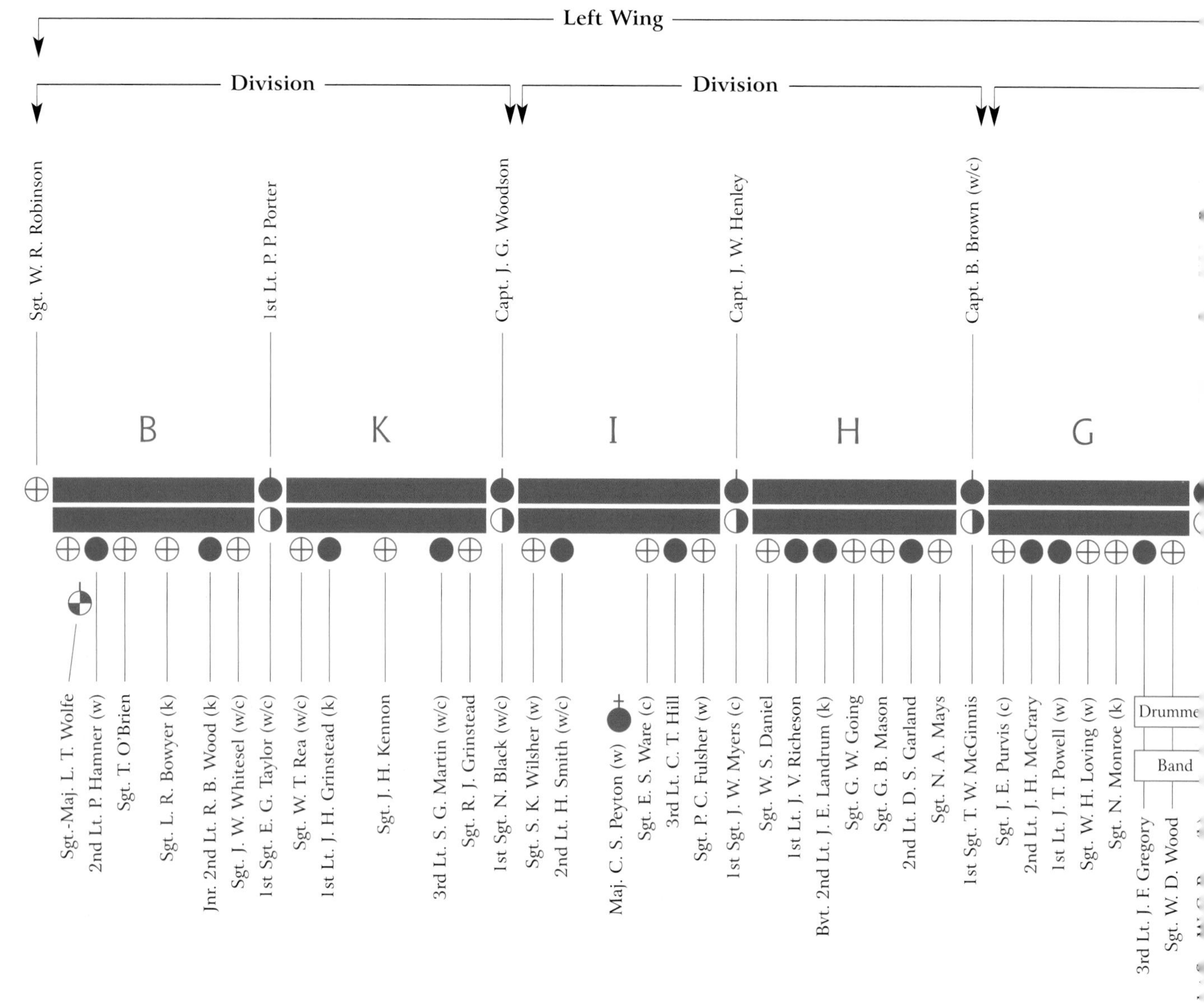

Left Wing

Division

Division

Sgt. W. R. Robinson

1st Lt. P. P. Porter

Capt. J. G. Woodson

Capt. J. W. Henley

Capt. B. Brown (w/c)

B K I H G

Sgt.-Maj. L. T. Wolfe
2nd Lt. P. Hamner (w)
Sgt. T. O'Brien
Sgt. L. R. Bowyer (k)
Jnr. 2nd Lt. R. B. Wood (k)
Sgt. J. W. Whitesel (w/c)
1st Sgt. E. G. Taylor (w/c)
Sgt. W. T. Rea (w/c)
1st Lt. J. H. Grinstead (k)
Sgt. J. H. Kennon
3rd Lt. S. G. Martin (w/c)
Sgt. R. J. Grinstead
1st Sgt. N. Black (w/c)
Sgt. S. K. Wilsher (w)
2nd Lt. H. Smith (w/c)
Maj. C. S. Peyton (w)
Sgt. E. S. Ware (c)
3rd Lt. C. T. Hill
Sgt. P. C. Fulsher (w)
1st Sgt. J. W. Myers (c)
Sgt. W. S. Daniel
1st Lt. J. V. Richeson
Bvt. 2nd Lt. J. E. Landrum (k)
Sgt. G. W. Going
Sgt. G. B. Mason
2nd Lt. D. S. Garland
Sgt. N. A. Mays
1st Sgt. T. W. McGinnis
Sgt. J. E. Purvis (c)
2nd Lt. J. H. McCrary
1st Lt. J. T. Powell (w)
Sgt. W. H. Loving (w)
Sgt. N. Monroe (k)
3rd Lt. J. F. Gregory
Sgt. W. D. Wood

Drumme

Band

The Confederate battle flag of the 19th Infantry Regiment. It was captured by Union troops close to the Copse of Trees at the high water mark of Pickett's charge.

Notes

- While every effort has been made to place known individuals in their likely location in accordance with the Confederate version of Hardee's drill and tactics manual, they cannot be guaranteed.
- This regiment did not have a full band, although some musicians/buglers were retained. The position of a band and the buglers is shown.

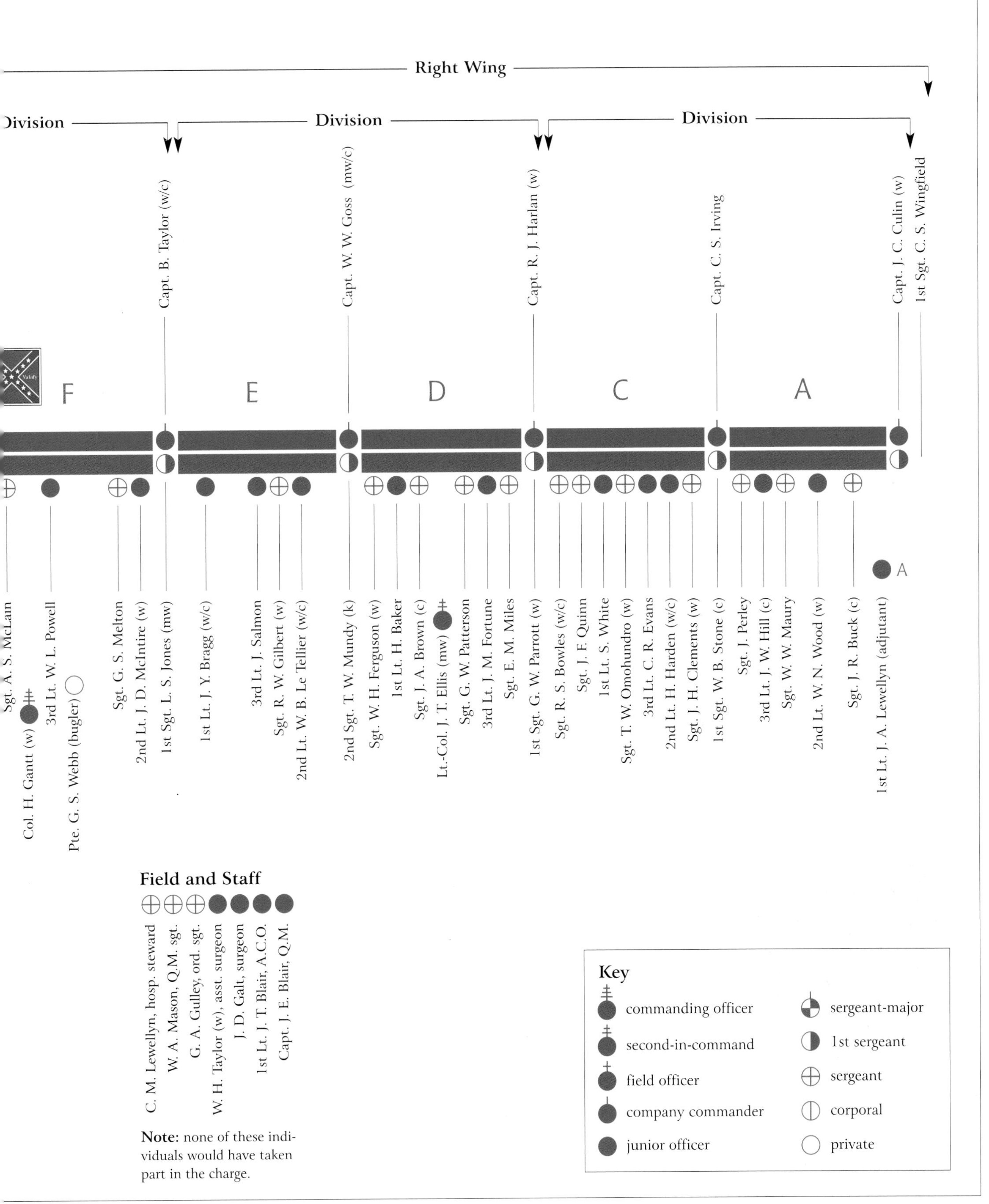
Right Wing
Division
Division
Division
F
E
D
C
A
Capt. B. Taylor (w/c)
Capt. W. W. Goss (mw/c)
Capt. R. J. Harlan (w)
Capt. C. S. Irving
Capt. J. C. Culin (w)
1st Sgt. C. S. Wingfield
Sgt. A. S. McLain
Col. H. Gantt (w)
3rd Lt. W. L. Powell
Pte. G. S. Webb (bugler)
Sgt. G. S. Melton
2nd Lt. J. D. McIntire (w)
1st Sgt. L. S. Jones (mw)
1st Lt. J. Y. Bragg (w/c)
3rd Lt. J. Salmon
Sgt. R. W. Gilbert (w)
2nd Lt. W. B. Le Tellier (w/c)
2nd Sgt. T. W. Mundy (k)
Sgt. W. H. Ferguson (w)
1st Lt. H. Baker
Sgt. J. A. Brown (c)
Lt.-Col. J. T. Ellis (mw)
Sgt. G. W. Patterson
3rd Lt. J. M. Fortune
Sgt. E. M. Miles
1st Sgt. G. W. Parrott (w)
Sgt. R. S. Bowles (w/c)
Sgt. J. F. Quinn
1st Lt. S. White
Sgt. T. W. Omohundro (w)
3rd Lt. C. R. Evans
2nd Lt. H. Harden (w/c)
Sgt. J. H. Clements (w)
1st Sgt. W. B. Stone (c)
Sgt. J. Perley
3rd Lt. J. W. Hill (c)
Sgt. W. W. Maury
2nd Lt. W. N. Wood (w)
Sgt. J. R. Buck (c)
A
1st Lt. J. A. Lewellyn (adjutant)
Field and Staff
C. M. Lewellyn, hosp. steward
W. A. Mason, Q.M. sgt.
G. A. Gulley, ord. sgt.
W. H. Taylor (w), asst. surgeon
J. D. Galt, surgeon
1st Lt. J. T. Blair, A.C.O.
Capt. J. E. Blair, Q.M.
Note: none of these individuals would have taken part in the charge.
Key
commanding officer
second-in-command
field officer
company commander
junior officer
sergeant-major
1st sergeant
sergeant
corporal
private

The diagram shows approximately how the line of Wood's regiment, the center one of Garnett's Brigade, might have looked at that moment. Some 328 men, a third of a regiment's full strength, moved off in two ranks with a full complement of officers – thirty-eight (all dismounted) – giving a very generous 1:9 ratio of officers to enlisted men and with each company having at least three, although the regiment had already lost Lieutenant-Colonel Ellis, mortally wounded by a shell fragment during the long wait in the sun – the first of seventeen officers that would be hit in the next half-hour. The company commanders were on the right of their front rank with a covering first sergeant immediately behind. All the lieutenants formed part of the file-closer rank of supernumeraries at the rear. Their task was to guide and steady the line, keep the men moving and closed up as casualties occurred, and prevent men dropping back – if necessary by threats with their revolvers. There were forty-three sergeants in the line, thirteen under full establishment, the first sergeants posted behind the company commanders, the second sergeants as guides on the left of each company, with the remainder probably in the file-closer rank at the rear.The shortage of sergeants may be the reason that two corporals were detailed specifically to carry the colors in the center of the line.

With an average company strength of under thirty, as a number of casualties had already occurred due to the heat or enemy shells, and perhaps as many as forty-six officers and sergeants at the rear, the front rank of each company would not have held more than fourteen men. Moving forward shoulder to shoulder, the regiment's front would not have extended beyond 90–95 yards – a regiment 1,000 strong in line would have a frontage of over 300 yards. On the right flank was Company A and on the left Company B, which was as specified in the drill manual. Both these companies could have been deployed forward as skirmishers, but on this occasion there is little evidence that this happened unless a few had been detached from each company; indeed Lieutenant Wood in Company A makes no mention of it in his description of events that afternoon. Colonel Gantt strode forward some thirty paces behind the color guard with his adjutant behind the right flank, and the one-armed Major Peyton and Sergeant-Major Wolfe behind the left. It is most unlikely that any of the regiment's administrative staff took part in the attack, as none of them were casualties and men such as the quartermaster, the assistant commissary officer, the surgeon and his assistant had vital duties to perform behind the line.

Some of the 19th Virginia Infantry Regiment almost reached the Copse of Trees near the Angle on Cemetery Ridge, the high water mark, some say, of the Confederacy itself. When the remnants came back they left behind around 150 dead, wounded or captured comrades.

Federal Government Purchase of Foreign Rifles and Muskets

It was quickly realized that the war was not going to be a short one and that therefore the existing stocks of rifles and muskets would be woefully inadequate, and that even expanded home manufacture could never make up the deficit in time to equip huge armies. The U.S. government turned to foreign purchase. As an example of the scale, the following figures are taken from the 1862 annual Report of the Chief of Ordnance of purchases made in one year:

Austrian rifles	135,755	Belgian rifles	23,994
Austrian muskets	34,500	Belgian muskets	33,200
English Tower muskets	8,999	French rifles	48,108
English Enfield rifles	116,740	French muskets	4,850
Prussian rifles	6,409	Minie rifles	5,179
Prussian muskets	105,140	Other foreign rifles	203,831

The total is a staggering 726,705.

Union

The 20th Maine Volunteer Infantry Regiment, which was part of Vincent's Brigade, 1st Division, V Corps, was heavily involved in the defense of the extreme left flank of the Union line on Little Round Top on July 2. The regiment was somewhat isolated and involved in an hour-long, particularly tough fight amongst trees, rocks and across stone walls. It ended with the regiment making a spontaneous downhill advance with the bayonet that finally dispersed the attacking Rebels of the 15th Alabama. The diagram opposite shows the regiment in close column of companies, a common formation for units in reserve, as it might have been drawn up earlier that day waiting to be deployed. The companies, in two ranks, formed one behind the other at a distance of half their frontage – in this case some 10 yards. Here the company commanders are in front of their command with the first sergeants taking those officers' places on the right of the front rank. The 20th Maine was seriously short of senior, experienced field officers so a captain (Clark) was second-in-command and controlled the right wing companies (A, C, D, E, and F) while another captain (Spear) took charge of the left wing. Overall, however, the officer to soldier ratio of 1:14 was generous.

With an engaged strength of 386 it was well above the average Union regimental strength (298), but almost 100 less than the 15th Alabama at the start of the action. The 20th Maine apparently had no surgeon or assistant surgeon on its establishment – a rare and extraordinary situation. The regiment's "doctor" was a civilian, John Chamberlain, the youngest brother of Colonel Joshua Chamberlain and of his acting adjutant Thomas Chamberlain. John Chamberlain was an agent of the U.S. Christian Commission (see box, page 234) and had joined his brothers at Aldie during Lee's march north. He rode with the regiment to Gettysburg and it became his initial task during the battle to set up a small aid station with a few orderlies behind Little Round Top.

The internal structure of these two regiments from either side is virtually identical, the main difference being that proportionately the Rebels were better off for officers, particularly senior ones. Going into battle with two captains acting as second- and third-in-command and no surgeon would seem a significant disadvantage, although in the event it was not so.

INFANTRY FIREARMS AND OTHER WEAPONS

Procurement Problems and Solutions

At the start of the war the infantry of both sides was equipped with a confusing variety of firearms. Initially, owing to rapid expansion, many infantry regiments in both North and South were armed with old flintlock muskets dating back to the War of 1812 and beyond – even in November 1861 several Virginia militia

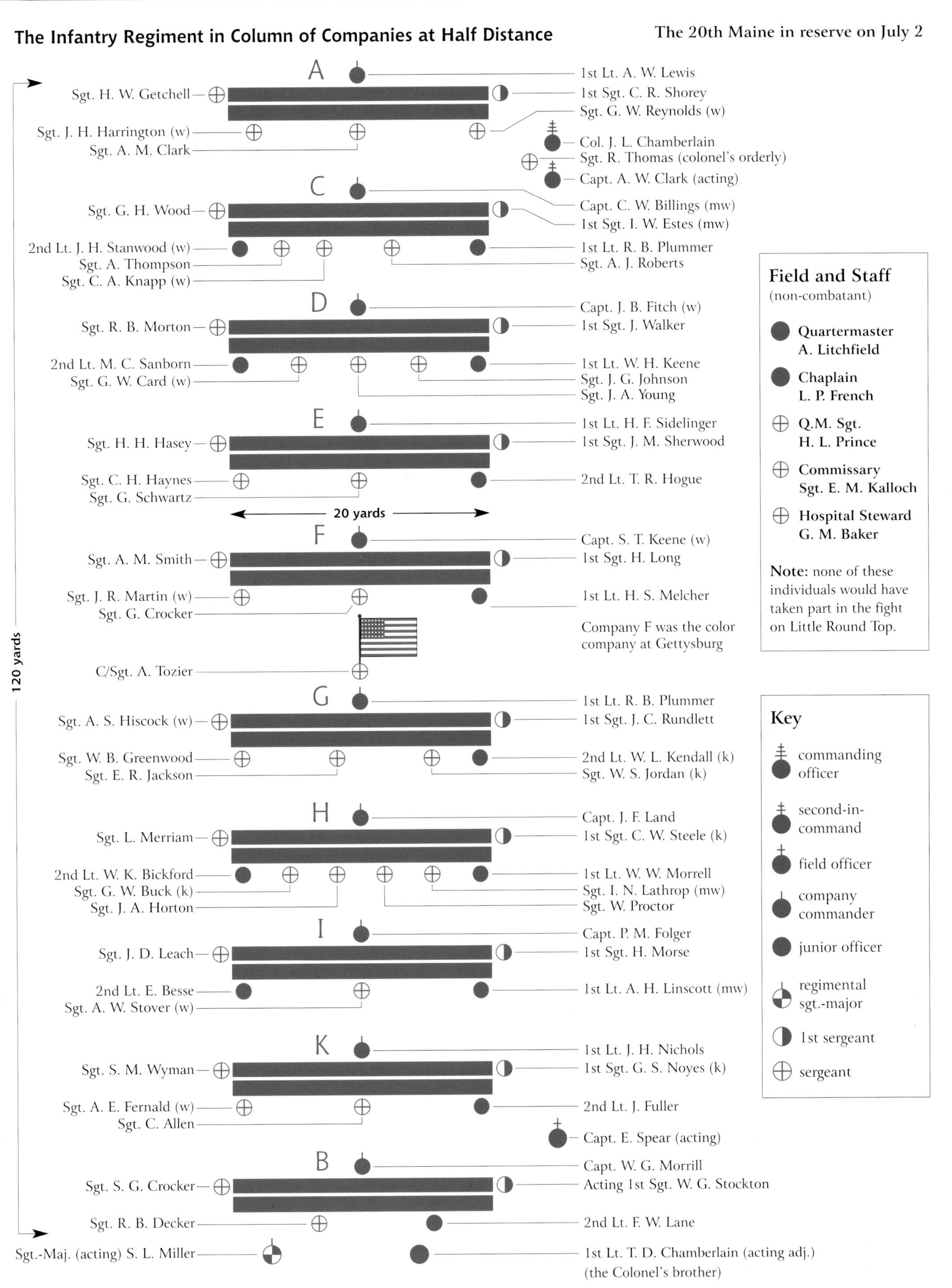
The Infantry Regiment in Column of Companies at Half Distance
The 20th Maine in reserve on July 2
A
1st Lt. A. W. Lewis
Sgt. H. W. Getchell
1st Sgt. C. R. Shorey
Sgt. G. W. Reynolds (w)
Sgt. J. H. Harrington (w)
Sgt. A. M. Clark
Col. J. L. Chamberlain
Sgt. R. Thomas (colonel's orderly)
Capt. A. W. Clark (acting)
C
Sgt. G. H. Wood
Capt. C. W. Billings (mw)
1st Sgt. I. W. Estes (mw)
2nd Lt. J. H. Stanwood (w)
Sgt. A. Thompson
Sgt. C. A. Knapp (w)
1st Lt. R. B. Plummer
Sgt. A. J. Roberts
D
Capt. J. B. Fitch (w)
Sgt. R. B. Morton
1st Sgt. J. Walker
2nd Lt. M. C. Sanborn
Sgt. G. W. Card (w)
1st Lt. W. H. Keene
Sgt. J. G. Johnson
Sgt. J. A. Young
E
1st Lt. H. F. Sidelinger
Sgt. H. H. Hasey
1st Sgt. J. M. Sherwood
Sgt. C. H. Haynes
Sgt. G. Schwartz
2nd Lt. T. R. Hogue
20 yards
F
Capt. S. T. Keene (w)
Sgt. A. M. Smith
1st Sgt. H. Long
Sgt. J. R. Martin (w)
Sgt. G. Crocker
1st Lt. H. S. Melcher
Company F was the color company at Gettysburg
C/Sgt. A. Tozier
120 yards
G
1st Lt. R. B. Plummer
Sgt. A. S. Hiscock (w)
1st Sgt. J. C. Rundlett
Sgt. W. B. Greenwood
Sgt. E. R. Jackson
2nd Lt. W. L. Kendall (k)
Sgt. W. S. Jordan (k)
H
Capt. J. F. Land
Sgt. L. Merriam
1st Sgt. C. W. Steele (k)
2nd Lt. W. K. Bickford
Sgt. G. W. Buck (k)
Sgt. J. A. Horton
1st Lt. W. W. Morrell
Sgt. I. N. Lathrop (mw)
Sgt. W. Proctor
I
Capt. P. M. Folger
Sgt. J. D. Leach
1st Sgt. H. Morse
2nd Lt. E. Besse
Sgt. A. W. Stover (w)
1st Lt. A. H. Linscott (mw)
K
1st Lt. J. H. Nichols
Sgt. S. M. Wyman
1st Sgt. G. S. Noyes (k)
Sgt. A. E. Fernald (w)
Sgt. C. Allen
2nd Lt. J. Fuller
Capt. E. Spear (acting)
B
Capt. W. G. Morrill
Sgt. S. G. Crocker
Acting 1st Sgt. W. G. Stockton
Sgt. R. B. Decker
2nd Lt. F. W. Lane
Sgt.-Maj. (acting) S. L. Miller
1st Lt. T. D. Chamberlain (acting adj.)
(the Colonel's brother)
Field and Staff
(non-combatant)
Quartermaster
A. Litchfield
Chaplain
L. P. French
Q.M. Sgt.
H. L. Prince
Commissary
Sgt. E. M. Kalloch
Hospital Steward
G. M. Baker
Note: none of these individuals would have taken part in the fight on Little Round Top.
Key
commanding officer
second-in-command
field officer
company commander
junior officer
regimental sgt.-major
1st sergeant
sergeant

Principal Infantry Firearms at Gettysburg

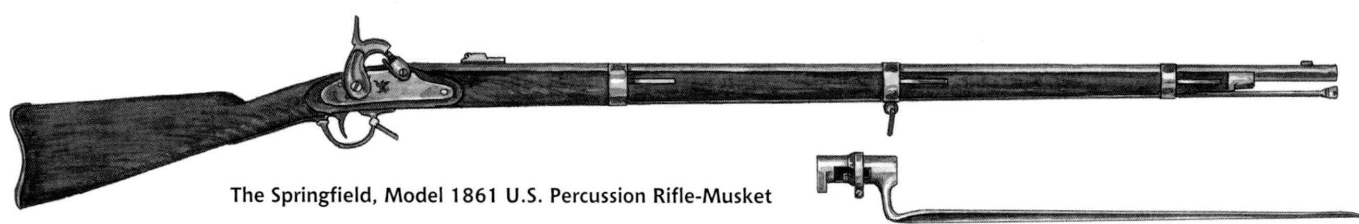

The Springfield, Model 1861 U.S. Percussion Rifle-Musket

The most widely used shoulder arm of the Civil War, seeing service in every major battle. It was made at the Springfield Armory in Massachusetts at a cost of around $15 and by 32 other private manufacturers. Its rifled bore, interchangeable parts, and percussion-cap ignition system incorporated the major prewar innovations into an accurate and dependable rifle. Approximately one million were made during the war and, although an improved 1863 model was produced, the 1861 model remained the basic infantry weapon of the war. It weighed 9.25 pounds, was 58.5 inches long, came with a 21-inch socket bayonet and fired a .58 conical Minie bullet at a muzzle velocity of 950 ft/sec. The front sight doubled as a bayonet lug and it had a two-leaf rear sight. Maximum range 1,000 yards, effective battlefield range up to 500 yards.

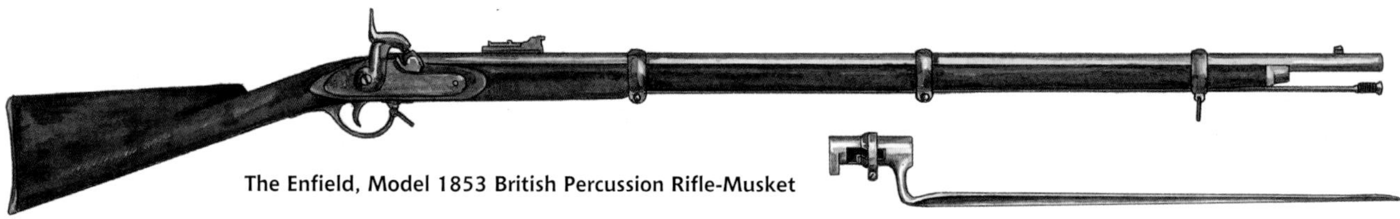

The Enfield, Model 1853 British Percussion Rifle-Musket

This British-made rifle-musket was originally issued to the British Army in the Crimean War to replace their smoothbore muskets. Great efforts were made by agents from both sides in the Civil War to purchase these weapons and it is thought some 800,000 were imported legally by the U.S. and illegally by Southern blockade-runners during the war. It proved a dependable and popular weapon, particularly with the Confederates. Although it got its name from the British Royal Small Arms Factory at Enfield, the owner, the British government, was sensitive about remaining neutral and so the rifle-muskets used in the Civil War were made at private factories in London and Birmingham. It weighed 9.20 pounds, was 55.25 inches long with an angular socket bayonet and fired a .577 conical bullet that was normally interchangeable with Springfield's .58. The 1856 model, which was a shorter version with a sword bayonet, was often called the "Sergeant's Rifle." Maximum range 1,100 yards, effective battlefield range up to 800 yards.

regiments were so equipped. The reason for this was that the manufacture of flintlocks had not ceased until the 1840s so there were still large stocks in the various arsenals. The smoothbore percussion musket was introduced in 1841. The use of a percussion cap instead of the old flintlock firing mechanism improved wet-weather performance and very marginally speeded up reloading. In the same year a muzzleloading rifle was produced; it became known as the "Mississippi" as the Mississippi Volunteers carried it during the Mexican War of 1846–48. Then in the early 1850s the U.S. Army adopted the rifle-musket firing the Minie bullet and consequently work began on rifling smoothbores to take this new ammunition. From 1855 all new U.S. weapons were rifled. The most common in use throughout the Civil War was the U.S. "Springfield", named after Springfield, Massachusetts, the site of the main U.S. arsenal after the Union authorities set fire to, and abandoned, that at Harper's Ferry in April 1861, destroying 17,000 finished muskets (however, the Confederates salvaged much machinery and many tools, which became the core of their ordnance effort at Fayetteville, North Carolina). The next most numerous were the British "Enfield" rifle-muskets, of which over 800,000 were bought by the Union and Confederacy during the course of the war.

In the South the limited supplies of rifle-muskets were soon exhausted so smoothbore percussion muskets converted from flintlocks became the general issue. When Major Josiah Gorgas was appointed chief of ordnance of the Confederate States Army in 1861 he found the Confederacy arsenals contained only 15,000 rifle-muskets and 120,000 inferior smoothbores. Compounding his problems was a lack of powder, there being just small quantities at Baton Rouge and Mount Vernon, Alabama, left over from the Mexican War. Some 70–80 percent of Rebel regiments marched to war in 1861 with smoothbores – some individuals and regiments continued to prefer them for several years thereafter. However, according to Colonel E. Porter Alexander, Longstreet's senior artillery battalion commander, by July 1863 the majority of Lee's infantrymen had a Springfield or Enfield, mostly the latter. According to Brigadier-General Crawford's Pennsylvania Reserves' inventory of the 3,000 firearms collected from the Gettysburg battlefield on July 2 and 3, over 80 percent of Confederate weapons were Enfields. The South had used every possible way of supplementing the meager prewar stocks. Initially many volunteers were instructed to bring their own squirrel guns, "Kentucky" hunting rifles or shotguns; manufacturing (copying existing models) was given priority and purchasing overseas with its associated blockade-running became a highly organized activity.

Once the war got under way and Confederate armies proved successful in the field, substantial quantities of serviceable weapons came into Rebel hands with the capture of Union arsenals – for example, two of Early's brigades re-equipped themselves from stocks abandoned by General Milroy in his hasty retreat from Winchester on June 15, 1863, early in the

Gettysburg campaign. To a victorious army go the spoils of war. Arms taken from prisoners and scavenging on battlefields became rich sources of weaponry for the Confederates in the first half of the war. A Rebel soldier stated that after Shiloh (April 1862) his regiment "swaped [*sic*] our very indifferent guns for their splendid Endfield [*sic*] rifles." Three months later at Gaines' Mill one of Jackson's "foot cavalry" recorded that the 21st Virginia Regiment (Jones's Brigade, Johnson's Division, Ewell's Corps at Gettysburg) had one company armed with Springfields, one with Enfields, one with Mississippi rifles and seven with smoothbores. But after the battle the whole regiment was equipped with "top class guns." Following Fredericksburg, Lee's men collected over 9,000 abandoned weapons, although a surprisingly small proportion was Springfields. However, five months later Colonel William Allan, the chief of ordnance of Ewell's Corps, was able to ensure all men in the corps were armed with .58 rifle-muskets from discarded weapons picked up on the Chancellorsville battlefield – many from XI Corps, whose German soldiers acquired the Rebel nickname of "Flying Dutchmen" after their rout by Jackson's surprise attack.

The Rifle-musket and Smoothbore Musket

At Gettysburg it was the muzzleloading, single-shot rifle-musket that dominated the battlefield. Most infantrymen on both sides carried one of the several varieties of this weapon. With the U.S.-manufactured Springfield in his hands, the average soldier felt he

Principal Infantry Firearms at Gettysburg

The Austrian, Model 1854 Lorenz Rifle-Musket

Both the earlier .54-caliber and the later re-bored .58 Austrian rifle-muskets were carried by 21 Union regiments at Gettysburg and by an unknown number of Confederate soldiers. Called the "Lorenz" as it was designed by Lt. Lorenz of the Austrian Army, it entered Hapsburg service in 1854. It was imported in large numbers during the war, with the Union purchasing over 226,000 and the Confederacy at least 100,000 as its .54 ammunition could be used in the "Mississippi" and vice versa. The earlier model had non-adjustable rear sights calibrated to hit a target up to 300 paces, but later versions had the leaf backsight adjustable up to 800. It had a 37.5-inch barrel and took a quadrangular socket bayonet. As noted below, opinions as to its value varied wildly from "although a little heavy, a fine piece" and a "wicked shooter" to "not worth much" and "miserably poor." The 14th Vermont was the only one of the five regiments in Stannard's Brigade to be entirely armed with the .54 Lorenz when it took part in the critical attack on Pickett's right flank at the height of the charge.

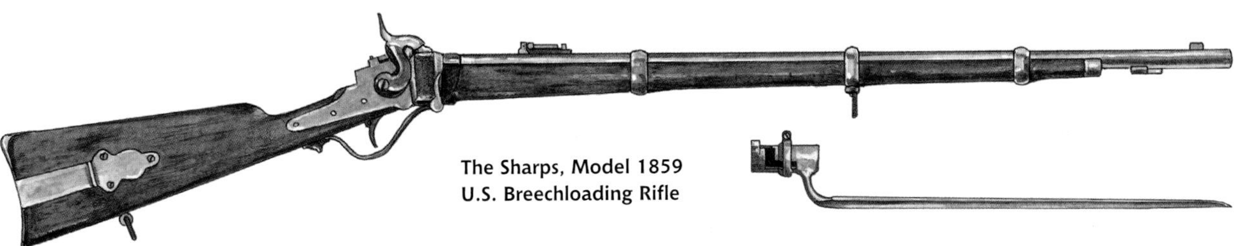

The Sharps, Model 1859 U.S. Breechloading Rifle

In 1848 Christian Sharps invented a rifle that loaded from the breech. The breechblock moved down when the trigger guard was moved down, a paper or linen cartridge was placed in the open breech and when the breechblock was raised again it tore off the paper, exposing the powder so the flame from the cap could ignite the charge. Its only drawback was that it leaked gas badly. The legendary Union sniper Private Truman "California Joe" Head was the first to be issued with the 1859 model for test and evaluation. It was so effective that Col. Hiram Berdan, a highly controversial "political" officer, ordered 2,000 for his U.S. Sharpshooters. It was light (8.75 pounds), .52 caliber with a barrel length of 30 inches, leaf backsight, long angular bayonet, and, with the special double-set triggers, cost $43. It was the best single-shot breechloader of the period, with a skilled marksman able to drop a man at 700 yards. However, its main advantage was that a soldier could fire up to nine shots a minute and could reload lying down – the ideal weapon for the skirmish line or for sharpshooters. The U.S. government missed the opportunity for large-scale manufacture of these weapons at the start of the war, but some 9,000 Sharps rifles (as distinct from carbines) were eventually purchased. The Confederates were later able to make up to 5,000 inferior copies at Richmond. At Gettysburg the 1st and 2nd U.S. Sharpshooters and the 14th Connecticut were armed entirely with Sharps rifles and the 2nd New Hampshire, 1st Massachusetts Sharpshooters and 13th Pennsylvania Reserves had half or more of their men so equipped – giving an approximate total of 1,100 among the infantry of Meade's army, although a few individuals may have purchased their own.

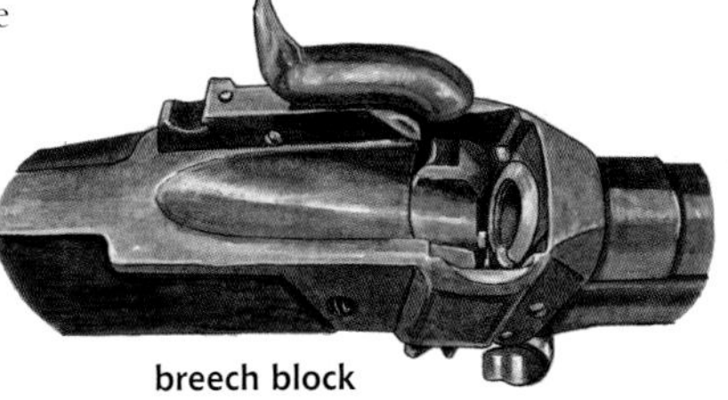

breech block

Principal Infantry Firearms at Gettysburg

The Mississippi, Model 1841 U.S. Percussion Rifle-Musket

The U.S. adopted the percussion system in 1841 and produced an infantry rifle-musket that year. This was a .54-caliber weapon with a 33-inch barrel. The new arm was popular, accurate and easy to handle, and its browned barrel finish, contrasting with the bright brass furniture, gave it a pleasing appearance. It owed its name to the successful use of the weapon by the Mississippi Volunteer Regiment commanded by Jefferson Davis at the Battle of Buena Vista in the Mexican War. About 25,000 were manufactured at the Harper's Ferry Armory but without provision for a bayonet. Beginning in 1855 many were rifled to take the .58 bullets, fitted with a lug to take a sword bayonet and the simple notch backsight was replaced with the leaf sight for longer ranges. It was copied by Confederate manufacturers and was carried by a substantial number of Rebels in July 1863.

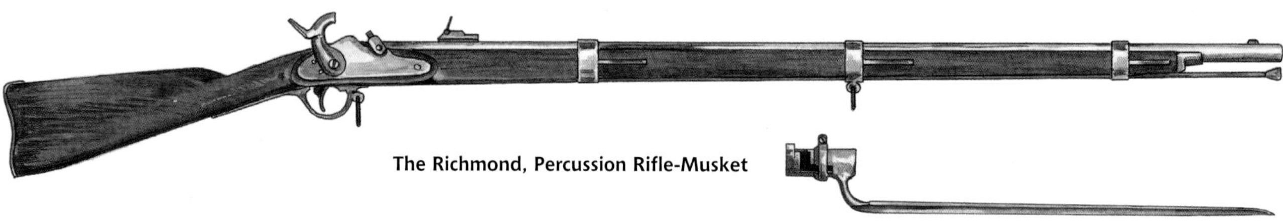

The Richmond, Percussion Rifle-Musket

Manufactured at the Richmond Armory from 1861–65 using equipment captured at Harper's Ferry, this weapon was produced in larger numbers than all the other Confederate arms during the Civil War. It closely resembled the 1855 Springfield but with a different two-leaf rear sight. The fore sight doubled as a bayonet lug and early production models used a lockplate with a distinctive full humpback design – reduced in later versions. It weighed 9 pounds, had a 30-inch barrel and fired the .58 Minie bullets with an effective battlefield range of 500 yards.

The Springfield, Model 1842 U.S. Smoothbore Musket

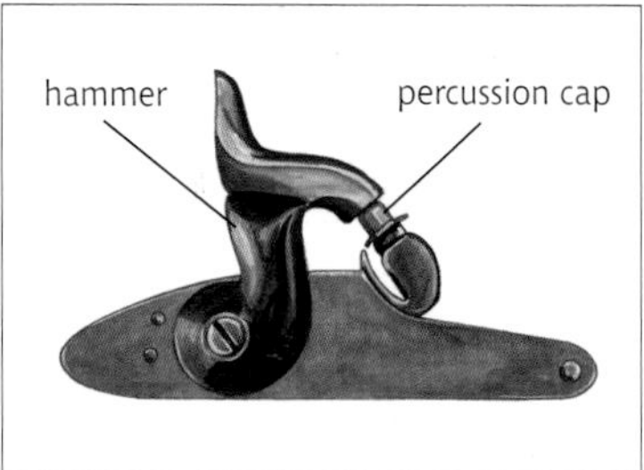

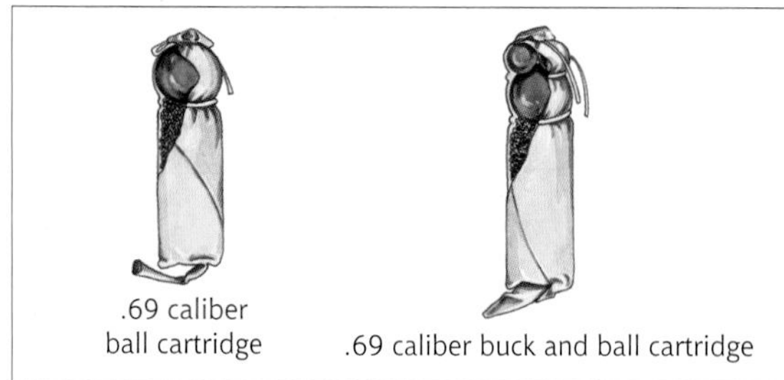

In the early days of the war many Union infantrymen were armed with a number of obsolete smoothbore muskets. Most of these weapons were made at Springfield or Harper's Ferry; others were of foreign origin. These muskets were of .69 caliber with a long 42-inch barrel and could fire either a single ball or a combination of the single ball and three smaller balls, this latter being the famous "buck and ball" cartridge, which effectively converted the musket into a form of shotgun. About 172,000 were made, of which some 10,000 were re-bored and converted to rifles in the prewar period. Although its effective range was only 100 yards it was still popular with some regiments and several thousand were used at Gettysburg. The 12th New Jersey Regiment was so armed and on July 3 was deployed just south of Zeigler's Grove, from where they delivered devastating "buck and ball" volleys, knocking over scores of their Mississippian attackers.

had the best weapon readily available at the time, with the British Enfield, preferred by some, coming a close second. The Confederates, using captured machinery, made an excellent copy of the U.S. Model 1855 rifle-musket firing the .58 Minie bullet called the Richmond rifle. The infantry also had a number of breechloaders (Sharps) and the cavalry breechloading carbines (Sharps and Burnsides) and repeaters (Spencers) (see Section Four: The Cavalry) on the battlefield. However, these significant technical developments – particularly the latter, which would soon change battlefield tactics for ever – had been rejected as insufficiently tested by Brigadier-General James W. Ripley, the Union chief of ordnance. Ripley had the chance at the start of the war to authorize the large-scale production and purchase of breechloading, single-shot rifles for standard issue. He failed to do so. Instead he went ahead with the "tried and tested," but now somewhat outmoded Springfield. This decision was not without its support at the time, as the consensus of expert opinion inclined toward the use of the muzzleloader, and the repeaters of the day were considered especially undesirable for military purposes. It was said that those already in use were complicated in their mechanism, liable to malfunction, difficult to repair and got through ammunition so rapidly that supplies were soon exhausted.

At Gettysburg eighty-one Union infantry regiments (33 percent) held a .58 Springfield as their only firearm. Another fifty-five (22 percent) were armed with the .577 Enfield and 29 (12 percent) carried a mixture of both. Nevertheless, a small minority was still armed with the old smoothbore musket. In the Army of the Potomac twelve regiments (5 percent) were armed solely with this weapon – notably four of the five regiments in Colonel Kelly's Irish Brigade, 1st Division, II Corps – while another thirteen had a mixture of various smoothbore and rifle-muskets (Springfields, Enfields, Austrian or French). Of these foreign weapons, the Austrian was the most common, coming in for heavy criticism from some quarters and praise from others. Lieutenant-Colonel Abert, an assistant inspector general in the U.S. Army, examined 800 such rifles and found only 100 serviceable. A Captain C. Piepho of the 108th Ohio Volunteers (not at Gettysburg) found the Austrian rifle-muskets "totally worthless . . . the locks of the said guns having springs of so weak a construction that many of the men had to snap the lock three or more times before the piece would discharge." However, the quartermaster of the 104th Pennsylvania Volunteer Infantry Regiment considered the Austrians "very superior weapons, although not so well finished as the American," and a soldier of the 5th New York Regiment considered them "short, light and very easily cleaned" – opinions were very subjective.

Four Union regiments carried the new "Sharps" breechloading .52-caliber, single-shot rifle, while another three had a mixture of Sharps and other weapons. In total at least 80 percent of Meade's infantrymen carried a muzzleloaded rifle-musket of some sort, including the Austrian .54 caliber, with the balance being equipped with smoothbores, other foreign weapons, Sharps breechloaders or a confusing mixture of all weapons – the 11th New Jersey had .577 Enfields, .577 Austrian and .58 Austrian rifle-muskets, and .69 smoothbore muskets, and the 4th Ohio had .58 Springfields, .577 Enfields, .69 U.S. smoothbore and .69 English smoothbore muskets.

Precise figures are not available for Lee's army, but at least 85 percent of his infantrymen carried a rifle-musket – Mississippi, Richmond, Austrian, Springfield or Enfield, with the majority being Enfields. Although the one Confederate sharpshooter battalion (3rd Battalion Georgia Sharpshooters) and a detachment of another (1st Battalion North Carolina Sharpshooters) were present at Gettysburg armed with the Enfield, only a few men in the former had the special sniper's rifle – the .45 Whitworth – costing $1,000 at 1863 prices. The Georgia sharpshooters would have made use of their Whitworths around the Peach Orchard and Stony Hill on July 2, but the duties of provost guard at Hill's Corps headquarters would probably have kept the North Carolinians at more mundane work. At around noon on July 3 Lieutenant-General Ewell, the Confederate corps commander whose men had taken Gettysburg two days before, was riding down a street in the town when his wooden leg was hit by a sharpshooter firing from around 1,000 yards away – to which he responded, "It don't hurt a bit to be shot in a wooden leg."

Sir Joseph Whitworth, one of the premier firearm designers of the era, had designed what today's military would call a sniper rifle and it became a firm Rebel favorite. The veteran sharpshooter Isaac Shannon stated, "I do not believe a harder-hitting, harder-kicking, long range gun was ever made than the Whitworth rifle." It is claimed that it was a sharpshooter with a Whitworth who killed Major-General Sedgwick (VI Corps commander at Gettysburg) at a range of over 1,000 yards while placing artillery in position at Spotsylvania Court House in May 1864. Major-General Reynolds was killed by a single shot to the head while commanding the Federal forces resisting the Confederate advance down the Chambersburg Pike early on July 1, but no Rebel sharpshooter units were present at the time. The Whitworth rifle fired a .45 six-sided bullet from a 33-inch barrel with a 1:20 twist at a speed of 1,200–1,400 feet per second out to an extreme range of over a mile. The bullet was unusually long, its length being 2.5 times its diameter, and fired by 85 grains of black powder. It had a variety of sights, some more sophisticated than others, ranged out to 1,200 yards. Some had a simple telescopic sight fixed on the left side of the weapon.

The problem with all muzzleloaders, be they rifles or smoothbores, was the very fact that they were muzzleloaders and therefore loading was a fiddly, time-consuming business. Three shots a minute was supposed to be the rate for a trained soldier, but in action it was more likely to drop quickly to two. An equal inconvenience was that to load reasonably quickly you had to stand up, or at least kneel – the former being a decidedly unhealthy position to adopt when being shot at. Soldiers under fire want to lie down and while doing so be able reload as necessary. The reloading of a muzzleloader while prone is possible, but it takes far longer and ramming becomes doubly difficult. Many men at Gettysburg undoubtedly did reload while lying down. A grim example of what could be achieved in dire circumstances with sufficient determination occurred during the Confederates' final attack on Culp's Hill on July 3. A Rebel soldier of the 1st Maryland was hit in the stomach, rolled over onto his back and struggled to reload his musket. Men of the 147th Pennsylvania who were about to finish him off were restrained by their officer. They then watched as the wounded soldier finally finished the reloading. He removed the ramrod from the barrel, cocked the hammer, put the muzzle of the piece under his chin and then, with the end of his ramrod, pressed the trigger.

The rifle-musket's increased range – its significance at Gettysburg

Before examining the technicalities of loading drills and firing methods of the infantry weapons in use at Gettysburg, the question of the significance of the increased range of the rifle-musket over the smoothbore merits examination. The effective range of the smoothbore had not changed since Waterloo in 1815. A soldier aiming and firing his smoothbore at an enemy over 100 yards away in a battle situation was going to knock him down about once in every thirty shots. If the target had advanced to within 50–70 yards of the firer, then the chances of a hit increased dramatically to one in three, or much better if loaded with "buck and ball" (see page 103) ammunition. At less than 50 yards, and if firing his shot as part of a volley from his company or regiment, then the results were likely to be devastating. Both controlled volleys and continuous firing at close range with a musket, rifle or smoothbore against exposed targets had great killing power. The bodies piled up across the Wheatfield, in Devil's Den, the Slaughter Pen, on the slopes of Culp's Hill or Little Round Top and just short of the Angle or Copse of Trees are overwhelming proof of that – the point being that the great majority of these men, who fell within striking distance of their enemy, had been hit by bullets (Minies) from the longer-range rifle-musket as well as by balls from smoothbores.

The grooves in the barrel spun the bullet, giving the rifle-musket a theoretical range of 1,000 yards or more at which it could penetrate 3.25 inches of pine plank. If fired coolly and carefully by a well-trained soldier at 500 yards, there was a good chance of scoring a hit on a stationary target with one shot out of two. On a battlefield, however, where the target moved and often fired back, the effective range was cut to 300 yards. Nevertheless, this still gave the rifle-musket a considerable effective range advantage over the smoothbore's 100 yards.

A number of authors and historians have considered that the rifle-musket's increased range rendered the close-packed infantry assault in lines, as seen at Gettysburg and on many other battlefields, as verging on futile – the tactics of the Napoleonic era were now outmoded. In other words, a frontal assault across open ground, such as Pickett's charge, against infantry that could open fire effectively at 300–500 yards, could never succeed. The theory of the "rifle revolution" is fine, the reality rather different. It does not allow a realistic assessment of many other factors that existed on battlefields of the nineteenth century, up to and including 1863, and some in modern times. Consider the following:

- Officers on both sides were trained to restrain the fire of defending soldiers in the main line until the range was short enough to ensure maximum losses, preferably with controlled volley firing. Advancing troops seldom fired at the long ranges even in open ground, as to do so meant halting to reload or pushing on with an empty weapon – better to save one's shot until closing in and then try to rush the position over a short distance.
- The terrain frequently dictated the range at which fire could be opened. Folds in the ground, low hills, woods, trees, buildings and rocks all obscured the view, making fields of fire short. If the target could not be seen there was no point in pulling the trigger. Much of the firing and fighting at Gettysburg was at close range because of these terrain features. The Rose Farm woods around the Wheatfield, the scrub and boulders of Devil's Den, the trees covering much of Little Round Top and all of Culp's Hill, and even the undulations of the ground between Seminary and Cemetery Ridges dictated the distances at which successful fire could be opened, irrespective of the range of the rifle or musket.
- Smoke from infantry weapons and artillery fire obscured the battlefield. Black powder caused clouds of smoke to drift across Civil War battlefields, particularly during prolonged artillery duels. Combine this smokescreen with some of the

The Effect of Keeping Rifle-musket Sights at 300 yards as Enemy Approaches

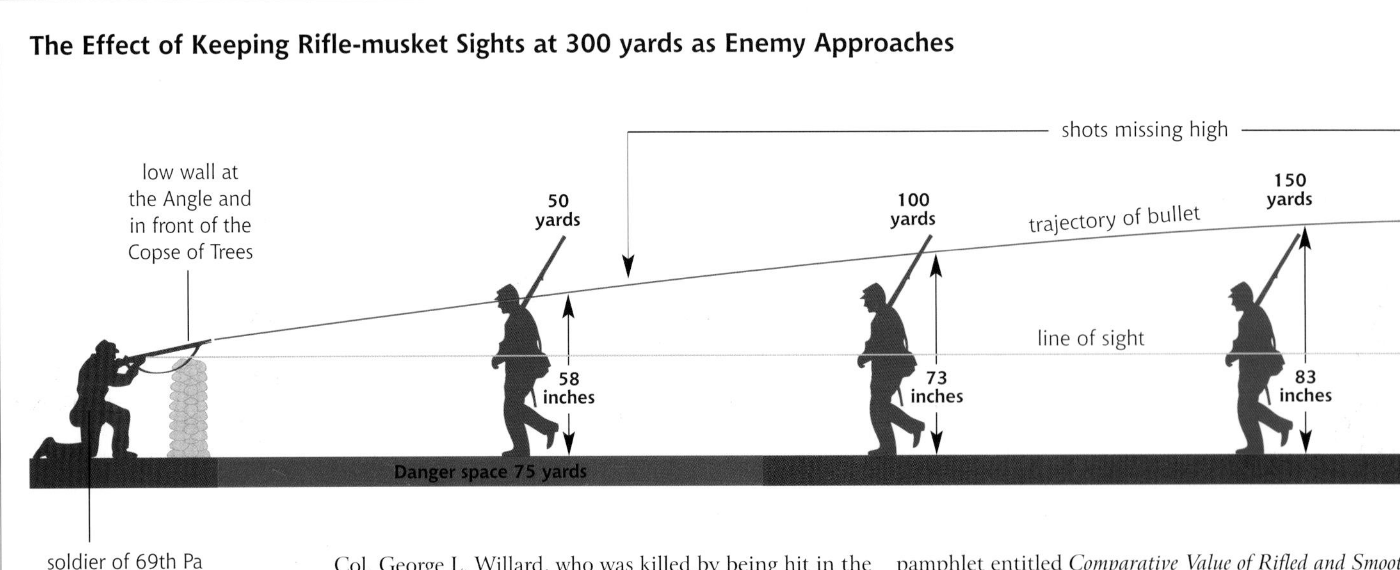

Col. George L. Willard, who was killed by being hit in the face by an artillery round on July 2 when leading his brigade (3rd Brigade, 3rd Division, II Corps) in a successful counterattack against Barksdale's Brigade, was an ardent supporter of the smoothbore. Writing in a pamphlet entitled *Comparative Value of Rifled and Smoot[h] Bored Arms* about infantry defending against cavalry, Willard makes the point that a soldier opening fire against charging cavalry at 500 yards must elevate his sights accordingly. However, as the horse covers over

Hit Rates for the Rifle-musket and Smoothbore Musket

The results of test firing to compare the accuracy at various ranges of the rifle-musket and smoothbore are shown below. These tests were carried out in ideal conditions with no dangerous distractions to the firers, but nevertheless point to the general and rather obvious conclusion that at ranges up to 100 yards it did not much matter what weapon the soldier was using, but if the man with the smoothbore loaded buck and ball then at such a short range that was the better weapon. In the table the number of hits is out of fifty firings and the figures under the various ranges in yards show the range of hits, lowest to highest. There was one ball and three buckshot in each buck-and-ball cartridge.

	100 yards	200 yards	300 yards	500 yards
Rifle-musket	48–50	32–41	23–29	12–21
Smoothbore	37–43	18–24	9	
Smoothbore (buck and ball)	79–84 (buckshot)	19–31		
	31–36 (ball)	18–22		

terrain features mentioned above and often it would not have been profitable for infantrymen, even those armed with Springfields or Enfields, to open fire above 100–150 yards.

- The rifle bullet's trajectory rose above the point blank at longer ranges; in other words, it followed a curved path and would come plunging down, having gone high over targets at a closer distance. Thus hitting a target at 100 yards or more required a reasonably accurate estimate of distance and consequent adjustment of the sights. Often a flustered firer desperate to reload would not have the ability, time or inclination to guess ranges and fiddle with his sights. If a Federal soldier of the 69th Pennsylvania Infantry kneeling behind the wall at the Angle set his rifle-musket sights at 300 yards to hit Confederates just as they approached the Emmitsburg Road, steadied his rifle on the wall and took careful aim at the belt buckle (midriff) of his target, he had a reasonable chance of a hit. However, as the enemy clambered over the fences and pressed forward and our Yankee soldier scrambled to reload, there was a sporting chance he would forget to adjust his sights. In that case, if he still aimed in roughly the same place on his next target, his shot would probably just miss the top of the Rebel's head. As the range shortened and with the sights still set at 300, the firer would continue to miss high with his enemy 250 yards distant until only 75 yards away – see the illustration below. It was simpler and safer to have the sights down at the start and open fire at close range.
- As there was an almost total lack of live firing practice, most soldiers learned their shooting on the battlefield where the drills emphasized volley firing at closer ranges. Some soldiers, such as those in the Union's Irish Brigade, deliberately kept their smoothbores for the very reason that their flat trajectory was fine when most firing was going to be at close range anyway, the barrels did not foul so quickly as those of rifles (see page 109), and they could load with "buck and ball" (see page 103) for a shotgun effect.

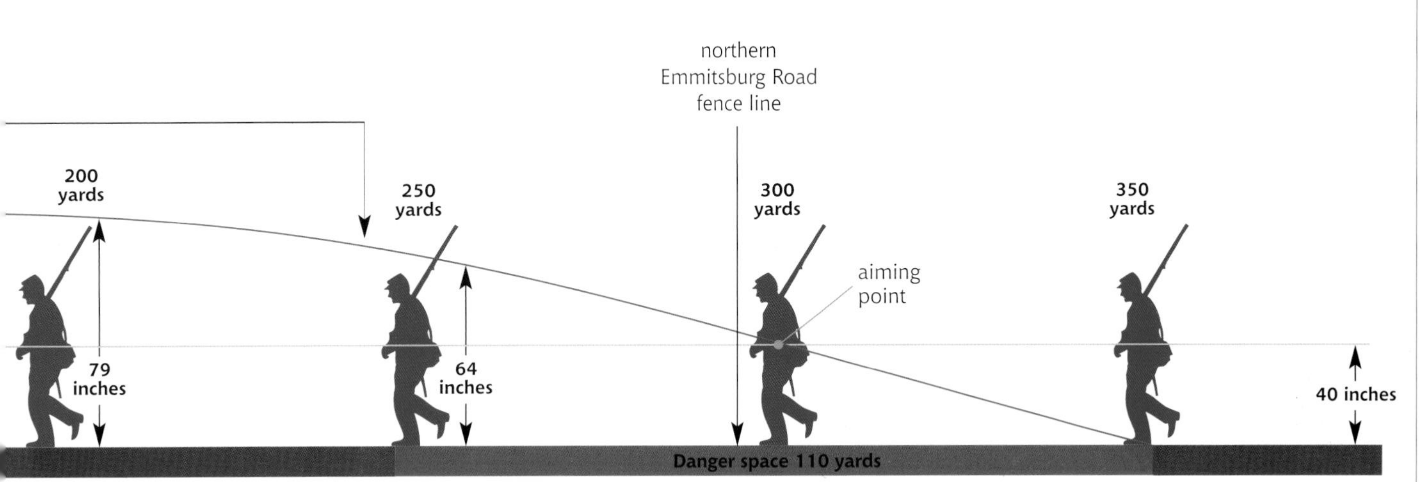

yards a second, the cavalryman is only in the danger zone at that range r 7 seconds before sights must be altered. Because of this, Willard ated that a soldier "will wisely do away with the ELEVATED SIGHT, d wait until the enemy are within point blank range . . . from this int, and in proportion as the distance decreases, the smoothbore, used against masses, acquires a real superiority over the rifled musket. The soldier armed with the first, if he aims directly at the line which gallops towards him . . . sees his chances of hitting increase with each second whilst the one armed with the rifle musket, sees them diminish in the same proportion unless he changes his sight before every shot."

Skirmishers and snipers excepted, most infantrymen at Gettysburg found themselves involved in rushed and flustered firing at ranges from 200 yards down to a few feet. Paddy Griffith, in his *Battle Tactics of the American Civil War*, gives the results of his extensive research into the ranges at which fire was opened in Civil War battles as follows:

- 1861–62 – average range 122 yards.
- 1863 – average range 127 yards. Relating this to Gettysburg, it would mean the defenders of the Angle mostly opened fire as, or after, the attackers climbed the Emmitsburg Road fences and began to ascend the final slope – a highly probable event as casualties inflicted before then would mostly have been caused by artillery fire.
- 1864–65 – average range 141 yards.

At Seven Pines, admittedly a battle fought in close country, the average range dropped to 68 yards. In all these instances the average range is well below 200 yards, a distance at which it does not much matter whether you are firing a rifle-musket or a smoothbore. Some of the best examples of fire being withheld until very close range at Gettysburg occurred on July 2 and 3 during the intense fighting for Culp's Hill – said to have involved some of the most sustained musketry firing of the entire war. On July 3 a blistering fire by the 5th Ohio and 147th Pennsylvania, who withheld their volleys until the attackers were only 100 yards away, destroyed the final attack by Steuart's Brigade across the Pardee Field. Private David Mouat in the 29th Pennsylvania, who were about 100 yards to the north, later wrote that his regiment held their fire until the Rebels had closed to 50 yards when the "whole line up and let them have it." Add together all these factors and instances (there are many more examples from all three days) and the extra accuracy at longer ranges of the rifle-musket was probably of negligible overall importance at Gettysburg. As a former infantry soldier, the present writer can vouch for the fact that on today's battlefield the footsoldier with his high-powered automatic rifle seldom opens fire much beyond 250 yards – seeing, aiming and hitting an enemy beyond that distance is often too problematic and best left to heavier or indirect-fire weapons.

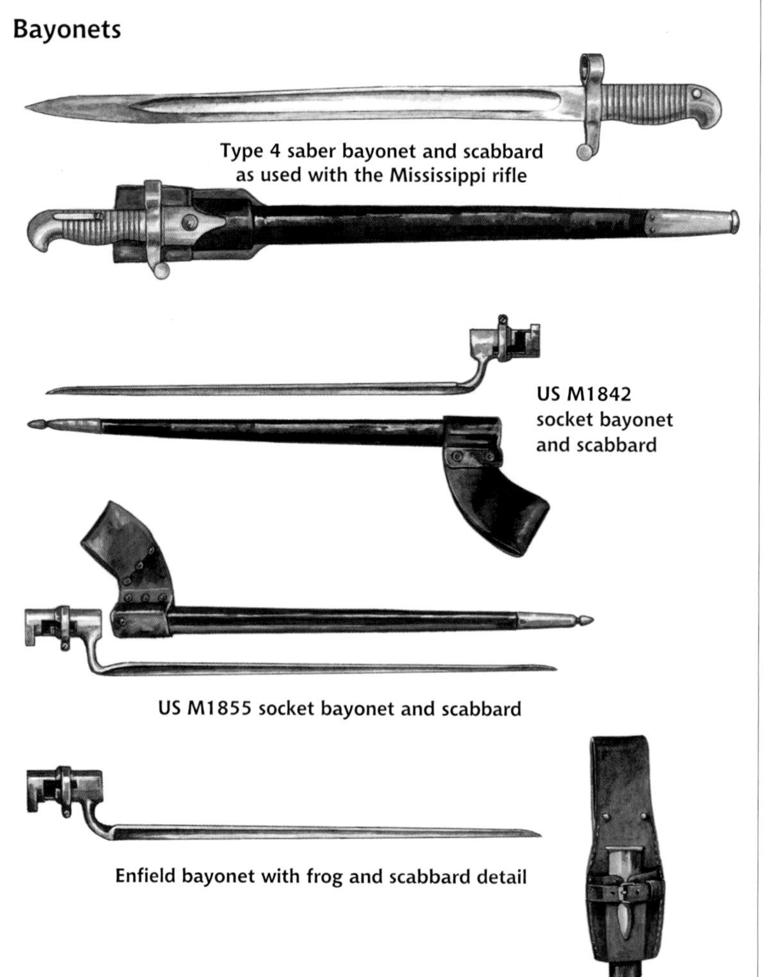

Revolvers

Although most mounted officers and many junior officers in both armies carried revolvers, they were principally a cavalryman's weapon and are therefore discussed in Section Four: The Cavalry.

Bayonets

Bayonets carried at Gettysburg were mainly of the socket type for the Springfield and Enfield rifle-muskets and sword bayonets for the Mississippi – as shown in the illustration below. It was of much more practical use off the battlefield than on it, frequently doing duty as a can opener, entrenching tool, candleholder, tent peg or roasting spit. Although it was invariably fixed before an attack, a bayonet seldom drew enemy blood. The Confederate Brigadier-General John Gordon, commanding the Georgia Brigade in Major-General Early's Division, whose command drove Barlow's Union Division off Blocher's Knoll and then through Gettysburg on July 1, had this to say on the subject: "The bristling points and the glitter of the bayonets were fearful to look upon as they were leveled in front of a charging line, but they were rarely reddened with blood." On the Union side the sentiments were the same. A colonel noted in his diary, "Corporal Selby killed a rebel with his bayonet there, which is a remarkable thing in a battle and was spoken of in the official report." At Gettysburg only about one percent of casualties were caused by bayonets or swords.

Swords

In both armies the sword was usually an indication of rank rather than a useful weapon of war – the soldiers' name for them was "toadstabbers." As noted of bayonets above, the number of sword-inflicted casualties at Gettysburg was minute. All officers carried a sword, although General Lee rarely did so in the field, and they were much in evidence at Gettysburg, as on other battlefields, held aloft and waved by officers exhorting their men. Brigadier-General Armistead secured immortality just before being mortally wounded and captured by raising his hat on the point of his sword as he led his men over the stone wall near the Angle at the climax of Pickett's charge. One of the rare examples of a sword doing serious damage occurred on the evening of July 2

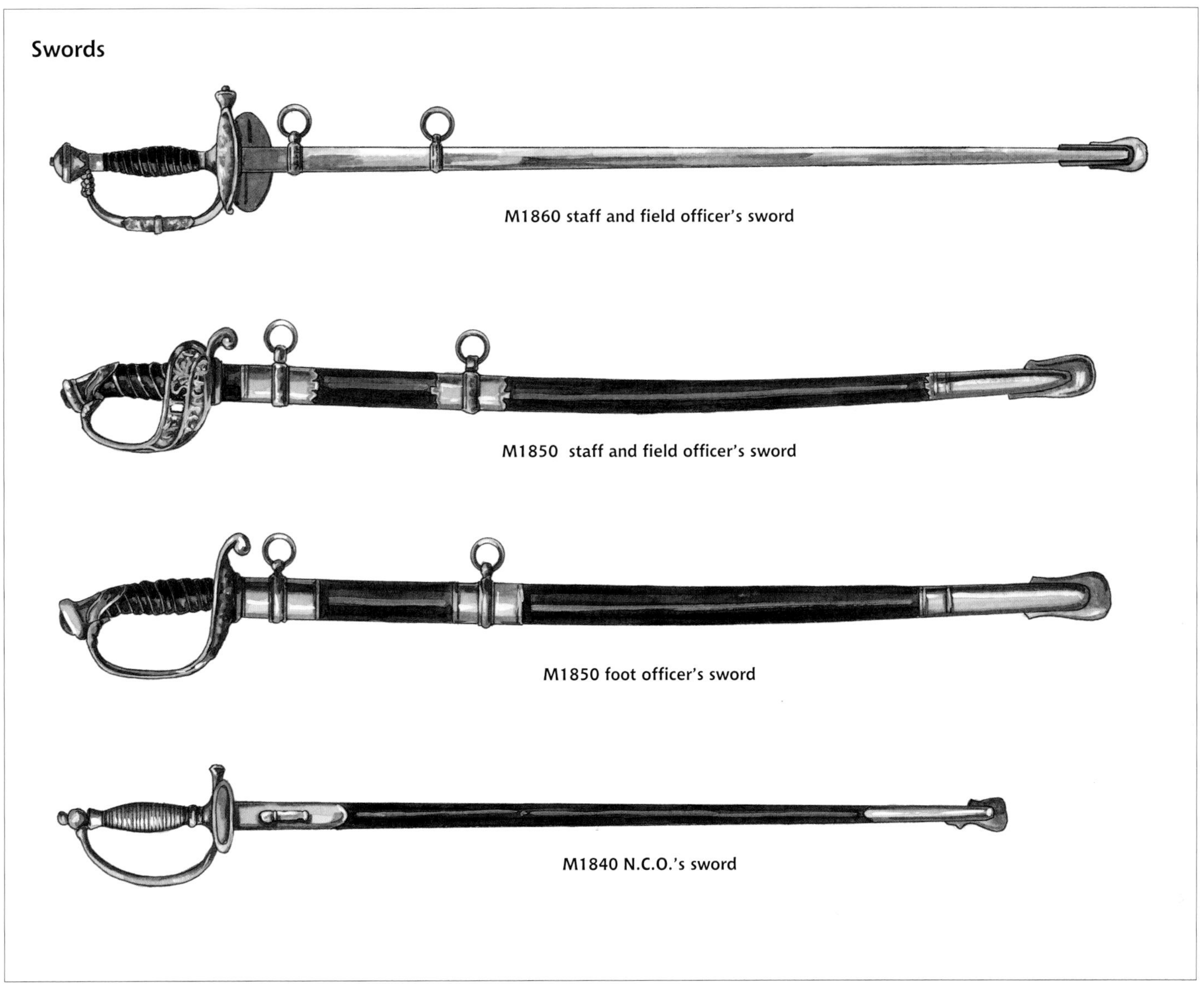

M1860 staff and field officer's sword

M1850 staff and field officer's sword

M1850 foot officer's sword

M1840 N.C.O.'s sword

when Colonel Archibald Godwin led forward his 57th North Carolinians as part of the assault on the Union line along the Brickyard Lane at the foot of the eastern slopes of Cemetery Hill. The colonel crossed the wall not far from the present 33rd Massachusetts Regiment's monument and was confronted by a large Yankee wielding a clubbed musket, a blow which he deflected with his left arm, at the same time chopping down with his sword and splitting the man's skull in two.

The Union infantry officer's sword generally had a slightly curved blade some 34 inches long with an ornate brass guard and hilt, a twisted wire-wrapped grip and a black leather scabbard with decorative brass mountings. Union infantry sergeants were issued with 32-inch straight swords with a brass hilt and ribbed grip in imitation wire wrapping. Since many of Lee's sergeants did not want to distinguish themselves by wearing even rank chevrons, few bothered to carry a sword. Confederate officers often picked up good-quality swords on the battlefield, as Southern-made weapons were usually of an inferior manufacture, slightly shorter than Union ones, with hilts often crudely cast and grips often bound round with black oilcloth and wound round with plain untwisted wire. Confederate scabbards too were more roughly sewn and much plainer.

INFANTRY AMMUNITION

The estimated total expenditure of rifle-musket and musket ammunition at Gettysburg is between 3 and 4 million, with the greater number being fired by Meade's army as it was defending and thus had more opportunity to fire. Bullets caused some 90 percent of the casualties. A Dr. Henry Janes, responsible for the 21,000 wounded left on the battlefield, stated he found only 204 men with injuries compatible with artillery fire.

The quartermasters and ordnance sergeants of both sides had six calibers of ammunition to worry about at Gettysburg:

.58 for Springfields, Richmonds and some Austrian rifle-muskets
.577 for Enfields, but it was interchangeable with .58
.54 for Mississippis and some Austrian rifle-muskets
.52 for Sharps breechloaders
.69 for rifle-muskets
.69 for smoothbore muskets (ball and "buck and ball")

Indenting for and supplying the right amount of the right type to the right regiment was a matter that merited careful thought. Quartermasters of regiments armed with Springfields, Enfields or a mix of both (such as the 20th Maine) could issue either .58 or .577. But with the 7th New Jersey, for example, things were more complex. It was armed with Springfields, Enfields, smoothbores and some Austrian .54s, so fairly exact proportions of at least three different types of cartridge were required. In these circumstances efforts were made to simplify matters by ensuring that at least each company in the regiment had the same type of firearm, although even this was not always possible. Considerable re-boring of muskets took place so that most would take either a .58 or .69 type of ball.

The main types of ammunition were as follows.

The Minie Bullet

This was not a ball, as it is often termed, but a conical-shaped bullet. Prior to the introduction of the Mine bullet, rifles had been used with difficulty in combat due to the problem of having to force the bullet down the grooves of the barrel – initially a wooden mallet was issued to British riflemen for this purpose. It made for slow loading, and with fouling accumulating in the barrel not many shots could be fired before it needed cleaning, causing yet further interruption and delay. The Minie bullet was originally designed by Captain Claude-Etienne Minie of France and subsequently improved in the United States. Since the Minie was smaller than the diameter of the barrel, it could be loaded more quickly and easily. The conical lead bullet had a cavity in its base so that when fired the expanding gasses from the ignited powder would push the sides of the soft lead bullet against the bore of the barrel and into the rifling. In this way the bullet was spun as it exited the muzzle, giving it a more stabilized flight, and increasing its accuracy and range. It also gave the Minie a distinctive whizzing noise as it passed close by – and if you heard it, you knew that it had missed you.

U.S. armories manufactured Minie bullets of .577 to .58 calibers for Springfields, Enfields and some Austrian weapons, .54 caliber for Mississippi and other Austrian rifle-muskets, and .69 for re-bored smoothbores. The bullets were called "3-ring Minies" as they had three rings, or grease grooves, cut into the circumference round the base – the bullets were greased during manufacture to reduce friction. Some of these bullets weighed over an ounce and caused horrendous wounds, graphically described as a "terrible, crippling, smashing invasion of the sacred machine, splitting bones like green twigs and extravasating blood in a vast volume of tissue about the path of the projectile." A limb hit invariably meant amputation, and a Minie bullet in the stomach was a certain agonizing death. By far the most common bullet or ball used at Gettysburg, the Minie was chosen by the 7th New Jersey as the most dominant feature of the monument erected on the site where its commander Colonel Louis R. Francine was killed east of the Peach Orchard – this despite the regiment being armed with a mixture of four different caliber weapons.

There was also the "Williams" Minie bullet, which had a hole in its base in which were fitted a lead disc and plug holding a zinc washer. When the weapon was fired, the washer jammed up against the base of the bullet and expanded, scraping the bore clean. It was fired by the Springfields and Enfields, was wrapped in pink paper instead of brown, and was issued on a scale of 1:10 in the cartridge packets.

The .69 Ball

This was the ammunition for the old U.S. Model 1842 muzzle-loading smoothbore musket. The ball (it was a "ball" rather than bullet or conical shaped) was even larger than the Minie and thus caused similarly ghastly wounds, but without the grooved barrel the effective range was reduced to about 100 yards.

Common Infantry Ammunition Used at Gettysburg (actual size)

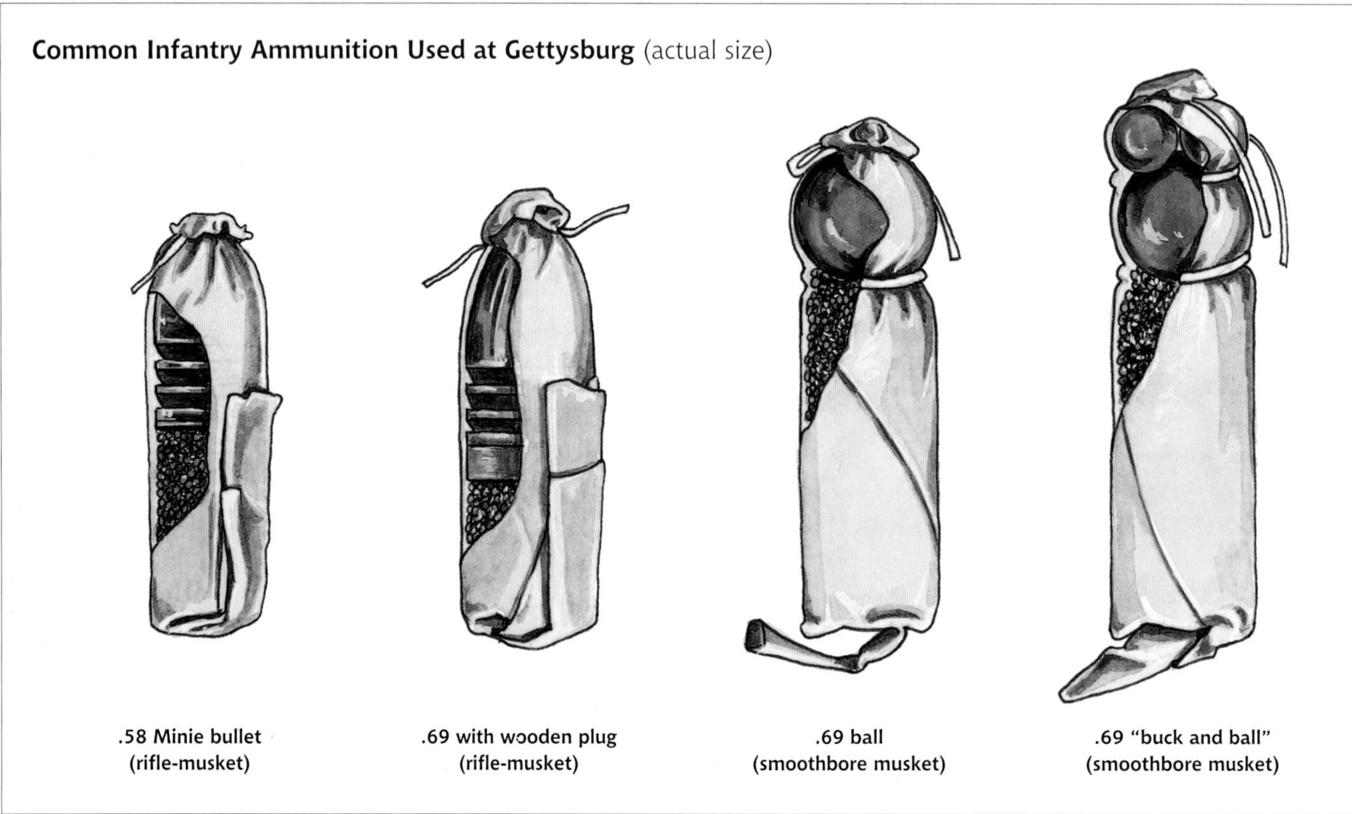

.58 Minie bullet (rifle-musket) — **.69 with wooden plug (rifle-musket)** — **.69 ball (smoothbore musket)** — **.69 "buck and ball" (smoothbore musket)**

The .69 "Buck and Ball" and Buckshot

This cartridge had the normal .69 ball with three .22 balls on top so that on firing they spread out like a shotgun cartridge. Fired in volleys at ranges below 100 yards, these were devastating missiles and knocked attackers down in swathes, although the .22 balls were not so damaging. This ammunition was popular with all soldiers armed with smoothbores at Gettysburg and was particularly useful among trees, boulders, or across the Wheatfield, or defending the stone wall at the Angle. A variation was to have the cartridge loaded entirely with buckshot, usually twelve smaller balls, creating a proper shotgun cartridge with which missing was difficult at close range even with rough alignment rather than proper aiming.

Percussion Caps

These small copper covers, inlaid with one half grain of fulminate, were placed over the nipple of the rifle or revolver before firing. The hammer striking on the outer surface of the cap caused a spark to ignite the charge in the cartridge. They were somewhat fiddly to handle, particularly when stressed, in a hurry or on the move, and were easily lost. The demand for caps was astronomical. They were punched out by machines from thin sheets of copper at a rate of 3,000 every hour and then the fulminate was pressed into the base. Small boys were often used to sort, count and varnish them by hand, a well-practiced boy supposedly being able to handle 7,000 in an hour. The North made or purchased some 1.25 billion percussion caps during the war.

Ammunition Supply and Consumption

Supply

Details of the system of supply by the use of depots, railways and wagon trains are given in Section Five: Other Arms and Services, so information here is confined to estimates of what infantry small arms ammunition was available to both sides at Gettysburg. By 1863 ordnance staff had been permanently established at officer level from brigade upwards and with an ordnance sergeant in regimental headquarters. Part of their job was estimating, indenting and accounting for ammunition supply. Ammunition was carried on wagons designated specifically for the purpose, with different wagons carrying infantry and artillery supplies. Each official army wagon (there were plenty of commandeered civilian wagons and carts), 10 feet long and usually drawn by six mules, could take an average load of 3,000 pounds, or around 25,000 rounds of small arms ammunition in wooden boxes. This represented the reserve ammunition additional to that carried by the soldier. Ammunition wagons (infantry and artillery) were usually grouped into trains on a divisional basis, with another train carrying the army reserve. These trains were kept separate from ambulance, baggage or supply trains and had priority on the roads. Just before Gettysburg Meade sent all his trains back to his base at Westminster except those carrying ammunition (and ambulances), which came forward (as did Lee's) as close to the battlefield as possible, in many cases only a few hundred yards behind the firing line. From there, under the direction of the ordnance staff officers, they were sent forward to replenish their units as required.

So how much infantry ammunition was available at Gettysburg? It is impossible to be precise, but a reasonable estimate can be made. A few weeks after the battle, Meade's assistant adjutant general issued General Order Number 83, which dealt in considerable detail with the entitlement of transport for all formations – in other words, how many wagons they could have and what they should carry. Although issued after the battle, it is likely that it represents, at least approximately, the situation in July. Paragraph 4 stated: "To every 1000 men, cavalry and infantry, for small arms ammunition, 5 wagons." This book has adopted Busey and Martin's engaged figures for all strengths; for Union infantry this is, in round numbers, 74,500. If ammunition wagons carried 25,000 rounds, then Meade's nineteen divisional trains (infantry ammunition) and army reserve train might have held over 9,000,000 rounds between them – say 420,000 with each division and 1,000,000 with the reserve, making an overall total of about 360 infantry ammunition wagons. As each Union infantry soldier was carrying forty rounds in his cartridge box and another twenty in his pockets or knapsack, it means almost another 4,500,000 was taken onto the battlefield over the three days by Yankee infantry. This gives a possible total of up to 13,500,000 rounds available, or about 180 per man – two-thirds being in the trains.

The Confederate Ordnance Manual stipulated that an army in the field should carry 200 rounds per man, divided between the soldier and the trains – not much difference from the Union estimates above. With 57,000 infantrymen with Lee at Gettysburg, this gives a total figure of 11,400,000. However, in early 1863 the Southern Ordnance Department had issued an order that the practice of issuing an extra twenty rounds per man on the eve of battle should cease, the reason being that the forty rounds in the cartridge boxes were considered more than adequate and the extra twenty were easily lost or damaged – the Confederacy was anxious to cut back on wastage. It is therefore reasonably safe to assume that Lee's infantry went into action with forty rounds apiece, which, using the overall figure of 11,400,000 above, would mean 2,280,000 rounds with the troops and 9,120,000 in the trains. However, this would give the infantry of the Army of Northern Virginia more ammunition man for man than the Army of the Potomac, and this is surely not correct.

There are two reasons for thinking this figure is too high. First, the South could not compete with the manufacturing capacity of the North and ammunition production was no exception. Ammunition had to be conserved; wastage and spoilage were problems necessitating high-level action to reduce them, such as that noted above. Additional, rigorous measures were taken to inspect and account for ammunition. Reports were required from ordnance officers every two weeks to account for every round. Disciplinary action had even had to be taken to stop the practice of cutting up cartridge boxes to repair shoes, thus exposing the contents to the elements – wet cartridges were unusable. The second reason is that Colonel Josiah Gorgas, the South's chief of ordnance, had made a careful study of ammunition expenditure in several battles and found that it was never as much as anticipated. Ordnance returns after First Manassas showed an expenditure of 19–26 rounds per man, indicating the 200 basic load was excessive. At Chancellorsville expenditure ranged from 25–30, again showing that sixty rounds per man overall was more than sufficient. Assuming this to be the case at Gettysburg, then Lee's infantry went into action with forty rounds each and another twenty in the wagons. That meant a total of 3,420,000 rounds, 2,280,000 with the soldiers and another 1,140,000 in the wagons – two-thirds in the cartridge boxes and one-third in reserve, the reverse of the Army of the Potomac. Supposing these figures are correct, it would give each of the nine infantry divisional trains four small arms ammunition wagons with another four or five in the army reserve. This was probably cutting things too fine, but ammunition of all types was scarce in the Confederacy. Major James Dearing, the commander of Pickett's artillery battalion, wrote that "there was no rifle ammunition in Richmond when we left and it is sent to us now as fast as it is prepared."

Consumption

How many shots the infantry fired during those three days at Gettysburg is an intriguing question. Equally interesting was how many shots did it take to hit a man – how many were wasted? To arrive at an approximate answer to the first, an assessment of the intensity and duration of the firing is necessary; with the second, the number of shots fired must be related to the casualties inflicted.

Of the intensity of much of the musketry fire throughout the battle there can be no doubt. In the north on July 1 the close-range clashes along McPherson's Ridge, around his farm and at the railway cut – where regiments such as the 24th Michigan and 26th North Carolina exchanged volleys at 20 yards and no fewer than thirteen color-bearers of the 26th and ten of the 24th went down – are examples of such intensity. Also in the north, the prolonged fighting for possession of Culp's Hill on both July 2 and 3, much of it in darkness and all of it in thick woods, saw what were surely some of the fiercest and lengthy firefights of the entire war. A soldier in the 60th New York on the steep slope immediately south of the summit of Culp's Hill later recalled that, as the Rebels advanced on the evening of July 2, "Not a shot was fired at them until they got within about 15 rods [80 yards]. Then the order was given (Fire!) and we did fire, and kept firing. If ever men loaded and fired more rapidly than the 60th did on that occasion, I never saw them do it." The following day Corporal James Hyde of the 137th New York noted the condition of the trees on Culp's Hill, "The limbs were cut from the trees . . . on some trees there was not a piece of bark left as large as your hand" (some of the damage was caused by artillery). A year later many trees on the hillside were dead or dying from the damage suffered during the fighting (see photograph, page 324). At times both attackers and defenders slogged it out within a few feet of each other. The color of the 149th New York had eighty shot holes in it and the staff was snapped twice by musketry. Undoubtedly there were times when both sides faced acute ammunition shortages and the casualty rate, particularly for the attacking Confederates, was appalling.

In the center on Day Two, the so-called "Sickles' salient" along the Emmitsburg Road, the Peach Orchard and the Wheatfield all witnessed the devastating effect of musketry (and artillery fire). This was seen again on a grand scale in the repulse of Pickett's charge the next day. On the latter occasion it was musketry fire that put over 800 holes in a 16-foot length of fencing (see page 106), and it was mostly close-range musketry fire that piled up Confederate bodies so thickly in front of the Angle and Copse of Trees that a person could step from body to body without touching the ground.

In the south it was the Devil's Den, the Slaughter Pen, whose very names indicate what happened there, and the struggle for Little Round Top where evidence of the weight of fire delivered from the infantry abounded. A civilian walking over Little Round Top and into the valley between the hill and Devil's Den two days after the battle observed, "I counted . . . over forty dead bodies within a circle of fifty feet in circumference . . ."

A good indication of the rate of fire is the frequency with which units became short of, or ran out of, ammunition. There is ample evidence of this, particularly among the Union infantry who were defending for virtually the entire battle and therefore, being mostly static, had more time for reloading and firing than did attacking Confederate units. Only when both sides slugged it out by exchanging fire at close range for a prolonged period did ammunition expenditure become excessive for Yankees and Rebels. Three examples of ammunition shortages will suffice. The first occurred on July 1 during the Union I Corps' stubborn defense of both McPherson's and Seminary Ridges. By early afternoon the Union regiments were running out of ammunition and the wagons of the divisional ammunition train were ordered forward. Amazingly, these wagons had been left in the charge of a sergeant, Ordnance Sergeant Jerome A. Watrous of the 6th Wisconsin (Iron Brigade). Watrous brought his wagons right up to the firing line just behind McPherson's Ridge in what became known as "The Mule Train Charge" (see photograph opposite). The second example involves the 20th Maine on Little Round Top on July 2. Like most of their comrades, the soldiers started the action with sixty rounds each, but after one and a half hours of fighting, which included scrabbling around rummaging in the pockets of the dead and wounded, they were down to the last few rounds. Additionally, it is highly likely that many rifle-muskets were by then unserviceable due to fouling. These two factors were stressed by the commander of the 20th Maine, Colonel Joshua Chamberlain, when he wrote later of "our ammunition being totally exhausted and many of our arms unserviceable." It was at this moment, with no immediate prospect of replenishment, that bayonets were fixed and the remnants of the regiment swept down the slope to throw back their attackers (15th Alabama) at last. Third, on Culp's Hill some Union regiments could be pulled out of the line for brief periods as Greene's Brigade was reinforced by six regiments from Wadsworth's Division, thus allowing some of Greene's men to withdraw for brief periods to clean weapons and restock with ammunition.

All this goes some way toward illustrating the intensity of the infantry fighting at Gettysburg and toward helping give an approximate answer to the questions posed above. The relevant factors can be summarized as follows:

- The Union infantry initially went into battle with sixty rounds each, the Confederates with probably forty.

- There were occasions when this was clearly insufficient, particularly for the Union troops who were mostly defending. At one extreme is Private Milledge of the 66th Ohio, who claimed to have fired 200 rounds during his time on Culp's Hill – possible, but exceptional. Brigadier-General John Geary claimed his men fired off 277,000 rounds on Culp's Hill. With 3,900 men engaged, this would mean the average man fired some seventy shots. Lieutenant James G.

The Union Mule Train Charge, July 1

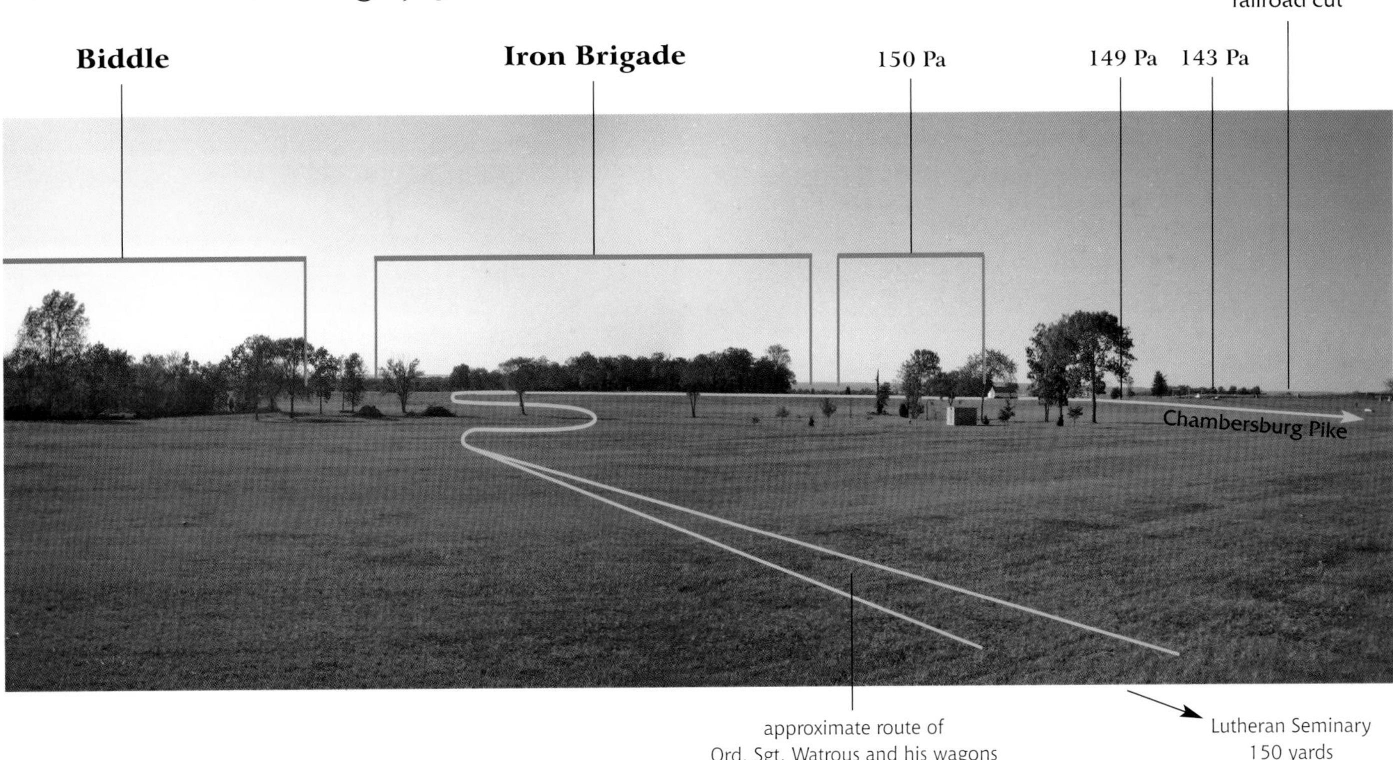

By mid-afternoon on July 1, repeated attacks by the Confederates under Maj.-Gens. Heth and Rodes had left the Union defenders along McPherson's Ridge and the railroad cut desperately short of ammunition. The divisional ammunition train of 10 mule-drawn wagons under the command of Ord. Sgt. Jerome Watrous was ordered forward from behind the Lutheran Seminary. Watrous had his teams whipped up into a gallop and led them past the Seminary and across the open field, under heavy shellfire, toward the firing line of the Iron Brigade in the Herbst Wood. There he rode along behind the line, with ammunition boxes being thrown from the wagons while he followed on foot, smashing them open with the back of an ax. Some 75,000 rounds were delivered before the mules headed back toward the town, eventually joining the Chambersburg Pike. Several mules were hit and all the wagons were riddled with holes.

Rosengarten, the ordnance officer for I Corps, estimated that 228,000 rounds of small arms ammunition were expended on July 1, which, with about 11,500 infantry, would give an average expenditure of over 190 per man. This is far too high and must include all ammunition actually issued, with no account being taken of what was not fired, lost on casualties, wasted, or captured by the advancing enemy.

- There were plenty of instances when ammunition was short or ran out during intensive fighting and was replenished by various means, indicating that large numbers of Union troops found their sixty rounds insufficient for a three-day battle. Nevertheless, set against this was that many of the 13,000 Union infantrymen in VI Corps may not have fired at all and the remainder only a few times.

- The Confederates went into action with fewer rounds than their Union opponents but all their divisions were heavily engaged at some time during the three days. On Culp's Hill there is evidence that some of their regiments ran out of ammunition and had to resort to bringing loose rounds forward in blankets from wagons parked east of Rock Creek. Also, a Major Jones of the 26th North Carolina mentions that his men were running low but were able to replenish stocks from the bodies of enemy killed or captured during the taking of McPherson's Ridge and Gettysburg town on July 1.

- Other forms of expenditure apart from firing are seldom mentioned, but were a feature on all battlefields to a greater or lesser extent. They include wastage due to cartridges getting wet, damaged, or lost, sometimes by a soldier putting them on the ground to speed up handling and then having to move quickly and forgetting or being unable to pick them up. Many rounds were collected from the dead or wounded to alleviate shortages, but equally many were not. A half-filled cartridge box that remains on a dead or injured soldier is ammunition lost to the fight, as is one that stays with the walking wounded or stretcher case on his way back. Similarly, as an infantry unit without ammunition is useless and must withdraw, it was not unknown for soldiers to hasten that situation by deliberately throwing ammunition away. Undoubtedly tens of thousands of rounds were lost at Gettysburg in these ways and an allowance should be made for this when estimating the number actually fired.

So how many shots were fired at Gettysburg? With the Army of the Potomac, assuming the 13,000 infantrymen in VI Corps fired very few (they had only 242 casualties) and that some was wasted or lost to the battle, then an average of forty-five rounds for the rest of the infantry appears reasonable. This gives a total of some 2,767,000. With the Confederates, as virtually all the infantry were engaged at some point, and the number of instances of units running short was smaller than for the Union infantry, it appears that an average of around thirty (the Confederate Ordnance Department calculated twenty-six) is likely, giving a total of 1,710,000 fired. Therefore an estimate of the number of rounds actually fired from rifle-muskets or smoothbores during the three days would be 4,477,000 – say 4,500,000.

How many of these rounds hit a human target? Although some 10 percent of recorded casualties were caused by artillery or other means, it is assumed that at least 10 percent of missing/captured were wounded, so these may cancel each other out. Using only the number of dead and wounded figures from Busey and Martin's *Regimental Strengths and Losses at Gettysburg*, a total of 30,615 casualties were inflicted by some 4,500,000 shots, giving a ratio of 1:147, say 1:150. Considering the decimated trees and peppered fencing, this overall proportion of hits to misses is probably about right.

Firing Drills and Fire Control

Like movements on the battlefield, the firing of a rifle-musket was reduced to a drill. The sequence of actions was hammered home with every recruit by continuous repetition, then more repetition. This is still the case in a modern army: the handling and firing of weapons must become second nature, as in action there is no time to wonder what to do if a weapon stops firing – reaction must be instinctive. The problem for most of the infantrymen at Gettysburg was that, while they knew how to handle their rifle-musket, they had not had much, if any, previous live firing practice. Many learned their shooting on the battlefield and it is possible that most of the newly recruited nine-month men in the regiments of Major-General Doubleday's 3rd Division of I Corps, for example, had never actually fired their arms before Gettysburg. If not they certainly had plenty of opportunity during those three days in July, as they were involved in fierce fighting on July 1 defending Seminary Ridge and then on July 3 repelling Pickett's and Pettigrew's attack. Assuming an empty weapon, the sequence for firing was as illustrated in the diagram opposite.

The most effective way of defeating an attack was for the defenders to control their fire. Their officers would aim to conserve fire until the enemy was at close range – say 100 yards away – and then to concentrate fire in volleys, but at the same time always endeavoring to have some men with loaded weapons. As the historian of the 121st Pennsylvania put it when describing how the regiment, deployed on McPherson's Ridge on July 1, opened fire against the attacking Carolinians: "[The enemy] had reached within a few yards of the top of the ridge, when the men arose and delivered their fire directly in their faces, staggering them and bringing them to a stand." As the reader will discover, Gettysburg is packed with examples of frontal assaults being broken up by sustained musketry fire at close range. This type of control was not always easy to achieve in the noise, smoke and confusion of battle and required strict fire discipline.

Let us consider the options open to Colonel Dennis O'Kane, commanding the 69th Pennsylvania Infantry, a regiment which, after heavy fighting on the first two days, was, by the time it faced Pickett's charge, down to around 220 all ranks. At around 3:15 p.m. on July 3 the regiment was crouched behind the low stone wall in front of the Copse of Trees with its right flank about 35 yards south of the Angle, watching in amazement the spectacle of 12,000 Confederates advancing to attack. Fire control and good shooting were going to be vital for the Union defenders. The divisional commander, Brigadier-General John Gibbon, rode along behind the line shouting, "Do not hurry, men, and fire too fast. Let them come up close before you fire, and then aim low and steadily." The brigade commander, Brigadier-General Alexander Webb, told his men to hold their fire until the enemy had crossed the Emmitsburg Road – they would then be about 200 yards away. With the withdrawal of their skirmishers, the Emmitsburg Road fences were a convenient marker for the Union troops defending the northern part of Cemetery Ridge. As the Rebels broke them down or scrambled over them it was an obvious moment to open fire. That this was the case is evidenced by the fact that the wooden fence slabs were so perforated that in places the holes were barely half an inch apart. Over 800 balls had hit one strip of fencing 16 feet long and 14 inches wide. These were shots that missed at a range of 200–250 yards, which says a lot for the accuracy of the firing at comparatively close range. Be that as it may, Colonel O'Kane went further by insisting his men conserve ammunition and not fire until they could see the "whites of their eyes" – well below 100 yards. Lieutenant Frank Haskell of Gibbon's staff later wrote of this moment:

> The click of the locks as each man raised his hammer, to feel with his finger that the cap was on the nipple; the sharp jar as a musket touched the stone upon the wall when thrust, in aiming, over it; and the clinking of the iron axles, as the guns were rolled up by hand a little further to the front, were quite all the sounds that could be heard. Cap boxes were slid around to the front of the body; – cartridge boxes opened; – officers opened their pistol holsters. Such preparation, little more, was needed.

Although the 69th had made little effort to improve the defensive qualities of the wall, it had made a very positive effort to increase its firepower in terms of speeding up firing and its effectiveness. Hundreds of Confederate and Union weapons from the previous day's fighting – both rifle-muskets and smoothbores – had been discarded on the slope in front. These were gathered up and distributed among the companies so that, according to Robert Whittick of Company E, each man had between six and twelve pieces beside him. To boost the firepower even more, many men had extracted the balls from the "buck and ball" ammunition and substituted loads of twelve buckshot.

In theory, Colonel O'Kane had several options as to the actual method of opening fire. Assuming the 69th was in two ranks, they were:

- A single volley by all 200 or so rifle-muskets. This would produce an extremely destructive blast of Minie bullets (the 69th had no "buck and ball" smoothbores for their first volley) if delivered at less than 100 yards, but all the regiment would be unloaded at the same time. Reloading would

Rifle-musket Loading Drills

1. A paper cartridge is taken from the cartridge box.

2. The cartridge is torn open with the soldier's teeth – the reason a man with missing front teeth could not be enlisted.

3. The exposed black powder is poured down the barrel.

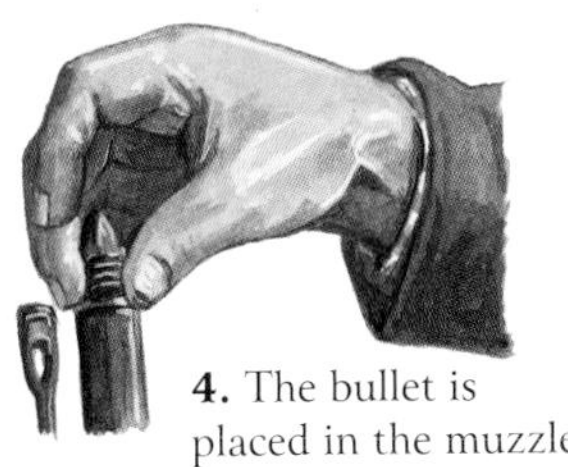

4. The bullet is placed in the muzzle.

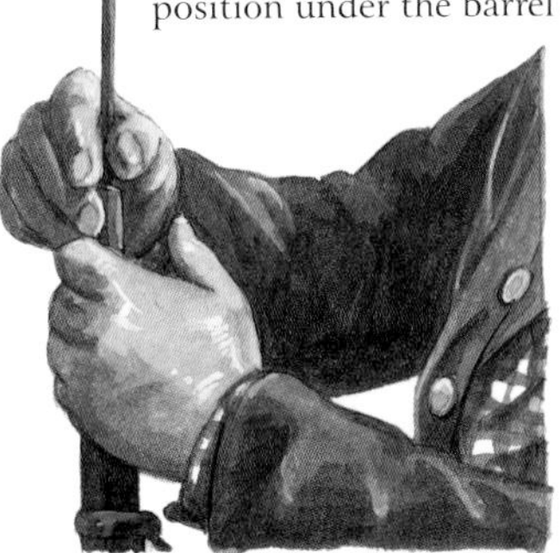

5. The metal ramrod is taken from its position under the barrel and used to ram bullet and powder to the bottom of the barrel. The ramrod is replaced, the hammer pulled back to half-cock, the old percussion cap removed.

6. A new copper percussion cap is taken from the cap box.

7. The cap is pressed down over the cone and the hammer pulled back to full cock – the soldier is ready to fire.

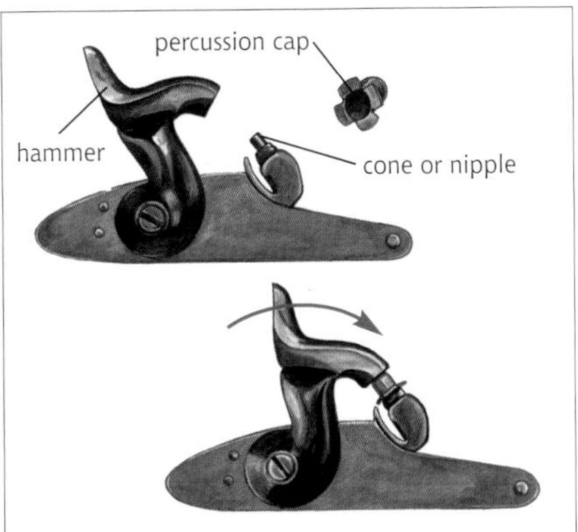

When the trigger is pulled the hammer flies forward and strikes the cap, which explodes, sending a flash through the cone into the barrel. There the powder explodes and propels the bullet.

8. The soldier aims and fires.

normally have taken 25–30 seconds, so only one more volley could be fired before the surviving Rebels got in amongst them. With the 69th this was not the situation, as they could snatch up one of the loaded spare muskets beside them and fire again within a matter of 4–5 seconds. However, the noise and smoke of battle and human nature being what it is, rather than a second volley it is more likely the men would resort to firing at will, with each man firing as soon as he had grabbed another gun. This would produce a ragged but continuous and deadly hail of lead while the enemy struggled to cover the last 75 yards. Unsurprisingly, not many made it.

- Volleys could be fired by ranks. The front rank, in this case around 100 men, would fire first and then reload while the second took their turn at firing. We know Colonel William R. Creighton, commanding the 7th Ohio behind the barricades on Culp's Hill, ordered his men to hold their fire and then ordered firing by ranks, which was well executed and halted the Rebel attack. It could be an effective way of controlling fire so that the interval between volleys would be only 10–15 seconds. In Colonel O'Kane's case, however, it is possible that the second rank was crowded into the first so that there was, in reality, one thick line of 200 men stretched along some 250 feet of wall.
- Firing by companies. This could start with either flank company. With the 69th, starting from the right, this would see Company I firing first, after which it would progress through A, F, D, H, C, E, B, K to G. By the time Company G had fired, Company I would be ready to fire again. If he followed the drill book, the first company commander would start proceedings with the shouted order: "Company I – ready – aim – fire – load." The advantage of this method was that there was no pause, the enemy being always under controlled fire. A variation was for alternate companies to fire a volley, that is Companies I, F, H, E and K first, and then the remainder. As the 69th had plenty of spare weapons to hand, it is unlikely that either of these methods was used.
- Firing by file. In this case firing would commence with the right-hand file (two men) of the right- (or left-) hand company with the next file taking aim the instant the first brought down their pieces to reload, and so on to the left. This is effectively a *"feu de joie"* in which fire ripples down the line in one long continuous volley. By the time the last man has fired, the first is able to fire again and the process is repeated.

Assuming the 69th Pennsylvania had 200 men in the line and that each had an average of five preloaded muskets besides his own, and that fire was opened immediately after the attackers had crossed the Emmitsburg fences 200 yards from the wall, it is possible to estimate the number of shots that could have been put down by this regiment before the Confederates could reach the defenders. If the attackers came on at a brisk walk initially and then at a run for the last 50 yards, they would cover the 200 yards in about two minutes. Within that time each defender could have fired seven times (once with his own rifle-musket, five times with his spares and once again after reloading). Thus 1,400 bullets/balls plus hundreds of buckshot – say at least 2,000 rounds – could have been delivered over a frontage of about 80 yards. That is the theory – such a volume of fire at close range, coupled with artillery firing canister, should have destroyed the attackers. But, as we know, this was not the case: some Rebels crossed the wall and hand-to-hand fighting occurred.

Problems in Firing

It is unclear if the 69th Pennsylvania did wait until they saw the whites of their assailants' eyes, but it is certain the accuracy of their firing, and that of their comrades spread out along Cemetery Ridge that afternoon, would have been adversely affected by a variety of problems commonly faced by infantrymen.

Maintaining accuracy

With the exception of the 69th Pennsylvania and any other Yankee soldiers who had the foresight to have collected spare muskets, the first shot fired was likely to be the most accurate, with subsequent shots tending to be less so. With the first shot the barrel would be clean and the loading procedures carried out carefully and precisely without undue haste. Once that shot had gone difficulties could accumulate, particularly for inexperienced troops, until finally, in extreme cases, the firer could no longer use his weapon until remedial action had been taken.

Human errors

The adrenalin rush, the fear, noise, smoke, confusion, comrades collapsing with blood pouring from dreadful wounds, and the sight of an enemy still coming on induced a frantic need for haste. With this life-and-death urgency for speed in reloading came the hugely increased risk of fumbling and making mistakes. Under normal conditions, three shots a minute was a reasonable expectation with the rifle-musket, but it was a rate of fire that was not sustainable for long during periods of intense fighting. The better drilled the soldier, the less likely he was to make errors; however, there can have been few infantrymen at Gettysburg who did not make, or see made, one or more of the following human errors:

- Forgetting to remove the ramrod from the barrel before firing. A soldier of the 19th Maine involved in counterattacking the Confederates as they swarmed over the wall at the high water mark of Pickett's charge said afterward that in the smoke "the only man of my regiment I could see fired off his ramrod." A ramrod was as lethal as any bullet but subsequent loading was impossible – the best solution was to pick up a discarded weapon or another ramrod.
- Putting the cartridge down the barrel ball first, or neglecting to tear off the paper and thus inserting an unopened cartridge. The same soldier in the 19th Maine stated that in his excitement, "I got a cartridge in wrong end first." In both cases this meant the weapon could not be fired, and removing the cartridge was a lengthy process, one that could not be undertaken with the enemy closing in. Again, if possible, snatching up an abandoned musket was the only answer.
- Forgetting the rifle-musket was already loaded and ramming another cartridge down the barrel. Firing in these circumstances could cause a burst barrel with injurious consequences for the firer. Seemingly this was a common error at Gettysburg. After the battle Union forces collected

some 35,000 rifle-muskets and muskets from the battlefield, of which 12,000 had two charges, 6,000 between three and ten, and one had twenty-two. These statistics are perhaps suspect, in that after pushing three or four cartridges down the barrel it would be obvious what had happened, as the ramrod would go only part way down. As for twenty-two cartridges, one wonders if so many would actually fit in the barrel and, if so, if such gross overloading might have been done deliberately. Nevertheless, accurate or not, these figures show that this error was commonplace.

- Forgetting to put the percussion cap in place on the nipple, resulting in a misfire.
- If a bayonet was fixed, then spiking your right hand (there was no such thing as a left-handed musket, so everyone fired from the right shoulder) due to over-hasty use of the ramrod.
- If fire was opened over 300 yards with the rifle-musket it was easy to forget to adjust the sights as the enemy got closer. As discussed on page 99, this could result in many shots going high.
- Poor aiming. This was extremely common and was the primary reason why officers sought to ensure that, if at all possible, fire was held until the range was such that it was difficult to miss. The enemy fired back, the enemy moved, the firer was in a frantic hurry and often frightened – all these factors combined to make accurate shooting problematic. Again, the tendency of a hastily aimed shot, perhaps combined with a failure to pull the butt well into a bruised shoulder, caused the shot to go high. One of the most frequent instructions yelled through the smoke and din of battle by officers and N.C.O.s was "Aim low! Aim at the knees!"
- The sheer physical discomfort of a prolonged engagement could have inevitable consequences for the accuracy and frequency of firing. Noise deafened, the smoke blinded, and biting the cartridge dried the mouth, leaving you with a gritty tongue and teeth. Every time you fired the butt slammed into your shoulder and particles of half-burned powder stung your face. A soldier surviving a long firefight unwounded would still be suffering from a badly bruised shoulder, partial deafness, blackened cheeks, stinging eyes, a headache and a raging thirst.

The Rebel Yell and the Yankee Hurrah

The Rebel yell was originally raised at First Manassas on July 21, 1861. At Gettysburg it was heard continuously throughout the three days of fighting. It was described by many as a high-pitched shout, supposedly a variation on the Southern foxhunter's cry. A Yankee surgeon considered it was a succession of "yelps, staccato and shrill," while a *New York Herald* correspondent reported it as "shrill, exultant, savage . . ." A Southern soldier, J. Harvie Drew, of the 9th Virginia Cavalry, interpreted it as "Who—who—ey! Who—ey! Who—ey! Woo—who-ey! Who—ey!" He considered it derived from:

> Hollering, screaming, yelling from one person or another to their dogs, or at some of the cattle on the plantation, with accompanying reverberations from hilltops, over valleys and plains, were familiar sounds throughout the farming districts of the South in days gone by.

Its effect on the battlefield was undeniable. A Colonel O. M. Roberts, one-time commander of the 11th Texas Infantry (not at Gettysburg), described its effect in battle:

> when the command was given "Forward, charge!" it, too, would be rapidly passed, and then simultaneously the Texas "rebel yell" burst out from the whole line, as all together they dashed at double quick toward the enemy. The effect of the yell was marvelous . . . Such yells exploded on the air in one combined sound have been heard distinctly three miles off across a prairie, above the din of musketry and artillery.

The Rebel yell was quite different from the more disciplined cheer of the Yankees. The same Harvie Drew has given us his version of their shout as "Hoo-ray! Hoo-ray! Hoo-ray!" with the first "hoo" uttered with a short, low and indistinct tone, and the following "ray" shouted with a long, high tone.

Technical problems

In addition to human errors, problems with the weapons themselves could diminish the effectiveness of a unit's firepower, namely:

- Fouling accumulating in the barrel. Despite the Minie bullet being designed to slip easily down a barrel, and despite the use of the Williams "cleaning cartridge" when available, ten or twelve shots would see many weapons with barrels clogged, with black powder fouling to the extent that it was difficult to force cartridges down. The only solution was to clean the barrel. Done properly, this was a lengthy business, involving pouring hot water down the barrel to loosen the dirt and using the ramrod with a piece of cloth attached (often a piece torn off a shirt) to remove it. Weapon cleaning was, therefore, the first priority of soldiers of both sides during a lull in the fighting or at night. Private George Carr with the 149th New York on Culp's Hill recalled that the regiment's Enfields "were so foul that a ball could not be driven home without difficulty, and the barrels so hot as to be painful to the touch." At the other end of the battlefield, in the struggle for Little Round Top, Private Valerius Giles in the 5th Texas, whose ramrod had got stuck in the barrel due to fouling, resorted to banging the end of the ramrod on a rock to drive it home. An additional hindrance to ramming cartridges down a dirty barrel was wet, slippery hands. July 1 was hot and humid and some men of the 47th North Carolina, attacking from McPherson's Ridge toward Seminary Ridge, had this problem, their sweaty palms being unable to grip the metal ramrod tightly. They found the best quick solution was to wipe the ramrod in the dirt or dust.
- The percussion cap falling off the nipple (or forgetting to put it on), which if not noticed would mean the weapon would not fire when the trigger was pressed. To have this happen with an enemy in front of you would have been more than disconcerting.
- The barrel overheating due to constant firing. This could make the weapon (as noted by Private Carr above) literally "too hot to handle" and made the pouring of powder down the barrel a hazardous undertaking.
- Finally, there was the obvious reason for fire slackening – shortage of ammunition (see pages 103–105).

UNIFORMS AND EQUIPMENT

Detailed illustrations of both Union and Confederate uniforms appear between pages 256 and 257.

Union Uniforms

Because of the huge influx of manpower in the early months of the war, both North and South experienced difficulties with clothing and equipping their armies. Although the Northern industrial capacity had, by 1863, caught up with the demand for uniforms, this had not been the case earlier when they had been made of a material called "shoddy" – the origin of the word we still use to describe poor-quality goods. A contemporary writer described it as consisting of "the refuse stuff and sweeping of the shop, pounded, rolled, glued, and smoothed to the external form and gloss of cloth." In wet weather the soldiers found "their clothes, overcoats and blankets, scattering to the winds in rags, or dissolving into their primitive elements of dust." However, after the first year or so these supply contracts were cleaned up and Union troops had relatively little ground to grumble about the quality of the clothes issued from the quartermaster.

By far the most common campaign jacket worn at Gettysburg was the short, dark blue, wool-flannel so-called sack coat with its turnover collar and four brass buttons down the front. It was comfortable and quickly became the utilitarian fatigue jacket or blouse that saw service in every theater of the war. Federal clothing depots and at least a dozen private government contractors eventually produced it. Many junior officers also wore this sack coat, whereas the senior commanders favored the knee-length, dark blue frock coat. Initially trousers had also been dark blue, but by December 1861 they had been replaced by the cheaper, sky blue, kersey-cloth version held up by suspenders – belt loops were not in use. Although issued with overcoats for the winter weather, they were certainly not in evidence during the summer and many soldiers jettisoned them anyway as being too burdensome to carry.

All infantrymen need to look after their feet, the first requisite for this being strong, comfortable footwear. Generally the Union soldier was somewhat better off in this respect than his enemy down south. The most common issue were Jefferson boots, or as they were often called, bootees or "gunboats." They were ankle length, made of cowhide and fastened with a leather lace.

The most common headgear for the soldier was the Model 1858 forage cap, often called the "bummer's cap," and its cousin the kepi. The forage cap had a narrow leather visor and a high crown with a round, flat top that flopped forward at a sharp angle. The kepi was a French-style forage cap with a lower crown that tilted forward at a smaller angle. These caps became the most distinctive uniform item of the Civil War. As with all soldiers' headgear, including the modern beret, it was worn in a great variety of styles, most of which involved altering the angle of the peak or the size of the crown. The peak flipped up gave a jaunty appearance, straight ahead could be the "chasseur" cap, and sloping down the "McDowell" style. Often, but not always, the front or crown had a brass infantry hunting horn with the regimental number in the center. Although the forage cap was worn throughout the Army of the Potomac by the great majority, some Union infantrymen preferred the comfort of a wide-brimmed slouch hat and this was certainly the case with the officers. The five regiments of the Iron Brigade at Gettysburg were the only ones still to be wearing the distinctive tall black hat – the so-called Hardee hat with its brim turned up on the left side, unit insignia at the front and ostrich plume on the right. It had been the standard Union infantryman's hat at the outbreak of the Civil War, but long before Gettysburg it had been rejected by most of the army as being uncomfortable, hot and heavy; it had, however, become a badge of honor for the Iron Brigade. Early in the action on July 1, as the Confederates pushed down either side of the Chambersburg Pike, the appearance ahead of the black hats confirmed that they were opposed by veteran troops rather than militia units as had first been thought.

A number of regiments modeled themselves on the original Zouaves of the French colonial armies. Their various uniforms were distinctive, if not gaudy, usually featuring bright red or blue baggy trousers; short, blue, highly decorative jackets; cummerbunds, white gaiters and a turban or fez-type cap. Such elaborate dress was fine on parade but did not wear well in the field, gaiters being just one item quickly abandoned – or converted to use as a coffee filter. The actual design and color was dependent on the wishes of the benefactor of the regiment, who obtained funds from local

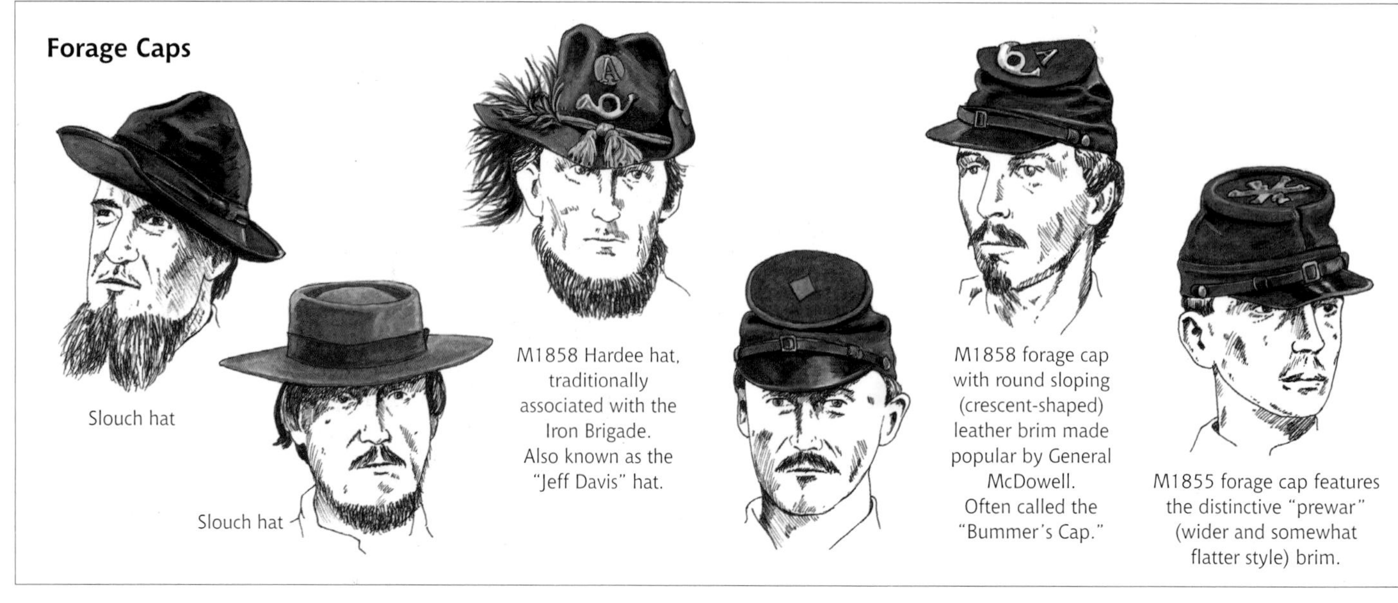

Forage Caps
Slouch hat
Slouch hat
M1858 Hardee hat, traditionally associated with the Iron Brigade. Also known as the "Jeff Davis" hat.
M1858 forage cap with round sloping (crescent-shaped) leather brim made popular by General McDowell. Often called the "Bummer's Cap."
M1855 forage cap features the distinctive "prewar" (wider and somewhat flatter style) brim.

Union Infantryman in Heavy Marching Order

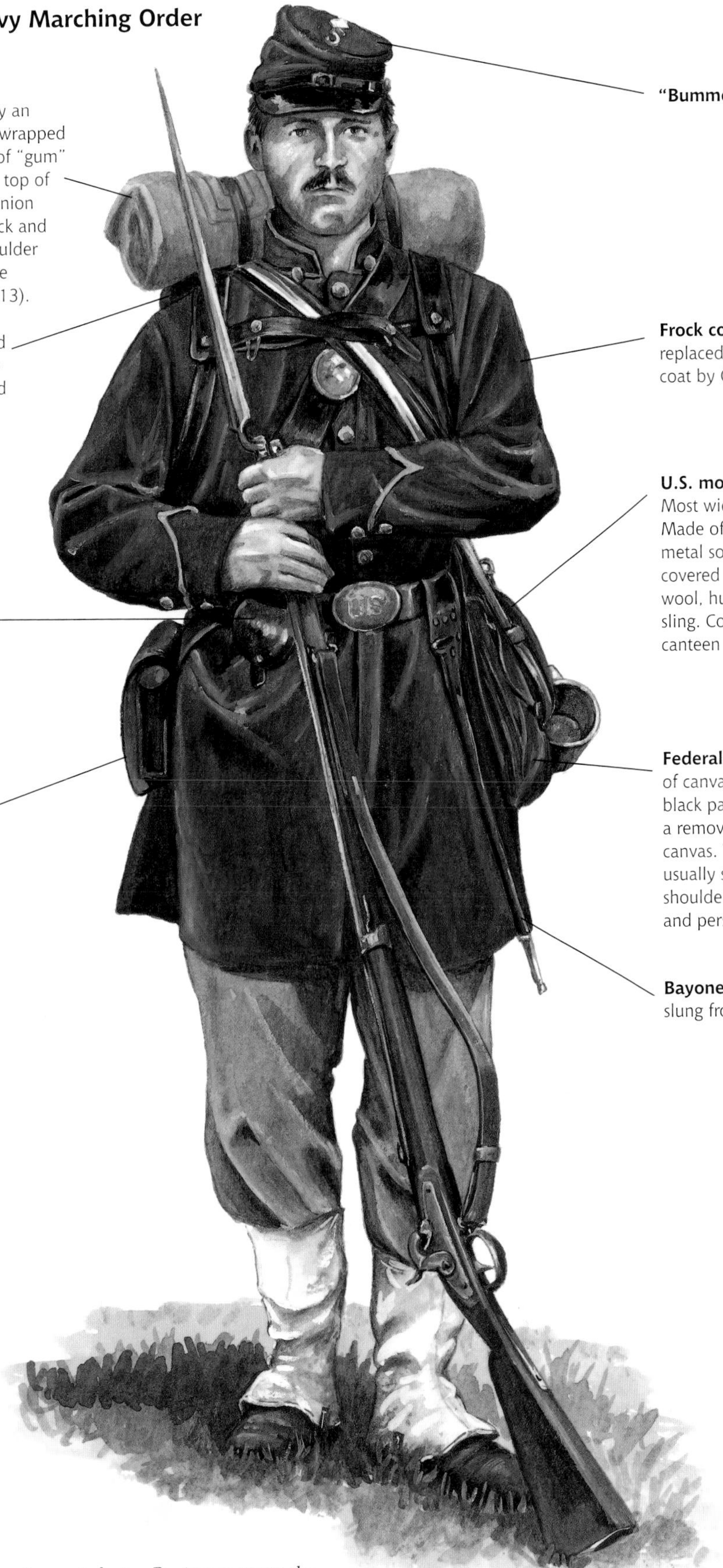

Blanket roll. A blanket (occasionally an overcoat) with personal belongings wrapped inside and covered with a waterproof "gum" blanket was sometimes strapped on top of the knapsack. By Gettysburg most Union soldiers had abandoned the knapsack and carried the blanket roll over the shoulder and across the chest, as shown in the Confederate illustration (see page 113).

Knapsack made of black rubberized cloth or painted canvas. These were an improvement on those supported by a wooden frame, which were heavy, uncomfortable, and mostly discarded. Unit designations were often painted on the knapsack.

Leather cap pouch. Worn on the belt at the front. A small piece of fleece kept the little copper percussion caps from falling out when the pouch was open.

Leather cartridge box. Contained 40 cartridges in two tinned metal containers. The cartridges were issued in packets of 10 with 12 percussion caps. Inside the flap was a tool pocket with cleaning patches.

"Bummer's" forage cap.

Frock coat. Mostly replaced by the sack coat by Gettysburg.

U.S. model 1858 canteen. Most widely used of the war. Made of two pieces of tinned metal soldered together and covered with gray, blue or brown wool, hung from white cotton sling. Cork stopper secured to canteen by cord or chain.

Federal-issue haversack. Made of canvas waterproofed with black paint. Buttoned inside was a removable bag of unpainted canvas. The haversack was usually slung over the right shoulder and contained rations and personal items.

Bayonette scabbard slung from belt on left side

This infantryman from the 5th New Jersey Infantry Regiment wears the regulation uniform of the Union Army. Many items of uniform carried into the field were left to brigade commanders to decide, the rest being deemed surplus and put into the regimental store. The 5th had been ordered to wear their frock coats during the Gettysburg campaign even if the majority of the Union Army wore the four-buttoned sack coat.

towns and wealthy friends. The problem was not so much the initial outlay but funding replacements for damaged or worn-out uniforms. By the time of Gettysburg the distinctive Zouave dress had largely disappeared. However, a few Union regiments became Zouaves long after formation, an example being the 146th New York, which adopted the new uniform in June 1863, just before the battle. One regiment, the 155th Pennsylvania, celebrated its origin by having its memorial on the summit of Little Round Top clothed entirely in Zouave uniform, although whether that is an accurate representation of how it fought is uncertain. Perhaps more likely was that it merely retained the jackets, as depicted on the memorials of the 23rd, 72nd and 95th Pennsylvania Regiments.

Confederate Uniforms

The South had great difficulty in producing uniforms that were in any way "uniform." New recruits in the early months of the war wore their civilian clothes or old militia uniforms for training. Dress regulations of June 1861 tried to regularize issues to recruits as a double-breasted gray coat, with sky blue trousers and cap, but production could never meet demand. It took many months for the Confederate War Department to organize a supply system to issue clothing and equipment to all the volunteer regiments. Despite the efforts of clothing depots established at Atlanta and Columbus in Georgia, Raleigh in North Carolina, and Richmond in Virginia, the Confederate soldier suffered from shortages throughout the war. The result was that the average Rebel regiment looked a somewhat motley crew in terms of dress. A Northern correspondent described Rebel prisoners captured during the Peninsular campaign of 1862 as follows:

> Some were wrapped in blankets of rag-carpet, and others wore shoes of untanned hide. Others were without shoes or jackets, and their heads were bound in red handkerchiefs. Some appeared in red shirts; some in stiff beaver hats; some were attired in shreds and patches of cloth; and a few wore the soiled garments of citizen gentlemen; but the mass adhered to homespun gray, or "butternut," and the coarse blue kersey common to slaves. In places I caught glimpses of red Zouave breeches and leggings; blue Federal caps, Federal buttons, or Federal blouses . . .

The butternut color referred to was a brown of various shades. The vegetable dye used to make cloth gray was found to change it to anything from a whitish tan to dark brown after prolonged exposure to the sun – which explains why Confederate jackets and trousers varied from pale blue-gray to dark brown. The British observer Colonel Wolseley, watching Confederate troops on the march, commented:

> Several regiments were to a man clothed in the national uniform of gray cloth, whilst others presented a harlequin appearance, being dressed in every conceivable variety of coat, both as regards color and cut. Gray wideawake hats, looped up at one side, and having a small black feather, are the most general head-dress; but many wear the Yankee black hat or casquette of cloth. That which is most unmilitary in their general appearance is the long hair worn alike by officers and men. They not only allow their locks to hang down the backs of their coats, but many pass them behind their ears as women do.

A typical soldier's uniform consisted of a short-waisted jacket, trousers and cap. The jacket and trousers were made of a coarse material called "jean" – a mixture of wool and cotton that was tough and durable but far too hot in summer.

Even more than their Yankee opponents, Rebel infantry suffered from a lack of serviceable boots or shoes. Generally the soldiers preferred shoes with broad soles and big, flat heels instead of boots, which were heavy, twisted the ankles and were difficult and time-consuming to put on and remove, especially when wet – modern infantrymen would probably still agree. Shoes and boots were so valuable that special missions were undertaken to procure them. They were often pulled from the feet of the dead and used by prisoners to barter for food or tobacco. It was not unknown for Rebel infantry without shoes, or with badly fitting ones, to be organized into separate units to march on the grassy roadsides. According to his 1878 account of events, lack of shoes and the consequent sore and bleeding feet in his division was of concern to Major-General Henry Heth when he reached Cashtown on June 29 en route to Gettysburg. He wrote, "I reached Cashtown, eight miles from Gettysburg . . . My men were sadly in want of shoes. I heard that a large supply of shoes were stored in Gettysburg." However, this was the first time he had emphasized this as the main reason for sending Brigadier-General Pettigrew's Brigade down the Chambersburg Pike to Gettysburg on June 30. In reality it was just a reconnaissance in force – finding shoes would be a bonus. In any case, Heth's men would have been out of luck as Gettysburg had no shoe factory. Major-General Early's Division had already passed through the town on June 26 and his requisition for 1,500 pairs of shoes produced nothing. The Union Cavalry 1st Division commander, Major-General John Buford, ended his dispatch to his corps commander dated June 30 in Gettysburg with the words, "Facilities for shoeing are nothing" and then added, seemingly erroneously, "Early's people seized every shoe and nail they could find."

Confederate headdress was almost as varied as the uniform, but there was a preference by officers and enlisted men for the soft-brimmed slouch type, as it was practical for providing warmth and shade from the sun (it also made a useful foraging basket for holding eggs or blackberries). It was made of thick felt, it was comfortable and available in many styles and colors. However, the gray forage cap was the general issue, although it was not uncommon to see a faded blue version obviously "donated" by a Yankee quartermaster via a body on a battlefield.

Officers' dress was supposedly laid down by regulations promulgated in June 1861. They stipulated a gray, double-breasted frock coat with two rows of seven brass buttons and a standing collar of a color varying according to the branch of service. Generals and staff officers were to wear dark blue trousers and other officers light blue. There were the usual fussy details as to numbers of buttons, stripes down the trousers and rank insignia for the various grades – see the illustrations on page 86. A copy of the French kepi was adopted for officers, dark blue for generals and staff, gray for the juniors. Many Confederate officers, particularly company officers, decided that the frock coat made them obvious targets on the firing line and adopted the short jacket like their soldiers.

Zouave regiments were very rare in the Confederate Army and there were none at Gettysburg. A battalion of "Louisiana Tigers" raised in New Orleans was originally a Zouave unit, but by 1863 they had been disbanded and the personnel assigned to other Louisiana regiments.

Confederate Infantryman in Light Marching Order

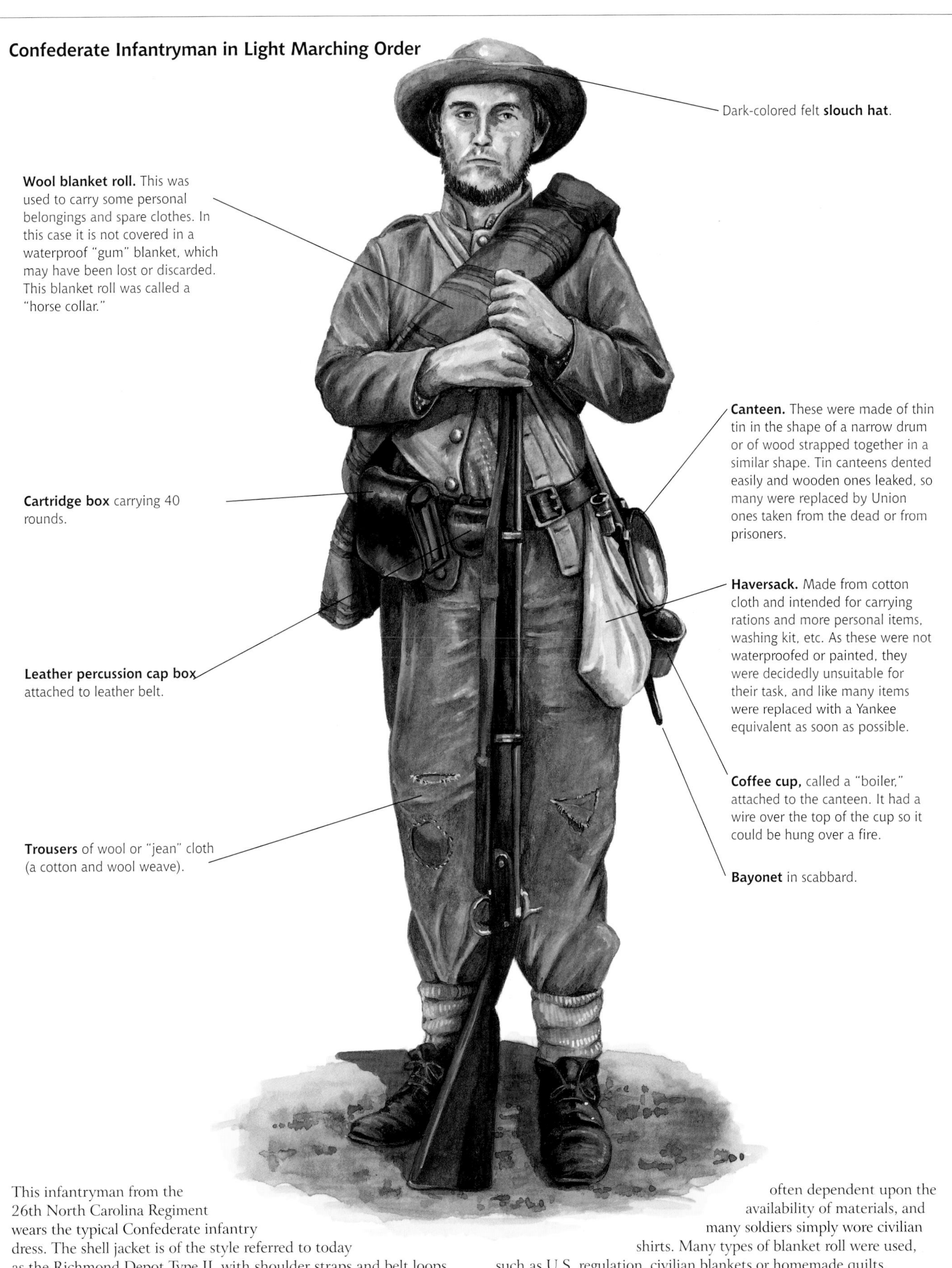
Dark-colored felt **slouch hat**.
Wool blanket roll. This was used to carry some personal belongings and spare clothes. In this case it is not covered in a waterproof "gum" blanket, which may have been lost or discarded. This blanket roll was called a "horse collar."
Canteen. These were made of thin tin in the shape of a narrow drum or of wood strapped together in a similar shape. Tin canteens dented easily and wooden ones leaked, so many were replaced by Union ones taken from the dead or from prisoners.
Cartridge box carrying 40 rounds.
Haversack. Made from cotton cloth and intended for carrying rations and more personal items, washing kit, etc. As these were not waterproofed or painted, they were decidedly unsuitable for their task, and like many items were replaced with a Yankee equivalent as soon as possible.
Leather percussion cap box attached to leather belt.
Coffee cup, called a "boiler," attached to the canteen. It had a wire over the top of the cup so it could be hung over a fire.
Trousers of wool or "jean" cloth (a cotton and wool weave).
Bayonet in scabbard.

This infantryman from the 26th North Carolina Regiment wears the typical Confederate infantry dress. The shell jacket is of the style referred to today as the Richmond Depot Type II, with shoulder straps and belt loops. His trousers are made of a "jean" cloth fabric, but captured Union blue trousers were also common. The Confederate-issue shirt was often dependent upon the availability of materials, and many soldiers simply wore civilian shirts. Many types of blanket roll were used, such as U.S. regulation, civilian blankets or homemade quilts. Knapsacks were also common and it was not unusual to see Confederate soldiers with both blanket roll and knapsack.

Union Infantryman's Equipment

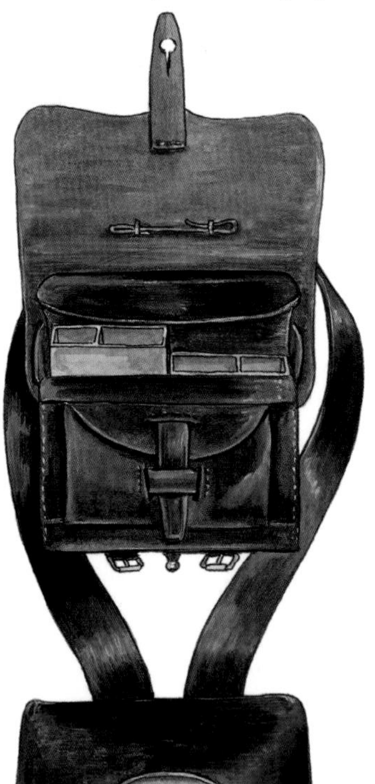

U.S. M1855 cartridge pouch with tinned liners to hold paper cartridges. A cast brass oval U.S. plate is affixed to the flap.

U.S. oval brass belt buckle

Decorative brass eagle plate worn on the cartridge belt

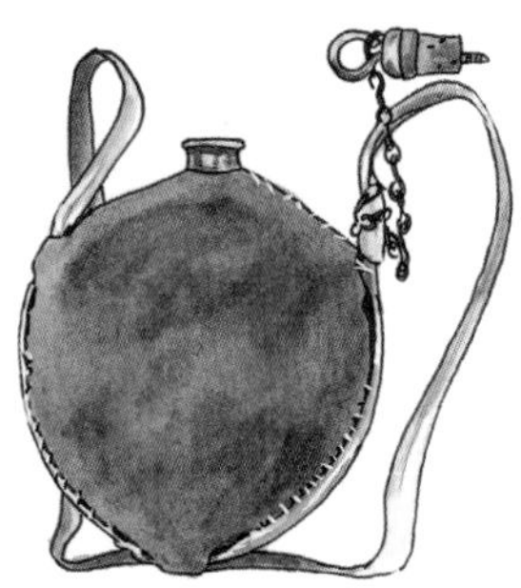

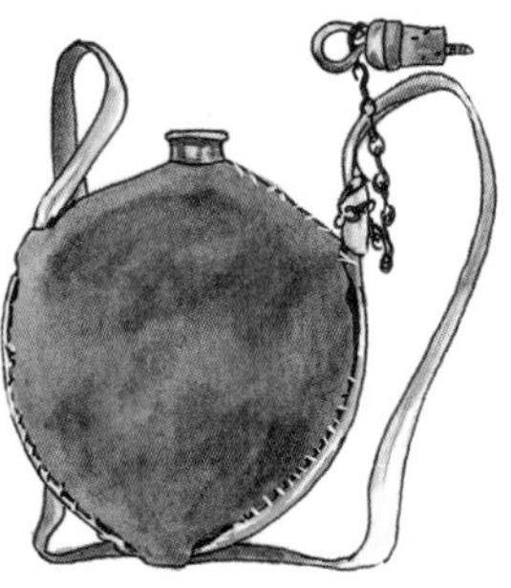

U.S. M1858 "Smoothside" canteen with light blue cloth cover

U.S. M1862 canteen, a modification of the 1858 pattern with seven concentric reinforcing rings. It was commonly known as the "Bullseye" canteen.

Cap pouch

U.S.-issue haversack, a canvas bag painted with a black water-repellent tar. Confederates used similar bags, some without the black tar. Rations, as well as cooking and eating utensils, were kept inside the haversack. Also shown is the removable muslin inner bag.

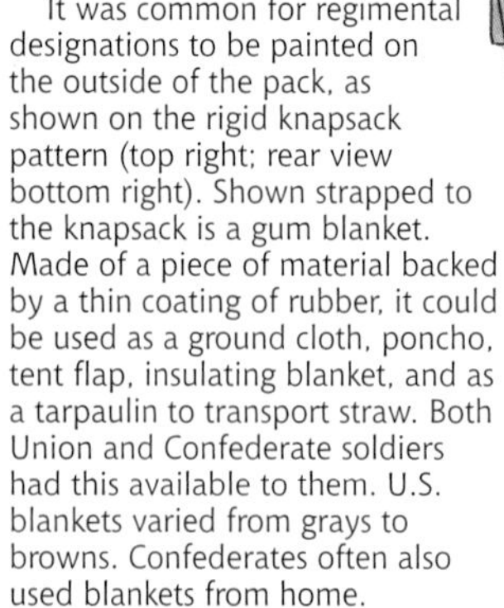

The U.S. M1858 double-bag knapsack was made of black painted canvas. Shown here are front and rear views (left and below left; also see open view illustration, Confederate equipment opposite). The interior of the knapsack was formed by two bags approximately 12 inches square. Things such as the gum blanket, shelter half, extra clothing, and personal items were carried in this pack. This is just one of many models used by both Union and Confederate troops.

It was common for regimental designations to be painted on the outside of the pack, as shown on the rigid knapsack pattern (top right; rear view bottom right). Shown strapped to the knapsack is a gum blanket. Made of a piece of material backed by a thin coating of rubber, it could be used as a ground cloth, poncho, tent flap, insulating blanket, and as a tarpaulin to transport straw. Both Union and Confederate soldiers had this available to them. U.S. blankets varied from grays to browns. Confederates often also used blankets from home.

Equipment

Personal equipment and accoutrements may have varied slightly in shape and color between Lee's and Meade's infantrymen at Gettysburg, but they served the same purpose in both. A soldier's initial issue included a haversack, knapsack, canteen, gum blanket (Union only), wool blanket, leather belt, cartridge box, percussion cap pouch and bayonet scabbard. The Rebels took particular pride in carrying the bare minimum. One soldier recalled:

I wore a cartridge box and bayonet holder on my belt. Extra cartridges were placed in pockets. Around my shoulder hung my woolen blanket and a captured Yankee gum (poncho) in which I wrapped my

Confederate Infantryman's Equipment

Confederate-manufactured cartridge pouch
(exterior above, interior below)

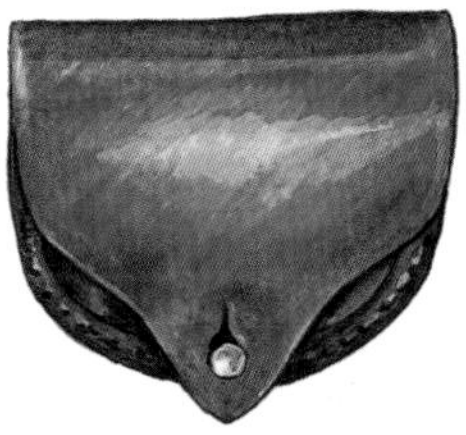

Cap pouches

Wooden drum canteen made from cedar or cherry wood

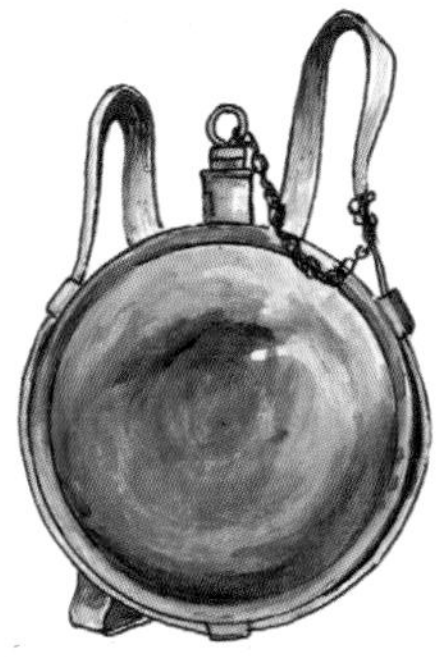

Confederate-issue drum canteen

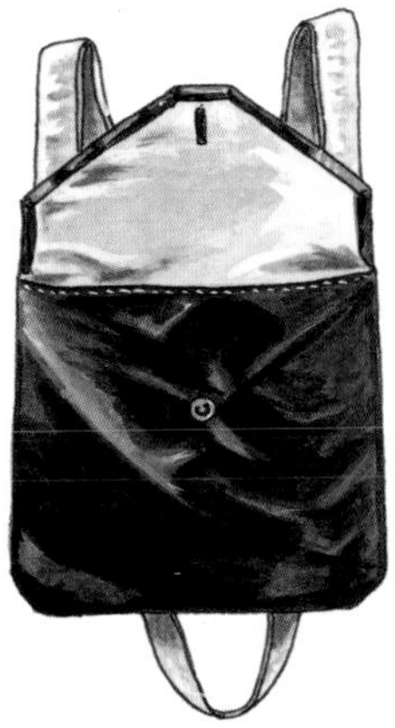

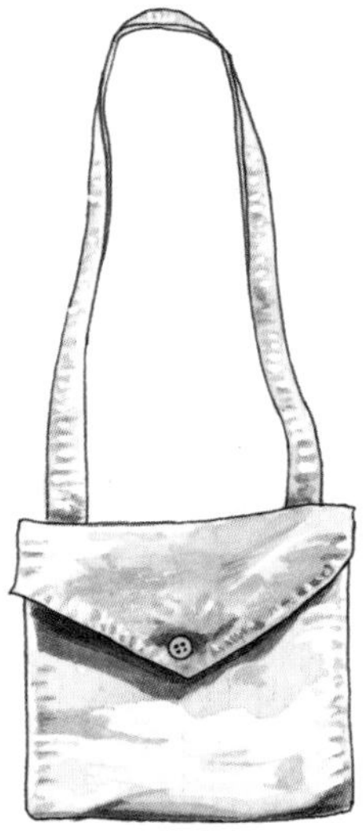

Haversacks

Oval South Carolina plate

Oval Texas plate

Oval CS plate

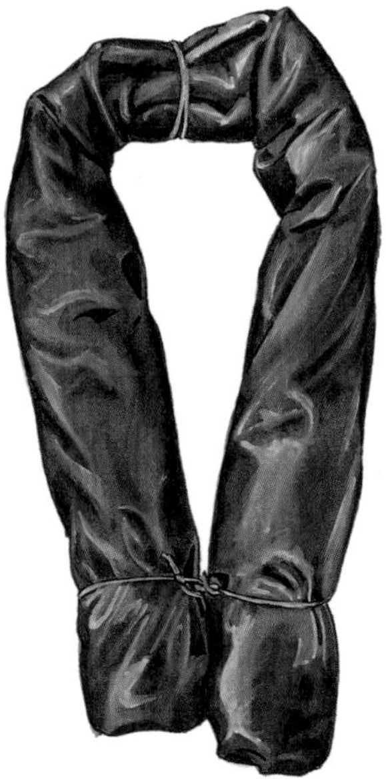

Blanket roll. The one shown is simply a gum blanket, but it could also be formed of an ordinary blanket or carpet.

US M1858 double-bag knapsack (shown open). It consisted of two bags; the first was closed with four flaps, and the other had a flap with leather straps that could be tied shut.

few belongings – a comb, a toothbrush and powder. I also had a haversack in which my plate, knife, spoon and fork rested with what meager rations we received. I tied my coffee boiler to my canteen to be ready to scoop up water at the first well or creek we passed.

Surprisingly, he makes no mention of how he carried his percussion caps or that it was not uncommon for Confederates to carry captured U.S. knapsacks with the Union regiment's number still on them. Details of equipment are shown in the illustrations above.

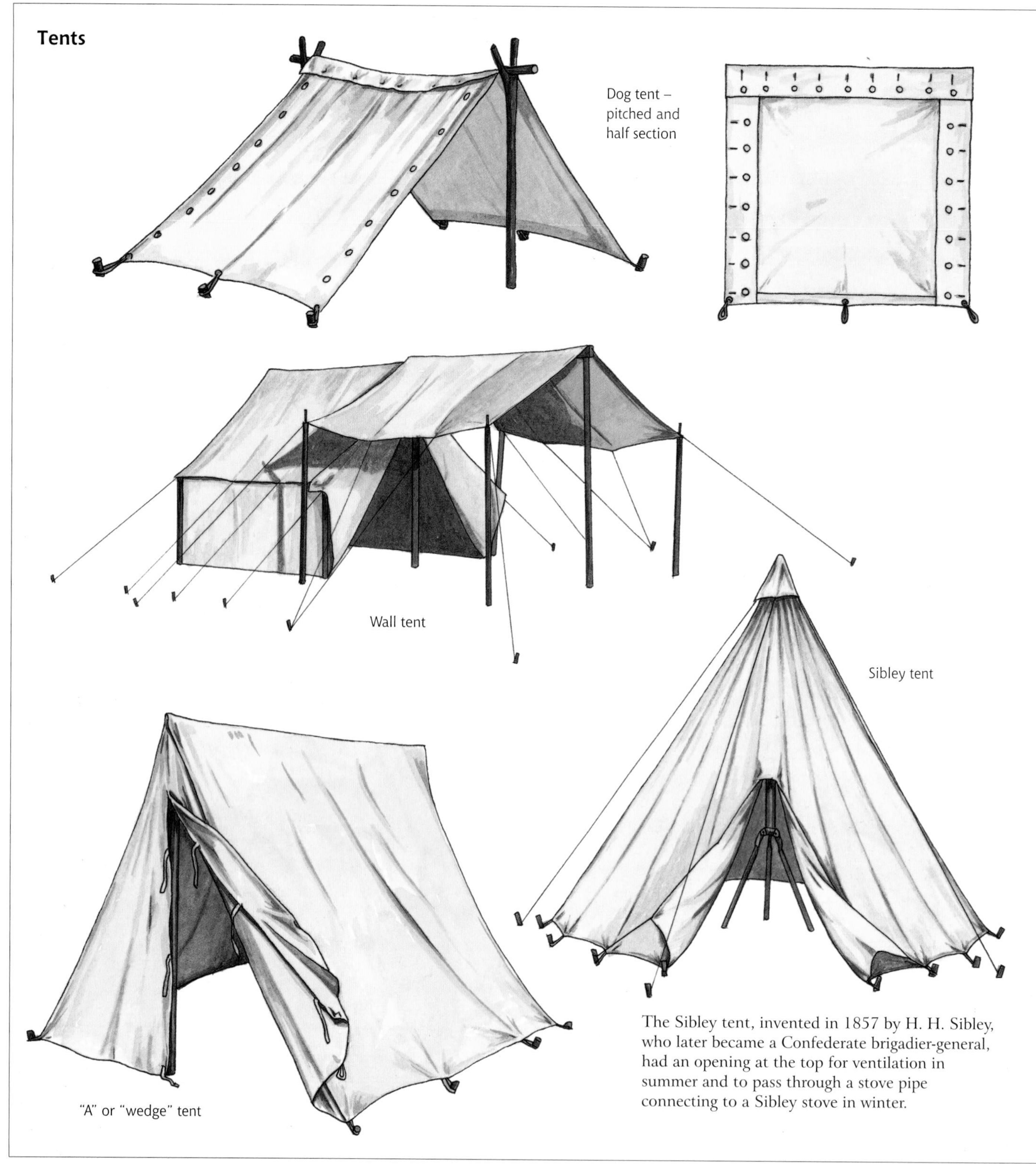

The Sibley tent, invented in 1857 by H. H. Sibley, who later became a Confederate brigadier-general, had an opening at the top for ventilation in summer and to pass through a stove pipe connecting to a Sibley stove in winter.

INFANTRYMEN ON THE MARCH

Among an infantryman's skills the ability to march long distances, often at a rapid pace and carrying all the equipment needed to fight, ranks high. The necessary stamina comes with training, care of the feet and the enforcement of strict march discipline to minimize the discarding of equipment and, a potentially crippling problem on the line of march, straggling. In this campaign infantry soldiers in both armies marched over poor roads either in sweltering heat or under drenching rain. They carried, initially at any rate, roughly the same 50–60 pounds of rifle-musket, 40–60 rounds of ammunition, equipment, knapsack, spare clothing, three days' rations, canteen, blanket and poncho in what was termed "heavy marching order." By the time they reached the battlefield many were down to "light marching order," having abandoned all nonessentials such as knapsacks and, in a few instances, even essentials such as ammunition.

Camping and Tentage

On campaign an overnight camp or bivouac followed a more or less regular routine. On arrival pickets would be posted and men would be detailed to forage for food if possible, but particularly for firewood – farmers' fences were an irresistible temptation to many (see box, page 221). Fires would be lit – weather permitting – coffee brewed and the evening meal cooked. Sometimes soldiers grouped themselves into messes to combine and share rations, often with one man selected as cook. However, it was more likely the men cooked as individuals in the field. Shelter for the Union soldier in 1863 was a "dog tent." Each soldier was issued one half of a tent, consisting of a rectangular piece of canvas that could be buttoned to another to form a small tent. It was called a "dog tent" because it was thought only large enough for a dog to crawl in and stay dry. Its main advantage was the speed with which it could be erected. All that was required was a straight stick as ridgepole (another use for a piece of fencing) and two more as tent poles (rifles stuck in the ground by bayonets would also suffice). Confederates were not issued with shelter tents, although some regiments were given a variation of the dog tent that could be used to make a lean-to shelter. More often they had nothing but a sodden blanket to wrap themselves in. The Rebels therefore particularly prized captured Yankee tents, especially the rubber blankets that made excellent groundsheets or overhead cover.

There were several types of larger tents, such as the four- or six-man wedge tent or the Sibley bell tent, which would be found in a permanent camp but were too bulky and heavy to take up wagon space on campaign. The exception to this was the "wall tent," which was used as a headquarters office, as accommodation for senior officers, or as a hospital tent.

The various types of tent are illustrated opposite.

Distances and March Rates

Discounting the retreat and follow-up after the battle, both armies had approximately the same starting point – the area around Fredericksburg and Falmouth on the Rappahannock River – and both the same finishing point – Gettysburg. Nevertheless, as far as distances were concerned, because Lee's men took a long, left-hook route westward through the Blue Ridge Mountains, over the Shenandoah River and then northward up the valley, with some units touching the Susquehanna River before turning back to Gettysburg, the Army of Northern Virginia put more miles behind them than the Army of the Potomac. Although some regiments and many individuals may have marched much further, Ewell's Corps covered the greatest distance of either army by a substantial margin. It penetrated Pennsylvania as far as the banks of the Susquehanna opposite Harrisburg and Columbia, 30 miles north and northeast of Gettysburg respectively. By the time it went into action on July 1 it had marched at least 220 miles. When Hill and Longstreet reached the battlefield via the Shenandoah Valley and Chambersburg, they had covered over 175 miles. Meade's men, however, had mostly marched due northeast of the Blue Ridge and thus covered an average of around 120 miles, although none of these estimates takes into consideration the countless detours and countermarches that were the inevitable lot of every infantryman, whether Rebel or Yankee.

However, it is not just the measuring of miles on a map that counts. The weather, the condition of the roads, how much movement across country is required, and how many obstacles – such as rivers – have to be crossed are all factors of vital importance in assessing a march in terms of time and distance. A marching speed for a large body of infantry on reasonable roads in fine weather is 2.5 miles an hour (this was known as "common time" and translated into about 70 yards a minute on the battlefield). Frequently, at the end of June, regiments were ordered to "quick-time" or even "double-quick" as the battlefield approached. The former meant about 2.8 miles an hour or 82 yards a minute; the latter, which was a fast run, 5 miles in the hour or 150 yards a minute.

The weather and poor roads ensured that good marching conditions rarely existed in Maryland and Pennsylvania in June 1863. Lee's invasion officially began on June 3 when Lafayette McLaws' Division broke camp and started for the army concentration area around Culpeper Court House. Not until June 10, with two-thirds of his army grouped around Culpeper, did the invasion march begin in earnest. From June 10 to July 1 inclusive is twenty-two days, giving an average daily march of 10 miles for Ewell's Corps and 8 for Hill and Longstreet. Some days there was no marching at all; on others hours were spent sitting by the roadside waiting for other troops, guns or wagon trains to pass before the march could be resumed. But as the days passed, the pace often had to be forced and distances of over 20, even 30, miles were achieved – although the old army phenomenon of "hurry and wait" was everywhere evident.

Meade's reaction to the invasion did not start until June 12, when he began to move north to keep his army between the enemy and Washington. From June 12 to July 1 is twenty days, which gives an average day's march of only 6 miles. In neither case do these hypothetical averages do justice to the actuality. For both armies the really serious marching effort took place during the last ten days of June. Then marching was often required in pouring rain, over roads ankle-deep in mud, in high temperatures and with an urgent need to catch up or concentrate. During this period many regiments on both sides were marching 20–30 miles a day, which sometimes involved several hours of marching in the dark before a halt was called (on the night of June 14/15 the Union VI Corps marched throughout the entire night). For many soldiers, memories of the utter exhaustion, the heat, the thirst, bleeding and blistered feet, and of men straggling or collapsing were almost as vivid as those of the battle.

Such was the case for the men of Union Major-General Hancock's II Corps. On June 29 they had started marching at 8:00 a.m. and continued well into the night, covering some 30 miles. When they halted after fourteen hours, many of the soldiers were in a shocking state and many more had not made it at all. Because he was behind schedule, Hancock had driven his men exceptionally hard. A general rule of any march was that after wading a stream the troops would be allowed a few minutes to wring out their socks and dry their feet. Hancock did not permit this and marched his men fast with soaking socks that quickly produced scores more men hobbling along, crippled with burst blisters. Straggling became chronic, the numbers growing to such an extent that they overwhelmed the efforts of the provost guard to force them forward. One soldier remembered that "the day began with a route march and ended with go as you please."

A Typical Union Infantry Brigade's March to the Battlefield

Note A new, inexperienced brigade consisting of nine-month men for whom Gettysburg would be their only battle. Nicknamed the "Paper Collar" Brigade, it had spent its time in the Washington defenses and was fully equipped with the regulation uniform and equipment. Stannard, however, was an experienced commander, having fought at 1st Manassas, Williamsburg, and in the Peninsular and Antietam campaigns.

The brigade was to follow and overtake the A.P., already two days' march ahead, and report to Maj.-Gen. Reynolds, commanding I Corps. It was to be the rearguard of the army during the move north.

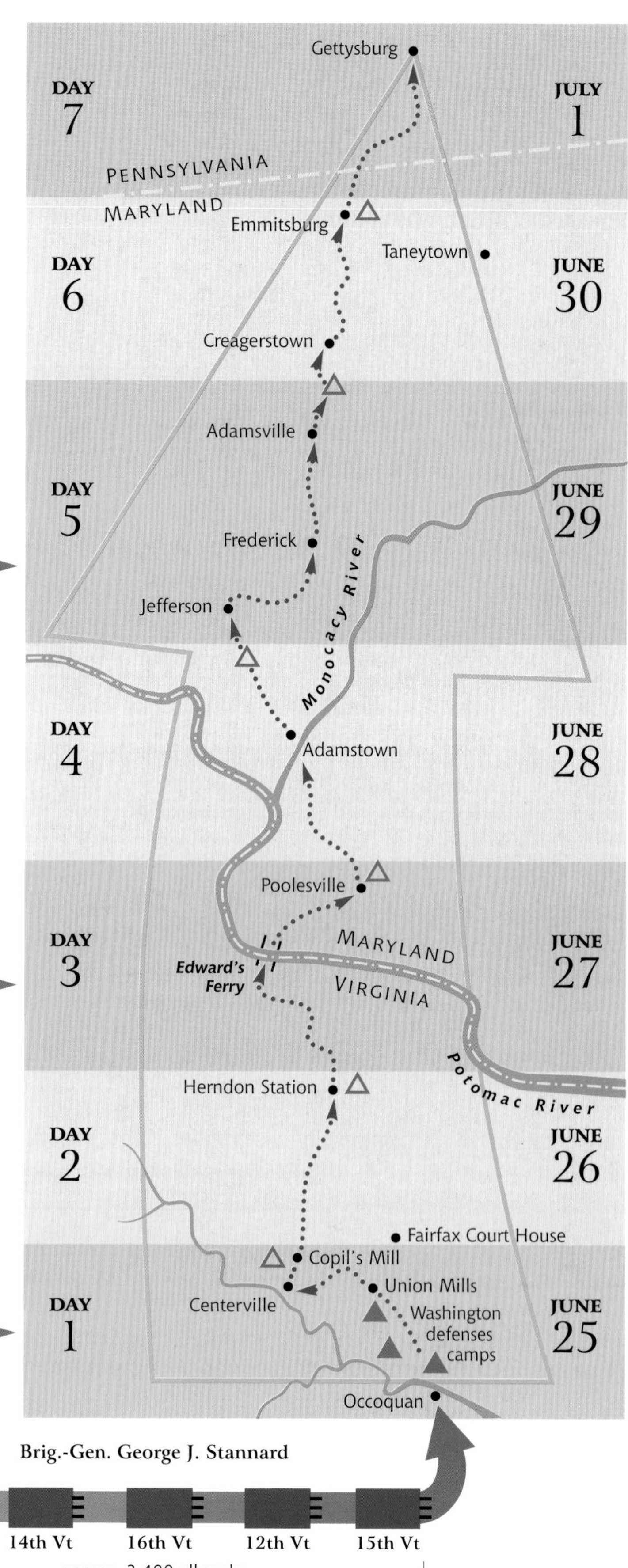

Day 5 March began at 7:00 a.m. The brigade was learning the need to march light the hard way. For several days now kit was being discarded. Heavy wool blankets, overcoats, some knapsacks, even extra shoes and cooking utensils littered the line of march. Rations were now getting short as wagons were well to the rear. Beans and pork had all been consumed and the men were on what they called "marching hardtack." A long halt of 3–4 hours at Frederick for the usual reason. Many men purchased food from the residents. There was a big fuss when some men of 13th Vermont stole some cheese from a nearby sutler's wagon. Some 90 men were left in Frederick due to the state of their feet. The brigade finally camped between Adamsville and Creagerstown.

Day 3 Reveille 3:00 a.m. and on the road at 5:00 a.m. At 9:00 a.m. the brigade halted to allow III and VI Corps baggage trains to pass. Reached the Potomac by mid-afternoon and crossed over the pontoon bridge. The brigade halted and many men bathed their blistered feet in the water. That night the brigade encamped at Poolesville.

Day 1 Breakfast of boiled pork and beans at 5:00 a.m. Ordered to leave all unnecessary kit (knapsacks) and clothes behind. This order was soon rescinded and the men marched with knapsacks and three days' rations in haversacks and seven in the wagons. Many men still carrying overcoats. After waiting for VI Corps wagons to pass, the brigade left the Union Mills area around 4:30 p.m., with the 13th Vermont having marched up from Occoquan.

As they started, so did the rain. Marched through Centerville and went into wet bivouac at Copil's Mill, about a mile north of the town.

3rd Brigade, 3rd Division, I Corps

13th Vt 14th Vt 16th Vt 12th Vt 15th Vt

approx. 3,400 all ranks

△ overnight campsite

Day 7 The 12th and 15th Vermont were left behind as train guards when the march from Emmitsburg began at around 10:00 a.m. with the 13th Vermont leading. After two hours they rested, brewed coffee, and ate crackers. They moved on in the afternoon, which was very hot with occasional showers. About 8 miles south of Gettysburg they heard Maj.-Gen. Reynolds had been killed. The brigade pressed on toward the sound of gunfire. About 4 miles south of the town, with the noise of battle in their ears, they halted again. It was then discovered that, although strictly forbidden, many men had lightened their loads by discarding ammunition. This was replenished and the brigade arrived on the battlefield after 7:00 p.m. and were positioned just SE of Cemetery Hill.

Day 6 On the march by 7:00 a.m. Rumors rife that Hooker had been sacked and Meade in command, with the Rebels near Gettysburg. Much stopping and starting as they neared the Pennsylvania border due to wagons, ambulances and guns on the road. Nevertheless, at times units at the end of the column had to resort to double-quick to keep up. More rain, and more soldiers dropped out. However, the brigade had gained a day due to sheer determination to keep going, despite bleeding feet, lack of sleep and food, the mud, the rain and the exhaustion. Maj.-Gen. Doubleday rewarded their efforts with a new nickname, "The Flying Brigade."

Day 4 More waiting to allow trains to pass. March started around 7:30 a.m. By now considerable suffering with bleeding, blistered feet made worse by pebbles and stones under the mud. The Q.M.s had refused to issue new shoes as men were shortly to be discharged, and now the old ones began to disintegrate or be sucked off in the mud. Some men marching barefoot and beginning to straggle. Some officers allowed the worst affected to take turn riding their horses. It was now hot and humid as well as wet. Stannard was informed that I Corps H.Q. was near Emmitsburg. Brigade waded across the Monocacy River and pressed on into the night before halting a few miles short of Jefferson after a 20-mile march.

Day 2 After a miserable night reveille was at 5:00 a.m. in pouring rain. Soggy breakfast followed by more waiting for VI Corps wagons and artillery to pass. Soldiers picked berries, boiled coffee (with difficulty), sat on their knapsacks wrapped in their gum clothes. By evening had only reached Herndon Station.

Stannard's Brigade had marched well over 100 miles in six days, averaging 18 miles a day under taxing conditions of continuous rain, mud, high humidity and short rations. Three regiments had continued for another day. For inexperienced, unfit troops it was a very commendable effort, marred only by a few instances of drunkenness and the throwing away by some of much of their ammunition. The brigade had started out with around 3,400 men, but with the two regiments doing train guard and some falling out en route, only 1,950 went into action at the battle.

On July 2, the 13th Vermont was engaged in the evening when it charged from Cemetery Ridge and drove off Wright's Brigade. On July 3 the brigade's attack on the right flank of Pickett's charge played a decisive part in defeating Lee's final assault. The brigade lost 351 men or 18% of its engaged strength.

An example of distances covered in the last few days before the battle is provided by the 20th Maine Infantry, whose marching schedule for the six days prior to their arrival late on July 1 was:

June 26	20 miles
June 27	19 miles
June 28	resting in camp near Frederick
June 29	15 miles
June 30	25 miles
July 1	23 miles
Total	**102 miles**

A Confederate Army corps of 20,000 men, mostly infantry, on a single road and with the men marching closed up and four abreast would produce a column at least 4 miles long. Add on another 2 miles for the inevitable spreading out, plus another 4–6 miles for the hundreds of artillery wagons and ordnance, supply, ambulance and baggage trains, and a 12–14 mile unmanageable snake is created. The leading regiment would be arriving at its destination while the last group of wagons had barely started. Lee had three such corps for the invasion; Meade had seven smaller ones to counter it. A factor of paramount importance in moving armies of this size is sound planning and effective staff work. As many roads as possible had to be used, the routes had to be selected, the orders of march and timings decided, complex movement orders written and delivered to commanders. A misunderstood order, a delayed start, a column of wagons on the wrong road or a column crossing from one road to another could cause chaos even in fine weather on good roads. The Gettysburg campaign is full of such snarl-ups, which took hours to untangle. Hancock's march, mentioned above, is an example. His march should have started at 4:00 a.m., but a clerk had failed to deliver the movement order so the march began four hours late, which resulted in Hancock ruthlessly forcing the pace and neglecting proper march procedures, thus crippling large numbers of his men.

On the March to Gettysburg

The Gettysburg campaign tested the marching ability of the infantry of both armies to the limit. This was particularly so toward the end of June, when Lee and Meade sought to concentrate for the clash both knew was inevitable. The following paragraphs give an idea of what it was like to be a soldier in butternut or blue on the roads of Virginia, Maryland and Pennsylvania during that time. Jacob Hoke, a resident of Chambersburg, watched Ewell's Corps march through the town on its way north. He later wrote:

> First . . . comes a brigade or two of cavalry [in this case Jenkins' Brigade, which had passed through several days earlier]. After an interval of probably a day, the different regiments composing a brigade, and the various brigades composing a division, and the several divisions of a corps, pass with their immense trains of artillery, caissons, forges, ambulances and ammunition wagons. These wagons are each drawn by four or six horses or mules, and in passing along the macadamized streets they make that grinding noise which indicates immense weight of freightage. In some circumstances herds of fifty to one hundred cattle are driven along for the use of the men. Scattered here and there along the line at the heads of brigades, are

The Confederate Infantryman's Shoes

The main problem in providing soldiers of the A.N.V. with shoes was lack of leather, which led to manufacturers skimping by using leather only for the soles and canvas for the uppers, which soon disintegrated with hard marching. There was even resort to wood for the soles, some with iron horseshoe-shaped plates on the heels and toes. Shoes bought in Britain were found to be even worse, as they were lined with stiff paper, which guaranteed they fell to pieces after a good soaking. Shoes manufactured in Richmond were made, according to one officer, "with the face of the skin next the animal turned out, which is contrary to the practice of the best makers and contrary to the arrangement of nature." A soldier wrote that shoes were:

> generally made of green or at the best half-cured leather, they soon took to roaming; after a week's wear the heel would be on the side, at an angle to the foot, and the vamp, in turn, would try to do duty as a sole. It was impossible to keep them straight, and to judge by your tracks you could hardly tell whether you were going or coming. They conformed to the weather also. While hot and dry they would shrink like parchment, and when wet they just "slopped" all over your feet.

The situation became so critical that in the winter before Gettysburg Lee combed every regiment for shoemakers. These men had no other duty except shoemaking, some even being sent to Richmond to procure tanned leather for the task. Throughout the Gettysburg campaign and battle, soldiers, particularly Southern ones, were on the lookout for "winning" shoes or boots. A useful source was the feet of the dead of either side, or prisoners. Surprisingly, however, Major-General Johnson's initiative on June 29 in ordering the removal of 126 pairs of shoes from the feet of paroled Union militiamen and issuing them to the Stonewall Brigade was considered highly dishonorable by the ungrateful recipients.

There is a long established myth that the main reason Heth sent Pettigrew's Brigade down the Chambersburg Pike on June 30 and again on July 1 was to search for shoes in Gettysburg. Heth states in his report that Pettigrew was sent for supplies, particularly shoes. However, Heth knew Early's Division had been through the town on June 26 so there would not be much left of anything, certainly shoes (and Gettysburg did not have a shoe factory). In the years that followed the battle there was considerable witch-hunting for scapegoats on whom to pin the Confederate failure and for bringing on the battle too soon. For this latter Heth was in the frame and it is feasible that he emphasized that shoes were the reason he attempted to march into Gettysburg.

> bands of musicians. "Dixie," "My Maryland," and the "Bonnie Blue Flag" were the favorite pieces played. The passage of a corps usually occupied from a day to a day and a half . . .
>
> The Confederate infantry as they marched through Chambersburg presented a solid front. They came in close marching order . . . Their dress consisted of nearly every imaginable color and style, the butternut largely predominating. Some had blue blouses, which they had doubtless stripped from the Union dead. Hats, or the skeletons of what had once been hats, surmounted their partly covered heads. Many were ragged, shoeless and filthy . . . They were, however, well armed and under perfect discipline. They seemed to move as one vast machine.

A Union corps, apart from the uniforms, would look virtually the same. The exact order of march of divisions would be specified in the previous night's movement order and brigade commanders would have similarly instructed their regiments. It was usual to change the order daily so that each brigade and regiment took turns as the advance or rear guard. The advance guard brigade would have skirmishers ahead and flankers out on either side of the route. These were a single file of soldiers marching some 150–200 yards on either flank of the column. They protected the flanks and, if the column was attacked, would become the skirmishers when it turned left or right into line to meet the threat. At the head of the first division rode the commander and his staff, usually accompanied by a small mounted escort, one of whom would carry the rectangular divisional color (Confederate formations had not developed a similar system at this level). Each following brigade would be led by its commander, staff and triangular flag-bearer and, if available, brigade bands would head the leading regiments. John D. Billings, a Union artilleryman, painted an illuminating vignette of a Yankee infantry regiment on the march:

> You can easily count the regiments in a column by their United States colors. A few of them, you will notice, have a battle flag bearing the names of the engagements in which they have participated. Some regiments used the national colors for a battle-flag, some the state colors . . .
>
> You will have little difficulty in deciding where a regiment begins or ends. It begins with a field officer [the colonel, lieutenant-colonel or adjutant, often all three] and ends with a mule. Originally it ended with several army wagons; but now that portion of regimental headquarters baggage which has not gone to the wagon-train, is to be found stowed about the mule, that is led by a contraband [former

A Young Lady Welcomes the Rebels

On June 26, as his division arrived in Greencastle, Major-General Pickett had an encounter with a young lady. He was riding with the 53rd Virginia Infantry Regiment under Colonel William R. Aylett at the time, and the band was playing "Dixie." A young woman rushed onto her verandah frantically waving the United States flag, which she proceeded to wrap around her waist as a skirt. She danced around, flaunting the flag and herself and at the same time shouting "Traitors! Traitors! Traitors!" Colonel Aylett later stated that, "Struck by her courage and loyalty, Pickett, with hat off, gave her a military salute, my regiment presented arms, and we cheered her with a good old-fashioned rebel yell . . ." At this unexpected response from the enemy, the lady stopped shouting and let her flag fall, saying, according to Pickett, "Oh, I wish I had a rebel flag. I'd wave that too."

> slave]. Yes, the head, ears and feet which you see are the only visible externals of a mule. He is "clothed upon" with the various materials necessary to prepare a "square meal" for the colonel and other headquarters officers.

Confederate regiments also made use of pack mules and additionally had a gaggle of slaves at the rear, mostly carrying surplus kit for their officer masters. Billings neglected to mention that pioneers would head a regiment if serious obstacles were likely to be encountered, or that also in the rear marched the surgeon, his assistant and several hospital corpsmen, and, if there was one, the chaplain. Finally, behind the division would come the provost guard, supposedly sweeping up stragglers, although as discussed below this became a near impossible task. As noted by Billings, by mid-1863 the regimental baggage wagons under the quartermaster were grouped in a divisional train behind the marching troops. They moved in the same order as the regiments and theoretically could be brought forward when the regiments went into bivouac.

March Conditions

It was the combination of the distances marched and the weather that caused so many men to collapse and straggle. The heat, frequently 90 degrees in the shade, and high humidity, which often alternated with drenching rain, was particularly oppressive for men burdened with 50-pound loads, sweating in woolen uniforms, and struggling to maintain the pace with empty canteens. Tens of thousands of feet stirred up clouds of drifting dust. The columns had no escape from this affliction, which coated their clothing, hair and caked their faces, giving them a white mask, only disturbed by the streams of sweat coursing down their cheeks and necks. As Private John Haley in the 17th Maine put it:

> The air was almost suffocating . . . the dust in the road was scalding . . . the soil of Virginia was sucked into our throats, sniffed into our nostrils, and flew into our eyes and ears until our most intimate friends would not have recognized us . . . All day long we tugged our weary knapsacks in the broiling sun, and many fell out to fall no more.

The same sun crippled the Confederates. Captain Dooley, 1st Virginia Infantry, wrote:

> Terrible had been that march along the scorched and blazing plains of Virginia . . . Choking, blinding were the clouds of dust that rose from beneath the army's unsteady tread; parching was that unquenchable thirst which dried the tongue to its very roots. The men fell by tens, twenties, nay, hundreds along the dusty roadsides.

According to one account, by the time Major-General Newton's divisional rearguard reached Dumfries at 5:00 p.m. on June 15, some of the regiments had less than a third of their men present. In the 20th Maine by late afternoon men would be falling out continuously with foot trouble and exhaustion, although many struggled gamely on to rejoin the regiment in bivouac during the night.

In order partially to relieve their suffering, many men abandoned equipment, even ammunition, along the line of march.

Slaves on the March

It is seldom recorded that Lee's army marching north that summer of 1863 was accompanied by thousands of black slaves – probably between 6,000 and 10,000. Many were accompanying their masters to do much of the manual labor of setting up camp, foraging for firewood or food and cooking – Union prisoners on July 3 reported seeing long lines of slaves baking corn for the troops at the front. Slaves were to be seen on the line of march as a gaggle perhaps twenty or thirty strong at the rear of each regiment; according to Private John T. Smith, the 13th Alabama had at least twenty-five with the regiment. Major-General Pender had a personal slave called Joe who, the general claimed in a letter to his wife, "enter[ed] into the invasion with much gusto and is quite active in looking up hidden property." Many thousands more were present with the A.N.V. under lease arrangements between their owners and the government, most of them employed as laborers or wagoners driving and maintaining the huge fleets of wagons in the divisional and reserve trains that accompanied the army.

The advancing Rebels, particularly the mounted units of Jenkins and Imboden, rounded up many freeborn or runaway blacks (contrabands) living in Pennsylvania who did not flee in time. Jacob Hoke, the civilian who watched the Confederates march through Chambersburg, recounted in his book *The Great Invasion*:

> These poor creatures . . . sought concealment in the growing wheat fields about the town. Into these the cavalrymen rode in search of their prey, and many were caught – some after a desperate chase and being fired at. In two cases, through the intersession of a friend who had influence with Jenkins, I succeeded in effecting the release of the captured persons.

Rachel Cormany, who observed the Rebels as they passed through Chambersburg, described the activities of Jenkins' men in her journal on June 16:

> [They were] hunting up the contrabands and driving them off by droves . . . Some of the colored people who were raised here were taken along – I sat on the front step as they were driven by just like we would drive cattle. Some laughed and seemed not to care – but nearly all hung their heads.

Colonel William S. Christian, commanding the 55th Virginia Infantry, wrote to his wife on June 28, "We took a lot of negroes yesterday. I was offered my choice, but as I could not get [take] them back home I would not take them. In fact my humanity revolted at taking the poor devils away from their homes." Some slaves managed to take the opportunity of deserting while in Pennsylvania, particularly after the battle during the Confederate retreat. To quote Hoke again:

> A number of colored persons also made their escape from the army while in Pennsylvania, some of whom are yet living there. Said the writer to one of these soon after the war, "Where were you born, Sam?" "I was born in Georgia, sah," replied my sable friend. "How did you get up here?" I inquired. "I come Norf wid my young master; I was his servant, and he was an offisser, and when he got wounded at de battle of Gettysburg I just dun run away."

Schematic View of Union 1st Division, III Corps on the March to Gettysburg

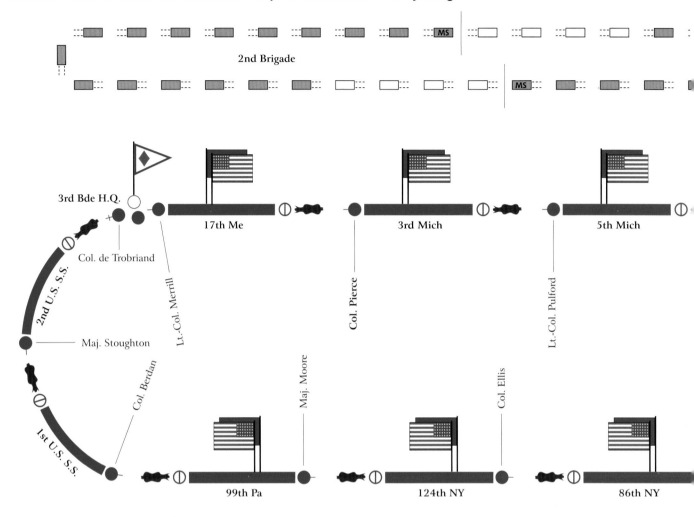

MS

2nd Brigade

MS

3rd Bde H.Q.

Col. de Trobriand

17th Me

Lt.-Col. Merrill

3rd Mich

Col. Pierce

5th Mich

Lt.-Col. Pulford

2nd U.S. S.S.

Maj. Stoughton

Col. Berdan

1st U.S. S.S.

99th Pa

Maj. Moore

124th NY

Col. Ellis

86th NY

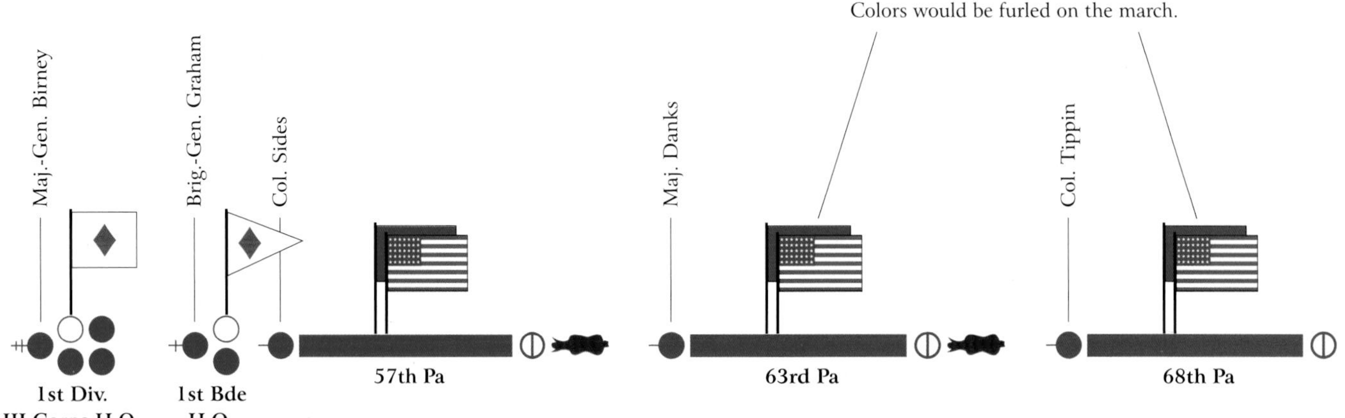

Notes

• This division left Hartwood Church on June 11 and marched some 130 miles via Bealton Station, Manassas Junction, Centerville, Edward's Ferry, Jefferson, Frederick and Emmitsburg, arriving Gettysburg (less 3rd Brigade, who arrived July 2) late on July 1. It was a tough march, the weather wet and humid, the roads terrible, with many men suffering from bleeding feet.

• The division is shown at its engaged strength of 5,100, although it would hav started out stronger. Many men were detached on duties with the trains and elsewhere – the 17th Maine had almost 100 detached by July 2.

• The order of march of the brigades was supposed to change daily. An average s of 2.5 miles an hour was considered good, with the marching troops of this divisi spread over at least 1.5 miles and the 60 wagons another two-thirds of a mile.

• By 1863 regimental bands had been largely abolished, but it is assumed at leas one brigade band would have been formed, if only to enliven the march.

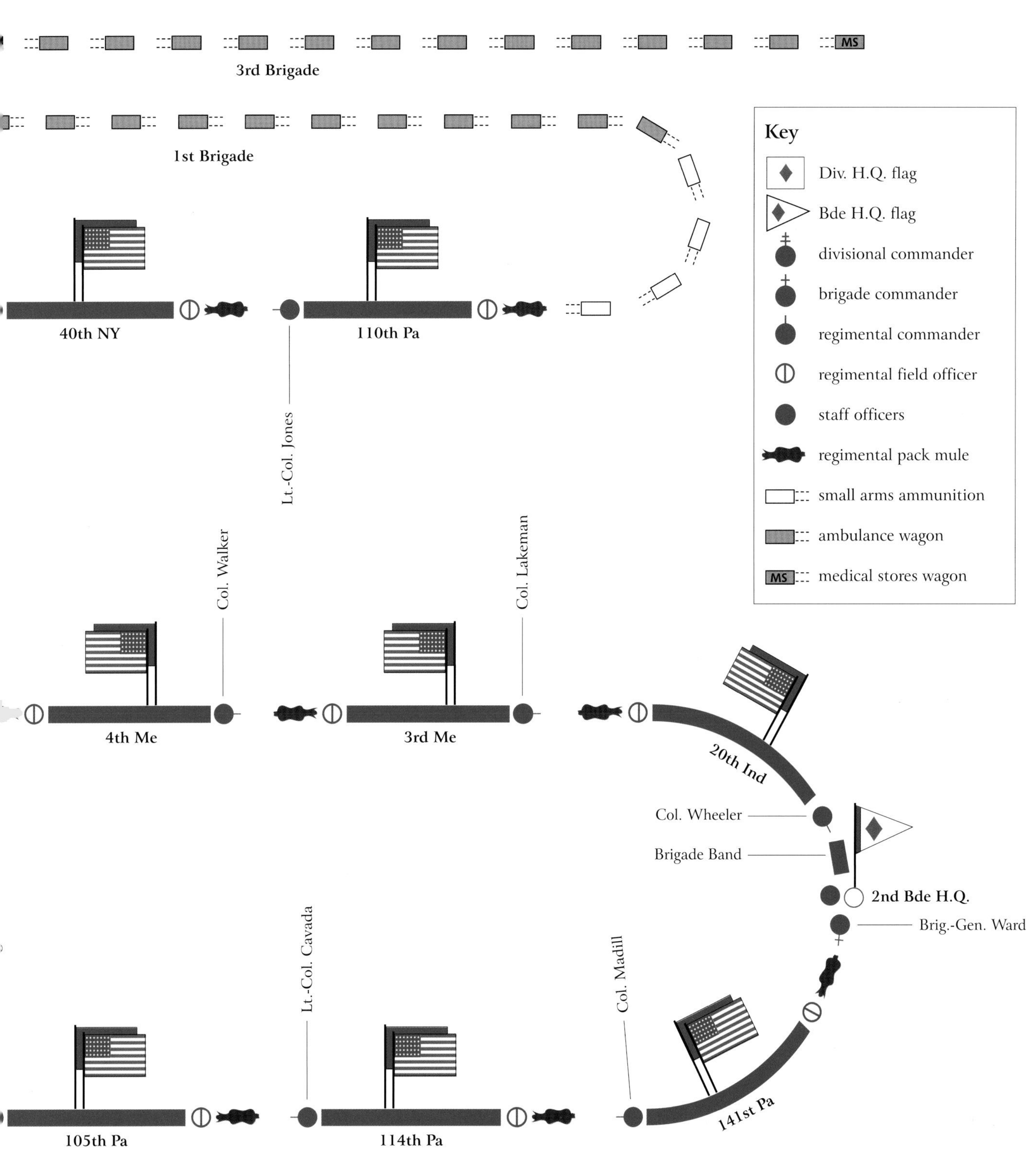

't was usual for the commander (or adjutant) to lead the ‑imental column with the troops marching four abreast ‑h the national and regimental colors in the center and a ‑d officer at the rear. Behind him most regiments had the ‑gle pack mule led by an African American allowed to ‑ompany the troops on the march. Note how easy it is for ‑ivilian observer to count the flags to get the number of ‑iments and thus report enemy strengths and locations.

• A divisional wagon train followed each Union division. Within this train each brigade had its own ambulance wagons and ordnance wagons carrying small arms ammunition under the brigade ordnance officer. The numbers shown here are an average estimate (see page 230). This train remained with the division on, or very near, the battlefield to the rear of the firing line. All divisional baggage wagons (tents, camp equipage), subsistence and commissary wagons (food and fodder) and quartermaster's wagons (stores, clothing, etc.) were grouped in the corps supply train. At Gettysburg these corps trains were centralized at one huge park at the Westminster railhead some 25 miles from the battlefield.

Captain David Acheson of the 140th Pennsylvania Infantry admitted, "I can hardly bear the heat . . . I threw away everything but my haversack and canteen, and would have dropped them if I could not have kept up the regiment." John Billings again:

> If you were to follow the column after, say, the first two miles, you would find various articles scattered along at intervals by the roadside, where a soldier had quietly stepped out of the ranks, sat down, unslung his knapsack or his blanket roll, took out what he had decided to throw away, again equipped himself, and, thus relieved, hastened on to join his regiment. It did not take long for an army to get into light marching order after it was once fairly on the road.

The main cause of soldiers collapsing with varying degrees of heatstroke and dehydration was insufficient drinking water. In these conditions one canteen was hopelessly inadequate. Major-General David Birney, a divisional commander in the Union III Corps, later stated, "the country is barren of good water, and men would gather on the road side, lapping up like dogs anything like liquid." Stannard's nine-month men were under emphatic orders from their commander not to leave the line of march at any time to fetch water. At one brief halt in Maryland, Lieutenant Stephen F. Brown of 13th Vermont, with a soldier, collected as many empty canteens as they could carry and went to a nearby stream to fill them, only to find it guarded by a sentry. The sentry reminded the lieutenant of the general's orders but Brown ignored him, filled the canteens, left his name and returned to his grateful men. He was soon arrested and relieved of his sword. In this instance Stannard had placed the sentry because the brigade would shortly arrive at Frederick where water would be available. Brown later rejoined the 13th Vermont.

Then there was the rain; and then there was mud. While streams, wells, and rivers were life-savers in the intense heat, heavy rain turned the roads and tracks into quagmires sometimes knee deep, causing many men to lose their shoes and socks or to hang them round their necks to avoid such loss – either way hundreds of soldiers walked barefoot on the rough, stony roads. Blisters burst, feet bled and men fell out or hobbled painfully along, well behind their regiment. As depicted in the diagram on page 126, men took to walking off the road on grass or softer ground to relieve the pain. At the end of one day's march, Private R. S. Robertson wrote to his parents, "Weak, sore and worn out after a long and weary march . . . This is the hardest marching on record since the war began and we are completely used up. The sides of my feet are covered with large blisters and the soles are so sore, I can scarcely bare my weight . . ."

River crossings could be a welcome relief for filthy, aching bodies and empty canteens, but they could also be unpleasant, if not hazardous, undertakings. If no pontoon bridge had been assembled, then the troops waded across. If the bottom was treacherous or the current swift and cavalry available, then a line of horsemen would be placed in the water downstream, charged with catching any infantryman who lost his footing. If no enemy was nearby and time permitted, the first thing the men did on reaching the river was to strip and wring out such clothes as needed it, which was always trousers, drawers and socks – sometimes everything. When a regiment was over the river and moved off, it was not uncommon to see rifle-muskets used as clothes lines from which were suspended shoes, socks and perhaps a shirt. Corporal Edmund D. Patterson, 9th Alabama, did not enjoy his crossing of the Shenandoah on June 19 at Front Royal. The pontoons were still on the wagons and there was a long wait as regiments took it in turn to wade over. Patterson wrote in his journal:

> It was no pleasant task crossing the river at that time. I pulled off my boots, socks, pants and etc., thinking I might keep them a little dry, but by the time I had cut my feet on the sharp rocks, and fallen down a time or two, I regretted it. The bank on this side of the river is steep and by the time we crossed it had become perfectly slippery and I had to go up it on all "fours." Some of the boys would nearly reach the top and then an unlucky slip would send them down "sousing" into the river again. The rain poured down in torrents and the cussing of some of the boys was fearfully serious.

The crossing of the Potomac from Virginia to Maryland was a symbolic and special occasion for most Southerners. It was swollen by the recent rains when the men of McLaws' and Hood's Divisions crossed on June 26, although Thomas Wade of the 15th Georgia described it as a "little over one knee deep and 200 yards wide." Be that as it may, thousands removed their trousers, shoes, socks and underwear, tied them with their belts to their muskets and waded

The Union's "Mud March," January 20–22, 1863

Much is made of the marching difficulties due to mud (and heat) faced by both armies as they converged on Gettysburg in June 1863, but the situation was nothing compared to Major-General Burnside's infamous march at the beginning of the year. On that occasion, after the bloody repulse of his frontal attacks at Fredericksburg the previous month, Burnside decided to make a turning movement downstream in another attempt to cross the Rappahannock. However, this plan was vetoed by the President, so Burnside decided instead to outflank Lee's left by enveloping it via Banks's Ford. The movement got under way on January 20. Within two days it was abandoned due to the weather.

The army, with its great wagon trains of pontoon boats, artillery and supplies, made a good start clearing their camps and moving up the river. By mid-afternoon it was drizzling; by nightfall it was sheeting down relentlessly. It was not to stop for two days. The next day the mule-drawn wagons carrying the pontoons churned the road into a quagmire. The wagons sank to their axles; the guns sank until only their muzzles were above the mud. The exhausted horses floundered, as did the men, as each slippery step through the ooze dragged at their shoes and weighed them down. One soldier described his surroundings as "a river of mud. The roads were rivers of deep mire, and the heavy rain had made the ground a vast mortar bed." Triple teams of mules hitched to the wagons and guns failed to move them and still the rain cascaded down in torrents. On the opposite bank, watching Confederate pickets were highly amused by their enemy's struggles. Large signs were erected at the river's edge reading "This way to Richmond" and "Burnside's Army Stuck in the Mud." By noon on the 22nd Burnside admitted defeat and ordered his soldiers back to their camps.

over whooping and yelling like schoolchildren. On the south bank, while waiting to cross, whole regiments sang "All Quiet Along the Potomac Tonight." On the north bank bands welcomed the men by thumping out "Maryland, My Maryland" over and over again, while a crowd of curious onlookers from Williamsport, including a number of young ladies, assembled to see the fun. The sight of so many semi-naked men would surely not be forgotten.

Stannard's Union brigade crossed the Potomac dry-shod over the pontoon bridge at Edward's Ferry on June 27, but when it arrived at the Monocacy River it was found to be muddy, fast flowing and without a bridge. One incident that caused considerable mirth among the men of the 13th Vermont was watching the commander of Company A get a ducking. An Irishman from County Tipperary, Captain John Lonergan slipped in mid-stream and went under. On scrambling ashore to the laughter of his men he remarked, "Too much liquid on the outside, and not enough on the inside, or it would never have happened."

Marching Rations

Most men were issued with three days' "marching rations" at the start of a march, with the expectation, seldom realized, that these would be replenished from the supply trains thereafter. The Union ration consisted of one pound of hard bread or cracker (hardtack), threequarters of a pound of salt pork, $1^1/_2$ pounds of fresh meat (from the slaughter of cattle on the hoof), sugar, coffee and salt. All this was stowed in the haversack, which meant it was often soaked, although this had little effect if the cracker was old and rock hard. Hardtack (Union regiments usually issued nine or ten per man) was a flour-and-water biscuit or cracker that had a reasonable flavor when fresh, but if stored for many years would become like granite. It was variously called "tooth-dullers," "worm castles," or "sheet-iron crackers." The requirement for recruits to have good front teeth was to ensure they could bite the paper cartridge, but they also needed strong molars to cope with hardtack past its prime. One soldier told a splendid story of a mule munching on hardtack. The mule, he wrote:

> received it joyously, and set to work; he worked away at it for a while on one side of his mouth, then deftly transferred it to the other side and tried again. A kind of worried look came into his eyes, and finally, laying his ears well back on his head, he made a determined effort to crush it, but finding all his efforts useless, he dropped it on the ground and paid no further attention to it.

Hardtack could be eaten plain, toasted over a fire, crumbled into a soup or – and this was thought the best way – crumbled and fried with pork or bacon fat to make a dish called "skillygalee."

The Rebel soldier's diet was somewhat different and often less in quantity than that of his Yankee counterpart. The average Confederate subsisted on bacon, cornmeal, molasses, peas, vegetables, rice, usually a coffee substitute, and tobacco. One of the principal reasons for invading the North was so that the Confederates could have access to the rich farming countryside of Maryland and Pennsylvania. Virginia had become an empty breadbasket and Lee intended to ease the burden by supplying his army through foraging and requisitioning; both of these are discussed in greater detail in Section Five: Other Arms and Services. Many in Lee's army wrote home of the lush pastures, tidy fields, fat cattle and large barns of the Northern states. One soldier put his opinion neatly when he wrote, "they has [some] of the finest land in the world and some of the ugliest women I ever saw." Another agreed with him, remarking, "I have not seen a really pretty girl since I have been in Penn." Foraging, which could very often merge into pilfering, was an overriding feature of the Confederate march north. Most Rebels regarded ruthless foraging as a legitimate payback for the previous poor behavior of the Yankees in Virginia. Lee, however, was determined to prevent, or at least curtail, looting and issued two General Orders to that effect. The first, dated June 21, stressed on pain of punishment that requisitioning was authorized only by the "chiefs of the commissary, quartermaster, ordnance and medical departments of the army." Payments had to be made in Confederate currency (which was worthless to Northerners) or receipts issued. The second, six days later at Chambersburg, indicated that Lee, although expressing general satisfaction with the conduct of his troops, was aware that lapses were occurring. The relevant paragraph reads:

> The commanding general therefore earnestly exhorts the troops to abstain with most scrupulous care from unnecessary or wanton injury to private property, and he enjoins upon all officers to arrest and bring to summary punishment all who shall in any way offend against the orders on this subject.

When Major-General Pender's Division encamped near Fayetteville on June 28 guards were positioned around the town to prevent looting. Nevertheless, in countryside where there seemed "enough

Brigadier-General Wadsworth's "Bull Train"

Not long after the "Mud March," Wadsworth, commanding the 1st Division, I Corps, had the idea of supplementing the capacity of the wagon trains by making use of the numerous carts and antiquated wagons that the army acquired with the daily delivery of escaping slaves. Wadsworth's idea was to form them into a special supply train, to be drawn by steers selected from the corps' cattle herds and broken in for the purpose. The intention was to load the carts with rations, send them forward to the troops, issue the rations, then slaughter the oxen for fresh meat and break up the carts for wood for the cooking fires – seemingly a highly practical idea. A Captain Ford was put in charge of the project and worked all winter adapting the wagons and breaking in the steers to yokes and draft. Feeding the steers unsoaked hardtack caused a number to swell up and die, but the captain persevered and by the time Chancellorsville was fought the "Bull Train," as it was called, was supposedly ready, although it remained in camp for that battle.

When the Union Army embarked on its march to Gettysburg, Captain Ford's train started off at the rear of I Corps' wagon train. What had not been thought through was the fact that wagons drawn by mules or horses easily outpaced the plodding oxen and so an ever-widening gap opened up between the proper wagon train and the "Bull Train." Despite the yelling and lashing of the drivers, by the end of the first day Captain Ford's train had dropped back 3 miles, making it highly vulnerable to Confederate raiders. Matters did not improve, and before the Potomac was reached the supplies had been redistributed and the steers had rejoined the herd – the general's scheme had failed.

The 19th Virginia Infantry Regiment on the March to Gettysburg

This diagram shows the regiment in a likely order of march, with the colonel, lieutenant-colonel and adjutant leading. Pioneers might have been in front to clear obstacles, with a regimental band had the regiment possessed one. Company commanders led their companies, with the other officers and most sergeants at the rear. At the rear of the regiment came the field officer, sergeant-major, the surgeon and his assistant, and, if present, the chaplain. Finally, almost certainly, at least one pack mule led by a slave. Note the men are no longer in parade-ground four-abreast formation but mostly walking individually, with a number (probably those without shoes) at the side of the road on the grass or easier ground away from the mud.

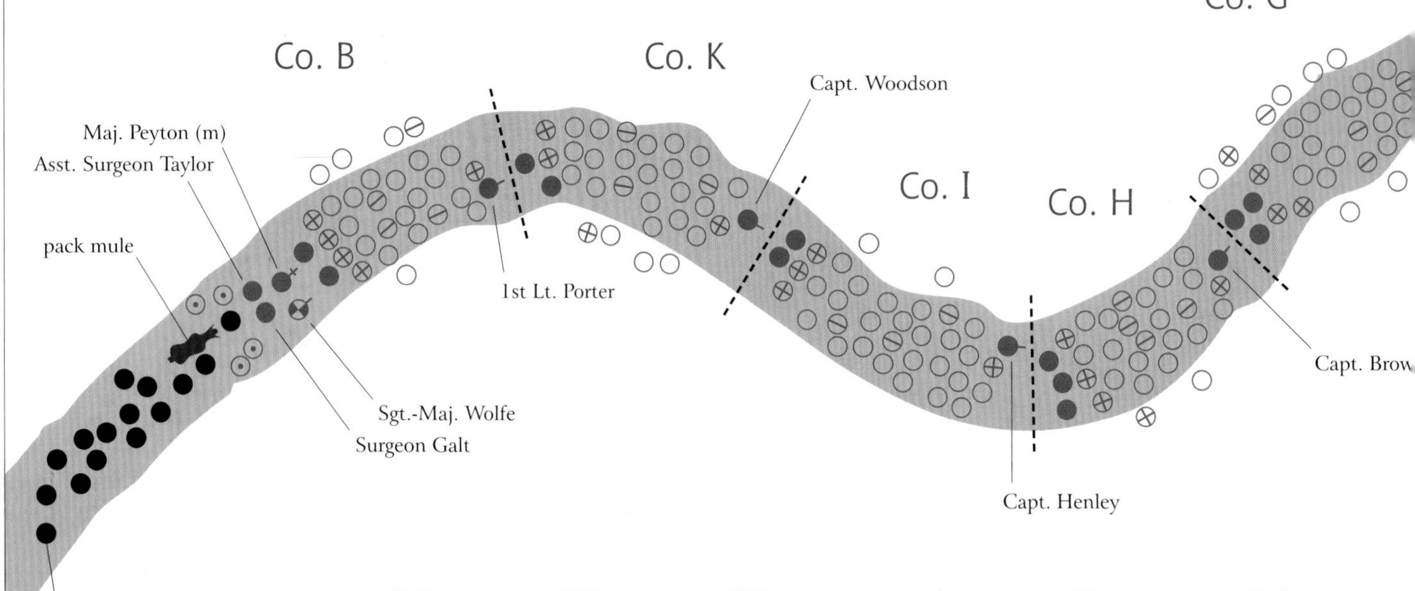

Trailing behind most Confederate regiments was a group of slaves – some of whom escaped after the battle. They were mostly officers' servants. Also at the rear were several men of the Ambulance Corps carrying a medical haversack and one or two stretchers.

The regimental wagons (at least six, probably more) were not on the line of march with the regiment. Under the regimental quartermaster, along with the wagonmaster and teamsters, they were grouped to form a baggage train that followed the division under the orders of the divisional quartermaster. Each wagon could carry up to 3,000 pounds at about 2.5 miles an hour on a reasonable road. These wagons contained forage for the six mules, cooking utensils for the soldiers, hospital stores and some officers' baggage. Confederate wagons were often captured U.S. Army wagons with "U.S." still painted on the sides. They were supplemented by all forms of carriages and carts requisitioned as necessary.

wheat to supply the world," it could not be stopped entirely. Horses were collected by the score, while many of the surly "Dutch" inhabitants seemed only too happy to hand over goods free out of fear – as a soldier in Brigadier-General Lane's Brigade put it, "they know how their soldiers have behaved in Virginia and they fear that ours will retaliate." Private William Daniel, 2nd South Carolina Infantry, expressed himself well satisfied with what the countryside provided – one way or another – "our men feasted themselves on cherries of which the country affords the greatest abundance, mutton, chickens, turkeys, &." Rachel Cormany, resident of Chambersburg, watched as Confederates poured through the town on June 27. She was not impressed:

> While I am writing thousands are passing – such a rough dirty ragged rowdyish set one does not often see . . . Many have chickens as they pass – There a number are going with honey – robbed some man of it no doubt – they are even carrying it in buckets . . . they are poorly clad – many have no shoes on. As they pass along they take the hats off our citizens heads and throw their old ones in exchange.

Union regiments marching north experienced food shortages as their rations ran out and their supply wagons failed to catch up. Although short on pork and beans, the average soldier had plenty of U.S. dollars in his pockets with which to purchase food if the generosity of the inhabitants was insufficient. In most towns, Union soldiers were welcomed warmly as saviors and considerable amounts of milk, butter, cookies, fresh bread as well as cooked meals were handed out as the troops marched passed. Nevertheless, a number of the townsfolk were not above making a dollar or two and most Yankees were willing to part with their money, often at well above the going rate, in exchange for a full stomach.

An instance when the welcome by the local populace got out of hand occurred in Frederick on June 28, the day Hooker was replaced by Meade. Large numbers of Union troops, feeling entitled to some rest and recuperation, descended on the town. The

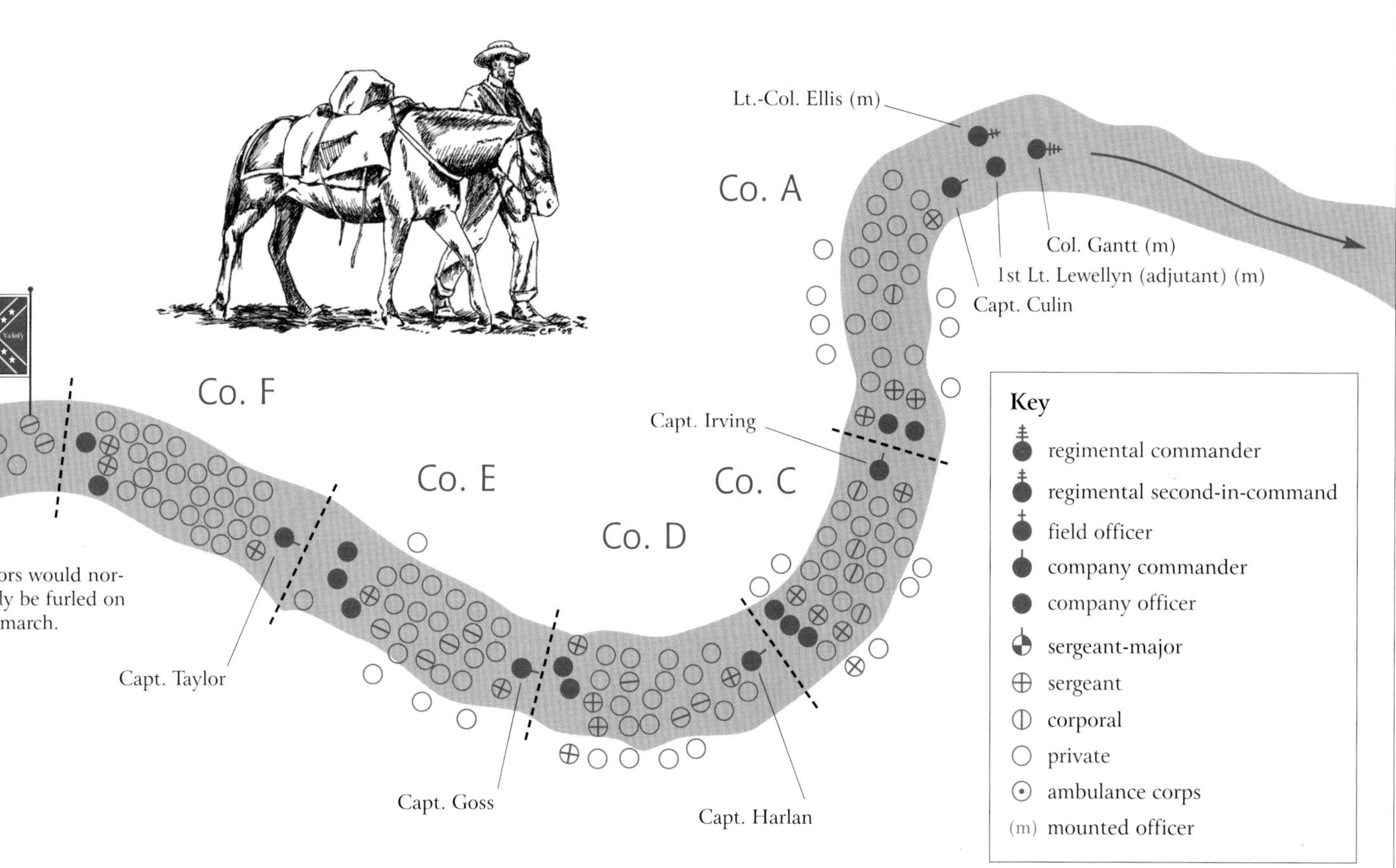

Notes

• This regiment was part of Brig.-Gen. Garnett's Brigade, in Pickett's Division, which had not seen action since Sharpsburg the previous September. This was to change dramatically at Gettysburg, as its only role in the battle was to take part in Pickett's famous charge on July 3. The 19th Virginia began the advance with 328 all ranks and came back having suffered almost half that number in casualties, including 21 out of 38 officers.

• The serious marching for the regiment took place over 10 days – June 16–27, with two rest days (22nd and 23rd) – when it marched from near Culpeper Court House to Chambersburg, a marching distance of 130 miles. The march was conducted in extreme heat alternating with heavy rain and muddy roads. To the casual observer the regiment did not look impressive, as many men were without shoes or blankets, wearing threadbare jackets and patched pantaloons. Despite strict orders to the contrary, there was some pillaging, with "an abnormal amount of chickens and fresh meat being cooked around campfires at night." Memories of the march included raging thirsts, caused by the soaring temperature on the 22-mile march on June 17 which saw many men dropping out, and at every stream soldiers jostling and scrambling for water "like a flock of sheep, frightened and confused." On June 20 a number of men were swept away during the crossing of the swollen Shenandoah River. Five days later, after wading the Potomac, Garnett's Brigade formed three sides of a square to watch the execution of Private John Riley who had accepted money as a substitute, deserted and repeated the process three times (see box, page 33).

bars were opened, rye whisky flowed, the provost lacked the means (mounted troops) or will to take action and the good citizens of Frederick encouraged the merrymaking. Corporal Joseph Lumbard, 147th Pennsylvania, noted, "A short distance North of Frederick we passed a very large brewery, a detail of men had taken out the liquor and emptied the casks in the streets [to destroy it], and whilst passing this place a number of the boys got down on their knees and drank up the beer out of the gutters." The ensuing intoxicated chaos in Frederick was inevitable. According to the *Boston Morning Journal* of July 4, hundreds of men were "lying about the streets, on the door steps, under fences, in the mud, dead drunk . . ." Major-General Slocum (XII Corps) sent Meade a dispatch stating that when he left the town there were "a great number of men from every corps lying about the streets beastly drunk." Meade reacted immediately, ordering the commander of the 2nd Pennsylvania Cavalry to assist the provost marshal in cleaning the place up.

Similar scenes had occurred in Williamsport, 25 miles to the west, when Hood's Division of Rebels marched through two days earlier and "liberated" whiskey was handed out. The barrels were placed beside the road, tops removed, and men dipped their cups in as they passed. John Stevens, 5th Texas (Hood's Division), recorded the effect of these generous helpings of raw spirit:

> there were more drunk men . . . than I think I ever saw in my life . . . some cried some hooped and yelled. Some cussed and swore, others ripped and tore . . . It kept us sober boys busy to keep the drunk ones from killing each other. Some soon fell by the wayside helpless . . . Some others were not seen for 15 hours afterwards and when they caught up with their commands, they were quite sober but their eyes looked like burnt holes in a blanket.

Coffee

Then, as now, few Americans can survive long without coffee. The addiction in fact originated in the Civil War. During the war by far the most important staple on soldiers' minds became the acquisition of coffee. Men fought for it, traded for it, and looted it off the dead, wounded or prisoners. The beans were pounded between rocks or crushed with the butts of rifles to obtain the grounds for a strong brew. Most Union troops were reasonably well supplied with coffee, the official ration being 28 pounds per soldier per year, whereas the Confederates seldom managed to issue their ration of 21 pounds per man. The Rebels were therefore frequently forced to improvise with substitutes made from peanuts, potatoes, parched corn or rye, peas or chicory. It is claimed that Colonel Alexander, Longstreet's acting artillery chief, downed a mug of sweet-potato coffee just prior to ordering the start of the barrage that prepared the way for Pickett's charge. John D. Billings, the former Union artilleryman, recalled, "What a Godsend it seemed to us at times! How often after being completely jaded by a night march . . . have I had a wash, if there was water to be had, made and drunk my pint or so of coffee and felt as fresh and invigorated as if just risen from a night's sound sleep!" It was quite common on an exhausting march for men to fall out for a "brew" and then, refreshed, set out to rejoin the regiment. The term "coffee cooler" meant a coward or shirker – a man who stayed behind his advancing unit until his coffee had cooled enough to drink. A Confederate was not above throwing his tobacco ration at a Union picket in the hope of getting coffee in exchange. After a suitable pause a packet of coffee beans would usually come arching back.

To understand how precious was the coffee (and sugar) ration to the soldiers, one can do no better than quoting Billings' description of the distribution system within a company on active service:

It was usually brought into camp in an oatmeal sack; a regimental quartermaster receiving and apportioning [it] among the ten companies . . . Then the orderly sergeant . . . must devote himself to dividing it. One method . . . was to spread a rubber blanket on the ground, – more than one if the company was large, – and upon it were put as many piles of coffee as there were men to receive rations; and the care taken to make the piles of the same size to the eye, to keep the men from growling, would remind one of a country physician making his powders, taking a little from one pile and adding it to another. The sugar that always accompanied the coffee was spooned out at the same time on another blanket. When both were ready they were given out, each man taking a pile . . .

The manner in which each man disposed of his coffee and sugar ration after receiving it is worth noting. Every soldier of a month's experience in campaigning was provided with some sort of bag into which he spooned his coffee; but the kind of bag he used indicated pretty accurately . . . the length of time he had been in service . . . a raw recruit . . . would take it up in a paper, and stow it away in that well known receptacle of all eatables, the soldier's haversack, only to find it a part of a general mixture of hardtack, salt pork, pepper, salt, knife, fork, spoon, sugar and coffee by the time the next halt was made . . . But your old veteran . . . took out an oblong plain cloth bag, which looked as immaculate as the every day shirt of a coal-heaver, and into it scooped without ceremony both his sugar and coffee, and stirred them thoroughly together.

March Discipline

As noted above, there were numerous incidents of straggling in both armies, caused by lack of shoes and crippled feet, exhaustion and heatstroke, foraging and pilfering, drunkenness and outright desertion. Many units fought at Gettysburg at much below their strength at the start of the march north. This was because the engaged strength – the actual infantry fighting strength – was reduced not only by straggling, sickness and desertion en route but also by the detachment of men to the artillery, to various administrative duties at headquarters, or to the trains – including complete regiments being detailed as train guards. An example of this is Stannard's five-regiment brigade, which started out around 3,400 strong but went into action with 1,950 due to two regiments guarding trains (about 1,200 men) and another 250 lost to various causes on the march or to duties other than fighting.

March discipline was not all that it should have been in many units. While the Union regiments were marching in their own territory, and often enthusiastically welcomed, so their behavior toward private property and local inhabitants was generally good – except when drunk. The same cannot always be said of the Confederates. The problem was that Union soldiers had seriously misbehaved while campaigning in the South and now the Rebels were in enemy territory many men felt entitled to behave likewise, particularly as they were marching through a land of plenty. Lee's General Orders to curb ill-discipline were not strictly enforced in some regiments. While senior officers (majors and above) tended to do their best to maintain march discipline, the company officers, who were much closer to their men, tended to turn a blind eye to what was going on.

Apart from the unit's officers, march discipline was also one of the responsibilities of the provost guard, who were charged with sweeping up stragglers and making arrests as necessary. Meade's provost guard was under the Provost Marshal General, Brigadier-General Marsena R. Patrick, who had around 1,500 men to police the march of over 100,000 men scattered across a considerable area; of these 1,500, fewer than half (about 700) were mounted (2nd Pennsylvania Cavalry, two companies of the 6th Pennsylvania Cavalry, and a small detachment of the Oneida New York Cavalry). There was no equivalent, formalized post of provost marshal in the Army of Northern Virginia. In Lee's headquarters provost matters were part of the Inspector General Colonel Robert H. Chilton's brief. In the past the practice had been for a senior commander to be appointed provost marshal for the campaign in addition to his command functions, an example being Brigadier-General Lewis Armistead during the Antietam operations. Alternatively, it could be left for divisional commanders to appoint from their staff on an ad hoc basis officers specifically responsible for preventing straggling and for guarding prisoners. However, from June 4, 1863 the provost guard for Lee's army was the five companies of the 1st Virginia Battalion (Irish Battalion) under Major David B. Bridgeford. Not only was this hopelessly inadequate for the tasks involved, but it was an infantry unit and thus quite incapable of policing a long march. Additionally, during the Gettysburg campaign four companies of this battalion were left at Winchester, with the fifth stationed at Gordonsville. Confederate march discipline was entirely in the hands of regimental and brigade commanders.

Lack of a provost guard, sympathetic company officers, and marching through a rich, hostile countryside combined to ensure looting and pilfering were far more prevalent offenses in the Army of Northern Virginia than in the Army of the Potomac. As a soldier from the 3rd Carolina put it: "The officers in command issued some very stringent orders with reference to the destruction of private property, but the soldiers paid no more attention to them than they would to the cries of a screech owl." Major-General Hood's Texans were renowned for their liking of liquor and general light-fingeredness. As Lee once said, "Ah, General Hood, when you Texans come about the chickens have to roost mighty high." After crossing the Potomac a quarter of a pint of celebratory whiskey was issued to Hood's men and the effect, combined with deep mud, was unstoppable straggling the following day. Although a trifle exaggerated, the situation was neatly described by a soldier who commented later that they had marched in three states, and some in four – the states of Virginia, Maryland and Pennsylvania, and a large number in the state of intoxication. Those units marching toward the rear of the army did not fare so well, as the men ahead did a good job of eating up everything in sight and "leaving only enough food to eat one good meal a day." This is not surprising, if there is truth in the comment of a soldier who maintained that, "Last night Wofford's brigade of this division [McLaws'] stole so much that they could not carry the rations they drew."

While some units had a poor reputation for straggling and stealing, others made stringent efforts to maintain discipline and punish those caught out. Brigadier-General Armistead enforced a tough, no-nonsense regime, as did Major-General Early, who caught four men pilfering near York and had them tied together and marched around, preceded by a band playing the Rogue's March and carrying a banner with the words, "These men have disgraced themselves by pillaging women's gardens and henhouses." A soldier in Brigadier Anderson's Brigade caught stealing a chicken was forced to march 2 miles carrying a heavy pole across his shoulders.

INFANTRY TACTICS AT GETTYSBURG

Tactics are all about the various techniques, methods and ruses used in attacking or defending against an enemy. No battle can be won decisively unless one side or the other attacks. A good defense can prevent defeat, throwing back an enemy assault, but unless the defender resorts to an attack at some stage the result of the battle will be indecisive. Such was Gettysburg in its tactical sense. If an attack is to achieve lasting or decisive results it has to be physical. Fire alone never won great victories. Infantry must physically drive an enemy from his ground, occupy his position and repel any counterattacks. This often involves an infantry bayonet charge, not that bayonets often cross – they seldom do – but at some stage, to succeed, attacking infantry must rush forward to close with the defenders. At Gettysburg the Confederates took the role of attacker. Throughout the first three days of July, Lee's men made attack after attack, which on the first day eventually succeeded in pushing Meade's leading formations back but failed to achieve lasting results on the remaining two.

To the attacker go several advantages. He can chose where and when to attack – he holds the initiative. He can concentrate his attack in terms of numbers opposite what he considers the enemy's weak point or points. To give his attack the maximum chances of succeeding, it should come as a surprise to the defender. Stonewall Jackson's favorite military dictum was "mystify, mislead and surprise" – the first two resulting in the third. Surprise can come in many forms. The attack may be in overwhelming numbers, at an unexpected place, from an unexpected direction, at an unexpected time, under cover of darkness, or be mounted unexpectedly quickly. The more of these factors that the attacker combines in his assault, the more assured success becomes. According to military theory, an attacker should endeavor to assemble at least a 2:1, preferably 3:1, superiority over the defender at the point chosen to attack. This concentration includes both manpower (infantry) and firepower (artillery). This is all theory, easy to describe but extraordinarily difficult to put into practice on a battlefield, but nevertheless is the ideal for which to strive.

For Lee at Gettysburg it is probably fair to say that in all his attacks of brigade strength or over he never achieved real surprise. On July 1 he achieved numerical superiority and so drove the Yankees back, but there was little in the way of surprise. On the following day he again outnumbered the Union troops of III Corps in Sickles' salient, but not dramatically so, and reserves were close at hand, so without surprise only a push back was achieved. On July 3, with Pickett's charge, not only was there no surprise but also he never seriously outnumbered his opponents along Cemetery Ridge in either infantry or artillery. The result was failure. Of course countless

Cherry-picking

One item of food was available in abundance along the line of march – cherries. It was the time of year when cherry trees were laden with ripe fruit. An article in *The Gettysburg Magazine*, issue 31, by Thomas L. Elmore contains a graphic account of cherry-picking at its best:

> Individuals and even entire units could not resist the delicious temptation. One unit commander gave the necessary orders, "Halt, stack arms, cherry trees, charge!" and hundreds of soldiers ran to the trees and began climbing. "It was impossible to keep the men from breaking the small limbs and picking cherries as they marched," wrote another officer, although some citizens requested and received a guard to protect their fruit. A South Carolina veteran was so impressed that he sent back samples: "I send you some cherry seed which you must plant. The fruit is the large white cherry, as large, if not larger, than a partridge egg." While the loss of cherries would not ruin a farmer, family members could still become enraged when faced with the loss. In one case two women ran out of a house to berate a soldier in unintelligible German, but their cause was ultimately hopeless, or in this case fruitless, judging from the exuberant reaction of the men when encountering those luscious cherries.

The Company Fund Fiddle

When Union troops were on operations for extended periods they could not be issued with their full camp ration entitlement – rice, beans, candles, soap, potatoes, vegetables, etc.; they had to exist on marching rations. The unissued rations then reverted to the government and the soldiers lost out. However, there was such a thing as a Company Fund controlled by each company's commander. It was within the regulations for the company commander to receive the cash equivalent of these missing rations from the brigade commissary, with the expectation it would be passed on to the soldiers. It had to be claimed from the commissary with all the correct forms, which most company commanders had neither the time nor inclination to be bothered with. Nevertheless, many officers did claim the money but conveniently forgot to pay it out.

other factors went into why things turned out as they did, but in very simplistic terms Lee failed to combine superior numbers with surprise. Big battalions can win on their own, though they must be very big; even with small numbers surprise can be decisive (as at Chancellorsville); but to be sure of lasting, overwhelming success the two need to come together.

For a defender it is all about selecting suitable ground for the defense – a position that offers secure flanks, obstacles to an attacker but few concealed approaches, ground behind which your troops can get shelter and concealment, and behind which reserves can be positioned so they can quickly reach a threatened area. If an attacker knows your position in general terms but cannot locate where your position is weakly held, cannot see all your deployment and does not know whether you have strong reserves or where they are, it becomes much more difficult for him to achieve surprise. If the defender can ascertain where the main attack is to be made and can reinforce that area, then he is five-tenths of the way to defeating it. Again in simplistic terms, this is what Meade was able to do on July 2 and 3. He had an excellent defensive position on a low ridge with flanks anchored on hills; he concealed his reserves and was able to rush them to the threatened spot – the Sickles' salient on the 2nd and the center of Cemetery Ridge on the 3rd. His handling of the defense was skilful but it was not enough to crush Lee. To do that he needed to do more than launch local, smallscale counterattacks (several such regimental attacks succeeded): he needed to switch his entire army from defensive to offensive mode.

Basic Formations

Line

Most of the actual fighting at Gettysburg, whether offensive or defensive, was with the unit or formation deployed in a line. In attack it provided a less vulnerable target to all types of fire than a closely formed column and it could, if necessary, quickly produce a good volume of fire to the front. Within regiments, companies formed in two ranks (see diagram below) with the colors in the center and supernumerary officers and sergeants at the rear to keep the men moving and prevent skulking. Brigades and divisions could also advance in lines. These could be a single long line (see diagram below), or there could be one or two regiments or brigades following behind the leading line as supports. When Hood's Division formed up to attack the Union left on July 2 it had two brigades, each with its regiments in line, in the first wave, with two brigades similarly formed to follow in a second wave – see the diagram opposite. Later the same day another Confederate division, Anderson's, deployed for its attack with all five of its brigades in line (see diagram opposite below); it stretched for over a mile. Union defenders also invariably fought in lines, with regiment after regiment, brigade after brigade fighting alongside each other. The line lends itself to defending linear obstacles or boundaries such as fences, walls, roads, streams, barricades and edges of woods. From Culp's Hill along Cemetery Ridge to Little Round Top or along the Emmitsburg Road, Union units not in reserve deployed in lines to facilitate the maximum volume of fire at an advancing enemy.

Line Formations

A regiment in line

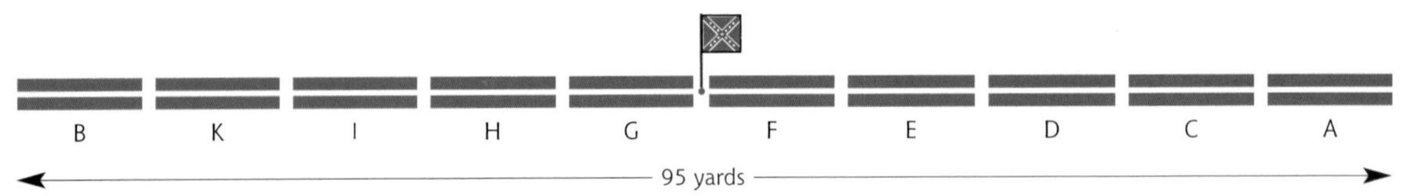

19th Virginia Infantry Regiment

Notes

- By far the most common formation when advancing to attack, or defending a linear obstacle such as a wall or fence line.
- Companies are formed up side by side in two ranks with supernumary officers and N.C.O.s in a third rear rank. The color party is in the center.
- The diagram shows the 19th Virginia Infantry Regiment formed up ready to take part in Pickett's charge on July 3. A detailed diagram of this regiment is on pages 90–91.

A brigade in line

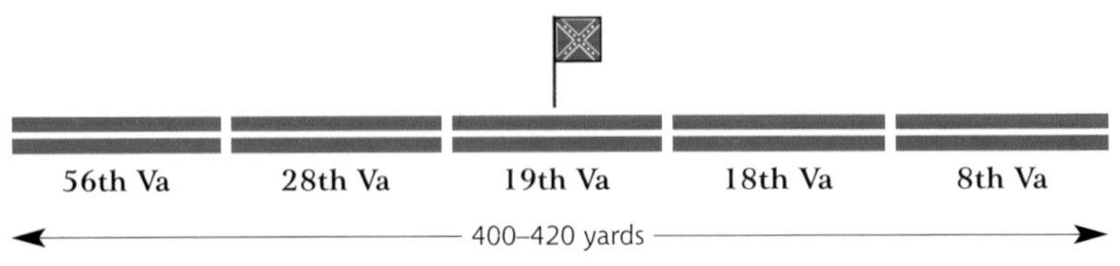

Garnett's Brigade

Notes

- This formation with all regiments in one line was frequently adopted at Gettysburg by a brigade leading an attack by a division. It was quite slow moving and difficult to control, particularly if obstacles had to be crossed. Halts were sometimes needed to maintain and adjust alignment.
- The diagram shows Brig.-Gen. Garnett's Brigade formed up as the left forward brigade of Pickett's Division prior to its advance on July 3.

Line Formations

A divisional deployment for an attack in two lines or waves

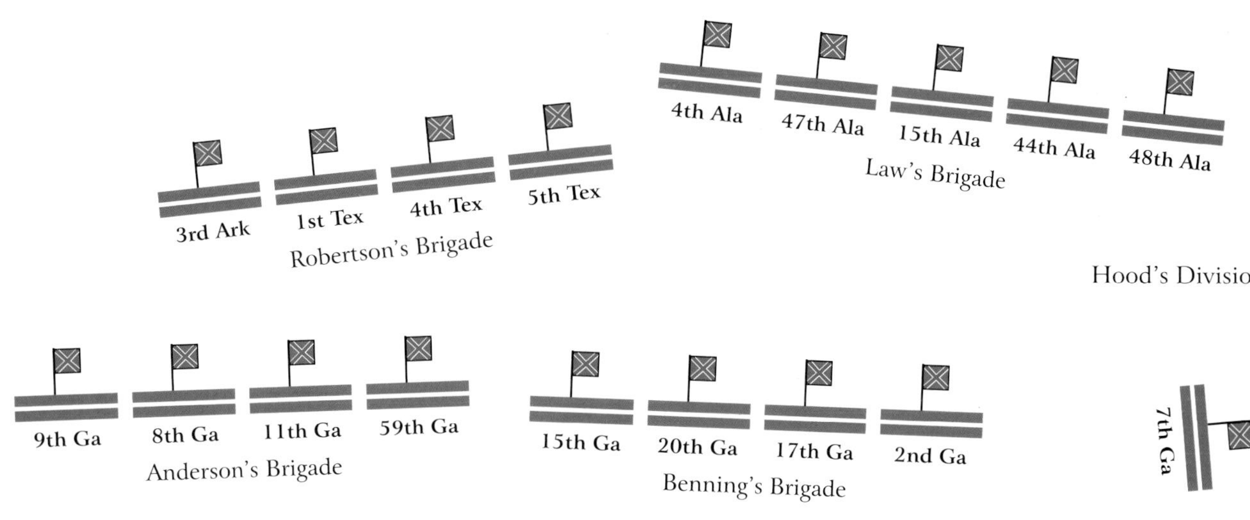

Notes

• This shows a division deployed to advance in two lines each of two brigades. Each brigade is in line, as is every regiment in the brigades. The object of the second wave is to follow up the first, support it, reinforce it, or push through it to continue the attack. The 7th Georgia in this instance has been detached from Anderson's Brigade and placed on the flank across the Emmitsburg Road.

• The diagram depicts Maj.-Gen. Hood's Division deployed on the south end of Seminary Ridge prior to attacking Devil's Den and the Round Tops. In this case the brigades are not exactly aligned, as they conformed with stone walls along the edge of Biesecker's Wood on Warfield Ridge.

A division deployed in single line

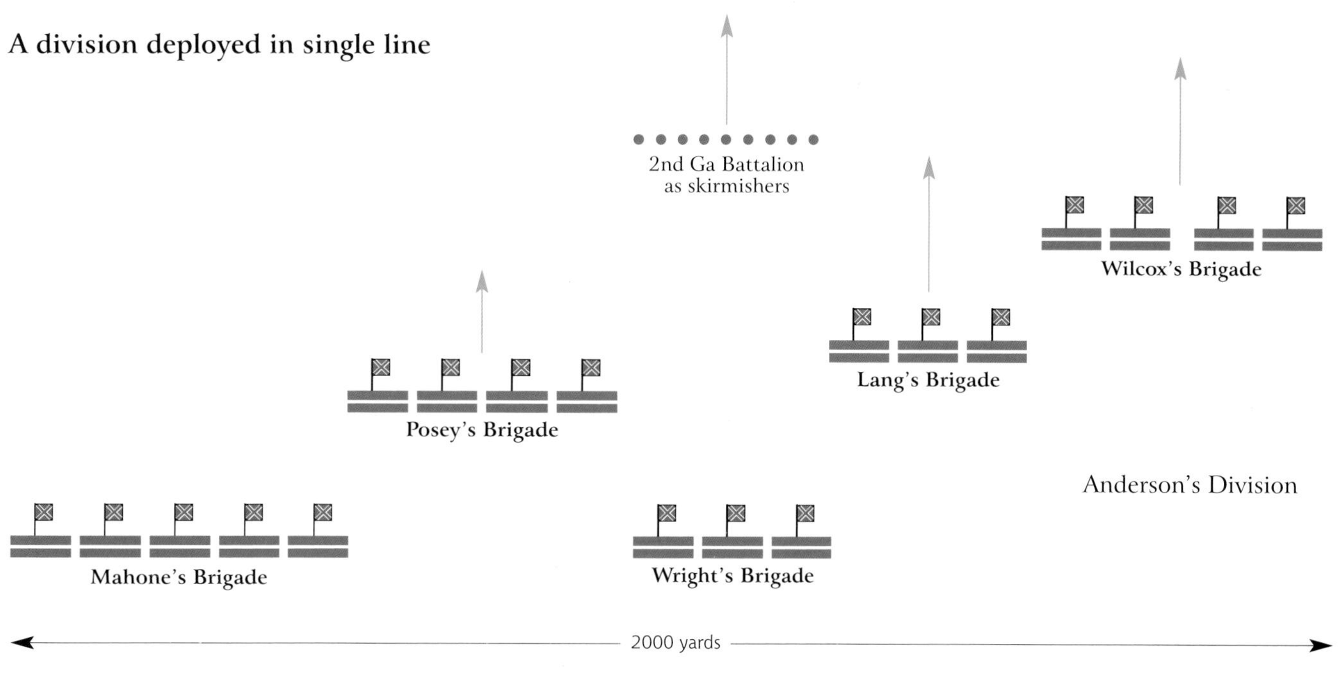

Notes

• It was possible, as this diagram shows, to launch a divisional attack with all five brigades in line and with no supporting or follow-up waves. In this case Maj.-Gen. Richard Anderson's Division of over 7,000 men was spread over a frontage of more than a mile. With regiments in two ranks, it meant about one man every 1.5 yards – a very thin line. The irregular line was due to brigades conforming to terrain features – mostly the edges of woods.

• In the event, the attack took place late on July 2 and developed into more of an attack in echelon from the right with the left brigade, Mahone's, never advancing at all.

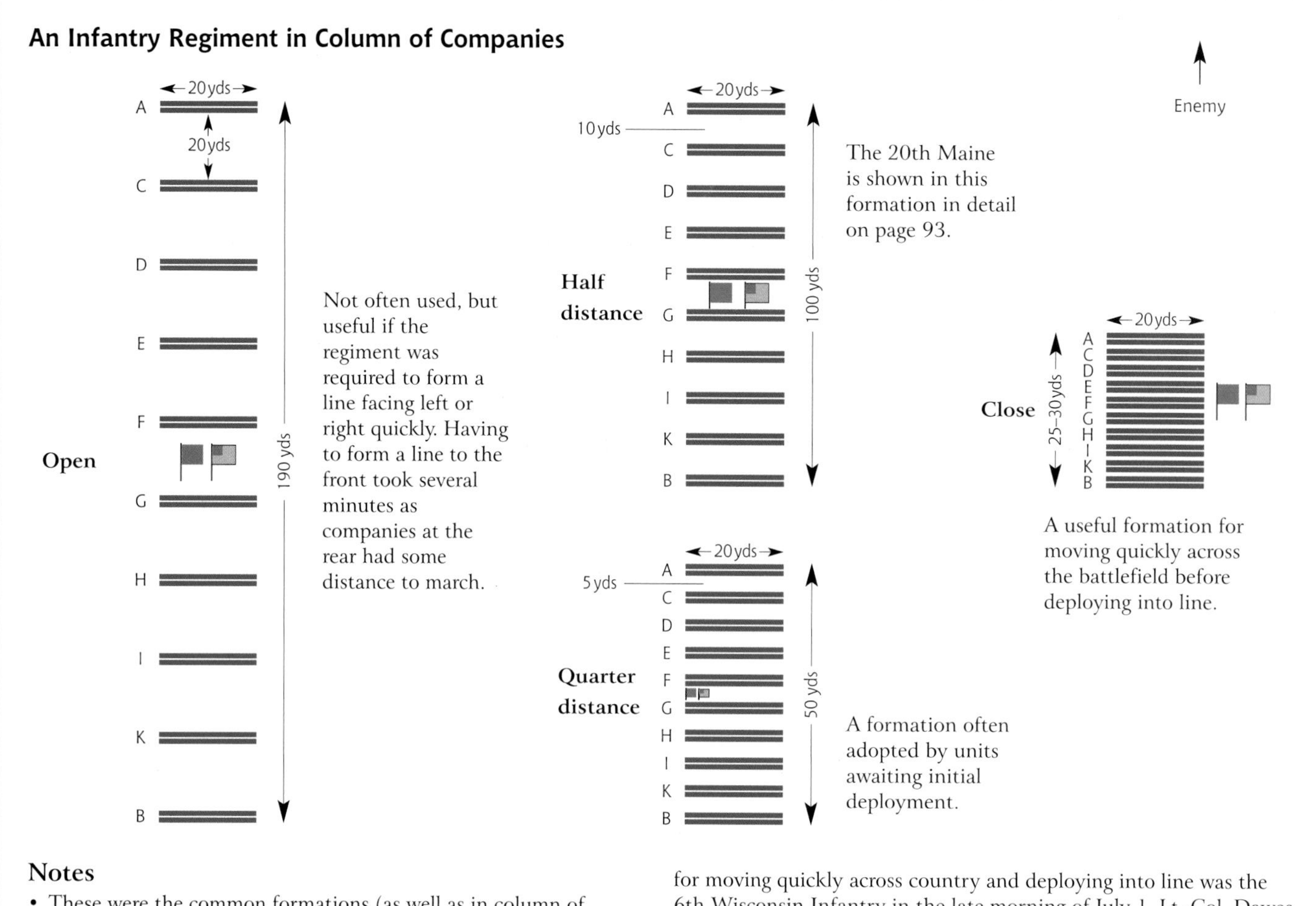
An Infantry Regiment in Column of Companies
Enemy
Open
20yds
20yds
A
C
D
E
F
G
H
I
K
B
190 yds
Not often used, but useful if the regiment was required to form a line facing left or right quickly. Having to form a line to the front took several minutes as companies at the rear had some distance to march.
Half distance
10yds
20yds
100 yds
The 20th Maine is shown in this formation in detail on page 93.
Quarter distance
5yds
20yds
50 yds
A formation often adopted by units awaiting initial deployment.
Close
20yds
25–30yds
A useful formation for moving quickly across the battlefield before deploying into line.

Notes

- These were the common formations (as well as in column of divisions) adopted by units when maneuvering around the battlefield, as they were easily controlled, comparatively fast moving and less subject to disruption by obstacles.
- A good example of the use of the close or quarter-distance column for moving quickly across country and deploying into line was the 6th Wisconsin Infantry in the late morning of July 1. Lt.-Col. Dawes double-quicked his regiment in column of companies from west of the Lutheran Seminary to the Chambersburg Pike, where he deployed into line along the road to help throw back a successful Confederate attack.

Columns

The simplest column was the column of route, or marching column, used to move troops as quickly as possible from A to B. If an enemy appeared to its front it could take a while for this type of column to deploy forward into line, although it could instantly turn left or right into line. This was the formation in which both armies marched to Gettysburg, where an example of its use was Vincent's Union Brigade on July 2, which was detached from its division and double-quicked in column of fours to Little Round Top.

A regiment in column of companies had each company in line in two ranks formed up one behind the other. The distance between the companies varied from open (the distance being the same as the company frontage) to close (every company almost treading on the heels of the one in front) – see diagram above. These columns were seldom used for fighting as they could generate very little fire to the front. They were, however, comparatively easy to control and allowed for much quicker movement around the battlefield. We see them used mostly by Union forces at Gettysburg in getting into position, in shifting reserves behind the main firing line or just waiting in reserve to be given their task.

Another variation was the column of divisions. This does not mean a huge column with divisions one behind another, but the grouping of two companies within a regiment and calling them divisions – a regiment thus having five divisions (see diagram of the 19th Virginia Infantry Regiment, pages 90–91). A brigade could be formed in line, with each regiment side by side but with all the regiments in divisional columns. This is how Colonel Kryzanowski's Brigade waited in reserve just north of Gettysburg on the afternoon of July 1 (opposite above). Such a formation is a mass of men and an attractive target for guns, as Kryzanowski's soldiers discovered.

Changing formation

Tactical maneuvers were based on General Winfield Scott's *Infantry Tactics or Rules for the Exercise and Manoeuvres of the United States Infantry*, issued in 1835. The book was a translation of a French manual based on Napoleonic drills and tactics and its general structure remained the basis for all Civil War manuals. Officers, N.C.O.s and soldiers had to know their drill, which meant the differing formations, when best to use them and how to change from one to another without generating chaos. Most changes of formation involved getting from one type of column to line, or vice versa, to meet changing terrain or tactical circumstances. The diagram opposite gives two simple examples – changing from marching column, via column of companies, to line facing the same direction, and just one way of changing from marching column straight to line, also facing the same direction.

A Brigade Deployed in Line with Regiments in Double Column of Companies (or Divisional Columns)

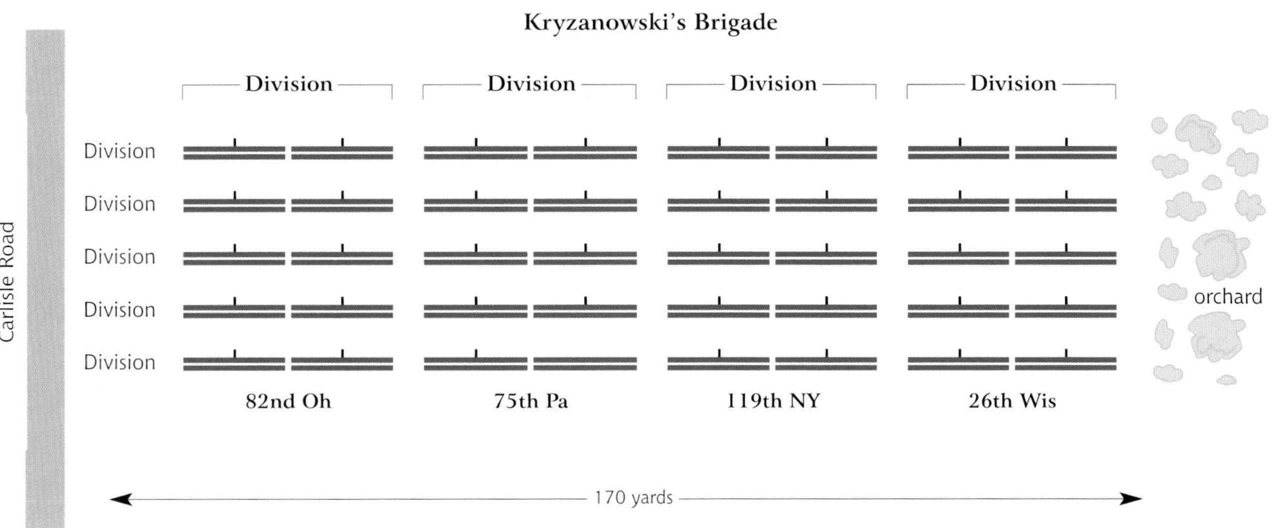

Notes

- The 58th NY were on detached duties until late afternoon July 1.
- This diagram shows a brigade of some 1,400 men formed up in a solid mass formation in reserve awaiting a decision on deployment. Each regiment is in double column of companies. This was the formation adopted by this brigade in reserve just north of Gettysburg during the afternoon of July 1. In this position they received some losses from Confederate guns on Oak Hill. They eventually moved forward, initially in this formation.

Examples of a Regiment Changing Formation

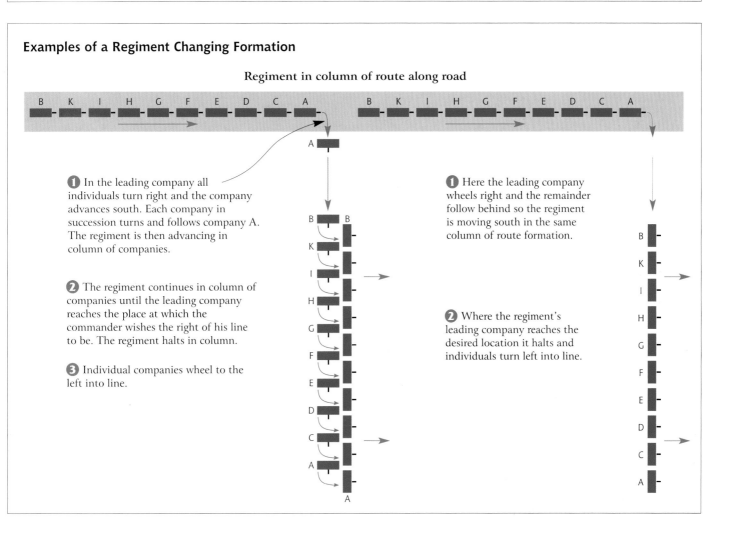

Regiment in column of route along road

B K I H G F E D C A B K I H G F E D C A

❶ In the leading company all individuals turn right and the company advances south. Each company in succession turns and follows company A. The regiment is then advancing in column of companies.

❷ The regiment continues in column of companies until the leading company reaches the place at which the commander wishes the right of his line to be. The regiment halts in column.

❸ Individual companies wheel to the left into line.

❶ Here the leading company wheels right and the remainder follow behind so the regiment is moving south in the same column of route formation.

❷ Where the regiment's leading company reaches the desired location it halts and individuals turn left into line.

Grand Tactics (the tactics of the generals)

Frontal attacks

The objective here is to smash a hole in the defense, exploit it, and drive the enemy from his position by the ferocity of the assault. A purely frontal infantry attack is likely to succeed only if some or all of the following features are present:

- the attacker has overwhelming numbers
- the attack achieves surprise of some sort (unexpected, time, direction, place, speed or in darkness)
- the attack is well supported by reserves and supports in follow-up waves
- the flanks are secure
- there is strong and effective artillery support
- the enemy is poorly positioned and exposed to heavy fire
- enemy morale is low
- the attacking commander is able to exploit unforeseen opportunities

At Gettysburg the Army of Northern Virginia attacked on all three days of the battle. By the end of Day Three virtually every Rebel infantryman had been involved in at least one major attack, many in two. There had been four divisional attacks on July 1 – Heth, Pender, Rodes and Early; six more on July 2 – Hood, McLaws, Anderson, Early again, Johnson and a half-hearted effort by Rodes again. Then on the final day a three-divisional assault – Pickett, Pettigrew (Heth again) and Trimble (Pender again) – preceded by a separate one by Johnson again. By the time the last shot was fired, Lee had launched fourteen divisional attacks. In the event, with two significant exceptions, both on July 1, all these attacks resulted, primarily, in frontal assaults. Only on July 2 did purely frontal attacks (although the Confederates attacked both sides of the infamous Sickles' salient, the actual assaults were invariably frontal) eventually succeed in driving back, not destroying, Sickles' men and their reinforcements. The reasons that this tactic proved so unrewarding and costly will become clear in the later sections, but it had a lot to do with the factors listed above.

A Frontal Attack: Part of Early's Divisional Assault, July 2

Looking down the southern half of Brickyard Lane from near the 68th New York monument. The fence line was defended by four Union regiments, totaling some 1,100 men, against three Confederate regiments with some 1,250. It was a classic frontal attack against a defensive line in two ranks firing volleys at close range. Almost certainly the firing here was by ranks within each regiment, but in the center it was not sufficient to halt the attack. The 54th and 68th New York gave way, although the others held their ground. There was some bitter hand-to-hand fighting along this road in the fading light, during which there was a rare example of a sword being used to kill. See Map 57.

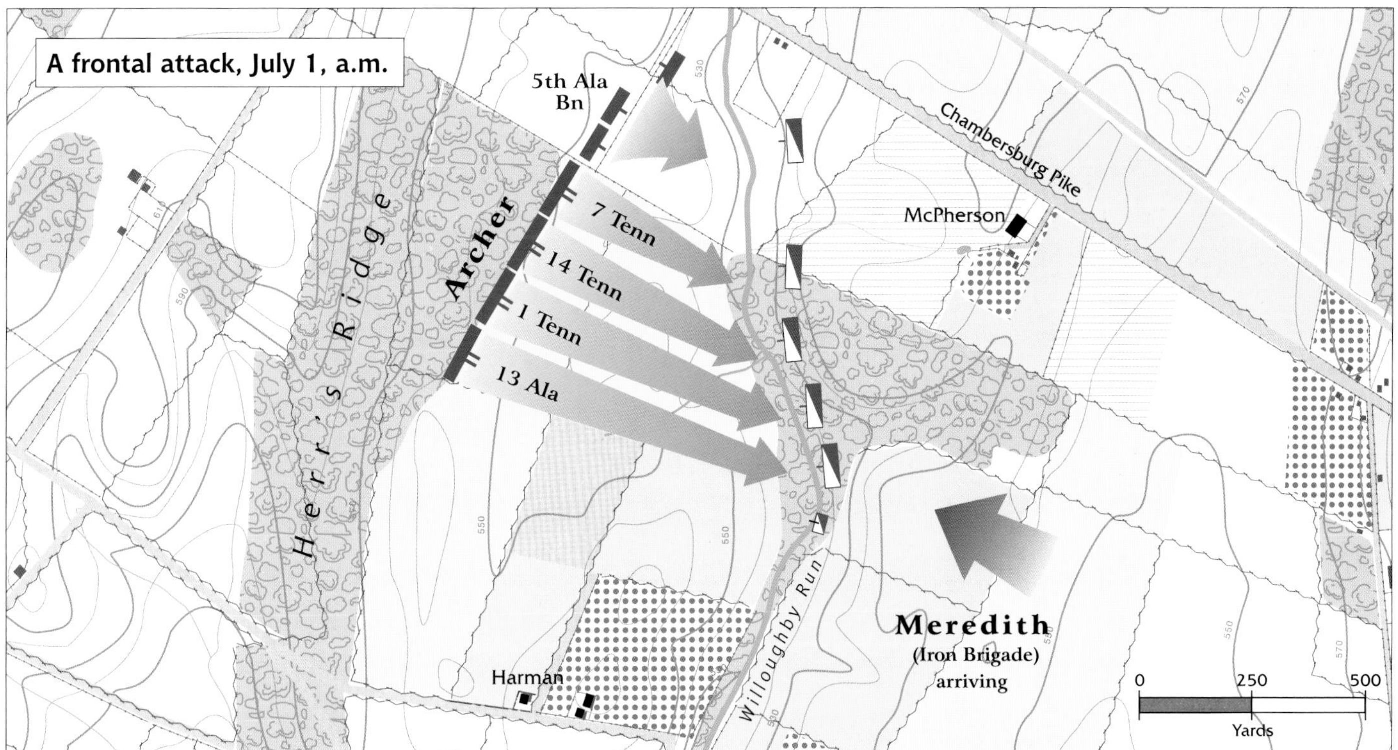

Notes

- The Confederates (Archer) launched a typical frontal advance/attack with all four regiments and his battalion in a double-rank line extending for over 600 yards.
- The attack was initially against dismounted Union cavalry. These were soon replaced by the Iron Brigade, which drove the Rebels back over the Willoughby Run and captured Archer.

Flank attacks

Military history is full of examples of the effectiveness of striking an enemy in his flank (or rear). An individual struck in his side while grappling with somebody to his front is unlikely to recover. Thus it is with an infantry unit or formation. It is most effective if it is unexpected so that the unit has no time or means to do anything to check or counter it. At Gettysburg it was Perrin's and Lane's Carolinians sweeping round the exposed left flank of the Union defenders on Seminary Ridge on the first day that secured the position and drove those Yankee regiments back through Gettysburg. A more dramatically successful flank attack was that carried out by the 13th and 16th Vermont Infantry against the right flank of Pickett's Division just as it closed with the defenders near the Angle and the Copse of Trees. It was a decisive blow. This was followed by the 16th Vermont, joined by the 14th, attacking the left flank of the late-arriving brigades of Lang and Wilcox with similar results. Lee intended a major flank attack by the divisions of McLaws and Hood on what he thought to be the left flank of Meade's army on July 2. Regrettably for the South, the flank was not where it was thought to be.

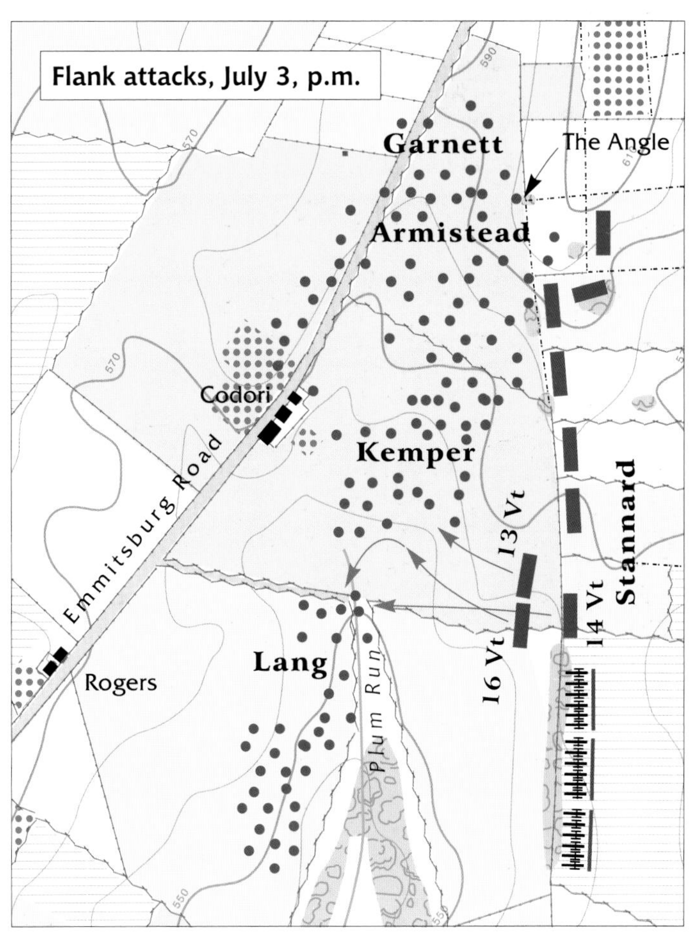

Notes

- This was effectively a double flank attack by Stannard's Brigade, with the 13th and 16th Vermont advancing in line, swinging right and delivering a massive volley into the right flank of Kemper's already disorganized brigade.
- This was followed by the advance of the 14th Vermont to strike the left flank of Lang's Brigade in conjunction with the 16th Vermont, which turned around and attacked for the second time.

Counterattacks

If well timed, a counterattack, even by a comparatively small number of men, can produce impressive results. An attacking force has usually suffered losses, including loss of commanders, during its advance; formations may be disrupted, men exhausted and confused as the final objective is reached. An unexpected counterattack at this moment is difficult to deal with. Two examples can be seen at Gettysburg. On July 1 the immediate counterattack against the advancing Archer's Brigade by Meredith's Iron Brigade as soon as it arrived on the field drove the Confederates back through the Herbst Wood, over Willoughby Run and resulted in the capture of the Confederate brigade commander (Archer). The second daring, but dreadfully costly, counterattack took place on Cemetery Ridge on the second day. An advance by Richard Anderson's Division was under way, while Wilcox's Brigade had crossed the Emmitsburg Road and was approaching the ridgeline. Union reserves had not yet arrived to plug a hole in the defenses and the only unit immediately available was the 1st Minnesota Infantry (the only regiment from that state present at Gettysburg). It charged forward and, although sacrificing some 60 percent of its strength, the Confederate advance was stalled for long enough to allow more Union troops to deploy and subsequently drive off the main attack.

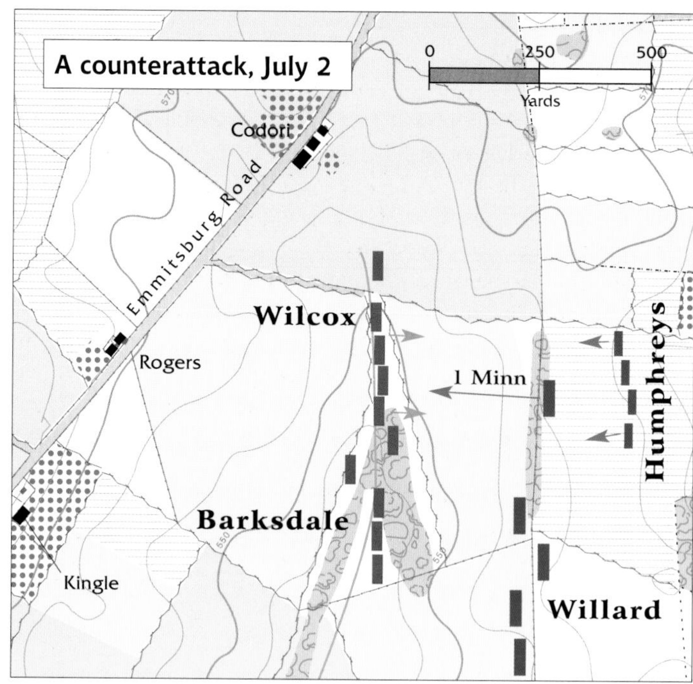

Notes

- The Confederates had driven Sickles from his salient and the Union withdrawal to Cemetery Ridge had become disorganized. There was a gap in the defenses that Wilcox's Rebels were approaching.
- The only unit immediately available was the 1st Minnesota Infantry who were ordered forward. The counterattack successfully checked the Confederate advance, although the cost to 1st Minnesota was very high.
- Sufficient time was gained for other Union units to be brought forward and the attack repulsed.

Refusing a flank

This is a tactic much used by defenders whose flank is threatened. It is the bending back of the defensive line so that it faces the new threat with the aim of avoiding being attacked in flank or rear. The most extreme example occurred on July 2 on Little Round Top. Here, in a bid to avoid being outflanked, the 20th Maine on the southern end of the Union line refused its left flank to such an extent that the regimental line took on a V shape, with soldiers almost fighting back to back. Another example, on a bigger scale, was deployment of the Union Iron Brigade and Stone's Brigade for the defense of McPherson's Ridge against Daniel's Confederate Brigade attacking from the north and the threat from Heth's Division in the west. It was the appearance of Confederate infantry on Oak Hill on the afternoon of July 1 that caused Stone to refuse his right flank by shifting two (and later three) of his regiments to positions along the Chambersburg Pike, facing north at right angles to the Iron Brigade, which was facing west.

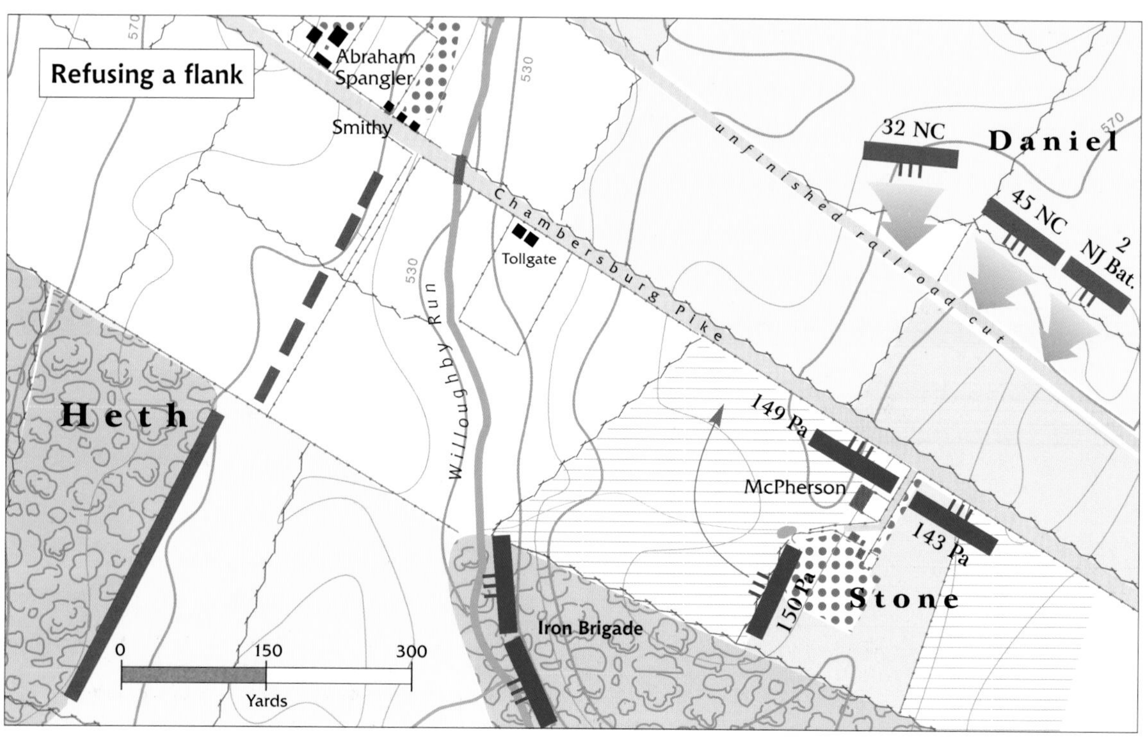

Notes

- The appearance of Confederates on Oak Hill (off the map to the north) meant that the right flank of the Union line along McPherson's Ridge facing west was exposed. Col. Stone refused his right flank by placing two regiments along the Chambersburg Pike to face the new threat.
- As the Confederate attack developed, Stone also swung his third regiment, the 150th Pennsylvania, onto the left of his line along the road. In the event, this first Rebel attack from the north was beaten off.

Feint attacks

The object here is to put in an attack on one part of the enemy line to make him believe it is the main effort. His reserves will then be drawn away and committed before the main assault in an entirely different place achieves surprise. Success is invariably dependent on the vigor of the feint attack and its timing in relation to the main effort – there must be proper coordination between the two attacks, which in turn means careful planning and even more careful supervision by the commanders and their staff.

A striking illustration of how piecemeal attacks allow the defender the luxury of switching reserves came on July 2. No fewer than six Confederate infantry divisions attacked from one end of the "fishhook" to the other – all starting at different times over a period of nearly five hours. In summary they were:

4:30 p.m. Hood advanced on the Round Tops

5:30 p.m. McLaws attacked the Peach Orchard and Rose Woods

6:15 p.m. Anderson attacked the Union position along the Emmitsburg Road

7:30 p.m. Johnson attacked Culp's Hill

8:00 p.m. Early attacked East Cemetery Hill

9:00 p.m. Rodes made an unenthusiastic advance along Long Lane toward Cemetery Hill

One wonders what might have happened if the timings had been better coordinated and Meade had been unable to keep rushing reserves to meet developing threats.

The nearest Lee came to employing feint attacks came on two occasions on the third day: the continued furious frontal assaults by Johnson's reinforced division on the almost impregnable defenses atop the steep slopes of Culp's Hill, and the massive attack by the divisions of Pickett, Pettigrew and Trimble on Cemetery Ridge. The former drew Union reserves to the right, including the return of XII Corps and units of I and VI Corps. These repeated, fruitless and costly attacks lasted from around 5:00 a.m. until the end of the morning. Lee's final assault came in the afternoon after a lengthy artillery bombardment. By this time the heroic efforts on his extreme left wing (actually to the rear of the Union position along Cemetery Ridge) had long since petered out and Meade was free to concentrate on defeating his enemy's main effort. There was no coordination of timings on the Confederate side, with the result that each attack could be defeated in detail.

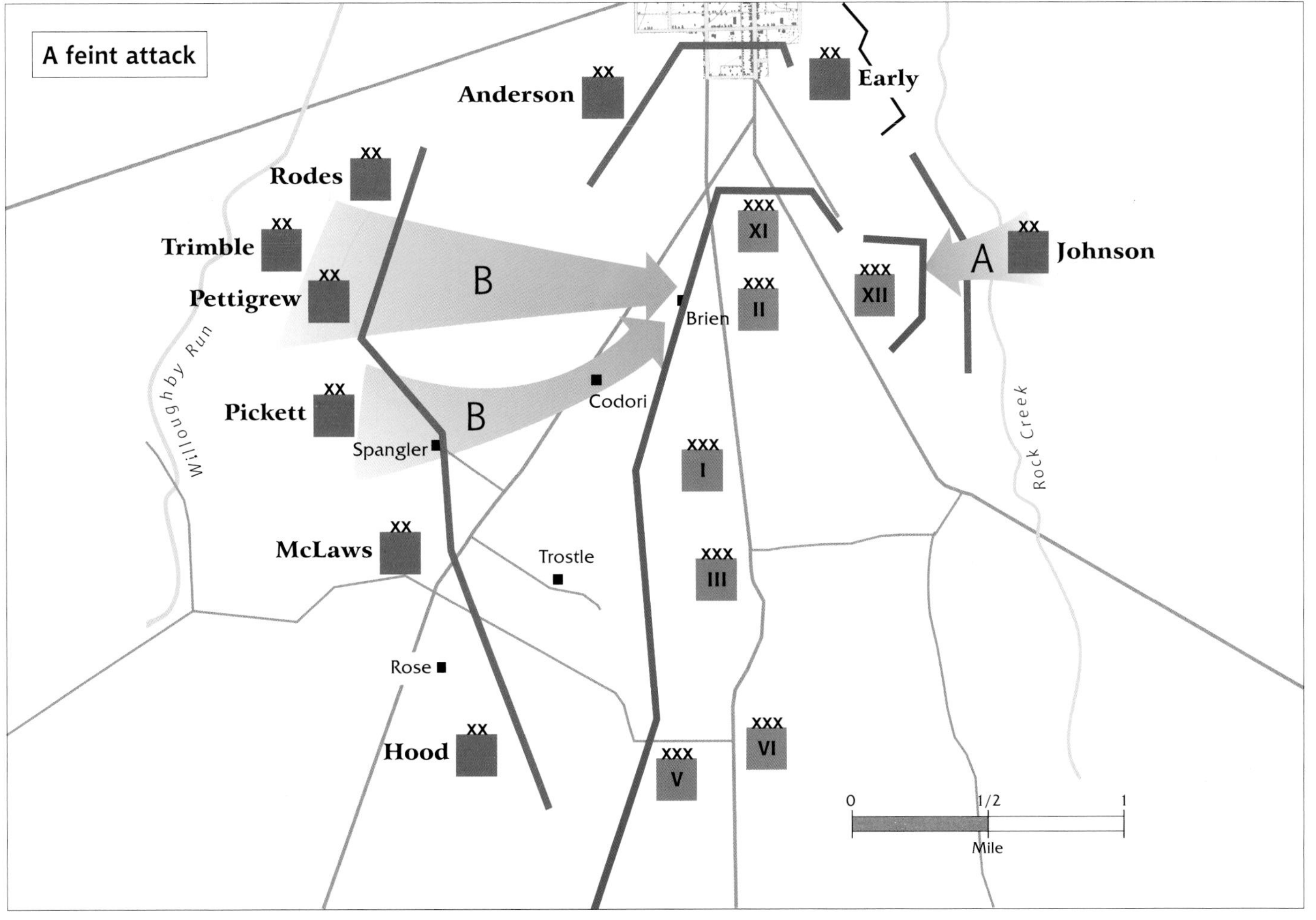

Notes

• This simplified map illustrates how on July 3 Johnson's attack at **A**, which continued all morning and took place almost exactly in the rear of where Lee's main assault would be mae, had great potential as a feint to draw off Union reserves.

• The main three divisional attacks at **B** did not get under way until around 3:00 p.m., long after Johnson's had failed.

• This failure to coordinate the two attacks was one of the numerous factors that ruined the Rebel's day on July 3.

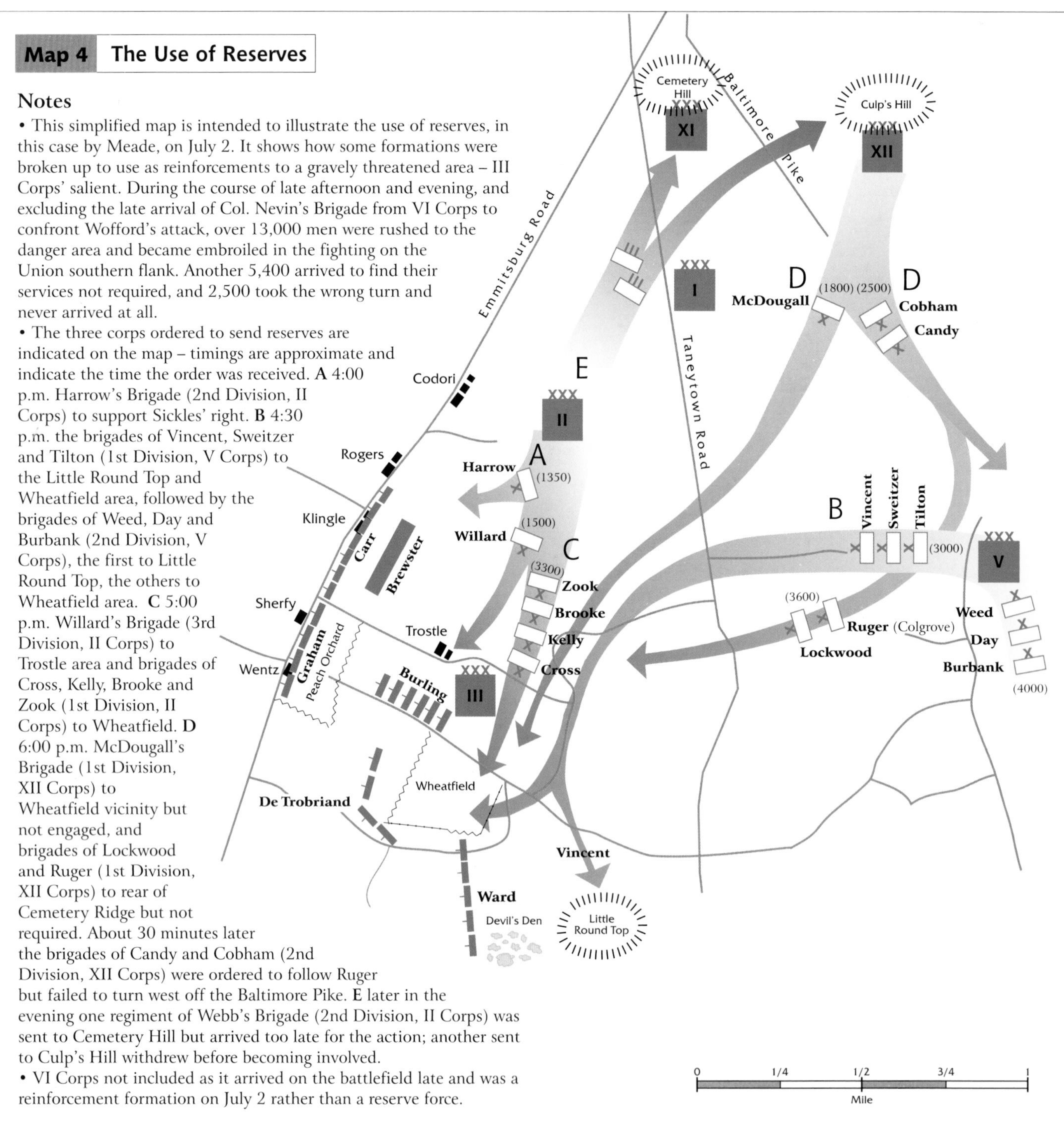
Map 4 The Use of Reserves
Notes
• This simplified map is intended to illustrate the use of reserves, in this case by Meade, on July 2. It shows how some formations were broken up to use as reinforcements to a gravely threatened area – III Corps' salient. During the course of late afternoon and evening, and excluding the late arrival of Col. Nevin's Brigade from VI Corps to confront Wofford's attack, over 13,000 men were rushed to the danger area and became embroiled in the fighting on the Union southern flank. Another 5,400 arrived to find their services not required, and 2,500 took the wrong turn and never arrived at all.
• The three corps ordered to send reserves are indicated on the map – timings are approximate and indicate the time the order was received. A 4:00 p.m. Harrow's Brigade (2nd Division, II Corps) to support Sickles' right. B 4:30 p.m. the brigades of Vincent, Sweitzer and Tilton (1st Division, V Corps) to the Little Round Top and Wheatfield area, followed by the brigades of Weed, Day and Burbank (2nd Division, V Corps), the first to Little Round Top, the others to Wheatfield area. C 5:00 p.m. Willard's Brigade (3rd Division, II Corps) to Trostle area and brigades of Cross, Kelly, Brooke and Zook (1st Division, II Corps) to Wheatfield. D 6:00 p.m. McDougall's Brigade (1st Division, XII Corps) to Wheatfield vicinity but not engaged, and brigades of Lockwood and Ruger (1st Division, XII Corps) to rear of Cemetery Ridge but not required. About 30 minutes later the brigades of Candy and Cobham (2nd Division, XII Corps) were ordered to follow Ruger but failed to turn west off the Baltimore Pike. E later in the evening one regiment of Webb's Brigade (2nd Division, II Corps) was sent to Cemetery Hill but arrived too late for the action; another sent to Culp's Hill withdrew before becoming involved.
• VI Corps not included as it arrived on the battlefield late and was a reinforcement formation on July 2 rather than a reserve force.
Cemetery Hill
XI
Baltimore Pike
Culp's Hill
XII
Emmitsburg Road
I
D
McDougall
(1800) (2500)
D
Cobham
Candy
Taneytown Road
E
Codori
II
Rogers
Harrow
A
(1350)
Klingle
Carr
Brewster
Willard
(1500)
C
(3300)
Zook
Brooke
Kelly
Cross
B
Vincent
Sweitzer
Tilton
(3000)
V
(3600)
Ruger (Colgrove)
Lockwood
Weed
Day
Burbank
(4000)
Sherfy
Graham
Peach Orchard
Trostle
Wentz
Burling
III
Wheatfield
De Trobriand
Vincent
Ward
Devil's Den
Little Round Top
0 1/4 1/2 3/4 1
Mile

Use of reserves

Herein lies another key factor in generalship on the battlefield. The maintenance of a reserve at all times, the ability to move it quickly, the use of it to deal with an unexpected threat or to exploit success (not to reinforce failure) can quickly decide the issue. At Gettysburg the attacking Confederates were operating on exterior lines (along the outer rim of a circle – fishhook), whereas Meade could switch reserves from one flank to the other or to the center far more quickly (across the diameter of the circle). Reserves for the Confederates tended to be second or third waves of infantry advancing 200–800 yards behind the leading line, the idea being that they should be available to maintain the momentum of the assault by pushing through the leading wave if it was held up. In practice, following lines tended to merge with the leading one, reinforcing it perhaps, but with considerable mingling of units and loss of control. The best example of this was the merging of units from Pettigrew's, Trimble's and Pickett's Divisions along the Emmitsburg Road and in front of the Angle and Copse of Trees on the afternoon of July 3. Throughout the second and third days, Meade was able to keep switching reserves at will to where they were needed. It was a crucial battle-winning factor for him.

Minor Tactics (the tactics of the colonels and captains)

Skirmishers

Skirmishers played an important role in most Civil War battles and Gettysburg was no exception. They were often used by both sides some 200–500 yards in advance of their main line to see off or absorb the fire of enemy skirmishers. Union defenders pushed a line of skirmishers forward to give early warning of an enemy advance; to delay and inflict losses on such an advance; and to block and delay enemy skirmishers, thus preventing them inflicting casualties on the main line of defenders. If pushed back they would join the main line. Attacking Confederates were usually preceded by a skirmish line whose function was to drive in the enemy skirmishers, thus exposing the main line to skirmish fire before the main assault went in. Similarly they were to absorb the fire of the enemy, shielding the main attacking regiments following some 200 yards behind. Skirmishers could also be deployed ahead of the leading regiments in a long advance to contact or to protect the flanks of an attack.

The procedure followed when an infantry regiment provided men as skirmishers was to use two companies, normally the two flank companies, both of whom would fall back to their positions on the flanks of the advancing line as the attack approached close to the enemy position. Sometimes an entire regiment would be used to skirmish ahead of a brigade advance. On the skirmish line they were trained to operate in groups of four men about 5 yards apart and supporting each other, making use of cover and firing slowly and deliberately as individuals. Officers and N.C.O.s controlled the line from behind by observing and shouting orders or by use of a bugler. In theory, some groups of four were held back as supports, and further back still a reserve platoon of perhaps fifteen men would be available.

There are numerous examples of their use during the battle. There were continuous clashes between skirmishers of both sides on the southern outskirts of Gettysburg itself late on July 1 and on the following day. Confederate skirmishers from Johnson's Division, including most of the 1st North Carolina Regiment, caused problems early on July 2 as they were able to annoy the XII Corps defenders of Culp's Hill. Brigadier-General Ruger, then commanding the 1st Division of XII Corps, made good use of skirmishers after dark on July 2, sending them forward to test whether the division's breastworks on Culp's Hill were occupied by the enemy. They were, and the resultant information persuaded Ruger to delay his attack until daylight the next morning. An example of a regiment deploying skirmishers ahead of its own advance is the 150th Pennsylvania, who rushed forward to support the Union line on McPherson's Ridge on July 1. Company B was sent ahead as a skirmish line and was subsequently reinforced by Company G as reserves. No fewer than four companies (B, D, E and F) of the 19th Maine were acting as skirmishers throughout the morning of July 3 in front of Cemetery Ridge. They had at least seven hours out in the open fields, most of it under a broiling sun, and suffered from heatstroke as well as from the fire of Confederate skirmishers. As one soldier remarked, "The heat in the glaring sun was intolerable, and we had been without food or water since the morning before . . ." (see box, page 476).

Sharpshooters

As far as Gettysburg is concerned, there was little difference in the tactical employment of specific sharpshooter units and ordinary infantry regiments deployed as skirmishers – sharpshooters skirmished and infantrymen on the skirmish line on many occasions acted as sharpshooters. The name "sharpshooter" derives from the Sharps breechloading rifle with which U.S. sharpshooter units were armed. They were selected for their shooting skills and supposedly had to be able to fire ten consecutive shots all to within 5 inches of the bull from 200 yards. However, when Colonel Hiram Berdan's men were practicing in January 1863, they managed only 57 percent hits on targets up to 5 feet square from 180–250 yards – hardly worthy of a marksman rating. Their shooting ability was supposed to be put to use tactically on the battlefield to make the skirmish line more effective in terms of inflicting casualties. In today's military parlance, they were to act as snipers: to conceal themselves and, with a combination of accurate shooting and patience, endeavor to pick off officers (as noted on page 97, Major-General Sedgwick, VI Corps commander at Gettysburg, was killed by one in May 1864), gun crews, horses and enemy sharpshooters. Major-General Reynolds was killed by a shot through his head on July 1 and forever afterward it was said to be the work of a Confederate sharpshooter. More likely he was shot by a skirmisher from Brigadier-General Archer's Brigade or by a stray bullet.

Some examples of the use of sharpshooters during the battle were:

- The Yankees had the 1st and 2nd Regiments of U.S. Sharpshooters under Colonel Hiram Berdan. On the morning of July 2 four companies of the 1st Sharpshooters (Companies D, E, F and I), about 100 men under the immediate command of Lieutenant-Colonel Casper Trepp, together with some 200 more from the 3rd Maine Infantry Regiment, were sent forward in a skirmishing role to reconnoiter Pitzer's Wood on Seminary Ridge. It was this reconnaissance that made contact with Wilcox's Alabama infantry of Major-General Anderson's Division – not Longstreet's Corps, as is often alleged.

- The Confederates used the steeple of the German Dutch Reformed Church at the junction of Stratton and High Street in Gettysburg as a place in which to install marksmen (not from a designated sharpshooter unit). They had a clear view of Union troops on Cemetery Hill half a mile away. They opened up a long-range fire on Captain Michael Wiedrich's Battery, hitting Lieutenants Nicholas Sahm and Christian Stock plus several horses. Wiedrich turned a gun on the steeple, hitting it and silencing the marksmen.

- Rebel sharpshooters on the upper floor of Farnsworth House attracted considerable return fire – the chipped brickwork is still visible.

- Private Charles Stacey, an excellent shot in the 55th Ohio Infantry, took up a position near a fence line close to the Emmitsburg Road on the morning of July 2. Lying behind some scrub, Stacey was able to remain in the same position for three hours, during which time he fired off twenty-three well-aimed shots. He was subsequently captured and imprisoned at Belle Isle, but his gallantry was rewarded thirty years later with the Medal of Honor.

- Major Eugene Blackford commanded a battalion of Confederate sharpshooters from the 5th Alabama Infantry, whose men were heavily involved with sniping from a block of houses on Main Street on July 2 and 3.
- Confederate sharpshooters or skirmishers were ensconced among the boulders of Devil's Den where they did considerable damage firing up at Little Round Top.
- The 3rd Georgia Sharpshooter Battalion was deployed as skirmishers in advance of Brigadier-General Wofford's Brigade when it attacked Union positions along the Emmitsburg Road on July 2.

Fire control

This has been discussed in detail on pages 106–108 with regard to defending troops. Fire control for the attackers, in this case mostly Confederate infantry, poses some slightly different problems. A regiment advancing to attack with fixed bayonets and loaded muskets must do so without firing, at least until it gets within 200 yards of the enemy. Now a decision must be made on whether to fire or press on. To stop and fire a volley at this stage would largely be a waste of ammunition and would mean either a pause to reload or continuing with unloaded weapons. In theory it would be better to keep advancing until 30–40 yards from the objective, fire a quick volley and then rush in with the bayonet. In practice, if under heavy fire, an attacking line that stopped to fire often did so at some convenient obstacle such as a fence line. Having the need to reload and having found some, albeit flimsy, shelter, it was very difficult for commanders to get all their men forward again together. The tendency was for a firefight to develop with the consequent loss of momentum – the assault had been halted.

At Gettysburg there are scores of examples of firefights between lines of infantrymen sometimes only 20 yards apart, particularly in the woods on Culp's Hill or Little Round Top. However, the best example of numerous attacking infantry under heavy fire going to ground and not advancing again occurred on July 3 during the massive Confederate attack on Cemetery Ridge. Here the Emmitsburg Road, particularly to the north of Codori Farm, was within 200–300 yards of the Union line and was an obvious landmark at which the defenders opened maximum rifle-musket fire. The Rebels were checked and scrambled over the fences. The fierce fire, heavy losses and confusion as units became intermingled meant that numerous men decided thus far and no further.

Breastworks/entrenchments

The spade and the ax played their part in the fighting at Gettysburg. The Civil War saw extensive use of trenches and field fortifications well before Gettysburg. Trench systems proliferated in the defenses of Washington, Richmond, Fort Donaldson and in the offensive system dug by McClellan in the Peninsula. Skilful use of even hasty barricades and natural or manmade obstacles invariably boost the ability of defenders to give a good account of themselves and obstruct, delay or defeat an attack. The Gettysburg battlefield was well endowed with potential barricades in the form of miles of heavy wooden fencing and low stone walls. Hills like Culp's Hill and the Round Tops, and areas like Devil's Den were covered in loose rocks and boulders, all excellent material for building breastworks.

Union regiments made considerable use of their spades and axes in preparing their defensive positions. The most striking examples were the elaborate trenches and breastworks constructed during the night of July1/2 by Brigadier-General John Geary's men on Culp's Hill. They were undoubtedly a critical factor enabling Greene's lonely brigade to hold the hill on July 2 against continuous attacks by greatly superior numbers. The combination of frontal attacks uphill against determined defenders firing at close range from behind strong barricades proved virtually unbeatable. There was also extensive use of stone walls and boulders at the other end of the battlefield on Little Round Top and in Devil's Den. Another factor assisting the Union defenders, though to a lesser extent, was the barricades using fence rails and low stone walls running north–south along the western face of Cemetery Ridge; these provided some protection from both artillery and rifle-musket fire. The best-known stone wall on the battlefield was the one running in front of the Copse of Trees and forming the Angle.

For the Confederates it was mostly the fences that proved a hindrance to their advances. In places pioneers or skirmishers ahead of an attack threw them down, but generally they became an obstacle to be knocked down or clambered over by advancing troops. This not only delayed the assault but made easier targets of the soldiers, who had to bunch up to get through gaps or climb over, and invariably units had to pause once over the obstacle to adjust the line. The best example of this was the effect of the fences on either side of the Emmitsburg Road; they formed a convenient defensive line for Sickles' men when defending along the road on July 2, but caused considerable inconvenience to Pickett's, Pettigrew's and Trimble's men the next day in their long walk toward Cemetery Ridge.

The bayonet charge

The Rebels fixed bayonets prior to almost every attack they made during the battle; it was an automatic drill – load your musket, fix your bayonet. Every assault was therefore a potential bayonet charge. The sight of long lines of thousands of bayonets glinting in the sun coming ever closer was guaranteed to set a defender's heart rate rocketing. The bayonet was, and is, largely a weapon of morale, relying on the fear of fighting hand to hand with cold steel undermining a defender's resolve to stay put as the attack closes in. At Gettysburg death or wounds inflicted by a bayonet were negligible – less than one percent. Either the attackers were driven off; or they stopped short of their objective to engage in a firefight; or the defenders hastily withdrew; or many of the protagonists in close combat preferred to wield their muskets as a club. Very few bayonet charges resulted in bayonet fighting.

For a defending regiment to resort to a bayonet charge as a counterattack was something of a last resort, but could nonetheless prove effective. The Iron Brigade's driving Archer's men back across Willoughby Run on July 1, the charge of the 1st Minnesota to halt Wilcox's advance on Cemetery Ridge on July 2, and the charge of the 20th Maine on Little Round Top to drive off the 15th Alabama are clear examples of defenders resorting to successful bayonet charge counterattacks. With the 20th Maine, however, there was a strong element of the "last resort" in their charge, as many men were out of, or nearly out of, ammunition, while other muskets were becoming unusable due to accumulated fouling.

SECTION THREE

The Artillery

The relatively open battlefield made Gettysburg the scene of probably the fiercest artillery clashes of the Civil War. On July 2 the first hour of the action against Sickles' salient was a massive artillery duel between hundreds of gunners on both sides, each attempting to silence their opponent's cannon prior to the Confederate attack aimed at the apex of the Union salient at the Peach Orchard. The next day saw what was to be the biggest single artillery bombardment ever witnessed on American soil – in preparation for another of Lee's infantry assaults and this time involving over 12,000 men in his final fling to knock Meade off Cemetery Ridge.

A total of 631 (Confederate 273, Union 358) artillery pieces were engaged at Gettysburg. They were deployed over some 25 square miles of battleground, playing a crucial role in the struggle, if not always as lethal as might be expected. However, the effect on morale of large numbers of guns opening fire, with the subsequent continuous crashing and the drifting smoke, was considerable. They were an inspiring sight, giving the impression of power and great destructiveness. Infantrymen, even if not on the receiving end, were invariably impressed. One who fought at Antietam said:

> a battalion of artillery with guns at full gallop swept into position, opening in volleys. It was a grand and inspiring sight to witness batteries going headlong into action, – the neighing of horses, the rumbling of caissons, the halt, the furious cannonade, the officers on their chargers with swords gleaming in the sunlight, with buglers clanging out the order, the passing of ammunition, the ramming, the sighting, the firing and the swabbing, – the guns booming in chorus like heaven-rending thunder.

As with infantry weapons, the Union started the war with a distinct advantage over their enemies in the South. They could count on over 4,000 pieces, of which some 163 were field pieces left over from the Mexican War. Almost another 8,000 cannon of all types were issued to Union armies between 1861 and 1866. The Union's Cold Spring Foundry, on the other side of the Hudson River from the U.S. Military Academy at West Point, could produce twenty-five guns and 7,000 projectiles a week. During the war over 1,700 guns and almost 3 million projectiles left its gates. It was the same with the production of gunpowder. At full capacity the Union mills could produce over 500 barrels every day, with the main Du Ponts mill manufacturing more than the total output of the other thirteen factories. These early advantages in the manufacturing capacity of Northern foundries and factories was complemented by a well-trained professional corps of artillerymen in the U.S. Regular Army.

The Confederates had a tough time trying to catch up – something they never completely achieved, particularly with regard to equipment and ammunition, including fuses. Colonel E. Porter Alexander, the acting commander of Longstreet's Corps Artillery Reserve at Gettysburg, had this to say about Rebel disadvantages at the start of hostilities:

> The drawbacks upon its efficiency at the beginning of the war were very serious, and came both from its organization and from its equipment. The faults of its organization were recognized and gradually overcome within eighteen months. The deficiencies of equipment, the result of causes many of which were beyond control, continued with but partial mitigation to the end of the war. The batteries were generally composed of but four guns, which is not an economical arrangement; but as no objection was made to it, either by army headquarters or at the War Department, and as the scarcity of both horses and ordnance equipment made it difficult to get, and more so to maintain a six-gun battery, it resulted in that few six-gun batteries were put in the field, and nearly every one of these was eventually reduced to four guns.

At Gettysburg only four Confederate batteries out of sixty-eight (barely 6 percent) had six pieces, one in each of Pickett's, Hood's and Richard Anderson's Divisions. However, in the Army of the Potomac six-gun batteries were the norm, with only fourteen out of the sixty-five engaged (21.5 percent) having four – one each in I and II Corps, two each in V, XI and XII Corps and the Cavalry Corps, plus four in the Army Reserve.

In the South in 1861 the only foundry for casting cannon was the Tredegar Iron Works at Richmond (see box, page 143). Although a number of others were started during the war, the Confederates came to rely heavily on captured enemy pieces and equipment. In the latter half of the conflict it was common to find A.N.V. artillery units with all guns having the U.S. stamp on them. Some Rebel ordnance officers estimated at least two-thirds of their ordnance once belonged to "Uncle Sam." A Confederate prisoner passing some Union artillery commented, "I swear, Mister, you all has got most as many of these here U.S. guns as we'uns has." A Southern officer observed, "The combination of Yankee artillery with Rebel infantry would make an army that could be beaten by no one."

A four-gun battery of Confederate 3-in ordnance rifles deployed at the regulation interval of 14 yards. Note the gun limbers are close behind their piece for speed of loading, although, in practice, this was not alway possible or sensible.

TERMINOLOGY

For the better understanding of the artillery arm, certain terms need explanation. The meanings are for Union artillery but generally, unless specifically excepted, they apply to the Confederate service as well.

Guns

These are relatively long-barreled cannon designed to fire projectiles at a high velocity and nearly flat trajectory. They are direct-fire weapons, where the gunner must see the target before firing. Out of the Union's 358 artillery pieces at Gettysburg, 214 were guns of various types; the Confederates, out of their total of 273 artillery pieces, had 141 guns engaged.

Howitzers

Howitzers are shorter-barreled cannon with a chamber at the base of the bore to take a small charge. Their muzzle velocity is less than that of the gun and therefore their range is shorter. The projectile's trajectory is more of an arc, the idea being to lob it over enemy defenses or hit troops hidden from view by rising ground. However, this is indirect fire, and with the limited range of the pieces in the Civil War the gunner had at least to be able to see the area in which the enemy was concealed in order to fire effectively.

Gun-howitzers

A gun that, despite having no chamber, is capable of firing at a relatively high angle, although not one comparable with a howitzer. The familiar 12-pounder "Napoleon" was a gun-howitzer.

Company

The official term for the sub-units in an artillery regiment. However, this was easily confused with infantry companies, so the commonly accepted term of "battery" (see below) was almost universally used. "Company" was not officially changed to "battery" in the Union Army until 1866.

Battery

Derived from the French *batter* meaning "to beat," as in the use of early artillery to beat down the walls of a castle. Strangely, units of the 5th U.S. Artillery were officially called "batteries" from that regiment's creation in 1861. The 1866 Order noted above merely brought all other artillery regiments into line with common practice.

"Battery" can also be used for a group of guns of any number or size operating together. For example, when Lieutenant-Colonel McGilvery cobbled together a number of guns in a line defending the center of Cemetery Ridge on July 2 when the Rebels threatened to break through, that group of guns could legitimately be termed a "battery."

The term "battery" rather than "company" will be used throughout this book.

Consolidated Batteries

It was not uncommon for two batteries to be merged together because of losses in men and guns. At Gettysburg two of several examples on the Union side were the merging of Batteries F and K of the 3rd U.S. Artillery, and C and F of the Pennsylvania Independent Artillery, both having six pieces. Historians sometimes mistake such batteries as two and thus credit them with more pieces than they had. The Confederates, with mostly only four pieces in a battery, did not have to resort to these mergers.

Battalion

This term, when applied to artillery, had a particular meaning in the Confederate Army but not the Union. It meant a formally

Confederates Capture Forty Cannon

Three days of Confederate infantry attacks, a number of which closed with the Union defenders before cannon could withdraw, resulted in forty cannon falling into Rebel hands. They included guns from Brown's, Bigelow's, Cushing's, Smith's, Turnbull's, Walcott's, Watson's and Weir's Batteries. However, as the Confederate attacks were eventually driven off and the retreating infantry made few attempts to take the guns, they took only seven with them when they finally left the field on July 4.

established unit of between four and six batteries under a single, not necessarily senior, commander. For example, at Gettysburg McLaws' Divisional Artillery Battalion of four batteries was commanded by Colonel Henry C. Cabell, whereas a Captain Willis J. Dance was the commanding officer of a five-battery battalion in the Artillery Reserve of Early's Corps.

Brigade

The Union Army grouped artillery batteries into brigades of between four and eight batteries, usually from different regiments. At Gettysburg they could be commanded by an officer as senior as a colonel (I Corps Artillery Brigade, Colonel Charles S. Wainwright) or as junior as a first lieutenant (XII Corps Artillery Brigade, Lieutenant Edward D. Muhlenberg).

Foot Artillery

This was the official term for what was commonly called "heavy" artillery. These units normally manned coastal or river fortifications, mounting large, immobile guns. None was present at Gettysburg.

Field Artillery

The official term for batteries assigned to operate with infantry or cavalry units, but often incorrectly called "light" artillery. The usual field pieces included 6- and 12-pounders, 10-pounder Parrotts, 3-inch ordnance rifles and the Model 1857 12-pounder gun-howitzer or "Napoleon." Field artillery was divided into mounted and horse artillery.

Mounted Artillery

This confusing term was officially used for field batteries operating with infantry. The confusion arises as not all the detachments were mounted in the sense of riding their own horses. Officers, sergeants, buglers and drivers were mounted in the proper sense, but the remainder – the corporals, cannoneers and wagon drivers – were mounted (that is, did not walk) only when they climbed onto a limber, caisson or wagon. Field (mounted) artillery made up the great bulk of the batteries on both sides at Gettysburg throughout the three days.

Horse Artillery

The official term for field artillery assigned to operate with cavalry. In order to keep up with the cavalry, every member of the battery rode his own horse and thus could accurately be considered "mounted." The term "horse artillery battery" was frequently abbreviated to "horse battery." Very few horse artillery batteries were engaged on the main battlefield at Gettysburg. An exception was Battery A of the 2nd U.S. Artillery under Lieutenant John H. Calef, which fought as part of Buford's delaying action along the Chambersburg Pike on July 1.

Light Artillery

Field artillery is often considered and called "light artillery." This is incorrect as technically the term is limited to "Horse Artillery." The "light" refers to speed, not the size or weight of the guns. Numerous Union and Confederate batteries incorporated the word "Light" in their titles, but unless they were formally assigned to a cavalry unit and every member rode a horse, then they were not light batteries no matter what they called themselves. Examples from the Union were the 1st New York Light Artillery, Battery L in I Corps Artillery Reserve, and the 1st Maryland Light Artillery, Battery A in the Army Artillery Reserve. A Confederate example was the Norfolk Light Artillery, Blues' Battery in Heth's Division. None of these was horse artillery and they were therefore not strictly entitled to incorporate "light" in their title.

BATTERY ORGANIZATION

The internal organization of artillery batteries of both armies was basically the same, the differences being in the number and type of pieces in the battery and the number of men serving the battery in various capacities. It was these differences that made the average Union battery a stronger unit in terms of firepower and manpower than a Confederate one. Of the sixty-five Union batteries that participated in the action, fifty were six-gun batteries, fourteen four-gun and one two-gun, giving an average of 5.5 guns per battery. Of these only one had mixed ordnance and that was the 2nd Battery, Connecticut Light Artillery, commanded by Captain John W. Sterling in the Army Artillery Reserve.

The Confederacy's Tredegar Iron Works

The North's huge advantage over the South in industrial capacity is widely recognized. In 1860 it produced some 90 percent of all industrial goods, thirty times as many shoes, thirty-two times as many firearms and thirteen times as much iron – the raw material for the manufacture of rifled cannon. Struggling to compete, the main iron works supplying artillery to Lee's army was the Tredegar Iron Works at Richmond. Joseph R. Anderson, a West Point graduate and engineer who had only completed a year's military service before the Civil War, took control of the works in 1841. He entered Confederate service in 1861, but was wounded during the Seven Days Battles, resigned his commission and returned to manage the works.

The demands made on the works included not only the manufacture of cannon for field service, but also the production of 8-inch, 10-inch and 15-inch guns for coastal defenses, railroad supplies and armour plate for warships. As with other private factories that sprang up in the South, Tredegar could only ever work at around 30 percent capacity due to a chronic shortage of raw materials – and at times skilled labor. To obtain tin, copper, coal, coke and above all pig iron for cannon presented neverending difficulties. In the early part of the war the pig iron was of such poor quality that the field pieces, mostly smoothbore howitzers, were often more dangerous to the gunners than to the enemy. Major-General Daniel H. Hill, who was responsible for the defense of Richmond during the Gettysburg campaign, wrote to George W. Randolph, Confederate Secretary of War, in April 1862: "Our shells burst at the mouth of the gun or do not burst at all. The metal of which the new guns are made is of the most flimsy and brittle character and the casting is very bad." Without captured cannon the Confederate artillery would not have been able to compete on the battlefield.

Confederate Artillery Batteries and Pieces Engaged at Gettysburg

Unit	Batteries	12-pdr Naps	10-pdr Parrotts	20-pdr Parrotts	3-in ord rifle	6-pdr gun	12-pdr how	24-pdr how	Navy rifle	Blakely rifle	Whitworth rifle	Total pieces
1st Corps												**87**
Hood	4	11	4	–	2	1	1	–	–	–	–	19
McLaws	4	2	6	–	4	–	4	–	–	–	–	16
Pickett	4	12	3	2	1	–	–	–	–	–	–	18
Reserve	10	14	–	3	7	–	6	4	–	–	–	34
2nd Corps												**79**
Johnson	4	6	5	2	3	–	–	–	–	–	–	16
Early	4	8	2	–	6	–	–	–	–	–	–	16
Rodes	4	6	4	–	6	–	–	–	–	–	–	16
Reserve	8	8	5	4	14	–	–	–	–	–	–	31
3rd Corps												**84**
Heth	4	4	2	–	7	–	2	–	–	–	–	15
Pender	4	7	1	–	2	–	6	–	–	–	–	16
Anderson	3	3	5	–	–	–	5	–	4	–	–	17
Reserve	9	16	2	–	14	–	2	–	–	–	2	36
Cavalry												
Stuart	6	2	4	–	11	–	3	–	–	3	–	**23**
Totals	**68**	**99**	**43**	**11**	**77**	**1**	**29**	**4**	**4**	**3**	**2**	**273**

Notes

The Confederate ordnance type was mixed within most batteries, making ammunition supply something of a nightmare. There was an almost equal division between rifled (140) and smoothbore (133) pieces.

Union Artillery Batteries and Pieces Engaged at Gettysburg

Unit	Batteries	12-pdr Naps	10-pdr Parrotts	20-pdr Parrotts	3-in ord rifle	12-pdr how	James rifle	Total pieces
I Corps								
Artillery Reserve (Wainwright)	5	12	–	–	16	–	–	28
II Corps								
Artillery Reserve (Hazard)	5	12	4	–	12	–	–	28
III Corps								
Artillery Reserve (Randolph)	5	18	12	–	–	–	–	30
V Corps								
Artillery Reserve (Martin)	5	12	6	–	8	–	–	26
VI Corps								
Artillery Reserve (Tompkins)	8	18	18	–	12	–	–	48
XI Corps								
Artillery Reserve (Osborn)	5	16	–	–	10	–	–	26
XII Corps								
Artillery Reserve (Muhlenberg)	4	10	10	–	–	–	–	20
Army Artillery Reserve (Tyler)	19	44	10	6	40	2	4	106
Cavalry Corps (Pleasonton)	9	–	–	–	46	–	–	46
Totals	**65**	**142**	**60**	**6**	**144**	**2**	**4**	**358**

The Confederate battery organization was more complex in that, of the sixty-eight present fifty-four had four pieces and most of these had mixed ordnance. The Rebel situation is best shown in tabular form:

	Same ordnance	Mixed ordnance
6-gun batteries	–	4
5-gun batteries	–	2
4-gun batteries	17	37
3-gun batteries	2	4
2-gun batteries (sections)	1	–
1-gun batteries (sections)	1	–
Totals	**21**	**47**

Within the mixed batteries there was a variety of combinations of ordnance, the most common being smoothbore (Napoleons) with rifled cannon – either Parrotts or 3-inch ordnance rifles. Five batteries had three types of ordnance and one six-gun battery had four different types (Captain Hugh M. Ross with three 10-pounder Parrotts, one 12-pounder Napoleon, one Navy rifle and one 12-pounder howitzer). Details of the number of batteries and different types of cannon in both armies are shown in the boxes opposite.

With regard to manpower the Union battery was also the strongest, with an average strength of 107 men, whereas an average Confederate battery mustered 92. For the Yankees this was well short of the full war establishment for a six-gun battery of five officers and 150 men – a paper figure that was seldom more than wishful thinking. However, the strongest Union battery, the 5th Battery, New York Light Artillery, under Captain Elijah D. Taft, mustered 146 at Gettysburg and there were a number of others above 130. The smallest Union battery, with four cannon, was Battery C, 1st New York Light Artillery, commanded by Captain Almont Barnes, which had 62 all ranks. For the Confederates, their strongest six-gun battery was Captain James Reilly's Battery D, 1st North Carolina Artillery, with 148 men. The four-gun Warrenton (Virginia) Battery, commanded by Captain James V. Brooke, was the smallest with 58 men.

Mounted Battery of Maneuver

Maneuver personnel

A battery of maneuver consisted of the guns with their attached limbers and caissons as depicted in the diagram on pages 148–49. This was the fighting battery – guns plus first line ammunition – and normally excluded the quartermaster sergeant, stable sergeant, battery wagon, forge, ambulance wagon, their drivers, artificers, cooks and extra men held to replace losses. If all posts were filled, the battery of maneuver had 104 all ranks made up as follows:

1 x captain (mounted)
4 x lieutenants (mounted)
6 x sergeants (mounted)
12 x corporals
36 x drivers
42 x cannoneers
2 x buglers (mounted, only one shown on diagram)
1 x guidon (mounted)

Note that 50, almost half, were mounted, thus the requirement for horses was 86 of which 14 would be saddle (although most officers provided their own mounts) and 72 draft horses.

Administrative personnel

These men included some, or all, of the following:

1 x quartermaster sergeant (mounted)
1 x stable sergeant (mounted)
2–6 x artificers (mounted)
8–10 drivers/teamsters

Initially up to 30 extra men were needed as replacements (Captain John Bigelow's 9th Massachusetts Battery, Army of the Potomac Artillery Reserve, had 28 such men on September 3, 1862). An additional 10 (including two spare) saddle horses and up to 25 draft horses were required for drawing the battery wagon, forge, ambulance and providing replacements for losses.

Battery Structure

A six-gun battery consisted of the six guns, numbered from 1–6, with the no. 1 normally on the right of the line and no. 6 on the left, although this alignment was frequently disrupted in action. The six detachments, also numbered from 1–6, each consisted of the gun, its limber and caisson. Two detachments made a section, with the three sections making up the battery being called "right section," "center section" and "left section." When the enlisted men (cannoneers and drivers) attached to a piece were paraded without their guns, limber, caissons and horses, they constituted a platoon commanded by the sergeant.

Duties

Captain – battery commander (mounted)

A captain had overall command of the battery, with responsibility for training, serviceability of guns, ammunition and equipment, discipline and operational performance. He was usually the chief recruiter, with responsibility for keeping his battery up to strength with horses, frequently using influence outside normal requisitioning. At Gettysburg only thirty-six (55 percent) of the Union's sixty-five batteries were commanded by captains, the remaining twenty-nine being under lieutenants. However, of the sixty-eight Confederate batteries only three (4 percent) were not commanded by captains. The command of a battery of from four to six guns, hundreds of rounds of artillery ammunition, over 100 men, more than 100 horses with all the associated equipment, tools and harnesses was a highly responsible task – far more so than that of the infantry captain with perhaps only fifty men. Artillery officers frequently bemoaned the glacial promotion within their corps, which was due, in part, to the relatively light casualty rate compared with their infantry counterparts. During the battle only five Union battery commanders were killed (6.7 percent) and only three Confederates (4.4 percent). It was the battery commander who selected the best position for his guns in the area assigned to him by his battalion or brigade commander. And it was he who, having assessed the situation, gave the first order regarding the type of ammunition to be used. Although a primary task in action for all officers, chiefs of piece and gunners was to observe the fall of shot and order any necessary adjustments, the battery commander often earmarked an officer specifically for this duty.

First and second lieutenants – section chiefs (mounted)

These three officers each had command of a section of two guns (detachments). They were also given administrative duties within the battery, such as requisitioning, and they were sometimes detached with their guns on picket or special tasks with a small unit of infantry. In action they sometimes dismounted so that they could better direct the fire of, or give orders to, their guns. The senior lieutenant took command if the captain was absent.

Second lieutenant – chief of the line of caissons
The junior officer in the battery had command of, and responsibility for, all the caissons and ammunition carried on them. The personnel under his direction included the chiefs of caisson (see below), drivers and any extra-duty men assigned to him. He was often also appointed battery adjutant (staff officer). In battle his primary role was to keep the guns supplied with ammunition and ensure maximum protection for the caissons, teams and men from enemy fire. At the same time he had to position them as close as possible to the gun line to facilitate resupply – usually conflicting requirements. On July 2 Lieutenant Charles E. Hazlett managed to get his guns up the steep, wooded and boulder-strewn eastern slope of Little Round Top. On the summit there was no room for the caissons, which had to be positioned down the slope, well protected from fire but requiring many men and much muscle to haul heavy ammunition to the guns

First sergeant – orderly sergeant (mounted)
The senior N.C.O. in the battery, the forerunner of the battery (or company and squadron) sergeant-major. He worked for the battery commander and had considerable responsibility for daily administration, calling the roll, maintaining duty rosters for guards and fatigues, overseeing equipment repair, horse grooming, training, instructing the sergeants in their duties and overall discipline. In battle he remained alongside the battery commander, ready to fulfill any duties he might be given. If the battery was short of an officer, the first sergeant would take on the duties of chief of caissons, or if casualties were high he could command a section of guns. If he was chief of caissons for some time the likelihood was he would be elected as the junior second lieutenant and confirmed in his appointment.

Quartermaster sergeant (mounted)
He was responsible for the drawing and issue of clothing, personal equipment, rations, small arms and ammunition to the men. These duties included keeping records of all receipts and issues. He was in charge of all details concerning the battery wagons and teamsters, which included the drawing of supplies in bulk from the nearest quartermaster's depot. In action he was normally left out of battle, remaining with the battery supply and baggage wagons in the appropriate divisional train. However, in action there was necessarily considerable flexibility over the tasks assigned to senior NCOs. At Gettysburg the 9th Massachusetts Battery was short of an officer and the first sergeant was absent recruiting. This meant that Quartermaster Sergeant James W. Reed was wounded in the neck while commanding the line of caissons.

Some Union six-gun batteries had a commissary sergeant or a stable sergeant in addition. The 9th Massachusetts Battery had Stable Sergeant Nelson Lovell, who was in charge of the spare horses and forage and was initially located near Spangler's Farm while the battery was in action near the Peach Orchard and Wheatfield, but who later rode forward on his own initiative to assist in what had become a desperate fight. He took charge of a gun in the battery's stand in front of Trostle Farm.

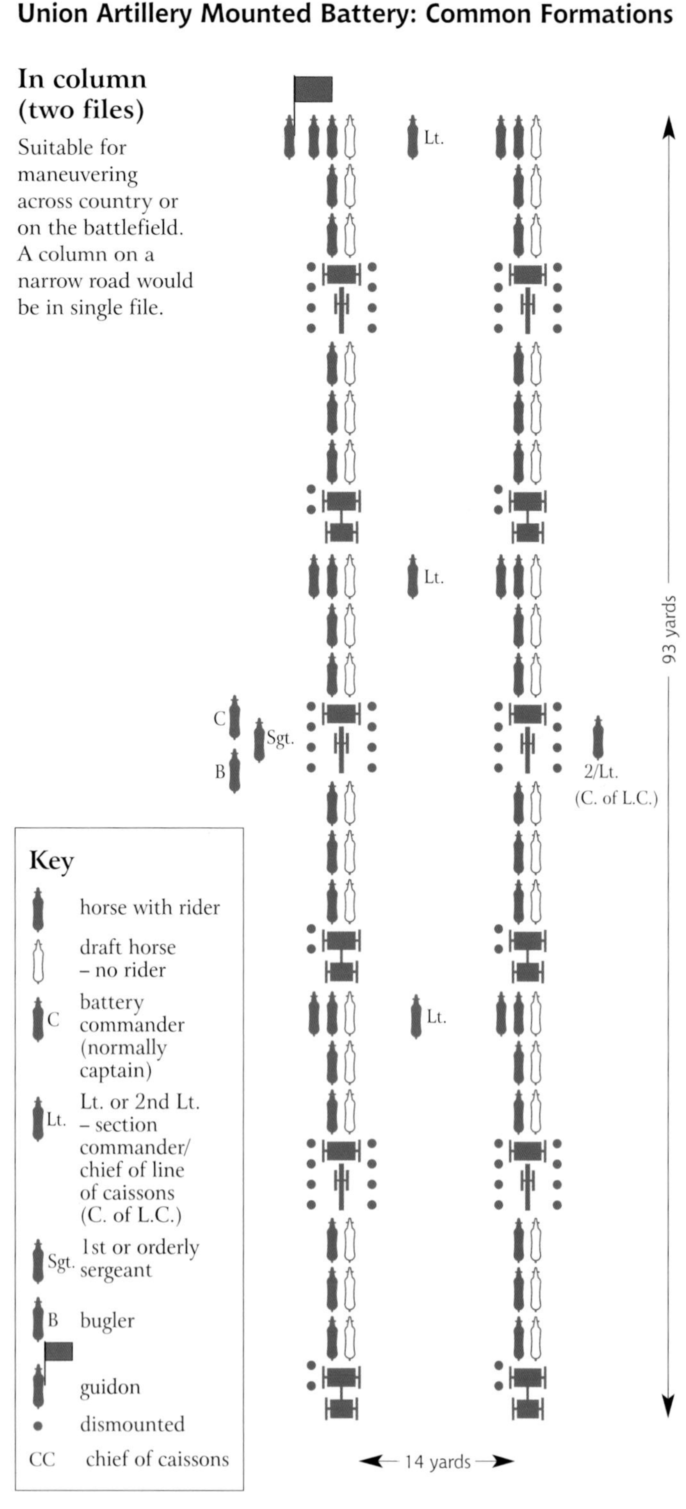

Sergeants – chiefs of piece (mounted)
These sergeants were ranked in order of seniority – second, third, fourth and so on. Each sergeant was a platoon commander, with responsibility for one cannon, twelve horses and their harness, and all the cannoneers and drivers in one detachment. He was responsible for their training and for ensuring that cannoneers and drivers could switch roles. In action he was dismounted, leaving his horse with the drivers, and controlled the actions of his detachment in accordance with the shouted orders of his section commander. He

In line

Common formation on the parade ground and on the battlefield when awaiting orders to deploy "in battery."

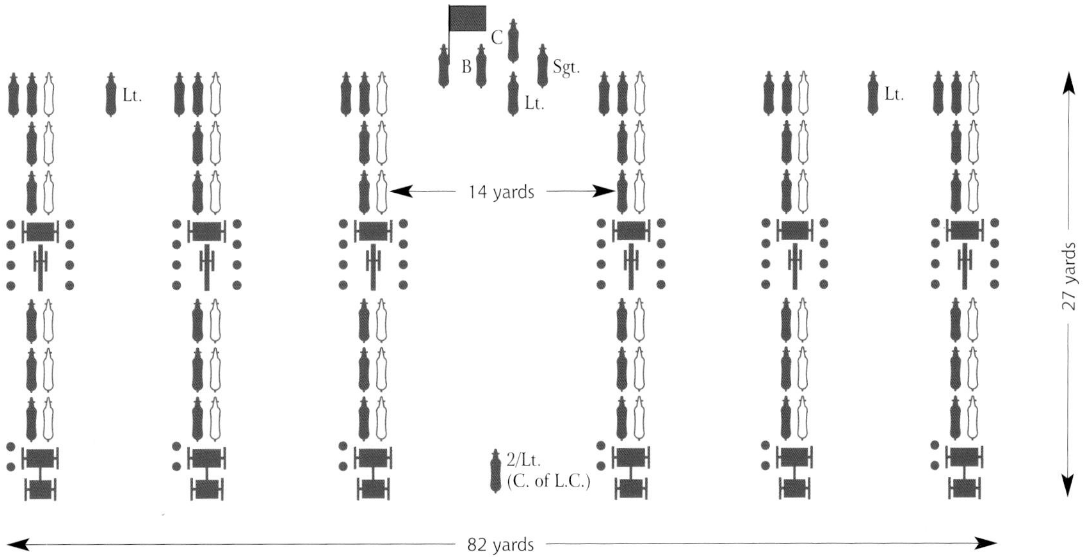

In battery

A battlefield formation with the battery prepared to fire. The distances are flexible and the guns may be much closer, depending on the ground. If the position is to be occupied for some time, the limber may be unhitched and the team taken to the rear.

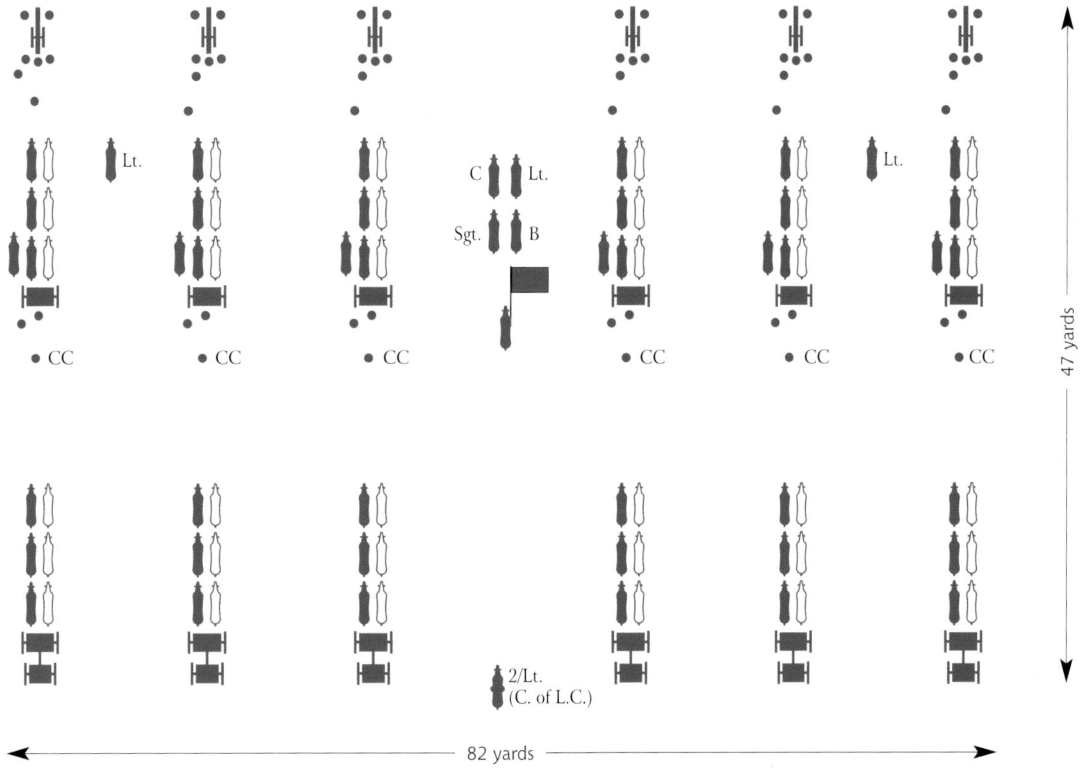

paid particular attention to ensuring the gunner selected the correct target, range and appropriate projectile. In addition he would be checking with the chief of caissons to ensure a smooth replenishment of empty ammunition chests, and supervising the cutting free of injured or dead horses and replacing them – initially from the limber or caisson teams. If senior ranks were few, a sergeant could command a section of two guns. A Gettysburg example was Sergeant Daniel Whitesell, in charge of the center section of Battery C, 5th U.S. Artillery, under Captain Gulian V. Weir.

Corporals – gunners

A mounted battery had twelve corporals; the six senior were gunners. Each had responsibility for the men and equipment in one gun detachment. In action he obeyed the commands of his sergeant (chief of piece), aimed and sighted the cannon and shouted orders to the cannoneers, such as "Case, two degrees, three seconds," which told no. 6 the correct projectile to use – this particular instruction indicted an estimated range to the target of slightly over 700 yards. In particular he would determine the rate of fire.

Mounted Artillery – Six Union Cannon Deployed "In Battery" (ready to fire)

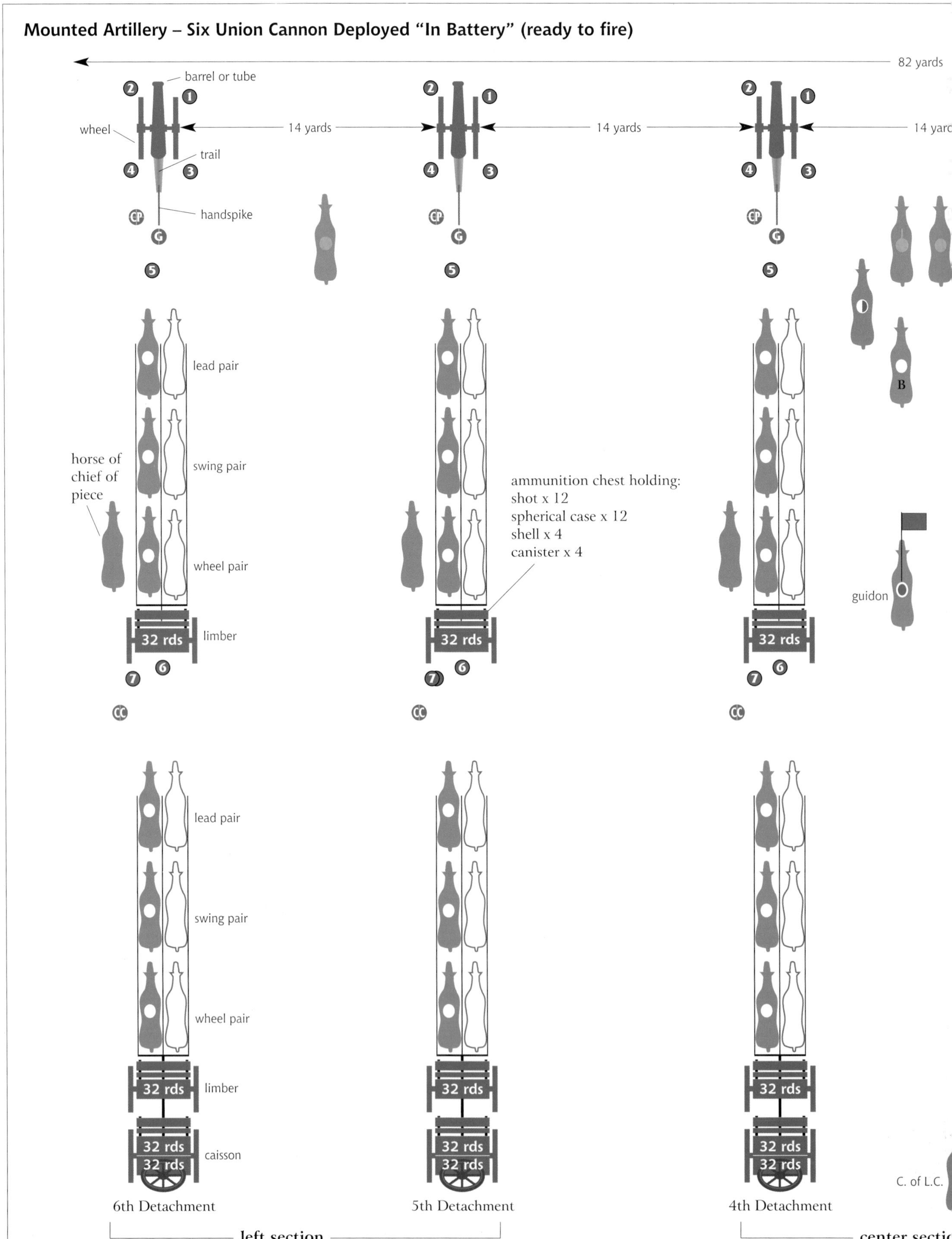

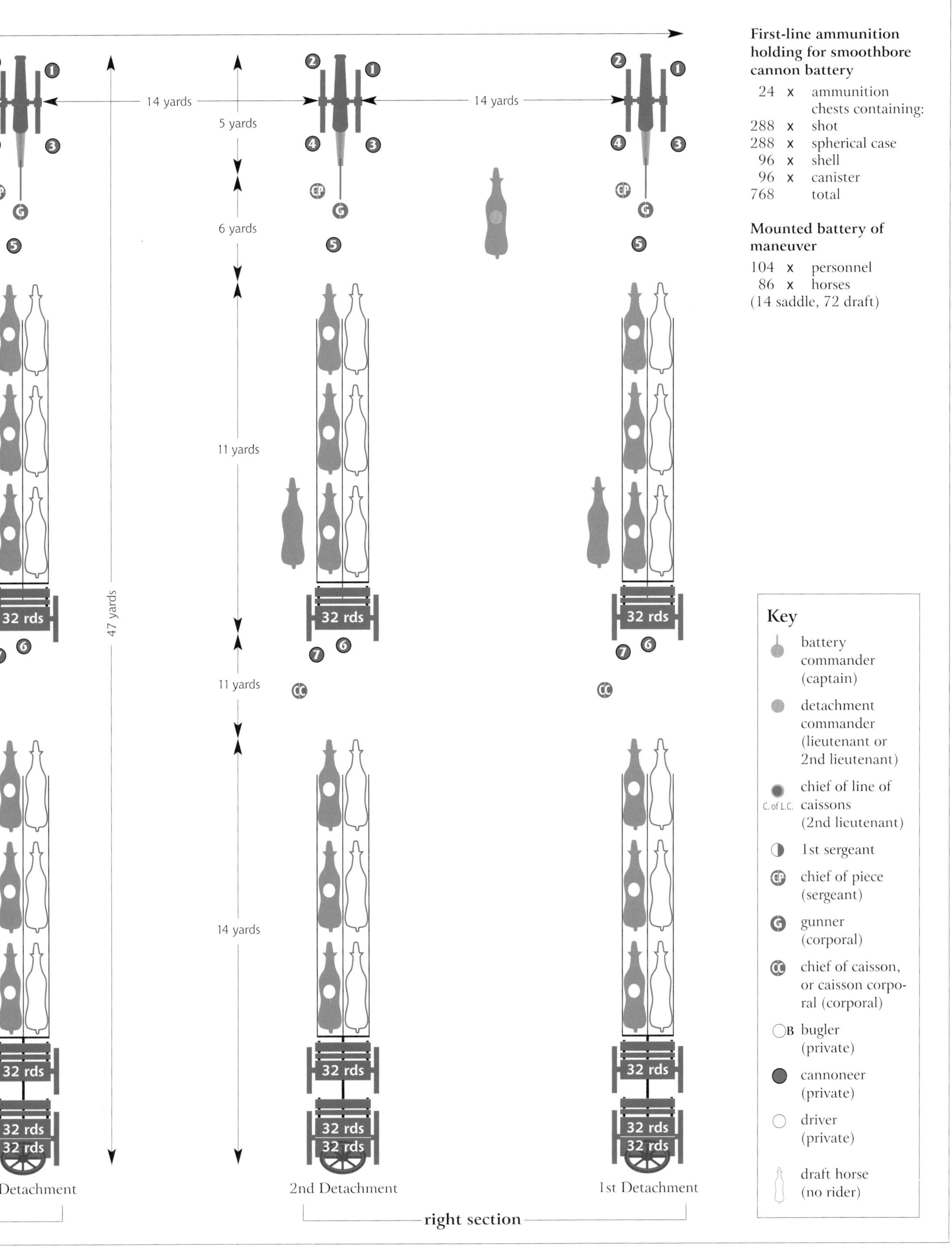

First-line ammunition holding for smoothbore cannon battery

24 x ammunition chests containing:
288 x shot
288 x spherical case
96 x shell
96 x canister
768 total

Mounted battery of maneuver

104 x personnel
86 x horses
(14 saddle, 72 draft)

Key

- battery commander (captain)
- detachment commander (lieutenant or 2nd lieutenant)
- C. of L.C. chief of line of caissons (2nd lieutenant)
- 1st sergeant
- CP chief of piece (sergeant)
- G gunner (corporal)
- CC chief of caisson, or caisson corporal (corporal)
- B bugler (private)
- cannoneer (private)
- driver (private)
- draft horse (no rider)

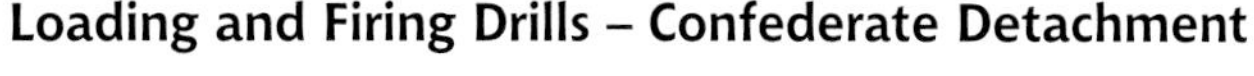

Loading and Firing Drills – Confederate Detachment

When in action, the cannon would be driven into position, the cannon removed from the limber by the cannoneers and brought to bear on the likely target. The gunner and cannoneers would position themselves as shown.

- On the command "Commence firing" by verbal order, signal or bugle, the gunner communicated the orders he received for the kind of ammunition to be fired for each shot to no. 6 at the limber and, if shell or spherical case, the range or time. He was equipped with a fuse gauge and hausse (pendulum) sight. He gave the command "Load." If the firing were slow, he checked each fuse as it was brought forward to ensure it was the required length – if not he corrected it with his fuse gauge.
- No. 6 at the limber box took the appropriate projectile, prepared the fuse if necessary, using his fuse gauge and the Table of Fire (page 163) glued inside the lid of the limber chest, and then handed the round to no. 7, who took it to no. 5.
- No. 3 held a priming wire and had a thumbstall over his thumb. On the command "Load" he covered the vent to keep air from any embers that might be present. No. 1 then sponged the bore with a wet sponge to remove any embers, at the same time checking to see that the vent was covered. If not, he shouted "Stop vent" and ceased sponging until it was covered.
- No. 2 received the round from no. 5, who had been handed it by no. 7. No. 2 then placed the round in the muzzle, ensuring the seam of the cartridge did not come under the vent. No. 1 then rammed the round down the bore and he and no. 2 stood back.

Key

- **G** the gunner (corporal) gave executive orders and pointed and sighted the piece
- **1** swabbed bore and rammed load
- **2** inserted charge and projectile into muzzle
- **3** tended vent and pricked cartridge
- **4** primed and fired the piece
- **5** carried round to no. 2
- **6** issued ammunition and prepared fuse
- **7** received round from no. 6 and carried it to no. 5

- The gunner then stepped up to the breech, placed the hausse sight in its seat and aimed the piece by making adjustments with the elevating screw and giving directions to no. 3, who moved the trail with the handspike, assisted by nos. 1 and 2 as required. No. 5 returned to the limber for another round that had been prepared by no. 6 and handed to no. 7.

- When satisfied with the aiming the gunner stepped back, at the same time removed the hausse sight and shouted "Ready" or raised both hands as a signal. On this command no. 3 pricked the cartridge through the vent to open a hole in the bag and covered the vent as soon as the primer was inserted. No. 4, having inserted his lanyard hook into the ring on a priming tube, dropped the tube into the vent and stepped back as far as possible while holding the lanyard with enough slack that it could be tightened without his moving position. No. 6 was preparing rounds for firing, cutting fuses as directed, assisted when necessary by no. 7. When no. 7 handed the round to no. 5 he told him the range or time on the fuse, and no. 5 reported it to the gunner before handing it to no. 2.

The Patron Saint of Artillerymen

The Louisiana State memorial consists of a 9-foot-long reclining figure of an artilleryman representing the Washington Artillery of New Orleans and standing over him a second 10-foot-high female supposedly representing "The Spirit of the Confederacy." However, the woman is also claimed to be St. Barbara, the patron saint of artillerymen. She lived in Asia Minor around A.D. 300, the daughter of a rich nobleman who was infuriated when his daughter converted to Christianity. Her father took her before the Roman prefect, who condemned her to death by beheading, her father carrying out the sentence. The story is that, as he returned home, he was struck by lightning and his body consumed by fire and thereafter Barbara came to be regarded as the saint to call upon for protection in a storm. With the introduction of gunpowder and the frequent loss of life due to accidental explosions, St. Barbara also gained the additional role of patron of artillerymen.

- The gunner stepped clear of the wheel to get the best view to observe the fall of the shot and ordered "Fire." No. 3 yanked the lanyard to fire the piece. No. 5 handed another round to no. 2 and the process began again until the order "Cease firing" from the detachment or battery commander or by bugle.

In this diagram the cannon has been detached from the team, as would be likely if it was to be in position for some time so that the team could be withdrawn a short distance, if possible into cover.

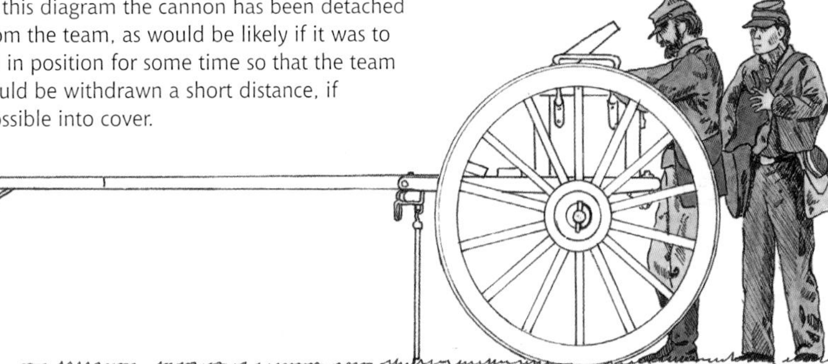

Corporals – chiefs of caisson
These were normally the six junior corporals whose duty was the care of the limbers and caissons, in particular the loading and packing of the ammunition. For this reason they were often called "caisson corporals." They were responsible for ensuring the drivers took proper care of their horses and harness, but operational control was by the chief of the line of caissons or the chief of piece. In action they remained with the caisson and prepared the ammunition for transfer to the forward limber.

Privates – cannoneers
Their primary duty was the actual loading and firing of the cannon. Each was assigned and trained in a primary position according to the numbers that described the duties of each different gun position (see the Loading and Firing Drills diagrams, pages 150–51). However, they were also trained to be competent in any position or as a driver. In action they received their orders from the gunner, with the chief of piece supervising the overall actions of the detachment. On the march they walked alongside their piece, only riding on the limber or caisson when speed was essential for deployment, and lent a shoulder to the wheel or hauled on a rope to get their cannon through the mud or up a steep slope.

Privates – drivers
These were the riders who rode and controlled the teams that moved the cannon and caissons. Each limber and caisson on campaign normally had a team of six draft horses. A driver had two horses and their harness in his care. He rode the left-hand horse but was responsible for feeding, watering and grooming both. These men were usually chosen for their skill with horses, although they were trained to take a place in a gun detachment if needed. In action they brought the ammunition into position as directed by the sergeant (chief of piece). The caisson drivers were directed into position by the chief of the line of caissons (normally an officer), often under fire. During the battle they tried to keep the horses calm, removed harnesses from downed animals and remained alert to the possible need to move position quickly. On July 3 the Union drivers with the caissons just behind the crest of Cemetery Ridge had to endure the intense bombardment of Confederate guns preparing the way for Pickett's attack, much of which burst over them. In these circumstances the usual procedure was for the drivers to lie down holding the reins in their hands. Drivers under heavy artillery fire had immense difficulty in controlling their horses, many of whom plunged and kicked in desperate attempts to get away.

The Funeral of Private Edwin H. Babson, 9th Massachusetts Battery

Soldiers killed on the battlefield rarely had the dignity and solemnity of a proper individual military funeral; more likely the best they could expect was a hastily dug grave, often a communal one, with none of their comrades present. However, given time, a death before battle merited a full-blown military send-off such as described by Sergeant Levi W. Baker of Captain John Bigelow's 9th Massachusetts Battery some three weeks before the battle:

> 10 June. Edwin H. Babson died of congestion of the lungs, caused by fever and ague. He was sick but two days. He was nineteen years old, an excellent soldier, liked by all, officers and men. He was the first we laid away, and we gave him a comrade's burial. At sunset his remains were laid on a caisson, covered with the flag and drawn by six horses, led by comrades, to the grave under an apple tree near headquarters. The procession was led by the guard detailed for the day, and a regimental band of the post, and followed by all the company. "Slowly and sadly we laid him down," and as his remains were lowered, the customary salute was fired from revolvers. The grave was marked by a tablet of red sandstone, well carved and lettered by one of our own men. His remains were afterwards removed to Massachusetts.

Privates – teamsters or wagoneers
These men were under the control of the quartermaster sergeant and were assigned to drive and take care of the battery wagon, forge and sometimes an ambulance wagon, usually drawn by four or six mules. An important part of their duty was the protection of their wagons, particularly the baggage wagons, from thieves in the form of hungry or marauding infantrymen! The teamsters and extra men assigned to the battery were responsible for the care of spare horses belonging to the battery. On the march they were to be found at the rear of the battery column or, more usually, further to the rear in the divisional train. Despite their comparatively safe job, teamsters often received a corporal's pay.

Privates – artificer and farrier
These men were skilled specialists and were paid at a higher rate than the other privates. The artificer and farrier traveled with the forge and battery wagon that contained their tools. The former was responsible for repairs to the wooden and iron parts of the battery carriages and wagons, while the latter had the daunting task of shoeing the horses and mules.

Privates – extra men
Most batteries had extra men (the 9th Massachusetts Battery had fifteen in September 1862) above the minimum required to enable the battery to be operational. They were assigned to the detachments for training as cannoneers and drivers, and were used to fill positions vacant due to sickness, furlough or battle casualties. They were normally under the overall supervision of the chief of the line of caissons, but they formed a useful pool of manpower for both the first sergeant and the quartermaster sergeant for fatigues and picket or guard duties. Their position was not an official one and individuals could expect to be rotated into more permanent positions.

Privates – musicians (mounted)
A battery usually had one or two musicians (mounted buglers). They were part of the battery commander's staff and as such remained with the battery headquarters at all times. During a normal day, routine activities were announced by up to ten bugle calls. In battle the common calls heard above the din of firing were "In Battery," "Commence Firing" and "Cease Firing." The bugler would be likely to get other duties within the headquarters, such as clerk or orderly.

Probably the most famous bugler at Gettysburg was Private Charles W. Reed, the bugler of the 9th Massachusetts Battery, who saved the life of Captain Bigelow, his battery commander, when the battery was overrun near Trostle Farm on July 2. Many years later he received the Medal of Honor for his gallantry. See Section Ten: Day Two.

Privates – guidons (mounted)

The soldier carrying the battery guidon was, like the musician, permanently attached to the battery commander's staff. His main function was, in the dust and confusion of battle, to act as a marker on which the guides (sergeants) could position and align their detachments. He acted on the orders of the battery commander and when arriving at a position on which the battery was to form "in battery" (get ready to fire), the guidon would halt either on the right or in the center of the proposed position. Once the battery was in position he would station himself in the center of the limbers, about 20 yards in the rear of the guns. Like the bugler, he was likely to be given clerical and orderly duties. In camp the guidon was kept furled and housed in the commanding officer's tent or quarters.

CANNON AT GETTYSBURG

Strictly speaking, all the artillery pieces at the battle should be classified as field artillery, as all the batteries in both armies were assigned to operate with either the infantry or cavalry. However, to differentiate between them the artillery batteries working with the former will be referred to by their correct title of "mounted" batteries and those with the latter will be called "horse" batteries – there were no "foot" batteries at Gettysburg. There were eleven different types of ordnance on the battlefield, of which the most common were the 12-pounder gun-howitzer (referred to as the Napoleon), the 3-inch ordnance rifle and the 10-pounder Parrott. The characteristics of each type are discussed below.

Model 1857 12-pounder Gun-howitzer (Napoleon)

This was probably the most popular, certainly the best known, field piece of the Civil War. The Napoleon was named after the French Emperor Napoleon III, who in the early 1850s instructed his ordnance department to design a cannon with which he could standardize his field artillery. His uncle, Napoleon I (an artilleryman by training), had a few heavy 12-pounders with his Imperial Guard at Waterloo; he nicknamed them his "Beautiful Daughters." The new cannon impressed a U.S. military mission that toured Europe during 1855–56 and recommended it be adopted by the American service. Although this was agreed, only five Napoleons were purchased between 1857 and the start of the Civil War. Four were given to Battery M, 2nd U.S. Artillery at Fort Leavenworth, Kansas, under the command of a Captain Henry J. Hunt. They were the only Napoleons on the field at First Manassas, where Hunt used them to cover the flank of the retreating Union Army. It was Hunt, now a brigadier-general and Meade's chief of artillery at Gettysburg, whose coordination and control of the Union artillery on July 2 and 3 was a major factor in withstanding repeated Rebel assaults (see box, page 155).

The 1857 Model Napoleon was a muzzleloading, smoothbore cannon, versatile in terms of firing all four of the different types of ammunition, lighter than previous models but every bit as strong and reliable. However, Union artillery ammunition expenditure returns for Gettysburg indicate that only Meade's 12-pounder Napoleons fired solid shot at the battle and it is quite likely this was also the case with Lee's Napoleons. This cannon was popular with the cannoneers, as the barrel was made of bronze (commonly called brass) and so there was far less chance of its bursting on firing – not uncommon with some iron guns. It had a bore of 4.62 inches and a muzzle velocity of 1,400 feet per second. Using a charge of 2.5 pounds and with the barrel at a 5-degree elevation, this cannon could fire a 12-pound solid iron cannonball out to 1,680 yards (the distance of first graze). However, it was most effective when firing ball or shell at ranges from 400 to 1,200 yards, and with canister (a highly effective anti-personnel weapon) below 350 yards. At 1,000 yards a solid shot would penetrate about one foot of oak. The barrel with its carriage weighed 2,445 pounds, light enough to be hauled by men for short distances (Captain John Bigelow's Napoleons from the Union Army's Artillery Reserve were dragged back by hand over 300 yards during their retirement from Sickles' salient on July 2), although the normal method of movement was, as with other pieces, by a six-horse team. Bigelow's cannon, like all Napoleons manufactured in the North, were distinguishable from those made in the South by the bulge or swelling at the muzzle, something missing from Confederate Napoleons.

Lee had ninety-nine Napoleons (and one outdated 6-pounder) at Gettysburg; Meade had 142.

These three Napoleons on Barlow's (Blocher's) Knoll represent the six of Lt. Baynard Wilkeson's Battery G, 4th U.S. Artillery, which defended this hill on July 1 in support of Brig.-Gen. Barlow's Division. Note how the copper in the bronze barrels has turned them green with age, making Napoleons on today's battlefield easy to recognize. Wilkeson was mortally wounded on this knoll by a shell that killed his horse and almost severed his right leg. He completed the amputation by cutting through the remaining sinew with a penknife. He died later from loss of blood and shock at the field hospital set up in the alms house alongside the Harrisburg Road. A total of 241 out of 631 (38%) of these cannon were engaged at the battle. The bugler is atop the 153rd Pennsylvania Infantry monument.

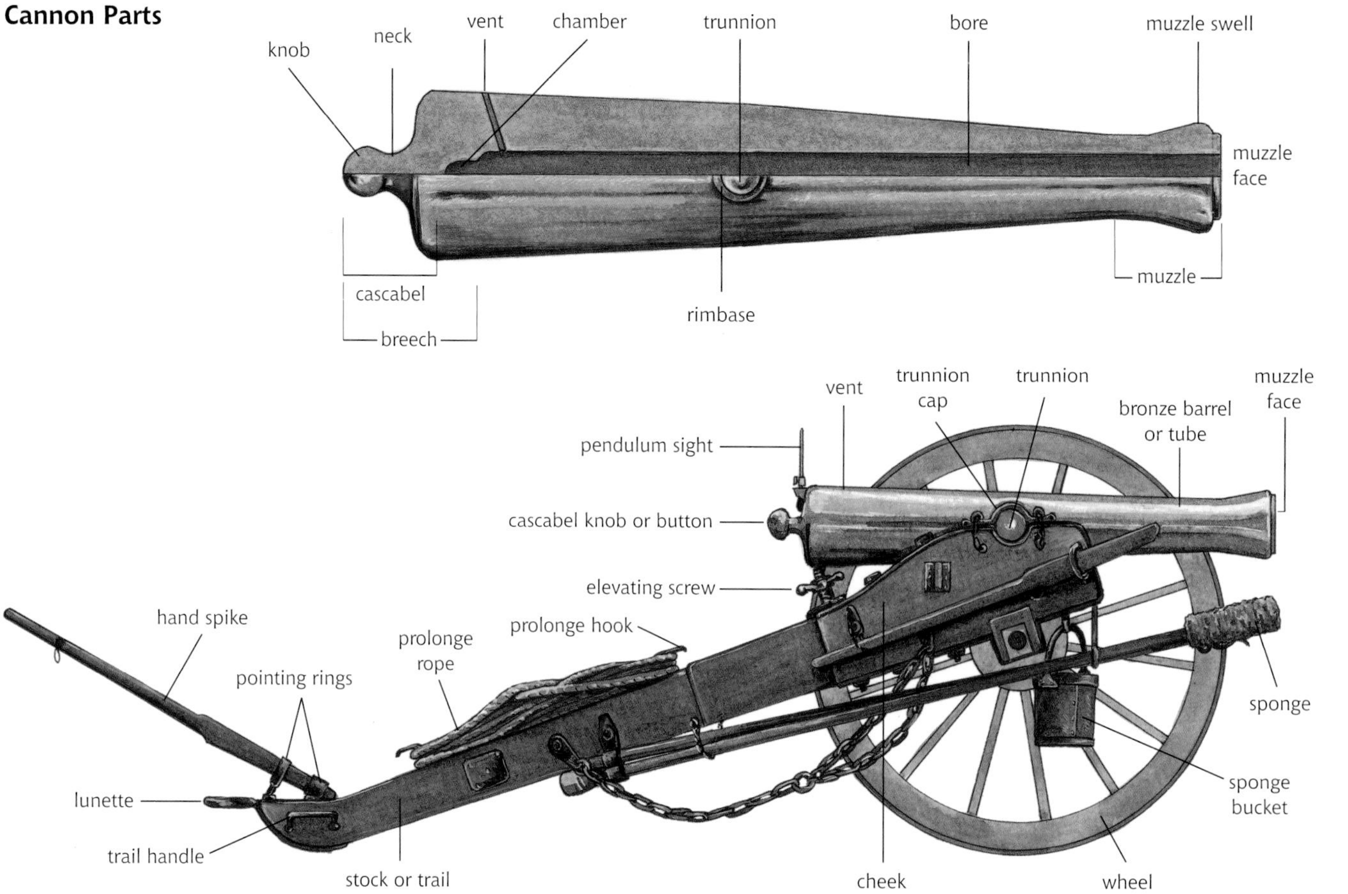

Cannon Parts

knob
neck
vent
chamber
trunnion
bore
muzzle swell
muzzle face
cascabel
breech
rimbase
muzzle

vent
trunnion cap
trunnion
bronze barrel or tube
muzzle face
pendulum sight
cascabel knob or button
elevating screw
prolonge hook
prolonge rope
hand spike
pointing rings
sponge
sponge bucket
lunette
trail handle
stock or trail
cheek
wheel

3-inch Ordnance Rifle

Adding rifling to a cannon barrel made it more difficult and expensive to manufacture, and increased the length of the tube, but it greatly increased the range and accuracy of the piece. The 3-inch ordnance rifle, originally called the "Griffen Gun" after its designer, John Griffen, was the most widely used rifled cannon of the war. It was extremely durable, as the barrel was made of wrought iron and, when finished, was sleek and completely smooth. With wrought iron there was no fear of burst barrels. When the tubes were tested in 1856 in front of representatives of the U.S. Ordnance Department, Griffen challenged them to burst a piece! Only after 500 shots, and finally firing it with a charge of 7 pounds and thirteen balls filling the entire barrel, did they succeed. A burst barrel occurred only once during the entire Civil War, and then it was at the muzzle (the less dangerous end for the cannoneers) when firing double canister in the Battle of the Wilderness. Another advantage was its comparative cheapness. The North produced over 1,000 during the war at a cost of about $350 each. Cannon for the South were made by Richmond's Tredegar Iron Works and by another manufacturer in Rome, Georgia.

The tube weighed only 820 pounds (its lightness was the reason it became the exclusive cannon of the fast-moving horse artillery) and used a black powder charge of only one pound, but produced a muzzle velocity of 1,215 feet per second. With maximum elevation of 16 degrees, the rifling enabled firing out to an extreme range of over 4,000 yards (almost 2.5 miles), although the maximum effective range at lower elevation (5 degrees) was about 2,000 yards. It had a fearsome reputation for accuracy at long distances.

A 3-inch ordnance rifle cannon marking the position of Capt. Robert H. Fitzhugh's Battery K, 1st New York Light Artillery on Cemetery Ridge, July 3. The six cannon belonged to Brig.-Gen. Tyler's Artillery Reserve and came into action south of the Copse of Trees in time to help repulse Pickett's charge. A total of 221 (38%) of these cannon were engaged at Gettysburg. Note the smoothness of the barrel, a characteristic of these guns.

A Confederate soldier was quoted as saying, "The Yankee three-inch rifle was a dead shot at any distance under a mile. They could hit the end of a flower barrel more often than miss, unless the gunner got rattled." It fired all projectiles except solid shot.

Brigadier-General Henry Jackson Hunt, 1819–1889

Early life
A somewhat stern, stuffy individual of the old U.S. Regular Army, Hunt, with his bushy black beard, was forty-four years old at Gettysburg. His father had been an infantry officer, serving much of his time on the frontier in the west. As a boy of eight he had been with his father on the expedition that established Fort Leavenworth, but within two years his father died. Henry Hunt attended West Point and graduated in 1839, at twenty, into the artillery. He fought initially as a lieutenant in the Mexican War but his outstanding dash and courage at the Battles of Contreras and Churubusco won him the brevet rank of captain and, at Chapultepec, major. Made substantive captain in 1852, he was selected in 1856 as a member of a three-man board that revised field artillery drill and tactics for the army. It was officially published as *Field Artillery Tactics* by the War Department in 1861 and was used by the Union (and Confederate) artillerists throughout the Civil War.

The Civil War
Hunt was probably the most gifted and professional artillerist of the war. He was the acknowledged expert on the science and tactics of gunnery. He sought to have artillery accepted as a separate arm of the service alongside the infantry and cavalry, commanded and coordinated by senior artillery officers under the commanding general rather than scattered in small packets under infantry brigade commanders. He had a gunner's eye for the ground and how best to position batteries in order to get maximum effectiveness when they opened fire. His four overriding tactical principles were the massing of batteries; the maximum concentration of fire onto targets; that artillery's priority target in defense was the enemy infantry, not counterbattery fire; and that firing should always be slow and deliberate – anything over one shot a minute was excessive. On one occasion when he saw a battery firing too quickly he shouted at the officer, "Young man, are you aware that every round you fire costs $2.67?" Not only was a slow rate of fire likely to be more accurate and conserve ammunition, but Hunt was always suspicious that firing off rounds quickly implied the gunners wanted to quit the gun line and move to the rear to replenish. Hunt would insist that cannon remained in position while the caissons went back for ammunition.

Early in the war he prepared Harper's Ferry for "defense or destruction." He was promoted major in the U.S. 5th Artillery in May 1861 and distinguished himself at First Manassas when his four guns, out on the left flank, broke up the Confederate pursuit. After organizing the artillery for the defense of Washington, he became a colonel on the staff of Major-General George B. McClellan in the Peninsula and commanded the Artillery Reserve. At Malvern Hill, where he had two horses shot under him, his use of massed artillery fire (at one stage he used sixty cannon as though they were one battery) at close range to smash the attacking Rebels prompted the Confederate General D. H. Hill to proclaim, "It was not war – it was murder." On September 15, 1862 he was promoted brigadier-general of volunteers. He fought at Antietam as chief of artillery – a battle the Confederates called "artillery hell." At Fredericksburg his 147 guns emplaced on Stafford Heights forced Lee to abandon any thought of counterattacking the Union forces across the Rappahannock River. However, at Chancellorsville Hunt was out of favor with the army commander, Hooker, and was confined to administrative duties rather than having direct control of the Army Artillery Reserve. The ill-coordinated Union artillery at this battle was a factor in Hooker's defeat. Hooker acknowledged this when he restored Hunt to command three days later.

At Gettysburg
July 1. Hunt's new commander, Meade, had more confidence in him than Hooker and allowed him considerable latitude in directing the artillery during the battle, although Hunt was never given specific instructions on this point. After the war, when asked by the Joint Committee on the Conduct of the War, "When were you restored to the full command of the artillery?" he replied, "General Meade took command on the twenty-eighth of June, I think, and moved the next morning. I had no opportunity then of saying anything whatever to him about my position." Hunt was not on the battlefield during July 1 but remained at Taneytown with Meade. They both arrived on Cemetery Ridge after midnight on July 1.

July 2. During the darkness Meade and Hunt carried out a reconnaissance of the whole position along Cemetery Ridge to Little Round Top and then to the Union right where the Baltimore Pike crossed Rock Creek. Hunt supervised the deployment of over 100 guns during the early morning. At about 11:00 a.m., after returning from Culp's Hill, he was sent by Meade to visit III Corps' commander (Sickles) who was having difficulty deciding how to implement his deployment orders. Hunt and Sickles rode forward together to inspect the position, about threequarters of a mile in front of Cemetery Ridge, that Sickles considered a better one for his corps. Hunt, however, could not give Sickles his consent ("Not on my authority") for such a change of orders. Sickles moved anyway. During much of the severe fighting in the afternoon, which eventually saw Sickles driven from his salient, Hunt was fully occupied positioning the Artillery Reserve and controlling ammunition supply. At one stage during the day Hunt was almost badly mauled by a herd of stampeding horned cattle. He described his experience thus:

> A herd of horned cattle had been driven into the valley between Devil's Den and Round Top, from which they could not escape. A shell had exploded in the body of one of them, tearing it to pieces; others were torn and wounded. All were stampeded, and were bellowing and rushing in their terror, first to one side and then to the other . . . cross I must, and in doing so had my most trying experience of that battle-field.

He spent most of that night with Brigadier-General Tyler, commander of the Artillery Reserve, supervising the reorganizing of batteries that had suffered losses, repairing damage and replenishing ammunition in the limber chests.

July 3. In the early hours Hunt was on Culp's Hill checking battery positions for the bombardment of Rebel troops that had gained a foothold at the base of the hill. He then oversaw the arrangements of the massed batteries along Cemetery Ridge to meet the expected Confederate assault. His strict orders to the batteries not to engage in a lengthy counterbattery duel were overridden by Major-General Hancock, commanding II Corps. This was to lead to a long feud between the two after the war. Nevertheless, his guns played a crucial role in throwing back Longstreet's attack on the Union center.

After Gettysburg
Hunt continued as chief of artillery of the Army of the Potomac for the remainder of the war and he was in charge of the Union batteries that battered the Petersburg defenses in 1864. He remained in the army after the war, commanding a frontier district and the Department of the South from 1880 until 1883 when he retired. He became Governor of the Soldiers' Home in Washington D.C., where he died of pneumonia, aged seventy, in 1889.

Its disadvantages were those of all rifled cannon, namely the high velocity often meant the projectile burying itself in the ground before exploding, with the consequent loss of lethality. Also the small caliber (3 inches) meant its performance with canister was less rewarding than with a smoothbore. As much of the firing at Gettysburg against infantry was within best canister range (350 yards), the Army of the Potomac probably had too high a proportion of rifled cannon (214 out of 358) for the best tactical mix. Early in the war Major-General McClelland tried to reduce the ratio of rifles to smoothbores to 1:2. He was unsuccessful. Brigadier-General Hunt realized their limitations and after Fredericksburg tried, also in vain, to replace some rifles with smoothbores.

It was the four 3-inch rifles of Lieutenant John H. Calef's Battery A, 2nd U.S. Artillery, that fired the opening Union artillery shot at Gettysburg. In 1864 when Calef handed in his four guns he noted their serial numbers. The "opening gun," number 233(1862), now stands at the foot of Major-General Buford's statue at the spot where the shot was fired (see box, page 340). All forty-six cannon with the Union Horse Artillery were 3-inch ordnance rifles, but only nine of the nineteen pieces operating with Stuart's Confederate Cavalry Division at the battle were of this type.

Lee had seventy-seven 3-inch ordnance rifles at Gettysburg; Meade had 144.

Parrott Rifled Cannon

This was another type of rifled, muzzleloading cannon firing projectiles varying in size from 10–250 pounds, although only 10- and 20-pounders were present at Gettysburg, the great majority being the former. Designed by Captain Robert P. Parrott, who had resigned from the army in 1836 to take charge of the West Point Foundry in Cold Spring, New York, all this family of cannon are recognizable by the thick reinforcing band of wrought iron, in the case of the 10-pounder about 13 inches wide, covering the breech and reinforce that was the point of greatest pressure during firing. However, this was not entirely satisfactory, as the tube was still made from cast iron, which tended to crack with hard use, resulting in the barrels occasionally bursting at the muzzle without warning. All Parrott had done was to move the potential bursting point forward to a marginally less lethal area. This defect made the cannon decidedly unpopular. A Private Augustus Buell, Battery B, 4th U.S. Artillery (a Napoleon battery), commented, "so long as the Parrott gun held together it was as good as any muzzle loading rifle" and, "if anything could justify desertion by a cannoneer, it would be assignment to a Parrott battery."

The 1863 Model was slightly modified by increasing the bore from 2.9 to 3 inches to make its ammunition the same size as that used in the 3-inch ordnance rifle, and the muzzle swell of the 1861 Model was eliminated. The 10-pounder could be produced quickly and cheaply at a cost of $187 each, so the Parrott became the workhorse of the artillery in the early years of the war, and continued to be produced in quantity even after the introduction of the 3-inch ordnance rifle. However, the end of the war also saw the end of the Parrott – it was never used again.

The 10-pounder had a barrel weight of only 900 pounds, high muzzle velocity, great accuracy and, with a one-pound charge and 6 degrees of elevation, could fire at distances up to 2,400 yards (the 20-pounder 3,000 yards). With extremely high elevation (35 degrees) it could reach out beyond 3 miles. As with all rifled cannon, its effectiveness at close range with canister was not that of a smoothbore, although a bolt fired at 400 yards could penetrate wood almost 6 feet thick; however, like the 3-inch ordnance rifle, the Union Parrotts at Gettysburg did not hold or fire solid shot.

Lee had forty-three 10-pounders and eleven 20-pounders at Gettysburg; Meade had sixty of the former and six of the latter.

Howitzers

Howitzers were bronze, smoothbore cannon with tapered powder chambers that allowed the use of a small charge of one pound. The resultant low muzzle velocity gave the 12-pounder an effective range of only up to about 1,100 yards – making them easy targets against longer-range artillery. Firing was at a higher elevation than with guns, as the projectile was intended to follow a high trajectory to attack targets hidden behind cover. It could fire all ammunition except solid shot and the Model 1841 12-pounder was probably the most effective field piece of the war at ranges below 400 yards, and due to its lightness (under 800 pounds) was highly suitable for accompanying infantry in the advance. As will be seen below (pages 475–76), Confederate Colonel Alexander wanted to use howitzers to go forward in support of Pickett's Division in its charge on July 3, but due to a misunderstanding this did not happen.

The Army of the Potomac had only two 12-pounder howitzers at Gettysburg, both in the Army Artillery Reserve. The Army of Northern Virginia, however, had a total of twenty-nine 12-pounders and four 24-pounders – a comparatively high 12 percent of the pieces engaged. The Confederates mostly sought to overcome the howitzers' lack of range by mixing them with other types of cannon. In practice this usually meant either one or two howitzers in a four-gun battery – an example being Major William T. Poague's battalion, whose four batteries each contained either one or two howitzers. Perhaps surprisingly, two of Lee's batteries were composed entirely of howitzers, although they were part of the strongest artillery battalion in the army – Colonel E. Porter Alexander's. Captain Fickling had four 12-pounders and Captain Moody four 24-pounders which Alexander had seemingly earmarked for close

Four 10-pounder Parrotts formed two sections of Capt. James E. Smith's 4th New York Independent Battery on the top of Devil's Den. Smith deployed them here on July 2 and was then engaged in a lengthy artillery duel with Confederate guns supporting Maj-Gen. Hood's divisional attack. Eventually Smith was forced to leave three intact cannon behind to be captured by the advancing Texans. Note the reinforced breech, necessary to reduce the chances of the cast iron bursting. Despite this, the barrel was burst, although nearer the muzzle. A total of 103 (16%) were engaged at the battle.

12-pounder Whitworth Breechloading Gun

This gun could also be used as a muzzleloader.

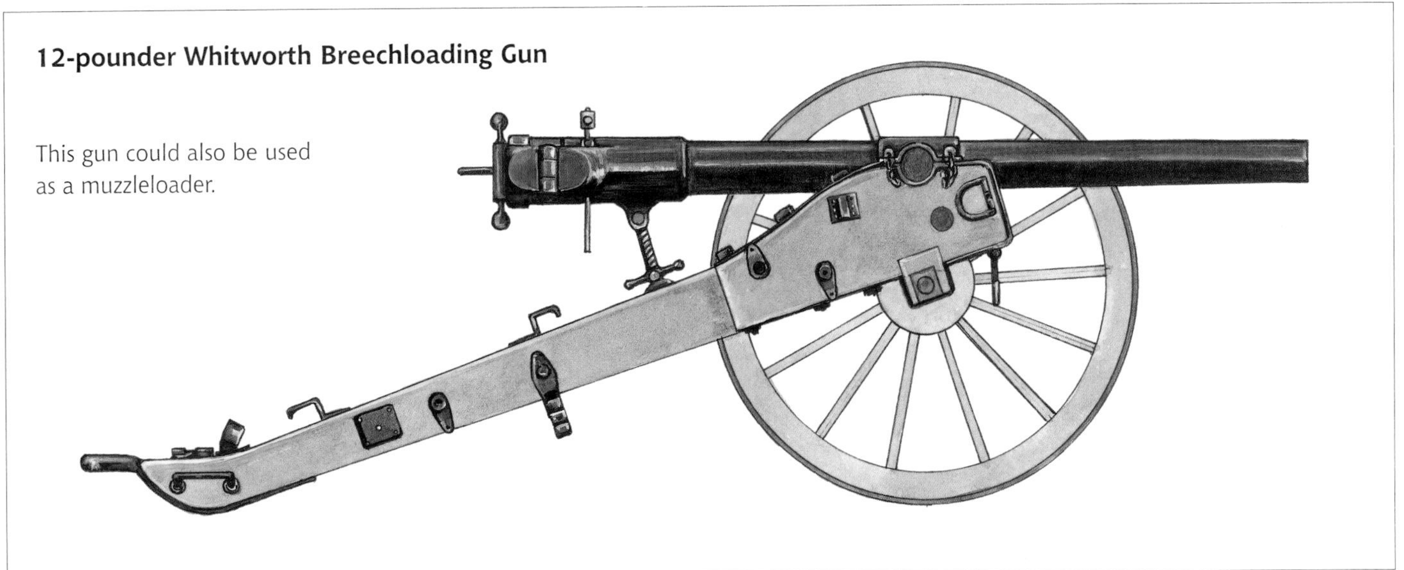

infantry support of Pickett's Division on July 3, as their lack of sufficient range would have precluded their taking part in the main preliminary bombardment.

Lee had thirty-three howitzers at Gettysburg; Meade had two.

Whitworth Rifled Cannon

The Whitworth breechloading cannon was an English-model gun imported by the Confederacy during the early months of the war before the blockade was tightened. It was a very rare cannon in the Civil War, but an interesting precursor to modern artillery in that it was breechloaded and had extraordinary accuracy over enormous range. Because the projectile did not have to be rammed down the barrel, tighter rifling was possible, which enabled it to reach out to an extreme range of well over 5,000 yards (making it the artillery's sniper rifle), although effective firing was up to around 2,500 yards. However, the rifling was not of the conventional grooves but rather was a 2.75-inch spiral hexagonal shape. Although explosive shell was made for the Whitworth, the shape of the projectile did not permit a sufficiently large powder cavity for this type to be effective; so solid shot in the form of 12-pound bolts was its principal ammunition – the only ammunition fired by these cannon at Gettysburg. This projectile made a recognizable howl as it hurtled through the air, causing those at the receiving end to yell "Whitworth!" as the bolt tore overhead. The Confederates' two Whitworths at Gettysburg were positioned on Oak Hill on July 3, firing at Cemetery Hill as part of the preparatory bombardment for Longstreet's attack. This was a range of some 4,000 yards, within their capability but well beyond their effective range. At that distance, with the smoke of firing, it is doubtful if the gunners saw much of their target. In addition, Colonel Alexander complained that the Whitworth's "breechloading arrangements, however, often worked with difficulty, and every one of the six [held by the Confederacy] was at sometime disabled by the breaking of some of its parts," and its efficiency "was impaired by its weight and the very cumbrous English carriage on which it was mounted." This weakness was again exposed at Gettysburg when one of the Whitworths on Oak Hill, damaged by Union fire on July 1, was put out of action again on July 3 when its breechloading mechanism broke.

Lee had two at Gettysburg; Meade had none.

Other Rifled Cannon

The Confederates had three other variations of rifled cannon:

The Blakely

Designed by Captain Theophilus A. Blakely and imported from England, this muzzleloading cannon fired a variety of ammunition, including flanged and studded projectiles, usually of copper or brass, which fitted into the grooves in the tube. The 12-pounder was made of steel and iron with a bore of 3.4 inches and a tube weighing 800 pounds. With a charge of 1.5 pounds it could fire out to 2,000 yards effectively. However, its recoil was alarmingly powerful and not infrequently damaged its carriage. Colonel Alexander again:

> The only advantage to be claimed for this gun is its lightness, but this was found to involve the very serious evil that no field-carriage could be made to withstand its recoil. It was continually splitting the trails or racking to pieces its carriages although made of unusual strength and weight.

Coupled with this, the fact that it performed better on a diet of English ammunition ensured the Blakely quickly became obsolete.

Lee (Stuart) had three with his cavalry; Meade had none.

The 3-inch Navy rifle

These cannon were originally cast for naval use and therefore normally had an underlug instead of trunnions, but for use by the army at Gettysburg they must have been converted to fit the standard artillery carriage by having the underlug removed and trunnions added. In terms of caliber, range and general characteristics they were identical with the 10-pounder Parrott and in some instances are referred to as "Navy Parrots."

At Gettysburg Captain Hugh M. Ross had one and Captain John T. Wingfield had three; the Army of the Potomac had none.

The James rifle

The Union Army Artillery Reserve had four James Rifles at Gettysburg. They were the only rifled bronze cannon on the field. They threw a 12-pound projectile up to 1,700 yards effectively. They formed part of Lieutenant-Colonel McGilvery's gun line along the southern part of Cemetery Ridge on July 3.

ARTILLERY EQUIPMENT AND IMPLEMENTS

Carriages

The primary function of the carriage was to hold the cannon in place while it was aimed and fired. It also enabled the piece to be moved easily. At Gettysburg the no. 2 carriage was used for the 1857 Napoleons, 3-inch ordnance rifles and 10-pounder Parrotts. All gun carriages, limbers and caissons (see below) were made of oak. A gun carriage consisted of two cheeks bolted together and to the trail. The cheeks supported the cannon by its trunnions, and in turn rested upon the axletree supported by two wheels. The back of the trail rested on the ground. The carriage dissipated the force of the recoil by rolling along the ground. On hard ground it could jump back several feet, but on soft soil the trail tended to dig in, making careful re-aiming necessary. At the end of the trail was an iron ring called a lunette, which was the means by which it was attached to the limber. Two pointing rings just forward of the lunette held a handspike, which provided leverage

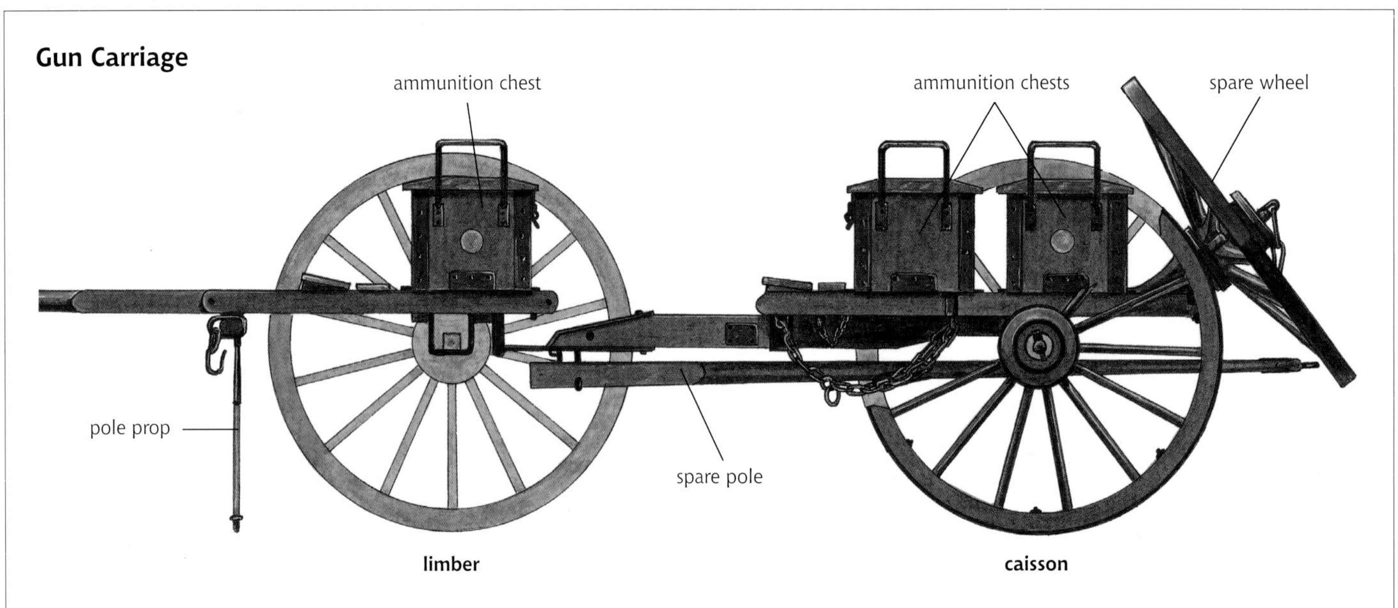

A Nasty Wound

Sergeant John Merrell, Battery H, 1st Ohio Light Artillery, kept a diary of the events in his battery during the battle. He described how his gun kept firing for an hour, by which time it was so hot it had to be replaced. They were under heavy fire from shells as well as muskets. Merrell stated that a Minie ball struck Sergeant George Ritchie in the abdomen, which was a polite way of saying in his groin. In fact Ritchie had been hit in the penis, the ball cutting its apex. Happily he recovered, returned to his battery, was later promoted first lieutenant, survived the war, married and fathered two sons and a daughter.

A limber with ammunition chest (above) and a caisson with three ammunition chests plus spare wheel (right), both positioned on Cemetery Ridge near the Angle.

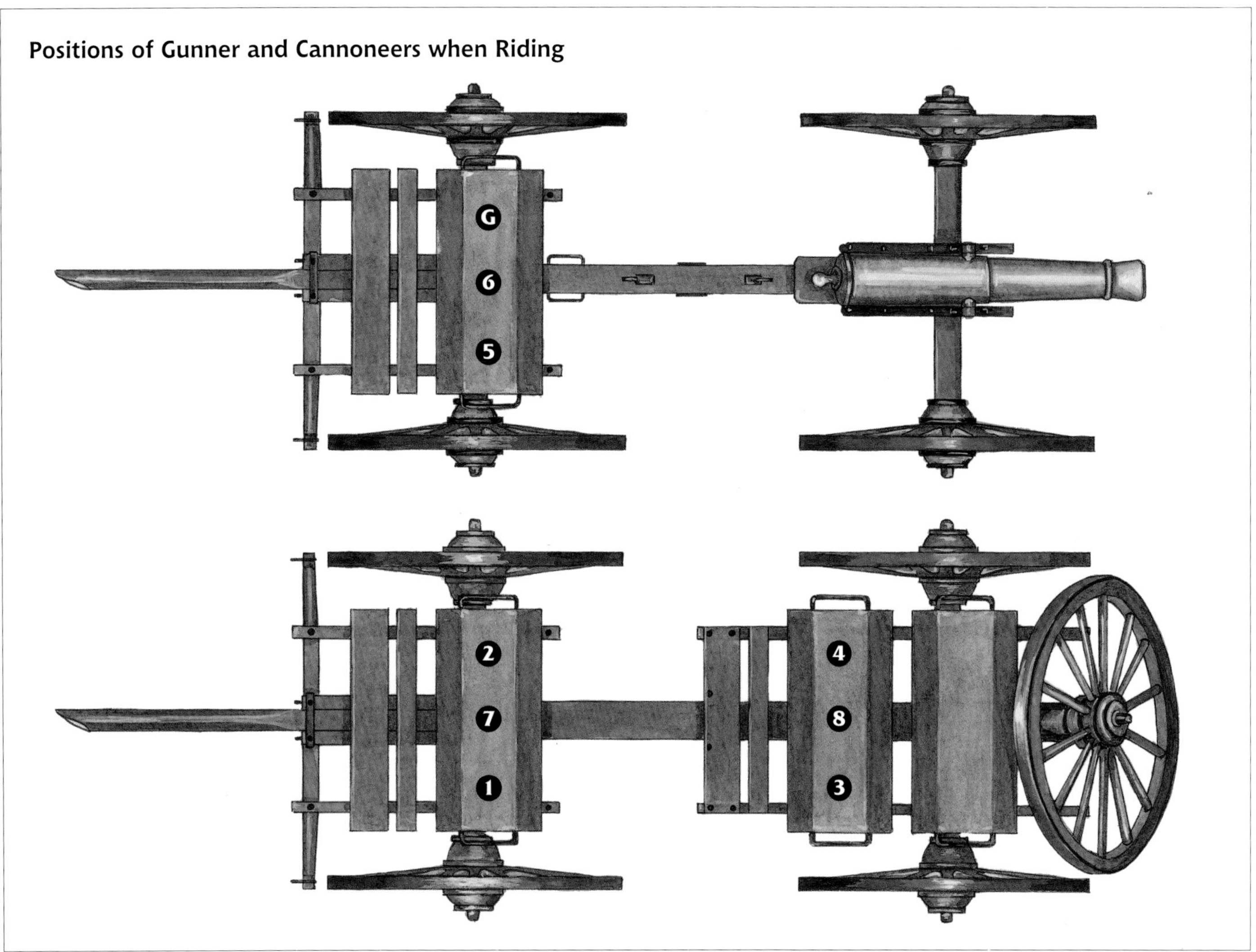

Positions of Gunner and Cannoneers when Riding

by which alignment could be adjusted. Forward from the pointing rings were two hooks around which was wound the prolonge, or towing rope (see below). The two wheels (the same size and interchangeable with all field artillery equipment) had iron tires and fourteen spokes that were dished slightly inwards to make the wheels springier on rough ground. This dishing improved the cornering of the vehicle and had the effect of throwing mud outward, away from men and horses close behind the carriage – an unpopular characteristic with infantry on the sides of the road. In addition, two handspikes, two sponges, a worm, and a sponge bucket were attached to the carriage.

Limber

A two-wheeled cart consisting of an axle with its wheels surmounted by a framework for holding an ammunition chest and receiving a pole for the horse team. At the rear of the axle was a pintle hook to receive the lunette on the end of the trail of the gun carriage. When the carriage and limber had been hooked up, the result was a four-wheel cart. Fully loaded, the combination of Napoleon cannon and limber had a draw weight of 3,865 pounds. The limber ammunition chest could serve as a seat for three cannoneers, but in order to spare the horses cannoneers would ride only when fast movement was really necessary. A grease (tar) bucket and two leather water buckets were slung underneath the limber and a tarpaulin strapped on top of the ammunition chest, which also served as a welcome seat cushion. Cannoneers seated on these chests had a jolting, bone-jarring ride, clinging desperately to the ammunition chest handles. Not only were they sitting on all the gunpowder, but if thrown off when moving at speed broken bones were inevitable and the cannoneer had to roll clear of the pounding hoofs and bouncing wheels of any following cannon or caissons.

Caisson

A two-wheeled platform intended to transport ammunition in two chests identical to that on a limber. It had a trail, or stock, like that on a gun carriage terminating in a lunette so that it could be hooked up to a limber for movement. Attached to the rear was a spare wheel weighing 180 pounds, making the total load exceed that of a gun and limber. Because this caused more teams to break down pulling caissons than pulling guns, in 1863 the Confederate Artillery Board recommended only one spare wheel per section (every two guns). Slung underneath was a spare limber pole and spaces were provided for an ax, long-handled shovel, pickax and spare handspike. The caisson was normally attached to a limber, with the whole forming another four-wheel cart carrying three ammunition chests. If necessary, up to another six cannoneers could sit on these ammunition chests – but this made the total weight excessive. An additional grease (tar) bucket and two water buckets were carried on the caisson's limber.

Battery Wagon

The battery wagon, also attached to a limber, was a long-bodied cart with a rounded top carrying all the equipment needed for maintenance within the battery. The wagon contained such items as paint, oil, spare gunner's tools, axes, over 200 pounds of spare harness, spare trail and wheel spokes, scythes, picks, spades and fodder in a rack at the rear. The chest on the battery wagon limber contained a set of saddler's and carriage-maker's tools. The total weight of the wagon with stores was almost 1,300 pounds, which was drawn by six draft horses.

Battery Forge

The forge was a portable smithy to which was attached the inevitable limber, with its chest on which the blacksmith sat, to allow it to be towed by another team of six draft horses. The limber chest contained the smithy's tools plus some 200 pounds of horseshoes and 50 pounds of nails. The forge consisted of firebox, bellows, coal, anvil, spare iron, and more shoes.

There is at least one example of smithies making repairs right up in the firing line at Gettysburg. On July 2 the recoil of one of the 3-inch ordnance rifles of Captain Rigby's Battery A, 1st Maryland Artillery, broke an axletree. On seeing this Lieutenant A. N. Parsons (Battery A, 1st New Jersey Light Artillery) told Rigby to have his gun dragged back into a hollow and bring his forge forward to where his own forge was sheltered by a large rock. There, with shells bursting nearby or screaming overhead, the combined team of smithies had the axle repaired and the gun back in action within an hour.

Implements

Worm

An ash staff with a large corkscrew fixed to one end, used to insert down the barrel to remove debris after frequent firing.

Handspike

A staff with iron at one end that was inserted in the pointing rings on the end of the trail to give leverage to move the trail and thus make adjustments to the alignment of the cannon.

Sponge and rammer staff

A long ash pole with a wool-covered sponge at one end and a rammer head at the other. It was used by cannoneer no. 1 for sponging out the barrel after firing and for ramming home the charge before firing.

Vent prick or priming wire

Pointed metal rod with a loop at the opposite end used by cannoneer no. 3 to thrust down the vent to pierce the charge in the bore.

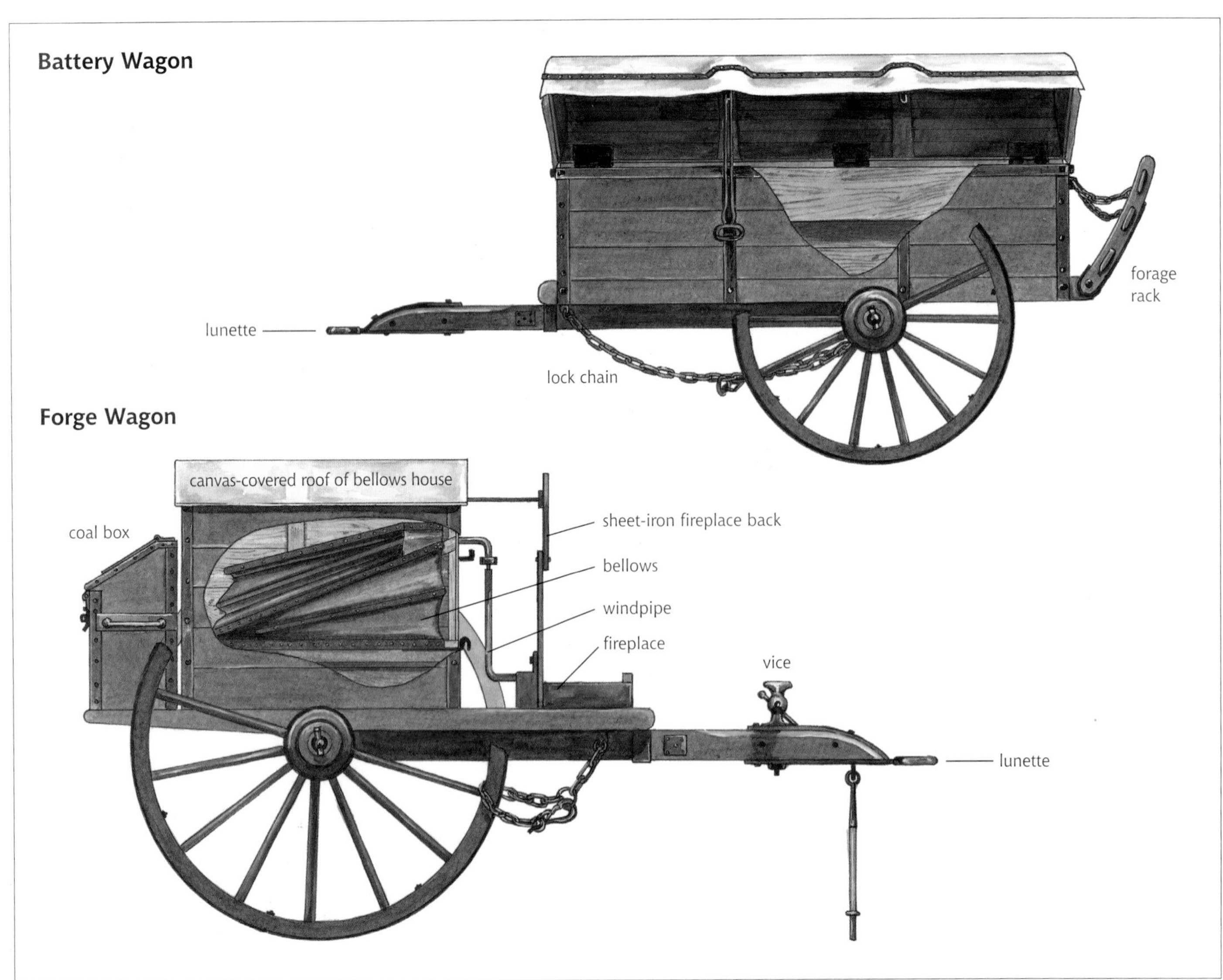

Artillery Equipment

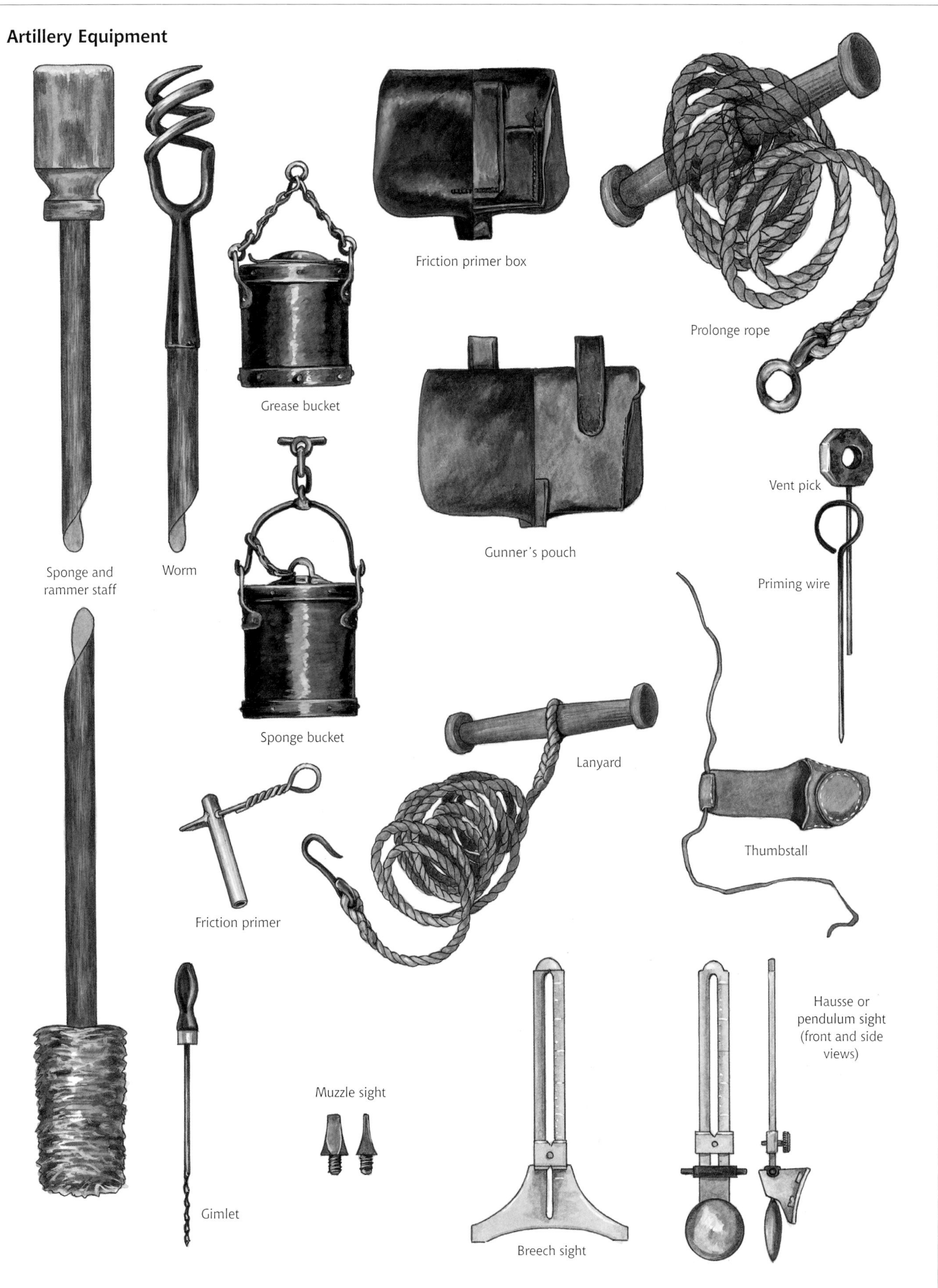
Sponge and rammer staff
Worm
Grease bucket
Friction primer box
Prolonge rope
Gunner's pouch
Vent pick
Priming wire
Sponge bucket
Lanyard
Thumbstall
Friction primer
Muzzle sight
Gimlet
Breech sight
Hausse or pendulum sight (front and side views)

Thumbstall
A covering to protect the thumb of cannoneer no. 3 while he had his thumb pressed over the vent opening during loading. It was made of buckskin with horsehair stuffed under the thumb pad.

Friction primer
A small tube filled with rifle powder that was inserted in the vent by cannoneer no. 4 at the moment of firing as the means of igniting the charge in the bore. The lanyard was hooked to the wire eye and a sharp pull drew the serrated end of the wire through a friction composition similar to a match head. The composition ignited and lit the fine musket powder in the shaft, the flame instantaneously igniting the powder in the bore. For a Napoleon, forty-eight friction primers and, for emergencies, 2 yards of slow match and four port-fires were carried.

Lanyard
A 12-foot length of cord with a toggle at one end and hook on the other. Cannoneer no. 4 attached the hook to the wire eye of the friction primer in the vent.

Hausse (pendulum) sight
This free-swinging sight was carried by the gunner (corporal) and attached to a seat on the side of the barrel at the breech end. It consisted of an upright piece of sheet brass with a movable slide that traveled along a graduated scale on the side. At the lower end of the sight was a lead-filled brass bulb, which allowed the sight to remain upright regardless of rough ground or the angle of the trunnions. The gunner looked through the sight down the barrel and through the top of the muzzle sight to the target. There was a different sight made to fit each cannon type. This sight was more effective when used in heavy siege or coastal guns than under the varied conditions of a battlefield.

Muzzle sight
A small iron sight that was screwed into the muzzle swell on guns and the middle of the muzzle ring on howitzers.

Prolonge
A piece of hemp rope 12 feet 7 inches long with a hook at one end and a toggle at the other. Two rings were attached at equal distance in the middle of the rope. The hook and toggle could be passed through the rings and hooked together to shorten the rope as required. It was used to drag the cannon by hand if need be.

Gimlet
Used for removing a plug or broken friction primer from the vent.

Vent punch
If an obstruction in the vent could not be removed with the gimlet, the vent punch was used to drive it into the bore.

Sponge bucket
This was made of sheet iron with a wooden cover. It was attached to the right side of the carriage and used to carry the water for sponging out or cleaning the barrel.

The Importance of Water for Guns

In the heat of action, on a hot day and with heavy firing, water to sponge the guns was often of more critical importance than drinking water for the cannoneers. With only one or two leather buckets available, it was important that nothing was spilled or the bucket accidentally knocked over. Without a wet sponge, firing would be exceedingly dangerous. Lieutenant Charles E. Hazlett commanded the six 10-pounder Parrotts of Battery D, 5th U.S. Artillery on Little Round Top on July 2. Early on, the water bucket of one cannon was pierced by a bullet near the bottom, causing the water to run out before a shot was fired. Private Thomas H. Scott described how Hazlett's ingenuity overcame the problem:

> Our battery covered the top [of Little Round Top] from right to left, and we had good shelter for our limbers in the rear, and the first thing the commander did was to order the swing and wheel drivers to the front to take our place as fast as we were killed or wounded. He also ordered up the caissons and ordered the battery wagon and forge drivers to get the camp kettles filled with water and brought to the guns, so we could have water to drink and sponge our pieces with . . .

Grease bucket
Also made of sheet iron with a metal cover, it held tar used as axle grease.

ARTILLERY AMMUNITION AT GETTYSBURG

There were four types of artillery ammunition in use at Gettysburg – namely, solid shot, shell, spherical-case shot (shrapnel) and canister. Each of these projectiles was attached to a block of wood called a "sabot" which fell away after firing. For the guns and 12-pounder howitzers the cartridge was a bag made of woolen material free of any cotton, containing the charge of gunpowder with the projectile attached to the same sabot, making what was called a round of "fixed ammunition."

Solid Shot

For smoothbores, cast-iron solid shot was the familiar spherical cannonball; for rifled cannon the elongated projectile was called a "bolt." With solid shot the weight in pounds was used to designate the caliber of the cannon to which it belonged, although a complete fixed round for a 12-pounder weighed 15.4 pounds. Solid shot was used for battering walls, fortifications, in counterbattery fire and against massed troops. It was more accurate than other types of ammunition and ranged further. On hard ground there was the added advantage of possible ricochets. Ricocheting shot kept low and did not lose its lethality until after the third bounce. Conversely, if it struck soft ground on a slope it would bury itself and cause no harm, which was not infrequently the case at Gettysburg. Solid shot could be a fearsome killer of men and horses in the right circumstances. Artillery officers liked firing it into tightly grouped formations, such as columns of infantry, where one shot at the right angle could plough through twenty ranks with ease, bowling men over like so many helpless skittles.

Solid shot represented 37.5 percent of the ammunition carried with the average smoothbore (Napoleon) battery at the battle. Of the usual thirty-two rounds in the 12-pounder's chest, twelve were solid shot.

Spherical-case Shot (Shrapnel)

Brigadier-General Henry J. Hunt, Meade's chief of artillery, called spherical-case "long-range canister." It was a hollow cast-iron shot filled with musket balls (seventy-eight for a 12-pounder) and embedded in melted sulphur or resin. Because these projectiles were intended to burst in the air over or among troops in the open rather than penetrate before exploding, the outer casing was thinner than that of a shell, and a weaker charge was used. The selection of the right fuse was particularly difficult if the target was troops exposed in the open but advancing quite rapidly, as was frequently the case at Gettysburg – a common situation for Union gunners.

Smoothbore Artillery Ammunition

Solid shot attached to wooden sabot with tin straps

Arrangement of tin straps on a shell with an opening to allow for a fuse

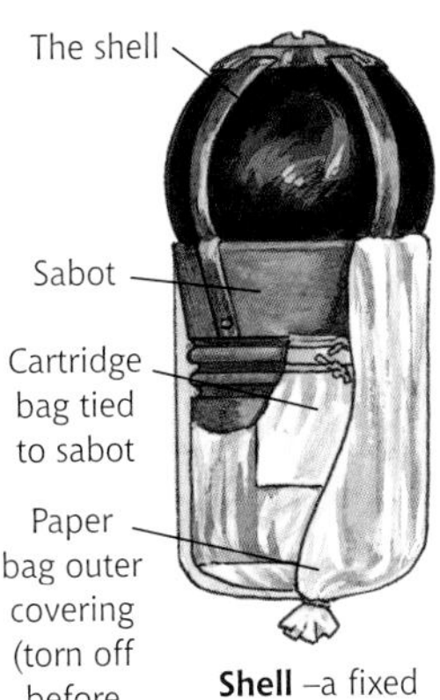

Shell –a fixed projectile as packed in limber/caisson ammunition chest

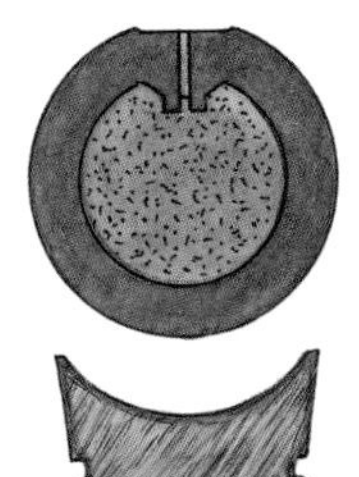

Cross-section of shell with a sabot

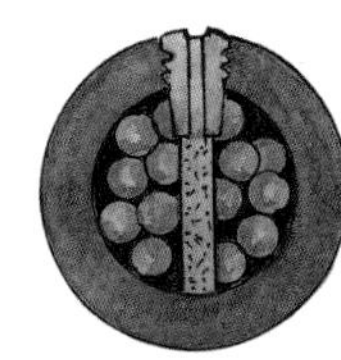

Interior of spherical case showing 4.5-ounce burster charge and musket balls

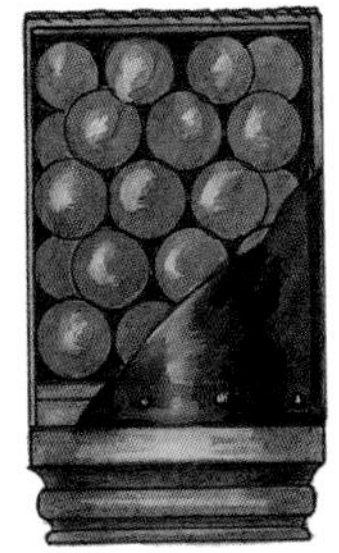

12-pounder canister round showing interior with large cast-iron shot

Tapered sabot for howitzers – necessary as the powder chamber was smaller than the bore

Fixed canister with paper bag covering the cartridge

The four types of artillery ammunition in use at Gettysburg. The "sabot" was a block of wood which fell away after firing.

Not only must the range be estimated accurately but also the gunner must remember to select different fuses as the enemy closed. These difficulties made it best used against stationary troops, or those moving slowly.

Case shot represented 37.5 percent (the same as solid shot) of ammunition with a 12-pounder Napoleon battery – again twelve out of the thirty-two rounds in the limber chest, but possibly up to 60 percent for rifled cannon (see below).

Shell

As its name implies, a shell was a hollow iron projectile containing a bursting charge of black powder that was ignited by a fuse lit by the flash of the propellant charge. There were two types. First, the timed fuse shell of which more were carried and fired at Gettysburg than the second type. It was designed to target troops in the open. The key to effective firing lay in selecting the fuse with the appropriate burning time for the range of the target – a task open to error, although a range/fuse table was pasted inside the lid of all smoothbore ammunition chests. The second type was a percussion shell that burst on impact. The outer casing was sufficiently thick to penetrate earthworks or wooden buildings without breaking, making it particularly suitable against troops deployed under cover or in woods. However, the small bursting charge of only half a pound of powder in a 12-pounder shell meant that its effect was often psychological rather than physical.

Shells represented only 12.5 percent or four out of thirty-two projectiles carried in the ammunition chests of Napoleons.

TABLE OF FIRE. LIGHT 12-POUNDER GUN. MODEL 1857.

SHOT. Charge 2½ Pounds.		SPHERICAL CASE SHOT. Charge 2½ Pounds.			SHELL. Charge 2 Pounds.		
ELEVATION In Degrees.	RANGE In Yards.	ELEVATION In Degrees.	TIME OF FLIGHT. Seconds.	RANGE In Yards.	ELEVATION In Degrees.	TIME OF FLIGHT In Seconds.	RANGE In Yards.
0°	323	0°50′	1″	300	0°	0″75	300
1°	620	1°	1″75	575	0°30	1″25	425
2°	875	1°30′	2″5	635	1°	1″75	615
3°	1200	2°	3″	730	1°30′	2″25	700
4°	1325	3°	4″	960	2°	2″75	785
5°	1680	3°30′	4″75	1080	2°30′	3″5	925
		3°40′	5″	1135	3°	4″	1080
					3°45′	5″	1300

Use SHOT at masses of troops, and to batter, from 600 up to 2,000 yards. Use SHELL for firing buildings, at troops posted in woods, in pursuit, and to produce a moral rather than a physical effect; greatest effective range 1,500 yards. Use SPHERICAL CASE SHOT at masses of troops, at not less than 500 yards; generally up to 1,500 yards. CANISTER is not effective at 600 yards; it should not be used beyond 500 yards, and but very seldom and over the most favorable ground at that distance; at short ranges, (less than 200 yards,) in emergency, use double canister, with single charge. Do not employ RICOCHET at less distance than 1,000 to 1,100 yards.

CARE OF AMMUNITION CHEST.

1st. Keep everything out that does not belong in them, except a bunch of cord or wire for breakage; beware of loose tacks, nails, bolts, or scraps.
2d. Keep friction primers in their papers, tied up. The pouch containing those for instant service must be closed, and so placed as to be secure. Take every precaution that primers do not get loose; a single one may cause an explosion. Use plenty of tow in packing.

(This sheet is to be glued on to the inside of Limber Chest Cover.)

Reproduction of the Table of Fire (glued to the inside of the limber chest cover)

Canister

This was close-range artillery ammunition reserved for soft targets (humans or horses) at 350-yard range or less. It was very effective if fired into the edges of a wood about to be attacked by

The appalling effect of a direct hit by a shell on a Confederate soldier.

infantry. The canister resembled a large shotgun cartridge in that it consisted of a tin cylinder attached to a sabot and filled with cast-iron shot (or any small lumps of metal). Canisters for guns contained twenty-seven shots (for howitzers forty-eight), all packed in four tiers in sawdust. As with solid-shot ammunition, no fuse was required. As the projectile left the barrel, the pressure of the charge and the relaxation of the confining pressure of the barrel caused the canister to disintegrate, allowing the balls to be hurled forward in an ever-increasing cone. This made missing difficult at ranges under 200 yards. If the artillerymen were getting really worried at that range they could, and did, load with double-shotted canister. In this case only one round would be fixed ammunition; otherwise there would be two cartridges in the barrel with unpleasant consequences for the cannoneers if fired. For this reason it was usual to hold one or two unfixed canister rounds in an ammunition chest.

There was only a 12.5 percent holding (four rounds in a chest of thirty-two) of canister rounds in a Napoleon battery at Gettysburg, which was found to be inadequate by a number of defending Union batteries on July 2 and 3, but of which the

Confederate Artillery Ammunition Problems

From the start of the war the Southern artillery had been plagued, not only by the insufficient quantity of ammunition but also by its poor quality. The situation had not changed by July 1863. A major factor in the generally less than effective Confederate artillery bombardments during the battle was defective ammunition that either exploded prematurely, too late, or not at all. Add to this frequent wastage due to poor packing and the problems of having several different calibers in the same battery, and the size of the handicap becomes clear. There were three difficulties:

• **Fuses.** The Bormann fuse was the one most commonly in use at Gettysburg for smoothbore cannon, but the Confederate factories had not been very successful in copying it. According to Colonel Porter Alexander, only about 20 percent of the A.N.V.'s Bormann fuses worked properly during the entire war. In 1866 he wrote:

> Repeated attempts were made to improve the manufacture, but they accomplished nothing, until after the battle of Chancellorsville the Bormann fuse continued in use, and premature explosions of shells were so frequent that the artillery could only be used over the heads of the infantry with such danger and demoralization to the latter that it was seldom attempted. Earnest requests were made to the Ordnance Department to substitute for the Bormann fuse, the common paper-fuses, to be cut to the required length and fixed on the field . . . These requests . . . were at length successful in accomplishing the substitution. The ammunition already at hand, however, had to be used up, and its imperfections affected the fire even as late as Gettysburg.

This problem affected the firing of shell and spherical-case ammunition, most effective against troops in the open at medium to long range. Two Gettysburg examples: Colonel J. Thompson Brown's guns bombarding Cemetery Hill were unable to neutralize the enemy satisfactorily as they had been unable to use shell. Brown reported in August 1863: "had we been able to continue our fire with shell, the result would have been entirely satisfactory; but, owing to the proximity of our infantry to the enemy, and the defective character of some of the shell, the batteries were compelled to use solid shot [not usually in a good anti-personnel role]."

Captain Willis Dance, firing from Seminary Ridge, said much the same thing: "In this position it was impossible to say what damage was inflicted on the enemy, because, for fear of injuring our infantry in front, we were ordered to fire only solid shot . . ."

• Mixed calibers. As has been mentioned, it was always something of a logistical nightmare for Confederate ordnance officers ensuring the right amount of the right type of ammunition was stocked in the ammunition chests. Also the similarity in size of the 3-inch ammunition and the 2.9-inch could cause serious difficulties. First Lieutenant John M. Gregory, ordnance officer of Ewell's Corps, reported several instances of this and of defective friction primers:

> [In] Jones' battalion, the ammunition of the 3-inch (banded) gun, or navy Parrott, is mixed up with the 2.9-inch 10-pounder Parrott in such a way as to cause great inconvenience. Two guns were rendered unserviceable after firing 12 rounds, from the shell lodging in the bore.
>
> Lieutenant Osborne, ordnance officer, Carter's battalion, reports also that some of the 3-inch Parrott ammunition was issued to him for the 2.9-inch Parrott ammunition.
>
> Lieutenant [John] Seldon, jr., ordnance officer First Virginia Artillery also reports that he received some 3-inch Parrott ammunition. He reports that he could not use the Confederate States fuse with Yankee ammunition.
>
> Lieutenant Fontaine reports that the friction primers were very defective from improper filling, and also from the top part not being properly closed.

• Poor packing. Again quoting Lieutenant Gregory:

> The artillery ammunition lately received from Richmond is packed in such miserably weak boxes that they are always bursting, and, in consequence, several boxes have been so damaged as to render the ammunition entirely unserviceable. Besides, there is great danger of explosion in the wagons from the loose powder.

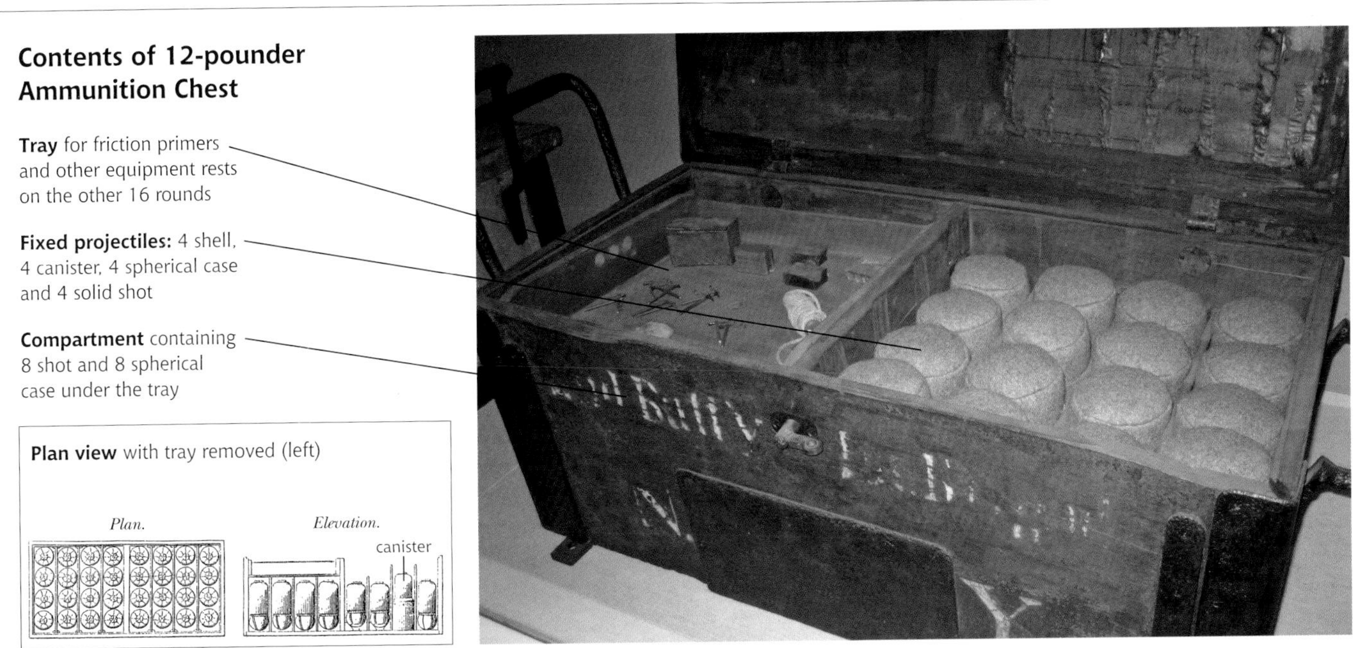

attacking Confederates had little use. An example of the, at times, critical shortage of canister in some Union batteries occurred on the evening of July 2 when Early's attack partially succeeded in breaking through the Union line along Brickyard Lane. Up the slope on East Cemetery Hill behind the infantry line, the six 3-inch ordnance rifles of Battery F and G, 1st Pennsylvania Light Artillery, under Captain R. Bruce Ricketts, ran out of canister and resorted to firing spherical case without fuses, called "rotten shot," as it burst at the muzzle, scattering the balls rather like canister.

Fuses

Solid shot and canister both operate on the same principle as musket fire: the projectiles are simply flung at the enemy by exploding a charge of powder behind them. Shell and case shot are more complex in that they are required to explode on, near or above the target. For this a fuse is needed. During the Civil War there were, as noted above, two types of artillery fuse – time and percussion fuse.

Time fuses

The most common and successful (because it was reliable and waterproof) in use at Gettysburg was the Bormann fuse, of Belgian origin. Within a squat threaded cylinder of metal was a groove running round the circumference; a channel at one end of the groove led to the center of the fuse, which was in turn perforated to communicate with the charge inside the shell. The top of the fuse was sealed with a thin sheet of tin, graduated up to 5.25 seconds. The cannoneer at the limber chest (see pages 150–51) would screw the fuse into the shell and punch a hole at the required number of seconds – the fuse being lit by the flame of the discharge. The Confederates, however, had real problems when they undertook to copy and manufacture these fuses early in the war. The use of these Southern-made fuses by Rebel artillery generated many complaints concerning its quality (see box opposite). By Gettysburg the manufacturing problems had been mostly overcome but quantities of the defective fuses were still with the Army of Northern Virginia and had to be used in the battle. Many Confederate artillerymen preferred the old form of paper fuse, packed with a composition of mealed powder, which could be cut to the required length and inserted into a wooden plug in the hole in the shell. Paper fuses were color-coded – yellow burned for five seconds, green for seven and blue for ten.

Percussion fuses

This type of fuse exploded on impact. This entailed the use of a mechanism involving some sort of slider or spring and striker. Their complex and often delicate construction made them somewhat unsuitable for prolonged field service, as there was always the worry that their mechanism might become armed during transportation or loading.

Artillery caisson and dead mule.

Ammunition Holdings

Union

Below is an estimate of the first-line ammunition (ammunition immediately available and not part of the army and corps artillery reserve trains) by type held in the ammunition chests carried on the limbers and caissons of the engaged artillery of the Army of the Potomac at Gettysburg. Because numerous batteries on both sides ran low on, or out of, ammunition during the three days and had to be replenished from reserves, it is useful to have some idea of the quantity available to battery commanders when they first came into action, assuming they had restocked before deploying. The calculations are based on the figures contained in *Field Artillery Tactics*, signed in Washington on March 1, 1863 by Secretary of War Edwin M. Stanton, which confirmed that the normal practice was for each ammunition chest for smoothbore cannon to hold 32 projectiles (solid shot 12, spherical case 12, shell 4, canister 4). Estimates for rifled cannon are more difficult, as the breakdown by type of projectiles in the chests was still to be finalized in the light of battlefield experience, although it was determined that they would contain fifty rounds. However, it is clear from expenditure returns that rifled cannon did not fire (nor presumably hold) any solid shot at Gettysburg. Each cannon had one chest on its limber and three more on the caisson/limber available to it.

Army of the Potomac – Estimated Initial First-line Artillery Ammunition Holdings

	Fixed solid shot	Fixed spherical-case shot	Fixed timed and percussion shell	Fixed and unfixed canister	Total
12-pdr gun-howitzer (Napoleon)					
Holding per limber chest	12	12	4	4	32
Holding per cannon (4 chests)	48	48	16	16	128
Holding per battery (6 cannon)	288	288	96	96	768
Army holding (142 cannon)	**6,816**	**6,816**	**2,272**	**2,272**	**18,176**
Rifled cannon (3-in ordnance rifles, 10- and 20-pdr Parrotts and James rifles)					
Holding per limber chest	–	20	25	5	50
Holding per cannon (4 chests)	–	80	100	20	200
Holding per battery (6 cannon)	–	480	600	120	1,200
Army holding (214 cannon)	**–**	**17,120**	**21,400**	**4,280**	**42,800**
12-pdr howitzer					
Holding per limber chest	–	20	15	4	39
Holding per howitzer (4 chests)	–	80	60	16	156
Army holding (2 howitzers)	**–**	**160**	**120**	**32**	**312**
Total first line ammunition (358 cannon/howitzers)	**6,816**	**24,096**	**23,792**	**6,584**	**61,288**

Notes

- Only the Napoleons carried solid shot, while overall the holdings of case shot and shell were about equal. Only about 11% of the total holding was canister.
- The average first-line holding of all types of ammunition per cannon was 171.

Note: totals have been rounded up or down to the nearest hundred:

Fixed solid shot	6,800
Fixed spherical-case shot	24,000
Fixed shell (timed and percussion)	24,000
Fixed canister	6,600
Total	**61,300**

These holdings indicate that the type of firing was expected to be mostly at medium range (350–1,200 yards) with 78 percent of stocks being spherical case or shell and only 11 percent each for solid shot and canister.

This gives an average overall first-line holding per gun (358 engaged) of 170 rounds, but it was not equally divided: a smoothbore (Napoleon) had 128 rounds per gun and a rifled cannon 200, with batteries holding 768 and 1,200 respectively.

To arrive at an estimated total holding for the army, these figures must be added to the ammunition held in the wagons of each corps' artillery train and the Army Reserve train, including the "secret" additional stock of twenty rounds per gun (about 7,000 rounds) that Brigadier-General Hunt had added. Of this extra stock, Hunt wrote: "I had moreover, on my own responsibility, and unknown to General Hooker, formed a special ammunition column, attached to the Artillery Reserve, carrying twenty rounds per gun, over and above the authorized amount, for every gun in the army." Hunt stated in his report that the Army of the Potomac started the battle with 270 (including the extra twenty) rounds per gun, or 96,660, say 97,000, in total. Whether he included the III Corps artillery train that had been left behind by Major-General Daniel Sickles is not clear, but these figures assume he did. Of this ammunition, some 61,300 was up front with the guns, with the balance of 35,700 being held in wagons in the various reserve trains. Assuming the reserve stocks were held in the same proportion as the first-line (shell and case 39 percent each; shot and canister 11 percent each), then the estimated number of the different types of ammunition would be as shown below in round figures:

	First line	Reserves	Total
Solid shot	6,800	3,900	10,700
Spherical-case shot	24,000	13,900	37,900
Shell	24,000	13,900	37,900
Canister	6,600	3,900	10,500
Total	**61,400**	**35,600**	**97,000**

These figures give an average army holding of 270 rounds per piece.

According to the report of Lieutenant Cornelius Gillett, ordnance officer of the Artillery Reserve train, he spent the entire night of July 2 "sending out wagons and issuing to batteries . . . the wagons which had been unloaded were ordered to the rear, and I sent about seventy teams . . . [back] to Westminster." He then summarized his issues at Gettysburg as follows:

To Major McGilvery	4,030
To Brigadier-General Hunt	360
To batteries	7,474
To supply train Second Corps	2,825
To chief of artillery Third Corps	3,000
To supply train of Eleven Corps	1,500
Total issued at Gettysburg	19,189

He then added, "I had remaining on hand 4,694 rounds . . ." From this it would seem the Artillery Reserve train initially held some 24,000 rounds, although this seems too high a figure.

The holdings of the types of ammunition with each cannon had implications for the rate and length of time a gun or battery might expect to be able to fire without replenishment. For example, a Napoleon smoothbore had only twelve solid shot in the gun limber, which at a moderate rate of two shots a minute would last only six minutes. At this rate a gun would fire off its entire first-line solid shot ammunition (forty-eight rounds) in twenty-four minutes; similarly spherical case. Some twelve minutes' firing at a fast rate of four rounds a minute would see the gun and battery out of this type of ammunition. With only four rounds of canister per limber, the enemy closing in, guns firing as rapidly as possible with some double-shotted, a Union battery would exhaust its holding in well under five minutes. All of which goes to emphasize how vital was the adequacy and smooth functioning of ammunition resupply, together with the need to conserve ammunition. Numerous batteries on both sides ran out of ammunition at some time during the three days; some had to be temporarily withdrawn and replaced because of it, while some resorted to firing off ammunition not best suited to the target – for example spherical case instead of solid shot, or without fuses instead of canister.

Confederate

Lee's Army of Northern Virginia seldom had sufficient reserves of artillery ammunition – Gettysburg being no exception – and there were very serious problems with the quality (see box, page 164). The quantity and quality of the ammunition were two of several shortcomings that prevented the softening-up bombardment of the Union line prior to the final Pettigrew–Trimble–Pickett attack on the last day from achieving its objective (see Section Eleven: Day Three). Colonel Alexander had this to say about the Rebel system of artillery ammunition supply in general:

> No ordnance-wagons accompanied the [artillery] battalions, the total supply of reserve ammunition being concentrated into one train under the ordnance-officer on the staff of the chief of artillery of the corps. These trains never exceeded one wagon to three guns, which was sufficient when within a day's march of a depot of supplies, but compelled the greatest saving in the use of ammunition when on active campaigns. Indeed, the limited resources of the Confederacy, the scarcity of skilled workmen and workshops, and the enormous consumption, kept the supply of ammunition always low. The Ordnance Department in Richmond was never able to accumulate any reserve worth mentioning, even in the intervals between campaigns, and during active operations the Army of Northern Virginia lived, as it were, from hand to mouth . . . The order "save your ammunition" was reiterated on every battlefield, and many an awful pounding had to be borne in silence from Yankee guns, while every shot was reserved for their infantry.

What do Colonel Alexander's remarks mean in terms of Confederate artillery ammunition holdings at Gettysburg? It is certain that overall, gun for gun, Lee's gunners had fewer rounds per piece than Meade's. Rebel ammunition chests for their smoothbore and rifled cannon would mostly be of the same design and hold similar amounts to those of the Yankees. However, the loading of the chests was not necessarily identical. Andrew's *Mounted Artillery Drill*, dated April 10, 1863, a Confederate publication, contains the results of an Artillery Board that recommended, presumably from battlefield experience, that holdings of the ammunition chests of 12-pounder smoothbores (Napoleons) be somewhat different from the standard Union practice. The board recommended 8 solid shot, 16 spherical case, 4 shells and 3 canister – all fixed ammunition. Additionally, there should be two more canister rounds, unfixed, loaded with .69 musket balls to be used in conjunction with other projectiles (i.e. double canister), thus making five canister in all – a total of 33 rounds (Union 32). It is uncertain whether these loadings had been adopted by June, but for the purposes of estimating Confederate holdings it is assumed they were.

For rifled cannon this board recommended the four chests with each cannon be loaded as follows:

- Gun limber, caisson limber and forward chest on the caisson each with 36 spherical case, 18 shells, 6 canister and no solid shot. Total per chest: 60 projectiles.
- The rear chest on the caisson containing only 36 rounds – 24 spherical case and 12 shells. This was almost certainly designed to reduce the weight of the caissons.

A fairly typical four-gun battery with two Napoleons and two 10-pounder Parrotts, such as Captain Hugh H. Garden's Palmetto (South Carolina) Light Artillery, would, on this basis, have 264 smoothbore and 432 rifled ammunition, totaling 696 rounds in its chests as first-line holdings.

Army of Northern Virginia – Estimated Initial First-line Artillery Ammunition Holdings

	Fixed solid shot	Fixed spherical-case shot	Fixed timed and percussion shell	Fixed and unfixed canister	Total
12-pdr gun-howitzer (Napoleon) + 1 x 6pdr					
Holding per limber chest	8	16	4	5	33
Holding per cannon (4 chests)	32	64	16	20	132
With mostly mixed batteries, estimates not practical per battery	–	–	–	–	–
Army holding (100 cannon)	**3,200**	**6,400**	**1,600**	**2,000**	**13,200**
Rifled cannon (3-in ordnance rifles, 10- and 20-pdr Parrotts, Navy, Blakely, and Whitworth rifles)					
Holding per limber (60 limber chests)	–	36	18	6	60
(36 limber chests)	–	24	12	–	36
Holding per cannon (140 cannon)	–	60	30	6	96
Army holding (140 cannon)	**–**	**8,400**	**4,200**	**840**	**13,440**
12- and 24-pdr howitzer					
Holding per limber chest	–	20	15	4	39
Holding per howitzer (4 chests)	–	80	60	16	156
Army holding (33 howitzers)	**–**	**2,640**	**1,900**	**528**	**5,068**
Total first-line ammunition (273 cannon/howitzers)	3,200	17,440	7,700	3,368	31,708

Notes

• Only the Napoleons held solid shot but, unlike the Union artillery, well over twice as much spherical case was held than shell of both types. Only 11% of total holding was canister.

• The average first-line holding of all types of ammunition per cannon was about 117.

Note: totals have been rounded up or down to the nearest hundred:

Fixed 12-pdr smoothbore	3,200
Fixed spherical-case shot	17,500
Fixed shell (timed and percussion)	7,700
Fixed canister	3,400
Total	**31,800** (say 32,000)

As with the Union artillery, the Confederates seemingly anticipated most firing to be at medium ranges and accordingly held a large preponderance of spherical case and shell (almost 79 percent) and only around 10 percent each of solid shot and canister.

These figures give an overall average first-line holding per piece of 117 (say 120) rounds, compared with the Union 170. As Lee's batteries were mixed, it is impractical to compare battery holdings, but as far as gun types were concerned, Confederate smoothbores probably had around 132 rounds with the gun at the start of the battle, but only 96 with the rifled cannon – the reverse of Union artillery.

It was in the corps reserve ordnance trains that holdings were likely to be particularly thin. A wagon drawn by six mules on dirt roads could haul a load of about 3,000 pounds. The average weight of a fixed projectile was 15 pounds, so a wagonload of artillery ammunition would be around 200 projectiles or twenty-five boxes (ammunition was normally packed in wooden boxes containing eight rounds of the same type – very heavy at 120 pounds). Assuming Colonel Alexander's one wagon for every three guns to hold for Gettysburg, this would mean ninety wagons with an approximate holding of about 18,000 rounds in the reserve ordnance trains, or sixty-six rounds per gun. This reflects Alexander's statement that Lee started the campaign "with a good deal less than 100 rounds per gun extra." In a letter dated March 17, 1877 Alexander was more specific when referring to the reserve trains at the start of the campaign:

> I am very sure that our ordnance trains did not carry into Pennsylvania a reserve supply of more than 100 rounds per gun additional, and I don't believe they had over 60 rounds to a gun. I have never seen the figures, but I was myself chief of ordnance of the army from August 1861, to November 1862, and was very familiar with the extent and capacity of the ordnance trains. When nearer Richmond we seldom had a reserve of over 50 rounds per gun, the difficulty of transportation always limiting us to the utmost economy in its use, and in the trains devoted to its carriage.

It would seem therefore that sixty-six rounds per gun in the corps reserve trains are about right. On this basis the estimated total of artillery projectiles available to the Army of Northern Virginia would have been about 50,000, or an average of 186 rounds per gun for 273 guns actually engaged.

However, for Gettysburg there was also a small army ordnance train. Kent Masterton Brown, in his book *Retreat from Gettysburg*, quotes from a recent discovery by Wes and Sam Small of Gettysburg from *The Report of Ordnance Stores on Hand* that Lee's Army Reserve ordnance train had a mere 3,810 projectiles (some fourteen shots per piece), 2,720 friction primers, 640 fuses and two barrels of cannon powder. It was broken down as follows:

	Shell	Case	Shot	Canister
Napoleon	528	1152	168	58
10-pdr Parrott	448	512	–	36
20-pdr Parrott	152	–	–	–
3-in ordnance rifle	32	–	–	–
12-pdr howitzer	230	210	–	40
24-pdr howitzer	48	–	–	16
Whitworth	–	–	72	–
Blakely	12	96	–	–
Totals	**1,450**	**1,970**	**240**	**150**

There were also only 70,250 musket caps, 40,000 rounds of .69, and 22,000 rounds of .54 ammunition – not quite enough to give every infantryman one shot each! This amount of artillery ammunition represents only 476 boxes (at eight rounds each) or some twenty wagonloads – a desperately small reserve ordnance train. Lee had ordered another ordnance train before the campaign but had no idea of its whereabouts at the start of the battle – it did not arrive until July 6, by which time Lee was in full retreat. Assuming all caissons with the batteries were full and that this really was all Lee had in the Army Reserve train, then he fought Gettysburg with not quite 40,000 rounds, or 146 per gun. In view of the number of batteries that ran dry on July 3, it is feasible that the holding was indeed this low.

Artillery Ammunition Expenditure

Union

Brigadier-General (then Colonel) Hunt issued detailed Artillery Orders dated September 12, 1862, part of which read:

> The proper expenditure of ammunition is one of the most important duties of an Artilleryman. An officer who squanders the whole of his ammunition in a short engagement proves himself incapable of appreciating the due effect and use of his arm, and incurs the heaviest of responsibility.

It is even more difficult to estimate expenditure of artillery ammunition for both sides than it is to calculate approximate holdings. Generally expenditure was very high overall, with battery commanders frequently sending back to replenish from reserve wagons, particularly at night. Some ammunition was lost when caissons were hit and exploded and commanders, aware of dwindling stocks over the course of three days' fighting, often ordered that firing either cease or that it be at a slow, deliberate rate, sometimes as low as one shot every two minutes. On occasion ammunition was wasted on minor clashes when it should have been conserved. An example is the artillery exchanges that started as early as 8:00 a.m. on July 2 between Confederate gunners and Major-General Hancock's II Corps' batteries over possession of Bliss Farm – for both sides an unnecessary side-show that simmered and flared up at intervals all day. Up to 100 guns were involved during the day, with a substantial expenditure of ammunition and the loss (by Lieutenant H. Cushing's Battery A, 4th U.S. Artillery) of several limbers of ammunition. There was a similar problem the next day when Hancock countermanded the army chief of artillery's instructions not to reply to the Confederate bombardment. By doing so he seriously depleted the long-range ammunition in his corps. According to Captain Patrick Hart (15th New York Artillery), when the Confederate infantry advanced "Hancock['s] arty was as silant [*sic*] as the grave."

Then, more ominous, Major Thomas W. Osborn, commanding the Artillery Reserve Brigade of the Union XI Corps, later wrote that he had seen a battery throwing ammunition away so they could report it exhausted and retire for more. Some batteries were more heavily involved than others. On July 1, for example, only the Union guns with I and XII Corps were engaged and none of Longstreet's Confederate Corps. However, despite the lack of action on the first day, by the end of the battle Longstreet's guns had been in action longer than those of the other two corps. Some examples of the wide variety of expenditure illustrate the problem:

- On July 1 the four 12-pounder Napoleons of Captain Lewis Heckman's Battery K, 1st Ohio Light Artillery, fired some 113 rounds in just thirty minutes – 28 rounds per gun at the comparatively slow rate of about one shot every minute.
- In the fighting around the Peach Orchard on July 2 the ten 12-pounder Napoleons belonging to Captains Ames and Hart of the Army Artillery Reserve were all withdrawn with empty caissons.
- On July 2 Captain John Bigelow's six 12-pounder Napoleons fired 92 of the 96 rounds of canister held with the guns in the defense of the "Plum Run line."
- Also on July 2, Captain R. Bruce Ricketts, commanding the 3-inch ordnance rifles of Battery F and G, 1st Pennsylvania Light Artillery, later stated: "On that second day we fired about 500 rounds, all we had, and more, for, at the last, we received a few rounds from the adjoining battery. About 25 rounds were used prior to 4 p.m. and about 475 rounds after that hour, from four guns and three only at the last . . . We expended in all 1050 rounds, about five tons (during the battle)."
- Major Osborn, in his report to Brigadier-General Hunt, stated, "I am unable to give any definite estimate of the amount of ammunition expended during the engagement. After we had exhausted the supply with the batteries, I replenished from our [XI Corps] train. Colonel Wainwright [I Corps Artillery Reserve commander], on the p.m. of the 1st, also replenished from our train, and, *after this source was exhausted* [author's emphasis], I drew from the reserve train of the army."

A consolidated report on the Army of the Potomac's expenditure of artillery ammunition at Gettysburg shows that five corps (I, II, III, VI and XII) fired a total of almost 20,700 rounds. For these corps the report includes a breakdown of the types of ammunition used but only a total for XI Corps (4,993) and the Artillery Reserve (11,184), with an incomplete report for V Corps and none for the Cavalry Corps. The table below shows the breakdown of expenditure for I, II, III and XII Corps, but not for the forty-eight cannon of VI Corps, as the report shows they fired only 315 rounds between them, so to include them would distort the average for the great bulk of the Union guns. The report clearly indicates that only Napoleons fired solid shot, thus confirming that the rifles' caissons probably did not hold this ammunition.

Army of the Potomac – Return of Artillery Ammunition Expenditure, I, II, III and XII Corps

	Number of cannon	Solid shot	Spherical case (shrapnel)	Shell – timed and percussion	Canister	Total rounds	Corps total
I Corps							
12-pdr Napoleons	12	544	530	192	219	1,485	
3-in ordnance rifles	16	–	1,090	1,768	172	3,030	
10-pdr Parrots	–	–	–	–	–	–	
Corps total	**28**	**544**	**1,620**	**1,960**	**391**	**–**	**4,515**
II Corps							
12-pdr Napoleons	12	732	730	244	244	1,950	
3-in ordnance rifles	12	–	1,425	1,977	462	3,864	
10-pdr Parrotts	4	–	625	625	150	1,400	
Corps total	**28**	**732**	**2,780**	**2,846**	**856**	**–**	**7,214**
III Corps							
12-pdr Napoleons	18	522	343	111	35	1,011	
3-in ordnance rifles	–	–	–	–	–	–	
10-pdr Parrotts	12	–	533	510	174	1,217	
Corps total	**30**	**522**	**876**	**621**	**209**	**–**	**2,228**
XII Corps							
12-pdr Napoleons	10	232	361	60	100*	753	
3-in ordnance rifles	–	–	–	–	–	–	
10-pdr Parrotts	10	–	354	525	100*	979	
Corps total	**20**	**232**	**715**	**585**	**200**	**–**	**1,732**
Totals	**106**	**2,030**	**5,991**	**6,012**	**1,656**		**15,689**

*estimated

Notes

- The above figures include only those corps that submitted detailed reports.
- No solid shot was fired by any rifled cannon.
- About equal amounts (38%) of spherical case and shell were fired, 13% of solid shot and 11% of canister.

Note: Figures have been rounded up or down to the nearest fifty:

Solid shot	2,050
Spherical-case shot	6,000
Shell (timed and percussion)	6,000
Canister	1,650
Total	**15,700**

This shows some 76 percent of all firing in these corps was either spherical case or shell in equal proportions.

The above figures give a corps average expenditure of 3,925 rounds, which figure these estimates will use for V Corps, halving it for the Cavalry Corps.

The overall estimate of Union Army ammunition expenditure is calculated as follows:

I Corps	4,515
II Corps	7,214 – by far the highest corps expenditure
III Corps	2,228
V Corps	3,925 – a corps average
VI Corps	– these 48 guns are not included as they fired only 315 rounds
XI Corps	4,993
XII Corps	1,732 – the lowest corps expenditure
Artillery Reserve	11,184 – indicating how heavily these 106 guns were involved on July 2 and 3 to reinforce the Union line
Cavalry Corps	1,963 – half an infantry corps average
Total	**37,754 (say 38,000)**

This total gives an average expenditure per Union piece actively engaged at Gettysburg (310, excluding VI Corps' 48 guns) of 123 rounds.

Confederate

Unfortunately the present writer has been unable to find any consolidated Confederate report of ammunition expenditure. However, some recorded examples of individual batteries or battalions give an indication of the fluctuating amounts.

- In the three days' fighting the Confederate Major William Pegram's Battalion in Hill's Corps Artillery Reserve, consisting of twenty pieces of Napoleons, 3-inch rifles, Parrotts and howitzers, reportedly fired 3,800 rounds. This is an average of 190 rounds per piece – well above the average.

- In contrast, Major David McIntosh's Battalion of sixteen pieces in the same corps reserve fired a total of 1,249 rounds, mostly shells, with an average per gun of seventy-eight.
- Lieutenant-Colonel John Garnett's Battalion of fifteen pieces in Heth's Division was not engaged on July 1 but fired off 1,000 rounds during the remaining two days at the low average rate of sixty-six per piece.
- In Longstreet's Corps Captain Edward S. McCarthy commanding the 1st Richmond Howitzer Battery of two Napoleons and two 3-inch rifles reported he had fired 600 rounds from the rifles and 264 from the Napoleons in two days. The rifles' firing 300 rounds each was well above the average.
- Also in Longstreet's Corps, Captain Basil C. Manly's Battery A of 1st North Carolina Light Artillery reported firing 1,146 rounds during the whole campaign – although the great bulk would have been at the battle – from his two Napoleons and two 3-inch rifles, making 132 each.
- Confederate Lieutenant John M. Gregory, Chief of Ordnance in Ewell's Corps, submitted a detailed report of ammunition expenditure. In it he states that for the period of the battle sixty-five guns were engaged and fired 5,851 rounds at an average of 90 per gun.

The average from these six random examples shows that Confederate guns fired around 115 rounds each during the battle. Using this figure, the total expenditure for the Army of Northern Virginia would be very approximately 31,395 (say 31,400).

Rates of fire

For both sides conservation was supposedly a key principle during the three days of battle. Conservation meant not firing unnecessarily at long ranges; using appropriate ammunition for the range and type of target; and firing deliberately, slowly, with accurate judging of ranges and careful, unhurried aiming. Rapid fire and double-shotting were reserved for close-range emergencies. Colonel Alexander, appointed de facto artillery chief for Longstreet's attack on July 3, had this to say on ammunition expenditure: "During the previous afternoon [July 2], we had 62 guns in action from 1 to 4 hours, & had refilled our chests from the trains. Our reserve wagons I knew must be very nearly empty of all but canister [the Confederates had few, if any, opportunities to fire canister at Gettysburg]."

An example of well-controlled firing, with the rate appropriate for the situation, is illustrated by Captain A. Judson Clark, commanding the six 10-pounder Parrotts of Battery B, 1st New Jersey Artillery, on the afternoon of July 2. His controlled response to the heavy Rebel gunfire of their pre-attack softening-up bombardment was to open fire first by single guns, then by section, then by half-battery and finally two rounds of battery fire. After careful observation of the strike, and when satisfied as to the effectiveness of the firing, he ordered "Fire at will" – the guns firing continuously and independently at a deliberate rate when ready. That afternoon this battery was engaged for around two hours, during which time they fired 1,342 rounds – an average of 224 rounds per gun, or each gun firing one shot every two minutes; a slow rate, but nevertheless one that consumed considerable quantities of ammunition in a comparatively short time. At the end of the day Sergeant William Clairville, who cut a notch in a stick for every round his gun fired, counted 241 notches. Artillery manuals indicate that Clark's one carefully aimed shot every two minutes was a slow rate.

EFFECTIVENESS OF ARTILLERY FIRE

It is generally accepted that the effect of artillery fire during the Civil War was psychological as much as physical – probably more so, with the percentage of casualties caused by gunfire seldom exceeding 10 percent, often less. Nevertheless, gunfire had a powerful effect on morale, not only for those on the receiving end. When told that his battery position on Little Round Top was a poor one for guns, the battery commander Lieutenant Charles E. Hazlett responded, "Never mind that, the sound of my guns will be encouraging to our troops and disheartening to the others." He was right.

Certainly fire boosted the morale of infantry waiting to advance to see their guns battering the enemy positions – the more guns, the more impressive it looked and sounded. Conversely, infantry under fire from enemy guns expected their own to reply, even though it might be tactically unsound to do so. The primary example of this at Gettysburg occurred on the afternoon of July 3 in the Union line on the southern sector of Cemetery Ridge. As mentioned above, when the full fury of the Confederate bombardment got under way, Major-General Hancock, commanding II Corps, rode down this part of the line insisting the Union batteries respond with counterbattery fire. This was contrary to Hunt's order that ammunition be conserved for the expected infantry assault. Hancock insisted that the morale of his infantry required that Union artillery reply and he gave direct orders to that effect to several batteries, two of which obeyed. However, they ceased firing when the artillery brigade commander, Lieutenant-Colonel Freeman McGilvery, countermanded the general's order after Hancock had moved on.

Direct evidence of the comparatively small physical effect artillery fire had on personnel at Gettysburg, and during the Civil War in general, comes from a Union officer, Surgeon Henry Janes, 3rd Vermont Infantry, who was responsible for some 21,000 wounded after the battle. On October 27, 1899, he published his observations in the *Baltimore Sun*. The relevant part is quoted in Gregory A. Coco's *A Concise Guide to the Artillery at Gettysburg*:

> The proportion of cases in which artillery men are able in the excitement of battle, to burst shells in exactly the right position in front of a line of battle to do much execution is very small, even at a range of only one mile . . .
>
> The execution done by artillery in battle is usually greatly overrated. During our Civil War, out of 245,790 shot wounds [to Union soldiers] 14,032 were caused by artillery, viz, 350 by solid shot, 12,520 by fragments of shells, etc., and 1,153 by grape and canister . . .
>
> Just before Pickett's celebrated charge at Gettysburg the Confederates opened upon our line with about 150 pieces of artillery, which were immediately answered by an equal number on our side, but among the 20,995 Union and Confederate wounded left under the charge of the writer on this battlefield there were only 204 wounds caused by artillery . . .

Confederate losses (see Section Twelve: The Aftermath) during the battle were, according to Busey and Martin's *Regimental Strengths and Losses at Gettysburg*, 22,846 and Union 23,051, totaling 45,897. However, this figure includes 11,199 missing and captured, some of whom, say a third, 3,733 – would be wounded. The estimated total killed and wounded figure therefore is 38,431. The estimated artillery ammunition expenditure for the Confederates was 31,400 and for the Union 37,000, giving a total of 68,400 rounds. Assuming 9 percent of casualties were inflicted by gunfire, then losses attributable to artillery amounted to 3,459. Therefore it took about twenty shots to hit one man.

The above statistics do not, however, take into account the damage done by gunfire to both horses and material. In this respect the Confederate artillery caused considerable loss of horses and ammunition caissons just behind the Cemetery Ridge crest on the afternoon of July 3. Hunt reported, "The enemy's cannonade, in which he must have almost exhausted his ammunition, was well sustained, and cost us a great many horses and the explosion of an unusually large number of caissons and limbers."

One of the six 10-pounder Parrotts of Capt. A. Judson Clark's 2nd Battery, New Jersey Light Artillery. This gun was positioned near the center of Cemetery Ridge on July 3 and was engaged in repelling Pickett's advance that afternoon. Codori Farm can be seen through the spokes of the right-hand wheel. The thick woods on the horizon to the right of the muzzle are Spangler Woods from which Pickett began his attack.

Types of fire

Direct fire

With direct fire the gunner had to see what he was firing at. Put simply, the shot went "directly" from the muzzle in a straight line to the target (but see "Point-blank fire" below). The rifled cannon at Gettysburg were high-velocity, direct-fire weapons and, while the 12-pounder Napoleons were classified as gun-howitzers, they too were direct-fire pieces in that the gunner needed to see his target even with high elevation of the barrel. Virtually all the artillery firing during the battle was direct fire of some sort as there were so few howitzers. Cannon were positioned so they could see the ground over which their enemy was likely to approach, gunners peered through their sights trying to align their piece correctly, while officers and N.C.O.s sought to observe the fall of shot and shout adjustments as necessary. All the ammunition in use could be employed in the direct-fire role, although perhaps the primary type was the round shot from the smoothbore or bolt from the rifle. It was the equivalent of the bullet from the musket. It had a flat trajectory, the solid iron ball skimming the ground at less than a man's height and smashing through anything in its path. Although a gun barrel could be elevated, giving the projectile a more curved trajectory at longer ranges, this negated the skimming and disemboweling effect as the shot tended to bury itself, particularly if the ground was soft.

Ricochet fire

This was the type of fire mostly, but not exclusively, used by guns firing solid shot or canister. The gunner aimed to hit the ground just in front of the target so that the ball (or balls) bounced, hitting the enemy at about chest height, and continued bouncing another two or three times before coming to rest. It was designed to maximize the bowling-alley effect. It was best used on dry, level ground – the gunner hoping for several bounces, as with a flat stone skimming across the surface of a pond.

If a 12-pounder smoothbore fired with the barrel horizontal, the ball would strike the ground (the technical term was "first graze") at about 325 yards. The next bounce would be at around 600 yards, with a third some 150 yards further on; thereafter it was probably rolling, but still capable of injuring anybody that got in the way. Out to the second bounce the ball was about chest height; after that it was the knees that were most vulnerable. An elevation of the barrel by one degree was enough to extend the distance of the first graze by something around 350 yards. Further elevation and the shot would be traveling above a man's height out to the first graze, which negated much of the lethality of the shot at short to medium range. Ricochet firing was more effective if the barrel was slightly depressed, the gun aimed in front of the target so that all grazes occurred within 400–500 yards.

At Gettysburg the use of ricochet firing was hampered by the softness of the ground, and it could not be used against targets on high ground such as Culp's Hill, Cemetery Hill, Devil's Den, or the Round Tops. However, it would have been feasible for some of the Union batteries to have employed it against the Pettigrew–Trimble–Pickett advance from Cemetery Ridge as the Confederates approached the Emmitsburg Road. One confirmed incident occurred on July 2 during Captain John Bigelow's final stand in the field close to the Trostle Farm. According to his bugler, Charles Reed, Bigelow ordered his four guns in the center and right to "commence . . . firing solid shot low, for a ricochet over the knoll" and into the infantry beyond.

Point-blank fire

The expression to fire at "point-blank" range is well known. Its modern usage means to shoot at extremely close range, from only a few feet (or even inches) from the target – a miss being impossible. There was a lot of point-blank fire at Gettysburg, but it was a technical term used by artillery professionals. If a gun fired with the barrel horizontal to the ground the trajectory of the round was a parabola. When the ball left the barrel it was forced very slightly above the line of sight (this being a straight line from the muzzle to the target). It occurred the instant the shot left the barrel and was called the "first point-blank primitive." The "second point-blank primitive" was the point at which gravity pushed the ball below the line of sight – for a 12-pounder about 300 yards. Thus for the artilleryman "point-blank fire" meant firing at any target between the first and second point-blank primitives – not quite so close as its modern meaning. With targets beyond this distance it was necessary to increase the elevation of the barrel to obtain a direct hit. This was the gunner's technical differentiation between "point-blank" and "direct" fire. With the former the barrel was simply horizontal; with the latter calculations were needed to get the right elevation for the range – the purpose of the Table of Fire inside the lid of the ammunition chests, as shown on page 163.

Indirect fire

This was artillery fire at targets out of sight of the gunners. Modern artillery fire is almost entirely indirect, with the target usually several miles away over the horizon. At Gettysburg it was still in its infancy and was largely the province of howitzers lobbing shells at high angles in a siege situation. Guns could, theoretically, use indirect fire with barrels at a high elevation and firing shells or spherical case, but it was not attempted at Gettysburg as ammunition was short and the effectiveness could not be observed. However, there was considerable unintended indirect fire on the third day. A high proportion of the thousands of rounds fired by the Confederate batteries at targets along the crest of Cemetery Ridge went high and burst over, or struck, the reverse slope of the ridge, hitting headquarters, horse teams, wagons and administrative personnel rather than the intended targets – the Union guns on the ridge and forward slope. As Brigadier-General Robert O. Tyler, commander of the Union Artillery Reserve, reported: "the enemy opened a terrific fire of artillery, which, passing over the crest of the hill, concentrated behind the lines where the reserve was lying."

Overhead supporting fire

This is artillery fire intended to support either attacking or defending infantry by firing over their heads at targets beyond them. This had been standard practice for well over 100 years but it was not to be recommended in 1863. The year before, Brigadier-General Hunt had issued written orders on the subject:

> It may be laid down as a rule that Artillery should not fire over our own troops. For this there are three good reasons. Accidents are liable to happen to the troops from the projectiles. It embarrasses their advance by battering the ground in front of them, and obliging them to hold back until the fire can be stopped or its range extended. It makes the men over whom the projectiles are passing uneasy, and may demoralize them. When it becomes necessary to fire over troops, solid shot, and in rare cases, shell should be used, and not canister nor shrapnel [spherical case]; the latter projectile being liable to burst too soon, and carry destruction among those over whose heads it was intended to pass ["friendly fire;" see box, page 173].

Gettysburg saw plenty of overhead artillery fire from both sides, with incidents of friendly fire on all three days. On July 1 the 7th Wisconsin (Iron Brigade) were retiring toward their batteries on Seminary Ridge when they came under canister fire from Union guns. Lieutenant-Colonel John Callis described it thus:

> Our own batteries that had been firing over our heads from the top of Seminary Ridge was so near that the . . . canister began to kill our own men [Hunt's orders, as we have seen, specifically forbade overhead fire with canister]; when I raised my saber above my head waving it, and at the top of my voice ordering the Capt. of the battery [possibly Captain Greenleaf T. Stevens of 5th Company, Maine Light Artillery] to cease firing. But amid the roar of musketry, and screeching of shot and shell through the air, he seemed not to hear me . . .

Modern communications between infantry and gunners mean that fire can be adjusted and errors corrected quickly (even so they still occur). On the Gettysburg battlefield this was not the case, as the 5th Texas Infantry discovered to their cost on July 2. The regiment was about to take part in a fourth attempt to storm Little Round Top. Confederate batteries were to support the attack by firing over the Texans' heads at the enemy on the hill. Private William A. Fletcher described what happened: "The guns were not elevated enough and were doing fine work on our position. The bursting and flying pieces of shell and rock put us in a panic condition . . ." The only way to stop the firing was for somebody to ride out to locate the batteries and tell them to stop. This was not easy with terrified horses and it took some minutes before two officers managed to mount and spur away. The firing was stopped eventually, and the Texans were much relieved to hear that the attack was cancelled.

On the morning of July 3 Doles's Confederate brigade was positioned in Long Lane, south of Gettysburg, and had come under fire from sharpshooters on the outskirts of the town. He requested Confederate guns just south of Fairfield Road to open fire on the houses concerned. Doles reported:

> The battery opened fire, its fire taking effect on my men. We waved our flag, and sent them word that they were firing on us . . . They did not cease firing . . . I make this statement for the purpose of putting on record my protest against such indifference and negligence on the part of those in command of these two batteries. I have made every effort to find out the batteries, and have failed so far.

ARTILLERY TACTICS AT GETTYSBURG

It was Brigadier-General John Gibbon of the Army of the Potomac, commanding the 2nd Division in II Corps, who wrote the manual of artillery tactics used by both sides during much of the war. Perhaps while enduring the Confederate bombardment on Cemetery Hill on July 3 he reflected ruefully that his enemy gunners were using his *Artillerists Manual* as their basic textbook. It was a highly scientific work, with plenty of complex mathematical formulae, and had been accepted as the official gunner's manual in 1859. The factors discussed below were all relevant to the positioning and use of artillery at Gettysburg whether deployed in an offensive or defensive role.

Siting

At Gettysburg this was often done by senior officers, usually chiefs of artillery and artillery brigade or battalion commanders. Battery commanders seldom had much choice over where to deploy their guns. Good gun positions had at least some of the following features.

Field of Fire

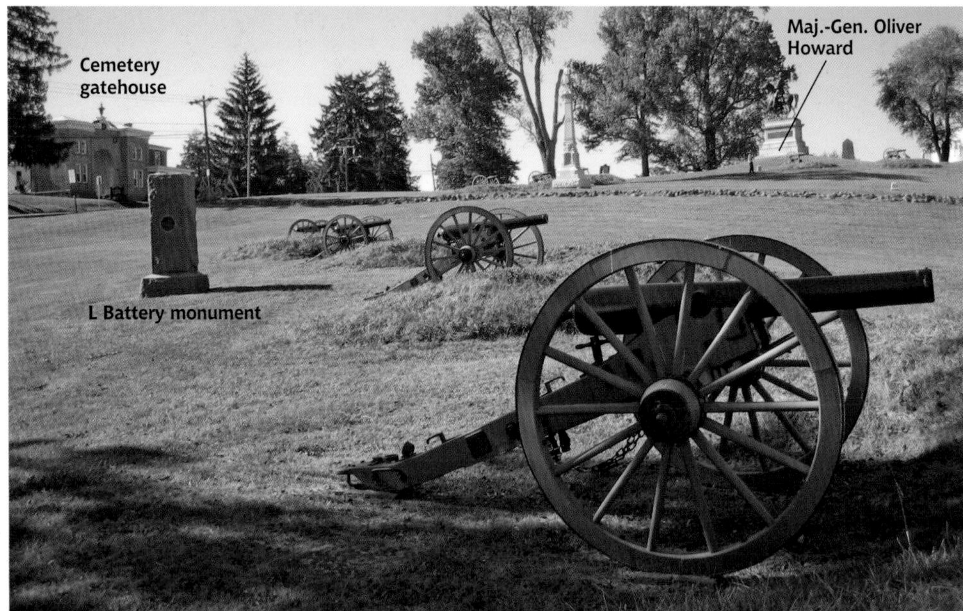

Left: Four of Lt. George Breck's six 3-in ordnance rifles, Battery L, 1st New York Lgt. Artillery on East Cemetery Hill, July 2–3.

Note

- Breck took commmand when Capt. Gilbert H. Reynolds was wounded.
- The entrenchments were dug by the battery on July 2 and 3.
- The guns are positioned on the crest of the hill firing east.
- Maj-Gen. Howard's XI Corps H.Q. was near the crest of the hill.
- This battery went into the action 124 strong and suffered 17 casualties (13.7%) during the two days of fighting.

Right: L Battery's field of fire looking east from the gun position above.

Note

- The wall running across the front marks Brickhill Lane, which was lined with four Union regiments on July 2 (from left to right: 68th NY, 54th NY, 41th NY and 33rd Mass). The white monument in the center is that of 41st NY.
- Most of the trees in the middle distance did not exist in 1863 so the battery had a good field of view and was protected by the infantry to the front, although it had to fire over their heads.
- On the evening of July 2, three North Carolina regiments of Early's Division attacked from the east. The battery was prevented from firing canister by the Union infantry in front.

Fields of fire

The gunners must be able to see as far possible, and on as wide an arc as possible, to their front. This usually meant placing batteries in the open, as indeed was the case at Gettysburg. As Brigadier-General Hunt wrote:

> A moderate elevation which gives a good view of the ground is the best position for Artillery. Too much elevation should be avoided [not often possible on hills such as Culp's, Oak, Benner's, Cemetery, Devil's Den and Little Round Top], since fire is more effective in proportion as the projectiles pass more closely to the ground. Ground covered by bushes, trees or other obstructions is not favorable to the use of artillery.

Cover from fire

Ideally, the best natural cover was that afforded by the crest of a hill that sloped gently toward the enemy. Guns could then be placed just behind the crest with their muzzles poking over the top. This was seldom practical, and many guns on hills or rising ground had to be positioned down the forward slope or on the crest itself. Most Union guns along Cemetery Ridge on July 2 and 3 provide good examples. However, in these circumstances some limbers and most caissons could be on the reverse slope out of the direct line of fire. Artificial cover in the form of entrenchments could be dug to give some protection to the cannoneers and gun. Pits could be dug to contain ammunition chests after the limber was unhitched. A good example of guns being at least partially dug in was L Battery, 1st New York Light Artillery, on East Cemetery Hill, as shown in the photograph above. These guns had a reasonably good field of fire to the front down a gentle slope, but they had to be located on the flat top of the hill in order to fire – see the photographs above.

Flank protection

Artillery batteries should have infantry flank protection otherwise they are extremely vulnerable to attack by fire or enemy infantry. Guns can normally take care of themselves to the immediate front, provided supporting infantry is available on the flanks. An example of a battery being placed in an exposed position by no less a personage than Major-General Hancock, the Union II Corps commander, is Captain Weir's Battery C, 5th U.S. Artillery, on July 2. Weir was ordered to a position southeast

Four of Lt. Alonzo H. Cushing's 3-in ordnance rifles together with their limbers sited just behind the Angle on July 3. Note the limbers are unhitched and close behind the cannon for easy ammunition supply. Cushing was killed near here after being hit in the shoulder, testicles and then through the mouth during the close-quarter fighting as Armistead led his Virginians over the wall. The monument to the left of the left-hand cannon marks where Armistead fell mortally wounded. It is the only Confederate monument on the Union side of the battlefield.

of Codori Farm, close to the Plum Run stream and well outside the protection of friendly infantry. Weir pointed out there was no Union infantry nearer than a few skirmishers in the farm who were engaging the enemy. Hancock overruled him, saying, "Go in there, I will bring you support." He was not able to do so before Weir was forced to retire.

Ammunition supply

There was usually a conflict between a gun position that gave a reasonable field of fire and the need to keep the limbers, caissons and horse teams close to hand but as much as possible out of harm's way. Provided the battery was not likely to move immediately, the limbers could be unhitched and the chief of caissons would try to withdraw them under cover nearby. However, his first priority was the speedy replenishment of ammunition to the guns so, as at Gettysburg, while the caissons might be under cover, the limbers and their teams had to be exposed just behind the guns. In extreme cases there was only enough room on a position to site the guns, so heavy ammunition had to be manhandled to the battery from some distance away. At Gettysburg this was the situation, with two sections (four 10-pounder Parrotts) of Captain James E. Smith's 4th New York Battery sited on the hill above Devil's Den on July 2. Smith was unable to position the limbers on the crest due to lack of space, and nearby infantrymen of the 124th New York witnessed artillerymen struggling to carry ammunition up to the guns – three of which were later captured. The same situation occurred on the summit of Little Round Top. There Lieutenant Charles E. Hazlett, commanding Battery D, 5th U.S. Artillery, found the slope was so steep and covered with trees and rocks that only four guns (10-pounder Parrotts) were, with a tremendous effort by men and horses, able to reach the top. For the limbers and caissons it was impossible; they remained further down the reverse slope, necessitating drivers being employed to hump ammunition to the summit.

Facility of movement

The battery site should be such that movement of the guns into or out of it in any direction is possible without undue delay – for a fast exit that meant the guns being limbered up on site. If necessary, ensuring this facility of movement might involve knocking down nearby walls or fences, or filling up ditches. To have guns overrun and abandoned in position due to difficulties of terrain was considered unacceptable. To quote Brigadier-General Hunt: "It is a disgrace to an Artillery officer if a gun, or even an opportunity of rendering service, should be lost through a neglect or want of forethought on his part." Part of the reason three guns of the 4th U.S. Artillery Battery were lost at Devil's Den was the difficulty of getting the teams forward quickly; also if Little Round Top had been taken Hazlett's cannon would probably have had to be abandoned.

Tactical Use of Artillery Fire

This depended on the target, its range, whether it was stationary or not, whether it was a hard target (buildings or entrenchments) or a soft one (humans or horses), the ammunition supply within the battery and the urgency of the situation. Based on the answers to these questions, the battery commander would decide on the type of ammunition to be used, the loading (whether double-shotted or not) and the rate of fire. He also had a choice as to how many guns to engage the target with. The whole battery could fire at will (as soon as individual pieces were ready – but this was heavy on ammunition), single guns, one section or half a battery could be used – there were several combinations.

As an example, if firing at enemy guns at a range of 1,200 yards, then the choice of ammunition would probably be round shot, which could both smash guns and kill or maim nearby cannoneers and horses. However, an artillery duel would not normally necessitate rapidity of fire, but rather called for accuracy, and so firing would be slow – perhaps only one shot every two minutes by each gun. Alternatively, a very slow rate might have no. 1 gun firing, then no. 2 a minute later and so on at one-minute intervals; thus a six-gun battery would take five minutes to fire six well-aimed shots and ammunition would be conserved. Only with a slow rate could proper accuracy be maintained, as it usually gave time for the smoke to clear between shots and so aim and range could be adjusted. If the target was advancing infantry at the same range (firing guns at infantry over 1,200 yards was really wasting ammunition; Gibbon considered artillery fire should not be used "beyond the limit of distinct vision"), then the choice was more likely to be spherical case, or a mix of case and round shot or shell, at least while the enemy was over 350 yards away. If the ground was favorable then this might be ricochet or grazing fire. Below 350 yards with the enemy still coming on, the firing would be speeded up and ammunition switched to canister if available or spherical case with fuses cut to one second. With infantry charging home from 150 yards away, the gunners would probably be loading double-shotted or even triple-shotted canister or a mix of shot and canister – as was the case with the Union batteries near the Angle and Copse of Trees as Armistead's Virginians charged home on the afternoon of July 3.

Frequently batteries would open fire in accordance with their brigade or battalion commanders' orders. The artillery supporting Pickett's Division on July 3 was commanded by Major James Dearing, who instructed his four batteries to fire by battery – that is, fire in turn, one round from each gun: "I at once brought my battalion in battery to the front, and commenced firing slowly and deliberately. To ensure more accuracy, and to guard against the waste of ammunition, I fired by battery." Guns, unlike infantry, would normally avoid firing volleys as advancing infantry could take advantage of the pause in between firing to double-quick forward, knowing they were safe for perhaps twenty or thirty seconds.

Concentration of fire

This was a principle of war that applied as much to artillery as to any other arm. Heavy concentrations of gunfire at a specific point or area could be devastatingly destructive, or at least devastatingly frightening, at the receiving end. Hence guns should not be too widely scattered but should be so placed that their fire could converge on important areas. The dispositions of Lee's army facilitated the concentration of his guns on the center of Meade's line. This was because he occupied exterior lines (the outer circumference of a half circle); thus, in theory, his artillery if correctly positioned could concentrate fire onto the center of the circle – Cemetery Ridge near the Copse of Trees. Union guns were forced to reply by firing from interior lines out toward the circumference of the half circle, making their efforts more scattered and less concentrated. That is probably an oversimplification, but it indicates the overall battlefield situation once the armies had fully deployed by July 2.

In most Civil War battles, including Gettysburg, the proportion of casualties inflicted by artillery fire was small, but the effect on morale was often considerable. It was not necessarily the number of killed or wounded that decided an issue but the terror, panic and demoralization caused by concentrated fire. Just the horrendous noise brought concussion, deafness and bleeding from the ears and noses of some cannoneers serving the guns. To Captain John E. Dooley, 1st Virginia Infantry, at the start of the combined Confederate and Union barrage on July 3, "the sky seemed to open and darken the air with smoke and death dealing missiles. I never forget those scenes and sounds. The earth seems unsteady beneath this furious cannonading, and the air might be said to be agitated by the wings of death." This huge concentration of Rebel guns on the part of the Union line that was the objective of Longstreet's attack is discussed in detail in Section Eleven: Day Three.

Counterbattery fire

Artillery fire designed to destroy enemy guns was, and remains, an important task for gunners on any battlefield. However, the general consensus at the time was that artillery was best employed on the battlefield against infantry or cavalry. Only if the opposing guns were exposed and there were no other available targets was it deemed worthwhile to indulge in counterbattery fire. Part of the problem was that it required pinpoint accuracy, which was possible only if the range was known precisely, or if time and ammunition could be spent on ranging shots that could be observed – if not, ammunition was likely to be wasted. Once a major infantry attack was under way it was a priority target for every gun within range.

Nevertheless, at Gettysburg counterbattery fire was a priority for many Confederate guns. This was because the Rebels were attacking and therefore wanted to neutralize the Yankee artillery in order to lessen the damage it would do to their advancing infantry. Conversely, Meade's gunners were, particularly on July 3, instructed to reserve their ammunition for the infantry attack. With some exceptions this was what they did. The Confederates correctly concentrated on counterbattery fire for their grand assault on the third day, but it failed to achieve its objective, the reasons for which are, as noted above, explained in Section Eleven: Day Three.

The best tactic for an artillery commander who wanted to destroy or force a withdrawal of enemy guns was to select an enemy battery and concentrate as many of his guns as possible on that target. Once that battery had been eliminated, fire would be switched to the next. The same principle applied to a battery firing in the counterbattery role. If at all possible the commander should concentrate his fire on one or two guns at a time. Other things being equal, six guns firing at one would quickly put it out of action and they would be able to turn on the next.

Enfilade fire

Enfilade fire was fire directed along a line from end to end, or as nearly so as possible. The naval term would be "raking fire" – fire that swept a ship from stem to stern. It was a gunner's dream to catch line after line of dense columns of advancing infantry with enfilade fire and smash them with solid shot, the balls tearing great gaps in the ranks as they bowled over dozens of men with horrendous injuries. Every battery commander sought to position his guns so that, if at all possible, any enemy attack could be caught in enfilade.

At Gettysburg there were plenty of opportunities for both sides to employ enfilade fire. On the morning of July 1 the Union I Corps was defending McPherson's Ridge, a mile west of the town, against ever increasing pressure from Lieutenant-General A. P. Hill's Corps advancing down the Chambersburg Pike and deployed opposite along Herr's Ridge, threequarters of a mile away. Initially the Confederates positioned the twenty cannon (five batteries) of Major William J. Pegram's artillery reserve battalion on the ridge astride the Pike; they were later reinforced by another sixteen pieces (four batteries) from Major David G. McIntosh's Battalion.

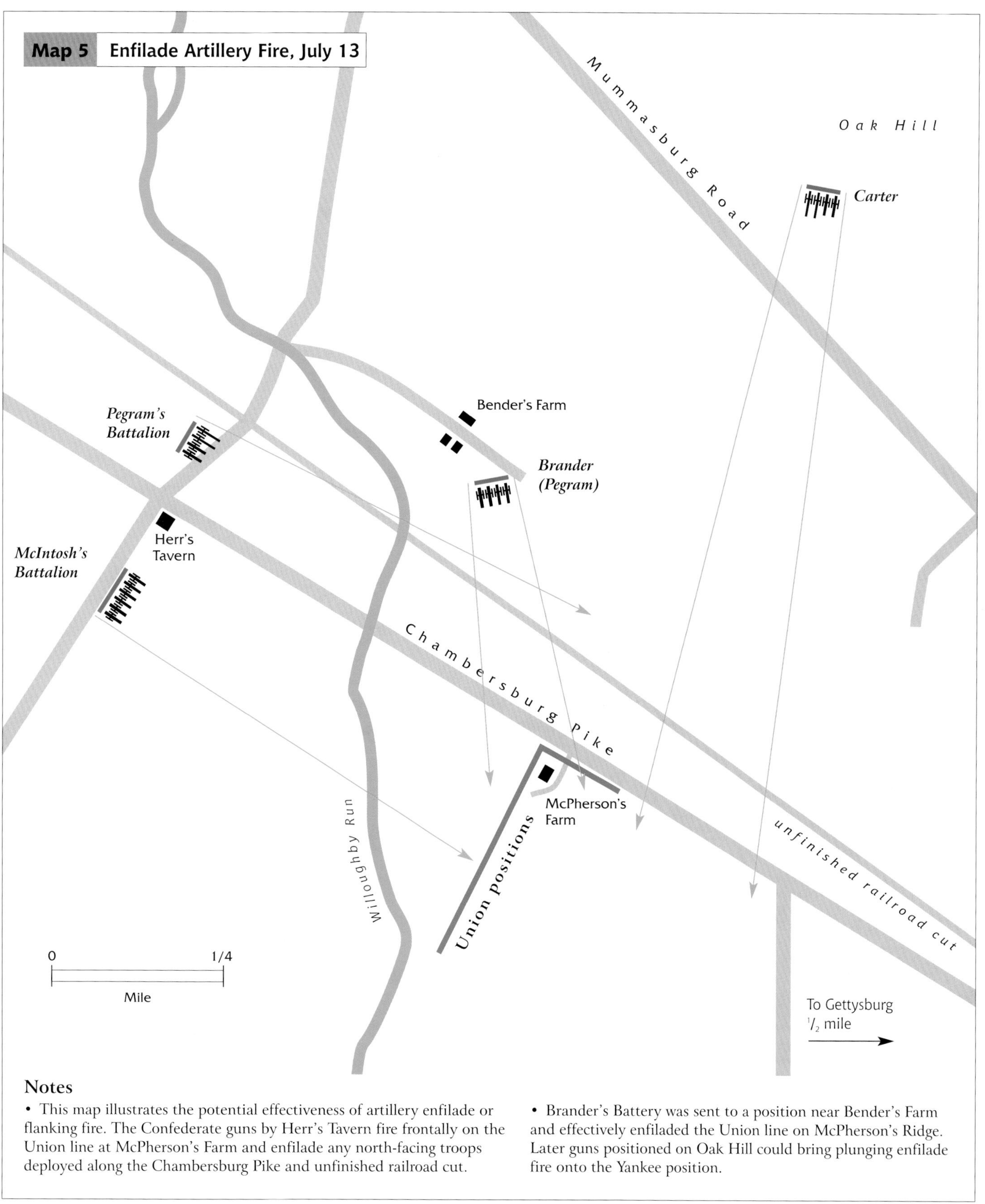

Notes

- This map illustrates the potential effectiveness of artillery enfilade or flanking fire. The Confederate guns by Herr's Tavern fire frontally on the Union line at McPherson's Farm and enfilade any north-facing troops deployed along the Chambersburg Pike and unfinished railroad cut.
- Brander's Battery was sent to a position near Bender's Farm and effectively enfiladed the Union line on McPherson's Ridge. Later guns positioned on Oak Hill could bring plunging enfilade fire onto the Yankee position.

They substantially outgunned the Union artillery opposed to them. Major Pegram increased his advantage by pushing Captain Thomas A. Brander's two Napoleons and two 10-pounder Parrotts forward on his left to deploy in battery near Bender's Farm (see Map 5 above), from which location he brought effective enfilade fire onto the Union infantry near McPherson's Farm. The situation became far worse for the defenders of McPherson's Ridge when Ewell's Corps advanced from the north and positioned guns on Oak Hill, thus completely outflanking and enfilading the Union position, which was ultimately forced to withdraw despite seeing off several Rebel infantry assaults. On July 3 two Whitworth rifles were moved to Oak Hill as it appeared an excellent position from which these long-range cannon could enfilade the main Union line on Cemetery Ridge. However, it was near their extreme range and, as noted above, one had its breech broken by its own recoil. More successful were Lieutenant-Colonel Thomas H. Carter's ten rifled cannon on either side of the railroad cut. Although only partially able to enfilade Cemetery Hill, their fire was effective.

Probably the best opportunity for the Rebels to use enfilade fire came on July 2 when the Union III Corps under Major-General Sickles had been pushed forward threequarters of a mile in advance of the main Union line on Cemetery Ridge. Along the Emmitsburg Road, at the Peach Orchard and then east toward the Wheatfield was a triangular salient – an open invitation to enfilade gunfire from the north and south.

Another chance – on a grander scale in terms of guns employed and distances involved – came for both sides on the following day. For the Confederates, deployed along the outer rim of a huge semicircle, it occurred when positioning their batteries for the preparatory bombardment prior to their final infantry advance. The 3-inch ordnance rifles and Parrotts of Ewell's Corps, positioned on Benner's Hill, had a magnificent enfilade shoot onto Cemetery Hill. Major Thomas Osborn, who was at the receiving end, described it thus:

> The gunners got our range at almost the first shot. Passing low over Col. Wainwright's guns they caught us square in flank and with perfect elevation. It was admirable shooting. They raked the whole line of batteries, killed and wounded the men and horses and blew up the caissons rapidly . . .

For the Union gunners, particularly those in the southern sector of Cemetery Ridge, the opportunity came to fire into the flanks of Pickett's lines of infantry as they crossed the open fields to assault the center of their line.

The Artillery "Charge"

This tactic involved artillery moving forward at best speed, with cannoneers sitting on the limbers or running alongside, in support of advancing infantry, probably on their flanks, so that they could halt when closer to the enemy to support the final assault with canister. It was a difficult concept, as it usually meant maneuvering the guns to within musketry range with all the attendant risks for both men and horses. The nearest artillery came to a charge at Gettysburg was on the second day, when Colonel Alexander led his battalion of six batteries in a 600-yard dash down the slope of the Seminary Ridge up to the Emmitsburg Road to follow up the retreating troops of Sickles' Corps. According to Alexander:

> I can recall no more splendid sight, on a small scale, – and certainly no more inspiring moment during the war, than that of the charge of these six batteries. An artillerist's heaven is to follow the routed enemy, after a tough resistance, and throw shells and canister into his disorganized and fleeing masses. Then the explosions of the guns sound louder and more powerful, and the very shouts of the gunners, ordering "Fire!" in rapid succession, thrill one's very soul. There is no excitement on earth like it . . . pieces and caisson went at a gallop, some cannoneers mounted, and some running by the sides – not in a regular line, but a general race or scramble to get there first.

Confederate Battery in Action
(two Napoleons and two 10-pounder Parrotts)

Captain Brander's Richmond (Virginia) "Letcher" Battery, part of Maj. William J. Pegram's Battalion in A. P. Hill's Artillery Reserve saw action on all three days at Gettysburg. On July 1 it was positioned on a hill east of Willoughby Run from where it enfilad

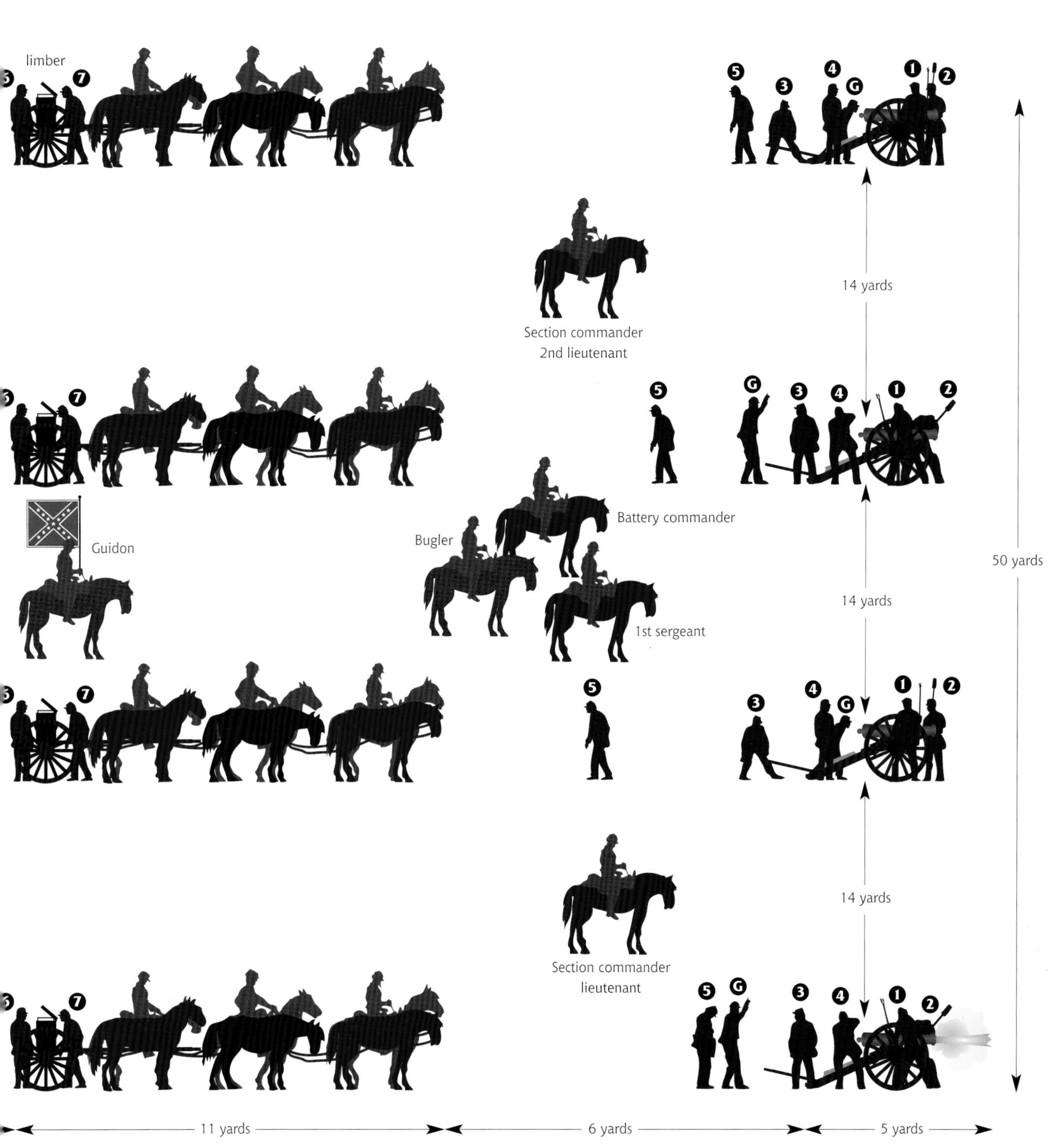

e Union position near McPherson's Farm although coming under avy return fire. On July 2 it was engaged in periodic artillery changes with Union batteries and on July 3 participated in the eparatory bombardment of Cemetery Ridge prior to Longstreet's final attack. The battery started the battle with 65 all ranks and suffered 17 casualties – the highest losses in the corps' Artillery Reserve. The battery's monument is on West Confederate Avenue, east of the road, in McMillan Woods.

A major part of the Confederate artillery plan for Longstreet's attack on July 3 was for as many guns as possible to advance on the flanks of the infantry to support them as they closed with the enemy. As will be seen in Section Eleven: Day Three, very few guns were able to do this, mainly due to running out of ammunition.

SUMMARY OF ARTILLERY STATISTICS

Comparative Statistics – Artillery Personnel

	Confederate	**Union**
Overall estimated strength	6,325	6,931
Percentage of army	9%	7%
Guns per 1,000 infantry	4.7	4.9
Strongest 6-gun battery	Bat. D, 1st NC Artillery: 148	5th NY Art. Res.: 146
Weakest 6-gun battery	Co. C, Sumter (Ga) Art. Bat.: 124	Co. D, 5th U.S. Art.: 75
Average battery strength	91	107
Total personnel loss	630	759
Average battery loss	9	11.7
Personnel loss as % of army loss	2.7%	3%
Highest total battery loss	Brooks Bat. (SC) Lt. Art.: 36	Bat A, 4th U.S. Art.: 38
Highest % battery loss	Brooks Bat. (SC) Lt. Art.: 51%	Bat. I, 5th U.S. Art.: 31%
Lowest total battery loss	9 batteries had none	13 batteries had none

Before discussing the part played by artillery chiefs and examining the roles played by artillery brigades and battalions on both sides, it may be useful to the reader to summarize the main overall statistics and conclusions described above.

- Numbers of cannon. Meade deployed 358 pieces of ordnance (mounted and horse artillery), which were actually engaged at some time during the three days in sixty-five batteries, almost all of which had six cannon of the same type of gun. Lee employed 267 in sixty-eight batteries, the great majority of which were four-gun batteries and of mixed ordnance.

- Types of cannon. There were two basic types at Gettysburg – smoothbore (12-pounder Napoleons and howitzers) and rifled cannon (3-inch ordnance rifles, 10- and 20-pounder Parrotts, and Navy, Blakely, James and Whitworth rifles). Forty percent of Union cannon were smoothbore with an effective range of about 1,700 yards; the remainder were rifled cannon, mainly 3-inch ordnance rifles, with effective ranges out to 2,500 yards. Union batteries were composed of guns of a uniform type. The Confederates were much more mixed, with 36 percent smoothbore Napoleons, 12 percent smoothbore howitzers, and a single 6-pounder gun; 28 percent 3-inch ordnance rifles, 20 percent Parrotts and the remainder Navy, Blakely or Whitworth rifles. Rebel batteries normally had a section of smoothbore guns for short-range work and another of rifled cannon for longer ranges.

- Ammunition holdings. Batteries on both sides ran short of ammunition during the battle and replenishment was often a problem, although the Union artillery reserves were better stocked and more easily accessible due to the army's occupying interior lines. Estimates show the Union artillery holding about 270 rounds per gun, totaling some 97,000 rounds. Of these, first-line ammunition immediately available to the batteries at the start (assuming all chests fully stocked) was about 61,400 rounds to which the reserve trains added another 35,600. Confederate estimates are less secure, but show a holding of around 50,000 rounds or nearly 190 per gun. Of these, first-line stocks amounted to 32,000 rounds and in the reserve train 18,000, although this latter could be as low as 3,800 if one Confederate return is accepted. If so, the total holding would be reduced to 35,800 rounds or about 130 per gun.

- Ammunition types. Four types were used – solid shot, spherical case, shell and canister. The Union gunners had 78 percent of their holdings divided equally between spherical case and shell, the remaining 22 percent also equally divided between solid shot and canister. Rebel gunners held some 55 percent of spherical case, 24 percent shell and the balance equally divided between solid shot and canister. For both sides, therefore, the great bulk of firing was using either spherical case or shell at medium ranges – out to a mile.

- Ammunition expenditure. For Meade's guns, total expenditure is estimated at about 37,000 rounds or an average of 120 per piece; for Lee's, a possible total of 31,400: an average of 115 per gun.

- Types of fire. Because of the need to conserve ammunition and ensure firing was as accurate as possible, artillery fire was predominantly deliberate, at a slow rate of one round every one to two minutes. Batteries would not fire volleys but rather individually at will in accordance with the orders of the battery commander. The object was to site the guns with a good field of fire, secure flanks and, if possible, withdraw the horse teams a short distance to the rear under cover. Although there was considerable counterbattery fire at Gettysburg (mostly by the Confederates), the priority target was always the infantry – this was particularly true of the Union guns, as they were almost entirely firing in defense of their position. Firing was to be as concentrated as possible, with all guns firing at one target to destroy or neutralize it before moving to the next. The ideal was enfilade fire into the flanks of an enemy.

- Artillery effectiveness. As with most large battles, the proportion of casualties inflicted by artillery was small, although their firing had both strongly positive and strongly negative effects on morale, depending on whether the infantry were watching their own guns fire or were at the receiving end. Assuming around 9 percent of casualties were the result of gunfire at Gettysburg, then it took some twenty shots to hit a soldier as distinct from a horse.

- With personnel there was little difference in the number of guns per 1,000 infantry – almost five each, which was high. Union batteries were, on average, stronger than their opponents', as most had six guns rather than four. In terms of casualties as a percentage of total losses, the two sides were almost equal with 2.7 for Confederates and 3.0 for Union artillerymen.

ARTILLERY COMMAND AND CONTROL AT GETTYSBURG

Confederate

Army Headquarters: Brigadier-General William N. Pendleton, Chief of Artillery; Captain George W. Peterkin A.D.C.

1st Corps

Hood's Division:	Major Mathias W. Henry, battalion commander
McLaws' Division:	Colonel Henry C. Cabell, battalion commander
Pickett's Division:	Major James Dearing, battalion commander
Artillery Reserve:	Colonel James B. Walton, chief of artillery
	Colonel E. Porter Alexander, battalion commander
	Major Benjamin F. Eshleman, battalion commander

2nd Corps

Johnson's Division:	Major James Latimer (mw);
	Captain Charles A. Raine, battalion commander
Early's Division:	Lieutenant-Colonel Hilary P. Jones, battalion commander
Rodes' Division:	Lieutenant-Colonel Thomas A. Carter, battalion commander
Artillery Reserve:	Colonel T. Thompson Brown, chief of artillery
	Captain Willis J. Dance, battalion commander
	Lieutenant-Colonel William Nelson, battalion commander

3rd Corps

Heth's Division:	Lieutenant-Colonel John J. Garnett, battalion commander
Pender's Division:	Major William T. Poague, battalion commander
Anderson's Division:	Major John Lane, battalion commander
Artillery Reserve:	Colonel R. Lindsay Walker, chief of artillery
	Major David G. McIntosh, battalion commander
	Major William J. Pegram, battalion commander
Cavalry Division:	Major Robert F. Beckham, chief of artillery

Gettysburg tested to the limit the new artillery organization, implemented after Chancellorsville (see pages 24–25), and found it wanting. The battle required, particularly on the third day, coordination of the whole of the artillery effort at army command level in the planning, execution and supervision of its operation. The potential problems, dealt with in detail in Section Eleven: Day Three, were ruthlessly exposed in the preparatory bombardment before Longstreet's attack. They included lack of an army artillery reserve; the lack of uniformity of ordnance within batteries; unreliability of projectiles; shortage of ammunition, coupled with the "disappearance" of the reserve train; inadequate artillery staff; and lack of clarity in the artillery command structure. These fault lines were exaggerated by an army chief of artillery who was seemingly uncertain in his own mind whether he was primarily a staff officer/adviser to Lee in all artillery matters, chief artillery liaison officer between the army commander and the corps commanders, or overall artillery commander with executive authority. In his own words, Brigadier William N. Pendleton described his role after the post-Chancellorsville reorganization:

> Having assigned the reserve artillery battalions [to the corps commanders] I have no special charge, but superintend all the artillery, and direct in battle such portions as may need my personal attention. This is a better arrangement, I think. My work will be much as it has been, but freer, as none of the petty details of one or two battalions will require my care.

The Order of Battle diagrams in Section One set out the detailed structure of the artillery at Gettysburg – an organization that came into being when the Army of Northern Virginia formed three corps from the original two after Jackson's death at Chancellorsville. Special Order No. 106, dated April 16, 1863, specified that each of the nine Confederate infantry divisional commanders was to have an artillery battalion permanently attached. In addition, the former Army Artillery Reserve was broken up and each of the three corps given an artillery reserve of two battalions under a corps chief of artillery. Thus a corps commander had five artillery battalions under command, each with the appropriate number of artillery field officers.

There was now no central artillery army reserve directly controlled by Lee or his chief of artillery, Pendleton. All the guns were committed to specific infantry formations; all the guns were therefore under the orders of senior infantry commanders who outranked the artillery officers in direct control of them. Divisional and corps commanders regarded the guns as theirs, to be used as they saw best to support their infantry, not necessarily in accordance with the needs of the army as a whole. Without an army reserve of guns, Pendleton, as he seemed pleased to announce, "had no special charge." To obtain a large concentration of fire from many artillery battalions or to rush extra guns to a threatened point, he had to rely on getting the timely cooperation of the corps commanders. While this was feasible, it would take time to plan, coordinate and execute and was altogether more likely to be problematic than if he had several battalions under his immediate control. In simple terms, too many officers – both infantry and artillery – could move batteries and battalions about, as one small example from July 2 illustrates. As McLaws' Division was waiting to attack toward the

Brigadier-General William Nelson Pendleton, 1809–1881

Early life

Aged fifty-four at Gettysburg, "Parson" Pendleton, as he was known to many, was only two years younger than Lee. Born in Richmond, he graduated at twenty-one from West Point into the artillery but resigned three years later – having spent much of that time in hospital, ill with what may have been yellow fever. When not sick, his military service involved garrison duties and teaching mathematics. On leaving the military he became a teacher at Delaware College in Pennsylvania for four years before becoming an Episcopal minister to heal his "depraved and unsanctified heart." He was rector at Frederick, Maryland and then Lexington, Virginia. In 1860 Pendleton, then over fifty, agreed to teach mathematics to a Lexington militia artillery battery. At the outbreak of war they elected him captain. In order to placate his religious conscience with his warlike position, he called his four cannon "Matthew," "Mark," "Luke" and "John" in what was then called the Rockbridge Artillery.

The Civil War

From early on "Parson" Pendleton was in the public eye as an eccentric military minister, who reputedly opened fire on the enemy with the words, "May God have mercy on their misguided souls – Fire!" He had been slightly wounded at First Manassas and his horse was shot from under him. His actions in this battle earned him considerable praise from no lesser personage than Stonewall Jackson. On the strength of this performance he was promoted colonel. He continued to preach and train, and his efforts were soon rewarded with further promotion in March 1862 to brigadier-general.

Pendleton proved to be far more the theorist and the administrator than the commander handling guns in the field. This was revealed to all at Malvern Hill, where he was in charge of the Artillery Reserve of fourteen batteries with huge potential firepower. Pendleton managed to bring just one of his batteries into action when the Rebel infantry urgently needed support. The next Pendleton performance was after the Battle of Sharpsburg (the Confederate name for Antietam) on September 17, 1862, a clash considered by many to be the bloodiest single day of the war, when he was tasked with using his reserve artillery to cover Lee's withdrawal over the Potomac. At midnight he woke Lee with the news that the Federals were over the river and all the guns lost. Stonewall Jackson put in a quick counterattack that drove the Yankees back and revealed that no guns had been lost – they had been, unbeknown to Pendleton, deliberately withdrawn the previous evening. His reputation would never recover from this embarrassment. One officer summed it up with the words, "Pendleton is Lee's weakness. He is like the elephant, we have him and we don't know what on earth to do with him, and it costs a devil of a sight to feed him."

Nevertheless Pendleton proved himself a capable administrator, working well on the reorganization of the Confederate artillery in late 1862 and into the following year. In the field again at Chancellorsville, once more his artillery reserve was poorly handled. Tasked with deploying his guns on Fredericksburg Heights against the Union VI Corps attack, he managed to pull out too early, losing eight cannon in the process. During the final reorganization of Lee's artillery before Gettysburg, the Army Artillery Reserve was abolished (a mistake, as it turned out) and Pendleton became chief of artillery but with no guns directly under his authority. As noted on page 181, it was an arrangement he liked – he had become an adviser and administrator.

At Gettysburg

July 1. Pendleton rode with Lee down the Chambersburg Pike toward the action on McPherson's Ridge. Twice that afternoon and evening Pendleton, who had been put in command of a number of guns, failed to open fire – first on the right of the Confederates during their advance on Seminary Ridge, and later, after moving forward, at the Union positions on Cemetery Hill.

July 2. Pendleton did little of note. He went on an early-morning reconnaissance which revealed little of significance and he did not play a part in the Confederate artillery preparations for Longstreet's delayed attack that afternoon.

July 3. Pendleton's positive contribution to the massive preliminary bombardment of Cemetery Ridge prior to Longstreet's attack was negligible. He approved Colonel Porter Alexander's deployment and so made no adjustments. His offer to Alexander of nine "howitzers" (they were rifled cannon) from Hill's Corps was accepted but through misunderstandings they went missing at the crucial moment. His main failing that day was in not ensuring the prompt resupply of ammunition to the batteries. His moving the reserve ammunition wagons further back without informing the gunners caused batteries to run out or short at a critical juncture. Pendleton had no proper role during the battle, unlike his opposite number a mile away on Cemetery Ridge; he had no army reserve to control and thus spent his time as an ineffective liaison officer between Lee and the corps commanders.

After Gettysburg

Surprisingly, Lee kept the "Parson" as his chief of artillery for the remainder of the war, although the position was primarily administrative. He lost his son, Major Sandie Pendleton, serving on Ewell's staff at Gettysburg, who was mortally wounded at the Battle of Fisher's Hill on September 23, 1864. Pendleton returned to Lexington and his Episcopal church after the war and died almost twenty years later in 1883. He was buried beside his son.

Peach Orchard, the corps commander, Longstreet, rode up and insisted McLaws post a battery at a gap in the treeline near where his infantry were positioned. McLaws protested it would draw fire and cause casualties to the infantry. Longstreet insisted and the battery was moved – with the infantry suffering as predicted. An infantry lieutenant-general ordering an infantry major-general to move a single battery commanded by an artillery captain, with the artillery command having no say in the matter.

At a higher level, taking artillery units from one corps and moving them into another's area in the heat of a battle inevitably caused problems of command and ammunition replenishment. And so it proved for the Confederates at Gettysburg, particularly on July 3.

Union

Note: a union artillery brigade equates to a Confederate battalion.

Army Headquarters: Brigadier-General Henry J. Hunt, chief of artillery; Lieutenant-Colonel Edward R. Warner, assistant inspector general (artillery); Captain John N. Craig, assistant adjutant general (artillery); Lieutenant C. F. Bissell A.D.C.

I Corps Artillery Brigade:
Colonel Charles S. Wainwright, chief of artillery

II Corps Artillery Brigade:
Captain John C. Hazard, chief of artillery

III Corps Artillery Brigade:
Captain George E. Randolph (w)
and Captain A. Judson Clark, chiefs of artillery

V Corps Artillery Brigade:
Captain Augustus P. Martin, chief of artillery

VI Corps Artillery Brigade:
Colonel Charles H. Tompkins, chief of artillery

XI Corps Artillery Brigade:
Major Thomas W. Osborn, chief of artillery

XII Corps Artillery Brigade:
Lieutenant Edward D. Muhlenberg, chief of artillery

Cavalry Corps:
1st Artillery Brigade: Captain James M. Robertson

2nd Artillery Brigade: Captain John C. Tidball

Army Artillery Reserve:
Brigadier-General Robert O. Tyler, chief of artillery

1st Regular Brigade:
Captain Dunbar R. Ransom (w), chief of artillery

1st Volunteer Brigade:
Lieutenant-Colonel Freeman McGilvery, chief of artillery

2nd Volunteer Brigade:
Captain Elijah D. Taft, chief of artillery

3rd Volunteer Brigade:
Captain James F. Huntington, chief of artillery

4th Volunteer Brigade:
Captain Robert H. Fitzhugh, chief of artillery

The Army of the Potomac fought Gettysburg with eighty-five more artillery pieces than its opponent; it had bigger batteries; the guns within the batteries were of the same type; ammunition supply was well organized; there was a large Army Reserve of nineteen batteries and all were under the overall control of a competent professional chief of artillery – Brigadier-General Henry Jackson Hunt. However, this had not always been the position.

As with the Confederate service, Chancellorsville had been the catalyst for change. Union batteries had not shone at that battle, partly due to their being allocated out to infantry divisions, which dissipated their firepower, and partly because of the serious lack of field officers (majors and above) in the artillery. The latter was due to the inordinately slow promotion within the artillery – as noted above – which led to many capable and ambitious officers transferring to the infantry or cavalry. To quote Hunt, "a policy which closes the door of promotion to battery officers, and places them, and the arm itself, under a ban, and degrades them in comparison with other arms of the service, induces discontent, and has caused many of our best officers to seek positions, wherever they can find them . . ." Not untypical was Major-General Abner Doubleday, commander of the 3rd Division in I Corps. He was commissioned from West Point into the artillery in 1842 and, despite service in the Mexican and Seminole Wars, was still a captain with almost twenty years' service when the Civil War started. In May 1861 he switched to the infantry as a major and later to the Infantry Volunteers and thus secured promotion to brigadier-general.

This lack of experienced senior officers had worried Hunt for months. His report after Gettysburg was forthright on the subject:

> In my report of the battle of Chancellorsville, I took occasion to call attention to the great evils arising from the want of field officers for the artillery. The operations of this campaign, and especially the battle of Gettysburg, afford further proofs, if such were necessary, of the mistaken policy of depriving so important an arm of the officers necessary for managing it . . . In the seven corps, the artillery of two were commanded by colonels, of one by a major, of three by captains, and of one by a lieutenant taken from their batteries for the purpose. The two brigades of horse artillery attached to the cavalry were commanded by captains [only one of the seventeen Confederate artillery battalions was not commanded by a field officer] . . . In no army would the command of the artillery of a corps be considered of less importance . . . than that of a brigade of infantry. In none of our corps ought the artillery commander to have been of less rank than a colonel, and in all there should have been a proper proportion of field officers with the necessary staffs. The defects of our organization were made palpable at Gettysburg, not only in the field, but in the necessary and important duties of reorganizing the batteries, repairing damages, and getting the artillery in condition to renew the battle . . .

Nevertheless, the Union artillery at Gettysburg had, in addition to more guns and uniformity of types of ordnance within them, three key advantages over Lee's gunners:

- Hunt far outshone his opposite number, Pendleton. Not only was he a thoroughly professional artilleryman but also he had been restored to executive authority, under Meade, to oversee the army's artillery and coordinate its efforts. Hunt ensured there was a much greater degree of competent centralized control, not only of the tactical use of the guns but also of their administration and ammunition supply.
- The Army Artillery Reserve, rather than being abolished after Chancellorsville as in the Army of Northern Virginia, had been doubled. At Gettysburg the reserve had 106 pieces in nineteen batteries divided among five brigades – 30 percent of the army's artillery engaged at the battle. This mass of firepower played a critical role in defeating Confederate attacks on July 2 and 3. It was grouped centrally and batteries were readily available to reinforce the line, plug gaps and on occasion save the situation at the height of a Rebel assault. The Artillery Reserve and its use was a key factor in the Union successes during the battle

- The third vital factor was ammunition supply. Prior to Gettysburg all reserve ammunition (artillery and small arms) for each division had been carried in the same train under the control of an infantry officer, quartermaster or staff officer, none of whom properly understood the needs of artillery. There was often confusion in battle, with trains not being where the guns most needed them or the chests not having the right quantities of the different types of ammunition. At Gettysburg all this changed. Each corps had its own separate artillery train under the direction of the corps chief of artillery, and there was a train specifically for the Artillery Reserve, also under the control of its chief of artillery (Brigadier-General Robert O. Tyler). Finally, Hunt had, without informing Meade, ensured that an extra twenty rounds per gun was carried with the reserve train. The only potentially serious problem arose on July 2 when Hancock's II Corps, which had managed to get only half its reserve artillery train to the field, began running out of ammunition. Hunt's extra supply saved a critical situation developing into something worse.

ARTILLERY HORSES

Horse or Mule for the Artillery?

"A horse for military service is as much a military supply as a barrel of gunpowder or a shotgun or rifle." Thus said Union Quartermaster General Montgomery C. Meigs in April 1862 when trying to persuade the Secretary of War to give authority to commandeer horses from Southern sympathizers in the Shenandoah Valley. Sufficient horses were a prerequisite for the movement of armies' guns and cavalry. More horses were needed for commanders, staffs and couriers. It is no exaggeration to say that without horses an army could not take the field. Areas of conflict were quickly denuded of horses as animals were requisitioned, commandeered or stolen. Private citizens went to ingenious lengths to hide their animals – one was found tied to the bedpost in a lady's bedroom. To capture enemy horses was a crucial task of any cavalry or foraging force. The Union armies captured many more than the Confederates, as for most of the war campaigning was in Rebel territory – Gettysburg being one of the few exceptions.

Horses were roughly divided into draft and saddle animals. Draft horses pulled cannon, caissons and some wagons, while saddle horses carried riders. In the field artillery half the horses performed both functions, as the left-hand horse of each pair pulling guns or caissons carried a driver.

At the start of the war it is estimated the Northern states held around 3.5 million horses, with only 1.7 million being in the Confederate states; the border states of Kentucky and Missouri had another 800,000. However, the horse was not the only draft animal available. Considerable use was made of mules, and to a much lesser extent, of buffalo. While the North had a preponderance of horses, the reverse was true of mules, with the South holding some 800,000, the North 100,000 and the two border states 200,000. So as far as draft animals were concerned there was, seemingly, an approximate balance between the two. This was not, however, the true picture, as mules were useless for drawing guns or caissons, or indeed anything that needed to be in or near the firing line. Mules were strong, surefooted and excellent load-carriers or pullers, but became demented under fire. Horses would kick, buck or rear, but mules went mad. They would kick and roll around on the ground, entangling harnesses and causing pandemonium. Nevertheless, they were used to carry mountain howitzers due to their surefootedness and the fact that these howitzers could be dismantled into individual loads. Confederate Brigadier-General John D. Imboden, then a colonel, had a battery of mountain howitzers carried by mules at the Battle of Port Republic in June 1862. He described what happened when shells burst overhead as his battery took shelter in a gully:

> The mules became frantic. They kicked, plunged and squealed. It was impossible to quiet them, and it took three or four men to hold one mule from breaking away. Each mule had about 300 pounds weight on him, so securely fastened that the load could not be dislodged by any of his capers. Several of them lay down and tried to wallow their loads off. The men held these down and that suggested the idea of throwing them all to the ground and holding then there.

For this reason mules were almost universally used for drawing the wagons of supply and ammunition trains.

The ideal artillery horse is described in *Field Artillery Tactics* as being, at the time of purchase:

> 5 to 7 years old; height 15 hands 3 inches, allowing a variation of 1 inch. They should be well broken to harness, free from vice [bad behavior], perfectly sound in every respect, full chested, shoulders sufficiently broad to support the collar . . . special attention should be directed to the feet, to see that they are perfectly sound and in good order, with hoofs rather large, and that the horse submits willingly to be shod.

A good draft horse cost the U.S. government about $150. With the demand from the military so great, many an unscrupulous dealer charged high prices for much older horses whose gray hairs had been dyed. As the war progressed, animals that met the attributes quoted above became rarities and inferior horses were hitched to countless guns and caissons.

Care and Feeding

All horses, but particularly artillery ones, required constant care and attention if they were not to succumb quickly to the grueling hardship and workload of continuous campaigning. In October 1862 Lee issued General Order No. 115, specifically targeted at the care of artillery horses. Officers were held responsible for the condition of battery horses and those guilty of neglect could expect punishment. No artillery horse was to be ridden except by artillerymen, whose duty it was to do so in action, and the chief of artillery was empowered to arrest any man using a horse other than in battery service. There were three basic components to good horse care: forage, water and grooming.

Forage

The daily allowance for forage was 26 pounds – 12 of oats, barley and corn, and 14 of hay. With some 7,280 Union artillery horses on the main Gettysburg battlefield (see "Statistics" below), the theoretical daily requirement for forage was a staggering 190,000 pounds. As wagons carried about one ton (2,000 pounds), ninety-five wagons (570 mules) would be needed for this purpose. The

Confederate need is estimated at 144,000 pounds or seventy-two wagonloads. Depots could not provide forage in these amounts over long periods, so armies depended on what could be squeezed from the countryside in which they were operating and so, in time, large areas were picked clean, causing particularly severe shortages of grain and hay. Lieutenant-Colonel Garnett, who commanded a Confederate artillery battalion at Gettysburg, reported after the retreat from the battle:

> I regret to state that, owing to the jaded condition of the horses, which had been but scantily supplied with forage since July 1, during all of which time they had not received a single feed of corn, I was forced to abandon two rifled pieces . . . the losses which my battalion has incurred during the recent campaign are especially heavy in horses, those now remaining being for the present almost totally unserviceable.

Horses were frequently on short rations, supplemented by grazing on grass, which was not a proper alternative to grain and in which, unlike cavalry, artillery horses hitched to cannon or caissons could seldom indulge – certainly not on the line of march. It was not unknown for battery soldiers to be sent on grass-cutting forays to feed their horses.

Water

Water was a commodity that had to be found for all horses every day – the minimum amount being 4 gallons. The problem became acute at the end of a day's march when the nearest stream or well could be some considerable distance away, or during a lengthy battle such as Gettysburg. Serious difficulties could arise if teams were unhitched and led to a distant source of water, as this immobilized the guns or caissons. Such action was at times unavoidable, but it was usually staggered so that at least half a battery always remained ready for action. An example of how this situation could lead to disaster occurred at the Battle of Stones River in December 1862. Just before a Confederate attack, half the horses of Battery E, 1st Ohio Volunteer Light Artillery were taken to a stream 500 yards from their position. This was a major contributory factor in the assault overrunning the stranded guns. At Gettysburg, with the recent rain, streams were running high and, although thirst became a torment for many in the open at midday, Willoughby Run, Pitzer's Run, Plum Run, Rose's Run and Rock Creek were within reasonable distance of most troops and horses during long lulls or at night.

Grooming

This included normal brushing and washing away mud or dust, but also meant particular attention to shoeing, care with the fitting of harness or saddle, the use of a folded blanket under the latter to prevent back sores and a soft leather pad under the collar to relieve tenderness.

On the March

Artillery horses on the march seldom moved across country to reach a battlefield – there were just too many obstacles to movement. Some of the factors that affected marching are discussed below.

Pulling capacity

A single draft horse, according to *Field Tactics*, could draw 1,600 pounds for 23 miles in a day – this supposes he was not being ridden and that the march was over reasonable surfaced roads. Artillery horses were supposed not to draw more than 600–700 pounds each. A 12-pounder Napoleon with its limber and full ammunition chest weighed just under 3,900 pounds (including drivers but not cannoneers) and a caisson and limber about 3,800. A six-horse team would therefore just be able to manage satisfactorily in good conditions.

Road conditions and steep slopes

The effect of poor roads, hills, mud or having to carry cannoneers, even for short distances, put immense strain on artillery horses, often already weakened by fatigue and inadequate forage, and dramatically reduced performance. Deep mud was the artillery horse's nightmare. With wheels sunk up to their axles in clawing mud, it would sometimes be necessary to abandon guns, as not even men heaving on the wheels together with extra horses on the traces could shift them. Any progress would be made only at the expense of utter exhaustion of men and animals. Similar problems occurred when a battery was confronted with a steep hill. The procedure was to halt carriages at the rear, unhitch one or two pairs of horses and add them to the teams pulling the carriages in front (it was impossible to hitch more than ten horses to one gun) for the grinding drag ahead. However, with ten horses it was difficult to get the animals pulling together. Frequent rests were needed when wheels were locked. When descending a sharp incline, the drivers remained mounted to control the teams while the cannoneers hung onto a drag rope to help check the descent. For a steep descent in really difficult conditions the wheels of the carriage were locked, the cannoneers used the drag rope and only the three wheel-horses were left in the carriage, the others being taken out and led at the rear. Crossing a ditch usually involved the use of the prolonge for pulling and the handspike for leverage. When it was necessary to move a gun or caisson along a steep hillside where there was a danger of its overturning, a drag rope was fastened to the lower side, passed over the top of the gun, and held by two or three men walking on the upper side of the slope.

Breakdowns or accident en route

When this happened to a cannon's carriage it was pulled off the road for repairs while those behind closed the gap and continued. Its caisson also halted, always remaining with the gun, although if it was a caisson carriage that broke down its cannon continued the march leaving the caisson behind to catch up when possible.

Road space

Cannon and caissons took up considerable road space. Their standing instructions were to keep closed up with as little as 2 yards between the rear of a caisson and the heads of the leading pair of the following gun. Assuming in ideal conditions this was possible, then a cannon and limber drawn by six horses followed immediately by its caisson would take up about 30 yards of road space; a six-gun battery occupied 180 yards – say 200 yards. On this basis, Meade's Artillery Reserve of 106 pieces on the march would occupy at least 1.8–2 miles. The average Confederate battery with four guns would require around 120 yards of road. Thus Colonel Porter Alexander's battalion of twenty-four pieces would need about 720 yards.

March rates

These were dependent on the type of road or track, the condition of the teams, the weight of the load pulled, the weather and condition of the roads, the type of country (hilly or flat) and the number of unavoidable delays due to congestion, waiting for marching infantry, or tangling with endless supply trains. The daily marches of artillery were often longer than that of a cavalry unit over the same ground, as they must make more detours and avoid bad ground that led horses could easily pass over. One animal being injured or going lame put extra strain on the remainder of the team and slowed progress. Generally a battery would endeavor to march at the same rate and cover the same distance as the troops to which it was attached, which under good conditions could be 20 or more miles in a day. *Field Artillery Tactics* states that "Average daily marches at the natural rates are, for infantry, 15 miles, performed in six hours; for cavalry 17 miles in six hours; for artillery 16 miles in ten hours . . . each arm moving at its natural rate in an ordinary country" – not a common situation on active operations.

Losses

As with soldiers, losses of horses due to sickness or exhaustion far outnumbered those caused by enemy action. The life expectancy of a horse during the Civil War was said to be about eight months. Glanders, a contagious disease that affected the respiratory tracts of mules and horses, was probably the biggest killer, and it was common for worn-out animals to be shot. However, on the battlefield horses were often far more difficult to kill than men, it being not uncommon for a horse to be hit by several high-impact Minie balls before collapsing. James R. Cotner, in his article "Horsepower Moves the Guns" in the March 1996 issue of *America's Civil War*, gives a graphic example of how much punishment horses could take before being killed:

> At Ream's Station in August 1864, the 10th Independent Battery, Massachusetts Volunteer Light Artillery fought from behind a low makeshift barricade, with its horses fully exposed only a few yards behind the guns. The battery was fighting with five guns, and in a short time the five teams of horses came under fire. Within minutes only two of the thirty animals were still standing, and these all bore wounds. One horse was shot seven times before it went down, and struggled back up, only to be hit again. The average number of wounds suffered by each horse was five. The Confederates were firing from a cornfield approximately 300 yards away.

At Gettysburg, Union artillery horse losses have been put at 881, or about 12 percent of the total. Colonel Alexander recalled that he lost 116 horses out of 312 (37 percent) from his reserve battalion in two days' fighting, and that 80 percent of these were caused by artillery fire, which is understandable as few, if any, of his guns came within range of musket fire. Union Major-General Alexander S. Webb, who won the Medal of Honor for his actions at Gettysburg, also told Alexander after the war that he lost 27 out of 36 horses in about ten minutes when in position on Cemetery Hill. If 36,500 is taken as the approximate number of horses present at Gettysburg (see "Statistics" below) and 12 percent the approximate percentage killed, then roughly 4,400 died in all, including cavalry, staff, escort horses, etc.

Statistics

The establishment for horses for a six-gun battery was as shown below, with the figures for four guns (Confederates) in parenthesis, as, due to an acute shortage of horses, the majority of Southern guns, caissons and battery wagons were drawn by only four horses. The figures exclude cavalry actions away from the main battlefield.

	Draft	Saddle	Total
Gun carriages	36 (16)	–	36 (16)
Caissons	36 (16)	–	36 (16)
Battery wagons	6 (4)	–	6 (4)
Forges	6 (4)	–	6 (4)
Sergeants	–	8 (4)	8 (4)
Artificers	–	6 (2)	6 (2)
Buglers	–	2 (2)	2 (2)
Spare (very variable)	10 (6)	2 (2)	12 (8)
Totals	**94 (46)**	**18 (10)**	**112 (56)**

Note: These figures do not include horses for between two and five officers, but the number of artificers was often less than shown.

Using the above figures, the estimated number of artillery horses on the main battlefield (excluding all horse artillery except those with Major-General Buford) was:

	Draft	Saddle	Total
Union (58 batteries)	5,452	1,044	6,496
Confederate (63 batteries)	2,898	630	3,528
Totals	**8,350**	**1,674**	**10,024**

Assuming all supply and artillery trains were mostly pulled by mules, the estimated number of horses of all types present at Gettysburg, including the cavalry actions, is as follows:

	Mounted artillery	Horse artillery	Cavalry	Staff/Others	Total
Union	6,496	1,692	11,077	3,000	22,265
Confederate	3,528	807	7,578	2,250	14,163
Totals	**10,024**	**2,499**	**18,655**	**5,250**	**36,428 (say 40,000**

Add in the mules pulling the trains, and the total number of animals that brought the armies to Gettysburg probably exceeded 90,000.

SECTION FOUR
The Cavalry

The impression is sometimes given that cavalry on both sides played a very minor role at Gettysburg. While it is true that on the main battlefield it was only on July 1 that one Union cavalry division (1st Division under Major-General John Buford) was fully engaged in a crucial and skillful delaying role west of the town, as far as the campaign as a whole was concerned cavalry played a critical part. There were some fifty cavalry clashes and skirmishes, from the largest full-scale battle of the Civil War on June 9 at Brandy Station to the much smaller action at Falling Waters on July 14, which saw the rearguard of Lee's retreating army cover his recrossing of the Potomac. At Brandy Station some 15,000 cavalry (and some Union infantry) fought all day, sometimes dismounted and at others charging and countercharging with drawn sabers into hand-to-hand melees in traditional cavalry style. As the Confederate advance north progressed, horsemen fought each other at Aldie (June 17), Middleburg (June 19), Upperville (June 21), Hanover (June 30) and Hunterstown (July 2). During Lee's withdrawal after the battle it was Union cavalry that pursued and harried, and opposing cavalry that delayed, screened and protected the long columns of infantry, guns and wagons as they struggled south. At Williamsport on the Potomac it was Major-General J. E. B. "Jeb" Stuart's Division that screened the Army of Northern Virginia from July 7–12, giving it the time to prepare entrenched positions covering the ford and ferry. At the end of the Gettysburg campaign there was no longer any truth in the old army jibe, "Whoever saw a dead cavalryman?"

On the fringes of the Gettysburg battlefield itself, three significant engagements took place. Late on July 2 the Union 2nd Cavalry Division under Brigadier-General David M. Gregg advanced down the Hanover Road threatening the extreme left of the Confederate line. The Rebels were compelled to send their Stonewall Brigade to hold Gregg at Brinkerhoff Ridge some 4 miles east of the town. The detachment of this brigade and its involvement in what was only a skirmish meant that Major-General Ewell's attacking force, which assailed Culp's Hill during the evening and into the night of July 2, was appreciably weakened. The next day, in the same area around Rummel Farm, later known as East Cavalry Field, it was also Gregg who this time thwarted Stuart's attempt to attack the rear of the Union line as Longstreet's famous infantry assault went in on Cemetery Ridge. Finally, late on July 3 on the Confederate's extreme right, Brigadier-General Judson Kilpatrick launched a futile, costly cavalry attack across broken country against Rebel infantry and guns. The result was a bloody repulse and the death of Brigadier-General Elon J. Farnsworth who, in obedience to Kilpatrick's senseless order, led the charge.

CAVALRY PRIOR TO GETTYSBURG

Confederate

A Southerner was, on average, considered the superior horseman mounted on a better horse, especially early in the war. Roads in the rural South were often poor and horses were usually used for individual transportation rather than for drawing the carriages and streetcars of the more urbanized North, where a generation of townsmen had become more accustomed to sitting behind rather than on horses. Thus, in the South there was a greater proportion of men who regarded the horse as a necessary part of everyday life. Many Southerners were accomplished riders from boyhood. Horse owners in Confederate states also owned slaves so were free from the tedium of feeding, grooming, and cleaning out stables. Although many Northern farmers could ride, they mostly kept their horses for pulling a plough. In the South, long before the war, young men often organized themselves into mounted militia companies, many with exotic names. Apart from the popular social attributes of such units, they taught the basics of drill and how to charge with the saber, provided "slave-catcher" patrols and constituted the force to be called on in case of a serious slave uprising. Additionally, at the start of the war, Southern horses tended to be faster-moving and thus better suited to cavalry work than the slower, more heavily built draft horses of the North – the reason being that almost every Southern town had its racecourse and over time the sport had developed a superior stock of fleet-footed animals. As one Rebel horseman put it, "probably no nation ever went to war richer in its cavalry raw material."

The Southern cavalry recruit had to come with his own horse, for which he was paid a per diem allowance. The horse was valued at mustering and, if it was killed in action, the trooper was entitled to that amount in compensation. The snag was, from the soldier's point of view, that no money was paid if the horse died from fatigue or sickness – both far more common than death in battle. If a cavalryman's mount died from any cause he had to replace it, which often meant returning home and being absent from his unit for weeks – he was usually allowed sixty days. If he failed to provide another mount he was forced to transfer to the infantry or artillery. As the war progressed and horses became scarce and far more expensive, this system proved to be a serious drain on cavalry manpower in the South, which, coupled with inferior firearms and horse furniture, ensured the Southern cavalry lost its edge during the period 1863–65. Major Henry McClellan, Stuart's assistant adjutant general, wrote:

> two causes contributed steadily to diminish the numbers and efficiency of the Confederate cavalry. The Government committed the fatal error of allowing the men to own their own horses, paying them a per diem for their use, and the muster valuation in cases where they were killed in action; but giving no compensation for horses lost by any other casualties of a campaign . . . Toward the close of the war many were unable to remount themselves, and hundreds of such dismounted men were collected in a useless crowd, which was dubbed "Company Q." The second cause was the failure or inability of the Government to supply good arms and accoutrements. Our breechloading arms were nearly all captured from the enemy and the same may be said of the best saddles and bridles. From these causes, which were beyond the power of any commander to remedy, there was a steady decline in the numbers of the Confederate cavalry and, as compared with the Federal cavalry, a decline in efficiency.

Despite the evident disadvantages of this system, no attempt was made to change it; indeed as late as May 25, 1863 Confederate General Order No. 67 stated: "Whenever a cavalryman fails and refuses to keep himself provided with a serviceable horse, he may, upon the order of the corps commander, be transferred into any company of infantry or artillery in the same army he may select." At least he had a choice of regiment.

Nevertheless, for the first half of the war it was the Confederate cavalryman who was the acknowledged superior in horsemanship, daring, effectiveness and leadership. The exploits of Jeb Stuart and John Mosby in the East and the raiding of Nathan Bedford Forrest and John Hunt Morgan in the West far outshone their Northern opposites and generally established a distinct psychological advantage. However, by mid-1863 the Union cavalry had caught up. It proved its increased competence at Brandy Station and reinforced this throughout the Gettysburg campaign and on the battlefield itself on July 1. For the remainder of the war the Confederate cavalry's shortage of both horses and breechloading carbines, and its indifferent equipment reversed its previous superiority.

The South organized their cavalry in large fighting formations from the beginning of the conflict. On September 24, 1861 Jeb Stuart was promoted brigadier-general and given command of the newly formed Cavalry Brigade with six regiments. In May the next year the brigade was expanded to include the Wise, Hampton and Cobb Legion Cavalry and Critcher's Virginia Battalion, plus a battery of horse artillery under Captain John Pelham. In July the Cavalry Division was formed with two brigades and Stuart promoted major-general. By the end of that year two more brigades had been added and the newly promoted Major Pelham commanded five batteries of horse artillery. By then Stuart had command of some 600 officers and some 8,550 enlisted men – a truly formidable force of experienced horsemen. Details of the composition of this division as it was engaged at Gettysburg can be found on page 84 of Section One: Orders of Battle. In summary, at the start of the campaign Stuart had twenty-six regiments in six brigades and six horse batteries – over 9,000 all ranks. Of these, one brigade (Brigadier-General Beverly H. Robertson's) was not engaged during those three days. In addition, operating independently of Stuart was the mounted infantry brigade of Brigadier-General John D. Imboden with some 1,100 men. Lee began his advance north with the largest mounted force ever at his disposal.

Union

At the war's beginning the North had the theoretical advantage of owning five regiments of regular cavalry, although their leadership was massively diluted when 104 of the 176 officers resigned to go South. In the opinion of the United States commanding general, Winfield Scott, improvements in weapons had outmoded cavalry. He therefore considered that when President Lincoln made his first appeal for volunteers, only one additional regiment of cavalry need be authorized. Poor performance in action and the realization that the war was likely to be long, however, soon highlighted the inadequacy of the cavalry. In August 1861, after Major-General George B. McClellan took command of the Union Army, this policy was changed and a major recruitment drive instituted. At the end of 1861 the Union cavalry strength stood at 4,744 regulars and 54,654 volunteers; by the war's end there would be 160,000.

To recruit this large number of volunteers quickly, local political and civic leaders were empowered to raise companies, and often entire regiments. In return, these individuals were usually rewarded for their efforts by being given officer rank – not a surefire way of appointing cavalry leaders. The method of recruiting was, of necessity, hasty and slapdash. An Ohio cavalry officer explained: "The method of obtaining enlistments was to hold war meetings in schoolhouses . . . The recruiting officer, accompanied by a good speaker, would attend an evening meeting which had been duly advertised. The latter did the talking, the former was ready with blank forms to obtain signatures and administer the oath." Anyone between the ages of eighteen and forty-five could enlist with the briefest of medical examinations. A further requirement for cavalry was that the recruit "should not exceed in weight one hundred and sixty pounds, should be active and strong, physically sound and with a natural fondness for horses and experience in handling them." As noted above, most Northerners were not horsemen and records indicate that as few as 10–20 percent of cavalry enlistments were farmers, even in rural areas. An officer from New York was struck by recruits' "great inferiority, mentally and physically, when compared with either infantry or artillery." Company officers were mostly elected civic leaders or veterans who had seen some military service in the Mexican War of 1846-48. Virtually all, however, would have to be trained from scratch alongside the privates.

A regular cavalryman maintained it took two years to produce a seasoned trooper mounted on a properly schooled horse. A graphic description by Captain Vanderbilt in the *History of the Tenth New York Cavalry* illustrates the problems with training green men and horses:

> Such a rattling, jingling, jerking, scrabbling, cursing I never heard before. Green horses – some of them had never been ridden – turned round and round, backed against each other, jumped up or stood up like trained circus horses. Some of the boys had a pile in front of their saddles, and one in the rear, so high and heavy it took two men to saddle one horse and two men to help the fellow into his place. The horses sheered out, going sideways, pushing the well-disposed animals out of position, etc. Some of the boys had never ridden anything since they galloped on a hobbyhorse, and they clasped their legs close together, thus unconsciously sticking their spurs into their horses' sides . . .

He then went on to describe what happened when the commanding general set a cracking pace on the march:

> Blankets slipped from under saddles and hung from one corner; saddles slipped back until they were on the rumps of the horses; others turned and were on the underside of the animals; horses running and kicking; tin pans, mess-kettles, patent sheet-iron stoves the boys had seen advertised in the illustrated papers and sold by the sutlers of Alexandria – about as useful as a piano or folding bed – flying through the air; and all I could do was to give a hasty glance to the rear and sing out at the top of my voice, "c-l-o-s-e u-p!" Poor boys! Their eyes stuck out like those of maniacs. We went only a few miles, but the boys didn't all get up till noon.

Such green troopers were roughly handled by an enemy eager to demonstrate their superiority and seize their enemies' superior arms and equipment. At First Manassas Union troops were chased from the field by Confederate "Black Horse Cavalry." This was followed by the havoc of Jeb Stuart's ride around McClellan's army encamped on the Chickahominy in June 1862, and Mosby's raids on Union trains, railroads and poorly defended outposts. These successes and others established in the minds of most in the North and South that Union horsemen were no match for their mounted opponents. One consequence of these continual reverses was to make the Union cavalry something of a butt of derogatory jokes by their infantry comrades, such as, "There's going to be a fight boys; the cavalry's running back!"

However, by early 1863 Union cavalry had learned many lessons, the troopers were well armed and equipped and had gained experience and confidence in raids of their own. Also a huge cavalry depot was established at Geisboro Point, near Washington, to train, equip, and supply men and horses. When Major-General Hooker took command of the Army of the Potomac in January 1863 he embarked on a complete overhaul of his mounted arm. He consolidated the forty regiments, which had largely operated with, and under the command of, infantry corps, into a Cavalry Corps of three divisions, giving the army a powerful, mobile and offensive force for the first time. At Kelly's Ford on March 17 Brigadier-General William Averell, with around 2,000 Union cavalry, challenged about 800 Confederate horsemen under Brigadier-General Fitzhugh Lee for ten hours and eventually pushed them back – some Virginians fleeing in panic. It was the first time Union troopers had shown they could stand up to – defeat, even – Rebel cavalry. Casualties were comparatively light, but Stuart lost his gallant artillery commander, Major Pelham. Unfortunately for the Union cause, Hooker's reorganization was to some extent negated by the appointment of several cavalry commanders of dubious ability, the most notable of whom was Major-General George Stoneman, given overall command of his cavalry. Stoneman led his force round Lee's army near Fredericksburg in an endeavor to cut communications with Richmond and cause mayhem in Lee's rear. It did no such thing and the great majority of Union cavalry were absent when Stonewall Jackson crashed into Hooker's right flank at Chancellorsville in May 1863. One cavalry brigade that was at Chancellorsville was commanded by Brigadier-General Alfred Pleasonton, who dispersed some Confederates he claimed were attempting to block Hooker's retreat. This dubious claim was accepted by Hooker when trying to put some sort of gloss on his defeat. When Stoneman disappeared to Washington for treatment for his piles, Pleasonton took his place and it was he who commanded the Union cavalry at Gettysburg.

At Brandy Station Union cavalry did well in surprising Stuart's division and holding them to an expensive draw in what was to become the largest cavalry battle of the Civil War. Although Stuart lost only 500 men to Pleasonton's 900, his invulnerable reputation was badly tarnished and those that gave the result some thought realized that Union cavalry were no longer going to be a pushover. This battle was the opening drama of the Gettysburg campaign. The details of Pleasonton's Cavalry Corps, as engaged during the three-day battle, are given in Section One: Orders of Battle. In summary, he commanded three divisions composed of thirty-three regiments (including three small regimental detachments) divided into six brigades, all supported by nine batteries of horse artillery. About 11,850 men of all ranks saw action, of which 775 were horse artillerymen.

REGIMENTAL STRENGTH AND ORGANIZATION

Union

The original U.S. cavalry regiment had an establishment of over 1,100 men divided into three battalions, each of two squadrons, each of two companies (called troops at Gettysburg). A colonel commanded with a lieutenant-colonel as his second, three majors commanding the battalions and captains the companies (the senior being the squadron commanders). However, with the huge expansion of the volunteer cavalry, things had changed considerably by Gettysburg. Brigadier-General Phillip Cooke's *Cavalry Tactics*, issued in November 1861, saw a regiment divided into two battalions (or wings) with just two majors on establishment. Later the squadron designation was dropped and troops became the sub-units.

The largest Union regiment at the battle was the 5th Michigan Cavalry with 645 all ranks divided into twelve troops designated A–M (omitting J) of an average strength of 54 men. The regiment with the smallest representation was the tiny detachment of 42 men in the Oneida New York Cavalry that provided close security at Meade's headquarters (see box, page 279). Discounting the Oneida, the smallest regiment was the 1st New Jersey Cavalry with 199 men commanded by a major. The average strength of a Union regiment engaged at the battle was about 350, with 29 to a troop. Although in theory a regiment could still split into battalions of four troops if necessary, this rarely happened. Pleasonton's cavalry had ten regiments commanded at the battle by majors (seven) or captains (three). Brigadier-General Wesley Merritt's Brigade had five regiments with not a single colonel or lieutenant-colonel among them – two were commanded by majors, three by captains.

The 8th Illinois Cavalry (nicknamed "the Big Abolition Regiment") was a fairly typical regiment, engaged from the start of the battle west of the town in the skillful delaying action of Major-General Buford's Division. Its muster rolls for April 30–June 30 show 25 officers and 536 enlisted men; this gives an average troop strength of about 46. However, once those absent, sick or on detached duties had been taken off, only some 470 actually fought with the regiment on the battlefield, with the twelve troops averaging 38 (excluding regimental headquarters and administrative personnel). To illustrate how this typical regiment was organized just prior to the battle, the details of the headquarters, troops and those probably left out of the fighting are given in the table below for each troop using the muster rolls signed on June 30.

Muster Roll of the 8th Illinois Cavalry, June 30, 1863

Regimental headquarters (tactical – engaged in the action).

Commanding officer	Major John L. Beveridge
Second-in-command	Major William H. Medill (mw July 6)
Sergeant-Major	Samuel W. Smith
Chief Bugler	Private George W. Bartholomew
Standard/Guidon	Private H. Mulley

Regimental headquarters (administrative – probably not directly engaged in the fighting)

Quartermaster	1st Lieutenant James T. Berry
Commissary	1st Lieutenant Bradley L. Chamberlain
Veterinary Surgeon	George E. Corwin
Assistant Surgeon	Theodore W. Stull
Quartermaster Sergeant	Robert W. Gates
Saddler Sergeant	William D. Hazlett
Hospital Stewards	George R. Wells, Andrew J. Willing
Blacksmith	Private Peter Vanderipe
Assistant Blacksmith	Private Gilbert Mott

Troop A

Troop Commander	2nd Lieutenant Lyman G. Pierce
1st Sergeant	Sergeant Harvey A. Humphrey
Quartermaster Sergeant	David H. Fillmore
Sergeants x 3	Thomas J. Brown, Joseph Phillips, Leonard Smith
Corporals x 5	John Durrant, Jr., Richard I. Gallagher, Alonso Hall, Bernard Martin, Benton Van Dyke
Blacksmith	Private John Lewis
Privates x 25	

Troop B

Troop Commander	1st Lieutenant John A. Kelly (absent sick July 8)
1st Sergeant	Sergeant George W. Corbit
Sergeants x 6	Adin F. Cowles, Dyre D. Dunning, Harrison Hakes, James W. Maynard, Charles W. Morse, Edward B. Wright
Corporals x 7	Orris A. Bishop, Cyrus H. Cronk, James M. Howe, Denis H. Remington, Andrew A. Reynolds, George M. Roe, William Weed
Buglers x 2	Privates William L. Campbell, Hiram S. DeWitt
Blacksmith	Private George McGregor
Privates x 31	

Troop C

Troop Commander	1st Lieutenant Daniel D. Lincoln
1st Sergeant	Sergeant Truman Culver
Commissary Sergeant	Simon V. Hoag
Quartermaster Sergeant	Alfred McCrear
Sergeants x 4	Charles S. Gilbert, Herman Hazard, Portus J. Kennedy, Ebenezer R. Buckley
Corporals x 5	George Daniel, Charles H. Henshaw,
Buglers x 2	Privates William C. Kier, Philip Riley
Farrier	Private Harvey P. Baker
Blacksmith	Private Freeman B. McClintock
Saddler	Private Henry Brown
Privates x 35	

Troop D

Troop Commander	Captain Henry J. Hotopp
Troop Officers x 2	1st Lieutenant Carlos H. Verbeck, 2nd Lieutenant William C. Hazelton
1st Sergeant	Sergeant Andrew Dunning
Commissary Sergeant	Sergeant Garrett P. Durland
Quartermaster Sergeant	Sergeant William E. Higgins
Sergeants x 2	Charles S. Clark, Asa W. Farr (w July 6)
Corporals x 7	Clark R. Barnes, William Beye, Henry Englekind, Joel A. Northrup, Anthony Plank, Herman Rehling, Perry Tanner
Bugler	Private Dedrick Mund
Saddler	Private David Laning
Privates x 28	

Troop E

Troop Commander	Captain Daniel W. Buck
Troop Officers x 2	1st Lieutenant Amsasa E. Dana (commanded the troops providing the pickets that first clashed with the Rebels on the Chambersburg Pike on July 1), 2nd Lieutenant Marcellus E. Jones (fired the first shot of the battle – see box, page 193)
1st Sergeant	Sergeant Alexander McS. Riddler
Commissary Sergeant	Sergeant Sewell Flagg (w July 6)
Quartermaster Sergeant	Sergeant Samuel Bend
Sergeants x 4	Frank Crosby, Thomas S. Heines, Edward Wayne, Owen Whittaker
Corporals x 6	Herbert Cooley, Darwin Dense, Edgar A, Hardy, Abram A. Kinsey, William Pinches, Levi S. Shafer
Bugler	Private Morgan Hughs
Blacksmith	Private Lewis Strouse
Saddler	George Fosha
Privates x 33	

Troop F

Troop Commander	2nd Lieutenant Edward Russell
1st Sergeant	Sergeant Joseph Clapp
Commissary Sergeant	Sergeant Charles W. Sprague
Quartermaster Sergeant	Sergeant Giles Buskirk
Sergeants x 4	Jesse C. Allen, George B. Hewes, (w July 1), George W. Huntoon, Harry A. Pearsons
Corporals x 5	Joseph W. Cook, Abraham Haner, Alvey P. Searle, William H. Sheperd, William E. Smith (k July 9)
Buglers x 2	Privates Otis Alford, Thomas J. Lett
Blacksmith	Private George Ellis
Farrier	Private Henry C. Smith
Saddler	Private John W. Doolittle
Privates x 23	

Troop G

Troop Commander	Captain Dennis J. Hynes
Troop Officer	2nd Lieutenant George F. Warner
1st Sergeant	Sergeant Louis H. Rymer
Commissary Sergeant	Sergeant Charles Schriber
Quartermaster Sergeant	Sergeant Harvey J. Sheldon
Sergeants x 4	Marquis W. Cassidy, William Goudy, Sheldon Morgan, William N. Palmer
Corporals x 5	A. Judson Annis, Thomas J. Clute, James C. Edminton, Jesse B. Grassford, Michael E. Wright
Bugler	Private Dennis Delaney
Blacksmith	Private James Morris
Saddler	Private Lewis C. Pray
Privates x 37	

Troop H

Troop Commander	1st Lieutenant Edmond DeWitt Dowd
1st Sergeant	Sergeant John W. Delaney (w July 9)
Sergeants x 3	Silas M. Finch, Charles Goodspeed (w July 1), John C. Smith
Corporals x 3	Francis E. Hubbard, John Kewley, Addison V. Teeple (w July 8)
Blacksmith	Private William B. Pierce
Farrier	Private Charles L. Sullivan
Saddler	Private George McCollom
Privates x 24	

Troop I

Troop Commander	Captain A. Levi Wells
Troop Officers x 2	1st Lieutenant Azor W. Howard, 2nd Lieutenant Thomas Grimley
1st Sergeant	Sergeant Zaccheus Hays
Commissary Sergeant	Sergeant Willard Cummins
Quartermaster Sergeant	Sergeant Henry A. Sheldon
Sergeants x 3	James A. Bell, Francis M. Gregory, John M. Williams
Corporals x 8	Oscar Bowdish, Loren Carver, Aaron W. Chase, Appollos S. Fuller, William H. H. Halburt, Roswell C. Humphrey, Michael J. Kelly, Joseph Pfifer
Buglers x 2	Privates Lester W. Folsom, Henry F. Marks
Blacksmith	Private Albert Cool
Saddler	Oscar L. Gardner
Privates x 22	

Troop K

Troop Commander	1st Lieutenant Darius Sullivan
1st Sergeant	Sergeant John A. Kinley
Commissary Sergeant	Sergeant Charles D. Brown
Sergeants x 4	Joseph Bushnell, Richard Duckworth, Sylvester B. Freelove, Richard C. Vinson
Corporals x 4	John Beckwith, Charles Greenville, Harley J. Ingersoll, Alfred Van Fleet
Blacksmith	Private Samuel Pettingill
Privates x 27	

Troop L

Troop Commander	Captain John M. Waite
Troop Officer	2nd Lieutenant Judson A. Stevens
1st Sergeant	Sergeant Charles Bradley
Quartermaster Sergeant	Sergeant Rodger S. Horton
Sergeants x 2	Josiah E. Richardson, Aaron W. Rundle
Corporals x 6	George Archer, Arick H. Burzell, Amos R. Cole, Joseph E. Dixon, William A. McHenry, Samuel G. Workman
Buglers x 2	Privates James H. Ewing, Warren A. Washburn
Blacksmith	Private Charles L. Dunham
Privates x 35	

Troop M

Troop Commander	2nd Lieutenant John Sargent
1st Sergeant	Sergeant Adam C. Fowler
Sergeants x 6	Benjamin F. Cook, David A. Fisher, L. John Himber, Isaac R. McCulloch, Reuben T. Prentice, Ralph B. Swartout
Corporals x 3	Frank H. Campbell, Mervin D. Overacker, William C. Wilson
Buglers x 2	Abel C. Crooker, Albert Gifford
Blacksmith	Private Ezra A. Perry
Privates x 33	

This muster roll is for one of the few cavalry regiments to be actually engaged on the main battlefield. However, as stressed by Busey and Martin in *Regimental Strengths and Losses at Gettysburg*, the total strength of twenty-five officers and 536 enlisted men was not the strength of fighting on July 1. Rather it reflected the number entitled to pay as at June 30. The number actually engaged the next day – present on the battlefield, equipped and performing their duties – is estimated as 470 all ranks. This means some sixty-six men were on the payroll but absent from front-line duty with the regiment; these would include stragglers, sick, men under arrest and those detached on other duties – for example Private David Diffenbaugh, the regiment's only fatality at Gettysburg, was killed while attached to brigade headquarters. His name, along with that of Lieutenant Jones, is recorded on the 8th Illinois monument sited at the intersection of Buford Avenue and the Mummasburg Road, where John Forney's Farm was located during the battle.

The regimental headquarters has been divided into what in modern terms are the tactical headquarters and the administrative headquarters staff. The former would be controlling the regiment in action, the latter personnel would mostly perform their duties either immediately behind the front line (medical and veterinary personnel), or further back with the wagons/train (quartermaster, commissary, farriers, blacksmiths and saddlers). With the 8th Illinois the only strange omission in the tactical headquarters is the lack of an adjutant, usually a lieutenant. His was a crucial appointment as the commander's staff officer and in this case it is entirely possible that another officer performed these duties in addition to his normal ones. Similarly with the administrative personnel, the 8th Illinois lists an assistant surgeon but no surgeon – it was normal practice to have both. Note the number of soldiers whose duties involved looking after the horses – four at regimental headquarters and twenty-one specifically appointed as blacksmiths, farriers or saddlers within the twelve troops. Troops C, F and H had all three; none of the remainder had a farrier but all except D had blacksmiths. The key individual was the blacksmith, closely followed by the saddler (one sergeant and seven among the troops); however, it is likely that the troops lacking such specialists on their payrolls had assistants performing these duties. Only three troops had farriers – presumably they were something of a luxury and really more of an assistant to the blacksmith.

Command and control at troop level was somewhat thin in that seven had only one officer. Troop H seems particularly badly off, with only one officer, a first sergeant and three sergeants – no quartermaster or commissary sergeants. Assuming all the officers were present on the battlefield, then the ratio of officers to enlisted men was 1:23. The leadership establishment for a full-strength troop allowed for a captain, first lieutenant, second lieutenant, first sergeant, quartermaster and commissary sergeants, five sergeants and eight corporals. None of the troops in the 8th Illinois had all these posts filled, although all had first sergeants. Certainly in troops short of key individuals – such as quartermaster or commissary sergeants – ordinary sergeants would have performed these essential duties and their places would have been taken by corporals.

Casualties amounted to thirty-nine for the period July 1–14. These consisted of eleven killed or mortally wounded, twenty-six wounded and two missing (both deserted). However, losses during the battle (in effect on July 1, as the regiment was not engaged on the next two days) amounted to only seven – one killed, five wounded and one missing. This represents a mere 1.5 percent, which is minimal considering the regiment was in the forefront of the delaying action on the left flank of McPherson's Ridge and later on Seminary Ridge.

The 8th Illinois Cavalry's Monument

This is a unique monument in several ways. First, it is the only one to have a regulation cavalry saddle as its main feature. It is a complete replica of the McClellan saddle (see illustration, page 199) and includes all the items essential to a cavalryman, such as his blanket roll, saddlebags and haversack. Second, it names Lieutenant Marcellus E. Jones as the man who fired the first shot of the battle as the enemy crossed the Marsh Creek bridge (see box opposite). Third, on the other side is the name of the only soldier of the regiment to be killed at Gettysburg. Private David Diffenbaugh was a member of the 8th Illinois, but his name does not appear on the regiment's muster roll of June 30 as he had been assigned as orderly to the brigade commander, Colonel Gamble.

Confederate

The structure of a Confederate cavalry regiment was based on that of the Union Army except that the Rebels had ten companies (troops) designated A–K, omitting J. The cavalry company was originally supposed to have 80–100 men, thus making the Confederate regiment 800–1,000 strong. Like the infantry, this establishment strength was theoretical and never achieved on campaign. The largest Confederate cavalry regiment at Gettysburg was the 6th Virginia Cavalry in Brigadier-General William E. "Grumble" Jones's Brigade with 552 all ranks – each of its ten companies averaging fifty-five men. The smallest was the 39th Virginia Cavalry Battalion (half a regiment) with 122 men doing escort duties. There were twenty-six cavalry regiments or battalions engaged at the battle, with an average strength of some 290 men.

CAVALRY WEAPONS

Union

Breechloading carbines

There is little doubt that the Union cavalry trooper was the best-armed soldier on the Gettysburg battlefield. Not only did he have his revolver and saber but a breechloading, rifled carbine that enabled him to fire three times as fast as any muzzleloader. At 300 yards, in ideal conditions, a 24-inch pattern could be made with twenty shots; although it was possible to fire at greater ranges it was primarily a short-range weapon. It was the ideal cavalry weapon. Not only was it shorter than a rifle-musket and so easier to handle on a horse, but also the breechloading facility largely overcame the difficulty of reloading while mounted. Finally, it gave the cavalry the option, frequently adopted, of fighting dismounted against infantry when necessary. It was a Sharps that supposedly fired the opening shot at Gettysburg (see box opposite and Map 6). Lieutenant Marcellus Jones, 8th Illinois Cavalry, was with a forward picket on the morning of July 1 when he saw Rebel infantry some distance away on the Chambersburg Pike. He borrowed the carbine of Corporal (later sergeant) Levi Shaffer, rested the barrel on a fence rail and fired.

It is important not to confuse the breechloading Sharps rifle with the carbine. The former was an infantry weapon with which six Union regiments were fully (1st and 2nd U.S. Infantry) or partially (1st Minnesota, 1st Massachusetts, 2nd New Hampshire and 14th Connecticut) armed at Gettysburg. Both weapons were .52 caliber, and with both the breechblock was lowered by pushing forward a lever that doubled as a trigger guard. This gave access to the chamber for loading a paper or linen cartridge. As the breechblock closed it cut open the end of the cartridge with a sharp edge to facilitate ignition when the hammer, which had to be cocked manually, struck the percussion cap. Its main drawback was that when the cartridge was cut some black powder leaked out and built up in the fore stock and could cause a secondary explosion when the percussion cap was struck. This could result in minor burn injuries to the soldier, a broken fore stock and useless carbine. Meticulous cleaning was essential.

Their inventor, Christian Sharps, patented both the rifle and carbine in 1848 and the U.S. government bought over 9,000 of the former and 80,500 of the latter during the war. No fewer than twenty-eight of the thirty-three Union cavalry regiments at Gettysburg were at least partially, if not mainly, armed with the Sharps carbine. Every trooper in the five regiments of the reserve brigade (Merritt) in Buford's 1st Division had one.

The second most common, if not popular, breechloader with the Union cavalry at the battle was the .54 caliber Burnside carbine. It had been patented as early as 1856 by an A. E. Burnside, a Rhode Island arms manufacturer who later became Major-General Burnside, commander of the Army of the Potomac that went down in defeat to Lee at Fredericksburg. Its range and effectiveness were much the same as the Sharps, but its loading mechanism was slightly different in that the breechblock was rotated into a vertical position by pressing two trigger guards together and lowering. It fired a brass cartridge – an advantage, as the Confederate manufacturers found it difficult to copy and so captured Burnside carbines were useless to the Rebels. During the war the U.S. government purchased over 55,000 Burnsides along with 22 million cartridges. Twelve of the thirty-three Union regiments carried at least some Burnsides at Gettysburg – it being the only longarm of the 12th Illinois, 1st New Jersey and 7th Michigan.

Much less numerous were the Gallagher and Merrill breechloading carbines. They were normally used only if Sharps or Burnsides were not available. Both were .54 caliber, but the latter was originally intended as a sporting weapon so was not sufficiently rugged for army use – the hammer and sights were fragile and broke off easily. The Rebels captured large numbers of Merrills while they were being delivered along the Baltimore and Ohio Railroad, and as they fired paper cartridges they could make use of them. At Gettysburg the 3rd West Virginia was armed with Gallaghers and the 3rd Indiana partially so, while the 17th Pennsylvania was the only regiment equipped with Merrills.

Only two Union cavalry regiments (the 5th and 6th Michigan in Brigadier-General Custer's Brigade) possessed the weapon that was to become the most sought after and famous of the war – the Spencer breechloading repeater rifle. This .52-caliber rifle fired seven rounds as fast as the soldier could pull the trigger and eject spent rounds. The weapon was loaded by a tubular magazine that passed through the stock. A spring fed the copper-rimmed cartridges toward the breech. It was operated by pulling down on the trigger guard lever, as with the Sharps. This dropped the breechblock and extracted the fired shell. Closing the lever pushed another round into the chamber. The hammer was then cocked manually with the thumb. These weapons were fired for the first time by the 5th Michigan Cavalry (Wolverines) on the afternoon of July 3 near the Rummel Farm on East Cavalry Field, some 3 miles east of Gettysburg, against advancing dismounted skirmishers of the 9th and 13th Virginia Cavalry. An article by Wiley Sword in the *Gettysburg Magazine*, issue 20, in 1998 describes the effect of their opening fire:

> Posted behind a rail fence, the Wolverines waited until the advancing rebels approached to within 100 yards. At the sound of the first volley from the fence line, a Confederate officer yelled, "Now, for 'em boys, before they can reload!" Yet the deadly rifles blazed again and again. "Many a Reb fell, either dead or wounded," noted an excited witness . . . In a few minutes the attack was over. The Wolverines called out to the surviving gray cavalrymen to come in or be shot; and thereafter "one lean Johnny . . . asked to see our guns," noted Lt. Sam Harris of Company A. "You's load in the morning and fire all day," the prisoner grimly remarked.

Who Fired the First Shot?

The circumstances of Lieutenant Marcellus E. Jones's claim to firing the first shot at Gettysburg are recounted in the notes to Map 6, "Union Picketing System," on page 207. The stone commemorating this event is still preserved today, although well outside the boundary of the Gettysburg National Military Park. The four sides of the stone are inscribed as follows:

First shot at Gettysburg, July 1, 1863, 7:30 A.M.

Fired by Captain M.E. Jones with Sergeant Shafer's carbine, C. E, Eighth Regiment Illinois Cavalry

Erected by Captain Jones, Lieutenant Riddler, and Sergeant Shafer

Erected 1886

Note: Jones's rank on the June 30 muster roll is second lieutenant and that of Shafer, corporal. Riddler was then a first sergeant.

The second main claimant was Corporal Alpheus Hodges of the 9th New York Cavalry. He maintained that he was at a vedette post at the Chambersburg Pike bridge over the Willoughby Run at around 5:00 a.m. when he went forward to investigate approaching riders. Having decided they were Rebels, he started to return when they fired at him and he returned fire, upon which they withdrew. This account does not seem to stack up. First, the bridge in question is only 1.5 miles from the town center – far too close for the outer line of vedettes west of Gettysburg. Second, it is behind (east of) Gamble's pickets. He had vedettes across the Chambersburg Pike and along Wisler's Ridge all night, so how did these Confederate riders get through the 8th Illinois line undetected? Finally, the Confederates had no cavalry scouting ahead of their advance down the Chambersburg Pike at that time of the morning. The likelihood is that Hodges was on the Newville Road where the 9th New York had its picket line and he fired at someone much later – he may perhaps have moved across to where the Mummasburg Road crossed the Willoughby Run, although years later he emphatically rejected this possibility after visiting the site. The Gettysburg Battlefield Memorial Association accepted Hodges' version and erected a monument to the regiment east of the present Buford Avenue some 200 yards south of its junction with the Mummasburg Road.

The third main claimant to have fired the first shot was Private F. E. Whitney, Company B, 17th Pennsylvania Cavalry. Like the other two, he claimed to be picketing the Chambersburg Pike when he fired at advancing Rebels at around 6:00 a.m. As his regiment was not picketing that pike it would seem that at best Whitney got confused with his road names. The 17th Pennsylvania vedette line included the Carlisle and Harrisburg roads to the north and northeast of the town.

On the evidence, it would seem that Jones's claim should stand and that the other two were confused over their locations and the timing of events.

Cavalry Weapons at Gettysburg

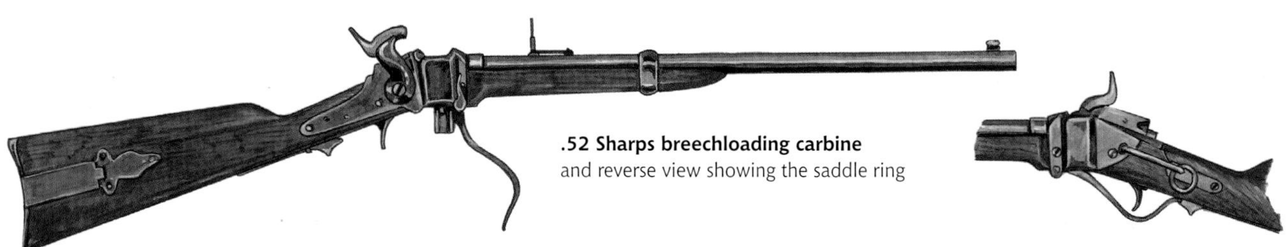

.52 Sharps breechloading carbine
and reverse view showing the saddle ring

The saddle ring allowed the cavalryman to clip the weapon to his shoulder strap (carbine belt), and prevented its loss should he be thrown from his horse.

Note
When pushed forward the trigger guard lowered the breechblock, giving access to the chamber for loading the linen cartridge.

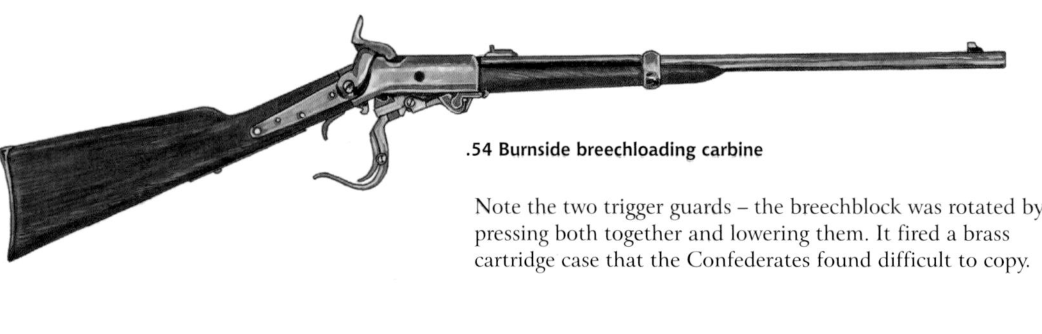

.54 Burnside breechloading carbine

Note the two trigger guards – the breechblock was rotated by pressing both together and lowering them. It fired a brass cartridge case that the Confederates found difficult to copy.

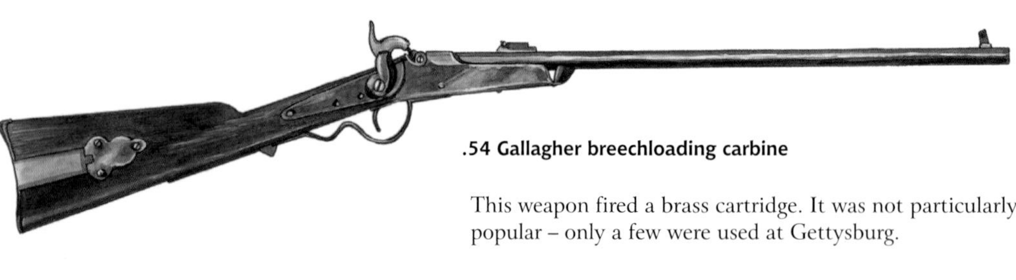

.54 Gallagher breechloading carbine

This weapon fired a brass cartridge. It was not particularly popular – only a few were used at Gettysburg.

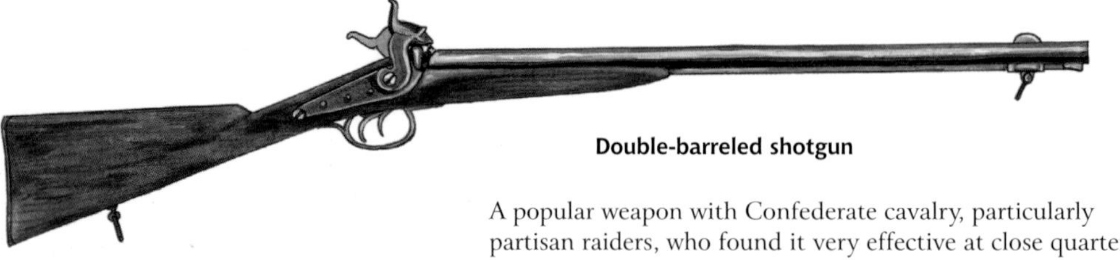

Double-barreled shotgun

A popular weapon with Confederate cavalry, particularly partisan raiders, who found it very effective at close quarters.

It was not until mid-1863 that Spencer repeating carbines began to become available from the rifle manufacturers in New Haven, Connecticut, so none had been issued to the troopers at Gettysburg. Although prone to stoppages caused by the copper cartridge case sticking in the chamber when the weapon overheated, and by its short range and low muzzle velocity (the cartridge contained only 45 grams of powder), it would become the most effective small arm of the war. A Union soldier was later to say, "I think the Johnnys are getting rattled; they are afraid of our repeating rifles. They say we are not fair, that we have guns that we load up on Sunday and shoot all the rest of the week."

Some Cavalry Revolvers Used at Gettysburg

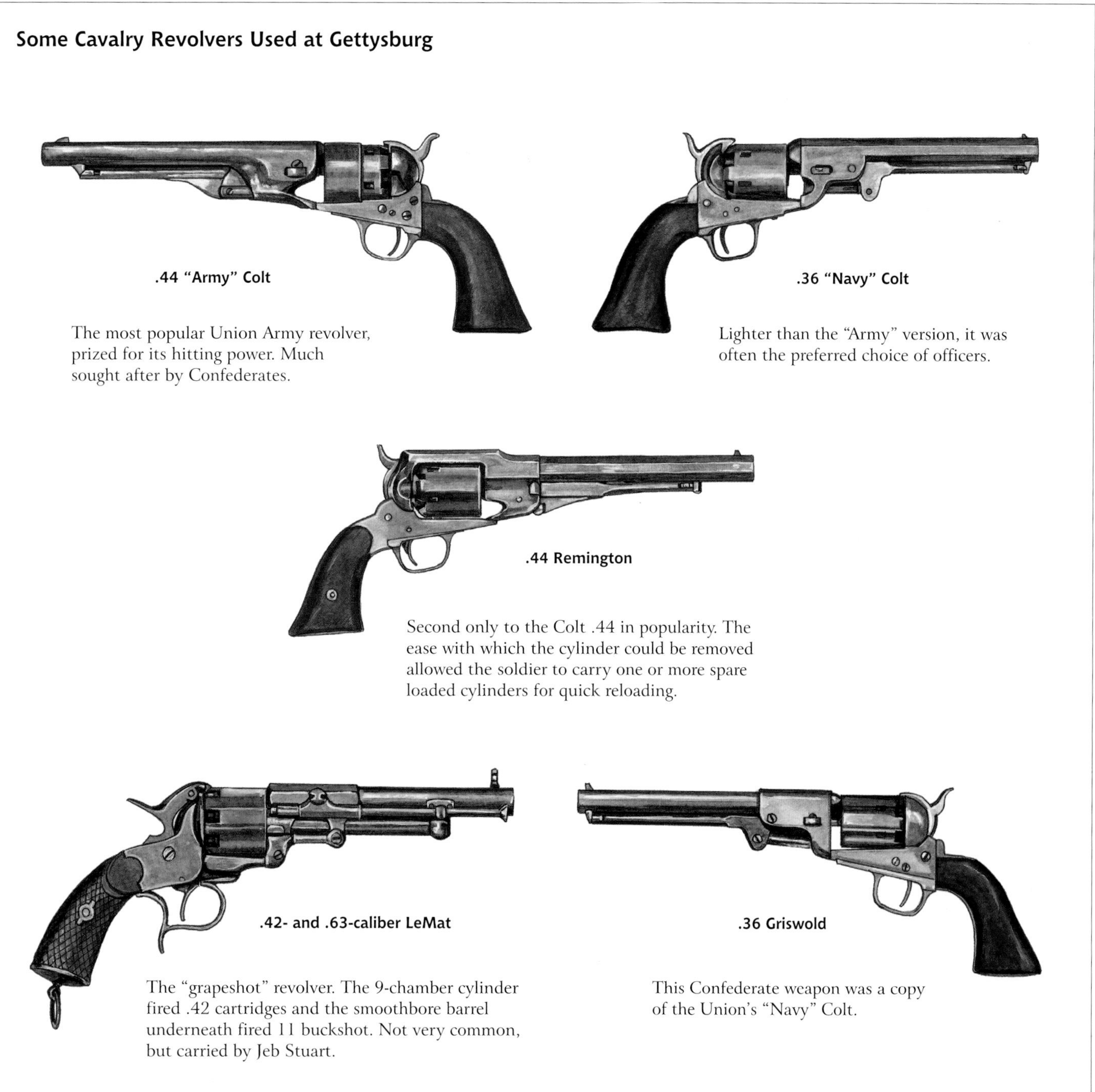

.44 "Army" Colt

The most popular Union Army revolver, prized for its hitting power. Much sought after by Confederates.

.36 "Navy" Colt

Lighter than the "Army" version, it was often the preferred choice of officers.

.44 Remington

Second only to the Colt .44 in popularity. The ease with which the cylinder could be removed allowed the soldier to carry one or more spare loaded cylinders for quick reloading.

.42- and .63-caliber LeMat

The "grapeshot" revolver. The 9-chamber cylinder fired .42 cartridges and the smoothbore barrel underneath fired 11 buckshot. Not very common, but carried by Jeb Stuart.

.36 Griswold

This Confederate weapon was a copy of the Union's "Navy" Colt.

Revolvers

The second most popular weapon after the breechloading carbine, certainly among Union troopers, was the revolver carried in a belt holster. With its rapid rate of fire it was the ideal weapon for use in a close-quarter melee. There were many varieties, but the most common with the cavalry in 1863, as well as with infantry and artillery officers, were the six-shot models made by the Colt Firearms Company and invented by Samuel Colt himself. Other models, such as the Remington, Whitney, Allen, Savage and Starr, were also used but in smaller numbers. The 1860 Colt six-shot, single-action percussion came in two calibers. The heavier .44 was the "Army" model and was popular for the powerful punch it delivered – the bullet could penetrate seven pine boards each threequarters of an inch thick, each separated by a one-inch space, at 16 yards. The lighter .36 version was often the choice of officers and was called the "Navy" Colt. Both fired paper-wrapped cartridges, inserted into the cylinders and rammed with an attached loading lever that swung beneath the barrel. Percussion caps were placed on each nipple behind each cartridge.

After the Colt the next favorite was the Remington, which also came in "Army" and "Navy" models. Its increasing popularity as the war progressed was due to the ease with which the cylinder could be removed from the gun (to do this with a Colt meant removing the barrel first). This allowed quicker reloading – a soldier could carry one or more spare loaded cylinders, pop out the empty and reload immediately with another six shots. There was also the question of cost – a Colt was sold to the government for $25, the Remington for $12!

Revolvers inevitably had a few technical drawbacks. Percussion caps could come apart during firing, getting between the cylinder and frame of the weapon and jamming its action. Caps could simply fall off causing a cylinder to misfire; and it was possible for a single cap to cause a "chain fire" in which all six cylinders fired at once, possibly exploding the gun in the firer's hand.

Between January 1, 1861 and June 30, 1866 the U.S. government acquired and issued 129,730 Army and 17,010 Navy Colt revolvers, and 125,314 Army and 11,901 Navy Remingtons. At Gettysburg, of the thirty-three Union cavalry regiments present and engaged, eighteen were armed with the heavy "Army" Colt .44, another eight had both the .44 and "Navy" .36, while the remainder had a mix of Colts and Remingtons. In addition, the 1st Ohio had a few Whitney .36s and the 8th Pennsylvania a handful of Allen .44s.

Sabers

The Civil War cavalryman's third weapon – troopers of both sides were the best armed of all branches of the army. Every mounted Union soldier had his saber, either the more common Model 1840 heavy saber known as the "wrist-breaker," or the similar, but lighter, 1860 version. Both were based on an earlier French model featuring a slightly curved blade, brass hand guard, and leather hand grip bound with twisted wire with a leather saber knot attached to the guard that was wound round the wrist in action to prevent its being dropped. Scabbards were of iron and sometimes covered with leather or similar material. At the start of the war most sabers had blunt blades when issued, so if swung rather than thrust they were mere bludgeons, perhaps breaking bones or bruising an adversary but unlikely to kill or seriously wound him. However, by 1863 most cavalrymen's sabers had sharpened blades. Although close combat with sabers was something of a rarity during the war, the Gettysburg campaign, and cavalry actions on the periphery of the main battlefield, saw several traditional mounted clashes between saber-wielding troopers. The first occasion was at Brandy Station on June 9 and then again on July 3 at East Cavalry Field; on both occasions all-out charges took place, resulting in desperate melees with saber and revolver – although even then it was the revolver that caused the most serious wounds. Nevertheless, cavalry of both sides expected to fight (as distinct from move) dismounted as often as mounted and by mid-1863 many troopers attached their sabers to their saddles so they would not be hampered when operating on foot.

Cavalry Saber and Basic Equipment

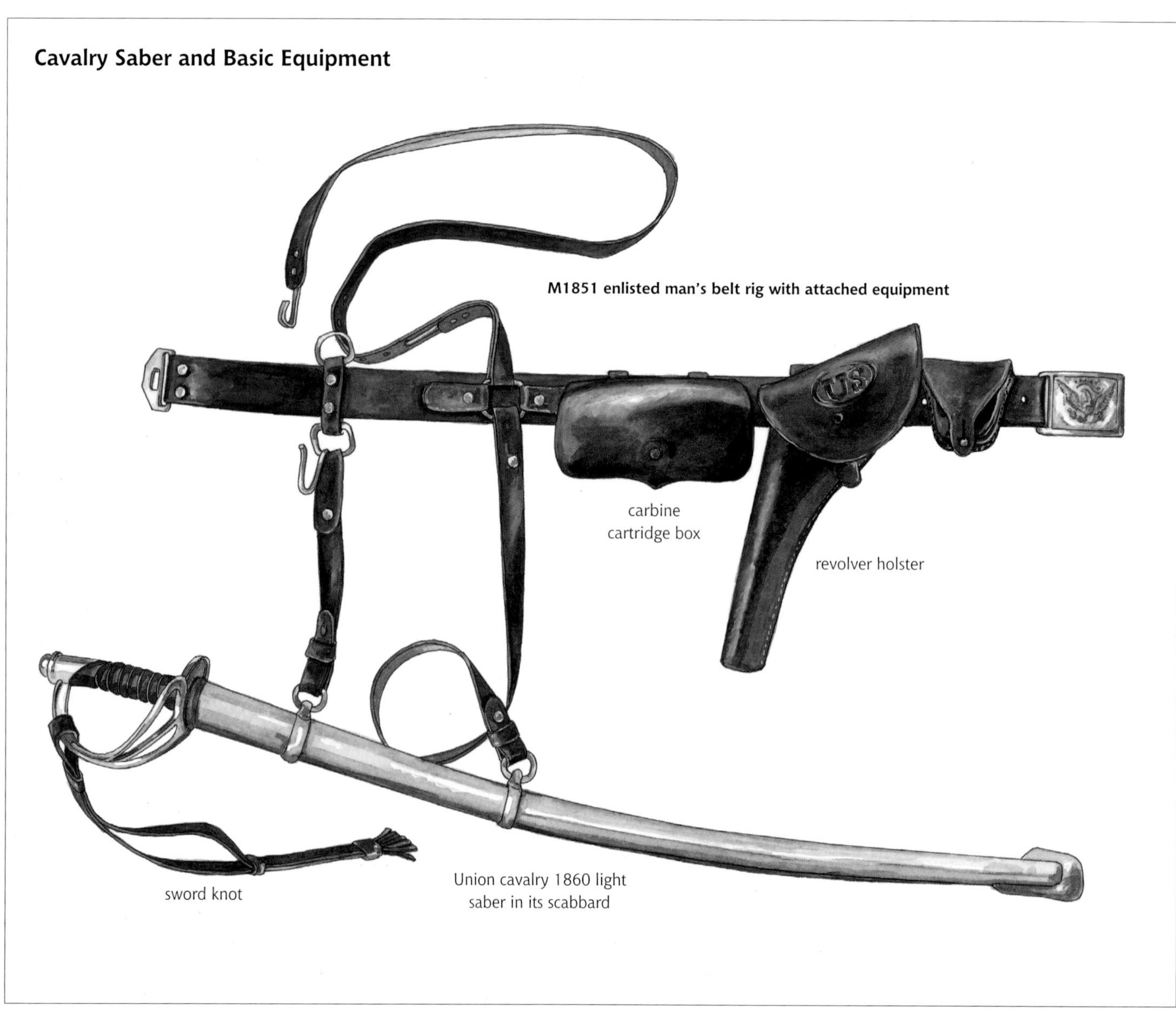

Confederate

Longarms

Confederate cavalry had a surprising mix of muskets, rifles and carbines. One civilian observer wrote, "Much of the Southern cavalry was ridiculously equipped. In one regiment I have seen four or five different kinds of rifles and shotguns, all sorts of saddles, some with rope stirrups, many of the saddles without blankets; all sorts of bridles, and in fact a conglomerate get-up fairly laughable." Although something of an exaggeration, this statement was based on truth, and it was generally true that Stuart's horsemen faced the enemy with a motley collection of arms.

Most of Lee's cavalrymen used single-shot, muzzleloading carbines that were cut-down versions of various rifle-muskets. However, the most sought-after weapon was the breechloading Sharps carbine with which many of their Yankee enemies were armed. Not only was it the ideal cavalry or mounted infantry firearm, but also, as noted above, it fired linen cartridges, which, unlike metal-rimmed ones, could be manufactured in the South. Thus most Rebel Sharps were captured, although the South did attempt to produce their own copy – the "Richmond" Sharps. It was not a success and only about 5,000 were manufactured; Lee described it as "so defective as to be demoralizing to our men." A number of Confederate cavalrymen eschewed muzzleloading muskets or carbines in favor of the double-barreled, sawn-off shotgun: its spread of shot made it difficult to miss and it was devastatingly lethal at close range. Unlike with the Union cavalry at Gettysburg, there is no equivalent record of the type and number of weapons carried by Rebel regiments.

Revolvers

The revolver was a popular, indeed essential, weapon for all Confederate mounted troops, many of whom carried several stuck in their belts. Numerous foreign-made revolvers were imported by both sides, the Confederates purchasing several thousand of the five-shot "Kerr" revolver. Perhaps the most exotic was the LeMat, developed before the war in New Orleans, Louisiana, by Dr. (later Colonel) Alexandre LeMat. It was called the "grapeshot" revolver, as it was able to fire both conventional .42-caliber cartridges and .63-caliber buckshot. The LeMat had a nine-chambered cylinder, weighed about 4 pounds and had a second, smoothbore barrel under the main one taking eleven buckshot. A quick flick of a small lever on the hammer nose allowed the selection of the desired barrel. The Confederacy purchased only some 3,000, as they never attained the popularity of the Colt or Remington, although several senior Confederate generals, including Jeb Stuart and P. G. T. Beauregard, carried it.

The South did manufacture some of their own revolvers, although probably fewer than 10,000 during the entire war. Confederate arms-makers all suffered from a lack of sufficient materials. Steel was unavailable and brass and iron usually substituted. Brass was particularly scarce and the bells of many Southern churches were donated to be melted down, with some ending up in pistol frames. The most successful manufacturer was Griswold and Gunnison, whose factory (operated by twenty-four people of whom twenty-two were slaves) at Griswoldville, some 70 miles south of Atlanta, produced around 3,500 revolvers in a two and a half year period. These "Griswolds" were .36-caliber copies of the Navy Colt. However, as with muskets and rifle-muskets, the average Rebel cavalry regiment had an inconvenient mix of revolvers and pistols. An example is the 34th Virginia Cavalry (more irregular mounted infantry than proper cavalry) in Brigadier-General Albert Jenkins' Brigade, which led Lee's advance into Pennsylvania, whose troopers were armed with Army and Navy Colts, Remingtons, Whitneys, Adams, Griswolds and at least one Savage revolver.

Sabers

The basic Confederate saber was a somewhat crude copy of the Model 1840 U.S. Army weapon, often with brass or leather scabbards rather than iron. There was considerable skepticism among the Southern cavalry about the usefulness of sabers in action, with the majority regarding them as an unnecessary encumbrance. Major John S. Mosby, Stuart's great friend, a scout during the Gettysburg campaign and later a renowned partisan leader, had this to say on the subject:

> We had been furnished with sabers before we left
> Abingdon but the only real use I ever heard of their being
> put to was to hold a piece of meat over the fire for frying.
> I dragged one through the first year, but when I became a
> commander I discarded it . . . the saber is of no use
> against gunpowder.

Nevertheless, many Rebels troopers did carry a saber, although it was tied to the saddle rather than slung on their belt so they could operate effectively on foot. The British observer Lieutenant-Colonel Arthur Fremantle, riding with Longstreet's Corps, noted: "Unlike the cavalry with Bragg's army, they [A.N.V.] wear swords, but seem to have little idea of using them – they hanker leg and the saddle, which has a very funny appearance; but their horses are generally good, and they ride well."

Despite a lack of enthusiasm among many of his partisans and mounted infantrymen for the traditional sword-wielding charge, Stuart had a liking for the saber and its use. He encouraged the old-fashioned cavalry spirit, with its emphasis on dash and daring, and the full-blooded, thundering charge. This was echoed in his cavalry officer corps, and indeed among most of the men in the cavalry regiments. As one of them stated, "Dismounted fighting was never popular with the Southern trooper, who felt he was only half a man when separated from his horse." The saber was used extensively in several mounted clashes during the Gettysburg campaign, including Brandy Station and on East Cavalry Field, but a successful all-out cavalry charge on the main battlefield against infantry and guns was, in virtually all circumstances in 1863, a thing of the past. Certainly there was only one attempt at Gettysburg, on July 3, when the Union Brigadier-General Farnsworth attempted such a tactic in totally unsuitable conditions; it ended in disaster.

UNIFORMS AND EQUIPMENT

Union

As with weapons, the Yankee trooper was invariably better dressed and equipped than his Rebel opposite number. The general issue to a trooper in the early stages of the war included cavalry cap; dark blue blouse (fatigue tunic, reaching below the hip); short, dark blue jacket trimmed with yellow (the cavalry color); one pair of light blue trousers with a yellow stripe down the outer leg; two flannel shirts, two pairs of drawers, two pairs of stockings, a pair of boots and an overcoat. The "correct" uniform hat was the stiff, broad-brimmed infantry Hardee type with the right side of the brim folded upward. However, as in the infantry, this was soon replaced by the soft forage cap (see illustrations, page 110), often with the regimental number and the crossed sabers symbol of the Cavalry Corps at the front. Officers had rank badges on their shoulder boards. With the rough wear on campaign, many troopers wore items of civilian clothing, usually shirts, and there was a considerable variety of calf-, knee- or thigh-length boots complete with spurs. Cavalrymen's uniforms, particularly boots, generally lasted longer then those of the infantry, for obvious reasons. Strangely, no heavy riding gloves were issued, forcing men to buy their own, as this was almost an essential item.

Equipment had to be provided for man and horse, the latter having to carry it all plus the trooper. As with all inexperienced soldiers, the tendency was to try to carry too much, but for the horseman to do so quickly exhausted his mount, forcing him to dismount. This was a problem in the earlier part of the war and with new recruits, but life in the field taught numerous lessons and cavalrymen, like their marching comrades, learned to strip down to essentials. By Gettysburg the trooper retained his leather belt on which to hang his saber, revolver holster, cartridge box for carbine ammunition, sometimes a smaller one for revolver rounds and cap box – to lose your belt presented serious difficulties – and carbine sling. The revolver holster was normally worn on the right hip with the butt end pointing to the front to allow the weapon to be easily drawn with the left hand, as the trooper was trained to shoot with his left and control his horse with the reins in his right hand. A common alternative to the revolver cartridge box was to carry one or two spare preloaded cylinders for quick reloading. In addition, the trooper had a rawhide "McClellan" saddle, a sleeping blanket that doubled as a cushion under the saddle, poncho, saddlebags (for forage), a canteen and a haversack. The supposedly waterproof haversack contained personal items, spare ammunition and the trooper's rations; it was worn slung over the shoulder or attached to the saddle, as was the canteen. Finally there was a picket pin with a 30-foot rope (for grazing his horse), leather "boot" in which to rest the muzzle of the carbine, and a feedbag. All this still amounted to a substantial load – though not supposed to weigh more than 60 pounds.

The 1859 McClellan Model saddle was certainly the most comfortable and therefore popular saddle of the time. Over thirty years after the collapse of the Confederacy the British purchased large numbers for use in the Boer War and the U.S. Cavalry used it until they abandoned horses. It was designed by the first commander of the Army of the Potomac, Major-General George B. McClellan, based on his experiences as a captain in the Crimean War of 1853–56. The saddletree was made of wood, with a leather seat over a black rawhide cover with a curved metal plate reinforcing the wooden pommel. The rider had to sit very upright and could not exert much grip with his legs, and it was almost impossible to rise in the saddle when trotting. A McClellan saddle forms part of the 8th Illinois monument west of Gettysburg (see box, page 192).

Confederate

Whether he fought for the North or South, a cavalryman required the same basic uniform and equipment. Stuart's horsemen wore much the same mixture of short gray or butternut jackets, civilian clothes, a variety of hats (with the slouch hat being popular), tall riding boots, and gauntlets – although the latter two were not issued. Dress regulations were promulgated in 1861 but were gradually abandoned as the war lengthened. Officers had better-quality gray jackets, sometimes double-breasted, with their rank denoted by bars on the collar and the thickness of elaborate whorls and twists of yellow piping on their sleeves ("Austrian knots"). Stuart set an extraordinary example of flamboyance with his dress (see pages 268–69) and some cavalry officers attempted to follow his example.

According to the Confederate Ordnance Department's *Field Manual*, a cavalryman needed the following for his horse: "1 bridal, 1 watering bridle, 1 halter, 1 saddle, 1 pair of saddle bags, 1 surcingle, 1 pair of spurs, 1 curry comb, 1 horse brush, 1 picket pin and 1 lariat (1 link and nose bag when specially required)." As for all cavalrymen, belt, cartridge boxes, revolver holster (although many stuck several in the waist belt), haversack and canteen were essential items. As with most things, except perhaps the horses, the South generally had mediocre equipment. This was especially true of their cavalry saddle, which was both unsightly and uncomfortable. As the Southern cavalryman supplied his own horse, so he initially had to provide his own saddle. These tended to be the light English model, which was fine for gentle riding around the farm but lacked durability and made horses' backs and riders' backsides sore when used continuously for long periods. Another drawback was that it lacked any place to hang camp kettles, fodder bags, or other items of personal kit. As with so many things, most troopers sought to capture a Union McClellan saddle at the earliest opportunity and the Confederate Ordnance Department sought to copy it, although, as with weapons, the result was not on a par with the genuine article.

CAVALRY ON THE MARCH

The most famous, some would say infamous, cavalry march of the Gettysburg campaign was that conducted by Stuart's three brigades around Meade's army and his late arrival on the periphery of the battlefield. His troopers and their mounts had covered 210 miles in eight days, an average distance of 26 miles a day (see also Section Seven: The Road to Gettysburg). Before examining some aspects of this march in detail, certain basic considerations pertaining to cavalry on the march need explanation.

March Rates

At a walk, cavalry were expected to cover 4 miles in the hour along reasonable roads or tracks. Thus, in eight hours of marching a regiment might hope to cover 30 miles or more. This is well in excess of the infantry's 20 miles at 2.5 miles an hour. At a slow trot, 6 miles would be covered in an hour, but this rate could not be kept up continuously for extended periods; however, in reasonably flat country, alternating with walking and given rest periods, it could extend a day's march to up to 40 miles. At a maneuver (brisk) trot a horse would be moving at 8 miles per hour. However, this was primarily a battlefield (tactical) march rate when there was a need to hurry when approaching action or maneuvering for position in the face of the enemy. A maneuver gallop developed a speed of 12 miles per hour and was used only on the battlefield when the situation demanded considerable extra speed in getting into position or in the early stages of a charge. A flat-out, extended gallop would produce a speed of some 16 miles an hour and was reserved for the final stages of a charge.

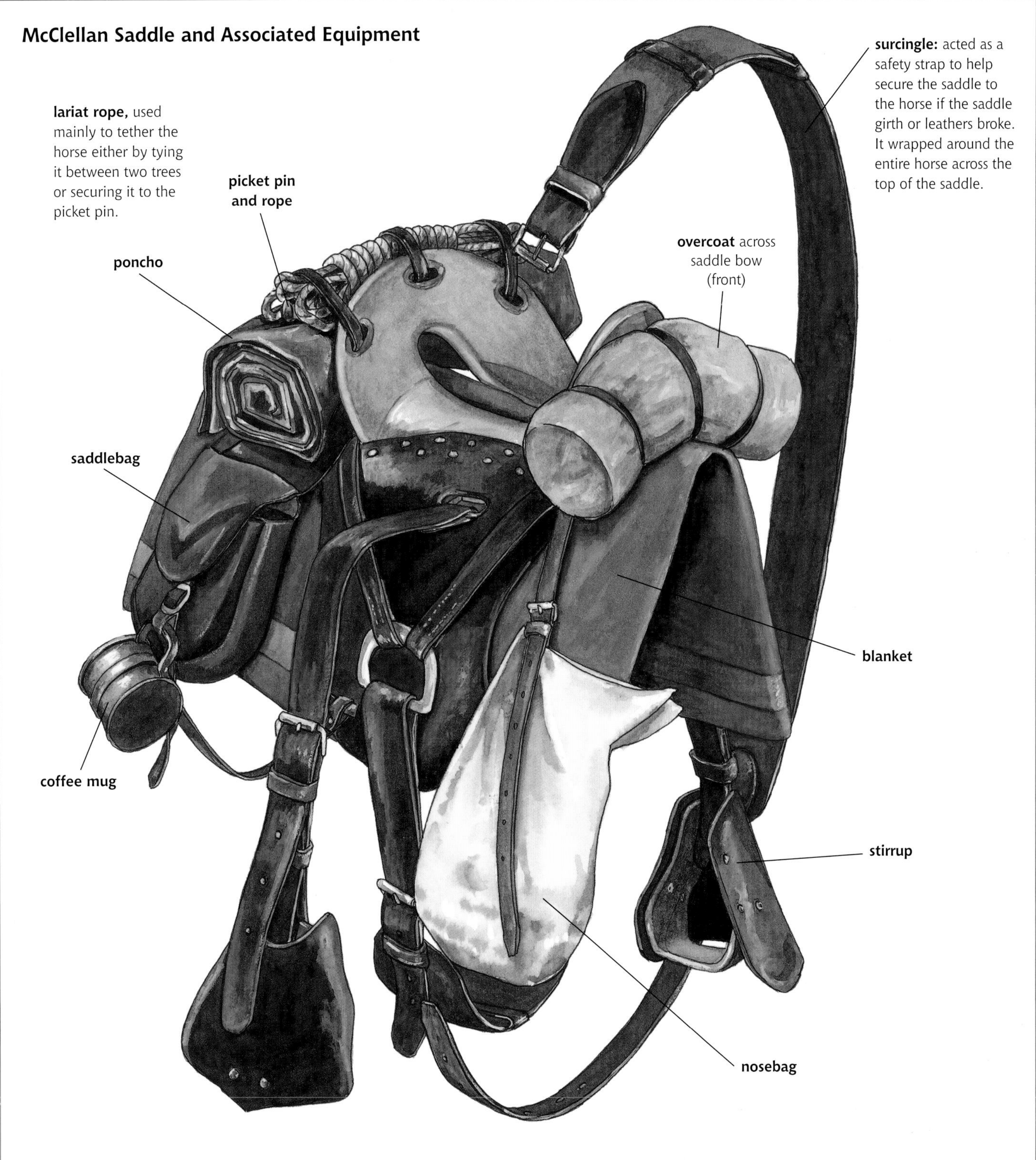
McClellan Saddle and Associated Equipment
lariat rope, used mainly to tether the horse either by tying it between two trees or securing it to the picket pin.
picket pin and rope
poncho
saddlebag
coffee mug
overcoat across saddle bow (front)
surcingle: acted as a safety strap to help secure the saddle to the horse if the saddle girth or leathers broke. It wrapped around the entire horse across the top of the saddle.
blanket
stirrup
nosebag

March Formations

On a reasonable road where width permitted it, a regiment of cavalry would normally be in column of fours. Narrow roads, tracks or defiles could reduce this to twos or even single file. It was also normal practice for some horsemen to be deployed as "flankers" about 150–200 yards off the road on either side paralleling the line march. If the column was attacked from a flank, it could quickly turn left or right and the flankers would provide a screen of skirmishers.

Column Lengths

The official road space allowed for a horse was 3 yards with another yard added for the gap between each animal. Provided a unit was marching in fours, the theoretical length of the column was its total strength in yards. Thus Confederate Colonel Lawrence Baker's 1st North Carolina with 407 men would, in column of fours, occupy about 400 yards of road. Using this formula, Wade Hampton's brigade of 1,751 all ranks would extend for just over a mile (allowing for 50-yard gaps between regiments), and Stuart's command of

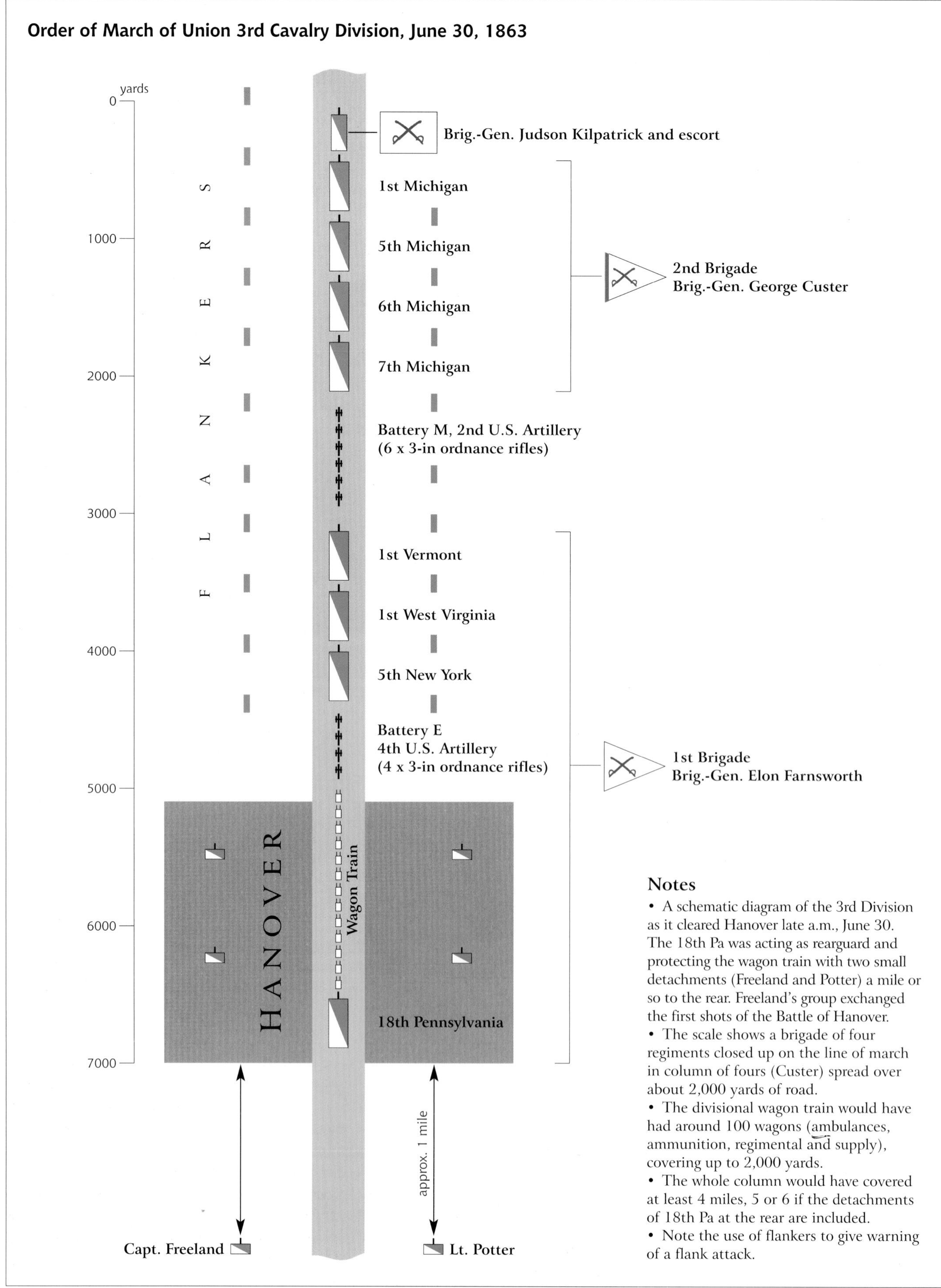
Order of March of Union 3rd Cavalry Division, June 30, 1863
yards
0
1000
2000
3000
4000
5000
6000
7000
F L A N K E R S
Brig.-Gen. Judson Kilpatrick and escort
1st Michigan
5th Michigan
6th Michigan
7th Michigan
2nd Brigade
Brig.-Gen. George Custer
Battery M, 2nd U.S. Artillery
(6 x 3-in ordnance rifles)
1st Vermont
1st West Virginia
5th New York
Battery E
4th U.S. Artillery
(4 x 3-in ordnance rifles)
1st Brigade
Brig.-Gen. Elon Farnsworth
HANOVER
Wagon Train
18th Pennsylvania
approx. 1 mile
Capt. Freeland
Lt. Potter
Notes
• A schematic diagram of the 3rd Division as it cleared Hanover late a.m., June 30. The 18th Pa was acting as rearguard and protecting the wagon train with two small detachments (Freeland and Potter) a mile or so to the rear. Freeland's group exchanged the first shots of the Battle of Hanover.
• The scale shows a brigade of four regiments closed up on the line of march in column of fours (Custer) spread over about 2,000 yards of road.
• The divisional wagon train would have had around 100 wagons (ambulances, ammunition, regimental and supply), covering up to 2,000 yards.
• The whole column would have covered at least 4 miles, 5 or 6 if the detachments of 18th Pa at the rear are included.
• Note the use of flankers to give warning of a flank attack.

sixteen regiments in three brigades on their march round Meade would need 6,000 yards (3.4 miles) on a single road.

In practice things were not so simple. Column of fours was not always possible; straggling occurred; on long marches regiments tended to spread out; and large cavalry columns often had artillery batteries and numerous wagons accompanying them adding to their length and reducing their speed. The key to keeping columns of troops (not just cavalry) to manageable lengths and ensuring reasonable progress was to use as many parallel roads or tracks as possible, even if that meant increasing the distance to be covered by some units. Guns and wagons had to use roads or tracks but cavalry and infantry could move across country or through open woods, thus cutting corners.

Wagon Trains

If a cavalry column was compelled to keep to the pace of a wagon train, then its progress was automatically slowed to 2.5 miles an hour – the best speed of mule-drawn wagons along a reasonable road. Stuart's Division (three brigades), in addition to its own ammunition and ambulance wagons, captured 125 Union wagons, filled largely with fodder, at Rockville on June 28. Stuart's insistence on retaining rather than destroying them not only reduced his march rate but substantially lengthened his column, as for all practical purposes wagons could only move in single file. Six mules pulling a wagon occupied about 20 yards of road. Allowing 5 yards for gaps, this meant the 125 wagons added over 3,000 yards (1.77 miles) to his column. His ten guns, limbers, caissons and attached wagons would add another 400 yards, thus giving his command a total closed-up length of about 3 miles. In practice, as was the case when the brigades snatched some rest between Westminster and Union Mills on the night of June 29, the men were occasionally stretched out along 7 miles of road. See page 223 and box, page 311.

Horse Management

It is worth emphasizing the obvious fact that Civil War armies could not function without the horse. Horses moved guns, ambulances, generals, staff officers, and couriers as well as cavalry. Add in the tens of thousands of mules drawing wagons and the scale of an army's dependence on animals is clear. But, like the men who rode or drove them, they suffered from sickness and fatigue. Far more horses died of disease or were broken by overwork than were killed by the enemy. Good horse management, constant care and attention to feeding, watering, grooming, shoeing and resting were the first priority of every cavalryman or horse artilleryman. The Union Major-General William T. Sherman made this plain when he instructed: "Every opportunity at a halt during a march should be taken advantage of to cut grass, wheat, or oats and extraordinary care be taken of horses upon which everything depends." The memoirs of Isaac Norval Baker, who rode with Company F of the 18th Virginia Cavalry in Imboden's Brigade during the retreat from Gettysburg, recorded in graphic detail what happened to horses that had, due to intense and prolonged operational pressures, not received the care they needed:

> We fed our horses on sheaf wheat and the beards made our horses tongues sore and ulcerated. Our regiment was about the last to cross the river [Potomac], we went in camp about a mile or so south of the river with orders to unsaddle our horses. Our horses' backs were raw with ulcers one or two inches deep and full of maggots. The green flies had put up a big job on us, our blankets were full of maggots and rotten, our saddles had from a pint to a quart of maggots in them and we had to run them out with hot water and soap and it was months before the horses backs were cured.

Some March Difficulties

Most difficulties are best illustrated by Stuart's eight-day march around the Army of the Potomac (June 25–July 2 inclusive). He took with him around 5,150 men, including over 300 horse artillerymen. They were divided into three brigades – Chambliss with four regiments, Hampton with six, and Fitzhugh Lee also with six – and three horse artillery batteries with ten guns. If strung out along a single route in column of fours this column would have been 3.4 miles in length once the captured wagon train was included; in practice the distance was often much more due to straggling and exhaustion. As noted above, the average (and quite respectable) distance covered each day was 26 miles. That this was maintained was largely due to continuous marching, often through the night, with the bare minimum of rest, horses plodding listlessly with many of their riders asleep in the saddle. Twenty-six miles was a fair eight-hour march with some halts along the way, but Stuart's troopers were often scarcely out of the saddle for 24 hours or more at a time. Stuart realized the drag that the extra wagons had on his progress and attempted to lessen it by paroling most of the 400 prisoners and reducing the mule teams from six to four animals. This did little to speed things up. Precious time was spent swinging round to the east of the enemy; and on numerous minor diversions such as chasing the wagons, dismantling tracks on the Baltimore and Ohio Railroad at Hood's Mill, destroying a bridge at Sykesville, cutting telegraph lines, and skirmishing with Yankees at Rockville, Cooksville, Westminster, Hanover (an all-day action on June 30) and Carlisle, as well as escorting nearly 2 miles of wagons. To one officer the train seemed "strung out to infinity" and was termed "a source of unmitigated annoyance." Major Henry B. McClellan of Stuart's staff described the situation with the captured wagon train during the night march on June 30:

> The mules were starving for food and water, and often became unmanageable. Not infrequently a large part of the train would halt in the road because a driver toward the front had fallen asleep and allowed his team to stop. The train guard became careless through excessive fatigue, and it required the utmost exertions of every officer on Stuart's staff to keep the train in motion.

Stuart later described how "whole regiments slept in the saddle . . . In some instances they fell from their horses, overcome with physical fatigue and sleepiness." On one occasion he himself announced, "I am perishing for sleep," and collapsed by a haystack. By the time the leading brigade (Fitzhugh Lee) and Stuart reached Carlisle late on July 1 after an all-night march and found the garrison unwilling to surrender, many men were, as one officer related, "overcome and so tired and stupid as almost to be ignorant of what was taking place around them." A trooper of the 9th Virginia felt "weak and helpless." Another was seen asleep leaning against a fence despite artillery firing only 10 yards away.

The Horses – Neglected Heroes

No Civil War army could move or fight without horses (and mules). In terms of numbers, more than twice as many horses as soldiers perished on the battlefields, or died of overwork or disease. An estimated 1.5 million horses died during the war, compared with more than 620,000 men. Replacement of animals became an ever-growing problem for both sides, one that the North was better able to handle than the South, especially from 1863 onward.

Winter, exacerbated by hard campaigning, had left the Army of the Potomac in dire need of replacements in early 1863, even though the government had provided some 285,000 remounts for the cavalry alone since the start of the war. With the average artillery horse's working life lasting seven months, and that of a cavalry horse much less, shortages were inevitable. The North had set up a large remount and training depot just outside Washington, but demand invariably exceeded supply. The cost of a good horse in the North at the outset of the war was around $125; at the end it was $200. (This was cheap in contrast to the Confederacy, however, where by 1865 a cost of $600 was not exceptional.) In late May 1863, just two weeks before the Gettysburg campaign got under way, Pleasonton complained that sick and overworked horses meant that his command was "not fitted to take the field," while the other two divisions could barely mount half their commands. Buford's Division required 2,000 remounts. This meant that some 40 percent of the army's cavalry were either without horses while they awaited replacements or were unfit to take the field. A huge effort during the latter part of May and early June, however, saw most of the Union cavalry remounted.

At least the North had a well-organized central remount depot, a facility lacking in the South. By mid-1863 the Confederate system of individuals providing their own replacements was acknowledged as virtually unworkable and great emphasis was placed on requisitioning horses and rounding up or capturing those of the enemy. Requisitioning became increasingly important once the Confederates had entered Northern territory. Stuart took about 1,000 from the area around Hanover, but still, after the crippling ride north, over half his force had convalescent horses on July 3, while many of those recently captured were untrained as riding horses – a distinct problem in a cavalry fight. That Stuart was able to secure so many horses does not reflect well on the compliance by the Army of the Potomac to General-in-Chief Halleck's instructions, dated June 25, 1863:

> Major-General Hooker,
> *Army of the Potomac*:
>
> The immense loss and destruction of horses in your army, and the difficulty of supplying this loss, render it necessary that you should impress every serviceable animal likely to fall into the hands of the enemy. There are many animals in Loudoun County and the adjacent parts of Maryland. These should be seized, to save them from the enemy, as well as to supply yourself.
>
> H. W. HALLECK,
> *General-in-Chief*

As the Army of Northern Virginia moved into Maryland and Pennsylvania, the requisitioning of horses was high on its priority list. On June 29 a Dr. J. L. Suesserott visited Lee's headquarters in Chambersburg to plead that his neighbor might keep just one blind horse. He was successful – but not for long, as he explained:

> I visited General Lee at his headquarters, near Chambersburg, for the purpose of having a blind mare, the property of one of my neighbors, exempted from capture. All of the other available horses having been either captured or removed to safe quarters [hidden], I wanted to have the use of this one for the purpose of having my corn plowed. After having stated to the general the object of my visit, and while the paper was being prepared

Hardly surprising, therefore, that when men and animals finally arrived in the vicinity of the main battlefield on the afternoon of July 2 they were utterly spent and considerably less numerous than when they started out. As a soldier of the 4th Virginia Cavalry wrote in his diary: "July 2. This makes the fifth night without sleep with the exception of four hours. Traveling all the time. July 3 (At Gettysburg). Only some twenty men with Company "D" out of fifty-six who started. Our raid is at an end. It makes ten days."

However, it was not only Rebel cavalry that suffered. The march north had been much the same for both armies in terms of numbing fatigue, sleep deprivation and endless hours on the road, either struggling through mud or choking in a permanent cloud of dust kicked up by tens of thousands of feet and hooves. Two incidents described by Union cavalry officers well illustrate march conditions. First, an officer of the 2nd New York Cavalry (not present at the battle) in Buford's Division:

> [Troopers soon learned to sleep in the saddle] either leaning forward on the pommel of the saddle, or on the roll of coat and blanket, or sitting quite erect, with an occasional bow forward or to the right or left, like the swaying of a flag on a signal station, or like the careenings of a drunken man. The horse of such a sleeping man will seldom leave his place in the column, though this will sometimes occur, and the man wakes at last to find himself alone with his horse which is grazing along some unknown field or woods. Some men, having lost the column in this way, have fallen into the enemy's hands. Sometimes a fast-walking horse in one of the rear companies will bear his sleeping lord quickly along, forcing his way through the ranks ahead of him, until the poor fellow is awakened, and finds himself just passing by the colonel and his staff at the head of the column!

A second officer of the 17th Pennsylvania Cavalry, also in Buford's Division, described the scene on the line of march just before dawn on June 29:

> The column halted before the light of day with orders to dismount and stand to horse . . . an hour passed and the gray dawn . . . lighted up a picture I can never forget. The men, who were completely exhausted, had slipped the bridle rein over their arms and lay down in a bed of dust (8 inches deep) that almost obscured them from sight. Their jaded steeds seemed to know they should not move, and propping themselves with extended necks and lowering heads, stood like mute sentinels over their riders dead in sleep.

. . . The order for the safety of the horse having been finished and given me, I left and made rapid strides toward town, only to find that the Medical Purveyor of the Confederate Army had taken the horse and my corn . . .

It was not just numbers of horses, or lack of them, that caused headaches for both armies, but the means of feeding and watering them. Lack of sufficient daily nourishment, coupled with long periods of overwork in rain, snow and mud, were the root cause of much animal sickness such as "hoof rot," "grease heel" and "scratches." A report on XI Corps' animals "lost, killed or abandoned" since June 12 shows the following:

	Horses	Mules	Total
Abandoned from exhaustion	55	12	67
Abandoned from lameness	16	3	19
Abandoned from glanders	3	–	3
Captured by the enemy	13	26	39
Animals strayed or stolen	7	2	9
Animals died on the march	15	7	22
Animals drowned crossing Potomac	–	2	2
Animals killed in battle	98	–	98
Totals	**207**	**52**	**259**

It is not clear exactly what period these figures cover, but they illustrate the variety of ways animals were lost on campaign. The report makes no mention of another way in which horses disappeared – this time illegally. On June 20 the Quartermaster General (Montgomery C. Meigs) wrote to the chief quartermaster of the Army of the Potomac (Ingalls):

I am informed that on the route of the march of the Eleventh Corps a large number of horses and mules were abandoned. It is said, though I know not on what authority, that some 1,100 were abandoned on the route [north to Gettysburg] . . .

Quite a large number of horses and mules branded "U. S." are found in possession of sutlers and other civilians, and are being seized on this side of the river. I am told that many of these persons show what purport to be certificates of officers or quartermasters that they have sold these horses or mules to persons claiming them.

As no officer has the right to sell a Government horse or mule until condemned and branded (C), these certificates will be disregarded and the animals seized . . .

In the summer of 1862 a Confederate depot for overworked horses was set up at Winchester where the animals could recuperate. A horse required 12 pounds of grain (preferably oats) a day and another 10 pounds of hay to maintain health while being worked hard. This meant hundreds of wagons were needed to carry fodder for the cavalry, artillery and staffs – the horses pulling ambulances and mule-drawn supply wagons were supposed to carry fodder for their own needs. However, keeping horses properly fed from supply trains alone during a campaign such as Gettysburg was an impossibility. Alternatives were sought to replace or supplement what was carried forward. Capturing enemy wagons was one of them. The 125 wagons seized by Stuart on the outskirts of Washington and taken with him on his march were mostly stuffed with grain, and while they may have been a hindrance with regard to speedy movement they at least helped solve one of his problems. Another rich haul was the 6,000 bushels of grain taken when Winchester fell to Ewell in mid-June. Allowing a horse to graze was a common way of supplementing or even replacing grain. However, some 80 pounds of pasturage only had the nutritional value of 26 pounds of hay or grain. In May Lee's horses were surviving on less than 3 pounds of grain a day. A major advantage in invading Pennsylvania in June and July was that it would be harvest time for hay, oats and feed corn, and there would be plenty of grass in the fields.

THE CAVALRY'S ROLES AND TACTICS

There have always been differences of opinion over whether cavalry regiments in either army fought following the traditional European model, where the primary battlefield aim was to charge with sabers flashing, or as mounted infantry (dragoons) who used horses for movement but fought on foot, or whether they were trained to do both with more or less equal facility. In truth, cavalry on both sides could fight in both roles if circumstances demanded it and they were armed accordingly with rifle/carbine, revolver and saber. Although Stuart's men preferred to use revolvers rather than sabers in a melee, he himself favored the latter and endeavored to inculcate the mounted attack – the charge – as the decisive tactic on the battlefield, particularly against a mounted enemy. In this thinking he was supported by the majority of his senior commanders and his troopers, who were decidedly uncomfortable when separated from their horses.

Nevertheless, the Confederate cavalry at Gettysburg was more divided along "specialist" lines than the Yankees. One of Stuart's troopers stated that the brigades of Jenkins and Imboden "were called cavalry but were essentially mounted infantry and only effective as such . . . The Confederate cavalry proper hardly considered those forces as actually belonging to the army, but rather as a species of irregular auxiliaries." Imboden's command was certainly considered as a mounted infantry formation, as it contained the 62nd Virginia Mounted Infantry and the small company of Virginia Partisan Rangers, which in total formed over half the brigade. Although Jenkins' regiments were all nominally cavalry units, they were more irregular than regular in that their forte was raiding and foraging rather than formal mounted maneuvers or tactics. In reality, Confederate cavalry were more akin to European light cavalry – more at home scouting, skirmishing or raiding but able to wield their sabers if necessary.

The Union cavalry at Gettysburg, with their breechloading Sharps rifles, revolvers and sabers, were clearly armed for both roles. That they were quite capable of putting up a good fight with their side arm and saber was demonstrated by the numerous charges at Brandy Station and East Cavalry Field (Rummel Farm). Alternatively, they were effective as mounted infantry in delaying the Rebel advance down the Chambersburg Pike on July 1. The problem with dismounting to fight was what to do with the horses. In practice, the answer was for one man in four to be left out of the action as a horse-holder some way behind the firing line. This was a very substantial reduction in manpower, equivalent to suffering, if only temporarily, 25 percent losses. However, this disadvantage was more than compensated for in Meade's cavalry as all had the ability to fire rapidly with their Sharps, having left their sabers fixed to their saddles. Both sides employed this technique, although perhaps the Confederates more so in the Western theater of operations – being armed with muzzleloaders put them at a serious disadvantage once they dismounted. It was in the West that on one occasion the Rebels impressed the British observer Colonel Fremantle with their horse-handling:

> We found [Brigadier] General Martin giving orders for the withdrawal of the cavalry horses in the front and for the retreat of the skirmishers. It was very curious to see three hundred horses suddenly emerge from the wood just in front of us, where they had been hidden – one man to every four horses, riding one and leading the other three, which were tied together by their heads. In this order I saw them cross a cotton field at a smart trot, and take up a more secure position . . . The way in which the horses were managed was very pretty . . . They were never far from the men, who could mount and be off to another part of the field with rapidity, or retire to take up another position, or act as cavalry [attack with sabers] as the case may require.

The cavalry's tasks in the Civil War, in approximate order of importance, were:

- reconnaissance and screening
- defensive delaying actions
- pursuit and harassment of retreating enemy
- offensive action
- raiding against enemy lines of communications and foraging

The Gettysburg campaign and battle saw numerous examples of each.

Reconnaissance and Screening

These two roles were by far the most important. The first involved obtaining information on the enemy's strengths, locations and intentions; the second was the prevention of the enemy securing that information. Only cavalry had the mobility for these tasks, although there were other supplementary ways of gaining operational intelligence (see Section Six: Command and Control). The critical importance of these roles in the lead-up to the battle for both sides will be discussed more fully in Section Seven: The Road to Gettysburg; it is sufficient here to note the extent to which Lee was inhibited in his actions by Stuart's inability to keep him informed or screened prior to the battle while engaged on his march round Meade.

The tactics of reconnaissance were based on patrolling, on scouting, on probing, on exploring roads and tracks, towns or villages. Patrols covered wide areas or arcs and often needed the back-up of larger bodies of cavalry to force a way through the enemy screen. It was just as important for the commander to know there was no enemy in a certain area, or it was weakly held, as to know that a place was swarming with the opposition. Information was not just needed on enemy troops but also on topographical features – the state of the roads, the availability of local supplies or fodder, the depth of a river, and the location of fords or bridges.

Cavalry screens were the reverse side of the reconnaissance coin. Mounted formations often had both roles, probing the enemy for information and at the same time blocking (screening) his efforts to gain intelligence. Such were the tasks of Stuart's Rebel and Pleasonton's Yankee horsemen strung out along opposite banks of the Rappahannock River in early June. As the campaign started and Lee first began concentrating around Culpeper Court House, then moving his infantry (Ewell's Corps) east and then north, Stuart's overriding task was to screen the movement and prevent Hooker realizing what was happening.

Partisan Rangers

These irregular bands of mounted troops were authorized by the Confederate government to operate behind enemy lines in territory that had been overrun by Union forces. For example, in March 1862 Virginia authorized between ten and twenty companies, each under a captain who had to provide arms and equipment. Companies could be grouped into units of four, six or ten, commanded by a major, lieutenant-colonel or colonel respectively. One of the best organized and disciplined ranger units was that commanded by Major John S. Mosby, who began his war service as a private in "Grumble' Jones's 1st Virginia Cavalry. As a lieutenant he began scouting for Stuart in early 1862 and was given permission to raise his rangers in January 1863. In March of that year he captured Union Brigadier-General Edwin H. Stoughton at Fairfax Court House when he surprised him in bed and woke him with a slap on the backside! Mosby was of considerable value in providing information to Stuart during the Gettysburg campaign (see Section Six: Command and Control).

Mosby's unit was something of an exception, as many partisan rangers were little more than bandits. They were usually a law unto themselves and inclined to raid friend and foe alike. These units were raised to operate in their own states and this, together with their loose discipline and tenuous overall control, attracted many recruits, who saw the units as a splendid way to fight from home and gain plenty of loot. The Confederate authorities belatedly sought either to convert them to regular cavalry or to disband them. Lee was asked for his opinion and replied as follows:

> Experience has convinced me that it is almost impossible, under the best officers even, to have discipline in these bands of Partisan Rangers, or to prevent them becoming an injury instead of a benefit to the service, and even where this is accomplished the system gives licence to many deserters & marauders, who assume to belong to these authorized companies & and [*sic*] commit depreciations on friend and foe alike. Another great objection to them is the bad effect upon the discipline of the army from the constant desire of the men to leave their commands & enjoy the great licence allowed in these bands.

All such units were officially disbanded in April 1864 and the men ordered to form regular cavalry units. Some avoided this fate and continued operating, one of which was Mosby's 43rd Virginia Battalion of Virginia Cavalry, which was not disbanded until April 20, 1865.

A Confederate Colonel Is Captured

On June 30, during the clash at Hanover, Union Private Abraham Folger of the 5th New York Cavalry had been captured by the commander of the 2nd North Carolina Cavalry, Lieutenant-Colonel William Payne. Folger later described how he managed to reverse the situation in a unique and amusing manner:

> While charging in the edge of the town and getting separated from my regiment I was made a prisoner by Lieutenant Colonel William H. Paine [Payne], commanding the 2nd North Carolina Cavalry, and was being taken to the rear. On the main road, just outside the town, was situated a tannery, the vats of which were under cover and very close to the street.
>
> I was walking along beside the colonel's orderly and as we came near these tannery vats I saw a carbine lying on the ground. When I came up to it I quickly took it. Seeing it was loaded I fired and killed Paine's horse, which in its death struggle, fell over towards the vats, throwing Paine head first into one of them, the colonel going completely under the tanning liquid.
>
> Seeing the colonel was safe enough for the moment I turned my attention to his orderly, who, finding his pistol had fouled and was useless was about to jump his horse over the fence to the right and escape that way if he could, but not being able to do so, concluded he had better surrender. The reason I did not fire upon him was that the last shot in the captured carbine was fired at the colonel's horse. As the orderly did not know this, it was my play to make him think instant death awaited him if he attempted to escape. So I took him in and disarmed him, and made him help get the colonel out of the tanning liquid.
>
> His gray uniform, with its white velvet facing, his white gauntlet gloves, face and hair, had all become completely stained so that he presented a most laughable sight.
>
> I then mounted the orderly's horse, and marched them before me to the market place, where I turned them over to the authorities.

A screen was also charged with giving early warning of an enemy's approach and usually consisted of cavalry (or infantry) outposts of varying strength called "pickets" strung out across the front or flanks of the main force. On occasion this line could stretch for up to 50 miles. However, important though it was, picketing was tiring for both men and horses. It was also often a boring duty that absorbed very large numbers of horsemen. For these reasons the Confederates tended to use more infantry pickets and conserve their cavalry for more mobile duties whenever possible. If a squadron of two troops was deployed on outpost duty, the line of pickets would be organized similarly to that shown on Maps 6 and 7. Up to half the squadron would be held in reserve as the "Grand Guard" (for relieving pickets, patrolling, deploying as skirmishers, and dealing with the unexpected). About 500–1,000 yards forward or to the flanks of the Grand Guard, depending on the ground, would be the line of pickets, each consisting of thirty or more men under an officer. Each picket also held back a reserve of up to half its strength. The remainder were pushed 400–500 yards forward and spread out as single horsemen vedettes (sentries) to cover the sector allotted. At Gettysburg vedettes were doubled up. Private Thomas Kelly, 8th Illinois, recounted, "About 700 men were detailed from the four regiments of our brigade for picket duty. The order was for double posts, and two men were placed on each post with a corporal or sergeant." This doubling up of the usual single vedettes was confirmed by Kelly when he added,

Lee's Horse at Gettysburg – Traveller

Traveller was Lee's favorite warhorse and, with occasional rest periods, was ridden by him throughout most of the war. The iron-gray horse was born in 1857 in Greenbrier County, now in West Virginia. He was first called Jeff Davis by Andrew Jackson, who raised him. He was renamed Greenbrier by his next owner, Captain Joseph M. Broun, quartermaster of the 3rd Virginia Infantry. Lee bought the horse from Broun for $200 in late 1861 and renamed him Traveller. The horse weighed 1,100 pounds and stood 15.3 hands high. Traveller had few vices, but was spirited and could at times be nervous. At Second Manassas, while Lee was at the front reconnoitering dismounted and holding Traveller by the bridle, the horse was startled by some movement and plunged, pulling Lee down on a tree stump and breaking both his hands. Lee went through most of the remainder of the campaign in an ambulance wagon; when he did ride a courier rode in front leading his horse.

After the war Traveller accompanied Lee when he took the post of President of Washington College. When Lee died in 1870 Traveller was led behind the hearse, following the caisson with his master's boots reversed in the stirrups, his saddle and bridal draped in black crepe. The following summer Traveller stepped on a rusty nail, developed lockjaw and had to be put down, aged thirteen. He was initially buried behind the main building of the college (renamed Washington and Lee University after Lee's death), but his body was unearthed by persons unknown and his bones bleached for exhibition in Rochester, New York, in 1875 or 1876. In 1907 a Richmond journalist paid to have the bones mounted and returned to the college and they were displayed in the Brooks Museum, in what is now Robinson Hall. The skeleton was several times vandalized by students carving their names on it. In 1929 the bones were placed in the basement museum of the Lee Chapel, where they stood for thirty years, deteriorating with exposure. Finally, in 1971, Traveller's remains were buried in a wooden box encased in concrete and placed next to the Lee Chapel on the Washington and Lee Campus, only a few feet away from the Lee family crypt where his master's body lies.

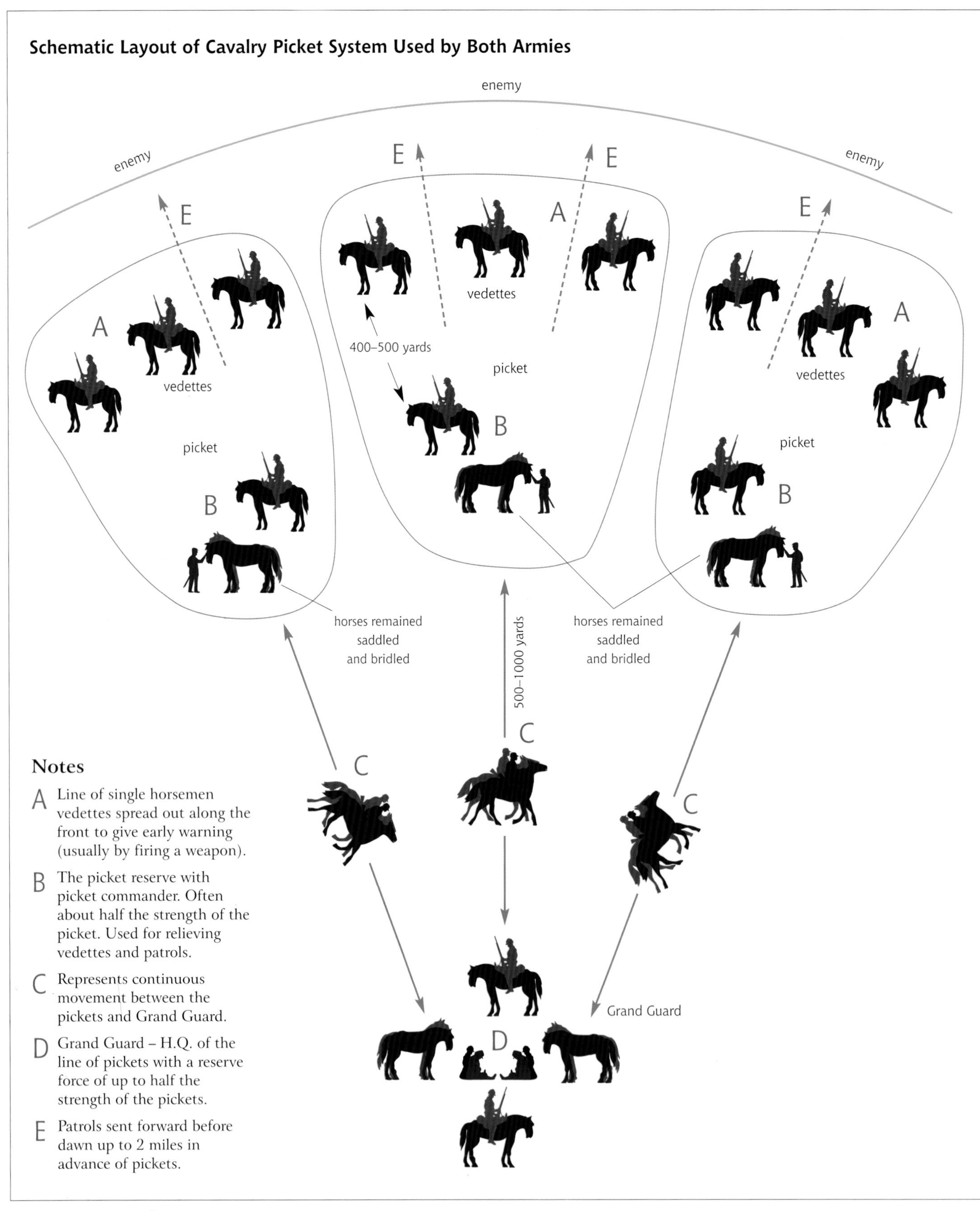
Schematic Layout of Cavalry Picket System Used by Both Armies
enemy
enemy
enemy
E
E
E
E
A
A
A
vedettes
vedettes
vedettes
400–500 yards
picket
picket
picket
B
B
B
horses remained saddled and bridled
horses remained saddled and bridled
500–1000 yards
C
C
C
C
D
Grand Guard
Notes
A Line of single horsemen vedettes spread out along the front to give early warning (usually by firing a weapon).
B The picket reserve with picket commander. Often about half the strength of the picket. Used for relieving vedettes and patrols.
C Represents continuous movement between the pickets and Grand Guard.
D Grand Guard – H.Q. of the line of pickets with a reserve force of up to half the strength of the pickets.
E Patrols sent forward before dawn up to 2 miles in advance of pickets.

"On the morning of July 1 I relieved the post at 6 o'clock with trooper Jas. O Hale and Sergeant [actually then a corporal] Levi Shafer." There would be continuous patrolling between the vedettes and before-dawn patrols would sometimes probe forward for up to 2 miles along likely enemy approaches. In theory, the pickets would be on duty for twenty-four hours before being relieved and, according to Kelly, with individuals doing two hours on duty at the post and four off resting. On operations with reduced manpower this was more likely two on and two off. See Map 6.

Map 6 Union Picketing System – 8th Illinois Cavalry across the Chambersburg Pike

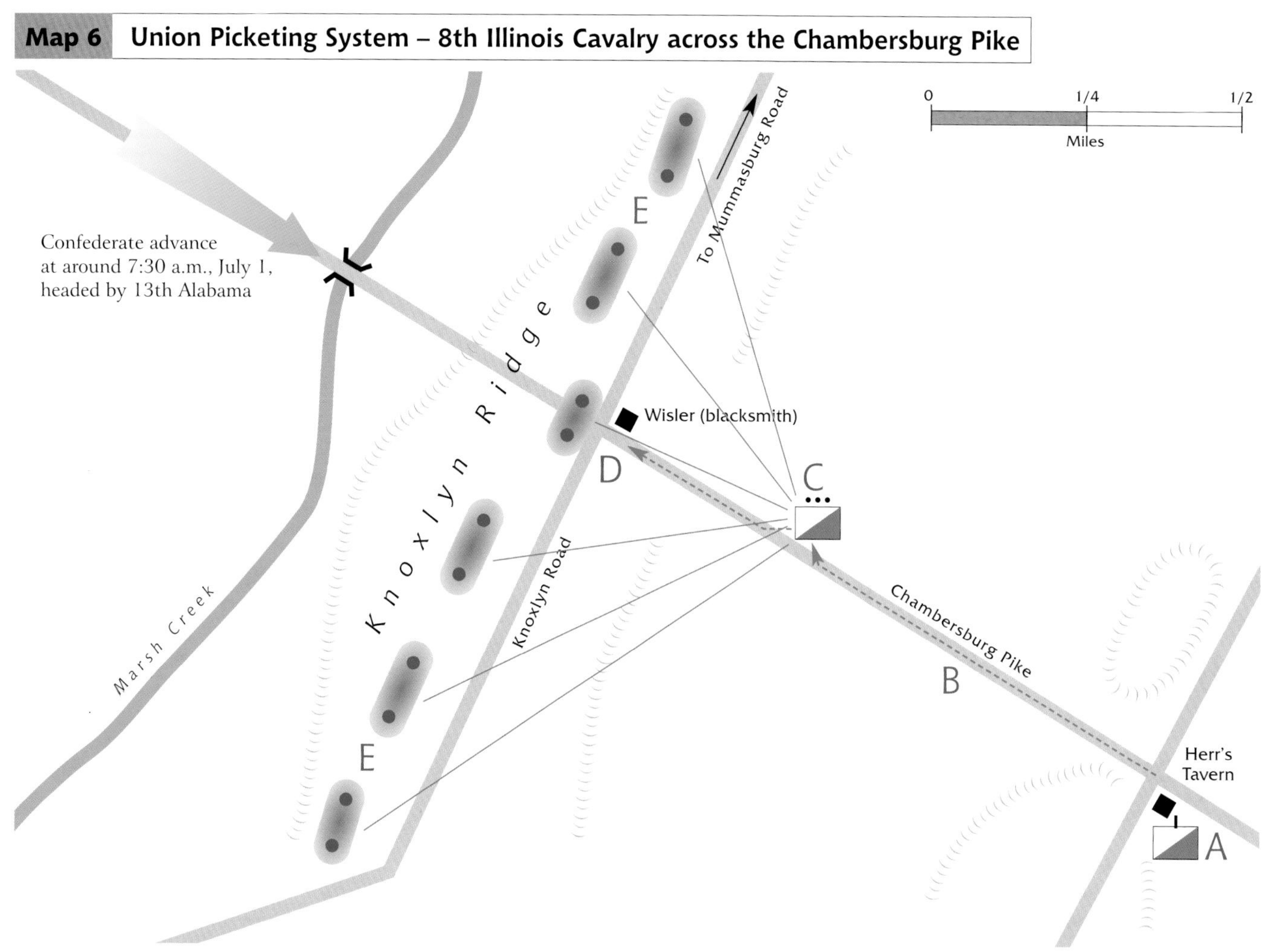

Notes

A Capt. Daniel W. Buck, commanding Troops E and H, was given the task of providing the pickets across the 8th Illinois sector, centered approximately on the Chambersburg Pike. Their combined available strength did not exceed 80 all ranks. Buck established his base/headquarters at Herr's Tavern, about 2 miles west of the town center. He ordered Lt. Marcellus E. Jones (June 30 muster roll shows him as a 2nd Lt.) with 35 men of E Troop to establish the picket and vedette line. Buck's location at the tavern became the "Grand Guard" or main reserve for the picket.

B Jones with his 35 men (the number he stated he had) moved forward.

C Jones established his picket headquarters and reserve position on the reverse (eastern side) of Knoxlyn Ridge close to the pike. His plan was to establish a line of vedette posts along the ridge overlooking Marsh Creek and to locate his main no. 1 post on the Pike itself. He decided, in addition to the post on the Pike, to have two posts to the north and three to the south. Because the enemy were expected at any time, Jones increased the size of each vedette from a single man to two, with an N.C.O. in charge of each. As Jones required a reserve for patrolling and to relieve the vedettes at regular intervals, it is likely that half of his 35 men remained in reserve and 17 or 18 N.C.O.s and men formed the vedettes. Frequent patrols were sent from this location to check the vedette line.

D No. 1 vedette post, located on the pike close to Wisler's blacksmith's shop, some 500 yards in advance of Jones's picket headquarters. It had a clear view along the Pike over Marsh Creek. The names of the troopers providing the two vedettes at 6:00 a.m. on July 1 are unknown, but we do know from Pte. Thomas Kelly's account that they were relieved at that time by himself, Pte. James O. Hale and Cpl. Levi Shafer (his rank on the June 30 muster roll, but probably promoted soon afterwards and remembered as a sergeant). It was from here that about an hour later Lt. Jones borrowed Shafer's carbine to fire the first shot of the battle (see box, page 193) as the Rebels approached the bridge over the creek some 600 yards away.

E The vedette line (six posts of two men each) spread about half a mile north and threequarters of a mile south of the Pike along the ridge. Each man was about 200 yards from his neighbor but supposedly able to see him. The plan shows only the single troopers. There would also be five or six sergeants or corporals, either with one of the vedettes, moving between them, or acting as an additional post themselves. On sighting the enemy a vedette was supposed to fire a shot to alert the others and the picket commander – the 8th Illinois battlefield memorial depicts this. On this occasion, however, it was a messenger from the vedette on the Pike who galloped back to warn Jones of the Confederate approach. Jones yelled to a trooper, "Tell Alex [1st Sgt. Alexander Riddler] to get out the entire command; the Johnnies are coming." Jones went forward and fired his famous shot.

Defensive Delaying Actions

Mounted cavalrymen find themselves at a serious disadvantage when acting on the defensive. It is virtually impossible to aim properly sitting on a horse, reloading is awkward and a mounted man provides a large target. Cavalry were meant to attack. To stand on the defensive was to surrender the advantages of movement and momentum. The answer to this difficulty was to fight defensively while dismounted, and to move and act offensively, preferably when mounted. This meant arming and training cavalrymen appropriately. The breechloading rifle or carbine combined with the revolver and saber gave a man on a horse the ability to act on the defensive and the mobility to undertake successful delaying actions. Such a horseman was not necessarily just a mounted infantryman, as he retained his attacking role, his ability to charge and wield his saber and fire his revolver effectively in a melee.

Gettysburg furnishes a classic example of successful delaying tactics by cavalry – but helped by the lack of urgency or speed on the part of the Rebels. Early on July 1, 2,750 men from two brigades of the Union 1st Cavalry Division under Major-General John Buford delayed the 7,500 infantry of Major-General Heth who were advancing on Gettysburg from the west down the Chambersburg Pike. Buford made sound defensive use of the four successive ridges that blocked the Rebel line of march west of the town. However, although the Union cavalry were handled skillfully, and although they forced the leading Confederate formation to deploy, there was no serious pressure on them until they had fallen back to McPherson's Ridge. Firing their breechloading carbines at twice the rate of their enemy and lying prone to reload, Buford's men had little problem in checking their slow-moving attackers – numerous Confederate regiments halted and waited in column on the Pike for a considerable time. During the hour and a half after the first contact, the Union cavalry suffered virtually no losses. Buford's decision to hold firm for longer on McPherson's Ridge or, if forced back, Seminary Ridge, was made in the knowledge that Union infantry were about to arrive.

Cavalry were also able to skirmish (either mounted or dismounted) and were frequently employed in other defensive duties, such as escorting generals, providing provost guard, or protecting wagon trains. At Gettysburg several regiments had troops detached for escort or provost duties at army or corps headquarters; these included the 1st Maine, 1st New Jersey, 1st Pennsylvania, 6th U.S., and 17th Pennsylvania. Buford's Division was withdrawn from the battle on July 2 and went back to Westminster to guard the army trains. On the Confederate side, Imboden's Brigade spent the period of the battle guarding supply trains at Chambersburg but was later involved in heavy fighting while defending and escorting them and ambulances during Lee's retreat.

Meade's Horse at Gettysburg – Old Baldy

Baldy was born and raised on the western frontier and at the start of the Civil War was owned by Major-General David Hunter, but his name during this period is unknown. He was purchased from the government by Meade in September 1861 for $150 and named Baldy because of his white face. Despite his uncomfortable pace, he became Meade's favorite horse and he rode him throughout all his battles during 1862 and 1863. It is said that Baldy was wounded anywhere from five to fourteen times during the war, starting at First Manassas when he was hit on the nose by a piece of shell. He was wounded in the right hind leg at Second Manassas and again at Antietam, where he was hit in the neck and left for dead. At Gettysburg, on July 2, a bullet that passed through Meade's right trouser leg hit him in the stomach. He staggered and refused to move. Meade commented, "Baldy is done for this time." He was led to the rear and, amazingly, eventually recovered. In 1864 Baldy was on duty at the Siege of Petersburg when he was struck in the ribs by a shell fragment. At this point Meade decided he should be retired.

He was sent to the farm of Meade's staff quartermaster, Captain Sam Ringwalt, in Downington, Pennsylvania, but was later relocated to Meadow Bank Farm, owned by a friend of the Meade family. Baldy was, despite all his wounds, still reasonably active in retirement and Meade was able to ride him in several memorial parades. However, like Traveller (see box, page 205), Baldy outlived his master and so became, also like Traveller, the "riderless horse" in the general's funeral procession in November 1872. Baldy lived another ten years but by then was too feeble to stand and had to be put down, aged thirty. On Christmas Day of that year his remains were disinterred and decapitated and the head sent to a taxidermist. Today, Baldy's head is mounted on a plaque in a glass case and is on show in the Meade Room of the Civil War and Underground Railway Museum of Philadelphia.

Pursuit and Harrassment of Retreating Enemy

Lee's retreat from Gettysburg to the Potomac during the period July 4–14 contained some of the most desperate fighting of the campaign, much of it involving the cavalry of both sides. An army in retreat needs cavalry to provide information, to form rearguards, to delay or disperse its pursuers and to escort its vulnerable ammunition or supply trains. Conversely, the pursuer needs to make maximum use of the mobility of his cavalry to intercept, cut off, harass and attack his adversary. Only a successful pursuit can bring about the complete destruction of a beaten army. Lee succeeded in avoiding the break-up of his army after Gettysburg. That he brought it back over the Potomac at Williamsport and Falling Waters on July 13 and 14 had a lot to do with the skill and fighting qualities of Stuart's cavalry and the mounted infantry of Imboden's Brigade. Stuart redeemed himself during the 50-mile retreat, as his actions in fending off attacks bought sufficient time for Lee to dig in around Williamsport and Hagerstown and then escape across the Potomac. Despite the efforts of the Union cavalry under Buford, Kilpatrick and Gregg in pursuit and the clashes at Monterey Pass, Emmitsburg, Greencastle, Smithsburg (all on July 5), Hagerstown (July 6), Williamsport (July 6) Funkstown (July 7 and 10), Boonsboro (July 8), Beaver's Creek Bridge (July 9) and Falling Waters (July 14), one of the major criticisms of Meade has remained his failure to trap Lee before he crossed back into Virginia. A detailed discussion of this final period of the campaign and the cavalry's role in it are contained in Section Twelve: The Aftermath.

Map 7 Buford's Vedette Lines, June 30–July 1, and Reserve or Fall-back Position, July 1

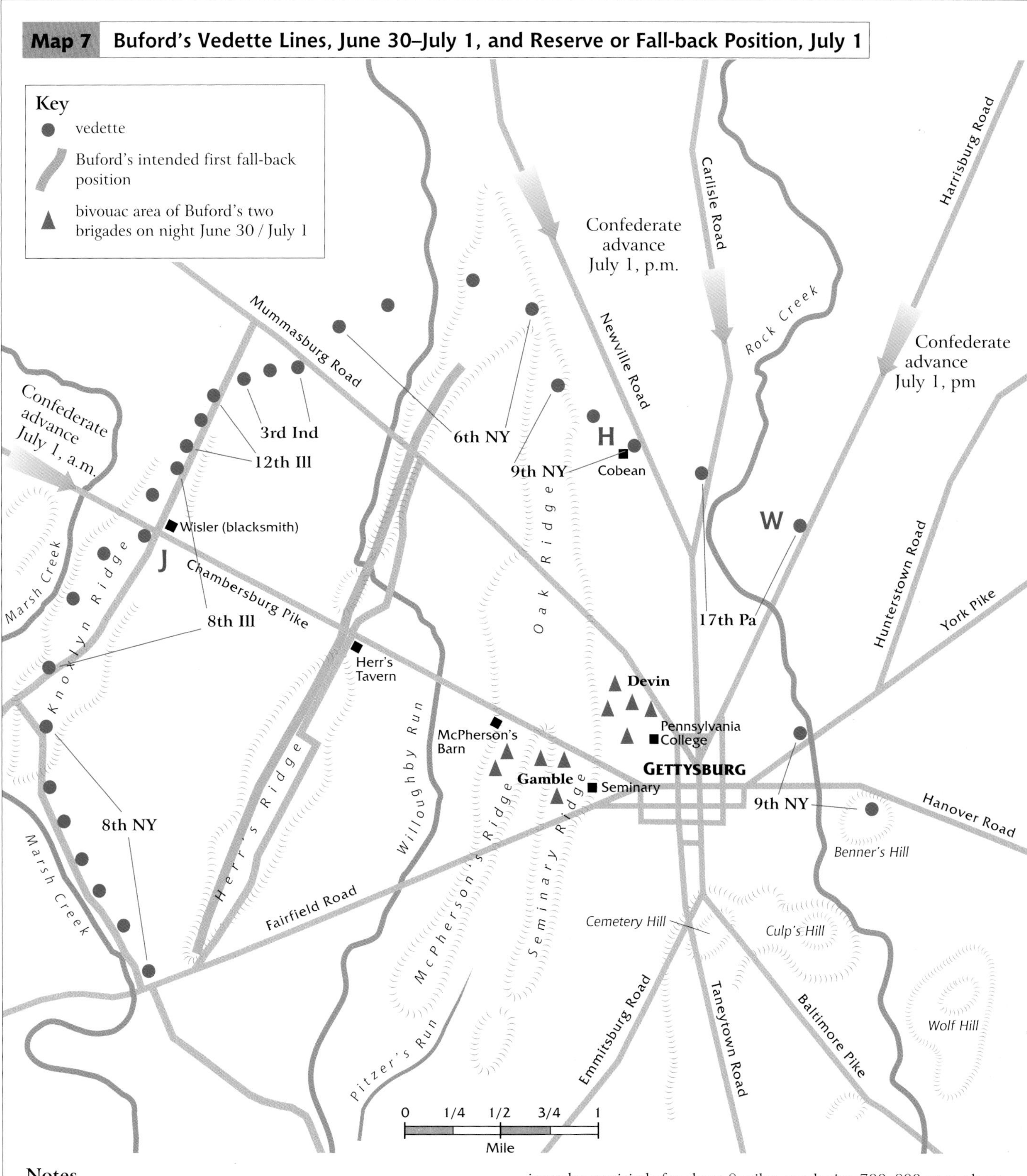

Notes

• This map shows the approximate layout of Buford's 1st Cavalry Division from the late afternoon of June 30 to about 7:30 a.m. on July 1 and the intended first fall-back position if attacked from the west. Confederates had been sighted west of Gettysburg out along the Chambersburg Pike on June 30. It was known that the enemy was concentrating around Cashtown and more were north of Gettysburg. It was therefore considered that the western approaches should be most heavily picketed. This task was given to Gamble's Brigade, while Devin's watched the north and east. The pickets stretched in an irregular semicircle for about 8 miles, employing 700–800 men, about 20% of the division, although a maximum of half would be on watch at a time. In the west the vedette line was 3 miles from the center of town, but in the east the closest was a mere quarter of a mile away on the York Pike. The positions of the picket reserves and "Grand Guards" behind the vedette line are uncertain and so not shown.

• Also shown are the locations of the three main claimants to firing the first shot of the battle: J (Lt. Jones), H (Cpl. Hodges) and W (Pte. Whitney). As noted in the box on page 193, Jones's claim is almost certainly the correct one.

Offensive Action

Napoleon would have put offensive action at the top of the list of his cavalry's tasks, particularly his heavy troopers in their helmets and cuirasses or his lancers, who delighted in running down fleeing infantry. Interestingly, the 6th Pennsylvania Cavalry had exchanged their lances for Sharps carbines as late as May 26. However, by 1863 offensive action in terms of the charge had slipped down the list. Not all old-fashioned cavalry charges in the Gettysburg campaign were cavalry-versus-cavalry affairs. Of the many charges made at Brandy Station, the two by the former lancers of the 6th Pennsylvania stand out. The first was made against artillery batteries and resulted in a vicious saber fight among the enemy guns. Major Henry C. Whelan described it:

> We dashed at them squadron front with drawn sabers, and as we flew along – our men yelling like demons – grape and canister were poured into our left flank and a storm of rifle bullets on our front. We had to leap three wide ditches, and many of our horses and men piled up in a writhing mass in those ditches and were ridden over . . . We dashed on, driving the Rebels into and through the woods, our men fighting with the saber alone, whilst they used principally pistols. Our brave fellows cut them out of the saddle and fought like tigers, until I discovered they were on both flanks, pouring a cross fire of carbines and pistols on us, and then tried to rally my men . . .

Later in the battle the same regiment, supported by the 6th U.S. Cavalry, charged a Rebel position defended by the 10th Virginia Cavalry and protected by a low stone wall. Despite heavy fire from guns and rifles, the attackers reached their objective only to be driven off by a countercharge of the 9th Virginia Cavalry, which forced them back in confusion. The 6th Pennsylvania suffered the highest casualties of any Union regiment at Brandy Station, and their performance so impressed their divisional commander, Buford, that he reported to his corps commander Pleasonton, "These men did splendidly yesterday."

Nevertheless, both these instances illustrate how difficult it was to gain significant results from a cavalry charge unsupported by the other two arms, and how vulnerable the horsemen were to flank attacks or a well-timed counterstroke when they were disorganized on blown horses. Similarly, charges were often handicapped by the closeness of the country – in this case ditches and a stone wall, the former causing considerable losses, the latter protecting the defenders.

Cavalry could, and did, take the offensive on foot as well as mounted, and in towns as well as in more open fields. Two examples of fighting in built-up areas occurred during the Confederate withdrawal from Gettysburg. The first was in the streets of Hagerstown on July 6. This clash saw horsemen of both sides charging each other down the main streets of the town, ending in a fierce and bloody melee in the town square. The second was the action at Boonsboro on July 8 when the Rebel 7th Virginia smashed into the 6th U.S. Cavalry as it was marching up the National Road. A running fight ensued and the Union regiment was badly cut up, losing fifty-nine men to the Virginians' eleven.

Revolver Skills

Even at close range it requires considerable practice to shoot accurately with a revolver; this is particularly so when riding a horse. With the big-caliber weapons used in the war there was a considerable kick, with the revolver tending to jump after each shot. William Quantrill, who led an independent band of Rebels in Kansas, and his bushwhackers were renowned for their revolver skills. They discovered that by reducing the powder charge in their cartridges by one half they could eliminate much of the kick, thereby increasing accuracy, but without making any appreciable sacrifice of striking or carrying power. The best shot in Quantrill's band, and also the fastest on the draw, was Ol Shepherd, who had only one eye. It was said he could "cut a one-forth [*sic*] inch rope in two at twenty paces, and with his hand never raised higher than his hip." All these bushwhackers prided themselves on their shooting ability and constantly practiced to improve it. As a group, Quantrill's guerillas were probably the most formidable bunch of revolver fighters of the war – and afterward when they turned their skills to crime.

Raiding Enemy Lines of Communication and Foraging

Long-distance strategic raids deep into enemy territory and across the lines of communications of armies were a popular military operation for cavalry on both sides during the war. Their objectives were to damage enemy infrastructure – railroad tracks or stores, supply depots, bridges and cut telegraph lines. Additionally, and this was what made them attractive to the participants, there were endless opportunities to forage and loot. This aspect, along with terrifying civilians, destroying property and generally causing mayhem, resulted in the formation of several Rebel partisan guerrilla gangs. The most notorious was led by William C. Quantrill, who for almost four years terrorized the Kansas–Missouri border (see box below).

For the first two years it was the Confederates who predominated in carrying out large-scale raids. Apart from Jeb Stuart, Nathan Bedford Forrest was perhaps the most famous Rebel raider – he rose to be a lieutenant-general. An extraordinarily strong man, on receiving a near fatal pistol wound from a disgruntled subordinate he succeeded in holding his assailant's pistol hand, used his teeth to pry open his penknife and with his free hand stabbed his attacker fatally in the stomach. Forrest's raiding in Tennessee a year before Gettysburg caused two entire infantry divisions to be tied down protecting the Nashville–Stevenson railroad. Later in the war his operations against Major-General Sherman during the Atlanta campaign led the Union general to exclaim in frustration, "That devil Forrest . . . must be hunted down and killed if it cost ten thousand lives and bankrupts the Federal treasury." Forrest survived and lived to become the first Grand Wizard of the Ku Klux Klan. Stuart became famous for his two audacious raids around the Army of the Potomac in 1862. However, his ride around it in June 1863 was not primarily a raid.

By 1863 a more competent and confident Union cavalry had taken up strategic raiding seriously. Major-General George Stoneman's raid during the Chancellorsville campaign was a colossal failure and merely deprived Hooker of the cavalry he needed for the battle itself. More successful by far was Benjamin Grierson's raid in the Vicksburg campaign. It was a strategic masterpiece, diverting critical Confederate forces away from Ulysses S. Grant's army; Grant said of it, "It has been one of the most brilliant cavalry exploits of the war, and will be handed down in history as an example to be imitated."

For the Gettysburg campaign, perhaps foraging should be ranked equal top of the Confederate cavalry's priority duties. The need to supply the Army of Northern Virginia with every conceivable item of food, fodder and equipment, as well as with horses, was one of the, if not the, paramount reasons for the invasion of Pennsylvania by Lee in the summer of 1863. This subject will be explored in greater depth in Section Seven: The Road to Gettysburg; sufficient to say here that Longstreet's entire corps missed the Chancellorsville battle as it had been sent south in April primarily to collect food for the men and fodder for the horses. Brigadier-Generals John Imboden and "Grumble" Jones both had foraging missions in Western Virginia before the Gettysburg campaign got under way. Both these brigades also had foraging as a priority task in the two weeks before the battle.

CAVALRY COMMAND AND CONTROL AT GETTYSBURG

Confederate

Divisional Headquarters

Major-General James Ewell Brown Stuart – divisional commander
Major Henry B. McClellan – chief of staff
Major Johann Heinrich August Heros von Borcke – assistant adjutant general (w. June19)
Major Andrew R. Venable – assistant inspector general
Major Norman R. Fitzhugh – quartermaster
Captain William W. Blackford – chief engineer
Captain John E. Cooke – chief of ordnance
Lieutenant Frank S. Robertson – engineer
Lieutenant G. M. Ryalls – provost marshal

A.D.C.s

Captain J. L. Clarke
Captain Henry C. Lee
Captain R. B. Kennon
Lieutenant Christwell Dabney
Lieutenant Robert H. Goldsborough (c)
Lieutenant H. Hagen
Talcot Eliason – surgeon
Captain Justus Scheibert – Pomeranian observer

Lee's overhaul of the structure and command of the Army of Northern Virginia after Chancellorsville did not much effect the cavalry, although there was an acute shortage of both manpower and horses. The preparations for the Gettysburg campaign saw Stuart's division increased from four brigades to six with the addition of Brigadier-General William E. "Grumble" Jones with around 1,550 men and the much smaller (960) brigade under Brigadier-General Beverly H. Robertson. Brigadier-General John D. Imboden's mounted infantry was to operate independently and was never part of Stuart's command. However, his brigade commanders were by no means equal in ability or in their relationship with their divisional commander. As this had a bearing on the conduct of cavalry operations prior to the battle (see Section Seven: The Road to Gettysburg) a few words on each is needed.

Brigadier-General William E. "Grumble" Jones

Jones was an extremely profane, morose, quarrelsome and complaining (thus his nickname) thirty-nine-year-old West Point graduate of 1848. His early career was mostly with mounted rifle units fighting Indians in the Pacific Northwest. His bad-temperedness developed after losing his wife in a shipwreck shortly after their marriage. He left the army in 1857 to become a farmer. At the outbreak of the war Jones formed a cavalry company and was elected its commander. He was something of a martinet but quickly proved himself courageous and an able tactician. He was a fighter, and his military ability (Cedar Mountain, Groveton and Second Manassas) ensured quick promotion. He had reached brigadier-general by September 1862 when he inherited the veteran, all-Virginia, "Laurel" Brigade and did particularly well at Brandy Station, holding his own in a day of intense fighting against superior numbers.

Although Stuart admired Jones's ability (he considered him the finest outpost officer in the army), he detested him personally. Captain William Blackford of Stuart's staff later wrote that Jones regarded Stuart "with intense jealousy when placed under his command, a feeling which ripened afterwards into as genuine a hatred as I ever remember to have been in my experience in life." The feeling was so intense that Jones asked to be relieved of command when he learned of his assignment to Stuart's Division; the request was refused. In a similar vein, Stuart requested that Jones be transferred to the infantry. This was also rejected with the words that Stuart should not let his "judgment be warped" by ill feelings. Nevertheless, Stuart declined to take Jones with him on his ride round Meade, leaving him and Robertson to guard the rear of the army as it marched up the Shenandoah Valley into Maryland and Pennsylvania.

Jones was killed on June 5, 1864 while personally leading a charge in the Rebel rout at Piedmont.

Brigadier-General Beverly H. "Bev" Robertson

A thirty-six-year-old, bald, gray-bearded, disagreeable-looking former West Point graduate, Robertson served with the 2nd U.S. Dragoons in the West throughout his early career. This soldiering had been in New Mexico, Kansas and Nebraska, fighting Apaches at Tornado del Muerto and Sioux at Blue Water. In March 1861 he was promoted captain but was dismissed from the Union Army in August after accepting a commission in the same rank in the Confederate Army. Prior to Gettysburg Robertson had been serving in North Carolina under Major-General D. H. Hill, a situation that neither found amicable. One member of Stuart's staff described Robertson as "an excellent man in camp to train troops, but in the field, in the presence of the enemy, he lost all self-possession, and was perfectly unreliable." He performed poorly at Brandy Station when he withdrew from Kelly's Ford, and again at Middleburg and Upperville his actions were uninspiring. Put briefly, Robertson "was more at drilling than he was at fighting." Lee himself remarked, "What to do with Robertson, I do not know." On June 24 Stuart made that decision. He had no wish to have Robertson under his immediate command so ordered him to join "Grumble" Jones's strong brigade as Lee's rearguard – as the senior of the two, Robertson would be technically in command. In the event Robertson was not involved in the main battle, only arriving in time to take part in Lee's withdrawal.

His remaining war service was undistinguished. At one stage he was relieved of his command "owing to mutinous remarks to his brigade," his resultant assignment being the Department of South Carolina for "the reorganization and instruction of cavalry troops." After the war he became an insurance broker in Washington, dying in 1910, aged eighty-three.

Major Johann Heinrich August Heros von Borcke

Von Borcke is worth a note even though he did not quite make the battle. He was a 6-foot 4-inch, blond-haired, giant Prussian volunteer who arrived at army headquarters during the Battle of Seven Pines a year prior to Gettysburg and was later attached to Stuart's staff. On arrival he spoke not a word of English but was seemingly quick to learn, soon gaining the obvious nickname of "Von" and a reputation for fancy uniforms, including a plumed hat that resembled Stuart's. Longstreet's chief of staff, Lieutenant-Colonel G. Moxley Sorrel, described Borcke's appearance on first arrival as an "ambulating arsenal":

> [a] double-barreled rifle was strapped across his back, a Winchester carbine hung by his hip, heavy revolvers were in his belt, right and left side; an enormous straight double-edged sharp-pointed cuirasseur's [*sic*] saber hung together with sabertasche [*sic*] to his left thigh, and a short "*couteau de chasse*" [hunting knife] finished up his right side. Besides, his English army saddle bore two large holsters, one for his field glasses, the other for still another revolver, bigger and deadlier than all the others . . . When I next saw him he had discarded – taught by experience – all his arsenal except his good saber and a couple of handy pistols.

Von was badly wounded by a bullet in his neck at the cavalry clash at Middleburg on June 19, which put him out of action for a long time. He eventually returned to duty, and was with Stuart at his death at Yellow Tavern in May 1864. He was promoted lieutenant-colonel in December 1864. At the end of the war he returned to Prussia, where he fought in the war with Austria in 1866 before finally retiring to his castle in East Prussia. There he advertised his lifelong passion for the Rebel cause by flying the Confederate battle flag from his battlements and calling his daughter Virginia. He died in Berlin in 1895.

Brigadier-General Albert G. Jenkins

A thirty-two-year-old Southern aristocrat, blue-eyed with a good physique and long brown beard, Jenkins had no military experience prior to the war. However, he was quickly elected captain of the "Border Rangers," the first cavalry company of Cabell County, Virginia. By August 1862 he was a brigadier-general leading his brigade on a 500-mile ride through West Virginia, which gained him a somewhat dubious reputation as a successful raider and marauder rather than a conventional cavalry leader. He lived up to this reputation when he led Major-General Robert Rodes' Division (Ewell's Corps) in the advance up the Shenandoah Valley. He failed to trap the enemy at Martinsburg and his men were blamed for much of the horse-stealing, violence to property, and fraud that was part of the foraging required to keep the advance moving. Rodes was furious with his behavior at Chambersburg, where Jenkins fled from what turned out to be a tiny group of Union scouts without attempting to ascertain the enemy's strength. His brigade played no role at Gettysburg, as Jenkins was badly wounded by long-range shellfire while peering through his glasses on Blocher's Knoll and his regiments never reached their intended position on Lee's extreme left flank. Nevertheless, Jenkins' troopers were later involved in the cavalry battle at Rummel Farm on July 3. Jenkins eventually recovered and resumed command of his raiders, only to have his arm shattered at the Battle of Cloyd's Mountain in May 1864 – he died after his arm was amputated.

Brigadier-General Wade Hampton

Hampton was Stuart's second-in-command, a forty-five-year-old Southern plantation-owner reputed to be the largest slave-owner in the South. He was immensely strong and a fine horseman who could supposedly make a horse groan with the grip of his legs. He had no military experience before the war, but at the outset formed at his own expense what was effectively a private army called Hampton's Legion. He fought and was wounded at both First Manassas and Seven Pines, but thereby gained a well-deserved reputation for courage and competence. Under Stuart's command he demonstrated his ability in no fewer than five raids, three of them of his own against the rear of Burnside's army in late 1862. By the summer of 1863 Stuart and Hampton had developed a high degree of mutual respect and the latter's six well-disciplined regiments formed the second strongest of the three brigades Stuart led to Gettysburg. Hampton was wounded in the head during a skirmish near Hunterstown on July 2, then three more times at Rummel Farm the next day – two more saber cuts to his head and a piece of shell in his right hip.

He eventually recovered and took command of the cavalry division on Stuart's death in May 1864; he was promoted lieutenant-general in February 1865. After the war he returned to his destroyed plantation and was subsequently elected for two terms as governor and then as a senator. He died in 1902, aged eighty-four.

Brigadier-General Fitzhugh "Fitz" Lee

Described as "the laughing cavalier," Fitzhugh Lee "had a prevailing habit of irrepressible good humor which made any occasion of seriousness in him seem like affectation." It was this lack of seriousness and barely adequate academic talents that almost got him dismissed from West Point when his uncle Robert E. Lee was superintendent. As a young lieutenant he survived being shot through the lungs by an Indian arrow in Texas in 1859. He resigned from the U.S. Regular Army in May 1861 to accept a commission in the Confederate Army and served on Ewell's and J. E. Johnston's staff during the Peninsular campaign. By July 1862 he was a cavalry brigadier-general, commanding a brigade at South Mountain and Antietam, and under Stuart during his raids in December of that year. Stuart had a high regard for him, writing "In my estimation no one in the Confederacy possesses more of the elements of what a brigadier of cavalry ought to be." On one occasion, however, he angered his divisional commander by arriving late at the Battle of Second Manassas – an event that led to Stuart's losing his plumed hat and cape. The ever high-spirited Fitz redeemed himself shortly afterward by leading a raid that captured Union Major-General John Pope's headquarters tent containing that general's dress uniform, which Fitz donned himself before strutting around his own headquarters, much to the amusement of his staff.

Lee was unable to command his brigade at the start of the campaign – he missed Brandy Station – as he had been somewhat incapacitated by a kick from a horse, although he kept up by traveling in an ambulance. He resumed command from Colonel Thomas T. Munford on June 24. Lee was heavily involved in the Rummel Farm clash against the Union cavalry on July 3 just east of the main battlefield. On the reorganization of the cavalry after Gettysburg, Lee received command of a division (as did Hampton) before he was twenty-eight. In March 1865, when Hampton was detached from the Army of Northern Virginia, Lee assumed command of the cavalry. After the war he spent many years farming in Virginia and was elected governor in 1885. He was appointed consul general to Cuba at the outbreak of the Spanish-American War in 1898 and died in Washington D.C. in 1905, aged seventy.

Colonel John R. Chambliss

Chambliss succeeded to command of the brigade after Brigadier-General William Henry Fitzhugh "Rooney" Lee (General Lee's second son and cousin of Fitz) was severely wounded in the leg and his senior colonel killed at Brandy Station. Thus he was very much a newcomer to brigade command at Gettysburg but, although lacking in active experience, he handled his men well at the Rummel Farm action on July 3. Chambliss proved an able cavalry leader and secured promotion to permanent command of his brigade in January 1864. He was shot through the body and killed at the cavalry action on the Charles City Road, near Richmond, in August 1864. Robert E. Lee wrote of his death, "His fall will be felt throughout the army, in which by his courage, energy and skill, he won for himself an honorable name."

Union

Cavalry Corps Headquarters

Major-General Alfred Pleasonton – corps commander
Colonel George A. H. Blake – commissary of musters (responsible for receiving muster rolls)
Lieutenant-Colonel Andrew J. Alexander – chief of staff and assistant adjutant general
Lieutenant-Colonel William H. Crocker – inspector general
Lieutenant-Colonel Charles G. Sawtelle – quartermaster
Lieutenant-Colonel Albert S. Austin – commissary of subsistence
Lieutenant-Colonel Charles R. Smith – chief of ordnance
Captain John Green – assistant inspector general
Captain Frederick C. Newhall – assistant inspector general
Captain V. E. von Koerber – topographical engineer
Captain Thomas Drummond – uncertain

A.D.C.s

Captain G. A. Crocker
Captain George A. Custer – promoted brigadier June 29
1st Lieutenants C. B. McClellan, C. B. Parsons, Clifford Thompson, James F. Wade, Leicester Walker and George W. Yates (thirteen years later Captain Yates was killed at the Battle of Little Big Horn while serving as a troop commander in the 7th U.S. Cavalry under Lieutenant-Colonel Custer)

Others

8, including:
1st Lieutenant Woodbury M. Taylor – Ambulance Corps
George L. Pancoast – medical director
George Mc. McGill – assistant surgeon

Total: 27 staff

The Cavalry Corps experienced a major shake-up in its senior commanders prior to and during the Gettysburg campaign. As explained above, Pleasonton got promotion to major-general and the job he had always craved – that of corps commander – after Chancellorsville in May. His place as the 1st Cavalry Division's commander went to John Buford, promoted major-general on June 1. At Brandy Station Colonel Benjamin F. "Grimes" Davis, a thirty-six-year-old ex-dragoon and veteran of the Apache wars, about whom it was said "he liked to fight the rebels as well as he liked to eat," was shot through the head. His place at the head of the 1st Brigade, 1st Division was taken by Colonel William Gamble. Pleasonton's reshuffling of units and commanders during June saw the disappearance of several foreign-born senior officers soon after the Brandy Station battle (Colonels Alfred Duffie, Luigi Di Cesnola and Sir Percy Wyndham), for whom he had a particular dislike, and Colonel John B. McIntosh taking over the 1st Brigade, 2nd Division.

Then, just three days before the battle, immediately following Hooker's replacement by Meade as army commander, four more promotions took place within the cavalry corps. The first saw the twenty-nine-year-old Brigadier-General Judson Kilpatrick appointed to command the new 3rd Division, which had previously been employed ineffectively among the Washington defenses. But most startling of all, three captains jumped three clear ranks to become brigadier-generals of volunteer cavalry – thereafter known as "the Boy Generals." They were entirely Pleasonton's personal choice for promotion, with no regard for seniority – he was determined to make the most of the go-ahead by Meade to recommend for promotion whomever he considered deserving. Pleasonton had recently written, "Give me 15,000 cavalry [and] let me place my own officers over it." Well, he got nearly 12,000 horsemen and carte blanche for promotions. The surprised and delighted young officers were Captain Wesley Merritt, who got the Reserve Brigade in Buford's 1st Division; Captain Elon J. Farnsworth, who took over the 1st Brigade in the 3rd Division; and Captain George A. Custer, who got command of the 2nd Brigade in the same division.

A few words on each Union cavalry brigade commander and the role he played in the campaign or battle are given below.

Colonel William Gamble

A forty-five-year-old Irishman, who had lived in America since boyhood, Gamble had several years' experience as a sergeant-major in the U.S. Dragoons. He had left the army in 1843 to become a civil engineer in Chicago. He was appointed a lieutenant-colonel in the 8th Illinois Cavalry in 1861 and looked every bit the image of a "Colonel Blimp" with his plump, red face and frizzy side-whiskers. He fought in the Peninsula and was severely wounded in the chest while leading a charge at Malvern Hill. As a brigade commander during the Gettysburg campaign, Gamble had a somewhat inauspicious encounter with the Rebels near Snicker's Gap on June 18, timidly withdrawing when faced with what he thought were superior numbers. He did better at Middleburg the next day. There he skillfully used his dismounted troopers with their breechloading carbines as skirmishers behind several fence lines to delay a Rebel advance that was eventually pushed back. It was a smallscale foretaste of what was to happen on July 1. He was in action again at Upperville on June 21 before, after another nine days and many nights of grueling marches, he finally led his brigade into

Gettysburg at 11:00 a.m. on June 30. The next morning it was his destiny to open the battle some 4 miles east of the town.

Gamble ended the war as a brigadier-general of volunteers and mustered out in 1866. However, he joined the Regular Army as a major four months later in the 8th U.S. Cavalry – only to die in the same year in the same rank.

Colonel Thomas C. Devin

Another Irishman, forty-one years old, balding and with a ruddy face, Devin had already won the nicknames of "Buford's Hard Hitter" and "Old War Horse" for his actions at Antietam and Chancellorsville. Before the war he had been a partner in a New York City paint, oil and varnish firm as well as a militia officer. It was in the latter capacity that he acquired a reputation as a competent cavalryman. When tested on his military ability by an officer from the War Department, that officer reported, "I can't teach Colonel Devin anything about cavalry; he knows more about the tactics than I do." Devin was appointed colonel of the 6th New York Cavalry in November 1861 and his regiment quickly became acknowledged as one of the best drilled in the army.

Devin's Brigade was at Brandy Station before taking part in the long march north to Gettysburg, where he arrived on the afternoon of June 30. There his vedette line was responsible for covering the approaches to the town in the north and east. Unlike Gamble in the west, Devin did not have any convenient ridges or streams to facilitate fighting a delaying action. Nevertheless, on July 1 when Ewell's Corps came pouring down the Newville and Carlisle Roads, he conducted skillful retreat and reporting tactics north of the town until the arrival of XI Corps infantry. Devin's Brigade was then regrouped on the York Pike protecting XI Corps' right flank.

Devin gained promotion to brevet brigadier-general of volunteers in August 1864 for his action at Fisher's Hill, ending the war as major-general of volunteers. He continued to serve in the Regular Army and died on active duty as colonel of the 3rd U.S. Cavalry in 1878, aged fifty-six.

Brigadier-General Wesley Merritt

Described by some as one of the "boy wonders" of the war, as he rose from captain in June 1863 to major-general by the end of the war at the age of thirty-one. A West Point graduate of 1860, Merritt served with the dragoons on the frontier until August 1861. After promotion to captain in the 2nd U.S. Cavalry, he served as A.D.C. to Brigadier-General Philip St. George Cooke when that officer commanded the cavalry of the Army of the Potomac. After a spell in the headquarters of the Department of Washington, Merritt again became an A.D.C., this time to Major-General George Stoneman, accompanying him on his less than glorious raid during the Chancellorsville campaign.

As a captain, Merritt had gained a reputation as a hard, unyielding disciplinarian but also as a tough, thoroughly professional cavalry officer – something belied by his boyish, beardless face. Pleasonton selected him for accelerated promotion on the eve of Gettysburg with the words, "It is necessary I have a good commander for the regular brigade of cavalry, and I earnestly recommend Captain Wesley Merritt be made a brigadier-general for that purpose. He has all the qualifications for it, and has distinguished himself by his gallantry and daring. Give me good commanders and I will give you good results." He thus became the third commander of the Reserve Brigade in less than three weeks. After Brandy Station Major Charles J. Whiting had been relieved for poor performance and his successor, Major Samuel H. Starr, had done no better at Upperville. A member of the 6th U.S. Cavalry wrote: "The men were pretty thoroughly disgusted with the affair [the clash at Upperville]. Major Starr, to whose want of judgment and feeble efforts on this occasion where properly chargeable . . ."

In the great cavalry clash at Brandy Station, Merritt, still a captain, had demonstrated his courage and swordsmanship in the midst of a desperate melee with the 9th Virginia Cavalry. In this vicious cut-and-thrust struggle he had his hat sliced from his head and received a sword cut on his leg. Merritt was promoted and took command of Buford's Reserve Brigade on June 29 but remained some distance from the battlefield during the first two days. It was only in mid-afternoon on July 3 that his troopers were unsuccessfully committed to action against Rebel infantry on Lee's extreme right flank astride the Emmitsburg Road (South Cavalry Field).

After Gettysburg Merritt was almost continuously in action for the remainder of the war – the battles, raids and skirmishes are too numerous to list. By war's end he was a major-general of volunteers. He continued to serve, principally engaged in fighting Indians in the West. Later he was appointed Superintendent of the U.S. Military Academy at West Point before commanding the first Philippine expedition in 1898 as a Regular Army major-general. Along with Admiral Dewey, he received the surrender of Manila. He finally retired in 1900 after forty years of active service, dying ten years later, aged seventy-six.

Colonel John. B. McIntosh

McIntosh has been described as "a born fighter, a strict disciplinarian, a dashing leader and a polished gentleman." Formerly a midshipman during the Mexican War, he was a businessman prior to the outbreak of the Civil War. His brother, a West Point graduate, became a brigadier-general in the Confederate service (much to John's disgust) and was killed at Pea Ridge in March 1862. By Gettysburg John McIntosh was held in high regard as the commander of the 3rd Pennsylvania Cavalry. He had fought at White Oak Swamp, South Mountain and Antietam as a junior cavalry officer before promotion in November 1862 to the command of a regiment. He fought well as a brigade commander at Kelly's Ford and Chancellorsville, and was the obvious person to replace Sir Percy Wyndham (relegated to command the remount depot near Washington after his regiment's mauling at Brandy Station) in command of the 1st Brigade of the 2nd Division at Gettysburg. He brought his newly equipped and remounted brigade from Wyndham's depot to join the army on June 28. His 3rd Pennsylvania led the charge into Westminster on June 30 but he was not engaged again until the battle just east of Gettysburg around Rummel Farm on July 3. In this clash his regiments were fully committed – at one point McIntosh personally led his staff into the fray.

McIntosh was badly injured by a fall from his horse in September 1863. After his recuperation he was severely wounded at the Third Battle of Winchester in September 1864, which resulted in the amputation of a leg. He continued in the army after the war and retired in the rank of brigadier-general in 1870. He died in 1888, aged fifty-nine.

Colonel John Irvin Gregg

A tall man of thirty-six and cousin of his divisional commander, John Gregg wore a long piratical beard that earned him the nickname of "Long John." He had seen action in the Mexican War, during which his abilities as a soldier saw him rise from private to captain. The next ten years were spent in the Regular Army before he entered the commercial world as an iron merchant in Pennsylvania. He was commissioned captain in the 3rd U.S. Cavalry in May 1861. After fighting in the Peninsula, Gregg was appointed colonel of the 16th Pennsylvania Cavalry late in 1862. From April the following year he was given the 3rd Brigade of the 2nd Division.

Gregg was heavily involved at Brandy Station and in the actions at Aldie, Middleburg and Upperville en route to Gettysburg. He was the only senior officer to voice his concerns about the elevation of the three captains to brigade command immediately before the battle. In a confidential memorandum he wrote that he doubted "any reason can be assigned by the most favorably disposed to warrant these appointments." On July 2 Gregg's brigade was held in reserve during the clash with the Rebel infantry over possession of Brinkerhoff Ridge, just 2 miles east of Gettysburg on the Hanover Road (see box, page 449). On July 3 Gregg saw some action en route to guard XII Corps' southern flank adjacent to Wolf's Hill. His regiments were not involved in the main cavalry engagement that day at Rummel Farm.

After Gettysburg and the subsequent Confederate retreat, Gregg's service took him to at least thirteen further actions, during which he was wounded three times (at Deep Bottom, Hatcher's Run and Amelia Court House) before finally being captured at Farmville. Fortunately his imprisonment lasted only three days, as he was released on Lee's surrender at Appomattox Court House on April 9, 1865, by which time Gregg was a major-general of volunteers. He continued to serve in the Regular Army as colonel of the 8th U.S. Cavalry, leading several expeditions against the Indians in the Mojave Desert, and another to survey and map the Texas Panhandle. He retired in 1879, dying in 1892 at the age of sixty-five.

Brigadier-General Elon J. Farnsworth

In July 1863 Farnsworth was a tall, gangly, mustachioed and impetuous young man of twenty-six who had had a varied and volatile career prior to his sudden meteoric rise to brigade command – a position he was destined to enjoy for a mere five days, as he was killed in the closing moments of the battle. His earliest employment was as a civilian forager with the U.S. Regular Army and as such accompanied it on the Utah Expedition (1857–58) to subdue the Mormons in Salt Lake City who had declared themselves exempt from U.S. laws. Later, as a student at the University of Michigan, he was renowned for his partying and pranks. In his third year he succeeded in getting expelled (along with seven others) when a drunken escapade resulted in a fellow student's dying after being thrown from a building. At the outbreak of war he was appointed first lieutenant and adjutant of his uncle's (John F. Farnsworth's) regiment, the 8th Illinois Cavalry. Within three months he was a captain. In early 1863 he had the pastor of the St. Paul's Church in Alexandria, Virginia, arrested for failing to read the prayer for the U.S. President. When several congregation members protested a scuffle broke out that was only subdued when Farnsworth threatened to shoot them!

Farnsworth served in all his regiment's campaigns. During the Chancellorsville operations he was one of Pleasonton's A.D.C.s. He had been personally selected for the post by the general, as Pleasonton was keen to keep in favor with Farnsworth's uncle, who had left the army to take his seat in Congress. During the Stoneman raid Farnsworth saved the horse artillery ammunition by floating them over a river. His leadership qualities were demonstrated at Brandy Station with his handling of the 8th Illinois when he was sent to assume command after heavy losses had left them without senior officers. Able though the young Farnsworth undoubtedly was, there was surely something of currying favor and personal advancement in Pleasonton's mind when he wrote to Congressman Farnsworth on June 23 that "Captain Farnsworth has done splendidly – I have serious thoughts of having him made a brigadier general . . . I am sadly in want of officers with the proper dash to command cavalry . . . do assist us until we get ahead of the Rebs." Five days later came the promotion. Farnsworth was forced to borrow a suitable uniform reflecting his one-star status from his benefactor.

Within two days of taking over his brigade Farnsworth was leading the charge that drove Stuart's men out of the small town of Hanover, 20 miles from Gettysburg. His men were lightly engaged at Hunterstown on July 2, but on the afternoon of the next day the unfortunate young brigadier-general was to charge just once too often. Details of the circumstances of his death can be found in Section Eleven: Day Three.

Brigadier-General George Armstrong Custer

Custer was to become a legendary hero of his nation. He was to have a brilliant Civil War record as an outstanding cavalry leader, a man promoted brigadier-general at twenty-three and major-general at twenty-five. From First Manassas to Lee's surrender, Custer took part in every battle fought by the Army of the Potomac except one. He was wounded only once, but was to have eleven horses killed under him. Nearly 6 feet tall, with a lean but strong physique and long golden curls, he had the *beau sabreur* temperament of a dashing Napoleonic cavalry officer. He deliberately cultivated that image, with his fancy black velvet jacket liberally covered in gold lace and with a double row of buttons grouped in pairs, blue shirt with large stars on each collar, and crimson necktie. This was topped off with a wide-brimmed black hat complete with gilt cord, rosette and silver star. At night he curled his locks round candles to keep his ringlets in shape.

For all his foppish, showman's dress, Custer was a daring, courageous and resourceful cavalryman. At West Point he failed to distinguish himself, graduating last in a class of thirty-four just after the start of the Civil War. He was commissioned into the 2nd U.S. Cavalry. However, several days after graduation he failed in his duty as officer of the guard to stop a fight between two cadets. He was courtmartialed but saved from punishment by the desperate need for officers at the outbreak of the war. He became A.D.C. to Major-General George B. McClellan and was present at Antietam and Chancellorsville; by May 1863 he was a first lieutenant and A.D.C. on Pleasonton's staff. On May 21 Pleasonton sent him on an amphibious raid deep behind Rebel lines. It was a huge success. Custer burned two schooners and a bridge, captured twelve prisoners, several boxes of shoes and thirty horses. On Pleasonton's promotion to corps command, Custer remained with him as A.D.C. and brevet captain. On his promotion to brevet brigadier-general on May 29, Custer assumed command of the 2nd (Michigan) Brigade – the Wolverines – in Kilpatrick's 3rd Division; he was the youngest general in the army.

At Brandy Station Custer, then still a lieutenant and A.D.C., was badly shaken when thrown by his runaway mount, which made a botched attempt at jumping a wall. At Aldie he was alongside his general when Kilpatrick led the 1st Maine into an all-out charge, but again Custer's horse ran away with him. The action at Hanover on June 30 against Stuart's horsemen was Custer's first chance to show his mettle as a brigade commander. He succeeded, while Farnsworth drove the enemy out of the town, in pinning and threatening the Confederate left flank, with the result that the Confederates retreated. The next day at Hunterstown, in yet another charge, Custer's horse fell wounded close to the enemy position. As its dazed rider struggled to his feet, he became the target for numerous Rebel marksmen. Custer's life was saved by the bugler of the 1st Michigan Cavalry, Norville Churchill, who galloped up and shot Custer's nearest assailant before galloping madly away with his general clinging on behind him. At Rummel Farm on July 3 Custer's Brigade was heavily committed in the battle and he personally led the 7th Michigan, his smallest regiment, in a desperate charge, the first of the battle, that scattered the 9th Virginia Cavalry before running out of momentum and being forced to flee by a well-timed counterattack. Custer survived unscathed. His brigade lost 257 men at Gettysburg, the highest number of any cavalry brigade at the battle.

Custer, as noted above, was continually in action for the rest of the war, rising to major-general and a cavalry divisional commander. His fearless aggression in battle earned him enormous respect and put him increasingly in the public eye. In July 1866 Custer was appointed lieutenant-colonel of the 7th U.S. Cavalry. In late 1867 he was courtmartialed and suspended for a year for being absent from duty during the campaign against the Southern Cheyenne. Back on duty in 1868, Custer spent the next eight years campaigning against Indians. As most readers will know, he met his match on June 25, 1876, on the Little Big Horn when he split his force into three and then contemptuously attacked a huge Indian village. It cost him and the men with him their lives, but gained him everlasting fame and started a controversy that still rumbles on today.

SECTION FIVE

Other Arms and Services

SUPPLY AND TRANSPORT, MEDICAL, SIGNALS

SUPPLY AND TRANSPORT

"An army marches on its stomach" is a well-known dictum attributed to Napoleon. It is an oversimplification, as an army requires much more than food if it is to fight, indeed survive. The Duke of Marlborough was nearer the mark when he wrote: "An army cannot preserve good order unless its soldiers have meat in their belly, coats on their backs and shoes on their feet" – he might have added ammunition in their pouches. Many men on both sides fought at Gettysburg without the meat and the shoes, while thousands of Rebels lacked the coat as well. There were at least 170,000 men and 75,000 animals (excluding the Union trains at Westminster and the Confederate wagons near Fairfield) involved in operations at and close to Gettysburg during those three days in July. The soldiers and animals needed water and feeding daily; the former also needed clothing, shoes, equipment, replacement arms, ammunition and medical supplies. Horses and mules required fodder and shoes as well as replacements for broken harnesses or saddles. Without horses the guns and cavalry could not move; without mules neither could the thousands of wagons carrying the armies' needs. To get the armies to Gettysburg was a mammoth exercise in supply, involving complex planning and constant supervision on a massive scale.

The solution to these problems lay with the Quartermaster, Commissariat and Ordnance (for ammunition) Departments of the respective armies. A soldier was supposedly entitled to his basic marching ration of a pound of hardtack and another pound of meat, plus sugar, coffee and salt daily. For Lee's army of 72,000 this equated to 144,000 pounds, or 72 tons, of food. For the three weeks up to and including the battle, 1,512 tons were needed. For Meade's approximately 94,000 men the figure was 94 tons daily and almost 2,000 tons for the three weeks – as an easy rule of thumb one ton of food per 1,000 men every day. For meat, great reliance was placed on beef, sheep or hogs on the hoof. It is estimated that twenty-five cattle were needed to feed twenty-five men for a month, which explains why huge herds were rounded up and taken overland (twenty herders were needed for 1,000 head of cattle), accompanying the troops on the march until they were butchered. If every man in the Army of Northern Virginia was to get his full meat ration during the month-long Gettysburg campaign, nearly 3,000 cattle required slaughtering. To keep the horses and mules healthy they needed a diet of not less than 12 pounds of grain a day, plus a similar amount of hay. Assuming some 75,000 horses were involved, their daily needs amounted to some 900 tons of grain and hay.

Neither men nor animals got anything like these quantities on a regular basis and suffered accordingly. Many men and horses of both armies went into battle at Gettysburg hungry and weak as a result of a combination of hard marching and insufficient, poor-quality rations or fodder. The exceptions were perhaps the Confederates in Ewell's Corps, who had done relatively well for food and other supplies since crossing the Potomac (leading elements on June 15) and spreading out on their main mission as the advance guard of the army – foraging. Meade's troops and horses certainly suffered from lack of food during the battle itself as his subsistence and commissary train of some 3,500–4,000 wagons, together with a huge herd of cattle, did not arrive at the forward base at Westminster 25 miles away until July 2. Most wagons sent forward on July 3 could not deliver supplies because of the fighting, so it would be the next day before thousands of men got their rations, having consumed what was in their haversacks several days before.

By early 1863 Virginia had suffered for months from the depredations of the Army of the Potomac camping, marching, foraging and fighting on its soil. The Yankees had been ruthless in their seizing of supplies of all kinds. They considered themselves an army of occupation entitled to take what they needed. Add to this the presence of the Army of Northern Virginia and it is easy to understand why Virginia had been stripped bare, with many of its farms ruined by the spring of that year. By April Lee had become seriously worried that his army was disintegrating for lack of food supplies and fodder. He scattered his cavalry and some artillery batteries far and wide in search of provisions, while Longstreet's entire corps was sent south, and thus missed Chancellorsville, largely because Lee's supply system could not sustain it. On April 16 he had written to President Davis concerning "the present immobility of the army owing to the condition of our horses and the scarcity of forage and provisions." A primary reason for Lee's marching north and taking the war out of Virginia and into the fat farms of Pennsylvania was so that his troops and animals could eat.

Supplies of all types had to be located or manufactured, procured/assembled, stored and delivered or collected. Without transportation and roads, railroads or rivers (lines of communication) none of these activities was possible. The organization and systems of supply used by both sides during the Civil War were almost identical because the South, as with many other military activities, tended to copy those of the North. This was because they were familiar to Confederate officers from the old U.S. Army who had resigned to come South at the outbreak of hostilities. The systems in use for the Gettysburg campaign, under the headings of "Supplies" and "Transportation" are examined below.

Supplies

By 1863 the logistical support system for both armies was divided among four military supply departments or bureaus reporting to the respective Secretaries of War. The Quartermaster General was responsible for the provision of clothing, equipment, pay, animals (but not cavalry horses in the Confederacy), forage and transportation; the Commissary General provided rations; the Chief of Ordnance weapons, ammunition and associated equipment; and the Surgeon General medical supplies. Each department was charged with the procurement and distribution of their respective commodities, but it was the Quartermaster General who had the everlasting headache of providing transport for all of them. An essential element of success in getting all types of supplies to the troops was effective cooperation between departments – a commodity frequently lacking, although at most depots the quartermaster and commissary were located together.

Supplies were centralized at depots of varying size and importance. The map opposite shows the main depots established at railheads relevant to the Gettysburg campaign; it does not attempt to show the many smaller field depots set up by the commanders of the geographic military districts, or in the course of a particular campaign. For the Confederates the main supply bases in the Gettysburg campaign were Richmond and Staunton (both off the map), with a forward railhead at Culpeper Court House coming into operation later, and Winchester, which became a base (but not a railhead) after its capture. Field armies normally drew their supplies from the forward depots/railheads on wagons for forward transportation and distribution to their units.

The logistical organizational structure was based on the various subordinate formations and units down to regiment. At Gettysburg at army headquarters Meade had a brigadier (Rufus Ingalls) as chief quartermaster; a colonel (Henry F. Clarke) as chief commissary of subsistence; a captain (Daniel W. Flagler) as chief of ordnance; and a major (Dr. Jonathan Letterman) as medical director. The relative importance of the duties of these logistical staff officers is roughly indicated by their rank, with the quartermaster and commissary officers having the greatest responsibility and the most taxing difficulties in their implementation. Lee's headquarters contained a lieutenant-colonel each as chief quartermaster (James L. Corley), chief commissary of subsistence (Robertson G. Cole) and chief of ordnance (Briscoe G. Baldwin), with a surgeon (Lafayette Guild) as medical director. Formations down to brigade all had logistics staff officers on their establishments, although by Gettysburg not all had been formalized by

Notes

- This map shows the huge advantage in terms of nearness of supply bases, and railroad links to them, of the Army of the Potomac when deployed along the Rappahannock River and around Fredericksburg before the start of the campaign in May and early June 1863. The Union's main supply bases were at the Washington D.C./Alexandria complex, Baltimore and Aquia. Maximum use was made of trawlers to tow barges laden with stores and equipment from Alexandria to Aquia to keep the army at Fredericksburg supplied. From these bases there were good, short railroad links ❶ forward to rail depots at Manassas Juntion and Culpeper Court House (before the Confederates occupied the area), or at Harper's Ferry for the troops at Winchester. As the Union forces moved north in June they had equally good railroad links ❷ to forward depots established at Frederick and Westminster. After July 6 Meade was able to benefit from the opening of the railroad as far as Gettysburg. ❸
- In contrast, Lee's army relied on the main base at Richmond and a forward railhead at Staunton over 60 miles southeast of Culpeper – this latter was only a temporary Confederate railhead for a comparatively short time in June, when it became Lee's assembly area from which he launched his invasion. Once the Army of Northern Virginia left Culpeper and moved into the Shenandoah Valley and thence northward, all supplies from Staunton had to be brought forward on slow-moving wagon trains – which is one reason why so much emphasis was placed on local foraging once north of the Potomac.
- The Rebels captured Winchester and Martinsburg on June 14–15 and with them secured 28 pieces of artillery, 300 loaded wagons, 300 horses, 6,000 bushels of grain and other quartermaster and commissary supplies – a rich haul. Thereafter Winchester became a forward Confederate supply base, although there was no rail link to Staunton 50 miles to the south. It was used as a major collecting point for cattle, horses and other supplies that were sent south – after the army had taken their requirements.

Key

main Union supply base

Union forward railhead/base

Gettysburg – Union railhead established from July 6

Culpeper Court House

Confederate forward base

Union railroad link to forward bases

temporary Confederate railroad link

approximate route of main body of Army of the Potomac to Gettysburg

approximate route of Army of Northern Virginia to Gettysburg

route of Early's Division to Gettysburg

❶❷❸ Union rail supply routes as the army moved north

❹ temporary Confederate rail link to the south

wwwwww main Confederate cavalry raids on Union rail communications

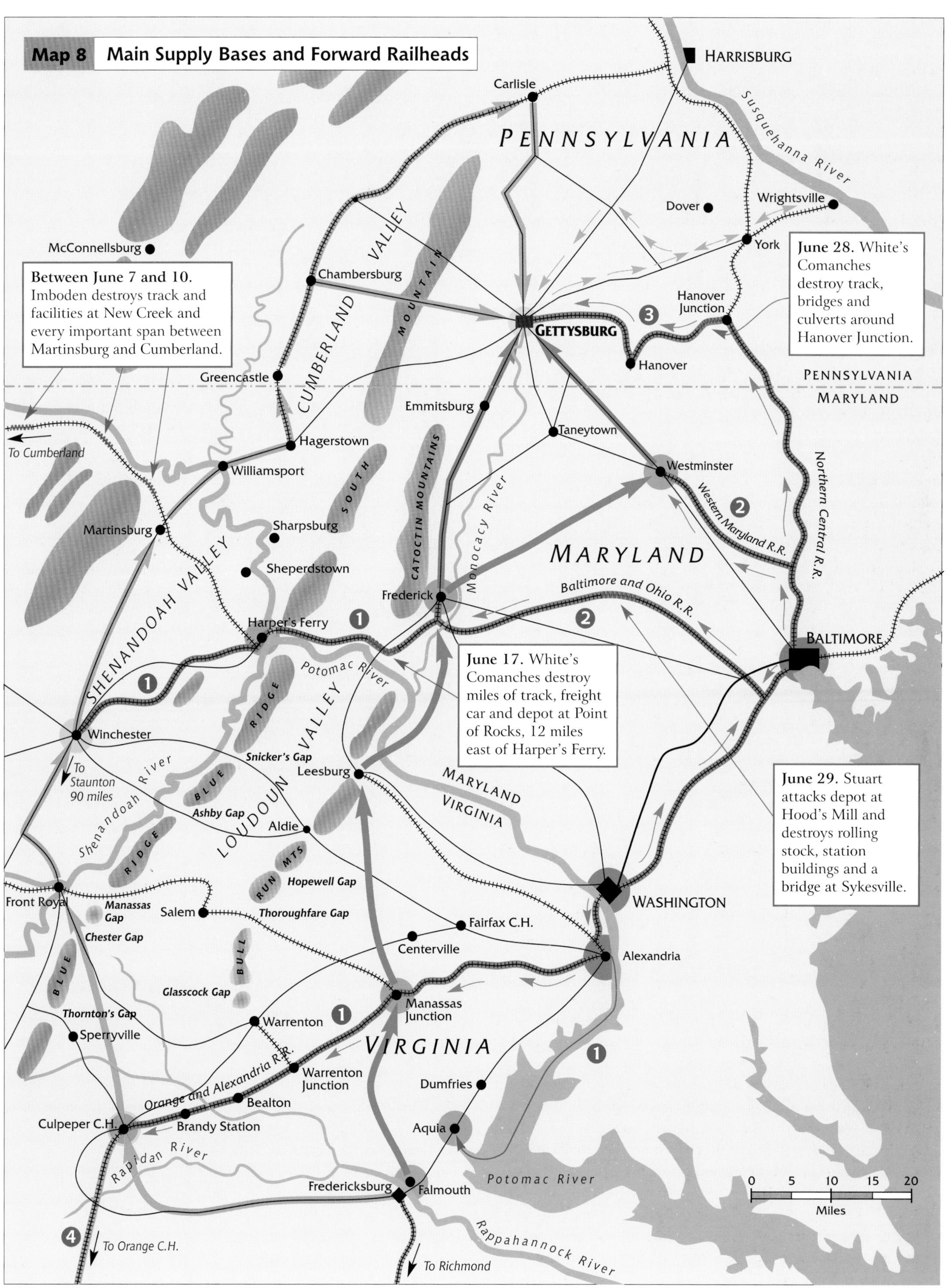
Map 8 Main Supply Bases and Forward Railheads
HARRISBURG
Carlisle
PENNSYLVANIA
Susquehanna River
Wrightsville
Dover
York
McConnellsburg
Between June 7 and 10. Imboden destroys track and facilities at New Creek and every important span between Martinsburg and Cumberland.
Chambersburg
CUMBERLAND VALLEY
MOUNTAIN
June 28. White's Comanches destroy track, bridges and culverts around Hanover Junction.
Hanover Junction
GETTYSBURG
Hanover
PENNSYLVANIA
MARYLAND
Greencastle
Emmitsburg
Taneytown
Hagerstown
To Cumberland
Williamsport
Westminster
Western Maryland R.R.
Northern Central R.R.
SOUTH
CATOCTIN MOUNTAINS
Monocacy River
Sharpsburg
Martinsburg
MARYLAND
Sheperdstown
Baltimore and Ohio R.R.
Frederick
SHENANDOAH VALLEY
Harper's Ferry
BALTIMORE
Potomac River
June 17. White's Comanches destroy miles of track, freight car and depot at Point of Rocks, 12 miles east of Harper's Ferry.
RIDGE
LOUDOUN VALLEY
Winchester
To Staunton 90 miles
Snicker's Gap
Leesburg
Shenandoah River
BLUE
MARYLAND
VIRGINIA
June 29. Stuart attacks depot at Hood's Mill and destroys rolling stock, station buildings and a bridge at Sykesville.
Ashby Gap
Aldie
RIDGE
BULL RUN MTS
Hopewell Gap
Front Royal
WASHINGTON
Manassas Gap
Salem
Thoroughfare Gap
Chester Gap
Fairfax C.H.
Centerville
Alexandria
BLUE
BULL
Glasscock Gap
Thornton's Gap
Manassas Junction
Sperryville
Warrenton
VIRGINIA
Orange and Alexandria R.R.
Warrenton Junction
Dumfries
Bealton
Culpeper C.H.
Brandy Station
Aquia
Rapidan River
Potomac River
Fredericksburg
Falmouth
0 5 10 15 20
Miles
To Orange C.H.
Rappahannock River
To Richmond

their respective governments. For example, in the Union Army at corps level a lieutenant-colonel was authorized as chief quartermaster and chief commissary, at division a major supposedly held the appointment of quartermaster and another of commissary, while at brigade captains acted as assistant quartermasters and assistant commissaries. In practice this was seldom the situation. At Gettysburg the only Union formation headquarters staff that specifically lists staff officers of the correct rank in all three major supply posts was the Cavalry Corps – it had lieutenant-colonels controlling the Quartermaster, Commissary and Ordnance Departments. With the Confederates it was usual for a major to hold these three key appointments at corps level. Nevertheless, despite the differences from authorized posts and ranks, every formation or unit from regiment upward had an officer whose duty it was to indent for, collect and distribute supplies, even if in addition to his other staff responsibilities and not specific in his title.

At regimental level the regimental quartermaster was frequently tasked with supervising all supplies including rations, but was usually assisted in these duties by senior N.C.O.s. At Gettysburg the 17th Maine, a typical Union infantry regiment, had a quartermaster (First Lieutenant Josiah Remick), a quartermaster-sergeant (John Yeaton), a commissary-sergeant (John F. Putnam) and a hospital steward (Nathaniel B. Coleman). There was no N.C.O. nominated to assist with ordnance. By way of comparison, the 19th Virginia Infantry's headquarters contained a captain as quartermaster (James E. Blair), a first lieutenant (John T. Blair, brother of the quartermaster) as assistant commissary, a quartermaster-sergeant (W. A. Mason), an ordnance sergeant (George A. Gulley) and a hospital steward (Charles W. Lewellyn).

Lack of space in this book precludes examining every problem besetting both sides in supplying their troops in the field, so as Lee's men were, at the start, suffering the most from inadequate logistical support, their difficulties, and how they sought to solve them, are enumerated below.

Shortages and the A.N.V.

By 1863 Virginia had run out of the means of sustaining the Army of Northern Virginia. It had been denuded by the seemingly everlasting presence of two opposing armies that had consumed the state's produce like a swarm of locusts. As early as 1862 Lee had been informed by Colonel Lucius B. Northrop, the commissary general in Richmond, that he was to cut his men's meat ration; he refused. In November an infuriated Northrop got the Secretary of War, George W. Randolph, to order Lee to comply. Lee's forthright objection was ignored. Transport difficulties prevented meat from being brought from elsewhere, and in January 1863 Northrop insisted the meager meat ration, down to a quarter of a pound a day, be supplemented by extra sugar rather than meat. Again Lee appealed in vain, with Northrop going as far as to complain that commanding generals "should not be permitted to issue any order respecting rations whatever." By April 1863, with only about 400,000 pounds of meat arriving in the previous three months, Lee's army was facing starvation. His frustration with this intractable problem is clear from his comment that "the question of *food for this army* gives me more trouble and uneasiness *than everything else combined*" (emphasis in original). His army was to march and fight throughout the summer months of that year by subsisting on a combination of local purchase, impressments, requisitioning, some delivery from depots, theft and capture of enemy stocks. It was entirely a hand-to-mouth existence with serious consequences for the health of the army. In March 1863 Lee's medical director, Dr. Lafayette Guild, directed that surgeons with all formations should encourage the collection of vegetables and greenery such as wild mustard, watercress, peas, and pickles to counter the outbreaks of scurvy that were becoming worryingly common throughout the army.

This chronic lack of supplies was a longstanding problem for Lee. When asked after the war why he had crossed the Potomac before the Sharpsburg (Antietam) campaign in September 1862 he replied, "Because my men had nothing to eat, I went to Maryland to feed my army." He had written to President Davis on September 12 that year from Hagerstown, Maryland:

> We have found in this city about fifteen hundred barrels of flour . . . the supply of beef has been very small, and we have been able to secure no bacon. A thousand pairs of shoes and some clothing were obtained in Frederickstown, two hundred and fifty pairs in Williamsport, and about four hundred pairs in this city. They will not be sufficient to cover the bare feet of the army.

In Virginia in 1863 Lee found himself still in the unenviable situation for any general, where a large army was likely to starve and a small one likely to be defeated. As noted above, Lee was obliged to scatter his cavalry in search of foodstuffs for both men and animals and to fight Chancellorsville with an entire corps away foraging for itself and the army in eastern South Carolina. Early that year Lee's quartermaster undertook to supply 45 tons of forage a day from North Carolina by rail – about half the army's requirement – but managed only 15. Every ton received by rail had then to be hauled in wagons another 70 miles to reach the animals that were to eat it.

Clifford Dowdey, in his book *Lee & His Men at Gettysburg*, suggests, "the Gettysburg campaign can be called the largest commissary raid in the history of modern warfare, and the desperate necessity was symptomatic of the collapse of Confederate resources." This was hardly an exaggeration. For every thought Lee gave to the strategy of his forthcoming invasion surely five were devoted to logistics, the securing and transportation of supplies ranging from food and ammunition to shoes for men, mules and horses. Once the campaign got under way, dependence on the normal method of supply trains following an army was supplemented by, indeed superseded by, massive foraging, requisitioning and the capture of enemy stocks.

Foraging and requisitioning

These activities also included impressment and outright theft. Impressment was the compulsory purchase of supplies, be they food, fodder, horses, cattle, hogs, chickens, wagons, carts, tools or equipment, from friendly civilians. It was not popular, as payment was usually well below the market price and thus the owner was cheated. Lee objected on moral grounds and preferred to appeal to the patriotism of local Southern farmers, which usually worked. Requisitioning from farms and towns in Northern territory was an entirely different matter, and was the primary method of provisioning during the Gettysburg campaign once Lee's troops entered Maryland and Pennsylvania. Leading the way, strapped to his saddle, was the one-legged Lieutenant-General Richard S. Ewell, commanding the 2rd Corps. He had led the Confederate advance by nearly two weeks and had been instructed to supply his command off the country when in Pennsylvania and at the same time to send all surplus south for the use of the rest of the army. In this Ewell was reasonably successful as his report later made clear:

> we reached Carlisle on the 27th [June], halting one day at Chambersburg to secure supplies . . . At Carlisle, General George H. Steuart . . . rejoined the corps, bringing some cattle and horses. At Carlisle, Chambersburg and Shippensburg, requisitions were made for supplies, and the shops were searched, many valuable stores being secured. At Chambersburg, a [wagon] train was loaded with ordnance and medical stores and sent back. Near 3,000 head of cattle were collected and sent back by my corps, and my chief commissary of subsistence, Major W. J. Hawks, notified [Lieutenant] Colonel R.G. Cole [Lee's commissary chief] of the location of 5,000 barrels of flour along the route traveled by the command . . . General Early levied a contribution on the citizens of York, obtaining among other things, $28,600 in United States currency, the greater part of which was turned over to [Lieutenant] Colonel Corley, chief quartermaster, Army of Northern Virginia; 1,000 hats, 1,200 pairs of shoes and 1,000 pairs of socks were also obtained here.

Ewell, with Jenkins' horsemen riding ahead, had done his best to strip the Cumberland Valley of anything useful to the army. During the week prior to the battle Ewell had sent his men raiding, requisitioning and destroying railroads and culverts from as far afield as McConnellsburg in the west to Wrightsville on the Susquehanna River 80 miles to the east. However, he had largely followed his commander's instructions with regard to the prohibition of outright looting and wanton destruction (apart from fence rails for campfires and Early's destruction of an iron foundry; see boxes below and page 222) of private property. However, hundreds of "Dutch" farmers and storekeepers would argue that requisitioning left them with little or no livestock or supplies in return for a fistful of unusable Confederate money, or a receipt that was unlikely to be honored even if the Rebels won the war, and was tantamount to robbery. On June 29 and 30, during the concentration of Lee's army toward the Gettysburg area, the task of escorting Ewell's huge wagon train crammed with two weeks' foraging and impressments was given to Johnson's Division. His route was through the Cashtown Pass and his enormous column seriously delayed the movement of other troops along the Cashtown–Gettysburg road.

An example of the requisitioning procedure, although not a very rewarding one, occurred in Chambersburg (probably the hardest-hit town of the campaign in terms of Rebel requisitioning) on June 28. Major Raphael J. Moses, Longstreet's chief commissary officer, who was to become a legendary and normally highly successful scrounger, carried it out. The British observer, Colonel Fremantle, later described Moses' activities that day:

> Major Moses tells me that his orders are to open the stores in Chambersburg by force, and seize all that is wanted for the army in a regular and official manner, giving in return its value in Confederate money or a receipt. The storekeepers have, doubtless, sent away their most valuable goods on the approach of the Confederate Army. Much also had already been seized by Ewell, who passed through nearly a week ago. But Moses was much elated at having already discovered a large supply of excellent felt hats

A Requisition by Ewell's Corps

To the authorities of Chambersburg, Pennsylvania:

HEAD-QUARTERS SECOND ARMY CORPS
June 24th, 1863.

By direction of Lieutenant-General R.S. Ewell, I require the following articles: 5,000 suits of clothing, including hats, boots and shoes; 100 good saddles; 100 good bridles; 500 bushels of grain (corn or oats); 10,000 lbs. sole leather; 10,000 lbs. horse-shoe nails; also the use of printing office and two printers to report at once. All articles except grain will be delivered to the Court-House Square, at 3:00 o'clock P.M., to-day, and grain by 6:00 o'clock P.M. today.

J.A. Harman
Major and C. Q. M. Second Corps D'Arm.

On the same day two further requisitions covering, among other things, harness leather, picket ropes, curry combs, 400 pistols, 50,000 pounds of bread, 500 barrels of flour, 11,000 pounds of coffee, the same amount of sugar, 25 barrels of beans and 25 of dried fruit. As we know, Ewell received virtually nothing from these demands.

Stealing Fence Rails

Fence rails were not supposed to be taken, but this was surely the rule that was most ignored by both sides during the march to Gettysburg. Fence rails were usually the only source of firewood for cooking or to use as poles for a bivouac tent. On June 13, in the Blue Ridge Mountains, the 3rd South Carolina bivouacked for the night in the open with a light rain falling. In the morning Colonel James D. Nance, in command of the regiment, summoned the company commanders to headquarters. One by one he asked each officer if his men had taken rails during the night, starting with Captain Richardson of Company A.

> "Did your men take any rails?"
> "Yes, sir."
> "Did you have them put back?"
> "Yes, sir."
> "Captain Garry, did your men use any rails?"
> "Yes, sir."
> "Did you have them replaced?"
> "No, sir."

All the officers down to Company K admitted their rails had not been put back, except for Richardson. The furious colonel harangued them on their crime and finished with the words,

"Now, gentlemen, let this never occur again. For the present you will deliver your swords to Adjutant Pope, turn your companies over to your next officer in command, and march in rear of the regiment until further orders."

Only Captain Richardson was absolved from this humiliation. The punishment only lasted a day, but it was not forgotten.

hidden away in a cellar, which he annexed at once . . .
Moses proceeded into town at eleven o'clock a.m. with an official requisition (from General Longstreet), for three days rations for the whole army in this neighborhood [Longstreet's Corps alone had some 21,000 men, so three days' rations was a minimum of 10 tons, probably a lot more]. These rations he is to seize by force, if not voluntarily supplied . . . Neither the mayor nor the corporation officers were to be found anywhere, nor were the keys of the principal stores forthcoming until Moses began to apply the ax . . . Major Moses did not get back till very late, much depressed at the ill success of his mission. He has searched all day most indefatigably, and had endured much contumely from the Union ladies, who called him a "thievish, little rebel scoundrel," and other opprobrious epithets. This did not annoy him so much as the manner in which everything he wanted had been sent away or hidden in private houses, which he was not allowed by General Lee's order to search. He has only managed to secure a quantity of molasses, sugar and whisky.

As with Ewell before him, in not taking from private households as distinct from stores, farms or commercial concerns, Major Moses was complying with Lee's General Order No. 72, dated June 21. That stipulated, "No private property shall be injured or destroyed by any person belonging to or connected with the army, or taken, excepting by the officers hereinafter designated." It then went on to designate the Commissary, Quartermaster, Ordnance and Medical Departments. Apart from the fact that the wording could be interpreted as allowing designated officers to remove goods from private property, there was no attempt to define all-embracing phrases such as "necessary supplies" or how to calculate "market value." Thus it was easy for requisitioning officers to take what they wanted and pay what they wanted in a currency useless to the recipient. In his book *The Great Invasion*, Chambersburg resident Jacob Hoke told of his experiences that day, and explained why Moses only got molasses "which General Ewell had kindly left us" from his store:

> These [molasses] we would have removed with our stock of dry goods, but the cellar was deep and the hogsheads heavy, and we were unable to draw them out. The Confederates [Moses' men], however, were equal to the occasion, and when thirty or forty of them took hold of the ropes, they soon had them all up in front of the store [for wagons to remove].

Hoke went on to say that careful note was made of everything taken while he stood by and agreed the number and weight of each barrel. He was even allowed to keep what he needed for his personal use. And "the following day Major Moses . . . rode around to each place plundered and paid for the things taken."

Despite Lee's order, not all requisitioning was carried out as meticulously in accordance with the rules as Major Moses' in Chambersburg. Most Rebels, officers included, were angry before they reached Northern soil, and with good cause. Union troops in the South had not been particular about private property. In the battles around Fredericksburg and elsewhere the Yankees had taken what they wanted and vandalized what they liked, regardless of ownership, and no payments were made or offered. Thus many, probably the great majority, of Lee's men marching through Maryland or Pennsylvania considered the time for retribution had arrived. This anger, reinforced by hunger and bleeding feet, meant that some requisitioning slid easily into looting, to which a minority of officers, mostly junior regimental ones, turned a blind eye. An example was Captain Edmund D. Patterson of Alabama, who was captured at Gettysburg and spent many months in a Yankee prison; he wrote in his diary on June 28:

> Some of the boys have been "capturing" chickens. It is against positive orders, but I would not punish one of them, for as Joe McMurray says, it's not half as bad as they did [to] his mother and sisters in Alabama, for they not only took such things, but took the rings from his sisters' fingers, and earrings from their ears, besides cursing and abusing them.

As noted above, the richest pickings in Pennsylvania went to the cavalry under Jenkins (and Imboden) leading the advance of Ewell's Corps, with his infantry a close second. Those following got the supplies that Ewell's men had overlooked, or that were sent back in wagons or on the hoof as surplus to his needs. Private John O. Casler, 33rd Virginia (Stonewall) Brigade, later recalled:

> General Lee had orders out that we were not to molest any of the citizens, or take any private property, and any soldier caught plundering would be shot . . . But our quartermasters managed to gobble up everything they came to. They would take the citizens horses [a top foraging priority] and wagons and load them up with provisions and goods from the stores; consequently we accumulated an immense train. The cavalry were in front and on our flanks, and they had a good chance

Early Burns an Iron Works

Lee had issued very forthright and specific orders that there should be no deliberate destruction of property by his troops while they were north of the Potomac. The only significant act in defiance of this order was the burning of the Caledonian Iron Works (including the furnace, saw mill, two forges and a rolling mill) on the orders of Major-General Early on June 26. These works were owned by a Radical Republican by the name of Thaddeus H. Stevens. In 1886, in a letter to the historian Professor J. Fraise, Richard Early gave his reasons for this act of destruction, which put several hundred people out of work:

> My reasons for giving the order were founded on the fact that the Federal troops had invariably burned such works in the South . . . notably among them the iron works of Hon. John Bell, of Tennessee . . . Moreover, in some speeches in congress, Mr Stevens had exhibited a most vindictive spirit toward the people of the South . . . This burning was simply in retaliation for various deeds of barbarity perpetrated by Federal troops in some of the Southern States . . .

Mr. Stevens had obviously infuriated Early, as not only did he lose his iron works but Early's men and others made off with some forty horses and mules, $10,000 worth of goods from the company store, iron bar valued at $4,000, a large amount of grain, used up 80 tons of grazing grass and destroyed all his fence rails. To finish things off, his workers' houses had their windows smashed. Apparently Mr. Stevens was amazingly philosophical about such a huge loss and was heard to congratulate the Rebels on doing such a thorough job!

of plundering and getting good horses. They made good use of it, too, and came out well supplied; but the infantry got nothing but what we could eat, but we got plenty of that. As soon as we would go into camp [bivouac] in the evening some of the soldiers would strike out into the country, before they had time to put out a guard, and would come back loaded with "grub" . . . cherries were ripe while we were in Pennsylvania, and there were a great many trees along the road. We stripped them both of cherries and limbs, leaving nothing but the trunks.

Capture of enemy supplies

This was an important adjunct to the more usual foraging but was never sufficient in itself to do more than provide a useful, but intermittent, boost to supplies. While Union troops were not averse to taking Rebel stocks, use of enemy supplies of all descriptions was more a Confederate specialty. On virtually every battlefield some Rebels went into action riding Union horses or wearing Union uniform jackets, hats and shoes, many scavenged from battlefields. Some fired Union bullets or shells from Union guns, and carried their supplies in wagons with U.S. painted on the canvas sides and often drawn by Union mules. During the campaigning in June 1863, prior to Gettysburg, there were three substantial Rebel captures of enemy supplies and equipment:

- On June 13 Rodes secured enemy supplies after a brief clash at Berryville, while the next day at Martinsburg he captured five cannon and caissons, 400 rounds of rifled artillery ammunition, some small arms and ammunition, 6,000 bushels of grain, various other commissary stores and two excellent ambulances.
- On June 14 and 15 Ewell took Winchester and the nearby Stephenson's Depot. The combined haul, despite the Union garrison sending 114 wagonloads of supplies to safety on June 11, was considerable. The list included 300 loaded wagons, 300 horses, 200,000 rounds of rifle/musket ammunition, and 23 artillery pieces (seventeen 3-inch rifles, four 20-pounder Parrotts and two 24-pounder howitzers).
- On June 28 Stuart's cavalry captured a large Union wagon train mostly carrying grain, but also bacon, sugar, hams and bottled whiskey, south of Rockville. The wild and exciting chase ensured the Rebel yell was heard within 4 miles of Washington. There were around 150 wagons but a number were wrecked when they overturned in their dash to escape – these were then burned but the mules retained. According to Stuart's report, "More than one hundred and twenty-five best United States model wagons and splendid teams with gay caparisons were secured and driven off. The mules and harness of the broken wagons were also secured." (See page 201 and box, page 311.)

Meade's opportunity to effect captures on a large scale occurred during the Confederate retreat from Gettysburg starting on July 4. Whether he was successful is discussed in Section Twelve: The Aftermath.

How successful was the Rebels' foraging?

Although Lee's aim of living off the farms and towns of Pennsylvania was largely successful in so far as food, fodder, some clothes and wagons were concerned, it is impossible to quantify accurately the total take for the various categories of supplies in the weeks leading up to the battle. The big disappointment was shoes for the soldiers and horses, particularly cavalry mounts. Even Gettysburg, a comparatively large town, failed to meet Early's demands on June 26. All he was able to secure were a few items when the stores were opened, along with some horseshoes and nails, plus U.S.$5,000 in cash.

Edwin B. Coddington, in his book *The Gettysburg Campaign*, quotes four sources that indicate a substantial haul at least in terms of cattle and sheep taken. First, Fitzgerald Ross, in his book *Citizens and Camps of the Confederate States*, claimed that the Confederates obtained enough supplies to sustain the army for several months, and also secured horses and wagons in "incalculable numbers" – although this could hardly apply to suitable cavalry horses. He also said the army butchered 300 cattle every day to ensure the men got an adequate meat ration – this number would supply only around 7,500 men at twenty-five men per animal – but he omitted to mention the large quantities of sheep, hogs and poultry that were consumed. Next, Major-General John Sedgwick's letter to his sister, dated July 26, 1863, in *Correspondence of Sedgwick*, II, states, "we captured twelve thousand head of cattle and eight thousand head of sheep that the enemy [Confederates] had driven from Pennsylvania." Third, G. W. Nichols' *A Soldier's Story of his Regiment*, written many years after the war, recounts how at a big bend in the Shenandoah River, near Mount Jackson, Virginia, he saw 2,000–3,000 acres of land packed with cattle and sheep. A herdsman told him there were some 26,000 cattle and 22,000 sheep taken from Maryland and Pennsylvania corralled there. Finally, Spencer Glasgow Welch, in a letter dated July 17, 1863, and published in *A Confederate Surgeon's Letters to his Wife*, wrote, "We gathered up thousands of beeves in Pennsylvania – enough to feed our army until cold weather."

It is impossible to know precisely how many animals were rounded up during the campaign by Lee's foraging efforts. However, judging by the above and by the fact that Winchester became a collecting point for thousands of animals not accompanying the army into Pennsylvania, a reasonable estimate would be up to 50,000 cattle, 30,000 sheep, 20,000 horses and mules, plus thousands of hogs. These figures would include the foraging that continued in the vicinity of Gettysburg during the three days of fighting. Damage claims by the citizens of Adams County show that hundreds of cattle, sheep, horses and hogs, along with flour, grain and wagons were commandeered by Lee's quartermasters and commissaries during the battle.

Transportation

The two basic requirements for any supply system were, and still are, procurement and distribution. For the former the prerequisites are availability and money, largely outside the scope of this book; the latter depends on means of transportation (a major responsibility of the quartermaster general of both armies). During the Gettysburg campaign supplies were transported by rail, river and road.

Rail (Map 8)

The Civil War saw the first large-scale use of railroads in wartime. This new mode of transportation was a critical factor in the outcome of several campaigns and battles. By the end of 1860 the nation possessed some 30,600 miles of railroad – about 8,500 miles in the seceded states and over 22,000 in the North. Not only were there more miles of track in the North but there were also more connecting branch lines, making for easier long-distance movement and greater flexibility. In the South the only route east to west from Richmond to the Mississippi was via Chattanooga and across southern Tennessee to Memphis – all other routes were circuitous and fraught with endless delays and other difficulties.

Both sides appreciated the critical importance of the strategic and tactical use of railroads. One boxcar carried up to 20 tons of stores or supplies. A flat car had the same carrying capacity but with greater flexibility as to the type of load. It could take two army wagons filled with supplies with room to stuff other stores under and between. Then there was the question of speed. Six mules pulled a wagon carrying 1.5 tons a distance of 2.5 miles an hour – on reasonable roads – but an engine could pull sixteen rail cars with a total load of over 300 tons and cover 15 miles in the hour.

For the North it was the great east–west route of the Baltimore and Ohio Railroad that was vital strategically for the movement of troops and supplies between distant theaters of operations, and tactically in supporting armies in Maryland and Pennsylvania. If Baltimore fell – and it was a possible distant objective of Lee's invasion – the Confederates would have cut the only railroad linking Washington to the rest of the Union. During the Gettysburg campaign the Baltimore and Ohio initially supplied the forward base at Winchester via a branch line from the larger one at Harper's Ferry. However, when these were lost as the Confederates advanced up the Shenandoah Valley in mid-June, Union supplies were easily switched to a railhead at Frederick. Nevertheless, throughout much of the war the North had a constant struggle to maintain this particular railroad from Confederate raids – during June 1863 it was attacked in several places by Imboden, White's Commanches and Stuart. By 1865 some 18,000 men were deployed protecting this vulnerable lifeline. See Map 8.

How to Destroy Railroad Tracks

There were three stages in the well-organized destruction of a length of rail track, requiring three separate parties, each with a different task. The first group spread out along the track with one man opposite each wooden tie (sleeper). At a given signal that section of line was raised on edge and tipped over. The ties were then pried loose from the rails and the first group moved on to the next section of track to repeat the process. Meanwhile, the second party piled up the ties and placed the rails on top before setting fire to the ties. When the rails were red hot, the third party took over with their pinchers and "railroad hooks" to twist the rails and bend them round trees. Unless it was bent into a very small U, a rail could be straightened quite easily, but a twisted rail would have to go back to a rolling mill. To damage rails successfully, the job had to be done thoroughly, and it required plenty of time and personnel – commodities not usually available.

The North used railroads ruthlessly and efficiently. In January 1862 Congress authorized the President to seize control of railroads and telegraph for military use whenever necessary, although most traffic was conducted in accordance with an early agreement on costs between the government and the northern railroad companies. A new war department entitled the U.S. Military Rail Roads (U.S.M.R.R.) operated any railroads seized by the military. Senior and experienced civilian railroad officials were commissioned into the army and continued to do their jobs in uniform. Daniel C. McCallum, formerly general superintendent of the Erie Railroad, was made a brigadier-general and became the director of the U.S.M.R.R. Brigadier-General Herman Haupt (a West Point graduate who resigned three weeks after commissioning in 1856), once chief engineer of the Pennsylvania Railroad, became chief of construction and transportation in the Virginia theater.

During the Gettysburg campaign Haupt controlled an organization of full-time construction and transportation experts to run the railroads in Virginia, Maryland and Pennsylvania. His department was divided into a Construction and a Transportation Corps, the former building and repairing, the latter running the trains. The Construction Corps consisted of professional engineers, skilled workmen and manual laborers (civilians paid $2 a day, putting them on the level of an infantry captain) who were provided with materials, tools and their own transport. The emphasis during the campaign was on speed of repairs of track and bridges. Prefabricated components were used and the military railroad yards in Alexandria had special teams working continually on straightening twisted rails for reuse.

Haupt's contribution to the success of the Army of the Potomac in June and July 1863, indeed for much of the war, was outstanding. The campaign began with the army situated at Falmouth, near the railhead at Aquia Creek on the Potomac River. Railroad cars loaded with full wagons could run straight through Washington to Alexandria, where they were loaded onto barges carrying eight cars apiece. Steam-powered tugs took the barges down the Potomac to Aquia Creek where the cars were reassembled into railroad trains that ran on to Falmouth. A sixteen-car train could run from Washington to Falmouth perhaps carrying as much as 300 tons in just twelve hours without any offloading. This vast accumulation of stores and supplies around the Falmouth area meant that, to prevent its capture, large quantities had to be destroyed when Hooker moved north. On June 14 soldiers of the Union VI Corps watched in amazement the wholesale destruction of war material, commissary stores and the dismantling of a hospital at Potomac Creek, 4 miles north of Falmouth. In a letter to his brother, dated June 20, 1863, Private Daniel Faust wrote:

> There was lots of things destroyed on this march. There was millions of dollars worth of tents and wagons and ammunition burned. The road was strewn with broken guns and such stuff. If a wagon upset . . . they just unhitched the horses [and mules] and set fire to [it] with the load on and all.

However, as Hooker's, or Meade's, men came north, railheads opened successively on the Orange and Alexandria (Manassas Junction), Baltimore and Ohio (Frederick), Western Maryland (Westminster) and, finally, on July 6, at Gettysburg via a branch from the Northern Central. The depot at Westminster was receiving a shuttle of fifteen trains a day during the battle. After the battle the decrepit Western Maryland was running at five times its normal capacity, delivering 1,500 tons of supplies a day to Westminster, while the Gettysburg line assisted in the evacuation of 16,000 wounded. Throughout Hooker's, and then Meade's, campaign of maneuvering, first north to confront Lee at Gettysburg and then during the pursuit, Haupt and the U.S.M.R.R. maintained virtually continuous support to forward railheads, each within comparatively short distances from the army.

While in the North the military use of railroads was paramount, the same did not always apply in the South, where it was largely "business as usual" for the railroad companies, with passengers and private freight shipped alongside military stores, sometimes taking precedence over them. Civilian officials, despite many attempts to get cooperation and coordinate rail transportation, continued to run their affairs as best suited the finances of the railroad company. Civilian control extended right up to a forward railhead, often leaving quartermasters and commissary officers at the mercy of these officials, sometimes to the army's detriment. While the Army of Northern Virginia was deployed around Fredericksburg and along the Rapidan River there was a direct rail link south to Richmond. However, much to Lee's frustration, it was inefficient and unreliable – hardly surprising, as its superintendent turned out to be a Federal agent! Once the campaign got under way, a Confederate forward railhead was established at Culpeper Court House, but that was the furthest north that a railhead could be used as the invasion progressed. North to Front Royal and thence to the next major depot set up at Winchester, supplies moved by wagon, at the pace of a mule.

Road

In June and July 1863, to move supplies from railhead to battlefield, first Hooker then Meade, and Lee relied on roads and tracks. The means of movement was the ubiquitous army wagon, sometimes pulled by horses, but far more often by mules. Although virtually any farm wagon, cart or carriage could be drafted into service, it was the four-wheel cart, about 10 feet long, topped by wooden hoops covered in canvas, that occupied the roads in their tens of thousands throughout the war. The standard Union wagon usually had the letters "U.S." and the corps badge and number or name of the formation to which it was attached painted on the canvas sides. A Rebel wagon train was invariably a more motley collection of vehicles than a Yankee one and included a mixture of civilian carts and army wagons, some with "U.S." still painted on. Early in the war teams of four horses were used to draw wagons, but mules (mostly six) were soon substituted as better animals for the task. Mules usually showed extreme nervousness under fire, although there were occasions, such as Sergeant Watrous's "Mule Train Charge," when they decided to perform admirably (see photograph, page 105). As John Billings neatly put it:

> The latter [the mule] was more particular as to the kind of service he performed. Like a great many bipeds that entered the army, he preferred to do his military duty in the safe rear. As a consequence, if he found himself under fire at the front, he was wont to make a stir in his neighborhood until he got out of such inhospitable surroundings.

Billings then went on to describe some of the attributes of the mule over the horse in military service:

> mules have a great advantage over horses in being better able to stand hard usage, bad feed, or no feed and neglect generally. They can travel over rough ground unharmed where a horse would be lamed or injured in some way. They will eat brush, and not be very hungry to do it, either. When forage was short, the drivers were wont to cut branches and throw before them for their refreshment. One mule driver tells of having his army overcoat partly eaten by one of his team – actually chewed and swallowed.

Other equally important reasons for exchanging horses for mules were the worsening shortage and increasing expense of horses, and their indispensable need on the battlefield itself. A wagon drawn by six mules had a capacity of 1.5 tons (3,000 pounds) on reasonable roads, less on rough tracks or up steep hills. Under good conditions they would travel 2.5 miles in the hour. In the early part of the war Union teamsters (drivers) were civilians, but due to their lack of discipline and their ineffectiveness, enlisted men "upon whom Uncle Sam had his grip" and who could not resign or "swear back" without penalty, later replaced them. Slaves supervised by wagonmasters

Pack Mules

That pack mules were the usual way of supporting small detachments is clearly evidenced by the instructions of the assistant adjutant-general of the Army of the Potomac, Brigadier-General Seth Williams, to I Corps, dated June 7, 1863.

> The commanding general directs that you detach from your command 600 infantry . . . the detachment to be absent from camp four or five days, and to be provided with three days rations in haversacks, empty knapsacks, one blanket, and 150 rounds of ammunition, to be carried on pack mules and the person. Two ambulances, properly supplied, will accompany the expedition, but no wagons . . .
>
> The pack mules to transport the ammunition and the shelter tents of the officers should come from the reserve mules supplied by the chief quartermaster for contingent uses to avoid, if possible, taking any from the wagon trains. Pack masters, ambulance attendants, &c., should accompany the detachment.

River (and sea)

Water transportation was well utilized by the North. Supplies and troops could be moved on the open ocean or on inland waterways. A superior navy gave the Union control of the coastline. Not only could a naval blockade be applied to reduce dramatically the Confederates' ability to obtain supplies from overseas but, conversely, shipping could carry entire armies with their supplies and land them at selected locations to invade the South. In 1862 use of the Potomac River, Chesapeake Bay and the James and York Rivers enabled McClellan to land his army at Fort Monroe on the tip of the Virginia peninsula and march to the gates of Richmond – and then withdraw again to Washington. Command of the sea gave the Union massive strategic and logistical advantages.

Rivers played an important role in the outcome of the Civil War. The great rivers such as the Mississippi, Ohio, Tennessee and Cumberland provided highways into the South in the west, while in the east the Potomac, York and James Rivers facilitated Union armies in threatening Richmond and keeping them supplied. In the west the loss of Fort Donelson in early 1862 gave the Union control of the Cumberland. But of far greater significance was the loss of Vicksburg on the day after Lee's defeat at Gettysburg. Grant's successful advance down the Mississippi and subsequent siege split the Confederacy in two. The South never really recovered from these two major setbacks occurring virtually simultaneously in the eastern and western theaters.

In the Gettysburg campaign the use of rivers as a means of supply was significant only when Hooker left the Falmouth area, when the Potomac was used as his main line of supply, with towed barges ferrying massive tonnages from Alexandria to Aquia Creek.

Mule Wagon

invariably drove Confederate wagons. On the march or when parked, wagon trains were guarded by units of either infantry or cavalry specifically given the task by division or corps headquarters, although it was the unit or formation quartermasters who were responsible for getting them to the right place at the right time.

Pack mules were also sometimes used when wagons were unavailable or when a detachment was sent on a mission away from the main area of operations (see box, page 225). Four mules could carry the rough equivalent of one wagon and could get to places a wagon never could. One was also usually to be seen plodding along at the rear of a marching infantry regiment, guided by a slave (Rebels) or African American or freed slave (Yankees), carrying extra kit for the officers. The present writer has found no mention of the substantial use of pack mules at Gettysburg other than the 216 listed with the Union XI Corps in Brigadier-General Ingalls' transport recapitulation dated June 1, 1863 (see page 230).

Mules – Cantankerous and Dangerous

Kentucky was the main source of supply of these tough, stubborn, sure-footed and hardworking animals. Although most mules were used in teams to pull wagons, they were also used as pack animals – there was usually at least one behind infantry regiments on the march – and they were used as such when wagons were unavailable, or in mountainous country where horses were seriously disadvantaged. The best accounts of life with mules are contained in *Hardtack and Coffee* by John D. Billings, who served in the Army of the Potomac. The following are quotes from his book on an animal without which neither army at Gettysburg could have been supplied or replenished.

> **Driving.** It was really wonderful to see some of these experts drive these teams [usually of six animals]. The driver rides the near pole mule, holding in his left hand a single rein. This connects with the bits of the near lead mule. By pulling this rein, of course the brutes would go to the left. To direct them to the right one or more short jerks of it were given, accompanied by a sort of gibberish that the mule drivers acquired in the business. The bits of the lead mules being connected by an iron bar, whatever movement was made by the near one directed the movements of the off one. The pole mules were controlled by short reins which hung over their necks. The driver carried in his right hand his black snake, that is, his black leather whip, which was used with much effect on occasion.

Kicking. These are a few samples, most all of which have reference to his great ability as a kicker. Unquestionably he had no equal in this field of amusement – to him. His legs were small, his feet were small, but his ambition in this direction was large. He *could* kick with wonderful accuracy, as a matter of fact. Mule-drivers tell me he could kick a fly of his ear, as he walked along in the team, with unerring accuracy. This being so, of course larger objects were never missed when they were within range. But the distance included within a mule's range had often to be decided by two or three expensive tests. One driver, whom I well knew, was knocked over with a mule's hind foot while standing *directly in front of him*. This shows something of their range.

Shoeing. It may be asked how he was shod if he was such a kicker. To do this, one of two methods was adopted; either to sling him up as oxen are slung, then strap his feet; or walk him into a noose, and cast him, by drawing it around his legs. Of course he would struggle violently for a while, but when he gave in it was all over for that occasion, and he was as docile under the smith's hands as a kitten.

When entangled. Being surer-footed and more agile than a horse, of course he gets into fewer bad places or entanglements; but once in, and having made a desperate struggle for his relief, and failing, he seems utterly discouraged, and neither whip nor persuasion can move him. Then, as in the shoeing, the driver can handle him with the utmost disregard of heels; but when once on his feet again, stand aside!

The Union Supply System

In 1863 overall control of the Union supply system was in the hands of two brigadier-generals. Brigadier-General Joseph P. Taylor was commissary general of subsistence. A highly experienced officer, by the time he died in 1864 he had served in the Subsistence Department for thirty-five years, a period that included the Mexican War. Brigadier-General Rufus Ingalls was chief quartermaster of the Army of the Potomac, a competent administrator and organizer who in his report on the battle had the following to say concerning the principles on which the army's supply trains functioned:

> In the forward movement our trains are never in the way of our troops; on the contrary, each corps has its train [nine in the Gettysburg campaign] which follows it on the march, and which forms its indispensable moveable magazine of supplies [of all types]. Wagon trains should never be permitted to approach within the range of battlefields. They should be parked in safe and convenient places out of risk, and well guarded. Troops should go forward lightly loaded, and without wagons except for extra ammunition [both small arms and artillery ammunition reserves were close behind the battle line, but Union troops went hungry during most of the three days' fighting]. If they are successful the trains can be brought up very quickly. If defeated they will find an unobstructed road, and will get back to their wagons soon enough.
>
> At the great battle of Gettysburg I had the trains of the whole army parked at Westminster, on the Baltimore Branch Railroad and pike, at a distance of 25 miles from the field, guarded by cavalry and artillery . . .

By no means everybody would agree with Ingalls that wagons never hindered the army's progress. Private George T. Stevens of the 77th New York in VI Corps was forthright about the problems caused by wagon trains:

> All day long the trains crowded by, four and five wagons abreast [guaranteed to cause chaos]; the drivers shouting and lashing their beasts to their greatest speed. No one who had not seen the train of an army in motion can form any just conception of its magnitude, and of the difficulties attending its movement. It was said that the train of the Army of the Potomac, including artillery . . . if placed in a single line . . . would extend over seventy miles.

A Union wagon train, clearly showing how much road space it occupied.

The Confederates' Use of Slaves

The thousands of African American slaves who marched north with the Army of Northern Virginia in June 1863 could be divided into two basic categories. The first were the officers' (and enlisted men's) personal servants, mostly coming from their own estates in the South. The second group were the teamsters and laborers traveling and working with the quartermasters' trains. The slaves were mostly engaged either by being leased by their owners to the Quartermaster's Department or compelled into service with the army by impressments. They had to have an identity document signed by their owner to prove their status in the army and they were required to wear civilian clothes.

It is doubtful if a Rebel headquarters could have functioned efficiently without the officers' servants. Many of these African Americans were free men and were paid a monthly wage by their master. Within a headquarters these servants pitched camp, broke camp, collected firewood, cooked, did laundry, groomed, fed and watered horses, together with numerous other mundane tasks needed to keep the routine of life functioning – something that often included foraging on their masters' behalf. Servants even got passes to return home on furloughs, sometimes traveling on their own, sometimes with their masters. It was usual for wealthy officers to have two or even more servants, many remaining loyal to their masters throughout the war. An example was Colonel Porter Alexander, whose task it was to oversee the preliminary bombardment by Longstreet's guns on July 3. Alexander had two servants: the first, Charley, was his personal servant/groom for most of the war; and the second was his wagon driver from Second Manassas until he was captured a few days before the final surrender at Appomattox. Alexander wrote of the first:

> I had hired for an [h]ostler & servant a 15 year old darkie named Charley – a medium tall & slender, ginger-cake colored, & well behaved & good dispositioned boy. In all the 3½ years I had him with me I had to give him a little licking but twice – once for robbing a pear tree in the garden of the Keach house, in which we were staying . . . & once in Pa. Just before Gettysburg, for stealing apple-brandy & getting tight on it.

Captain Jedediah "Jed" Hotchkiss, Ewell's topographical engineer at Gettysburg, was certainly exceptional when his concern over his rented servant's drunkenness led to his buying the man instead of just beating him. General Lee, meanwhile, wrote home about one of his slaves:

> Perry is very willing and I believe does as well as he can. You know he is slow & inefficient & moves much like his father Lawrence whom he resembles very much. He is also very fond of his blankets in the morning. The time I most require him out. He is not very strong either.

Many servants at a headquarters had their own horses or mules or had access to their master's mounts. They used this mobility to forage for their master (and themselves) – and even, on occasion, to visit a local girl. Although some took the opportunity to disappear during the aftermath of the Rebel defeat and during Lee's retreat, it was never an epidemic. Most black servants remained loyal despite the numerous opportunities to abscond. The servant of Major McLeod, 8th South Carolina Infantry, provided an exceptional example of loyalty to his master even after the latter's death. His name was July and he accompanied the ambulance carrying his gravely wounded master on the retreat. When the major died, July personally buried him and erected a marker before making his way to his master's family home to break the news of his death. He then guided the major's brother-in-law back to the grave so that his body could be brought home for final burial.

The second category of slaves was those working with the trains. They were far more numerous than the first, as they were to be found as teamsters driving, loading, unloading and maintaining the wagons of the reserve train and quartermasters' trains of the regiments, brigades and divisions. They also drove many ambulances and even some ordnance wagons. Slaves were used as general laborers for building bridges, repairing roads or rail tracks and sometimes, such as around Richmond, for digging trenches and building fortifications.

It will never be possible to know accurately how many slaves marched north with Lee that June, but based on the number of regiments, artillery battalions and the estimated number of wagons, the figure could hardly have been less than 7,000 and was probably nearer 10,000, a few of whom actually fought for the A.N.V.

Looking down on a wagon train crossing the Potomac at Edward's Crossing (Ferry), James Bowen of the 37th Massachusetts wrote:

> Far as the eye could reach vast wagon trains would march over hill or through valley, or were parked beside the road waiting their turn to join the procession, and the vivid panorama gave to many a beholder a truer realization of the magnitude of that branch of the army service.

These enormous and unwieldy Union transportation columns accompanying the army to Gettysburg consisted of some thirty-two separate wagon trains comprising:

- nine corps wagon trains, each with an ordnance train (artillery ammunition), subsistence, commissary and quartermaster's train and baggage train
- twenty-two divisional ordnance (small arms ammunition) and ambulance trains
- an artillery reserve ordnance train

After Chancellorsville, where the Union supply system had been chaotic, divisional quartermaster and commissary trains were integrated into corps supply trains, each under the corps' chief quartermaster. Within these new corps trains, divisional wagons were divided into separate smaller trains carrying headquarters, regimental and artillery baggage (tents, cooking utensils, camp equipage); subsistence and commissary; quartermasters' stores (clothing, equipment, etc.); headquarters (corps, division and brigade) wagons containing entrenching tools, fodder, subsistence, armorer's tools and musket parts, etc. At the rear of these corps trains would usually be a herd of cattle, sheep and hogs on the hoof.

On July 1 Meade ordered that "corps commanders and the commander of the Artillery Reserve will at once send to the rear all their trains (excepting ammunition wagons and ambulances) parking them between Union Mills and Westminster." The following day they were ordered still further to the rear and a vast city of wagons and animals assembled at the Westminster railhead to await the result of the battle. A witness described this huge gathering:

> The army wagons were everywhere, in the streets, in the fields, on the various roads, and a line of them constantly traveling to the Gettysburg turnpike . . . Night and day, the noise of the army wagons, the clanking of cavalry sabers [Buford withdrew to Westminster on July 2], and the braying of the mules could be heard and general noise and confusion prevailed everywhere.

However, divisional ordnance trains (small arms and artillery ammunition), the Artillery Reserve ammunition train and ambulances remained located close behind the forward troops. This proved critical for success in defending the Union position. On July 1, it will be recalled that the Union 1st Division train of I Corps carrying small arms ammunition was rushed forward to the firing line on McPherson's Ridge where Ordnance Sergeant Watrous tossed out boxes containing 25,000 rounds in what became known as "the Mule Train Charge" (see photograph, page 105). Similarly, on July 2, the speedy availability of rifle ammunition for the defenders of Culp's Hill enabled troops running short to replenish during lulls or at night. On that same day the ammunition train of the Artillery Reserve issued thousands of extra rounds to the guns deployed along Cemetery Ridge.

It is difficult to put precise numbers on the wagons that made up these corps trains, but a reasonable estimate can be made using three documents: Major-General McClellan's General Order No. 153, dated August 10, 1862, and Meade's General Order No. 83, dated August 21, 1863 (both of which concern the official number of wagons permitted for various supplies in each formation), and Brigadier-General Rufus Ingalls' "Recapitulation" list of the wagons and ambulances in the Army of the Potomac, dated June 1, 1863. Based on the two General Orders, the official Union wagon entitlement for various supplies and ammunition was as shown in the left-hand column of the table opposite. If using that official entitlement, the trains of I Corps at Gettysburg would have been composed of the wagons in the right-hand column.

Type of supplies	Wagon entitlement	I Corps wagons
Baggage (tents, camp equipage, cooking utensils, etc.)		
corps H.Q.s	4	4
division H.Q.s	3	9
brigade H.Q.s	3	21
gun batteries, 4–6 guns	2	10
infantry regiments		
700–1,000 men	6	–
500–700 men	5	15
300–500 men	4	60
fewer than 300 men	2	42
Entrenching tools, etc.		
each corps	6	6
Forage for ambulance animals		
each division	1	3
Armorer's tools, extra arms, etc.		
each division	1	3
Subsistence, fodder, Q.M. stores (clothes, etc.)		
each 1,000 men	7	84
each corps H.Q.	3	9
each division H.Q.	2	6
each brigade H.Q.	1	7
Small arms ammunition		
each 1,000 men	5	60
Hospital supplies		
each 1,500 men*	3	24
Ordnance trains (artillery)		
multiply number of 12-pounders by 122 and divide by 112		13
multiply rifled guns by 50 and divide by 140		6
each battery for subsistence and fodder	2	10
Theoretical total wagons in I Corps train		**392 (say 400)**

* See pages 234–36.

A sutler's store in camp. During the Civil War a sutler accompanied most regiments, supplying a variety of goods and necessities to the troops. See box, page 231.

The above table is only a guide to the sort of numbers of wagons and their loads likely to be found during the Gettysburg campaign, as the second General Order was issued after the battle, no doubt in light of experience and the need to reduce numbers. Almost certainly the numbers in the wagon trains moving north with the Army of the Potomac that June were greater (there is no mention of the regimental sutlers' wagons, for example), and we know that a few two-horse wagons were employed, as well as XI Corps having over 200 pack mules at the start of June (see below). Nevertheless, the figures at least indicate an approximate proportion of wagons devoted to different types of supplies, with 40 percent carrying baggage but only 30 percent subsistence and fodder, although with the latter the August 1863 Order stipulated that wagons carry enough for their own teams.

Strangely, there is no mention of ambulances as distinct from wagons carrying medical stores. Ambulance trains were a major component of army trains and normally followed their division along with ordnance (small arms) wagons. In the case of I Corps at Gettysburg, Ingalls' list (see below) shows sixty-seven ambulances with the corps on June 1 – the lowest number of any corps – making a possible overall total of 470–500 wagons.

The length of the I Corps train, with 400 wagons on a single road, would be around 4.5–5 miles, allowing 20 yards per wagon and team – add another threequarters of a mile for ambulances. Straggling would probably increase this again by half a mile. However, the corps train would have taken up less road space – about 3–3.5 miles – when diverted to Westminster. If all the wagon and ambulance trains of the army were to move along a single road, they would stretch for at least 60 miles.

Possibly as a direct result of Gettysburg experience, when unbeknown to Meade his chief of artillery had brought an extra twenty rounds per gun, Meade's August 1863 Order included under ammunition trains, "5th. For the general supply train of reserve ammunition of 20 rounds to each gun in the army, to be kept habitually with Artillery Reserve, 54 wagons."

The third useful document in estimating the transportation available to Hooker and then Meade is in the National Archives and is headed: "Recapitulation of the number of Officers and enlisted men, Cavalry and Artillery horses, Wagons and means of Transportation in Army of Poto." It is dated June 1, 1863, and signed by Brigadier-General Rufus Ingalls, Chief Quartermaster. Although it is dated a month prior to the battle, it gives a reasonable indication of the number of horses, mules, wagons and ambulances available to each corps. Relevant extracts are shown below, slightly rearranged from the original for clarity.

Artillery and cavalry horses have been excluded as the above figures relate to wagon trains. There is considerable variation between corps, as might be expected, but the average number of wagons per corps is 446 (excluding ambulances), which is not far from the 400 that was I Corps' entitlement if it had been operating under the August 1863 regulations.

There is no obvious explanation why the number of ambulances varies so much from corps to corps – certainly the figures do not represent the differences in the strength of the corps. However, they give an average of 110 ambulances per corps, or 40 plus per division, which from other sources appears about right. However, it is possible that the total number was increased during June as the quartermaster general of the U.S. Army put the number as 1,100 on July 4.

Supply wagon trains of all types totaling from 5,500 to about 6,300 (including ambulances) for the Army of the Potomac is a reasonable overall estimate. Of these, Meade sent around two-thirds to Westminster just before the battle (3,600–4,200). Some 4,000 wagons, around 30,000 horses and mules, together with herds of cattle and other animals, must have been a staggering sight and a quartermaster's nightmare to untangle. After this diversion, and following each division to the battlefield on the final leg of the march, were the ordnance (small arms) and ambulance wagon trains, composed of an average of 40–50 ambulances (including some medical supplies) and 10–12 wagons carrying musket/rifle ammunition, taking up some threequarters of a mile of road. Also en route were the wagons (formerly moving with the corps trains) carrying each corps' reserve, or second-line, artillery ammunition. An approximate ratio for artillery trains was one

Command			**Means of Transportation**			
	Horses	**Mules**	**Army wagons**	**2-horse wagons**	**Ambulances**	**Pack mules**
I Corps	393	2578	404	6	67	–
II Corps	670	2,795	496	7	117	–
III Corps	951	2,326	525	13	98	–
V Corps	879	2,621	496	7	166	–
VI Corps	1,001	2,933	557	11	167	–
XI Corps	1,100	1,549	414	10	83	216
XII Corps	897	1,480	365	12	94	–
Cavy. Corps	1,085	2,404	313	4	86	–
Subtotals	**6,976**	**18,686**	**3,570**	**70**	**878**	**216**
Arty Res.	489	1,307	291	3	15	–
Engineers	757	526	120	2	12	–
Provost	67	24	21	1	4	–
Army H.Q.	600	1,085	300	13	19	–
Totals	**8,889**	**21,628**	**4,302**	**89**	**928**	**216**

ammunition wagon for every three guns. The seven Union infantry corps at Gettysburg averaged thirty guns apiece, so their artillery trains would have around ninety wagons, each train a mile long. To these must be added about eighty-five wagons carrying projectiles (including the extra twenty per gun) for the Artillery Reserve, occupying another mile.

It is not possible to reconcile the number of mules to wagons, as there were undoubtedly a number of wagons drawn by draft horses as well as the ambulances and other two-horse wagons. There is no explanation why only XI Corps is shown with pack mules (four mules were supposedly equal to the load-carrying capacity of one wagon).

The Confederate Supply System

Transportation, as in the North, was a problem to be handled by the Quartermaster's Department. Although this agency worked hard, the basic difficulties were never properly solved. In a way this was probably the greatest single failure of the department – certainly other supply bureaus took this view. Their objection was that the Quartermaster's Department had control over their transport. Who would know better how to transport medicine than the Medical Corps for example? Each bureau felt its own needs to be much greater than any of the others and that it should therefore have priority over shipments, whereas the quartermasters tended to allocate priority to the movement of their own supplies. An extreme example was when the Commissary Department would impress all the freight cars in a given locality for the dispatch of foodstuffs, leaving nothing for the other services to use. However, at the same time the Quartermaster's Department would impress all the locomotives. The resultant tangle would cause frayed tempers and much needless delay.

At Lee's headquarters in June 1863 Lieutenant-Colonel James L. Corley was chief quartermaster with the unenviable task of overall coordination and control of the wagon trains. The Army of Northern Virginia was moving out of a state that had been denuded of supplies of every sort into Maryland and Pennsylvania in order to sustain itself, primarily by foraging, requisitioning and capture. This meant that a high proportion of the subsistence and forage wagons were, at the outset, empty, as requisitioning and foraging would fill them. As Lee moved up the Shenandoah and Cumberland valleys, wagons were filled, many more wagons requisitioned, supplies were used up and wagons refilled, as well as a

Sutlers

Sutlers were civilian storekeepers running a store that provided a wide variety of goods, including food, for sale to the soldiers. In camp there would be sutlers' tents, in the field on operations a mule-drawn wagon. There would usually be one sutler's wagon bringing up the rear of every regiment's baggage train. If this was the approximate number accompanying the armies to Gettysburg, then some 500 sutler's wagons (Union 300, Confederate 200) were mixed with the reserve supply and subsistence trains around Westminster and Fairfield.

Sutlers were officially recognized, and regulations governed their conduct and the soldiers' dealings with them. As one soldier wrote, "The law recognized the sutler and the orders shielded him. That was the theory. Everybody kicked and cursed him and plundered him. That was [the] practice." Undoubtedly a sutler's life was fraught with problems, particularly in the field. There was always the chance of being caught up in some action and perhaps losing one's livelihood, being captured – cavalry raiders were a constant worry – or even losing one's life (at least one sutler was killed).

To the soldier in need of supplies, the sutler's tent offered a tantalizing bounty – tobacco, candy, tinned meats, shoelaces, patent medicines, pies and newspapers, etc. But unscrupulous sutlers – a Dutch word meaning "to undertake low offices" – were legion, and often the soldier paid five times the true value of an item. Resentment of inflated prices and shoddy goods was high in both armies. One newspaper correspondent wrote that they were "a wretched class of swindlers and well deserved all their troubles." Thefts from a sutler's tent or wagon were common. En route to Gettysburg some cheese went missing from a sutler's wagon near the 13th Vermont Infantry and the irate victim reported the matter. This resulted in the regiment's parading to be searched by an officer. The guilty men belonged to Company G, but the inspecting officer passed them by with, according to Private Henry H. Stevens, the comment that "Company G did not know enough to steal cheese."

Charles Wellington Reed, Captain Bigelow's bugler, has left a classic account of what could happen to sutlers, in this case from the depredations of Union II Corps soldiers, when the troops were hungry.

> This afternoon we had a big excitement[.] [O]ur Sutler ever since the arrival of the army has been kept destitute of everything eatible [*sic*] and for the last two days we could purchase nothing. [W]ell after dinner our Sutler made his appearance from Washington with three wagon loads of stuff and was not half unloaded before an immense crowd had gathered from the 2nd Corps which arrived this morning[.] [N]ow and then one would make a grab and leave and others growing more bold entered the tent and the first thing Mr Sutler knew he was overrun and saw his property on the move. [He] is a fine fellow and has treated us well, so Captain had our battery turn out to the rescue[.] [T]hey marched up and wedged their way between the tent and the crowd and endeavored to have some order[.] [T]he thing worked fine for a while but the drawn sabers only made them worse[.] [S]uch yelling, howling and screeching, was truly bewitching. [O]ur fellows were getting hustled some, the ropes were cut and the tent going over in spite of all we could do[.] Lieut Whitaker [mortally wounded at Gettysburg] made a cut at a fellow who evaded the blow and then wrenched it out of his hand but Lieut drawing his revolver with a threat to shoot him the fellow dropt it and fled but not before he had given Lieut a severe cut across the hand just as the tent was falling and instant demolition was expected[.] General Hays rode up and dashing furiously amongst the crowd with drawn revolver scattered them right and left[.] [H] was followed by a battalion of infantry who immediately surrounded our belagured [*sic*] Sutler . . . Gen. Hancock had a roll call throughout his command and all who were absent were fined twenty cents and a sum of two hundred dollars turned over into the hands of our Sutler for damages . . . the famous Irish Brigade were the ones that caused the mischief.

large reserve of loaded wagons being built up, together with herds of animals on the hoof. The Army of the Potomac had much more uniform-looking wagon trains than the Rebels. A Confederate wagon train could include the standard army wagon, captured wagons with "U.S." on the sides, drays, carriages, buggies and farmers' carts all jumbled together. This mixing of different types increased as the invasion progressed and large numbers of civilian vehicles were incorporated in the trains. Lack of uniformity was also a feature of the Rebels' ambulance trains, where shortages of appropriate wagons led to the frequent use of supply wagons and other types of conveyance – much to the discomfort of the injured. Although the majority of Confederate wagons (except for ambulances, which invariably had horses) were drawn by six mules, many had four and some even two. Numerous draft horses were requisitioned from reluctant farmers, along with their carts – the unfortunate owners not only lost their livestock and corn, but their own horses and carts were used to carry them away.

There was a basic difference in the organization of the trains between the two armies. While both had quartermaster, subsistence, ordnance and ambulance trains, Lee had one each of these trains belonging to each division – they were not grouped into corps trains, as these would have been far too unwieldy, Confederate corps being far larger than Union ones. The Army of Northern Virginia had no corps reserve trains for quartermaster, subsistence or ambulances, only an ordnance train to supply the corps artillery battalion. However, by early July the army had accumulated vast quartermaster and subsistence trains, along with at least 5,000 cattle, about the same number of sheep and a large herd of hogs. Most of these formed the army reserve train grouped around Fairfield during the battle and put under Major John A. Harman, Ewell's chief quartermaster, for the eventual retreat. Even more than with the Union Army, it is extremely difficult to determine the number of wagons accompanying Lee on his invasion. The approximate official allowance that Lee had laid down the previous year for infantry, cavalry and artillery regimental baggage was one wagon for every 100 men, one for each headquarters, one for ordnance (small arms ammunition) and one for medical supplies. This would permit some 1,750 wagons for baggage, tents and camp equipage, although it was certainly reduced before the Gettysburg campaign. With ordnance wagons (artillery projectiles, forges, tools, etc.), one wagon for three guns was the usual rough method of allocation, giving around 90–100 wagons. The large divisions would each require up to 80–100 ambulance vehicles, totaling about 800. Thus far, this gives a total of 2,650 wagons, excluding subsistence. With these it is impossible to do other than make an educated guess. The Confederates had some 300 distinct units (regiments, batteries) and formation headquarters of various sizes. Assuming each would take an average of at least three wagons of subsistence/forage at the outset, with a high proportion empty, then the subsistence trains might have totaled about 1,000 wagons. This would give a total estimated number of 3,650 wagons. Many more were collected en route and during the battle itself, so by July 4, when Lee was organizing a retreat, he would have had perhaps 4,500 wagons and ambulances to get clear of the battlefield area – in single file they would have covered about 50 miles.

At Gettysburg Lee brought his wagon trains up comparatively close behind his army, unlike Meade who had sent all except the essentials some 25 miles to his rear. The procedure for the Confederates was usually to form divisional wagon parks alongside divisional field hospitals (see Map 9, page 243), perhaps 2 miles or more behind the forward line. From there ammunition or other requirements could be ferried forward under the quartermaster, commissary or ordnance officer as appropriate. There was also the large reserve subsistence train parked near Fairfield on the Marsh Creek, some 3 miles southwest of Lee's right flank. During the battle on July 3 Longstreet's Corps ordnance train was dangerously close to the action and was moved back – a move that was to cause much confusion and delay, as nobody in authority knew its new location.

MEDICAL SERVICES

Gettysburg saw at least 26,000 men wounded from both sides. This figure is almost certainly conservative but it will never be possible to know the exact number. The great majority of these men received initial medical treatment of some sort during the period July 1–4 at over 200 aid posts/dressing stations and field hospitals on or surrounding the battlefield, including in Gettysburg itself. When Lee retreated he was unable to take 6,800 wounded with him due to a combination of the seriousness of their wounds and lack of transport. He left behind about 100 medical personnel to attend them. Meade left a similar number of doctors (106) behind when he moved in pursuit. Perhaps understandably, when the pressure of numbers threatened to overwhelm Union field hospitals during the battle and in the days immediately following, many Rebel wounded took last place in the treatment queue, with the inevitable increase in suffering and deaths. Meade had around 650 medical officers on the field during the battle, Lee about 400 – both more or less the correct establishment figure. If one accepts that some 165,600 men were engaged at Gettysburg, then the ratio of doctors to soldiers was 1:158. The Army of the Potomac provided one medical officer for every 144 men, the Army of Northern Virginia one for every 179. This reflected the overall medical arrangements for the two armies. The Union was, as with most things military, better organized and equipped than the Confederacy. The latter generally had fewer doctors, fewer ambulances, greater shortages of medical supplies and was perpetually in want of suitable transport.

Some 75 percent of surgical operations performed during the Civil War were amputations. This was because three out of every four soldiers were hit in the limbs, and at that time amputation was the recognized treatment for compound fractures or severe laceration of a limb. Nevertheless, there was a difference of opinion among surgeons about the need to lop off so many limbs. However, in a field hospital when time was desperately short, immediate amputation invariably won the argument. An experienced surgeon could remove a limb in a matter of minutes – some at Gettysburg spent a whole week doing nothing else. Gunshot wounds were by far the most common, over 70 percent being to arms, legs, hands or feet. A man hit in the head, chest or abdomen had usually received a mortal wound. According to Union statistics, the average mortality rate for chest wounds was 62 percent and for the abdomen 87 percent. The result of this was that field hospitals carried out an elementary triage system whereby the "dressing" surgeons and a medical orderly would pass over the lightly and mortally wounded to get the others onto the operating table as soon as possible.

The Minie ball made a hideous wound, often changing shape as it entered the body, smashing bone and dragging in bits of clothing, skin, hair and dirt. Unlike a high-velocity modern bullet, there was seldom an exit wound. As one cynical surgeon commented, "When balls are lost in the capacity of the belly one need not amuse oneself by hunting for them." In practice this philosophy was proved a reasonably sound one, as of those men lucky enough to survive such a wound many did so with the ball still in them.

There was no understanding of the need for antiseptic conditions. A surgeon would use the same knife or saw all day, wiping his hands or instruments on his coat when they became too sticky. Bullets were frequently probed for with fingers, blood- and pus-soaked sponges just squeezed out in water, wounds would be packed with wet, unsterilized lint and bound with wet, unsterilized bandages. Splints were often cobbled together using fence rails or pieces of board. Patients were sedated with either ether or chloroform; if these were unavailable, with whiskey or brandy. The preferred method was to pour some chloroform onto a sponge or cloth and place it over the patient's nose and mouth until he was unconscious. After sedation the surgeon then "removes the limb, ligates the vessels and when all oozing has ceased, secures the stump by points of suture placed at intervals of one inch." For general pain relief, reliance was placed on opiates. Opium was usually administered in tablet form and sometimes morphine was rubbed in the wound – failing all else, more whiskey.

Tillie Alleman never forgot the horror of what she saw going on in Jacob Weikert's home:

> I saw the surgeons hastily put a cattle horn over the mouths of the wounded ones, after they were placed upon the bench. At first I did not understand the meaning of this, but upon inquiry, soon learned that that was their mode of administering chloroform, in order to produce unconsciousness. But the effect in some instances was not produced; for I saw the wounded throwing themselves wildly about, and shrieking with pain while the operation was going on.
>
> To the south of the house, just outside of the yard, I noticed a pile of limbs higher than the fence. It was a ghastly sight! Gazing upon these, too often the trophies of the amputating bench, I could have no other feeling, than the whole scene was one of cruel butchery.

Following an amputation, a soldier's most dreaded disease, hospital gangrene, might appear within days. It spread quickly from the size of a dime to an area up to 10 inches in diameter. The gray-colored, rotting tissue soon turned black, giving off a revolting odor. During the first two years of the war it was treated by cutting it away or burning it out with nitric acid till "you could see smoke rise, the flesh sizzle and crisp up, and all this time the patient screaming in agony." Fortunately, by Gettysburg a Dr. Middleton Goldsmith had introduced a more effective and less barbaric treatment. This involved applying lint

Amputations

The trademark of Civil War surgery was amputation. It accounted for some 75 percent of all operations. But primitive though the conditions were, thousands of men's lives were saved by the loss of a limb. Perhaps the most extraordinary example was the Confederate Brigadier-General Francis R. T. Nicholls, who lost an eye, an arm and a leg – the last at Chancellorsville leading the 2nd Louisiana Brigade, an injury that finally rendered him unfit for further service. Amputations performed within the first forty-eight hours after wounding were twice as likely to be successful as those done later.

The fatality rates for Union amputations are shown below (no similar statistics are available for the Confederates). Unsurprisingly, amputations involving a leg from hip to ankle caused the greatest percentage of deaths.

	Cases	Deaths	% Fatal
Fingers	7,902	198	2.5
Forearms	1,761	245	13.9
Upper arms	5,540	1,273	23.0
Toes	1,519	81	5.3
Shins	5,523	1,790	32.4
Thighs	6,369	3,411	53.6
Knee joints	195	111	56.9
Hip joints	66	55	83.3
Ankle joints	161	119	73.9

Surgeons at Work

Major-General Carl Schurz commanded the 3rd Division, XI Corps, and for a time acted as corps commander at Gettysburg. In the early twentieth century he published his *Reminiscences*, in which he gives a graphic description of surgeons at work.

> There stood the surgeons, their sleeves rolled up to the elbows, their bare arms as well as their linen aprons smeared with blood, their knives not seldom held between their teeth, while they were helping a patient on or off the table, or had their hands otherwise occupied, around them pools of blood and amputated arms or legs in heaps, sometimes more than man high. Antiseptic methods were unknown at the time. As a wounded man was lifted on the table, often shrieking with pain as the attendants handled him, the surgeon quickly examined the wound and resolved upon cutting off the injured limb. Some ether was administered and the body put in position in a moment. The surgeon snatched his knife from between his teeth . . . wiped it rapidly once or twice across his bloodstained apron, and the cutting began. The operation accomplished, the surgeon would look round with a deep sigh, and then – "Next!"
>
> And so it went on, hour after hour . . . a surgeon having been long at work, would put down his knife, exclaiming that his hand had grown unsteady, and that this was too much for human endurance – not seldom hysterical tears streaming down his face . . . Many of the wounded men suffered with silent fortitude, fierce determination in the knitting of their brows and the steady gaze of their bloodshot eyes . . . But there were, too, heartrending groans and shrill cries of pain piercing the air, and despairing exclamations, "Oh, Lord! Oh Lord!" or "Let me die!" or softer murmurings in which the words "mother" or "father" or "home" were often heard.

The U.S. Sanitary Commission and U.S. Christian Commission

The Sanitary Commission was founded in 1861 as the Civil War began, despite opposition from the Medical Department, and was the forerunner of the American Red Cross. Its purpose was to promote clean and healthy conditions in the Union Army camps and generally to help provide comfort to sick or wounded soldiers and sailors.

It staffed field and general hospitals, raised money, and worked to educate the military and government on matters of health and sanitation. Besides inspecting camps, drainage and food, it also distributed medical supplies, clothing and food and virtually every corps had its Sanitary Commission wagon with its store of beef stock, chewing tobacco, chloroform, bandages, etc. Staff included relief agents, inspectors, clerks, cooks and drivers. Many women volunteered to work with the Sanitary Commission. Some worked at camps organizing medical services or acting as nurses, while others raised money and helped with the administration. The Commission also provided food, lodging, pay, pensions and care for soldiers returning from service. It was a large-scale voluntary welfare service that can be likened to modern Veterans' Associations or the British Legion. In total it distributed about $15,000,000 worth of supplies.

At Gettysburg the Rev. Dr. Gordon Winslow was the U.S. Sanitary Commission agent responsible for inspecting Confederate field hospitals after the battle. While describing the Rebel surgeons as "intelligent and attentive," he went on to report that there was "often a deplorable want of cleanliness. Especially in barns and outhouses, vermin and putrid matter are disgustingly offensive."

On July 2 several Sanitary Commission wagons arrived and began distributing supplies. By July 12 another twelve wagons had arrived with more medical supplies and food, which was issued to authorized medical officers from a depot established in the White Run School on the Baltimore Pike. With the arrival of larger quantities of supplies by rail, this store was moved to the Fahnestock store and warehouse in the town, which became the center from which huge quantities of donated stocks were issued to the various hospitals of both sides. Gregory A. Coco provides a glimpse of the staggering variety of goods provided in his splendid book *A Strange and Blighted Land*. Among many other things he lists 10,000 towels and napkins, 110 barrels of bandages, 4,000 pairs of shoes and slippers, 7,158 woolen shirts, 3,500 fans, 1,200 pairs of crutches, 10,300 loaves of bread, 8,500 dozen eggs, 1,250 bottles of brandy, 500 pounds of preserved meats and 3,600 pounds of preserved fish. Many of the gifts had poignant messages pinned to them. Coco again gives some examples:

> On a bed quilt was pinned a card saying: "My son is in the army. Whoever is made warm by this quilt, which I have worked on for six days and most of all of six nights, let him remember his own mother's love."
>
> On a bundle containing bandages was written: "This is a poor gift, but it is all I had, I have given my husband and my boy, and I only wish I have more to give, but I haven't."

The Sanitary Commission was disbanded in 1866.

The U.S. Christian Commission (U.S.C.C.) was founded in New York in November 1861 with the objective of providing nursing care and promoting the spiritual and religious wellbeing of soldiers and sailors, particularly those facing death. The chairman was a George H. Stuart, a banker, who had spent much of his life supporting evangelical missions. Under his leadership the Christian Commission raised $3 million in cash, plus valuable donations of supplies. Men, women, even children, raised money, sewed clothes and created kits for soldiers from both North and South. The organization recruited over 5,000 volunteers to assist chaplains and surgeons in ministering to the needs of soldiers.

The Commission set up a temporary hospital at Westminster and their wagons brought supplies to the Union II, III and V Corps hospitals immediately after the battle. Eventually some fifty U.S.C.C. agents were working, with some at every corps hospital except the VI, where they set up a tent from which supplies were distributed. They also had representatives at the various buildings such as the court house, Seminary, Pennsylvania College and the several churches in town being used as hospitals. Two supply depots were established in Gettysburg, one at John Shick's store and the other at Adams Express Company close to the railroad station. U.S.C.C. agents were often religious ministers who found that the soldiery did not always appreciate the emphasis they placed on prayer, repentance and conversion. One incredulous and dismayed preacher exclaimed, "Not a single one of the men from Georgia or Alabama had previously received the rite of baptism. No hereafter did these ignorant creatures of God believe in."

Believers or not, as the Adams *Sentinel* wrote on July 21, these agencies "have been doing noble work here . . . The thousands of

soaked in bromide to the area once the diseased tissue had been cut away. This reduced the cases of hospital gangrene dramatically.

Before turning to the detail of how the armies at Gettysburg organized their medical services, some of the highlights of Meade's medical director's report, dated October 3, 1863, provide a useful illustration of the transport problems his department faced prior to the battle and their effect. When referring to wagons being diverted to Westminster, Dr. Jonathan A. Letterman is writing about the four-horse divisional medical wagons carrying 20–22 hospital tents, medical and hospital supplies, stores, small items of furniture, bedding, basins, bed pans, etc., needed to set up and equip properly a tented field hospital capable of caring for hundreds of casualties. He wrote:

> It is scarcely necessary to say that if the transportation is not sufficient . . . the effect must fall upon the wounded . . .
>
> In the autumn of 1862, I investigated the subject [of transport] very carefully . . . with the view . . . to limit the amount necessary, and to have that amount always available. The transportation was one wagon to each regiment and one to each brigade [for Gettysburg 305]. This gave all that was required . . . This system worked well [at Chancellorsville] . . .
>
> On June 19 [1863], while the army was on the march . . . to some unknown point north of the Potomac River . . . the transportation of the department was cut down by Major-General Hooker on an average of two wagons per brigade [about 116], in opposition to my opinion expressed verbally and in writing. This reduction necessitated the turning in of a large portion of the supplies, tents, etc., which were necessary for the proper care of the wounded in the event of a battle. Three wagons were assigned to a brigade of 1,500 men [27 brigades out of 58 were over 1,500, so perhaps 143 medical stores/supply wagons were allowed],

A U.S. Sanitary Commission tent at Gettysburg.

wounded men . . . will ever bear in kind remembrance the untiring efforts of the members of the commissions."

Colonel John C. Chamberlain of the 20th Maine (see page 92) rode to Gettysburg as a member of the U.S.C.C. He arrived on the battlefield on the morning of July 2 in advance of the remainder of the Commission representatives, and after his spell helping with the 20th Maine spent his time visiting field hospitals. Below is an extract from a letter he wrote from Middletown, dated July 11, 1863.

> Then came the wounded; they were lying under every tree, the woods seemed full of them, they issued from every path and were scattered along the roadsides. They were wandering about searching for their respective hospitals. It was a very small proportion who could be accommodated in ambulances. Many of their hospitals I was able to point out to them after washing their wounds . . . This is the way I spent my time at Gettysburg – going round the hospitals, reading in the faces of the men their wants and trying to relieve them, speaking words of comfort and religious consolation, and gathering their dying messages to their friends at home.

There was no Southern equivalent of either of these organizations. While women in the South often sent supplies to help the Rebel troops, including medical supplies, and while there were nursing efforts in camps, there was nothing on the scale of the U.S. Sanitary Commission. The nearest volunteer civilian organization was probably the Richmond Ambulance Committee, whose objective was to give direct support to the army. Volunteers participated in transporting the wounded in most major battles. After Gettysburg they spent some three weeks moving wounded at Winchester.

doing away with regimental wagons. This method in its practical working is no system at all . . . [and it failed] to give the department the means necessary to conduct its operations.

On the 25th of that month, I directed Assistant Surgeon [Jeremiah B.] Brinton, U.S. Army, to proceed to Washington, and obtain the supplies I had ordered the medical purveyor to have put up, and there await orders.

On the 26th, he was ordered to proceed with them to Frederick. This step was taken to obviate the want of supplies consequent upon the reduction of transportation . . . Dr. Brinton arrived at Frederick on June 28, the day after the arrival of headquarters there, with 25 army wagon loads of such supplies as would most be required in case of a battle. The train with these supplies followed that headquarters until we reached Taneytown.

On July 1, the trains [including Dr. Brinton's wagons] were not permitted to go further, and, on the 2d, were ordered farther to the rear, near Westminster . . . It was ordered that "corps commanders and the commander of the Artillery reserve will at once send to the rear all their trains (excepting ammunition wagons and ambulances), parking them between Union Mills and Westminster."

On the 2d, these trains were ordered still farther to the rear, and parked near Westminster, nearly 25 miles distant from the battlefield. The result of this order was to deprive the department almost wholly [XII Corps had managed somehow to disregard this order] of the means for taking care of the wounded until the result of the engagement of the 2d and 3d was fully known . . . Its [the order's] effect was to deprive this department of the appliances necessary for the proper care of the wounded, without which it is as impossible to have them properly attended

> to as it is to fight a battle without ammunition. In most corps the wagons exclusively used for medicines moved with the ambulances, so that the medical officers had a sufficient supply of dressings, chloroform, and such articles until supplies came up, but tents and other appliances, which are as necessary, were not available until July 5.

The shortages of supplies and the enormous strain put upon surgeons is well documented by Union Dr. John S. Billings, working in the 2nd Division, 1st Corps field hospital near the Lightner Farm (see Map 9, page 243). On July 6 he wrote to his wife:

> I have been operating all day long and have got the chief part of the butchering done in a satisfactory manner. I am utterly exhausted mentally and physically, having been operating night and day and am still hard at work. I have been left here in charge of 700 wounded with no supplies and have my hands full. Our division lost terribly. Over 30-percent were killed and wounded.

On July 10 he described how: "the orderly has just scrubbed all the blood out of my hair with castile soap and bay-rum and my scalp feels as though a steam plow has been passed through it."

Dr. Billings did not exaggerate. His division suffered the highest percentage overall loss (56.4 percent) of the entire army. There were 91 killed, 616 wounded and 983 missing/captured. I Corps treated 2,400 wounded, including about 260 Rebels. Billings was one of the outstanding surgeons of the war, going on to become the Deputy U.S. Surgeon General for thirty years, and founding the Surgeon General's Library, which later became the National Library of Medicine at Bethesda, Maryland.

Lee's medical services had to try to cope with the same horrendous number of casualties as their enemy but with substantially fewer medical officers, properly equipped ambulances and medical supplies. The Medical Department had been one of the first elements of the Confederate Army to be raised. As early as February 1861 its Congress had authorized its establishment and a year later introduced a formal field organization that largely followed that of the U.S. Army. In brief, the scheme issued in May 1862 permitted a medical director for an army, a medical director for a corps, a chief surgeon for a division and a senior surgeon for a brigade. Each regiment (infantry, cavalry or battalion of artillery) would have a surgeon, assistant surgeon, a hospital steward, two medical orderlies and two men from each company acting as stretcher-bearers and attendants for the wounded, and two ambulance wagons. This somewhat ad hoc system of providing stretcher-bearers was in operation at Gettysburg. Colonel Fremantle, the British observer with Longstreet's Corps, noted of McLaws' Division, "In rear of each regiment were from twenty to thirty negro slaves, and a certain number of unarmed men carrying stretchers and wearing in their hats the distinctive red badges of the ambulance corps [although it was not a formally established corps]." At brigade level the senior surgeon responsible for supervising the medical arrangements for his brigade was not relieved of his regimental duties. The Union system was better organized by Gettysburg in that they had a separate Field Ambulance Corps (see page 238). Medical officers were not given high ranks. Dr. Letterman, the medical director of the Army of the Potomac, was ranked only as a major. Corps directors were captains and divisional chief surgeons either captains or lieutenants, and assistant surgeons lieutenants. There was also another grade of acting assistant surgeon. In the Union Army they were civilian doctors hired on contract without any formal rank, although they were rated as officers.

Medical Staff

Regimental surgeons and assistant surgeons

At the outbreak of the war the U.S. Regular Army had thirty surgeons and eighty-five assistant surgeons, of whom twenty-four went south and became the nucleus of the Confederate medical services. By the end of the war there were some 11,000 of them in all, with the South mustering over 4,000. Their duties in camp mostly involved looking after sick soldiers rather than injured ones, as disease was by far the greatest killer throughout the war, far outstripping battle deaths and casualties. In a major battle such as Gettysburg the usual practice was for the regimental surgeons to work at the divisional or corps field hospitals while the assistant surgeons followed their regiments, accompanied by a medical orderly, to set up a forward aid post as close behind the line as possible commensurate with reasonable security. At the field hospital the medical director would allocate the best and

Confederate Surgeons

Dr. Hunter McGuire was the medical director of Stonewall Jackson's Corps at Chancellorsville and A. P. Hill's Corps at Gettysburg. In 1889 he gave an address on the subject of the Confederate medical services in which he had the following to say concerning their surgeons:

> The hardships he endured and the privations to which he was subjected soon transformed him from a novice to a veteran, and, I can say with truth that before the war ended some of the best military surgeons in the world could be found in the Confederate Army. His scanty supply of medicines and hospital stores made him fertile in expedients of every kind. I have seen him search fields and forest for plants and flowers, whose medicinal virtues he understood and could use. The pliant bark of a tree made for him a good tourniquet; the juice of the green persimmon [sweet tomato-like fruit of an American tree] a styptic [a substance causing blood vessels to contract and thus stem the flow of blood]; a knitting needle, with its point sharply bent, a tenaculum, and a pen-knife in his hand a scalpel. I have seen him break off one prong of a common table-fork, bend the point of the other prong, and with it elevate the bone in a depressed fracture of the skull and save life. Long before he knew the use of the porcelain-tipped probe for finding bullets, I have seen him use a piece of soft pine wood and bring it out of the wound marked by the leaden ball . . . Many a time I have seen the foot of the operating table raised to let the blood go, by gravitation, to the patient's head, when death from chloroform was imminent, and I would add that, in the corps to which I was attached, chloroform was given over 28,000 times, and no death was ever ascribed to its use.

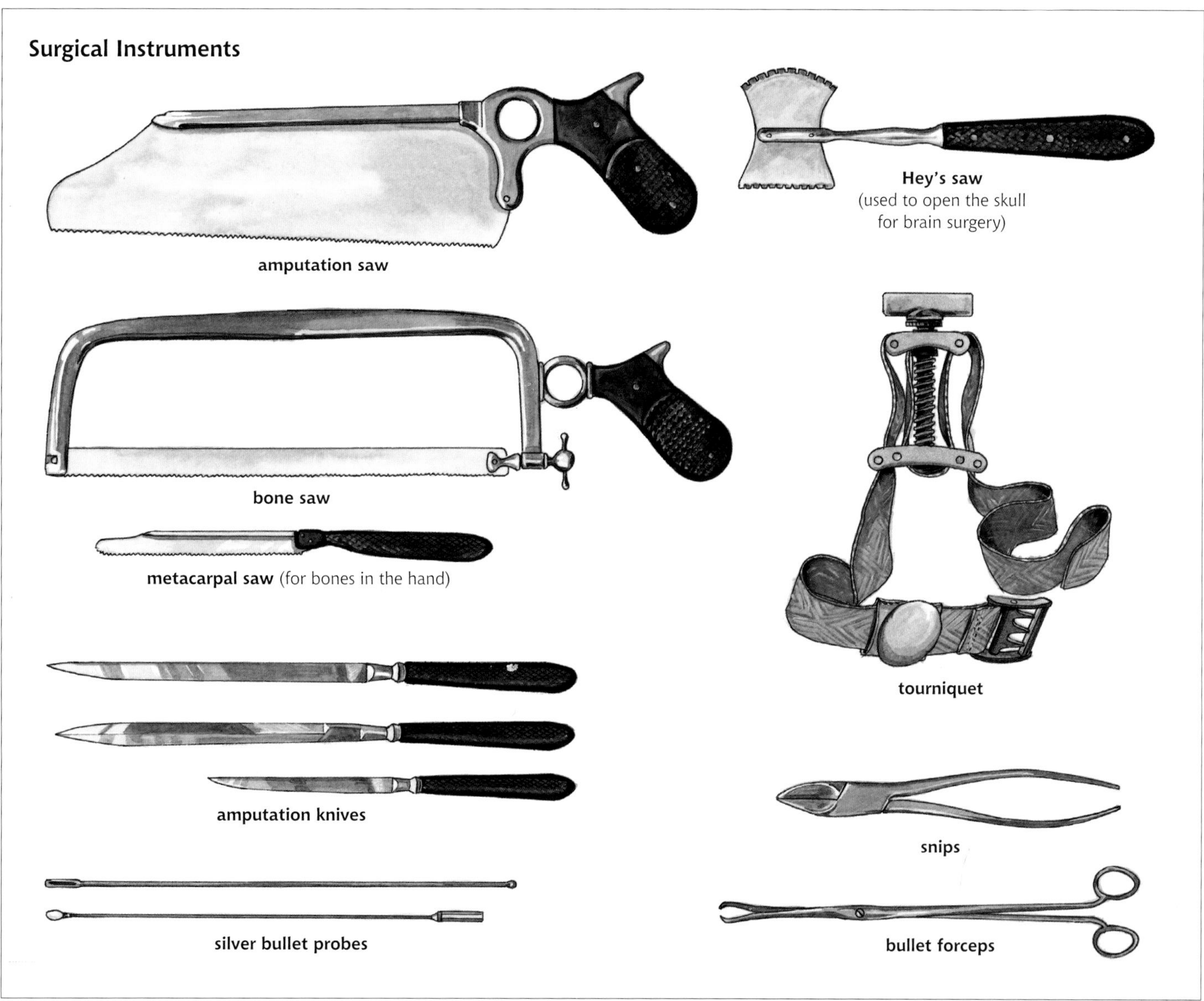

most experienced surgeons (usually three or four at a divisional hospital) to perform operations while the others became "dressing surgeons," whose task was the immediate post-operation care of the casualties, maintenance of patients' records – nature of wound, treatment received, etc. – and to ensure proper interment of those who died.

Surgeons had a regimental medicine chest, amputating and pocket cases of instruments, the latter known as "the surgeon's field companion." These cases included amputating knives, saws, forceps, catheters, lancets, needles, different types of syringes, splints, dental instruments, tourniquets and a trepanning set (cylindrical saw for removing part of the skull). The assistant surgeon going forward with the troops would carry a much reduced set of instruments, as his task was merely to give immediate life-saving first aid and get the wounded man to a field hospital. This involved staunching bleeding, applying initial bandages, administering a stiff swig of whiskey and organizing and directing stretcher-bearers and walking wounded back to the ambulance collecting point, or direct to the divisional/corps field hospital. He was assisted in these duties by a medical orderly, who carried a larger and heavier knapsack (up to 20 pounds when full) called the "hospital knapsack' which contained additional instruments, dressings and medicines that might be needed in an emergency on the march or in action.

Hospital stewards

These men were the equivalent of first sergeants and were paid as such, as their duties were onerous and important. In battle their location was in the field hospitals. The regimental surgeon usually chose them from the men of the unit whom he considered reasonably educated and of good character. Regulations required a steward to be "temperate, honest, and in every way reliable, as well as sufficiently intelligent, and skilled in pharmacy, for the proper discharge of the responsible duties likely to be devolved upon him." These duties were largely administrative, such as supervising the erection of the hospital tents, the hospital cooks and orderlies (nurses). He was responsible, under one of the surgeons, for maintaining medical records and the security and dispensing of medicinal whiskey. On occasion he also assisted in performing minor operations and even prescribing drugs. In the Union Army his rank was distinguished by an emerald-green half-chevron, yellow edged, which bore a 2-inch-long caduceus (staff with two entwined snakes and two wings on top). A Confederate steward often wore the black chevrons of a first sergeant.

The U.S. Ambulance Corps

The collection and transportation of the wounded was a major problem during the first part of the war due to the failure to make any proper provision for moving them to field hospitals set up in the rear of the battlefields. This was the cause of much unnecessary suffering and death. Reportedly, after the First Battle of Bull Run in July 1861, not a single casualty reached Washington 27 miles away in a military ambulance, many being compelled to walk. It was not until Major-General George B. McClellan, then commanding the Army of the Potomac at Harrison's Landing, Virginia, issued General Order No. 147 on August 2, 1862 that proper order was brought to the system – although an Ambulance Corps Act was not finally passed until March 1864. Until then the corps was not an official part of the Regular Army. General Order 147 set out an organization based on the following – all officers being mounted:

- At corps level a captain, whose duties were to command all the ambulances and transport carts in the corps under the general directions of the medical director. He was to keep the medical director informed of the state of the ambulances, horses and equipment and ensure all personnel were trained in their duties of stretcher-bearers. Before a battle the captain would be informed by the medical director as to the division of the ambulances. He would select suitable places as close to the firing line as possible, commensurate with reasonable security, as ambulance collecting points to which serious casualties would be brought for transporting to field hospitals. During the action he was personally to check that casualty evacuation by ambulance was effective.
- At divisional level a first lieutenant would have similar responsibilities, as well as being acting assistant quartermaster for the divisional ambulance corps. This must have been somewhat onerous, as he was obliged to sign and account for the ambulances, carts, horses and harness, etc., and was held responsible for deficiencies. He had under his orders a mobile (cavalry) forge, a blacksmith and saddler.
- At brigade level there was to be a second lieutenant with responsibilities for the ambulances and men assigned to his brigade.
- At regimental level there were to be three ambulances (mostly two-horse; the four-horse wagons normally carried the medical supplies, tents, etc.) and a transport cart, the former with a driver and two Ambulance Corps men, the latter with just a driver, all under a mounted sergeant. Each ambulance would have two stretchers. A corps headquarters would qualify for two ambulances and an artillery battery for one.

The casualties of Union Ambulance Corps at Gettysburg amounted to one officer and four privates killed and seventeen injured.

Countless extraneous factors ensured that the actual situation in the field was rarely as it should be. As noted on page 230, the number of ambulances varied considerably from corps to corps within Meade's command, although this was substantially the organization in use at Gettysburg. I Corps, with, according to

Brigadier-General Ingalls, 67 ambulances, had the fewest and VI Corps the most with 167 – the average for the army being 110 per corps. If the General Order 147 formula is applied to I Corps, then with a corps headquarters, thirty-two infantry regiments and five artillery batteries, there should have been 103 ambulances with Major-General Reynolds on July 1 – he was seemingly well below his entitlement. VI Corps, with its headquarters, thirty-seven infantry regiments and eight batteries, should have been accompanied by 121 ambulances – Major-General Sedgwick had more than his theoretical entitlement. However, if General Order 147 is used to calculate the corps average, the figure is 113 – very close to Ingalls' 110.

The Confederates never had a recognized ambulance corps. At regimental level the assistant surgeon would have an orderly and two men per company detailed to act as stretcher-bearers under his instructions. During the early part of the war when almost every regiment had a band, the bandsmen were required to carry the stretchers in battle – Bandsman Julius Leinbach, 26th North Carolina Infantry, wrote: "We had considerable experience in giving first aid to the wounded, and I, for one, got myself to believe I could amputate a man's leg as well as some of the doctors." Nevertheless, this was not a very satisfactory arrangement, as bandsmen were not directly commanded by the medical officers and were more often required to practice music than medicine. By Gettysburg the number of bands had dwindled and both Lee and Meade had adopted a system of permanently assigned ambulance men for the duty.

Ambulance Wagons

By mid-1863 the Army of the Potomac had largely replaced the two-wheeled ambulances, which were notorious for jolting and jarring their passengers unmercifully, with the four-wheeled version called the "Rucker" ambulance, which was heavier and decidedly more comfortable. It was drawn by two horses and crewed by a driver and two stretcher-bearers. In the locked box under the driver's seat were supposed to be three bed-sacks, six cans of beef stock, a leather bucket, three camp kettles, a lantern and candle, six tablespoons, six tin tumblers and, hopefully, 10 pounds of hardtack. It was designed to carry two wounded men lying down, but could be adapted to take three or even four. It was a well-sprung wagon with two leather-covered seats reaching the whole length on the floor. Hinged to the inner sides of these seats was another leather-covered seat that could be let down so that men could sit facing each other or three or four men could lie lengthways in a tier or bunk-bed arrangement (see the diagram opposite). On each side of the wagon was hung a canvas stretcher.

As noted above, each Union division had an average of something over forty of these ambulances at Gettysburg. The Rebels, however, had to make do with far less sophisticated vehicles. They had one genuine ambulance wagon called a "Chisholm," but they mostly had to make up numbers with supply wagons, civilian carriages and buggies, especially during the retreat after the battle. It was a common occurrence in both armies suffering from transport shortages for ambulance wagons to be used for other than their proper purpose and specific regulations forbidding this were not universally followed. In a Union circular dated June 18, 1863, Hooker reduced the number of wagons permitted with the trains and ordered that "The use of ambulances for carrying baggage for citizens, women &, on marches must be stopped. If division, brigade or other commanders violate this rule, corps commanders will cause the ambulances to be taken from them and turned in, and the officers court-martialed . . ." Neither was it unknown for ambulance horses to be commandeered on the battlefield for other more pressing purposes, an example being Brigadier-General Maxcy Gregg and his staff officer Major Alexander C. Haskell, who replaced their wounded mounts by unharnessing two ambulance horses on the Antietam battlefield.

Battlefield Casualty Evacuation

The sequence of getting a wounded soldier from the firing line to, if necessary, a base hospital perhaps 100 miles from the battlefield is shown in the diagram on page 240, using the 4th Michigan Infantry on July 2 as an example. The Confederates at Gettysburg used the same system, although it was not uncommon for field hospital staff to receive assistance from the quartermasters' staff as their trains were parked nearby.

Medical Inspectors and Purveyors

Both sides established a medical inspectorate under a medical inspector general with a staff of medical inspectors and assistants whose duties involved ensuring that medical regulations were complied with. This entailed visiting camps and hospitals checking on the personal hygiene, water supply, sanitation, cleanliness and medical records. Medical inspectors were attached to armies in the field, Meade's being a Dr. John H. Taylor. An example of a more unusual duty was the use by Dr. Guild, Lee's medical director, of Surgeon R. J. Breckinridge, Guild's medical inspector, "to proceed to the hospitals near the army where our sick and wounded have been sent since the battle at Gettysburg, and to have all those who are fit for duty returned to their regiments."

Medical purveyors ordered and directed medical stores, supplies and drugs. They were physicians, or sometimes pharmacists, whose task was to ensure supply of all the physical medical needs to enable hospitals to function in the field and in the rear. The provision and distribution of drugs was a key requirement of the purveyor's department. As in so many other areas of procurement, it was the South that had the more acute difficulties due to their lack of sufficient manufacturing capacity. Considerable quantities of drugs were bought overseas and smuggled in through the Union naval blockade. Hasty improvization helped improve output – including the cultivation of opium poppies in the Carolinas and California. On June 25 the Army of the Potomac's medical director (Letterman) became concerned that, with a battle likely, and insufficient transport, there were not enough medical supplies available with the army. He instructed "Assistant Surgeon [Jeremiah B.] Brinton, U.S. Army, to proceed to Washington, and obtain the supplies I had ordered the medical purveyor to have put up, and there await orders." They arrived on July 4.

Casualty Evacuation – Firing Line to Base Hospital

4th Michigan Infantry Regiment deployed in woods west of Stony Hill, July 2.

Regimental aid post
Established initially near the eastern edge of the wood immediately behind (east of) Stony Hill.

Divisional ambulance collection point
Set up near Wheatfield Road on reverse (eastern) slope of Stony Hill. Normally sited by divisional quartermaster as part of his transport responsibilities.

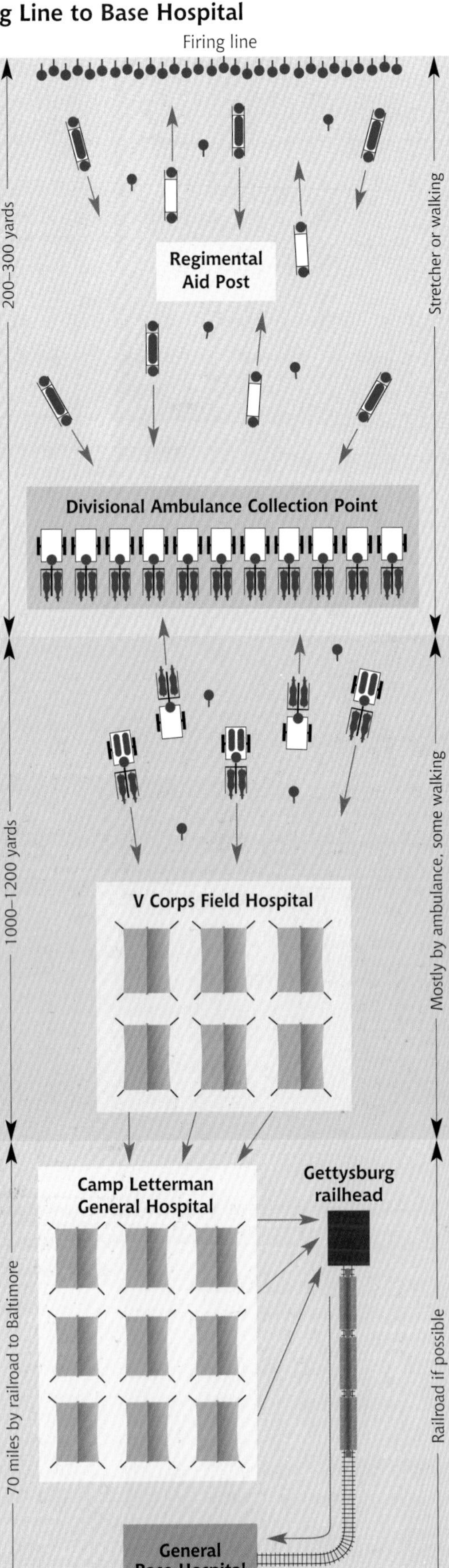

• The 4th Michigan belonged to the 2nd Brigade (Sweitzer), 1st Division (Barnes), V Corps (Sykes). It went into action 342 strong, suffered 165 casualties, of which 64 were wounded.

• **Aid post**
Staff: The assistant surgeon and one or two orderlies.

Task: Sending stretcher-bearers forward to collect casualties. Immediate action to staunch bleeding, remove obvious foreign bodies, administer liquor for shock and direct walking wounded to field hospital. Send stretcher cases to ambulance collection point.

• **Ambulance collection point** (1st Division)

Staff: 1st Lt. Joseph C. Ayer, Ambulance Corps. 3 x 2nd lts., 11 sgts., 33 drivers, 66 stretcher-bearers (9th Mass sent to Brinkerhoff Ridge).

Task: Transport wounded from A.C.P. to corps field hospital from all 11 regiments in the division.

Vehicles: 33 ambulances, probably all two-horse.

V Corps field hospital
First set up around Jacob Weikert Farm on the Taneytown Road.

Later, early on July 3, moved SE and positioned around the Jane A. Clapsaddle dwelling south of the Baltimore Pike.

• The initial location of this field hospital was behind (east of) Little Round Top on the Taneytown Road and there was an hour's delay in getting ambulances to it while it was located by Ayer.

Staff: Medical Director Surgeon John J. Milhau, up to 11 surgeons from the regiments and H.Q. staff, 11 hospital stewards, orderlies, cooks, etc.

Task: Care of the seriously wounded and sick, performing operations (mostly amputations). Asst. Surgeon John S. Billings recalled some 750 wounded being received on July 2 and working all night.

Vehicles: Medicine wagons. The total number is uncertain, but it could have been up to 10, although Billings recalled only three. Several forge wagons. Most, if not all, supply wagons had been sent to Winchester.

Camp Letterman
Set up by mid-July on the York Pike, 1.5 miles east of Gettysburg, and acted as a general hospital until it closed four months later.

Base hospitals
These were opened up to large numbers of wounded, mostly in Baltimore, and some in Washington and Alexandria.

NOTE
The Confederates had a base hospital at Winchester but there was no rail link.

• There was considerable delay in getting wounded and sick back to base hospitals by rail. Meade's medical director, Letterman, had been told the Gettysburg railhead would be able to take them on July 6, but Letterman reported "that this [railroad] was not in good running order for some time after that date."

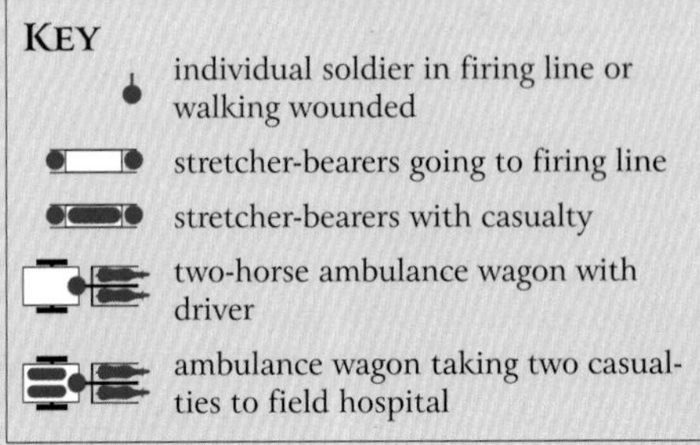

KEY
individual soldier in firing line or walking wounded
stretcher-bearers going to firing line
stretcher-bearers with casualty
two-horse ambulance wagon with driver
ambulance wagon taking two casualties to field hospital

The Lutheran Theological Seminary

This former theological seminary in Gettysburg is Schmucker Hall, more commonly known as the "Old Dorm" as its rooms were used primarily as a dormitory, classrooms and offices. Built in 1832, its most striking feature is the copper-roofed cupola that has oxidized to the familiar green color. It was initially only a large aid station for Union troops on July 1, and the cupola provided an excellent observation post for a Union signals station from the day before. The signals officer, Lieutenant Aaron B. Jerome, claimed that Major-General Buford also used it for a time as he watched events unfolding to the west. Some temporary breastworks were put up in front of the building by Union defenders, but it was overrun by the Rebel attack of the late afternoon of July 1. Later during the battle it was hit by Union artillery firing from Cemetery Hill.

First Lieutenant Jeremiah Hoffman, 142nd Pennsylvania Infantry, was wounded on July 1 and found himself in the Lutheran Seminary after it had been captured by the Confederates. Writing later, he gave a detailed account of events in the building:

> My first recollection of the hospital at Gettysburg Seminary is that our [Union] doctors had no instruments. They were taken prisoner, and in the hurry and excitement of the battle, neither of the parties recollected it was necessary to attend the wounded. The Rebels had to attend to their own and the Union doctors found it much more safe to hide in the cellars and behind large trees than to stand and argue the point of international law as to the exemption of doctors, while acting in their professional capacity, from the fate of ordinary prisoners . . .
>
> On that same day, the Fourth, they brought his body [First Lieutenant Andrew G. Tucker, the acting adjutant of the 142nd] downstairs in a blanket. They roughly lined his grave with fence palings and buried him beside the Col. [Colonel Robert P. Cummins] . . . They were holding the body over the grave when the head slipped over the edge of the blanket and the Lieutenant's beautiful jet black hair dragged over the ground. The thought of his mother and sisters was called up, and surely it cannot be called unmanly that a few tears stole down my cheeks.

After the fighting the Seminary became a major hospital when its brick buildings were supplemented by a number of tents erected nearby. Although it was then a Union hospital, it treated a number of Confederate wounded, including Generals Kemper and Trimble. At its peak twenty-one surgeons were operating and between 600 and 700 casualties were treated from both sides. The heavy rain after the battle caused the basement to flood and about 100 of the worst cases accommodated there were evacuated to the fourth floor.

The building now houses the Adams County Historical Society and is a popular tourist site.

Field Hospitals

The field hospital was the magnet to which all, apart from the very lightly wounded or those unable to get help, were drawn in battle. They came on foot, on stretchers, half-carried by comrades, slumped over a horse's neck and by ambulance, all following small hospital marker flags that indicated the route – yellow for the Yankees and red or yellow for the Rebels. Larger flags (the Union ones having a large green "H" in the center) were flown above field hospitals to indicate their location. That some Confederates used red instead of yellow flags is evidenced by a red lady's petticoat being flown from the cupola of the Lutheran Seminary when it came under artillery fire to show that it was being used as a hospital. Similarly, when John Cunningham's farm on the Marsh Creek was taken over on July 2, the owner was told to provide something red to indicate its use as a hospital – nothing red was immediately available so a pair of white panties was flown instead!

At Gettysburg field hospitals were set up 1–3 miles behind the fighting (see Map 9 opposite), the sites selected by the medical directors of the corps or divisions – in the case of the Confederates in close consultation with the chief quartermasters, whose wagon trains were invariably parked nearby. Under the charge of the senior surgeon, they were staffed by headquarters and regimental surgeons, hospital stewards, orderlies, nurses and cooks. Extensive use of farms, barns, outbuildings and sheds was the predominant means of getting casualties under cover during the battle, as the Union wagons with most of the tents were at Westminster, and the Confederates were under-resourced in this respect. A corps field hospital could be spread over a very large area and would comprise divisional hospitals within it, encompassing numerous separate farms and buildings as well as some tents. Around 175 farms and houses were commandeered by both sides to form part of field hospitals outside Gettysburg (Gregory A. Coco, in his book *A Vast Sea of Misery*, provides a list of their locations). In the town about another fifty buildings were used, many by both sides as Gettysburg changed hands on July 1.

Field hospitals were grim, indeed horrific, places – and Gettysburg's was as grim as any. The Schwartz Farm (see Map 9) formed an important part of the Union II Corps field hospital after its fourth and final move on July 22 – the other moves had been due to being too close to incoming artillery fire and the flooding of Rock Creek and White Run. It treated well over 3,000 casualties, including nearly 1,000 Rebels, many from Pickett's Division. It consisted of 156 acres of farmland and woods with a small orchard. The brick farmhouse and brick barn formed the main hospital, but use was also made of the nearby carriage and wagon sheds and corncrib. One of the best descriptions of a field hospital was written by the chief nurse who served there. It appeared in the *Gettysburg Compiler* on March 15, 1887 and is quoted in full in Kathy Georg Harrison's book *Nothing But Glory*.

> The old farmhouse was only one of half a dozen occupied by the men of Hancock's corps, but it was a type of them all. Its every room was a chamber of death and the boards of the shambling porch that girded it were stained with the blood of the men for whom there was no room inside. The shade of a vine-clad trellis gave these poor fellows partial shelter from the scorching heat. West of the farmhouse, and only a stone's throw from the vine-clad porch with its freight of human misery, stood the old barn. This was devoted exclusively to the wounded of the Confederate Army, and while the soldiers of the North were dying for lack of care it was not strange that these poor creatures were left in even worse condition . . .
>
> The smaller of the barn doors had been unhinged to serve as surgeon's tables, and there on the threshing-floor and haylofts of peaceful husbandry war had garnered its awful harvest of death and agony . . . Every available inch of space was occupied. The men lay close to each other, side by side in long rows, as compactly as when a few days before . . . they had marched shoulder to shoulder across the Emmitsburg Road . . . as compactly as we laid their mangled bodies a few days later, in the long trenches of the stubblefield. The cattle pens, too, still reeking with the litter of the barnyard, were as densely packed with victims as the threshing floor above, and I noticed with horror, as I assisted the dressing of a bleeding wound, that the blood of the patient filtered through the

Notes

• Around 175 separate locations served as some sort of field hospital on or near the battlefield. This map attempts to show only the general location of divisional or corps field hospitals, together with those of the Confederate quartermasters' trains. The latter were invariably located close to the field hospital on sites selected by the divisional quartermaster and medical director in consultation. The only Union train shown is the ordnance train of the reserve artillery, as their quartermaster trains were at Westminster and the position of the other ordnance trains is not known for certain – other than that they were brought as close as possible to the formations they supplied.

• Field hospitals incorporated farms, outbuildings and barns as well as tents. This map shows only one main farm or house to represent each hospital. The Union I and XI Corps were forced to move their hospitals out of the Lutheran Seminary, Pennsylvania College and numerous buildings in Gettysburg late on July 1. Most were taken over by the Confederates. Similarly, II and III Corps pulled back on July 2 when Sickles was pushed out of his salient. Many hospitals treated wounded prisoners from the opposing side. This was particularly the case when the Rebels drove the Yankees from their positions north and west of Gettysburg on the first day. The situation was reversed after the battle as thousands of wounded Confederates were left behind (with many of their own surgeons) when Lee withdrew.

• The Confederate hospital in and around the Samuel Cobean property, the so-called "Second Corps Field Hospital," was really an additional hospital to the divisional ones of Ewell's Corps. It was set up by Dr. Hunter McGuire, Ewell's medical director, using a surgeon from each of the three divisions under Dr. Harvey Black.

• In Gettysburg town some of the buildings used as hospitals included the Adams County Court House, Adams Express Office, Christ Lutheran Church, Gettysburg Railroad Depot, Washington House Hotel, Union (Public) School, St. Francis Xavier Roman Catholic Church, Alexander Spangler Warehouse and a number of private houses.

• Confederate wounded in Longstreet's and Hill's Corps had a long and painful journey of 2–3 miles back to their divisional hospitals from where they fell on July 2 and 3. By July 2 all Union field hospitals were grouped along Rock Creek, White Run and the Baltimore Pike – the army's main line of communication to the southeast.

• Camp Letterman, named after Dr. Jonathan Letterman, medical director of the Army of the Potomac, was opened on July 22. It was a huge complex, with eventually over 500 tents and 30 surgeons. It is estimated that over 4,000 men, many of them Rebels, had been treated there by the time it closed on November 20.

• When Issac Lightner returned to his home, which had been used by the 3rd Division of I Corps as a field hospital, he and his family found the dreadful stench so bad they could not live there again.

Key

Union Corps Hospital

Union Divisional Hospital

Union Hospital in building or buildings, or first location of hospital

Union Hospital later taken over by Confederates

Confederate Divisional Hospital

Confederate prisoner-of-war holding areas

Confederate wagon trains located beside divisional hospitals

Union Artillery Reserve wagon train

Map 9 Main Field Hospital and Confederate Divisional Wagon Train Locations

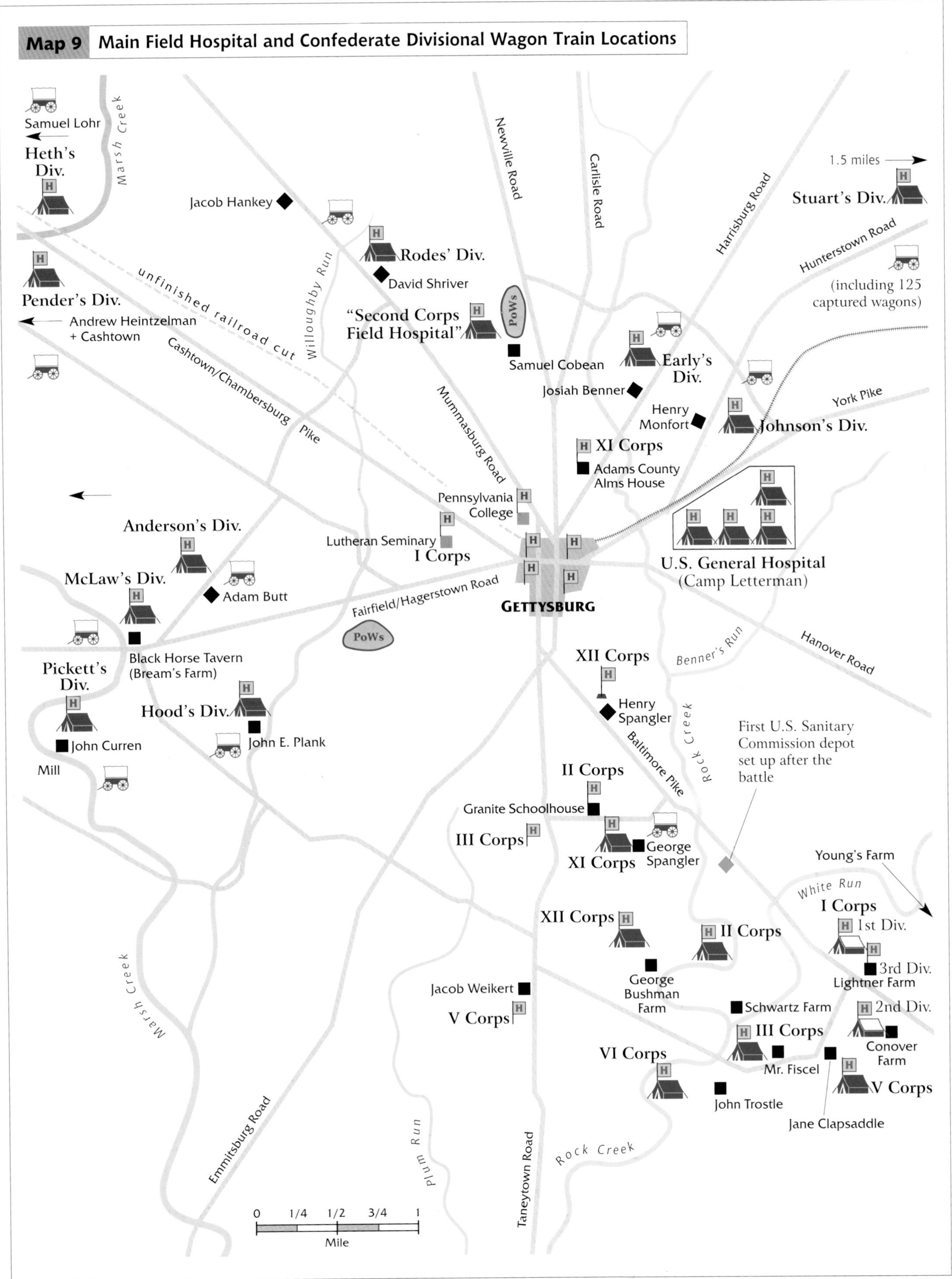

Samuel Lohr
Heth's Div.
Marsh Creek
Jacob Hankey
Rodes' Div.
David Shriver
Newville Road
Carlisle Road
Harrisburg Road
1.5 miles
Stuart's Div.
Hunterstown Road
(including 125 captured wagons)
Pender's Div.
unfinished railroad cut
Willoughby Run
"Second Corps Field Hospital"
PoWs
Andrew Heintzelman + Cashtown
Cashtown/Chambersburg Pike
Samuel Cobean
Early's Div.
Josiah Benner
Mummasburg Road
Henry Monfort
York Pike
Johnson's Div.
XI Corps
Adams County Alms House
Pennsylvania College
Lutheran Seminary
I Corps
Anderson's Div.
McLaw's Div.
Adam Butt
U.S. General Hospital (Camp Letterman)
Fairfield/Hagerstown Road
GETTYSBURG
PoWs
Black Horse Tavern (Bream's Farm)
Pickett's Div.
XII Corps
Benner's Run
Hanover Road
Hood's Div.
Henry Spangler
John E. Plank
John Curren
Mill
Rock Creek
Baltimore Pike
First U.S. Sanitary Commission depot set up after the battle
II Corps
Granite Schoolhouse
III Corps
George Spangler
XI Corps
Young's Farm
White Run
I Corps
1st Div.
XII Corps
II Corps
3rd Div.
Lightner Farm
George Bushman Farm
Jacob Weikert
V Corps
Schwartz Farm
2nd Div.
III Corps
Conover Farm
VI Corps
Mr. Fiscel
V Corps
John Trostle
Jane Clapsaddle
Marsh Creek
Emmitsburg Road
Plum Run
Taneytown Road
Rock Creek
0 1/4 1/2 3/4 1
Mile

cracks and knot-holes of the floor and dripped upon the sufferers below.

As night came on darkness threw a kindly mantle over such repulsive sights, but the horror of the situation was hardly less acute. The only illumination of the place came from the sickly yellow glow of an army lantern . . . The men – restless, suffering and unable to sleep – tossed and moaned and raved in wild delirium. The weather-beaten barn resounded with a horrid chorus of curses, imprecations and groans that sounded doubly awful at night, and the old army lantern's glimmering light wrought weird, fantastic shadows among the cobwebbed rafters of the roof.

The sheer volume of work meant that hundreds of desperately injured men had to lie in filth and with the agonies of their wounds and thirst for many hours, if not days. Confederate casualties had to lie the longest, with the result that deaths among them were high as it was those with the most serious wounds who had been left behind. Even with amputations being performed throughout the twenty-four hours by exhausted surgeons, there were not enough tables or surgeons to cope. Dr. Bushrod W. James described the situation at II Corps hospital:

Every surgeon in the hospital was kept nearly a week amputating limbs, probing for and removing bullets, or sewing, bandaging

Field Hospitals – Senior Staff

The main field hospitals on or very near the battlefield, together with, in the case of the Confederates, the divisional supply trains, are listed below with the names of the officers in charge and the approximate number of casualties treated in them during the fighting and afterwards.

Army of Northern Virginia

Army Headquarters Chief Quartermaster: Lieutenant-Colonel James L. Corley; Medical Director: Dr. Lafayette Guild

Longstreet's 1st Corps Chief Quartermaster: Major John D. Keily Jr.; Medical Director: Dr. John S. D. Cullen

Hood's Division Divisional Quartermaster: Major Moses B. George; Chief Surgeon: Dr. John T. Darby. Casualties treated: about 1,550

McLaws' Division Divisional Quartermaster: Major Abram H. McLaws (brother of the divisional commander); Chief Surgeon: Dr. Frank W. Patterson. Casualties treated: about 1,550

Pickett's Division Divisional Quartermaster: Major Robert T. Scott; Chief Surgeon: Dr. Magnus Lewis. Casualties treated: about 280, but many more were captured after Pickett's charge fell back and were treated in the Union II Corps hospital

Ewell's 2nd Corps Chief Quartermaster: Major John A. Harman; Medical Director: Dr. Hunter H. McGuire

Johnson's Division Chief Quartermaster: Major George D. Mercer; Chief Surgeon: Dr. Robert T. Coleman. Casualties treated: around 1,300

Early's Division Chief Quartermaster: Major Charles E. Snodgrass; Chief Surgeon: Dr. Samuel B. Morrison. Casualties treated: about 800

Rodes' Division Chief Quartermaster: Major John D. Rogers; Chief Surgeon: Dr. W. S. Mitchell. Casualties treated: over 1,400

Hill's 3rd Corps Chief Quartermaster: Major James G. Field; Medical Director: uncertain

Heth's Division Chief Quartermaster: Major Alexander W. Vick; Chief Surgeon: Dr. Henry H. Hubbard. Casualties treated: over 1,500

Pender's Division Chief Quartermaster: Major Nathaniel E. Scales; Chief Surgeon: Dr. Pleasant A. Holt. Casualties treated: about 1,300

Anderson's Division Chief Quartermaster: Major Arthur Johnston; Chief Surgeon: Dr. Henry DeS. Fraser. Casualties treated: approximately 1,100

"Second Corps Field Hospital" Medical officer in charge: Dr. Harvey Black. Casualties treated: possibly 200 casualties

The above gives a total number of Confederate casualties treated during the battle of 10,780, to which must be added almost 1,800 treated in Union hospitals. In all, perhaps 12,500 wounded Rebels, many of whom subsequently died, were treated.

The Army of the Potomac

Army Headquarters Chief Quartermaster: Brigadier-General Rufus Ingalls; Medical Director: Dr. Jonathan Letterman

I Corps Chief Quartermaster: Lieutenant-Colonel James J. Dana; Medical Director: Surgeon J. Theodore Heard. Casualties treated: 2,400, including some 260 Confederates

II Corps Chief Quartermaster: Lieutenant-Colonel Richard N. Batchelder (uniquely for a quartermaster, in 1895 he was awarded the Medal of Honor for gallantry against Mosby's guerrillas in October 1863); Medical Director: Surgeon Alexander N. Dougherty. Casualties treated: about 3,260 including 950 Rebels – many captured after the repulse of Pickett's charge

III Corps Chief Quartermaster: Lieutenant-Colonel James F. Rusling; Medical Director: Surgeon Thomas Sim. Casualties treated: about 2,550, including about 260 Rebels

V Corps Chief Quartermaster: Lieutenant-Colonel William H. Owen; Medical Director: Surgeon John J. Milhau. Casualties treated: about 1,675, including some 75 Rebels

VI Corps Chief Quartermaster: Lieutenant-Colonel Cornelius W. Toles; Medical Director: Surgeon Charles O'Leary. Casualties treated: about 315, including a few Rebels (this corps saw very little action compared with the rest of the army)

XI Corps Chief Quartermaster: Lieutenant-Colonel William G. Le Duc; Medical Director: Surgeon George Suckley. Casualties treated: about 1,500, including nearly 100 Rebels

XII Corps Chief Quartermaster: uncertain; Medical Director: Surgeon John McNulty. Casualties treated: around 1,325, including 125 Rebels

Artillery Reserve Field Hospital Medical Director: Surgeon Joseph D. Osborne. Casualties treated: about 200

Cavalry Corps Chief Quartermaster: Lieutenant-Colonel Charles G. Sawtelle; Medical Director: Surgeon George L. Pencoast. Casualties treated: over 300

The approximate total number of casualties treated in Union field hospitals on the battlefield was 13,500. The combined total of men being treated by one side or the other in one of the field hospitals or dressing stations surrounding the battlefield is around 26,000. When the Confederates retreated on July 4 they left behind some 6,800 wounded in Yankee hands.

The kitchen at Camp Letterman.

> and dressing the wounds of those who were too badly mangled and shattered to be aided in any more hopeful manner. Every hour the improvised operating tables were full, and many of the poor fellows had to be operated on lying on the damp ground.

Tents were initially in short supply as the wagons had to come up from Westminster and it was not until July 9 that many Confederate wounded were finally moved under proper shelter. One of these men recalled the revulsion felt for the hordes of flies and maggots:

> Great green flies in swarms of millians [*sic*] gathered in the camp, grown unnaturally fattened on human blood . . . Fever-smitten, pain-racked, there came to us another terror: we were being devoured while living by maggots – creeping, doubling, crawling in among the nerves and devouring the soldier while yet alive. The noise they made as they doubled and twisted, crept and crawled was that of hogs eating corn.

SIGNALS

The two opposing signal corps in the war were the U.S. Army Signal Corps, which began with the appointment of Major Albert J. Myer as its first signal officer just prior to the war, and the Confederate States Army Signal Corps, a much smaller group of officers and men, using similar organizations, techniques and equipment as their Yankee enemy. Both used strategic and tactical communications, including electromagnetic telegraphy (field telegraph) and aerial telegraphy (flag or "wigwag" signaling). Signal Corps duties included not just communications but battlefield observation, intelligence gathering and, on occasion, directing artillery fire. The Confederate Signal Corps also included an espionage function. The Union service was usually effective on the battlefield but suffered from political wrangling in Washington, particularly with the civilian-led U.S. Military Telegraph Service (U.S.M.T.S.). This was largely responsible for strategic long-distance telegraphic communications and consisted of commercial companies that had been federalized under the U.S.M.T.S. Colonel Myer, as he then was, was to be sacked from his position as head of the U.S. Signal Corps for his attempts to control all electromagnetic telegraphy within the corps – although he still held his appointment for the Gettysburg campaign.

Myer began his career as a medical officer and served as such in the Mexican War, where, it is said, he got his first ideas on signaling by watching Comanche Indians signaling with their lances to other Indians on nearby hills. He eventually devised a system for which he took out a patent and in 1858 a board, presided over by a Lieutenant-Colonel Robert E. Lee, was convened to look into his ideas. The board was less than enthusiastic. Nevertheless, Myer continued his experiments the following year. Assisting with these trials was a Second Lieutenant Edward Porter Alexander, the future signal, engineer and artillery officer and the man who was to coordinate the Rebel artillery barrage on July 3. Later that year Congress passed a bill that authorized:

> the manufacture or purchase of apparatus and equipment for field signals $2,000: and that there be added to the staff of the army one signal officer, with the rank, pay and allowance of a major of cavalry, who shall have charge under the direction of the Secretary of War, of all signal duty, and all books, papers and apparatus connected therewith.

In 1861 Major Myer, with a party of two officers and sixteen men, was in New Mexico practicing and testing his system. During one expedition one of the columns was commanded by a Captain Lafayette McLaws, who was able to see first hand the value of signalers and their flags – it was to be McLaws who, two years later, halted the Confederate outflanking movement of Longstreet's Corps when he realized they were about to become visible to the Union signal station on Little Round Top. By June 1861 Myer had established a Camp of Instruction at Red Hill in Georgetown for the training of signalers for an expanding branch of the army – although it was not until March 1863 that the corps was recognized by Act of Congress. It established a Signal Corps during the "present rebellion" that included a chief signal officer with the rank of colonel, a lieutenant-colonel, two majors,

Officers of the Union Signal Corps, Army of the Potomac.

a captain for each corps or military department, and as many lieutenants, not to exceed eight, per corps or department as the President deemed necessary. Myer was promoted colonel.

By mid-1863 a Union Army headquarters would typically have:

1 captain – chief signal officer
1 lieutenant – adjutant and officer in charge of records
3 quartermaster – ordnance and property officers
3 sergeants – clerks
2 sergeants – in charge of reserve camp, depot and stores
6 soldiers – assistant clerks, flagmen and escorts
4 soldiers – responsible for stores and repairs
3 soldiers detailed from each corps – guards and in charge of depot trains on the march

An army corps would have a captain, eight lieutenants (based on a three- or four-brigade division), six to eight sergeants and about forty or more soldiers – a total of around sixty personnel. By the end of the war the U.S. Signal Corps numbered about 300 officers and 2,500 men.

Porter Alexander, Myer's former assistant, resigned from the U.S. Army on May 1, 1861 to join the Confederate Army as a captain of engineers, one of whose tasks was to train recruits to form a Confederate signals service. As General Beauregard's chief of engineers and signals at First Manassas, he gained lasting recognition when he sent a wigwag signal to a brigade commander, Colonel Nathan Evans, "Look out for your left, your position is turned." The warning was in time for Evans to counter the move. This was the first time in American military history that a signals unit had transmitted information in battle – flag signaling had proved its worth. After that battle Alexander was appointed the Confederate Army's chief of ordnance. His comments were:

> I remained in charge of the signals also but could not give it a great deal of personal attention. I instructed my brother J.H. in the system & soon afterwards lieutenancies were given to most of the men I had trained, & they were distributed about in our army & sent to other armies to introduce the system everywhere. A general signal officer for the Confederacy was wanted & I was offered the position with the rank of colonel, but I declined being unwilling to leave the field. It was accordingly given to a Col. Norris, who had been a signal officer at Norfolk & was an excellent man.

By Gettysburg Alexander was a colonel, but commanding an artillery battalion in Longstreet's Corps, while Lee's headquarters had no designated signals officer, although there was a signals detachment.

The Confederate Signal Corps was formally established in April 1862, a year ahead of the Union service. It was to consist of one major, ten captains, twenty lieutenants, twenty sergeants and 1,500 men detailed from all branches of the army. A signals officer was authorized for the staff of each corps and division. The Confederate Signals Corps came under the Adjutant General's Department in Richmond, the chief signal officer being Colonel William Norris. All personnel were instructed in the cipher system, entrusted with key words, and in the use of the electronic telegraph. When occasion required, they became messengers and agents going into enemy lines and cities, or even going overseas to communicate with agents or secret friends of the Confederate government. They ordered supplies and conveyed them to their destination often by running the naval blockade along the eastern seaboard. It was the duty of Colonel Norris to wait on President Davis every morning with the cipher dispatches from army and department commanders. By the beginning of 1863 the Secretary of War reported: "The Signal Corps has been filled and organized and is now in effective operation. It justifies the expectations entertained of its utility and contributes materially to the dispatch of orders, the transmission of intelligence, and the general safety of the Army."

The Confederate Signal Corps performed duties and used equipment very similar to its Northern counterpart, with some exceptions. Electric telegraphy was not used in tactical battlefield communications due to a shortage of telegraph wire and trained operators. Also their wigwag system, although performed with similar flags, had slightly different codes and flag movements. The main difference, however, was the use of corps personnel in espionage duties – see Section Six: Command and Control.

Wigwag Signaling

Two basic types of signaling were used in the Civil War: visual signaling using either flags, torches or rockets, and the telegraph. The former was called wigwag signaling and was based on the concept of signal stations on high ground which could see each other so that messages could be passed from one to another and repeated (relayed) along a chain of stations to the intended recipient. Its disadvantages included its dependence on good weather for visibility and the slowness in transmitting messages – on average it took a minute for three words. The stations could be either observation stations, watching and reporting enemy activity, or communications stations whose task was merely to pass on messages. A station could perform both tasks, and often did. Observation was a crucial function and played an important part in keeping Meade informed during Gettysburg – see page 250. Five months after the battle, Brigadier-General George A. Custer wrote to Captain Norton, Meade's chief signal officer, stressing the importance he attached to observation: "An army can have no better outpost, from which to watch the movements of the enemy, than a signal station; and with a practical signal officer at such a position, no force can move without being detected."

In the Union Signal Corps, knowledge of the code that translated letters into numbers, which corresponded to a particular flag movement, was restricted to officers; all Union signal officers had to memorize the code. It was usually the sergeant in the party who acted as flagman, making the appropriate number signals (see below) as the officer called them out. Although in 1863 Union flagmen themselves were not given the code, most had learned it by endless repetition. The Confederates did not limit official knowledge of the codes to the officers, so any soldier could send a message if necessary.

The code most commonly used included just two symbols, which made it simple to use. For example, to make the number "1" the flag was waved from the vertical to the left and instantly returned to the vertical. To indicate the number "2" it was waved to the right and returned to the vertical. If the flagman made the signal for a "1" and followed it immediately by a "2" then it would read as number "12," which the code might show to be the letter "O." Similarly, two successive waves to the right would read "22" or letter "N." Three waves to the right and one to the left, or "2221," stood for the word ending "tion." Waving the flag directly to the front and bringing it back to the vertical signaled the number "5." At the end of each word a "5" was signaled; at the end of a sentence "55," and at the end of a message "555." When torches (called "flying torches," as they were waved about) or lanterns fueled with turpentine were used at night the same movements were made as with a flag but because the man was not visible a point of reference was needed. This was provided by the so-called "foot torch" at which he stood while making signals.

Because of the need to see from a signal station and the need to have as uniform a background as possible, such as the sky, suitable positions were very visible and exposed to enemy observation and fire. The two most effective yet obvious stations at Gettysburg were the cupola of the Lutheran Seminary and Little Round Top. The latter was plainly visible to the Confederates and was subjected to heavy rifle-musket and artillery fire, forcing the signalers to take shelter, and on July 3 compelling them to cease signaling and rely on couriers for almost two hours.

The other essential items of equipment were the telescope and binoculars. The first was extremely powerful and gave a magnification of thirty times. It was normally used to read signals from a distant station – it is claimed that on a clear day this could be 20 miles away. The second were more a general observation tool as their magnification was less but they gave a wider field of vision.

"Wigwag" Signal Flags

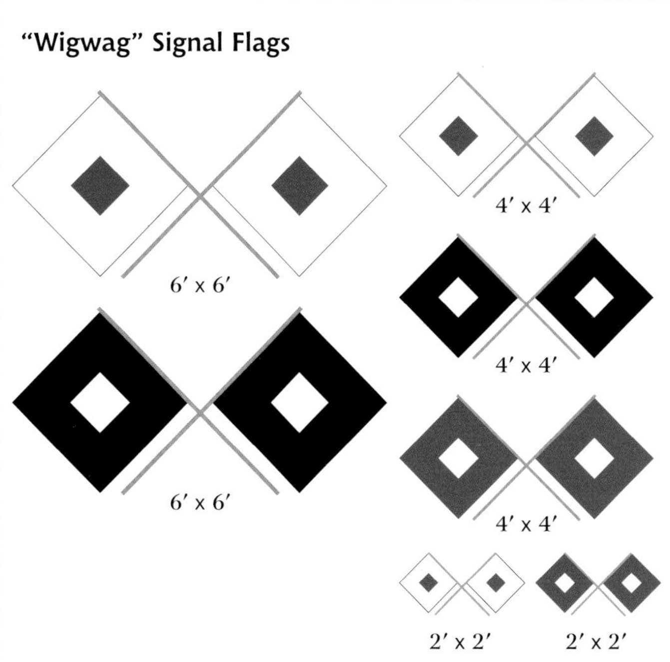

Notes

- Wigwag signaling was performed during daylight with a single flag tied to a hickory staff constructed in 4-foot jointed sections. Red, black and white were the only colors used.
- The 4-foot flags attached to 12-foot staffs were the ones most often used, although 2-foot flags were used if the flagman wanted to avoid enemy attention. The red flags were generally for use at sea or on coastal defenses.

Field Telegraph

Telegraph trains were introduced by Myer to support telegraphy for mobile operations. Horse-drawn wagons carried telegraph sets and supplies, such as reels of insulated copper wire and 200 iron lances, for setting up temporary field lines – a practice called "flying telegraph lines." Each train consisted of two wagons equipped with 5 miles of wire and a telegraph instrument. By Gettysburg this instrument was the Beardslee Patent Magneto-Electric Field Telegraph Machine, named after its inventor, George W. Beardslee of New York (his son, Captain F. E. Beardslee, commanded the Union telegraph train during the Gettysburg campaign). It required no battery as it used a hand-cranked generator and was based on a dial indictor, a circular index plate bearing the letters of the alphabet and a pointer that turned to the letter to be transmitted. A similar pointer spelled out the message at the receiving end. There was, however, much more to it than just cranking a handle. A whole set of procedures had to be followed and some operators found it too complex. The Beardslee machine was carried in a wooden box, the whole weighing around 100 pounds. Apart from complexity, its disadvantages were that the generator could not produce enough power to transmit messages more than 8 miles, and there was a tendency for the sending and receiving pointers to get out of synchronization, garbling the signal. At Chancellorsville the Union Army commander, Hooker, south of the Rappahannock, could not be connected to his chief of staff, Butterfield, over 10 miles away on the other side of the river using the field telegraph. Using both electrical and visual signals, the Signal Corps took three hours to deliver messages between them. The system broke down completely when Hooker and Butterfield overloaded the system and the Military Telegraph had to take over. Even then the inadequacy of the field communications contributed to Hooker's defeat.

By 1863 the Union had about thirty field telegraph trains in use and, despite their poor showing at Chancellorsville, they proved a valuable asset in the latter part of that year, although Meade's field telegraph trains were not used at Gettysburg. This was unusual in that it was routine to connect corps by telegraphic communications at this stage of the war. At Fredericksburg and

Wigwag Method

An article written in 1889 by a former Union Civil War signalman provides a clear account of the practicalities of wigwag signaling.

> When a message is about to be sent, the flagman takes his station upon some elevated object and "calls" the station with which he desires to communicate by waving the flag or torch slowly to and fro. The operator seated at the glass [telescope], watches closely the distant flag, and as soon as it responds by dipping, he is ready to send his dispatch. Holding the written message before him, he calls out to the flagman certain numbers, each figure or combination of figures standing for a letter. The flagman indicates each separate figure by an ingenious combination of a few simple motions . . . There are a few syllables which are indicated by a single stroke of the flag; otherwise the word must be spelled out letter by letter. Experienced signal officers, however employ many abbreviations by omitting vowels, so that scarcely a single word, unless a very unusual one, is spelled out in full.
>
> The rapidity with which all this is executed by experienced operators is astonishing. The flag is kept in such rapid motion that the eye of the inexpert can scarcely follow . . . An ordinary message of a few lines is dispatched in ten minutes; a whole page of foolscap occupies about thirty minutes in the transmission . . . The distance also through which signals can be transmitted without an intermediate station is surprising. [Messages were sent] regularly from Ringgold to Summerville, on Lookout Mountain, a distance of eighteen miles . . . But these instances required remarkably favorable conditions of the atmosphere, locality, etc. Ordinarily, messages were not sent a greater distance than six or eight miles.

The longest recorded distance for successful wigwag signaling was from Maryland Heights, overlooking Harper's Ferry, to Sugarloaf Mountain, a distance of 24 miles.

Chancellorsville this had been the position. After the battle, during the pursuit, field trains were again used to connect most corps telegraphically, although much of the credit for this is probably due to the arrival of signals reinforcements from Washington under an energetic Captain William Nicodemus (later he became chief signal officer at Washington as a colonel). During the battle the field trains had been sent to Frizellburg about 18 miles southeast of Gettysburg down the Taneytown Road. Meade's chief signal officer, Captain Lemuel Norton, had this to say about these trains in his report dated September 18, 1863:

> On July 1 general headquarters remained near Taneytown . . . In the evening I was made acquainted by the general commanding with the line of defense to be occupied by the army [the Pipe Creek line – a possible defensive position covering the Taneytown Road and Baltimore Pike some 15 miles southeast of Gettysburg] in case the enemy made an irresistible attack on our position, and directed by him to "examine the line thoroughly, and at once upon the commencement of the movement [to the Pipe Creek line] extend telegraphic communications from each of the following points, viz, general headquarters, near Frizellburg, Manchester, Union Mills, Middleburg, and the Taneytown Road."
>
> In order that these instructions might be promptly and successfully fulfilled, signal telegraph trains were sent to Frizellburg, and everything held in readiness to extend the wire at a moment's notice to the points desired . . .

Signalers Under Fire

Sergeant Furst, a flagman on Little Round Top on July 3, wrote the following description of his day:

> July 3rd. Were up before daylight. Began to signal in direction of Gettysburg at daybreak. Held our station all day, but were much annoyed by the enemy's sharpshooters in and near the Devil's Den. Have to keep under cover to protect ourselves. The large rock piles up all around us serve as good protection. Today there have been seven men [signalers] killed near our station by the enemy's sharpshooters: hundreds on all sides of us by the enemy's severe cannonading [Major Mathias W. Henry's guns of Hood's Division were firing at Little Round Top]. Up to near noon there has been considerable skirmishing along the line. A little later the whole of the artillery on both sides opened up and shell flew fast and thick. A good many have been struck near our station, but we are able to keep up communication [mostly by courier]. The fight upon the right is said to have been very severe, but our troops have held their positions and repulsed the enemy at every point.

Later that year, when control by the Signal Corps of the field telegraph was in doubt, numerous officers stressed its virtues to the army in the field. On November 12, 1863 Captain McClure, acting chief commissary of I Corps, wrote to Captain Norton (still the chief signal officer of the Army of the Potomac):

> It is with pleasure that I attest the great utility of the signal telegraph as used in this army under your direction. I recollect one instance when the line was more than twenty miles in length and where I transmitted messages by it with perfect success. Corps headquarters were at Guilford, and Army headquarters were at Fairfax at the time. The flags could not be used owing to dense woods and want of positions, but the line worked like a charm. In my opinion it is of great benefit to the army as now conducted.

The next day Meade himself wrote: "I should be very sorry to see the field telegraph separated from the Signal Corps as, I understand from you, is now proposed . . ." There was an ongoing and heated conflict over its control in Washington with the chief of the Military Telegraph, Anson Stager. The deciding moment came when Colonel Myer advertised in the official *Army and Navy Gazette* for scarce, skilled operators to apply for commissions in the Signal Corps. This was entirely unauthorized and infuriated the Secretary of War, Edwin M. Stanton, to the extent that he removed Myer from his post and turned all telegraph apparatus over to Stager.

A Union wagon train of the Military Telegraph.

The U.S. Military Telegraph (U.S.M.T.)

This organization was formed early in the war, and despite its name employed civilian operators, although its senior managers were given commissions in the Quartermaster's Department so that they could disburse government funds and property. Its head was (Colonel) Anson Stager, an official of the Western Union Telegraph Company (after the war he became its vice-president). President Lincoln took control of the nation's commercial telegraph lines in February 1862 and they became available for use by Stager's organization. Although the U.S.M.T. was technically under the Quartermaster's Department, in practice it was controlled by Secretary of War Edward M. Stanton, who was well informed on telegraph affairs, as he had been a director of the Atlantic and Ohio Telegraph Company. He placed the telegraph office next to his own in the War Department, and one of his biographers described his operators as "Stanton's little army." Myer was to find Stager a powerful adversary (he has been described as a "stubby, whiskered, ill-tempered conniver") in the struggle he would lose to keep telegraphic communications control within the army. The Military Telegraph was supposed to serve the needs of the army and yet it functioned independently of army commanders. Only the civilian operators knew the cipher codes – even President Lincoln was denied access to them.

Throughout the campaign, the Military Telegraph was the means by which the General-in-Chief (Halleck) in Washington communicated with the army commander (Hooker and then Meade). Despite the destruction of telegraph lines by Rebel cavalry at every opportunity, there was no period of over thirty-six hours when communication was impossible. Below are two examples of messages sent by this means, the first by Hooker prior to the battle; the second from Meade afterwards.

> SANDY HOOK, June 27, 1863 – 1 p.m. (received 3 p.m.)
> Maj.-Gen. H.W. Halleck, *General-in-Chief:*
>
> My original instructions require me to cover Harper's Ferry and Washington. I have now imposed on me, in addition, an enemy in my front of more than my number. I beg to be understood, respectfully, but firmly, that I am unable to comply with this condition with the means at my disposal, and earnestly request that I may be at once relieved from this position I occupy.
>
> JOSEPH HOOKER, *Major-General*

Note: this message took only two hours to be received.

> HEADQUARTERS ARMY OF THE POTOMAC
> July 4, 1863 – 7 a.m.
> (received 7.20 p.m.)
>
> Major-General HALLECK:
> *Washington:*
>
> This morning the enemy has withdrawn his pickets from the positions of yesterday. My own pickets are moving out to ascertain the nature and extent of the enemy's movement. My information is not sufficient for me to decide its character yet – whether a retreat or maneuver for other purposes.
>
> GEO. G MEADE, *Major-General*

Note: this message took much longer (over twelve hours) as it had to go by courier to the nearest Military Telegraph because there was no field telegraph operating at Gettysburg at that time.

Instructions to Signal Officers

Official U.S. Army Signal Corps instructions went into great detail over how signal stations in the field should operate.

> Officers at each signal station must take care that a look-out through the glass [telescope] is kept at each station so constantly that no signal can be shown, at any time, at the communicating station, for more than ten minutes without receiving an answer. For this reason, when not at the glass himself, he will cause his men, or any one on duty at the station, to keep a regular "glass-watch," assigning the men by turns, and fixing particular hours for each, that responsibility for neglect may be easily traced. These details will relieve each other every two or four hours, day and night. The watchmen on duty must be seated at the glass; and before assuming his station must, with the aid of the soldier last on duty, make certain he knows the exact position of the observed station, and that it is plainly in the field of the glass. This precaution is particularly necessary at night, when the least movement of the glass may have thrown the station out of view. All land marks being then invisible, there is nothing by which to detect the error; and signals might be long shown in vain at one station, while the glass not bearing upon them is attentively watched at another.

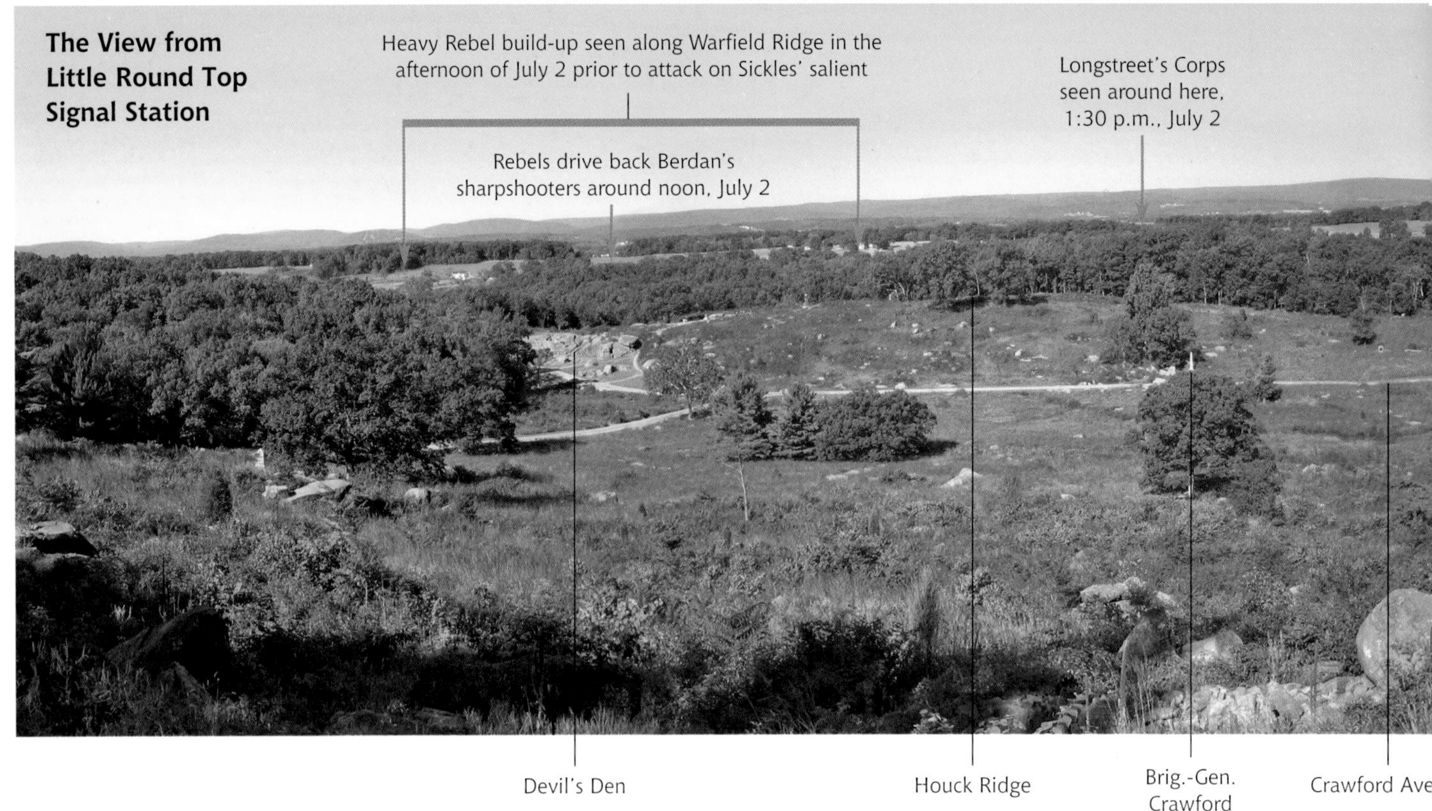

Gettysburg – Battlefield Signals

There is insufficient space in this book to examine the quite extensive use made of both telegraphic and wigwag signaling during the campaign before and after the battle, although it will be touched on in Sections Six, Seven and Twelve. The remainder of this section is devoted to the role it played, predominantly for the Army of the Potomac, during the battle itself.

Gettysburg presents an excellent example of the effective use of wigwag signaling both for communication and for conveying intelligence. However, it was all somewhat one-sided, as although the Rebels used the cupola of the Lutheran Seminary after the capture of Gettysburg town, Lee did not have a signal officer at his headquarters, seemingly relying mainly on couriers for receiving information and giving instructions. Although corps commanders and some divisions had signal officers (Longstreet's Corps, Captain Jacob H. Manning; Ewell's Corps, Captain Richard E. Wilbourn – the same Wilbourn that supported the wounded Jackson at Chancellorsville; and Hill's Corps, Captain Richard H. T. Adams), their activities were not planned or coordinated by Lee's headquarters, and so were used mostly for internal communication within the formation as the opportunity presented itself. Although some, but not all, senior commanders mention in their reports signal officers providing useful service during the retreat, there seems little available evidence of significant messages being transmitted by flag during the period July 1–3 by Confederate signalers. In his article "The Confederate Signal Corps at Gettysburg" in the *Gettysburg Magazine*, David Winfred Gaddy writes:

> Thanks to the papers preserved by Hood's signal officer, Lt. Eli Duvall, three brief signal messages sent on July 2 can be entered into the record . . . The first of the three, in the order in which they appear in Duvall's notebook, was from Signal Sergeant Buchanan, Duvall's assistant, to the I Corps signal officer. It says, simply, "July 2, 1863. To Capt. Peyton T. Manning: The [signal] line is open to the left from where you left me." Next . . . Signed by Maj. John W. Fairfax of Longstreet's staff, and also dated July 2, says: "To Genl. Lee. We are doing well." The response was, "Genl. Lee: To Maj. Fairfax: I am delighted to hear it – press on."

Within the Army of the Potomac it was a different story. On July 1 four signal stations were used as first Buford's Cavalry Division and then I and XI Corps battled to keep the advancing Rebels from taking the town. In this they were unsuccessful and the stations established in the Lutheran Seminary, Pennsylvania College and Adams Court House were abandoned. With the arrival of XI Corps the fourth station was set up on the high ground of Cemetery Hill – the location around which the Union forces rallied after their retreat on the first day. The other four stations were set up on July 2 at Meade's headquarters at the Leister House, on Culp's Hill (or rather Stevens' Knoll, a spur of Culp's Hill), Power's Hill (which served briefly as Meade's headquarters on July 3) and Little Round Top. During July 2 and 3 the key stations were at Meade's headquarters and on Little Round Top, the latter having an extensive view over much of the battlefield to the west, northwest and north along Cemetery Ridge (see the photograph above).

The locations of these signal stations are shown on Map 10, page 252.

Lutheran Seminary cupola

A splendid viewpoint with views in all directions. Occupied on July 1 by Lieutenant Aaron B. Jerome, signals officer of Major-General Buford's Cavalry Division. During the course of the day

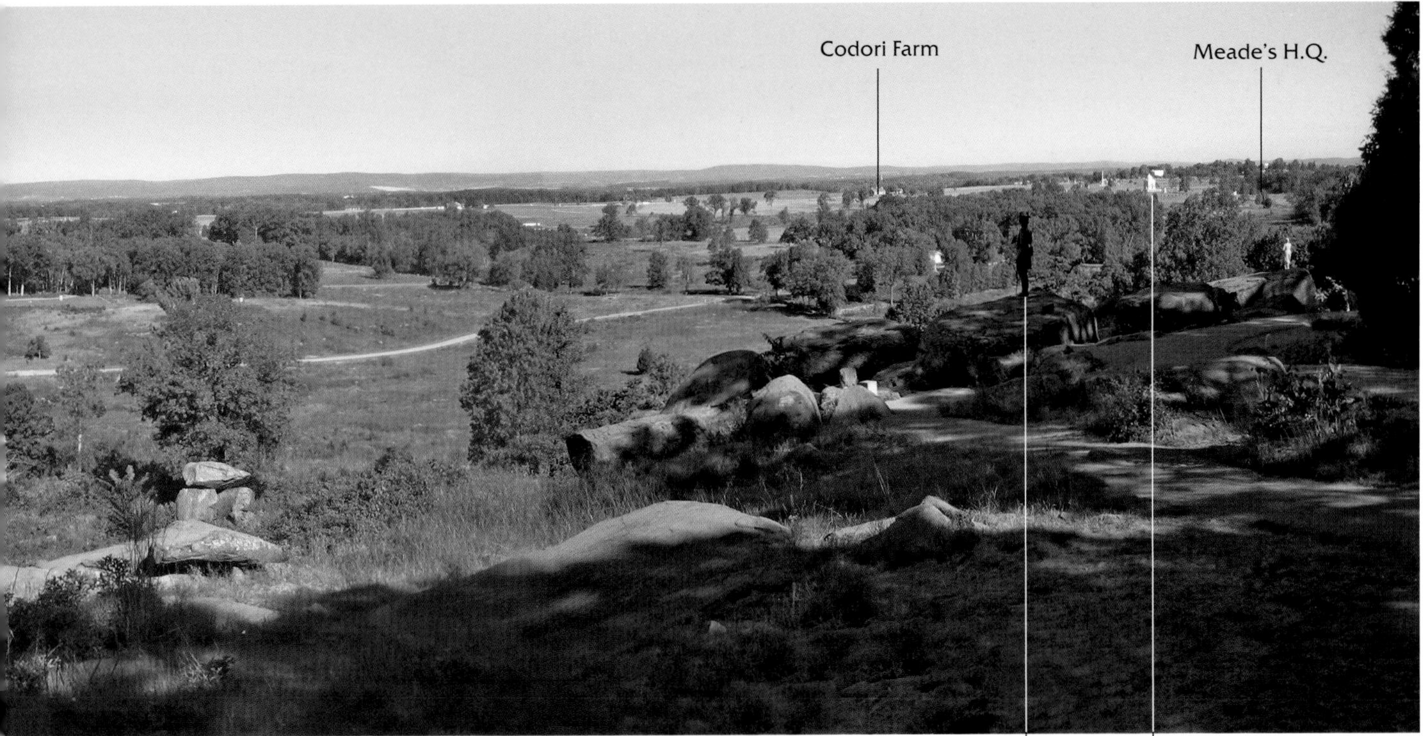

he sent a number of reports/observations by courier and flag, mostly to the station on Cemetery Hill. Important ones included:

- Around 7:00 a.m. to General Buford by courier reporting the advance of Confederate troops down the Chambersburg Pike. This brought Buford forward to the cupola to assess the situation.
- At about 8:30 a.m. he sighted the arrival of Union troops (Cutler's Brigade), leading the advance of I Corps up the Emmitsburg Road at a distance of about 2 miles. This confirmed Buford in his determination to keep delaying the Rebels east of the town.

Pennsylvania Hall, Gettysburg College
Lieutenant Jerome with his signals detachment occupied the cupola on June 30 on the arrival of Buford in the town. The following morning he moved forward to the Seminary but later, during the heavy fighting of July 1, Jerome moved back to the hall. From there he was in contact by flag with the Cemetery Hill station – then the headquarters of Major-General Howard, who had assumed overall control in the area after Reynolds' death. It was probably from here that Jerome sent the following by flag sometime shortly after 1:00 p.m.:

> General Howard
>
> Over a division of the rebels is making a flank movement on our right; the line extends over a mile, and is advancing, skirmishing. There is nothing but cavalry to oppose them.
>
> A. B. Jerome
> First Lieutenant, Signal Officer

Adams County Court House
This was the last station used by Lieutenant Jerome and it was from here that he was forced to withdraw as the Union forces were driven back through Gettysburg.

Cemetery Hill
This station was first set up when Howard left a reserve (Brigadier-General Steinwehr) on the hill when he deployed north of the town on July 1. It was first occupied by Captains P. Babcock and T. R. Clark (XI Corps). It was also used by I Corps (First Lieutenants J. C. Wiggins and N. H. Camp). Captain Lemuel Norton, Meade's chief signal officer, was with the army headquarters at Taneytown on July 1 and tried to contact the Cemetery Hill station (Howard) via a relay station he had posted on Indian Lookout (a high hill overlooking Emmitsburg). These efforts failed until communications were established using torches via Indian Lookout and Little Round Top around 11:00 p.m. This line was kept open throughout the battle, although Captain C. S. Kendall and First Lieutenant L. R. Fortescue were captured by Stuart's cavalry at the Indian Lookout on July 6 during the Rebel retreat.

Meade's Headquarters (Leister House)
This was the central command station from July 2, receiving signals from all other stations, particularly Little Round Top. It was the location of Captain Norton except when touring the position to check on other stations. The officer directly responsible for this station was Captain D. E. Castle, who was left alone without even a flagman at Leister House when Meade moved to Power's Hill to escape the heavy bombardment of July 3. Castle resorted to signaling personally with a white bedsheet as a flag.

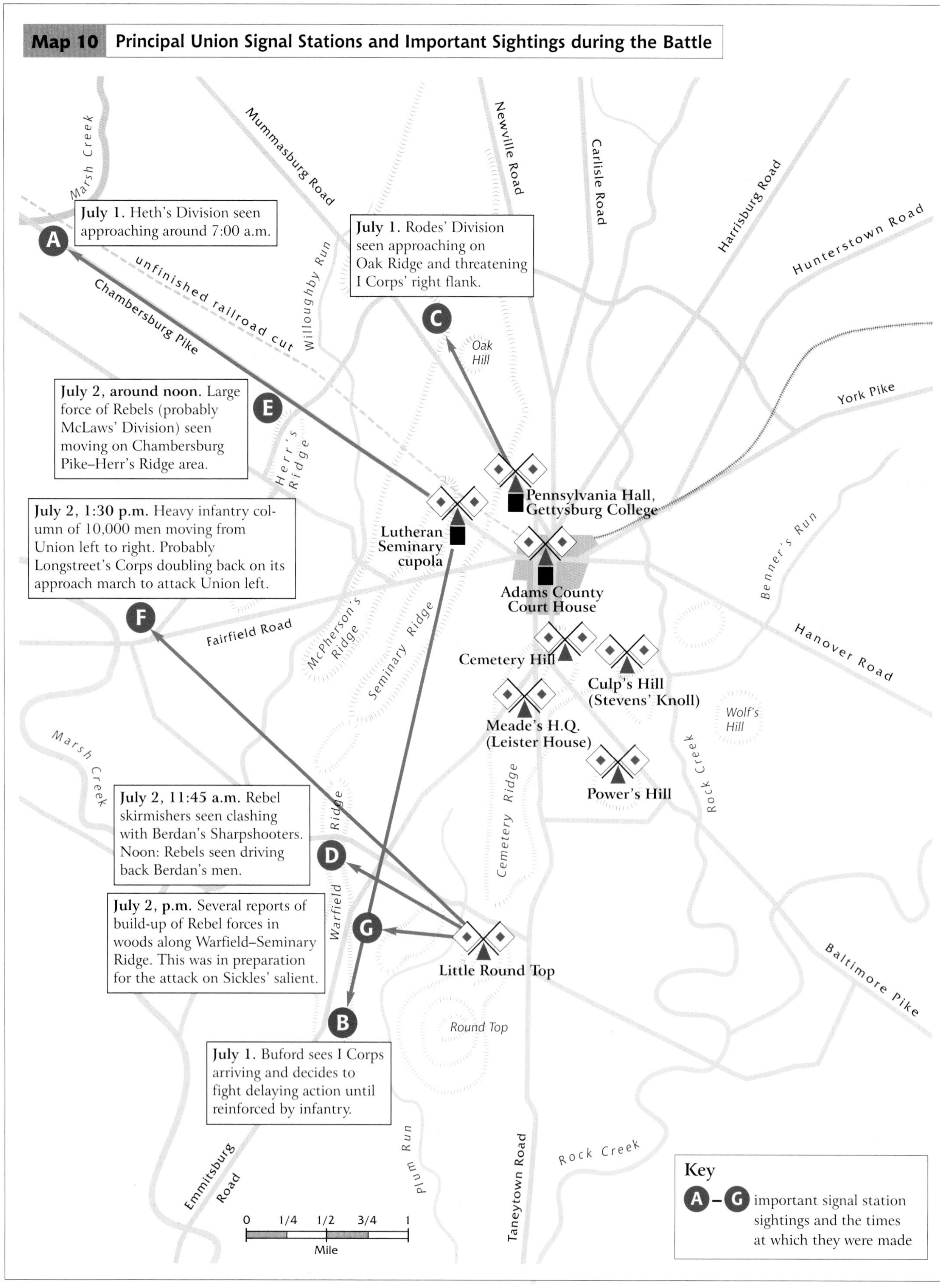
Map 10 Principal Union Signal Stations and Important Sightings during the Battle
July 1. Heth's Division seen approaching around 7:00 a.m.
July 1. Rodes' Division seen approaching on Oak Ridge and threatening I Corps' right flank.
July 2, around noon. Large force of Rebels (probably McLaws' Division) seen moving on Chambersburg Pike–Herr's Ridge area.
July 2, 1:30 p.m. Heavy infantry column of 10,000 men moving from Union left to right. Probably Longstreet's Corps doubling back on its approach march to attack Union left.
July 2, 11:45 a.m. Rebel skirmishers seen clashing with Berdan's Sharpshooters. Noon: Rebels seen driving back Berdan's men.
July 2, p.m. Several reports of build-up of Rebel forces in woods along Warfield–Seminary Ridge. This was in preparation for the attack on Sickles' salient.
July 1. Buford sees I Corps arriving and decides to fight delaying action until reinforced by infantry.
Marsh Creek
Mummasburg Road
Newville Road
Carlisle Road
Harrisburg Road
Hunterstown Road
York Pike
Unfinished railroad cut
Chambersburg Pike
Willoughby Run
Oak Hill
Herr's Ridge
Lutheran Seminary cupola
Pennsylvania Hall, Gettysburg College
Adams County Court House
Benner's Run
Hanover Road
Fairfield Road
McPherson's Ridge
Seminary Ridge
Cemetery Hill
Culp's Hill (Stevens' Knoll)
Wolf's Hill
Meade's H.Q. (Leister House)
Power's Hill
Rock Creek
Cemetery Ridge
Warfield Ridge
Little Round Top
Round Top
Baltimore Pike
Emmitsburg Road
Plum Run
Taneytown Road
0 1/4 1/2 3/4 1
Mile
Key
A–G important signal station sightings and the times at which they were made

Captain Norton's After-Action Report for July 2, 3 and 4

On July 2, I reported at an early hour at the point selected for headquarters of the army for that day, but found the signal officers, who had been previously assigned to the different army corps, already on the field, and through their exertions the general commanding had been placed in communication with nearly all the corps commanders.

Before 11 a.m. every desirable point of observation was occupied by a signal officer, and communication opened from General Meade's headquarters to those of every corps commander.

A station was established [intermittently] upon Round Top Mountain, on the left of our line, and from this point the greater part of the enemy's forces could be seen and their movements reported. From this position, at 3.30 p.m., the signal officer discovered the enemy massing upon General Sickles' left, and reported the fact to General Sickles and the general commanding.

At 5.30 p.m. [it was nearer 4.00 p.m.] the enemy opened a terrific fire, but our left was fully prepared for them, and the fight gradually extended to the whole front, so that every signal station was kept almost constantly working. The station at Round Top was once, and that at General Meade's headquarters twice, broken up by the rapid advance of the enemy and the severity of the fire, but were immediately re-occupied when the positions became tenable . . .

On July 3, the same positions were occupied by the signal officers as on the day previous . . . The station at General Meade's headquarters and that at General Howard's were rendered inoperative for a couple of hours by the furious attack upon our center, but both were again actively employed as soon as the tremendous fire moderated sufficiently to permit of messages being read and transmitted with accuracy . . . In the evening, the commanding general removed his headquarters to a strip of woods on the Taneytown Road, and another station was established at this point, still maintaining communication with those previously opened.

On July 4, at 5.40 a.m., the signal officer from a station on the college in Gettysburg reported to the general commanding "that the enemy had evacuated the position they held yesterday," and at 9.30 a.m. reported the new line occupied by them, and that they were retreating toward Hagerstown. This station was kept open all day, and information in regard to the movements of the enemy sent in by orderly. General Meade's headquarters were removed to the Baltimore pike, and this was made the terminus of all signal lines.

July 5. – All signal stations were this day discontinued, excepting those on Round Top Mountain, Cemetery Hill, court house and General Meade's headquarters.

Culp's Hill spur (Stevens' Knoll)

This was the area of XII Corps' station. It supported Brigadier-General Williams' headquarters, as Williams was acting as corps commander because Major-General Slocum regarded himself as the overall right-wing commander.

Power's Hill

This station supported Major-General Slocum's right-wing headquarters and was commanded by First Lieutenant J. E. Holland on July 2 – attached to XII Corps. It was to this station that Meade withdrew at around 1:30 p.m. on July 3 to escape the effects of the Rebels' heavy and prolonged bombardment prior to Pickett's attack.

Little Round Top

This station had a panoramic view of most of the battlefield fronting Cemetery Hill and could see all the signal stations in use on the second and third days of the battle. As such, it was the busiest outstation, sending frequent reports throughout July 2 and 3. Nevertheless, it was occupied only intermittently during July 2. The main sequence of events at this signal station was as follows.

Late on July 1 Brigadier-General John W. Geary's Division (XII Corps) was posted on the left of the Union line along Cemetery Ridge and the corps signal officer, First Lieutenant J. E. Holland, established a station on Little Round Top. Eventually, signaling by torch, contact was made with Emmitsburg (Indian Lookout) at around 11:00 p.m.

Between 5:00 and 5:30 a.m. on July 2 Holland packed up and departed when Geary's Division moved north.

Sometime later, Lieutenant Jerome arrived in support of Buford's troopers, who were in front of Little Round Top and protecting the left flank of the army. At 11:45 a.m. Jerome reported to army headquarters, "General Butterfield: Enemy skirmishers are advancing from the west, one mile from here." Ten minutes later: "General Butterfield: The rebels are in force, and our skirmishers give way. One mile west of Round Top Signal station the woods are full of them." He had watched Lieutenant-Colonel Casper Trepp's Sharpshooters clash with Brigadier-General Wilcox's Brigade in woods on Warfield Ridge, and be driven back. Shortly after this Jerome withdrew when Buford's cavalry was sent back to Westminster. The next to arrive was Captain Norton, who was visiting signal stations, accompanied by Captain P. A. Taylor from II Corps (in reserve behind Cemetery Ridge). They found Little Round Top unoccupied. After scanning the field carefully, considerable troop movement was spotted along the Chambersburg Pike and in the Herr's Ridge area. A joint signal was sent to II Corps:

> Round Top Mountain Signal Station
> July 2, 1863
> Capt. Hall:
> Saw a column of the enemy's infantry move into woods on ridge, three miles west of town, near Millerstown Road. Wagon teams parked in open field beyond the ridge, moved to rear behind woods. See wagons moving up and down on the Chambersburg Pike, at Spangler's. Think the enemy occupies the range of hills three miles west of the town in considerable force.
> Norton, Taylor
> Signal Officers

What they had seen was probably McLaws' Division coming down the Cashtown (Chambersburg) Pike and moving onto the Herr's Ridge Road leading south from the tavern. This was part of Longstreet assembling his leading two divisions preparatory to moving south behind the Herr's Ridge woods for their (unintentionally) late afternoon attack on the Union left. It is odd that this message was sent to II Corps rather than Meade's headquarters, but it may have been repeated to him.

Shortly after this, Captain Hall arrived on the hill and Norton left to return to headquarters. Hall was senior to Taylor so assumed command of the Little Round Top station, which was still without any infantry support. At around 1:30 p.m. Hall signaled to Butterfield at army headquarters:

> Round Top Mountain Signal Station
> July 2, 1863, 1.30 P.M.
> Gen. Butterfield:
> A heavy column of enemy's infantry, about ten thousand, is moving from opposite our extreme left toward our right.
> HALL

What he had seen was Longstreet's Corps doubling back on itself after arriving at the Black Horse Tavern and realizing their flank march to attack the Union left would be compromised by being seen from Little Round Top if they continued on that route. Some forty minutes later Hall sent a follow-up message: "Those troops were passing on a by-road from Dr. Hall's house to Herr's tavern, on the Chambersburg pike. A train of ambulances is following them." The Confederate column was by then hidden from view and Hall's second signal was merely adding further explanation by pinpointing, correctly, the road the Rebels were using when first reported. This signal confused the understanding of the situation for Meade, although the fault was not Hall's. At noon Meade had been told the woods a mile west of his left were full of the enemy – then nothing for an hour and a half. Next he was told 10,000 enemy were moving toward his right. Little wonder that at 3:00 p.m., when he telegraphed the General-in-Chief (Halleck) in Washington, he expressed his doubts with the words "He [the enemy] has been moving on both my flanks, apparently, but it is difficult to tell his exact movements . . . "

During the afternoon Hall sent additional messages concerning troop movement in the woods opposite his position. At about 4:00 p.m. Brigadier-General Gouverneur K. Warren, Meade's chief of engineers, arrived with two aides on the summit of Little Round Top, probably in response to Hall's signals that enemy activity was increasing. Warren was astounded to find no troops apart from signalers on the hill. Hall pointed out the Confederate build-up in the woods less than a mile away. If Warren needed convincing, a shell burst that wounded him slightly in the neck clinched the matter.

Later, at a time difficult to determine, Hall and Taylor left Little Round Top, possibly on the orders of Lieutenant-Colonel Charles Morgan, II Corps' chief of staff, to report to Major-General John Sedgwick (VI Corps). Sometime later this hilltop had yet another signals detachment arrive, this time forty-three men from VI Corps, under the command of Captain E. C. Pierce and accompanied by First Lieutenant George J. Clarke.

The morning of July 3 saw Little Round Top under close-range musket fire from the rocks of Devil's Den and this, together with artillery fire, made it extremely unhealthy for flagmen to stand up in the open and wave their flags. Thus most communication from this station that day was by courier. This was possible, as at about 11:00 a.m. First Lieutenants J. C. Wiggins and N. H. Camp from I Corps reinforced the station and so their detachment supplied additional couriers. At around 1:00 p.m. the thunderous bombardment of the Union line by the Confederate guns preparatory to Pickett's attack began. Around 2:00 p.m. General Warren visited the station again. According to Pierce's report:

> [Warren] directed us to keep a lookout on certain points, and to send messages every few minutes to Gen. Meade during the day. In this connection I wish particularly to place upon record the fact that the signalmen attached to Lieut. Wiggin's party and mine are worthy of all commendation for the bravery displayed by them in riding to and fro, through unexampled artillery fire, with important messages. During the afternoon of this day, after the enemy were repulsed from our right and center, Major-Generals Meade, Sedgwick, Sykes, Pleasonton etc., visited our station . . .

In the evening of July 3 Meade again moved his headquarters to a strip of wood along the Taneytown Road and a signal station was set up. On July 4 Captain Hall (II Corps) re-established signal stations in Gettysburg, first in the Court House and then in the cupola of Pennsylvania College. At 5:40 a.m. he reported "that the enemy had evacuated the position they held yesterday." Lee's retreat had begun.

Summary

In general the Signals Corps made some very positive contributions to the success of the Army of the Potomac at Gettysburg. Lieutenant Jerome provided valuable information to Buford on July 1 and warned Howard on Cemetery Hill of the impending attack from the north by Rodes. It was Jerome on Little Round Top that gave the first indication that the enemy was in strength to his west on Warfield Ridge on July 2. The presence of the signal station on Little Round Top brought about Longstreet's lengthy countermarch on the afternoon of July 2, which caused the major Confederate attack to go in much later than intended. It is also quite likely that Meade sent Warren to Little Round Top that same day in response to messages from the station about the build-up of the Confederates opposite. Warren then recognized its tactical importance and immediately had it occupied by infantry and guns.

Any criticisms probably revolve around the inexperience of Captain Norton, who had to take over his critical responsibilities after the capture of Captain Ben Fisher near Aldie on June 17. Perhaps a more forceful officer would have insisted on bringing forward the telegraph trains and instituted a better coordinated plan for both inter-corps and army headquarters communication, and the use of the signals reserves to provide intelligence. The value of Little Round Top as a station was obvious, but Norton never ordered its occupation, so the presence of a station there was somewhat intermittent, and it never made contact with the station on Jack's Mountain. This sugar-loaf mountain is some 600 feet high and very steepsided; it lies just southwest of Fairfield and 10 miles from Gettysburg, overlooking both the Fairfield Gap and Monterey Pass through South Mountain. This station had been occupied on the orders of Captain Norton at Emmitsburg en route to Gettysburg, had a commanding view of the Confederate approaches to the battlefield and could clearly see Little Round Top. The station was occupied by Captain C. S. Kendall and First Lieutenant L. R. Fortescue, who were able to contact Taneytown by flag but not Little Round Top. Kendall even sent a courier to Little Round Top, as he could see the enemy massing prior to Pickett's attack.

SECTION SIX

Command and Control

POLITICAL, MILITARY, STAFF AND INTELLIGENCE

POLITICAL CONTROL

President of the Confederacy: Jefferson Davis (1808–1889)

Jefferson Davis was the first and only President of the Confederate States of America and as such he was also the commander-in-chief of the army and navy. Unlike the North, the South had no general fulfilling the role of general-in-chief of the army until Lee was appointed to the position in February 1865, two months before the surrender.

Davis was born in 1808, in Kentucky, into very much a military family. His father and uncles all served in the American Revolution and his three elder brothers in the war of 1812, two of them being specially mentioned for gallantry at the battle of New Orleans. Jefferson Davis graduated from West Point in 1828 into the infantry. He served in the Black Hawk War of 1831 and for a time had charge of the Indian chieftain, Black Hawk, after his capture. In 1833 he transferred to the 1st Dragoons and was appointed adjutant. After two years' active service against the Pawnees, Comanches and other tribes, Davis eloped with General Zachary Taylor's daughter and resigned from the army to settle down as a cotton planter in Warren County, Mississippi. Within three months his marriage was cut short by the death of his wife from malaria.

As the years passed, his plantation prospered and in 1845 he remarried, this time to the socially prominent Varina Howell. He had become a vocal advocate of "States' Rights" and in the year of his marriage was elected to the U.S. Congress. On the outbreak of the Mexican War, Davis resigned from Congress and was appointed colonel of the 1st Mississippi Regiment of Riflemen. Under his command the regiment was perhaps the best drilled in the army when it joined General Taylor on the Rio Grande. Davis led his regiment in a successful charge on the Mexican redoubts at the Battle of Monterey in 1846. However, at Buena Vista he was seriously wounded, leading the Mississippi riflemen and Indiana Volunteers in the last charge of the battle which clinched the victory. Taylor's dispatch mentioned his courage and coolness under fire.

He returned to public life as a senator and in 1853 was appointed Secretary of War by President Pierce. His record in that capacity was excellent and he became one of the most powerful figures in Washington, although military paperwork relating to the peacetime garrisons of a small army was hardly a necessary qualification for the high command he was ultimately to achieve. His four successful years as Secretary confirmed him as an autocratic, efficient, but self-important bureaucrat. He served in the Senate until early 1861 when Mississippi seceded. He was inaugurated provisional President of the Confederacy in February 1861 and elected for a six-year term a year later.

As President he faced a monumental task, but his reserved and often severe manner alienated many who came in contact with him, including senior commanders like P. G. T. Beauregard and Joseph E. Johnston. He regarded himself as the only person capable of overseeing the generals commanding armies, deciding war policy and supervising the detail of its execution. In 1863 he was fifty-five and suffering from poor health, which included blindness in one eye caused by glaucoma twelve years earlier, and often a great deal of pain in his good eye, probably due to nervous strain and too much close paperwork There is no doubt he was suffering considerably at the crucial war strategy meeting with Seddon and Lee on May 15 (see Section Seven: The Road to Gettysburg).

Davis could be inflexible and indecisive at the same time, and was prone to keeping favorite generals in the field long after they had proved less than competent and had lost the confidence of their troops – Braxton Bragg being an example. Although fully committed to the cause of the Confederacy, Davis came to regard the establishment of a strong central authority as vital to its survival, despite his passionate rhetoric on behalf of States' Rights before the war. This brought him into conflict with individual states. His military grand strategy was largely based on the determination never to give up territory, with the resultant loss of initiative as he advocated rushing reinforcements to every perceived or actual threat. In General Beauregard's perhaps somewhat jaundiced opinion:

> We needed for President either a military man of high order, or a politician of the first-class without military pretensions. The South did not fall crushed by the mere weight of the North; but it was nibbled away at all sides and ends, because its executive head never gathered and wielded its great strength under the ready advantages that greatly reduced or neutralized its adversary's naked physical superiority.

Davis advocated continuing the struggle right up until his capture on May 10, 1865 while fleeing from Richmond with his Cabinet. He was imprisoned in Fortress Monroe for two years, but then released on bail. He was never charged and was able to retire to Beauvoir Plantation, Biloxi, Mississippi, where he worked on his memoirs, *The Rise and Fall of the Confederate Government.* Davis died in New Orleans on December 5, 1889, aged eighty-one. Elaborate funeral ceremonies were held in New Orleans and the flags on Southern state capitols were lowered to half-mast. His body was subsequently moved to Richmond for reburial.

Secretary of War of the Confederacy: James Seddon (1815–1880)

James Alexander Seddon was the fourth Secretary of War of the Confederacy when he was appointed in November 1862; he held the position until January 1865, by which time he had proved to be the best. His appearance was less than reassuring – a War Department clerk thought the forty-seven-year-old Seddon looked like "a dead man galvanized into muscular animation." Despite his sickly appearance, he was an able, determined and loyal Southerner. Nominally head of the War Department, by 1863 Seddon formed, along with the President and General Lee, an informal strategy board making the key planning and executive decisions for the South.

Seddon was born in Falmouth, Virginia, on July 13, 1815 (two days before Napoleon surrendered to the British). After graduating from the University of Virginia in 1835 he was admitted to the Bar and practiced law in Richmond. He had two spells in Congress and in 1861 was a member of the Peace Convention that tried to prevent the Civil War.

An intelligent, scholarly man, he realized his limitations on military matters and so his influence on the conduct of the war was marginal. When the grand strategy of the war was being debated after Chancellorsville, Seddon initially favored Lee's Army of Northern Virginia providing reinforcements to Vicksburg in the west to try to prevent its capture; Lee was able to prevent this by persuasion and to launch the invasion of the north that became the Gettysburg campaign.

After the Confederate surrender, photographs were taken of the Union prisoners in the infamous Confederate prison at Andersonville which resulted in public demands that those responsible be punished. It was eventually decided to charge Seddon, Lee and several other generals with "conspiring to injure the health and destroy the lives of United States soldiers held as prisoners by the Confederate States." However, in August 1865 President Andrew Johnson ordered that the charges against them all be dropped. Seddon died in Goochland County on August 19, 1880, aged sixty-five.

The Seat of Government: Richmond

The importance of Richmond to the South remained critical throughout the war. Its loss would have devastated the Confederacy, not so much from a political point of view, as the government could have moved, but for reasons of the economy, industry and morale. On the eve of war Richmond was the most industrialized city in the South. Located on the James River, it was a thriving market place with transport links connecting regional farmers to international markets. Five railroads radiated out from the city and along its crowded riverfront were flour mills, tobacco warehouses and a growing industrial complex at the center of which was the Tredegar Iron Works. This became the only facility in the South capable of turning out heavy ordnance or munitions (see box, page 143). Without this arsenal on Byrd Island and the laboratory and artillery works nearby, no Confederate army would have retained the ability to fight for more than a few months. During the three and a half years from July 1861 to January 1865, the Richmond facilities produced 1,300 field pieces, over 921,000 rounds of artillery ammunition, 323,000 infantry arms, 34,000 cavalry carbines, 6,000 pistols and well over 72 million rounds of small arms ammunition.

Understandably, Richmond became the focus for Northern attention in the eastern theater of operations – the popular cry in the Union Army at the start of the war was "On to Richmond!" It was an easy city to threaten, being only 100 miles from Washington, and the Union soon had control of the sea, enabling armies to be landed at Fort Monroe on the James peninsula only 35 miles away. However, although numerous efforts were made to capture Richmond, and numerous battles were fought on its doorstep, it never fell to Union arms.

As discussed below in Section Seven: The Road to Gettysburg, there was, in theory, the possibility that Hooker with the Army of the Potomac would move on Richmond virtually unopposed when Lee disappeared west and north into the Shenandoah Valley in June 1863.

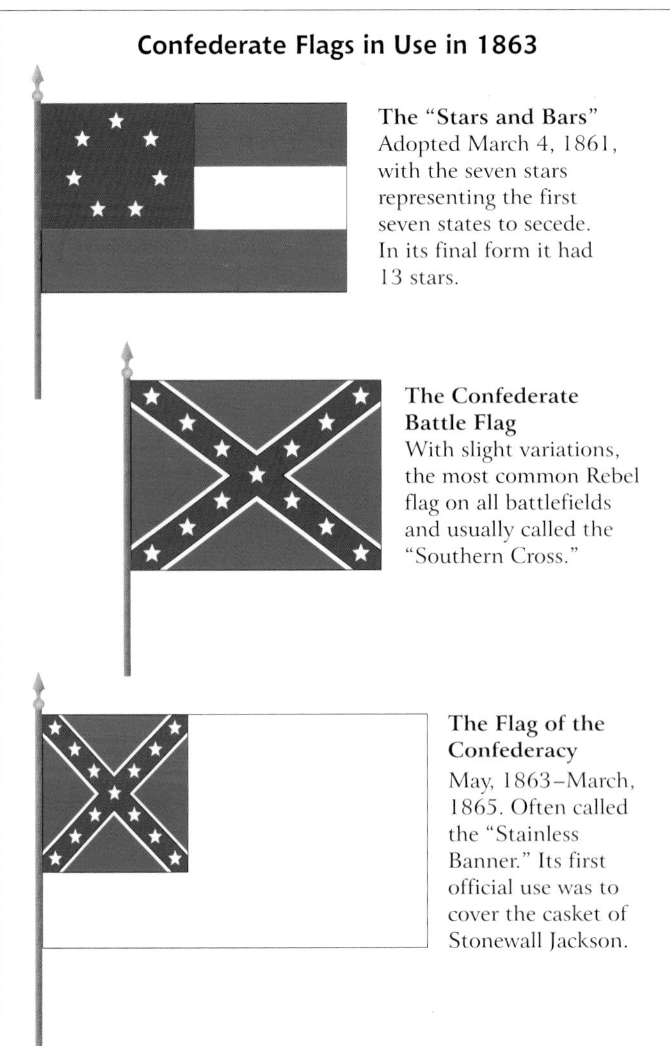

Confederate Flags in Use in 1863

The "Stars and Bars" Adopted March 4, 1861, with the seven stars representing the first seven states to secede. In its final form it had 13 stars.

The Confederate Battle Flag With slight variations, the most common Rebel flag on all battlefields and usually called the "Southern Cross."

The Flag of the Confederacy May, 1863–March, 1865. Often called the "Stainless Banner." Its first official use was to cover the casket of Stonewall Jackson.

Confederate Uniforms

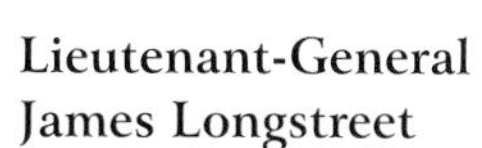

General Robert E. Lee
Lee usually wore a plain uniform with three stars on the collar because he disliked the heavily braided uniforms worn by most Confederate generals. Three stars in the Confederate Army indicated the rank of colonel (Lee's rank when he resigned from the U.S. Army); no one knows why he insisted on wearing this incorrect rank. He did occasionally wear the proper uniform, however, most notably when he surrendered to Ulysses S. Grant at Appomattox.

Major-General George E. Pickett
Pickett wears the regulation frock coat. According to regulations, the buttons should have been evenly spaced, but Pickett has them in groups of three, which was the Federal rule for general officers. The rank devices are placed on blue facings denoting infantry, a simple embroidered design on the cuff, and a red silk sash under his waistbelt. He has, however, retained his dark blue kepi-style cap. Generals had four stripes of gold embroidery up the front, sides and crown of their caps.

Lieutenant-General James Longstreet
Longstreet is shown wearing the regulation general's frock coat with two rows of buttons in pairs. The buff standing collar displays his rank devices of three embroidered gold stars within a laurel-wreath, and his cuffs display an "Austrian knot" made up of four widths of braid. Trousers are dark blue with two gold lace stripes on the outer seam. He has adapted his uniform for field use by dispensing with the regulation cap in favor of a broad-brimmed slouch hat, and wears a buff waist sash and Mexican War souvenir spurs.

Captain, 3rd Arkansas

Officers had considerable latitude in selecting their uniform and accoutrements, although the basic branch color was blue for infantry. This officer's double-breasted gray jacket has been created by cutting the skirts off his frock coat.

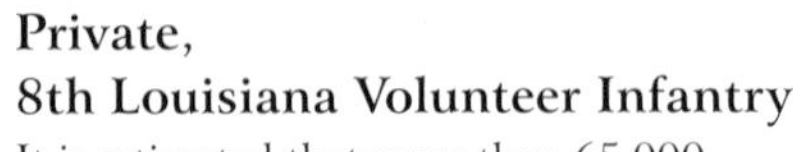

Private, 8th Louisiana Volunteer Infantry

It is estimated that more than 65,000 Southern blacks served in the Confederate ranks, and of these, some 13,000 were combatants. Although black musicians officially served in the ranks, the Confederate Congress did not officially authorize colored troops into the army until 1865. Free black musicians, cooks, soldiers and teamsters earned the same pay as white confederate privates. This illustration represents Private Charles F. Lutz, a "freeman of color" in Company F.

Sergeant, Color-bearer, 47th North Carolina Infantry

This man's jacket is of cadet gray cloth, trimmed around the collar, on the edges of the shoulder straps and at the cuffs with ½-inch dark blue tape. It has eight large buttons down the front, and two small ones on the straps and cuffs. His rank chevrons have been separately applied, each black velvet stripe ½ inch wide.

First Lieutenant, 2nd Virginia Infantry
Confederate officers had to supply their own uniforms, thus a variety of styles and trim prevailed. Rank was affixed to both sides of the collar, and the cuff sleeves were decorated with braid designs. In 1862 this sleeve braid became an optional item since the braid made an officer too easily distinguishable at a distance and thus a target.

Private, 3rd Georgia Volunteer Infantry
His frock coat is of the type issued by the Georgia Quartermaster Department in March 1863, with black facings. He is armed with a "Cook & Brother" rifle-musket, which was based on the Enfield two-band short rifle and was made in Georgia by two Englishmen working for the Confederacy.

Private, 4th Texas Infantry
Many of Hood's Texas Brigade were of Hispanic origin. The regiment received a large number of jackets, trousers, cotton shirts, shoes, socks and undergarments in the spring of 1863. The men had initially been issued with caps, but many Texans appear to have preferred their own hats, with the badge of the Lone Star embellished on them. This soldier is armed with the Enfield rifle with saber bayonet. Note the Texas Star buckle on his waistbelt.

Private, 5th Florida Infantry
One of the few items of clothing provided by the state of Florida to its troops was a blue forage cap. As part of the A.N.V. the 5th Florida received its clothing from the Richmond Depot, and this man wears the Type II jacket. The regiment was armed with both M1861 Springfield and M1853 Enfield rifle-muskets.

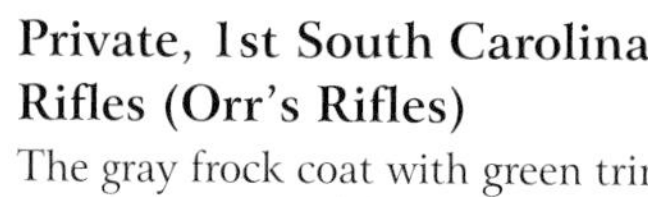

Private, 1st South Carolina Rifles (Orr's Rifles)

The gray frock coat with green trim in use at the start of the war had given way to the Richmond Depot Type II shell jacket by the time of the Gettysburg campaign. Orr's original headgear was the M1858 Hardee hat, but this too had either turned into a weathered slouch hat or been replaced with cap or civilian slouch hat. This private has retained the "Palmetto" emblem on his hat. He is armed with the Enfield rifle-musket.

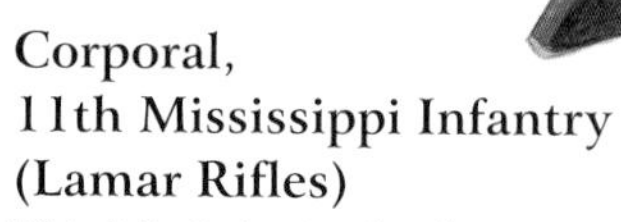

Corporal, 11th Mississippi Infantry (Lamar Rifles)

This Mississippian has been issued with a Richmond Depot Type II shell jacket that has been furnished with Mississippi state buttons. The jacket has a shoulder and a waist strap, but has no branch of service trim or piping. His belt and buckle is of the Georgia frame pattern. He is armed with an M1854 Austrian Lorenz rifle-musket.

Sergeant, 6th Alabama Volunteer Infantry

In July 1863 Sergeant Crawford Jackson (6th Alabama) described his uniform as "a black broad cloth coat, Alabama staff buttons, cut and trimmed in regulation style, a pair of gray trousers and slouch hat . . ."

Sergeant, 1st Maryland Battalion

The 1st Maryland went into action with its mongrel mascot dog, "Grace," leading the way. Unfortunately Grace was shot dead in the action at Culp's Hill on July 3.

Major-General J. E. B. Stuart
Many Confederate cavalry officers preferred the short, often double-breasted jacket. This had yellow-lined lapels which could be buttoned up in a variety of styles, as here revealing the lapel color. Stuart is depicted wearing his ostrich-plumed hat and high-topped leather riding boots. His personal armaments consisted of the French-manufactured M1860 cavalry saber and LeMat 1st model revolver.

Trooper, Phillip's (Georgia) Legion
This trooper wears a homespun single-breasted frock coat. His belt buckle is of state pattern and the belt of Confederate manufacture, but the rest of his accoutrements are of Federal origin. He has dispensed with his sword and instead carries a pistol, with a shotgun instead of a carbine.

Trooper, 1st Virginia Cavalry
When formed early in 1861 this regiment was clothed "hussar" style, but now, after the rigors of campaigning, this private wears another example of the Richmond Depot Type II jacket. The regiments of Stuart's Division were well armed and carried Sharps carbines slung by leather shoulder belts, the standard model U.S. cavalry saber and Colt Navy .36 caliber pistols.

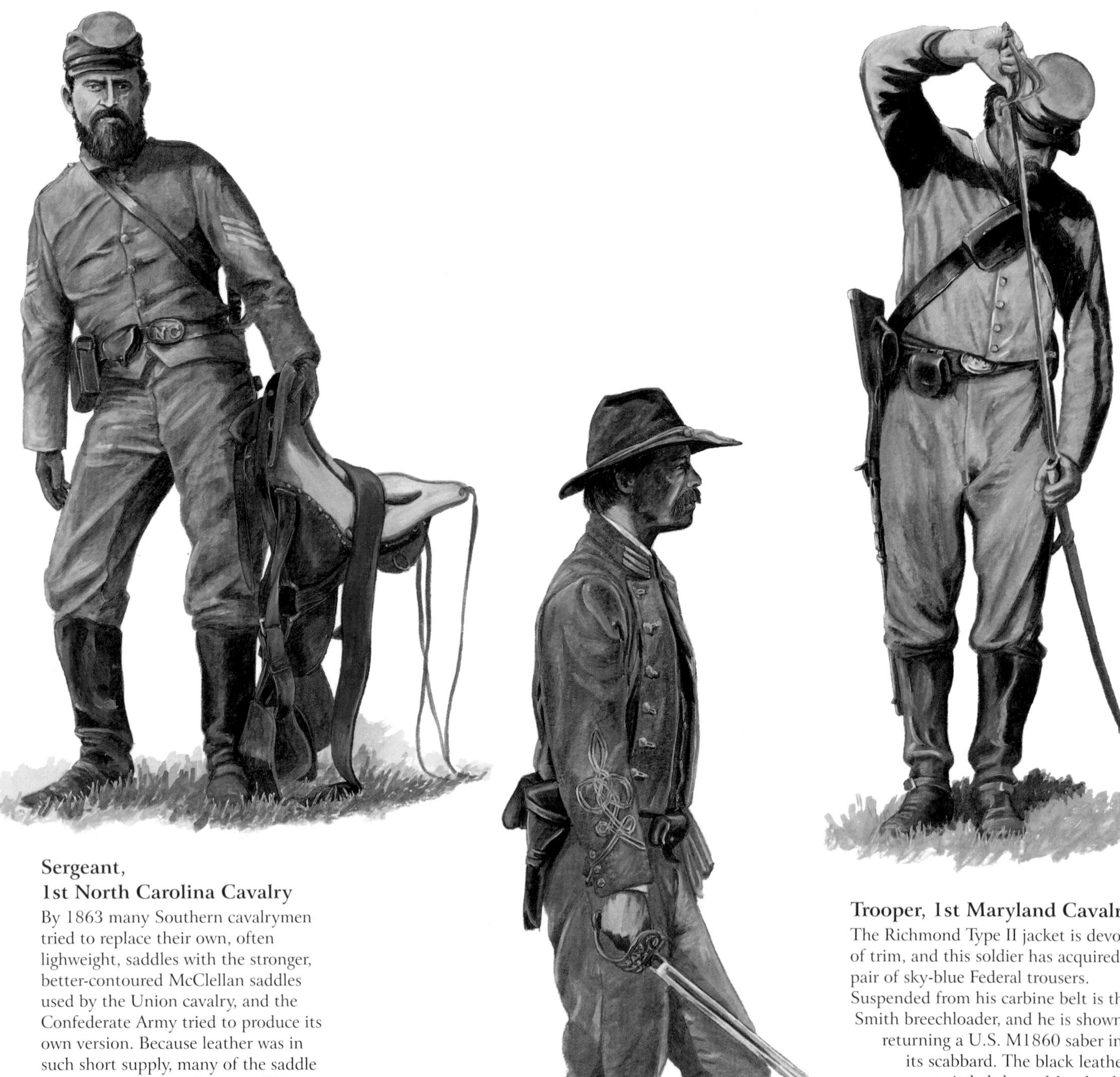

Sergeant,
1st North Carolina Cavalry

By 1863 many Southern cavalrymen tried to replace their own, often lighweight, saddles with the stronger, better-contoured McClellan saddles used by the Union cavalry, and the Confederate Army tried to produce its own version. Because leather was in such short supply, many of the saddle skirts were of painted canvas. This sergeant's Charlotte Depot jacket has six buttons down the front.

Trooper, 1st Maryland Cavalry

The Richmond Type II jacket is devoid of trim, and this soldier has acquired a pair of sky-blue Federal trousers. Suspended from his carbine belt is the Smith breechloader, and he is shown returning a U.S. M1860 saber into its scabbard. The black leather waistbelt has a Maryland oval buckle.

Captain, 1st South Carolina Cavalry

This captain wears the short double-breasted shell jacket. His side arm is the British Kerr .44-caliber revolver housed in its holster, and he is holding a non-regulation, steel-hilted imported officer's sword.

Confederate Slave

This figure represents General Lee's faithful servant William Mack Lee (see page 260), who is wearing an unofficial uniform jacket.

Ambulance Corpsman

This enlisted stretcher-bearer wears a plain civilian shirt, and is distinguished from other troops only by the red band on his hat. The badge was not described in army orders, and could have been any red cloth device, ranging from the hatband to a circle of cloth on the hat front, or an armband. The band displays the words "Ambulance Corps," which enabled him to leave the battlefield without written authority.

Lieutenant-Colonel – Surgeon

The regulation uniforms of Confederate surgeons and assistant surgeons consisted of a double-breasted gray frock coat with black collar and cuffs. The trousers were dark blue with black stripe edged with gold down each leg. This surgeon wears his rank insignia of two stars on his collar. There was no special sword pattern required for Confederate medical officers.

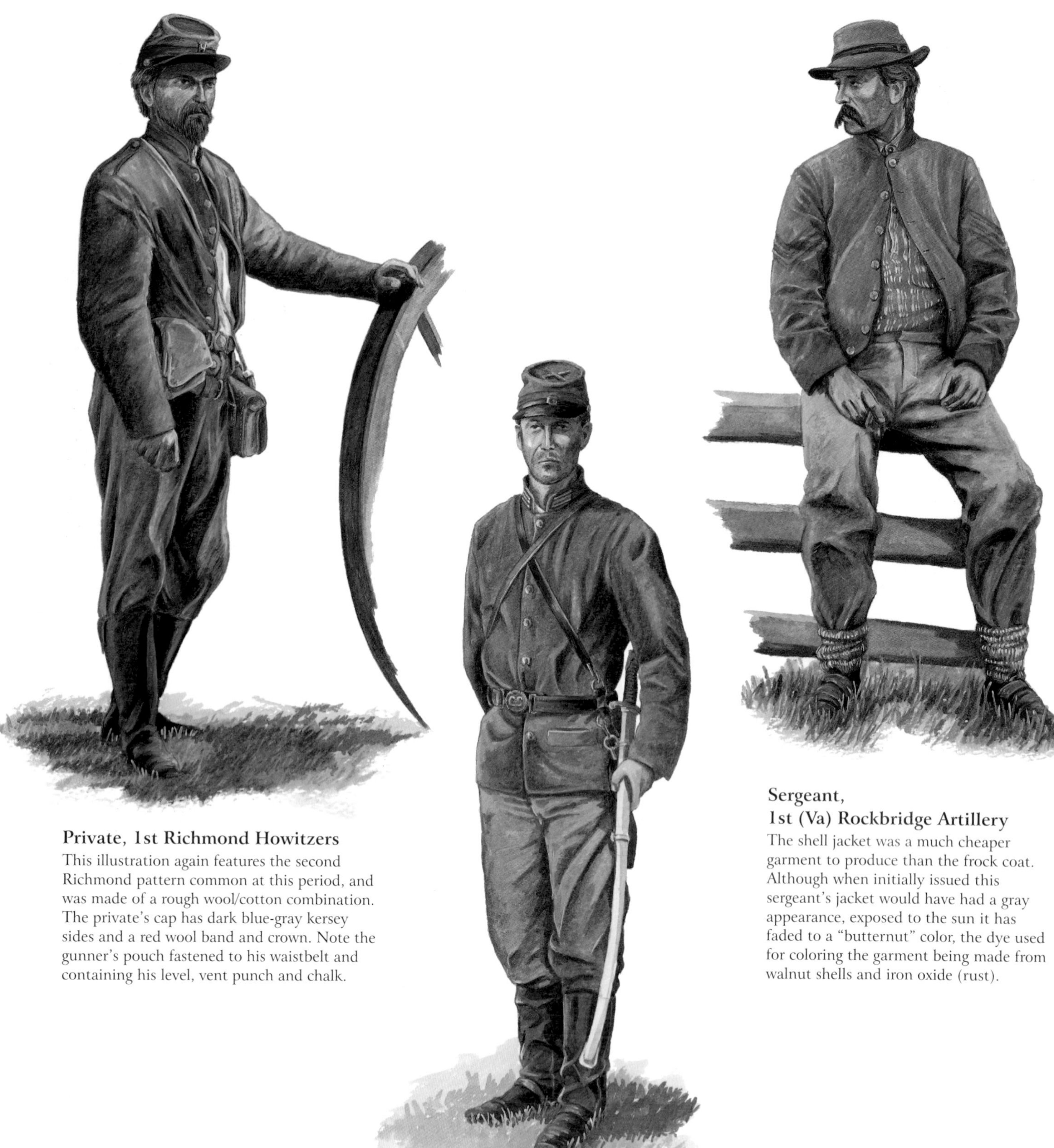

Private, 1st Richmond Howitzers
This illustration again features the second Richmond pattern common at this period, and was made of a rough wool/cotton combination. The private's cap has dark blue-gray kersey sides and a red wool band and crown. Note the gunner's pouch fastened to his waistbelt and containing his level, vent punch and chalk.

Sergeant, 1st (Va) Rockbridge Artillery
The shell jacket was a much cheaper garment to produce than the frock coat. Although when initially issued this sergeant's jacket would have had a gray appearance, exposed to the sun it has faded to a "butternut" color, the dye used for coloring the garment being made from walnut shells and iron oxide (rust).

Captain, Norfolk (Va) "Light Artillery Blues" Battery
Although they took their name from the dark blue uniforms originally worn by the unit, the Blues adopted Confederate gray and butternut in 1861. This officer wears a single-breasted coat with six buttons down its front. He is identifiable as belonging to the artillery only by the red background material on which his collar rank bars are mounted, and by the red band around the base of his kepi.

Union Uniforms

Major-General George G. Meade
Meade is shown wearing the regulation double-breasted frock coat with buttons arranged according to his rank, with black or very dark blue velvet collar and cuffs.

Colonel Joshua Chamberlain, 20th Maine
Chamberlain wears the regulation frock coat for a colonel. His shoulder straps bear the rank device of a silver eagle. His cap is decorated with a gold bugle horn with his regiment's number and on the crown a red Maltese cross – the badge of 2nd Division, V Corps. He is holding the M1850 field and staff officer's sword.

Brigadier-General John C. Robinson
Here the commander of 2nd Division, I Corps wears the regulation undress plain double-breasted frock coat. The badge on the felt hat consisted of the letters "U.S." in silver embroidery, surrounded by a gold embroidered laurel wreath. His shoulder straps are edged with gold embroidery, and bear the single silver star of his rank.

Private, 2nd Wisconsin (Iron Brigade)
The hats worn by the men of the Iron Brigade were the pattern 1858 army hat, known as the Hardee hat. Along with several other regiments of I Corps, the men had elected to continue to wear this headgear rather than adopting the forage cap. This soldier also wears white canvas leggings with which much of the army had been issued before Chancellorsville and also carries a knapsack.

Corporal, Flag-bearer, 69th New York State Volunteers
This was one of the all-Irish regiments in Union service with most of the men active in the Fenians, a group dedicated to the overthrow of British rule in Ireland. The dark blue waist-length jacket with light to medium blue trim and eight buttons was adopted in April 1861 as a substitute for the army regulation frock coat, and was issued by the state of New York to many of her regiments.

First Lieutenant, 1st Minnesota
This officer is dressed in the nine-buttoned single-breasted frock coat prescribed for captains and lieutenants. On the front of his jacket he wears a II Corps badge and he carries an M1850 officer's sword.

Private,
114th Pennsylvania Volunteers

This regiment (1st Division, III Corps) maintained its distinctive Zouave uniform throughout the war, with little modification to take account of the hardships of campaign. The soldier wears the Schuylkill Depot-issued jacket made to Collis's specification. The turban appears to have been more regularly worn by this regiment than by other Zouave units, who reserved their turbans for dress occasions.

Private, 84th New York
(14th Brooklyn Militia)

Though the jacket appears to be worn over a red vest, they were in fact a single garment, the jacket, with its false buttons, being sewn onto the vest. This uniform was inspired by the French *chasseurs à pied*. The regiment took great pride in its appearance and the men maintained the uniform throughout their service.

Private,
146th New York Volunteers

At the start of the war this regiment (2nd Division, V Corps) was issued with standard uniform, but the men were subsequently equipped as Zouaves when they joined the Army of the Potomac in November 1862 and a month prior to Gettysburg they received new Zouave uniforms. Although this private has opted to wear his forage cap, the usual headgear consisted of a fez or turban.

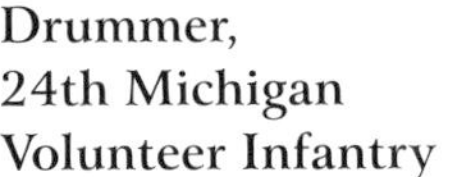

Drummer, 24th Michigan Volunteer Infantry

This man wears a standard-issue nine-buttoned frock coat. The regulation drum bears the Union coat of arms and state decoration, and is suspended from a white canvas sling.

Chaplain, 14th Connecticut

Army chaplains were essentially staff officers. According to orders of November 25, 1861, chaplains were to wear a "plain black frock coat with standing collar, and one row of nine black buttons; plain black pantaloons; black felt hat, or army forage cap." However, chaplains were rarely taken to task for wearing non-regulation uniform, and the standard of dress was a dark blue or black frock coat, often with black buttons instead of brass; dark blue trousers; a dark blue forage cap, often decorated with a gold crucifix within a wreath. Most supplied themselves with straight swords and black belts with buckles decorated with the same motif as the cap.

Sergeant, 2nd U.S. Sharpshooters

These men wore the standard frock coat and trousers, but made of rifle green instead of blue wool. Generally the regulation army blue flannel uniform was worn in the field, although the men retained their green caps. N.C.O.s wore green chevrons and trouser stripes on their blue uniforms. The buttons on an otherwise standard-issue blouse are black thermoplastic or gutta percha (hard black rubber). It should be noted that the government did not issue green chevrons or replacement buttons; it was necessary for the individual to purchase these from the regimental sutler. This soldier has retained the Prussian Army knapsack issued to both Sharpshooter regiments. Originally the men brought their own target rifles, though these were replaced first with Colt revolving rifles and, in May–June, 1862, with Sharps rifles.

Trooper, 1st Maine Cavalry

Whilst many cavalrymen wore the yellow-trimmed shell jacket, some preferred the single-breasted plain fatigue jacket devoid of trim as shown here. These jackets reached halfway down the thigh and were made out of a dark blue flannel material, fastened with four brass buttons. The regiment received six Burnside carbines per company in March 1862, but by the spring of 1863 had received the Sharps carbine, though they still retained their Burnsides.

Trooper, 6th Pennsylvania Cavalry (Rush's Lancers)

This man wears the regulation uniform, with one loop of lace and button on the collar. Until May, 1863 the regiment's principal weapon had been the lance, but this was replaced with the Sharps carbine. His cap has a horizontal leather visor, and is decorated with brass crossed sabers and his company number.

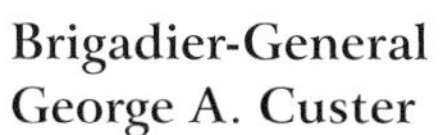

Brigadier-General George A. Custer

The Union's youngest brigadier-general was famed for his flamboyant dress sense, usually improvizing his own uniform, as shown in the illustration.

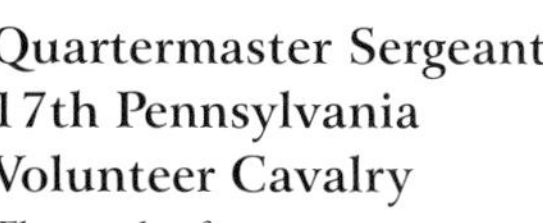

Quartermaster Sergeant, 17th Pennsylvania Volunteer Cavalry

The rank of company quartermaster sergeant was not a command position, as is conveyed by his unofficial chevrons – three strips with a single tie in worsted.

Trooper, 5th Michigan Cavalry
This trooper wears the regulation full-dress shell jacket, often worn on campaign with the forage cap. He is shown here firing the Spencer repeating rifle (the 5th and 6th Michigan Cavalry regiments were the first to be issued with this weapon).

First Sergeant, 9th New York
This sergeant wears gauntlet gloves. These were not issued to the enlisted men but were particularly useful when riding. He has removed the yellow trim to his regulation shell jacket and trousers. He is armed with a Smiths carbine which has been "broken" to permit reloading.

Bugler, 8th Illinois Cavalry
This jacket has a distinctive trim that clearly identifies the bugler from ordinary troopers, enabling officers to locate him easily in order to relay their commands. Note the double seam of yellow on his trousers and the ornate stitching on the top of his boots.

Hospital Steward

Equivalent in rank to a first sergeant, this steward wears the dress frock coat, trimmed with crimson, with only the green medical chevrons, edged with yellow, on his jacket, and his waist sash indicating his branch of service.

Assistant Surgeon

The badge on top of his cap identifies his corps by its shape and his division by its color. He wears the Old English letters "MS" (Medical Staff) on his shoulder straps – against regulations, but commonly seen. (His straps should have borne nothing but his rank bars.) His green sash and the all-metal M1840 sword peculiar to his branch further indicate his medical status.

Negro Cook, Army of the Potomac

Free blacks and "contraband" blacks were employed in the Army of the Potomac. As Union armies moved into the South, thousands of slaves fled to their camps. Although some officers sent them back to their masters, others allowed them to remain with their troops, using them as a workforce and dubbing them "contraband of war."

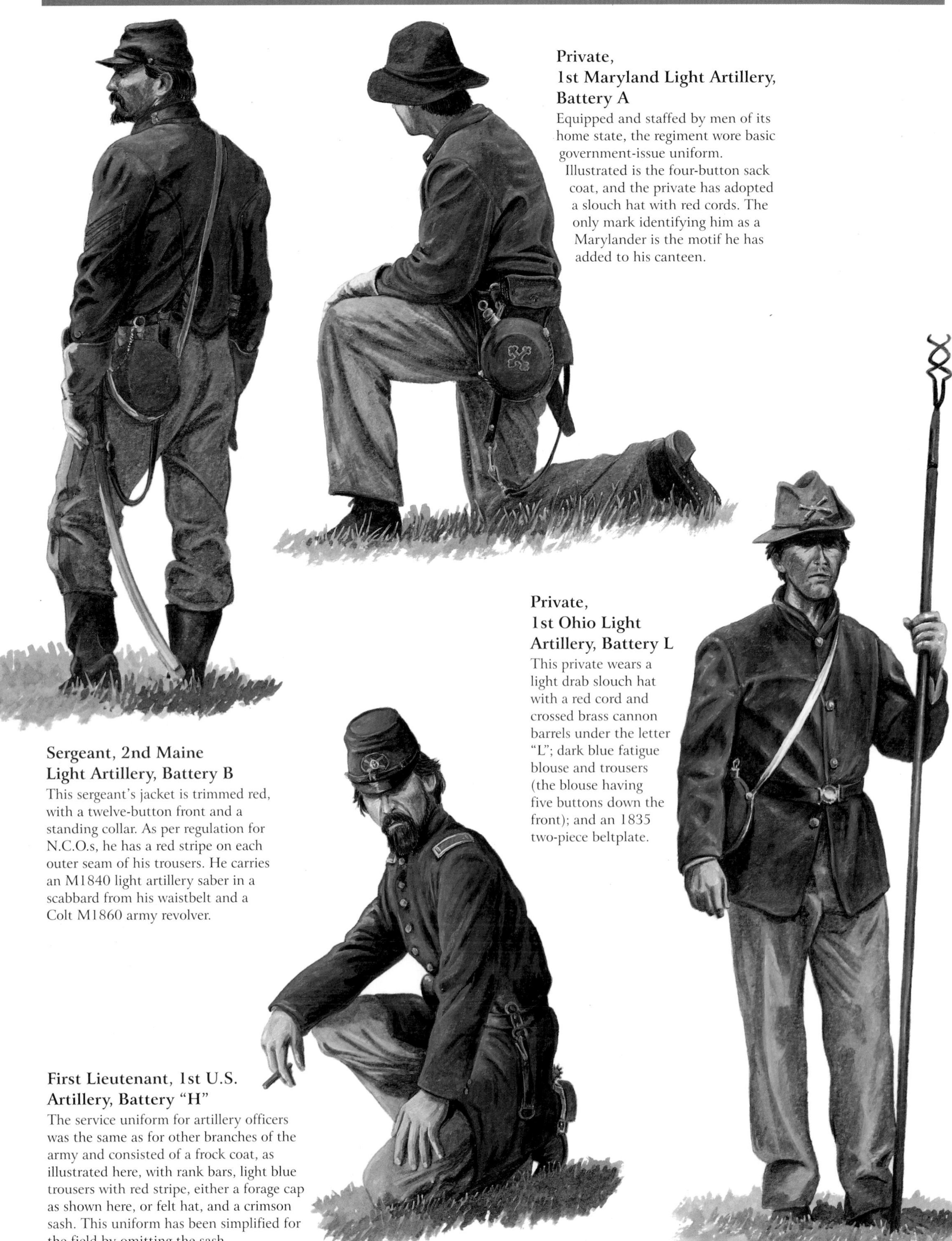

Private, 1st Maryland Light Artillery, Battery A

Equipped and staffed by men of its home state, the regiment wore basic government-issue uniform. Illustrated is the four-button sack coat, and the private has adopted a slouch hat with red cords. The only mark identifying him as a Marylander is the motif he has added to his canteen.

Private, 1st Ohio Light Artillery, Battery L

This private wears a light drab slouch hat with a red cord and crossed brass cannon barrels under the letter "L"; dark blue fatigue blouse and trousers (the blouse having five buttons down the front); and an 1835 two-piece beltplate.

Sergeant, 2nd Maine Light Artillery, Battery B

This sergeant's jacket is trimmed red, with a twelve-button front and a standing collar. As per regulation for N.C.O.s, he has a red stripe on each outer seam of his trousers. He carries an M1840 light artillery saber in a scabbard from his waistbelt and a Colt M1860 army revolver.

First Lieutenant, 1st U.S. Artillery, Battery "H"

The service uniform for artillery officers was the same as for other branches of the army and consisted of a frock coat, as illustrated here, with rank bars, light blue trousers with red stripe, either a forage cap as shown here, or felt hat, and a crimson sash. This uniform has been simplified for the field by omitting the sash.

President of the Union: Abraham Lincoln (1809–1865)

Abraham Lincoln, the sixteenth President of the United States, is considered by many to have been her greatest. He was born on February 12, 1809 in Hardin County, Kentucky. Of his upbringing he later said:

> My father . . . removed from Kentucky . . . to Indiana in my eighth year . . . It was a wild region, with many bears and other wild animals still in the woods. There I grew up . . . Of course when I came of age I did not know much. Still somehow I could read, write and cipher . . . but that was all.

Later his family settled in Illinois and Lincoln held various clerical jobs and was a partner in a grocery store in New Salem that failed and left him heavily in debt. He then studied law and spent eight years in the Illinois legislature. He was briefly a captain of militia in the Black Hawk War, but saw no action, claiming his only enemies were mosquitoes. He married Mary Todd in 1842 and they had four sons, only one of whom lived to maturity. However, when as President he became commander-in-chief of the U.S. Army, he had four brothers-in-law in the Confederate Army, and three of his sisters-in-law were married to Confederate officers. He served for two years (1847–49) in Congress but then retired from public life. In 1858, however, Lincoln ran against Stephen A. Douglas for senator. He lost the election, but in debating with Douglas he gained a national reputation that won him the Republican nomination for the presidency in 1860.

Although Lincoln had war powers that were virtually dictatorial, his wisdom in handling these for the good of the nation despite a divided Cabinet and a country torn by civil war were masterly. One of his greatest characteristics was his humanity. This is wonderfully illustrated by a letter he wrote in 1864 to a Boston widow, Lydia Bixby, whom he was (incorrectly) told had lost five sons in the war:

> Executive Mansion
> Washington, Nov.21, 1864
> To Mrs. Bixby, Boston, Mass.
>
> Dear Madam,
> I have been shown in the files of the War Department a statement of the Adjutant General of Massachusetts, that you are the mother of five sons who have died gloriously on the field of battle.
>
> I feel how weak and fruitless must be any words of mine which should attempt to beguile you from the grief of a loss so overwhelming. But I cannot refrain from tendering to you the consolation that may be found in the thanks of the Republic they died to save.
>
> I pray that our Heavenly Father may assuage the anguish of your bereavement, and leave you only the cherished memory of the loved and lost, and the solemn pride that must be yours, to have laid so costly a sacrifice upon the altar of Freedom.
> Yours very sincerely and respectfully
>
> A. Lincoln

Lincoln had been misinformed: Mrs. Bixby had lost only two sons in the war – Sergeant Charles N. Bixby was killed on May 3, 1863, and Private Oliver Cromwell Bixby on July 30, 1864. The others survived, although two had deserted to the enemy.

Lincoln's role in the opening moves of the Gettysburg campaign revolved around insisting that the overriding aim of the Army of the Potomac was the protection of Washington, and the replacement of Major-General Hooker by Meade only three days before the battle. These have been discussed above in the Prologue, and his reaction to the battle is given in Section Twelve: The Aftermath. His famous Gettysburg address is given in Appendix 1.

An actor called John Wilkes Booth assassinated Lincoln on April 14, 1865 – he was fifty-six year old. Booth leapt into the box in the theater where Lincoln was sitting and shot him in the back of the head with a .44 Deringer pistol, at the same time shouting, "*Sic semper tyrannis* [Thus always to tyrants]! The South is avenged!" Despite breaking his leg by falling as he jumped from Lincoln's box, Booth escaped on a waiting horse. He was run to ground hiding in a tobacco shed near Bowling Green, Virginia, on April 26. The shed was set on fire and Booth was shot in the neck while still inside. He was dragged clear but was paralyzed from the neck down and died within a few minutes.

Secretary of War of the Union: Edwin Stanton (1814–1869)

Edwin McMasters Stanton was a lawyer, politician, United States Attorney General (1860–61) and Secretary of War for most of the war and reconstruction period. He was born on December 19, 1814 in Steubenville, Ohio, the eldest of four children. He graduated from Kenyon College in 1833 and was admitted to the Ohio Bar three years later. In 1847 he moved to Pittsburgh, Pennsylvania, and in 1856 to Washington, where he had a lucrative practice before the Supreme Court. In 1859 he defended Daniel E. Sickles, then a politician and four years later the commander of the Union III Corps at Gettysburg, who was charged with murdering his wife's lover. Stanton got him acquitted by the first use of the temporary insanity defense in American history.

In 1860 Stanton was appointed Attorney General by President James Buchanan and is credited with changing Buchanan's position away from tolerating secession to denouncing it as unconstitutional and illegal. Stanton was a staunch Democrat and politically opposed to the Republican Abraham Lincoln, referring to him as the "original gorilla." Nevertheless, he accepted the position of Secretary of War "to help save the country" in January 1862 and proved a capable and hardworking administrator of the huge War Department. In doing so his imperious manner soon antagonized those directly under him. When one official was to be sent to Stanton to ask a favor, his reply was, "Don't send me to Stanton to ask favors. I would rather make a tour of a small pox hospital." Lincoln recognized his ability and was usually able to get his way when their opinions collided, but at times there was considerable pressure on the President to remove his unpopular Secretary. On one such occasion Lincoln responded, "If you will find another secretary of war like him, I will gladly appoint him." But his most laudatory, if somewhat exaggerated, comments on his Secretary came when he would not bow to Congressmen lobbying to make an appointment that Stanton had refused:

> His position is one of the most difficult in the world. Thousands in the army blame him because they are not promoted and other thousands blame him because they are not

> appointed. The pressure on him is immeasurable and unending. He is the rock on the beach of our national ocean . . . Gentlemen, I do not see how he survives, why he is not crushed . . . Without him I should be destroyed. He performs his task superhumanly . . . I cannot wrongly interfere with him.

Stanton held his post under President Andrew Johnson until 1868 when Johnson tried to sack him, but he barricaded himself in his office, claiming Johnson had violated the Tenure of Office Act, and initiated impeachment proceedings against him. Johnson lost office but Stanton resigned and returned to practice law. The following year President Grant appointed him to the Supreme Court but he died four days after confirmation by the Senate, aged fifty-five.

The Seat of Government: Washington D.C.

Washington remained a small city of a few thousand inhabitants, virtually deserted during the hot summer months, until the outbreak of the Civil War. It then became the Federal District of Washington D.C. and rapidly developed into the center of civilian and military leadership and logistics for the Union. The Army of the Potomac was created to ensure the protection of Washington, and the significant expansion of the Federal Government to administer the war ensured a rapid rise in its population, both civil and military. Throughout the war a ring of forts and a permanent military command tasked with its close defense protected the city. However, the only time it came under direct attack was in July 1864. On that occasion the Confederates under Jubal A. Early (he had been promoted to corps command two months before) tentatively attacked Fort Stevens. Early's advance on the city caused near panic as Lincoln summoned reinforcements from the Army of the Potomac, and civilian volunteers and administrative troops were hastily organized to man the defenses – Lincoln even proposed to General Grant that he return in person to conduct the defense. In the event, no serious assault was mounted and Early retired when he heard of the imminent arrival of VI Corps. Lincoln visited the fort during the action to watch the fighting and thus became the only U.S. President to come under fire during wartime.

The safety of Washington was always the underlying principle behind the strategic operations of the Army of the Potomac, and the Gettysburg campaign was no exception. Instructions from Washington in this regard were much the same to both Hooker and Meade. In brief they were:

- January 1863. Hooker was given the task of the defeat of Lee's army provided he kept "in view always the importance of covering Washington and Harper's Ferry either directly or by so operating as to be able to punish any force the enemy sent against them."
- June 5. Hooker's plan to attack A. P. Hill's Corps (the rear of Lee's army) south of Fredericksburg was rejected by Washington as lack of success might seriously endanger the city.
- June 15. Hooker was told he was free to operate against Lee as he saw fit, provided he kept the main Confederate force away from the city.
- June 27. Instructions to Meade as the new army commander included the words, "You will, however, keep in view the important fact that the Army of the Potomac is the covering army of Washington as well as the army of operation against the invading forces of the rebels."

MILITARY CONTROL – ARMY COMMANDERS

In both armies at Gettysburg officers, senior and junior, can be categorized broadly into either commanders or staff officers. The former received instructions, made plans, issued orders and supervised their execution. They took responsibility for the success or failure of the mission given to their army, formation, unit or sub-unit. Commanders ranged in rank from a general commanding an army down to a lieutenant or N.C.O. commanding a picket. Staff officers existed to facilitate control and administer the army. Their task was to ensure that the commander's instructions were issued, delivered and understood; they organized the supply of food, clothing, ammunition, and medical and communication assets. They were the oil that kept the military machine from grinding to a halt. At all headquarters from army to regiment, staff and administrative personnel played a key role. As with commanders, their ranks could vary from the highest (Major-General Daniel Butterfield, chief of staff to Meade) to the lowest (Commissary Sergeant John F. Putnam, 17th Maine).

The bulk of this section will examine the personalities and careers of the two army commanders, together with their methods of command and how their staff was organized at Gettysburg. Similarly, though much more briefly, each corps commander's career and his actions at Gettysburg will be summarized. Because the battle was preceded by a three-week campaign that culminated in three days of extensive fighting, and was followed by a ten-day retreat and pursuit, the numerous command decisions that affected the outcome of the campaign and battle are discussed in Sections Seven–Twelve.

Commander of the Army of Northern Virginia: General Robert E. Lee (1807–1870)

On April 18, 1861 President Lincoln offered a Colonel Robert E. Lee, an officer with over thirty years' service in the U.S. Army, command of that army's field forces at the outset of the looming Civil War. Lee declined. His home state, Virginia, had seceded from the Union and Lee tendered his resignation on the following day, writing to his sister on April 20:

> With all my devotion to the Union and the feeling of loyalty and duty of an American citizen, I have not been able to make up my mind to raise my hand against my relatives, my children, my home. I have therefore resigned my commission in the Army, and serve in defense of my native State, with the sincere hope that my poor services may never be needed, I hope I will never be called on to draw my sword . . .

Robert Edward Lee was born on January 19, 1807 at Stratford in Westmoreland County, Virginia, the son of a Revolutionary War hero nicknamed "Light Horse Harry" who later became bankrupt, had been to prison twice for indebtedness by the time Robert was two and disappeared on a boat to Barbados never to be seen again when his son was six. Poverty forced the family to move to Alexandria, Virginia, across the Potomac River from Washington. Robert E. Lee entered West Point in 1825, graduating second in his class four years later, after being appointed cadet adjutant. While there he also achieved the extraordinary distinction of not collecting a single demerit – a feat that earned him the nickname "Marble Model" and has never been equaled.

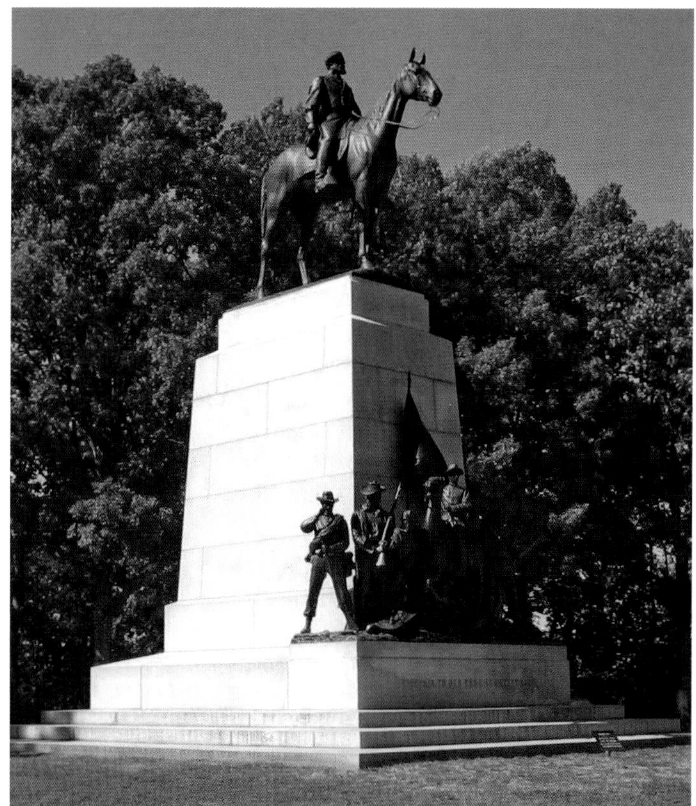

Equestrian statue of Lee at Gettysburg, situated to the east side of West Confederate Avenue, north of Spangler Woods. From a position some 300 yards to the east, near the Point of Woods, Lee watched Pickett's charge on July 3.

He was commissioned into the Engineers and as a young lieutenant married Mary Ann Randolph Custis, a direct descendent of Mary Washington, in 1831. With the outbreak of the Mexican War, Lee served with considerable distinction as a staff officer, was slightly wounded at Chapultepec and earned three brevet promotions. Following a stint in Baltimore Harbor he became Superintendent of West Point in 1852, but when the cavalry was expanded in 1855 Lee accepted the lieutenant-colonelcy of the 2nd Cavalry to escape the painfully slow promotion in the Engineers. In 1859 he took part in a dramatic event that contributed to the growing division between North and South. The radical abolitionist John Brown, with a small band of followers, raided the arsenal at Harper's Ferry, Virginia, seizing weapons and hostages with the object of starting an uprising among the slaves in that state. Lee was in command of the troops sent to deal with the situation. Brown was eventually cornered in the arsenal's engine house and taken prisoner (and later hanged) after a bloody shoot-out.

After resigning from the U.S. Army, Lee moved his family to Richmond and was given command of all military forces in Virginia as a brigadier-general. In September 1861 he was given his first field command in Western Virginia. However, his Cheat Mountain campaign resulted in a somewhat ignominious withdrawal when a Colonel Albert Rust failed to make an expected enveloping attack on the Cheat Mountain position. The public blamed Lee for being too cautious and he was, undeservedly, given his second nickname, "Granny" Lee. It was not a promising start, but President Davis retained enough confidence in him to appoint Lee as his military adviser in March 1862 after a period commanding Confederate garrisons along the Atlantic coast. From this position he was able to support Stonewall Jackson's brilliant Shenandoah Valley campaign. While at Richmond his engineering background came to the fore and he insisted on the construction of earthworks around the city, earning him yet another nickname – the "King of Spades."

When Joseph E. Johnston was severely wounded at Fair Oaks, just 6 miles east of Richmond, in the Peninsular campaign, Lee rode out to take command (June 1, 1862) of what Davis now renamed the Army of Northern Virginia. It would remain his command until virtually the end of the war. He fought the second day of the battle, but the initiative had been lost and Lee withdrew to the original Confederate positions. Later in the month he left a small force guarding Richmond while he crossed the Chickahominy and struck a Union corps north of the river. It was the start of what was called the Seven Days Battles (Oak Grove, Beaver Dam Creek, Gaines' Mill, Garnett's and Golding's Farm, Savage's Station, White Oak Swamp, Glendale, and Malvern Hill). By July 2, although Lee had failed to win any tactical victory, he had removed Major-General George B. McClellan's army from the very gates of Richmond – a desperately needed strategic triumph.

This success considerably improved his somewhat tarnished reputation. At the end of August he thoroughly defeated John Pope at Second Manassas, although McClellan checked him in his first invasion of Maryland, which culminated in the drawn battle of Antietam – "the bloodiest single day of the war" – in which Lee suffered some 13,700 casualties to McClellan's 12,400. At the end of the year an advance and frontal attack by Ambrose E. Burnside was brutally repulsed by Lee at Fredericksburg, and in May 1863 Joseph Hooker (Lee referred to him as "Mr. F. J. Hooker"), with a hugely superior army, was surprised and defeated at Chancellorsville – as described in the Prologue, at the cost of Lee's ablest lieutenant, Stonewall Jackson.

In June 1863 Lee was at the summit of his success as a general. He was the idol of the South (and still is today). Within less than a year he had saved Richmond and defeated five Union Army commanders in quick succession (McClellan twice, Pope, Burnside and Hooker), although at considerable, some would say disproportionate and debilitating, cost in manpower – see table, page 285. At Gettysburg, however, he failed. He personally accepted the blame to the extent of offering his resignation – which was refused. After Gettysburg Lee did not engage in any major campaign until May 1864 when Ulysses S. Grant moved against him. He repulsed Grant's direct assaults in the Wilderness campaign of May–June, but was not strong enough to push him back, and in July 1864 Grant began the long siege of Petersburg. Lee's appointment as general-in-chief of all Confederate armies came in February 1865 when the Confederacy had all but collapsed. On April 2 the Army of the Potomac finally broke through the Petersburg defenses and Lee's forces retreated – to surrender a week later at Appomattox Court House.

Lee was a Southern gentleman in the best sense of the word: upright, honest, caring, deeply religious and opposed to slavery. His personal prayer, which was memorized in later years by President Harry Truman, who used it throughout his life, contained the words: "Help me to be, to think, to act what is right because it is right; make me truthful, honest and honorable in all things; make me intellectually honest for the sake of right and honor and without thought of reward to me." Although his first concern was the welfare of his soldiers (in the Gettysburg campaign this meant their feeding), his honesty and religious conviction were behind his condemnation and prohibition of looting. Part of his Order on the subject read, "It must be remembered that we make war only upon armed men, and we cannot take vengeance for the wrongs our people have suffered without . . . offending against Him to whom vengeance belongeth."

Lee's opposition to slavery had led him to free the slaves he inherited from his wife's estate long before the war. One of them, William Mack Lee, chose to stay by the general's side throughout the war as his cook and personal servant, indeed friend and confidant. William Mack Lee, who became a Baptist Methodist minister in 1881, said of "Marse Robert": "I was raised by one of the greatest men in the world. There was never one born of a woman greater than Gen. Robert E. Lee." A somewhat biased and inflated opinion perhaps, but the sentiment was endorsed in a simpler manner by a Southern general who said of Lee, "As a soldier the men respected him, as a man they loved him." This affection for Lee was not confined to the Confederacy but was felt by men in the U.S. Army who had known him during the years before the war. Shortly after the final surrender, an Irish sergeant in Yankee uniform who had served with him on the frontier many years before visited Lee in his house. He was bringing a gift of food, which the general would only accept if it was passed to the wounded in hospital. The sergeant grabbed Lee in a bear hug and with tears rolling down his cheeks said, "Goodbye, Colonel. God bless ye. If I could have got over in time, I would have been with ye."

Lee's Final Address to His Troops

Hd Qurs Army of Northern Virginia
10th April 1865

General Order
No 9
After four years of arduous service, marked by unsurpassed courage and fortitude, the Army of Northern Virginia has been compelled to yield to overwhelming numbers and resources.

I need not tell the brave survivors of so many hard fought battles who have remained steadfast to the last, that I have consented to this result from no distrust of them. But feeling that valor and devotion could accomplish nothing that could compensate for the loss that would have attended the continuance of the contest, I determined to avoid the useless sacrifice of those whose past services have endeared them to their countrymen.

By the terms of the agreement, Officers and men can return to their homes and remain until exchanged. You will take with you the satisfaction that proceeds from the consciousness of duty faithfully performed and I earnestly pray that a merciful God will extend to you His blessing and protection.

With an unceasing admiration of your constancy and devotion to your country, and a grateful remembrance of your kind and generous consideration of myself, I bid you all an affectionate farewell.

R E Lee
Genl

By the summer of 1863 all officers and soldiers in the Army of Northern Virginia had absolute faith in their commander and in their own ability to "lick the Yankees" – it had been proved, albeit expensively, on several recent battlefields. Lee reciprocated this confidence. Years after the war Harry Heth probably got it right when he said, "The fact is, General Lee believed the Army of Northern Virginia, as it then existed, could accomplish anything." However, at Gettysburg a combination of overconfidence and an underestimation of the enemy's ability to fight was certainly one of many factors that went toward explaining the Rebel defeat.

At Gettysburg Lee was fifty-six years old, but looked older with his white beard and his handsome face showing signs of stress and fatigue. He was still an imposing figure, powerfully built and just under 6 feet tall. The British observer Colonel Fremantle described him as "the handsomest man of his age I ever saw." Lieutenant-Colonel Moxley Sorrel, Longstreet's staff officer, wrote that "his white teeth and winning smile were irresistible." He dressed in a long, gray, well-worn coat with only the three stars of gold braid on the collar suggesting anything of a military uniform. He wore blue trousers, high black boots, carried a red bandana and had a medium-brimmed dark felt hat, but carried neither sword nor revolver. In the spring of 1863 Lee had developed a heavy cold and fever, but he also complained of "a good deal of pain" in his chest, back and arms – indications that he may have been suffering from hypertension and had angina pectoris. That he was stressed was clearly evident on June 29 when Dr. J. L. Suesserott, a civilian, visited him in Chambersburg. The doctor wrote:

> I have never seen so much emotion depicted upon a human countenance. With his hand at times clutching his hair, and with contracted brow, he would walk with rapid strides for a few rods [a rod was 16.5 feet] and then, as if he bethought himself of his actions, he would with a sudden jerk produce an entire change in his features and demeanor and cast an enquiring gaze on me, only to be followed in a moment by the same contortions of face and agitation of person.

At that time Lee had every reason to be stressed, as he had just heard the previous day from a scout that Meade had crossed the Potomac, but there was still no sign of Stuart and his cavalry – he was becoming desperate for accurate information on his enemy. While his letter of August 8 in which he stresses his physical afflictions sounds a little like making an excuse for the Gettysburg failure, there is no doubt that Lee fought that battle when his health was impaired (see box opposite). He continued in command, however, and his health improved in that he had no more additional cardiac symptoms during the next six years.

Lee's method of command at Gettysburg will be evidenced in the later sections of this book dealing with the campaign, battle and retreat, when the problems he faced and the circumstances in which he made decisions are examined. Sufficient here to note that he had been accustomed to guiding rather than ordering his senior generals. His method was to use what in modern terms is called the "mission command" method of issuing orders. The subordinate is given general instructions on the objective to be achieved and is left to implement it as he sees best. The commander does not intervene unless there is a crisis, or unless the unexpected happens necessitating his intervention. Lee was accustomed – especially when he had Jackson as a corps commander – to giving his senior commanders their tasks and allowing them to implement them without direct supervision. At Gettysburg, with two new corps commanders (Hill and Ewell), Lee continued with this method and on two crucial instances issued instructions (to Stuart and Ewell) that arguably allowed the subordinate too much latitude in deciding what to do, what course to take.

Lee's Health at Gettysburg

There seems little doubt that Lee was less than a hundred percent fit at the battle. Chuck Teague, Vice President of the Civil War Round Table, assembled considerable evidence that Lee's health had been irreparably undermined by mid-1863 and that, while he had periods when he seemed to have recovered, these did not indicate that the underlying problems had gone. Using a number of sources, including Lee's letters to his wife, Chuck Teague published his findings in the *North and South* magazine of July 2003 and these are summarized below:

- In 1849 Lee contracted malaria, an illness that periodically returned throughout his life, and later, while commandant at West Point, he was seriously ill. The cause is unknown, but it was sufficiently unpleasant for Lee to state, "my health is failing fast, & if I could get hold of a Dr. sensible enough to see it . . .
- In 1855 he complained, "I fear my eyes will not hold out much longer."
- In 1860 while in Texas he had difficulty with the use of his right arm – the pain possibly related to cardiovascular problems.
- In March 1863 he admitted to his wife that he had "a very rickety position on his pins," and that he was "suffering from a heavy cold." By the end of the month this developed into sharp stabbing pains in his chest, back and arms, which, according to Lee, "came on in paroxysms . . . was quite sharp . . ." Modern medical opinion is that this was probably angina pectoris and a minor heart attack. Rest and medication brought some relief and Lee regained strength so that on April 24 he wrote to his son Custis, "my own health is improving." This was just as well, as within a few days he was immersed in the Chancellorsville campaign and was only two months away from Gettysburg.
- His untypical resting in a house rather than a tent at Gettysburg, and the observation of Imboden that Lee rode Traveler (a horse with an uncomfortable gait) slowly in approaching the town on July 1, perhaps add some weight to the notion that all was not well with him at that time.
- Several observers have commented on his appearance and behavior at Gettysburg. Dr. J. L. Suesserott of Chambersburg has been quoted on page 260, describing Lee's startling demeanor and obvious agitation. The Prussian Captain Scheibert contrasts Lee's calmness and self-possession at Chancellorsville with his appearance of Gettysburg, when he was showing visible signs of stress: "Lee was not at his ease, but was riding to and fro, frequently changing his position, making anxious enquiries here and there, and looking care worn." Colonel Fremantle, on the other hand, was surprised at Lee's passivity on July 2:

  > So soon as firing began, General Lee joined Hill just below our tree, and he remained there nearly all the time, looking through his field glass – sometimes talking to Hill and sometimes to Colonel Long of his staff. But generally he sat quite alone on the stump of a tree. What I remarked especially was that during the whole time the firing continued, he only sent one message, and only received one report.

- Colonel Long commented on Lee's uncharacteristic "degree of anxiety and impatience." Major Blackford of Stuart's staff, meanwhile, noted that on the evening of July 2 Lee appeared to be suffering from diarrhea:

  > I was a little surprised to see [Lee] come out of his tent hurriedly and go to the rear several times while I was there, and he walked so much as if he was weak and in pain that I asked one of the gentlemen present what was the matter with him, and he told me General Lee was suffering a good deal from an attack of diarrhea.

- After the battle, when Lee wrote to the President offering to resign, his letter contained the following:

  > I sensibly feel the growing failure of my bodily strength. I have not yet recovered from the attack I experienced the past spring. I am becoming more and more incapable of exertion and am thus prevented from making the personal examinations to the operations in the field which I feel to be necessary. I am so dull that in making use of the eyes of others I am frequently misled . . .

Lee died of his heart condition in 1870. There are very strong grounds for believing that during the Gettysburg campaign, particularly during the battle itself, his leadership and physical ability were handicapped by weakness and pain brought on by a combination of chest pains and diarrhea. Poor eyesight, the stress and anxiety of Stuart's absence, and the argumentative and seemingly uncooperative attitude of his corps commanders aggravated these disabilities. Lee was surely not at his best at Gettysburg.

Lee's control during the battle was largely a combination of personal visits or meetings with individual corps commanders, and reliance on his staff and couriers. His headquarters did not include a signal officer and there is little evidence that wigwag signaling played much part in controlling the widely dispersed formations – in an extreme case, a courier riding from east of Culp's Hill on the Rebel left would have to cover at least 5 miles to reach a unit in Devil's Den and could have taken up to an hour to complete the journey. This spreading out of the Confederate Army on July 2 and 3 was to make coordination and the synchronizing of events on the opposite flanks almost impossible to achieve.

To understand Lee's method of command at Gettysburg, it is useful to know his locations and movements, which are summarized below:

July 1

- Night June 30/July 1. Headquarters 25 miles west of Gettysburg in woods near Chambersburg. Here Lee had a meeting with Hill regarding the latter's wish to probe Gettysburg.
- July 1, a.m. Lee intended to move his headquarters to Cashtown. He rode forward with Longstreet and reached the small town by around 11:00 a.m. He then moved another 2 miles east of Cashtown, drawn forward by the sound of gunfire. At this stage he was anxious to avoid a general engagement until his army was concentrated and he was very agitated by Stuart's absence.
- Sometime before 2:00 p.m. Lee reached Herr's Ridge and conferred with corps commander Hill and then divisional commander Heth, who arrived for instructions.

- At around 2:15 Heth returned to seek Lee's permission to press the attack. At about 2:30 p.m. it was given – strangely, direct to Heth, thus bypassing his corps commander, who was close by.
- By 4:30 p.m. Lee was on Seminary Ridge and at 5:00 p.m. Longstreet arrived and suggested a wide right-flanking move to get between Meade and Washington.
- Sometime after 5:30 p.m. Longstreet departed and Lee rode through Gettysburg to meet with Ewell north of the town. Both Early and Rodes were present. A number of reasons were put forward, mainly by Early, as to why no attack could be made on that flank on July 1, nor any withdrawal of the corps to Seminary Ridge. Lee accepted this view.
- That evening Lee's headquarters was established just south of the Chambersburg Pike, close to the Lutheran Seminary. From there Lee changed his mind and sent instructions to pull Ewell's Corps back to Seminary Ridge. This brought Ewell hurrying to the headquarters arguing against such a move and assuring Lee he could attack Culp's Hill the next morning. Again Lee accepted.

The whys and wherefores of these orders and counterorders are discussed elsewhere. However, it is worth noting here that on July 1 Lee discussed events with all three corps commanders individually, but never met them together, never held a council of war to seek opinions and then make his decision before issuing orders, and was seemingly lacking in decisiveness when confronted with reluctant subordinates. Thus far he did not appear to be fully in control of events, nor indeed of his corps commanders.

July 2

- During the early hours of the morning Ewell was instructed to attack Culp's Hill when he heard Longstreet's guns open fire – this was later changed to making a demonstration with the attacking part left to Ewell's discretion.
- At about 4:00 a.m. Captain Johnston was sent to reconnoiter the Union left as Lee intended to attack that flank.
- At around 5:00 a.m. Longstreet returned to Lee's headquarters and was soon joined by his divisional commander, Hood, and also Hill, accompanied by Heth. At this informal gathering the forthcoming day's operations were discussed. When Johnston returned around 9:00 a.m., Lee gave orders direct to Longstreet's divisional commander, McLaws, who had joined the group and was to lead the attack.
- Around 10:00 a.m. Lee rode over to see Ewell before returning to meet Longstreet an hour later at Lee's headquarters.
- At about 11:00 a.m. Lee gave a direct order to Longstreet to use McLaws' and Hood's Divisions to attack the enemy left, but then agreed Longstreet could wait for Law's Brigade to arrive.
- At 4:30 p.m. when Longstreet's attack finally started, Lee positioned himself at his headquarters near the Seminary. He remained there throughout the attack, only sending or receiving one message.

As far as command and control were concerned, Lee still favored instructing his corps commanders individually rather than calling them in to receive orders for the day and coordinate their actions. This was a particularly bad day for coordination between the opposite wings of the army, as will be discussed in Section Ten: Day Two. Again, even with a corps commander present, Lee gave orders direct to a divisional commander, but then allowed a corps commander, already late, to delay moving off because a brigade was not yet up. Despite the long delay in Longstreet's attack, and its importance, Lee was content to sit watching events through his glass from a distance, making no attempt to check personally on events on his right.

July 3

- The night July 2/3 Lee spent at his headquarters issuing orders for the morning attacks by Ewell and Longstreet on both flanks (in practice a continuation of the previous day's attacks), although he did not meet with either.
- Sometime after daylight Lee rode over to Longstreet's headquarters in Pitzer's schoolhouse adjacent to Willoughby Run. There he found his corps commander, who, in view of Lee's non-specific order to envelop the enemy's flank, was still thinking in terms of moving round the Union left to get in his rear. Lee was forced to scrap his intended plan and think again, as fighting had already flared up once more on Culp's Hill long before Longstreet was ready to renew his attack.
- That morning Lee and Longstreet carried out a reconnaissance of Cemetery Ridge from the open ground opposite on Seminary Ridge, just north of Spangler Woods. The result was the afternoon's massive Confederate artillery bombardment (in which Lee again relied on delegating) and the grand assault that became known as Pickett's charge.
- Lee watched the attack from what is now known as the "Point of Woods," in the open near the eastern tip of Spangler Woods and 300 yards east of the Virginia Monument.

Once more, Lee did not see fit to summon his corps commanders to his headquarters on the night of 2/3 July. This might have ensured that everyone knew the plan, timings and objectives, and could discuss problems.

Overall during the three days, Lee's method of command had not worked well. He did not issue forthright orders directly to the commanders who were to implement them; he gave too much discretion to his corps commanders, and was taken aback by the experienced Longstreet's seemingly uncooperative attitude on July 2 – so much so that he again resorted to issuing orders direct to a divisional commander in the presence of his superior. His command philosophy was summed up later when he told a Pomeranian observer at his headquarters, "I think and work with all my powers to bring my troops to the right place at the right time," then adding that, having done that, "I leave the matter up to God and subordinate officers." It was a philosophy that failed him at Gettysburg. – God was impartial and neither his subordinates nor his staff were up to it.

After the war Lee returned to Richmond as a paroled prisoner but was later pardoned for his "treason." Somehow his application for restoration of his citizenship was mislaid, and it was not until the 1970s that it was found and granted. He refused several lucrative offers and instead assumed the presidency of Washington College (now the Washington and Lee University), in Lexington, Virginia. He never wrote his memoirs, although repeatedly asked to do so, preferring to let his army's record speak for itself. He died at Lexington on October 12, 1870, of the heart disease that had plagued him first in April 1863, and was buried in the chapel of the university that bears his name. Not long before his death he had written to his wife: "The warm weather has also dispelled some of the rheumatic pains in my back, but I perceive no change in the stricture in my chest. If I attempt to walk beyond a very slow gait, the pain is always there."

Commander of the Army of the Potomac: Major-General George G. Meade (1815–1872)

During the weeks of political intrigue and lobbying by Hooker's generals to get rid of him after Chancellorsville, Meade, who knew he was favored by some to replace Hooker, wrote to his wife:

> I do not . . . stand any chance, because I have no friends, political or others [this was not true] who press or advance my claims or pretensions, and there are so many others who are pressed by influential politicians that it is folly to think I stand any chance upon mere merit alone. Besides, I have not the vanity to think my capacity so pre-eminent, and I know there are plenty of others equally competent with myself, though their names may not have been so much mentioned.

On June 27, 1863 Major-General Hooker telegraphed Washington that he wished to be relieved of command of the Army of the Potomac. At three o'clock in the morning of June 28 a Major James Hardie, who had arrived at Frederick by special train from Washington, had Meade, then commanding V Corps, woken in his tent just outside town and handed him a secret Presidential Order. It contained the news that he was now the army commander – just three days before becoming engaged in the biggest setpiece battle of the war. At dawn Meade and Hardie rode over to Hooker's headquarters and found the outgoing commander awaiting them in full dress uniform. They conferred in Hooker's tent for a while, and then Meade emerged, found his son, who was an aide-de-camp at army headquarters, and announced, "Well George, I am in command of the Army of the Potomac."

George Gordon Meade was born on December 31, 1815 in Cadiz, Spain, where his father was serving as an agent for the U.S. Navy. The family moved to Philadelphia but financial difficulties necessitated further moves between Baltimore and Washington over a number of years. Young Meade's schooling suffered accordingly, but he gained a place at West Point in 1831. Although not particularly enamored with the military regime, he graduated nineteenth in the class of 1835 and was commissioned into the 3rd U.S. Artillery and sent to Florida at the start of the Seminole Wars. While in Florida he was struck down with a virulent fever that forced his transfer to the Watertown Arsenal in Massachusetts. Once fully recovered, Meade, disillusioned with the army, resigned to work for a railroad company as an engineer. On his twenty-fifth birthday he married Margaretta Sergeant, who in due course gave him a family of seven children. In order to improve his standard of living, Meade rejoined the army in 1842 and was appointed a second lieutenant in the Topographical Engineers. Posted to Texas in 1845, he was later transferred to General Winfield Scott's command and took part in the Mexican War as a staff officer before being brevetted to first lieutenant for gallant conduct at the Battle of Monterrey. The next ten years were mostly spent in surveying and design work for lighthouses on the east coast, except for a brief

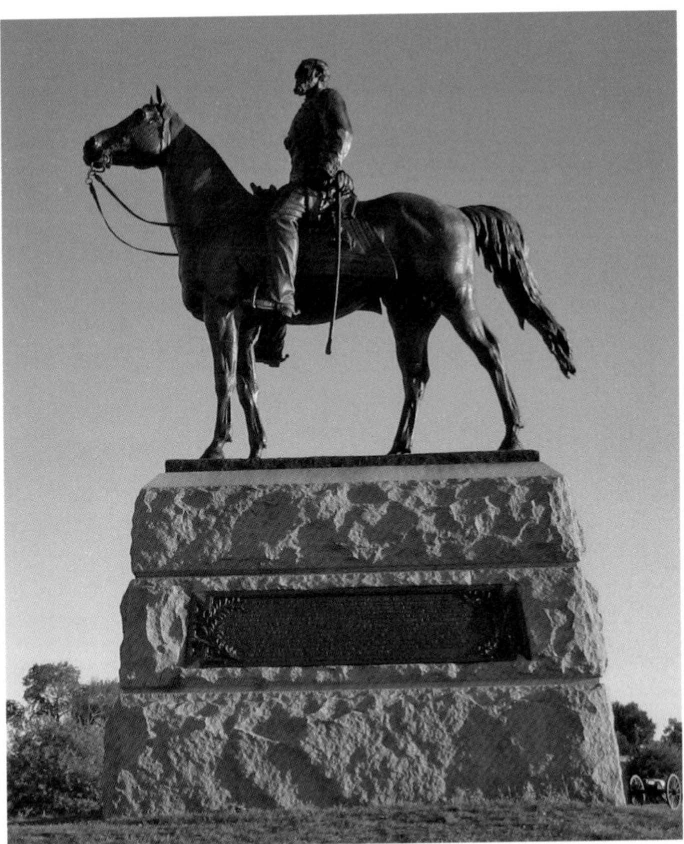

Meade's statue is located on Cemetery Ridge, 150 yards northeast of the Angle.

Meade's Announcement to the Army of His Acceptance of Command

Meade was not asked if he would take command of the Army of the Potomac, as were several other generals after Chancellorsville (see page 28). He had no option: it was a direction from the President. Meade announced the change as follows:

HEAD-QUARTERS
ARMY OF THE POTOMAC
June 28th, 1863

By direction of the President of the United States, I hereby assume command of the Army of the Potomac. As a soldier, in obeying this order – an order totally unexpected and unsolicited – I have no promises or pledges to make. The country looks to this army to relieve it from the devastation and disgrace of hostile invasion. Whatever fatigues and sacrifices we may be called upon to undergo, let us have in view the magnitude of the interests involved, and let each man determine to do his duty, leaving to an all-controlling Providence the decision of the contest. It is with just diffidence that I relieve in the command of this army, an eminent and accomplished soldier, whose name must ever appear conspicuous in the history of its achievements; and I rely upon the hearty support of my companions in arms to assist me in the discharge of the duties of the important trust that has been confided in me.

GEORGE G. MEADE
Major-General Commanding.

Major-General Henry Wager Halleck (1815–1872)

Halleck, who was general-in-chief in Washington from July 11, 1862 to March 12, 1864, had resigned from the army as a captain in 1854 at the age of thirty-nine. In August 1861 he was appointed major-general, becoming at a stroke the fourth senior officer in the army. His only field command was during the May–June period of 1862, when he took personal charge of the forces intent on capturing Corinth, Mississippi. To call Halleck's advance cautious was an understatement – it progressed at the rate of a mile a day and ended with entrenchment. At the end of a month he had covered 20 miles. Unsurprisingly, this snail-like approach ensured the Confederates were able to withdraw at their leisure.

Halleck was an academic soldier-turned-lawyer nicknamed "Old Brains," in part due to his pop-eyes and bulbous forehead. Apart from his miserable showing at Corinth, he spent his early war commanding military districts in the West. His forte was administration but, seemingly, whatever he touched he succeeded in making himself highly unpopular. The historian Kendall Gott has described Halleck as a department commander:

> Although he had impressive credentials, Henry Halleck was not an easy man to work for. The nature of his job and personality often provoked antagonism, hatred and contempt. Halleck's strengths were organizing, coordinating, planning and managing. He could also advise and suggest, and he sometimes ordered subordinates where and when to make a move, but he never was comfortable doing it himself. Halleck seldom worked openly, and as a department commander, he was always at headquarters, separated and aloof from the men. His decisions were the result of neither snap judgments nor friendly discussion, but calculated thinking. He was also prone to violent hatred and never cultivated close relationships. Overall he generated no love, confidence or respect.

Halleck was also noted for his inclination to blame others for his failures (not an uncommon characteristic among generals) and as well as being deeply resented by most field commanders was at the same time alleged to be the most unpopular man in Washington.

Nevertheless, Secretary of the Navy Gideon Welles's brutal summary of the man is unduly harsh. Welles said Halleck "originates nothing, anticipates nothing . . . takes no responsibility, plans nothing, suggests nothing, is good for nothing." At a meeting on June 16 Welles was equally derogatory. Halleck, he said, "sits and smokes, and swears, and scratches his arm and shakes it, but exhibits no mental capacity or intelligence . . ." Lincoln would never have kept Halleck for so long in such high office had he been that bad. The President found him extremely valuable for his management and administrative skills, and as a buffer between himself and top generals.

Halleck was a New Yorker who graduated from West Point in 1839 into the Engineers and earned a brevet promotion in Mexico. He worked on fortifications, taught at the Academy and wrote the *Report on the Means of National Defense, Elements of Military Art and Science* – hence his reputation as an academic. After resigning in 1854 he became a successful lawyer in San Francisco but retained contact with the military via the militia.

During the Gettysburg campaign Halleck rightly saw the foolishness of leaving a large garrison at the isolated town of Winchester, but his orders to withdraw almost all troops were ignored by the garrison commander, Major-General Robert C. Schenck (see page 300).When Winchester eventually fell to Ewell, Halleck was white with rage.

Halleck's next direct involvement in the campaign was his insistence that Harper's Ferry, or rather the Maryland Heights that overlooked it, should be garrisoned and strongly held – an eminently sensible decision. Hooker, however, was adamant that this garrison should join the Army of the Potomac to bolster his numbers (see page 311). The result of this clash was Hooker's resignation and Meade's appointment.

Halleck relinquished his top post to become chief of staff to Grant in March 1864, an appointment he retained until virtually the end of the war. He then commanded in Virginia and on the Pacific, later dying while commanding the Division of the South at Louisville, Kentucky, in 1872, aged fifty-seven.

spell in Florida in the 1850s during another Seminole confrontation. This was followed by a period surveying on the Great Lakes. The outbreak of the Civil War found Meade a forty-five-year-old captain whose active soldiering experience was decidedly limited.

Meade's age and lack of command experience was no bar to rapid promotion as he was appointed a brigadier-general of volunteers in the first summer of the war. He commanded a brigade in the Army of the Potomac in the Peninsular campaign. During the Seven Days Battles he fought at Beaver Creek and Gaines' Mill before falling, after being hit twice almost simultaneously, at Glendale. His wounds were serious. A musket ball struck him above his hip, clipped his liver, and just missed his spine as it passed through his body. The second bullet hit his arm, but Meade remained mounted until loss of blood compelled him to leave the field. After recovery in hospital and his return to active duty, Meade's brigade made a heroic stand on Henry House Hill to protect the rear of the retreating army after Second Manassas in August 1862. In this action his horse, Old Baldy, was wounded under him (see box, page 208). At the start of Lee's first invasion of Maryland, Meade was given command of the 3rd Division, I Corps. At South Mountain on September 14, where a spent piece of shell bruised his thigh, he so impressed his corps commander, Hooker, that the latter was heard to exclaim, "Look at Meade! Why, with troops like those, led in that way, I can win anything!" Three days later at Antietam, where his horse was again wounded, Meade took temporary command when his corps commander was hit. But it was at Fredericksburg (considered by some the worst day of the Army of the Potomac) that Meade confirmed his growing reputation for courage, personal leadership and drive. It was his division that provided the only success in a terrible day. His command was the only Union force briefly to break through the enemy line before being forced back for want of support. During the bitter fighting Meade received two bullet holes through his hat.

In 1863 Meade looked considerably older than his forty-seven years, with his thin face, grizzled beard, droopy pouches under his eyes, glasses, large nose and balding head. His men sometimes referred him to as "that damned, goggle-eyed, snapping turtle." He was certainly a "snapper" in that he had an explosive temper over any infringement of duty or incompetence. These bursts of sudden fury were usually brought on during the stress of action and his staff learned to fear them. Later General Ulysses S. Grant, who as general-in-chief of all Union armies knew Meade intimately, summed him up as follows:

> General Meade was an officer of great merit, with drawbacks to his usefulness that were beyond his control. He was brave and conscientious, and commanded the respect of all who knew him. He was unfortunately of a temper that would get beyond his control at times . . . No one saw this better than he himself, and no one regretted it more. This made it unpleasant at times, even in battle for those around him to approach him even with information.

There is little evidence that things got this bad at Gettysburg, although Sickles certainly felt the rough edge of Meade's tongue. Nevertheless, he could relax on less stressful occasions and chat amicably with his aides around a campfire, and he was a totally devoted family man who deeply regretted the separation that the war caused. His particular loathing was the press, and to a lesser extent civilians, of whom he could be extremely contemptuous. He never allowed journalists to speak to him, which they countered by never mentioning him in their newspapers except when something had gone wrong. Whereas Lee earned the respect and love of all under his command, Meade attracted the former but never the latter. He was respected for his fearlessness in battle, his energy, drive and straightforward determination to put duty first. And thus far in the war he had proved himself a competent leader on the battlefield.

Meade's style of command at Gettysburg was quite different from that of Lee. He was to spend hours in the saddle riding round, sizing up the position, allocating positions to his corps, checking and supervising. During the three days of fighting Meade made excellent use of capable subordinates such as Major-General John F. Reynolds, who was commanding the left wing of the army when the first clash occurred early on July 1, just west of Gettysburg town. When Reynolds was killed early in the day, Meade delegated great responsibility to his trusted friend Major-General Winfield S. Hancock, sending him forward to take command of the I, XI, and III Corps, although he was junior to both Howard and Sickles, thus making use of the extraordinary power given him by Secretary Stanton to make, irrespective of seniority, appointments, promotions or sackings of senior commanders on his own authority – a huge break with tradition. Meade was told, "You are authorized to remove from command, and to send from your army, any officer or other person you may deem proper, and to appoint to command as you may deem expedient." Meade had told Reynolds to hand over his II Corps to Brigadier-General John Gibbon, who was not the senior brigadier in the corps, and go forward to take charge of the situation at Gettysburg. Meade himself did not arrive from Taneytown until around midnight on July 1. He listened to his generals and agreed the decision to stand and fight on the ground they had selected and occupied. He toured the position on foot in the moonlight and then, before dawn, rode south along Cemetery Ridge and finally to Culp's Hill, indicating the positions the corps were to take up as they arrived and having a staff officer draw the positions on a map. By noon on July 2 his army was on the field except for the still marching VI Corps.

Unfortunately for Meade, he inherited two political manipulators from Hooker – Major-Generals Daniel Butterfield, his chief of staff, and Daniel Sickles, commanding III Corps. The former was to cause him grief later in the war, questioning his command decisions and courage. But it was Sickles who displayed serious insubordination that could have jeopardized the defense of Cemetery Ridge and thus the outcome of the battle on the afternoon of July 2. That he did so was partly Meade's fault in that, despite Sickles' twice querying his explicit orders as to his position in the line, Meade did not personally check that his instructions had been properly carried out until about 4:00 p.m. By then it was too late to make changes, as the Rebel attack on "Sickles' salient," almost threequarters of a mile forward of where he should have been, was starting. This was not the first time Sickles had given him trouble; Meade had reprimanded him severely shortly after taking command on account of the lack of urgency in III Corps' marching.

As noted in the previous section, Meade and his corps commanders made extensive use of their signal staff, and the army headquarters was kept busy sending and receiving wigwag messages throughout the battle. It was an effective means of control, in contrast to what was going on along Lee's line. The flag signaling supplemented the use of couriers and orderlies, who were continually dashing off with orders or up with reports from various parts of the line. This was particularly so during the latter part of July 2, once Sickles' error had been discovered and Meade was frantically involved in throwing reinforcements at his left to try to hold III Corps' vulnerable position.

The final illustration of Meade's battlefield command method came late on the second day after both sides had suffered huge losses and III Corps had been driven from its forward position. The key decision for Meade was what to do on the third day. Should he continue on the defensive in his present position, counterattack, or retire, perhaps to the Pipe Creek line in his rear? Meade summoned his famous "council of war" to seek the opinion of all corps commanders. Some might consider this a sign of weakness and indecision by an army commander, others that it was sensible to seek opinions before deciding. As it happened, all his senior officers voted to stay and fight where they were. Thus Meade had no problem making up his mind. But if opinions had differed widely, what then? History will never know what Meade was made of in those circumstances.

Following their severe losses, the Confederates retreated back to Virginia. President Lincoln and others heavily criticized Meade for lacking aggressive leadership in not pursuing the Rebels and crushing them with their backs to the rain-swollen, almost impassable Potomac River in mid-July – the validity of which is discussed in Section Twelve: The Aftermath. For the remainder of the fall of 1863 Meade led the army through an endless, meandering series of skirmishes, later called the Mine Run campaign, trying to outflank Lee's position in north central Virginia. However, despite his best efforts, Lee could not be brought to a major battle. On January 28, 1864 Meade received the official thanks of Congress for his victory at Gettysburg.

Meade continued in nominal command of the Army of the Potomac until the end of the war. However, General Grant was appointed commander of all Union forces during the winter of 1863/64 and elected to accompany the Army of the Potomac in the spring campaign. As the Wilderness campaign dragged on, the presence and directions of his superior officer, who was always at his side, curtailed Meade's control of the army. However, Meade accepted the situation and worked diligently in carrying out Grant's instructions. In recognition of his services he was promoted Major-General in the U.S. Regular Army in August 1864.

When Lee surrendered in April 1865 Meade was lying in an ambulance at army headquarters with a severe bout of sickness, headaches and fever, several miles from Lee at Appomattox Court House. When Grant rode off to accept the surrender, Meade still lay tossing and turning on his cot. However, news of the surrender acted as a potent medicine, as he instantly became very excited, jumped up and rode off on his favorite horse, Old Baldy, to announce the surrender to the troops.

After the war Meade was given command of the military districts on the east coast. He lived with his wife and family in Philadelphia until October 31, 1872 when he was suddenly struck down by a violent pain in his side. His old wound from Glendale had probably caused internal problems, and when pneumonia set in he faded quickly and died on November 7, 1872, aged fifty-six. He is buried in Laurel Hill Cemetery in Philadelphia.

MILITARY CONTROL – GENERAL OFFICERS

The Army of Northern Virginia

Lee's army at the battle consisted of some 71,700 all ranks engaged either on the field itself or in the nearby cavalry clashes during the period July 1–3. The army was organized into three corps, ten divisions and forty-two brigades. The total number of general officers (brigadier-generals up to generals) in positions of command at the outset of the battle was forty-nine. There was another "spare" major-general (Trimble), who was later given a command to replace a casualty, and one brigadier-general on the staff at army headquarters (Pendleton), giving a total of fifty-one general officers present. This figure excludes the two cavalry commanders (Imboden and Robertson) who were some distance away and not involved in the fighting. The ratio of generals to troops was therefore fractionally over 1:1,400. By comparison, the French at Waterloo had 1:860 but the Anglo-Allied 1:2,600 and the Prussians about the same.

The army commander was a full general; the three corps commanders lieutenant-generals, each commanding around 21,000 men; and the nine infantry divisional commanders all major-generals, commanding divisions with an average strength of 6,780 – all much larger formations than the equivalent in the Army of the Potomac. With brigades the situation was different in that the average size of an infantry brigade was similar to the Union brigades, and of the thirty-seven infantry brigades six were commanded by colonels, as was one of the five cavalry brigades. Thus, at the start of the battle colonels commanded some 17 percent of Confederate brigades – a proportion that was to rise rapidly as the fighting intensified.

The situation with regard to casualties of officers commanding formations at the start of the battle is best shown by a table:

	Killed/ mortally wounded	**Captured**	**Wounded**
Major-Generals	Pender	–	Heth Hood
Brigadier-Generals	Armistead Barksdale Garnett Semmes	Archer	G. T. Anderson Hampton Jenkins J. M. Jones Kemper Pettigrew Robertson Scales
Colonels	Avery		
Totals	6	1	10

One of the original divisional commanders was killed and two other major-generals were wounded. Of the brigadier-generals, four were killed, one captured and eight wounded, and one colonel commanding a brigade was killed. Of the fifty-two divisional or brigade commanders at the outset of the fighting seventeen (33 percent) became casualties.

As senior commanders fell, so the next senior officer present assumed command. Added to the casualties in the table above should therefore be one major-general wounded and captured (Trimble), one colonel killed (Marshall), and six colonels (Aylett, Fry, Gibson, Lowrance, J. G. Mayo Jr. and Terry) and one lieutenant-colonel (Luffman) wounded. In summary, the Confederate casualties among senior officers while commanding either a division or a brigade totaled twenty-six.

Brief biographical notes on Confederate corps and cavalry commanders are given below.

Lieutenant-General James Longstreet (1821–1904)

Longstreet, known as "my war horse" by Lee and "Old Pete" by soldiers, commanded the 1st Corps of almost 21,000 men and eighty-seven guns at Gettysburg. A West Point graduate of 1842, he had fought in the Mexican War and was wounded at Chapultepec while carrying his regiment's colors. He married in 1848, and his wife eventually bore him ten children. Much of his prewar service was in a series of dusty, dull frontier outposts with Longstreet serving as paymaster while developing his skill as a poker player.

He was made a brigadier-general at the outset of the war and commanded his brigade at First Manassas. By October 1861 he was a major-general commanding the 3rd Division – from major and paymaster in the U.S. Army to the command of a Rebel infantry division in a few months was meteoric by any standard. His aide at this time, Thomas Goree, considered Longstreet's "forte as an officer consists in the seeming ease with which he can handle and arrange large numbers of troops, as also with the confidence and enthusiasm with which he seems to inspire them." He was well known for his calm and unruffled manner under fire. At Sharpsburg a witness described him as being "as cool and composed as if on dress parade." He commanded his division at Fair Oaks and Seven Pines in the Peninsular campaign but failed to engage fully. He took part in the Seven Days Battles, but failed to attack promptly at Second Manassas. He did well at Antietam and was promoted to corps command as a lieutenant-general in October 1862. At Fredericksburg his men threw back wave after wave of frontally attacking Yankees and it was probably this battle that confirmed his belief in the strength of the tactical defensive.

Longstreet had lacked much enthusiasm for the Gettysburg campaign and throughout the weeks prior to the battle was under the erroneous impression that Lee had taken his advice to attack strategically but fight defensively. At Gettysburg his corps did not arrive until early on July 2, although Longstreet had met Lee the evening before on Seminary Ridge when he urged a move round Meade's left flank. On July 2 he was ordered to attack what was thought to be the exposed Union left, but the assault started late, at around 4:30 p.m., and he became embroiled in the vicious and costly fighting for the Peach Orchard, the Wheatfield and Devil's Den. On July 3, with the arrival of Pickett's Division, Longstreet was in command of the Rebels' final and failed assault on the enemy's center – an attack he was opposed to making.

In September 1863 he was sent to the West to support Bragg, fighting at Chickamauga, Wauhatchie and in the Knoxville campaign. On returning to the East he joined Lee for the Wilderness campaign but was seriously wounded in the neck by "friendly" musket fire.

After the war Longstreet became a Republican and relied on political appointments for a living when Southern sentiment turned against him as Gettysburg became regarded, not necessarily correctly, as the turning point of the war and Longstreet was considered largely responsible (almost certainly unjustifiably) for the defeat. He died in 1904, aged eighty-three. The *Dictionary of American Biography,* 1928, probably sums Longstreet up fairly: "Slightly below middle height, board-shouldered and somewhat heavy in his prime . . . Essentially a combat officer . . . an almost ideal corps commander . . . he did not posses the qualities necessary to successful independent command, and his skill in strategy was not great."

Lieutenant-General Richard "Dick" Stoddert Ewell (1817–1872)

Ewell commanded the Rebel 2nd Corps (formerly Stonewall Jackson's command) of some 20,600 men and seventy-nine guns at Gettysburg. In *Lee's Lieutenants*, Douglas Freeman describes him as:

> Bald, pop-eyed and long beaked, with a piping voice that seems to fit his appearance as a strange, unlovely bird; he probably has stomach ulcers and chronically complains of headaches, sleepless nights [he often slept curled round a camp stool] and indigestion; but quickly shows that he has a chivalrous, fighting spirit along with a sharp tongue and odd sense of humor.

Nicknamed "Old Bald Head" by his men, Ewell was one of the most profane men in the army and something of an eccentric. His favorite food was frumenty – wheat boiled in milk with sugar – but his most famous eccentricity was that, after many years as an old army bachelor, he finally married a widow, Mrs. Lizinka Brown, whom he insisted on introducing as "My wife, Mrs. Brown."

Ewell was a Virginian, a West Pointer who graduated from the class of 1840 into the dragoons, a veteran of Indian fighting and the Mexican War, and a superb horseman. He resigned from the U.S. Army as a captain in April 1861 and was immediately appointed colonel in the Confederate States Army. By June he was commanding a brigade at First Manassas and early in 1862 he was promoted major-general, handling his division with considerable skill under the watchful eye of Stonewall Jackson in the latter's famous Shenandoah Valley campaign. He did well during the Seven Days Battles but was badly wounded out in front of one of his regiments at Second Manassas. The bullet shattered his knee and the leg had to be amputated. There followed a long period of recovery during which he married and missed the battles at Sharpsburg, Fredericksburg and Chancellorsville.

Ewell reappeared, complete with wooden leg, in May 1863 as a lieutenant-general and corps commander. His appointment as Jackson's replacement was popular with his men, who admired his record as a courageous fighter, his honesty and generosity of spirit. His wound and marriage had two obvious consequences. The former meant he traveled on the march in a buggy, walked with crutches, and had to be lifted onto his horse (called Rifle) and strapped in the saddle. The latter brought about the moderation of his spectacular language. If there were any doubts as to the wisdom of his promotion, they would have concerned his physical handicap and how he would perform in a semi-independent role without the explicit orders and guidance of Jackson.

Such doubts were quickly dispelled as Ewell led the Army of Northern Virginia into Maryland and Pennsylvania in June. He handled his corps with skill, roundly defeating the Yankees at Winchester and at the same time amassing substantial supplies through extensive foraging while moving through enemy territory. At Gettysburg, however, the doubts over his competence at that level reappeared. Given discretionary orders by Lee, Ewell's failure to take Cemetery Hill on July 1, a lack of coordination in his attacks on the Union right on July 2 and again on the third day have led some to blame him for the overall loss of the battle. Although Ewell later stated, "it took a dozen blunders to lose Gettysburg, and I committed a good many of them," he was certainly being too hard on himself; the allegations are discussed in depth in the sections on the battle itself.

In 1864 he was relieved of his field command due to poor health and put in charge of the defenses of Richmond. After the war he retired to a farm in Tennessee, dying there in 1872, aged fifty-five.

Lieutenant-General Ambrose Powell Hill (1825–1865)

Hill, at thirty-seven, was the youngest of the Confederate corps commanders at Gettysburg, where he commanded the 3rd Corps of almost 22,000 men and eighty-four guns – the largest corps on the field. By 1863 this Virginian merchant's son, who was known to his soldiers as "Little Powell," had proved himself one of the ablest of the Rebel divisional commanders through his aggressive tactics and hard marching, to the extent that his previous command was known as the "Light Division." His men knew action was likely if they saw their general had donned what he called his red "battle shirt." His finest hour had come at Antietam (Sharpsburg) in September 1862 when Lee had got into difficulties but was saved by the last-minute arrival of Hill and his division after a 17-mile forced march from Harper's Ferry. Lee's words in his report after the battle, "and then A. P. Hill came up," went into Southern folklore and the history books. Jackson on his deathbed called Hill's name, and Lee on his was supposed to have mumbled, "tell Hill he *must* come up."

Hill was a West Point graduate of the class of 1847, but unfortunately a youthful indiscretion with a young lady left the cadet with gonorrhea, which was in the advanced stages by Gettysburg – something, along with bouts of typhoid and yellow fever in earlier years, that goes a long way to explaining his lackluster performance on this occasion. Commissioned into the artillery, Hill saw action in the Mexican War and against the Seminole Indians. At the outbreak of the Civil War, First Lieutenant Hill resigned from the U.S. Army and was immediately appointed colonel of the 13th Virginia Infantry. Hill fought at First Manassas, was a divisional commander for the Seven Days Battles, did well under Jackson at Cedar Mountain but poorly at Second Manassas. He made his name at Antietam, but briefly jeopardized the Rebel line at Fredericksburg before being lightly wounded at Chancellorsville after taking command of the corps when Jackson was hit.

In May 1863 Lee had Hill promoted to lieutenant-general and given the newly formed 3rd Corps for the Gettysburg campaign – this in spite of his well-known habit of feuding with his superiors; he had previously been put under arrest by both Longstreet and Jackson. However, Lee believed Hill's ability was well established. In October 1862 Lee had said, after recommending Jackson and Longstreet for promotion, "Next to these two officers, I consider A. P. Hill the best commander with me. He fights his troops well and takes good care of them." Six months later, when considering further promotions, Lee's praises were slightly more restrained. Perhaps recalling Fredericksburg, he recommended Hill to President Davis with the words, "I think on the whole [Hill] is the best soldier of his grade with me."

Unfortunately for the Army of Northern Virginia, Hill was not at his best at Gettysburg, where his performance was pedestrian and uninspiring. On July 1, as the advance elements of the armies clashed in an encounter engagement, it was Hill's Corps that embroiled the army in a full-scale battle that Lee did not initially want. On July 2 Hill was with Lee for much of the time, but when action finally got under way late in the afternoon he showed little interest in ensuring that Anderson's Division's support of Longstreet's attack on the Union left was properly supervised and coordinated – Wright's Brigade actually reached Cemetery Ridge but was not supported. On July 3 Hill was sidelined and had little to do as two of his divisions (Heth and Pender) were transferred to Longstreet for the final massive attack on the enemy center. The probability is that Hill's sickness was sapping his usual enthusiasm and this, coupled with the close proximity of Lee, was enough to make him content to do the minimum during the battle.

Hill put in another poor performance in the Wilderness campaign but then suddenly revealed his old flair during the defense of Petersburg, where his leadership was once more exceptional. In view of the fact that he was almost certainly dying of venereal disease complications by 1865, the Union bullet through the heart that killed him on April 2, only a week after returning from sick leave, was probably something of a mercy.

Major-General James Ewell Brown "Jeb" Stuart (1833–1864)

Although not a corps commander at Gettysburg, Jeb Stuart, at the age of thirty, commanded over 8,000 cavalrymen and twenty-one guns and was probably the most famous cavalry leader of the war. More importantly, he played a critical and contentious role in the ten days prior to the battle. By mid-1863 Stuart was known for his mastery of reconnaissance, offensive cavalry operations and raiding. His attitude to cavalry battlefield tactics was perhaps best summed up in his own words: "I strive to inculcate in my men the spirit of the chase." Despite this "tally-ho" philosophy, he had become the eyes and ears upon which Lee depended for information on the enemy and for screening the movements of the Army of Northern Virginia. From many months of experience, Lee knew Stuart's information would be timely and accurate – when deprived of it, as he was at a critical juncture of the Gettysburg campaign, Lee was groping in the dark.

Born at Laurel Hill Plantation, Virginia, Stuart attended West Point, graduating in 1854 (when Robert E. Lee was commandant) into Mounted Rifles in Texas. He fought the Comanches, surviving a bullet fired into his chest at point-blank range, and later acted as Lee's A.D.C. during the crushing of John Brown's raid on Harper's Ferry. He married the daughter of Philip St. George Cooke in 1854 – Cooke later became a Union general, so the extraordinary situation arose of Stuart fighting on the opposite side to his father-in-law.

Although comparatively short with a square frame and a flowing beard to mask his receding chin, Stuart became known as the "Beau Sabreur of the Confederacy." He was deeply religious (he never drank or smoked and was known as a "Bible Class man" at

Two Opinions of Jeb Stuart

A civilian lady, horrified by Stuart's dandified and flamboyant appearance and behavior at the two reviews of his cavalry division at Culpeper Court House immediately prior to the cavalry battle at Brandy Station, wrote anonymously to President Davis:

> President, allow a true Southern lady to say, General S's conduct since in Culpeper is perfectly ridiculous, having repeated reviews for the benefit of his lady friends, he riding up and down the line thronged with those ladies, he decorated with flowers, apparently a monkey show on hand and he the monkey. In fact General Stuart is nothing more or less than one of those fops, devoting his whole time to his lady friends' company.

Stuart's aide, Major Henry B. McClellan, has left an altogether different view of his commander's behavior. On the evening of June 23 Stuart was camped at Rector's Cross Roads, nearly 3 miles west of Middleburg. Persistent, heavy rain appeared to have set in for the night. McClellan recalled that Stuart could easily have found shelter in a building but refused, insisting his oilcloth and blanket be spread under a tree. McClellan remonstrated but Stuart replied, "No, my men are exposed to this rain, and I will not fare any better than they."

West Point) but also extraordinarily vain, keen to promote his self-image and thus particularly sensitive to press criticism. He carefully cultivated his inflated cavalier image with red-lined cape, yellow sash, hat with ostrich plume cocked on one side, elbow-length gauntlets, thigh-high boots, red flower in his lapel and golden spurs. Many, particularly infantrymen, regarded such an appearance as tasteless, if not ridiculous.

Captain Stuart resigned from the U.S. Army in May 1861 and was appointed a lieutenant-colonel of infantry in the Confederate Army. He quickly rose to colonel (1st Virginia Cavalry), then brigadier-general in September 1861, and major-general commanding the Cavalry Division in July 1862. Stuart led his regiment at First Manassas, participating in the pursuit. He led the cavalry of the Army of Northern Virginia in the Peninsular campaign and the Seven Days Battles, Second Manassas, Antietam, Fredericksburg, Chancellorsville, Gettysburg and the Wilderness campaign. Stuart was also a raider. Twice he had circumnavigated the Union Army under McClellan, once in the Peninsular campaign and again after the Battle of Antietam. After Second Manassas he attacked General Pope's supply base (capturing his dress uniform) in his rear at Catlett's Station. While of no lasting strategic significance, these raids enormously boosted Southern morale while depressing that of the North.

At the start of the Gettysburg campaign, Southern morale was sky-high. Lee and his army considered themselves more than a match for any larger Yankee force. In no branch of the army was this feeling more ingrained than in the cavalry. However, the campaign did not begin well for Stuart. On June 9 he was surprised at Brandy Station – an engagement that developed into the largest cavalry battle of the war (although the Union forces included some infantry). It ended in a draw, but Stuart's image was tarnished and derided in the newspapers – much to his embarrassment and annoyance (he and his officers were alleged to have spent too much time "rollicking, frolicking and running after girls" at a ball the previous night; see boxes opposite and page 298). During the following three weeks Stuart screened the initial movement of the army into the Shenandoah Valley and towards the Potomac River crossing. Then, acting on discretionary orders, he once more encircled the enemy, but in the process deprived Lee of his primary source of intelligence while marching through hostile territory. His exhausted and depleted division did not arrive in the vicinity of the battlefield until late on July 2. On the next day Stuart failed to launch an effective attack on the Union rear as he was blocked by Union cavalry and fought to another draw. Brandy Station and Gettysburg marked the end of the perceived and actual supremacy of Southern horsemen over their Northern opponents.

During Grant's drive on Richmond in the spring of 1864, Stuart halted Philip Sheridan's cavalry at Yellow Tavern on the outskirts of the city. On May 11 Stuart was shot at close range in the stomach and died the following day after twenty-seven hours of agony; he was thirty-one. His wife and two children survived him. His widow, Flora Cooke Stuart, wore the black of mourning for the remaining forty-nine years of her life. An equestrian statue of Stuart was dedicated on Richmond's famed Monument Avenue in 1907. It faces north, which indicates that the rider died in the Civil War. The U.S. Army named two models of World War II tanks (the M3 and M5) as "Stuarts," and there is a Stuart High School in Falls Church, Virginia, whose sports team is called "The Raiders" in honor of his Civil War escapades.

THE ARMY OF THE POTOMAC

The first major difference in the general-officer structure of the two armies was that none of the Union armies had an officer above major-general – even the general-in-chief (Halleck) in Washington was the same rank. At Gettysburg a Union major-general could command any formation from army to division. Command was based on seniority, although Meade had been authorized to promote and appoint on merit – something out of the question until then. At the battle, apart from Meade, there were thirteen major-generals – one chief of staff (Butterfield), eight corps commanders and four divisional commanders. Of the nine corps and twenty-two divisions in the Army of the Potomac, major-generals commanded all the former, with an average strength of 11,250. With the latter, however, averaging 3,750, eighteen were commanded by brigadier-generals. At brigade level, of the fifty-eight infantry and cavalry brigades, twenty-seven had brigadier-generals in command but thirty-one (53 percent) only rated colonels. This seeming anomaly was partly explained by the far smaller size of Union corps and divisions than the same Confederate formations, as explained in Section One: Orders of Battle. The total number of general officers in command of infantry and cavalry formations at the start of the battle was fifty-eight, plus six on the staff. This gives a ratio of generals to troops of 1:1,467 – not that different from the Confederates (1:1,400).

Casualties among those officers initially in command of brigades or higher formations were as shown in the table below:

	Killed/ mortally wounded	**Wounded**
Major-Generals	Reynolds	Hancock
		Sickles
Brigadier-Generals	Farnsworth	Meredith
	Weed	Paul
	Zook	Stannard
		Gibbon
		Webb
		Graham (and captured)
		Barnes
		Barlow (and captured)
Colonels	Cross	Stone
	Willard	Brooke
	Vincent	Smyth
Totals	7	13

Thus a total of twenty senior commanders out of eighty-nine (22.5 percent) were either killed or wounded. To these can be added two staff officers (Butterfield and Warren). Another colonel was killed (Sherrill) after taking command of his brigade during the battle and a further five were wounded (Chapman Biddle, Coulter, Leonard, Root and Wister).

Major-General John Fulton Reynolds (1820–1863)

Reynolds, who had declined the command of the Army of the Potomac after Chancellorsville, commanded I Corps of over 12,200 men and twenty-eight guns and was additionally appointed by Meade (previously his senior as a corps commander) to command the left wing of the army (I, III and XI Corps, screened by Buford's cavalry) during the approach to Gettysburg. Born in Lancaster, Pennsylvania, Reynolds went to West Point, graduating in 1841 into the artillery. Service over the next eighteen years included fighting the Seminoles, the Mexican War, where he was commended for gallantry at Monterrey and Buena Vista, and the Utah Expedition, before ending as commandant of West Point at the outbreak of war.

Reynolds was tall, slim and well tanned, with dark hair and a well-trimmed beard; he was an excellent horseman. By mid-1863 he was a well-respected commander although his war service on the battlefield had not been particularly remarkable – in fact, it was somewhat limited. In August 1861 he commanded a brigade of Pennsylvania Reserves in the Washington defenses and then during the Seven Days Battles, where his brigade repulsed A. P. Hill's Light Division at Mechanicsville. The next day, however, after the fighting at Gaines' Mill, he fell asleep and was captured – the height of ignominy. After six weeks in Richmond's Libby Prison he was exchanged. He did better at Second Manassas, where as a divisional commander he held onto Henry Hill with some outstanding personal leadership that allowed Pope to withdraw. He missed Antietam, although his division was present under Meade. He commanded a corps at Fredericksburg, but despite some hard marching to try to support the threatened right flank at Chancellorsville he did not arrive in time to prevent XI Corps from collapsing under Jackson's attack.

At Gettysburg he arrived at around 10:00 a.m. on July 1 to find Buford delaying the Rebel advance on the town. He rushed his corps forward to support the cavalry and summoned XI Corps to join him. However, shortly afterward he was shot, probably by a skirmisher from Archer's Brigade, while forward on McPherson's Ridge supervising the battle. The bullet passed through the back of his head and into his brain. He fell from his horse on his face and when his aides turned him over he smiled, gasped once and died. He was the only corps commander from either army to be killed at Gettysburg.

Major-General Abner Doubleday (1819–1893)

Doubleday commanded the 4,700 men of the 3rd Division of I Corps. He was the senior divisional commander on the battlefield and took over command of the corps on the death of Reynolds early on July 1. Prior to Gettysburg his career had been dull and mediocre. Born into a prominent New York family, he worked for two years as an engineer before attending West Point. He graduated in 1842 into the artillery and served in the Seminole and Mexican Wars without any particular distinction. In April 1861 at Fort Sumter he became famous as the first man to lay a Union artillery piece and fired the opening shot of the war.

He commanded a brigade at Second Manassas, a division at South Mountain (Antietam), Fredericksburg and Chancellorsville, where his performance varied between pedestrian and satisfactory. When Meade, who loathed Doubleday, knew he was to take over his 3rd Division he maintained he was pleased, as his old division would "think a great deal more of me than before." By then the rotund Doubleday was known as "Old Forty-Eight Hours" due to his plodding, deliberate methods. Gettysburg, however, was quite different. With huge responsibility thrust on him after his corps commander's death, Doubleday acted with decision and unaccustomed speed. As the Rebel pressure built up first in the west and then to the north of Gettysburg, he constantly brought up reserves, switched troops, regiments even, to counter each threat as it developed. He stubbornly defended McPherson's then Seminary Ridges against ever-increasing numbers until around 4:00 p.m. By the time the corps was forced back through the town it had suffered huge losses and was something of a broken reed for the remainder of the battle. Doubleday's action had bought time for the occupation of good defensive terrain by the rest of the army. He was justifiably furious when Meade replaced him as corps commander with Major-General John Newton, largely on the unfounded allegation by Major-General Howard that it was Doubleday's command that had fallen back first.

Gettysburg was really the end of Doubleday's war in terms of battlefield command, as he saw out the rest of his time in administrative posts. He continued to serve after the war, wrote two books and died of heart problems in New Jersey in 1893, aged seventy-four.

Major-General Winfield Scott Hancock (1824–1886)

Hancock commanded just over 11,200 men and twenty-eight guns in II Corps. Well over 6 feet tall, he made an impressive sight in his uniform with mustache and small goatee beard. Friendly, a natural leader, Hancock was widely known and respected for his courage and tactical ability. He invariably positioned himself in the thickest of the action and thereby inspired great confidence in those he commanded – helped by a bull-like roar and bursts of profanity that often announced his presence. When he appeared on Cemetery Hill during the I and XI Corps' confused retreat through Gettysburg on July 1, a witness of his arrival said, "soldiers retreating stopped, skulkers appeared from under their cover, lines were reformed." Another never forgot "the inspiration of his commanding, controlling presence, nor the fresh courage he imparted."

Hancock was born and raised in Norristown, Pennsylvania, and entered West Point at sixteen, graduating in 1844. There followed the usual years of boring frontier-post routine, interspersed with occasional excitement in the Mexican War, fighting the Seminoles and the Utah (Mormon) expedition in the 1850s. When the Civil War broke out Hancock was a thirty-seven-year-old captain and chief quartermaster of the Southern District of California in Los Angeles. By the fall of 1861 he was a brigadier-general. He fought well in the Peninsular campaign: "Hancock was superb today," said McClellan's report on the Williamsburg action. He fought at Antietam and as a divisional commander at Fredericksburg, where he led his men in one of the futile uphill charges with the accompanying slaughter that characterized that Union defeat. He performed brilliantly in covering Hooker's retreat at Chancellorsville and was given a corps command only six weeks before Gettysburg.

Hancock's personal leadership on arrival on Cemetery Hill late on July 1 was certainly a factor in rallying the depleted remnants of I and XI Corps. When his II Corps arrived on July 2 it was posted in the center of the line along Cemetery Ridge. When Sickles was wounded during Longstreet's attack, Hancock was put in command of the entire defense from Cemetery Hill to

Little Round Top. His leadership was inspirational, dashing along the line encouraging, moving regiments, plugging gaps, summoning reinforcements and directing desperate counterattacks, such as that of the 1st Minnesota. On July 3 Pickett's charge was aimed at Hancock's sector and he once again was at the front, issuing orders and directing the defense – although he had a difference of opinion with Colonel Hunt when he insisted, against Hunt's orders, that Union guns respond to the massive Confederate bombardment that preceded Pickett's advance. In the final stages of the Rebel assault Hancock was hit in the thigh and badly wounded. It was a wound that never really healed properly and severely restricted his further active service.

He remained in the army after the war and ran for President as "Hancock the Superb" in 1880, being narrowly defeated by James Garfield. He died, still in service, in 1886 of an infected boil, aged sixty-two.

Major-General Daniel Edgar Sickles (1825–1914)

Sickles commanded III Corps of 10,675 men and thirty guns at Gettysburg. A thoroughly disreputable individual, if physically courageous, he was a political general who had risen to his high rank almost entirely through influence and scheming. Sickles was born in New York City, the son of a patent lawyer. As a young man he qualified as a lawyer but quickly gained a notorious reputation as a drunkard, womanizer and later as a murderer. Elected to the New York State Assembly in 1847, Sickles scandalized society by escorting prostitutes into the legislative chamber. In 1852 he married a girl of sixteen. When sent to Britain as secretary to a minister, he shocked his hosts by refusing to drink the health of Queen Victoria at a banquet. He was constantly in debt and refused to curb his womanizing, but when he found his wife had taken a lover, Philip Key, he calmly shot him dead and then surrendered himself to the authorities. Tried for murder, he was defended by the future Secretary of War Edwin Stanton and acquitted on the grounds of temporary insanity – the first time this defense had ever been used in America.

At the outbreak of the war Sickles raised a regiment, or rather what soon became five regiments, which he named the "Excelsior Brigade," and which he regarded as his own personal property – although he had no means of paying its upkeep. At Gettysburg the 1,837-strong Excelsior Brigade (70th, 71st, 72nd, 73rd, and 74th New York, plus the 120th New York which had by then been added to the original five) formed the 2nd Brigade, 2nd Division, III Corps – still under Sickles' command. His brigade formed part of Brigadier-General Joseph Hooker's division at the battles of Williamsburg (May 1862) and Second Manassas (August 1862), although on both occasions Sickles was absent pulling political strings in Washington and trying to ingratiate himself with the President. This absence did not stop his promotion to major-general in November, when he took over Hooker's division when that officer became a corps commander. From civilian to major-general in two years was quite an achievement. At Fredericksburg Sickles' division, fortunately for its members, was kept in reserve. When Hooker took over the Army of the Potomac he ensured his friend Sickles got the III Corps, becoming the highest placed "political" general in the army. It was not a popular promotion with the other corps commanders – all West Pointers – who came to regard the headquarters of this upstart politico as a cross between a bar and a brothel. His first major battle was Chancellorsville, where he ended up on rising ground at a place called Hazel Grove. There he fought a stubborn and successful defensive battle until Hooker ordered his withdrawal – accomplished at a heavy price.

At Gettysburg, III Corps arrived on the field on July 2 and were ordered to take position at the southern part of the line. Sickles' performance has become one of the great controversies of the battle. With complete disregard for his orders, he advanced his position about threequarters of a mile in front of the line to occupy some slightly rising ground around the Peach Orchard – Hazel Grove probably being at the forefront of his mind. The "Sickles' salient" thus formed became the focus of the most bloody fighting on July 2; it is discussed further in Section Ten: Day Two. In the late afternoon Sickles was struck a glancing blow by a cannon ball that shattered his right knee, necessitating an amputation a few hours later.

He retired from the army in 1869 and was later made Minister to Spain by President Grant. True to form, an affair with Queen Isabella ensured an ignominious and speedy exit from the country. He was later appointed to the New York Monuments Commission but was dismissed in 1912 for mishandling the funds. He died two years later of a stroke, an embittered and crippled old man of eighty-nine.

Major-General George Sykes (1822–1880)

Sykes commanded V Corps at Gettysburg with just over 10,900 men and twenty-six guns. He was only forty-one and the most junior corps commander at the battle, as he had only been elevated to the position on June 28, stepping into the shoes of Meade on his sudden appointment as army commander. He was born in Delaware and graduated from West Point into the infantry in 1842. While a cadet he acquired the nickname "Tardy George" due to his methodical, somewhat slavish attention to regulations. It was a name that stayed with him and he was sometimes described as "having the slows," but in a mental rather than a physical sense. Young Sykes fought the Seminoles in Florida and throughout the Mexican War, and then spent many years in a series of frontier forts up to the start of the Civil War. Sykes was a dedicated "Old Army" regular whom one officer described as follows:

> It would have been hard to find a better officer in the Army than Sykes . . . he was so thoroughly and simply a soldier, that knew little of politics and cared less. [And was] one of the coolest men in danger or confusion that we had in the whole army.

Sykes was a small, somewhat thin man with a largish nose and full beard. He did well leading a regiment at First Manassas and was given a brigade of regulars in the Peninsular campaign. By June 1862 he had a division, "Sykes' Regulars" they called themselves, which fought well defending its position at Gaines' Mill in the Seven Days Battles. Sykes was in reserve at Antietam but was promoted to major-general in November 1862. Although present at both Fredericksburg and Chancellorsville, his division was only lightly engaged.

At Gettysburg V Corps arrived on the battlefield on the morning of July 2, having spent much of the previous thirty-six hours forced-marching from Union Mills. Initially held in reserve behind the left, at around 5:00 p.m. Sykes was ordered to support Sickles, whose exposed forward salient was coming under huge pressure. As he came forward Sykes refused to split his command, but Major-General Warren diverted Colonel Strong Vincent's brigade onto Little Round Top. Both brigades from both Barnes's and Ayres' Divisions were sent to the Wheatfield area, from where they were eventually forced to withdraw back onto Cemetery Ridge. Little Round Top was held with the help of a counterattack by Crawford's Division. The corps' losses were severe and only McCandless's Brigade was engaged on July 3.

Sykes was not employed again in any important role at that level, ending the war in the West in Kansas. He continued to serve as colonel on the frontier, where he died of cancer in 1880, aged fifty-eight.

Major-General John Sedgwick (1813–1864)

At Gettysburg Sedgwick commanded the largest corps in the Army of the Potomac, VI Corps, with over 14,000 men and forty-eight guns; strangely, due to circumstances, it was also the corps that suffered by far the lowest number of losses. Thus far in his career Sedgwick had been a highly rated commander with a huge amount of active soldiering behind him. A farm boy from the Connecticut Berkshires, he was the grandson of a Revolutionary War veteran who had fought under Washington at Brandywine and Valley Forge. After graduating from West Point in 1837, Sedgwick was seldom out of the firing line. His speciality was Indian fighting. He fought the Seminoles, Cheyennes, Kiowas and Comanches, and took part in the movement of the Cherokees west of the Mississippi on the "Trail of Tears." During the Mexican War he earned three brevet promotions for gallantry in the battles at Vera Cruz, Cerro Gordo, Churubusco and Chapultepec.

Sedgwick began the Civil War as a cavalry colonel before getting command of an infantry brigade in August 1861. Within six months he was commanding a division (2nd Division, II Corps) and in the summer of 1862 led it at Yorktown, Seven Pines and Glendale where he was wounded twice (Seven Days Battles). On recovery he was promoted major-general and was in action again at Antietam in September 1862. There his division gained lasting fame and virtual destruction when attacked on three sides in West Woods. Sedgwick was in the thick of the action and was hit three times (in the leg, wrist and shoulder) before he would leave the field. His recuperation was prolonged, causing him to exclaim, "If I am ever hit again, I hope it will settle me at once [his wish would be granted]. I want no more wounds." At Chancellorsville in May 1863 Sedgwick was commanding VI Corps opposite Fredericksburg with orders to take Marye's Heights. He did so against less than stubborn opposition but was halted when he reached Salem Church and was almost cut off before succeeding in scrambling back over the Rappahannock.

At Gettysburg he was a fifty-year-old bachelor, with a grizzly gray beard, known affectionately to his soldiers as "Uncle John," wearing a blue coat without rank insignia and a black slouch hat. On the night of July 1, VI Corps was still 35 miles from the battlefield near Manchester. The march began at 10:00 p.m. that night and continued throughout most of the next day, with the huge column spread over nearly 10 miles. Sedgwick's leading regiments arrived on the field around 5:00 p.m. and the corps was placed in reserve. Shortly thereafter Sedgwick suffered the indignity and frustration of having his corps broken up into packets that were rushed to support various parts of the field. He was heard to observe, "I might as well go home." By July 3 Sedgwick was in the extraordinary position of having one brigade on the left of the line and another 2 miles away on the right. His men saw little actual fighting and only suffered 242 casualties. Sedgwick had not been tested as a corps commander.

On May 9, 1864, at Spotsylvania, Sedgwick got his earlier wish: he was killed outright when a bullet struck him under his left eye. He was fifty-one.

Major-General Oliver Otis Howard (1830–1909)

At just thirty-two, "Old Prayer Book" Howard was the youngest corps commander at Gettysburg and he commanded XI Corps, the smallest corps, with some 9,240 men and twenty-six guns. However, on the march north his greatest concern was not numbers but rather low morale, indiscipline and his soldiers lacking confidence in themselves and their commander. This was largely due to their being surprised and rolled to ruin by Jackson's flank attack at Chancellorsville, the corps' first major battle. Composed mainly of "Dutchmen" – German-born immigrants – the corps was referred to by many as "Howard's Cowards" or the "Flying Dutchmen."

Howard was born in Leeds, Maine, the son of a farmer. He graduated from West Point in 1854 but remained to teach mathematics and study theology with the idea of becoming a priest. The outbreak of the Civil War led to Lieutenant Howard abandoning plans for the ministry and accepting the appointment of colonel of the 3rd Maine Volunteer Regiment. He commanded a brigade in the Union debacle at First Manassas, and two months later found himself a brigadier-general when only five months earlier he had been a lowly lieutenant. In June 1862 his right arm was hit twice in the elbow at Fair Oaks (Peninsular campaign), necessitating amputation. After recovery he led another brigade at Antietam, where it was caught in the same ambush in West Woods as Sedgwick's 2nd Division and was decimated, with Howard having to take command of the division when Sedgwick was wounded. In November he was made a major-general and the next month led his command into more slaughter on the slopes of Marye's Heights, Fredericksburg. When XI Corps commander Major-General Franz Sigel resigned in April 1863 his command was given to Howard. Then came Chancellorsville. By mid-1863 the unfortunate Howard had been dogged by defeat – First Manassas, the West Woods and Fredericksburg disasters, then being surprised and his corps running at Chancellorsville.

XI Corps started their march to Gettysburg from Emmitsburg at around 10:00 a.m. on July 1, but their commander galloped ahead into the town only to learn that Reynolds was dead and he was now the senior commander on the spot. He immediately selected Cemetery Hill as his headquarters. As his two leading divisions arrived in the early afternoon they were initially deployed just north of the town, but as the Rebel threat from that direction became clear they moved into line at right angles to Doubleday's I Corps fighting west of Gettysburg. Barlow's Division moved further north than was intended onto Blocher's Knoll. Eventually Howard's exposed right was turned and both corps crushed by sustained assaults that forced the Yankees into a panicky retreat through the town. As the remnants struggled up Cemetery Hill, where Howard had established his reserve (Von Steinwehr's Division), they were met by their general waving his sword and yelling, "Rally here, men: rally here! Form a line here! Go no further, but rally here!" Rally they did and remained in that location for the rest of the battle. Meanwhile a disappointed Howard had had his overall command on the battlefield taken by Hancock, who arrived with Meade's authorization, although Howard still took responsibility for forming the defensive line east of the Baltimore Pike. On the evening of July 2 Howard's men drove off Early's attacks on Cemetery Hill but not before several Rebel regiments had got among the Union guns.

Howard's line was not attacked on July 3 but XI Corps had suffered appalling losses during the first two days – well over 3,000, of whom about 1,500 were captured. When Howard selected Cemetery Hill as the place for his reserve he had undoubtedly chosen the vital ground, but his deployment north of the town has been criticized as being too extended, on poor defensive ground and with an exposed right flank.

Howard took his corps to the West in September 1863 to join the Army of the Cumberland and fight at Lookout Mountain and Missionary Ridge in the Chattanooga campaign. He commanded IV Corps in the Atlanta Campaign and in July 1864 succeeded to the command of the Army of the Tennessee. His performance in the West was decidedly more successful than it had been in the East.

After the war Howard devoted himself to the welfare of black people, founding the Howard University for them in Washington. He remained in the army, was involved in Indian fighting as commander of the Departments of the Columbia and the Platte, and became peace commissioner to the Apaches. He also served as Superintendent of West Point and commanded the Division of the East before retiring in 1894. He died of heart failure in 1909, aged seventy-nine.

Major-General Henry Warner Slocum (1827–1894)

Slocum commanded the nearly 9,800 men and twenty guns of XII Corps, and at thirty-six was the senior Union general at Gettysburg, senior even to Meade, the army commander. Slocum was a careful, cautious man; capable, but a stickler for order and detail. However, once battle was joined, and if acting under clear orders, he was one the army's hardest fighters and his command never lost a gun or a color throughout the war – a considerable achievement considering the number of actions his men fought in. Born near Syracuse, New York State, he graduated from West Point in 1852, seventh out of forty-three, and joined the artillery. Like virtually all his contemporaries, Slocum served against the Seminoles but mostly filled in the endless months of frontier duty studying law. He left the army in 1857 to practice law in Syracuse, but the start of the war saw him colonel of the 27th New York Volunteers.

He was badly wounded in the leg leading his regiment at First Manassas. In October 1861 he was given a brigade in the Army of the Potomac, which he commanded at Yorktown (Peninsular campaign). He commanded the 1st Division of VI Corps with some success in the desperate fighting at Gaines' Mill (the third of the Seven Days Battles) in June 1862 and within days became a major-general. At South Mountain (Antietam campaign) he ordered an assault against the wishes of his superior and overran the enemy position, capturing four battle flags. He was promoted to commander of XII Corps in October 1862. This spectacular rise from command of a regiment to a corps within twelve months set a record and came despite his experience in a senior position being limited. XII Corps missed Fredericksburg but was hotly engaged at Chancellorsville in May 1863. Slocum had been in charge of three corps as they marched to outflank the Rebel position, but timidity on Hooker's part in halting the movement negated this initial success.

At Gettysburg he earned his subsequent nickname of "Slow Come" by his refusal to march immediately to the sound of the guns on July 1. By virtue of his seniority, Slocum had been appointed right-wing commander (V and XII Corps) during the army's move north and when summoned urgently by Howard he dithered at Two Taverns only 5 miles away, being inclined to think the army might still divert to the Pipe Creek line in accordance with Meade's circular of that name. Consequently his corps did not reach the battlefield until about 6:00 p.m. on July 1, when Geary's Division was sent to Little Round Top and Williams' toward the right, while Slocum rode forward to take overall command from Hancock and Howard as the senior commander on the spot; Meade subsequently assumed command around midnight. Early on July 2 Geary and Williams were both posted on Culp's Hill. At this point the command setup of XII Corps became confused, as Slocum still considered himself a wing commander rather than a corps commander and thus handed over XII Corps temporarily to Brigadier-General Alpheus Williams. This led to confusion when Meade summoned XII Corps late on July 2 to support the left of the line under attack from Longstreet. The move resulted in only one brigade (Greene's) being left on Culp's Hill to face an assault by a Rebel division (Johnson's) that secured a foothold on the hill that night. Slocum's two divisions were ordered back to drive the Rebels out early next day. The position lost on the 2nd was retaken on the 3rd, and for the rest of the morning Slocum's men successfully defended Culp's Hill in some of the most intense fighting of the battle.

Slocum was transferred to the West and eventually commanded the Army of Georgia in Major-General William T. Sherman's famous "March to the Sea" through the Carolinas. He returned to his law practice after the war, served three terms in Congress and on the Board of the Gettysburg Monument Commissioners. He died in 1894, aged sixty-seven.

Major-General Alfred Pleasonton (1824–1897)

Pleasonton commanded the Cavalry Corps of over 11,800 men and sixteen guns; with the exception of VI Corps, this was the largest in the army. He had reached this powerful and vital position through years of currying favor with politicians and the newspapers. His aim in life was to ensure that he received the credit for every minor success and escaped the blame for any failure large or small in order to secure personal advancement. He was a small man with a waxed mustache who swaggered around in dandy uniforms carrying a riding crop and wearing a silly straw hat, making sure the press heard his boastful lies and fanciful stories of his military activities. To make matters worse, his men knew him to be a coward who led from the rear, but at the same time to be a ruthless disciplinarian. In one officer's opinion, he was "pure and simple a newspaper humbug . . . [who] does nothing save with a view to a newspaper paragraph." Another considered that "Pleasonton's late [recent] promotions [he had risen from brigade to corps commander in two months after Chancellorsville] were bolstered up by systematic lying" – he was later dubbed the "Knight of Romance." According to another he exercised a "tyrannical & illegal exercise of military authority."

Pleasonton graduated from West Point in 1844 and served in Mexico, against the Seminoles and in the Kansas border disturbances. During the Seven Days Battles he jumped from major to brigadier-general on the authority of McClellan, at whose headquarters he was serving with a cavalry regiment. After Second Manassas, Pleasonton was given the cavalry division. At Antietam some of his horsemen secured a bridge – a comparatively minor incident during which Pleasonton was well to the rear. However, in his report it was made out to be of huge significance for which he, Pleasonton, was responsible. During Lee's invasion of Maryland in 1862 Pleasonton's cavalry were unable to penetrate the Rebel screen and gain useful information. Nothing daunted, Pleasonton resorted to exaggeration and speculation in his reports, writing that Lee's army was over 100,000 strong – he had in fact crossed the Potomac with 40,000. In early 1863 Hooker promoted Stoneman over Pleasonton to command the Cavalry Corps. During the Chancellorsville campaign Stoneman dashed off south on what proved to be an ineffective raid, leaving behind Pleasonton with one brigade. One of the regiments was involved in a stiff fight at Chancellorsville, which Pleasonton embellished in his report to the extent of claiming that it was his men who killed Jackson. At the same time he claimed to have personally helped assemble and deploy twenty-two guns whose fire checked the enemy – in fact he placed one battery. Such was the extent to which he hoodwinked Hooker about his ability that when President Lincoln visited the army a few days later Hooker introduced Pleasonton with the words, "Mr. President, this is General Pleasonton, who saved the Army of the Potomac the other night." His reward came on May 22 when he was promoted major-general and given the Cavalry Corps.

At Gettysburg Pleasonton remained well out of harm's way at Frederick, Maryland, while Buford first scouted and then delayed the Rebel advance on July 1. The next day he removed Buford's Division from the battlefield, although it had suffered only 127 casualties, and then neglected to replace it. Thus Meade's left was unprotected during the crucial fighting at that end of the line. On July 3, during the cavalry clash on East Cavalry Field, Pleasonton was nowhere to be seen, although he did try to remove a brigade from the action just when it was most needed.

Surprisingly, Pleasonton retained command of the cavalry for another year, until removed by Lieutenant-General Ulysses Grant. After the war Pleasonton was disgusted to find he was a mere major again and resigned in 1868. He worked for a while in the Inland Revenue Service and later became a railroad president before retiring in 1888. He died nine years later at the age of seventy-three.

MILITARY CONTROL – THE STAFF

The staff categories and organization in both armies were similar, as commanders followed the system in which they had been trained in the old Regular Army, although the number of categories in various formations changed with their size and the preference of the commander. In general terms, the staff at a headquarters was divided into three categories – General Staff, Special Staff and Personal Staff. The staff officers shown below are those found at the army headquarters of both Lee and Meade at Gettysburg, but personnel with similar duties would be found at most lower headquarters down to regimental level.

General Staff

Chief of Staff (C.o.S.)

This was the senior staff officer, whose duties could include standing in for the commander, issuing instructions in his name, coordination of headquarters staff and activities, administration and movement. His duties and authority varied according to his relationship with the army commander. In Confederate armies there was no official position of chief of staff, but in practice the title was used.

Assistant Adjutant General (A.A.G.)

In the field these officers were the representatives of the Adjutant and Inspector General Departments in Washington or Richmond. Their rank could vary from brigadier-general at the headquarters of the Army of the Potomac to the lieutenant appointed adjutant of a regiment. At a large army headquarters there might be two or three A.A.G.s, but of differing ranks. They were general-purpose staff officers and could be given a variety of duties in the field. Their primary responsibility was for personnel administration, including promotions, leave, casualties, records, logs, strength accounting, discharges, absentees, transfers, etc. All these generated a vast amount of paperwork, including all correspondence, returns and the issue of orders on behalf of the commander. On operations some paperwork was still essential, but these officers were also used on operational duties such as delivering orders or messages, liaison with other commanders, movement control, reconnaissance and acting as guides along the line of march. Basically they got anything not specifically the responsibility of another branch of the staff.

Assistant Inspector General (A.I.G.)

Assistant inspector generals (A.I.G.s) were responsible for the other half of the Adjutant and Inspector General's Department duties – inspection. Their powers permitted them to inspect the readiness of units for operations, including their state of discipline. This included inspecting and reporting on their training, the state of their arms, clothing, equipment, accommodation, food, documentation, returns, compliance with regulations and the ability of the unit's officers. They were empowered to examine every facet of a unit's existence. On June 11, 1863 the acting assistant adjutant general of the Union III Corps sent orders to the 1st Division to be prepared to march containing this passage on inspector's duties:

> All surplus baggage and everything likely to impede the march or movements of the troops must be sent to the rear. You will require the officers of the

> inspector-general's department to thoroughly and carefully inspect the baggage, ambulances, baggage wagons &c., in your command, to make sure that the order is complied with, and, if necessary, to accomplish that end, your command will be drawn up in marching order.

On disciplinary matters, while the judge advocate and A.A.G. dealt with the legal side of courts martial, it was the A.I.G. who organized the firing party if the sentence was death. In the field it was the A.I.G. who liaised with the provost marshal with regard to prisoners, straggling or looting. In practice, at corps or divisional level it was not uncommon for the A.A.G. and A.I.G. duties to be the responsibility of one officer; indeed, even when the duties were divided between two, commanders often tended to regard them as interchangeable.

Chief Quartermaster
There was a representative of the Quartermaster's Department at every level down to regiment, in some cases even to the quartermaster sergeant of a company. His duties have already been examined in detail in Section Five: Other Arms and Services, so it is sufficient here to remind the reader that the quartermaster was responsible for supplying his formation or unit with clothing, equipment, cavalry horses (not the Confederates), artillery horses, pay and – the most troublesome duty of all – the provision of transport for all branches of the army.

Chief Commissary
There was normally a commissary officer on the staff of all formations down to, and including, brigades, with a senior N.C.O. at regimental level. Their duty was purely that of procuring and issuing food. As illustrated in Section Five, on operations this involved requisitioning along the line of march, rounding up cattle and hogs on the hoof, payment for items received or the issue of receipts and accounting for all issues to units – a thankless and demanding task.

Medical Director
There was a medical director on the staff at army and corps headquarters, usually chief medical officers at division and brigade, and surgeons and assistant surgeons with the regiments. Their duties are discussed in detail in Section Five, but revolved around the treatment of sick and wounded, burials, the provision of ambulance trains, the setting up of field hospitals, casualty evacuation and providing all the necessary medical supplies, tentage and equipment.

Special Staff

Chief of Artillery
At Gettysburg there was only one chief of artillery at army headquarters of both armies, other senior artillery officers being commanders of artillery brigades, regiments or the artillery reserve. At an army headquarters the chief of artillery normally had one or two junior general staff officers, such as A.A.G.s, A.I.G.s and A.D.C.s to assist him. He was responsible for advising the army commander on all artillery matters, tactical and administrative, and at the same time as the senior artillery officer issuing orders to, and supervising the employment of, the army's guns.

Chief of Ordnance
This staff officer – and there was one to be found at the headquarters of all formations with a senior N.C.O. at regimental level – had responsibility for the supply and repair of arms, guns, ammunition and all associated equipment, such as caissons, mobile forges, and the command and control of ordnance trains in the field. Once a campaign was under way, their primary task was to ensure that ammunition of all types was readily available as close to their troops or guns as possible and to supervise the resupply in action.

Chief of Engineers
Probably the most important function of the senior engineer officer with a field army was that of coordinating or carrying out topographical reconnaissance. The commander needed to have information on the state of roads, bridges, fords, the state of the flow of rivers, sites for pontoon bridges, the extent and density of woods, features suitable for defensive positions and works, and the capacity of the countryside to provide the army's needs. In a static situation, he would then oversee the construction of field works, trenches, breastworks, saps, the location of mines and siege works in general. Another critical task was that of mapmaking, for which there was a huge demand. In early 1863 Lee sent Captain Jedediah Hotchkiss, Stonewall Jackson's chief engineer and a skillful topographical engineer, to make a map of the Valley of Virginia and to extend it as far as Harrisburg, Pennsylvania, and Philadelphia in preparation for what developed into the Gettysburg campaign.

Chief of Signal Corps
Responsible for ensuring the army commander had communications with subordinate commanders, usually by wigwag signaling, and by telegraph to either Washington or Richmond. Details of the Signal Corps' involvement are discussed in Section Five.

Personal Staff

Aides-de-Camp (A.D.C.s)
Regulations permitted general officers to appoint two or three A.D.C.s, or personal staff officers, depending on the size of the headquarters. Their ranks varied from major at army headquarters to lieutenant at brigade. They invariably accompanied their general when he was promoted or transferred and became very much his military family. It was not uncommon for this to be almost literally the case, as generals tended to appoint their relatives or the sons of family friends. At Gettysburg Meade's son, Captain George Gordon Meade Jr., was one of his A.D.C.s and became involved with Sickles' flouting of his deployment instructions. On the Rebel side First Lieutenant Walter Keith Armistead was an A.D.C. to his father, whom he saw mortally wounded and captured in Pickett's charge. Duties of A.D.C.s were not defined by regulations, but in practice their battlefield use was in carrying messages. This was a crucial and dangerous duty that differed from a soldier courier taking a message in that the A.D.C. was often entrusted with verbal messages. To do this effectively he had to know his general's intentions, explain the order and answer queries from the recipient. When not in the field, the duties of the more junior A.D.C.s were anything but onerous and in many cases negligible.

Military Secretary (M.S.)
The duties of this appointment were related to the personal and official correspondence, including written orders, of the army

commander. The M.S. was normally one of the senior officers at the headquarters and often combined these duties with that of the general's A.D.C.

Judge Advocate General (J.A.G.)

He was responsible for the convening and administration of courts martial. In the field these courts were primarily used to deal with cases of straggling, absence and desertion. Lee was so concerned with the problem that he recommended the establishment of permanent courts for each corps. They were appointed in December 1862.

Chaplains

With the formation of the United States Volunteer Army, the place of regimental chaplain gained in importance, although they could also serve in hospitals or on the staff of higher formations, including army headquarters. Chaplains of all denominations and ordinances were needed. Army chaplains were authorized to wear the uniform of captains of cavalry, with shoulder straps, sash and sword, and many did. In 1862 the law stipulated that a regimental chaplain was to be a duly authorized clergyman and that his rank should be "Chaplain, without command," listed on the staff rolls next below the surgeon.

Confederate chaplains were mostly elected by the soldiers of a regiment and then commissioned by President Davis. Most chaplains, North or South, were Methodists, Baptists or Presbyterians, with a few Lutheran and some Roman Catholic priests. The first of a handful of Jewish regimental chaplains was appointed in April 1863. He was Ferdinand L. Sarner, a native of Germany, who was elected by the 54th New York Infantry Regiment. The 54th were in XI Corps at Gettysburg, where Chaplain Sarner was severely wounded and hospitalized but while awaiting discharge papers felt better, discharged himself, and went home. Another Union chaplain to suffer at Gettysburg was Horatio S. Howell of the 90th Pennsylvania, who rather foolishly refused to surrender his sword to a Rebel soldier on the steps of Christ Lutheran Church on Chambersburg Street on July 1. He was shot dead for his stubbornness – but it is quite possible his assailant did not realize he was a chaplain as he dressed like a line officer, sometimes even wearing a revolver.

Chaplains' duties included leading religious services, consoling those facing death, helping the sick and injured, and often running a camp library, writing letters for illiterate soldiers and taking charge of regimental mail. Soldiers of both sides had no time for chaplains who could not withstand the hardships of campaign life or who proved battle shy. Private Edward Edes wrote in 1862, "I have lost all confidence in the chaplain. He lied to me about carrying the mail and he does nothing at all but hang around his tent and sort the mail . . . I think he is nothing but a confounded humbug and nuisance." However, if a chaplain showed courage and dedication to his duties he soon won the respect of the men. A soldier of the 100th Indiana wrote of Chaplain John A. Brouse, "Without thought for his personal safety he was on the firing line assisting the wounded, praying with the dying, doing all that his great loving heart led him to do. No wonder our boys love our gallant chaplain."

Some undoubtedly joined for the money – $140 a month for Union chaplains and $85 for their Southern counterparts. It is estimated that Union authorities appointed some 3,000 chaplains during the war and the Confederates 600–1,000. On either side this was not enough for every regiment to have its own chaplain; many shared a brigade chaplain such as Father William F. Corby, chaplain to the Irish Brigade at Gettysburg. Father Corby's statue on Cemetery Ridge is close to the spot at which he climbed onto a boulder to give a brief address and absolution to the kneeling Irish Brigade on July 2, just prior to its being launched into the cauldron of the Wheatfield.

Provost Marshal (P.M.)

The P.M.'s responsibilities, which he carried out with the aid of the units nominated as the provost guard, included suppression of looting, preventing straggling, escorting, guarding and some interrogation of prisoners, regulating the movement of troops and civilians and the execution of sentences of imprisonment or capital punishment. In battle the provost guard was often deployed behind the line to turn back or arrest soldiers skulking in the rear with no good reason. In the Army of the Potomac the P.M. was administratively responsible for the Bureau of Military Information (B.M.I.) – see page 283.

Lee's Provost Guard

Lee had problems guarding prisoners at Gettysburg, as none of his designated provost guard was present: he therefore had to use other troops for this duty. His acting provost marshal was Major David B. Bridgford, commanding about 250 men of the 1st Virginia Infantry Battalion, of which companies A–D had been designated provost guard on June 4, 1863. They remained at Winchester for the entire campaign, with Bridgford as provost marshal of the town after its capture. His Company E was at Gordonsville. In addition, according to Colonel John S. Hoffman's (Smith's Brigade, Early's Division) report dated August 4, 1863, both the 13th and 58th Virginia Regiments from his brigade had also been left at Winchester to guard the 1,600 prisoners. The 13th Virginia remained there, not rejoining the brigade until July 23. The 58th Virginia escorted the prisoners to Staunton. On June 22 four companies were sent with them to Richmond, not rejoining the regiment until the 28th. The regiment then provided the escort for Lee's long-awaited and urgently needed ordnance train, which arrived at Cashtown on July 6.

Other Headquarters Personnel

Clerks

In the field clerks were kept to the minimum, but each senior staff officer at army headquarters, including the chief quartermaster, commissary and medical director, would have two or three as reports, returns and considerable other correspondence had still to be produced. An army commander would have more and there would be several clerks at corps headquarters. Much of this paperwork, such as orders, regulations and instructions, had to be copied to numerous recipients.

Couriers/orderlies/escorts

These soldiers were mounted and their duties were interchangeable. Primarily employed as messengers (couriers), they carried written messages but also acted as horse-holders for staff officers (orderlies) and bodyguards (escorts) for the general and sentries for the headquarters camp area. See box, page 279.

Servants (slaves in the A.N.V.)

Their tasks included pitching camp, packing up camp, cooking, laundering, foraging, grooming and feeding horses, and a host of other tasks that sustained the daily routine of the headquarters.

The Parole System

Lacking a means of dealing with large numbers of prisoners, the Federal and Confederate governments relied on a system of parole and exchange of prisoners. It called for prisoners to give their word not to take up arms against their captors until they had been formally exchanged for an enemy captive of equal rank. Parole was supposed to take place within ten days of capture. If he gave his word, the prisoner was freed. Sometimes parolees went home; sometimes they waited near their commands until the exchange could be arranged. The system grew increasingly complex and cumbersome as the number of parolees grew. The prospect of being sent home encouraged many men to allow themselves to be captured. Some were lost to the army when they failed to return to their units. Special parole camps – in reality detention centers – were introduced by the Federal authorities; their poor food and sanitation caused much resentment, as did giving the parolees non-combat roles or even sending them West to fight the Indians!

A formula for exchanging prisoners was devised by which so many privates equated with officers of different ranks as follows:

1 general	=	46 privates
1 major-general	=	40 privates
1 brigadier-general	=	20 privates
1 colonel	=	15 privates
1 lieutenant-colonel	=	10 privates
1 major	=	8 privates
1 captain	=	6 privates
1 lieutenant	=	4 privates
1 N.C.O.	=	2 privates

If a hospital was captured then it was usual practice to parole all inmates. A simple parole paper, as shown on the right, was signed and given to the prisoner and a copy kept by the signing officer.

HEAD-QUARTERS RODES' DIV.
. . . . 186 . .
. . . . a citizen of
. . . . is hereby
released on condition that he will give no information concerning or serve in any capacity whatever against the Confederate States, until regularly exchanged for a citizen of the Confederate States.
. . . .

Examples of parole at Gettysburg include Stuart's paroling of the 400 men captured with the wagon train on June 28 and the parole after the battle of several thousand Yankee prisoners who had been collected in a holding area near Samuel Cobean's farm on the Newville Road. One of the largest paroles of the entire war came with the capture of Vicksburg, which fell on July 4. On that occasion Major-General Ulysses S. Grant paroled 31,600 Rebels.

ARMY HEADQUARTERS

A comparison of the headquarters of both armies at Gettysburg reveals a large discrepancy in size, with Meade's totaling 1,529 staff and Lee's only 108. The Army of the Potomac certainly had a more elaborate headquarters staff, but the wide difference was due to the Union provost guard equating to well over two strong regiments, while Lee's provost guard was not even present. Similarly the 1st Massachusetts Cavalry providing Meade's escort was 250 strong against the ninety-one men in Companies A and C of the 39th Virginia Cavalry Battalion. Finally, all the Signal Corps staff (about forty-five) of the Army of the Potomac are included, while the numbers of signal staff with the Army of Northern Virginia are not known, but would probably be around twenty. The numbers in both headquarters are listed below.

Comparative Size of Army Headquarters

Sub-Unit	**Number**		**Comment**
	Union	**Confederate**	
Field and staff officers	50	17	
Signal Corps	45	20	(estimate; includes all personnel with the army)
Escorts/couriers	42 [1]	91 [2]	
	250 [3]	–	
Provost Guard	1,142 [4]	– [4]	
Total	**1,529**	**128** [5]	

1. The Oneida New York Cavalry under Captain Daniel Mann.
2. Companies A and C, 39th Virginia Cavalry Battalion. Company C under Captain Samuel B. Brown formed Lee's personal bodyguard.
3. Eight companies 1st Massachusetts Cavalry.
4. Eight companies 8th U.S. Infantry (148 men); four companies 93rd New York Cavalry; 2nd Pennsylvania Cavalry (489) under Colonel Richard B. Price; two companies 6th Pennsylvania Cavalry; and fifteen men from regular U.S. cavalry detachments.
5. The Order of Battle diagram shows 108, but this figure includes an estimated twenty signalers.

Lee's Headquarters

The British observer Lieutenant-Colonel Garnett Wolseley has given the best description of Lee's headquarters in the field.

> [It] consisted of about seven or eight pole tents . . . In front of the tents were some three or four wagons, drawn up without any regularity, and a number of horses roamed loose about the field. The servants – who were, of course, slaves – and the mounted soldiers called couriers . . . were unprovided with tents, and slept in or under the wagons . . . No guards or sentries could be seen in the vicinity, no crowd of aides-de-camp loitering about . . . [Lee's] staff are crowded together two or three in a tent, none are allowed to carry more than a small box each, and his own kit is but very little larger . . .

At Chambersburg, just before the battle, a soldier described the headquarters as follows:

> The general has little of the pomp and circumstance of war about his person. A Confederate flag marks the whereabouts of his headquarters, which are here in a little enclosure of some couple of acres of timber. There are about a half-a-dozen tents and as many baggage wagons and ambulances. The horses and mules for these, besides those of a small – very small – escort, are tied up to trees or are grazing about the place.

At Gettysburg Brigadier-General Imboden's description was even briefer: "half a dozen small tents . . . a little way from the roadside." However, as noted above, Lee's headquarters at the battle included Widow Thompson's home on the opposite side of the road (the Chambersburg Pike) in which he slept briefly on the night of July 1.

The table below lists the staff of both army headquarters at Gettysburg. Where a name appears in parenthesis it is the officer to which that staff officer normally reported rather than to the army commander or chief of staff.

Principal Army Headquarters Staff

General Staff	Confederate	Union
Chief of Staff	Col. Robert H. Chilton (and I.G.)	Maj.-Gen. Daniel Butterfield
A.A.G.	Col. Walter H. Taylor (and A.D.C.)	Brig.-Gen. Seth Williams (and M.S.)
	Maj. George B. Cook (and A.I.G.)	Maj. Simon F. Barstow
		Capt. John N. Craig (Hunt)
A.I.G.	Col. Charles Venable (and A.D.C.)	Col. Edmund Schriver
	Col. H. L. Peyton	Lt. Col. Edward R. Warner (Hunt)
Chief Q.M.	Col. James L. Corley	Brig.-Gen. Rufus Ingalls
Chief Com. Sub.	Col. Robert G. Cole	Col. Henry F. Clarke
Med. Dir.	Surg. Lafayette Guild	Maj. Jonathan Letterman
Special Staff		
Chief of Artillery	Brig.-Gen. William N. Pendleton	Brig.-Gen. Henry J. Hunt
Chief of Ordnance	Col. Briscoe G. Baldwin	1st Lt. John R. Edie (acting)
Chief of Engineers	Capt. Samuel R. Johnston	Brig.-Gen. Gouverneur K. Warren
		1st Lt. Mitchell (engineer)
Chief of Signals	–	Capt. Lemuel B. Norton
Personal Staff		
M.S.	Col. Armistead L. Long	see Williams above
A.M.S.	Col. Charles Marshall (and A.D.C.)	
A.D.C.s	Maj. T. M. R. Talcott (and A.G.G.)	Maj. Benjamin C. Ludlow
	1st Lt. George W. Peterkin (Pendleton)	Maj. James C. Biddle
		Capt. George G. Meade Jr. (Meade's son)
		Capt. Addison G. Mason
		Capt. William H. Paine (Warren)
		1st Lt. Paul A. Oliver
		1st Lt. C. F. Bissell
		1st Lt. Ronald S. Mackenzie (Warren)
		1st Lt. Chauncey B. Reese (Warren)
J.A.G.	Maj. Henry E. Young (and A.I.G. and A.G.G.)	–
Chaplain	–	–
P.M.		Brig.-Gen. Marsena R. Patrick
D.P.M. (B.M.I.)		Col. George H. Sharpe
		Capt. John McEntee
Foreign Observer	Capt. Justus Scheibert (Pomeranian)	–

Lee's Headquarters

- In Lee's letter to President Davis dated March 21, 1863 he reveals a not very high opinion of his staff generally:

  > The greatest difficulty I find is in causing orders and regulations to be obeyed. This arises not from a spirit of disobedience, but from ignorance. We therefore need a corps of officers to teach others their duty, see to the observance of orders, and to the regularity and precision of all movements. This is accomplished in the French service by their staff corps, educated, instructed and practiced for the purpose.

- When Lee took over command of the army in the Peninsula in 1862 his principal staff officers (Chilton, Long, Taylor, Marshall, Venable and Talcott) were totally lacking in staff experience or training. Chilton had been paymaster general in the old army and then worked in the adjutant general's office in Richmond, and although he was intelligent and conscientious he never mastered the operational side of being an effective chief of staff. However, Lee retained him until early 1864 to run the administrative side of the headquarters. Of the A.D.C.s Taylor had been a businessman, Marshall a lawyer, Venable a mathematics professor and Talcott an engineer officer. As shown in the above table, all were expected to undertake additional duties on top of that of delivering orders, giving instructions based on Lee's intentions, and carrying out reconnaissance. They learned on the job and at the battle their performance was mediocre and patchy.
- It bears repeating that Lee had no Signal Corps officer at his headquarters. There is no obvious reason for this other than his preference for use of couriers and A.D.C.s. Similarly, he had no provost marshal at Gettysburg (see box, page 276) or staff chaplain. Also lacking was an equivalent of Meade's Bureau of Military Information (B.M.I.) – see page 283 – or group of dedicated spies or scouts. The 1st Virginia Infantry Battalion (Lee's provost guard under Major Bridgford) had been given as one of its responsibilities the building up of an order of battle of the Union Army by recording the names, regiments, brigades, divisions and corps of prisoners and deserters by Special Order No. 151, dated June 4 and signed by Major Taylor, and was to be left at Winchester.
- Lee believed in having the minimum staff accompany him in the field and his personal escort was just the ninety-one men of Companies A and C, 39th Virginia Cavalry Battalion, commanded by Major John H. Richardson. Company C, under Captain Samuel B. Brown, became known as "Lee's Bodyguard" or the "Guides, Scouts, Couriers, Detectives and Scamps," and remained with Lee for the duration of the war. Company B, under Captain George W. Randolph, was sent to Ewell's Corps, but no further companies were recruited until Company D in November 1863. It was not unknown for Lee to ride around the battlefield almost alone. Colonel Alexander (Longstreet's de facto artillery chief on July 3) was surprised to see a solitary Lee join him at the guns covering Pickett's retreat. Such behavior did not make for speedy communications or effective control.
- By mid-1863 Lee's headquarters was invariably tented. While some convenient buildings might be used, Lee personally

Couriers and Escorts

Every headquarters from division upwards had at least some mounted couriers who were responsible for taking messages, in addition to staff officers (mostly A.D.C.s) similarly employed. Lieutenant-Colonel Moxley Sorrel, Longstreet's acting adjutant general, stated that the number of couriers permitted at infantry headquarters was six per corps, four a division and two for a brigade. This number was not realistic, as headquarters tended to need considerably more. Cavalry certainly required more than the infantry, and Stuart's large division had, according to Captain Charles M. Blackford, at least forty couriers, Stuart being personally accompanied by ten or twelve. Meade's army headquarters would have many more, as he had a considerable cavalry contingent permanently at his headquarters – the most famous being the Oneida (NY) Independent Cavalry Company.

The Oneida Cavalry was formed in Oneida Village, Madison County, New York, by the forty-nine-year-old businessman Daniel P. Mann and was mustered into service on September 4, 1861. This company holds a unique position in the history of the Civil War, in that it is the only unit to have served at the headquarters of every commanding general of the Army of the Potomac. It furnished couriers, escorts and orderlies for Generals George B. McClellan, Ambrose E. Burnside, Joseph Hooker and George Meade. Not only did the unit members become highly experienced couriers, renowned for their reliability, but they were also adept at picketing, patroling, raiding and reconnaissance. At Gettysburg Captain Mann commanded just over forty men; despite its dangerous duties, the unit suffered no losses. In 1905 the New York State erected and dedicated a monument in its honor near the site of Meade's headquarters.

Couriers could be provided by either detaching one or two troops from a regiment or breaking up a whole regiment for these duties. Some examples of the former at Gettysburg include the fifty-seven troopers of 1st Maine attached to I Corps headquarters; the troop of thirty-two of 1st New Jersey with VI Corps; and the two troops from the 17th Pennsylvania, one attached to V Corps, the other to XI Corps. The South also used detachments from cavalry regiments but, in addition, recruited specially formed courier units. These were authorized a year before Gettysburg and were intended to supply scouts, guides and couriers. One such unit was the 39th Virginia Cavalry Battalion raised by Major John H. Richardson. Lee was fully in favor of these specialist units, as they released cavalrymen back to their regiments. Company C of the 39th Virginia, under Captain Samuel P. Brown, was attached to Lee's headquarters in March 1863. It remained with Lee until the end of the war and was called "Guides, Scouts, Couriers, Detectives and Scamps" by his staff. Although there were establishments laid down for the number of couriers allowed at each headquarters, these were seldom followed, as the minimum size was at least one troop.

Couriers also often doubled up as escorts for the commander. Sending a trooper with important orders or messages was a somewhat risky business; they had key resposibilities that they had to carry out in hazardous circumstances and usually on their own. They needed initiative, a keen sense of direction and the ability to navigate across unfamiliar countryside. They could get lost, killed or injured, or, worst of all, might pass on a garbled message. For these reasons it was normal for important orders to be sent by several couriers, each leaving at a different time, which was recorded. Generally, however, couriers of both sides performed their duties well. Stuart often praised one of his couriers in his battle reports – eventually promoting the man to officer rank and putting him in charge of all his couriers. The theory was that officers delivered verbal messages while troopers handled only written ones, but this rule was frequently ignored. A Gettysburg example during the Confederate retreat was when Stuart sent Private Robert Goode, 1st Virginia Cavalry, "a trusty and intelligent soldier to reach the commanding general by a route across the country, and relate to him what I knew as well as what he might discover en route."

Perhaps an exceptional example is quoted in J. Boone Bartholomees Jr.'s book *Buff Facings and Gilt Buttons.* A newly arrived courier, Private Gill, reported personally to Stonewall Jackson at the start of the Seven Days Battles a year before Gettysburg. He recorded what followed:

> I told him [Jackson] I had come to report as a courier by order of Captain [Sandie] Pendleton, and was ready to receive any orders he might give me . . . General Jackson's first order directed me to go to each Brigade headquarters and deliver to each commanding officer positive instructions to move their respective commands that evening not later than 9 o'clock on the road to Louisa C[ourt] H[ouse], and when in line to await further orders.
>
> I got back to headquarters about 10 o'clock. I had had some ten brigade commanders to interview, which was no easy task for a green courier like myself. I accomplished the work, however, and reported to General Jackson that the army was moving in accordance with his instructions.

favored living in a tent. Lieutenant-Colonel Wolseley, a British observer, commented, "A large farmhouse stands close by, which in any other army would have been the general's residence *pro tem*, but as no liberties are allowed to be taken with personal property in Lee's army, he is particular in setting an example himself." While the house on the north side of the Chambersburg Pike (Widow Thompson's house) was undoubtedly part of his headquarters accommodation at Gettysburg, there was also a group of tents on the opposite side of the Pike. However, despite his preference for using a tent, on the night of July 1 Lee did use a bed in Widow Thompson's house instead of his usual cot under canvas. This suggests he may not have been feeling well at the start of the battle (see box, page 261).

Meade's Headquarters

- By mid-1863 it was the established practice that when a general was promoted or transferred he took over the staff at his new headquarters, but that he could bring his personal staff of A.D.C.s and could change the chief of staff if practical. With Meade taking command at such sort notice he accepted Hooker's staff without qualms, with the exception of Major-General Daniel Butterfield, Hooker's chief of staff. Butterfield was reasonably efficient but was deeply involved in politics and had several friends working with influential newspapers. One of the first things Meade did on taking command was to sound out three officers as immediate replacements for Butterfield. They were Major-General Andrew A. Humphreys (commander 2nd Division, III Corps), and Brigadier-Generals Gouverneur

K. Warren (Chief Engineer) and Seth Williams (A.A.G.). None accepted the post, so Butterfield remained and, to his credit, served satisfactorily during the battle before being wounded on July 3; he relinquished his post to Humphreys on the 8th. He was subsequently sent to the West, where he resumed his old job as chief of staff to his friend Hooker.

- Meade made immediate use of his new power to promote by wiring General-in-Chief Halleck requesting the elevation of three cavalry captains to brigadier-general (George A. Custer, Elon J. Farnsworth and Wesley Merritt). They were immediately approved.
- The main differences between the two army headquarters was the size of the Union commander's and his having Colonel Sharpe coordinating the activities of the B.M.I., whose spies were able to provide much useful information during the weeks prior to the battle (see below). This information was usually passed to Butterfield, who combined it with cavalry reports before passing it to Hooker or Meade. The other significant advantage at the battle was the ability of Meade's headquarters to keep in contact with his corps commanders by wigwag throughout July 2 and 3.
- Meade was also able to use, and have confidence in, two experienced brigadier-generals (Warren and Hunt) to conduct reconnaissance and supervise the positioning and actions of formations during critical phases of the fighting.

MILITARY INTELLIGENCE

The use of the word "intelligence" in the military sense is something of a misnomer in terms of the Civil War. In the modern military, intelligence is information that has been assessed, interpreted and evaluated by intelligence staff before being submitted to the commander. In the Civil War what most commanders were receiving was "information" without interpretation and evaluation. In most headquarters on either side it was the commander who had to decide on its reliability, value and the use to which it might be put. A commander primarily wanted information on three things concerning his enemy: composition and strength, location, and intentions – this last being the most difficult to obtain. Information on where there was no enemy – negative information – was often just as useful as positive information. The other, equally important, side of the coin was preventing the enemy getting information on your forces and activities – counterintelligence. A commander also required supplementary information on such matters as the terrain, state of the roads, crossing places of rivers or whether the area of operations would be able to supply food and fodder.

A commander needed timely information. The use of fast-riding couriers and the telegraph made this possible, with the latter being of particular value to Hooker, and then to Meade, in the run-up to the battle, as evidenced by the speed with which telegraphic messages were passed to and from Hooker's/Meade's headquarters during June. To take just one example, at 12:30 p.m. on June 28 Halleck telegraphed Meade at Frederick that Fitzhugh Lee's cavalry had crossed the Potomac near Seneca Creek; at 2:30 p.m. the same day Meade replied that he was sending two brigades to investigate. On the battlefield at Gettysburg Lee was informed at around 9:00 a.m. on July 2 that the Round Tops were unoccupied and Meade's left flank was therefore exposed. He based his plan to attack on this assumption, but for various reasons the infantry attack did not start until 4:30 p.m. – little wonder the early-morning intelligence was dramatically out of date.

For the Gettysburg campaign and battle, like any other, a commander had a wide variety of potential sources of information. They included cavalry patrols, signal stations, scouts, spies, prisoners, deserters, civilians, escaped slaves or "contrabands" (Union

Henry Thomas Harrison

Due to the diligent research of the great-grandson of Longstreet's famous spy "Harrison," the man who brought the news of the Army of the Potomac's move north to Frederick to Lee on June 28, details of his life are now known. Harrison was born near Nashville, Tennessee, in 1832 and in May 1861 mustered into the 12th Mississippi Infantry (State Militia) as a private. But by September he was discharged and started on his scouting/spying activities, initially for Major-General Earl van Dorn near Manassas. In February 1863 he reported to the Confederate Secretary of War, James A. Seddon, and the following month was assigned to Longstreet and dispatched to spy for Major-General D. H. Hill in North Carolina. He was, however, arrested within a short time and held captive for a month before convincing the Yankees that he was an innocent civilian trying to avoid conscription. In April 1863 Harrison reported to Longstreet at Franklin, Virginia, and two months later was sent to Washington specifically to obtain information on the movements of the Army of the Potomac.

Early in the morning of June 28 Harrison reported to Longstreet near Chambersburg, Pennsylvania, with details of the Yankees' move north and of their location around Frederick, Maryland. His information was quite detailed in that he explained that two Union corps were last known to be at Frederick, another close by and two more near South Mountain, leaving two unaccounted for. He also informed Longstreet that Meade had just replaced Hooker as army commander. Harrison was sent, along with a Major John Fairfax, to inform Lee. According to Fairfax, Lee, who was inclined to be skeptical of spies, listened "with great composure and minuteness to Harrison's information" and he quoted Lee as saying, "I do not know what to do. I cannot hear from General Stuart, the eyes of the army." Nevertheless, orders were issued for the concentration of the Army of Northern Virginia.

In September 1863 Harrison left Longstreet to report back to Richmond. Within a short time he married Laura Broders in, of all places, Washington, before leaving for a honeymoon in New York. Thereafter he continued his spying activities for the remainder of the war.

In 1865 he took his wife and daughter to Mexico, but after marital problems left home to go gold prospecting in Montana. It was the start of a twenty-five-year disappearance from his family during which his wife, assuming him dead, remarried. In 1900, however, he reappeared and made an attempt to visit his daughter, which was rebuffed. For ten years he worked as a detective in Cincinnati before finally retiring to Covington, Kentucky. He died there in October 1923, aged ninety-one. He is buried in Highland Cemetery, Fort Mitchell, Kentucky.

Ulric Dahlgren

It was during the Gettysburg campaign that Captain Dahlgren made his name as a resourceful, daring, indeed reckless, scout for the Army of the Potomac. For most of the earlier part of the war he had been a staff officer, and while on the staff of Major-General Franz Sigel had seen action at Cedar Mountain, Second Manassas and in the Washington defenses during the fall of 1862. In November of that year he led sixty horsemen over the Rappahannock in a three-day raid that penetrated into the town of Fredericksburg and captured over thirty prisoners. It was a promising start to his career as a scout and raider. In March Dahlgren joined Hooker's staff as an A.D.C. and carried dispatches during the Battle of Chancellorsville.

At Brandy Station on June 9 Dahlgren joined the 6th Pennsylvania Cavalry in a desperate charge on Rebel guns. His account reads, in part:

> Major Morris commanded the regiment, and I was riding very near him, when just as we were jumping a ditch, some canister came along, and I saw his horse fall over him, but could not tell whether he was killed or not, for at the same instant my horse was shot in three places. He fell, and threw me, so that I could see nothing for a few moments. Just then the column turned to go back – finding that the enemy had surrounded us. I saw the rear passing me, and about to leave me behind, so I gave my horse a tremendous kick and got him on his legs again. Finding he could still move, I mounted and made after the rest – just escaping being taken.

His activities from then on were frenetic. On June 11 he was scouting the Rappahannock all day; on June 13 he carried dispatches to Major-General Reynolds, one of which attached him to that general for his advance northward; on June 16 he was sent to Washington with a letter for the President; and a few days later was scouting the advancing Confederate infantry. On June 30 Dahlgren took command of a scouting party consisting of a sergeant and ten cavalrymen, together with Sergeant Milton Cline and four scouts from the B.M.I. Dressed in civilian clothes, the party set out for the rear of the Rebel Army. After a stop in Funkstown, Maryland, they marched toward Greencastle on July 1. The next day they discarded their civilian clothes and rode into the town square, where their arrival was the signal for wild scenes of welcome by a joyous townsfolk. According to Jacob Hoke, "Hats flew in the air and cheer followed cheer. Even the old and staid ministers forgot the proprieties and many wept for joy." Dahlgren then proceeded to clear the streets and prepare to ambush a party of Confederates approaching the town. At the appropriate moment Dahlgren's men charged with drawn sabers into the startled Rebels, capturing over twenty and, more importantly, two couriers with mailbags from Richmond. Inside was a letter from President Davis turning down a request from Lee that Confederate coastal garrisons be combed to produce a force to move north from the Carolinas and be positioned near Brandy Station as a reinforcement for Lee's army, and another potential threat to Washington.

Dahlgren, realizing the importance of this information, galloped the 30 miles over mountain roads to Gettysburg, arriving at Meade's headquarters very early on July 2, sometime after his meeting with his generals had broken up and the decision to stay and fight for a third day had been taken. Nevertheless, this was crucial information that told Meade his adversary was on his own – no Rebel reinforcements could be expected; this, coupled with the knowledge that Lee had only one fresh division (Pickett) available on the field, must have been very reassuring.

At the start of the Confederate retreat Dahlgren was involved in a second Greencastle expedition, which included a successful attack on part of Imboden's wagon train. However, he was badly wounded in the foot on July 6 during the fighting in Hagerstown. It was a wound that led to the amputation of his lower right leg. For his courage and resourcefulness Dahlgren was promoted colonel – he was then still only twenty-one. He did not fully recover until early 1864, when he was chosen to help lead a hair-brained scheme of Judson Kilpatrick's to raid Richmond and release Union soldiers held prisoner on Belle Isle and in Libby Prison. He led some 500 troopers on the raid, which ended in disaster with his being ambushed and shot dead by the 9th Virginia Cavalry. It was a tragic waste of a young officer of immense talent who would surely have risen to the top of his profession.

only), newspapers, observation from balloons (Union only), and intercepted signals (wigwag), dispatches, telegrams or letters. For the most part, individual commanders in the field arranged their own information-gathering activities. Army commanders, district commanders and some corps commanders all made use of scouts, spies, civilians and the interrogation of prisoners or deserters. A good example in the Gettysburg campaign was Longstreet's hiring and paying for his own spy, Henry Thomas Harrison, who brought news of the location of the Army of the Potomac to Longstreet early on June 28 (see box opposite). However, by June 1863 the Army of the Potomac had the benefit of a specific intelligence cell in its headquarters, something the Army of Northern Virginia was completely lacking. This was Colonel George Sharpe's Bureau of Military Information (B.M.I.). This, combined with Lee's dependence on an absent and out-of-touch Stuart during the critical days before the battle, explains at least in part why Meade was much the better informed on his enemy at Gettysburg. As Lee was to later admit, "the battle of Gettysburg . . . was commenced in the absence of correct intelligence."

To help the reader assess the relative value of the sources used by both sides in the run-up to the battle, each is explained in more detail below.

Cavalry

Cavalry units were the most common means by which an army commander sought tactical information and denied it to the enemy. Small patrols backed up by larger units were ideal for probing enemy positions to test reaction and identify the opposition, observing enemy camps, watching roads, interrogating civilians, counting marching columns of men, guns or wagons, or catching the occasional enemy courier. In conjunction with this, their mobility enabled them to spread out quickly along a river line or range of hills to prevent enemy patrols from securing information; this was known as screening. They were well suited to reporting on the terrain, on fords or bridges. And, if need be, cavalry units were able to fight for information or to attack enemy patrols. Although not accepted by a number of cavalry commanders as such, obtaining information was the primary role of cavalry.

In terms of numbers, both armies in the Gettysburg campaign were well endowed with the mounted arm. At the outset Lee had around 11,000 (including Robertson and Imboden) and Meade nearly 12,000. Although about 3,000 of Lee's men were more mounted infantry than cavalry, this did not greatly hinder their information-gathering capacity if well led and given appropriate orders. One effect of this near equality in numbers was that in the early phases of the campaign cavalry screens tended to cancel each other out and there were frequent small cavalry-versus-cavalry clashes, and not so much accurate information from this source about what was happening behind the screens. During the critical days from June 25 to July 1, Lee was totally out of touch with Stuart, the man on whom he was accustomed to depend for tactical information; it was to be a huge disadvantage.

Prisoners and Deserters

In any war there are prisoners and deserters. Although the former vastly outnumber the latter, it is the deserter who is generally the most willing to supply useful information on questioning; indeed many are eager to divulge all they know. Prisoners must be subjected to interrogation, a process that can be friendly and persuasive or aggressive and brutal. Although in the Gettysburg campaign it was the task of the provost marshal to guard and interrogate prisoners, and this was done whenever practical, it was often cavalry who made the capture and therefore had the initial opportunity to glean information. The difficulty with prisoners, and "deserters" who were planted, was that unless their information could be verified from independent sources there was no guarantee that it was not deliberately misleading. Despite this, it was deserters (and prisoners) who informed on the build-up of Rebel cavalry at Brandy Station and told Pleasonton of Ewell's departure from Fredericksburg, his presence at Culpeper and of subsequent Confederate movements in the Shenandoah Valley. The seeming ease with which information was extracted from Rebel prisoners was in part due to Colonel Sharpe's interrogation technique, including the promise that if the information given was proved correct the prisoner would be sent north for employment as a civilian.

The Army of the Potomac was in most respects the best organized for dealing with prisoners and their questioning. It attempted to keep track of where they were taken, what unit they belonged to and to record the information they gave. As with all pieces of information, those supplied by prisoners or deserters had to be collated and comparisons and deductions made. A Gettysburg example occurred late on July 2, just after Meade and his generals had decided to remain and defend Cemetery Ridge again the next day. The report on captured Rebels arrived and was compared with the information provided by spies on Lee's order of battle. The result was that Meade knew that every enemy formation had been engaged on either or both of the first two days – except for Pickett's Division. With just this exception he knew Lee had no fresh troops. It reinforced Meade's decision to stay.

Major-General Buford Serves Out Quick and Rough Justice

Private John Kelly of the 2nd U.S. Cavalry left an account of the hanging of a Rebel spy on June 27 at Frederick.

> On being brought before General Buford the prisoner was searched, and on his person was found a rough sketch of our camp, with a memorandum of the number of troops, horses, mules, wagons and artillery, and the route we were expected to take on our march. He was immediately escorted under guard by [Lieutenant John] Mix, the Provost-Marshal, to division headquarters. While on his way there, suspecting he had got himself into a bad scrape, he told a very plausible and pitiful story as to his poverty, with a wife and large family of small children depending upon him for support. The Provost-Marshal listened very attentively until he was all through, when, pointing out a lone tree a little to the left, he quietly remarked, "See that tree over there?" "Yes" the Johnnie saw it. And Mr Mix smilingly assured him that he would be hanging from that tree inside of five minutes. On arriving at Buford's headquarters the Provost stated the fellow's case, producing the paper found on him, and enquired how the prisoner should be disposed of. The General mused a few moments; then, looking from the prisoner to Mix, he remarked: "Well, if we send him a prisoner to Washington, it's ten to one that he will be back inside of a month with a commission in his pocket." He perused the paper again . . . [and said] "I guess you had best hang him." And hang him they did until the army had all passed by . . .

The Confederate's initial plan was for the 1st Virginia Infantry Battalion, as provost guard under Major Bridgford, to process prisoners and deserters. The usual sequence was questioning at brigade level or higher before being handed over to Bridgford, who would, after further investigation, have them escorted to Richmond, probably via Gordonsville, Virginia, where there was a small intelligence station operated by Company E of Bridgford's battalion. Lee may even have personally questioned selected prisoners. A Private D. G. Otto, who was captured while working for the B.M.I. and later exchanged, told Colonel Sharpe that Lee had questioned him. A valuable capture by Major John S. Mosby's rangers (working for Jeb Stuart) occurred on June 18 when two of Hooker's staff (Major William R. Sterling and Captain Benjamin F. Fisher, his chief signal officer) were caught. They were carrying messages that revealed the location of two Union corps and orders for the Union cavalry.

Scouts, Spies and the Bureau of Military Information (B.M.I.)

It was often difficult to distinguish between a scout and a spy, each of whom played important roles in the campaign, as both tended to operate as individuals, frequently behind enemy lines. In general, however, the scout wore uniform while the spy did not – or he wore his enemy's as a disguise.

Confederate scouting and spying

• **Scouting.** For the Gettysburg campaign Lee relied primarily on his cavalry commander to organize and control scouting activities. It was on the cavalry and Stuart's partisan rangers under the twenty-nine-year-old Major Mosby that Lee depended for tactical intelligence on the strength, location and intentions of the Union forces. Instructions to scouts included:

> observing the Federal army in camp, so as to be able to anticipate a movement; hanging upon the flank of the [Union] army, when in motion, reporting line of march and number of corps; and crossing the lines into Washington and beyond, bearing dispatches, interviewing certain parties and securing information.

According to Captain Thomas N. Conrad, "General 'Jeb's' scouts were to his superior officer [Lee] the very eyes and ears of the army . . ."

Unfortunately, at the critical time – the six days before the battle – Stuart was not in contact with army headquarters, nor indeed with any of the corps commanders. However, prior to this, in mid-June, Mosby, with his Company A, 43rd Battalion Virginia Partisan Rangers, was actively raiding and gleaning information in northwest Virginia and across the Potomac into Maryland. On June 10, as Ewell began his march, Lee instructed Jenkins, whose horsemen provided the vanguard of the army, to "keep your scouts out and collect all information of the strength & position of the enemy forces at Winchester, Berryville, Martinsburg and Harper's Ferry . . ." Similar orders went to Imboden's mounted infantry operating on Ewell's left flank in West Virginia, "to communicate any intelligence which may aid him [Ewell] in his operations . . ." The 35th Virginia Cavalry (White's Comanches), detached from "Grumble" Jones's brigade, was also tasked with scouting for Ewell.

Some four months before the campaign got under way, Lee had initiated a different type of scouting – seeking topographical information – when he sent Stonewall Jackson's engineer officer, Captain Jed Hotchkiss to survey and map the Valley of Virginia (see page 275).

• **Spying.** Most Confederate spying activities revolved around the "Secret Line" run by Major William Norris, head of the Confederate Signal Corps, and independent agents such as Captain Thomas Conrad and Lieutenant Benjamin F. Springfellow.

The Secret Line used agents, couriers and sympathetic civilians in Northern territory to bring information to Richmond. An officer who served in this organization described the operation:

> Every afternoon a courier would arrive in Richmond . . . bringing files of newspapers, letters and reports in cipher from parties in Canada and various portions of the United States. So regular was this service . . . the authorities in Richmond were in posession of Washington and Baltimore newspapers of the day before. The New York papers came a day later.

Jeb Stuart controlled two very successful individual spies. The first was Captain Thomas N. Conrad, a former headmaster and chaplain of the 3rd Virginia Cavalry with a talent for disguises that included dressing as a Union padre in order to operate behind enemy lines. As early as 1861 Conrad had established agents in Washington whom he claimed included clerks employed by the War Department who were able to pass on a complete order of battle of McClellan's army during the Seven Days Battles. The following year Conrad established a communications link of couriers between Washington and Richmond with a relay station just south of the Potomac called the "Eagle's Nest." In June 1863 Stuart sent Conrad into Washington, from where he operated from a Southern sympathizer's house within two blocks of the White House (it was called the Van Ness Mansion).

The second individual was Lieutenant Benjamin F. Springfellow, who won himself a place on Stuart's staff early in the war. He described his role as being "what is called in military language a Scout . . . My business was to get information; but my taste, and tempting opportunities, often led me to assume the character of a Partisan. I often indulged in capturing Picket Posts; engaged in raiding parties on wagon trains . . ." In early 1863 Stuart, on Lee's instructions, sent Springfellow into Washington to set up another spy ring independent of Conrad's network. This he succeeded in doing.

Union scouting and spying

• **The Bureau of Military Information (B.M.I.).** This was the U.S. Army's first professional military intelligence-gathering organization and it proved a major asset to both Hooker and Meade during the weeks prior to Gettysburg. It was set up in February 1863 by Hooker to replace the departed Pinkerton and his detectives. For administrative purposes it came under the provost marshal, Brigadier-General Patrick, but was controlled and tasked by Colonel George H. Sharpe. Sharpe appointed two assistants, a civilian John C. Babcock (he became Sharpe's deputy) and Captain John McEntee, to recruit and run teams of scouts and spies. The B.M.I. supported the Army of the Potomac, its task being to obtain information from all sources, analyze and interpret it, and present it to the army commander through the chief of staff (Butterfield) as intelligence.

Babcock had previously worked for Pinkerton as a mapmaker and had provided several excellent maps for the then army commander, McClellan. Babcock was Sharpe's principal interrogator, analyst and report writer. McEntee, a former quartermaster sergeant who had risen to captain during the battles of 1862, was also a report writer and interrogator, but was primarily tasked with leading scout and spy teams in the field. By May 1863 the B.M.I. unit working with the Army of the Potomac had risen to about twenty operatives and had become the primary source of information for the army commander.

One Union spy who made notable contributions throughout the war was Elizabeth Van Lew, known to many as "Crazy Bett" for her eccentricities. She resided in Richmond and ran a large and successful spy ring, which included a freed slave who worked in the White House to eavesdrop on President Davis and his visitors.

• **The Cavalry.** During the Gettysburg campaign Pleasonton's cavalry took second place to the B.M.I. in providing accurate and timely information to Hooker. This was despite specific orders from Halleck to the cavalry in mid-June:

> The commanding general relies upon you with your cavalry force to give him information of where the enemy is, his force, and his movements. You have a sufficient cavalry force to do this. Drive in pickets, if necessary, and get us information. It is better that we should lose men than to be without knowledge of the enemy, as we now seem to be.

In addition, Hooker sent clear guidance to Pleasonton on how he should cooperate with the B.M.I. team under McEntee, whom he was sending to his headquarters: "Captain McEntee . . . thoroughly understands the whole organization of the rebel army, and is sent out to join you. After you have examined any prisoners, deserters or contrabands brought in, the general desires you will give him a chance to examine all of them . . ."

Pleasonton did not carry out either of these instructions effectively. As will be seen in Section Seven: The Road to Gettysburg, he was more concerned with fighting than scouting, and Stuart's cavalry screen provided more than a match for the Yankees' timid probing. And McEntee was to tell Sharpe, "they [the cavalry] do not like to have an officer with them who makes a report of the same matters that they report."

• **Signal Stations.** Union forces made good use of signal stations for observation duties as well as communications during the Gettysburg campaign. By far the best example was the Union station on Maryland Heights, overlooking Harper's Ferry, under Captain Nathum Daniels. A defensive position was established on the Heights by the Harper's Ferry commander Brigadier-General Daniel Tyler, on the approach of Ewell's Corps in mid-June. On June 17 Captain Daniels of the Signal Corps arrived and established links with army headquarters via relay stations at Sugar Loaf Mountain, Maryland, and Leesburg, Virginia. According to Tyler, when the weather was clear the signal station could see as far as Williamsport, Martinsburg and Leesburg – an arc of nearly 20-mile radius covering numerous Potomac crossing points.

On June 20 Daniels reported that the "enemy has been crossing to the Maryland side all day . . . [and that] 30,000 to 40,000 troops [were] in and around Sharpsburg." On the 23rd Tyler reported:

> The signal officer just reports that the atmosphere is clear, and that he can see a line of troops 10 or 12 miles long moving from the direction of Berryville towards Shepherdstown Ford. It looks as if Lee's movement is toward Hagerstown and in[to] Pennsylvania. General Ewell, I am sure, passed through Sharpsburg yesterday in an ambulance.

This was superb, accurate information. The Confederates were to make a serious error in ignoring the Maryland Heights signal station.

Civilians, Newspapers and Slaves

Civilians

Civilians supplied considerable information, most of it useful, during the weeks prior to the battle. As the Army of Northern Virginia marched through Pennsylvania, the citizens organized spy groups in numerous communities to scout the enemy's composition and progress. It was an easy job for a civilian to watch and count a column of men, guns or wagons marching through a town. A division or corps with its train took several hours to pass and each regiment was easily counted by the number of flags carried. In these circumstances quite accurate estimates of numbers could be obtained, although it was unwise for a commander to put reliance on civilian information not corroborated by another source. Lee was always somewhat skeptical of civilian informants, much preferring experienced scouts or spies, stating that "reports from civilians however intelligent and honest cannot be relied on."

On the Union side, on June 24 Babcock sent a message to Sharpe that a civilian source (students from St. James's Boys School, near Hagerstown) reported:

> Gen. Ewell's corps with 70 pieces of artillery as having passed through Hagerstown[,] the last passing yesterday morning going towards Chambersburg. Gen. Ewell passed up yesterday morning. They report no force between Hagerstown and Frederick . . . No force at South Mountain . . . Longstreet and A.P. Hill are crossing [the Potomac] rapidly.

This information was substantially correct, although Ewell's Corps had seventy-nine guns at the battle. On June 28 Meade sent Halleck an amazingly detailed and informative statement from a blacksmith, Thomas McCammon, from Hagerstown which is quoted in full in the box on page 312.

Newspapers

Journalists were permitted to visit military camps with little or no restriction. They published what they saw and what they gleaned from friendly informants and overheard conversations. Both sides, therefore, made plentiful use of newspapers as there was no effective press censorship, although Hooker certainly tried in General Order No. 48, dated April 30, 1863, to prohibit the publication of crucial information.

> 1. Under no circumstances should be published the location of any corps, division, brigade or regiment, and especially is the location of my headquarters never to be named except during a fight.
> 2. That official reports when furnished without the sanction of the War Department, may never be published . . .

Despite this, and while much of what was published was exaggeration and speculation, there were frequently gems of useful information. An example came in April 1863 when *The Chronicle* published the surgeon general's figures of the number of sick and the percentage of the army these represented, enabling Richmond to calculate the strength and composition of the Army of the Potomac. When the *New York Herald* published details of movements of the army on June 18, Hooker complained to Halleck:

> So long as the newspapers continue to give publicity to our movements, we must not expect to gain any advantage over our adversaries. Is there no way of stopping it? I can suppress the circulation of this paper in my lines, but I cannot prevent their reaching it to the enemy. We could well afford to give millions of money for like information of the enemy.

Southern newspapers also published information of value to the North, despite an earlier agreement that they could avoid censorship if they refrained from passing on rumors or anything that might aid the enemy. One example was on June 9, when Pleasonton received a message from headquarters stating "The Richmond papers say that Lee's army is in motion" – it was concentrating around Culpeper.

Although newspapers could be something of a double-edged sword, as they could be used to spread disinformation, Lee made every effort to have Northern newspapers delivered as often as possible, and agents were tasked with obtaining and forwarding them by courier.

Slaves

Runaway slaves or contrabands sometimes proved useful sources of information. McEntee used at least one who had run away from his brigade at the U.S. Ford on the Rappahannock River. From him it was learned that his brigade was under orders to march and that the army's destination was Maryland via the Shenandoah Valley. This was corroborated by information from another contraband that Stuart's cavalry at Culpeper was having its horses shoed and supplies were arriving in preparation for a move. On June 10 two slaves captured at Brandy Station supplied crucial information that Lee, Longstreet and Ewell were at Culpeper and Hill still at Fredericksburg. One stated that three days' rations were to be issued and after that they were to feed themselves in Pennsylvania.

SECTION SEVEN

The Road to Gettysburg

THE CONFEDERACY IN MAY, 1863

An Overview (Map 11)

Richmond, Virginia, was one of the first state capitals in the new republic and State House on Shockoe Hill, overlooking the falls of the James River, still houses the oldest legislative body in the United States. It was built for Thomas Jefferson in white marble with an imposing entrance at the top of wide stone steps under a portico supported by eight pillars. Modeled on a Roman temple (the main building looks much like the Pantheon in Rome), it was opened for business in 1788. In 1863 it contained the offices of President Davis. On May 15 General Lee had been summoned there to attend one of the most critical meetings of the war with his President and the Secretary of War, Seddon. They were in effect the unofficial inner Cabinet that ran the war, making the overall political and military strategy. Now, after two and a half years of fighting, the Confederacy was in trouble – particularly in the West. These three men had to decide overall strategic priorities and produce an agreed plan of how to prosecute the struggle for the remainder of the year. The President would present the resultant decisions to the official Cabinet for endorsement several days later.

Although the politician, civil servant and soldier had differing opinions on how to proceed, at the outset of the meeting all three understood the situation in which the Confederacy found itself in mid-1863. The key problem areas are outlined below.

Manpower

In 1860 there were 23 million people in the twenty-two Northern states but only 9 million, of whom 3.5 million were slaves, in the eleven Southern ones. This huge discrepancy had obvious implications for the long-term prosecution of the war, particularly in regard to industrial capacity and the ability to keep large armies in the field. Although Lee had mostly been winning victories over the previous twelve months, they had been expensive in terms of casualties and, in one case, the Seven Days, pyrrhic. While overall the actual losses were similar for both sides, in percentage terms the Confederates had lost more heavily and from a far smaller manpower base.

Losses for Both Armies Prior to Gettysburg

Battles	Confederate	Union
Seven Days (July, 1862)	19,739 20.7%	9,796 10.7%
Second Manassas (August, 1862)	9,108 19%	10,096 13.3%
Antietam (September, 1862)	11,724 22.6%	11,657 15.5%
Fredericksburg (December, 1862)	5,300 7.3%	12,700 12.0%
Chancellorsville (May, 1862)	12,821 21.0%	17,278 13.0%
Total casualties	**58,692**	**61,527**

With the exception of Fredericksburg, where the Rebels remained on the defensive in a strong position against futile frontal attacks, Lee was losing about 21 percent in every battle while his opponents lost only 13 percent. It was a statistic the South could not sustain, as Lee himself appreciated. On June 10, at the outset of the Gettysburg campaign, he was to write to his President as follows:

> While making the most we can of the means of resistance we possess . . . it is nevertheless the part of wisdom to carefully measure and husband our strength, and not to expect from it more than in the ordinary course of affairs it is capable of accomplishing. We should not therefore conceal from ourselves that our resources in men are constantly diminishing, and the disproportion in this respect between us and our enemies, if they continue united in their effort to subjugate us, is steadily augmenting. The decrease of the aggregate of this army as disclosed by the returns affords an illustration of this fact. Its effective strength varies from time to time, but the falling off in its aggregate shows that its ranks are growing weaker and that its losses are not supplied by recruits.

The Union naval blockade

The U.S. Navy far outmatched anything the South could muster and by mid-1863 the blockade had been considerably tightened. Although blockade-running had been reduced to a fine art, with some skillful and courageous Southern captains successfully slipping through the net, it was not nearly as porous as it had been in the early years. This blockade had not only severely curtailed the purchase and importation of war materials but it had also cut off much worthwhile contact with foreign governments and sympathizers. One of the fast-fading hopes had been that foreign support might, with Southern military successes, not only help sustain resistance but put pressure on the North to recognize the Confederacy. From the outset of the war it had been realized by most that the advantages in manufacturing, productive capacity, sea power and the production of iron and munitions would give the North huge advantages that would increase the longer the war lasted. As an illustration of how the economy was being squeezed, by 1863 inflation had risen in the South to such an extent that $10 had the purchasing power that $1 had had three years earlier.

Military geography

As Map 11 (opposite) shows, the Confederacy was (ignoring Florida) roughly an irregular rectangle some 1,500 miles wide and 500–600 miles deep.This whole area was surrounded to the north and west by Northern territory and to the east and south by the sea, which was controlled by the Northern navy. This meant the South was operating, in grand strategical terms, on "interior lines" and the North on "exterior lines." The former meant that, theoretically, the numerically weaker South could reinforce a threatened area more quickly than the North, as the Confederates were inside the rectangle while its enemies were operating around the outside. However, the advantage of interior lines belongs to the army that can move more quickly from A to B, not necessarily the army that has the shortest distance to go.

While in the early years of the war the South operated geographically on interior lines, by May 1863 this advantage was fast disappearing, and certainly by the fall of that year had gone. The reason was largely down to railroads. As discussed in the previous section (see page 223), the North had a network of over 22,000 miles, the South a mere 8,500. The ability to move men and materials quickly that this gave the North was a war-winning factor. Couple this with the North's navy, which enabled its armies to be moved and landed along hundreds of miles of coast or within 60 miles of Richmond, and it is clear that Union forces could, on occasion, move, operate and be supplied with greater speed than the Confederates.

The possession of interior lines has, throughout military history, often given a numerically smaller force the ability to delay one advancing enemy army with a detachment while switching reserves to achieve greater strength against another separate enemy some distance away. To counter this, the force on exterior lines must keep up the pressure from several directions at once and thus crush the enemy in the center. As will be discussed below, during the Gettysburg campaign it was Lee's smaller army that operated on exterior lines in both the march into Pennsylvania and on the battlefield itself, and one of the key reasons for the Rebel defeat was their failure to coordinate attacks from different directions simultaneously.

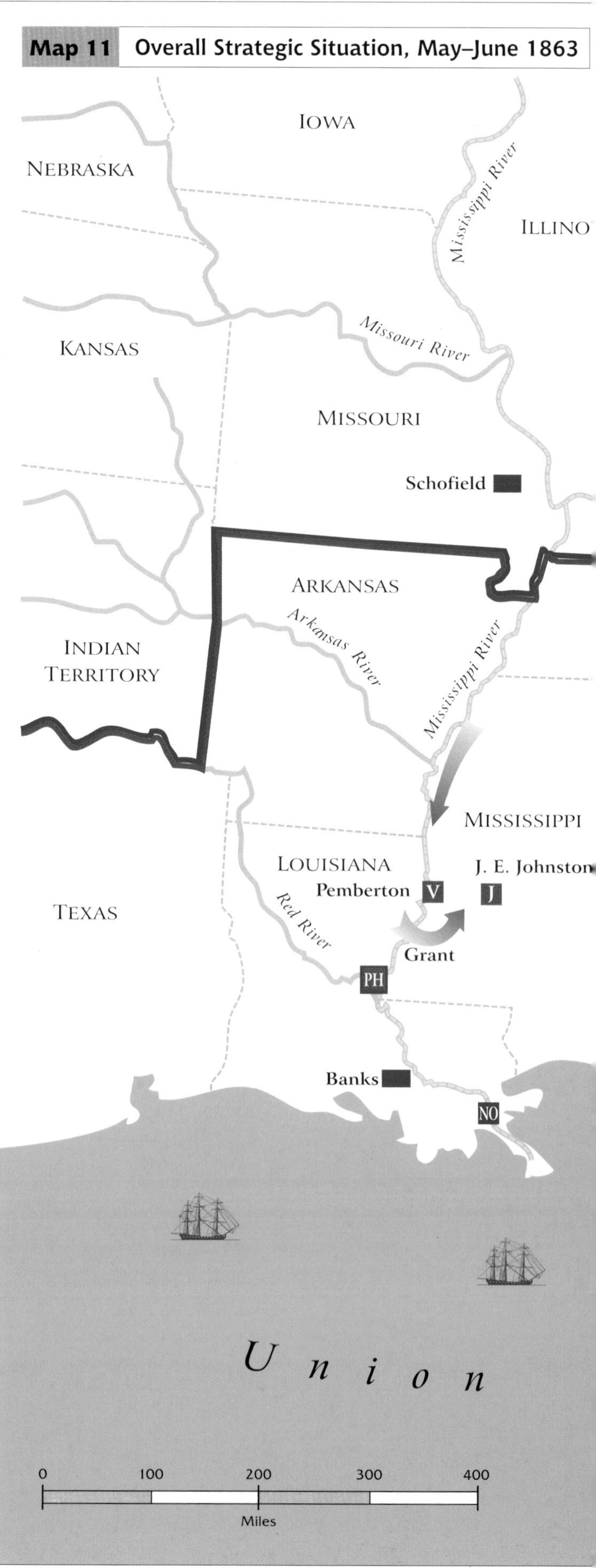

NEW YORK
NEW JERSEY
PENNSYLVANIA
Susquehanna River
G
OHIO
NDIANA
MARYLAND
Potomac
W
DELAWARE
WEST VIRGINIA (1863)
Hooker
F
Lee
R
Burnside
River
KENTUCKY
James River
VIRGINIA
Roanoke River
TENNESSEE
N
Rosecrans
Tennessee River
Bragg
C
NORTH CAROLINA
D. H. Hill
SOUTH CAROLINA
A
ABAMA
GEORGIA
Beauregard
Ch
S
FLORIDA
Naval
Blockade
Key
A Atlanta
Ch Charleston
C Chattanooga
F Fredericksburg
G Gettysburg
J Jackson
N Nashville
NO New Orleans
PH Port Hudson
R Richmond
S Savannah
V Vicksburg
W Washington D.C.
Union foothold on southern coast

The overall military situation

As Map 11 makes clear, by May 1863 the Confederacy was under severe pressure from all sides, including the sea – she was surrounded. There was something of a stand-off in the East with the Army of the Potomac under Hooker facing the Army of Northern Virginia under Lee across the Rappahannock. Along the east coast a number of important toeholds had been established by Union forces and required watching. To the north, Tennessee had been invaded, the Confederates had lost the railroad center at Nashville, and the even more important railroad center at Chattanooga was threatened by Rosecrans – although in mid-May there was also a stand-off between him and the Rebels under Bragg. A successful Union thrust in this area would take Chattanooga and put the last major Southern railroad center at Atlanta in danger. But it was in the West that things had become dire for the South.

The Civil War had three theaters of operations. From the Atlantic to the Appalachian Mountain chain was the "East;" from the Appalachians to the Mississippi was the "West;" and from the Mississippi to the Pacific was the "Trans-Mississippi" (Arkansas, Texas and Louisiana). This last theater can be disregarded in terms of significant military operations or importance. Nevertheless, as Davis, Lee and Seddon sat down to discuss the situation, it was the West that worried the two civilians most – indeed it was what had triggered the meeting in the first place. The Union offensive in the West under Major-General Grant had cost the Confederacy New Orleans; Port Hudson was surrounded; and Grant, with naval as well as military forces, had secured the line of the Mississippi River, with the exception of the fortress city of Vicksburg, which was in danger of being surrounded and besieged at any moment. If Vicksburg fell (it did so on July 4), the Confederacy would be split in two. The loss of the Trans-Mississippi states would not be critical, but if Vicksburg went so did 30,000 soldiers with their arms and equipment. Add this to the loss of much of Tennessee and New Orleans with their factories and foundries, as well as the disruption of the weak rail network through the loss of key junctions, and the South's ability to sustain its armies, already suffering from acute shortages of supplies and equipment, was further weakened. The possibility of victorious Union forces in the West pushing east and then swinging north – as happened when Sherman took Atlanta in 1864 and with his subsequent famous march from Atlanta to the sea – first squeezing, then crushing the Confederacy, was a seriously disturbing prospect.

Friday, May 15: the Crucial Meeting

The decisions taken on this day led to the Battle of Gettysburg some six weeks later. The problems facing the Confederacy outlined above were well known to each of the three men. Recent victories in the East had kept that theater relatively quiet for the moment, whereas in the West a military setback that could have grave consequences looked increasingly likely. What was the answer? What military strategy, if any, could either retrieve the situation in the West or at least offset the Union success there? Opinions differed. Details of what transpired at the meeting were not recorded, only the fact that it took place was noted by the War Department clerk, John B. Jones. Nevertheless, from subsequent actions and correspondence it is not difficult to set out the gist of the discussions.

Two overall strategic options were under consideration: to reinforce the West from the East and seek to reverse the situation there, or to take the offensive in the East. The possibility of remaining on the strategic defensive was not considered. The proposal to take the offensive in the West had been proposed by Longstreet some weeks earlier. He envisaged taking his corps, or at least two divisions (Hood and Pickett) to the West, combining with Johnston's and Bragg's forces and driving Rosecrans from Tennessee, then marching to the Ohio – hopefully thus drawing Grant away from Vicksburg. Longstreet had missed Chancellorsville as he had been unable to return from his large-scale foraging expedition in the South in time, but on his way back after the battle he visited Secretary Seddon and presented him with his proposal as being the best way of halting the worsening situation in the West.

Earlier in the month Seddon had already put forward to Lee a similar plan (although somewhat watered down, in that only Pickett's Division would be sent). This version had originated from General Pierre G. Beauregard, the officer who had commanded the attack on Fort Sumter that opened the war, then commanding the troops watching the coast from South Carolina to Florida. Lee had countered it on the grounds that he would have to withdraw the remainder of his army into the Richmond defenses – guaranteed to frighten the government. However, Longstreet's visit meant that the idea of reinforcing the West at the expense of the East was still very much alive in Seddon's mind when he sat down at the meeting. Indeed, the meeting had been called to resolve this very issue.

Longstreet was Lee's senior corps commander and confidant, and as such it was important they should agree strategy. In order to do so, Lee met with Longstreet in the days before the meeting to put across his view that an offensive in the East had a far better chance of success and of achieving long-term benefits for the Confederacy. Longstreet was persuaded. When writing to Senator Wigfall (an influential supporter of the West first proposal) before the meeting he stated:

> When I agreed with the Secy & yourself about sending troops west I was under the impression that we would be obliged to remain on the defensive here . . . [now there] is a fair prospect of forward movement. That being the case we can spare nothing from this army to re-enforce the west . . . If we could cross the Potomac with one hundred & fifty thousand men [it should] either destroy the Yankees or bring them to terms.

The person ultimately responsible for the final decision was President Davis. The urgency of the situation was underlined on May 14 when Richmond received the news that Jackson, the state capital of Mississippi, was lost – Mississippi was the President's home state. At the start of the meeting Lee had to convince both his President and the Secretary that an early offensive in the East was the better option.

Lee's plan was not new. He had mooted it in April, before Chancellorsville, as the best way of alleviating the pressure in the West, but it had been forestalled by that battle. The meeting ended with his proposal being accepted by the others. He was the South's premier general, with a string of recent victories to his credit, so his opinions carried enormous weight. Although we will never know precisely what arguments he used, they surely included the following:

- If Lee had to send men to the West, then there could be problems with his holding the line of the Rappahannock if Hooker attacked again. Lee's information was that his adversary was being reinforced and any reduction in his, Lee's, numbers would probably mean a withdrawal into the Richmond defenses with the possibility of a siege that would have only one ending. This was probably his most powerful argument.
- Sending troops to the West was now likely to be too late. Reinforcements would take too long to get there on the tortuous railroad links, and would come under the command of Johnston, in whom neither Lee nor Davis had any confidence. The likelihood was that troops would end up being of little use to stop the rot in the West, and of no use at all in the East because of their absence.
- Lee was an ardent exponent of offensive warfare. He was usually an attacking general, both strategically and tactically. Despite his frequent acknowledgment of the need for the Confederacy to husband its manpower resources, he believed the South, and his army in particular, needed to keep the initiative, to keep mobile and keep the enemy conforming to his movements. He again pressed forcefully his idea of an advance into Maryland and Pennsylvania. Such a move would disrupt Hooker's plans and compel the Army of the Potomac to withdraw from the Rappahannock to protect Washington, and it would give relief to an exhausted Virginia, which had been the battleground of large armies for over two years. The farmland north of the Potomac would be a land of plenty for his hungry troops. As Lee was later to say, "An invasion of the enemy's country breaks up all of his preconceived plans, relieves our country of his presence, and we subsist while there on his resources."
- The Army of Northern Virginia was highly experienced; many of its members were veterans of several victories, so overall morale could not be higher. The British observer Fremantle commented, "the universal feeling in the army was one of profound contempt for an enemy whom they have beaten so constantly . . ." Now was the time to strike with this army, not break it up or confine it to static defense. All would have agreed that an invasion of the North would bring about a major battle, with Lee having every confidence he could win it, and with such a victory there was every chance of threatening Washington, encouraging foreign recognition of the Confederacy, boosting the peace movement in the North and at the very least offsetting what looked like the imminent loss of Vicksburg.

President Davis had left his sickbed to attend the meeting, but he was not easily convinced that an invasion of the North in the East was prudent. At first he did not, as Lee later revealed, "like the [idea] of a movement northward." His worry was that it would expose Richmond to a Union advance, as its principal shield would have gone. Lee countered that, with a carefully concealed start, he would be well on the way to, or possibly over, the Potomac before Hooker knew for certain what was happening. In those circumstances Lincoln would pull Hooker back to protect his capital. These arguments won the day. On May 16 the Cabinet, with the exception of the Postmaster, John Reagan, who requested another meeting on May 17, approved the plan. A second vote again approved it and Lee returned by rail to his army. The march that ended at Gettysburg would go ahead.

Lee's Plan (Map 12)

Lee's aim was bring on a decisive battle with the Army of the Potomac in as favorable circumstances as possible. He had no clearly defined geographic objective such as Washington or Baltimore. His outline plan was to invade the North via the Shenandoah and Cumberland (an extension of the Shenandoah) Valleys into Maryland and Pennsylvania up to, and possibly over, the Susquehanna River. Lee was well aware that this move would soon draw Hooker north to protect Washington by interposing the Army of the Potomac between the capital and himself. Lee then wanted his battle, but he wanted it on ground of his choosing, when he had the initiative, knew his enemies' locations and when his own army was concentrated. An important part of this plan, as we have seen, was to secure food and fodder for his troops and dramatically reduce his dependence on supply trains from his railhead at Staunton.

Security

Lee's primary requirement for the success of the march north was security. Certainly until he was north of the Potomac he needed to prevent Hooker from being certain of his army's whereabouts. This depended on deception. At the same time Lee needed to know the movement and locations of his enemy. For both these essentials he must rely primarily on his cavalry under Stuart. Until then Stuart had dominated the tactical reconnaissance effort on all Lee's battlefields. The Confederate invasion of Maryland in 1862 had been Lee's only unsuccessful campaign prior to Gettysburg, but it had been the unfortunate loss of a critical order that had turned events against the Rebels then, not Stuart's handling of the cavalry. The Confederate cavalry and its commander were supremely confident of being the master of their Union opposite numbers. Although Hooker had reorganized his cavalry into a corps in its own right, they had a mediocre commander, Pleasonton having got the job over the far more able Major-General John Buford, his junior by eleven days.

Army strengths

Lee was taking the offensive, invading Northern territory and seeking a decisive battle – he was poking a stick into a hornet's nest. He knew full well that Lincoln's reaction would be to safeguard Washington and that would be Hooker's overriding task. But he was also acutely aware that the Confederates were losing the numbers game and that the probability was that he would be outnumbered from the outset by at least 20,000–25,000 men. In practice the campaign started with the Army of Northern Virginia's mustering nearly 83,000 men against an Army of the Potomac with a call on over 110,000. By the time the battle was joined these numbers had shrunk to around 72,000 and 94,000 respectively – these being men actually engaged between July 1 and 3. These figures meant Lee needed his army concentrated and with a good picture of his enemy's location and strength before he committed it to battle.

Lee had the option of attacking across the river at or near Fredericksburg but the prospect was unappealing and almost certain to result in more serious and unaffordable losses for no decisive gain. As he put it, "Unless it [Hooker's army] can be drawn out in a position to be assailed" it would eventually take the offensive with greatly superior numbers and push the Army of Northern Virginia back into the Richmond defenses.

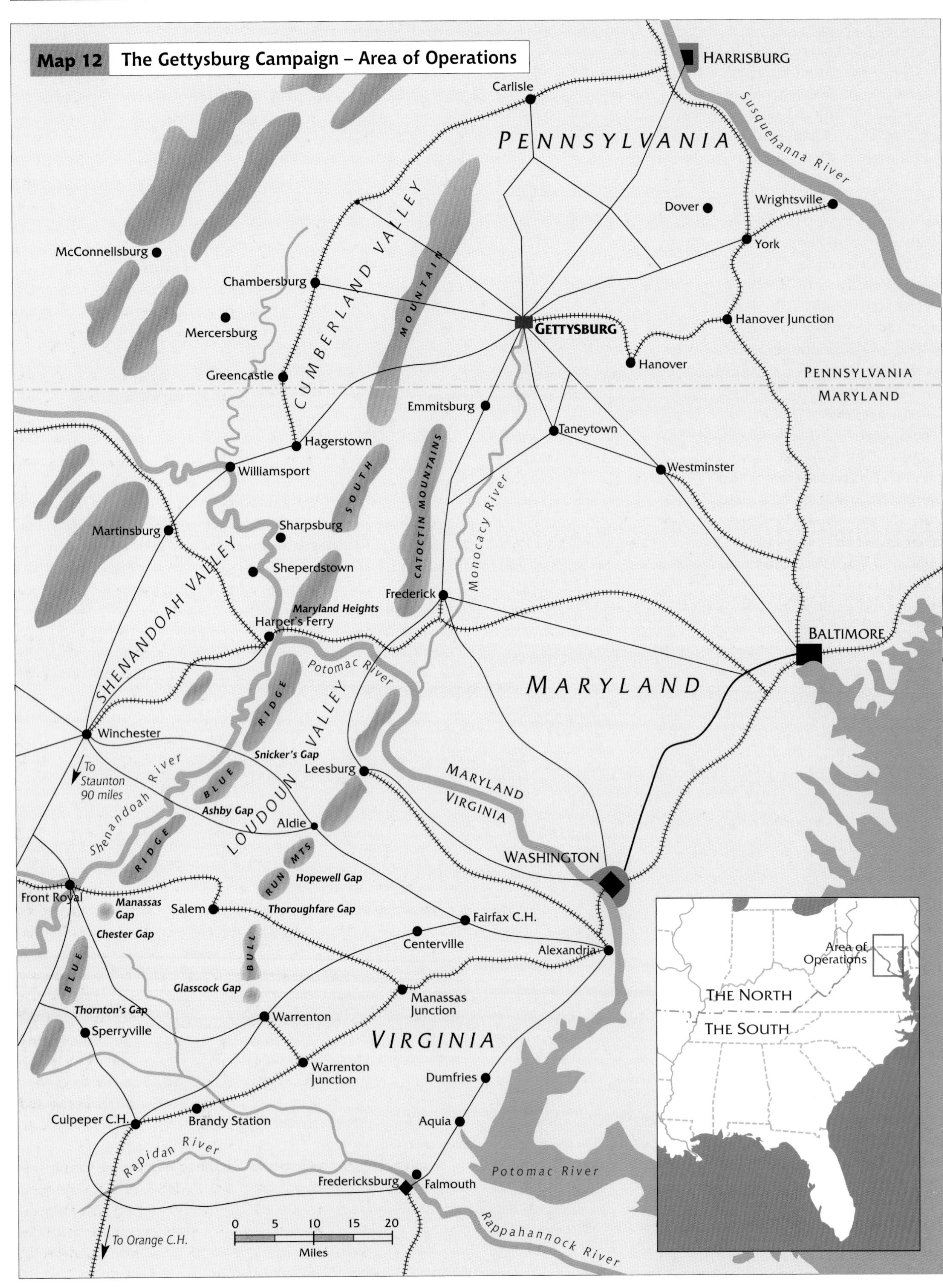
Map 12 The Gettysburg Campaign – Area of Operations
HARRISBURG
Carlisle
PENNSYLVANIA
Susquehanna River
Wrightsville
Dover
York
McConnellsburg
Chambersburg
CUMBERLAND VALLEY
MOUNTAIN
Mercersburg
GETTYSBURG
Hanover Junction
Hanover
Greencastle
PENNSYLVANIA
MARYLAND
Emmitsburg
Taneytown
Hagerstown
Westminster
Williamsport
SOUTH
CATOCTIN MOUNTAINS
Monocacy River
Martinsburg
Sharpsburg
Sheperdstown
Frederick
SHENANDOAH VALLEY
Maryland Heights
Harper's Ferry
BALTIMORE
Potomac River
RIDGE
MARYLAND
LOUDOUN VALLEY
Winchester
Snicker's Gap
To Staunton 90 miles
Leesburg
MARYLAND
VIRGINIA
Shenandoah River
BLUE
Ashby Gap
Aldie
RIDGE
RUN MTS
WASHINGTON
Hopewell Gap
Front Royal
Manassas Gap
Salem
Thoroughfare Gap
Fairfax C.H.
Chester Gap
Centerville
Alexandria
BULL
Area of Operations
BLUE
Glasscock Gap
Manassas Junction
THE NORTH
THE SOUTH
Thornton's Gap
Warrenton
Sperryville
VIRGINIA
Warrenton Junction
Dumfries
Culpeper C.H.
Brandy Station
Aquia
Rapidan River
Potomac River
Fredericksburg
Falmouth
Rappahannock River
0 5 10 15 20
Miles
To Orange C.H.

Crossing the Potomac

Lee would be operating on exterior lines during the march north in that moving from the Fredericksburg area via Culpeper Court House to the Shenandoah Valley, and thence north over the Potomac and up the Cumberland Valley, would mean his marching round the circumference of the circle, of which Washington and Baltimore were the center. Hooker would be marching inside this circle with shorter distances as far as protecting his capital was concerned. However, if Lee could cross the Potomac with Hooker still mostly to the south of it, then, in terms of time and distance, the ability to concentrate more quickly could well pass to the Confederates – provided they knew what Hooker was doing. Equally, until Hooker (later Meade) knew for sure all the Rebels were north of the Potomac he could not be certain they were not intending to threaten Washington directly – another important reason for Lee, that is Stuart, to operate a tight screen in the early stages of the campaign.

The invasion route

The Shenandoah–Cumberland Valley was an ideal route for the invasion. Not only did it provide a corridor that led directly to Pennsylvania and the Susquehanna River, but its most vulnerable eastern flank was protected by a double chain of mountains for over 100 miles and a large river for over 50. It was more than 70 miles from Lee's main railhead base at Staunton to Front Royal, another 55 to Williamsport on the Potomac and another 55 to Carlisle. For 170 miles Lee's extremely extended line of communication would have natural obstacles protecting its vulnerable flank. From east to west these obstacles were the Bull Run Mountains south of the Potomac and the Catoctin Mountains to the north; some 10 miles to their west was the longer chain of the Blue Ridge and its northern extension South Mountain; finally there was the Shenandoah River and the Potomac from Harper's Ferry to Williamsport. In any Confederate advance it was important to secure river crossings, and even more critical was the need to hold the gaps in the mountain chains. Once the Rebels marched toward and entered the Shenandoah Valley, Thornton's, Chester, Manassas, Ashby, Snicker's, Thoroughfare and Aldie Gaps became vital points for Rebel cavalry to hold in order to prevent Union horsemen from obtaining information about their enemy's movements. The series of sharp cavalry clashes in the Loudoun Valley in the third week of the campaign (see page 303) were the result of Pleasonton's attempts to penetrate Stuart's cavalry screen.

Supplies

The exceedingly long line of communication back to the railhead at Staunton meant that they were potentially vulnerable to attack and disruption. Mile after mile of plodding wagon trains would be tempting targets that required protection by escort troops and, more importantly, by the use of cavalry to secure and hold the mountain gaps as the trains moved up to and over the Potomac. Once north of the river, feeding off hostile countryside could begin in earnest and supplies, carts, wagons and horses requisitioned, reserves built up and livestock on the hoof collected. As noted above, Winchester became a forward base and collecting point after its capture and, with the exception of ammunition supply, the need for wagon trains toiling up from Staunton was hugely reduced.

Lee's Preparations

Lee returned to Fredericksburg on May 17 to prepare for his offensive. During the next two weeks he had two primary concerns, both brought about by the battle at Chancellorsville at the start of the month: namely the needs to reorganize his command structure and to reinforce his army.

The reorganization involved the forming of a third corps so that the Army of Northern Virginia had smaller and less cumbersome formations, and the appointment of two new corps commanders, one to replace Jackson, the other to command the new corps. These changes have been discussed in detail in the Prologue (see pages 20–26), but in summary saw Jackson's 2nd Corps go to Ewell and the 3rd Corps to A. P. Hill – both these officers receiving promotion to lieutenant-general. Longstreet retained the 1st Corps. The urgent need to replace the losses at Chancellorsville led to acrimonious communications between Lee and D. H. Hill in North Carolina concerning the return by Hill of four of Lee's veteran brigades under Robert Ransom, John R. Cooke, Micah Jenkins and Montgomery Corse (these last two Pickett's), which had been loaned to Hill to bolster his defense of the Atlantic coast. Lee, who was the overall commander of the department, could have ordered Hill to send these brigades but instead issued his customary discretionary orders: "I desire you to send to me & rely upon your good judgment to proportion the means to the object in view." Hill took advantage of such vague instructions and declined to send any brigades back – claiming he needed them in the South. It was the first example in the campaign of potential problems arising from Lee's fondness for discretionary orders. Both the President and Secretary of War became embroiled and the result was that Lee got none of his experienced brigades and commanders but two new, inexperienced ones instead (James J. Pettigrew and the President's nephew, Joseph R. Davis). This meant that Lee would not start out with the numbers he wanted and that on July 3 Pickett would advance to the attack with three brigades instead of five. Would they have made a difference to that last attempt to storm Cemetery Ridge and to the battle's outcome?

HOOKER'S SITUATION AND THINKING IN MAY, 1863

On the other side of the Rappahannock Hooker had replacement problems similar to Lee's, in that he had lost heavily at Chancellorsville and large numbers of his army were due for discharge, although morale generally among the soldiers was still reasonably high. After the disaster at Fredericksburg in December 1862 men had deserted in droves, with about one soldier in ten being listed as a deserter and Major-General Carl Schurz writing to Lincoln that he should "not be surprised to see this great army melt away with frightful rapidity." This was unduly pessimistic, but desertion was certainly a serious problem. However, after Chancellorsville desertion was minimal, as most men realized that, although defeated, they had inflicted as much damage as they received.

A much bigger problem was the huge number of Union soldiers due to be mustered out at the end of their engagement. Over 30,000 men were due to leave over the next two months. This amounted to some fifty-three infantry regiments or nearly three corps. The spring of 1863 saw the service of the two-year volunteers ending, along with that of the nine-month men who had enlisted during the crisis period in the fall of the previous year. At the end of April official figures showed 111,650 active-duty infantry available to the Army of the Potomac, but two weeks later Hooker claimed to have only 80,000 ready to march. Halleck, who insisted none could be spared from the Washington defenses, stonewalled demands for reinforcements. Some were ultimately provided, but a number (over 8,000 infantrymen) did not arrive until a matter of days or hours before the battle and even during it – Willard's Brigade joined II Corps at Gum Spring on June 25; Crawford's Division joined V Corps at Frederick on June 28 (the day Meade took command); Stannard's Brigade joined I Corps at Gettysburg late on July 1; two regiments of Lockwood's Brigade joined XII Corps at Gettysburg on July 2, and a third regiment, 1st Maryland, joined on July 3.

The turmoil in the high command of the Army of the Potomac and the series of attempts by plotters to oust Hooker have been discussed in the Prologue (see pages 26–28); they meant Lee's opponent was to go into action knowing he did not have the confidence of most of his corps commanders – a situation fraught with potential difficulties. Nevertheless, Hooker had set up the Bureau of Military Information (B.M.I.) in February and this was functioning well under the control of Colonel Sharpe; in the coming weeks it was to provide more accurate intelligence on Confederate activities than his cavalry. His cavalry had been reorganized and a cavalry corps of some 12,000 men created by early June. Although many horses were worn out, the new corps was superior in equipment and was potentially the equal of the Rebels' mounted arm in most respects except in the top leadership – Pleasonton came a very poor second to Stuart. Hooker had also centralized his artillery so that each corps had its own brigade and, what was to prove invaluable at Gettysburg, there was an Army Artillery Reserve.

Hooker had no specific plans for June except that he was considering some form of offensive over the river with what, despite its recent losses and the problem of time-expired men, was a fine army. He was thinking the opportunity might come if Lee moved and thus at least partially opened the road to Richmond. But there was no way he could undertake such a bold stroke without the sanction of Lincoln, and he would need timely information on his enemy's movements.

THE CAMPAIGN

Phase I: May 25–June 9 (Maps 13 and 14)

From late May up to and including the first day's fighting at Gettysburg on July 1, the decisions and movements of both armies were largely dependent on the quality of intelligence given to their respective commanders. At the start of this period both armies were eyeing each other across the Rappahannock; it was the physical barrier that separated them and had to be considered in any movement planning by Hooker or Lee. Its bridges and fords were key points that were picketed by both Rebels and Yankees, often within shouting distance of each other. In the early summer of 1863 the water was fairly low so that large bodies of troops, horses, wagons and guns could cross at the main fords, but only where there was a good approach down the steep banks. The tendency was for each army to keep extending their pickets and patrols further and further upriver, leapfrogging each other on opposite banks to ensure any attempt to cross was spotted.

Union activity

On May 25 Hooker was in Washington, unsuccessfully pleading with Halleck for reinforcements. Two days later he had information that the Army of Northern Virginia was stirring. It came from Colonel Sharpe, his B.M.I. spymaster at army headquarters. His informants reported considerable activity. The most convincing was from a deserter who stated that the Rebels were under marching orders – "an order from General Lee was very lately read to the troops announcing a campaign of long marches & hard fighting in a part of the country where there would be no railroad transportation." This was supported by information that Hood's and Pickett's Divisions had rejoined Longstreet; that Stuart's cavalry had been reinforced and was concentrating around Culpeper Court House; while the *Richmond Herald* of May 22 suggested that events at Vicksburg would "soon be eclipsed by greater events elsewhere. Within the next fortnight the campaign of 1863 will be pretty well decided. The most important movement of the war will probably be made in that time." All this was good, accurate information, which produced the deduction that Lee was about to march west and then probably north to take the offensive.

The next day Hooker was certain no march had yet started, the enemy camps being as "numerous and as well filled as ever." However, subsequent reports of enemy skirmishers having crossed the Rappahannock prompted Hooker to take some precautionary moves to bolster his right. He reinforced his cavalry assembled around Bealeton, telling them to drive the Rebels back across the river and at the same time instructed Meade, then commanding V Corps, to replace the cavalry pickets at the lower fords with infantry.

Confederate activity

Lee's intention was to use the Culpeper Court House as an assembly area for his entire army less Hill's Corps, which was to remain in the Fredericksburg defenses for as long as possible in order to confuse Hooker as to his exact intentions. The movement north would be led by Ewell's Corps with a mission to clear the Shenandoah of Union troops (there was a division of several thousand at Winchester under Major-General Robert H. Milroy and a garrison at Harper's Ferry) and secure the crossing sites along the Potomac at Sheperdstown, Virginia, and Williamsport, Maryland.

Notes

Hooker was aware that Lee was on the move westward, but he needed to know for sure which route Lee was going to take after crossing the upper Rappahannock. If he kept south of the Potomac, then a direct attack on Washington was a probability. If he marched up the Shenandoah, crossed the Potomac and into Pennsylvania, then the threat to Washington was less likely. In any event, information on the locations of enemy corps and movements was essential before Hooker could know how best to move to check Lee's advance.

- From the map it is easy to see how Lee would be operating on exterior lines and would have much further to march than Hooker, on interior lines, if Washington–Baltimore was the Rebel's objective. Given reasonably accurate information, Hooker would have little difficulty in interposing his army between Lee and Washington–Baltimore if the Confederates chose the short (B) or medium (C) left hooks.
- For Lee, the key to gaining a strategic advantage lay in preventing Hooker gaining the information he needed. Lee was to take the long left hook and in this case he needed to ensure that Hooker remained uncertain of his true intention until he, Lee, was north of the Potomac.
- Once the campaign got under way it would be the cavalry of both sides that would play the key role until the armies met on a battlefield.

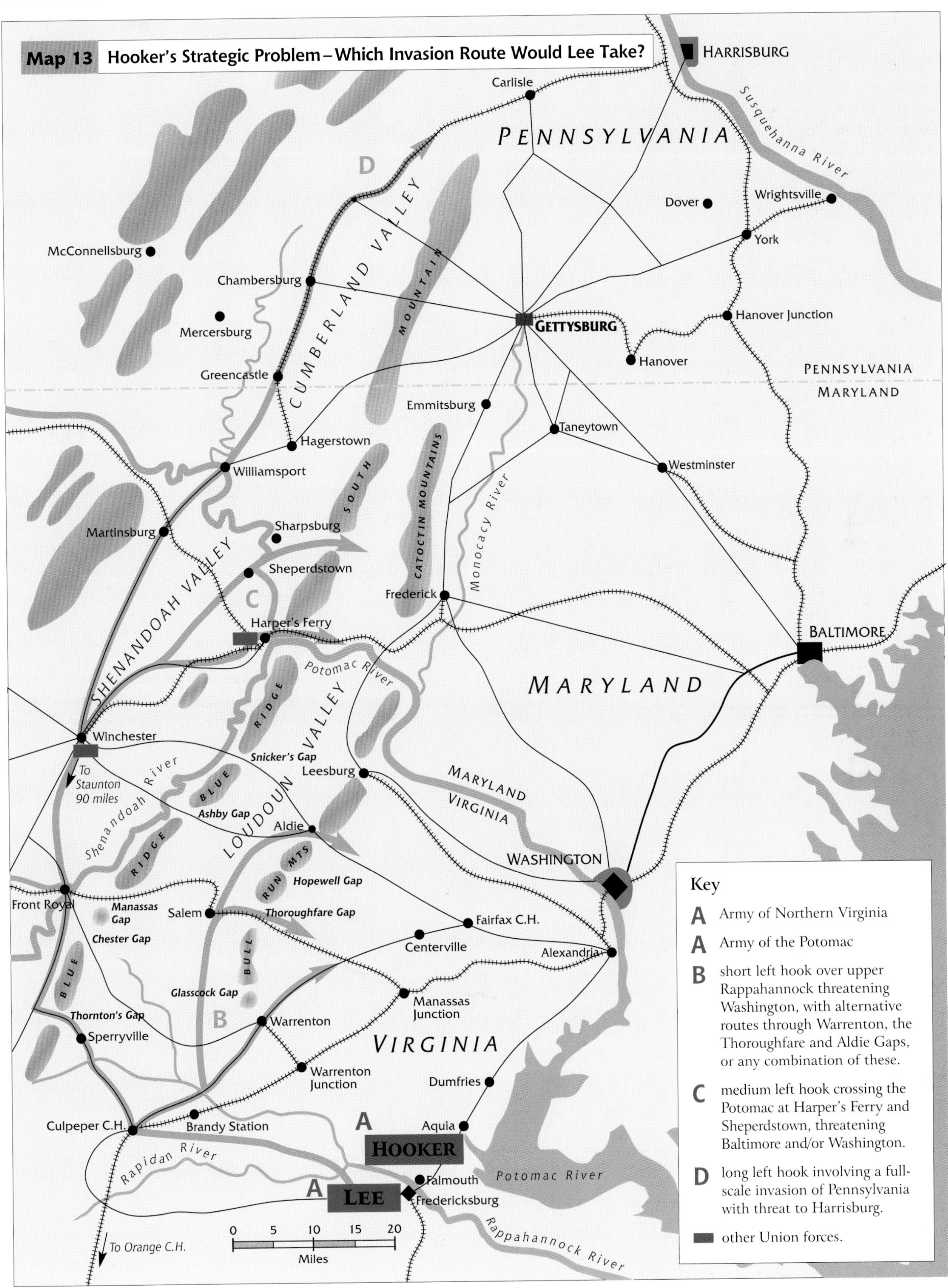
Map 13 Hooker's Strategic Problem–Which Invasion Route Would Lee Take?
HARRISBURG
Carlisle
PENNSYLVANIA
Susquehanna River
D
CUMBERLAND VALLEY
MOUNTAIN
Wrightsville
Dover
York
McConnellsburg
Chambersburg
Mercersburg
Hanover Junction
GETTYSBURG
Hanover
Greencastle
PENNSYLVANIA
MARYLAND
Emmitsburg
Taneytown
Hagerstown
Williamsport
Westminster
SOUTH
CATOCTIN MOUNTAINS
Monocacy River
Martinsburg
Sharpsburg
Sheperdstown
SHENANDOAH VALLEY
C
Frederick
Harper's Ferry
BALTIMORE
Potomac River
MARYLAND
RIDGE
LOUDOUN VALLEY
Winchester
Snicker's Gap
To Staunton 90 miles
Shenandoah River
Leesburg
BLUE
MARYLAND
VIRGINIA
Ashby Gap
Aldie
RIDGE
RUN MTS
WASHINGTON
Hopewell Gap
Front Royal
Manassas Gap
Salem
Thoroughfare Gap
Fairfax C.H.
Chester Gap
Centerville
Alexandria
BULL
BLUE
Glasscock Gap
Manassas Junction
Thornton's Gap
B
Warrenton
Sperryville
VIRGINIA
Warrenton Junction
Dumfries
Culpeper C.H.
Brandy Station
A
Aquia
HOOKER
Rapidan River
Falmouth
Potomac River
A
LEE
Fredericksburg
0 5 10 15 20
Miles
To Orange C.H.
Rappahannock River
Key
A Army of Northern Virginia
A Army of the Potomac
B short left hook over upper Rappahannock threatening Washington, with alternative routes through Warrenton, the Thoroughfare and Aldie Gaps, or any combination of these.
C medium left hook crossing the Potomac at Harper's Ferry and Sheperdstown, threatening Baltimore and/or Washington.
D long left hook involving a full-scale invasion of Pennsylvania with threat to Harrisburg.
other Union forces.

Initially Hill's Corps would fix the Yankees opposite Fredericksburg and Longstreet would do the same at Culpeper, but both would eventually follow Ewell north, with Hill being the last to leave. The responsibility for keeping Hooker in the dark rested with Stuart and his five brigades of horsemen at Culpeper. The initial phase, as far as Lee was concerned, was getting his army north of the Potomac before his enemy could react to stop him.

June 3 saw the first move of the Gettysburg campaign when McLaws' Division (Longstreet's Corps) broke camp and began its march to Culpeper. At the same time Ewell's Corps was given two days' rations and told to be ready to march at short notice. Hill's Corps remained in its camps. By June 5 five of Lee's nine divisions were strung out over 30 miles between Culpeper (Hood) and just south of Chancellorsville (Early and Johnson). At that moment a halt was called, as there had been a reaction from Hooker at Falmouth. In a letter to President Davis dated June 7 Lee explained what had happened:

> On the afternoon of Friday, the 5th instant, the enemy made open preparations [building a pontoon bridge] to cross the Rappahannock at the old position at the mouth of Deep Run. After driving back our sharpshooters, under a furious cannonade from their batteries, by a force of skirmishers, they crossed a small body of troops, and occupied the bank of the river. It was so devoid of concealment, that I supposed the intention was to ascertain what forces occupied the position of Fredericksburg, or to fix our attention upon that place while they should accomplish some other object. I thought it prudent to send that night to Gen. Ewell to halt his march until I could see what the next day might develop, and placed A. P. Hill's corps in position to meet any attack that might be made the next morning.
>
> After watching the enemy's operations Saturday (6th), and being unable to discover more troops than could be attended to by A. P. Hill, and no advance having been made by them, I sent forward to Gen. Ewell to resume his march and left Fredericksburg myself in the evening. My conclusion was that the enemy had discovered the withdrawal of our troops from Fredericksburg, and wished to detain us there while he made corresponding changes.

Union activity

It had proved impossible to prevent Hooker being aware that many of the Rebels were moving westward toward his right. On June 4 Colonel Sharpe reported, "There is a considerable movement of the enemy. Their camps are disappearing at some points." Hooker was also aware of the Rebel cavalry massing at Culpeper and suspected this might be in preparation for another of Stuart's strategic raids behind Union lines. At 3:00 p.m. on June 5 Halleck, in Washington, telegraphed Hooker with information regarding the threat posed by Stuart: "Prisoners and deserters brought in here state that Stuart is preparing a column of from 15,000 to 20,000 men, cavalry and artillery for a raid. They say it will be ready in two or three days." Meanwhile on the same day Hooker had two pontoon bridges thrown across the Rappahannock and ordered a division of Sedgwick's VI Corps over the river the next day to make a reconnaissance in force. This operation was what caused Lee to halt Ewell's march.

A pontoon bridge with Union artillery crossing.

Marching Orders for a Union Detachment

The following order, dated June 7, from the Assistant Adjutant General at Hooker's headquarters, for 600 men (in the event two companies of 2nd and 7th Wisconsin) to be detached from I Corps to join the cavalry for the operation that led to the Battle at Brandy Station, shows the considerable detail that staff at headquarters went to in sending a minor movement order to a corps commander.

It is desired that the command selected should be well disciplined and drilled, and capable of performing rapid marches, and that the officers should be drawn from those noted for energy and efficiency. You will please report the name of the officer you may designate to command the detachment . . . so that its effective fighting force may not be less than that indicated above.

You will please instruct the commander of the expedition to select such a route as will prevent the enemy on the opposite side of the river from observing his movement, and to take into custody all citizens he may meet on the way, to prevent them from informing against us.

Hooker hoped to take advantage of Lee's dividing his force and to strike over the river at Lee's right, thus threatening a direct advance on Richmond which lay only 60 miles to the south. The same day he telegraphed President Lincoln for authority to proceed, setting out the intelligence he had received and his conclusions. His assessment of his enemy's intentions in this letter was remarkably accurate.

> [the purpose of Lee's movement is] to enable the enemy to move up the river with a view to the execution similar to that of Lee's last year [his Maryland campaign]. He must either have in mind to cross the Upper Potomac, or throw his army between mine and Washington . . . To accomplish either he must have been greatly reinforced . . . from Charleston.
>
> Under instructions from [Halleck] dated 31 January, I am instructed to keep "in view always the importance of covering Washington and Harper's Ferry, either directly or by so operating as to be able to punish any force of the enemy sent against them." In the event the enemy should move, as I almost anticipate he will, the head of his column will probably be headed toward the Potomac, via Gordonsville [25 miles south of Culpeper] or Culpeper, while the rear will rest at Fredericksburg.
>
> After having given the subject my best reflection, I am of the opinion that it is my duty to pitch into his rear, although the head of his column may reach Warrenton before I can return. Will it be within the spirit of my instructions to do so?

The response from Washington was immediate and negative from both the President and Halleck. Lincoln's major concern was his capital and he feared Lee might be deliberately enticing Hooker to attack the strongly entrenched position at Fredericksburg while the main force came north of the river elsewhere. If Hooker did attack as he proposed, Lincoln considered that he might become "entangled upon the river, like an ox jumped half over a fence and liable to be torn by dogs both front and rear, without a chance to gore one way or kick the other." Halleck put it in more military terms but agreed it would be extremely unwise for Hooker to attack at Fredericksburg, instead suggesting he attack Lee's "moveable column" first. By this time Hooker had received a report from Major-General Sedgwick, some of whose troops were by now over the river, that he could make no progress without bringing on a major battle. He was told to keep one division (Howe's) on the south bank. Hooker's plan had been firmly vetoed – little did he know only one Rebel corps opposed him.

On June 6 Hooker turned his attention to his right flank and the Rebel cavalry threat. He reported his intentions to Halleck as follows:

> As the accumulation of the heavy rebel cavalry force at Culpeper may mean mischief, I am determined if practicable to break it up in its incipiency. I shall send all my cavalry against them stiffened by about 3,000 infantry. It will require until the morning of the 9th to gain [reach] their position, and at daylight on that day it is my intention to attack them in their camps.

Hooker's orders to Pleasonton were to "cross the Rappahannock at Beverley and Kelly's Fords, and march directly on Culpeper . . . to disperse and destroy the rebel force assembled in the vicinity of Culpeper, and to destroy his trains and supplies of all descriptions."

For his task Pleasonton had about 7,900 horsemen and 3,000 infantry under command, but it seems Hooker lacked confidence in his cavalry commander's tactical skills, as he instructed Pleasonton to keep the infantry together, "as in that condition it would afford you a moving *point d'appui* to rally on at all times, which no cavalry force can be able to shake."

Confederate activities

Meanwhile Stuart, with almost 10,000 horsemen and six batteries of horse artillery, was preparing for a grand review of his division to be held on June 5 at Brandy Station. The evening before, numerous civilian guests arrived from nearby counties and on special trains from Richmond to attend a gala ball. The review was a spectacular affair (see box, page 296) but Lee, who was to have been the guest of honor, was still at Fredericksburg, keenly watching the preparations for the advance across the river of Sedgwick's Division.

On June 7 Lee's five divisions (Hood, McLaws, Early, Johnson and Rodes) continued to move toward the area of Culpeper and were all in the vicinity by nightfall. Pickett's Division was summoned from Hanover Junction (35 miles to the south) and Hill's Corps remained at Fredericksburg. On the same day Lee issued orders to the two cavalry brigades not under Stuart's command. Brigadier-General "Grumble" Jones was to lead Ewell's Corps' advance up the Shenandoah and in preparation for this was given a warning order to concentrate near Strasburg or Front Royal by June 10, "with a view to cooperate with a force of infantry." He

Stuart's Review of His Cavalry, June 5, 1863

The best description of this elaborate review is contained in Edward G. Longacre's *The Cavalry at Gettysburg*, from which this extract is taken:

> Beginning at 10:00 a.m., a two-mile-long column of cavalrymen and horse artillerists marched in review across a wide, level plain. As did each of his officers, Stuart, at the point of the column, sported his best attire, including a new slouch hat, cocked at a rakish tilt, a black ostrich plume jutting from the brim. Behind him came his staff, trailed by sixteen cannon and four [five] brigades of horsemen, a guidon rippling in the van of each regiment. As the procession moved forward, damsels left the audience to scatter flowers across its path while, on the sidelines, three bands thumped and tootled away. The effect was imposing in the extreme – especially to the participants . . .
>
> After the march-past, Stuart called for maneuvers by regiments and brigades, which drew forth even louder exclamations of praise. To cap his spectacle, he presided over a sham battle, his cannon firing blank rounds from half a dozen positions, and his horsemen thundering past the guns, raised sabers jutting toward an invisible foe. The effect, concluded one horse artilleryman, was "inspiring enough to make even an old woman feel fightish."

was also told to obtain information on the enemy at Winchester, Charlestown and Berryville and to "keep your horses fresh . . . and have your whole command prepared for active service." Imboden's Brigade, which was making a nuisance of itself in West Virginia, was told to stir up trouble in Hampshire County as soon as possible, to keep Lee informed and, of particular importance, to "obtain for the army all the cattle you can . . . [and] collect recruits for your brigade, both cavalry and infantry."

The cavalry clash at Brandy Station, June 9 (Map 14)

Stuart's plan for June 9, which involved a very early start to cross the Rappahannock and screen the northward march of the infantry, was shattered by an attack across the Beverley Ford by the right wing of the Union cavalry under Brigadier-General John Buford at about 4:30 a.m. Pleasonton had split his force into two wings: the right under Buford, which consisted of his own division and that of Brigadier-General Wesley Merritt's Reserve Brigade (temporarily commanded by Colonel Charles Whiting; and the left under Brigadier-General David Gregg, composed of Colonel Alfred Duffie's 2nd Division and Gregg's own 3rd Division. Each wing had 1,500 infantry under command. During the night of June 8 Pleasonton's force moved into position on the east bank of the river, Buford's wing at Beverley Ford and Gregg's near Kelly's Ford some 6 miles to the southeast. Their orders were to advance simultaneously at first light, with Buford heading for Culpeper, Gregg joining him at Brandy Station and Duffie making for Stevensburg to act as flank guard.

On the left things got off to a bad start with Duffie getting lost and not crossing Kelly's Ford until 6:00 a.m., thus delaying Gregg's crossing for three hours. It was better in the north where the right wing, headed by Colonel Benjamin "Grimes" Davis's Brigade, splashed across the ford under cover of a mist, to the astonishment of the 6th Virginia Cavalry pickets, who fired only a few scattered shots before retiring in haste. Rebels and Yankees had been mutually surprised. Buford pressed forward and Stuart, on Fleetwood Hill, sent couriers galloping in all directions to summon reinforcements to support Jones. Meanwhile a furious series of charges and countercharges took place around the St. James's Church road junction, nearly costing the Confederates a battery of guns, but by 10:00 a.m. Buford faced a strong Rebel line and something of an exhausted stalemate had developed.

However, by noon Gregg, after performing a wide left-hook maneuver, had reached Brandy Station and turned to attack Stuart's rear at St. James's Church, his leading brigade commanded by Colonel Sir Percy Wyndham. Lieutenant Frank Robertson on Stuart's staff later stated, "The only time in my fourteen months service with Gen. Stuart that he seemed rattled was when Frank Deane, one of his couriers, dashed up and told him the Yankees were at Brandy Station." Stuart initially refused to believe it and was in the process of sending an officer to check when a second courier arrived shouting, "General the Yankees are at Brandy!" At first only a solitary 6-pounder howitzer that had returned for ammunition on Fleetwood Hill could be found to respond to this crisis and was brought into action by Major Henry McClellan, who was on his own at Stuart's headquarters. However, Stuart, who was at the front near St. James's Church, made use of his interior lines and Buford's temporary disorganization to switch the 11th Virginia

The Order of Battle for Brandy Station

Union forces
(Major-General Alfred Pleasonton)

1st Division (Brig.-Gen. John Buford)
1st Brigade (Col. Benjamin F. Davis)
2nd Brigade (Col. Thomas C. Devin)
Reserve Brigade (Maj. Charles J. Whiting)
Attached infantry (Brig.-Gen. Adelbert Ames)
86th New York
2nd Massachusetts
33rd Massachusetts
3rd Wisconsin

2nd Division (Col.Alfred N. Duffie)
1st Brigade (Col. Luigi P. Di Cesnola)
3rd Brigade (Col. J. Irvin Gregg)

3rd Division (Brig.-Gen. David M. Gregg)
1st Brigade (Col. Judson Kilpatrick)
2nd Brigade (Col. Sir Percy Wyndham)
Attached infantry (Brig.-Gen. David A. Russell)
2nd Wisconsin (2 companies)
7th Wisconsin
5th New Hampshire
81st Pennsylvania
6th Maine

Confederate forces
(Major-General J. E. B. Stuart)

Hampton's Brigade (Brig.-Gen. Wade Hampton)
Fitzhugh Lee's Brigade (Col. Thomas Munford)
W. F. "Rooney" Lee's Brigade (Col. John R. Chambliss)
Robertson's Brigade (Brig.-Gen. Beverly H. Robertson)
Jones's Brigade (Brig.-Gen.William E. "Grumble" Jones)

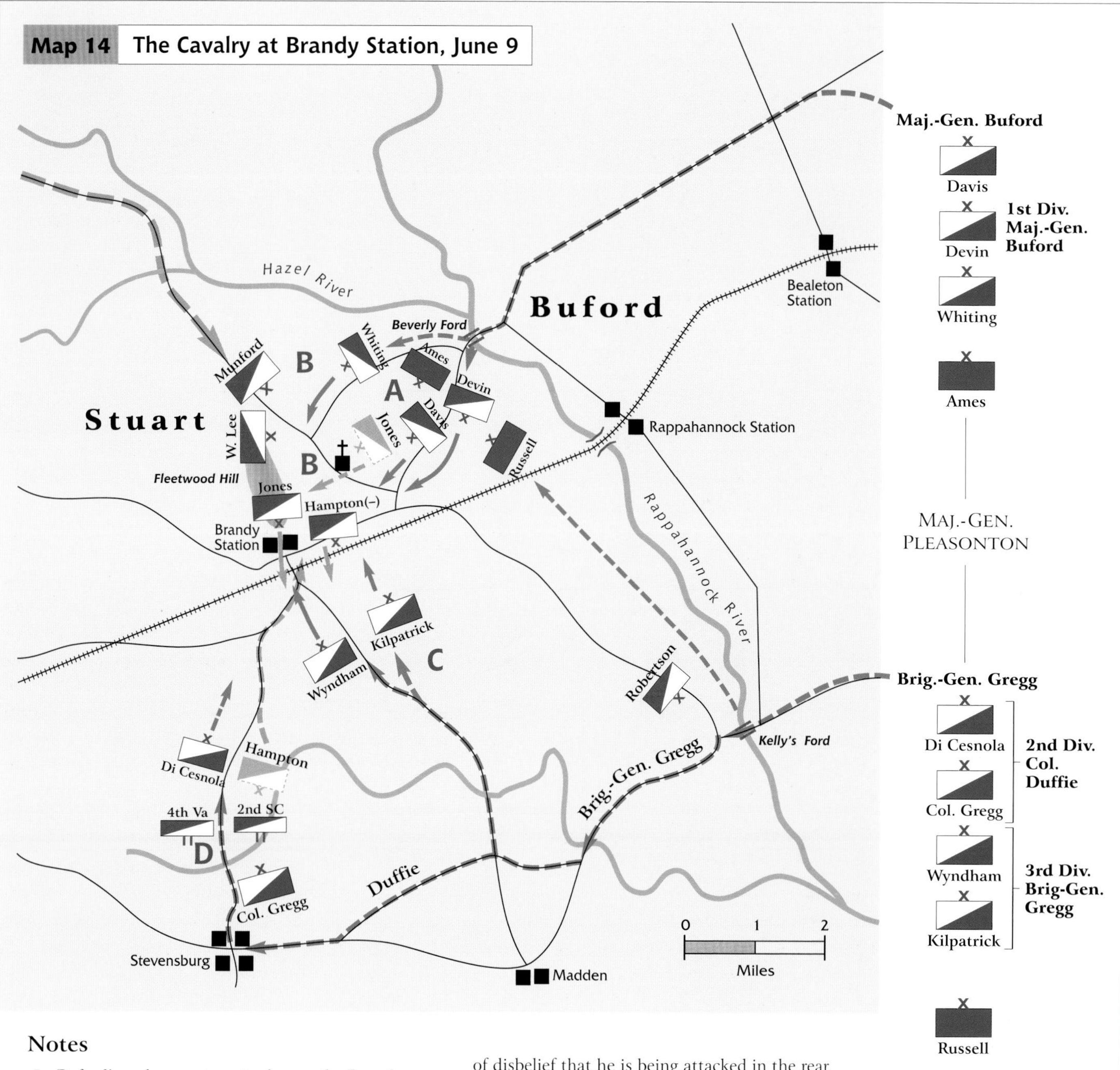

Notes

A Buford's early-morning attack over the Beverly Ford surprises the Rebel pickets. The attack, led by Davis, involves heavy fighting with Jones and W. Lee around, in front of and to the north of St. James's Church. Stuart summons help from Munford (Fitzhugh Lee, the usual brigade commander, was sick) to the northwest and Hampton from the south. Hampton hurries back, leaving two regiments in the south.

B As Stuart falls back toward Fleetwood Hill there is more chaotic and desperate fighting as reinforcements from both sides are committed. A series of charges and counter-charges takes place, with much clashing of sabers and banging of revolvers. Eventually Buford retires to regroup.

C After a delayed start behind Duffie, Brig.-Gen. Gregg's column, led by Wyndham, arrives at Brandy Station (bypassing an inexplicably passive Robertson), causing Stuart a moment of disbelief that he is being attacked in the rear. However, with the pressure easing to his front, Stuart is able to switch Jones and Hampton to counter the new threat. More desperate fighting takes place as Kilpatrick joins the battle before Gregg is checked. Buford is unable to launch further attacks, so Stuart is able to avoid being crushed between the two attacking wings. The battle is a tactical draw, but Pleasonton orders a withdrawal back over the Rappahannock as the cavalry fight for Fleetwood Hill is a stalemate and he has heard of approaching Rebel infantry. The battlefield is left in Stuart's possession.

D Duffie's march starts very late and thus delays Gregg coming behind him. Duffie reaches Stevensburg as planned, but is slow in marching to the sound of the guns. He is delayed by Hampton's two regiments and arrives too late to be of much use.

Key

- Union approach route
- Union attacks
- Confederate approach route or line of withdrawal
- Confederate attacks
- Confederate original position
- St. James's Church

Cavalry and 35th Virginia Battalion (White's Comanches) from confronting Buford and rush them to check Wyndham's advance on Fleetwood Hill. Although their counterattack was ragged and piecemeal, it delayed Wyndham's advance for long enough for more Rebel regiments under Wade Hampton to arrive. The battle then developed into a desperate struggle for the high ground of Fleetwood Hill. The fighting was bitter and disjointed. Charge and countercharge followed each other in quick succession, with control and organization on both sides almost totally lost. One New York cavalryman described the chaos: "Then followed an indescribable clashing and slashing, banging and yelling . . . We were so mixed up with the rebels that every man was fighting desperately to maintain the position until assistance could be brought forward." It was one of the most fearsome cavalry melees of the war.

Gregg was finally forced back south across the railroad, where he was joined by Duffie from Stevensburg, but the attack was not renewed. Back at St. James's Church Buford was preparing, somewhat belatedly, to advance again, but before he could do so Gregg had been pushed back. With this threat removed Stuart was able to consolidate his position on Fleetwood Hill facing Buford. There was some further fighting when Buford attacked Stuart's left, but the Rebels held their ground. By late afternoon both sides had had enough and with the approach of Confederate infantry Pleasonton withdrew his troopers and at around 7:00 p.m. recrossed the Rappahannock, before moving to the area of Warrenton Junction. Stuart's losses amounted to about 500 and Pleasonton's 900.

Comments

It had proved impossible for Lee to prevent Hooker from getting a fair inkling that some major operational move was imminent. The scouts and spies from Sharpe's B.M.I. coupled with extensive interrogation of prisoners and deserters had produced a reasonably accurate general intelligence picture. However, the problem of discovering Lee's actual strategic intentions remained. At this early stage of the campaign Hooker considered it likely that a large-scale cavalry raid into Maryland launched on his right flank was about to take place. He also thought this might be a prelude to another invasion of Maryland over the upper Potomac similar to that of 1862. It was a reasonable deduction on the information he had so far.

Hooker's answer to the likelihood of Lee's marching north and west was to attack across the Rappahannock at or near Fredericksburg, thus threatening an advance on Richmond. This would, he hoped, catch Lee off balance with his army strung out and would certainly bring a halt to his move to the northwest – Hooker's preliminary reconnaissance in force on June 5 did exactly that. However, Lincoln and Halleck, far too worried about their capital to authorize such a bold move, quickly overruled this plan.

The battle at Brandy Station was a tactical draw – but with both sides claiming they had the better of it. The Confederates had initially been surprised and, had Gregg's advance not been seriously delayed, Stuart would have in all probability been defeated by simultaneous attacks from front and rear. As it was, he was able to handle the situation with considerable tactical skill, switching forces from one front to another to check the Union attacks, and at the end of the day remained in possession of Fleetwood Hill. Pleasonton withdrew his force from the field and had obviously failed to achieve his objective to "disperse and destroy the rebel force assembled in the vicinity of Culpeper." This was not how he saw it. In a message sent by Hooker to Lincoln the next day he said, "Gen. Pleasonton reports that he had an affair with the rebel cavalry yesterday near Brandy Station, which resulted in crippling him so much that he will have to abandon his contemplated raid into Maryland, which was to have started this morning." A typically exaggerated Pleasonton after-action report, designed to boost his own standing with his military and political masters.

The Brandy Station clash was the largest cavalry action of the war (although some Union infantry was involved), but it produced no strategic results for either side. Lee's march was delayed only by a day and Hooker's plans and intentions were unaffected. However, the battle marked the coming of age of the Union cavalry. They had proved themselves the equal of the Rebels in close-combat fighting, and although they withdrew it was not as a defeated force. A Confederate officer, Major Henry McClellan, was later to say: "It [Brandy Station] made the Federal cavalry. Up to that time confessedly inferior to the southern horsemen, they gained on this day that confidence in themselves and their commanders which enabled them to contest so fiercely the subsequent battle-fields." This was certainly to be borne out at Gettysburg.

It was Stuart's reputation and ego that suffered. He had been caught napping; he had been initially outmaneuvered and, but for good fortune and great gallantry coupled with intense fighting from his hard-pressed horsemen, might well have been defeated. The Southern press had a field day at his expense (see box).

Stuart was not accustomed to having derogatory remarks published about him, and they undoubtedly hurt. Whether or not they influenced him in deciding to make his controversial ride around the Army of the Potomac two weeks later as a way of restoring his prestige as the world's most dashing and successful cavalry leader is debatable, but it is difficult to eradicate the notion that it played some part in his actions.

Brandy Station – Stuart's Bad Press

It has sometimes been suggested by authors that one of the reasons Stuart opted to ride around Meade instead of sticking to Lee's right flank was his desire to regain some of the public esteem that he felt he had lost as a result of the bad press he received after the battle at Brandy Station. The newspapers were uninhibited in their comments, but the insinuation that they influenced Stuart's decisions is probably unjustified as he was not aware of the extent of the press criticisms until after the campaign was under way. The *Richmond Dispatch* stated that Stuart had been ignominiously surprised, almost routed, the latter being avoided only by chance. The *Charleston Mercury* considered he spent too much time "rollicking, frolicking and running after girls" (all of which Stuart enjoyed) instead of attending his duties. It blamed the near defeat at Brandy Station on the after-effects of the partying at Culpepper Court House following Stuart's grand review parade. The *Richmond Examiner* exclaimed:

> this puffed up cavalry of the Army of Northern Virginia has been twice, if not three times, surprised [referring to Kelly's Ford as well as Brandy Station] . . . such repeated accidents can be regarded as nothing but the necessary consequences of negligence and bad management . . . the country pays dearly for the blunders which encourage the enemy to overrun and devastate the land.

And the *Richmond Whig* considered Stuart was lax and overconfident and must redeem himself by renewing combat with the enemy as soon as possible.

Phase II: June 10–June 24 (Maps 15–19)

Union activity

The day after Brandy Station, Hooker reported his assessment of the situation to Lincoln. He was unconvinced by Pleasonton's optimistic opinion that he had forestalled Stuart's likely raid and again proposed taking advantage of Lee's move west to attack south.

> I am not so certain that the raid will be abandoned from this cause. It may delay the departure for a few days. I shall leave the cavalry, which is all I have mounted, where they are near Bealeton, with instructions to resist the passage of the river by enemy forces . . . If it should be the intention [of Lee] to send a heavy column of infantry to accompany the cavalry on the proposed raid, he can leave nothing behind to interpose any serious obstacle to my rapid advance on Richmond . . . I do not hesitate to say that I should adopt this course as being the most speedy and certain mode of giving the rebellion a mortal blow.

That night (June 10) the President again forbade any such move with the words: "I think Lee's army, and not Richmond, is your sure objective point . . . follow his flank . . . shortening your lines while he lengthens his. Fight him too when opportunity offers. If he stays where he his, fret him and fret him."

Also on June 10 the Union War Department announced the creation of a new department, the Department of the Susquehanna, commanded by Major-General Darius Couch (recently resigned from III Corps), to contain Union troops in eastern and central Pennsylvania – not under Hooker's control.

Confederate activity

On June 10 Lee ordered Ewell to begin his march to the Shenandoah Valley. The corps trudged through the Chester Gap two days later to join up with Jenkins' mounted brigade at Front Royal – both heading for Winchester. The advance proper had begun, although Longstreet's Corps, now complete with the arrival of Pickett on June 11, waited at Culpeper, while Hill remained in the entrenchments above Fredericksburg. The Army of Northern Virginia had begun to spread out and Stuart's screening mission to keep prying enemy eyes away from what was happening became critical. From June 10–15 Stuart threw out a strong line of outposts stretching from Culpeper to the Blue Ridge, and his aggressive patroling kept Pleasonton in a state of uncertainty.

On June 12 Ewell's men were on the road by 4:30 a.m. with Rodes' Division in the lead, followed by Johnson and then Early. The citizens of Front Royal were delighted to see them and the column easily splashed across the knee-deep water of the Shenandoah before camping for the night near the river. Ewell was approaching Winchester, where Milroy had some 5,000 men and Colonel Andrew McReynolds commanded a detachment of 1,800 at Berryville, 10 miles to the east. Ewell planned to use Johnson's and Early's Divisions (about 12,000 men) to take Winchester while Rodes (8,000) and Jenkins (1,200) took on Berryville. However, the next day Jenkins messed up Rodes' plan to surprise Berryville and, although Rodes tried to cut off the Yankees' retreat, by the time the Rebel yell was heard as the infantry charged the defenders had gone to rejoin Milroy. Also on June 13 both Johnson and Early had preliminary skirmishes south of Winchester and by nightfall had driven the Yankees back to the southern outskirts of the town. That day saw little movement by Longstreet's Corps. At Fredericksburg Hill noticed signs that Hooker was starting to withdraw from the river. The next day the Second Battle of Winchester (the first had been won by Stonewall Jackson in May 1862) was fought, with Longstreet still in camp around Culpeper and Hill beginning his long march west to the Shenandoah, while Jenkins crossed the Potomac at Williamsport chasing a Union supply train – 150 miles separated the leading elements of the Army of Northern Virginia from its rearguard.

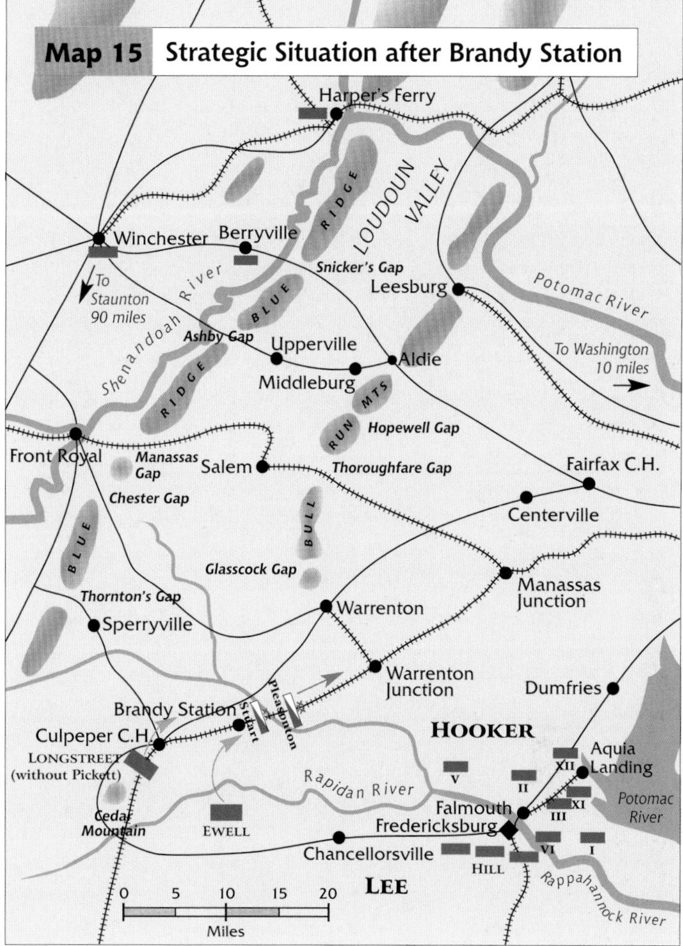

Notes

- Stuart has held his ground at Brandy Station and Pleasonton has withdrawn toward Warrenton Junction. Both Longstreet (less Pickett's Division, which has yet to rejoin from the south) and Ewell's Corps have arrived in the vicinity of Culpeper Court House, while Hill remains at Fredericksburg to block the route to Richmond and confuse Hooker as to Lee's intentions.
- Hooker remains in the Falmouth area with one division of VI Corps (Howe's 2nd Division) south of the Rappahannock. He is convinced Lee is shifting toward his right and that Stuart has planned a large-scale raid toward Washington. His wish to attack in force across the river toward Richmond has been vetoed by President Lincoln – a course of action that would almost certainly have brought Lee's movement to a halt.

Union activity

Because Pleasonton had failed to drive off Stuart at Brandy Station he was unaware that two Confederate corps were assembled in the Culpeper area. His report that "the enemy is in strong cavalry force here. We have had a severe fight" was hardly news to Hooker – it was the reason for Pleasonton's mission in the first place. The degree of uncertainty remaining in Hooker's headquarters is illustrated by the exchange of messages between Major-General Butterfield (Hooker's chief of staff) and Pleasonton. On June 11 Butterfield suggested that Stuart might still be planning a raid. On June 13 Pleasonton reported that Confederate troops had been seen marching through Sperryville, possibly toward the Blue Ridge. In reply Butterfield conjectured that the enemy might be attempting to move up the Bull Run Mountains and come back through the Thoroughfare Gap toward Manassas (option B on Map 13).

Although Hooker was still unsure of Lee's ultimate route or objective, it was clear that the enemy was likely to threaten Washington and his position at Falmouth was no longer suitable for its defense. Forbidden to attack southward, Hooker's only option was to move north in order to keep his army between the capital and Lee. On June 13 he gave orders for that move to begin. He divided his force into two wings, one under Major-General Reynolds consisting of I, III, V and XI Corps to march on Centerville, and the other under his own command composed of II, VI and XII Corps and reserve artillery to head initially for Dumfries. The cavalry were ordered to protect the left flank by sending a brigade each to the Thoroughfare Gap and Warrenton and another to picket the upper Rappahannock.

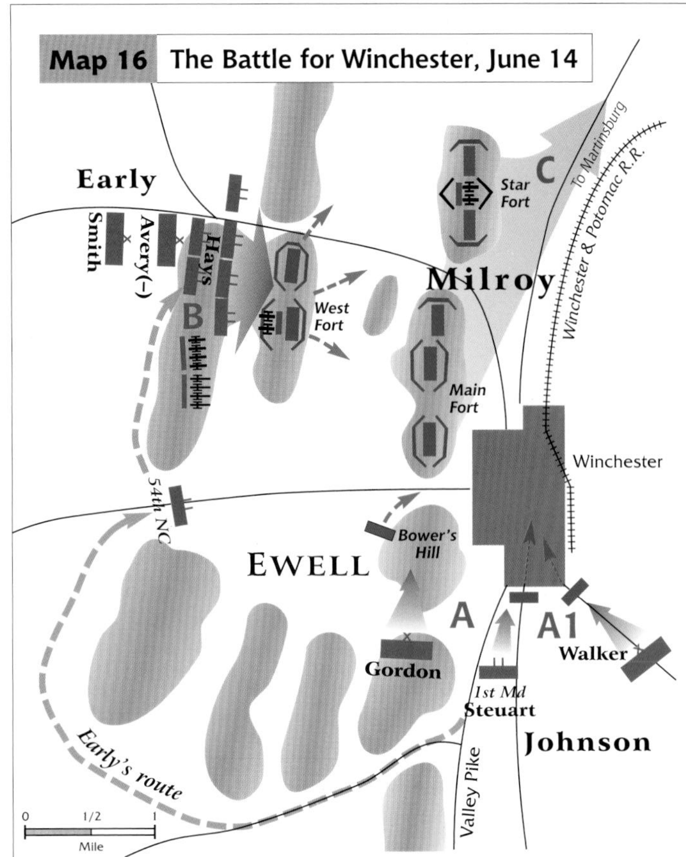

Notes

A Gordon's Brigade takes Bower's Hill and Ewell makes it his H.Q. early on June 14.

A1 Walker makes a noisy demonstration with Gordon on Bower's Hill to distract the Union forces, while Early makes his flank march.

B Early positions his men, unseen by the defenders of West Fort, on a ridge that dominates the Union defenses from the west. A 45-minute surprise bombardment destroys the enemy guns and a spirited charge by Hays's Brigade captures the fort.

C The route taken by Milroy when he withdraws his division during the early hours of June 15.

The battle for Winchester, June 14–15 (Maps 16 and 17)

Control of the Winchester/Berryville/Harper's Ferry garrisons, which belonged to VIII Corps, did not rest with Hooker. These troops were under the Middle Department, commanded by the notoriously political Major-General Robert C. Schenck, based at Baltimore. Schenck's primary role was the protection of the Baltimore and Ohio Railroad. His 2nd Division, under the equally political and extremely unpopular Milroy, was at Winchester, with a brigade at Berryville under McReynolds. There was also a large part of Brigadier-General Benjamin F. Kelley's 1st Division at Harper's Ferry watching the mountain pass through which the Potomac flowed and also the crucial railway bridge. At the end of April Halleck telegraphed Schenck to raise a matter that he had first discussed in January – why did he maintain an isolated post at Winchester? In Halleck's view it added nothing to the close defense of the railroad and was vulnerable to being cut off. In his wire he wrote, "As I have often repeated to you verbally and in writing, that is no place to fight a battle. It is merely an outpost that should not be exposed to an attack in force." It was not an order but strong advice, which Schenck had no difficulty in ignoring. On May 8 an exasperated Halleck instructed Schenck that he should withdraw the Winchester garrison to Harper's Ferry. True to form, Schenck failed to oblige. Not until June 14, the day Ewell's main attack went in, did Halleck threaten to dismiss Schenck with the words, "Unless there is a more prompt obedience of orders, there must be a change of commanders." On the same day Lincoln involved himself by wiring direct to Schenck to "Get General Milroy from Winchester to Harper's Ferry if possible. He will be gobbled up if he remains, if he is not already past salvation." He was indeed well past salvation.

Lincoln also sought Hooker's opinion of what was going on in the valley around Winchester and Martinsburg, and asked if Hooker could assist Milroy, who seemed to be surrounded – although Lee's army appeared considerably spread out: "If the head of Lee's army is at Martinsburg and the tail of it on the Plank road between Fredericksburg and Chancellorsville, the animal must be very slim somewhere. Could you not break him?" Hooker's response late that night showed he knew less about what was happening at Winchester than his President. He even asked:

> Will the President allow me to inquire if it is his opinion that Winchester is surrounded by rebel forces? . . . I do not feel like making a move for an enemy until I am satisfied as to his whereabouts. To proceed to Winchester and have him make an appearance elsewhere, would subject me to ridicule.

To which Lincoln snapped back: "You have nearly all the elements of forming an opinion whether Winchester is surrounded than I have [*sic*] . . . It is quite certain that a considerable force of the enemy is thereabout, and I fear it is an overwhelming one compared with Milroy's."

With the telegraph to Winchester down, Milroy had no way of knowing of the consternation his predicament was causing in

Washington. His defense was based on three forts (West, Main and Star) immediately north of the town (see Map 16), all of which if resolutely defended might prove costly to take. The Confederate's main assault on Winchester and its defenses went in on June 14. After taking Bower's Hill with Gordon's Brigade of Early's Division during the morning, Ewell adopted the summit as his headquarters. From there General Early noticed a ridge less than half a mile to the west of West Fort, which dominated it. Artillery on that ridge could cause chaos among the defenders. Thus a plan of attack evolved. Early would spend most of the afternoon of June 14 moving round to the west, occupy the ridge and bring up his guns to just below the crest, while Johnson's Division distracted the Yankees to the south of the town with constant skirmishing – surprise being a key element of the plan.

Surprise was achieved, despite Milroy's spending the day in a basket hoisted by block and tackle to the top of the flagstaff in Main Fort. Armed with a spyglass, he watched events but failed to spot the well-concealed flank march of Early's Division. One of his staff officers described this extraordinary observation post:

> All day, under a burning sun, did General Milroy keep his position in the lookout, and with a glass anxiously scan the surrounding countryside for signs of the enemy, but none were manifested, and it became generally the settled belief that they had passed on up the Valley to Harper's Ferry . . .

Thus it was something of a shock when, at 5:00 p.m., twenty Rebel guns opened a massive surprise bombardment, completely outgunning the defenders of West Fort. This forty-five-minute barrage was followed by a furious charge of the Louisiana Tigers of Hays's Brigade. The Rebels fought their way through the entanglements and overran the fort. The Yankees had had enough, many throwing down their arms to surrender while large numbers fled via the back of the fort. Meanwhile Early, who had been watching events from Bower's Hill, was struck in the chest by a spent bullet. He was only badly bruised and continued to command, much to the frustration of his surgeon.

During the night Milroy finally decided that evacuation was the only sensible option. Orders were given for a 2:00 a.m. start, but he insisted that all wheeled vehicles, including ambulances and artillery (abandoned guns were to be spiked), were to be left behind to avoid making a noise. In the Confederate camp it was fairly obvious that the Yankees were likely to pull out during the night and Ewell issued orders to cut them off. His plan envisaged Johnson's Division making a night march to cut the Martinsburg Pike about 3 miles north of the town. If necessary Early and Gordon would attack the forts at dawn to drive the Yankees into the ambush – Rodes was not available, as he was already on his way to Martinsburg having failed to catch McReynolds at Berryville. Johnson set off with Williams and Steuart, leaving Walker to follow later after disentangling himself from Winchester. Although Johnson had a good guide who led the column around difficult ground, there was inevitably straggling, confusion and loss of control, and considerable noise. By 4:00 a.m. Johnson had arrived at a railway cutting close to the Martinsburg Road near Stephenson's Depot at the same time as the Union cavalry advance guard, followed by Elliott's infantry brigade.

A furious and chaotic firefight ensued as Elliott gallantly attacked the railway cutting to clear the route for the rest of the marching column. Driven back once, he reorganized and tried again. Steuart was in trouble, but Williams arrived in time to extend and support the Confederate line to the left. A desperate battle developed at the road bridge, in which Private Owens of the 1st Maryland Artillery was later to win a posthumous Medal of Honor. The darkness, smoke and confusion were the cause of the friendly-fire incident when the advance of the 87th Pennsylvania was halted by a deadly volley from the 18th Connecticut. A powerful attack by the Rebel brigade under Walker drove back and scattered Ely's Brigade, and the arrival of McReynolds was too late to stop the rot. The charge of the 13th Pennsylvania Cavalry was decimated by gunfire and McReynolds' attempt to turn the Rebel left came to naught.

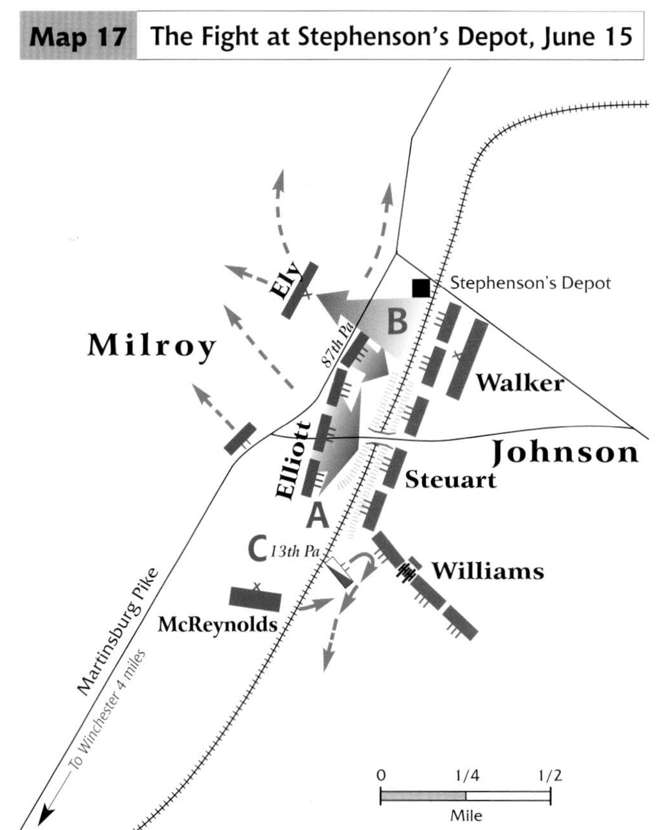

Map 17 The Fight at Stephenson's Depot, June 15

Notes

- Ewell's plan for the 15th was to cut off the Union withdrawal by placing Johnson's Division across the Martinsburg Pike NE of the town and launching an attack at dawn by Early and Gordon's Brigade on the forts.
- Johnson took 13 regiments – Williams' and Walker's Brigades and three regiments of Steuart's.
- The fight took place in the dark and there was a chaotic melee along the railroad as both sides' forces arrived on the scene and were pushed straight into the action.

A Steuart's regiments line railroad cut and are attacked by Elliott – fierce fighting in the dusk ensues.

B Walker arrives in time to drive off Ely's Brigade.

C McReynolds' Brigade is the last to arrive and attempts to outflank the Rebel left. A gallant cavalry charge by the 13th Pa is routed by artillery fire and McReynolds' late move is thwarted.

------> direction of Milroy's flight

Milroy, who had a horse killed under him and injured his hip, abandoned the struggle and scurried away to safety at Harper's Ferry. His command was scattered in all directions, with many surrendering on the spot. Johnson reckoned he personally captured thirty "with his opera glass." Those that got away were later dubbed "Milroy's Weary Boys." Gone were 4,500 men (mostly prisoners escorted to Richmond by the 54th North Carolina), 300 wagons, 300 horses, 200,000 rounds of rifle-musket ammunition, several thousand rifle-muskets, four 20-pounder Parrotts, seventeen 3-inch rifles and two 24-pounder howitzers. Halleck was apoplectic when given the news. He instantly telegraphed Schenck: "Do not give General Milroy any command at Harper's Ferry. We have had enough of that sort of military genius. If you have not already done so, send all your small posts and available troops there. That place must be held." Brigadier-General Daniel Tyler, who had just arrived after evacuating his position at Martinsburg (for which he was later courtmartialed), became the commander.

Confederate activities

After the loss of Winchester, Lee could only assume that Hooker was fully aware of his movement of a large force into the Shenandoah Valley. On June 15 Jenkins' horsemen, followed by Rodes' Division, crossed the Potomac at Sheperdstown, with Jenkins reaching as far north as Greencastle. That same day Lee set Longstreet and Hill in motion for the Shenandoah, the former to enter the valley via Ashby and Snicker's Gaps, the latter through Chester Gap at Front Royal. This meant that Longstreet would initially march west of the Bull Run Mountains up the Loudoun Valley while Hill followed west of the Blue Ridge up the Shenandoah. This would, Lee hoped, help to confuse Hooker over his real intentions. Stuart's cavalry was to screen Longstreet's movement and ensure no Union horsemen penetrated the Gaps to find out what was happening behind them.

On June 16 Stuart adopted a more aggressive posture, moving his main force into the Aldie area, where from June 17 to 21 he would clash with Pleasonton's forces in a series of intense cavalry actions at Aldie (17th), Middleburg (19th) and Upperville (21st); see opposite. Although these actions prevented Pleasonton from entering the Shenandoah Valley, it was no easy task. Stuart's troopers were pushed back to the Blue Ridge Gaps before the Yankee cavalry withdrew to the east. At one stage the situation became so critical that Longstreet diverted infantry into the mountain passes in case Stuart failed to hold. Each time Stuart faced Union horsemen he was finding it increasingly difficult to best them.

On June 17 Lee gave instructions to Ewell:

> I think the reports you have on the forces at Harper's Ferry must be exaggerated. I wish you to move Rodes' division on as far as Hagerstown and operate in the enemy's country according to the plan proposed. Give out that your movement is for the purpose of enveloping Harper's Ferry. Take what is necessary for the army and give the citizens of Maryland Confederate money or certificates. Repress marauding. Do not expose yourself. Keep your own scouts.

On the same day he wrote to Longstreet:

> I have heard nothing of the movements of Gen. Hooker either from Gen. Stuart or yourself, and therefore can form no opinion of the best move against him. If a part of our force could have operated east of the [Blue Ridge] mountains, it would have served more to confuse him, but as you have turned off into the valley and I understand all the trains have taken the same route, I hope it is for the best . . . You had better, therefore, push on, relieve Ewell's division as soon as you can and let him advance into Maryland . . . I shall go from here [Markham on Manassas Gap railroad] to the Valley.

With his army stretched out over 100 miles, Lee was showing concern over the whereabouts of the Union Army. Nevertheless, by June 20 Lee could be content that his plan appeared to be working well. Ewell's Corps, with the exception of Early, was over the Potomac; Longstreet had entered the Shenandoah Valley via the Ashby and Snicker's Gaps and was approaching that river; while Hill's leading division (Anderson) was a few miles southeast of Winchester with Pender bringing up the rear at Chester Gap. That day he wrote to Imboden to congratulate him on his success in collecting so many cattle and destroying bridges on the Baltimore and Ohio Railroad. On June 22 Lee was confident enough to send Ewell into Pennsylvania to march up the Cumberland Valley and fan out his divisions up toward the Susquehanna, with Stuart's cavalry earmarked to guard Ewell's exposed right flank. The only problem was still a lack of information on Hooker's move north – Stuart had been too preoccupied with defensive screening in the Loudoun Valley to know what was happening further east.

Union activities

Hooker's worries at this stage were threefold. First, he needed reinforcements urgently, or by the end of June, he believed, he would be down to fewer than 90,000 men. This problem was exacerbated by his generals reporting, erroneously, that Lee outnumbered him – Hancock reckoned Hill had 20,000–30,000 men, while Pleasonton reported that Ewell and Longstreet had 70,000 between them, plus Stuart's 10,000 cavalry. Halleck was unsympathetic. Second, Hooker felt "the necessity of having one commander for all of the troops whose operations can have an influence on those of Lee's army." He wanted control over the Military Department of Washington (Major-General Heintzelman) and the Middle Department (Major-General Schenck). Halleck sidestepped the issue. Third, he wanted freedom from Halleck's uncooperative interference. In particular, he was in acrimonious communication with Halleck over the fate of Harper's Ferry. On June 16 he telegraphed the President, "You have long been aware, Mr. President, that I have not enjoyed the confidence of the major-general commanding the army, and I can assure you so long as this continues we may look in vain for success . . . " Hooker had crossed the line. Lincoln's respone put him in no doubt of his place: "I now place you in strict military relation to Gen. Halleck, of a commander of one of the armies, to the General-in-Chief of all armies . . . I shall direct him to give you orders, and you to obey them."

Hooker knew of the loss of Winchester and Ewell's thrust north of the Potomac, but he was still uncertain of the destination of both Longstreet and Hill. Sergeant Milton Cline, the B.M.I. scout, had got into and out of the Loudoun Valley during the cavalry fighting there and confirmed the presence of these two corps. But would they follow Ewell over the Potomac or await his return and turn east toward Washington? Hooker had to know which before he took his army north of the river.

By June 17 the Army of the Potomac was grouped around and to the north of Centerville. There the great majority remained as Pleasonton clashed with Stuart in the Loudoun Valley. His efforts, however, gave Hooker no firm intelligence.

Confederate and Union activities in the Loudoun Valley

On June 16 Hooker told his President, "You may depend on it we can never discover the whereabouts of the enemy, or divine his intentions, so long as he fills the country with a cloud of cavalry. We must break through that to find him." Halleck considered "The information sent here by General Pleasonton is very unsatisfactory," and went so far as to communicate directly with Pleasonton on the matter. His words are worth repeating:

> [General Hooker] depends upon you with your cavalry force to give him information of where the enemy is, his force and his movements . . . Drive in pickets, if necessary, and get us information. It is better that we should lose men than to be without knowledge of the enemy, as we now seem to be.

In obedience to these instructions Pleasonton advanced from Manassas on June 17. He sent one regiment of fewer than 300 men (1st Rhode Island Cavalry), under the recently demoted Colonel Duffie, via the Thoroughfare Gap to Middleburg and took a division (D. Gregg) to Aldie. Just west of Aldie the road branched, with one road leading to Ashby and the other to Snicker's Gaps. Sitting astride these roads was Munford's (Fitzhugh Lee's) Brigade of Virginian horsemen. Leading the Union advance was Judson Kilpatrick, who proceeded to launch a series of piecemeal charges that led to some fierce, close-quarter saber and revolver fighting. At one stage Munford was on the point of withdrawing when two more of his regiments arrived, so at the end of the day he still blocked these crucial roads. One of Kilpatrick's forlorn-hope attacks involved the 4th New York, whose commander, Colonel Di Cesnola, was under arrest. On hearing his regiment was to charge, Di Cesnola, under provost escort, rode up to Kilpatrick to beg permission to lead the attack, with or without side arms (being under arrest he had neither saber nor pistol). Kilpatrick handed Di Cesnola his own saber, remarking, "Colonel, you are a brave man; you are released from arrest." As he handed over the sword he added, "Bring it back bloody." The attack made no headway, and Di Cesnola was captured and spent ten months in Libby Prison in Richmond – and presumably Kilpatrick lost his sword. Kilpatrick had lost some 300 men, and Munford in his report claimed "never to have seen as many Yankees killed in the same space of ground in any fight." Although the Confederates withdrew, their losses amounted to only about 120 – no Union troopers reached the Gaps.

On the basis of this action, Pleasonton boastfully and erroneously declared that no Confederate infantry worth mentioning were east of the Blue Ridge – in ignorance of the fact that Longstreet's Corps was then encamped in Stuart's rear. Meanwhile, to the south, the solitary 1st Rhode Island Cavalry succeeded in getting itself surrounded at Middleburg on the evening of June 17. After a stubborn resistance that lasted until the early hours of the next day, most of the survivors surrendered.

June 18 began well for Stuart. Major John Mosby had been operating behind enemy lines and the previous day had captured Major William R. Sterling of Hooker's staff and Captain Benjamin Fisher, his chief signals officer. They were carrying dispatches to Pleasonton that revealed the location of two Union infantry corps, orders for Pleasonton to penetrate the Blue Ridge Gaps and the deployment of Union infantry in support of the cavalry. In accordance with his instructions, Pleasonton continued his frontal skirmishing westward toward the Ashby and Snicker's Gaps on June 18, 19 and 20. On June 19 there was another action at Middleburg on the Ashby Gap road, where Stuart repelled a series of frontal attacks, mostly with dismounted troops behind stone walls supported by guns, in which a squadron of the 10th New York lost all but five of its men. Eventually Stuart pulled back to the next ridge and the fighting ceased for the day. The following day Pleasonton, reinforced by an infantry division, tried again to break through Stuart's screen, this time at Upperville, only 4 miles from the Ashby Gap. The result was another day of furious fighting, much of it at close quarters. By evening Stuart had been pushed back to the Gap, which was securely held with the help of some of Longstreet's infantry. Pleasonton pulled his troopers back to Aldie to regroup.

These Loudoun Valley clashes had cost the Confederates over 500 men and the Union forces nearly 900, while both sides had exhausted men and horses. A trooper of the 6th Pennsylvania thought that "all the fighting since the battle of Chancellorsville has been done by cavalry . . . and if they keep this up much longer that branch will be almost extinct."

Hooker was now fully aware that Lee's infantry was moving through the Shenandoah Valley but was still uncertain of their intentions. Hooker was getting information from Brigadier-General Dan Tyler, commanding at Harper's Ferry. Late on June 22 Tyler reported the information he had received from the signal post on Maryland Heights:

> The enemy has been crossing to the Maryland side [at Sharpsburg] all day, and are yet bringing over artillery and baggage wagons. Lieutenant Martindale says that many of the camps are gone that were here yesterday. We counted two hundred wagons on the road moving toward Boonsborough . . . I think there are now 30,000 or 40,000 troops in and around Sharpsburg.

Confirmation of what Hooker needed to know was supplied on June 24, not by his cavalry, but by the B.M.I., who informed him that the enemy was crossing the Potomac in force. John Babcock reported that Lee's army was at Sheperdstown and that "Longstreet and A. P. Hill are crossing rapidly." Hooker issued marching orders.

Confederate activity

On June 22 and 23 an exchange of orders, ideas and messages occurred between Lee, Longstreet and Stuart. Additionally, Lee reported to President Davis on the situation as he saw it, coupled with a repeated request for reinforcements. The messages to his generals resulted in one of the most controversial decisions of the campaign being made by Lee's cavalry commander, Stuart (discussed in detail on page 314). The messages, with crucial parts in bold, were:

- June 22, Lee to Stuart via Longstreet, written at Berryville.

> I judge the efforts of the enemy yesterday [at Upperville] were to arrest our progress and ascertain our whereabouts. Perhaps he is satisfied. **Do you know where he is and what he is doing? I fear he will steal a march on us**

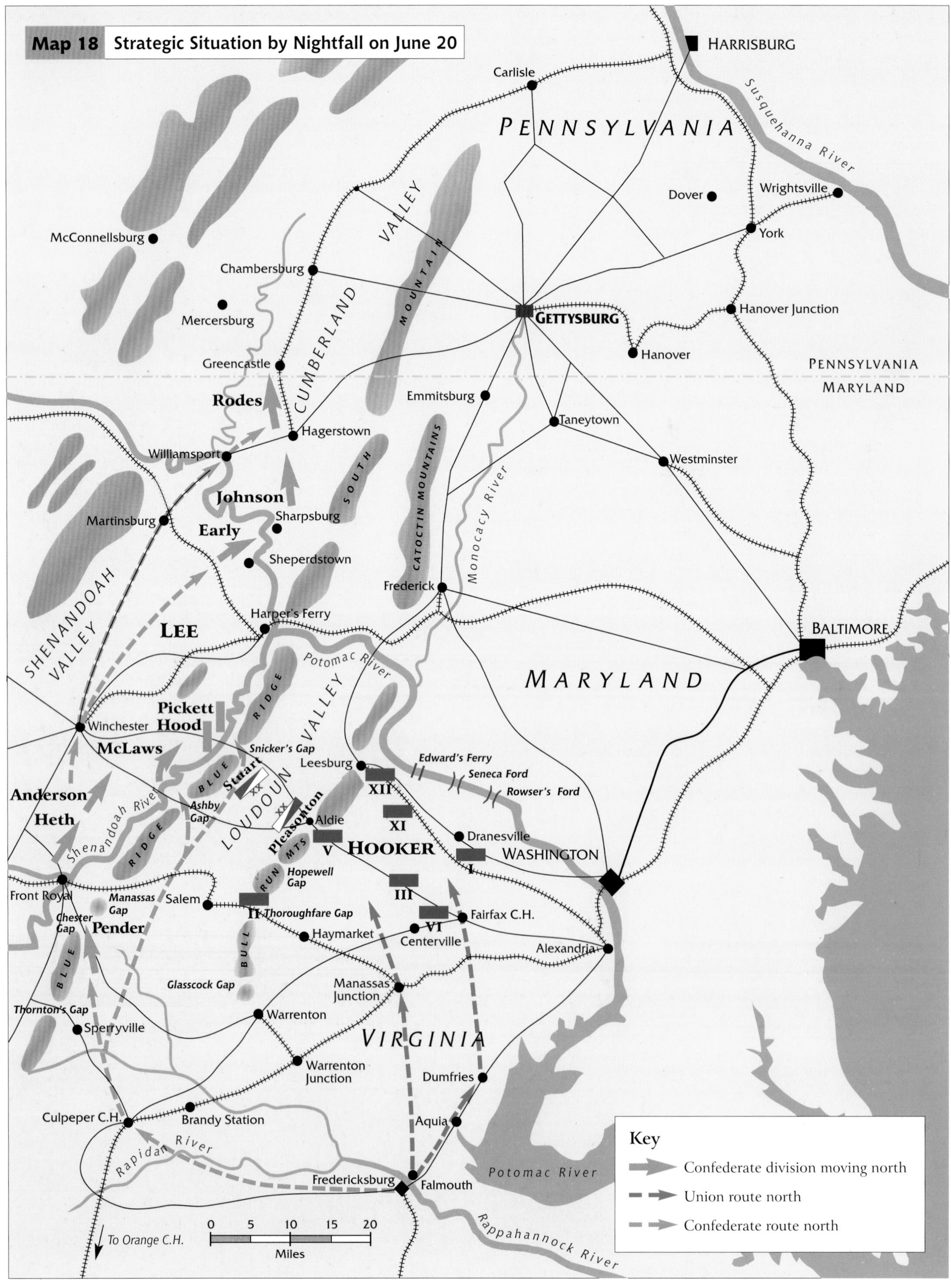
Map 18 Strategic Situation by Nightfall on June 20
HARRISBURG
Carlisle
PENNSYLVANIA
Susquehanna River
Wrightsville
Dover
York
McConnellsburg
Chambersburg
CUMBERLAND VALLEY
MOUNTAIN
Mercersburg
GETTYSBURG
Hanover Junction
Hanover
Greencastle
PENNSYLVANIA
MARYLAND
Emmitsburg
Rodes
Hagerstown
Taneytown
Williamsport
Westminster
SOUTH
CATOCTIN MOUNTAINS
Monocacy River
Johnson
Sharpsburg
Martinsburg
Early
Sheperdstown
SHENANDOAH VALLEY
Frederick
Harper's Ferry
LEE
BALTIMORE
Potomac River
MARYLAND
RIDGE
Pickett
Hood
Winchester
LOUDOUN VALLEY
McLaws
Snicker's Gap
Leesburg
Edward's Ferry
Seneca Ford
Rowser's Ford
XII
BLUE
Stuart
Anderson
Ashby Gap
Heth
Shenandoah River
Pleasonton
Aldie
XI
RIDGE
Dranesville
HOOKER
WASHINGTON
MTS
V
I
RUN
Hopewell Gap
III
Front Royal
Manassas Gap
Salem
II
Thoroughfare Gap
Fairfax C.H.
Chester Gap
Pender
VI
Haymarket
Centerville
Alexandria
BULL
BLUE
Glasscock Gap
Manassas Junction
Thornton's Gap
Warrenton
Sperryville
VIRGINIA
Warrenton Junction
Dumfries
Culpeper C.H.
Brandy Station
Aquia
Rapidan River
Potomac River
Fredericksburg
Falmouth
Rappahannock River
To Orange C.H.
0 5 10 15 20
Miles
Key
Confederate division moving north
Union route north
Confederate route north

and get across the Potomac before we are aware. If you find he is moving northward and that two brigades can guard the Blue Ridge and take care of your rear you can **move with the other three into Maryland, and take position on General Ewell's flank, keep him informed of the enemy's position and collect all the supplies you can for the use of the army . . .**

- June 22, Longstreet to Stuart, timed 7:45 p.m. Lee's letter to Longstreet, which accompanied the one he was to forward to Stuart, is lost. However, Longstreet makes reference to its contents and refers to route possibilities for Stuart not mentioned in Lee's letter to Stuart himself. Longstreet wrote:

General Lee has enclosed this letter for you, to be forwarded to you, provided you can be spared from my front, and provided I think you can move across the Potomac without disclosing our plans. **He speaks of your leaving via Hopewell Gap and passing by the rear of the enemy. If you can get through by that route, I think it will be less likely to indicate what our plans are, than if you should cross by passing to our rear . . .**

N.B. – I think that your passage of the Potomac by our rear, will in a measure disclose our plans. You had better not leave us, therefore, unless you can take the proposed route in rear of the enemy.

- June 22, Lee to Ewell. In addition to the letter authorizing Ewell to march for the Susquehanna to threaten Harrisburg, the state capital of Pennsylvania, Lee wrote a second time to Ewell, stating:

I also directed General Stuart, should the enemy have so far retired from his front as to permit of the departure of a portion of the cavalry, to march with three brigades across the Potomac, **and place himself on your right and in communication with you, keep you advised of the movements of the enemy, and assist in collecting supplies for the army.** I have not heard from him since. I also directed Imboden, if opportunity offered, to cross the Potomac and perform the same offices on your left . . .

Notes

• As the Confederates went into camp on the night of June 20 some 70 miles separated Rodes near Hagerstown from Pender at the Chester Gap. Stuart was involved in several clashes with the Union cavalry as they tried to penetrate through the Gaps in the Blue Ridge Mountains. With the help of some infantry from Longstreet, Stuart succeeded but, like Pleasonton, he was too preoccupied with fighting to find out what was happening behind the enemy horsemen. Lee had succeeded in getting his army into the valley and was well on his way north. Although he knew Hooker had left Falmouth and also marched north, he was beginning to be concerned over his precise whereabouts.

• Apart from his problems with Halleck, and lack of sufficient reinforcements, Hooker's overriding concern was to discover the intentions of Longstreet's and Hill's Corps. In obedience to his masters in Washington, he had moved his army north so that it was blocking any direct march toward his capital, but he needed to know for certain that all Lee's forces had crossed the Potomac before he did likewise. Meanwhile most of his army waited in their camps. On June 20 a B.M.I. scout provided the information he required – it was time to move.

This proposal of moving round the rear of the enemy army is said to have been put to Lee by Stuart at Berryville on the night of June 21. In his report submitted in August, 1863, Stuart stated:

I submitted to the commanding general the plan of leaving a brigade or so in my present front, and passing through Hopewell, or some other gap in the Bull Run Mountains, attain the enemy's rear, passing between his main body and Washington, and cross into Maryland, joining our army north of the Potomac.

- June 23, Lee to Stuart, timed 5:00 p.m. This crucial message contained Stuart's final instructions.

If General Hooker's army remains inactive, you can leave two brigades to watch him, and withdraw with the others, but should he not appear to be moving northward, I think you had better withdraw this side of the mountains [into the Shenandoah Valley] tomorrow night [June 24], cross at Shepherdstown the following day [June 25] and move over to Frederickstown [Frederick].

You will, however, be able to judge whether you can pass around their army without hindrance, doing them all the damage you can, and cross the river east of the [Blue Ridge] mountains. In either case, after crossing the river, you must move on and feel the right of Ewell's troops, collecting information, provisions, etc.

Give instructions to the commanders of the brigades left behind, to watch the flank and rear of the army, and, (in the event of the enemy leaving their front) retire from the mountains west of the Shenandoah [River], leaving sufficient pickets to guard the passes, and bringing everything clean along the Valley, closing the rear of the army.

As regards the movements of the two brigades of the enemy moving toward Warrenton, the commander of the brigades to be left in the mountains must do what he can to counteract them, but I think the sooner you cross into Maryland, after tomorrow [June 24], the better.

- June 23, Lee to President Davis. This message clearly shows that Lee expected Hooker to cross the Potomac shortly.

Reports of movements of the enemy east of the Blue Ridge cause me to believe that he is preparing to cross the Potomac. A pontoon bridge is said to be laid at Edwards Ferry [east of Leesburg], and his army corps [XII Corps] that he has advanced to Leesburg and the foot of the mountains have been successfully repelled by General Stuart with his cavalry . . .

General Ewell's corps is in motion toward the Susquehanna. General A. P. Hill's corps is moving toward the Potomac; his leading division [Anderson] will reach Shepherdstown today. I have withdrawn Longstreet west of the Shenandoah, and if nothing prevents, he will follow tomorrow.

- June 23, Lee to President Davis.

The season is now so far advanced as to render it improbable that the enemy will undertake active operations on the Carolina and Georgia coast . . . I see no benefit to be derived from maintaining a large force on the southern coast during

> the unhealthy months of the summer and autumn, and I think that a part, at least, of the troops in North Carolina, and those under General Beauregard, can be employed at this time to great advantage in Virginia.
>
> If an army could be organized under the command of General Beauregard and pushed forward to Culpeper Court House, threatening Washington from that direction, it would not only effect a diversion most favorable to this army, but would, I think, relieve us of any apprehension of an attack upon Richmond during our absence . . .

This letter and a subsequent one along the same lines two days later were in vain – it was too late.

Comments

Lee's campaign had got off to a good start. By June 24 half his army had crossed the Potomac and Ewell was well on his way toward the Susquehanna. He was still unsure of Hooker's precise locations, but knew he was also marching north, probably to cross the Potomac to keep his army blocking any move on Baltimore or Washington. Stuart had fought his defensive screen actions successfully in the Loudoun Valley and no Yankees had penetrated the Gaps. Hill's Corps had caught up with and overtaken Longstreet. It was time to issue instructions for the next phase of the campaign – operations north of the Potomac. In particular Lee needed to redeploy and reassign his cavalry as he moved deeper into enemy territory with an ever-increasing need for flank security and information on enemy movements and locations.

Hooker was disappointed with Pleasonton's failure to obtain useful information about the location of the main body of his enemy. The B.M.I. had come to his assistance, however, and he was clear that any major battle was now going to take place north of the Potomac, so he hastened to get there.

Lee had planned the deployment of his cavalry with some care. He had seven brigades, including his mounted infantry. Out in front was Jenkins' Brigade plus White's Comanches; on the left, the least threatened area, Imboden; at the rear two brigades (to be decided by Stuart); and on the right, the vulnerable right, between the Army of Northern Virginia and the Army of the Potomac, three brigades under Stuart.

Just how best to get Stuart forward onto Ewell's exposed right flank had been the subject of discussion involving Lee, Longstreet and Stuart. It all depended on whether Hooker was going to cross the Potomac in the next few days. If he was not, then Stuart's easiest and quickest route was to follow Longstreet up the Shenandoah, cross the Potomac near Sharpsburg or Shepherdstown and then move to the Frederick area – route A1 on Map 19. It was Lee's first suggestion. However, if the Army of the Potomac was on the move, then crossing the river via route A2 (round or through Hooker's marching corps) was thought feasible and recommended to Lee by Stuart during their meeting at Paris, a village just east of Ashby Gap, on June 18. Major Mosby had spent some time behind Union lines and returned to Stuart on the evening of June 22. He later wrote, "I had located each corps and reported it to Stuart. They were so widely separated that it was easy for a column of cavalry to pass between them. No corps was nearer than ten miles to another corps." He suggested that Stuart could pass through the Union Army by taking the Hopewell Gap (only manned by a small Union picket) and could be across the Potomac at Seneca Ford, a distance of about 30 miles, in a day's march. The Union corps were certainly widely dispersed, but it is highly unlikely that Mosby had located every corps and, even if he had, the information could only be useful if the enemy remained stationary. Mosby was dispatched again to find out if this was still so. Lee had accepted this route as a possibility and Longstreet favored it on the grounds that it would be more likely to confuse the enemy as to the Rebel Army's real destination. Mosby returned on June 24 to state that Hooker's men were still in their camps.

As discussed below, route A3 was the one taken by Stuart. Lee's orders left the final decision to him – but the paramount object in Lee's mind was to get his main cavalry force onto Ewell's right flank as soon as possible. The question of who was to blame for Stuart's late arrival on the battlefield and his being out of touch with the army for a week is discussed under "Controversies" below (pages 313–14).

Time and distance calculations must have been important factors in Lee's mind when considering Stuart's march north. Stuart

Notes

- Ewell, with Jenkins' Brigade, has reached Chambersburg in the Cumberland Valley en route toward Harrisburg and the Susquehanna. Imboden is moving onto the left flank of the army. Hill is crossing the Potomac at Sharpsburg, having overtaken Longstreet who has been supporting Stuart in the Blue Ridge Gaps. Longstreet is still in the Shenandoah Valley. Stuart's main force is assembled near Salem with Robertson and Jones in the Blue Ridge Gaps. Lee is content with progress so far, apart from some uncertainty over the detailed locations of Hooker's army, although he is aware that it has moved north toward the Potomac.
- The Army of the Potomac is spread out over a considerable area, with Pleasonton's cavalry guarding the left flank in the Loudoun Valley. For the men it was mostly another restful day in their camps – there had been little movement for five days – as Hooker pondered Lee's intentions.
- As soon as possible Lee wants Stuart to position himself on Ewell's vulnerable right flank. He needs his main cavalry force in the area A–A east of the Catoctin Mountains and South Mountain. Stuart is told to leave two brigades to follow the army up the Shenandoah and protect the rear. Lee's intention is to have a cavalry brigade leading the advance (Jenkins), another on the left flank (Imboden) and two at the rear (Stuart to decide which). Stuart is to be on the vital right flank once the army is over the Potomac, screening, protecting and above all providing information on the whereabouts of the enemy as they too come north of the river.

A1 The route Lee wanted Stuart to take if he found Hooker stationary. He was to march up west of the Shenandoah, cross the Potomac and position himself around Frederick. It was also still an alternative when Stuart found his intended route blocked.

A2 The route via Hopewell Gap and around or through the enemy's marching columns. This possibility had been discussed between Lee, Longstreet and Stuart before June 24. Mosby, Stuart's scout, thought the route perfectly possible and it was favored by Longstreet as being more likely to confuse the enemy than just following him up the Shenandoah.

A3 The approximate actual route taken by Stuart to the Potomac. After a clash with the rear of Hancock's II Corps he decides to swing south and east to march right around the Union Army.

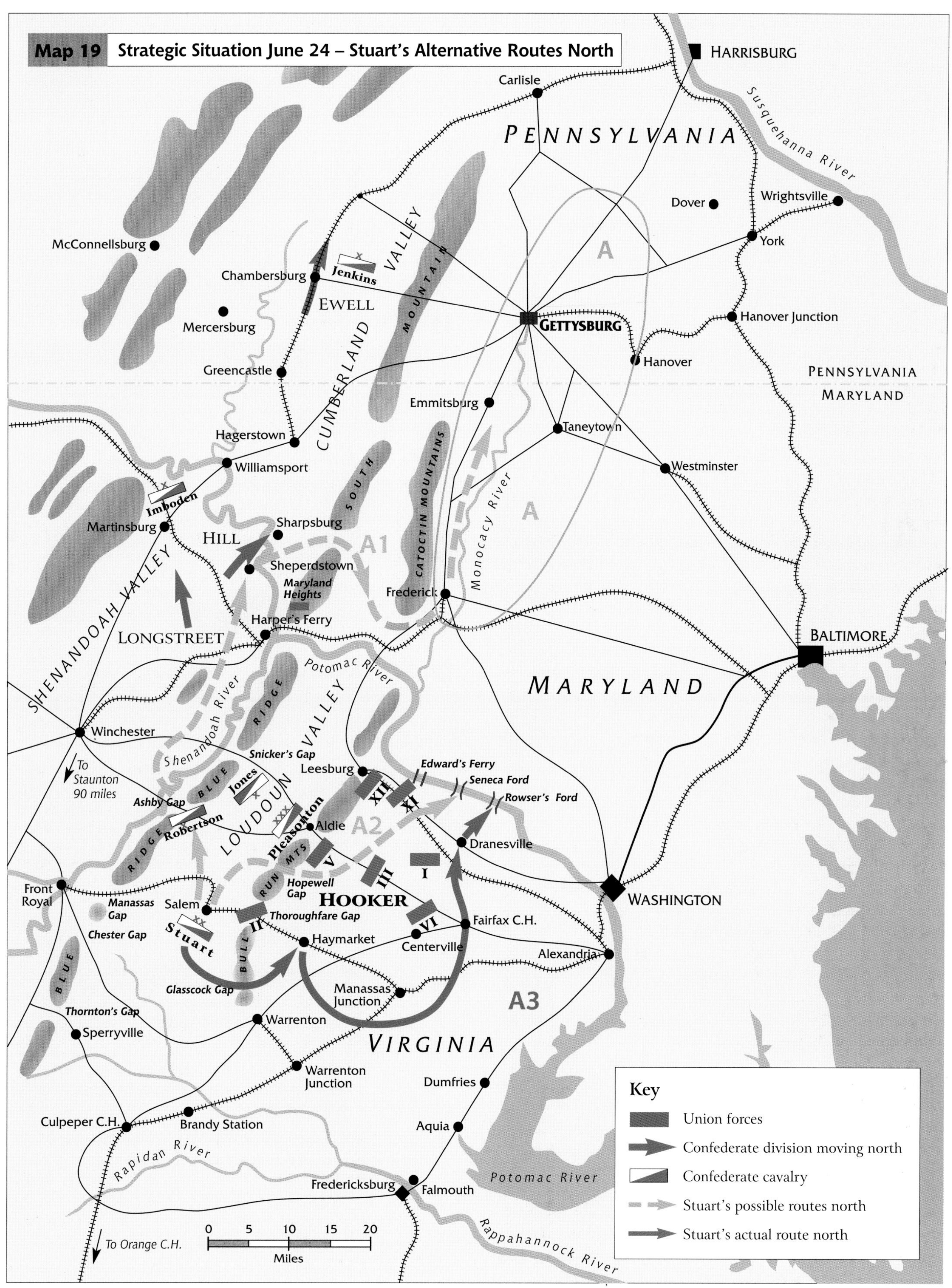
Map 19
Strategic Situation June 24 – Stuart's Alternative Routes North
HARRISBURG
Carlisle
PENNSYLVANIA
Susquehanna River
Wrightsville
Dover
York
McConnellsburg
Chambersburg
Jenkins
EWELL
CUMBERLAND VALLEY
SOUTH MOUNTAIN
Mercersburg
GETTYSBURG
Hanover Junction
Hanover
Greencastle
PENNSYLVANIA
MARYLAND
Emmitsburg
Taneytown
Hagerstown
Williamsport
Westminster
CATOCTIN MOUNTAINS
Monocacy River
Imboden
Martinsburg
Sharpsburg
HILL
Sheperdstown
Maryland Heights
Frederick
SHENANDOAH VALLEY
Harper's Ferry
LONGSTREET
Potomac River
BALTIMORE
MARYLAND
Winchester
Shenandoah River
BLUE RIDGE
LOUDOUN VALLEY
To Staunton 90 miles
Snicker's Gap
Jones
Leesburg
Edward's Ferry
Seneca Ford
Rowser's Ford
Ashby Gap
Robertson
Pleasonton
Aldie
XII
XI
LOUDOUN
Dranesville
BULL RUN MTS
V
III
I
Front Royal
Manassas Gap
Hopewell Gap
HOOKER
WASHINGTON
Salem
Thoroughfare Gap
Stuart
II
VI
Fairfax C.H.
Chester Gap
Haymarket
Centerville
Alexandria
Glasscock Gap
Manassas Junction
A
A1
A2
A3
Thornton's Gap
Warrenton
Sperryville
VIRGINIA
Warrenton Junction
Dumfries
Culpeper C.H.
Brandy Station
Aquia
Rapidan River
Potomac River
Fredericksburg
Falmouth
To Orange C.H.
0 5 10 15 20
Miles
Rappahannock River
Key
Union forces
Confederate division moving north
Confederate cavalry
Stuart's possible routes north
Stuart's actual route north

was near Salem, and Lee wanted him moving by June 24. Cavalry at a walk was expected to cover at least 30 miles in a day – with some trotting, 40 miles was reasonable – provided there were no unforeseen delays. Route A1 to Frederick was 60–70 miles – a two-day march – so Lee could expect Stuart in the Frederick area on June 26, or on the 27th at the latest. Similarly, route A2, which was only 50–60 miles, should be covered in about two days. Thus Lee knew he would be out of touch with his cavalry commander for two or three days at the most – no contact after that and he would be seriously worried.

Phase III: June 25–June 30 (Maps 20 and 21)

Confederate activity

When Stuart received Lee's and Longstreet's messages containing his commander's instructions, he had two decisions to make. The first was which two of his five brigades to leave guarding Lee's rear and the Blue Ridge Gaps; the second what route to take on his march north to get onto Ewell's right flank? For the former Stuart decided to post Robertson (with the four guns of Captain Moorman's Lynchburg (Virginia) Battery) and Jones (with Captain Chew's four guns of the Ashby (Virginia Battery) at the Blue Ridge Gaps – all under Robertson's command, as he was the senior of the two. These detachments amounted to almost 3,000 men. Undoubtedly Stuart wanted his best brigade commanders with him on his risky ride and he had little confidence in Robertson, who "was more at drilling than fighting" and had put up a poor performance at Brandy Station. It was in leaving Jones behind under Robertson that Stuart probably made an error of judgment. Not only was his brigade much stronger than Robertson's, but also Jones was regarded by Stuart as his finest outpost officer – and thus best fitted to have overall command at the Blue Ridge. Because of Robertson's seniority, the only way this could have happened was to keep Robertson under Stuart and send Chambliss to the Blue Ridge under Jones. He could not send Hampton, as that would have meant Robertson would be his second-in-command – unthinkable.

Stuart gave Robertson detailed instructions about his duties (see box, page 313) before setting out with the three brigades of Chambliss, Hampton and F. Lee, plus the six guns of Captain Breathed's 1st Stuart Battery – well over 5,000 horsemen. He had chosen the route through the Union forces, but instead of going via the Hopewell Gap in the Bull Run Mountains he headed for the Glasscock Gap (reaching it early on June 25) about 15 miles further south, thus adding a considerable distance to his route to the Potomac crossings.

The notes to Map 20 give an outline of Stuart's progress round the Army of the Potomac. As early as June 25 he found his intended route to Dranesville and the Seneca Ford blocked by Hancock's II Corps, which was now on the march. At that stage a decision had to be taken. He could swing south and further east, or withdraw the way he had come into the Shenandoah Valley and make for the crossing of the Potomac at Shepherdstown. He decided on the former, although he was unlikely to be able to march west of Centerville as his after-action report states he wanted to. By June 26 horses were starting to break down through lack of grain and more halts were necessary for grazing. On the same day, Hooker's army was crossing the Potomac; Robertson, if he had not been so incompetent, should have discovered this and informed Lee. By the 27th Stuart reached

Notes

1. **June 24.** Stuart assembles his three brigades of over 5,000 men and six guns at Salem and after midnight heads for the Glasscock Gap, which he passes through early on the 25th, reaching open country and hoping to march through or round any Union forces.

2. **June 25.** Stuart clashes with the rear of II Corps and realizes his intended route is blocked. He decides to continue to try to get round the enemy rather than follow Longstreet up the Shenandoah. He swings south and camps at Buckland. On that day Hooker is well spread out, occupying many roads north with his leading elements already over the Potomac.

3. **June 26.** A long march until midnight, when the column camps at Wolf Run Shoals on the Occoquon River.

4. **June 27.** Stuart's force is split into two columns for the day's march – Fitz Lee taking the easterly route and Stuart moving on Fairfax C. H. There are minor skirmishes at Burke's Station (F. Lee) and Fairfax C. H. (Stuart).

5. **June 27.** The columns reunite at Dranesville during the afternoon.

6. **June 27.** By midnight Stuart has crossed the Potomac at Rowser's Ford with the mass of Hooker's army already over the river and still between him and Lee, with whom he his unable to communicate.

7. **June 28.** Stuart advances on Rockville in two columns during the morning.

8. **June 28.** A running skirmish develops as Stuart pursues and captures a Union supply train. He takes 400 prisoners (soon paroled) and 125 wagons that join his column. The chase continues to within 5 miles of Washington.

9. **June 28.** The wagons slow the march, although the fodder in them is welcome for the half-starved horses. Stuart is forced to undertake another night march past Cooksville. Meade is well north of the Potomac and Stuart is unable to receive any information from, or send any to, his commanding general, who by this time is becoming worried at Stuart's disappearance and silence.

10. **June 29.** Stuart takes the morning to tear up railroad tracks and destroy the bridge at Sykesville.

11. **June 29.** Stuart clashes with Union cavalry at Westminster and occupies the town by late afternoon.

12. **June 29.** The column, now spread out over several miles, advances to Union Mills. Both men and horses are utterly exhausted, with many of the former asleep in their saddles.

13. **June 30.** After an all-day action against Kilpatrick's Union division at Hanover, Stuart is forced to withdraw even further to the east, to Jefferson, before he can turn north again.

14. **June 30.** After another long night march Stuart reaches Dover at dawn, with many in his command, men and horses, on the point of collapse, causing considerable straggling. After a short rest the column moves off again at around noon.

15. **July 1.** Still trying to locate Ewell, Stuart reaches Carlisle by late afternoon and has a minor clash with the defenders. After midnight Stuart finally receives a message from Lee telling him to march on Gettysburg where a battle has been in progress all day.

16. **July 2.** Stuart's much-depleted division finally reaches the vicinity of Gettysburg in the afternoon.

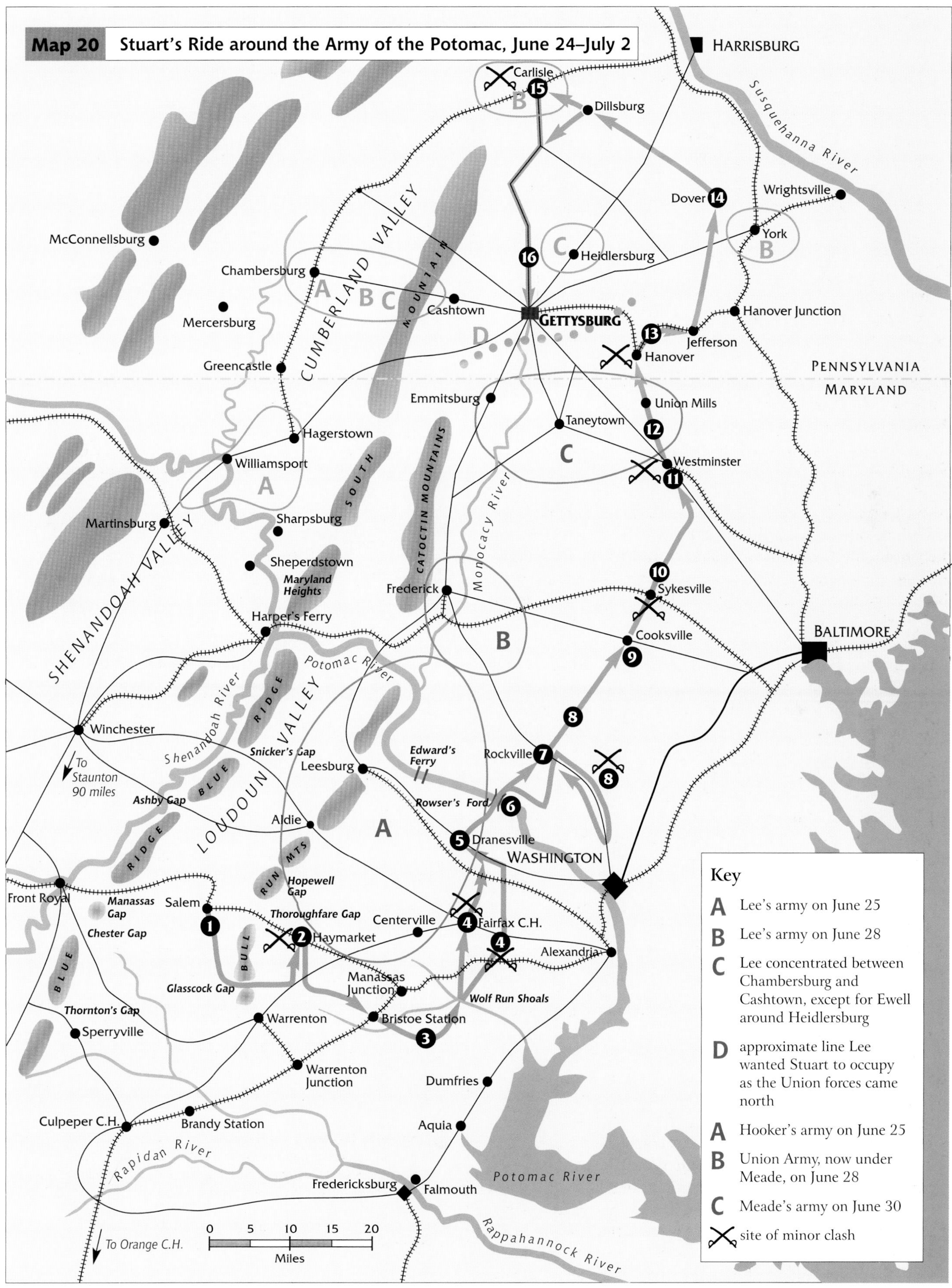

Map 20 Stuart's Ride around the Army of the Potomac, June 24–July 2

Fairfax Court House, where he captured a number of sutler's wagons. From there he sent Lee a message – which never arrived:

> I took possession of Fairfax C.H. this morning at nine o'clock, together with a large quantity of stores. The main body of Hooker's army has gone towards Leesburg, except the garrison of Alexandria and Washington, which has retreated within the fortifications.

This news of Hooker's movements would have been welcome to Lee, who was beginning to show some anxiety over Stuart's whereabouts, although the knowledge that his cavalry commander had only reached Fairfax Court House when he, Lee, was in the Cumberland Valley with the Army of the Potomac between them would surely have been disconcerting. Stuart pressed on and managed to cross the Potomac at Rowser's Ford; it was an exhausting and dangerous crossing. The next three days saw steady, if slow and exhausting progress northwards. The march was delayed, though not excessively so, by the capture of the wagons at Rockville and the chase toward Washington and their incorporation into Stuart's column (see pages 201 and 223; also box opposite). The need to rest men and animals, the clash with Union cavalry at Westminster, the destruction of railroad track and the bridge at Sykesville on June 29, and finally an all-day fight with Kilpatrick at Hanover on June 30 caused much more serious slowing. On July 1, still trying to find Ewell at Carlisle, Stuart received a message saying he was urgently needed at Gettysburg where a battle had begun. Not only was Stuart going to arrive too late, but also his command was utterly spent and numerically much weaker than ten days earlier. On July 2 a member of Company D, 4th Virginia Cavalry (quoted in Section Four, page 202), recorded in his diary five consecutive nights without sleep due to continuous marching and noted that by the time they finally reached Gettysburg, of the fifty-six men who started off in his company, only about twenty remained.

Stuart's Unwelcome Clash with II Corps, June 25

Stuart's A.D.C. Lieutenant Theodore S. Garnett Jr., describes the unexpected meeting between Stuart's column and Hancock's infantry and wagons on June 25 at the start of his ride around the Union Army:

> When morning [of June 25] dawned we found ourselves on the eastern slope of the Bull Run Mountains, and not far from the little town of Buckland. Across the plain, to our left, were the white tops of an immense wagon train, which, at the distance of two or three miles, presented the appearance of a huge flock of sheep. Here then we thought was the object of our silent march over the mountains. All that remained to be done was to "charge the camp."
>
> We moved cautiously on toward the train, and when near enough to attack, it was discovered that it was guarded by at least a division of infantry. They [the wagons] had taken the alarm and were hurrying off as fast as whip and spur could carry them – the infantry marching on the flank. We paid our respects to them, however, by running up a battery of horse artillery and blowing up a caisson for them, killing some of their horses and making their exit as unpleasant as possible.

Union activity

On June 25 Hooker ordered the army into Maryland. Reynolds was given authority over the left wing consisting of his own I Corps, Sickles' III and Howard's XI Corps, plus Stahel's cavalry brigade. The march orders took them over the Potomac at the two pontoon bridges at Edward's Ferry. More marching followed the next day for the entire army, in accordance with a carefully scheduled timetable to get the long columns over the river. By the end of the day the last formation over the bridges was VI Corps. It was catch-up time for the Army of the Potomac and the next three days saw some of the longest and most exhausting marching of the campaign, much of it in drenching rain with little sleep and no shelter.

The Weather During the Gettysburg Campaign, June 25–July 3

June 25 *morning:* cloudy but fine, roads in good condition
afternoon: showers, dust turning to mud
night: steady rain all night, creating deep mud and slippery roads

June 26 morning and afternoon: cold rain, roads very muddy, making difficult marching
night: more rain

June 27 *morning and afternoon:* showers but sky clearing, roads still muddy
night: cold but clear

June 28 *morning:* showers in Maryland, roads still muddy; Early encountered stifling heat and dust in north around York
night: intermittent rain or drizzle

June 29 *morning and afternoon:* drenching rain creating mud 4 inches deep in places; some sunshine boosted temperature and humidity; better weather in north.

June 30 *morning and afternoon:* some light rain, overcast but generally brighter and warmer

July 1 *morning:* some light rain initially, but later sunshine and high humidity; some heavy rain on South Mountain and at Emmitsburg
afternoon: intensely hot and humid, causing men to fall out from the heat and exhaustion; bright sunshine at Gettysburg – hot
night: mostly bright moonlight

July 2 *morning:* scattered drizzle, very still with some fog patches and heavy dew
afternoon: temperatures in the 80s, causing considerable thirst and heat exhaustion; VI Corps, still on the march, had to contend with several inches of dust on the roads and intense heat
night: cool and damp

July 3 *morning:* initially some cloud but later strong sunshine with temperature reaching mid-80s
afternoon: getting hotter, making Pickett's charge even more of an ordeal; later heavy rain in evening.
night: several drenching showers

It was on the 27th that Hooker visited Harper's Ferry on his way to Frederick; there he found 10,000 Union troops that he considered he should absorb immediately into his force, as they were, in his opinion, serving no purpose at their present location. His request to Halleck was rejected with the words, "Maryland Heights [overlooking the town] have always been regarded as an important point to be held by us . . . I cannot approve their abandonment, except in case of absolute necessity." Hooker, however, went so far as to hand instructions concerning the Harper's Ferry troops joining his army to Major-General William H. French, commanding the Harper's Ferry Dictrict. French telegraphed Halleck of this and received the reply, "Pay no attention to General Hooker's orders." As noted above, the failure of Lee to take these Heights enabled the signals station there to send critical information about Lee's movement into Maryland. It was this final spat with Halleck that triggered Hooker's resignation wire to Washington and his removal from his position on June 28. Now Major-General George Gordon Meade was in command – the sixth and last general to lead the Army of the Potomac.

By the end of June 28 the Army of the Potomac was assembled around Frederick and its new railroad line of communication was established to Baltimore and Washington; despite the damage done by Stuart on June 29, a new line was soon opened up to Westminster as the army moved further north. (This short, direct line of communication was in contrast to Lee's situation, as he was largely to live off the country through which he marched – except for ammunition resupply. He had written to Davis on June 25 that he had had to abandon his communications, as he did not have "sufficient troops to maintain . . . them.")

Meade had been given the powers denied to Hooker. Halleck, who loathed Hooker, wrote to Meade giving him authority over "All forces within the sphere of influence of your operations will be held subject to your orders . . . Harper's Ferry and its garrison are under your direct orders." Meade took over at the moment when B.M.I. sources provided an uncannily accurate count of Lee's army as it had passed through Hagerstown heading north (see Thomas McCammon's report, box, page 312). According to Colonel Sharpe, fewer than 80,000 men and 275 guns marched through the town. The actual engaged strength of the Confederates (including cavalry) at the battle was just under 72,000 with 271 guns. Meade issued marching orders for a dawn start on June 29. The army would head north from the Frederick area toward Pennsylvania, spread out over a 20-mile front from Emmitsburg in the west to Manchester in the east. The next day Meade wrote to his wife:

> We are marching as fast as we can to relieve Harrisburg, but have to keep a sharp lookout that the rebels don't turn around us and get to Washington and Baltimore in our rear . . . I am going straight at them, and will settle this thing one way or the other. The men are in good spirits; we have been reinforced so as to have equal numbers with the enemy . . .

Chasing the Wagon Train at Rockville, June 28

Lieutenant Theodore S. Garnett Jr., Stuart's A.D.C., later recounted the capture of the Union wagon train on June 28. Interestingly, there were initially about 150 wagons in the train, of which 125 were captured intact and (controversially) taken with Stuart.There is no apparent reason why, with so much grain in the wagons, Stuart's horses suffered from hunger from then on.

> As we neared Rockville the rear of an immense wagon train was just passing through on its way to Washington. A squadron of the Ninth, which was still in advance [according to Major McClellan, Stuart's staff officer, a Lieutenant Thomas Lee and a few men of the 2nd South Carolina led the chase], was ordered by General Stuart to push ahead at a gallop, and not to draw rein until they had overhauled the leading wagon of the train. The men dashed on and then a scene ensued which baffles description. The drivers of the train – six mule teams to each wagon – were of course exceedingly alarmed, and in some instances cut their mules loose or overturned the wagons. Others jogged leisurely along, only waiting until the front wagon should stop; some set fire to their wagons, and I suppose thirty were destroyed in this way. The whole train numbered one hundred and seventy-five wagons [150?], and was the post supply train running between Washington and Hooker's army. Soon the front wagon was overhauled and the whole train was in our hands. The dome of the capitol was distinctly visible from the spot at which this wagon was halted.

Confederate activities

Lee's intention during this period was to continue north to the Susquehanna and Harrisburg, the Pennsylvania capital. By June 28 he was seriously worried by his lack of contact with Stuart and consequent lack of information. It was the arrival of Longstreet's scout, Harrison, on the evening of that day with information that Hooker's army (Lee was not to know until June 30 that Meade had taken command) had crossed the Potomac on June 25 and 26 that caused Lee, with some initial doubts, to change his plan. He ordered the immediate concentration of his army in the Chambersburg–Cashtown area. If the enemy had crossed the river two or three days ago, they could now be very close – and Stuart's absence had become critical. Lee did not want to fight a battle without his cavalry screen in place nor before he had his whole army under his immediate control.

Comments

From June 24 to July 2 Lee had no contact with his main cavalry force on his vulnerable right flank. He almost certainly expected to be out of contact for two days, three at the most, but the lack of accurate information on his enemy's locations and movements, particularly on his crossing the Potomac on June 25 and 26 and in the last days of that month, ensured that Lee was operating in the dark at the critical time when the armies approached each other. The arguments over who was to blame for this, Lee or Stuart, are summarized below under "Controversies" (see pages 313–14).

Although Lee did not have precise operational knowledge of his enemy's whereabouts, he nevertheless was aware of what Hooker was doing in general terms, as is evidenced by the following:

- In his report of July 31 he wrote that his objective was "the transfer of the scene of hostilities north of the Potomac . . . and that in any event that [Union] army would be compelled to leave Virginia." That was what Lee expected to happen all along.
- On June 18 he told Davis, "the enemy has been thrown back from the Rappahannock, and is concentrating, as far as I can learn, in the vicinity of Centerville. The last reports of the scouts indicate he is moving over toward the upper Potomac." As early as this he knew that the Union Army was on the move.

A Civilian Informs on the Rebels

Meade forwarded this report to Halleck on June 28, 1863:

> Thomas McCammon, blacksmith, a good man, from Hagerstown, left there on horseback at 11 a.m. today. Rebel cavalry came first a week ago last Monday [June 15]. General [A. G.] Jenkins having 1,200 mounted infantry, said to be picked men from Jackson's men, and 300 or 400 cavalry of his own. The cavalry went back and forth out of Pennsylvania, driving horses and cattle, and the first infantry came yesterday a week ago [June 20] – General Ewell's men. He came personally last Saturday [June 20], and was at the Catholic church Sunday, with General Rodes and two other generals. On Monday [June 21] he [Ewell] left in the direction of Greencastle, in the afternoon, Rodes having left the same morning. Rebel troops have passed every day, more or less, since; some days only three or four regiments or a brigade, and some days, yesterday [June 27] for instance, all of Longstreet's command passed through [Hagerstown] excepting two brigades. Saw Longstreet yesterday [June 27]. He and Lee had their headquarters at Mr. [James H.] Grove's, just beyond the town limits towards Greencastle last night, and left there this a.m. [June 28] at 8 o'clock. Think A. P. Hill went through last Tuesday [June 23]. Heard from James D. Roman, a prominent lawyer and leading Confederate sympathizer, who was talking in the clerk's office last night; said that their officers reported their whole army, 100,000 strong, now in Maryland or Pennsylvania, excepting the cavalry. Mr. [William] Logan, register of wills, and Mr. [William H.] Protzman, very fine men in Hagerstown, have taken pains to count the rebels, and could not make them over 80,000. They counted the artillery; made it two hundred and seventy-five guns. Some of the regiments have only 175 men – two that I saw, 150. Largest regiment that I saw was a Maryland regiment that was about 700. Don't think their regiments would range 400. Great amount of transportation; great many wagons captured at Winchester. Horses in good condition. Ewell rides in a wagon. Two thousand comprise the mounted infantry and cavalry. Saw Wilcox's brigade wagons in town yesterday [June 27] or day before. Saw Kershaw's wagons in town yesterday. Kershaw's brigade is in McLaws' division, Longstreet's corps. The Union men in Hagerstown would count them and meet at night. Officers and men in good condition; say they are going to Philadelphia. Lots of Confederate money; carry it in flour barrels, and give $5 for cleaning a horse; $5 for two shoes on a horse rather than 50 cents United States money.

This report is extraordinarily detailed and reasonably accurate except for the counting of numbers. Not even 80,000 marched through Hagerstown, the total being around 66,000 along with 250 guns – remembering that the cavalry of Stuart, Imboden, Jones and Robertson were not among the columns moving through the town at that time.

- The next day he wrote, "indications seem to be that his [Hooker's] main body is proceeding toward the Potomac, whether upon Harper's Ferry or to cross the river east of it is not yet known."
- On June 20, from Berryville, he wrote, "The movement of the main body . . . is still toward the Potomac, but its real intention is not yet discovered."
- Two days later, Lee said to Stuart, "I fear he will steal a march on us, and get across the Potomac before we are aware."
- On June 23 he told Davis, "Reports of movements of the enemy east of the Blue Ridge cause me to believe that he is preparing to cross the Potomac. A pontoon bridge is said to be laid at Edward's Ferry . . ."
- On June 25, the day Hooker began to cross the river, Lee reported to his President, "I think I can throw General Hooker's army across the Potomac."

Lee wanted Hooker north of the Potomac and he wanted to give him battle there. On June 25 he knew his plan was working. What he wanted now was confirmation that his enemy was north of the river and operational intelligence on his movements – this was his cavalry's priority task, and one it spectacularly failed to carry out.

In contrast, Hooker and then Meade were comparatively well informed about Lee's movements from June 21 onward, not by the cavalry but by the B.M.I. and its scouts, spies and civilian informants. Hooker had made a major contribution to the Army of the Potomac when he established the B.M.I. cell under Colonel Sharpe at his headquarters. Generally speaking, intelligence on Lee's army and its movements in the week prior to the battle was uncannily accurate.

The change of command of the Army of the Potomac just days before a major battle went remarkably smoothly. Apart from Sickles, a Hooker man, Meade was well supported by his corps commanders. In his march north from June 28, Meade made good use of his interior-lines position and moved his army to guard Washington and Baltimore. At the same time he marched north on a wide front, making use of several routes, with cavalry screening flanks and rear (his best cavalry commander, Buford, was positioned on his most vulnerable flank, the west). He was well balanced to react in the direction of any serious threat, but with the primary objective of finding and fighting his enemy.

Mosby's advice that it would be easy for Stuart to slip between the Union corps because they were well spread out and stationary on June 24 was accurate for that date. Unfortunately, it was rendered invalid the next day due to the continued movement of Longstreet and Hill to begin crossing the river. This was reported to Hooker, who gave orders to break camp and march north. Thus did Stuart find his route blocked on June 25 by the marching columns of II Corps. Had Lee not moved, the chances are that Stuart might have got between the enemy camps.

If Jones or Hampton rather than Robertson had been in command of the cavalry left guarding the Blue Ridge Gaps, it is likely they would have kept Lee informed of the enemy's crossing of the Potomac on June 25 and 26. Despite Stuart's instructions to Robertson (see box opposite), he was content to sit idle on static picket duty until June 29, when he withdrew to Berryville, some 65 miles south of Chambersburg, where Lee was located. Lieutenant-Colonel Thomas Marshall, 7th Virginia Cavalry (Jones's Brigade), noted: "June 24 – Still on picket, and until June 29, upon which day moved in rear of the brigade to camp near Berryville, Clarke County [Virginia]." As at Brandy Station, Robertson had failed, and in a similar fashion.

CONTROVERSIES

The two main controversies of the campaign prior to the battle itself were: should Lee have conducted a strategic offensive campaign or remained on the defensive; and who was to blame for Lee's lack of information in the week prior to the battle – Lee or Stuart?

Should Lee Have Conducted a Strategic Offensive?

The arguments that Lee was justified in taking the offensive into Maryland and Pennsylvania in June, 1863 are summarized below.

Lee was an offensive general; his preference was to take the war or the battle to the enemy. In midsummer 1863, the Army of Northern Virginia had recently won two outstanding victories at Fredericksburg (defensive) and Chancellorsville (offensive), so confidence in their commander and morale were sky-high. The Rebels felt they could thrash the Yankees any day, no matter what the odds against them. Southern citizens felt the same, and not to take the war to the enemy would surely have been condemned with a massive outcry in the press against any such timidity. The public was quick to denounce passive generals. Lee understood this mood of self-belief among his soldiers and it reinforced his own confidence in them and in the idea that offensive operations were necessary to succeed and sustain civilian morale.

Lee was convinced that an offensive into Northern territory was the only way of securing the initiative and keeping his enemy off balance. An attacker has the choice of where, how and with what forces he attacks; the defender often does not know for certain where the blow will fall until it happens, and then he must react. Lee believed that, to win the war, success in the East was of paramount importance. With the huge manpower and industrial resources of the North, a long war would mean Southern defeat. He believed the only way to achieve victory was to demoralize the North before exhausting his own resources. He needed successes on the battlefield; he needed to inflict heavy losses to make his opponents feel that the sacrifices demanded were too high, that their goal of conquest of the South was not worth the effort. Only by an offensive grand strategy did Lee believe such a result was achievable. Only by being seen to be attacking and winning would the South have any chance of foreign recognition. In Lee's own words, "If we can defeat or drive the armies of the enemy from the field, we shall have peace." Lee sought the big, decisive victory – something that was probably impossible with such large armies engaged – and the best way to achieve this was usually to attack.

Stuart's Orders to Robertson

Stuart issued the following orders to Robertson on leaving him in command of the Confederate forces guarding the Blue Ridge Gaps:

> Your own and General Jones' brigades will cover the front of Ashby's and Snicker's Gaps, yourself, as senior officer, being in command. Your object will be to watch the enemy; deceive him as to our designs, and harass his rear if you find he is retiring. Be always on the alert; let nothing escape your observation, and miss no opportunity which offers to damage the enemy. After the enemy has moved beyond your reach, leave sufficient pickets in the mountain, withdraw to the west side of the Shenandoah, place a strong and reliable picket at Harper's Ferry, cross the Potomac, and follow the army, keeping on its right and rear. As long as the enemy remains in your front in force, unless otherwise ordered by General R. E. Lee, Lieutenant-General Longstreet, or myself, hold the gaps with a line of pickets reaching across the Shenandoah by Charlestown to the Potomac. If in the contingency mentioned, you withdraw, sweep the valley clear of what pertains to the army, and cross the Potomac at the different points crossed by it. You will instruct General Jones from time to time as the movements, progress, or events may require, and report anything of importance to Lieutenant-General Longstreet, with whose position you will communicate by relays through Charlestown. I send instructions to General Jones, which please read . . .

Robertson did none of these things, merely sitting at the Gaps long after Hooker had departed and crossed the Potomac.

Apart from these general factors in favor of an offensive, Lee saw an invasion of the North in June, 1863 as the best way of avoiding a siege of Richmond, of drawing his enemy away from Virginia. To remain on the defensive behind the Rappahannock invited the build-up of the Union forces opposite and their eventual offensive. On June 8 he wrote:

> I am aware that there is difficulty and hazard in taking the aggressive with so large an enemy in its front, entrenched behind a river where it cannot be advantageously attacked. Unless it can be drawn into a position where it can be assailed, it will take its own time to prepare and strengthen itself to renew its advance on Richmond.

Lee was well aware that the security of Washington would ensure that the Army of the Potomac followed him north. There was also the urgent need to supply his ragged and hungry soldiers.

The counterarguments, that Lee's mistake was to take the strategic offensive at that time, are based on the following points.

To win, the North had to conquer the South – invade the Confederacy, defeat its armies and take Richmond. For the South to win it had only to make such an undertaking too costly in blood and treasure. With the huge mismatch between the opposing sides in manpower and resources, it was imperative that the South conserved her assets and avoided costly battles. The argument was that a defensive grand strategy, coupled with some judicious offensive operations, was the best way of prolonging the war, inflicting expensive defeats on the enemy and wearing down the North's will to continue.

Although by mid-1863 the South had gained a number of victories, or at least draws, against the odds, these had not come cheaply. In every battle, except one, or series of battles fought by Lee in the year prior to Gettysburg, the South had lost more heavily than the North as a percentage of the numbers engaged (see table, page 285). The only battle in which the Rebels inflicted higher proportionate losses on the Yankees was Fredericksburg, where they had been entirely on the defensive. The South could not afford such expensive attacking battles as her losses were mostly irreplaceable, whereas the North's were not. Losses on the battlefield, through sickness and the steady, unstoppable flow of deserters, had cost the Confederacy at least 100,000 men in the twelve months prior to Gettysburg. For this reason alone, the argument goes, Lee, who acknowledged the problem, should have adopted a defensive strategic posture in June, 1863.

The bridge at Hanover Junction burned by Stuart's cavalry during the campaign.

Comments
One of the most effective operational strategies, particularly for the weaker side, is to take the initiative strategically or operationally but to fight defensively – make your opponent attack you on ground of your own choosing. Other things being equal, in the Civil War the tactical defensive had the edge. This was invariably the case when repelling frontal attacks. Lee had a strong case for assuming the strategic offensive in the summer of 1863, but he was fully aware that he needed to conserve his shrinking manpower. He needed and sought a decisive battle, but he could not afford massive losses. Prior to starting the march north, Lee had discussed operational strategy with Longstreet and Longstreet later claimed that it had been agreed that a strategic offensive should be linked to a tactical defensive if at all possible on ground of their choosing. That is not what happened at Gettysburg.

Who Was to Blame for Lee's Lack of Information?

Stuart was an extremely experienced and successful cavalry commander. He knew that his cavalry were his general's eyes and ears and that Lee depended on him for timely operational information on the main body of the enemy. Screening his own army and at the same time aggressively probing for the enemy's whereabouts and movements, and passing that information on, was always his primary function when operating under the general overall control of army headquarters. Stuart was well aware of this in June, 1863. During the crucial period as the two armies approached each other at the end of the month, Stuart failed to fulfill this primary cavalry function – there is no argument about this.

The three orders he received from Lee are given in full on pages 303–305. On June 22 Stuart was specifically asked where the enemy was and what he was doing. He was told that Lee was worried Hooker might cross the Potomac before Lee was aware of it. He was told to take position on Ewell's right flank and to keep him (Ewell) informed. He could also gather supplies. Stuart could have been in no real doubt as to his main duty.

The second letter from Lee on the same day was mostly concerned with the route Stuart should take. Longstreet favored moving round or through the Hopewell Gap, as did Stuart himself (largely on the advice of his scout, Mosby), provided he could get through. There was no change to his primary task.

On June 23 the final order from Lee gave Stuart discretion as to the route he should take, but again emphasized, "you must move on and feel the right of Ewell's troops, collecting information, provisions etc . . ." This was the classic "mission command" that Lee was accustomed to give his senior commanders. Stuart's primary objective is abundantly clear; how he gets there, how he carries it out is up to him – he must use his judgment. Lee was happy for Stuart to take the route through or round the enemy provided he could do so "without hindrance."

Lee expected to be out of contact with his cavalry commander for two or three days. Clearly, considering the distance involved, Stuart could not afford lengthy delays. He chose to go around and through the enemy, as on June 24 he believed them to be well spread out and stationary. On June 25 he marched through the Glasscock Gap instead of the Hopewell Gap, for reasons that are unclear, thereby immediately adding a substantial distance to his planned route to the Potomac crossing. On the same day he found his route blocked, not by stationary camps but by marching columns of infantry heading north. This was decision time for Stuart. Should he go back and take the easy route up the Shenandoah or continue his ride around the enemy and go further south and east? He chose the latter.

With hindsight, we know this was a bad decision. At the time Stuart must have known that to carry on trying to find a way around was fraught with the risk of delays and would quite possibly add many miles to the journey, thus tiring men and horses. He knew the need for haste, and he knew his primary mission to get ahead of Hooker's army and screen his own army's advance. By pressing on, many would consider he was foolhardy to say the least. Stuart had ridden around the enemy successfully before and it had gone a long way to establishing his reputation as a dashing cavalry leader – something that had been publicly tarnished when he was caught by surprise at Brandy Station. Perhaps there was an element of polishing up this reputation in his decision to continue the ride.

It very quickly became apparent that he had made a dubious decision. Delays followed each other in quick succession, with the ever-increasing need to rest and graze his horses; the chasing, capture and incorporation into his column of 125 enemy wagons and 400 prisoners (soon paroled); further clashes with the enemy at Westminster and Hanover (an all-day engagement); and the destruction of telegraph lines, railroad tracks and bridges. Things had gone seriously wrong by June 28. When he was chasing the wagons to within a few miles of Washington, the Army of the Potomac was over that river and grouped around Frederick between him and Lee at Chambersburg. Ewell, whose flank he was supposed to be protecting, was more than 80 miles away at Carlisle! From then on Stuart had no hope of fulfilling his primary task, and all his desperate efforts to catch up merely exhausted his men and animals, seriously reducing the number of effective horsemen he had available for when they finally arrived for the last day of the battle.

Comments

Lee has been blamed on two counts. First, that his discretionary orders about the route allowed Stuart to make the ride he did and that he clouded the issue of Stuart's role by adding instructions to gather supplies, etc.; and second that Lee did not make proper use of the cavalry he had left with him.

As regards the former point, Lee was dealing with a commander he trusted implicitly. He had made clear Stuart's primary mission, and had repeated it at least twice and, as was his custom, left the detailed means (in this case the route) to Stuart. There was no reason at the time for Lee to think he needed to insist on a specific route, as he had every confidence that Stuart was quite capable of deciding this for himself. There are perhaps some grounds for criticizing Lee for adding in instructions to gather supplies. However, it was abundantly clear that these were secondary to gaining Ewell's right flank and providing information on the enemy. It was obvious that these duties should not be rated as important as the primary one. Lee also stated that he favored his main cavalry force riding around the enemy provided it could do so *without hindrance*. That this was problematic in the circumstances at the time was surely obvious to Stuart, and on June 25 almost certainly impossible.

As for the second point – that Lee did not use the cavalry he had with him to best advantage – the brigades of Jenkins and Imboden were committed to screening the advance and left flank respectively, so that left the two brigades that Lee instructed Stuart to leave to guard the left rear and follow the army up the valley. Stuart took the three best brigades with him, giving Robertson command of his own and Jones's Brigades, which would be left behind. Stuart knew Robertson's limitations full well and gave him careful instructions. That Robertson failed to do anything worthwhile was not surprising, but should Lee have stepped in to use these brigades, some 2,500 men, when he failed to have any contact with Stuart – say by June 28?

At that time Robertson and Jones were still in the Gaps some 70 miles south of Lee at Chambersburg. To get a message to them would take at least a day and a half of hard riding, and another day and a half for these troopers to join the army. Three days, probably more, would be needed to have these brigades deployed in front of the army in the Gettysburg area. At this time Lee was hourly expecting news from Stuart, so it was only on June 29 that he summoned these two brigades to join him. Not until July 1 did they begin to move – they had missed the battle!

Stuart, understandably, felt that he needed his best brigades with him on such a critical mission, but leaving Robertson in command, even with detailed orders, proved a mistake, although at the time it appeared, for Stuart, to be the best option.

The fundamental reason for Lee's lack of information in the days prior to the battle appears to be that his faith in his cavalry commander was, in this instance, and most unusually, misplaced. His system of mission command had broken down, as it was to do again in the forthcoming battle.

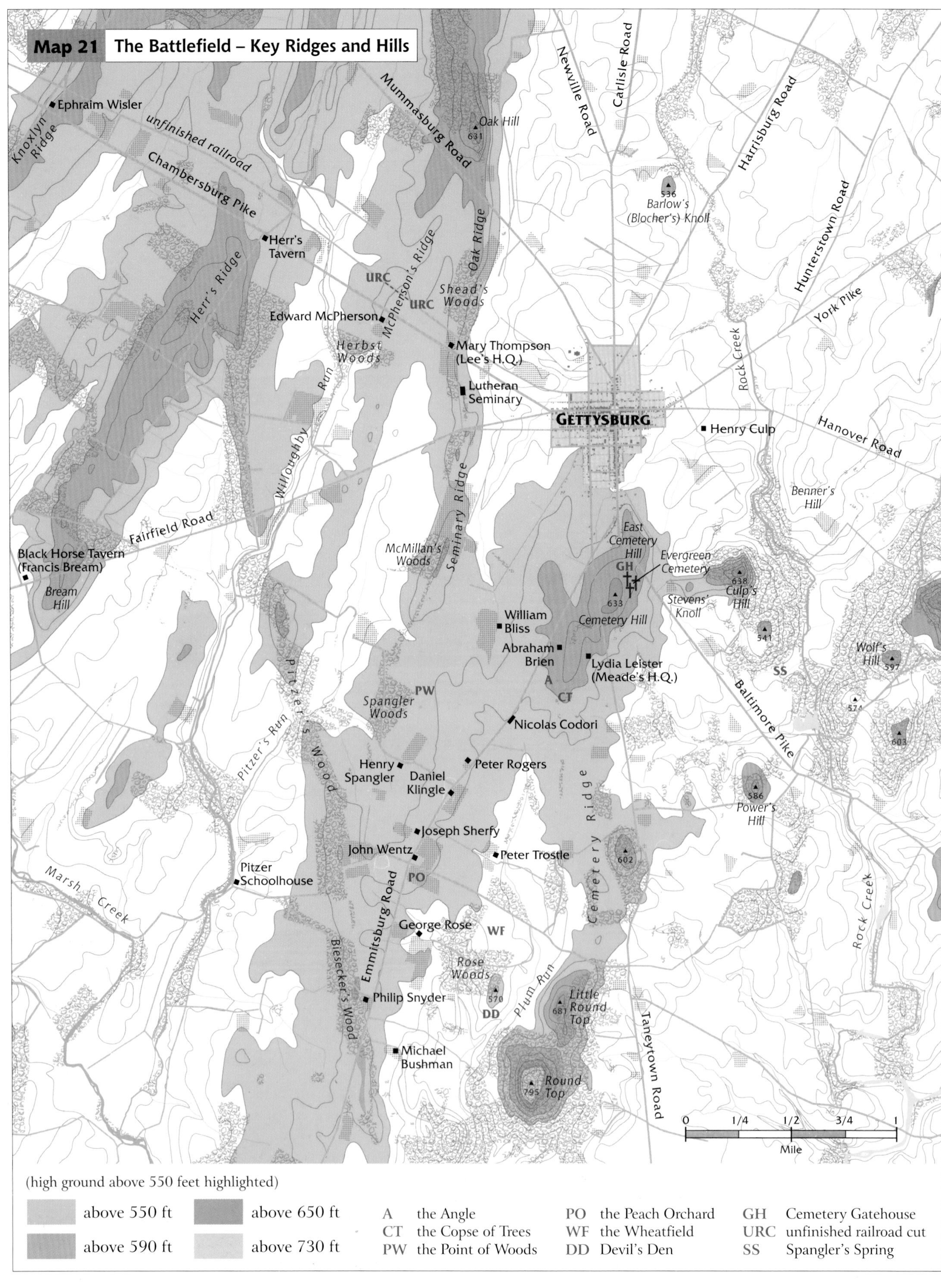

Map 21 The Battlefield – Key Ridges and Hills
Ephraim Wisler
Knoxlyn Ridge
unfinished railroad
Chambersburg Pike
Mummasburg Road
Oak Hill
631
Newville Road
Carlisle Road
Harrisburg Road
536
Barlow's (Blocher's) Knoll
Hunterstown Road
Herr's Tavern
Herr's Ridge
URC
McPherson's Ridge
Oak Ridge
Shead's Woods
York Pike
Edward McPherson
Herbst Woods
Mary Thompson (Lee's H.Q.)
Rock Creek
Lutheran Seminary
Willoughby Run
GETTYSBURG
Henry Culp
Hanover Road
Benner's Hill
Fairfield Road
Seminary Ridge
East Cemetery Hill
GH
Evergreen Cemetery
Black Horse Tavern (Francis Bream)
McMillan's Woods
Bream Hill
633
638
Culp's Hill
Stevens' Knoll
Cemetery Hill
541
William Bliss
Abraham Brien
Lydia Leister (Meade's H.Q.)
Wolf's Hill
597
SS
A
CT
PW
Spangler Woods
Baltimore Pike
574
Pitzer's Woods
Pitzer's Run
Nicolas Codori
603
Henry Spangler
Peter Rogers
Daniel Klingle
Cemetery Ridge
586
Power's Hill
Joseph Sherfy
John Wentz
Peter Trostle
602
Pitzer Schoolhouse
PO
Marsh Creek
Emmitsburg Road
George Rose
WF
Rock Creek
Rose Woods
Biesecker's Wood
Plum Run
570
DD
Philip Snyder
Little Round Top
681
Taneytown Road
Michael Bushman
Round Top
795
0
1/4
1/2
3/4
1
Mile
(high ground above 550 feet highlighted)
above 550 ft
above 590 ft
above 650 ft
above 730 ft
A the Angle
CT the Copse of Trees
PW the Point of Woods
PO the Peach Orchard
WF the Wheatfield
DD Devil's Den
GH Cemetery Gatehouse
URC unfinished railroad cut
SS Spangler's Spring

SECTION EIGHT

The Battlefield

Gettysburg is America's most famous and most celebrated battle; for many Americans it marked the turning point in, or high tide of, the Civil War. Although the premise is arguable, Lee's defeat at Gettysburg meant the Confederacy was doomed, whereas a crushing victory for the South at that time might, just might, have ensured that the Confederacy survived. The battlefield is visited by upward of 2 million people every year. They come to walk the ground, to explore and ponder where the climactic events of those three days took place. They come to find a particular regimental monument, marker or cannon among the 1,870 that are scattered over the field, or to stand on the spot where President Lincoln made his Gettysburg Address some four months after the battle. Nearly 150 historic buildings dot the fields or line the streets of the town, which itself formed part of the battlefield.

Fighting took place over some 20,000 acres and lasted for three days. This large area of land comprises the center of Adams County, of which Gettysburg is the county seat. The family of William Penn originally purchased the land from the Iroquois Indians in 1736 when neither Adams County, Pennsylvania State nor the United States existed. Within a few years 150 families, many settlers from Ireland fleeing English persecution, arrived in an area known by its small river – Marsh Creek (see the southwest corner of Map 21). One such man was Samuel Getty, who established a tavern there in 1761. By 1786 his son James had laid out a small town of 210 lots with a central town square surrounding his tavern. Thus was Gettysburg born.

When the armies converged on it in the summer of 1863, Gettysburg was prospering: a little town surrounded by fertile fields of ripening corn, wheat, oats and hay, with a liberal sprinkling of peach and apple orchards, together with woods of maple, oak and chestnut. Most of its farmers fled with their families at the first rattle of musketry or crash of cannon on July 1, only to return a few days later to find their homes and livelihood destroyed. Timber fences of the post-and-rail or worm (zigzag) variety or low stone walls bounded most of the fields and the roads and tracks that crisscrossed the battlefield. Both provided obstacles to movement and defensive barricades on which to steady a musket or shelter behind during the fighting.

The battlefield at Gettysburg was not one chosen in advance by either side. Both Lee and Meade wanted a decisive encounter, but they wanted it on ground of their own choosing, as terrain features inevitably play a major part in any battle. The ground over which fighting takes place largely dictates battlefield tactics. Hills, ridges, valleys, undulations, rivers, woods and buildings can all be used by commanders to enhance the defense of a position or facilitate an attack. Equally, the misuse of ground can easily lead to disproportionate casualties, lack of surprise and a bloody repulse. At Gettysburg, although both army commanders knew a battle was imminent, neither knew for sure where it would take place until late on July 1. Although Meade was comparatively well informed on his enemy's whereabouts, as late as June 30 he sent his artillery chief, Brigadier-General Henry J. Hunt, to reconnoiter a possible defensive line along the Pipe Creek, some 12 miles southeast of Gettysburg in Maryland. At the same time Lee, with no information from his cavalry, had no wish to bring on a major battle before he had concentrated his army. The clash at Gettysburg, therefore, was an encounter battle that developed in a piecemeal fashion as each side brought more troops to the front. Ground, however, was to play a major part for both sides. On the first day it became a question of senior commanders on the spot seizing and holding, or attacking, important features. By the early hours of July 2 it was the holding of a key feature (Cemetery Hill) by Union forces that decided Meade to deploy for a defensive action – at least initially.

As the battle developed, it was the ground occupied by the Army of the Potomac that gave its line the famous "fishhook" shape. This in turn gave Meade the tactical advantage of interior lines. It meant that troops or couriers had little over 2 miles to cover if moving from Culp's Hill in the north of the Union line to Little Round Top in the south. A Rebel regiment would have to move around the outer edge of the fishhook; there were no shortcuts, and the distance would be nearer 5 miles as the Army of Northern Virginia was operating on exterior lines. As the fighting progressed this had important, indeed crucial, tactical implications.

The remainder of this section will provide background notes on the terrain features, farms and buildings that played a prominent part in events or were the scene of a significant incident. Although not repeated when describing every place, it should be remembered that virtually all buildings were used to shelter wounded or as makeshift dressing stations.

WEDNESDAY, JULY 1

Ridges and Hills

Knoxlyn Ridge

Gettysburg was protected from the Rebel advance down the Chambersburg Pike from the northwest by a series of four ridges. They all blocked the approach to the town at right angles to the Pike and formed the key features of Buford's successful delaying action, which was to have a profound effect on events that followed. Lieutenant Marcellus Jones, 8th Illinois Cavalry, fired the first shot of the battle from Knoxlyn Ridge from close to Wisler's blacksmith shop at the crossroads. This ridge was the site of the cavalry vedette line of Colonel Gamble's Brigade (Buford's Division) and saw the first check to the Confederate advance. Had Buford used this ridge as his first fall-back position instead of just for vedettes, then the Union cavalry's delaying tactics might have been even more effective and more prolonged – but this is speculation.

Herr's Ridge

Exactly a mile further down the Pike toward Gettysburg the Rebels came up against Herr's Ridge, which blocked progress from north of the Chambersburg Pike to the Fairfield Road 2 miles to the southwest. On its eastern side, south of the Pike, was a large wood which later in the morning provided good cover for Heth's troops as they prepared to attack toward the town. The ridge got its name from Herr's Tavern (the site of Captain Black's cavalry picket reserve), located at the northern end of the ridge on the Pike. It dominates all the land to the east and west, but is itself overlooked by Oak Hill over a mile to the northeast. This ridge was the scene of vigorous skirmishing as Gamble's men forced Major Van de Graff's 5th Alabama Infantry Battalion to deploy and move forward. The first Rebel casualty of the battle occurred here when Private C. L. F. Worley of Company A of the battalion had his thigh smashed by a bullet; it resulted in an agonizing amputation, as he refused chloroform. This fall-back position was held by Gamble's men for about an hour before they withdrew to the next convenient stop line – McPherson's Ridge. Herr's Ridge then became the assembly area for the Rebel infantry of Heth's Division for its series of assaults on McPherson's Ridge. It offered a good platform for Confederate guns, which were grouped astride the Pike for their duel with a Union battery some 1,200 yards away. In the early afternoon an anxious Lee observed the action from this ridge and finally authorized Heth to press on with his attack.

McPherson's Ridge

Named after the owner of the farm close to the Chambersburg Pike, this ridge was mostly open and to the south of the Pike extends for well over a mile in a southwesterly direction, but to the north merges into the higher southwest-pointing spur of Oak Hill. At the foot of the western slope, facing the Confederate advance, was Willoughby Run with a scattering of trees along its course. Immediately south of the farm (only the barn of which exists today) and straddling the ridge was Herbst Wood (often erroneously called McPherson's Woods). An important feature of this ridge was that it is broad and has a shallow swale, or dip, running down its center, thus forming two low ridges. The struggle for the ridge saw some intense fighting between Brigadier-General Archer's Confederate Brigade and the Union Iron Brigade, and the struggle for its possession became prolonged and bloody as further reinforcements arrived from both sides. In this area Union Major-General Reynolds was killed and Confederate Major-General Heth wounded. Amongst the trees of Herbst Wood the grizzled seventy-year-old civilian veteran of the War of 1812, John Burns, was wounded while banging away at the attacking Rebels with his ancient flintlock musket.

Gettysburg, photographed from Cemetery Ridge in July 1863 showing the tents of a military camp.

John Burns, the Gettysburg resident who turned out to fight the Rebels on the first day.

Seminary Ridge (North)
The northern end of this ridge was the last of the four defensive ridges blocking the Confederate approach to the town from the west. It got its name from the Lutheran Seminary that stood on its northern end, threequarters of a mile west of the town square. To the north of the Chambersburg Pike it merges into the wooded slopes of Oak Ridge. To the south it extends for over 3.5 miles, the final 1.5 miles being called Warfield Ridge. On this ridge the Army of Northern Virginia formed its main battle line for the struggle that took place on July 2 and 3. The northern portion was the final position for the Union defense of the town in the west. It was along the narrow north–south road that passed the Lutheran Cemetery to join the Chambersburg Pike with the Fairfield Road that on July 1 Union guns were massed to support the defending Union infantry brigades of Stone, Meredith and Biddle. Not until late afternoon were the defenders forced to abandon this ridge under the combined threat of a flank attack in the south coupled with the collapse of XI Corps north of the town.

Oak Hill and Ridge
Dominating its surroundings in all directions except to the north, Oak Hill was decisive terrain. In particular it overlooks the plain north of Gettysburg and both McPherson's and Seminary Ridges, which extend like two arms from Oak Hill and Oak Ridge. When the Rebels of Rodes' Division arrived on the hill they were able to identify the exact location of the Union right flank to the south and the whereabouts of their comrades opposing them. Oak Hill provided a splendid enfilade shoot for the eight Confederate guns that Rodes pushed forward over the crest of the hill, while the woods along the ridge to the north and on the hill itself provided good cover in which Rebel infantry could form up.

Blocher's (Barlow's) Knoll
Blocher's Knoll is the only piece of comparatively high ground in the plain north of the town, topping over 530 feet above sea level but only 70 feet above Rock Creek, which flows at the bottom of its eastern slope. Its elevation above the surrounding fields gave it a slight advantage for occupying artillery, but with no feature nearby from which it could be supported, its defensive value was somewhat illusory. It is located almost exactly a mile north of the town square. The Union divisional commander Brigadier-General Francis C. Barlow was to make a desperate stand on this feature during the afternoon of July 1 before being driven back in confusion.

Cemetery Hill and East Cemetery Hill
This large, broad hill, rising to over 600 feet, proved to be one of the, if not the, deciding terrain features of the battle. Part of it extends northeast across the Baltimore Pike and is called East Cemetery Hill. Both are crowned with a number of small pastures and stone walls. Cemetery Hill and its extension dominate the town, only half a mile to the north, and all the roads leading to it. Running south from it for 1.75 miles is Cemetery Ridge, which formed the backbone of the Union defensive line on July 2 and 3. Cemetery Hill was the location on which the battered and retreating I and XI Corps rallied in the late afternoon and evening of July 1, and which the victorious Confederates failed to take after rampaging through Gettysburg. By the following morning Cemetery Hill had become reinforced, barricaded with earthen barricades ("lunettes") constructed to protect cannon positioned on its eastern slope. This hill formed the northern anchor on which the Union defense rested for the remainder of the battle.

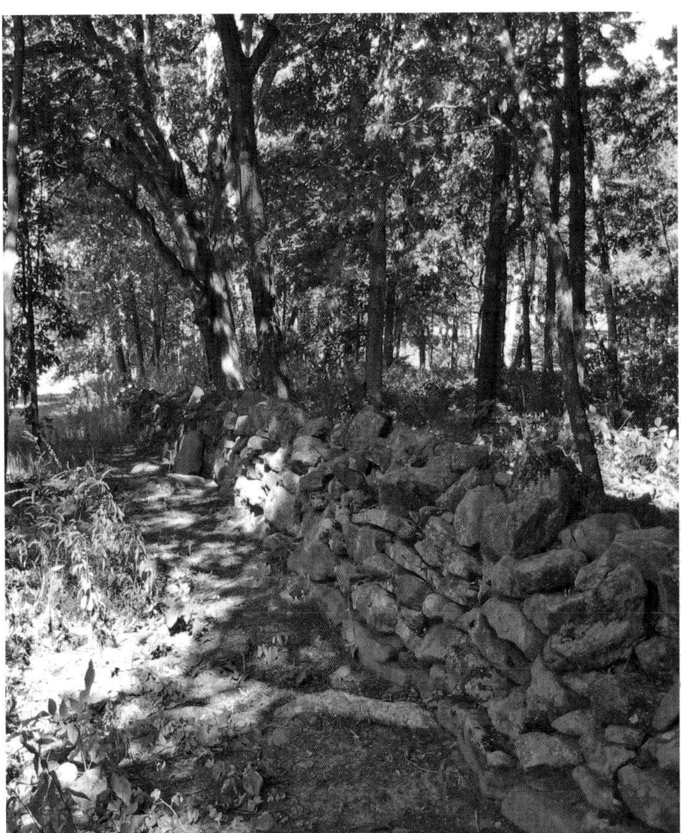

A good example of the sort of stone wall that was built up by Union troops to improve their defenses on several parts of the battlefield. This shows the wall along the eastern edge of Pardee's Field (see pages 460–61).

Notes

• This map shows the entire battlefield as it was in 1863. Included are some contour lines, woods, orchards, streams and fences/walls with places of importance named.

A	the Angle	PO	the Peach Orchard	GH	Cemetery Gatehouse
CT	the Copse of Trees	WF	the Wheatfield	URC	unfinished railroad cut
PW	the Point of Woods	DD	Devil's Den	SS	Spangler's Spring

McPherson's Farm, caught up in the fierce fighting on the first day of the battle.

Farms and Buildings

McPherson's Farm

Edward McPherson's farm consisted of the house and outbuildings – barn, wagon shed, hog pen and small garden. It was situated on the south side of the Chambersburg Pike at the northern end of the ridge of the same name and just a mile from the center of town. Close by to the south were "woodlots" (woods) owned by the neighbor, John Herbst. At the time of the battle a tenant, John Slentz, occupied the farm. He had made good use of his 95 acres, 65 of which were planted with wheat, oats, corn and grass, the remainder being woods and pasture. He maintained a kitchen garden and an orchard close to the house. According to records in the Gettysburg National Military Park, Slentz also owned three cows, six calves, four hogs, three turkeys and some forty chickens – a prosperous and not untypical Pennsylvania farm. Soon after firing started, Slentz, his wife and five children all fled to the safety of the basement of the Lutheran Seminary. This was just as well, as the farm was in the center of the desperate struggle for McPherson's Ridge that occupied the greater part of July 1. The Rebels used the farm as a field hospital after the battle moved on. Today only the barn remains; it was restored in 1978 by the National Park Service, but the peaceful, reflective atmosphere of so much of the battlefield is not present here, destroyed by the roar of traffic down what was the Chambersburg Pike and is now Route 30, and by the car park and large notice advertising visitor information.

The Lutheran Seminary

This magnificent building, the "Old Dorm," with its high cupola, is located near the northern end of Seminary Ridge to which it gives its name. It affords a splendid view over the shallow valley separating it from McPherson's Ridge about 600 yards to the west. From the cupola the view is extended considerably, and for this reason it was used as an observation post by Major-General Buford and by his signal officer Lieutenant Jerome to report the battle developing to the west. Hasty barricades were put up in front of the building, which became the center of the Union line in the late afternoon when that part of Seminary Ridge was attacked by Pender's Division. It was taken over as a Union aid station on July 1 before being overrun by the final Rebel attack. On subsequent days it was hit by shells fired from Cemetery Hill.

In the late morning of July 1 Emanuel and Mary Zeigler, the steward and matron of the Seminary, with their five children, fled to a relative's home near Two Taverns, 5 miles southeast of Gettysburg. Their teenage daughter Lydia later recalled her return: "Oh, what a homecoming! Everything we owned was gone – not a bed to lie on, and not a change of clothing. Many things had been destroyed, and the rest had been converted to hospital purposes." She was right. After the battle it became a fully developed field hospital with more than twenty surgeons treating up to 700 wounded from both sides. See also box, page 241.

A Shirker Amongst the Wounded

After the war, First Lieutenant Jeremiah Hoffman, 142nd Pennsylvania, recalled the hospital in the Lutheran Seminary:

> As usual in such places, there was some mean skulkers hiding among the wounded. There was a lounge [bed] in the corner and on it lay a man groaning dreadfully . . . I often put myself into agony by turning far enough to reach him my canteen. He was one of the mean growlers whom the nurses did not care to assist. It must have been on the second day of the fight when a shell burst under the entry door quite close to our room. The entry and adjoining rooms were filled with smoke, and the cry was raised, "The building is burning." The poor fellows who were badly hurt began to drag their bodies toward the door . . . when some of them were rudely pushed by the skulking dog on the lounge. He jumped up and ran down into the cellar the very picture of fright and not in the least bum.

The Battle Comes to Town

John Rupp and his wife Caroline occupied a house and ran a tannery business on Baltimore Street, near the southern edge of the town. Writing to his sister, Anne, about two weeks after the battle, John paints a vivid picture of what it was like to be caught up in the fighting in Gettysburg. The spelling is in the original and appeared in an article by Timothy H. Smith in the *Gettysburg Magazine*, issue 19, published in 1998:

> We have all escaped bodily injury. My property sustained very slight injury indeed, considering the heavy cannonading of boath armies from Thursday morning [July 2] to until Saturday morning [July 4]. When the battle commenced . . . we took our children and went over to Mr. Welty's celler . . . After the fire ceased, we came home and all slept on the floor that night [July 1] Thursday morning when the battle again began we went to our own celler [and] stayed thair that day. In the night of Thursday father [Henry Rupp] came and took Caroline and the children up to his house. Was then in the cellar by myself, that Thursday night, and all day Friday and Friday night until Saturday morning . . .
>
> The Rebs had my Tannery in thair possession for four days thay used the shop for a fort. It was full of Rebs firing on our pickets up at Welty's fence. . . Our men occupied My porch, and the Rebs the rear of the house, and I the celler. So you can see I was on neutral ground. Our men knew I was in the celler, but the Rebs did not. I could hear the Rebs load thair guns and fire. Thair was one of our men killed under my big oak tree in the lot, and one in Snyders meadow close to our house . . . I sustained no loss in Stock, but the Rebs broke all the glass in and sash in the shop. I gathered up a double handful of Minie Balls in my dweling after the battle . . . If you could have heard the shells fly over our house from boath sides. It was awful . . . Our house is pretty well riddled, thay balls passing through our bed steads, no shell struck it . . . Every church and hall is taken for Hospitals . . .
>
> I remain your brother
> John Rupp

The Rupp House, number 451 Baltimore Street, now houses the Friends of the National Parks, Gettysburg, a charity devoted to restoring the battlefield and monument preservation. A door from the tannery with bullet holes in it is displayed in the Gettysburg National Military Park Visitor Center.

Mary Thompson's House

This house is situated on the north side of the Chambersburg Pike, almost 350 yards north of the Lutheran Seminary and about threequarters of a mile from the center of Gettysburg. As such, it witnessed much of the fighting for both McPherson's and Seminary Ridges. It later became part of Lee's headquarters for the remainder of the battle, although the general himself preferred a tent nearby.

Other Significant Features

The railroad cut

The Gettysburg and Hanover Railroad ended at Gettysburg. By July 1863 the continuation of the railroad bed to the west had been excavated, but no stones, ties or rails laid. This unfinished track cut through Seminary Ridge and through the eastern and western ridges that together comprised McPherson's Ridge. It proved to be both a helpful and a hazardous obstacle for each side as the intense and bloody fight for McPherson's Ridge developed. The central cut, in places up to 20 feet deep, through the eastern branch of McPherson's Ridge was the scene of the surrender of some 230 men of the 2nd Mississippi and 55th North Carolina Regiments after the cut was charged by the 6th Wisconsin.

Gettysburg – the Town

By 1863 Gettysburg had around 450 buildings housing 2,400 inhabitants and was a prosperous commercial center. It boasted several local industries and businesses, such as carriage-makers, shoemakers, tanneries and merchants. Twenty-two shoemakers are listed in the 1860 census, but no shoe factory – so the Confederates' hunt for large quantities of shoes was always doomed to fail (see box, page 120). Additionally, there were several hotels, taverns, a railroad depot, a court house, the county jail, banks, school, churches, the Lutheran Theological Seminary and a college. Gettysburg was also the center of a spider's web of no fewer than eleven roads coming from every direction of the compass.

There were 190 African Americans living in the town (8 percent of the population), mostly in the west and southwestern part near which much of the fighting took place. As the approach of the Rebels brought with it the prospect of capture and enslavement, many fled; as resident Salome Myers put it, "the town is pretty clear of darkies . . . Darkies of both sexes are skedaddling." Their white employers hid some who remained and one was known to have spent two days in a church belfry.

On July 1, before the Confederates overran the town, many of its citizens, including children, watched events from the roofs of their houses. Once the town fell (Union skirmishers held onto the southern outskirts throughout the battle) there was danger from shelling and sharpshooters, so most citizens took shelter, although a number took in wounded from both sides and gave them care, food and lodging. Some went to great lengths to hide Union soldiers from Rebel patrols, in at least one case providing civilian clothes to disguise him. Immediately after the battle many citizens became involved in the care and sustenance of the wounded as all public buildings and some private houses became temporary field hospitals or aid stations.

There was no house-to-house battle for possession of Gettysburg, but rather a series of pockets of resistance by some Union forces as the great majority of I and XI Corps fled through the streets, with considerable numbers being taken prisoner. Those that got away rallied on Cemetery Hill, which became the lynchpin of the Union defense for the next two days. The most serious attempt to stop the rot took place just north of the town at John Kuhn's brickyard. Here three regiments (27th Pennsylvania, 134th and 154th New York) of Colonel Charles Coster's brigade made a stand for a short while against the hugely superior numbers of Early's Division (see box, page 381).

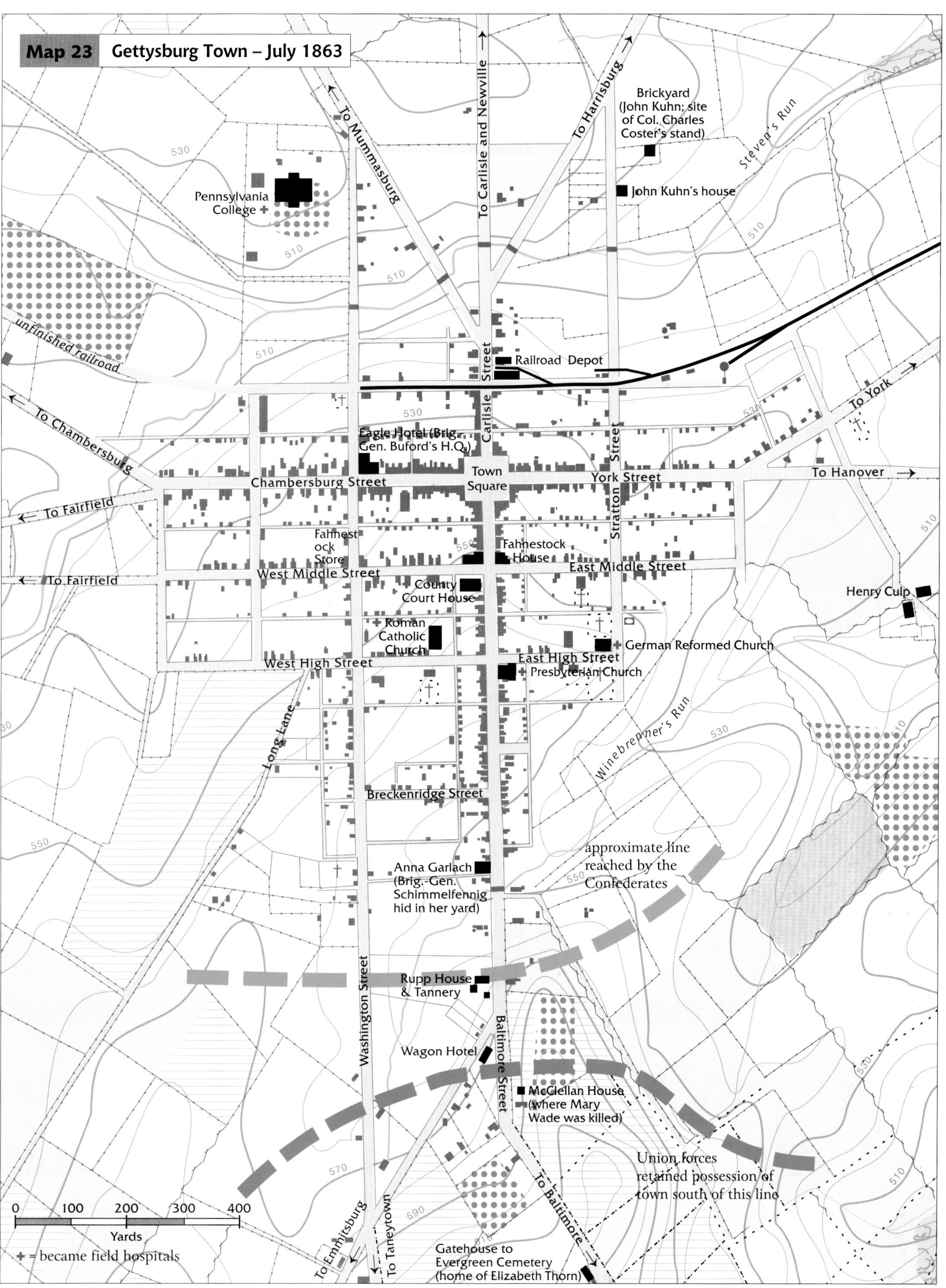
Map 23 Gettysburg Town – July 1863
To Mummasburg
To Carlisle and Newville
To Harrisburg
Brickyard (John Kuhn; site of Col. Charles Coster's stand)
Steven's Run
John Kuhn's house
Pennsylvania College
unfinished railroad
Railroad Depot
Carlisle Street
To York
To Chambersburg
Eagle Hotel (Brig. Gen. Buford's H.Q.)
Town Square
Chambersburg Street
York Street
Stratton Street
To Hanover
To Fairfield
Fahnestock Store
Fahnestock House
West Middle Street
East Middle Street
County Court House
Henry Culp
Roman Catholic Church
German Reformed Church
West High Street
East High Street
Presbyterian Church
Winebrenner's Run
Long Lane
Breckenridge Street
approximate line reached by the Confederates
Anna Garlach (Brig.-Gen. Schimmelfennig hid in her yard)
Rupp House & Tannery
Washington Street
Baltimore Street
Wagon Hotel
McClellan House (where Mary Wade was killed)
Union forces retained possession of town south of this line
To Baltimore
To Emmitsburg
To Taneytown
Gatehouse to Evergreen Cemetery (home of Elizabeth Thorn)
0 100 200 300 400
Yards
+ = became field hospitals

THURSDAY, JULY 2 AND FRIDAY, JULY 3

Ridges and Hills

Cemetery Ridge

This became the backbone of the Union line upon which Meade based his defense for the second and third days of the battle. It was the shank of the fishhook. The ridge begins on the southwestern edge of Cemetery Hill and extends south for 1.5 miles to join Little Round Top. It slopes gradually down from the north to the south and was mostly clear of trees, but with the northern half in particular crisscrossed with fences and low stone walls. It provided an excellent defensive position, well suited to both infantry and artillery. Most defenders could use the reverse slope for protection and concealment of reserves, which could be moved quickly from one point to another using the Taneytown Road while remaining hidden from the Rebels on Seminary Ridge – a facility of which Meade made good use during July 2. The ridge was anchored in the north on Cemetery Hill and in the south on Little Round Top. This meant its flanks could not be effectively turned without either of the two hills being taken first. Without first securing one or other of these hills, an attacker was forced to assault Cemetery Ridge frontally – which is what Lee tried unsuccessfully on both days.

Seminary Ridge

If one includes Oak and Warfield Ridges, which are really part of the same feature at the northern and southern ends respectively, then Seminary Ridge, at over 4 miles in length, is the longest on the battlefield. As discussed above, the northern part was used by the Union as a final defensive position west of the town on July 1. For the remainder of the battle, all the ridge south of the Chambersburg Pike, and including Warfield Ridge, became the main Confederate position for Hill's and Longstreet's Corps. It provided Lee's assembly area and start line for his massive infantry attacks on Cemetery Ridge some threequarters of a mile to the east. The ridge has a much steeper slope on its western side and it is this side that is covered throughout much of its length with dense woods. Its forward (eastern) slope was more open and provided the gun positions for the Rebels' cannon and the prolonged bombardment that preceded Pickett's charge on July 3. Lee was able to move troops behind (west of) the ridge without their being seen from the signal station on Little Round Top except when they used the road over the shoulder of Bream Hill near the Black Horse Tavern. The reverse slope and the woods provided shelter from view and artillery fire for the Rebel infantry in reserve or awaiting the order to advance.

Culp's Hill, Lower Culp's Hill and Stevens' Knoll

This rocky, steep-sided, heavily wooded hill rises nearly 640 feet above sea level and 180 feet above Rock Creek, which flows at the foot of its eastern slope. Culp's Hill extends south for about a quarter of a mile, culminating in another, lower summit called Lower Culp's Hill, some 80 feet above the creek. To the west a low ridge connects Culp's Hill to East Cemetery Hill with a small rise, Stevens' Knoll, in the center. It was the line from Lower Culp's Hill running through Culp's Hill and then bending west over Stevens' Knoll to Cemetery Hill that formed the "hook" of the fishhook – with Lower Culp's Hill being its point. This feature was not taken by the Rebels on the evening of July 1 and it became one of the most heavily fortified parts of the Union line, with extensive barricades and entrenchments constructed in the woods. It was defended by XII Corps and subjected to a series of determined assaults by Johnson's Division on the evening of July 2 and to a lesser extent the next day. Culp's Hill and Lower Culp's Hill saw some of the most intense close-quarter fighting of the battle, with the Confederates struggling up steep slopes through the woods to assault well-barricaded positions. Much of this fighting took place in the dark. The bullet- and shell-scarred trees have long gone, but the earthworks can still be traced in places.

Power's Hill

An isolated, steep-sided hill, mostly covered in woods, just under a mile east of the center of the Union line on Cemetery Ridge. It dominated the Baltimore Pike, which ran southeast at the foot of its eastern slope, and overlooks most of the reverse (eastern) slope of Cemetery Ridge and Hill. It therefore provided an excellent observation post over most of the Union positions. As such, it was the site of Major-General Slocum's XII Corps headquarters, a signal station and for a time on July 3 was Meade's headquarters when he was driven from Leister House by Confederate shelling. It was not the scene of any fighting.

The Round Tops

Round Top, or Big Round Top, as it is often called, marks the southern tip of Cemetery Ridge and is some 2.5 miles from Cemetery Hill. It was the highest and steepest hill on the battlefield, but was covered entirely by woods, which meant little could be seen from its slopes or summit and it was totally inaccessible for artillery. It was unoccupied by Union troops on July 2 but its slopes were used by some of Hood's Division to launch their attack on Little Round Top. On July 3 Round Top was occupied by the men of Colonel Joseph Fisher's Brigade (3rd Division, V Corps).

Little Round Top, immediately north of, and connected to, its larger sister, played a key role in the fighting on July 2. Belatedly occupied by Union forces and belatedly attacked by the

The effect of musket fire on the trees on Culp's Hill.

Round Top seen from the entrenchments on Little Round Top.

Confederates on the same day, this hill was the scene of some extraordinarily bitter fighting. Nearly 700 feet above sea level, with steep sides but largely free of woods on its western slope, it offered splendid views to the west and northwest. It was plentifully strewn with rocks and boulders, which gave cover to its defenders and facilitated the building of low barricades. However, its small, steep-sided summit precluded its use by more than a battery of guns and even they could not depress their barrels to fire on attackers at close range due to the convex slope and large boulders. It was with great difficulty that the four guns, but not the limbers, of Lieutenant Charles E. Hazlett's battery were hauled to the top. For this reason Little Round Top did not seriously dominate Cemetery Ridge to the north, although viewed from the Rebel positions it appeared to do so. It did, however, provide the site of a highly effective Union signal station. It also marked the extreme left flank of the Union line on July 2 and was the scene of intense fighting, including the legendary struggle between the 20th Maine and 15th Alabama. The statue of Brigadier-General Warren now surveys the field from the summit of what has become one of the most visited sites on the battlefield.

Farms and Buildings

Bliss Farm

A typical Pennsylvania farm with house and large, fortress-like red barn, surrounded by fenced fields. The farm was owned by William Bliss, who with his wife, two daughters and hired hand had left before the fighting started. This was just as well, as it was situated midway between the opposing lines half a mile southwest of Cemetery Hill and 400 yards from the Emmitsburg Road. Its position meant skirmishers continually disputed its possession. The barn in particular made a secure firing point for sharpshooters and it changed hands several times. It became the scene of heavy fighting late on July 2 and was taken by the Rebels of Anderson's Division during their attack late that afternoon (see box, page 399). On July 3 continuous skirmishing for its possession during the morning so annoyed Brigadier-General Hays that he ordered the 14th Connecticut to burn it down – which they did. It was the only farm on the battlefield to be completely destroyed. It was never rebuilt.

Henry Culp's Farm

Situated less than half a mile east of the town, this farm of some 240 acres was established by Christopher Kolp (Culp) in 1787. By 1863 the extended Culp family formed an important part of the Gettysburg community, with the original farm being owned by Henry Culp. Henry was married to Anna Raffensberger, whose parents owned Raffensberger Hill, now known as East Cemetery Hill. The farm was behind Confederate lines for most of the battle and escaped damage, although it was around it that the Rebels formed up to launch their attack on East Cemetery Hill on the evening of July 2. It was to this house that the mortally wounded Confederate brigade commander Colonel Isaac E. Avery was brought after this attack.

Lydia Leister's House

Lydia Leister was a widow with six children who owned a 9-acre smallholding just over a mile from the center of town, just off the west side of the Baltimore Pike. At the start of the shooting she fled with her children to shelter in a friend's house. Her home was chosen by Meade as his headquarters in the early hours of July 2, as it was conveniently situated in the center of his line and on the reverse slope of Cemetery Ridge. Late on the same day it was here that Meade held his famous conference with his corps commanders, at which it was unanimously agreed to stay and fight. It suffered severely in the Rebels' massive early-afternoon bombardment on July 3, forcing Meade temporarily to abandon it in favor of Power's Hill. The house was badly damaged by shelling but used as a makeshift field hospital after the battle. Lydia Leister rebuilt her property and prospered, later selling her home to the Gettysburg Battlefield Memorial Association. She died in 1893.

Abraham Brien's Farm

Abraham Brien was a free black farmer with a wife and three children who had purchased his 12 acres in 1857. He kept a cow, horse, planted wheat and barley, and maintained a peach and apple orchard adjacent to the house. His property was a mile from the center of Gettysburg and about 150 yards east of the Emmitsburg Road on the forward slope of Cemetery Ridge. Brien left with his family on July 1 when he heard the Rebels were coming, as he feared capture and enslavement. Brigadier-General Alexander Hays used the farm as his headquarters. Close to the reconstructed house (which visitors can see inside) is the high water marker of the 11th Mississippi, indicating the furthest point reached by that regiment on July 3. After the battle Brien returned to rebuild his life and claimed over $1,000 in compensation for the damage to his property – he received $15. He sold up in 1869 to work in a hotel in town, dying in 1875.

The Evergreen Gatehouse

This was the gatehouse to the Evergreen Cemetery on Cemetery Hill and in July 1863 it was occupied by the Thorn family. However, at the time of the battle Peter Thorn, the cemetery caretaker, was a corporal serving in the 138th Pennsylvania Infantry, which was at Harper's Ferry and Washington during the Gettysburg campaign. His wife Elizabeth, who was six months pregnant, undertook his caretaker duties. Living with her in the gatehouse were her parents and her three young sons.

On July 1 Major-General Howard placed a division in reserve on Cemetery Hill and Captain Wiedrich's Battery, 1st New York Light Artillery, was posted near the Gatehouse. Elizabeth Thorn later recounted what happened as Union troops started knocking on her door: "I took a butcher knife and stood before the oven and cut hot bread for them as fast as I could." She put tubs of water outside the door and her children kept them filled. "All the time our little boys were pumping and carrying water to fill the tubs. They handed water to the soldiers and worked and helped this way until their poor little hands were blistered." Elizabeth later accompanied a mounted officer to show him the roads leading into town from the east and northeast (the York, Hanover and Harrisburg roads). She was impressed by the way the officer made her walk on the "safe" side of his horse to protect her from stray bullets. While she was away a shell fragment smashed an upstairs window and buried itself in the ceiling. Late that night (July 1) Elizabeth was asked to prepare a meal for Major-Generals Howard, Slocum and Sickles.

> The . . . supper of the three generals was made up of two good sized dough cakes I had made, pan cakes, three pieces of meat I had, apple butter and coffee. I . . . said nothing while they ate. When they moved back their chairs I asked whether we ought to move out of the [gate]house. Gen. Howard answered, saying that we had better stay where we were and that as soon as there was any danger he would send us word.

The next day the family was advised to move out and after a long walk down the Baltimore Pike sheltered in Daniel Sheaffer's Farm.

When Meade finally arrived on the field shortly after midnight it was at the Gatehouse that he met with his corps commanders (Howard, Slocum and Sickles). After the battle Elizabeth helped with the burial of over 100 dead. Both Peter and Elizabeth Thorn died in 1907 and are buried in "their" Evergreen Cemetery.

The Brien House on Cemetery Hill, photographed not long after the battle.

Nicholas Codori's Farm

Nicholas Codori, a Frenchman from Alsace, had immigrated to America in 1828 and apprenticed himself to a local butcher before starting his own business. He did well, fathered eleven children and, at the outbreak of the Civil War, purchased the imposing farmhouse on the Emmitsburg Road 1.5 miles from the town center. As such it was situated almost precisely in the center of the battlefield of July 2 and 3. The Codori family sheltered in the basement during the fighting. On the evening of July 2 Anderson's men swept past either side of the house in an attack that took Brigadier Ambrose Wright's Georgians up to the Union line. The next day it was the turn of Pickett's Division. Again, their advance took them on either side of the house, with the division using it as a marker to incline to their left as it converged on the Copse of Trees. It is said that Pickett watched the final charge from the house. For months after the battle the house served as the Gettysburg Catholic Church, as the one in town was full of wounded. The Codori family continued to live in the house until 1983.

Peter Rogers' Farm

Peter and Susan Rogers occupied this farm with their adopted daughter, Josephine Miller. Peter was sixty-eight years old with long, silver hair and had cheered on the Union I Corps troops as they marched up the Emmitsburg Road on July 1 with the words: "Whip em boys, this time, if you don't whip em now, you'll never whip em." Some of the men brought chickens and Josephine began to bake bread. Peter's house was a small, white frame building on the Emmitsburg Road a quarter of a mile south of the Codori property and was at the center of the battle on both July 2 and 3. On July 2 it was part of Sickles' salient and on the front of the Union line, with the 11th Massachusetts Infantry posted close by. It was taken by Rebels in their attack during the afternoon and came under artillery fire from both sides during the battle. On July 3 Colonel David Lang's tiny Florida Brigade swept past the house as part of the Pickett assault.

Over a year after the battle the house was visited by a Mr. Isaac Moorhead, who described what he saw and was told by the grandson of the owner:

> [Shells had] entered the house from Cemetery Hill and [Little] Round Top, one bursting in a bureau and pinning a portion of the contents to the log walls, where they still remained. A piece of shell was stuck in the leaf of a table. A minie ball struck just over the clock. A rebel sharpshooter was killed on top of the house, and tumbled down in front of the door. Another died of exhaustion on the steps. Many were found dead in the yard. In a field behind the house several were buried; the feet of one stuck up through the ground. His skull was bare.

Peter Rogers was shot in the stomach in late 1864 after an argument over some flowers, but against the odds for that type of wound he survived and the culprit was jailed. Rogers died in 1870, aged seventy-five. When Sickles attended the fiftieth anniversary of the battle in 1913 he selected the Rogers' house as his headquarters where he met many veteran visitors.

Daniel Klingle Farm

Daniel Klinge was both a shoemaker and a farmer. He and his family lived in a small log house surrounded by orchards, with a barn and outbuilding, on the Emmitsburg Road some 400 yards south of the Rogers' Farm. As such, it was in the center of Sickles' line along that road. Klingle was still in residence on July 2 when Union troops of the 16th Massachusetts took up positions in the house and to the north, with the 11th New Jersey on the south side. Klingle was urged to leave, but his initial response was, "If I must die, I will die at home." However, he was persuaded to take his family to safety at a friend's house near the Rock Creek. En route he had an argument with a Union officer who snatched his hat from his head and wanted to take it without payment. He left his family near Little Round Top and returned to his house to retrieve some clothing, but the fighting was too close so he turned back. When close to Little Round Top he was summoned to the summit by a Union officer (possibly a signal officer) to help identify several terrain features. He then took his family on to Rock Creek. Meanwhile, his house had been made into something of a strong point, with sharpshooters at the windows and rifle-muskets protruding through gaps in the logs. It became a target for shellfire and was overrun in the evening by Longstreet's assault, which eventually forced Sickles to retire after some extremely bitter fighting. In 1933 the bones of two Confederate soldiers were unearthed in the bean patch. The house still stands.

The Cemetery Gatehouse, clearly showing battle damage.

Joseph Sherfy Farm

The Sherfy Farm was occupied by Joseph, his wife Mary, three sons, three daughters and mother-in-law Catherine Heagen. It was located about 300 yards north of the intersection of the Emmitsburg Road and the Millerstown Road, now known as the Wheatfield Road. The barn was alongside, to the west of the Emmitsburg Road, with the house set back to the northeast. Joseph Sherfy also owned the soon to be famous "Peach Orchard" (see page 330) some 400 yards to the south, as well as the extensive orchards between the Peach Orchard and his house on the opposite side of the Emmitsburg Road, together with another behind his house. His farm was primarily a fruit farm and he had a small fruit-canning business. Like most of the farms and buildings along the Emmitsburg Road, the Sherfy property was incorporated into Sickles' defensive salient and as such suffered considerable damage. The farm was occupied initially by the 57th Pennsylvania Infantry with Union guns in the flower garden. It bore the full force of Barksdale's Mississippians when they launched their assault late on July 2. The barn, while still sheltering some wounded, was burned down the next day and, like so many buildings in the area, it was surrounded by dead and wounded from both sides. Inside, one observer noted, "the house was terribly used up by shell . . . Four feather beds . . . were soaked with blood and bloody clothes and filth of every description was strewn over the house." For many years after the battle passers-by could see a 12-pounder cannon ball embedded in the trunk of a cherry tree in the yard.

Henry Spangler's Farm

Henry Spangler and his wife Sarah had their property on either side of a lane that led to the Emmitsburg Road, about a quarter of a mile to the southeast. In the opposite direction it led to the Fairfield Road. There were the usual outbuildings and a substantial orchard nearby, and 200 yards to the northwest were Spangler Woods. In between the farm and the woods was a swale. It was this swale that was to conceal the Rebels under Brigadier-General Cadmus M. Wilcox on the evening of July 2 when they advanced to attack Sickles' salient. It also provided some cover for Kemper's Brigade when it formed up at the start of Pickett's charge. The house was not in the center of the fighting, as were those of Codori, Rogers, Klingle, Sherfy and Wentz, and thus did not suffer the destruction meted out to them.

John Wentz Farm

Situated in the northeast corner of the intersection of the Emmitsburg Road and the Wheatfield–Pitzer Schoolhouse Road, surrounded by peach orchards, the Wentz property was at the apex of Sickles' salient and thus the target for McLaws' divisional attack late in the afternoon of July 2. John, seventy-three, his wife Mary, seventy-two, and daughter Susan, aged twenty-four, had left prior to this major assault and heavy preparatory bombardment. Union guns were posted on either side of the

The aftermath of Captain Bigelow's last-ditch defense of the corner of the field in front of Trostle's Farm, with numerous dead horses still lying where they fell.

small frame house and by the more prominent barn, with infantry of the 68th Pennsylvania under Colonel Andrew H. Tippin close by. It was the Rebels of Barksdale's Brigade that eventually swept through the area and Union forces were driven back. Strangely, the house was relatively unharmed, but a number of Union wounded sheltering in the cellar were captured. It was the barn that suffered considerable damage and was burned down on July 3.

George Rose Farm
George and Dorothy Rose owned the property, but in July 1863 John Rose managed it with the help of another tenant family. There were 230 acres, which included what was to become the blood-soaked "Wheatfield," some 400 yards east of the stone house and massive stone barn. The farm, woods and Wheatfield were the scene of intense fighting on July 2, and Union troops nearby claimed to have heard the farm bell ring as bullets struck it. The house was hit by shellfire (the owner kept a 12-pounder ball as a souvenir) and was used after its capture as an aid station by Dr. James B. Clifton of Brigadier-General Semmes' Brigade. This did not prevent the destruction of the property inside the house. Mr. I. O. Sloan, a U.S. Christian Commission representative, described the damage:

> Here everything was torn to pieces. Many shells had passed through the house. The enemy had destroyed all the furniture. Clothing was scattered about, drawers emptied and everything torn [presumably for bandages], and broken, and thrown into the utmost confusion. I should judge from the dead bodies we saw in the yard that South Carolina chivalry had been at work [Brigadier-General Joseph B. Kershaw's Brigade had over 2,000 men from that state].

The number of dead in the farmyard and immediate vicinity was huge. John Howard Wert, who visited the battlefield on July 6, described the dead around the farm:

> In the garden of the Rose house. . . nearly one hundred rebels were buried. All around the barn, even within the house yard, within a few feet of the doors, were, in numbers, the scantily buried followers of the Confederate cause . . . Two hundred and seventy-five were buried behind the barn; a rebel colonel was buried within a yard of the kitchen door.

These corpses were mostly from Kershaw's Brigade, which had attacked through Rose's property into the woods and on to the Wheatfield under murderous Union fire.

Peter Trostle Farm
This farm is one of the most famous on the battlefield. At the time Abraham Trostle, who had leased it from his father Peter, occupied it. With him were his wife, Catherine, and their children. The property, situated in almost the exact center of the battlefield about a third of a mile east of the Emmitsburg Road, consisted of a new, wood-frame house, large barn, wagon shed, corn crib, apple orchard, a summer kitchen under construction and 134 acres of land. It was a prosperous farm that extended to the Emmitsburg Road in the west, the Plum Run in the east and the Wheatfield in the south; its fields yielded a good crop of rye, wheat and corn. Beside the buildings was a narrow east–west lane connecting the farm to the Emmitsburg Road in the west.

On July 2 Major-General Sickles advanced his corps to the Emmitsburg Road and formed his defensive salient. He selected the yard of Trostle's as his headquarters and the family was advised to depart – which they did in a hurry, leaving a meal prepared on the table that was quickly eaten by Sickles' staff. A major Rebel attack, preceded by a heavy artillery bombardment, began around 4:30 p.m. and at its height Sickles was severely wounded in the leg and carried from the field – there is a marker there today. Many of Sickles' troops used the lane past the farm in their retreat that evening, including those engaged in the fighting withdrawal by Captain John Bigelow's 9th Massachusetts Light Battery. Bigelow fought his guns in a final stand in the corner of the field across the lane from the house. Bigelow was wounded and four of his guns were lost but recovered later. Marking the spot where this stand took place is a granite replica of a limber chest and two cannon. The buildings were all badly damaged and Trostle lost everything he owned. The barn has a hole near the roofline made by a cannonball that now resides in the Gettysburg Museum.

Michael Bushman Farm

The Reverend Michael Bushman owned the 175-acre farm at the southern end of the battlefield, some 250 yards east of the Emmitsburg Road. It had the usual barn outbuildings and peach orchard, and was approached by a lane from the Emmitsburg Road. On the afternoon of July 2 Hood's Division formed up on the right of the Rebel line beside and almost parallel to the Emmitsburg Road before attacking due east toward the Round Tops. The Bushman Farm was then occupied by skirmishers from the 2nd U.S. Sharpshooters (Berdan) and was directly in the path of Brigadier-General Jerome B. Roberston's Texan Brigade, in particular Colonel Robert M. Powell's 5th Texans. The advance moved off at the double-quick at about 4:30 p.m., supported by artillery fire and followed closely by the divisional commander. Confederate skirmishers drove Berdan's men from the farm and the Texans came under heavy cannon fire. As the attackers moved through the orchard south of Bushman's barn, a shell burst overhead, wounding General Hood in the right arm. The Rebels pressed forward and became embroiled in the bloody and prolonged struggle for the Rose Woods, Devil's Den and Little Round Top, leaving the farm to the rear of the Confederate line where, like every other battlefield building, it was taken over as a temporary field hospital. The house and barn are still intact and the old faceted stone walls show signs of musket-ball hits.

Black Horse Tavern (Bream's Farm)

This large (400-acre) property was owned and run by Francis Bream with his wife Elizabeth. It was located some 3 miles east of Gettysburg on the Fairfield Road and was thus not on the battlefield itself. However, it played its part in the action. First, it was located at a crossroads, the southern branch of which led up over the shoulder of Bream Hill on its way over Willoughby Run to the southern end of the battlefield. As it crested the rise, it was visible from the summit of Little Round Top. This was the route taken on July 2 by Longstreet's Corps in its long, supposedly outflanking march, to roll up the Union left. As these troops reached Bream Hill it was realized that they were visible from the Union signal station on Little Round Top and the entire corps was countermarched, adding considerable distance and time to its journey. The second part played by the tavern was its use as a major field hospital for McLaws' Division, a role it continued to play for six weeks after the battle.

Other Notable Features

Woods

As shown on Map 21, the battlefield is liberally endowed with woods, particularly down Seminary Ridge from Oak Hill in the north to where Biesecker's Wood touches the Emmitsburg Road over 4 miles to the south. The map shows the woods as they were in the summer of 1863, and visitors should be aware that today's woods are thicker and in places larger than during the battle. Most woods at the time were clear of underbrush and so visibility, although restricted, was reasonable over short distances. In general, these woods running south from Oak Hill, such as the McMillan, Spangler, Pitzer and Biesecker Woods, concealed the Confederate troops from view, if not always from fire, as they assembled and formed up prior to attacking. The "Point of Woods" – the eastern corner of Spangler Woods – was Lee's location as he watched the Pickett–Pettigrew–Trimble attack on July 3. Cemetery Ridge was only sparsely wooded. However, Culp's Hill on the Union right was very heavily wooded, as was the eastern half of Little Round Top and the whole of Round Top at the southern end. Culp's Hill woods were the scene of intense fighting and, along with the steepness of the slopes, were more of a blessing to the Yankee defenders than to the Rebel attackers. The woods on Little Round Top did not have any bearing on the fighting for that position, while those on Round Top were a major restriction to visibility and prevented the hill from becoming an important feature in the battle. Apart from the woods on Culp's Hill, the only other woods that saw serious infantry fighting were the Rose Woods in the south.

The Damage to the Trostle Farm

This farm was occupied by Union troops during July 1 and later used as a temporary field hospital. The damage caused was typical of the properties that had the misfortune to be on the battlefield. The following is an extract from Gregory A. Coco's excellent book, *A Strange and Blighted Land*, which details the claim made in 1874 by Catherine Trostle, her husband Abraham having been declared insane:

> The soldiers damaged or appropriated most of the crops on the place, consisting of hay, wheat, oats, corn and grass, they also stole vegetables, some cattle and a hog. The men destroyed rail fencing which was used for fuel, and ate the stored meat and potatoes, and took many household and personal things. The land was greatly injured by troops who cut roads through the fields, and by the passage of artillery vehicles and guns. The structures themselves were often struck by shells and balls, which went "crashing through the building and causing great destruction to its contents." In addition 16 dead horses [mostly belonging to Captain Bigelow's 9th Massachusetts Battery] were left "close by the door," and about 100 more around other parts of the farm. The land was fought over several times, driving away or killing the cattle, fowl, cows and other stock.
>
> Their losses included: 20 tons of hay in barn $300; 6,400 [fence]rails, $512; house and barn used for hospital purposes and damaged by shells, $200; three cows and one heifer killed, $40; one bull, $20; one hog, $15; one sheep, $5; 50 chickens, $12.50; two hives of bees, $14; 15 barrels of flour, $120; family clothes, $20; two barrels of hams and shoulders, 200 pounds, $40; one saddle and two bridles, beds and bedding, $50; 32 acres of grass, $650; one acre of potatoes, $50; one acre flax, $15; 4 acres of barley, $50; 8 acres of oats, $80; 9 acres of corn, $360; and 27 acres of wheat, $600.

The total claim amounted to $3,153.50, of which Catherine was unlikely to receive more than a tiny fraction, if any.

Streams

The heading is "streams" rather than "rivers," as they were not wide, were easily fordable through shallow water throughout their length and did not generally present an obstacle to movement – certainly for infantry or cavalry – and so did not have much influence on the tactics of the battle. Although a slight exaggeration, the battlefield boundary in the west was the Willoughby Run and in the east Rock Creek, as both ran a roughly north–south parallel course.

The only stream that saw considerable fighting on July 2, and whose water at times flowed red while its banks were littered with dead, was the Plum Run. It began life just south and east of the Codori Farm, flowing approximately southeast of the Trostle Farm and the Wheatfield, west of Little Round Top through "Devil's Den," and thence along the foot of the western slope of Round Top. Where it ran between Little Round Top and Rose Woods became known as the "Valley of Death."

Orchards

Virtually every farm had its peach or apple orchard; many had both. They were a feature of the battlefield, although not one of much tactical importance. The only orchard that will be forever associated with Gettysburg is the Peach Orchard owned by Joseph Sherfy (see page 327). This rectangular orchard was situated in the southeastern corner of the intersection of the Emmitsburg and Millerstown (Wheatfield) Roads, and measured some 300 yards along its northern and southern sides and about 150 yards on the eastern and western sides. At the time of the battle the fruit was still green on the trees. What made it so important was that Sickles selected it as the apex of his corps' forward defensive position, threequarters of a mile in advance of the Union line. He chose it because the orchard was the highest point on a low ridge that ran along the Emmitsburg Road. He made it the site of four Union gun batteries. The position was exposed to flanking fire and eventually overrun after a bitter struggle on July 2, followed by the rapid retreat of Sickles' Corps. The orchard was shattered by gunfire and branches that had been ripped from the trees were scattered throughout the orchard. The orchard today is on the same ground, but it is much smaller than it was in 1863 and has now been replanted.

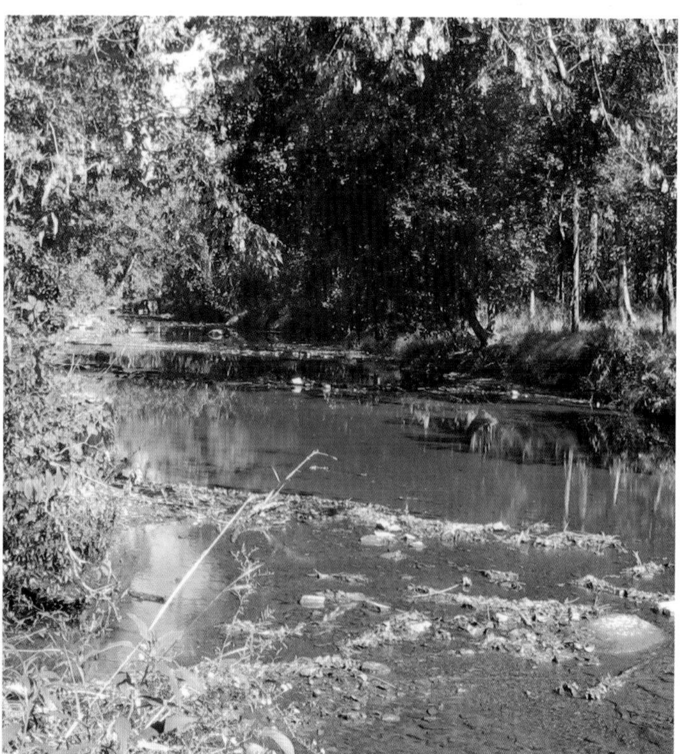

Rock Creek, looking east from near the 28th Pennsylvania Infantry monument. It was across this shallow stream that Steuart's and Walker's Brigades attacked Culp's Hill – advancing from right to left.

Devil's Den

Devil's Den is situated 450 yards west of Little Round Top at the southern end of a forested ridge that separates the Plum Run valley from the Wheatfield. From the summit a good view is obtained over the Philip Snyder and Bushman Farm areas. A veteran of the battle described it as:

> a wild, rocky labyrinth which, from its weird, uncanny features, has long been called by the people of the vicinity the "Devil's Den." Large rocks from six to fifteen feet high are thrown together in confusion over a considerable area and yet so disposed as to leave everywhere among them siding passages carpeted with moss. Many of the recesses are never visited by the sunshine, and a cavernous coolness pervades the air within it.

Such an area was ideal for skirmishers, sharpshooters and soldiers seeking protection from showers of shells and bullets. On July 2 it marked the extreme left of Sickles' salient and was held by the four guns (there was no room for six) of Captain James Smith's Battery that were the subject of repeated attacks by the 1st Texas and 15th Georgia Infantry Regiments through a triangular field just north of Devil's Den. Eventually Smith was overrun and had to abandon all four guns to the triumphant Texans. The area between Devil's Den and the Round Tops became known as the "Slaughter Pen." The dead of both armies littered the area for at least a week after the fighting. Today the Devil's Den boulders are clambered over by scores of visitors every day, as it is one of the most popular battlefield sites.

The Angle and the Copse of Trees

These two very insignificant features, only 100 yards apart, have become the most visited sites on the battlefield and the scene of countless reunions, ceremonies and re-enactments right up to today. They are said by many to mark the "high water mark of the Rebellion." The Angle is merely a 90-degree bend in a low rock wall that ran below the crest of Cemetery Ridge, 220 yards east of the Emmitsburg Road and a mile south of the town, on land tenanted by Peter Frey. The Copse of Trees, 100 yards to the southeast, is a small group of scrub oak trees, 80 yards south of the Angle and set back about 50 yards from the stone wall running south from it. The stone wall marked the front line of Brigadier-General Alexander Webb's Brigade of Brigadier-General John F. Gibbon's Division. Kneeling behind the wall between these two points were the 71st Pennsylvania on the right and the 69th Pennsylvania on the left, with four of Lieutenant Alonzo H. Cushing's guns between them. Lee had picked out the clump of oak trees as the marker upon which the divisions of Pickett–Pettigrew–Trimble would converge on the afternoon of July 3. The attack was thrown back, but only after scores of men, led by Brigadier-General Lewis A. Armistead (he was mortally wounded and captured), had clambered over the wall and onto Cemetery Ridge – the only troops to do so that day, hence the site becoming known as the "high water mark."

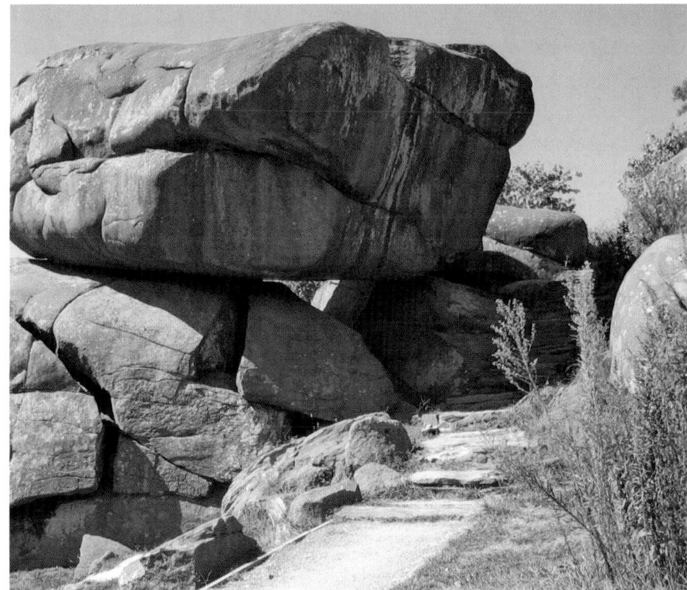

The entrance to Devil's Den, showing the size of the massive boulders that offered protection from bullets and shellfire.

After the Rebel charge had receded, the slope from the Emmitsburg Road to the wall between the Angle and Copse of Trees was covered with the dead and dying. Colonel Charles S. Wainwright, commanding the artillery brigade in the Union I Corps, described the scene:

> There was about an acre or so of ground here [in front of the Angle] where you could not walk without stepping over the bodies, and I saw perhaps a dozen cases where they were heaped one on top of the other. A captain lay thus across the body of a lieutenant-colonel. Both, especially the latter, were very handsome men. A wounded reb told me the colonel's name, but I have forgotten it . . .

The Wheatfield

The Wheatfield is one of, if not the, most bloodied parts of the battlefield. When at last McLaws' Division took it late on July 2, it had changed hands six times in a see-saw of desperate fighting, much of it at close range and at times hand to hand. When the fighting moved on, over 4,000 Confederate and Union dead and wounded littered the 19 acres of George Rose's wheatfield. The rectangular field borders the road – now called the Wheatfield Road but in 1863 known as the Millerstown Road – that connects the Emmitsburg Road to the Taneytown Road. Each side measures about 400 yards, except in the east where it is nearer 300. On all sides except the east woods surround the field, although they are thicker today than in 1863. Two generals were mortally wounded at the Wheatfield, one Rebel and one Yankee. The former was Brigadier-General Paul Semmes, who was shot in the leg and died eight days later when the wound became badly infected. The latter was Brigadier-General Samuel K. Zook, who was shot in the stomach and died in a field hospital on the Baltimore Pike soon after midnight.

Today the Wheatfield is the site of numerous Union brigade and regimental monuments. Particularly impressive is the Irish Brigade's monument, of green granite topped by a Celtic cross and adorned with the likeness of an Irish wolfhound – a traditional symbol of Irish loyalty. In 1888 a group of veterans returned to dedicate their monument. The last two lines of the inscription read:

> *'Tis ours to raise this cross on high above the Irish dead,*
> *Who showed mankind the way to die, when Truth and Freedom led.*

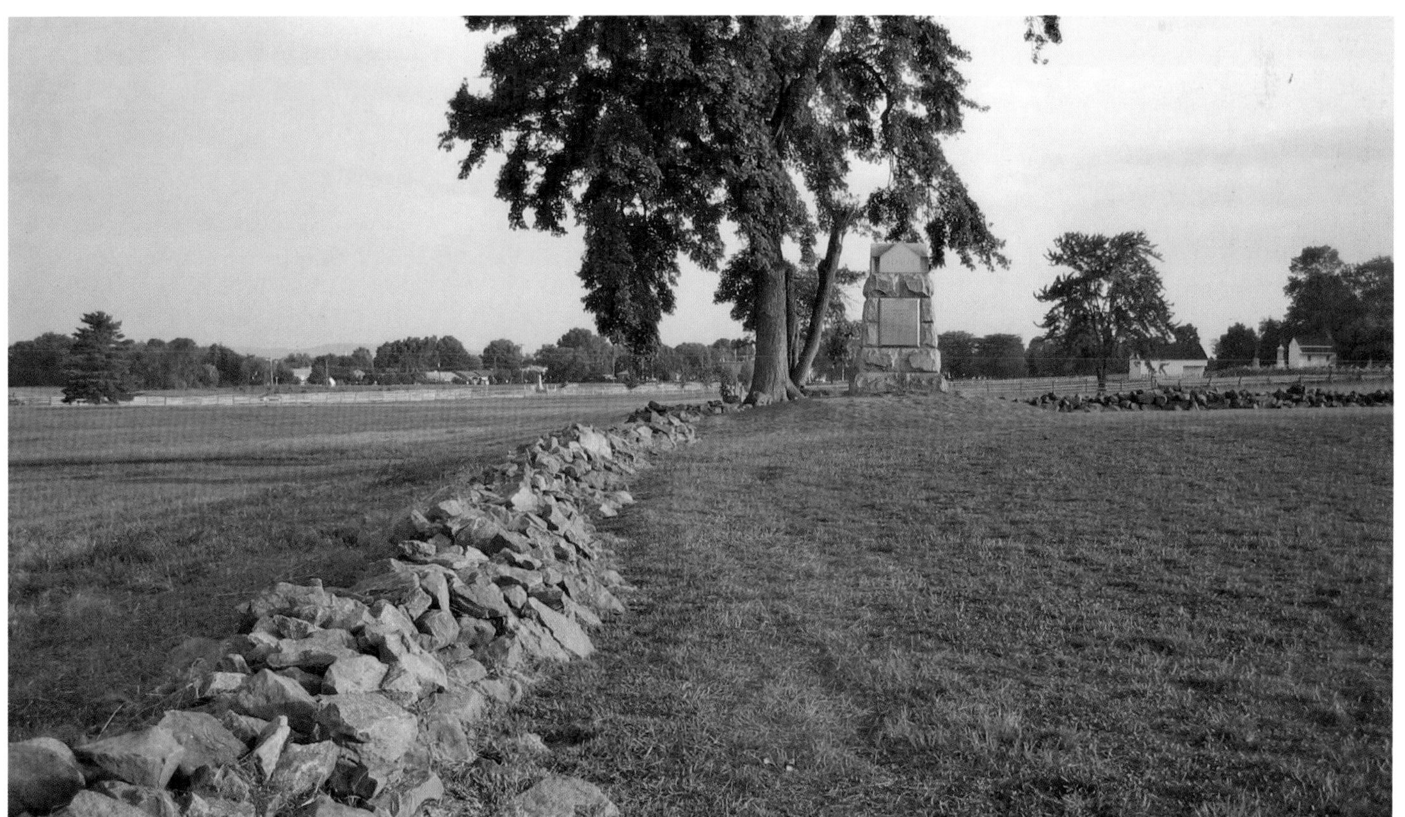

Looking north along the line of the stone wall leading to the Angle (corner), marked by the tree. The buildings on the right are Brien's barn (left) and his house (right).

Spangler's Spring

This natural spring is located at the south end of Culp's Hill, flanked in the east by a meadow bordered by Rock Creek, to the south by Power's Hill and 400 yards to the west by the Baltimore Pike. It had been used by farmers and animals for many years prior to the battle and brought welcome refreshment to the Yankees of XII Corps when they arrived at Culp's Hill on July 2. When most of these troops were sent south to support the Union left, the entrenchments on the slopes of the hill north of the spring were taken over during the night by Rebels of Brigadier-General George Steuart's "Maryland" Brigade. There was ferocious fighting the next morning when the returning Union forces counterattacked. Both sides reinforced and the struggle continued with fighting at extremely close range. Eventually, by late morning, the Rebels were driven back.

After the war the legend that there were temporary truces in the fighting so that soldiers from both sides could come to drink or fill canteens at the spring became established. The veracity of this is doubtful in view of the bitter fighting, but it persists to this day. The spring now has a concrete and stone cover to prevent damage by visitors.

The Emmitsburg Road

Of all the roads that converged on Gettysburg, the most well known is the Emmitsburg Road, as it ran diagonally southwest from the town through the center of the battlefield. Like all the other routes, it brought troops hurrying to the scene on June 30 and July 1, but unlike the others it saw some of the most desperate fighting on July 2 and became a key feature in Lee's final assault on July 3. In 1863 it was an unsealed, comparatively minor road, bordered on both sides by fences, mostly post and rail except for a worm fence along the east side from just north of Brien's farm to the Codori property, and again on both sides south of the Peach Orchard. The section running across the battlefield was 2.5 miles long, stretching from its junction with the Taneytown Road in the north to the Biesecker Wood in the south.

The road's most important tactical feature was that it followed a very slight ridge from the Codori Farm to south of the Peach Orchard, which was itself the highest point along the road. It was this rising ground that persuaded Sickles to move his corps forward, contrary to his orders, on July 2 and post his front line along the 1,000-yard stretch of the Emmitsburg Road from just north of the Rogers' Farm to the Peach Orchard. This portion of the road witnessed much of the afternoon struggle by Longstreet's Corps to smash Sickles' salient. The following day the swales to the west of the road provided some brief and occasional shelter from the Union artillery to the advancing divisions of Pickett, Pettigrew and Trimble when they launched their final attack on Meade's center. The reaching of this road by the Rebels was for many the watershed of the attack. After the delay in climbing over or through the two fences, there was no swale to shelter the attackers for the remainder of the assault, and the fences provided a convenient marker for the Union defenders to redouble their fire as their target came within effective musket range. The Emmitsburg Road was as far as many dead, wounded or living reached in that attack.

Jennie Wade – the Only Civilian Killed at Gettysburg

Mary Virginia Wade, called Jennie by friends (and history), was twenty years old in July 1863 and lived in the family home on Breckenridge Street. She had an elder sister, Georgia, and three brothers, John (Jack), Samuel and Harry. Her great-grandfather and grandfather had both fought in the Revolutionary War; her father, now in a mental hospital, had been a captain in the 80th Pennsylvania Militia; and her brother Jack had just joined the Union Army. The previous year her sister Georgia had married John L. McClellan, who was already in the Union Army, and moved to rented accommodation in a house on Baltimore Street at the foot of Cemetery Hill. Jennie was herself engaged to a Corporal Jack Skelly, who, unbeknown to Jennie, had been badly wounded and captured in the action at Stephenson's Depot on June 15 – he died on July 12, mercifully without knowing of Jennie's death.

As the noise of the fighting got nearer on July 1, Jennie locked up and ran with her small brother Harry and Isaac (a crippled child she was looking after) to her sister Georgia McClellan's house. However, as the Rebels pushed south through the town and reached the Rupp Tannery only 200 yards away, the house the family were sheltering in came under fire as Union sharpshooters used the roof. When men were wounded nearby, Jennie left the house to give them comfort and water. On July 2 the intensity of the firing increased and a 10-pounder Parrott shell smashed through the roof but luckily failed to detonate, then ploughed through a wall before lodging in the top of the southern wall – where it remained for fifteen years.

Jennie busied herself baking bread for the Union troops nearby. At dawn on July 3 she and her small brother Harry left the house in search of wood to bake more bread. By seven o'clock the firing began again in earnest, shattering every remaining window in the north-facing wall of the house. One bullet smashed the bedpost and showered splinters over the bed where Georgia was resting with her young baby without injuring either. Georgia heard Jennie say, "If there is anyone in this house that is to be killed today, I hope it is me, as George has that new baby." At 8:30 a.m. a bullet penetrated the outer door, then another door between the parlor and the kitchen, where Jennie was kneading dough, struck her in the back and entered her heart, killing her outright.

Jennie is buried in the Evergreen Cemetery and in 1901 her statue was dedicated in the presence of Georgia McClellan.

SECTION NINE

The Battle – Day One

WEDNESDAY, JULY 1

PROBLEMS AND PLANS

Lee (Map 24)

On the night of June 30/July 1 Lee's headquarters was in a stand of woods east of Chambersburg. His primary problem – lack of information on the whereabouts and movement of his enemy – had become progressively more acute since late on June 28. He knew they were over the Potomac and, although initially skeptical, now accepted that the Army of the Potomac was centered on Frederick some 30 miles to the south. As was his strategic intention, he had succeeded in drawing his opponent north of the river and he must have assumed Meade was likely to continue marching north. If so, then a clash of some sort was likely any time from June 30 onward. It followed that Ewell's Corps must be summoned back to join the main body of his army immediately. That is what Lee did, and by late June 30 two of Ewell's Divisions (Rodes and Early) were camped near Heidlersburg, only 8 miles north of Gettysburg and 15 from Cashtown. July 1 should see the Army of Northern Virginia reunited. However, Lee needed mounted troops to screen his advance and, more importantly, to probe toward Gettysburg and Hanover and southeast toward Taneytown, Fairfield and Emmitsburg. As he was unfamiliar with the country, Lee also needed information on the roads and tracks east of the South Mountain.

A glance at Map 24 reveals the extraordinary deployment situation that had developed with the Rebel cavalry by early on June 30. Stuart was 30 miles east of Greenwood and about to have an all-day clash with the Union cavalry under Kilpatrick that would drive him still further east as he sought to link up with Ewell at Carlisle via Dover, totally unaware that Ewell had been ordered south to the Cashtown/Gettysburg area. At Hanover Stuart was only 12 miles east of Gettysburg, so had he marched west instead of east after his fight with Kilpatrick he would have arrived in Buford's rear just as he faced Heth on the morning of July 1 – Lee would have had his cavalry just in time and Gettysburg would not have been fought as it was. Robertson and Jones were still south of the Potomac at Martinsburg, at least 40 miles from the Gettysburg/Cashtown area, and were therefore useless to Lee. Imboden and his mounted infantry were 5 miles east of Chambersburg at the rear of the army, 18 miles from Cashtown and with the direct route to the front blocked by infantry and trains; and anyway, they were not competent to perform the screening duties Lee so desperately needed – they were earmarked as baggage guard. Then there was Jenkins and his brigade under Ewell's command. Due to some error of Ewell or his staff, Jenkins was not told of Ewell's recall south until the day after the infantry, so on the evening of June 30 Jenkins was at Petersburg behind Ewell's infantry when he should have been scouting their advance – a task given to the 230 horsemen of the 35th Virginia Cavalry Battalion (White's Comanches), attached from Brigadier-General William E. Jones. As the enemy approached, Lee's infantry had to do their own scouting, as there was not a friendly horseman to be seen where there should have been. Compare this with the disposition of the Union cavalry on the same day. Buford's Division leads the left wing of Meade's advance and Kilpatrick the right, while Gregg guards the rear. The contrast is stark.

By nightfall on June 30 the position as Lee saw it from his headquarters was:

- He had four of his nine divisions (Heth, Pender, Rodes and Early) within an easy march of Gettysburg, two approaching from the north and two from the west.
- Unfortunately, the other five would all have to use the same road (the Chambersburg Pike up the steep slopes through the Cashtown Pass) for their march to the town, with the inevitable snarl-ups, delays and confusion with the artillery columns and wagon trains. Pickett's Division at the rear would have to await the arrival of Imboden's horsemen before relinquishing rearguard duties, and Johnson's Division (Ewell's Corps) would add to the congestion at Greenwood. For the present, however, the men of these two corps had enjoyed two days' rest in their camps along the road.
- Lee was fully alert to the likelihood that a clash was coming, probably within two or three days, and that he must have his army concentrated before this happened. His instructions to his army were to avoid bringing on a major battle before this concentration had been effected. Of the enemy he knew nothing of the detail he needed – he was groping forward half

Notes

Meade, June 29

• When Meade took command on June 28 his information on Lee's locations was good but he remained uncertain of his intentions. With two enemy corps around Chambersburg and another near Carlisle and York, as well as Rebel cavalry on his right, there was the possibility of Lee attempting to turn that flank and threaten Baltimore. Alternatively, Harrisburg was the intended target – on June 28 this was indeed Lee's plan.

• Meade's orders for the 29th reflected this uncertainty. He continued to march north with his corps well spread out over a 20-mile front, operating on interior lines with the objective of finding and fighting his enemy, while at the same time keeping his army between Lee and Washington and Baltimore. Cavalry guarded the left flank (Buford), the right (Kilpatrick) and the rear (Gregg). By the end of the day his army covered a front from near Westminster in the east to Emmitsburg in the west.

Meade, June 30

• Throughout the 29th and the early part of June 30 Meade was out of direct telegraphic contact as a result of Stuart's activities, so he was unaware of Ewell's recall south. His orders for June 30 saw a continuation of the march north over a wide front. There was the cavalry clash between Kilpatrick and Stuart at Hanover. The left wing under Reynolds was headed in the direction of Gettysburg and Buford's cavalry arrived at the town. Meade now considered this the most likely area where the armies would meet. He issued orders to the effect that the troops were about to defend their homeland and that corps commanders were authorized to execute any soldier who "fails in his duty at this hour." At the end of the day the Army of the Potomac was deployed across a front of over 20 miles, from Manchester in the east to southeast of Fairfield in the west. Meade was dissatisfied with the progress of III Corps for the second day running and rebuked Sickles.

Lee, June 29

• By now Lee was seriously agitated and annoyed that he had heard nothing from Stuart. He anxiously awaited confirmation of the location of his main enemy force and its movements. On June 28, still with no news, Lee issued instructions for the continued march on Harrisburg and the Susquehanna. Ewell (Rodes and Johnson) was to take Harrisburg, supported by Longstreet, while Early crossed the river lower down, followed by Hill (A and B on map). Rail tracks were to be destroyed.

• Late on June 28 Longstreet's scout, Harrison, reported that the Army of the Potomac had crossed the river and was moving north. Lee, operating on exterior lines, suddenly found his overriding requirement was to concentrate – which in practice meant recalling Ewell immediately. Lee's first orders for June 29 summoned Ewell to Chambersburg, but he later changed his mind and ordered Ewell to march on Gettysburg via Heidlersburg, as keeping east of the South Mountain would greatly facilitate Ewell's link-up with Early's Division. This changed order was received too late by Ewell to make it worthwhile recalling Johnson, who was allowed to continue down the Chambersburg road but turning off through Scotland to Greenwood.

Lee, June 30

• The Army of Northern Virginia was endeavoring to concentrate in the Chambersburg–Cashtown area. The absence of recent information on the enemy's movements was acutely worrying for Lee. Early in the morning, three regiments from Heth's Division under Brig.-Gen. Pettigrew marched on Gettysburg looking for supplies (and hopefully shoes), but found Yankee troopers on the outskirts of the town so returned to Cashtown to report. By evening Hill's and Longstreet's divisions were camped along the Chambersburg–Cashtown road with Ewell at Heidlersburg, except for Johnson over 20 miles to the west at Scotland.

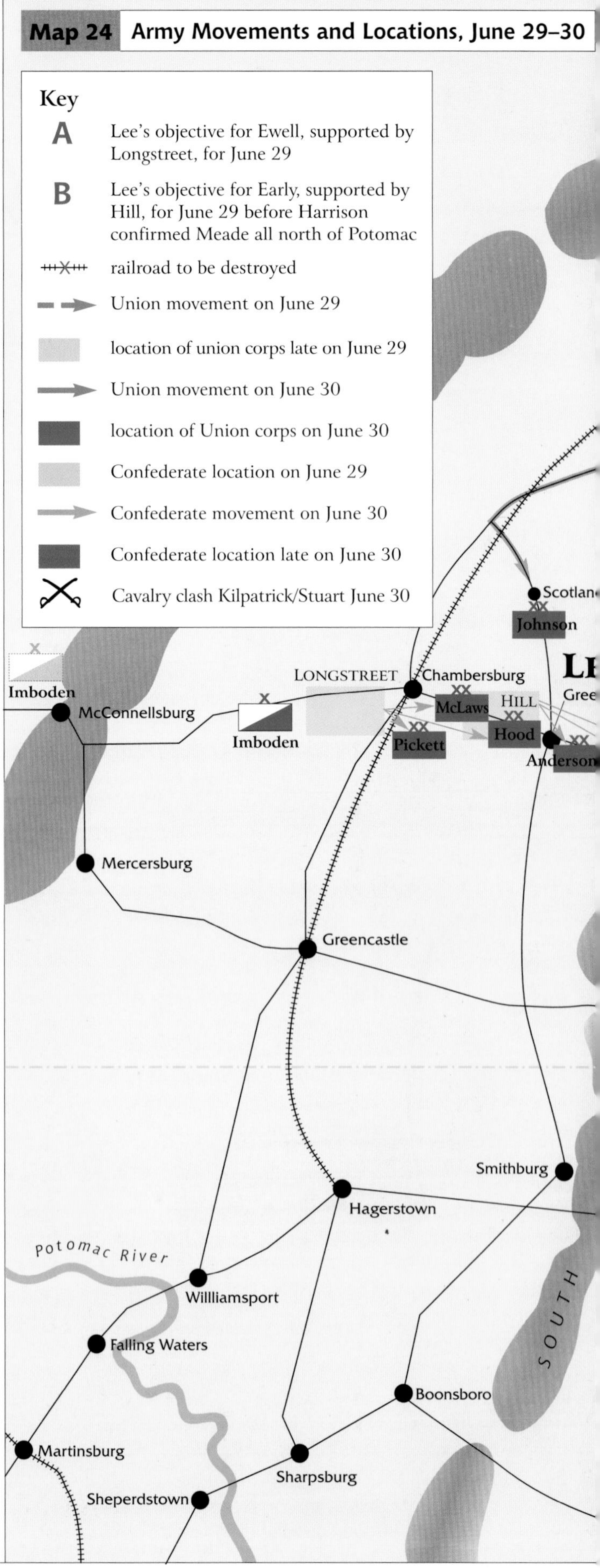

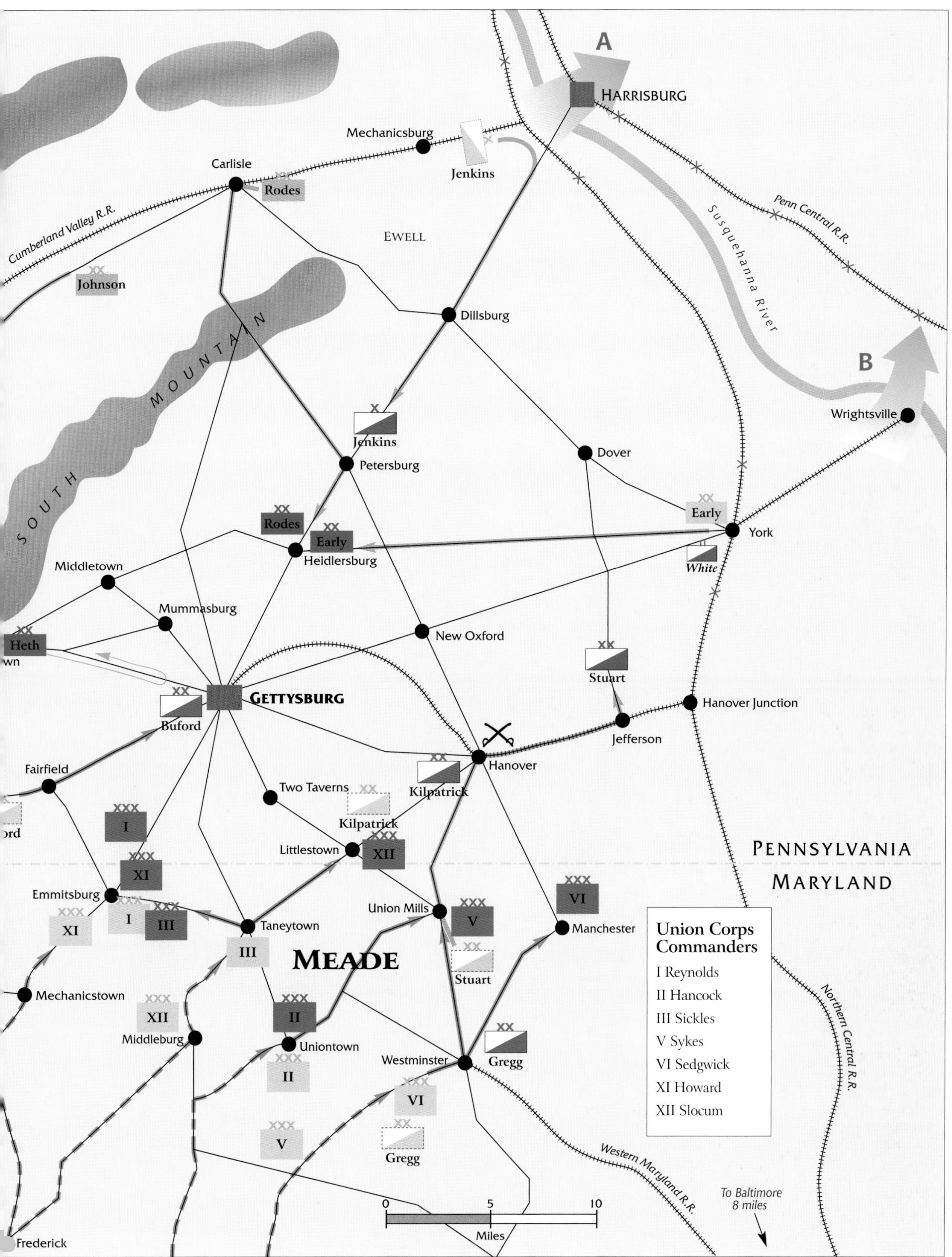
A
HARRISBURG
Mechanicsburg
Jenkins
Carlisle
Rodes
Cumberland Valley R.R.
EWELL
Penn Central R.R.
Susquehanna River
Johnson
Dillsburg
SOUTH MOUNTAIN
B
Wrightsville
Jenkins
Petersburg
Dover
Rodes
Early
Early
York
Heidlersburg
White
Middletown
Mummasburg
New Oxford
Heth
Stuart
GETTYSBURG
Buford
Hanover Junction
Jefferson
Hanover
Fairfield
Two Taverns
Kilpatrick
Kilpatrick
I
Littlestown
XII
XI
PENNSYLVANIA
MARYLAND
Emmitsburg
I
III
XI
Taneytown
Union Mills
V
VI
Manchester
III
MEADE
Stuart
Union Corps Commanders
I Reynolds
II Hancock
III Sickles
V Sykes
VI Sedgwick
XI Howard
XII Slocum
Mechanicstown
XII
Middleburg
II
Uniontown
II
Westminster
Gregg
VI
Northern Central R.R.
V
Gregg
Western Maryland R.R.
To Baltimore 8 miles
0
5
10
Miles
Frederick

blind. The only thing he knew for sure was that enemy cavalry (some of Gamble's troopers) had exchanged shots with an infantry flank guard from Heth's Division at Fairfield early that morning, and that later more enemy cavalry (again Gamble's men) had been seen by Pettigrew's reconnaissance approaching the town along the Emmitsburg Road. Heth refused to believe they had been more than a cavalry patrol and perhaps some militia. Hill was equally doubtful that there was serious opposition in the town. Hill passed this information to Lee along with his intention to send Heth early next morning to probe Gettysburg. Lee, who intended to move his headquarters to Cashtown on July 1, raised no objection.

- Previously Hill had gone so far as to state to Heth and Pettigrew, "I am just from General Lee, and the information he has from his scouts corroborates what I have received from mine – that is, the enemy is still at Middleburg [in Maryland] and has not yet struck their tents." To Heth's query whether his corps commander objected to his marching on Gettysburg again next morning, Hill had replied, "None in the world."
- It was also probably on this day that Lee received the information that his opponent was now Meade instead of Hooker, prompting the response, "Meade will commit no blunder in my front, and if I make one he will make haste to take advantage of it."

Although Lee wanted a battle and knew the enemy was near, he had wanted it on his terms, on the ground and at the time of his choosing, but with the absence of Stuart this was becoming increasingly unlikely to happen. Lee did his best to conceal his frustration at Stuart's failure to put in an appearance. While under this handicap his plan for July 1 was simple – proceed with caution, concentrate his army and avoid a general action until that was accomplished and he knew more of his enemy's whereabouts. His subordinates were so informed.

Meade (Map 24)

At 7:00 a.m. on June 28 Meade officially acknowledged his assumption of command to Halleck as follows:

> The order placing me in command of this army is received. As a soldier, I obey it, and to the utmost of my ability will execute it. Totally unexpected as it has been, and in ignorance of the exact conditions of the troops and position of the enemy, I can only now say that it appears to me I must move toward the Susquehanna, keeping Washington and Baltimore well covered, and if the enemy is checked in his attempt to cross the Susquehanna, or if he turns toward Baltimore, to give him battle . . .

To be woken at 3:00 a.m. to be told he was the fourth commander of the Army of the Potomac in eight months, and at a crucial stage of the campaign with the enemy deep inside Northern territory, must have been something of a shock, as Meade half acknowledged in his telegram to his commander-in-chief. It speaks highly of his resilience that he was quickly able to confront the situation and give orders. One problem was that as a corps commander he had not been kept informed of the movements of the other corps, the enemy locations or any campaign plan that Hooker might have had. The meeting with Hooker and then Butterfield just before dawn on June 28 undoubtedly filled in some information gaps, but it must have been a somewhat strained, if not embarrassing, occasion. Later Meade was to say of it that he received "no exact information about the condition of the troops and the position of the enemy" and that Hooker had provided "no intimation of any plan, or any views that he may have had up to that moment." Meade's first problem was to get up to date with the situation in respect of his own army and that of his enemy.

Although all his corps commanders (except Sickles, commanding III Corps) welcomed Hooker's replacement, there was a potential problem with the chief of staff, Major-General Daniel Butterfield. Butterfield was a Hooker man and, as the new army commander, Meade was entitled to bring his own staff from his corps headquarters and make fresh appointments as he saw fit. Initially Meade tried unsuccessfully, as discussed in Section Six: Command and Control (pages 279–80), to persuade three other generals (Williams, Warren and Humphreys) to take the post. Warren rightly made the point that Butterfield was better informed on all matters pertaining to the headquarters of the army and that another major change at that time would not be advisable. It speaks well of Butterfield that, despite knowing his days were probably numbered (Humphreys replaced him after the battle), he served Meade reasonably well at Gettysburg. In the event, the only officers Meade took with him to army headquarters were his personal staff. He did, however, as related above (pages 213 and 280), shake up the cavalry command and promote three captains (Merritt, Farnsworth and Custer) to brigade command – an unprecedented elevation.

His main problem was to get his army moving again, instill a sense of urgency, and endeavor to catch Lee, force a fight and at the same time block any threat to Baltimore. His plan to accomplish this was summarized in a long message to Halleck, timed 11:00 a.m., June 29, and sent by a courier who was killed the next day; the dispatch was found on his body.

> Upon assuming command of the army, and carefully considering the position of affairs and movements of the enemy, I have concluded as follows: To move today toward Westminster and Emmitsburg, and the army is now in motion for that line . . . If Lee is moving for Baltimore I expect to get between his main army and that place. If he is crossing the Susquehanna, I shall rely upon General Couch . . . holding him until I can fall upon his rear . . . I have ordered the abandonment of Harper's Ferry . . . While I move forward, I shall incline to the right [east] toward the Baltimore and Harrisburg road, to cover that, and draw my supplies from there [Baltimore] . . . my main objective being, of course, Lee's army, which I am satisfied has all passed on through Hagerstown toward Chambersburg. My endeavor [will] be . . . to hold my force well together, with the hope of falling on some portion of Lee's army in detail. The cavalry force between me and Washington [Stuart] . . . will be engaged by my cavalry [it was by Kilpatrick at Hanover on June 30] . . . My main point being to find and fight the enemy . . . I have hastily made up this dispatch to give you the information. Telegraphic communications have been cut off. I send this by courier, with the hope and expectation that it will reach you safely. Headquarters are tonight at Middleburg . . . There is rail communication from Baltimore to Westminster.

By the end of the next day Meade had received further information and considered he had solved at least one of his problems – preventing Lee crossing the Susquehanna and taking Harrisburg. Buford had entered Gettysburg and sent the following message to Pleasonton:

> I entered this place at 11:00 a.m. [his report says he arrived in the afternoon]. Found everybody in a terrible state of excitement on account of the enemy's [Pettigrew's] advance on this place. He had approached to within half a mile of the town when the head of my column entered. His force was terribly exaggerated by reasonable and truthful but inexperienced men. On pushing him back toward Cashtown, I learned from reliable men that Anderson's division was marching from Chambersburg by Mummasburg . . . toward York . . . Colonel Gamble has just sent me word that Lee signed a pass for a citizen this morning at Chambersburg. I can't do much just now. My men and horses are fagged out . . .

Buford then deployed his brigades to watch the roads leading to Gettysburg from the east and north.

But Meade's concern was that Lee might intend to march on through the Cashtown Gap and join Ewell in the Middletown–Mummasburg–Gettysburg area: Gregg had reported enemy infantry at Berlin and Reynolds had passed on Buford's message that Anderson was marching in that direction. His problem was to find out exactly where Lee was concentrating and cover his own left (the Fairfield–Emmitsburg area) and his right from the Hanover area. At 11:30 a.m. he sent a dispatch to Reynolds authorizing him to fall back to Emmitsburg, where he would be reinforced if the Confederates advanced and he felt a better defensive position was available in that area.

At 4.30 p.m. Meade sent a dispatch to Halleck from Taneytown that indicates he was worried by his lack of telegraphic communications, the physical state of his troops after the forced marching and uncertainty over the precise whereabouts of Ewell's Corps.

> Our reports seem to place Ewell in the vicinity of York and Harrisburg [Meade did not receive Brigadier-General H. Haupt's message of June 30 confirming that "Lee is falling back suddenly from the vicinity of Harrisburg" until the morning of July 1]. The cavalry [Stuart] . . . have passed on up through Westminster and Hanover, some 6,000 to 8,000 strong [overestimated]. I shall push on tomorrow [July 1] in the direction of Hanover junction and Hanover, when I hope by July 2 to open communications with Baltimore by telegraph and rail, to renew supplies. I fear that I shall break down the troops by pushing on much faster, and may have to rest a day. My movement, of course, will be governed by what I learn of the enemy. The information seems to place Longstreet at Chambersburg [correct] and A. P. Hill moving between Chambersburg and York [this relates to Buford's report of Anderson's Division marching to York via Mummasburg and was correct in that it indicated Hill moving east through the Cashtown Gap]. Our cavalry drove a regiment out of Gettysburg that a.m. Our cavalry engaged with Stuart at Hanover this a.m. Result not yet known.

Later that day he wrote to his wife:

> All is going well. I think I have relieved Harrisburg and Philadelphia, and that Lee has now come to the conclusion that he must attend to other matters. I continue well, but much oppressed with a sense of responsibility and the magnitude of the great interests entrusted to me. Of course in time I will become accustomed to this.

Shortly before midnight on June 30, when Meade had to make his decisions and issue orders for July 1, he had yet to receive the latest information from Buford to Pleasonton, timed 10:40 p.m., June 30, which stated:

> I have the honor to state the following facts: A. P. Hill's corps, composed of Anderson, Heth and Pender, is massed back of Cashtown, 9 miles from this place [correct]. His pickets, composed of infantry and artillery, are in sight of mine . . . Rumor says Ewell is coming over the mountains from Carlisle. One of his escort was captured to-day near Heidlersburg. He says Rodes, commanding a division of Ewell's, has already crossed the mountains from Carlisle [correct] . . . I have kept Gen. Reynolds informed of all that has transpired . . .

However, although Meade was well aware that a battle was imminent, he was still uncertain where it would take place. He had ordered light marching order for his troops and instructed all wagons except ambulances and ammunition wagons to Union Bridge, west of Westminster. His corps were positioned as shown on Map 24. The orders for July 1, which were both offensive and defensive, are summarized as follows (see Map 25):

- Orders to advance – issued before midnight on June 30. Army headquarters were to remain at Taneytown.The left wing, under Reynolds, was to continue toward Gettysburg, with I Corps marching to the town, XI Corps to follow within supporting distance and III Corps to head for Emmitsburg. II Corps was to proceed to Taneytown as a reserve, centrally placed to move toward Emmitsburg, Gettysburg or Hanover as the situation demanded. VI Corps was to remain at Manchester on the right flank, able to move quickly on Hanover. V Corps was to move to Hanover, and XII Corps to Two Taverns, centrally placed and within supporting distance of Emmitsburg, Gettysburg or Hanover. The cavalry was to watch the front and flanks. From these instructions it now seemed Meade half expected the clash to come on his left, possibly around Gettysburg – he would have two corps (I and XI) at or near the town and three more (II, III and XII) within 10 miles – four hours' marching time – of it.

With Buford's two brigades, Reynolds would have charge of over 24,000 troops positioned to check any major advance from Cashtown. If Lee attempted to outflank him via Fairfield and Emmitsburg, III Corps with II Corps in support could check him. On the right, should a threat emerge at Hanover, it would be met by V Corps supported by VI Corps at Manchester. In the light of what Meade knew at the time, it was a well-balanced, flexible interior-lines deployment.

- Subsequent orders for a withdrawal – issued after midnight on 30 June (see Map 25). These were based on a reconnaissance, carried out by Major-General Warren and Brigadier-General Hunt much earlier on June 30, of the so-called "Pipe Creek line" in Maryland.

> What became known as the Pipe Creek Circular makes strange reading, written as it was not long after Meade's marching orders to advance on July 1. The circular proposed a withdrawal of the army some 15 miles southeast of Gettysburg to the Parr Ridge, roughly along the line of the Pipe Creek, with the Union left at Middletown and right 18 miles away at Manchester, and with all supply trains concentrated at Westminster. Critics of Meade have alleged that his offensive spirit had evaporated or that he was dithering at a crucial moment. The reality was that he intended the move to be undertaken only if events made it necessary. It was a fall-back plan for use if circumstances prevented his being able to fight with advantage on ground of his choosing in Pennsylvania. Nevertheless, the sentence "that a general plan, perfectly understood by all, may be had for receiving attack, if made in strong force, upon any portion of our present position" left open the question of what constituted a "strong attack?" The next sentence, "Developments may cause the commanding general to assume the offensive from his present positions," made it likely that Meade was still in two minds what to do and was trying to ensure all options were left open.

The circular never reached Reynolds or Howard. This, according to Captain Stephen M. Weld on Reynolds' staff, infuriated the army commander as it was Meade's intention that all his corps commanders receive it on the evening of June 30. Weld stated that Meade later said he "had arranged for a plan of battle, and that it had taken so long to get the orders out that now it was all useless" and that Meade was "very much disturbed indeed." To be fair, Butterfield and his clerks had a mountain of paperwork to write out and copy to eight corps commanders, with the march orders in particular requiring detailed instructions as to timings and routes.

Yet another later message failed to reach Reynolds. In it Meade expressed doubts that Gettysburg was a suitable place to concentrate if Lee were doing so east of the town, and that, if the Rebels were concentrating at or west of the town, Meade knew too little about the surrounding countryside to judge whether it favored offensive or defensive operations. He wanted Reynolds' views on this.

However, at midnight on June 30 Meade knew much more about the dispositions and movements of his enemy than Lee did of his. In summary, his plan for July 1 now was to continue the advance northward but to anticipate that the clash could occur in the Gettysburg area. He had therefore grouped his left wing under Reynolds in that direction. Meade, who believed Lee's army was at least equal in strength to his own, was now hoping to fight a defensive battle on ground of his own choosing – hence his instructions to Reynolds and his Pipe Creek Circular. Ironically, this was also Lee's, and certainly Longstreet's, preferred option. The classic encounter battle was looming, with

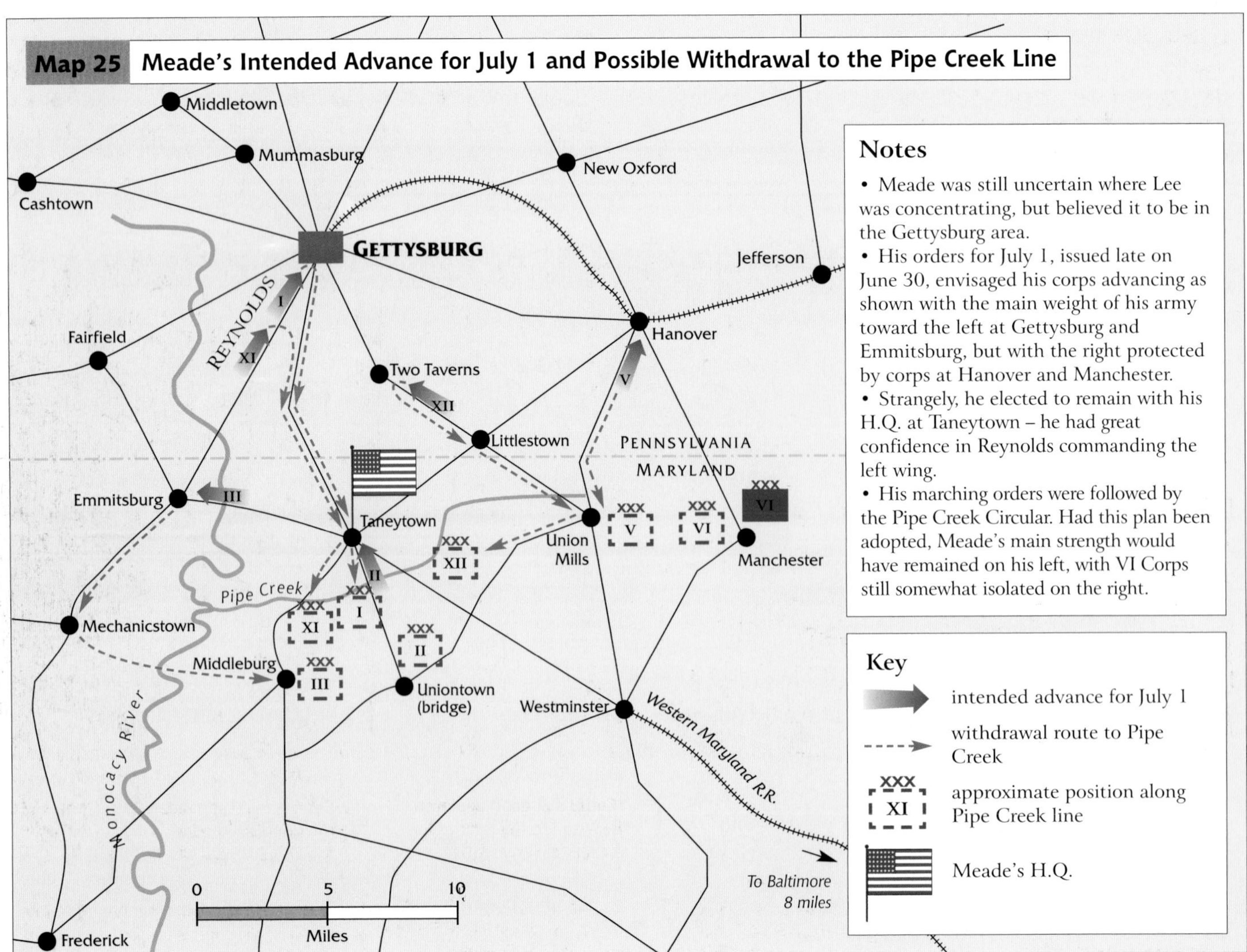
Map 25 Meade's Intended Advance for July 1 and Possible Withdrawal to the Pipe Creek Line
Middletown
Mummasburg
Cashtown
New Oxford
GETTYSBURG
Jefferson
Fairfield
REYNOLDS
I
XI
Hanover
Two Taverns
XII
V
Littlestown
PENNSYLVANIA
MARYLAND
Emmitsburg
III
Taneytown
Union Mills
Manchester
VI
Pipe Creek
II
Mechanicstown
Middleburg
Uniontown (bridge)
Westminster
Western Maryland R.R.
Monocacy River
To Baltimore 8 miles
0
5
10
Miles
Frederick
Notes
• Meade was still uncertain where Lee was concentrating, but believed it to be in the Gettysburg area.
• His orders for July 1, issued late on June 30, envisaged his corps advancing as shown with the main weight of his army toward the left at Gettysburg and Emmitsburg, but with the right protected by corps at Hanover and Manchester.
• Strangely, he elected to remain with his H.Q. at Taneytown – he had great confidence in Reynolds commanding the left wing.
• His marching orders were followed by the Pipe Creek Circular. Had this plan been adopted, Meade's main strength would have remained on his left, with VI Corps still somewhat isolated on the right.
Key
intended advance for July 1
withdrawal route to Pipe Creek
XXX XI approximate position along Pipe Creek line
Meade's H.Q.

Meade in two minds whether, if the enemy appeared in strength, to fight or to withdraw to the Pipe Creek line and Lee not wanting any major clash until he had all his army to hand. There is a military truism that "no plan survives the first shots." The first shots of the Battle of Gettysburg that were fired early on July 1 would seem to confirm this.

JULY 1 – AN OVERVIEW (Map 26)

It is not intended to describe the battle as fought on July 1 blow by blow, as this has already been done by countless authors. As with the subsequent two days of conflict, a general overview of the day's events will precede a more detailed look at the phases of the fighting on that day, followed by an examination of selected highlights. Each highlight will, where relevant, have subsections covering the ground, tactical significance, force comparison, command and control, plans and orders, an outline of events (normally covered by detailed maps), casualties and comments. The views, feelings and experiences of some of the participants will feature in the "boxes" that accompany the main text. At the end of this section some major controversies that have arisen since the battle will be outlined and discussed.

Shortly after 7:30 a.m., when Lieutenant Marcellus E. Jones of the 8th Illinois Cavalry fired the first shot of the battle, Confederate skirmishers in advance of Major-General Heth's Division, marching east along the Chambersburg Pike, deployed against Major-General Buford's cavalry pickets. Heth was engaged on a reconnaissance against what he thought was a local militia force. His corps commander, A. P. Hill, had advised Lee that the Union cavalry was in the area and the commanding general raised no objection to the probe to Gettysburg – although his corps commanders were still under instructions not to bring on a general engagement. On hearing of the Rebel approach, Buford initially deployed his horsemen on Herr's Ridge to delay the enemy advance. Under pressure, they pulled back to McPherson's Ridge where both cavalry brigades (Gamble and Devin) dismounted to offer serious resistance and gain time for the arrival of Union infantry.

This delaying action allowed time for Reynolds to hurry his I Corps (now under Doubleday) to McPherson's Ridge and summon XI Corps under Major-General Oliver Howard to Gettysburg. By 10:00 a.m. the leading brigade of Union infantry (Cutler) was arriving on the field, closely followed by the Iron Brigade. They deployed astride the Chambersburg Pike, and the Iron Brigade was able to throw back the Rebel (Archer's) attack south of the Pike, although the attack to the north (Davis) was initially successful. Only the timely use of a small reserve and some bitter fighting at the railroad cut finally drove the Confederates back to Herr's Ridge. During the early part of the fighting on McPherson's Ridge Reynolds was killed and Doubleday assumed command on the field until the arrival of his senior, Major-General Howard, commanding XI Corps. Behind Heth two more Rebel divisions (Pender and Anderson) were marching toward Gettysburg, while from the north another two (Rodes and Early) under Lieutenant-General Ewell were also approaching. The battle had been joined contrary to the intentions of both army commanders.

Around noon there was something of a lull, apart from artillery fire, during which both sides were rushing reinforcements to the scene and generals were making far-reaching decisions. The first to arrive was the leading division of Ewell's Corps, commanded by Major-General Rodes, who deployed onto Oak Hill, threatening to outflank the Union I Corps on McPherson's Ridge. However, poor leadership thwarted Rodes' attacks with heavy losses, especially to Iverson's Brigade. Meanwhile Howard had rushed two divisions of XI Corps (Schimmelfennig and Barlow) north of the town, with the third (Von Steinwehr) remaining in reserve on Cemetery Hill.

The Iron Brigade Rushes to Check the Rebels on McPherson's Ridge
Herbst Wood
Archer's Brigade advances to Willoughby Run in the valley the other side of McPherson's Ridge
Chambersburg Pike crests McPherson's Ridge
Davis's Brigade threatens the Union right north of the Pike
railroad cut (behind trees)
Meredith's Iron Brigade double-quicks into the wood to check Archer's advancing Rebels
Cutler's Brigade deployed here and to the right of the road to the railroad cut
Hall's 6 x 3-in ordnance rifles deployed here mid-morning, July 1
Lee's H.Q. marker

This view shows the Union situation around 11:00 a.m. on July 1. The Union line along McPherson's Ridge is threatened by the advance of Heth's Division, with Archer attacking south of the Chambersburg Pike and Davis to the north. The Iron Brigade arrives just in time to check and then push back Archer along the Willoughby Run. See also Map 27.

By about 3:30 p.m. a renewed attack by Heth from the west and repeated assaults by Daniel's Brigade of Rodes' Division from the north had finally driven I Corps off McPherson's Ridge back to its last defensive position west of Gettysburg along Seminary Ridge.

To the north of the town Brigadier-General Barlow had advanced to occupy Blocher's Knoll, thereby exposing his command to attack by Ewell's 2nd Division under Major-General Early. This attack caused Barlow's Division to collapse, while at approximately the same time there was an assault on I Corps' defensive line on Seminary Ridge that outflanked the position. With the Union front disintegrating in both the north and west, Howard summoned a brigade from Von Steinwehr's command under Colonel Coster to try to cover the chaotic retreat through the town of both Union corps. His gallant stand at the Kuhn Brickyard briefly checked but could not halt the Rebel onslaught that poured through the town. Many Union prisoners were taken, but the remnants rallied on Cemetery Hill and re-formed. By nightfall a hasty defensive position from Culp's Hill through Cemetery Hill to the northern end of Cemetery Ridge had been established.

Ewell, exercising the discretion given him by Lee, declined to attack the Union positions before dark, it being decided instead to renew the assault the following morning – thereby starting a controversy that still stimulates argument today.

Meanwhile Meade, on hearing of Reynolds' death, had sent forward his trusted friend Major-General Winfield Scott Hancock, II Corps commander, to assume command on the battlefield. He wrote a letter to this effect that Hancock took with him to show to Howard if necessary, as Howard outranked Hancock. Hancock arrived between 4:00 p.m. and 4:30 p.m., in time to see the retreat of XI and I Corps and to play a prominent role in organizing the defenses and deployment on Cemetery Hill (see Map 39). Dispatches from Howard and then one from Hancock convinced Meade that the battle he knew he must fight would occur at Gettysburg. All corps were ordered to march on Gettysburg. At 6:00 p.m. he telegraphed Halleck via Frederick as follows:

> The First and Eleventh Corps have been engaged all day in front of Gettysburg. The Twelfth, Third, and Fifth have been moving up, and all, I hope, by this time on the field. This

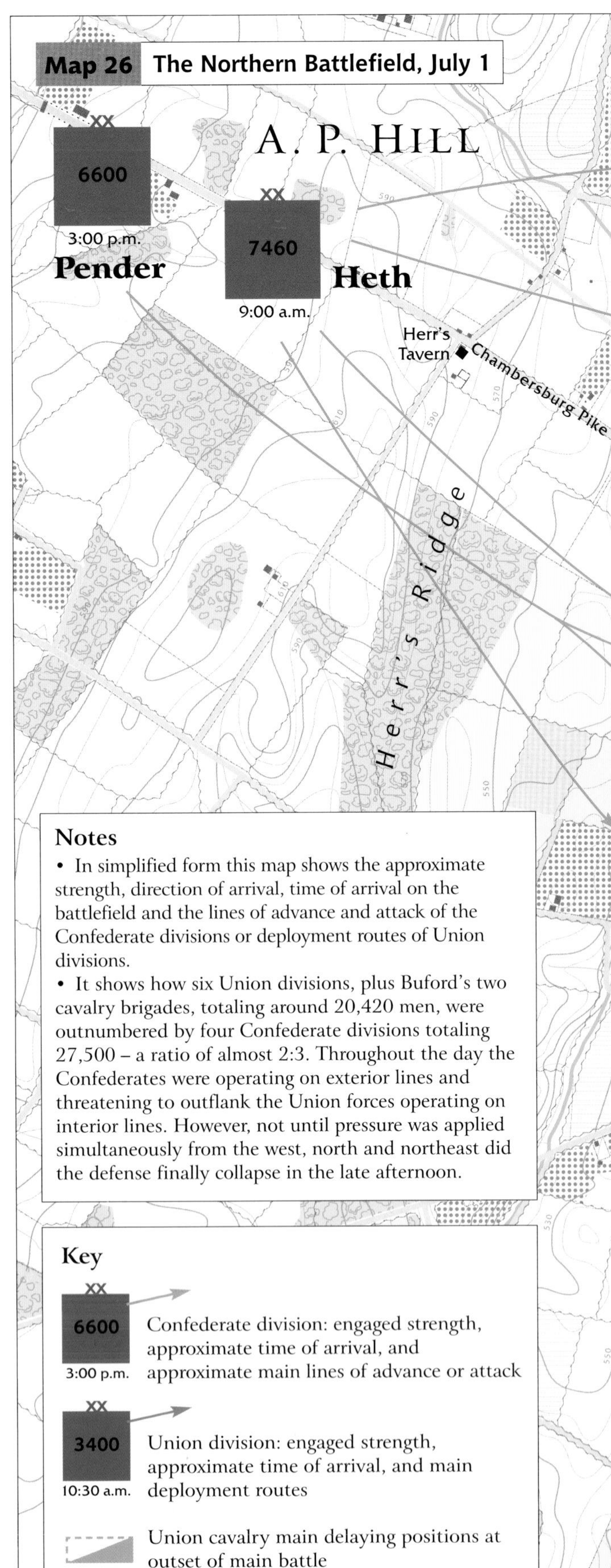
Map 26 The Northern Battlefield, July 1
A. P. HILL
6600
3:00 p.m.
Pender
7460
9:00 a.m.
Heth
Herr's Tavern
Chambersburg Pike
Herr's Ridge
Willoughby Run
Notes
• In simplified form this map shows the approximate strength, direction of arrival, time of arrival on the battlefield and the lines of advance and attack of the Confederate divisions or deployment routes of Union divisions.
• It shows how six Union divisions, plus Buford's two cavalry brigades, totaling around 20,420 men, were outnumbered by four Confederate divisions totaling 27,500 – a ratio of almost 2:3. Throughout the day the Confederates were operating on exterior lines and threatening to outflank the Union forces operating on interior lines. However, not until pressure was applied simultaneously from the west, north and northeast did the defense finally collapse in the late afternoon.
Key
6600
3:00 p.m.
Confederate division: engaged strength, approximate time of arrival, and approximate main lines of advance or attack
3400
10:30 a.m.
Union division: engaged strength, approximate time of arrival, and main deployment routes
Union cavalry main delaying positions at outset of main battle
(–) unit(s) detached

The Opening Gun at Gettysburg

Lieutenant John Calef commanded Battery A of the 2nd U.S. Artillery, attached to Buford's Cavalry Division and brought into action along the Chambersburg Pike early on the morning of July 1. His 3-inch Ordnance Rifle No. 233 fired the first artillery shot of the battle. When the memorial to Major-General Buford was dedicated on July 1, 1895, the tubes of the original four cannons that fired the opening salvoes were positioned at the four corners of the base of the statue. Major Calef was present and symbolically spiked each tube. Calef was a West Point graduate who won a brevet promotion for his gallantry at Gettysburg.

Calef's Battery claimed to have been the first unit to use the bugle call "Taps" at a military funeral over the grave of one of its cannoneers killed on the Peninsula. "Taps" was written by Major-General Dan Butterfield, Meade's chief of staff at the battle, who also designed the system of corps badges in use at Gettysburg. Butterfield now lies in the most elaborate tomb in the West Point cemetery.

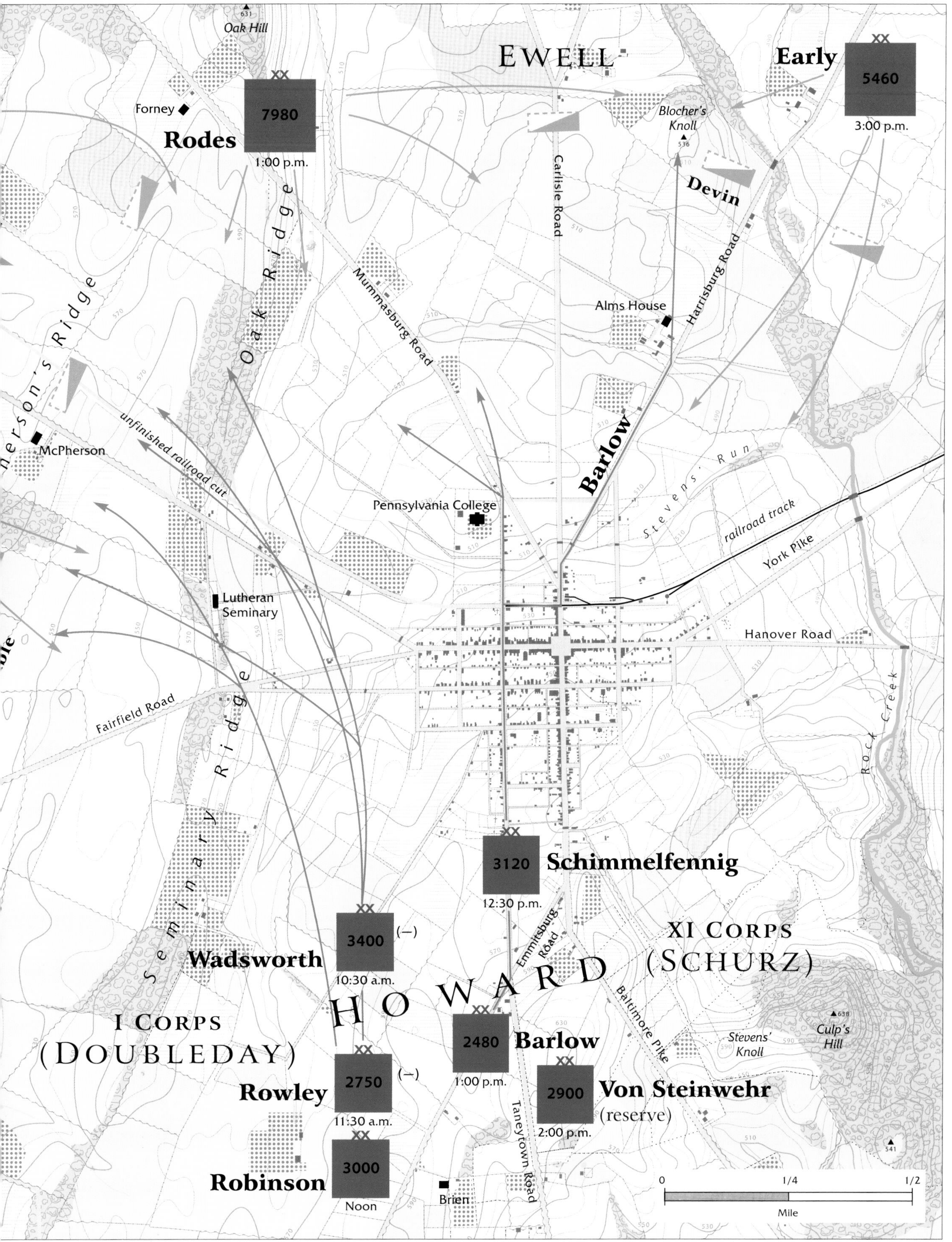

Oak Hill
EWELL
Early
5460
3:00 p.m.
Rodes
7980
1:00 p.m.
Forney
Blocher's Knoll
Devin
Carlisle Road
Oak Ridge
Mummasburg Road
Harrisburg Road
Alms House
McPherson
unfinished railroad cut
Barlow
Stevens' Run
railroad track
York Pike
Pennsylvania College
Lutheran Seminary
Hanover Road
Fairfield Road
Seminary Ridge
Rock Creek
3120
Schimmelfennig
12:30 p.m.
XI CORPS
(SCHURZ)
3400
(–)
Wadsworth
10:30 a.m.
HOWARD
Emmitsburg Road
Baltimore Pike
I CORPS
(DOUBLEDAY)
2480
Barlow
1:00 p.m.
Stevens' Knoll
Culp's Hill
2750
(–)
Rowley
11:30 a.m.
2900
Von Steinwehr
(reserve)
2:00 p.m.
Taneytown Road
3000
Robinson
Noon
Brien
0
1/4
1/2
Mile

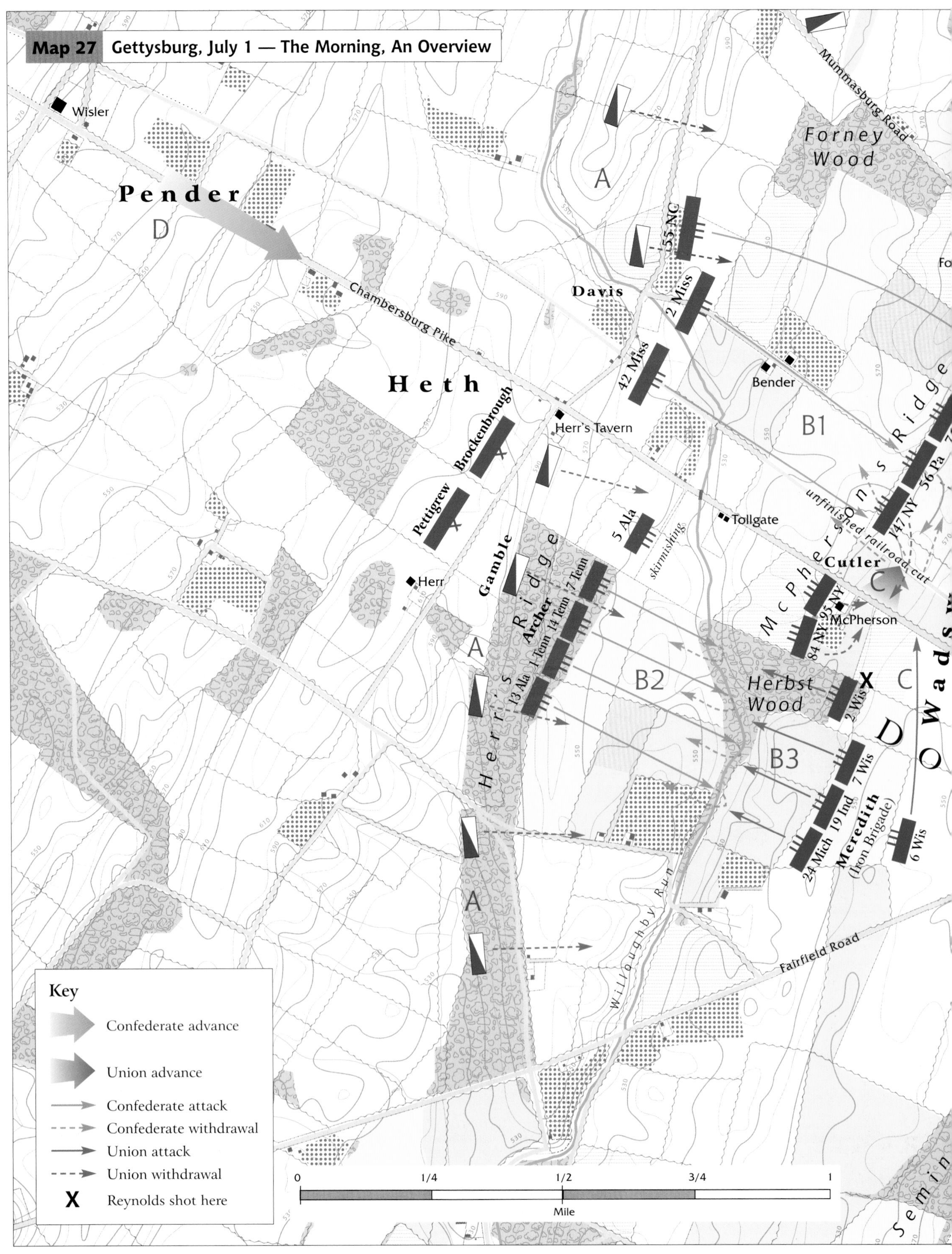
Map 27 Gettysburg, July 1 — The Morning, An Overview
Wisler
Pender
D
Chambersburg Pike
Heth
Davis
55 NC
2 Miss
42 Miss
A
Mummasburg Road
Forney Wood
Bender
B1
Herr's Tavern
Brockenbrough
Pettigrew
Gamble
5 Ala
skirmishing
Tollgate
unfinished railroad cut
McPherson's Ridge
147 NY
56 Pa
Cutler
C
McPherson
84 NY
95 NY
Herr
Herr's Ridge
Archer
7 Tenn
14 Tenn
1 Tenn
13 Ala
B2
Herbst Wood
2 Wis
X
B3
7 Wis
19 Ind
24 Mich
Meredith (Iron Brigade)
6 Wis
Wadsworth
Willoughby Run
Fairfield Road
Key
Confederate advance
Union advance
Confederate attack
Confederate withdrawal
Union attack
Union withdrawal
X Reynolds shot here
0
1/4
1/2
3/4
1
Mile

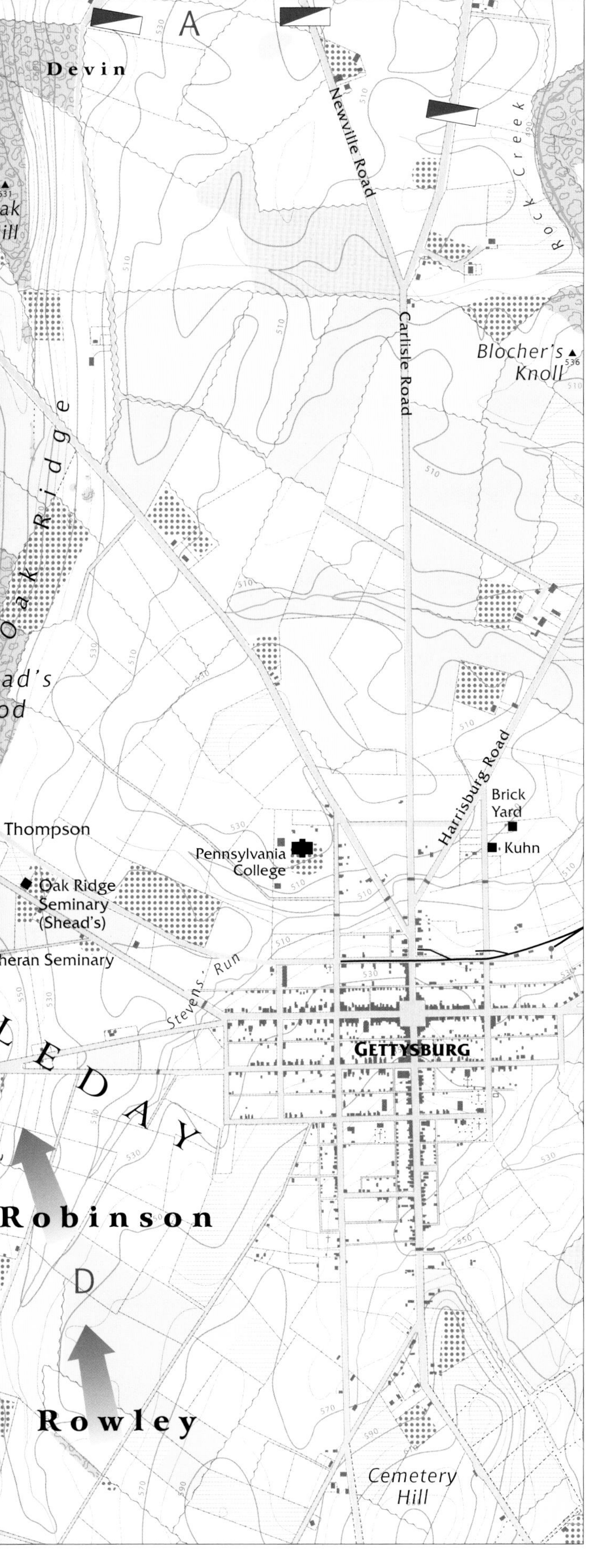

Notes

AAAA Buford's cavalry screen on Herr's Ridge and north of Gettysburg. This screen forced Heth's leading brigade to deploy and then fall back under pressure to McPherson's Ridge, where the Union cavalry made a determined stand. The arrival of Union infantry (Wadsworth's Division) just in time allowed the cavalry to withdraw to the flanks – Devin to the north and Gamble to the south.

B1/B2/B3 Heth deployed to attack McPherson's Ridge with two brigades – Davis north of the Chambersburg Pike (less 11th Miss guarding the train) and Archer south of it. At around 10:30 a.m. Davis advanced and was able to outflank and drive back three of Cutler's regiments, the northern two of which retreated in haste to Shead's Wood. Archer advanced a short while later in the south. However, the timely arrival of the Iron Brigade, which had double-quicked behind Cutler from the Emmitsburg Road, followed by an immediate charge into Herbst Wood and to the Willoughby Run, routed the Rebel assault and captured Archer. The Rebel attack north of the Pike had succeeded, that to the south had failed.

CC By 10:45–11:00 a.m. the Union line looked as though it was collapsing in the north with Davis sweeping in toward the Pike. The Union commander in the field, Maj.-Gen. Reynolds, had been shot dead in Herbst Wood and command of I Corps passed to Maj.-Gen. Doubleday. He rushed his only reserve (6th Wisconsin) to the Pike and it was able to check the Southerners with the assistance of the two regiments of Cutler's Brigade (84th and 95th NY), which had re-formed to face north. A spirited and very determined charge by the 6th Wisconsin, supported by these two regiments, on the unfinished railroad cut captured many Rebels and compelled the remainder to flee. This was the decisive moment of the morning's struggle, with McPherson's Ridge remaining in Union hands and a rebuffed Confederate division regrouping on Herr's Ridge.

DD The latter part of the morning saw the arrival of more infantry reinforcements for both sides. Lt.-Gen. A. P. Hill's second division under Maj.-Gen. Pender followed Heth down the Chambersburg Pike and moved up behind Herr's Ridge, bringing 6,600 men to the front. Meanwhile, the two other divisions of the Union I Corps under Brig.-Gens. Robinson and Rowley (the latter replacing Doubleday) arrived with some 5,750 men to bolster the defense of McPherson's Ridge.

At around noon there was a lull in the fighting except for a continued artillery exchange.

> leaves only the Sixth, which will move up to-night . . .
> A. P. Hill and Ewell are certainly concentrating; Longstreet's whereabouts I do not know. If he is not up tomorrow, I hope with the force I have concentrated to defeat Hill and Ewell. At any rate, I see no other course than to hazard a general battle. Circumstances during the night may alter this decision, of which I will try to advise you . . .

The circumstances did not alter and Meade arrived to assume command from Slocum at around midnight (by virtue of being the senior officer on the field until Meade arrived, Slocum was briefly and reluctantly in command of the army at Gettysburg).

THE MORNING See Map 27.

Highlight: The Struggle for the Railroad Cut, 10:45–11:30 a.m. (Maps 28 and 29)

This action was the culmination of the initially successful attack by the Rebel brigade led by the Southern President's nephew, Brigadier-General Joseph Davis, on Brigadier-General Lysander Cutler's 2nd Brigade, 1st Division, I Corps, defending McPherson's Ridge north of the Chambersburg Pike. Only the timely switching of the Union reserve regiment (6th Wisconsin) and another two forming front to flank (84th and 95th New York), followed by a desperate charge on the Rebels in the railroad cut, finally clinched the morning victory for the Yankees. There was some bitter fighting, resulting in heavy losses to both sides in a comparatively brief clash.

On the March to Gettysburg, July 1

Sergeant George A. Bowen of the 12th New Jersey Infantry, a regiment in the 3rd Division of II Corps, marched up the Emmitsburg Road to arrive on the battlefield after dark. His experience on the march must have been typical of most Union troops hurrying to the sound of the guns.

> We marched towards Gettysburg Pa. Where there had been some fighting there today. As we marched along the road we met the stragglers and Coffee Coolers, niggers, servants and all the non-combatants that follow an army, coming towards us getting away from the point of danger, they all had terrible stories to tell of what had happened at Gettysburg. The people along the road all are Union folks they come out to cheer us up and offer food of all kinds, but they do not have enough to go half around. It seems strange to be in a country where we are welcome and to feel we are among friends and well wishers. Arrived at Gettysburg [near Little Round Top] some time in the night. Had a good supper of fresh bread, fried Eggs and milk, all given me by some ladies along the road.

Bowen was later commissioned and ended the war as a captain.

The ground

The maneuvering and fighting took place within a square measuring about 600 yards on each side. The boundaries ran from the mid-point of the western edge of Shead's Wood due south and west for 600 yards, and then for another similar distance north and east respectively. Running approximately north–south through the center of this area was McPherson's Ridge. This ridge was itself composed of two parallel ridges about 200 yards apart, marked West and East Ridges on Map 28. McPherson's house, barn and outbuildings were on the reverse (eastern) slope of the western branch of the ridge, about 100 yards south of the Chambersburg Pike. The western ridge provided a good, albeit very exposed, gun platform for the Union artillery – initially Lieutenant Calef's horse artillery guns and then Captain Hall's 2nd Maine Battery. Its reverse slope offered cover from view for the movement of reinforcements and reserves from the Rebels on Herr's Ridge. However, Union troops in the swale between the ridges could not see what was happening less than 200 yards away on the eastern side of the eastern ridge – this had a bearing on the assembling of the regiments and the coordination of the Union charge on the railroad cut.

Crossing over or cutting through the two McPherson Ridges were the Chambersburg Pike and the unfinished railroad cut. Both ran from the northwest to the southeast and gradually converged on the town of Gettysburg. At the western end of the area of this action they were some 200 yards apart, at the eastern edge about 100. The Chambersburg Pike was a surfaced road with a post and rail fence along its south side and a worm fence on the opposite one. Both these fences provided obstacles to movement and soldiers climbing over became vulnerable targets to troops in the railroad cut. After the action numerous Union bodies were draped over these fences or slumped at their foot.

There were three "cuts" along the line of the unfinished railroad track, where it cut through the two McPherson Ridges and further east where it pierced the Seminary Ridge. They are marked "West," "Center" and "East" Cuts on Map 28. The East Cut was outside the area of this fighting. The cuts varied in depth from 20 feet in the center to only 2 feet or less at the extremities, with a length of between 100 and 150 yards. The shallower parts offered good cover from fire and good fire positions once occupied by Davis's men firing toward the Pike. However, where the cuts were deep with steep banks, some firers at the rim were knocked back down by the recoil of the shot, while many others found it too difficult to climb the banks anyway. Once Union troops reached the top of the bank they dominated those below and a party sealing the eastern end was in a position to bring devastating flanking fire along the length of the cut. Once this stage was reached the Rebels were forced to surrender in droves.

McPherson's Farm had an orchard to the south and a grass paddock to the east, with corn planted further east and to the west. The land between the Pike and railroad cuts from West Ridge eastward was grass and westward wheat. North of the cuts were large fields of standing wheat divided by worm fences.

Tactical significance

The overall significance of the Union success in the fight for the railroad cut was that it gave the Confederates a bloody nose, sending them reeling back to their start line on Herr's Ridge to the north of the Chambersburg Pike, just as the Iron Brigade had done to the south. It ensured a pause in the fighting – a lull – while both sides regrouped, the generals considered their next move and reinforcements arrived for both armies. It meant that McPherson's Ridge was still firmly held by I Corps and that this ridge was likely to be the scene of further heavy fighting if the Rebels renewed their advance. Nevertheless, there is an argument that pulling back to Seminary Ridge might have resulted in a stronger defense in the afternoon.

Force comparison

Overall, the struggle for the railroad cuts involved an infantry brigade on both sides. The first phase – which included the attack of Davis's Confederates on Cutler's regiments north of the Chambersburg Pike and saw all the Yankees north of the Pike forced to retreat – pitted three regiments against three regiments. The second phase, the defense and attack on the railroad cuts themselves, again involved the original three Rebel regiments defending against the assault of three different Yankee ones. Both brigades had one regiment missing from the action guarding trains (Davis the 11th Mississippi with nearly 600 men, and Cutler the 7th Indiana with 434). However, things were not as equal as these facts suggest. The statistics at the start of each phase are shown in the two below.

Phase One

Confederate (Davis)		Union (Cutler)	
2nd Mississippi	492	76th New York	375
42nd Mississippi	575	56th Pennsylvania	252
55th North Carolina	640	147th New York	380
Totals	**1707**		**1007**
Artillery – 2 batteries, 8 guns		Artillery – 1 battery, 6 guns	

Phase Two

The regiments on both sides had by this time suffered losses. In addition, a number of men in the 55th North Carolina and 2nd Mississippi had resorted to chasing the retreating Yankees into Shead's Wood and were not present with their regiments for this short final stage. This means the figures given below are more approximate estimates.

Confederate		Union	
2nd Mississippi	420	6th Wisconsin	344
		Brigade guard (part of 6th Wisconsin)	100
42nd Mississippi	520	84th New York	300
55th North Carolina	570	95th New York	230
Totals	**1510**		**974**
Artillery – 8 guns		Artillery – none	

- In phase one the Rebel attackers outnumbered their enemy by 700 men, the equivalent of about two regiments. Although they had more guns available in support, in practice they mostly concentrated their fire on the opposing artillery rather than supporting the infantry advance. Despite their greater numbers, two Confederate regiments (55th North Carolina and 42nd Mississippi) had no battle experience, with the latter only mustered into service in May. Both sides fought with equal courage, but in the end their numerical advantage was enough to enable the Rebels to outflank the Yankee right.
- In phase two the Confederates became the defenders while still outnumbering their opponents by over 500 men – yet they were defeated. In this case commanders had begun to lose control, with regiments intermingled, numerous soldiers still pursuing the retreating Union regiments and scores of men unable to fight or fire when they descended into the deeper parts of the cuts. Faced with a quick, determined assault, their advantage in numbers was not enough to avoid defeat.
- Artillery did not play a noticeable part for either side in phase one, although Hall's battery was able to inflict casualties on the 42nd Mississippi with canister rounds just before being forced to withdraw; and Pegram's guns were able to bring some enfilade fire down the line of the Pike when the 84th New York deployed to face north in the second phase.

Command and control

A number of command decisions and leadership issues directly influenced the outcome of the fight for the railroad cut. The officers primarily involved were, on the Confederate side, the divisional commander Major-General Heth and Brigadier-General Davis; and on the Union side Major-General Doubleday (then acting as I Corps commander) and three regimental commanders, Colonel Fowler, Lieutenant-Colonel Dawes and Major Pye.

Major-General Henry "Harry" Heth. The only officer in the Army of Northern Virginia who could lay claim to being a protégé of Lee. Both came from the same social background, West Point (although Heth graduated last in his class in 1847) and the old

The Iron Brigade Guard at the Railroad Cut

On July 1 Lieutenant Loyd G. Harris was commanding the Iron Brigade Guard of around 100 men, made up of detachments from each regiment in the brigade. The Guard was assigned to the 6th Wisconsin Infantry and as such participated in that regiment's charge on the railroad cut. Many years later Harris wrote of his experiences for the *Milwaukee Sunday Telegraph*.

> [Lieutenant] Colonel [Rufus R.] Dawes divided it [the Guard] into two companies, one on the right the other on the left of the regiment. Before this was executed, and while we having only a minute or so to catch breath after a double-quick of half a mile, I, feeling keenly my situation and obeying a sudden impulse, stepped in front of the men of the guard . . . and said: "I know how much you would like to be with your own commands, and I am just as anxious to join company C over there on the right of the 6th, but it cannot be so; do the best you can and I will do my duty toward you." Just then came the order to move "to the right" . . .
>
> To return to the charge of the guard with the 6th Wisconsin. When the enemy discovered us coming, they gave up the pursuit of Cutler's men and wheeled to the right to meet it. I could not help thinking, now, for once, we will have a square "stand up and knock down fight." No trees, nor walls to protect either, when presto! Their whole line disappeared as if swallowed by the earth. It was the old story of the sunken road at Waterloo. They had taken advantage of a deep railroad cut, a splendid position for them, and threatening death and destruction to any regiment that attempted to dislodge them. The 6th never hesitated. I did not hear Colonel Dawes command to charge, but I saw the colors moving forward; that was enough. I knew that the command had been given . . . The brigade guard on the right never faltered . . . On the left the fire was the worst I ever experienced . . .

The view down the railroad cut from the modern bridge, looking northwest toward South Mountain.

Regular Army. Heth was thirty-seven, handsome and socially charming, and well known as the only officer Lee called by his first name. He took part in the Mexican War and spent time in the 19th U.S. Infantry "chasing buffalo, Indians and Mormons." He was also a childhood friend of his corps commander, A. P. Hill, who had acted as groomsman at Heth's wedding in 1857. Like so many other regular officers, he resigned at the outbreak of the Civil War to join the Confederate service. As an independent brigade commander he was thoroughly routed at a small action in the defense of Lewisburg in the Allegheny Mountains in May 1862, although this did nothing to damage his reputation with Lee, who was to write of him to President Davis, "I have a high estimate of Genl. Heth." Heth was given command of a brigade in his old friend Hill's Light Division. He was slightly wounded at Chancellorsville and briefly served as acting divisional commander when Hill was also wounded. When Lee reorganized the army after that battle, Heth was promoted to command the new division in the 3rd Corps – again with Hill as his immediate superior.

Heth was the officer who launched the divisional attack that, in the event, brought on phase one of the Battle of Gettysburg. Under instructions to reconnoiter the town (looking for shoes was an idea promulgated years later) and not to bring on a general engagement, Heth proceeded to do exactly that. At the first resistance by Buford's mounted screen, Heth deployed his two leading brigades (Davis and Archer) and pushed the Union cavalry back to McPherson's Ridge. Resistance stiffened, however, and it was decision time for Heth. He rode forward to Herr's Ridge to survey the scene. In his report he stated: "it became evident that there were infantry [no, but he mistook dismounted cavalry for infantry], cavalry and artillery [correct] around the town." Such a force indicated something much stronger than militia or cavalry patrols. He had achieved his reconnaissance task and should have reported his findings to Hill. Heth knew that Lee did not want a major battle before the army was concentrated – even if this order had not been repeated on July 1, it had not been rescinded. Instead of halting the action, instead of reporting to his corps commander, Heth instructed his leading brigades "to move forward and occupy the town." It was the order that resulted in the Davis–Cutler fight for the railroad cut and was the initial Confederate contribution to the start of what developed into the Battle of Gettysburg. Although at noon it was still not inevitable, just under two hours later Lieutenant-General Richard Ewell would launch a second phase that made avoiding battle extremely difficult.

Brigadier-General Joseph R. Davis. If ever there was a case of nepotism and political clout securing rapid military promotion, "Joe" Davis was the classic example. A lawyer by profession, he had been elected to the Mississippi State Senate in 1860. At the outbreak of war he was thirty-six and had never worn a uniform in his life. In January 1861 he was a captain, in April a lieutenant-colonel and in August a colonel on his uncle's staff in Richmond. President Davis's first attempt to have him promoted brigadier-general in September 1862 was rejected by the Confederate Senate. However, it was not long before several of the senators who voted against it were offered suitable inducements to change their minds and a second vote was carried by 13 to 6. Davis commanded a brigade of Mississippians in North Carolina – a backwater with little excitement – in early 1863. The fight for the railroad cut was to be his first experience of battle.

Davis had two veteran regiments with significant battle experience (the 2nd and 11th Mississippi) and two with none (the 42nd Mississippi and 55th North Carolina). Unfortunately he had left the 11th Mississippi guarding the divisional train, so on July 1 his brigade went into action with a green commander, two equally green regiments out of three and at only threequarters its proper strength. Initially control was not difficult: Davis lined up the brigade and advanced toward the northern end of McPherson's Ridge, mostly through grass and wheatfields. The attack was surprisingly successful and when Davis's left overlapped the Union right and Yankees retired in haste, success looked certain. By this time, however, Davis had lost two regimental commanders (Colonels Connally and Stone) and his inexperience was revealed. Instead of halting and rallying his victorious regiments, control was lost and many men chased after the fleeing Yankees toward, and into, Shead's Wood. This was a crucial moment, requiring a firm grip to meet the new threat developing along the Chambersburg

Pike to the south. The wheel of Davis's Brigade to the right and its arrival at the railroad cut was disorganized, with regiments intermingled. Many officers had fallen, so control was at best tenuous; this, coupled with the unsuitability of the deeper parts of the cut for firing from, contributed to what had looked like a splendid success quickly dissolving into an ignominious surrender and flight.

Major-General Abner Doubleday. (See also page 270.) Doubleday was the senior divisional commander of the Army of the Potomac at Gettysburg and took formal command of I Corps on the death of Reynolds at around 10.45 a.m. He was a steady, experienced if ponderous commander – and he was loathed by Meade, who regarded him as a troublemaker. However, on the morning of July 1 Doubleday rose magnificently to the challenge of unexpected responsibility and decision-making. It was he who sent an aide (Lieutenant Benjamin T. Martin) galloping across to the 6th Wisconsin to halt the regiment as it was moving toward the left flank of the Iron Brigade to counter Archer's advance. Doubleday's decision to use the 6th Wisconsin and the brigade guard as his force reserve almost certainly saved the dangerous situation that quickly developed north of the Pike. Within minutes the staff officer returned with Doubleday's order that sent the 6th Wisconsin hurrying north to its confrontation at the railroad cut.

Colonel Edward B. Fowler, Lieutenant-Colonel Rufus R. Dawes and Major Edward Pye. The Union success in the actual fighting at the railroad cut owed much to leadership at regimental level. The three regimental commanders were Fowler of the 84th New York (14th Brooklyn Militia), and Pye, who took over the 95th New York when Colonel George Biddle was wounded – both in Cutler's Brigade; and Dawes commanding the 6th Wisconsin in the Iron Brigade. All three displayed fine leadership in the bitter and bloody fighting to prevent the collapse of the Union right. It was Dawes who double-quicked his men for 700 yards, changed formation into line and reached the Pike in time to check the Rebel rush, forcing them to take cover in the cuts. It was Dawes who got his men to clamber over the two fences that lined the Pike under intense fire, something he described as "a sure test of metal and discipline." It was Dawes who urged, encouraged and led his men in the charge on the cuts some 150 yards away across an open grass field. And it was Dawes who, just after ordering his regiment over the second fence, spotted Major Pye of the 95th New York on his left and dashed over, yelling, "Let's go for them Major" – an action to which Pye immediately responded by leading his men forward. Colonel Fowler was the senior officer of the two regiments from Cutler's Brigade (his 84th New York and Pye's 95th New York) that had been deployed south of the Pike facing west. When Archer advanced, only the 5th Alabama Battalion had deployed as skirmishers in front of them and thus neither regiment was heavily involved in the Iron Brigade's fight on their left. Fowler, realizing the danger developing on his right when he was fired on by Davis's Mississippians, withdrew both regiments from the line, realigned them facing north and advanced them to the Pike. Pye arrived in time to support the 6th Wisconsin in its charge and Fowler's men joined in a little later. It was undoubtedly the skill of these regimental leaders and the courage of their soldiers that saved the Union line from collapsing.

Plans and orders

Confederate. Heth, with the authority of his corps commander and under instructions not to bring on a general engagement, ordered his division to march on Gettysburg and occupy the town.

Union. Buford instructed his cavalry to delay the enemy advance until I Corps infantry arrived. Reynolds, as left-wing commander, decided to hold McPherson's Ridge strongly and, if at all possible, prevent the Confederates taking Gettysburg.

Outline of events

See Maps 28 and 29.

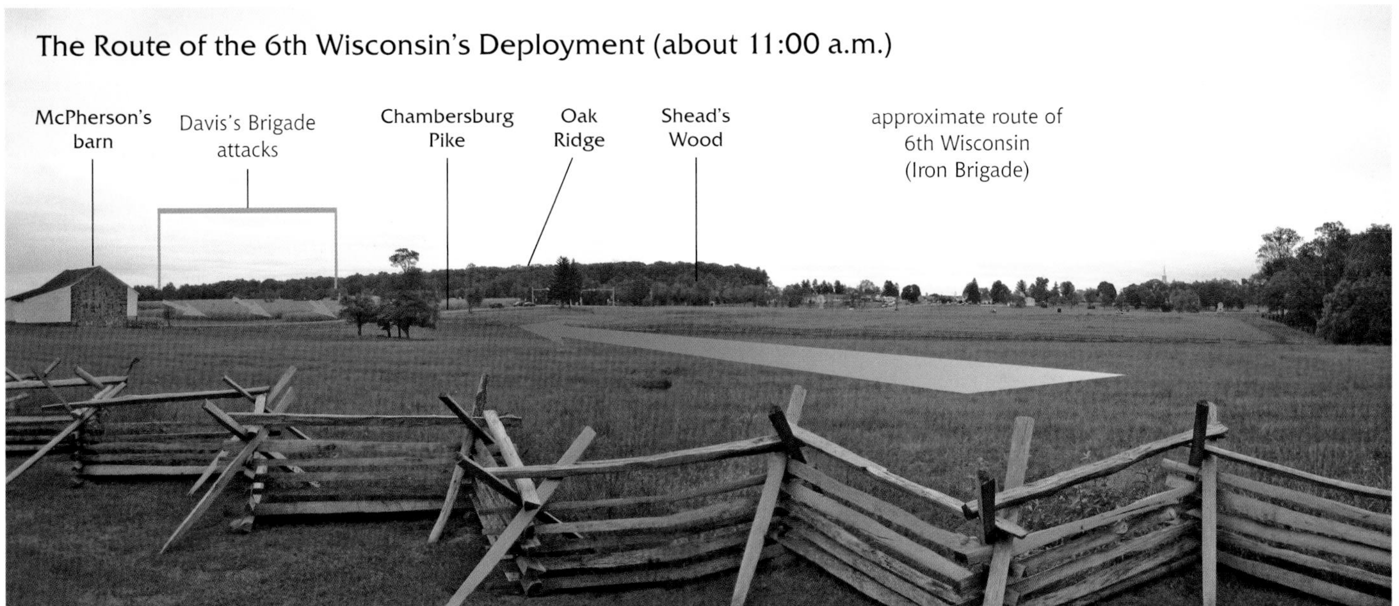

This photograph is taken from near the John Burns statue, looking toward Oak Ridge and the Chambersburg Pike. It shows the direction of the Confederate brigade attack under Brig.-Gen. Davis toward the unfinished railroad cut (beyond the Pike) and the Union right on McPherson's Ridge. It was the rapid advance of Lt.-Col. Rufus Dawes' 6th Wisconsin to the Pike and their charge on the railroad cut that led to Davis's regiment being driven back in some disorder.

A Rebel Evades Capture in the Railway Cut

Private David J. Hill, 2nd Mississippi Infantry, describes how he avoided capture when the 6th Wisconsin overran the railway cut.

> I found to my dismay that I was in a tight place, saw no chance of escape, was disgusted with the idea of surrendering and in fact became very much demoralized. I saw a bloody, muddy blanket lying on the ground also two wounded men lying near me. I tumbled down by them and covered myself with that blanket. I then went to practicing all maneuvers and moaning that I thought would become a badly wounded and suffering man . . . I got out as soon as I thought it safe to do so and the first man I met was a federal soldier wandering about as if dazed or lost and not knowing what to do. I saw that all one side of his lower jaw was torn off. I got him to a shade and fixed him down with his oil cloth, blanket and knapsack, then brought him a canteen of water and how pitiful to see him trying to drink by pushing the mouth of the canteen through the wound in his throat. I could do nothing more for him. He could not talk so I did not learn his name or what command he was of.

Although he escaped on this occasion, Hill was captured two days later.

Notes

AAA The 2nd Brigade (1st Division, I Corps) under Brig.-Gen. Cutler was the first Union infantry to arrive to relieve Buford's cavalry on McPherson's Ridge. Two regiments (95th & 84th NY) deployed south of the Chambersburg Pike and two to the north (76th NY and 56th Pa). The 147th NY was intended to follow them but was delayed by the move forward of the 2nd Maine Battery under Captain Hall, which deployed on West McPherson's Ridge and engaged Pegram's Battalion on Herr's Ridge. Uncertain where to go, the 147th waited on the reverse slope of the ridge along the lane leading to McPherson's farmhouse.

BBBB Davis's Confederate Brigade attacked and outflanked the 76th NY and threatened to overwhelm Cutler's position north of the Pike. After a brief wait, the 147th NY was rushed north to deploy with its left resting on the West Cut, supporting the right of Hall's guns. However, the Rebel attack was pressed home and, to avoid the line being rolled up from the right, Wadsworth, the divisional commander, gave the order for a withdrawal of Cutler's right to Shead's Wood (Seminary Ridge). The order failed to reach the 147th NY, who continued to hold out against overwhelming numbers. The regiment refused its right flank companies to face the Rebel assault from the north and on its right flank.

CCC On seeing the 147th in danger of being surrounded, Wadsworth repeated his withdrawal order. First Hall's battery and then 147th NY retreated in great haste, the infantry to regroup in the orchard near Mary Thompson's house, the artillery on Cemetery Hill.

DD Meanwhile Archer's Brigade had advanced a short while after Davis and the four leading regiments of Meredith's Iron Brigade deployed at the run toward Herbst Wood and Willoughby Run to confront this advance. The 6th Wisconsin was held back as the divisional reserve. It was soon to be rushed north to support Cutler's right.

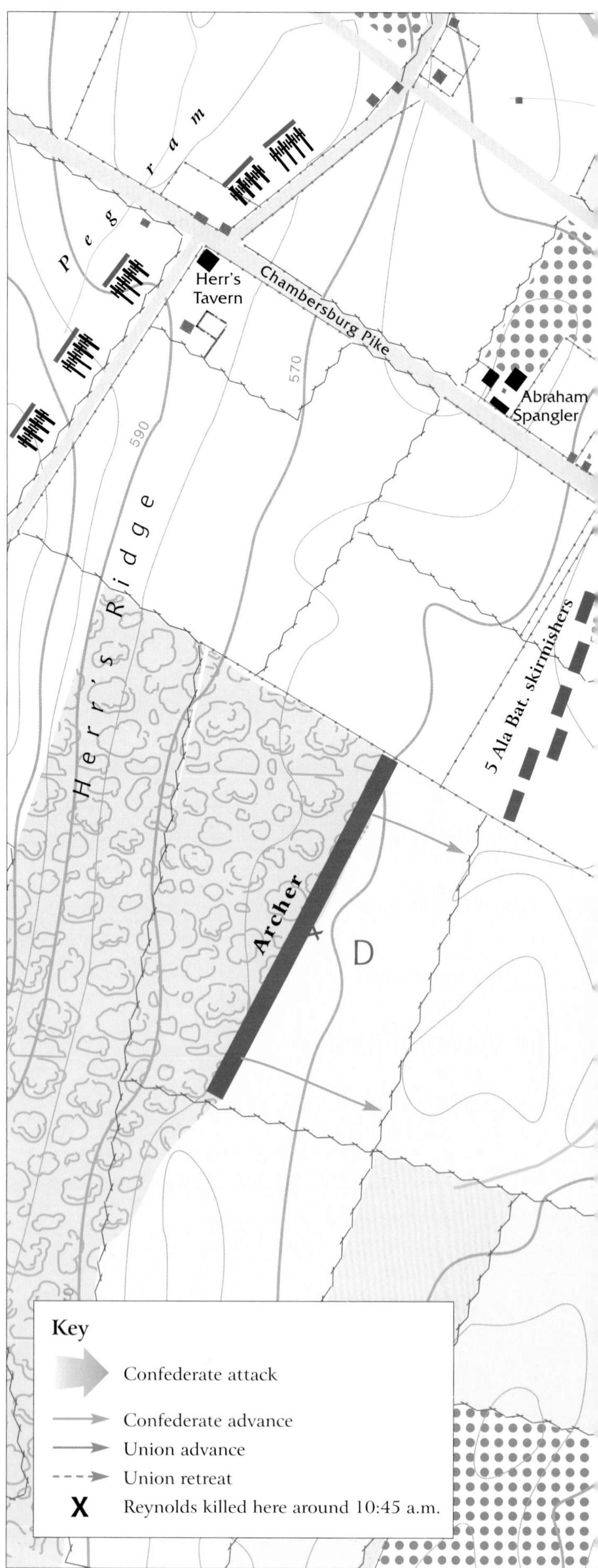

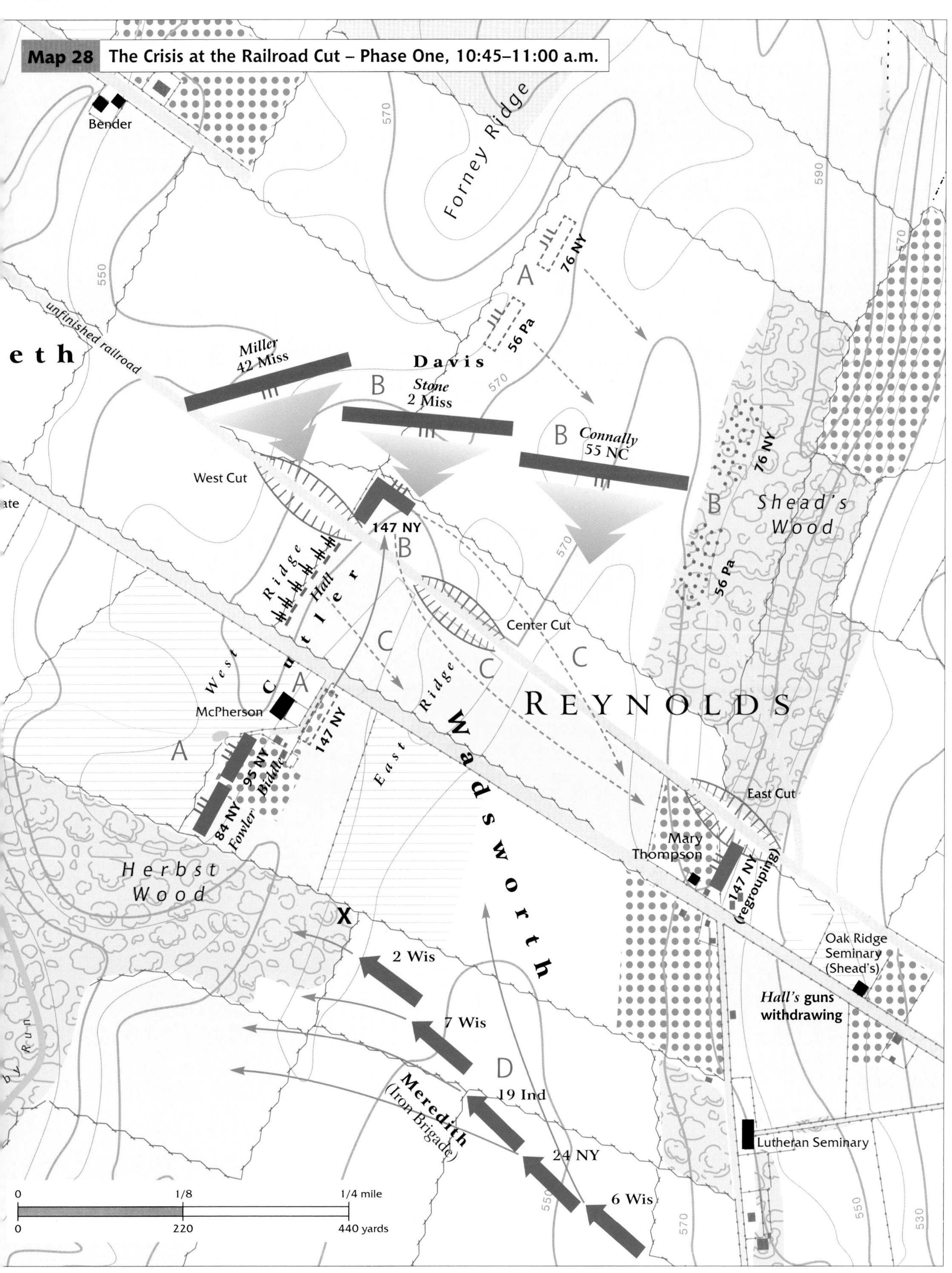
Map 28 The Crisis at the Railroad Cut – Phase One, 10:45–11:00 a.m.
Bender
Forney Ridge
unfinished railroad
Miller
42 Miss
Davis
Stone
2 Miss
Connally
55 NC
76 NY
56 Pa
West Cut
147 NY
Hall
Cutler
Ridge
West
McPherson
Center Cut
East Ridge
REYNOLDS
Wadsworth
Shead's Wood
95 NY
84 NY
Fowler
Biddle
Herbst Wood
2 Wis
7 Wis
19 Ind
24 NY
6 Wis
Meredith
(Iron Brigade)
East Cut
Mary Thompson
147 NY (regrouping)
Oak Ridge Seminary (Shead's)
Hall's guns withdrawing
Lutheran Seminary
0 1/8 1/4 mile
0 220 440 yards

Charging the Railroad Cut

Sergeant James P. Sullivan, a former Irish immigrant farm laborer, joined the 6th Wisconsin in 1861. He later described his experience in the railroad cut for a Milwaukee newspaper:

> In the road [Chambersburg Pike] our fellows straightened up their lines and waited for all hands to get over the fence and opened fire on the Johnnies, and then I found my gun would not go off . . . We climbed over the fence and I tried my gun again, and finding it had two loads in it I went to our Adjutant who was just in the rear of our company and said "Brooks, my gun won't go off." "Here take this," he said, and handed me one he had picked up . . . I went back into place in the line and fired it off, but when I loaded up and tried again it would not go, and then I knew my caps were bad. I went to Ticknor and told him my caps were bad. He said, "take Crawford's" pointing to a corporal of our company who had just dropped dead and we rolled him over and I took the cartridge box and buckled it on myself.
>
> As I turned around I saw Captain Ticknor start for the rear in a spread out staggering sort of way a few feet he fell . . .
>
> We were then within a few feet of the railroad cut and were ordered to fix bayonets and charge, which we did. Some of the Johnnies threw down their guns and surrendered. Some would fire and then throw down their guns and cry, I surrender, and some of them broke for the rear. I jumped into the railroad cut and a rebel officer handed me his sword and passed through the cut with the intention of stopping the Johnnies, who were climbing to the rear. Just as I climbed up the side of the cut a big rebel broke and run for the rear, and I called on him to halt, to which he paid no attention, and I flung the rebel sword at him with all my might, but I never knew whether I hit or not, for just as I turned to throw the sword, a bullet hit me on the left shoulder and knocked me down as quick as if I had been hit with a sledgehammer . . .
>
> After a while I began to feel better . . . I picked up my gun and tried to shoulder it, but found that me left arm was powerless so I went around to the other side of the cut where our fellows had a heavy line of prisoners . . . and took my place outside the rebs, intending to help guard them, but I felt sick and faint and the blood was running down inside my clothes and dropping from my pants leg and my shoe was full and running over.

The Fight for the 2nd Mississippi Infantry Colors

In the railroad cut a furious struggle developed for the colors of the 2nd Mississippi Infantry. The color-bearer, Private William B. Murphy, later described what happened:

> My color guards were all killed and wounded in less than five minutes, and also my colors were shot more than one dozen times, and the flag staff was hit and splintered two or three times. Just at that time a squad of soldiers made a rush for my colors and our men did their duty. They were all killed or wounded, but still rushed for the colors with one of the most deadly struggles that was ever witnessed during any battle of the war . . . there were over a dozen shot down like sheep in their madly [*sic*] rush for the colors. The first soldier was shot down just as he made for the flag . . . and at the same time a lieutenant made a desperate struggle for the flag, and was shot through his right shoulder. Over a dozen men fell killed or wounded, and then a large man [Corporal Frank Waller, 6th Wisconsin] made a rush for me and the flag. As I tore the flag from the staff he took hold of me and the color.

Corporal Waller was later awarded the Medal of Honor.

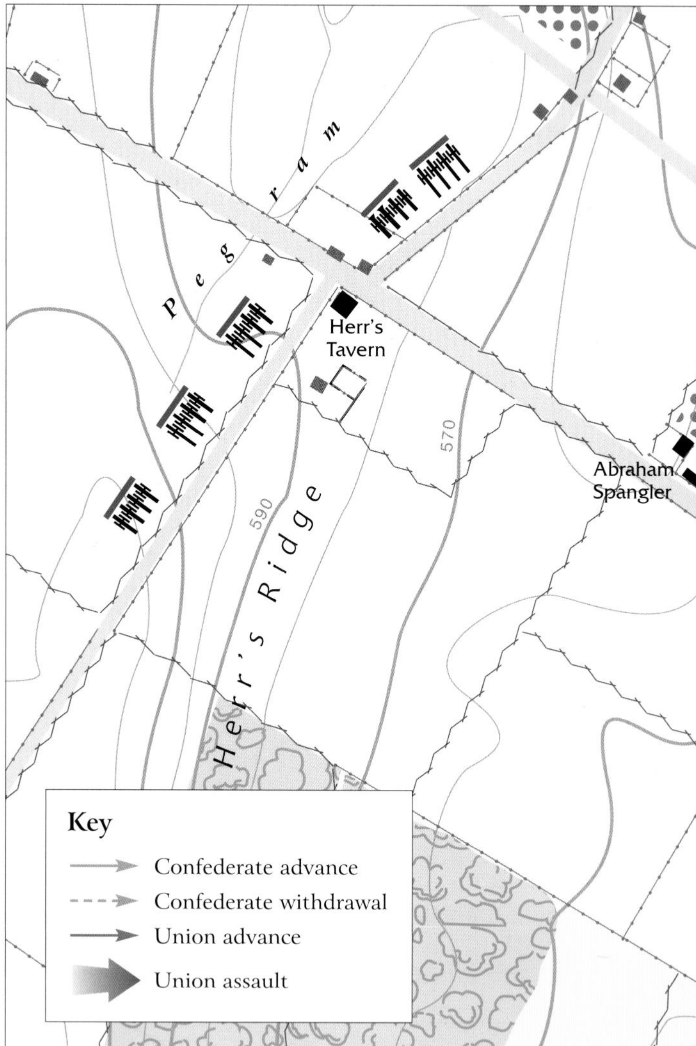

Notes

A The charge of the Iron Brigade into Herbst Wood drives back Archer's attack.

B1 Doubleday sends the 6th Wisconsin under Lt.-Col. Rufus Dawes to support Cutler's crumbling right. The regiment initially double-quicks in column of companies, wheels right heading east and then left turns into line and runs to the Chambersburg Pike, where it lies down and engages in a firefight with the advancing Rebels. The regiment is mostly on the reverse (eastern) slope of East McPherson's Ridge and thus Dawes cannot see what is happening to his left.

B2 Meanwhile, Col. Edward Fowler becomes convinced that he is about to be attacked on his right. As the Iron Brigade have taken the pressure off his front, he is able, as the senior of the two regimental commanders, to order the 84th NY (14th Brooklyn) and 95th NY to turn about and then move east and wheel left toward the Pike.

B3 As these moves take place, the Confederates swing toward the Pike and rush to the unfinished railroad cut, where most take cover and join in the fierce firefight across the 150 yards of grass separating the cut from the Pike.

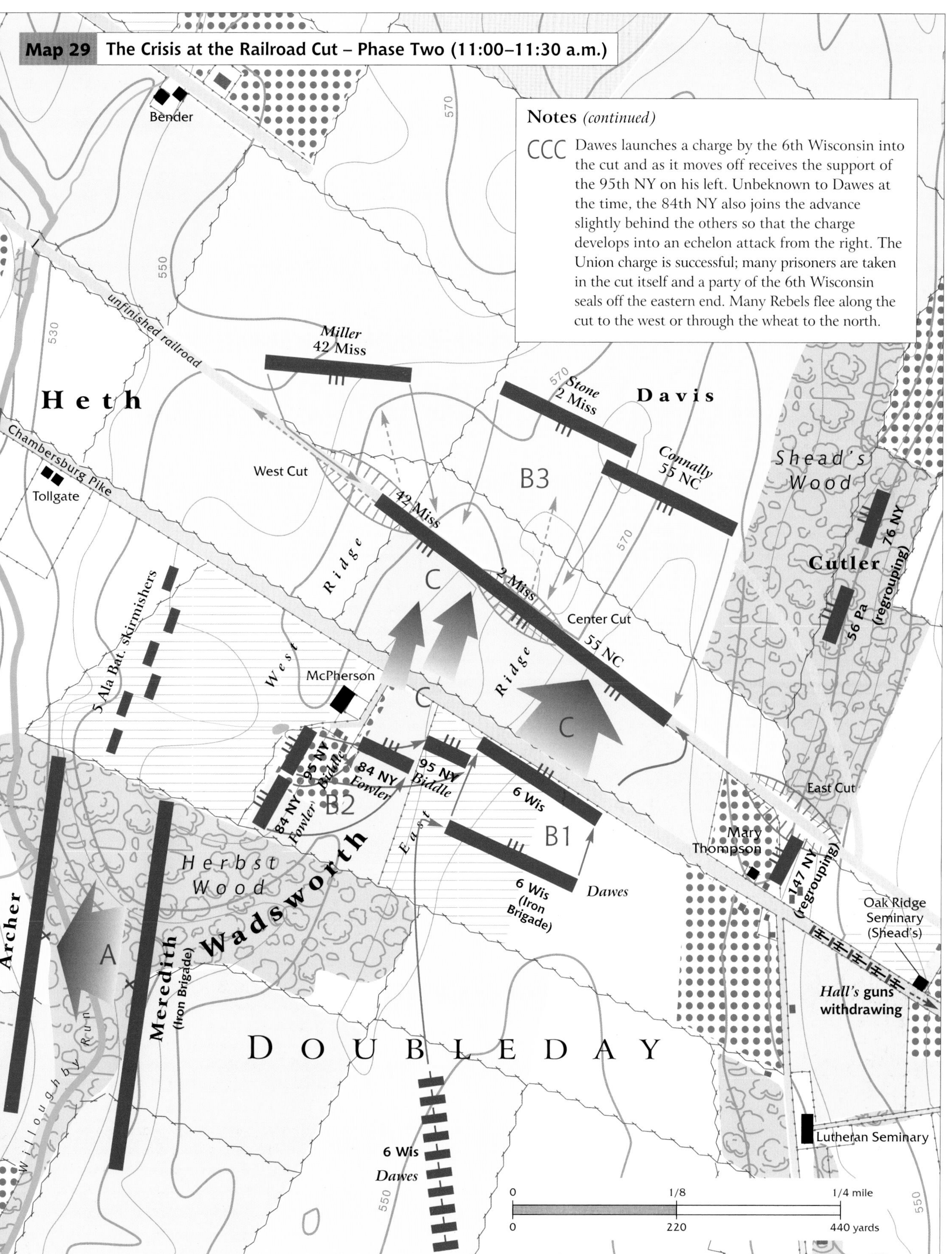
Map 29 The Crisis at the Railroad Cut – Phase Two (11:00–11:30 a.m.)
Notes (continued)
CCC Dawes launches a charge by the 6th Wisconsin into the cut and as it moves off receives the support of the 95th NY on his left. Unbeknown to Dawes at the time, the 84th NY also joins the advance slightly behind the others so that the charge develops into an echelon attack from the right. The Union charge is successful; many prisoners are taken in the cut itself and a party of the 6th Wisconsin seals off the eastern end. Many Rebels flee along the cut to the west or through the wheat to the north.
Bender
unfinished railroad
Miller 42 Miss
Heth
Chambersburg Pike
Tollgate
West Cut
42 Miss
Stone 2 Miss
Davis
Connally 55 NC
B3
Shead's Wood
76 NY (regrouping)
Cutler
56 Pa
2 Miss
Center Cut
55 NC
West Ridge
Ridge
5 Ala Bat. skirmishers
McPherson
95 NY Biddle
84 NY Fowler
95 NY Biddle
6 Wis
B1
B2
East
6 Wis (Iron Brigade)
Dawes
East Cut
Mary Thompson
147 NY (regrouping)
Oak Ridge Seminary (Shead's)
Hall's guns withdrawing
Herbst Wood
Wadsworth
Archer
Meredith (Iron Brigade)
Willoughby Run
DOUBLEDAY
6 Wis
Dawes
Lutheran Seminary
0 1/8 1/4 mile
0 220 440 yards

Results and casualties

It is difficult to estimate the losses sustained at the railroad cut as distinct from losses later in the battle. However, for both sides casualties were very heavy. The Confederates took about 1,700 men into the fight; at least 232 were captured in the railroad cuts and another 400 killed or wounded during the morning. The 2nd Mississippi lost its color and seven of its nine field officers were dead or wounded. Davis's Brigade came within an ace of achieving an outstanding success, but ended the morning having suffered a severe drubbing that cost it not far short of half its strength. It was rested on July 2 but was part of the Pickett–Pettigrew–Trimble charge on July 3, by which time it had been joined by the 11th Mississippi. The final casualty count at the end of the battle showed losses for the 2nd Mississippi of 47 percent, 42nd Mississippi 46 percent and the 55th North Carolina almost 65 percent – the fourteenth highest loss out of the 172 Rebel regiments at Gettysburg, the majority occurring on the morning of July 1.

According to Dawes, the 6th Wisconsin and brigade guard lost about 180 men in the actual charge on the cut. This is probably too high, as the regiment was involved in further fighting on Culp's Hill late on July 2 and early the next day, and its total losses for the battle are estimated at 168 (excluding the brigade guard) or almost 50 percent. A figure of 130–150 seems more likely. The gallant stand of the 147th New York cost it dearly, with only about 80 men rallying immediately after the action. It fought on subsequent days on Culp's Hill and by the end of the battle had suffered 78 percent casualties – the third highest percentage loss (along with the 16th Maine) of the 247 regiments in the Army of the Potomac. Overall, including Cutler's five regiments, Union losses were probably in the region of 800.

Comments

- The importance of outflanking one's enemy was evident. The advance by Davis started as a purely frontal attack, but when his superior numbers overlapped Cutler's regiments on their right they were forced to give way and a withdrawal was ordered. This swing south imperiled the right flank of the Union regiments south of the Pike and they had to react quickly and decisively to avoid losing McPherson's Ridge.
- The tactic of refusing a flank was used effectively, for a time at any rate, by the 147th New York just north of the West Cut as the regiment refused its right-flank companies when threatened from two directions simultaneously. Similarly, a little later, Colonel Fowler was able to change front entirely by withdrawing the 84th and 95th New York from facing west to facing north along the Pike to confront a new threat.
- This action illustrates how the timely rushing of even a small reserve to a critical point at the right moment can have far-reaching results. In this case it was Doubleday's sending the 6th Wisconsin north and the brilliant leadership and skill of its commander, Lieutenant-Colonel Dawes, which was the primary factor in checking the Rebel advance at the railroad cut. The move of this regiment to the scene was a good example of the importance of drill maneuvers on the battlefield. The 6th Wisconsin initially double-quicked in column of companies, then wheeled to the right facing east before finally turning left to bring the regiment into line facing its objective – in this case the Chambersburg Pike.
- The confrontation showed how determined low-level leadership, coupled with an old-fashioned infantry charge, even a frontal one, if delivered over a short distance, could be decisive if well timed. It was the charge of the 6th Wisconsin, supported by the 95th New York on its left with the 84th New York joining in a few minutes later, that took the railroad cut and forced the surrender and flight of so many of Davis's Brigade.
- How easy it was in the confusion of battle for important messages to go astray and thus jeopardize tactical maneuvers. The wounding of Lieutenant-Colonel Miller of the 147th New York just after he had received the order to retire meant the message never reached the companies and thus the 147th was isolated and nearly destroyed when the regiments to its right withdrew.
- Artillery (Captain Hall's 2nd Maine Battery) had to be positioned in the open on the crest of West McPherson's Ridge in order to fire. They were exposed to counterbattery fire from the more numerous guns on Herr's Ridge, but more important was the example of the vulnerability of gunners and horses to close-range rifle-musket fire when infantry support was withdrawn, in this case from their right. Captain Hall was extremely angry at what he saw to be lack of effective infantry support for his guns, compelling him to make a costly and chaotic retreat with the loss of one gun (later recovered).
- The charge on the railroad cut was the source of considerable controversy after the war. A lengthy argument developed over whether the credit for instituting and leading it should go to Colonel Fowler of the 84th New York or Lieutenant-Colonel Dawes of the 6th Wisconsin. As early as July 9 Fowler claimed the credit with the following statement in his report:

> At this time the Sixth Wisconsin Regiment gallantly advanced to our assistance. The enemy then took possession of a railroad cut, and I gave the order to charge them, which order was carried out gallantly by all the regiments . . . The advance was continued until near the cut, when I directed the Sixth Wisconsin to flank it by throwing forward their right, which being done, all the enemy within our reach surrendered . . .

This version was initially widely accepted and it was not until 1868 that Dawes, by then aware of Fowler's version, endeavored to set the record straight. On several occasions Dawes wrote on the subject, pointing out firmly that he initiated the charge and that Fowler did not order the 6th Wisconsin to charge – in fact, he never saw the 84th New York (14th Brooklyn) until they reached the cut after the 6th Wisconsin. In his memoir, published in 1890, he summed up his position:

> Colonel E. B. Fowler fourteenth Brooklyn, in his official report, had given the impression that he ordered the sixth Wisconsin regiment to make this charge. He gave us no orders whatever. I did not know he was on the field until the charge was over. I called Colonel Fowler's attention to the matter and he stated as an explanation that he sent an officer to give me such an order [in one of Fowler's versions he said he sent his adjutant]. Colonel Fowler was retreating his regiment when we arrived at the turnpike fence. He then changed front and joined our advance . . .

Colonel John A. Kellogg of the 6th Wisconsin was an aide to Cutler and watched the attack on the railroad cut. In 1865 he wrote: "the 6th commenced the movement, supported on the left by the 95th and the 14th [84th] on left of them. The 6th reached the cut about 3 minutes before any other regiment and captured the 2nd Mississippi and the other troops being a little behind . . ."

It would seem that Fowler was in the process of pulling back the 84th and 95th to avoid being outflanked when he saw the 6th Wisconsin advancing to the Pike. He halted and prepared to face north. He may indeed have sent his adjutant to contact Dawes, but if so he never arrived. When the 6th Wisconsin were aligned along the Pike Dawes would not have been able to see the 84th New York, as it was in the swale on the other side of East Cemetery Ridge. There can be little doubt that Dawes instigated the charge, shouting to Major Pye of the 95th New York on his immediate left moments before leading the charge of his regiment. A few moments later the 95th followed and shortly after that the 84th New York joined in. The attack was an echelon one from the right, with the 6th Wisconsin arriving at the cut having borne the brunt of the enemy fire.

THE LULL: NOON–2:00 P.M. (Map 30)

Apart from the unequal artillery exchanges between the massed Rebel guns of Pegram's then McIntosh's battalions on Herr's Ridge and the woefully inferior number of Union guns, for the infantry of both sides this was largely a period of regrouping and reinforcing. The Union regiments on McPherson's Ridge endeavored to seek cover from the shelling that drove away Calef's guns after a brief reappearance in his old position. For the generals it was a time for rethinking, making decisions and reorganizing their commands. Now is the appropriate moment to examine the thoughts and actions of these generals as they approached the battlefield or rode around it. As they held the initiative, the Confederates are discussed first.

Lee's Concern at Stuart's Absence

Evidence of Lee's ever-increasing worry at Stuart's absence is clear in the following quotation from Major-General Anderson's report. Anderson's Division was encamped near Cashtown awaiting orders on July 1, and in the late morning Anderson received word that Lee, whose headquarters was nearby, wished to see him. When Anderson approached he found Lee listening to the rumble of gunfire coming from the east. Lee looked worried, and after his conversation with Anderson he seemed to mumble more to himself than to anyone else:

> "I cannot think what has become of Stuart; I ought to have heard from him long before now. He may have met with disaster, but I hope not. In the absence of reports from him, I am in ignorance as to what we have in front of us. It may be the whole Federal army, or it may be only a detachment. If it is the whole Federal force we must fight a battle here; if we do not gain a victory those defiles and gorges through which we passed this morning will shelter us from disaster."

Major Henry McClellan of Stuart's staff was later to write: "It was the absence of Stuart himself that he felt so keenly . . . it seemed as if his cavalry were concentrated in one person, and from him alone could information be expected." Major-General Henry Heth had this to say on the same subject: "I saw General Lee several times between the 27th and 30th June. The first thing he would say showed his anxiety about his cavalry. 'Have you heard anything about my cavalry? I hope no disaster has overtaken my cavalry.' The last time I saw him before the 1st July he said, 'Any news to give me about General Stuart?' . . ."

Lee

On June 30 Lee had camped at Greenwood and while there had recalled both Ewell from the north and Robertson's cavalry from the south. On the morning of July 1 he rode toward the Cashtown Gap in the company of Longstreet, whose corps was still encamped near Chambersburg, in effect waiting to join the queue behind Anderson's and Johnson's Divisions for space on the Cashtown–Gettysburg Pike. Lee still thought the main body of the Army of the Potomac was around Middleburg in Maryland. Arriving at around 11:00 a.m., he was surprised to find Hill at Cashtown, despite the fact that two of his divisions were marching on Gettysburg. Hill could not throw much light on the situation, and probably with some feelings of embarrassment rode off to seek information. Lee remained for a while at Cashtown and rode over to Major-General Richard Anderson's camp to discuss the situation. His main worry at this stage was still the absence of Stuart. Anderson later recalled that Lee was "very much disturbed and depressed" and that he made it plain that "in the absence of reports from him I am in ignorance of what we have in front of us." He added, "If it is the whole Federal force we must fight a battle here." See box below.

A little later Major Campbell Brown of Ewell's staff arrived with the news that his commander had received Hill's earlier message that he (Hill) was marching on Gettysburg and that, using the discretion allowed him by Lee, Ewell had changed the direction of Rodes' and Early's Divisions toward that town. Lee asked Brown if Ewell had heard from Stuart. According to Brown, when he answered negatively Lee responded with some feeling that he "had heard nothing from or of him for three days, and that Genl. Stuart had not complied with his instructions" and has "gone off clear around Genl. Meade's army and I see by a Northern newspaper that he is near Washington [referring to Stuart's capture of the wagon train]." Nevertheless, Lee now knew that Gettysburg was almost certain to be the area of concentration of his army and he instructed Brown to return to Ewell and stress again that he should avoid bringing on a battle until the army was properly reunited. Brown later wrote, "General Lee then impressed on me *very strongly* that a general engagement was to be avoided until the arrival of the rest of the army." Telling Anderson to start marching, and leaving Longstreet to rejoin his corps, Lee continued his ride forward to see for himself what was happening.

Lee had been aware of the continuous booming of artillery for some time before he joined Hill in the vicinity of Herr's Ridge, close to the Chambersburg Pike about a mile southwest of Oak Hill, at around 1:30 p.m. Shortly afterward Heth arrived to explain what was happening and, as Ewell's guns were firing from Oak Hill, urged that now was the moment for him to renew the attack. It was decision time for Lee. Still uncertain of the strength of the opposition around Gettysburg, still unaware of the whereabouts of the bulk of the Union Army and with a third of his own army (Longstreet's Corps) still up to 20 miles away

Map 30 The "Lull" – Noon–2:00 p.m. (approximate locations at around 2.00 p.m.)
Wisler
Chambersburg Pike
Unfinished railroad
Mummasburg Road
Ramseur
Daniel
Hoffman
Forney Wood
Iverson
Thomas
Herr's Tavern
Pegram
Davis
Bender
Scales
McIntosh
HILL
Pender
Perrin
Heth
Brockenbrough
Tollgate
Wadsworth
Calef
McPherson
Stone
Meredith
Herbst Wood
I CORPS
Pettigrew
Cooper
Reynolds
C. Biddle
Lane
Harman
Fry (Archer)
Johnson (McIntosh)
Willoughby Run
C. Biddle (Rowley)
Fairfield Road
Key
Confederate advance
approximate Union advance
approximate Union withdrawal
0
1/4
Mile

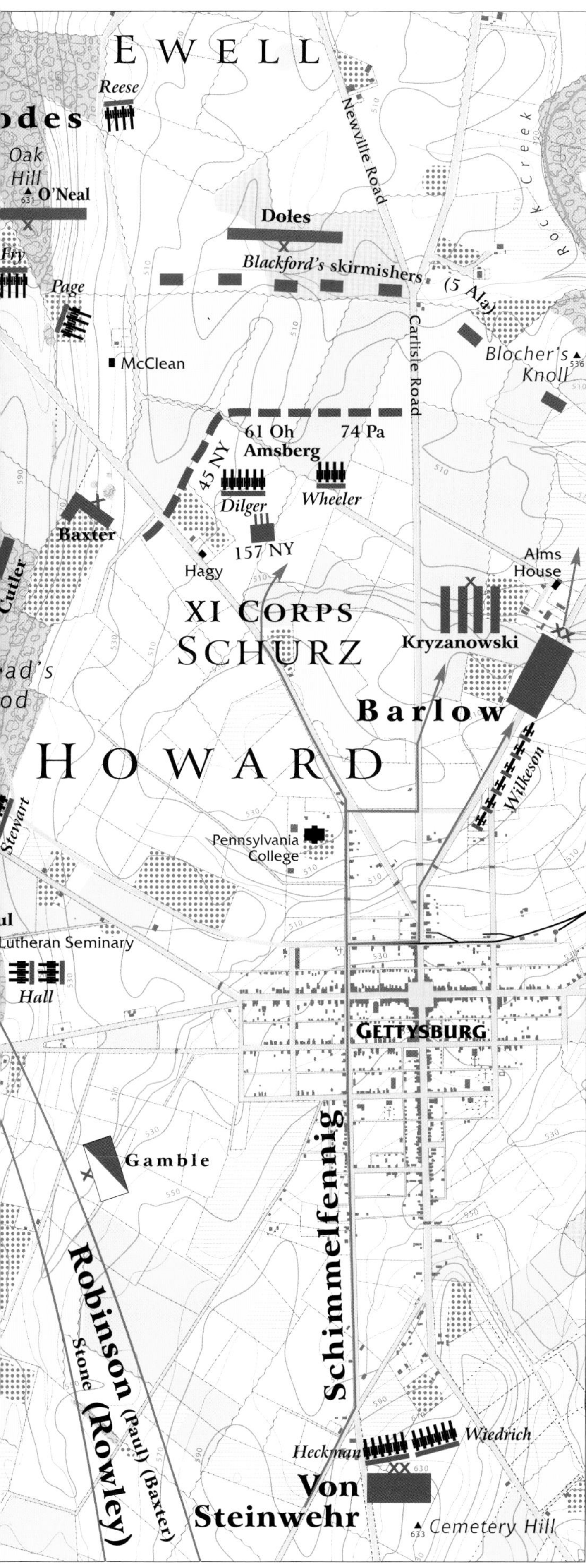

Notes

• During the period from about noon to about 2:00 p.m. there was a lull in the infantry fighting west of Gettysburg. However, there was no let-up in the artillery exchanges, with the massed Confederate batteries on Herr's Ridge making life particularly difficult for the Union regiments on McPherson's Ridge and forcing Calef's horse artillery, which had been ordered forward again, to retire for a second time.

• This was the time when reinforcements were arriving for both sides and readjustments made to the line. The significant events and approximate timings are listed below.

11:30 a.m.	• Meade at Taneytown receives Reynolds' message that he intends to "keep them [the Rebels] back as long as possible."
	• Howard at Cemetery Hill meets Schurz (now acting XI Corps commander).
	• 3rd Division, I Corps (Rowley) starts to arrive on battlefield by two different routes and deploys either side of the Iron Brigade (Meredith), although later Biddle's Brigade was withdrawn nearer to the Seminary Ridge.
NOON	• 2nd Division, I Corps (Robinson) arrives and is initially held in reserve near Lutheran Seminary.
12:30 p.m.	• 3rd Division, XI Corps marches through Gettysburg under Schimmelfennig and is ordered to occupy Oak Hill, but Rodes' Division has reached it first. Amsberg's Brigade is spread thinly between the Mummasburg and Carlisle Roads. Kryzanowski's Brigade remains massed in reserve east of the Carlisle Road.
	• Rodes' Confederate Division moves south along Oak Ridge toward Oak Hill.
1:00 p.m.	• 1st Division, XI Corps (Barlow) follows 3rd Division and moves to the right of Kryzanowski.
	• By this time Pegram's and McIntosh's artillery battalions are moved onto Herr's Ridge and Pender's Division has moved up behind Heth's.
	• Rebel guns (Carter and Fry) open fire from Oak Hill and leading elements of Rodes' Division begin arriving on Oak Hill.
	• Howard sends message to bring up III and XII Corps.
	• Doubleday, alerted by the Rebel guns, brings the depleted Cutler's Brigade forward to Shead's Wood and moves Baxter's Brigade onto Cutler's right, facing north. Paul's Brigade remains in reserve and is told to construct breastworks in front of the Seminary.
	• Meade finally learns of Reynolds' death.
1:30 p.m.	• Hancock leaves Taneytown for Gettysburg to take command on the field.
1:45 p.m.	• Lee arrives on Herr's Ridge to assess the situation.
2:00 p.m.	• 2nd Division, XI Corps arrives and is placed in reserve on Cemetery Hill.
	• O'Neal's Brigade (Rodes' Division) attacks.

near Chambersburg, Lee sent Heth back to his division with orders to refrain from attacking.

At about this time, at long last, Lee received news of Stuart's whereabouts. The news was not good. Stuart's staff officer, Major Andrew Venable, explained that Stuart was marching on Carlisle from Dover, trying to make contact with Ewell. Carlisle was 30 miles away, so it would be 24–36 hours before Venable could return to Stuart and Stuart's cavalry could reach Gettysburg.

It was not long after Rodes had launched his infantry attack from Oak Hill (at around 2:00 p.m. – see page 360), when Heth returned to report that some enemy were withdrawing from his front and to stress that he needed to attack, that Lee relented. He saw that, like it or not, battle had been joined in earnest and an opportunity had opened up, purely by accident, to inflict a defeat on an exposed portion of Meade's army. A simultaneous assault from west and north should crush the opposition, hopefully before fresh reinforcements arrived. But even then Lee briefly hung back, telling Heth to "wait awhile and I will send you word when to go in." Not long afterward (probably around 2:30 p.m.), as Heth later explained, "very soon an aide came to me with orders to attack." The actions of his subordinates and the fortuitous positioning of the forces on both sides had forced Lee's hand.

Ewell

Early on July 1 Ewell's two divisions were on the march from Heidlersburg to Cashtown. Rodes, accompanied by Ewell, was moving west via Middletown – destination Cashtown. Early broke camp later and was to march through Mummasburg toward the same place. At around 9:00 a.m. Ewell received a message from Hill that his corps was marching on Gettysburg. This immediately clarified the position for Ewell. Until then he had been frustrated and annoyed by Lee's instructions to bring his corps from Carlisle and York to either Cashtown or Gettysburg "as circumstances might dictate." It was this last phrase that was the problem, as Ewell was not used to discretionary orders, although the routes he had taken toward Cashtown, which was less than 10 miles from Gettysburg, were selected so that his divisions could easily change direction if necessary. Ewell promptly turned Rodes south through Middletown and Mummasburg, down what is known as the Carlisle Road, and Early was told to keep marching straight down the road from Heidlersburg (and Harrisburg). Both divisions would converge on Gettysburg and Ewell's Corps (less Johnson, who was to be stuck in train traffic for much of the day on the Chambersburg Pike) was, purely by accident, poised to arrive on the exposed northern flank of the Union forces engaged west of Gettysburg.

"Too Small and Too Young to be a Soldier"

A fifteen-year-old boy dressed in a cadet gray uniform marched on Gettysburg with the staff of Major-General Early on the morning of July 1. This was John Cabel Early, whose uncle was the divisional commander and who's father, Captain Samuel H. Early, served on his brother's staff. He later wrote this account of coming under fire for the first time that afternoon.

> As we neared Gettysburg we met General Early . . . Upon seeing me the latter said to my father that I was so much smaller than he had expected that he was afraid I would not do, but at any rate he wished my father to keep me out of the battle that was then impending. I was greatly crestfallen, but determined, so I just kept out of General Early's way . . . We marched up the road which leads directly into the main street of Gettysburg . . . Artillery firing on us had commenced and all our foot soldiers were lying down, but the officers were on horseback on the bank back of the road, my father and I with them. I proposed to my father that we also should lie down with the soldiers, but he laughed, and told me to keep my seat. The balls began to come thicker and closer to me mixed with grape or canister. One ball came so close that I thought it would take my head off, so I bent my shoulders to the horse's neck, whereupon my father teased me much, telling me that the ball was at least a mile off, also asking me how I thought I would like the life of a soldier. I replied with much feeling, that I wouldn't be surprised if Uncle Jubal was right and I was too small and too young to be a soldier.

When only a few miles from Gettysburg, the sounds of battle became audible to Ewell and Rodes as they rode along together. The two generals now spurred ahead to investigate. At about noon both rode forward onto Oak Hill to view the situation. They had stumbled upon the classic offensive position, whereby their enemy was fully engaged to his front and now Rodes had arrived, with the largest division in the Army of Northern Virginia, on his exposed flank Quick simultaneous attacks should easily crush the Union forces below. It was decision time for Ewell

Rodes urged attack and Ewell agreed to bringing up Lieutenant-Colonel Thomas A. Carter's artillery battalion and opening fire from Oak Hill to catch the enemy in enfilade. It was at 1:00 p.m., or thereabouts, that the eight guns of Captains William P. Carter and Charles W. Fry opened up and thereby announced to the Union generals below that Ewell's Corps had arrived – there would be no surprise attack from the woods on Oak Hill. Although Devin's Union cavalry had confirmed that Ewell was approaching and drawing close, until that moment the Union generals had been unaware that Oak Hill was in enemy hands – indeed Doubleday had wanted to occupy it with arriving reinforcements. The combined fire from Oak Hill and Hill's massed guns on Herr's Ridge was overwhelming, but their warning of impending disaster gave the Union forces more time to regroup and realign themselves to meet the threat. With the one-sided artillery duel in full swing, Major Brown rode up to Ewell with Lee's message re-emphasizing that he must not bring a general engagement. Again it was decision time for Ewell.

Seemingly Ewell had no trouble in taking what was almost certainly the right decision: to let the planned attack go ahead. Rodes occupied the high ground, the Yankees' flank was exposed and he could see, from his splendid viewpoint, both the enemy lines and those of Heth's troops spread out before him. A member of the 6th Alabama Infantry described the view as "the only time during the war that we were in a position to get such a view of contending forces. It seemed like a grand panorama with the sound effects of conflict added." Ewell overrode Lee's instructions and allowed Rodes' preparations for attack to continue. It was this decision, rather than Heth's first attack, that committed the Confederates to fighting the Battle of Gettysburg.

Meade

On July 1 Meade was still at Taneytown, over 12 miles south of Gettysburg. Early that morning he had received confirmation that Ewell had withdrawn southward from the Harrisburg area so it was a certain deduction

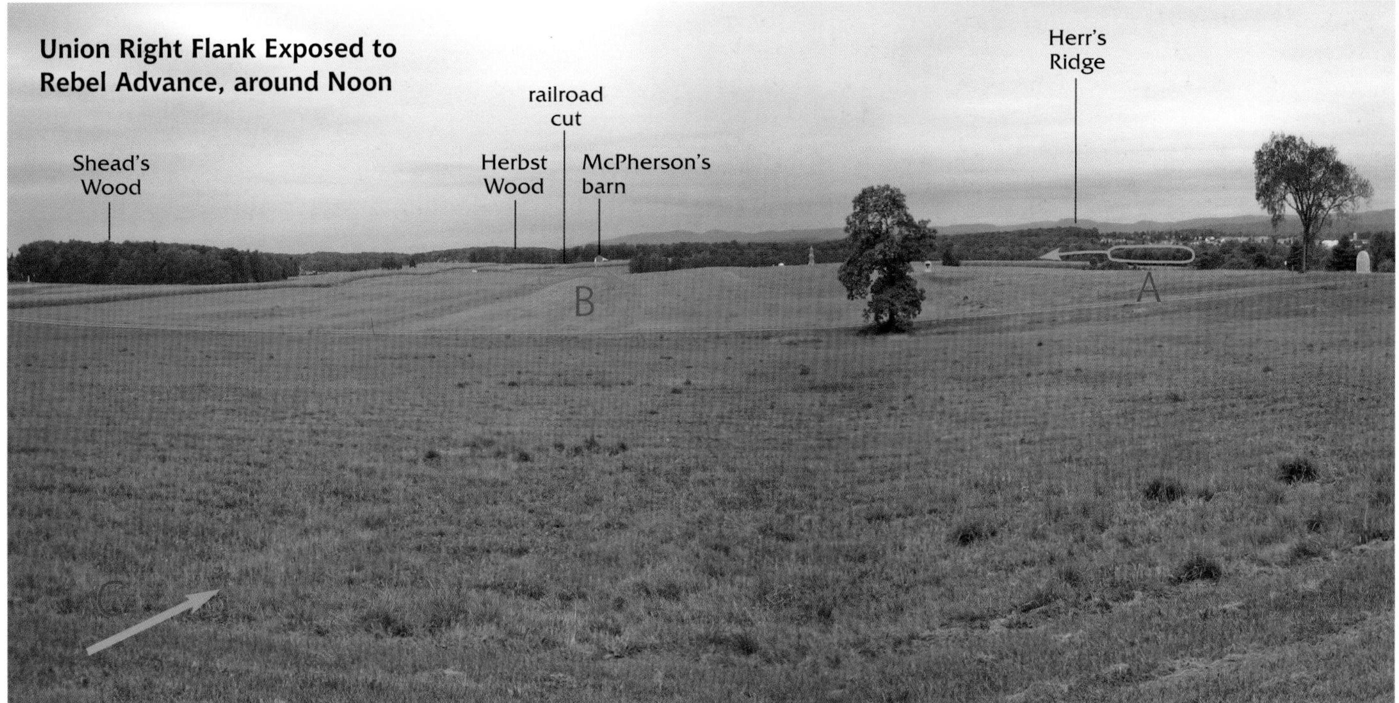

Heth's Confederates **A** failed during the morning to push Wadsworth's troops off McPherson's Ridge and from the railway cut. By noon Heth had two artillery battalions along Herr's Ridge, north and south of the Chambersburg Pike, massively outgunning the Union troops near McPherson's barn. The right flank of the Union positions **B** astride the Chambersburg Pike and railway cut. With the arrival, unnoticed, of Rodes' Division **C** on Oak Hill, the Union flank was exposed to enfilade fire and a flank attack. However, although the Confederate guns of Lt.-Col. Thomas A. Carter's battalion opened fire effectively, their doing so revealed the Confederate presence before the infantry attacks got under way. See also Map 30.

that Lee was concentrating his army. With Buford reporting Hill and Longstreet in the Chambersburg–Cashtown area probing east, the likely place of the Rebels' linking up was at or near Gettysburg. At 11:30 a.m. Reynolds' messenger (Weld) arrived to announce that fighting had started west of Gettysburg and that he, Reynolds, would "keep them back as long as possible." At noon Meade telegraphed his reaction to these new pieces of information to Halleck in Washington: "The news proves my advance has answered its purpose. I shall not advance any, but prepare to receive an attack in case Lee makes one. A battlefield is being selected to the rear . . ." He was in a quandary, and still inclined to be cautious, not wanting a battle on ground he had not seen and thus favoring a move to the Pipe Creek line for, hopefully, a better opportunity to counter Lee.

As he pondered Reynolds' news, Meade must have realized that his left-wing commander had not received the Pipe Creek Circular. Was Reynolds just fighting a delaying action? Was he going to withdraw under pressure down the Emmitsburg Road as his yesterday's orders had suggested he might? Or was he going to defend the approaches to Gettysburg until reinforcements arrived? If so, was the ground in the area occupied by Union forces suitable for developing defensive or offensive operations? Too many questions and no satisfactory answers. It was at this juncture that Meade castigated Butterfield for not getting his orders out promptly enough. All this planning, all these orders and his circular were now "all useless." However, Meade did little apart from signaling to Major-General Couch at Harrisburg to "throw a force in Ewell's rear" – an altogether useless gesture. Worse news was to follow.

At 1:00 p.m. news arrived of Reynolds' death. Howard was now in command at Gettysburg, something that did nothing to improve Meade's equanimity. It was decision time for Meade. Within half an hour the trusted Major-General Hancock was on his way to assess and take control of the situation – although he was junior to Howard. However, this was of no concern to Meade, who had the authority to appoint whomever he thought most fitted for the task; indeed the letter in Hancock's pocket made Major-General John Newton, from VI Corps, the acting commander of II Corps in Hancock's absence. Even at this stage Meade preferred to send a reliable subordinate to Gettysburg rather than go himself. He was still mentally uncommitted about where to concentrate his army, but if Hancock recommended it he "would order up all the troops [to Gettysburg]."

Howard

On the evening of the June 30 Howard, at Reynolds' request, had ridden over to meet him at Moritz Tavern, a mile south of Marsh Creek, to discuss the situation and the orders received so far. In the early hours of July 1, after returning to his headquarters, Howard's march orders for the day were delivered. Not long afterward, "Old Prayer Book" Howard had his XI Corps moving up the Emmitsburg Road in order to be in supporting distance of I Corps in accordance with those orders. Howard, with several staff, rode ahead to see for himself what was happening. He arrived near the Peach Orchard sometime between 10:00 a.m. and 10:30 a.m., when the fighting was developing quickly in the McPherson's Ridge area and the 1st Division, I Corps regiments were rushing to join the action. Howard was up to two hours ahead of his XI Corps.

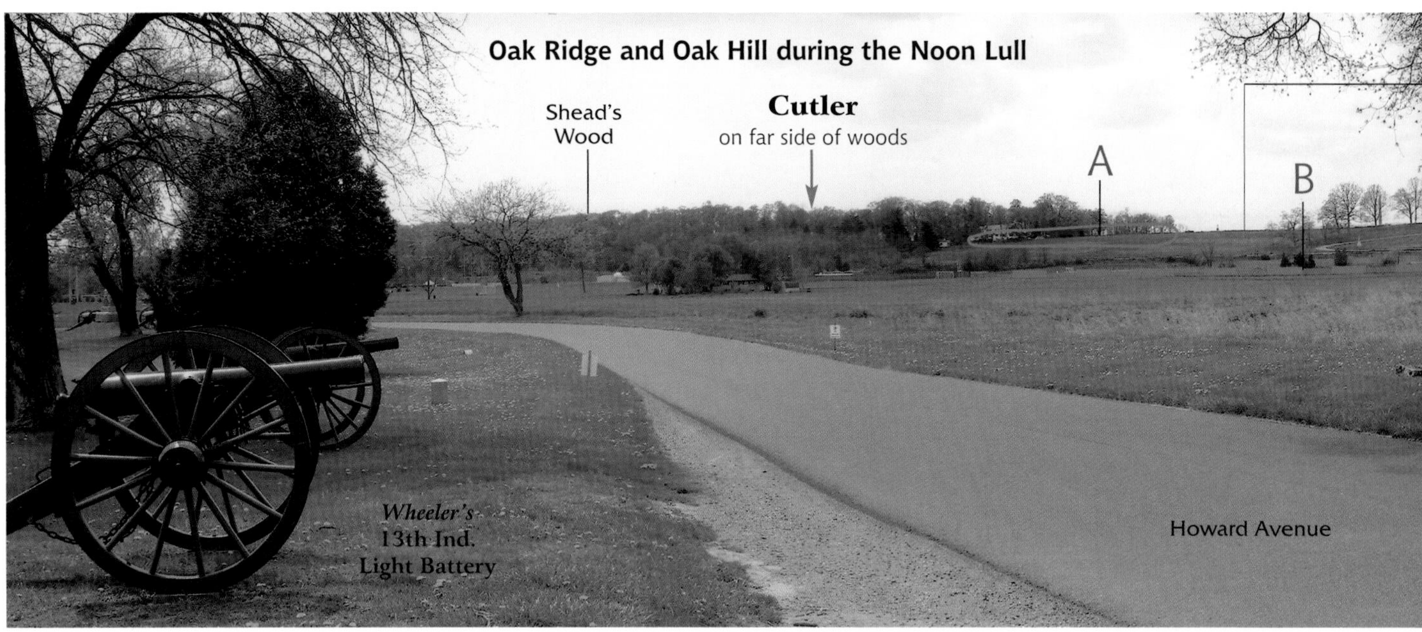

He continued up the Emmitsburg Road before turning his horse to the right to climb up Cemetery Hill. From there he had a fair view over the town and the fields to the north and west. Along with Culp's Hill to east, it was ground that cried out to be occupied by both infantry and guns. Turning to Colonel Theodore Meysenburg, Howard said, "This seems to be a good position, Colonel." The colonel replied immediately, "It is the only position, General." It is highly unlikely that an experienced commander like Reynolds had not also appreciated the value of these hills as a defensive position, but he had not told Howard about them, and while Howard was examining Cemetery Hill Reynolds was being shot only a mile away. Howard received the thanks of Congress for his selecting and then holding Cemetery Hill that evening. In the years following the war this caused some controversy, as a Captain Joseph G. Rosengarten of Reynolds' staff claimed that an aide, Captain Weld, had been sent to direct Howard to Cemetery Hill. Weld, however, had been sent to Meade, not Howard.

Howard then rode into the town and was ushered to the rooftop of the Fahnstock Store, where a view of events on McPherson's Ridge was obtained. It was while there that the news

Howard Learns of Reynolds' Death

Daniel Skelly was a Gettysburg teenager, employed as a clerk for the merchandizing firm of the Fahnstock brothers. He left a number of anecdotes of his exciting time during the battle (see also box, page 400).

On the morning of July 1, about 8 o'clock, in the company of my old friend Samuel W. Anderson . . . I walked out the Mummasburg Road north of the town just a short distance beyond the college building, where lay encamped in the fields, Col. Devin's Brigade . . . My companion and I went directly across the fields to Seminary Ridge, then known as the Railroad Woods by reason of the "Old tape-worm Railroad' being cut through it . . . The ridge was full of men and boys from town, all eager to witness a brush with the Confederates and not dreaming of the terrible conflict that was to occur on that day . . . I climbed up a good-sized oak tree so as to have a good view of the ridge west and northwest of us . . . We could distinctly hear the skirmish fire in the vicinity of Marsh Creek . . . Nearer and nearer came the skirmish line as it fell back before the advancing Confederates . . . Soon the artillery opened fire and shot and shell began to fly over our heads, one of them passing dangerously near the top of the tree I was on. There was a general stampede towards the town . . . The time was about 9 o'clock, or near it and our infantry had not come up yet. I was not long reaching the town and found the streets full of men, women and children, all under great excitement. Being anxious to see more of the battle, I concluded I would go up upon the observatory on the store building of the Fahnstock Brothers, situated on the northwest corner of Baltimore and West Middle Streets . . . The observatory was on the back of the building fronting on West Middle Street and . . . had a good view of the field where the battle was then being fought . . .

We [several other persons were present] had been up there quite a little time when I observed a general and his staff coming down Baltimore Street from the south of the town. Upon reaching the court house [opposite the store], they halted and made an attempt to get up into the belfry to make observations, but were unable to accomplish this. I went down into the street and going over to the court house told them that if they wished they could go up onto the observatory of the store building. The general dismounted and with two of his aides went with me up onto the observatory. Upon reaching the house-top, the general, with his field glasses, made a careful survey of the field west and northwest of the town; also the number of roads radiating like spokes of a wheel from the town. In the midst of it a scout [Skelly claims it was George Guinn, a member of Cole's Maryland Cavalry] came riding up West Middle Street at a full gallop, halted below us [and] called up, asking if General Howard . . . were there. General Howard answered in person, the scout called to him that General Reynolds had been killed and that he should come onto the field immediately.

Looking west from the position of Capt. John Wheeler's Battery toward Oak Ridge, stretching from Shead's Wood on the extreme left to Oak Hill on the right – a distance of about threequarters of a mile. **A** indicates the approximate position of O'Neal's Brigade and **B** the area occupied by Capts. Richard Page and Charles Fry – both engaged in an artillery duel with Wheeler and Dilger (off photograph to the left). **C** represents the approximate line of Blackford's skirmishers. **A** is the position of Baxter's Brigade from about 1:00 p.m., while **B** is the Union skirmish line provided by the 45th New York, 61st Ohio and 74th Pennsylvania. **D** indicates the area occupied by Doles's Brigade.

was brought to him that Reynolds was dead and he was therefore the senior officer on the field (see box opposite); according to Howard it was at 11:30 a.m. It was decision time for Howard. He instantly accepted the need to continue Reynolds' stubborn defense of the approaches to the town. He sent messages to Major-General Carl Schurz (3rd Division) that he was acting commander of XI Corps and to urge speed in getting to Gettysburg. Another aide galloped down the road to tell Brigadier-General Francis Barlow (commanding 1st Division, XI Corps). However, it seems he was somewhat dilatory in informing the nearest supporting formations – Sickles' III Corps and Slocum's XII Corps – merely telling them that Ewell was approaching from the north and that I Corps was engaged with Hill. Strangely, there was no mention of Reynolds' death, nothing about Howard's intention to defend the town nor whether he needed urgent support. Half an hour later he had doubts and sent another message to Slocum requesting help. By then he had returned to Cemetery Hill, where he established his headquarters. There he met Schurz, who had galloped ahead of his division, which he had handed over to Brigadier-General Alexander Schimmelfennig.

Both Howard and Schurz could see the urgency of the situation and the danger of the I Corps line being outflanked from Oak Hill, where activity had been spotted. As the leading elements of Schimmelfennig's (Schurz's) 3rd Division arrived at about 12:30 p.m., Howard sent it through the town and had it deploy in the open fields to the north with instructions to link up with I Corps on its left on Oak Ridge. Barlow's 1st Division was close behind, as it had been marching on a parallel road. It too was sent north of the town to form on the right of Schimmelfennig. Three of Major Osborn's five batteries (Captain Dilger and Lieutenants Wheeler and Wilkeson) were also rushed in great haste to the north. The remaining two (Captains Wiedrich and Heckman) were kept in reserve on Cemetery Hill where they were joined by Von Steinwehr's 2nd Division at about 2:00 p.m. A firm base had now been established on this dominating ground.

At about this time (2:00 p.m.) Howard finally got round to informing his army commander of what was happening. His message told Meade that the Union forces at Gettysburg were facing both Hill's and Ewell's Corps and that he had placed his troops west and north of the town. He also mentioned that he had summoned Sickles to "push forward" with his III Corps. This left open several questions. What was Howard's plan? Did he intend to hold Gettysburg? Did he need more reinforcements? He made no mention to Meade of his request to Slocum to come up.

After sending this message, Howard made his only visit to I Corps, to Doubleday on McPherson's Ridge just as the Rebel attacks were getting under way from Oak Hill. Howard's instructions to Doubleday were merely to stay in place, resist strongly and withdraw only if "forced back." From then on until the arrival of Hancock, although Howard had overall command, in practice Doubleday continued in tactical command of I Corps and Schurz of XI Corps.

Sickles

Major-General Daniel E. Sickles, commanding III Corps, was moving on Emmitsburg, 11 miles southwest of Gettysburg. Although the decisions Sickles made that day were not necessarily made during the noon lull, they are an interesting example of how a commander can find himself with conflicting orders and have difficult choices to make.

III Corps had been ordered by Meade to move through Emmitsburg, where it would be positioned to meet any threat developing from the east. At Emmitsburg Sickles sent an aide forward to Reynolds for further information and instructions. Just before he was shot Reynolds sent the aide back with the message, "Tell General Sickles I think he had better come up." Had Sickles done so then his corps would have arrived on the field by around 3:30–4:00 p.m. This did not happen, for while his aide was away Sickles received the Pipe Creek Circular, in which instructions were given that III Corps was to hold Emmitsburg. It was decision time for Sickles. Should he march to join Reynolds, his immediate superior, or stay where he was in accordance with his army commander's instructions? In a dilemma, Sickles sent again to Reynolds for clarification, but again while this messenger was away Howard's aide brought news of Reynolds' death and Howard's request for help. Sickles realized there was serious fighting taking place at Gettysburg so adopted a compromise solution. He left two brigades at Emmitsburg and marched north with the other four, informing Meade of his decision. When the army commander received this message he was still worried about the west flank and still wanted to keep the Pipe Creek possibility alive, so he sent a galloper with orders to "hold on as it [Emmitsburg] is a point not to be abandoned excepting in an extremity." By the time Sickles got this he was well on his way to Gettysburg and rightly ignored it. He was marching to the sound of the guns and, although he arrived too late to influence events around the town that day, it was a military maxim that was seldom wrong.

Slocum

By noon Major-General Henry W. Slocum's XII Corps had marched the 5 miles from Littlestown and was arriving at Two Taverns. At that point it was the same distance from Gettysburg and all soldiers heard the rumble of artillery fire from that direction. According to Edmund Brown of the 27th Indiana, "it sounded like one continual roll of thunder." Five miles was only a two-hour march so, had Slocum continued, nearly 4,780 men and twenty guns would have arrived on the battlefield in plenty of time to influence the afternoon's fighting. It was decision time for Slocum. Unfortunately for the Yankees at Gettysburg, the XII Corps commander was about to prove he had been well named – there was no immediate marching to the sound of the guns. XII Corps halted at Two Taverns as Slocum initially thought the cannonade was merely Buford's cavalry in action.

Slocum's most recent orders told him to go to Two Taverns and he was not inclined to budge without further orders from his army commander. Howard's 1:00 p.m. message informing him of the situation failed to move him. He did not even immediately send a staff officer ahead to check on the situation until alerted by a passing civilian that there was heavy fighting near the town. Only then did Slocum send an officer (Major Eugene W. Guindon) to find out what was happening. He returned to report serious cannonading. Some of Slocum's soldiers climbed onto barn roofs and reported seeing bursting shells and puffs of smoke. Not until 3:00 p.m., three hours after reaching Two Taverns, did Slocum finally get his men on their feet and head for the action, the noise of which got louder and louder as they tramped up the Baltimore Pike. At the same time, Howard dispatched Captain Daniel Hall explaining the urgency of the situation and asking if Slocum was moving up.

Part of Slocum's earlier reluctance may have been due to the fact that he outranked Howard but was not keen to take battlefield responsibility. At around 4:00 p.m. when Howard was ordering the general retreat through the town, he sent Major Charles Howard to Slocum with instructions to deploy his divisions on either side of the town and come forward to take command. Major Howard met the general on the Baltimore Pike near Power's Hill and, although Slocum deployed his command as requested, he declined to take over from Howard. According to Major Howard his response was, "I'll be damned if I will take responsibility for this fight." Some twenty-three years later Slocum wrote of this time: "My orders were to march to Two Taverns, and await orders from General Meade. The Twelfth Corps was in that position when we heard of the engagement at Gettysburg. We received no word from General Howard [requesting support], but started as soon as we heard of the battle."

Thus at the end of the two-hour noon lull it remained just I and XI Corps to face the renewed Rebel assaults. The commanders of the two corps within supporting distance (III and XII Corps) did not move until it was too late.

Summary

The noon lull had seen the Confederates considerably reinforced. Their gaining possession of the dominating ground of Oak Hill on the Union's exposed northern flank thus opened up a splendid attacking opportunity for crushing their enemy between advances from west and north. Lee had finally sanctioned this attack, which would get under way at approximately 2:00 p.m.

The Union forces had also reinforced, but to a lesser extent, while the position of only two small divisions of XI Corps in the open fields north of the town was conspicuously vulnerable. By 2:00 p.m. Howard's line was extended in a thin arc over 2 miles in length, curving round the town from south of Herbst Wood to the Harrisburg Road. No serious thought seems to have been given to using the lull to pull back to the much shorter line of the Seminary Ridge.

THE EARLY AFTERNOON

This was the period of the most intensive fighting of the day. It saw attacks by three of the four Confederate divisions on the field and a bitterly fought struggle for possession of McPherson's Ridge. By shortly after 3:30 p.m. XI Corps had lost Blocher's (later named Barlow's) Knoll and I Corps had finally been pushed off McPherson's Ridge to its final defensive position west of the town on Seminary Ridge. The battle neither army commander had specifically sought at Gettysburg was raging. A simplified overview of this period is shown on Map 31 and from it two highlights are examined in detail below, one a Rebel repulse and the other a Rebel success.

Highlight: The First Afternoon Attack by Rodes' Division from Oak Hill, approx. 2:00–2:40 p.m. (Maps 32–34)

The ground

The vital ground was Oak Hill, and its extension south to the Chambersburg Pike, Oak Ridge. North of the Mummasburg Road, which crossed the ridge about 250 yards south of Oak Hill, the ridge was mostly covered in woods and orchards, a finger of which almost touched the Mummasburg Road. These woods and Forney Wood some 400 yards west of Oak Hill and south of the road, offered excellent cover for an attacking force approaching from the north to form up and prepare to attack unseen by an enemy south of the road. The western slope of Oak Hill was more gentle than the eastern and there was some open ground that provided reasonable, if exposed, gun positions on the forward slope. The eastern side of Oak Ridge was steep and its slopes devoid of cover. From the edge of the woods on Oak Hill there was a splendid view to the southwest, south and particularly over the large expanse of open fields to the east and southeast to Gettysburg.

South of the Mummasburg Road, Oak Ridge, although lower than to the north, still dominated the area as far as the Chambersburg Pike. Some 400 yards of open ridgeline separated the Oak Hill woods north of the Mummasburg Road and Shead's Wood, which covered the eastern slope of the ridge as far as the unfinished railroad. The other feature of importance was Forney Ridge, which ran almost south for 600 yards from Forney Farm. It offered good cover from view and fire for any troops advancing southeast from the Forney Wood area over what were otherwise open fields of crops.

Tactical significance

When Rodes arrived on Oak Hill at around 1:00 p.m. the tactical significance of his position on the high ground was immediately obvious. As he later put it, "I found that by keeping along the wooded ridge . . . I could strike the force of the enemy with which General Hill's troops were engaged upon the flank, and . . . whenever we struck the enemy we could engage him with the advantage in ground." At that time his leading brigades had encountered Devin's cavalry patrols, left the road and were approaching from the north along the spine north of Oak Hill, under cover of the woods. The situation that Rodes (and Ewell) had stumbled upon presented at first sight a battle-winning opportunity. The right flank of the Yankees, which Hill's troops were engaging frontally, looked to be his for the taking. However, as Rodes and his corps commander watched, the situation began to change.

From the Union point of view, Oak Hill and Oak Ridge were just as important to secure and defend as they were for the Rebels to use as a jump-off point for an attack. Both Doubleday and Howard were well aware that Ewell was approaching from the north and realized the danger should Oak Hill be occupied by their enemy. Doubleday, worried about his exposed right (northern) flank, moved Baxter's Brigade of Robinson's Division to reinforce that flank during the noon lull. Howard rushed two divisions of XI Corps through Gettysburg with the intention of occupying Oak Hill with its 3rd Division (Schimmelfennig). In effect, a race for Oak Hill developed. The Rebels won, forcing XI Corps to adopt exposed positions across the fields north of the town to protect I Corps' rear. It was these movements that somewhat spoiled the scene for Rodes and Ewell, although they hastened to bring up the guns of Lieutenant-Colonel Carter's Battalion and open fire – thus announcing to all, Yankee and Rebel alike, that the leading formation of Ewell's Corps had arrived on the battlefield.

Force comparison

Rodes, with almost 8,000 men, had the largest division in the Army of Northern Virginia; it included an artillery battalion with sixteen guns. It was an extremely powerful force and, after the casualties inflicted on the Union forces during the morning's fighting, in terms of infantry it was at least equal to the three divisions of I Corps then in the field. The potential for a force of this size falling on the Union flank was enormous – no wonder both Rodes and Ewell, even though neither could know the exact numbers opposed to them, wanted to attack at once.

In the event, only a fraction of the Rebel division was actually engaged in the crucial first attack and thus the advantage in numbers was totally negated.

The assaults (there were two, although only one was intended) took place within thirty minutes between approximately 2:10 p.m. and 2:40 p.m. The first was initially between three regiments out of the five in O'Neal's Brigade, totaling just over 1,000 men, and Baxter's Union Brigade of 1,450, supported by the 45th New York from Amsberg's Brigade (3rd Division, XI Corps). When O'Neal advanced to attack from the woods on Oak Hill, the opposing forces were:

Confederate (O'Neal)		Union (Baxter)	
6th Alabama	382	12th Massachusetts	261
12th Alabama	317	83rd New York	199
26th Alabama	319	97th New York	236
Total	**1,018**	11th Pennsylvania	270
		88th Pennsylvania	273
		90th Pennsylvania	208
		Total	**1,447**

To the Rebel attack must be added the 317 men of the 5th Alabama who belatedly joined the attack after the other three regiments had been driven back. On the Union side, the 45th New York in Amsberg's Brigade, with 375 men and at least two guns from Dilger's Battery, were able to bring considerable fire to bear on O'Neal's attacking force. All in all, the attackers were outnumbered, possibly by as many as 500 men.

After O'Neal's failure, it was Iverson's Brigade that advanced to the attack. The defenders were again Baxter's Brigade, which had quickly switched to face west. This time, instead of support from the 45th New York, they had the benefit of flanking fire from some of Cutler's Brigade (1st Division, I Corps) positioned on the northern edge of Shead's Wood. The approximate numbers are tabulated below, with Baxter's regiments being rounded down slightly to reflect the light casualties suffered in the encounter with O'Neal:

Confederate (Iverson)		Union (Baxter)	
5th North Carolina	473	12th Massachusetts	250
12th North Carolina	219	83rd New York	185
20th North Carolina	372	97th New York	225
23rd North Carolina	316	11th Pennsylvania	260
Total	**1,380**	88th Pennsylvania	265
		90th Pennsylvania	200
		Total	**1,385**

This time the numbers were about equal, except that the defending Yankees had the numerical advantage as an indeterminate number of Cutler's soldiers added their fire support.

- The reasons that Rodes' attack was so dramatically watered down numerically are discussed under "Outline of events" on page 366. O'Neal sent 1,000 men to attack frontally a position manned by a force that outnumbered him by as many as 500 (although he would not know this at the time). The defenders were well positioned behind two fences that lined the Mummasburg Road and had the benefit of supporting musket and artillery fire on their right flank which hit the attackers in enfilade. Ideally, other things being equal,

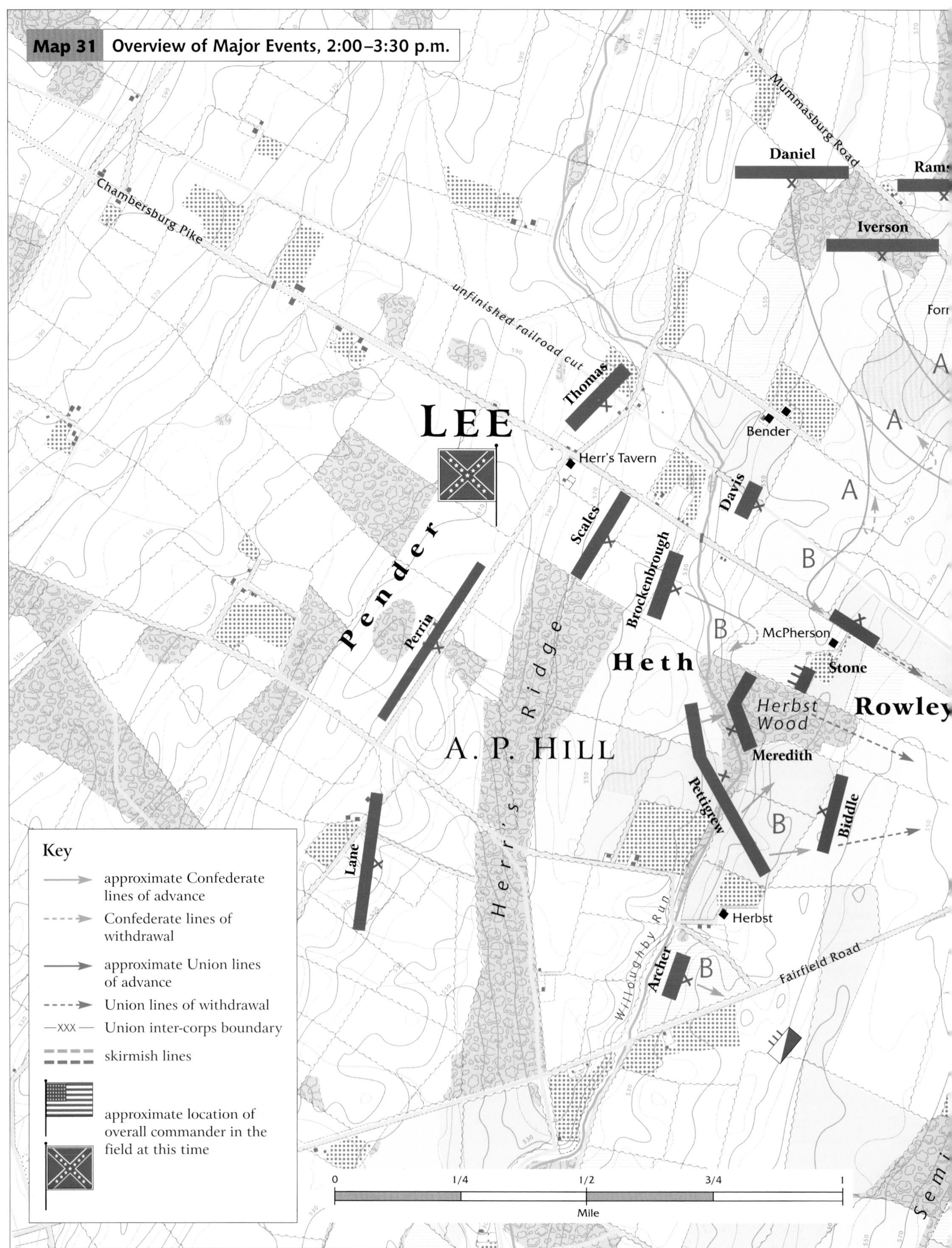
Map 31 Overview of Major Events, 2:00–3:30 p.m.
Mummasburg Road
Daniel
Iverson
Chambersburg Pike
unfinished railroad cut
Thomas
LEE
Herr's Tavern
Bender
Davis
Scales
Brockenbrough
Pender
Perrin
Herr's Ridge
Heth
McPherson
Stone
Herbst Wood
Rowley
Meredith
A. P. HILL
Pettigrew
Biddle
Lane
Herbst
Willoughby Run
Archer
Fairfield Road
A
B
Key
approximate Confederate lines of advance
Confederate lines of withdrawal
approximate Union lines of advance
Union lines of withdrawal
—XXX— Union inter-corps boundary
skirmish lines
approximate location of overall commander in the field at this time
0
1/4
1/2
3/4
1
Mile

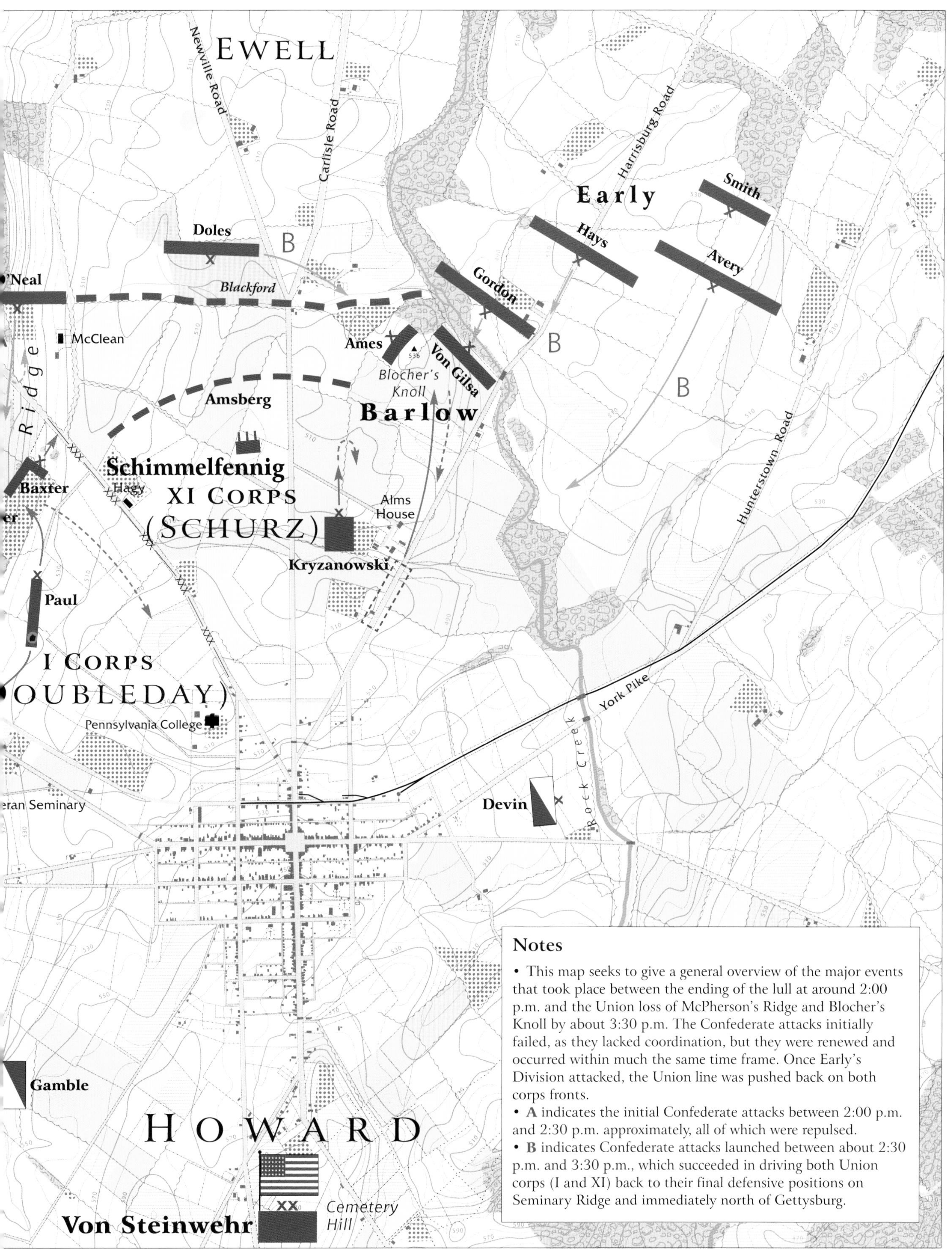

Notes

• This map seeks to give a general overview of the major events that took place between the ending of the lull at around 2:00 p.m. and the Union loss of McPherson's Ridge and Blocher's Knoll by about 3:30 p.m. The Confederate attacks initially failed, as they lacked coordination, but they were renewed and occurred within much the same time frame. Once Early's Division attacked, the Union line was pushed back on both corps fronts.

• **A** indicates the initial Confederate attacks between 2:00 p.m. and 2:30 p.m. approximately, all of which were repulsed.

• **B** indicates Confederate attacks launched between about 2:30 p.m. and 3:30 p.m., which succeeded in driving both Union corps (I and XI) back to their final defensive positions on Seminary Ridge and immediately north of Gettysburg.

an attacking force should outnumber defenders by two or three to one to give it a reasonable chance of success. Little wonder O'Neal's attack quickly turned into a disaster.

- With Iverson's attack, the numbers were about equal and the attack was again frontal but was defeated, in fact ended in catastrophe, due to being surprised by devastating fire at close range followed up by a spirited charge. The Union success was due more to good tactics than to numbers.

Command and control

The arrival of Rodes' powerful division on Oak Hill on the exposed northern flank of the Union defenses gave the Rebels an opening rarely seen on battlefields. That his initial attack failed miserably was primarily due to failed leadership, lack of coordination and misunderstandings between the Confederate commanders on the field. The Union commander with direct influence on the defense was the brigade commander, Baxter.

Major-General Robert Emmet Rodes. Rodes was the only non-West Point divisional commander in Lee's army. His career had started at the Virginia Military Institute (V.M.I.), from where he graduated with distinction in 1848. He stayed on at the V.M.I. as an instructor but left after two years when the post he wanted was given to Thomas (later Stonewall) Jackson. Thereafter he worked for several railroad companies as a civil engineer and executive in Alabama. Later he returned to the V.M.I. to take up a post teaching mechanics and engineering, but war broke out before he could assume his duties.

Rodes was commissioned as colonel of the 5th Alabama Infantry in May 1861 and led his regiment at First Manassas. In October of that year he was appointed brigadier-general and in the summer of 1862 commanded his brigade at Seven Pines, where he was wounded in the arm. Although not fully recovered, he fought again within a month at Gaines' Mill. About this time Longstreet commented favorably on his "coolness, ability and determination." Wounded again at Antietam, this time by a shell splinter in the thigh, he commanded his brigade at Fredericksburg and Chancellorsville. It was in the latter battle that Rodes played a prominent part in Jackson's crushing of the Union right flank. His battle cry heard over the din was "Forward men, over friend or foe!" After this battle the mortally wounded Jackson described Rodes' performance as "magnificent" and urged his immediate promotion. Lee made him a major-general on May 7, 1863.

By July 1863 Rodes was a rising star in the Army of Northern Virginia. His handsome face with drooping mustache and thick blond hair, along with his fighting record, made him a well-known figure in the army. On July 1 his division was on the march early and was soon diverted to march on Gettysburg from Middletown. At around 11:30 a.m., when some 5 miles north of the town, his advance guard clashed with Devin's vedettes. Pushing on down the Carlisle Road, the noise of battle became ever louder and when about 2 miles north of the town Rodes, thinking the wooded high ground (Oak Ridge) on his right was the dominating feature in the area, moved his division off the road onto it. His division then approached the battlefield along the ridge, which provided good cover but slowed progress considerably. He and Ewell rode ahead to check on the situation from the summit of Oak Hill. His eagerness to take advantage of the situation was endorsed by Ewell. As will be seen, Rodes' performance, particularly in the organization and supervision of his initial divisional attack, was decidedly deficient, although in fairness it must be said his subsequent attack was better coordinated and succeeded.

Colonel Edward A. O'Neal. O'Neal had no military experience before the outbreak of the war, having trained as a lawyer in northern Alabama and lived there all his life. He was one of the state's leading secessionist politicians and when Alabama seceded became a captain of a company called the "Calhoun Guards." Within a year he was colonel of the 26th Alabama Infantry, but had seen no action. He was soon to make up for this deficiency of experience, over the next year establishing a reputation for fearlessness, if not tactical ability. Serving in Rodes' Brigade in the Peninsula, he was wounded by a shell during the brigade's costly charge at Seven Pines but soon returned to duty. During the Seven Days Battles he was cited for gallantry at Gaines' Mill and again for "gallant conduct" by his acting brigade commander at Malvern Hill. He was hit in the thigh at the head of his regiment at South Mountain in September 1863, recovery from which took four months. In January 1863, when Rodes was appointed brigade commander, O'Neal as the senior colonel took over his brigade, although Rodes was unhappy at this promotion. It was O'Neal's lack of tactical ability, not his courage, that worried his seniors – a concern that was vindicated at Chancellorsville. At the start of Jackson's famous flank attack O'Neal neglected to advance his skirmishers well ahead of his brigade, with the result that the main line quickly overtook them and the whole attack came to a halt while O'Neal sorted the problem out. The next day O'Neal was wounded for the third time by what he termed "the fuse of a shell," although it only incapacitated him for a day.

O'Neal should not have survived as a brigade commander after this, but Lee was desperately short of senior officers and political influence, and the fact that he was the senior officer in the brigade secured his elevation to brigadier-general against the vocal protests of Rodes and the misgivings of Lee. O'Neal's official appointment letter, dated June 6, 1862, was in Lee's pocket throughout the Gettysburg campaign – he was sufficiently dubious of O'Neal's ability at brigade level to test him as a colonel for another campaign. O'Neal did not pass the test, although his attacking with only three of his five brigades was as much the fault of his divisional commander as it was his. Nevertheless, there was no excuse for O'Neal's not having horses either for himself or his staff at the moment when coordination and the passage of orders was critical during the preparation for the attack and its implementation. Then – surprisingly, considering his conduct in previous battles – O'Neal failed to lead his troops forward in person: an appalling failure for a brigade commander in the Civil War.

Brigadier-General Alfred Iverson, Jr. Iverson was, in some ways, even more unfitted to command his brigade at Gettysburg than O'Neal. His father, a friend of President Davis, had decided his son should follow a military career and accordingly sent him to a military school at Muskegee, Alabama. At the start of the Mexican War, when the young Iverson was only seventeen, his father took him out of school and got him commissioned as a second lieutenant in a Georgia regiment that he had raised. This experience was enough for him to obtain a regular commission in the U.S. Cavalry in 1855. The outbreak of the Civil War saw Alfred Iverson resign from the U.S. Army and President Davis give him command of the 20th North Carolina Infantry. His regiment did well in the

Peninsula at Gaines' Mill, although he was himself badly wounded early in the charge that saw his men take an enemy battery. After his recovery things started to go wrong for the young colonel.

At South Mountain in September 1862 his regiment, along with the rest of the brigade, fled the field after the brigade commander was mortally wounded. Three days later at Sharpsburg the brigade again broke and ran, although Iverson later rallied his regiment. Strangely, after being involved in these two fiascos, Iverson was promoted to brigadier-general and given command of the brigade in November 1862. At Fredericksburg his brigade was in reserve so its commander was not tested.

Iverson had not been a popular colonel of the 20th North Carolina. On his promotion he sought to have one of his friends brought in as his replacement, but all the field officers of the regiment signed a petition opposing the appointment. When Iverson refused to forward the petition, the officers sent it to army headquarters anyway. Furious, Iverson had all signatories placed under arrest – although none was actually removed from his post. Iverson's friend did not get command, but throughout the winter of 1862/63 he vetoed all subsequent appointees. In February 1863 he demanded, with the threat of resignation, that Stonewall Jackson grant his furlough. Jackson refused, telling him that with fighting imminent he would rather he leave the army entirely than take a furlough. Iverson remained. Even at Chancellorsville, where his brigade took part in Jackson's dramatic flank attack, there was controversy over his going to the rear in the midst of the fighting to look for support for his left flank; this was regarded by many of his officers as shirking.

On the first day at Gettysburg Iverson's performance was poor. He launched his first attack after telling his regiments to "Give them hell," while he remained in the rear as his brigade advanced. Thus he was not available to correct the unexplained 90-degree swing to the left and disastrous assault on a supposedly unoccupied stone wall that was not part of the original objective. Iverson did little to redeem himself with what was left of his men during the remainder of the battle. He was rumored to have been drunk, of hiding behind a chestnut log, of generally acting in a cowardly manner and of not deploying skirmishers; none of these accusations has been substantiated except for the fact that he did not lead his brigade into battle, as was his duty. After the campaign a number of officers refused to serve under him, the mortally wounded Colonel Daniel H. Christie of the 23rd North Carolina allegedly remarking that he would ensure "that imbecile Iverson" would never lead them again. The dying colonel succeeded, temporarily at least, as in July Lee removed him from command and made him provost marshal. He was later sent to Georgia to organize cavalry.

Brigadier-General Henry Baxter. Baxter was a miller from Michigan and forty-two years old at Gettysburg. His grandfathers had fought in the Revolutionary War, although he lacked any formal military education. Prewar militia experience saw him begin his service as a captain in the 7th Michigan. Baxter certainly had an iron constitution, as he was one of an exceedingly small number of men to survive not one, but two abdominal wounds and a third through the body. His first came as a captain leading his company in the Seven Days Battles; the second as a lieutenant-colonel at Antietam; the third at Fredericksburg in December 1862, by which time he was commanding the 7th Michigan, still a lieutenant-colonel. The authorities were impressed with his "follow me" style of leadership and rewarded him with brigade command in time for Chancellorsville, although his men saw little action.

At Gettysburg it was again his hands-on, personal leadership at the tactical level in a crisis that was instrumental in defeating first O'Neal's and then Iverson's Brigades in quick succession. After O'Neal's departure Baxter skillfully transferred four regiments from facing north to face the new threat developing in the west. It was his initiative that conceived the laying of an immediate ambush by concealing his men behind a convenient stone wall. As Iverson's Brigade staggered under the volley of hundreds of muskets at close range it was the brigade commander who led the charge that sent the Rebels reeling and produced a rich haul of prisoners. It was a magnificent defense of an exposed position. For the next two days Baxter was not seriously engaged, spending most of the time in reserve with his much depleted command in the rear of Cemetery Hill. Afterwards one of his colonels was to write, "I wish to say one word outside of my regiment in regard to Generals Baxter and Robinson. They were on every part of the field, encouraging and stimulating the men by their presence and bravery."

Plans and orders

Confederate. Rodes planned to attack from the area of Oak Hill and Forney Wood with the object of hitting the northern flank of the Union troops on Oak Ridge south of the Mummasburg Road and those he could see confronting Hill's troops in the McPherson's Farm area. As he watched from Oak Hill he saw a changing situation below, with the enemy debouching from Gettysburg into the plain north of the town and extending their line northward into what we know as Shead's Wood. Rodes, in his report, stated:

> a portion of the force opposed to General Hill changed position so as to occupy the woods [Shead's Wood] on the summit of the same ridge I occupied . . . Either these troops, or others which had hitherto been unobserved behind the same body of woods, soon made their appearance directly opposite my center [O'Neal's Brigade].

Rodes also became concerned for his own left flank as what were the leading elements of Schimmelfennig's Union Division began advancing north in the direction of Oak Hill. His left would be vulnerable at least until Early's Division appeared down the Harrisburg Road. There was an obvious need for speed as the attack had to get under way before the enemy could regroup and reinforce to face him in strength. He had five brigades with an average strength of just over 1,500, the smallest (Ramseur) with barely 1,000 and the largest (Daniel) with well over 2,000. He also had sixteen guns in his artillery battalion.

The outline plan – and there has been much debate about its exact objective and intentions, as Rodes' after-battle report is far from clear with regard to details – appears to have been as follows. A simultaneous attack on a two-brigade front with a third following en echelon on the right. O'Neal's Brigade to advance south down the line of Oak Ridge, crossing the Mummasburg Road and attacking the enemy to the south deployed on the ridge and in Shead's Wood. At the same time, on O'Neal's right, Iverson's Brigade, formed up in Forney Wood, would also advance south with the objective of attacking the enemy clearly seen around McPherson's Farm. This put just over 3,000 men in the leading wave, with a frontage of about half a mile, but with Iverson having further to advance (threequarters of a mile) than

O'Neal (less than a third of a mile). Artillery support was to be provided by the eight guns of Captains Carter and Fry. Echeloned to the right rear would be Daniel's large brigade (2,161 men), tasked with advancing to support Iverson or to continue the attack to his right. This brigade would also debouch from the Forney Wood and advance south across open fields toward the unfinished railroad and the Chambersburg Pike. Protecting the vulnerable left flank of the division would be Doles's small brigade (1,322), reinforced by the sharpshooters of the Alabama Brigade (O'Neal) under Major Eugene Blackford. Supporting the left flank would be Captain Page's and Captain Reese's Batteries, both of four guns. Ramseur's Brigade (1,027) would be held in reserve initially north of Forney Wood. This plan is recorded by Rodes in his battle report as: "being thus threatened from two directions, I determined to attack with my center [O'Neal] and right [Iverson, and possibly Daniel], holding at bay [with Doles's Brigade] still another force then emerging from the town."

The orders for the plan were issued verbally by Rodes and his staff but were complicated somewhat and the center weakened by his detaching the 3rd Alabama from the right of O'Neal's line and tasking it with advancing on the left of Daniel's Brigade. The sense of this is far from clear, as it created a large gap between this regiment and its parent brigade, but it may be there was insufficient room on Oak Ridge for O'Neal to deploy all his regiments; even so, they could have formed a second line. The effect was to remove the 5th Alabama from O'Neal's command and give it to Daniel. Rodes also, in addition to sending Blackford's skirmishers to the left with Doles, personally gave orders to the 5th Alabama to remain initially in reserve under his instructions on O'Neal's left as a link between him and Doles. Not only did this reduce O'Neal's attack from nearly 1,700 men to about 1,000, but also it seemingly confused O'Neal as to exactly which regiments he commanded and which he did not. Rodes reported on how the attack was supposed to get under way:

> I caused Iverson's Brigade [presumably by courier] to advance, and at the same moment gave in person O'Neal the order to attack, indicating to him precisely the point to which he was to direct the left of the four regiments then under his orders, the Fifth Alabama, which formed the extreme left of his brigade, being held in reserve under my immediate command, to defend the gap between O'Neal and Doles . . . Daniel was at the same moment instructed [presumably by courier] to advance to support Iverson, if necessary; if not, to attack on his right as soon as possible.

The intention, seemingly, was for the three advancing brigades to jump off at the same time. It is little wonder that O'Neal was confused, as what Rodes appears to have done was to take the 3rd Alabama and give it Daniel and take the 5th Alabama as his personal reserve, giving it orders as to its objective, but at the same time, according to his report, to regard O'Neal as still having command of four regiments. Rodes also gave Daniel discretionary orders about what to do in the middle of an attack. From a simple concept, the plan now had added complications. Like so many military plans, it was unable to survive the first shot.

Union. Baxter's plan was a simple holding one. He packed his 1,450 men into the two top sides of an inverted V, the total length of which was under 500 yards, its left side bounded by a stone wall and its right by the fence along the south side of the Mummasburg Road. This gave a density of about three men every yard. Perhaps half of these were able to bring fire to bear on O'Neal's attack, but at very close range. Baxter's planning as such was minimal, merely to take up the best defensive position possible, control the fire and later, as O'Neal's men disappeared, to bring his three north-facing regiments to face west.

Outline of events (Maps 32–34)

The first into action were the guns of Captains Carter and Fry, which had a good shoot into the Union troops along the Chambersburg Pike and in Shead's Wood (Stone's and Cutler's Brigades). They opened fire sometime after 1 p.m. while the infantry were sorting themselves out in their attacking formations and positions in the Oak Hill and Forney Woods. The gunfire alerted everyone that the Rebels were on Oak Ridge in force – the first casualty of the Confederate plan being the impossibility of achieving surprise. The second was the intention to have a simultaneous advance. Although Rodes' report would have the reader believe he launched the leading brigades at the same time, this did not happen. The first to jump off was O'Neal, probably at just after 2:00 p.m. Iverson had this to say about his start:

> During the cannonading . . . and not understanding the exact time at which the advance was to take place, I dispatched a staff officer to him [Rodes], to learn at what time I was to move forward, and received instructions not to move until my skirmishers became hotly engaged [which was not quite the answer Iverson wanted].
>
> Shortly afterward, however, I received an order from him to advance to meet the enemy, who were advancing to take the battery [this does not make much sense as no Union troops were anywhere near Carter's or Fry's guns at this stage]; to call upon Brigadier-General Daniel for support; that Colonel O'Neal's (Alabama) brigade would advance on my left, and that the batteries would cease fire as I passed them. I immediately dispatched a staff officer to inform Brigadier-General Daniel that I was about to advance, and one to notify my regiments, and to observe when the brigade on my left [O'Neal] commenced to move . . .
>
> Learning that the Alabama brigade, on my left was moving, I advanced at once . . .

What he neglected to mention was that he failed to deploy skirmishers or personally to lead his brigade forward.

Notes

- Rodes intended to attack the exposed northern flank of I Corps by surprise. This proved impossible, as Doubleday was alerted to the danger approaching via Oak Hill by cavalry patrols and Rebel guns opening fire, and thus hurried reinforcements (Baxter's Brigade, I Corps and soon afterward Paul's Brigade) to his threatened flank.
- Rodes intended to attack south astride and to the west of Oak Ridge, with two brigades simultaneously supported on the right by a third brigade (Daniel) en echelon. Poor coordination and delays resulted in a piecemeal attack. Instead of attacking with five regiments O'Neal attacked early and frontally with only three – only just over 1,000 men out of a division nearly 8,000 strong. The attack was quickly driven back, as was the belated advance of the 5th Alabama, by a hail of musketry from Baxter's men (**A**) and flanking fire from the 45th New York and Dilger's guns. This assault was quickly defeated before the other attacking brigade (Iverson) appeared on the scene.

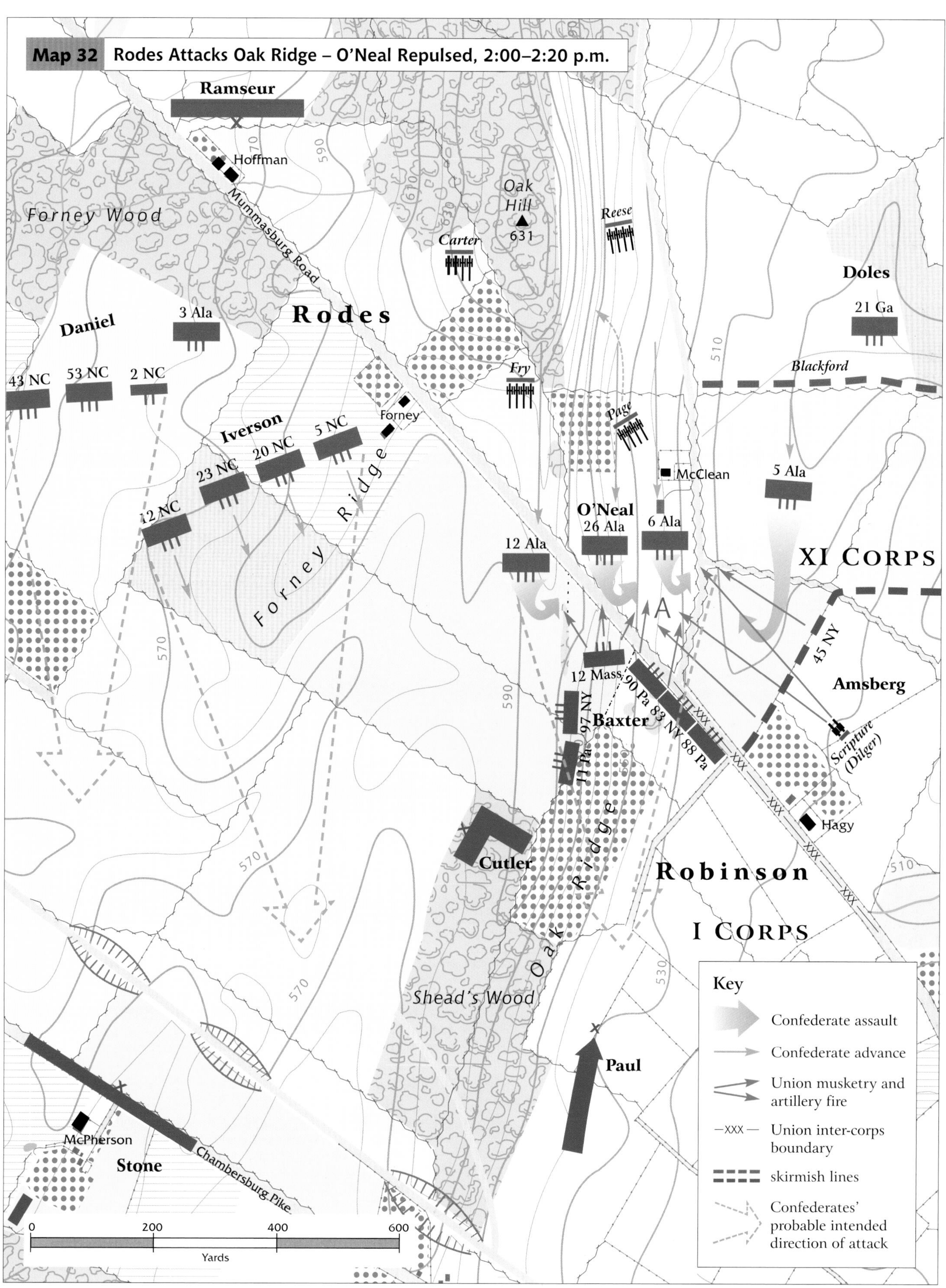
Map 32 Rodes Attacks Oak Ridge – O'Neal Repulsed, 2:00–2:20 p.m.
Ramseur
Hoffman
Forney Wood
Mummasburg Road
Oak Hill
631
Carter
Reese
Doles
21 Ga
Rodes
Daniel
3 Ala
43 NC
53 NC
2 NC
Fry
Blackford
Forney
Iverson
5 NC
20 NC
23 NC
12 NC
Forney Ridge
Page
McClean
5 Ala
O'Neal
26 Ala
6 Ala
12 Ala
XI CORPS
45 NY
Amsberg
12 Mass
90 Pa
83 NY
88 Pa
97 NY
Baxter
11 Pa
Scripture (Dilger)
Hagy
Cutler
Oak Ridge
Robinson
I CORPS
Shead's Wood
Paul
McPherson
Stone
Chambersburg Pike
0 200 400 600
Yards
Key
Confederate assault
Confederate advance
Union musketry and artillery fire
—XXX— Union inter-corps boundary
skirmish lines
Confederates' probable intended direction of attack

Many in O'Neal's Brigade were exhausted, particularly amongst the 5th Alabama, before they began their attack. When some distance north of Gettysburg they had been ordered off the road and up onto the ridge to their right, the 5th Alabama had been on the extreme left and had the farthest distance to go, and they had to move at speed. Colonel J. Hall, their commander, later wrote: "In places the regiment moved through full-grown wheat, in others over plowed ground. Through orchards, gardens, over wood and stone fences, which with the rapidity of the movement, fatigued the men, causing many of them to faint from their exhaustion." Corporal Samuel Pickens of the same regiment noted in his diary, "I was perfectly exhausted & never suffered so from heat & fatigue in my life. A good many fell out of the ranks being completely broken down & and some fainted."

When Rodes, probably not having much faith in O'Neal's ability, rode over to give him his orders personally, he found the brigade commander with the 5th Alabama and that neither he nor his staff had horses! Due to the difficulties in communication between the brigades and the distance between them, O'Neal advanced first, but not according to Rodes' report "in accordance with my orders as to direction . . ." It is far from clear just what objective Rodes had given them or how it could realistically have been much different from due south toward Baxter's men south of the Mummasburg Road. Like Iverson on his right, O'Neal failed to accompany his troops into action – having no horse was no excuse. After the leading three regiments had advanced, Rodes ordered the 5th Alabama to support them, but they arrived only in time to see the brigade being driven back and, after suffering severely, it withdrew northward. Within 15–20 minutes it was all over. The three regiments had been cut to pieces by frontal fire from Baxter's men and flanking fire from the left delivered by the 45th New York's rifle-muskets and Lieutenant Clark Scripture's (Dilger's Battery) guns firing canister. The attack barely made 200 yards before coming to a bloody halt and rapid retreat.

Iverson's Brigade stepped off, minus its commander, at about 2:20 p.m., just as O'Neal was being driven back. It had half a mile to march in extended lines before it reached the enemy along the Chambersburg Pike. This advance was through standing crops and could not be expected to progress at much more than 100 yards every two minutes – making the time to objective about 18–20 minutes. Initially, as they moved south from Forney Wood, Forney Ridge would have concealed them from observation by Baxter's men facing west on Oak Ridge. However, within perhaps 200 yards, the whole brigade began to wheel to the left and climb up to the crest of Forney Ridge. It is far from clear why this wheel took place. Was Iverson's objective really the unwooded, exposed part of Oak Ridge north of Shead's Wood that they actually attacked? Was this huge wheel originally intended? Would it have taken place if Iverson had been controlling the advance personally from the front? Was this a change of plan from the simple advance south? Did it occur by accident or on command? None of the after-battle reports answers these questions satisfactorily. Nevertheless, the wheel was made and the four regiments crested Forney Ridge over 400 yards from Oak Ridge, then moved down into the swale. They marched steadily forward toward what seemed to be an undefended stone wall. Their fate was worse than that inflicted on O'Neal. They were ambushed by Baxter's Brigade to their front and caught in the right flank by the fire of Cutler's men in Shead's Wood. They were totally surprised, brought to a

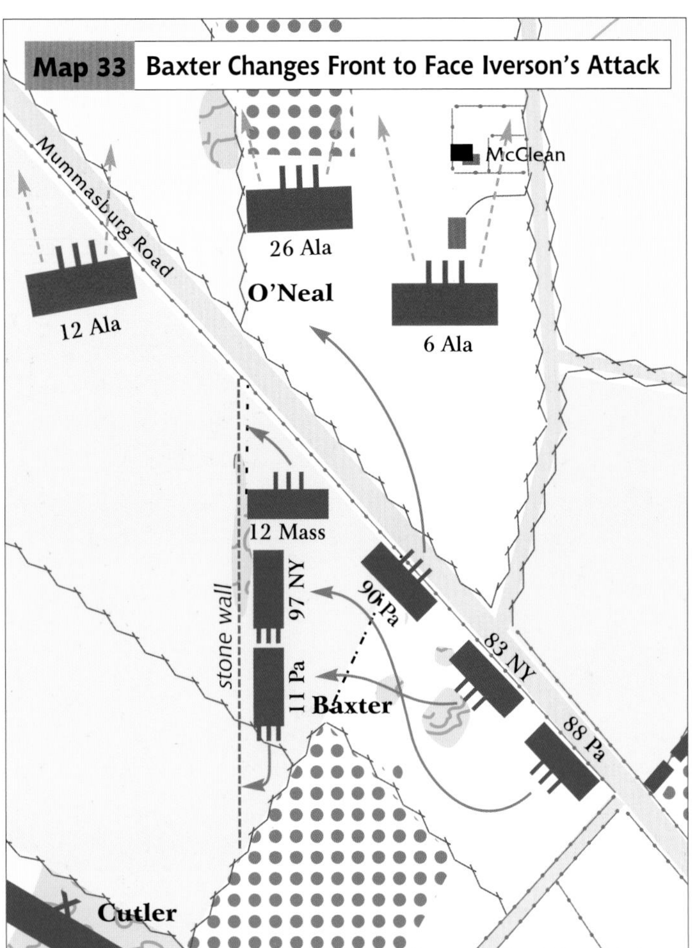

Notes for Map 33

As Rodes attacked piecemeal, there was a short period between O'Neal's retreat and Iverson's attack closing in that allowed Baxter to switch his brigade to face west, mostly concealed behind a stone wall (long disappeared). It was an excellent example at tactical level of a force on interior lines being able to confront and repulse one attacker and then turn to meet another. Conversely, it showed how, if attacking on exterior lines, it was essential the assaults were simultaneous.

Notes for Map 34

- With the retreat of O'Neal, Baxter was able to turn his brigade to face the looming threat in the west (Iverson). Much of his line was able to lie down and hide behind a stone wall, long since removed, that ran north–south from the Mummasburg Road to near the western edge of the large orchard on Oak Ridge. As Iverson advanced south and then swung to his left (area **A** on map), his brigade was concealed from view and fire by Forney Ridge. As they crested the ridge and moved into the swale (area **B**), the long lines of advancing infantry were exposed in the open but their enemy was invisible behind the wall.
- Baxter's men waited until the Rebels were very close before springing up and delivering a devastating hail of fire, supplemented by flanking fire from Cutler's men along the northern edge of Shead's Wood. This was followed by a spirited charge that routed Iverson and resulted in the capture of several hundred men. It was a near-perfect ambush, which had all but destroyed a Rebel brigade.
- Daniel's Brigade had not been able to support or participate in this advance and defeat, which had not lasted more than 15–20 minutes.

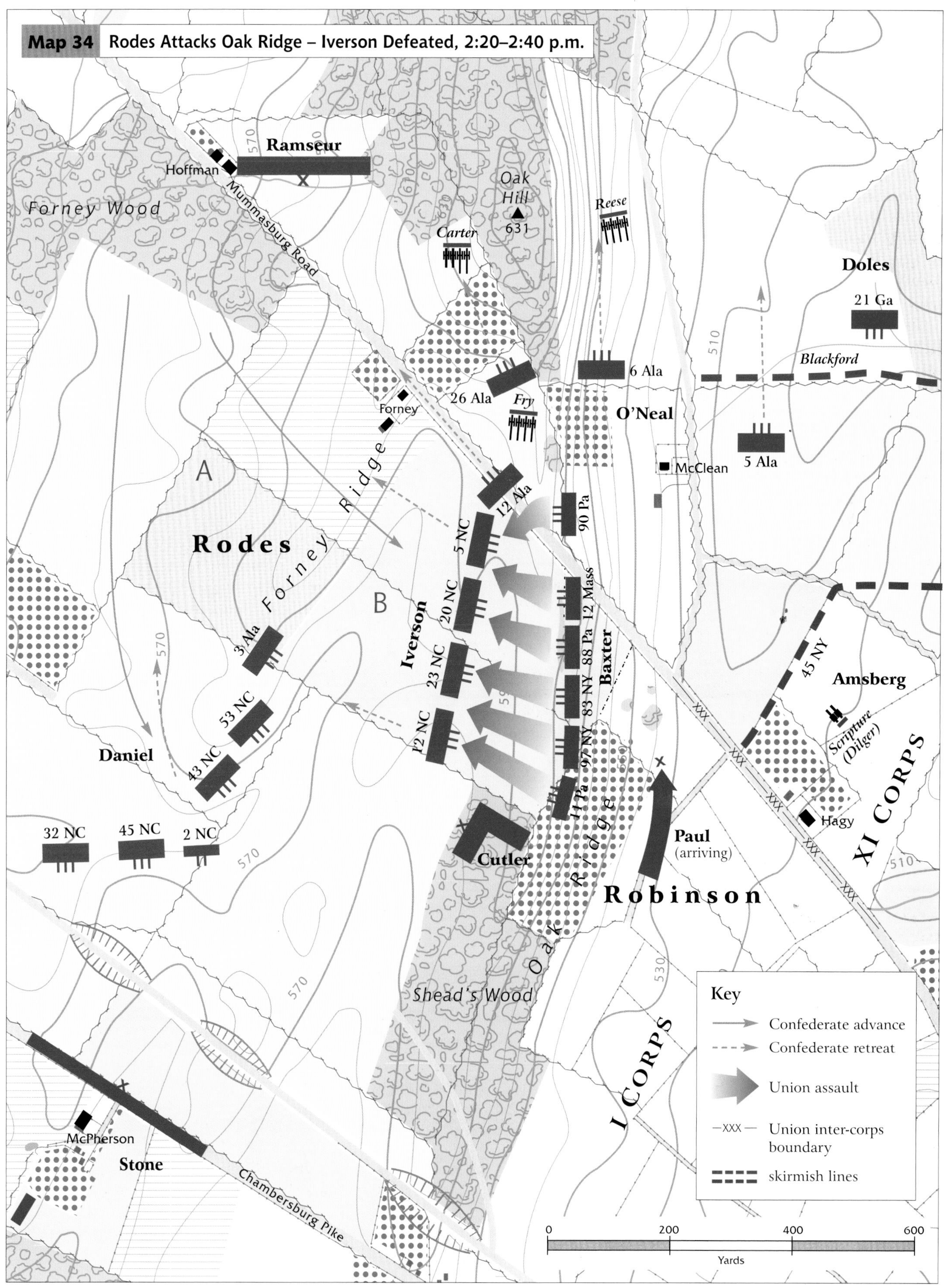
Map 34 Rodes Attacks Oak Ridge – Iverson Defeated, 2:20–2:40 p.m.
Ramseur
Hoffman
Mummasburg Road
Forney Wood
Oak Hill
631
Carter
Reese
Doles
21 Ga
Blackford
6 Ala
26 Ala
Fry
Forney
O'Neal
McClean
5 Ala
A
Forney Ridge
Rodes
12 Ala
5 NC
90 Pa
B
20 NC
12 Mass
Iverson
23 NC
88 Pa
Baxter
83 NY
3 Ala
53 NC
12 NC
97 NY
45 NY
Amsberg
Scripture (Dilger)
Daniel
43 NC
11 Pa
Oak Ridge
Hagy
XI CORPS
32 NC
45 NC
2 NC
Cutler
Paul
(arriving)
Robinson
Shead's Wood
I CORPS
McPherson
Stone
Chambersburg Pike
Key
Confederate advance
Confederate retreat
Union assault
Union inter-corps boundary
skirmish lines
0
200
400
600
Yards

shattering halt and then sent running by a spirited Yankee charge. Iverson's Brigade never recovered.

Daniel's Brigade advanced after, and en echelon behind Iverson's right. Unlike Iverson, it continued southward and, when he saw the difficulties faced by Iverson on his left, Daniel diverted two regiments (43rd and 53rd North Carolina) to support him in attacking Oak Ridge while the remainder moved against Cutler. These advances were brought to a costly halt. Rodes' first divisional attack had been thrown back with heavy losses.

The artillery exchanges on the western slope of Oak Hill had involved the Confederate batteries of Captains Carter and Fry firing into the flank of the Union troops engaged with Hill's Corps. Captain James H. Cooper's (Battery B, 1st Pennsylvania) and Captain Gilbert H. Reynolds' (Battery L and E, 1st New York) batteries replied, inflicting quite heavy losses on Captain Carter's men. On the exposed eastern slope the guns of Captains Page and Reese dueled with those of Captain Dilger (Battery I, 1st Ohio) and Captain Wheeler (13th New York). The Union guns dominated. Page's Battery was in an exposed position on a steep slope, each piece sited at a different level, "like seats in an amphitheater." Page's battalion commander, Lieutenant-Colonel Carter, had sent the guns here on Rodes' request, without personally seeing it. As losses mounted, Page reported his predicament to Carter, who galloped up to his divisional commander and his staff, furious, having just passed the gun position, and demanded, "General, what fool put that battery yonder?" An embarrassed silence followed, broken by Rodes saying quietly, "You had better take it away Carter."

Casualties

The losses tabulated below are those listed by Busey and Martin in their *Regimental Strengths and Losses at Gettysburg*. They indicate losses for the entire battle, although almost all occurred on July 1. On the Rebel side, only O'Neal's men were involved in any further serious fighting when they supported Johnson's Division in its attack on Culp's Hill on the morning of July 3. Baxter's Union Brigade was rushed around the battlefield, shifting its position numerous times on both July 2 and 3, but was never subjected to anything other than some artillery fire. However, a high proportion of Baxter's casualties would have occurred during its final defense of Oak Ridge and its retreat through Gettysburg during the collapse of the Union line later in the afternoon of the first day.

Iverson's Brigade suffered the really crippling losses; within a matter of minutes it virtually ceased to exist. Of the four regiments primarily involved, only the 12th North Carolina remained recognizable as a regiment, although even it lost over a third of its men. On the morning of July 2, Private Henry B. Berkeley of the Amherst (Virginia) Artillery went to look at the ground where Iverson's Brigade had been ambushed. He described what he saw in his diary:

> This morning on getting up, I saw a sight which was perfectly sickening and heart-rendering in the extreme . . . There [with]in a few feet of us, by actual count seventy-nine (79) North Carolinians laying dead in a straight line. I stood on their right and looked down their line. It was perfectly dressed. Three had fallen to the front, the rest had fallen backward; yet the feet of all these dead men were in a perfectly straight line . . . They had all been killed by one volley of musketry and they had fallen in their tracks without a single struggle.

The estimated losses of the regiments engaged are as follows:

O'Neal's Brigade	Killed	Wounded	Missing/ Captured	Total	%
3rd Alabama	17	74	?	91	26*
5th Alabama	26	116	67	209	65.9
6th Alabama	15	62	88	165	43.2
12th Alabama	17	66	?	83	26.2*
26th Alabama	8	57	65	130	40.8
Totals	**83**	**375**	**220**	**678**	**40***

*These totals should be slightly higher, but no figures are available for missing or captured personnel, of which there were some. For this brigade a total loss figure of 700, or 41 percent, appears reasonable.

Iverson's Brigade	Killed	Wounded	Missing/ Captured	Total	%
5th North Carolina	64	125	100	289	61.1*
12th North Carolina	12	60	7	79	36.1
20th North Carolina	41	94	118	253	68.0*
23rd North Carolina	65	120	97	282	89.2*
Totals	**182**	**399**	**322**	**903**	**65.2**

* The 5th North Carolina's losses were the sixth highest of all the 172 Confederate regiments at Gettysburg and those of the 23rd seventh and the 20th eleventh in terms of total numbers lost. The 97th New York's claim that Baxter captured 400 men is perhaps only slightly exaggerated. More accurate is the claim that the Rebels lost three colors.

Baxter's Brigade	Killed	Wounded	Missing/ Captured	Total	%
12th Massachusetts	5	52	62	119	45.6
83rd New York	6	18	58	82	41.2
97th New York	12	36	78	126	53.4
11th Pennsylvania	6	66	60	132	48.9
88th Pennsylvania	4	55	51	110	40.3
90th Pennsylvania	8	45	40	93	44.7
Totals	**41**	**272**	**349**	**662**	**46.6***

* The low number of men killed reflects the defensive position of these regiments, which were able to take shelter behind fences and latterly a stone wall. The high proportion of missing and captured reflects the large numbers of prisoners taken during the chaotic retreat through the town later on July 1.

Artillery losses on both sides, with the exception of Captain Page's Battery, were comparatively light. Those that did occur were mostly sustained on July 1 during the artillery exchanges of the afternoon. Total losses for the battle were:

Unit	Killed	Wounded	Missing/ Captured	Total	%
Confederate					
Captain Carter	5	3	2	10	9.7
Captain Fry	1	1	2	4	5.0
Captain Page	5	18	0	23	20.2
Captain Reese	0	0	0	0	0
Totals	**11**	**22**	**4**	**37**	**9.6**
Union					
Captain Dilger	0	13	0	13	10.2

Comments

- The importance of surprise on the battlefield was demonstrated in this incident. The Confederates had a possible chance of achieving it when Rodes' Division approached the field from the north through the woods on Oak Hill shortly after 1:00 p.m. However, opening fire with artillery before the infantry were ready to advance merely confirmed to the Union generals that the enemy had arrived. This, coupled with the time taken to shake out into a divisional attack formation and start the advance (at around 2:00 p.m.), precluded any likelihood of surprise. The Union forces, however, achieved a very successful defensive surprise when they ambushed Iverson's Brigade from behind a stone wall. It was the surprise effect of devastating musketry fire followed by a charge that routed the Rebels within minutes.
- Confederate control and coordination were poor from the start. The commanders of the leading two brigades were uncertain of the timing, and perhaps even of the objectives, of their advance. The result was a piecemeal attack that allowed Baxter, after dealing with one enemy, to move regiments to face and defeat another approaching from a different direction. It was a perfect example of a force operating on exterior lines (the Rebels) failing to ensure the two attacking brigades coming from different directions did so at the same time. Conversely, it illustrates how a force operating on interior lines (the Yankees) can succeed against threats from different directions.
- It was another example, out of many at Gettysburg, of the futility of frontal assaults over open ground against a determined enemy. Rodes' first attack lacked numbers, lacked surprise, was piecemeal, had no effective artillery support, lacked leadership from both brigade commanders and was frontal. The outcome could hardly have been different. Short-range rifle-musket fire, some of it flanking fire, destroyed both Rebel assaults.
- It showed how a bayonet charge, timed when the enemy was reeling from a blizzard of musket fire, could clinch the fight. Here Baxter's charge at the North Carolinians caught them at a huge disadvantage with few men capable of serious resistance. The result was an easy victory and hundreds of prisoners.
- As divisional commander, Rodes, although he redeemed himself somewhat a little later in the afternoon, must take overall responsibility for this failure, particularly for the lack of coordination at the start and for, in effect, removing two regiments (3rd and 5th Alabama) from his central attacking brigade. O'Neal may have used this as an excuse for his own poor leadership, but to take 700 men from an assault brigade of 1,700 was not sensible. Rodes has often been blamed for using two weak brigade commanders to lead the attack – he knew their limitations, and neither led their troops into battle. However, it is likely that, in order not to cause more delay and confusion, Rodes simply earmarked the leading brigades, Iverson followed by O'Neal, as the main attackers.
- Coming on top of the defeat of Heth's first attack on McPherson's Ridge, this repulse was a setback for Lee. The battle he did not really want at that time or in that place had started with two of his divisions being checked with substantial losses, and one brigade (Iverson's) wrecked.

Highlight: The Occupation, Defense and Loss of Blocher's Knoll, 2:15–3:30 p.m. (Maps 35 and 36)

The ground

It has always been a fundamental military principle that, other things being equal, commanders should occupy the high ground. High ground dominates its surroundings, it is likely to give good fields of fire and observation, and therefore can be more easily defended. It also offers reverse slopes behind which troop dispositions and movements can be concealed. A primary reason why Meade won Gettysburg was because he defended high ground that provided all of these things. No commander wants to be overlooked by his enemy. No commander likes the idea of having to attack an enemy occupying high ground. There were two instances at Gettysburg where a Union commander chose, on his own initiative, to move his troops forward to occupy higher ground and deploy forward of the main line of battle. On both occasions they turned out to be wrong and costly decisions. The first, on July 1, involved the 1st Division, XI Corps, under Brigadier-General Francis Barlow; the second, on July 2, involved the whole of III Corps under Major-General Daniel Sickles. In this section we are concerned with the former.

The threequarters of a mile gap north of Gettysburg between the north–south-running Oak Ridge in the west and Rock Creek in the east was open country, covered at the time of the battle by a patchwork of fields of standing crops and grass. There were undulations but no natural obstacle for a defender covering the approaches to the town to occupy. Artillery on Oak Hill dominated the entire area and could enfilade many Union troops deployed north of Gettysburg. A commander tasked with deploying east–west across this area would do so with considerable misgivings. Howard gave Schurz, the acting commander of XI Corps, this task early in the afternoon of July 1. His area of responsibility was a large V with the point at Gettysburg. The western arm was the Mummasburg Road, the eastern the Harrisburg Road. Down the center of the V was the Carlisle Road. The natural boundary on the right (east) was the tree-lined Rock Creek, several feet deep and with steep banks in places. To the left (west) the natural boundary was Oak Hill and Ridge, which by 1 p.m. was in Rebel hands.

Exactly half a mile north of the town square a small, unnamed stream ran from the Mummasburg Road due east to join Rock Creek. Immediately to its north, adjoining the Harrisburg Road, was a cluster of alms houses. To its immediate south was a slight rise in the ground from Kitsman's Farm in the west to Crawford's in the east. Occupying this low ridge, with the stream in front and alms houses on the right, offered, perhaps, just perhaps, a possible defensive line. It had the advantage of shortness – well under half a mile – something that to XI Corps (the smallest corps in the army) was surely an important consideration; it would enable an easier and stronger link-up with the right of I Corps near the Hagy Farm.

Schurz must surely have been even more anxious about covering as short a line as possible when Howard kept one of his divisions (Von Steinwehr) back as force reserve on Cemetery Hill. It meant he had to defend the northern approach with only some 6,340 men instead of 9,240. Nevertheless, when Schurz positioned his leading division (Schimmelfennig), he pushed forward a strong line of skirmishers that drove back Blackford's men, who

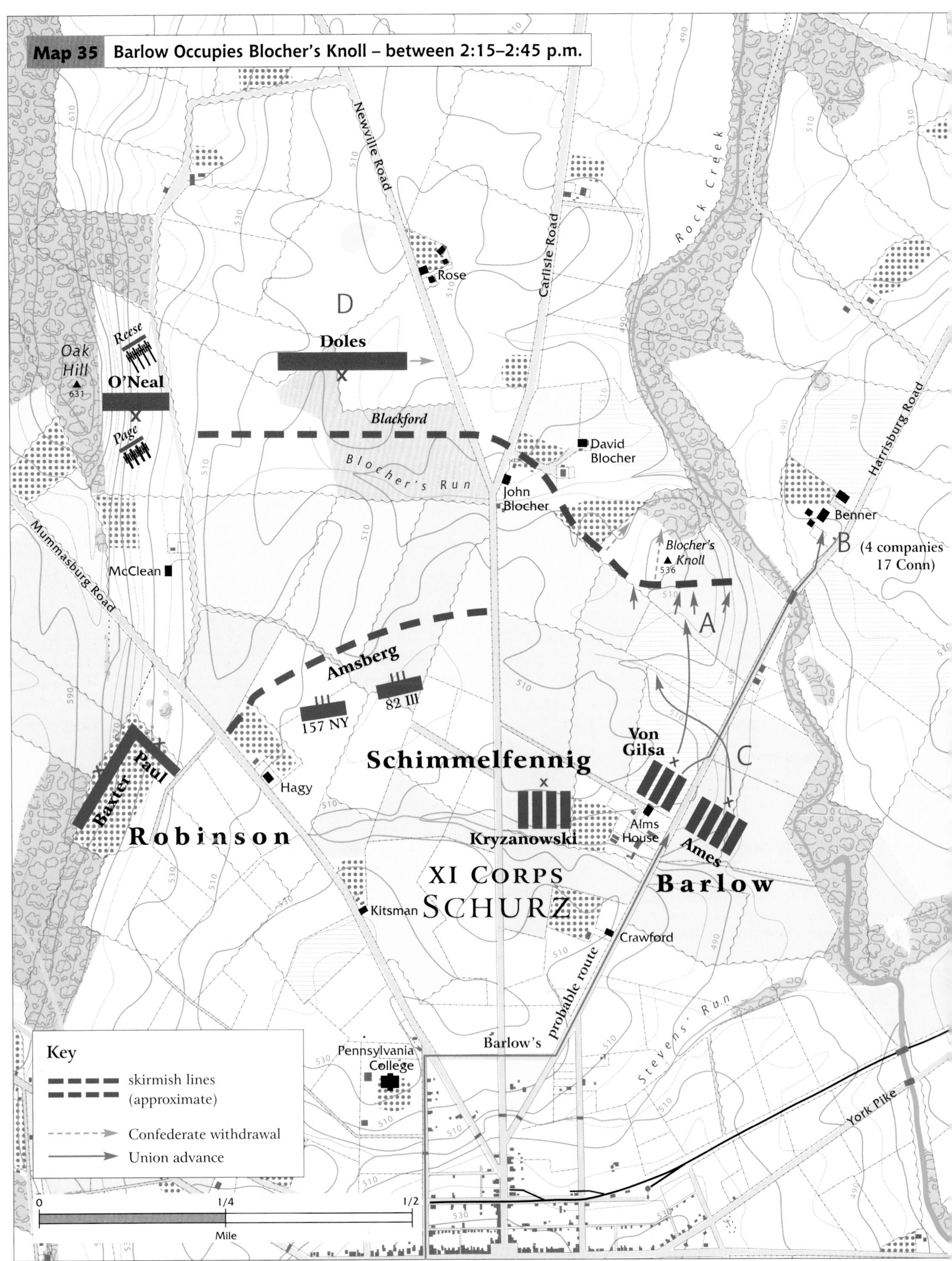

Map 35 Barlow Occupies Blocher's Knoll – between 2:15–2:45 p.m.
Newville Road
Carlisle Road
Rock Creek
Rose
D
Doles
Reese
Oak Hill
631
O'Neal
Page
Blackford
Blocher's Run
David Blocher
John Blocher
Benner
Harrisburg Road
B (4 companies 17 Conn)
Blocher's Knoll
536
A
Mummasburg Road
McClean
Amsberg
157 NY
82 Ill
Von Gilsa
C
Schimmelfennig
Paul
Baxter
Hagy
Robinson
Kryzanowski
Alms House
Ames
XI CORPS
SCHURZ
Barlow
Kitsman
Crawford
probable route
Barlow's
Stevens' Run
Pennsylvania College
York Pike
Key
skirmish lines (approximate)
Confederate withdrawal
Union advance
0
1/4
1/2
Mile

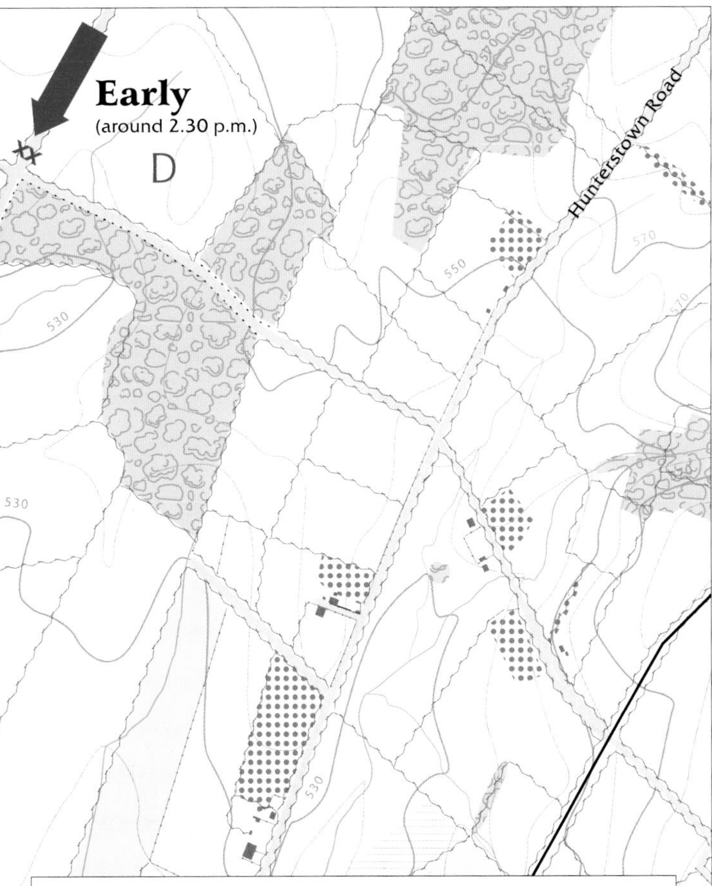

Notes

- This map shows the approximate deployment of both Union and Confederate forces north of Gettysburg shortly after O'Neal's and Iverson's first attacks on Oak Ridge had been driven off.
- The acting XI Corps commander (Schurz) has deployed Schimmelfennig's two brigades on either side of the Carlisle Road, with Amsberg's regiments stretched in a line of skirmishers across the 600 yards of fields between the Mummasburg and Carlisle Roads, his left being in the Hagy orchard. Two regiments (157th New York and 82nd Illinois) are in reserve. The other brigade (Kryzanowski) is in double column of companies east of the Carlisle Road between that road and the alms house orchard.
- Barlow's Division, the last to march through Gettysburg, has halted by the alms house and has Von Gilsa to the left of the Harrisburg Road and Ames to the right. To his immediate north Barlow sees Rebel skirmishers about a quarter of a mile ahead of him in the fields and on a small knoll of rising ground (Blocher's Knoll).
- Barlow either misunderstood or disobeyed his instructions to remain in his location, as he ordered forward Von Gilsa's Brigade to drive off the Rebel skirmishers and occupy the knoll; he did not wish it to be taken by the enemy and used as an artillery platform that would dominate his position (**A**). At about the same time he sent four companies of the 17th Connecticut under a Major Brady to take the bridge over the Rock Creek and then occupy the Benner Farm building (**B**). Within about 30 minutes he also sent his second brigade (Ames) forward to support Von Gilsa, along with his artillery battery (Wilkeson) (**C**).
- This controversial decision by Barlow opened up a substantial gap to his left,which was to be filled by Doles later moving to his left and attacking Barlow in conjunction with Early's attack, before Kryzanowski could advance to fill it (**D**).

A Narrow Escape for Captain Baron Von Fritsch

Von Fritsch, serving in the 68th New York Infantry in Von Gilsa's Brigade, 1st Division, XI Corps, left this account of his ordeal in Gettysburg town:

> Orders were shouted to fall back through Gettysburg on to Cemetery Hill, and it was high time to do so, as from all sides Confederate masses approached the town on the double quick . . . I rode behind our men into the town and saw many captured by Grey-coats everywhere.
>
> Passing a church on the outskirts, Surgeon Schultz, frightened to death, stopped me and asked if he would be taken prisoner, if caught. I said: "Put a white handkerchief on your arm, and attend to the wounded. There are lots of them in the streets."
>
> This delayed me and some twenty Confederates came rushing on, halloing [*sic*] me to surrender. One excited fellow got hold of Caesar's [his horse's] bridle with his left hand and was ready to plunge his bayonet into me with the right, screaming: "Surrender! Get down, you damned Yank!" "You be damned," I answered, and cut off his hand with my Saxon sword. Then I started off, gave spurs to my horse, but to my horror found myself in a yard, surrounded by high fence rails. They shot at me from behind and demanded surrender.
>
> "Marie!" I gasped, "save me!" And Caesar, with an enormous effort, jumped the fence and made off towards Cemetery Hill. Reaching the Arch, I dismounted and examined my horse; the poor fellow had been shot twice and the shoulder was badly scratched, but they were only slight flesh wounds. My left leg was wounded, and I felt the blood filling my right boot. My left shoulder strap had been shot away and the shoulder badly scratched. One bullet had damaged the back of my saddle, partially protected by a rubber blanket, and when I tried to replace my sabre, I found the scabbard bent. I had hurt my right knee badly on the fence, and torn off one of my stirrups.

The Last Minutes of Resistance on Blocher's Knoll

Major Thomas Osborn commanded the twenty-six guns (sixteen Napoleons and ten 3-inch ordnance rifles) of the reserve artillery battalion attached to the Union XI Corps. He describes going up to Blocher's Knoll shortly before it fell.

> I again returned to Wilkeson's Battery, where I met Wilkeson being carried to the rear by his men on a stretcher. One leg had been cut off at the knee by a cannon shot. He spoke to me and was cheerful and hopeful. I knew at a glance that the wound was fatal. There was no time for me to stop and, after talking with him, perhaps a quarter or half a minute, I left him. I never saw him again, as he died a few hours later . . .
>
> I soon hurried on to the front where I found the battery engaged in line with Barlow's division. The lines of battle were in the open field and very close together. The enemy's line overlapped ours to a considerable extent on both flanks. Lieutenant Bancroft was in command of Wilkeson's battery and doing good work. I knew that the two divisions must soon fall back or would be drawn back. I gave Bancroft what instructions were necessary and returned to get the other four batteries into satisfactory positions. A few moments after I left the line, General Barlow was seriously wounded and fell into the hands of the enemy.

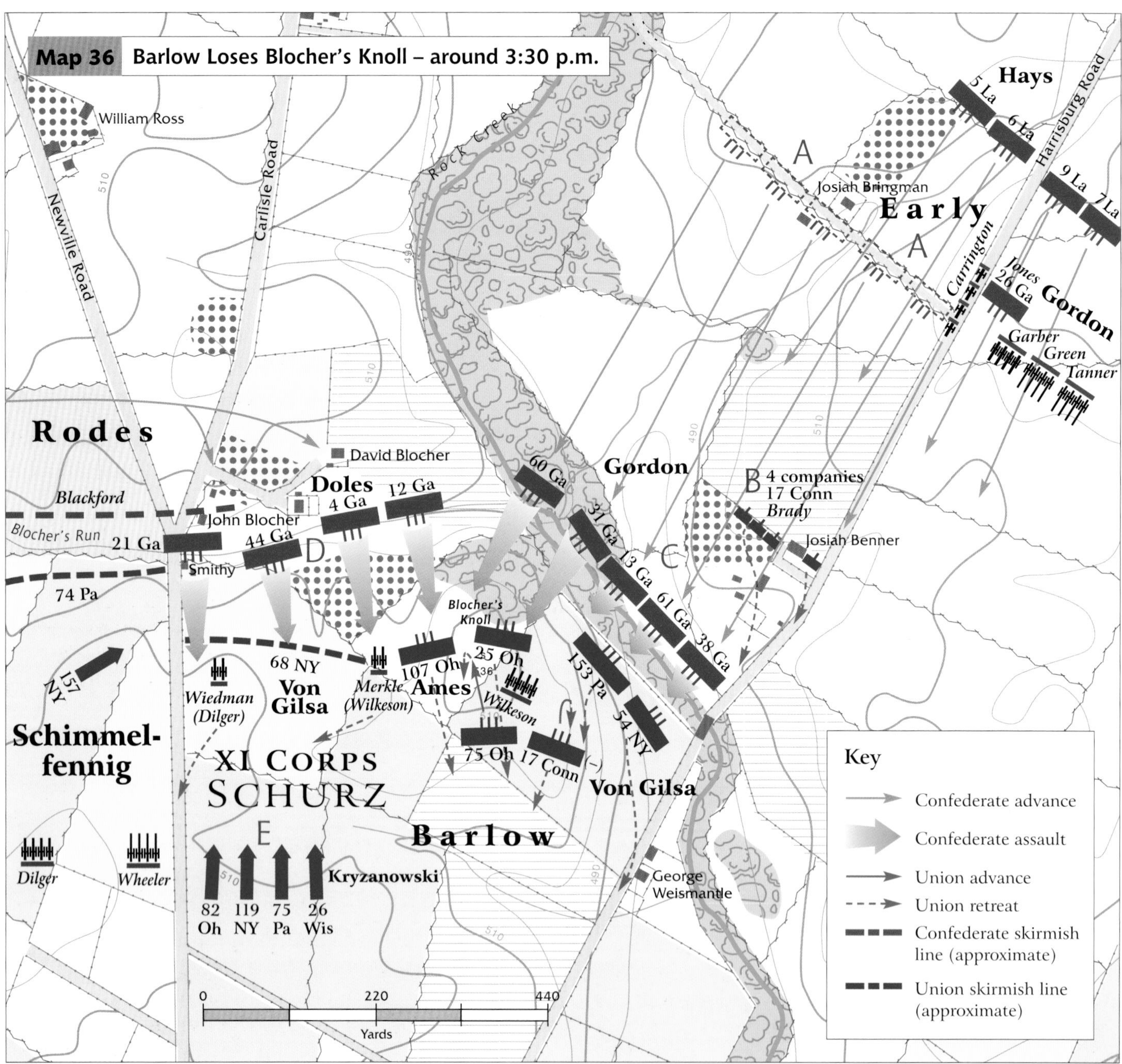

Notes

• At around 3.30 p.m. Early's Division launched its attack on Blocher's Knoll, occupied by Barlow's 1st Division of XI Corps. The initial assault was carried out by five regiments of Gordon's Brigade, which formed up along Bringman's Lane (**A**); the remaining regiment (26th Georgia) was tasked with supporting the guns of Jones's Battalion, which was engaged in softening up the Union position and dueling with Wilkeson's Battery on the knoll.

• After an advance of 500 yards, during which Maj. Brady's four companies from the 17th Connecticut in Benner's Farm (**B**) were withdrawn, the attackers splashed across Rock Creek and charged through the trees to assault the knoll (**C**). At almost the same time four regiments of Doles's Brigade from Rodes' Division that had moved to their left (east) deployed and assaulted across Blocher's Run and hit Ames's Brigade positions on the west and northwest of the knoll (**D**).

• Barlow had deployed in two thin lines, with the front line on the forward slope of the knoll and extending from the Harrisburg Road on the right to the Carlisle Road on the left. On the left the line was dangerously stretched, as the 68th New York had to be deployed as skirmishers. Barlow had the support of 16 guns from Wilkeson's, Wheeler's and Dilger's Batteries.

• After a brief fight, Von Gilsa's Brigade broke and retreated in great haste, despite Barlow's strenuous efforts to stop the rot. Both the 17th Connecticut and 75th Ohio (Ames's Brigade) from the second line were sent forward but, caught in a heavy crossfire, were unable to halt the general collapse of the defense as both Gordon and Doles closed in on the knoll.

• As Barlow's men ran for the rear, Barlow himself was hit and badly wounded (and later captured). At this time four regiments from Kryzanowski's Brigade (Schimmelfennig's 3rd Division, XI Corps) were advancing to support Barlow (**E**), as was the 157th New York from Amsberg's Brigade. They arrived too late and were in their turn overwhelmed and forced to return south, back to a line running west from the alms house. Blocher's Knoll, later known as Barlow's Knoll, had been lost within the space of 30 minutes.

had advanced some distance southeast of the Carlisle Road. The main body of the division halted just north of the unnamed stream and Amsberg's Brigade (just over 1,600 men) was sent forward to cover the ground from the Hagy orchard on the Mummasburg Road to the Carlisle Road, and to make contact with I Corps' right. It took three of Amsberg's five regiments to cover this arc, deployed as skirmishers. Kryzanowski's Brigade was kept back in double column of companies immediately to the east of the Carlisle Road, where they awaited the arrival of Barlow's Division.

When Barlow, accompanied by Howard, rode up the Harrisburg Road, he halted his brigades in column with Von Gilsa's Brigade near the alms houses and Ames's Brigade on the other side of the road. He surveyed the ground ahead of him. A quarter of a mile to the north was a small knoll of higher ground known as Blocher's Knoll. It was nothing spectacular, but it was some 70 feet higher than Rock Creek, which flowed along its eastern flank, and it appeared that it would offer a good platform for artillery, which, if occupied by the enemy, would render his position untenable. Barlow could not see from his position at the alms house that the northern slope on the knoll was mostly covered by a wood extending west from Rock Creek; but what he could see was that Rebel sharpshooters (some of Blackford's men), although they had been driven back, still occupied the knoll that, by a narrow margin, dominated his position. Barlow knew enemy were expected from the north, but as yet could see nothing of them.

Tactical significance

Once occupied by Barlow's Division, Blocher's Knoll became the extreme right flank of the entire Union defense line guarding the approaches to Gettysburg. This flank was "in the air;" any enemy approaching from the northeast down the Hunterstown Road or York Pike would render Blocher's Knoll untenable. If the knoll went, it was likely the whole Union line to the west would unravel – which is almost exactly what happened. Barlow's decision to move forward extended an already thin line, and the knoll became the focus of an all-out Rebel assault. The significance of its loss to Schurz was that it triggered the collapse of much of XI Corps' resistance north of the town, which in turn meant that, even with a stout defense by I Corps on Seminary Ridge, the enemy had succeeded in threatening its rear and a hasty, disorganized and at times panicky retreat was inevitable for both XI and I Corps.

Force comparison

The numbers compared here relate only to the forces actually engaged in the fight for Blocher's Knoll itself. On the Union side, Kryzanowski's Brigade of 1,230 men (the 58th New York was at Emmitsburg) was belatedly brought forward to assist Barlow but arrived too late to prevent the loss of the knoll. With the Confederates, Hays's Brigade (Early's Division) of 1,292 advanced behind Gordon to support him in the assault but was not required to participate in this part of the action. The fight took place between two Rebel brigades (Gordon's in Early's Division and Doles's in Rodes' Division) and the two Yankee brigades (Von Gilsa's and Ames's) in Barlow's Division. This meant the forces involved with the attack and defense of Blocher's Knoll were as follows:

Confederate		Union	
Gordon's Brigade		**Von Gilsa's Brigade**	
13th Georgia	312	54th New York	189
31st Georgia	252	68th New York	232
38th Georgia	341	153rd Pennsylvania	499
60th Georgia	299	**Total**	**920**
61st Georgia	288		
Total	**1,492**		
Doles's Brigade		**Ames's Brigade**	
4th Georgia	341	17th Connecticut	386
12th Georgia	327	25th Ohio	220
21st Georgia	287	75th Ohio	269
44th Georgia	364	107th Ohio	458
Total	**1,319**	**Total**	**1,333**
Grand total	**2,811**	**Grand total**	**2,253**
Artillery – 12 guns		Artillery – 16 guns	

- With the Confederates, the 315 men of the 26th Georgia did not participate in the attack as they were detailed to protect the gun line. Three batteries of Rebel artillery (Garber, Green and Tanner) took part in the preparatory bombardment of the knoll prior to the infantry (Gordon's) advance; the remaining battery (Carrington's) waited on the road to follow up the attack. However, the attackers received substantial artillery support from Rodes' Confederate batteries on Oak Hill.
- Note the smallness of Von Gilsa's Brigade with only just over 900 men, who were required to meet the initial shock of Gordon's almost 1,500, and the disparity between the 189 in the 54th New York and the 499 in the 153rd Pennsylvania. The latter was one of only two nine-month enlistment regiments in the Army of the Potomac (the other was the 151st Pennsylvania in Biddle's Brigade, 3rd Division, I Corps). Their enlistment had expired on June 22 but it was not until the regiment had reached the alms houses and was about to go into action that their commander, Major John Frueauff, explained that any man who did not want to go into battle should step out and it would be no disgrace – not a man moved. Von Gilsa's Brigade had only three regiments because the 41st New York had been left in camp and would not join until that night.
- Total numbers indicate that some 2,800 Rebel infantry attacked the knoll defended by 2,250 Yankees, giving the Rebels an advantage of 550 or perhaps two regiments. It was by no means a decisive superiority, but some very effective artillery fire from two directions supported the attackers.

Command and control

The man primarily responsible for the attack and capture of Blocher's Knoll – an action that triggered the start of the collapse of the Union right – was the Rebel divisional commander Major-General Early. The actual attacks were led by Brigadier-Generals Gordon and Doles (Rodes' Division) but neither had any particular command role other than just carrying out orders and the straightforward leading and encouraging of their regiments to drive forward the assault. However, the exceptional leadership of Gordon merits his inclusion here. The officer responsible for occupying and

The "Schoolteacher's Regiment"

"The Schoolteacher's Regiment" was the nickname of the 151st Pennsylvania Infantry, Biddle's Brigade, named after its colonel, Lieutenant-Colonel George I. McFarland, a former teacher. On the afternoon of July 1 this large regiment, with 467 men present, had been held back and was I Corps' last reserve when Biddle's Brigade gave way, exposing the flank of the Iron Brigade as the defense of McPherson's Ridge finally began to unravel. The regiment, led by McFarland, was ordered forward to stop the rot. This counterattack was to cost it most of its 72.2 percent casualties (the second highest of the 247 regiments in the Union Army), but it enabled both Biddle and the Iron Brigade to pull back to the Seminary Ridge – the final defensive line before Gettysburg. Lieutenant-Colonel McFarland has left an account of what happened:

> The enemy greeted me with a volley that brought several of my men down, where I had halted in position. Having previously cautioned the men against excitement and firing at random . . . I did not order them to fire a regular volley, but each man to fire as he saw an enemy on which to take a steady aim. This was strictly observed [the regiment was one of the few to have regularly practiced musketry] . . . Men fell thick and fast on our front [and] an attempt to flank us on our left was quickly stopped by our unerring oblique fire . . .
>
> I do not know how men could have fought more desperately, exhibited more coolness or contested the field with more determined courage . . .

The adjutant, Samuel Allen, was the fifth man to take the color when he finally bore it off the field. McFarland was knocked from his horse when shot through both legs as he encouraged his men. He was carried into the Lutheran Seminary but he did not receive treatment for two days, when his right leg was amputated below the knee. Miraculously he did not succumb to loss of blood or shock, but was crippled and in constant pain for the remainder of his life. After the war he went back to teaching and converted the McAlisterville Academy from a teaching college to an institution devoted to educating the orphans of Union soldiers who had lost their lives in the war, or the children of disabled ex-soldiers. McFarland died in 1891 aged fifty-seven.

defending the knoll was Brigadier-General Barlow. As with the attackers, Barlow's two brigade commanders, Colonel Von Gilsa and Brigadier-General Ames, were heavily involved in the fighting and performed with considerable gallantry but were not required to make any important command decisions at that time.

Major-General Jubal A. Early. Early was a forty-six-year-old bachelor at Gettysburg, well known as the only man who could get away with swearing in front of Lee – who called him "my bad old man." He certainly looked older than his years, with a balding head, unkempt gray beard and pronounced stoop. He was "bad" in that he was unpopular for his harshness, his overbearing attitude to subordinates and his general abrasiveness. Though a scholar and lawyer, he continually chewed tobacco, spoke ungrammatically with a rasp, and was excessively profane and dogmatic in his views.

Early was a Virginian who had graduated from West Point into the artillery in 1837 but spent only a year in the army before resigning to study law and become a Whig legislator (it seems the majority of senior officers on both sides had been a lawyer or politician or both at some time). He served in the Mexican War, where he contracted the arthritis that gave him his stoop. Although opposed to secession, he offered his services to his state at the outbreak of war and was appointed colonel of the 24th Virginia Infantry. He proved a battlefield leader of considerable talent, commanding a brigade at First Bull Run that secured him promotion to brigadier-general. He was shot through the shoulders at Williamsburg in the Peninsular campaign. He returned to duty to command a large new brigade (seven regiments) in Ewell's Division at the Battle of Malvern Hill, exactly a year to the day before Gettysburg; Early was, however, still suffering from his wound and had to be assisted onto his horse. He did well in the Second Manassas campaign and succeeded Lawton in command of Ewell's Division at Antietam, where, according to Stonewall Jackson, Early "attacked with great vigor and gallantry." Although still a brigadier-general, he was kept in command of the division and at Fredericksburg saved a dangerous situation from developing when he brought up his division at the run to plug a hole in Hill's line. At last, on April 23, 1863, Early was promoted major-general. At Chancellorsville he had the task of holding the lines above Fredericksburg while the rest of the army disappeared on the long flank march to attack Hooker's right. Almost driven from his position by the Union VI Corps assault, and forced to withdraw, he organized a spirited counterattack that drove the Yankees back.

A forceful, arrogant and successful commander, Early had but one military failing – lack of a good sense of direction. Not infrequently he failed to live up to his name and arrived late at his destination due to this shortcoming. He had problems finding the battlefield at First Manassas, struggled to launch his attack at Williamsburg on time and got bogged down unnecessarily in the swamps and woods around Malvern Hill.

During the Gettysburg campaign Early was still commanding what had formerly been Ewell's Division and had led the advance on York via Gettysburg, where he arrived on June 26, having torched the Caledonian Iron Works en route (see box, page 222). He then marched out along the York Pike. Disappointed by his recall from York, Early was moving west to rejoin the army on July 1 when he received the message to march on Gettysburg rather than Cashtown – this was not a problem, as he was already on the Harrisburg Road, which led directly to the town and, fortuitously, onto the flank of XI Corps. Riding ahead of the main column and not far behind White's Comanches, who were screening the advance, Early and his staff were met about 2 miles from the town by Lieutenant Thomas T. Turner of Ewell's staff with a dispatch informing him of the situation: that Rodes was fully engaged with the enemy and that he, Early, should "attack at once." Early moved off the road onto higher ground from which the town was visible. At about this time, Major Campbell Brown, also from his corps commander's staff, rode up with the same message – it was one of Ewell's standard staff procedures always to send two messengers at intervals with important dispatches.

From his vantage point Early could see enemy guns on Cemetery Hill and could tell that he had arrived on the flank of Union forces that appeared to be threatening Rodes' left. Early had already been instructed to attack, so he immediately summoned his brigade commanders to "double-quick to the front and open the lines of infantry for the artillery to pass." Although there is no evidence that Early had been pressing his brigades during their march that morning, once the enemy had been sighted and he saw the opportunity he had his division deployed at speed and into action within half an hour. This dispatch was facilitated by what would today be called good "battle procedure" in that he, as the overall commander, was at the head of his command on the march and accompanied by his staff. He was therefore in the right place to make a quick personal assessment of the situation, decide on a plan and send his couriers galloping away to bring up the troops required for the attack and clear the road for the guns to come up to the front at speed. It was a good example of the none-too-frequent smooth functioning of the Confederate command system at divisional level on the battlefield at Gettysburg.

Brigadier-General John Brown Gordon. Gordon was an inspirational leader. Although not a professional soldier, his natural leadership qualities, ability as an orator and outstanding courage in battle made him one of the Confederacy's foremost regimental and brigade commanders; and he became the war idol of Georgians for several decades after the war. In May 1864 he was promoted major-general, one of only three non-professionals to achieve that rank.

After graduating from the University of Georgia, he first practiced as a lawyer before becoming the manager of a coal mine in Alabama. At the outbreak of war he raised and commanded a company of mountaineers called the "Raccoon Roughs." At the time he was married with two small children whom he handed over to his mother to look after so that he could concentrate on soldiering – and so that his wife, Fanny, could accompany him in the field. She followed her husband devotedly and it became a standing joke that when Mrs Gordon was seen moving to the rear, a battle would be about to start. Such loyalty and faithfulness did not receive the blessing of Gordon's crusty old bachelor divisional commander. Early was reputed to have once said he wished to God that Fanny would be captured.

Union dead killed on July 1.

Gordon led his Raccoon Roughs at First Manassas and was elected colonel of the 6th Alabama in April 1862 in time for the Peninsular campaign. At Seven Pines, when his brigade commander (Rodes) was wounded, Gordon took over and led a charge into a hail of fire in which he was the only field officer to escape death; indeed, he remained untouched. Still commanding the brigade at Malvern Hill, he was in the thick of the action when he was temporarily blinded by dirt thrown into his eyes from a shellburst. When Rodes resumed command of the brigade, Gordon returned to his 6th Alabama. In September 1862 at South Mountain (in the Antietam campaign) his was the only regiment in the brigade to withstand the intense fighting – entirely due to its colonel's inspiring leadership. According to Rodes, he handled his regiment "in a manner I have never heard or seen equaled during this war." A few days later at "Bloody Lane" on the Antietam (Sharpsburg) battlefield, he survived five separate wounds, one of which hit him in the face and knocked him unconscious. Gordon was promoted brigadier-general in November 1862 but had not fully recovered from his wounds until the following April. At Fredericksburg, during the Chancellorsville campaign, it was Gordon's Brigade that led the counterattack to retake Marye's Heights and drive back the Union VI Corps – although in the event the Heights were unoccupied.

It was Gordon's Brigade that led the assault on Blocher's Knoll on the afternoon of July 1. A Captain Robert Siles described Gordon in the attack as follows:

> Gordon was the most glorious and inspiring thing I ever looked on. He was riding a beautiful coal-black stallion, captured at Winchester, that had belonged to one of the Federal generals in Milroy's army – a majestic animal [that] followed at a trot, close upon the heels of the battle line, his head right in among the slanting barrels and bayonets, the reins loose upon his neck, [General Gordon] standing in his stirrups, bareheaded, hat in hand, arms extended, and, in a voice like a trumpet, exhorting his men. It was superb, absolutely thrilling.

Major-General Carl Schurz. Born in 1829 in the village of Liblar on the Rhine near Cologne, Schurz was the son of a schoolmaster-cum-businessman and a farmer's daughter. The young Schurz studied history at both Cologne and Bonn Universities, where his gift for oratory became apparent. He became an enthusiastic and vocal supporter of the revolutionary movement then sweeping Germany. He was appointed a lieutenant, aged nineteen, in the revolutionary army when the revolution broke out in 1848 and was among the revolutionaries bottled up in the fortress of Rastatt when Prussian forces surrounded it. Fearing the consequences of capture, Schurz fled through the sewers just before the garrison surrendered, and escaped to Switzerland. With incredible skill and nerve, the young man soon returned to Germany in disguise and managed to rescue his former professor and revolutionary leader, Gottfried Kinkel, from Spandau prison in Berlin where he was facing life imprisonment. Both then fled to England. After a few months in Paris in 1851, Schurz was expelled as a dangerous alien and returned to England to get married and sail for America. Settling in Wisconsin in 1855, he soon became prominent in politics and used his skills as an orator in the anti-slavery debate. He earned the thanks of Lincoln for his vocal and passionate support in the 1860 election campaign, securing the appointment of Minister to Spain from July 1861 to April 1862. On returning to America, Schurz petitioned the President for a general's commission – a request that Lincoln initially refused but soon relented – and he was appointed a brigadier-general of volunteers. This was surely one of the, if not the, most political appointments to military high rank of the war, but done mainly to gain support for the war from the German-Americans, or the "Dutchmen" as the Rebels called them. By March 1863 he was a major-general (a promotion that caused an outcry from countless more senior and experienced officers), entirely untested at this level, indeed at any level of military command.

Schurz was first under fire at Freeman's Ford during the Second Manassas campaign, where his command performed poorly in an attempt to seize Stonewall Jackson's supply train. However, Schurz redeemed himself somewhat a little later at Second Manassas. At Chancellorsville he tried unsuccessfully to alert Howard to the dangers on the right flank and was thus outraged when his troops were vilified in the press after XI Corps' ignominious retreat. He went so far as to request an official inquiry to exonerate his troops.

At Gettysburg Schurz was thirty-four, wore thick glasses, had a large reddish beard, very little military experience and was regarded by most as a vocal and scheming political general with influence in Washington that went right to the President's office. On the afternoon of July 1 he found himself in an extremely testing situation when, as acting commander of XI Corps, he was given the task of rushing to check the advance of superior numbers of advancing Rebels threatening the army's exposed right flank north of the town. To make things more difficult, Howard allowed him to take only two weak divisions forward to do the job. Schurz had undoubtedly been thrown in at the deep end.

Unable to occupy Oak Hill as the enemy was there first, Schurz positioned the first division to arrive, Schimmelfennig's 3rd Division, north of the town on the left to link up with I Corps' right. One brigade (Amsberg) deployed between the Mummasburg Road on its left and the Carlisle Road on its right, and pushed forward a skirmish line with three regiments north and east of the Hagy orchard. The second brigade (Kryzanowski) remained in double column of companies to the right (east) of the Carlisle Road between that road and the alms houses. Barlow's Division arrived about half an hour later, marching up the Harrisburg Road, and was halted briefly on reaching the alms houses. Shortly thereafter Barlow ordered Von Gilsa's Brigade forward to drive off the Rebel skirmishers on Blocher's Knoll and occupy it. Later, on seeing Rebels (Doles) moving east and threatening his brigade on the knoll, Barlow sent Ames's Brigade forward to support Von Gilsa. Schurz was not present when these moves were made.

It is difficult to be certain what orders Schurz gave Barlow. However, he did order the initial dispositions of XI Corps. His objective was to protect Doubleday's right flank and be prepared to meet the expected arrival of the Rebels from the northeast. In his report Schurz stated, "I ordered General Schimmelfennig . . . to advance briskly through the town, and to deploy on the right of the first corps in two lines. This order was executed with promptness and spirit." With Barlow's orders, Schurz states:

> I had ordered General Barlow to refuse his right wing, that is to place his right brigade, Colonel Gilsa's, a little in the right rear of his other brigade, in order to use it against possible flanking movement by the enemy. But I now noticed that Barlow, be it that he had misunderstood my order, or that he was carried away by the ardor of the conflict, had advanced his whole line and lost connection with my third division on his left, and . . . he had instead of refusing, pushed forward his right brigade, so that it formed a projecting angle with the rest of the line.

Brigadier-General Francis C. Barlow. Barlow was only twenty-nine at Gettysburg and was loathed by his men as much he despised them. Barlow had no military experience before the war. Educated at Harvard, he had practiced law in Manhattan, but within five days of the fall of Fort Sumter had abandoned his wife of one day to enlist as a private. By the Peninsular campaign of 1862 he was the colonel commanding the 61st New York He saw action at Seven Pines and at Glendale during the Seven Days Battles, where he was conspicuous in leading his regiment in a successful bayonet charge. At Malvern Hill his regiment drove off repeated Rebel assaults. At Antietam he fell with shell fragments in his face and groin and his courage and determined leadership gained him his general's star. His wounds were slow to heal and it was not until April 1863 that Barlow, although still far from fit, assumed command of an XI Corps brigade. At Chancellorsville, where XI Corps was roundly defeated by Jackson's flank attack, Barlow's Brigade had the good fortune to be temporarily attached to III Corps (Sickles) and so avoided the stigma that went with the rout. Shortly afterward Barlow was given command of the 1st Division, XI Corps, which he was to take to Gettysburg.

Barlow was a fighter and a hard disciplinarian with a low opinion of the "Dutchmen" who formed his division: "These Dutch won't fight. Their officers say so and they say so themselves and they ruin all with whom they come into contact." He could be quite brutal in his treatment of his soldiers and had a particular hatred of straggling. Not only did he carry the enlisted man's heavy cavalry saber so that it would hurt when he whacked the backsides of stragglers, but he was known to employ a company of skirmishers with fixed bayonets at the rear of a marching column with orders to drive forward anyone who fell out. His appointment to command this division of German-Americans was in order to stiffen the discipline and fighting ability of the brigades that had run at Chancellorsville. On the march to Gettysburg Barlow had arrested one of his brigade commanders, Von Gilsa, for remaining at Middletown, Maryland, on June 27 until he received orders from his corps commander to move, rather than obeying his divisional commander's order to rejoin his division. However, Barlow, probably sensing serious trouble, reinstated the popular Von Gilsa before reaching Gettysburg. The mutual hostility between commander and commanded is neatly summed up by a soldier in Von Gilsa's Brigade who wrote, "With . . . Barlow banished to the Antipodes, our happiness would have been complete." And, "As a taskmaster he had no equal. The prospect of speedy deliverance from the odious yoke of Billy Barlow filled every heart with joy." They were delivered from his yoke when he fell seriously wounded and was captured on the first day of the battle – no doubt the cause for celebration by many.

Barlow was a gangling, slightly built man with a clean-shaven, boyish face – a rare sight in either army. He dressed with no apparent regard for the military code, often wearing a bright red, checked lumberjack's shirt under an unbuttoned uniform jacket.

His appearance, according to one observer, was that of "a highly independent mounted newsboy." Whatever he looked like, there was no disputing his ruthless, driving energy and taste for fighting.

His leadership at Gettysburg revolves around his decision to advance some 650 yards from the line he was supposedly to hold at the alms houses to occupy Blocher's Knoll. Once there, he was undoubtedly out on a limb and once under attack was vulnerable from two directions. In the event, Kryzanowski's Brigade had to be sent forward to plug the gap on Barlow's left, but arrived too late to prevent or delay the collapse of resistance on the knoll – indeed the fighting was over quite quickly once the Rebels closed with the defenders. For this error Barlow has been pilloried. Why did he decide to occupy the knoll? Was it against specific orders, as Schurz implied? Before reaching a judgment the following points need to be considered:

- According to the evidence available, Barlow had only one brief meeting with his corps commander, Schurz, before deploying. This took place as his division was entering Gettysburg. The two spoke at the intersection of the Taneytown and Emmitsburg Roads, before Schurz hastened north to complete the deployment of Schimmelfennig's Division. If that was the last occasion they met, it must have been then that Schurz told Barlow to refuse his right wing – that is, to place his right brigade, Von Gilsa's, a little in the right rear of his other brigade, in order to use it against possible flanking movement by the enemy. One wonders how, without having seen the ground, Schurz could be so specific that Barlow's right wing must be refused and that he must use Von Gilsa's Brigade for this purpose. There seems to be a whiff of hindsight in this statement.
- The overall commander on the field, Howard, rode north with Barlow to reconnoiter the positions of both his corps personally and he assuredly discussed the developing situation with the divisional commander. They were shelled from Oak Hill as they came north of the town. Howard, in his report, said that he rode to the knoll itself, but this can be discounted as Rebel skirmishers still occupied it. With enemy now on Oak Hill, any thought of seizing it was abandoned. According to Howard, "as soon as I heard of the approach of Ewell and saw that nothing could prevent the turning of my right flank if Barlow advanced the order [to seize Oak Hill] was countermanded." Did Howard countermand the order before leaving Barlow or was he told by courier later? It is uncertain, as they probably parted company sometime between 1:30 and 2:00 p.m. just as the noon lull was ending.
- Barlow disliked his position by the alms houses. To him the higher ground of the knoll cried out to be occupied. Rebel skirmishers were already in possession and he was worried that they would be followed by infantry and, of even more concern, guns. Enemy guns on the knoll would make his present position untenable – or so he thought. If he looked to his immediate left he saw Kryzanowski's men still in double column of companies a mere 250 yards away. Why were they still in that formation and vulnerable to artillery fire? Were they about to deploy and advance? Did Barlow know they formed a second line and the reserve after Amsberg's Brigade had deployed forward between the Mummasburg and Carlisle Roads? He would also have seen Rebel infantry moving east from the base of Oak Ridge (Doles's Brigade) and the battle flaring up as O'Neal attacked south from Oak Hill. There is a possibility that Barlow saw the taking of the knoll as an essential step, not only to deny it to the Rebels, but as a jump-off point to attack the enemy's left flank and as a better place from which to dominate the Harrisburg Road, from which direction he knew more Rebels were expected, and the bridge over the Rock Creek, itself an obstacle in places with banks that Early described as "abrupt and rugged." Very soon after his division arrived, Barlow dispatched Von Gilsa to drive away the enemy skirmishers and occupy the knoll.
- Afterwards Barlow, understandably, maintained he had done the right thing in advancing his division. In writing to his mother he said, "On arriving in the town Gen. Schurz ordered me to go through the town, form on the right of the 3rd Division (which was just preceding us) and engage the enemy. I went through and formed as directed." In later years none of Barlow's seniors at the time actually claimed that he disobeyed orders. Howard later stated that he "left Barlow to complete his march and deployment near the upper waters of Rock Creek." This could imply he expected Barlow to advance beyond the alms houses. In another account Howard described XI Corps' deployment extending "eastward over to, and beyond. Rock Creek." There was nothing to say this was not what was required. Even Schurz only said Barlow had "misunderstood" his order and "advanced his whole line;" it is possible the latter phrase could mean he (Barlow) should have advanced only one brigade as Schimmelfennig had done – which is exactly what he did initially.

There is little doubt that Barlow's advancing to the knoll opened up a good attacking opportunity for first Gordon's and then Doles's Brigades, but this was exacerbated by Kryzanowski not advancing to support sooner. We can never be sure that Barlow was disobeying his orders, whether the orders were clear or whether they were genuinely misunderstood. However, there is a reasonable argument that what he did was understandable in the circumstances at the time, although in the event the decision was an error.

Plans and orders
See Map 35.

Outline of events
See Maps 35 and 36.

Casualties
The losses of both sides in the action on Blocher's Knoll are, as usual, difficult to estimate. However, with the Confederates neither Gordon's nor Doles's Brigades were seriously engaged again. Gordon later wrote in his report, "the movements [of his brigade] during the succeeding days of the battle (July 2 and 3) I do not consider of sufficient importance to mention." Private Henry Thomas, 4th Georgia, Doles's Brigade, recalled, "we were not actually engaged again, though continually under annoying fire." Therefore it is reasonable to assume that the casualties of the regiments involved in the attack (the 26th Georgia was held back) for the whole battle were virtually all incurred on July 1 (including Doles's driving back Kryzanowski's Brigade).

Union losses were more complex. In Von Gilsa's Brigade, the 41st New York was not present, and in Ames's Brigade 100 men of the 75th Ohio were detached. Additionally, both brigades fought again on Cemetery Hill the following day. During the fight for Blocher's Knoll all Union regiments lost, then some were killed and many captured during the chaotic retreat through Gettysburg. In the tables below, a fifth of total Union losses have been omitted but all prisoners are assumed to have been taken on July 1.

Taking account of the above, the estimates of losses during the struggle for Blocher's Knoll and the subsequent retreat of Barlow's Division to Cemetery Hill are as given below:

Confederate Unit	Strength	Blocher's Knoll loss	%	PoWs	%
38th Georgia	341	133	39		
61st Georgia	288	111	38		
13th Georgia	312	137	44		
31st Georgia	252	65	26		
60th Georgia	299	59	20		
Gordon's Brigade	**1,492**	**505**	**34**		
12th Georgia	327	53	16		
4th Georgia	341	53	15		
44th Georgia	364	75	21		
21st Georgia	287	38	13		
Doles's Brigade	**1319**	**219**	**17**		
Total engaged	**2,811**	**724**	**26**		
Union					
54th New York	189	82	43	48	58
153rd Pennsylvania	499	169	34	46	27
68th New York	232	111	48	67	60
Von Gilsa's Brigade	**920**	**362**	**39**	**161**	**45**
17th Connecticut	386	163	42	96	59
25th Ohio	220	147	69	75	51
75th Ohio	169	149	55	96	64
107th Ohio	458	169	37	77	45
Ames's Brigade	**1,233**	**628**	**47**	**344**	**55**
Barlow's Division	**2,253**	**990 (say 1,000)**	**44**	**505**	**51**

- In estimating these losses the initial strengths, total loss and prisoner figures have been taken from Busey and Martin's *Regimental Strengths and Losses at Gettysburg*.
- Doles's Brigade lost comparatively few men in its fight with the Blocher's Knoll defenders, as the total of 219 includes those lost in driving back Kryzanowski. Gordon's Brigade lost a third of its strength in taking the knoll, with Barlow's Division losing about 1,000, or 44 percent of those engaged, of which half were prisoners taken on the knoll or in the town a little later.

Comments

- The importance of subordinate commanders having clear and unambiguous orders is illustrated by the Blocher's Knoll action. According to Barlow, he did as directed; according to Schurz, Barlow misunderstood his instructions and advanced his *whole* division. According to Howard, he left Barlow to complete his deployment beyond Rock Creek. Nobody seemed clear about what exactly Barlow was to do with his division, where he was to deploy once the occupation of Oak Hill was seen to be impossible. All these generals knew that more Rebels were expected from the northeast. The most telling argument for a misunderstanding and poor communication between senior commanders is that none of them blamed Barlow for outright disobedience to orders, even when writing about the action years later.
- Nevertheless, Barlow's occupation of the knoll turned out to be a mistake. His troops formed a salient on the exposed right flank of the Union line and thus were very vulnerable to attack on either side, or to outflanking – which is what happened. What Barlow did on July 1 was to be repeated on a far larger scale the next day when Sickles advanced his entire corps threequarters of a mile in front of the main Union line. Unlike Barlow, there was to be no doubt that Sickles had disobeyed orders.
- This comparatively smallscale engagement illustrates how effective are simultaneous attacks from different directions, even if they are frontal ones. Unless the defenders are supported (Kryzanowski was too late), they are usually crushed, outflanked and defeated.

THE LATE AFTERNOON AND EARLY EVENING

The late afternoon and early evening of July 1 saw the defeated Union I and XI Corps chased through Gettysburg by the victorious Rebels but able to rally on Cemetery Hill, where Howard had placed Von Steinwehr's Division on arrival earlier in the afternoon. The outline of these events and the detailed defensive positions are shown on Maps 38 and 39. The approximate situation of both armies on the field at around 8:00 p.m. is shown on Map 40.

CONTROVERSY

The Rebels' Failure to Take Cemetery and Culp's Hills

Among the numerous controversies that resulted from the fighting on July 1, one stands out as being of critical importance to the overall conduct of the battle for the next two days. It has generated arguments and counterarguments by participants and historians ever since. It is the failure of the Confederates to take either Cemetery Hill or Culp's Hill before dark – that is, by just after 8:00 p.m. Had they done so, the subsequent fighting would almost assuredly not have been at Gettysburg. This alleged failure to reap the full reward of success on Day One resulted in a "blame game" down the years that has continued to the present day. The controversy has revolved around whether Lee or Ewell, or both, were at fault and to what degree – the assumption being that had a coordinated attack been launched during the period 4:30–7:00 p.m. it would have succeeded. This is not necessarily a sound assumption. To reach a conclusion on this issue, the decisions of relevant commanders on both sides are explained briefly below, as nearly as possible on the basis of the situation at the time as they knew it.

Early

As his leading brigades chased XI Corps through the town, Early summoned "Extra Billy" Smith's Brigade, which had been in reserve, to rejoin the division, only to learn that Smith had moved to block the York Road as a large enemy force was approaching from that direction. Early was initially disbelieving and again sent for Smith to rejoin, only to have a courier gallop up to say that a

The 134th New York Infantry at the Kuhn Brickyard

This regiment, commanded by Lieutenant-Colonel Allan H. Jackson, was 400 strong when it was rushed, as part of Colonel Charles Coster's Brigade, to try to halt the victorious Rebels sweeping into the town from the north. Until then it had spent the afternoon as part of XI Corps' reserve on Cemetery Hill. There were four regiments in the brigade as it double-quicked up Stratton Street, but for some inexplicable reason Coster left the 300 men of the 73rd Pennsylvania Infantry at the railroad depot, thus reducing his force to some 924 men, of whom the untested 134th made up nearly half; in addition, fifty men from each regiment were detached and did not arrive until the following morning.

The brigade was ordered by Schurz to position itself in the John Kuhn Brickyard on the northeastern edge of the town. It deployed its three regiments in a line about 200 yards long behind a post and rail fence. On the left, with its left flank on Stratton Street, was the 27th Pennsylvania; in the center the 154th New York; and on the right the 134th, which thus became the right flank of the entire army. This regiment was bent back so that it faced northeast as the enemy advance threatened that flank. This was not the only problem; the position did not have a good field of fire, as rising ground on the left ran across much of the regiment's front. There was no time to find any alternative. Private Charles McKay of the 154th New York described the scene:

> I shall always remember how the Confederate line of battle looked as it came into full view and started down towards us. It seemed as though they had a battle flag every few rods . . . the men were told to reserve fire until the enemy were close enough to make our volley effective.

The two Rebel brigades belonged to Avery and Hays, with a combined strength of at least 2,400 men. A desperate fight ensued as the overwhelming numbers of Rebels closed in. The 134th were charged in front by the 21st North Carolina, while the 57th North Carolina swept round its exposed right flank so that the regiment was bent back with the right-hand companies almost facing the rear. Sergeant John Wellman of the 154th recalled how he saw the 134th "being doubled up and broken." Coster's order to retire was not initially received by the 134th on the right. According to its commander, Lieutenant-Colonel Jackson, "I was on the extreme right flank and did not receive the order till late; my wing suffered the most in consequence."

Once ordered to retreat there was a desperate scramble to get away through the clogged streets of the town. Corporal Robert O. Seaman of Company H and Sergeant John Carroll of Company B carried the colors of the 134th that day. Seaman was badly wounded in the right arm and Carroll took the colors; however, soon afterward he collapsed, shot through both legs. An officer of the 154th saved the national color while Carroll tore the silk regimental color from its staff and wrapped it round his body under his uniform before being captured. Many men were taken prisoner, although some found refuge. Sergeant Arthur W. De Goyler of Company H later wrote:

> I ran until I came to the foot of Main Street, where there is a large square. Here the bullets were flying like hail and the street was blocked up with men, artillery, ambulances and horses, so I ran into a yard and went into the house and sat down, as I was very tired and overheated. In the house were a good many of our wounded boys of the 134th. In a few minutes a rebel cavalryman [unlikely; possibly mistaken] came to the door and ordered all who were not wounded to come out. Just then the lady who lived in the house came into the room. Well, she told me to come with her, and with three others she took us upstairs and hid us away.

The men were reunited with their comrades on July 4. Lieutenant-Colonel Jackson and Private Levi More of Company C hid in the loft over the kitchen of a Mrs Henry Meals for two days and nights before being able to get back to Union lines.

This fight cost the 134th dearly. According to Henry F. Teller in a letter home, published in the *Evening Star and Times* dated July 10, 1863, only five officers and twenty-seven men mustered on Cemetery Hill that evening. They were amalgamated with the 154th, which had also been crippled, although the strength of the brigade picked up again slightly the next morning when the fifty soldiers from each regiment who had missed the fight returned.

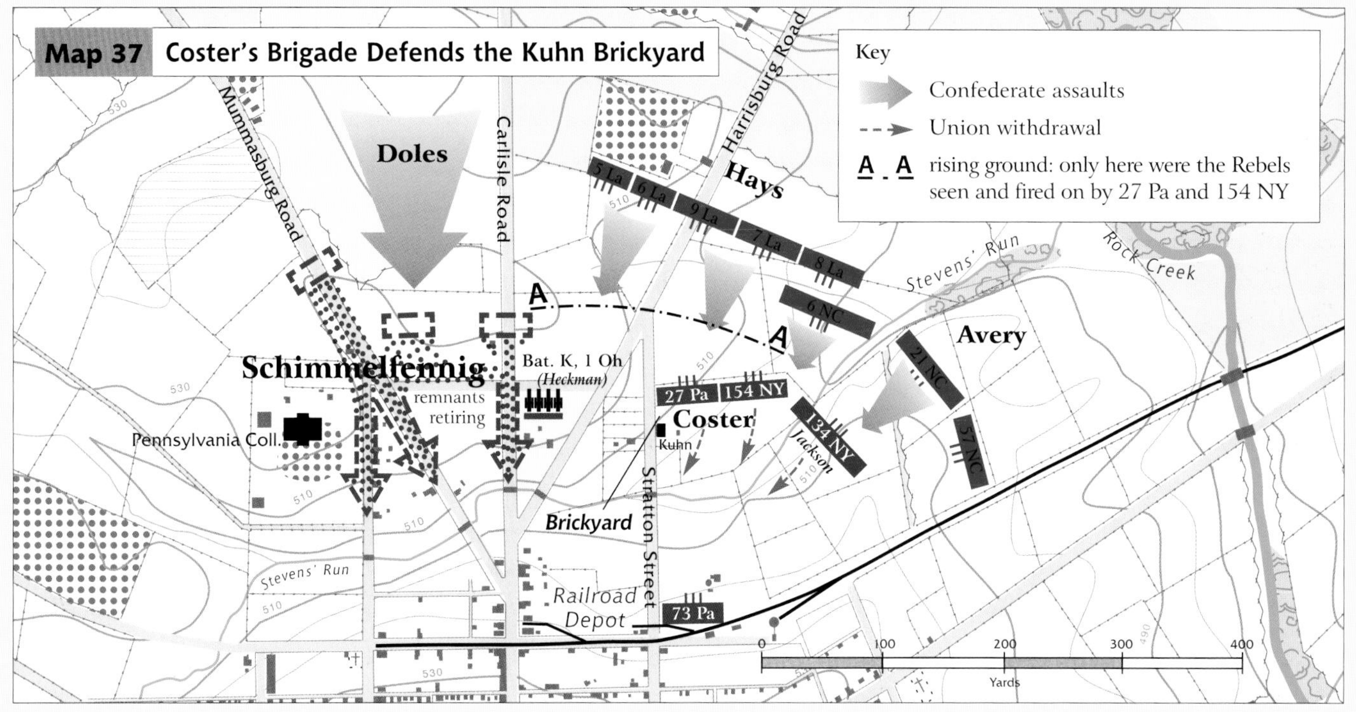

Notes

• The Union lines north and west of Gettysburg began collapsing around 3:30 p.m. XI Corps in the north went first; its retreat was more precipitate and more disorganized than that of I Corps, which was able to put up a more effective resistance along Seminary Ridge. However, once the town was reached, chaos reigned as units intermingled, officers lost control and the pursuing Rebels had a field day taking prisoners (over 3,500 for the day) before the survivors managed to regroup on Cemetery Hill.

• The attacks that finally brought the Confederates victory took place more or less simultaneously (although this was much more accidental than planned) within 30–40 minutes of each other. They began at about 3:30 p.m. with the loss of Blocher's Knoll (**A**) to Early (not depicted on Map 38), assisted by Doles's Brigade from Rodes' Division, and the third and successful assault by Daniel's Brigade on Cutler's troops in Shead's Wood (**A**). Within about 15–20 minutes Early and Doles followed up and pushed back Kryzanowski's belated attempt to support Barlow (**B**). Early then drove back Ames (who had taken over when Barlow was wounded and captured) from the alms house area (**B**), while further west Ramseur's Brigade had finally forced Paul off the Oak Ridge. By 4:00 p.m. Pender's Division was launched against strong Yankee resistance on Seminary Ridge, which, after a stiff fight, forced them back into the town. At much the same time Coster's Brigade, which had been rushed by Howard from Cemetery Hill, was putting up a last-ditch stand at the Kuhn brickyard on the northern outskirts of the town (**C**).

• Between about 4:00 p.m. and 4:30 p.m. Gettysburg was filled with Union troops (**D**), wounded and otherwise, trying to escape the yelling Rebels who poured in from the north and west.

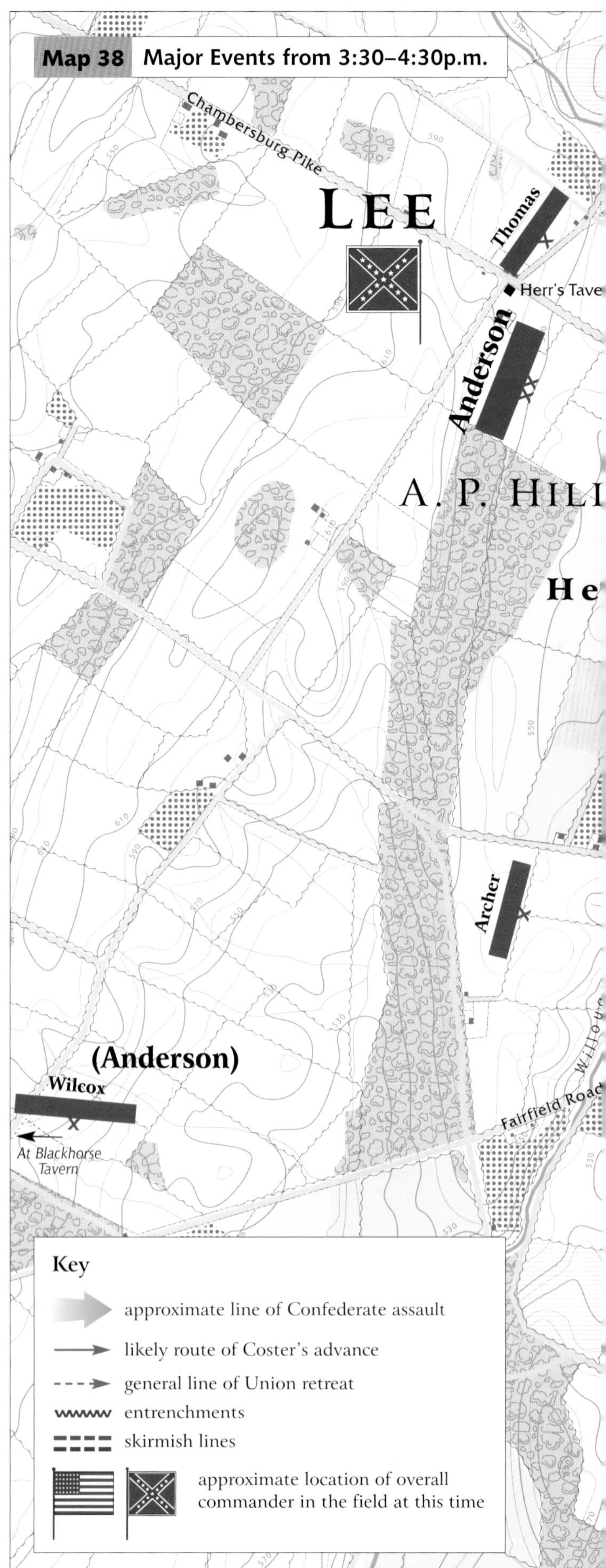

Brigadier-General Alexander Schimmelfennig in Hiding

Schimmelfennig was chased through Gettysburg town on July 1 after his division (3rd Division, XI Corps) had fallen back and became desperately involved in trying to avoid capture. His horse was shot and the general clambered over a fence into the back yard of Anna Garlach's house, which fronted onto Baltimore Street (see Map 23). However, Baltimore Street was swarming with Rebels, so he ducked down under a wooden culvert in Mrs. Garlach's yard behind the house. That night he crawled out and made himself a more comfortable hiding place between two swill barrels, a woodshed and a pile of timber. There he remained, undiscovered, throughout the entire battle, given occasional sustenance by Mrs. Garlach, who brought him milk and bread when she pretended to feed her pigs. It was not safe for him to emerge until July 4. Mrs. Garlach later described the incident:

> There was an old water course in our yard at the time, now converted into a sewer, and for twelve feet from the street [was] covered with a wooden culvert and General Schimmelfennig hurriedly crawled out of sight under this culvert . . .
>
> He remained in there until after dark . . . On the second day mother made a pretense of going to the swill barrel to empty a bucket. In the bucket however was water and a piece of bread and instead of these going into the barrel they went to the general in hiding . . .
>
> General Schimmelfennig was in hiding from the evening of the first day to the morning of July 4th . . . At the fence was a number of his own men. They thought he had been killed and when they saw him they went wild with delight.

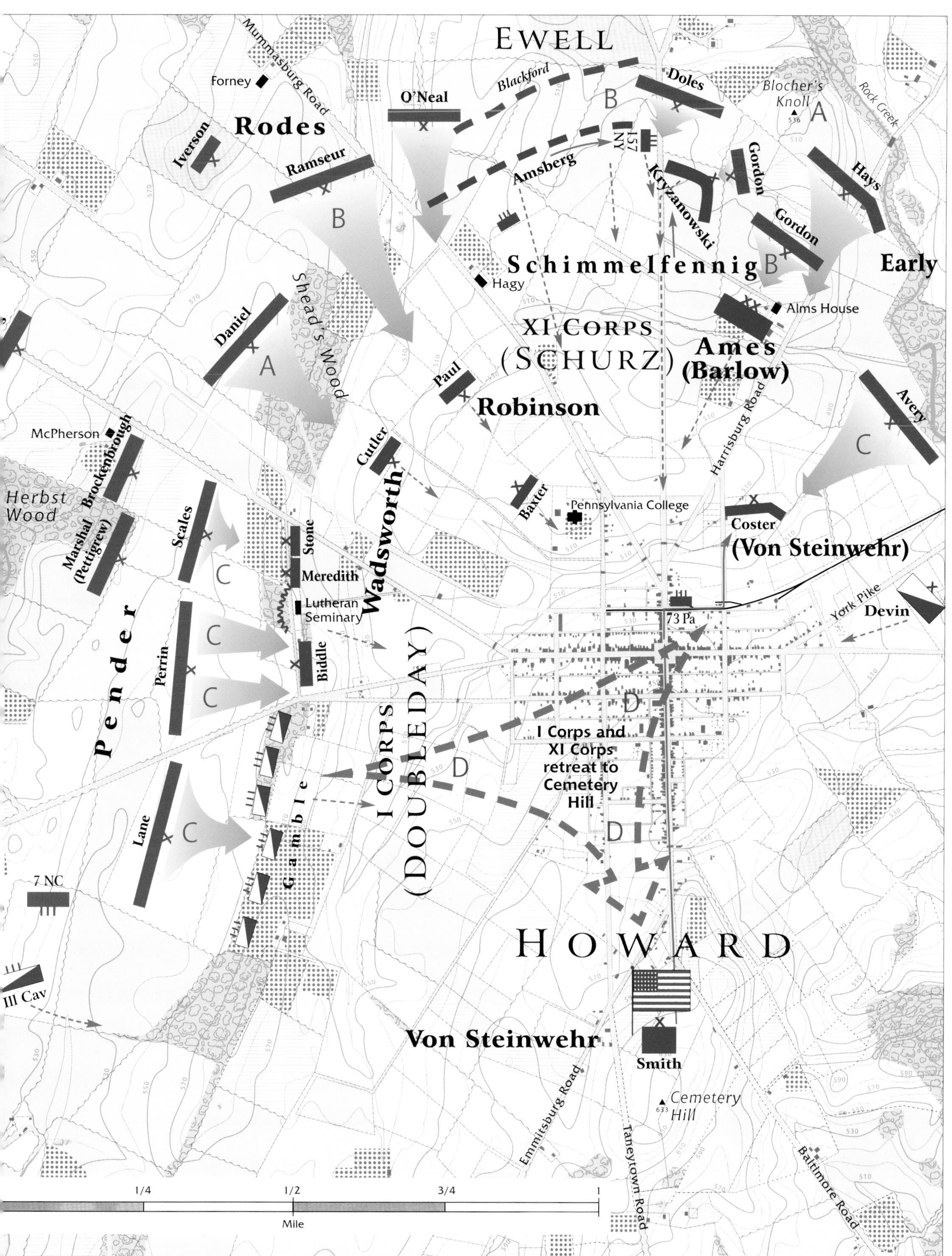
EWELL
Mummasburg Road
Forney
Rodes
O'Neal
Blackford
Doles
Blocher's Knoll
536
Rock Creek
Iverson
Ramseur
Amsberg
157 NY
Kryzanowski
Gordon
Hays
Gordon
Early
Schimmelfennig
Hagy
Alms House
Daniel
Shead's Wood
XI CORPS
(SCHURZ)
Ames
(Barlow)
Paul
Robinson
Harrisburg Road
Avery
McPherson
Brockenbrough
Cutler
Wadsworth
Baxter
Pennsylvania College
Herbst Wood
Marshal (Pettigrew)
Scales
Stone
Meredith
Lutheran Seminary
Coster
(Von Steinwehr)
York Pike
Devin
73 Pa
Pender
Perrin
Biddle
I CORPS
(DOUBLEDAY)
I Corps and XI Corps retreat to Cemetery Hill
Lane
Gamble
7 NC
HOWARD
Ill Cav
Von Steinwehr
Smith
Cemetery Hill
633
Emmitsburg Road
Taneytown Road
Baltimore Road
1/4
1/2
3/4
1
Mile

Union force of infantry, artillery and cavalry was advancing and threatening the left flank and rear of the division.

Decision. Early, despite still being skeptical, ordered Gordon to take his brigade to the York Pike and remain there, assuming command of Smith's Brigade as well as his own. Thus Early would have only two brigades (Hays and Avery) in Gettysburg. He then joined Ewell in the town square shortly before 5:00 p.m.

Ewell

Ewell, now accompanied by Early, rode south to the edge of town to observe the enemy situation. Hundreds of his own soldiers were milling about in every street, wounded were being carried into buildings, some firing was continuing on the southern outskirts and hundreds of Yankee prisoners were being herded to the rear. Units were intermingled and the impression was one of general confusion. Ewell knew he had two of his divisions, Rodes' and Early's, to hand and Johnson's about an hour's march away up the Chambersburg Pike. He knew that Rodes had suffered severely in the afternoon's fighting, Early less so, and Johnson not at all. However, both Rodes' and Early's men were extremely tired after much marching and fighting, and it would take some time for them to regroup and reorganize themselves. Nevertheless, Ewell was pleased with what

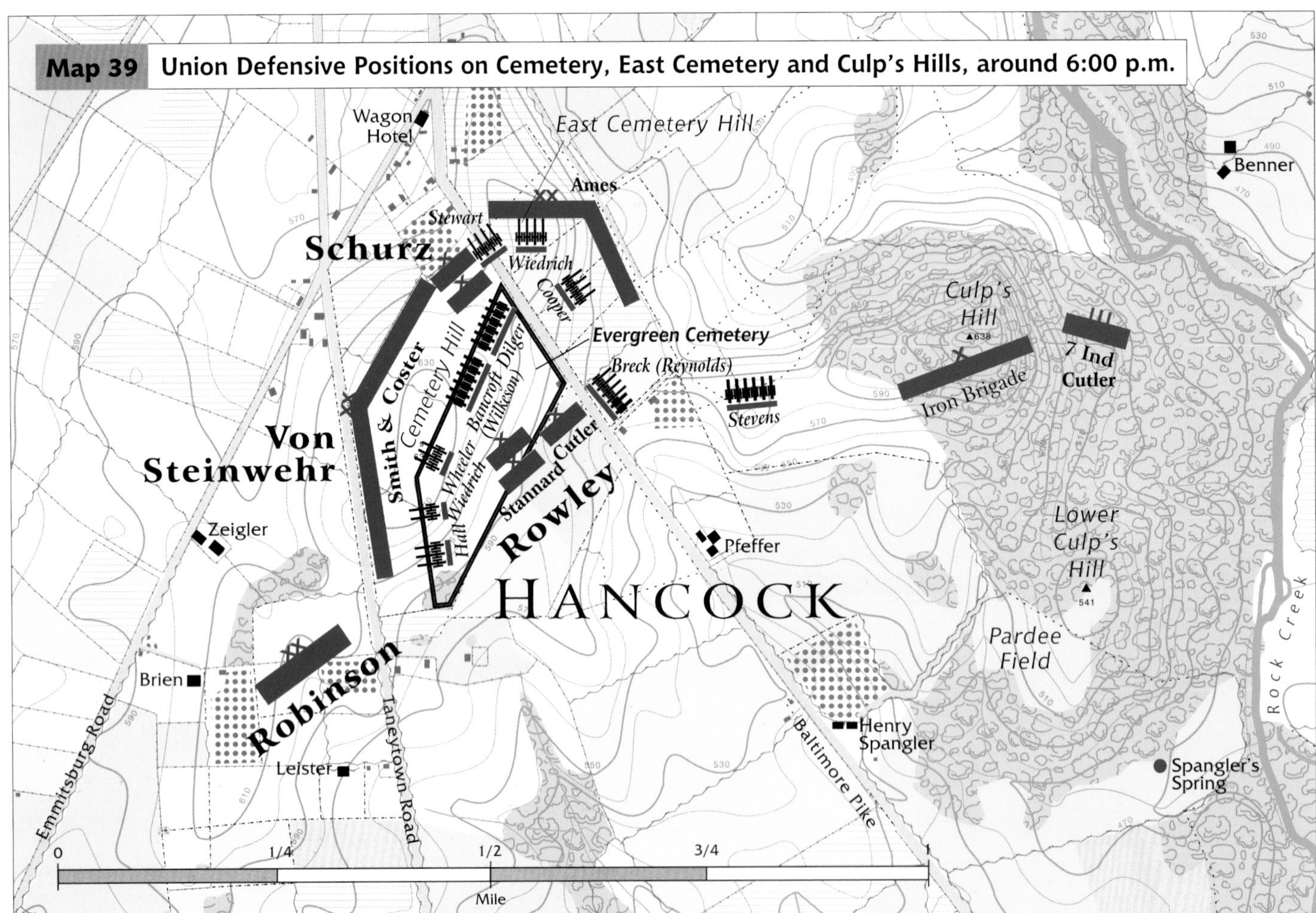

Notes

• By around 6:00 p.m. the Union defenses on Cemetery and Culp's Hills had been consolidated and some reinforcements had arrived, the largest being Stannard's Brigade (Rowley's Division) of nearly 2,000 men. In addition, the 7th Indiana, with some 375 men who had been guarding the trains at Emmitsburg, rejoined Cutler's Brigade, but was sent to support the Iron Brigade on Culp's Hill. Some 7,000 infantrymen were present.

• Despite these reinforcements, the strength of the position rested with the artillery rather than the infantry. During the day's fighting I Corps' artillery battalion, under Col. Charles Wainwright, had lost seven of his 28 guns, while XI Corps' artillery had lost three of its pieces. There were a total of 43 serviceable guns concentrated on Cemetery Hill, on which Stevens' Battery had been positioned on a small knoll (which now bears his name) on the ridge linking Cemetery Hill to Culp's Hill. The guns were deployed as listed at right:

East Cemetery Hill – Col. Wainwright
Stewart 4 × Napoleons
Wiedrich 4 × rifles (2 rifles were deployed in the Cemetery)
Cooper 4 × rifles
Breck (Reynolds) 4 × rifles, 1 × Napoleon
Stevens 6 × Napoleons – he had a good flanking shot at Rebels attacking East Cemetery Hill from his position on his knoll

Cemetery Hill – Maj. Osborn
Dilger 6 × Napoleons
Bancroft (Wilkeson) 6 × Napoleons
Wheeler 3 × rifles
Hall 3 × rifles
Wiedrich 2 × rifles

All these 20 guns were positioned inside the actual cemetery and, like Wainwright's, were able to fire over the heads of the infantry deployed lower down the slope.

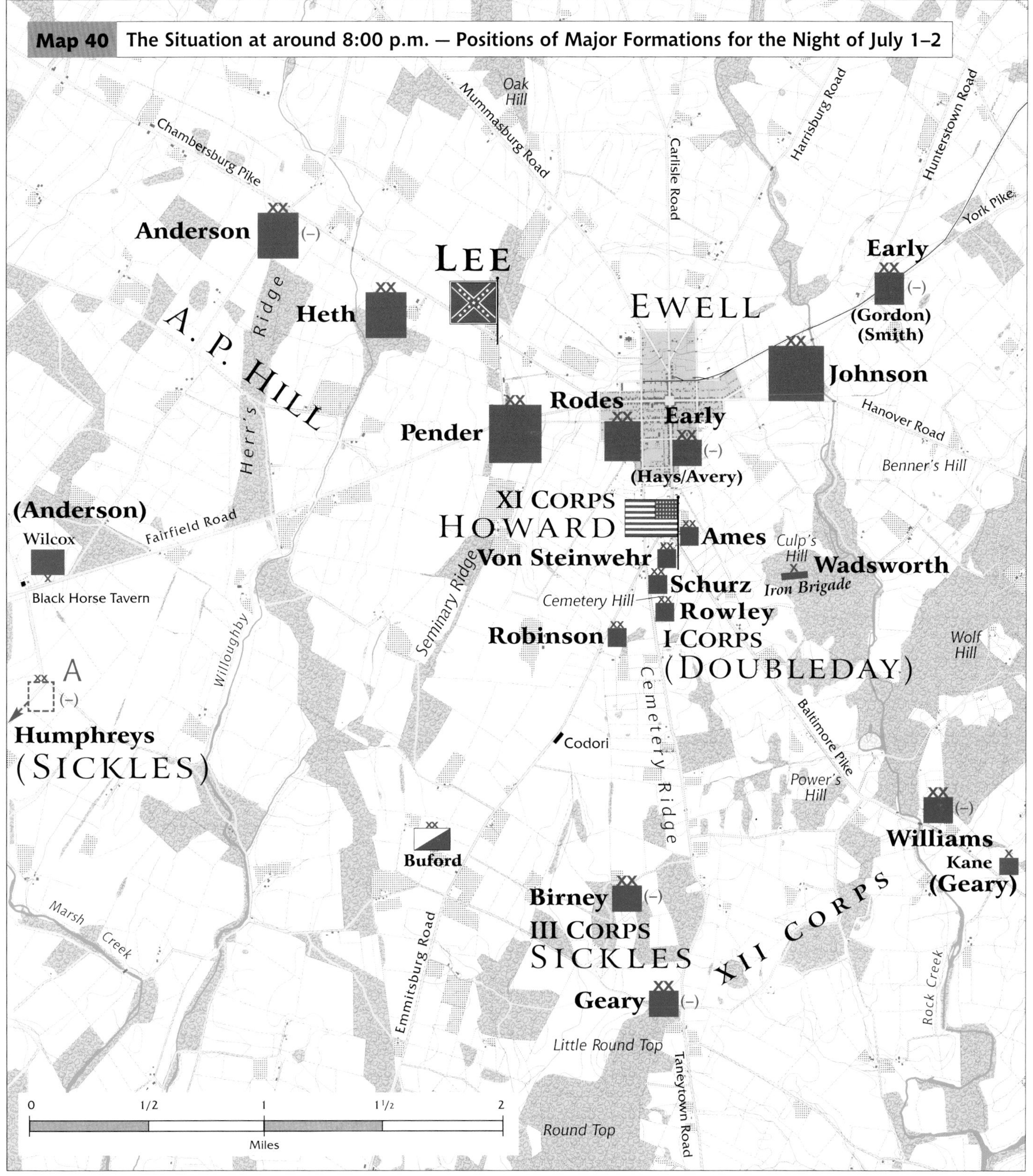

Notes

• This map shows the approximate situation at around 8:00 p.m., as darkness fell and fighting ceased. Both sides had suffered severe losses during the day. As always, it is impossible to be precise but research points to a total loss for the A.N.V. of around 7,000, with the A.P. suffering about 9,000, including many prisoners.

• Both sides had, by this time, brought further formations to, or near to, the battlefield. The size of the symbols on the map shows the relative size of the formation in very general terms. The (–) sign indicates that the formation at that location is incomplete – for example, both the divisions of Birney and Williams had a brigade absent at that time. **A** indicates that Humphreys advanced to that location but withdrew after meeting Confederates.

• Taking into account the estimated casualties, the approximate strength of the two forces is Confederates 34,000 and Union 26,300.

he had achieved. Although he had not followed instructions to avoid bringing on a major battle, he had, almost certainly rightly, taken the opportunity to attack the enemy in the flank – it had been the only sensible option, irrespective of Lee's orders. The Yankees had suffered heavily and were now disorganized and in retreat, although they seemed to be rallying on the high ground overlooking the town in the south, where artillery was also visible. (Rodes was later to describe it as "a formidable line of infantry and artillery immediately in my front.") The hill occupied by the Yankees (Cemetery Hill) was steep-sided and thus a naturally strong defensive position. However, Ewell was professional enough to know that a retreating enemy should be followed up relentlessly and not allowed to rally. To do so required time to reorganize his brigades and move them to suitable jump-off points outside the town. He would need to locate gun positions (there were none in the town) that could bring fire to bear on the Yankee guns and infantry positions. To succeed, an attack required a major effort and, to be sure of success, support from Hill's Corps on his right.

Decision. Ewell resolved, after consulting Early, to warn both him and Rodes to regroup their commands and prepare for another attack. He sent Lee's courier, Lieutenant James P. Smith, who was present with Ewell, back to Lee with the message that both Ewell and Early wanted to press ahead and take Cemetery Hill, but that to do so would require strong support on their right – from Hill's Corps. Shortly after this, Major Walter H. Taylor rode up with Lee's verbal message which, according to Lee's report, informed Ewell "to carry the hill occupied by the enemy, if he found it practical, but to avoid a general engagement until the arrival of the other divisions of the army . . ." – another of Lee's infamous discretionary orders that passed the buck back to Ewell.

Hancock Reports to Meade

Working with Howard, Major-General Hancock rallied the remnants of I and XI Corps on Cemetery Hill. At 5:25 p.m. Hancock scribbled a short report on the situation for Meade at Taneytown.

> GENERAL: When I arrived here an hour since, I found that our troops had given up the front of Gettysburg and the town. We have now taken up a position in the cemetery, and cannot be well taken. It is a position, however, easily turned. Slocum is now coming on the ground and is taking a position to the right which will protect the right. But we have, as yet, no troops on the left, the Third Corps not having yet reported; but I suppose that it is marching up. If so, its flank march will in a degree protect our left flank. In the meantime Gibbon had better march on so as to take position on our right or left, to our rear, as may be necessary, in some commanding position. General (Gibbon) will see this dispatch. The battle is quiet now. I think we will be all right until night. I have sent all the trains back. When night comes it can be told better what had best to be done. I think we can retire; if not we can fight here, as the ground appears not unfavorable with good troops. I will communicate in a few moments with General Slocum, and transfer the command to him. Howard says that Doubleday's command gave way. General Warren is here.

This last remark about Doubleday was untrue, but Meade disliked Doubleday intensely and this caused him to appoint Major-General John Newton to take command of I Corps with Doubleday, who had done well that day, reverting to his division – much to his annoyance.

Lee

At about the same time that Ewell was riding through Gettysburg, Lee was on Seminary Ridge considering his next move, still missing Stuart, still in half a mind to press his advantage but still hesitant to commit more troops without Longstreet's Corps on the field . . . There at around 5:00 p.m. Longstreet joined him and both carefully observed the enemy positions on Cemetery Hill. It was there that Lieutenant Smith found them and delivered Ewell's message that he wanted to attack but needed support on his right. According to Smith, Lee asked Longstreet if any of his troops were available but his response was "indefinite and non-committal." In any event, the leading division of Longstreet's Corps (McLaws) was several miles away up the Chambersburg Road, stuck behind Johnson's slow-moving wagon train, and could not have arrived before dark. There were, however, a substantial number of unblooded or comparatively unblooded troops available much nearer, all belonging to Hill's Corps. These were the 3,000 men of Thomas's Brigade (Pender), which had seen no action, and Lane's Brigade (also Pender), which had suffered only lightly. More importantly, by 5:00 p.m. Hill had over 7,000 men of Anderson's Division halted a mere 1.5 miles from Gettysburg beside the Chambersburg Pike. However, Lee had taken direct control of this division, perhaps because Hill was feeling ill that day and had not shown much sensible initiative so far, and had personally told Anderson, who had ridden forward to find out why he was halted, to remain where he was as Lee's only reserve.

It was while Longstreet was with Lee at this time that he assertively put forward the suggestion that Lee's best option was to move around the Union left and take up a strong defensive position between Meade and Washington, thus forcing him to attack. This, according to Longstreet, was the underlying strategy of the whole campaign – advance into enemy territory, threaten Washington or Baltimore, choose a defensive position and force the enemy to attack. What Longstreet wanted was another Fredericksburg. Lee was unconvinced and responded, "If the enemy is there tomorrow we must attack him." According to Longstreet's later correspondence on the subject, he responded, "If he is there, it will be because he is anxious that we should attack him . . ." There is no doubt Longstreet was most unhappy with the prospect of attacking a position he deemed "very formidable" – the words he used later that evening when discussing it with Colonel Fremantle, the British observer at his headquarters. Lee, it seemed, would have liked to take Cemetery Hill that evening but was fast becoming more inclined to think it too risky and favor waiting till the following day. This is evident from the somewhat half-hearted decision he then made.

Decision. Lee decided not to push Hill, who protested that his men were too exhausted and had suffered too much, into supporting Ewell, and to keep Anderson's Division in reserve. Not even the guns of Garnett's and Poague's battalions, which had been brought forward onto Seminary Ridge, were brought into action. Smith was sent back to Ewell with the message that no support would be available but that he should take the hill if possible and that he, Lee, would ride over to see him shortly. Ewell would have to manage on his own.

Ewell

Ewell was now aware that any further attacks would have to be made without assistance from Hill. Johnson's Division, with nearly 4,000 men, was approaching Gettysburg but, according to Johnson himself, who had ridden ahead of his men, would not be available for at least an hour – which meant light would be fading. Two brigades were out on the York Pike guarding against an unlikely, but just conceivable, threat against that flank, which left him with only two remaining brigades.

Meanwhile, Ewell had been looking hard at the high hill (Culp's Hill) half a mile east of Cemetery Hill. It dominated Cemetery Hill and appeared unoccupied. Now was the time to take it. Early's two brigades (Hays and Avery) were close at hand for the task and could be relieved when Johnson's Division arrived. Two staff officers were sent to check if the hill was indeed unoccupied. They returned later to say it was clear of the enemy – incorrect: they had somehow missed the remnants of the Iron Brigade, which arrived in the vicinity at that time but were probably hidden by the woods that covered the hill. Early protested strenuously against the proposal that his two brigades move to Culp's Hill. His men were exhausted and had been doing all the hard marching and fighting; it would be unreasonable to advance again – especially as Johnson's men had nearly arrived.

Decision. Ewell decided to do nothing. He considered the difficulties he faced in attacking Cemetery Hill that evening: no support from Hill; insufficient fresh troops; difficulty of positioning artillery to bring fire to bear; the possible threat to his left flank along the York Pike; the formidable slopes of the hill; and the fact that the Union troops appeared well prepared, with considerable artillery support. He used the discretion given him by Lee finally to abandon any thought of taking Cemetery Hill. He also accepted Early's arguments for doing nothing about Culp's Hill until Johnson arrived. When Johnson's men did arrive after skirting the town to the north, the last brigade not until dark, he moved his division eastward along the railroad track and halted just east of the town.

Lee

Lee rode into Gettysburg sometime after 5:30 p.m., possibly nearer 6:00 p.m. There, on the outskirts of the town, he met with Ewell, Early and Rodes, together with a gaggle of staff officers. It was potentially an important conference, as time was getting short if Lee was to insist on doing something about Cemetery Hill. However, Lee had apparently given up this idea, as he accepted the arguments put forward – mostly by Early – against such an attack and in no way censured Ewell for using his discretion not to attack. Lee then, according to Early's later account, wanted Ewell to launch an attack at dawn. Again it was Early who voiced most of the objections, claiming the hill was too steep, the enemy too strong and an offensive would be too costly. Once again Lee appears to have accepted this pessimistic prognosis. But he tried another tack. Perhaps with Longstreet's words still in his head, he suggested that if nothing could usefully be done on this flank it would be better to shift Ewell's Corps tonight back to the right and position it on Seminary Ridge where the rest of the army was concentrating. All his generals present disliked this idea – there were wounded to care for, booty to be collected and above all morale would suffer severely if the troops were forced to abandon Gettysburg and the positions they had won at so high a cost. A frustrated and bewildered Lee gave up.

Decision. Ewell's Corps was to remain where it was. The attack next day would probably be against the Union left, in which case Ewell was to launch a diversionary attack with the discretion of (according to Early) converting it to "a real attack on discovering any disorder or symptoms of giving way on the enemy's part." Lee left to return to his headquarters.

Lee

That night Lee's mind was in something of a turmoil. A night attack was now out of the question: his generals on the left were opposed to attacking at first light; Hill considered his men too exhausted to do anything useful at present; and Longstreet was against attacking here at all, wanting to shift the entire army round the Union left – a major strategic move. It was at this time, after returning from his meeting in Gettysburg, that Lee changed his mind with regard to moving Ewell's Corps back to Seminary Ridge. Colonel Charles Marshall, Lee's assistant military secretary, was sent to convey this order to Ewell. To say this caused consternation at Ewell's headquarters is a considerable understatement – the upshot being that Ewell was lifted into his saddle and strapped on for the 1-mile ride with Colonel Marshall to raise his objections with his commander-in-chief personally. It was a lengthy meeting, at which Ewell is presumed to have argued that if Johnson occupied Culp's Hill then the enemy position on Cemetery Hill would be untenable.

Decision. Lee was persuaded – another change of mind. Ewell's Corps would remain where it was. By the time Ewell returned to his headquarters, July 2 had arrived.

Comments – Ewell

Many Southern supporters and writers, and particularly those seeking to protect Lee's reputation as a general, have castigated Ewell for not following up his initial success by taking Cemetery and Culp's Hills on the evening of July 1. His failure, so the argument goes, was a major cause of the eventual Confederate defeat. Is this a fair judgment? To the present writer, definitely not. Ewell understood the need to follow up a retreating enemy, but he was accustomed to receiving specific orders as to what to do. As divisional commander under Jackson, this was how he had operated; now, as a newly appointed corps commander in a crucial battle with vital decisions to be made quickly, the buck had been passed to him by Lee: Ewell was to use his discretion over whether to attack. This put doubts in his mind. Had he been ordered to attack immediately, he would probably have done so with what he had available – several subordinate commanders, such as Gordon, were surprised that this did not happen.

Ewell had been given a choice. He considered the situation as he knew it at the time: Johnson's Division would probably not arrive in time to participate; the brigades immediately available (Hays and Avery) were tired and disorganized; Rodes had suffered heavily; and although Ewell tended to discount reports of a strong enemy presence on his left, he felt they could not be ignored. Then there was the steepness of Cemetery Hill, with a seemingly strong enemy position on its slopes and summit, and several batteries of guns in support, while his guns were not able to bring fire to bear from the Gettysburg area. The southern outskirts of the town were not a suitable place to form up for an attack, which meant moving east of the town. This would require more time and he needed to have taken the hill before dark (at around 8:00 p.m.). If an offensive was to be mounted quickly, he would have to make an uphill frontal attack against an enemy of unknown strength with tired troops. However, if he could have support from Hill's Corps on his right attacking from the west, then the entire operation would almost certainly succeed. Ewell's request for such support was rejected and he was given the option of attacking or not. Ewell decided that, in the circumstances at the time, Cemetery Hill would not be attacked that evening. Had he done so without support, the odds are that he would have failed.

There are firmer grounds for criticizing Ewell for not occupying Culp's Hill. It clearly dominated Cemetery Hill and appeared unoccupied – indeed it was to be reported as such (erroneously) by the officers who went to look – yet he did not insist it was occupied immediately by some of Early's brigades. At around 7:00 p.m. he told Johnson to occupy the hill if he found it unoccupied. Johnson did no such thing and on being reminded several hours later, sent a reconnoitering party up the hill. The 7th Indiana of Cutler's Brigade, which had been sent to reinforce the Iron Brigade, fired on Johnson's men in the dark, causing several casualties. By then the chance of taking the hill had gone. Ewell failed to make clear to Johnson the importance of securing this dominating feature and then failed to make sure he had at least tried. Although there would have been a fight for Culp's Hill, the Iron Brigade was in no condition to resist a determined attack by superior numbers. Culp's Hill in Rebel hands at the end of July 1 would have dramatically altered the odds in the Confederates' favor and might well have persuaded Hancock (by then in command of the Union forces on the battlefield) to recommend withdrawal to Meade rather than staying to fight.

Comments – Lee

From the moment Lee arrived at around 2:00 p.m. he assumed command of the Rebel forces on the battlefield and as such took responsibility for all major decisions. The latter part of the afternoon and early evening of July 1 was one of the most critical times in the battle, when decisions made would affect the outcome more than at any other time – although neither Lee nor anyone else could know that. It followed that, for Lee in particular, it would be looked upon as possibly the key moment in his military career. By 4:30 p.m. two enemy corps had been sent reeling and there were well over three hours of daylight left for fighting. As Lee was aware, an enemy in retreat must not be allowed time to recover, regroup, reinforce and prepare defensive positions – any reasonable risk was worth taking to ensure the Union forces did not have time to consolidate their positions on Cemetery Hill and the ridge running south from it, as he could see they were in the process of doing. By accident of positioning, coupled with hard fighting by his troops, Lee had achieved on Day One what he had always wanted – to defeat his enemy in detail. The ground was not of his choosing and he was still uncertain of the whereabouts of the remainder of Meade's army, but two of the seven Union corps had been beaten.

Instead of acting with firmness and decisiveness, however, Lee seemed assailed by doubts and indecision. He surely knew the importance of keeping up the momentum of the offensive – he was renowned as an offensive general – and after advancing to Seminary Ridge asked Hill if his two leading divisions could attack Cemetery Hill from the west, the very thing Ewell wanted. Lee had been on the field for several hours and should have known that only Archer's and Davis's Brigades had suffered so severely as to be too weakened to take the offensive again. That left six brigades, one of which had seen no action at all (Thomas). Despite this, Lee meekly accepted Hill's plea that his troops were not up to another attack. If Lee knew the condition and location of Hill's troops, why was he asking their commander if he could take Cemetery Hill – why did he not just tell him to do so?

Then there was the question of Anderson's 7,000 men sitting on their hands in reserve on Herr's Ridge, where Lee had told them to remain. Surely now was the time to bring forward the reserve to reinforce success. With a modicum of good staff work and a sense of urgency these brigades could have stormed Cemetery Hill, perhaps in conjunction with Ewell, before dark. Such an attack launched by 7:30 p.m. would almost certainly have succeeded. Lee seemed either to have forgotten this division or took the conscious decision not to use them, worried that Longstreet's Corps was still a long way off and Anderson might be needed for some unexpected emergency. Whatever the reason, it turned out to be an error of judgment.

Lee had not spoken in person to Ewell since June 10 and did not know him well. Yet when communicating with him at this critical juncture and knowing that he was new to corps command, Lee initially sent Ewell a verbal message telling him to take the hill occupied by the enemy if practical. Perhaps he was so caught up in discussions with Longstreet (who arrived about 5:00 p.m.) on what to do the following day (see also Section Ten) that he relied on a staff officer. Whatever the reason, Lee had once again avoided taking a decision, preferring to hand the responsibility to a subordinate. Hill declined to move; Anderson was available but not called upon; and Ewell would get no support, but was told to take the offensive on his own if he could. At a time that called for decisive leadership, for the issue of clear orders and for the fruits of the Confederate victory so far to be exploited, Lee was content to take counsel of his doubts.

His handling of the Ewell/Early/Rodes meeting was similarly weak. Instead of ordering a dawn attack by Ewell, he merely suggested it and then accepted all the various feeble objections put forward by his generals, presumably on the premise that Johnson would occupy/take Culp's Hill. With that idea abandoned, he again suggested rather than ordered that Ewell's Corps move back to the Seminary Ridge – he was almost certainly thinking of his plan for the next day, perhaps along with Longstreet's hankering for an attack or move round the Union left. The chorus of objections caused him to abandon this idea as well. Later that night he changed his mind and sent instructions that the move of Ewell's Corps would take place. After wasting about an hour arguing with Ewell when he rode over to protest, Lee capitulated again. Ewell would stay where he was and mount a diversionary attack that might develop into something more.

Perhaps it was ill-health that affected Lee's performance on July 1; whatever it was, he reacted to the quickly changing situation with tentativeness and indecision. It was his first experience of dealing with difficult subordinates and he exhibited a worrying inability to stamp his authority on them. Certainly he was lacking information that Stuart could have provided, and he was missing Longstreet's Corps, but when Lee saw his victorious troops pouring through Gettysburg at 4:30 p.m. it opened up a chance that he failed to take, although he had the troops available. To blame Ewell for failing to take Cemetery Hill that evening appears unjustified. Lee was the commander-in-chief; he was on the field; the responsibility was his.

SECTION TEN

The Battle – Day Two

THURSDAY, JULY 2

PROBLEMS AND PLANS

Lee

Lee cannot have got much sleep on the night of July 1 as he wrestled with plans for the coming day. There were a number of key factors that he undoubtedly turned over constantly in his mind during those hours of darkness.

First, Lee wanted to take the offensive. He was an offensive general, and the whole object of the campaign had been to take the offensive with a view to seeking a decisive battle on favorable terms. Now he had the initiative. On July 1 he had soundly defeated two enemy corps; however, during the night they would surely consolidate their strong position on Cemetery Hill and be reinforced – if it was Meade's intention to stand and fight. If his enemy was still there in larger numbers by dawn, then it would surely mean they were there to stay.

What Lee lacked was information on exactly how much of Meade's army was still on the march to Gettysburg, and where they were. Without Stuart and his horsemen he could never be sure. He knew he had faced I and XI Corps and a cavalry division on July 1, and he knew from Johnson's captured courier (presuming Ewell had passed on the information) that V Corps was but 5 miles away and XII Corps was very close. Lee also knew the longer he waited the more men Meade would deploy on the ridgeline ahead of him to the east. This difficulty was compounded by the fact that, although Longstreet was present in person, his corps was not. It would take several hours to get all three corps to hand and several more to get them formed up to attack. There could be no question of a dawn attack by Longstreet's troops, and neither Hill nor Ewell showed much enthusiasm for early attacks on their part. The enemy position was naturally strong and with every hour that passed the Yankees would make it stronger as more units arrived.

Sunrise and Sunset

Because so many activities, movements, marches and attacks were related to sunrise and sunset during the battle, these timings are given here to assist the reader in understanding the significance of when events occurred in relation to how close they were to daylight or darkness.

	June 30	July 1	July 2	July 3	July 4
Twilight begins	04:03	04:03	04:04	04:04	04:05
Sunrise	04:35	04:35	04:36	04:36	04:37
Sunset	19:33	19:33	19:33	19:32	19:32
Twilight ends	20:06	20:06	20:06	20:05	20:05

There was a full moon on June 30, but clouds obscured it on the night of July 1/2 when Meade made his early-morning reconnaissance of his position. The following night, however, had good moonlight.

Another major worry for Lee was the behavior of his corps commanders. He had accepted both Hill's and Ewell's objections to attacking at dawn (or very early on July 2) or, in Ewell's case, moving his command to the right and deploying on Seminary Ridge. He had not made up his mind sufficiently resolutely to overrule them. Then there was Longstreet, his one experienced corps commander, who was set against attacking at Gettysburg and strenuously advocated a strategic move by the whole army round the enemy left.

But the Army of Northern Virginia had never been stronger, had never been so confidant it could trounce any bunch of Yankees. Its morale was sky-high: it had just sent two enemy corps fleeing through Gettysburg and he, Lee, was convinced his soldiers could do anything he asked of them.

With these factors churning over in his mind, we can be fairly sure Lee considered, if only briefly, each of the following four options that night.

- To withdraw back to the South Mountain passes, there to take up a strong defensive position and await, first, the arrival of Stuart and, second, Meade's advancing to attack at a tactical disadvantage. Lee later said he dismissed this possibility as to "withdraw through the mountains with our extensive trains would have been difficult and dangerous." But it was only a matter of turning wagons around and heading back the way they had come – tiresome, yes, time consuming, certainly, but by no means impossible, and once through the South Mountains the wagons would be reasonably secure with the army and the mountains between them and the enemy. Lack of provisions and the ability to forage are sometimes put forward as arguments against this course, but they lack validity as Lee had about a week's supplies available, and foraging parties still roamed the countryside during the battle. Meade would certainly have followed up any retreat and would probably have been compelled by pressure from Washington to attack any position adopted by Lee – it was paramount the Rebels be driven from Northern territory for political as well as military expediency. But the real, overriding reason Lee rejected this option was surely that it meant surrendering the initiative. He was on the offensive, he had just defeated a substantial part of his enemy and to withdraw on July 2 would have had a hugely detrimental effect on his men's morale. To retire, even to turn at bay later, after such a hard-won fight was probably unthinkable.

- To follow Longstreet's advice and maneuver south and then southeast to threaten Washington, take up a defensive position and await attack. This was a strategic not a tactical plan. As we shall see, July 2 did involve attacks on Meade's left, but they were tactical not strategic moves. Longstreet's idea had the theoretical advantage that it would threaten Meade's lifeline, the Baltimore Pike. Meade would probably withdraw. His superiors in Washington would order him back out of the Gettysburg position. At 9:15 p.m. on July 1 part of a signal from Halleck read: "in a strategic view are you not too far east, and may not Lee attempt to turn your left and cut you off from Frederick? Please give your full attention to this suggestion . . ." This is almost exactly the maneuver Longstreet was advocating. The problem was that in the circumstances at the time, it was impractical and highly risky without Stuart's presence. To move the entire army without a strong cavalry screen would be marching blind, while the enemy, with his cavalry, could watch every move and either adjust his position accordingly or launch an attack. It would be impossible to conceal the move, as it would have to be made east of the South Mountains, which were only 6 or 7 miles west of Meade's position. It would be perfectly obvious to Meade what was happening, and the long columns of marching troops and wagon trains would prove a disastrously vulnerable target to attack. Lee would be offering his extended left flank to attack with few, if any, horsemen to protect it. If Meade elected to withdraw and conform to Lee's move, then being on interior lines he could slip back down the Taneytown Road and Baltimore Pike to another good position – as we know, he had one in mind along the Pipe Creek.
- To remain on the defensive in his present location on Seminary Ridge and strengthen the position by pulling Ewell back from Gettysburg and the area to the east of the town. This would shorten his line, make communication between his corps easier and quicker, and present the enemy with a strong position that they would eventually be obliged to attack. This would have been a variation on Longstreet's plan but would have been wholly in keeping with his idea of a strategic offensive linked to a tactical defensive. Such a plan would allow for the grouping of the entire army along Seminary Ridge – it would certainly have had Longstreet's backing. There was no shortage of supplies, as evidenced by the Rebels remaining for another three days on that ground and then successfully withdrawing the trains to the Potomac. The problem with it was that it surrendered the initiative to Meade, something Lee was instinctively loath to do, particularly as he had decisively got the better of him the day before.
- To continue attacking the Army of the Potomac in its present position. To maximize the chances of success against what was obviously a formidable position, the attack would need to be made as early as possible, hopefully before Meade's whole army was up. Lee was certainly inclined to this option on July 1 when discussing with Ewell and Early the possibility of a dawn attack on their front the next day and when he twice sought to bring Ewell back to Seminary Ridge – a move that would have facilitated several options.

By daylight on July 2 Lee had resolved in his mind his earlier and instinctive determination to attack – the other options had been rejected and he was determined to regain the momentum and initiative that had lapsed with the taking of Gettysburg late the previous afternoon. The questions he had to answer were: who was to make the attack, or attacks, and where would they strike? From his subsequent actions it is clear he favored locating and attacking the enemy's left flank. However, no instructions had been disseminated during the night so the issue of orders, the assembly of the troops, any necessary marching to jump-off positions and the deployment of supporting artillery and ammunition wagons still had to take place before any attack could be launched. All these activities take time and require good and speedy communications (aides and couriers dashing around as well as senior commanders consulting), along with a clear understanding by all of what is to happen if lengthy delays are not to be inevitable. The likelihood of an early attack, even a morning attack, depended on Lee's decisions and his instilling a sense of urgency in his subordinates, and on their willing and energetic co-operation. With the above in mind, Lee's actions, decisions, and movements that morning are enumerated below in likely chronological order, with the caveat that the timings can be only approximate but are probably within thirty minutes either way.

4:00–4:30 a.m.

Lee sent Captain Samuel R. Johnston, his engineer staff officer, on a reconnaissance of the Union left (see Map 41). Although he was something of a personal scout for Lee, and in his own words acted as "Reconnoitering Officer" on the general's staff, Johnston was being sent to do a cavalry job as Stuart was still missing – and Lee made no attempt to utilize Jenkins' Brigade, which was by then on the field with Ewell. As Johnston remembered his instructions, they were "to reconnoiter along the enemy's left and return as soon as possible." Hardly specific, but then Johnston was an experienced officer and had carried out many such duties previously. As he later wrote, "he [Lee] wanted me to consider every contingency." Major John J. Clarke, an engineer officer from Longstreet's headquarters, and two or three mounted escorts accompanied Johnston.

Lee also sent Colonel Armistead L. Long in the same direction, but his primary duty as Lee's acting assistant chief of artillery was to examine potential gun positions. He was out on Seminary Ridge at sunrise visiting Hill's positions and then Ewell's. Major Charles S. Venable, one of Lee's A.D.C.s and assistant inspector general, was dispatched to Ewell's headquarters around this time to discuss the possibility of an early attack on the enemy right.

Finally, Brigadier-General William N. Pendleton, chief of artillery, according to his report, rode out to the right accompanied

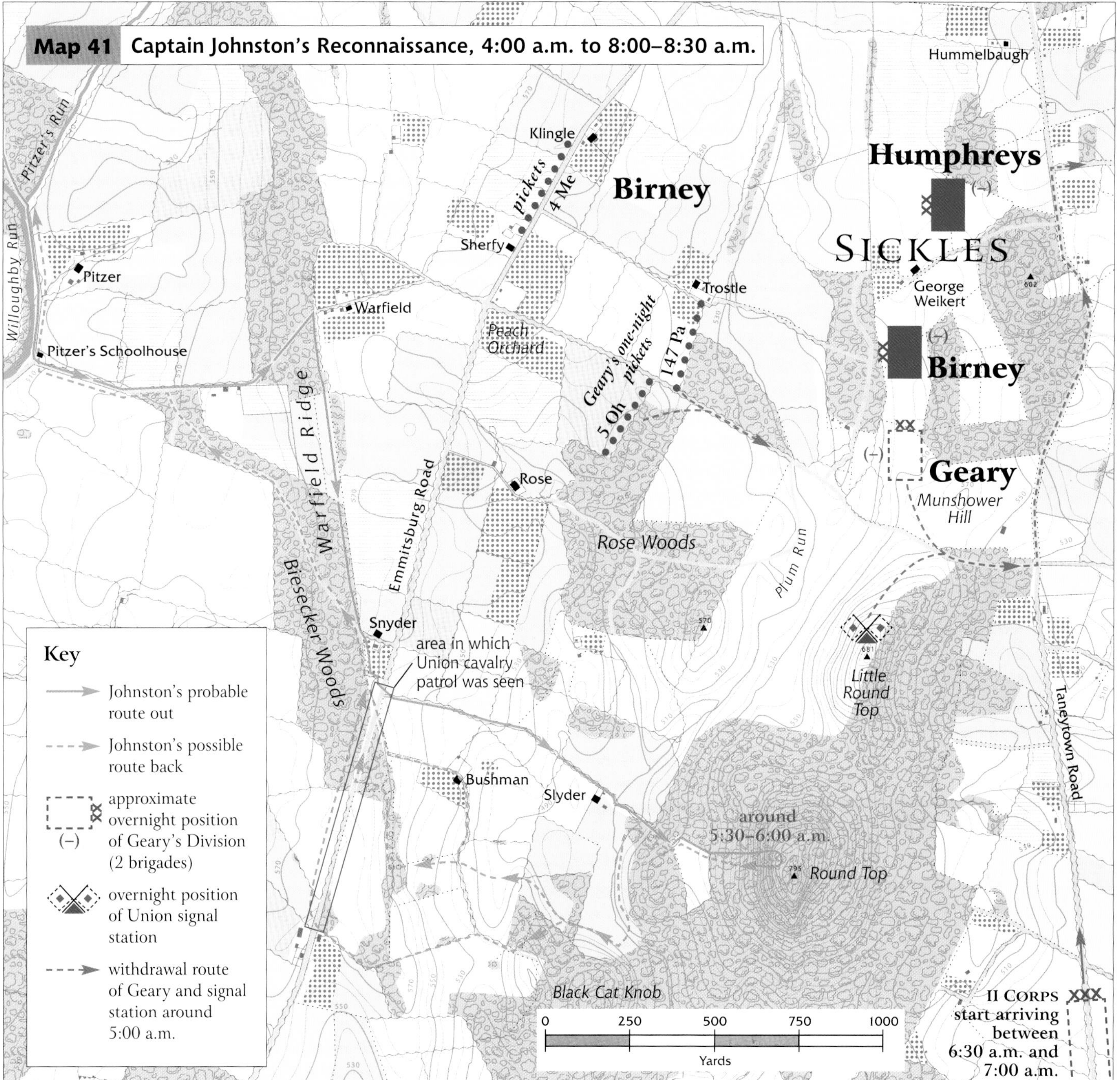

Notes

• This map shows the likely route taken by Capt. Johnston on July 2. He started out shortly after 4:00 a.m. and had returned about four hours later after covering at least 9 miles, possibly as many as 10. His task was to examine the enemy's left and ascertain if there were Union troops in the area of the Round Tops.

• Johnston was a very experienced reconnoitering officer in whom Lee had considerable trust. He was accompanied by a Maj. Clarke, an engineer officer from Longstreet's headquarters, and a small escort. The route out shows him reaching Round Top around 5:30 and staying for about half an hour. During that time he would not have seen any enemy activity in the vicinity, as by then Geary's Division, pickets and the signal station had withdrawn and were en route for Culp's Hill.

• Many accounts put Johnston on what we know as Little Round Top. This is most unlikely, as if he had been there he would have seen or heard activity in Birney's Division only 750 yards away, and this approach would have involved crossing large open areas between the Emmitsburg Road and Little Round Top, whereas he undoubtedly selected the most concealed route. Also, no one at the time regarded the two unnamed hills as separate features. Johnston referred, as did countless later reports, to "Round Top;" it was the dominating hill and used by Johnston, as he himself stated, as the marker for finding his direction during his outward journey.

• The early part of his return is less certain; the routes shown are possible alternatives. It remains a mystery as to why he never encountered more than three or four cavalrymen, as Buford's Division was protecting the Union left and had, supposedly, numerous pickets out.

• Johnston confirmed that he had reached "Round Top" when Lee enquired how far he had got. His report that there was no enemy in that area was correct at the time he made it – but its validity did not last.

by several staff and Colonel R. Lindsay Walker, chief of artillery of Hill's Corps. However, Walker's after-battle report makes no mention on any reconnaissance with Pendleton that morning. Pendleton achieved little, although on its return journey his party supposedly captured two stray Union cavalrymen drinking from the Willoughby Run.

4:30 a.m.
Longstreet and his staff, riding ahead of his leading division, arrived to see Lee at around this time. Together they rode over to observe Cemetery Ridge through their glasses from a vantage point near the Seminary. Later Longstreet wrote, "On the morning of the 2d I went to General Lee's headquarters at daylight and renewed my views against making an attack." It soon became apparent to Longstreet that Lee had every intention of doing just that. Longstreet did little to hide his annoyance, a fact well described by Lieutenant-Colonel Moxley Sorrel, his chief of staff:

> [Longstreet] did not want to fight on the ground or on the plan adopted by the General-in-Chief. As Longstreet was not to be made willing and Lee refused to change or could not change, the former failed to conceal some anger. There was apparent apathy in his movements. They lacked the fire and point of his usual bearing on the battlefield.

5:00–8:00 a.m.
During this period there was a considerable coming and going of generals and staff at Lee's observation post on Seminary Ridge, watched by a gaggle of foreign observers and the London *Times* correspondent Francis Lawley; several of them, including the British observer Colonel Fremantle, climbed nearby trees to get a better view of events. Lee spent much time seated on a log. Fremantle described the scene at one stage: "Just below us were seated Generals Lee, Hill, Longstreet and Hood in consultation – the two latter assisting their deliberations by the truly American custom of *whittling* sticks." At other times both Heth and McLaws were present. During this period Lee appeared anxious and spent considerable time gazing at the opposite ridge. According to Hood, writing years later, Lee told him, "The enemy is here and if we do not whip him he will whip us."

8:00 a.m. (or shortly after)
Johnston arrived back from his reconnaissance after about four hours' absence – longer than expected, as he had covered a considerable distance (at least 9 miles) and spent time going first to Lee's tented headquarters by Mary Thompson's house and then having to search for Lee on the Seminary Ridge. Writing to General McLaws almost thirty years later, Johnston described his arrival as follows:

> [Lee] looked up, saw me and at once called me to him, and on the map which he was holding I sketched the route over which I had reconnoitered. He was surprised at my getting so far, but showed clearly that I had given him valuable information. I was not interrupted in my narrative, and when through I stepped back . . .

In another letter he gave a little more detail:

> I found Generals Lee, Longstreet and A. P. Hill sitting on a log near the Seminary. General Lee saw me and called me to him. The three generals were holding a map. I stood behind General Lee and traced on the map the route over which I had made the reconnaissance. When I got to the extreme right of our reconnaissance on the Little Round Top [pointing to the hill on the map], General Lee turned and looking at me, said, "Did you get there?" I assured him I did.

The reference by Johnston in this passage written so long after the battle to "Little Round Top" does not ring true, as at the time of the battle it had no name and in most reports both hills are considered as one and referred to as "Round Top." The likelihood is Johnston reached what was later described as "Round Top" or "Big Round Top" (see "Controversies," page 450). The crucial point of this reconnaissance, however, was that Johnston had seen no large body of enemy in the vicinity of Round Top, and for Lee this indicated the Union line did not stretch that far south – Meade's left was seemingly in the air and vulnerable.

8:30–9:30 a.m.
With Johnston's return and the news that there were no enemy in the vicinity of the Round Tops it was decision time for Lee. At around 8:30 a.m. first Hood's and then McLaws' Divisions began arriving in the fields between Seminary and McPherson's Ridges, although Brigadier-General Evander Law's Brigade (Hood's Division) still had some way to march. Pickett's Division was well to the rear of the column, having started out from Chambersburg only after the arrival of Imboden's horsemen at around 2:00 a.m.

With these two divisions arriving, Lee called McLaws over to give him his orders. This was unusual, to say the least, as Longstreet was nearby and it was Lee's established practice to brief his corps commanders on what he wanted in general terms and let them get on with it. Now he was ignoring Longstreet and giving detailed orders to his subordinate in front of his superior. It was not calculated to improve Longstreet's already disgruntled, sulky mood. Lee had decided to use Longstreet's Corps to attack what he thought was the left flank of the Union line on the Emmitsburg Road just north of the Peach Orchard (see Map 42). Lee pointed out on his map the exact place he wanted McLaws to deploy. It was just south of the Peach Orchard facing up the Emmitsburg Road. He was to attack in a northeasterly direction with the road as his axis and roll up the enemy line. Lee's words were, "General, I wish you to place your division across this road [Emmitsburg Road], and I wish you to get there if possible without being seen by the enemy." He then added, "Can you do it?" McLaws replied in the affirmative but wanted to make a personal reconnaissance of the area with Johnston (he had misunderstood Lee and thought Johnston was about to go on his reconnaissance). He asked if he could go out with Johnston again and see for himself. At this stage Longstreet, who was obviously seething at the way he was being ignored, cut in and, speaking directly to McLaws, said, "No, sir, I do not wish you to leave your division." Then, pointing at the map, he told McLaws to deploy parallel to the Emmitsburg Road – the opposite of what his commander-in-chief had just indicated. Immediately Lee snapped, "No, General, I wish it placed just perpendicular to that." Longstreet had been put down in front of his subordinate and was being forced to make an attack he considered unwise to say the least. His mood blackened and he rejected yet another request by McLaws to make some sort of reconnaissance. Johnston was told to accompany Longstreet on the move south.

Lee instructed Hill that Anderson's Division should deploy on Longstreet's left and attack the center of the Union line.

Shortly after this Lee rode over to the left through Gettysburg to find Ewell to give him his part in the plan. Ewell was absent from his headquarters with Lee's staff officer, Venable. Lee spoke with Major-General Isaac Trimble (the general without a command) and, when Ewell and Venable returned, Ewell argued against an outright attack on Culp's Hill or a move of his corps to the right. Again, Lee did not force the issue, telling Ewell to launch a diversionary attack when he heard Longstreet's guns, and to convert the diversion to an all-out assault if he thought it feasible. Lee returned to his position on Seminary Ridge shortly before 11:00 a.m. and explained Ewell's role in the plan. At about 11:00 a.m. Lee also told Longstreet to move off. However, Law's Brigade was still in the process of completing an eleven-hour, 28-mile march – a feat that Longstreet was to describe as "the best marching done in either army to reach the field of Gettysburg." Longstreet claimed that he then requested Lee's permission to delay moving off until Law joined the division – a request he said Lee accepted. There is considerable doubt as to Lee's actually agreeing this delay, but Longstreet certainly waited for his brigade and Lee did not order him to move without it, so Lee had at least sanctioned it by remaining silent.

The Confederate plan for Thursday, July 2 was straightforward in concept. Longstreet's Corps, spearheaded by McLaws' Division would make a concealed march to the south and attack up the Emmitsburg Road from a jump-off point in dead ground south of the Peach Orchard. It was intended to roll up the vulnerable left flank of the Union Army, thought to be on the Emmitsburg Road. In support would be Hood's Division, and on the left Anderson's Division of Hill's Corps attacking the Union center with Heth's Division threatening to advance. At the same time Ewell was to launch a diversionary demonstration – which might develop into something more serious – on Meade's extreme right on Culp's Hill. Over 21,500 men were committed to the main attack, supported by at least five or six battalions of artillery. Ewell had over 17,000 men available to use as he saw fit to create the diversion.

Lee later described his plan as follows:

> I was determined to make the principal attack upon the enemy's left, and endeavor to gain a position from which it was thought that our artillery could be brought to bear with effect. Longstreet was directed to place the divisions of McLaws and Hood on the right of Hill, partially enveloping the enemy's left, which he was to drive in. General Hill was ordered to threaten the enemy's center, to prevent reinforcements being drawn to either wing, and co-operate with his right division [Anderson] in Longstreet's attack. General Ewell was instructed to make a simultaneous demonstration upon the enemy's right, to be converted into a real attack should the opportunity offer.

Comments

The key element of the plan was to hit the Union left flank, which was supposedly "in the air." It was based on Johnston's report that there was no sizeable force of Yankees on, or in the immediate area of, the Round Tops. Lee believed that not all Meade's corps had yet reached the battlefield and that his line did not stretch all the way down Cemetery Ridge to the Round Tops. He thought the Union left rested on the Emmitsburg Road somewhere between the Codori and Rogers' houses. There was no way Lee could know for sure how many troops were opposing him that morning as he had lacked cavalry to find out, and it was impossible to see what was on the reverse slope of Cemetery Ridge. He was relying on the accuracy of one captain's reconnaissance and his own gut feeling that Meade could not have yet concentrated his entire army.

Captain Johnston had reported not seeing any enemy on the Round Tops at around 5:30–6:00 a.m. but Lee was well aware that no attack could start until between 2:00 p.m. and 3:00 p.m. at the earliest, as he had sanctioned a delay in Longstreet's moving off on his long approach march until about noon. It would be at least nine hours after Johnston had been on Round Top that McLaws would start his attacks and Lee's plan depended on no more Union troops arriving and on Meade doing nothing about his vulnerable left flank. There was a distinct lack of urgency on Lee's part. He did not send Longstreet off on his approach march until he had returned from meeting Ewell, and then he allowed a further unnecessary delay of about an hour while Longstreet waited for Law's Brigade. In modern military parlance, "battle procedure" – whereby actions necessary in the preparation for battle take place concurrently – was sadly lacking.

The plan was an attack from exterior lines with the main assault being made on the enemy's extreme left and a diversionary one on his extreme right, separated round the arc by some 4.5 miles. As with any such attacks against an enemy operating on interior lines, they should be simultaneous in order to prevent the defender from switching reserves from quiet sectors to threatened ones. To ensure this, Lee had told Ewell to advance when he heard the guns open up in the south. Despite this, coordination and communication between the two ends of the Rebel line would be difficult due to the distance involved.

Lee's intention to attack up the line of the Emmitsburg Road was feasible only if the Union left was on that road; if it was mostly back on or just behind the Cemetery Ridge, such an attack would hit thin air and be exposed on the right to heavy fire and counterattack. A number of historians have tried to get round this problem by assuming it would be an oblique, angled advance involving some sort of wheel, or half wheel, to the right in order to attack Cemetery Ridge – an extraordinarily clumsy and convoluted maneuver. But there is no evidence of this; everything points to the fact that Lee and his generals thought the Union line was along the Emmitsburg Road from early that morning. There are five clear instances that this had been his thinking:

- Lee twice emphasized to McLaws that he was to form up across and perpendicular to the Emmitsburg Road.
- Lee's own report written in January 1864:

  > The enemy occupied a strong position, with his right upon two commanding elevations adjacent to each other, one southeast [Culp's Hill] and the other, known as Cemetery Hill, immediately south of the town, which lay at its base. His line extended thence upon high ground along the Emmitsburg Road, with a steep ridge in rear [Cemetery Ridge], which was also occupied.

- Longstreet's report: "The enemy having been driven back by the corps of Lieutenant-Generals Ewell and A. P. Hill the previous day, had taken a strong position extending from the hill at the cemetery along the Emmitsburg Road."

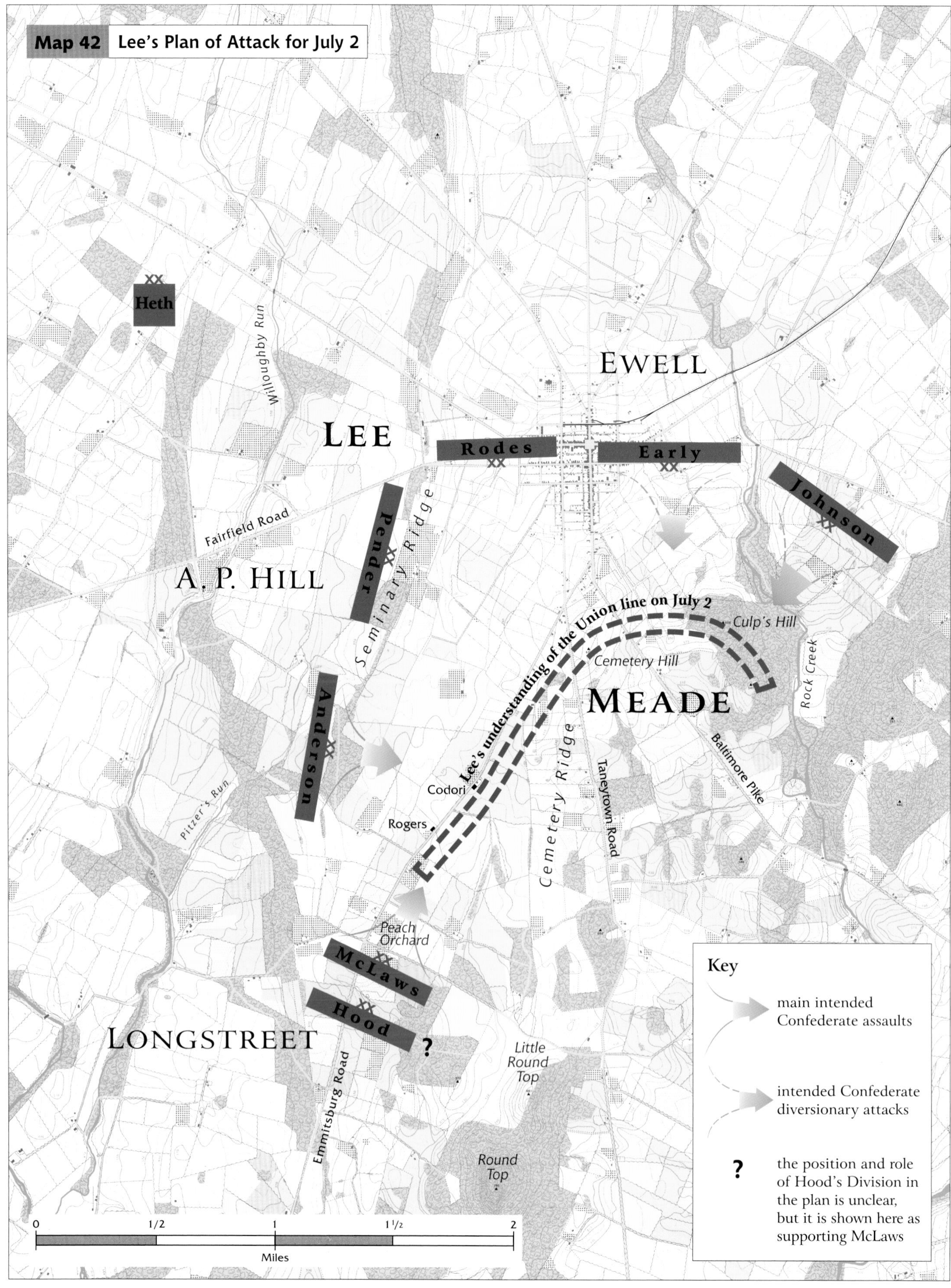
Map 42 Lee's Plan of Attack for July 2
Heth
Willoughby Run
EWELL
LEE
Rodes
Early
Johnson
Fairfield Road
Pender
Seminary Ridge
A. P. HILL
Lee's understanding of the Union line on July 2
Culp's Hill
Cemetery Hill
Rock Creek
MEADE
Anderson
Baltimore Pike
Cemetery Ridge
Taneytown Road
Codori
Rogers
Pitzer's Run
Peach Orchard
McLaws
Hood
?
LONGSTREET
Little Round Top
Emmitsburg Road
Round Top
Key
main intended Confederate assaults
intended Confederate diversionary attacks
? the position and role of Hood's Division in the plan is unclear, but it is shown here as supporting McLaws
0
1/2
1
1 1/2
2
Miles

- If Lee had not believed Meade's left flank rested somewhere near Rogers' house on the Emmitsburg Road rather than all along the Cemetery Ridge, there is surely no way a general of his ability would have ordered an attack that would immediately expose his right to massive enfilade fire and a smashing counterattack. Finding Yankees occupying the Peach Orchard at 4:00 p.m. came as a total surprise to Longstreet and his generals. Strangely, neither the clash between Wilcox's Confederate Brigade (Anderson's Division, Hill's Corps) and Berdan's U.S. Sharpshooters in Pitzer's Wood around noon, nor the move forward by Sickles' divisions to the Peach Orchard around 2:00 p.m. seem to have alerted the Rebel high command that all was not as they thought.
- Later, according to Hood, once the battle on the right flank was joined and he wanted to move his division round to the right, Longstreet countered it with the words, "Genl. Lee's orders are to attack up the Emmetsburg [*sic*] Road."

We now know that during the morning the Union line was mostly along the Cemetery Ridge and that no Union troops apart from some cavalry pickets and several forward-skirmishing regiments were deployed forward along the Emmitsburg Road until Sickles advanced to the Peach Orchard between 2:00 and 3:00 in the afternoon. Trying to reconcile an attack up the Emmitsburg Road with one on Cemetery Ridge – an attempt made unconvincingly by a number of historians – is, in the present author's view, unrealistic. Lee's intended plan for July 2 was approximately as set out on Map 42.

The above being so, it remains something of a mystery why Lee was so convinced the main Union defensive line was along the slight ridge that carried the Emmitsburg Road, as much of it was visible from Seminary Ridge and, although there was some serious skirmishing along its line, it in no way indicated that the bulk of Meade's army was deployed that far forward. From the angle at which Lee was observing the situation from the north of the line, it is conceivable that the line of the road seemed to represent the main Union line.

Notes

- Lee believed Meade's line ran along the Emmitsburg Road onto Cemetery Hill and thence to Culp's Hill. His plan was based on the Union left being "in the air" near Rogers' house, and that not all of the enemy corps were present.
- Johnson had reported the Round Tops area clear, so the plan was to roll up the Union left from the area south of the Peach Orchard with Longstreet's Corps, while Anderson's Division of Hill's Corps attacked the center. Ewell would make a simultaneous diversionary attack on the enemy right which might develop into a full-scale attack.
- Such an attack would have made no tactical sense if Lee thought Meade's line was back on Cemetery Ridge.
- The use of exterior lines by Lee is strikingly obvious from the map, as is the great distance between McLaws' and Johnson's Divisions.
- The rising ground around the Peach Orchard would conceal McLaws' and Hood's Divisions forming up in the swale to the south, and if their approach had been unseen the attack would have been a devastating one.

Meade

Meade spent July 1 at Taneytown, evaluating reports and assessing the situation as it developed at Gettysburg. By the early evening he appeared to favor a continuation of the fight at Gettysburg and concentrating his army at that point, based on reports from Howard and Hancock that the terrain was suitable. After the war, when addressing the Joint Committee on the Conduct of the War (J.C.C.W.), Meade explained his thinking at that time thus:

> Early on the evening of July 1, I should suppose about 6 or 7 o'clock, I received a report from General Hancock, I think in person [correct, he returned to Taneytown to report; see box, page 386], giving me such an account of a position in the neighborhood of Gettysburg, which could be occupied by my army, which caused me at once to determine to fight a battle at that point; having reason to believe, from the account given to me of the operations of July 1, that the enemy were concentrating there.

Having got the remainder of his army marching on Gettysburg (they would arrive from four directions along the Emmitsburg, Taneytown and Hanover Roads and the Baltimore Pike over a period of sixteen hours) and accepting that a battle would probably take place near Gettysburg, Meade left Taneytown late that evening. He was headed for the battlefield accompanied by his chief of artillery, Brigadier-General Henry J. Hunt, and his chief engineer, Brigadier-General Gouverneur K. Warren (two officers destined to play major roles in the coming battle and whom Meade trusted implicitly), and by Captain William H. Paine, an engineer on Warren's staff. The party arrived at the Evergreen Cemetery Gatehouse not long after midnight to be met by Major-Generals Hancock, Howard, Slocum and Sickles. Meade immediately discussed the situation with his generals and was relieved to hear they all considered the high ground south of the town made for a strong defensive position. Meade responded, "I am glad to hear you say so for it is too late to leave it."

At that moment Meade had one overriding problem to resolve, hopefully before daylight, but certainly within two hours of that time. That was to ensure that all available troops and artillery were deployed in good defensive positions, so that he had a continuous defensive line with a centrally placed reserve. Reinforcements would be arriving from different directions and at different times, and Meade needed to know where to place them. To do this he needed to look at the ground, know where exactly his divisions were located, assess the weak points that needed strengthening, and following from that where best to deploy the other corps as they arrived. Crucial to this process were the position and likely intentions of the enemy. Between 1:30 and 2:00 a.m. Meade, accompanied by Hunt, Captain Paine, Lieutenant Charles E. Bissell (another engineer on Hunt's staff) and Meade's son Captain George G. Meade Jr., rode out on a tour of the position in the moonlight. Their route took them first onto Cemetery Hill, then down the spine of Cemetery Ridge as far as the base of Little Round Top, before turning east, crossing the Taneytown Road, then proceeding as far as the Baltimore Pike before heading north to Culp's Hill (near which he had a brief meeting with Slocum concerning that officer's concerns about a gap on the right).

Apart from selecting favorable positions for his infantry divisions and artillery batteries, Meade surely gave considerable thought to the enemy's possible intentions and threats. From Cemetery Hill he could see the lights of hundreds of campfires in a huge arc stretching from the northwest of his position round the north of the town to the east. From this it appeared that the Rebel center was Gettysburg itself. Meade knew that the town and the area to the east were occupied by Ewell's Corps, while to the west of Gettysburg was Hill's Corps. The big question was, where was Longstreet? Had he now joined Lee? If so, and Meade had to assume he had, where was he, and how did Lee intend to use him? The odds were heavily weighted in favor of Lee resuming the offensive on July 2. It was something of a surprise that the Confederate success yesterday had not been immediately followed up. With daylight, and if Longstreet was now present, a renewed attack was virtually certain. It would be mounted as soon as possible, probably within two or three hours of daylight.

What Meade found was that the advice given him by his generals that the ground south of Gettysburg was eminently suitable for defense was correct. The distance from Culp's Hill on the right to the round-topped hills on the left was only 2 miles in a straight line. A defensive line between these two extremities would run west from Culp's Hill to Cemetery Hill then bend south along Cemetery Ridge, gradually losing height until it reached the Round Tops – thus forming what became known as the "fishhook." Such a position would give Meade all the advantages of interior lines and the ability to switch reserves quickly to threatened areas out of sight of the enemy. Enhancing this facility was the Taneytown Road, which ran the entire length of the position just below and east of the Cemetery Ridge crest. Strategically, the key to the position was the Baltimore Pike. Like the Chambersburg and York Pikes, it was an all-weather road capable of taking heavy traffic and it was Meade's link direct to his main base at Westminster 20 miles away. Westminster was his railhead for supplies from Baltimore, and the telegraph line from Washington also ended at Westminster. If Lee threatened to cut the Baltimore Pike, Meade would be in serious trouble, compelled to withdraw on Westminster, not only to preserve his communications with his base but also to ensure he kept his army between Lee and Baltimore and Washington. It was for just such a contingency that he had issued the necessary instruction for a possible withdrawal to the Pipe Creek line.

Still thinking strategically, Meade would have considered what moves Lee might make that would be most threatening to his link with Westminster – which of his flanks was most vulnerable to a Confederate turning movement? During the final phase of his march north Meade had been anxious about his left and a threat developing along the line Fairfield to Emmitsburg (see Map 24). This had also been a worry in Washington and Halleck had specifically warned him about it. In the event Meade had instructed Sickles to march on Emmitsburg and that officer had left two brigades at the town when he hurried north on July 1. This was the course that Longstreet was so keen to adopt. Now, however, Meade was more concerned with his right. He was fairly sure all Lee's army (which he was still convinced outnumbered him) had been, or was shortly to be, assembled to the east, north and west of Gettysburg. As he stood on Cemetery Hill he could see Rebel campfires burning a mile east of the town. If Lee attacked strongly on Meade's right with Longstreet's Corps, for example, or moved round Culp's Hill and east of Wolf's Hill, he would be within half a mile of the Baltimore Pike. Underlining the potential danger to his right was the fact that the troops defending it (I Corps) had suffered severely during the first day of the battle. (Meade replaced Doubleday as the corps commander – on the basis of his own poor opinion of him and Howard's malicious report that I Corps had broken – with Major-General John Newton, commander of the 3rd Division, VI Corps; he arrived on the field around 8:00 a.m. that morning to a sullen reception by both Doubleday and most of his soldiers, who rightly regarded the changeover as unjustified.) On the other hand, those fires northeast of Gettysburg seemed to mark the extreme left flank of his enemy. If so, it was in the air and possibly vulnerable to an attack by V Corps approaching up the Hanover Road.

On the completion of his reconnaissance, Meade established his headquarters in Lydia Leister's house just south of Cemetery Hill, close to the Taneytown Road, sheltered from direct fire and centrally placed to communicate quickly with all parts of his line. During the ride around the position Captain Paine, on instructions from Meade, had sketched an outline of the hills and ridges and marked the position that each corps was to occupy. His first task at

Meade's A.D.C.s

We have already seen that Meade's headquarters staff far exceeded that of Lee, and that in consequence his control over his formation was better than his opponent's.This advantage was greatly increased by Meade's operating on interior lines – not only did he have more staff, but they had much shorter distances to cover when delivering dispatches. Major-generals in the Union Army were entitled to four senior A.D.C.s and a variable number of acting ones. As army commander, Meade had a total of eleven whose primary duty was as messengers. They were: Lieutenant-Colonel Joseph Dickinson (also assistant adjutant general); Major James C. Biddle; Major Benjamin C. Ludlow; Captain John C. Bates; Captain Charles E. Cadwalader; Captain Emlen N. Carpenter; Captain Ulric Dahlgren (acting; see box, page 281); Captain Addison G. Mason; Captain George Meade, Jr.; Captain James Starr (acting); and First Lieutenant Frederick Rosencrantz (acting).

Notes

• This map shows the general positions of the 10 Union divisions that were on, or very close to, the battlefield in the early hours of July 2. Of these, two had suffered substantial losses during the first day's fighting and two had brigades detached on flank protection at Emmitsburg. While I and XI Corps had troops deployed in some form of defensive positions, III and XII Corps soldiers were, apart from pickets, mostly encamped in bivouac areas rather than deployed tactically. Candy's Brigade from Geary's Division sent two regiments forward as skirmishers (147th Pennsylvania and 5th Ohio) and they spent the night behind stone walls south of Trostle's Farm, as shown. This was roughly the position when Meade began his 2:00 a.m. reconnaissance of the position.
It remained much the same when Captain Johnston started on his reconnaissance of the Union left some two hours later. Note the signal station that had been established on the summit of Little Round Top, but no troops.

• Also shown are the nine divisions, two brigades and the artillery reserve that had yet to arrive in the area. These totaled about 38,750 men and 180 guns, or 48 percent of the army's manpower (discounting cavalry) and 57 percent of its artillery (discounting guns with the cavalry). These formations started arriving from around 7:00 a.m. and, apart from VI Corps, were present on the field by 11:00 a.m. VI Corps, the largest in the army, did not arrive until late afternoon, having had a crippling march of over 30 miles.

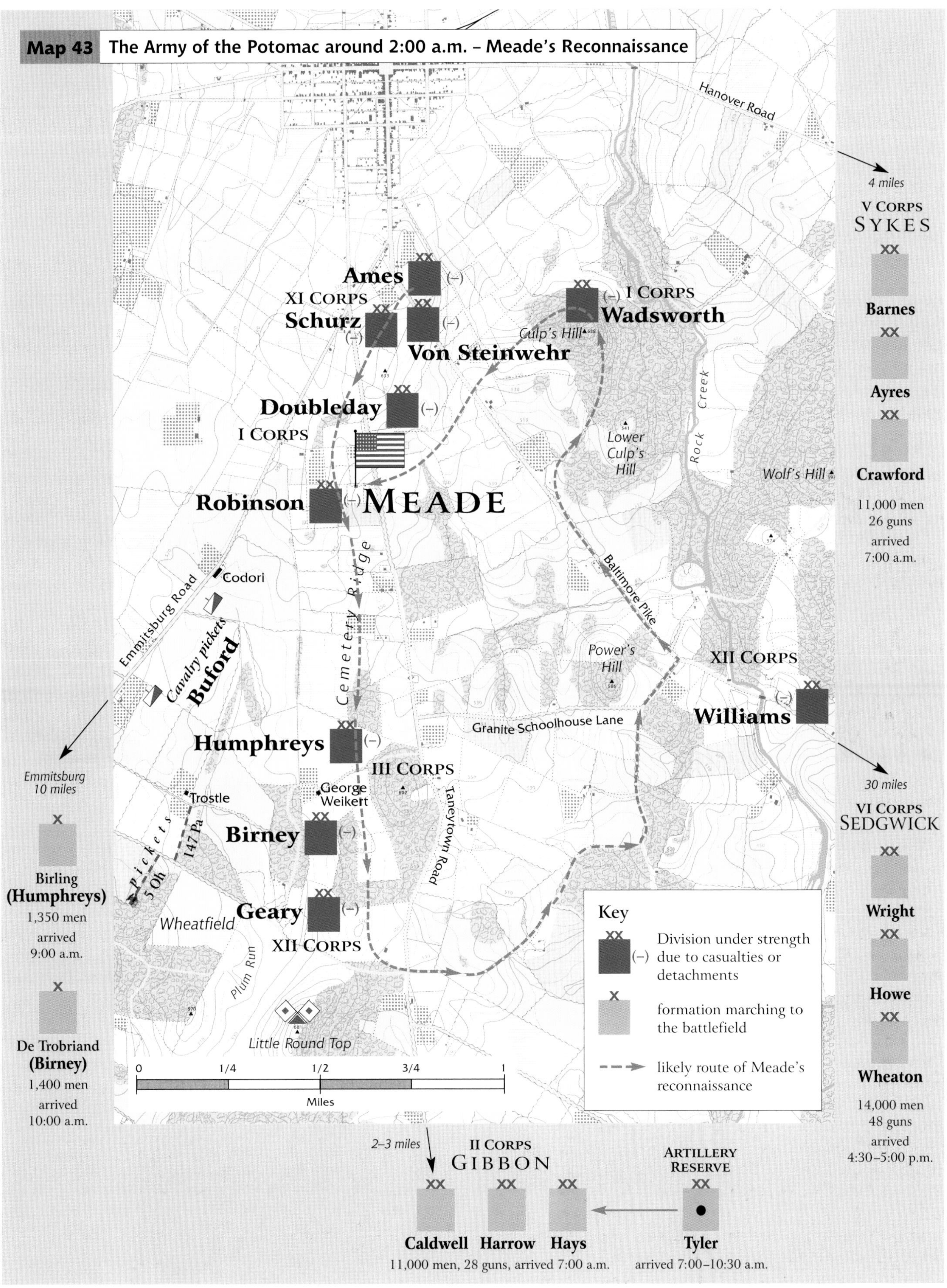

Map 43 The Army of the Potomac around 2:00 a.m. - Meade's Reconnaissance
Hanover Road
4 miles
V CORPS
SYKES
Barnes
Ayres
Crawford
11,000 men
26 guns
arrived
7:00 a.m.
Ames
XI CORPS
Schurz
Von Steinwehr
I CORPS
Wadsworth
Culp's Hill
Doubleday
I CORPS
Robinson
MEADE
Lower
Culp's
Hill
Rock Creek
Wolf's Hill
Baltimore Pike
Codori
Emmitsburg Road
Cavalry pickets
Buford
Cemetery Ridge
Power's
Hill
XII CORPS
Williams
Granite Schoolhouse Lane
Humphreys
III CORPS
Emmitsburg
10 miles
Trostle
George
Weikert
Taneytown Road
30 miles
VI CORPS
SEDGWICK
Birney
147 Pa
pickets
5 Oh
Birling
(Humphreys)
1,350 men
arrived
9:00 a.m.
Geary
Wheatfield
XII CORPS
Plum Run
Wright
Howe
Wheaton
14,000 men
48 guns
arrived
4:30–5:00 p.m.
De Trobriand
(Birney)
1,400 men
arrived
10:00 a.m.
Little Round Top
Key
Division under strength due to casualties or detachments
formation marching to the battlefield
likely route of Meade's reconnaissance
0 1/4 1/2 3/4 1
Miles
2–3 miles
II CORPS
GIBBON
ARTILLERY
RESERVE
Caldwell Harrow Hays
11,000 men, 28 guns, arrived 7:00 a.m.
Tyler
arrived 7:00–10:30 a.m.

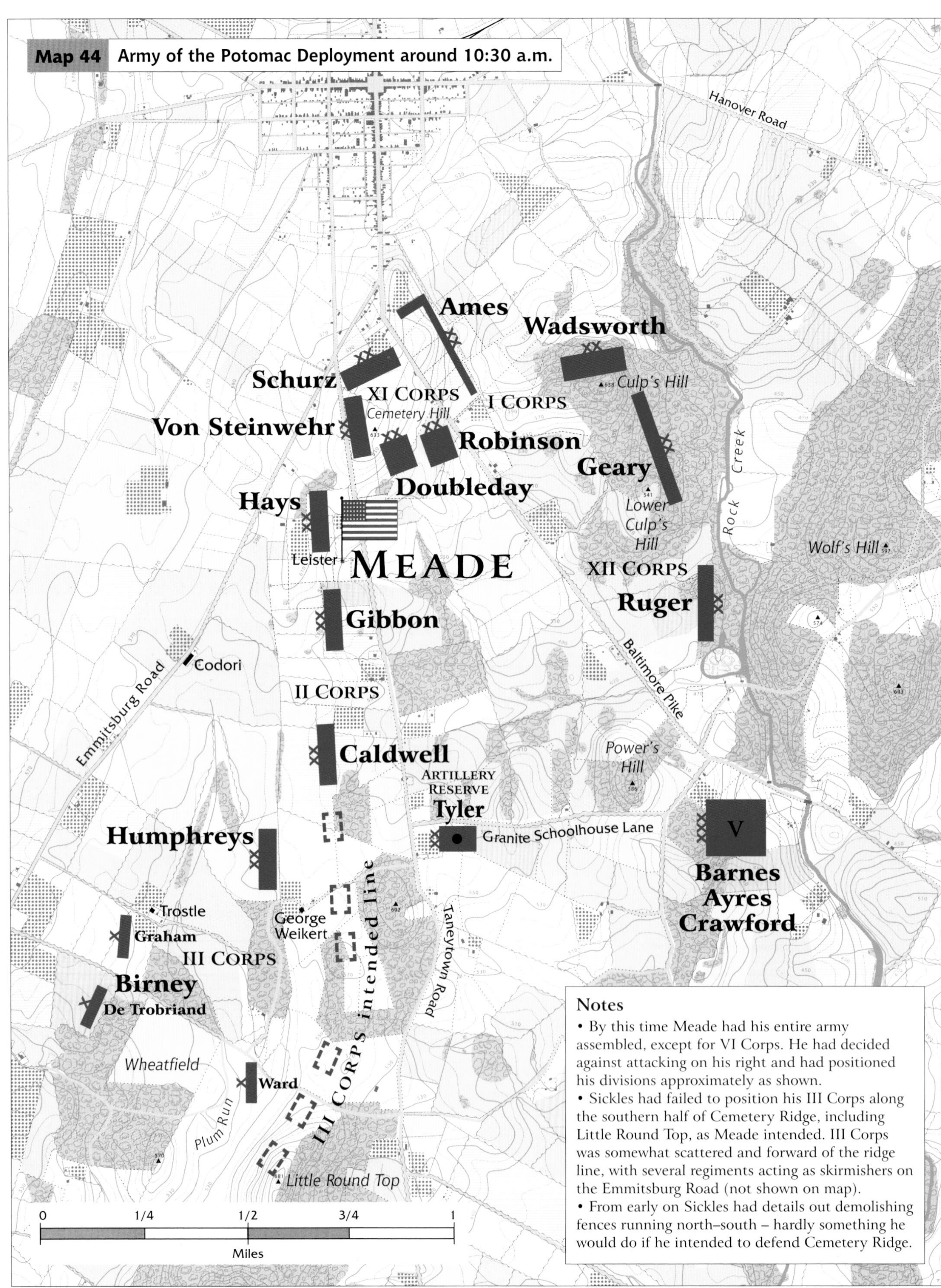
Map 44
Army of the Potomac Deployment around 10:30 a.m.
Hanover Road
Ames
Wadsworth
Schurz
XI CORPS
Cemetery Hill
I CORPS
Culp's Hill
Von Steinwehr
Robinson
Geary
Rock Creek
Doubleday
Hays
Lower Culp's Hill
Wolf's Hill
Leister
MEADE
XII CORPS
Ruger
Gibbon
Codori
Baltimore Pike
Emmitsburg Road
II CORPS
Caldwell
Power's Hill
ARTILLERY RESERVE
Tyler
Humphreys
Granite Schoolhouse Lane
V
Barnes
Ayres
Crawford
Trostle
George Weikert
III CORPS intended line
Taneytown Road
Graham
III CORPS
Birney
De Trobriand
Wheatfield
Ward
Plum Run
Little Round Top
0
1/4
1/2
3/4
1
Miles
Notes
• By this time Meade had his entire army assembled, except for VI Corps. He had decided against attacking on his right and had positioned his divisions approximately as shown.
• Sickles had failed to position his III Corps along the southern half of Cemetery Ridge, including Little Round Top, as Meade intended. III Corps was somewhat scattered and forward of the ridge line, with several regiments acting as skirmishers on the Emmitsburg Road (not shown on map).
• From early on Sickles had details out demolishing fences running north–south – hardly something he would do if he intended to defend Cemetery Ridge.

the Leister house was to make tracings for distribution to the corps commanders. During those early-morning hours Meade took or confirmed the decisions that made up his plan to hold the ground he had inspected, which are summarized below.

Meade's initial priority was to strengthen his right, particularly as heavy skirmishing broke out with Ewell's troops in this area shortly after dawn, heightening his worry that an early attack there was imminent. There was also still the possibility of launching an attack on the Rebel left. With this in mind Meade instructed that:

- I Corps (Newton from about 8:00 a.m.) to remain on Culp's Hill. Geary's Division (XII Corps) to support I Corps on Culp's Hill. This meant an early move for the division from its overnight camping ground just north of Little Round Top.
- XI Corps (Howard) was to stay in its locations on Cemetery Hill and East Cemetery Hill.
- On its arrival around 7:00 a.m., II Corps (Gibbon handed command back to Hancock) was initially placed in reserve just east of the Taneytown Road close to its junction with Granite Schoolhouse Lane. Within about an hour it was deployed in line along the northern part of Cemetery Ridge. Arriving behind II Corps was the Artillery Reserve of over 100 guns and all their associated wagons under Brigadier-General Robert O. Tyler. It was initially parked wheel to wheel immediately east of the Taneytown Road and just south of the Granite Schoolhouse Lane.
- V Corps (Sykes) approached the battlefield along the Hanover Road and turned south off the road on Brinkerhoff Ridge, about 2 miles east of Gettysburg. It joined up with Williams' Division (XII Corps), which had moved to the area from the Baltimore Pike after daylight and had become involved in skirmishing with Ewell's left flank. V Corps was then well positioned to advance on Ewell's exposed flank. However, Meade, on receipt of a report from Slocum and Warren that the tangled woods and hills in the area were unsuitable for an offensive operation, and the fact that VI Corps was still a long way off, abandoned the idea of attacking and ordered V Corps into reserve between Granite Schoolhouse Lane and Rock Creek. Williams' Division, now under Brigadier-General Thomas Ruger – Williams commanded XII Corps as Slocum still regarded himself as a "wing commander" – joined Geary on Culp's Hill and Lower Culp's Hill.
- Meanwhile III Corps (Sickles) had been ordered to replace Geary on Cemetery Ridge in a line from II Corps' left and extending south to the Round Tops.

By about 10:30 a.m. Meade's army was deployed as shown on Map 44. It was all present except for VI Corps, which would not arrive until late afternoon. Meade had reason to feel a little less anxious, especially as an early attack by Lee had not materialized – it would be another hour and a half before Longstreet reluctantly started his long march to the right. The only problem that was just becoming evident to Meade was that Sickles, with III Corps, was having problems getting his men into the locations Meade wanted.

THE MORNING AND EARLY AFTERNOON

On the Confederate side the morning was largely spent in finalizing plans for an offensive against the supposed vulnerable left flank of Meade's army; assembling Longstreet's Corps for its march south; the actual march; positioning the artillery batteries to support the attack; and adjusting the positions of Anderson's brigades on Seminary Ridge – Wilcox's Brigade of Anderson's Division had a brief fight in Pitzer's Wood with Union sharpshooters around 12:30 p.m. An early and lengthy clash of skirmishers developed for Bliss Farm, and Ewell's troops started a lively exchange of fire with Wadsworth's men on the Union right.

It was on the Union side that the more significant events took place. These all centered around Sickles and his III Corps.

A Raid at Bliss Farm

Lieutenant Charles E. Troutman, 12th New Jersey Infantry, took part in a raid on the Bliss Farm buildings to silence Rebel sharpshooters.

> Towards the evening a body of North Carolina sharpshooters had ensconced themselves in a house and barn about midway between the lines of the opposing armies, and were rendering it unsafe to work the batteries on our right and left front. A battalion of the regiment to which I was attached was ordered to dislodge them so down the slope we went . . .
>
> A captain of one of the companies running beside the writer was struck just above the right eye, and the noise of the bullet sounded exactly as that made by throwing a nail into a boot. It was zip, zip all the way across the meadows. Over the fence we went and through the barn yard knee deep in manure, and we were in the stable, but not an enemy was to be seen.
>
> A constant shuffling above told us, however, that the foe was still in possession, and so were we. It was certain death to charge up the ladder leading through a three-by-five hole in the loft above, but at last a venturesome youth, whose curiosity exceeded his fear, climbed up the ladder until his eyes were above the level of the upper floor. The sight he got satisfied him, for with a shout he loosened his hold and came down among us, accompanied by three Confederates, who, in making dash at him, had fallen through. I do not know how or why it happened, but this fortunate capture seemed to be the signal for the surrender of the whole force above, and throwing down their arms and accoutrements they descended into the stable. After gathering them together they were shown the general direction to the rear and away they went in huddled groups, with guards over the field strewn with our dead and wounded. A detail of fifteen men was then ordered to charge the house as we were convinced there was a body of sharpshooters there. We ran through the budding beauties of the garden through lilacs, rose bushes, and raspberry bushes, the berries of which the size of a man's thumb, were temptingly hanging. But there was more serious business on hand. A rattling, splitting sound and the picket fence went down and the remnant of us dashed into the kitchen door where twelve men were captured. Then we sat to a toothsome repast that had been prepared by the hungry North Carolinans whom we had interrupted. After capturing one more man who was discovered in an old fashion cupboard, we heard the sound of the recall and ran back over the meadow under a live archway of shells, regaining our lines.

Encounters with the Rebels in Gettysburg

After his retirement Daniel Skelly, the teenage clerk at the Fahnstock Store (see also box, page 358), wrote *A Boy's Experiences During the Battle of Gettysburg*, published in 1932. Some extracts for July 1–2 are given below.

When I went out in front of the house about 7 o'clock in the evening [July 1], the Confederate line of battle had been formed on East and West Middle Streets, Rodes Division of Ewell's Corps lying right in front of our house . . . In passing I want to pay a tribute to these veterans of the Confederate Army. They were under perfect discipline. They were in and about our yard and used our kitchen stove by permission of my mother . . . There was no noise or confusion among the Confederate soldiers sleeping on the pavement below our windows . . .

Day dawned on the second of July bright and clear . . . we were soon assured that if we kept within certain restrictions we could go about the town . . . Some time during the morning in front of my home on West Middle Street . . . I was in conversation with one of the Confederate soldiers, whose regiment lay along the street in line of battle, when he asked me if I had ever seen General Lee. I replied that I had not. "Well," he said, "here he comes up the street on horseback." The general rode quietly by unattended and without any apparent recognition from the Confederate soldiers along the street . . . I was later informed . . . that he had gone to the jail, presumably for conference [this was probably his morning meeting with Ewell] . . . About 4 o'clock an interruption was caused in our conversation [with a Confederate major] by a terrible cannonading off to the southwest of the town [Longstreet's guns had opened fire] and we separated, he joining his regiment in the street and I going to my father's house near the Fahnestock store.

About dusk, Will McCreary and I were sent on some errant [*sic*] down on Chambersburg Street and as we were crossing from Arnold's corner to the present Eckert corner, we were halted by two Confederate soldiers who had a lady in their charge. She was on horseback and proved to be the wife of General (Francis) Barlow who had come into the Confederate lines under a flag of truce looking for her husband, who had been severely wounded on July 1, and as she was informed, had been brought into town. She informed us he was with the family "named McCreary' on Chambersburg Street. We directed her to Smith McCreary's residence (though) she did not find the general there . . . for he had been taken from the field to the farmhouse of Josiah Benner on the Harrisburg Road . . .

Sickles Establishes His Salient

Sickles' action that morning and in the early afternoon had huge repercussions for how the Battle of Gettysburg was fought. What he did rendered the plans of both army commanders inappropriate and has stimulated heated debates over its rights and wrongs ever since. The events are outlined below with rough guides as to timings.

By 5:30 a.m. Geary's Division (XII Corps) had departed from its overnight position near the northern base of Little Round Top for Culp's Hill and so had the signal station on its summit. Sickles' Corps was in its overnight area south of the George Weikert and Trostle Farm. One of his divisional commanders, Birney, sent several regiments as far forward as the Emmitsburg Road to form a strong skirmish line. Sickles had been told by Meade that he was to occupy Geary's old position on Cemetery Ridge with his right on II Corps' left and his left on what we now know as Little Round Top. Sickles was expecting Burling's and De Trobriand's Brigades to march up the Emmitsburg Road that morning – they arrived between 9:00 and 10:00 a.m.

At perhaps 8:30 or 9:00 a.m. Meade sent his son, Captain George Meade Jr., to check that Sickles was in position and to receive any report on what was happening on the left. Captain Meade found III Corps' headquarters tents beside the Taneytown Road. He spoke to a Captain George E. Randolph, Sickles' chief of artillery, and was told the general was resting in his tent. Randolph went to speak to him and returned with the unwelcome news that the corps was not in position, as Sickles was uncertain where exactly he was supposed to be. As the army commander's A.D.C., Captain Meade should have insisted on seeing the general and pointing out the deployment required; his youth and inexperience probably explain why he failed to do so. Instead he returned to report to his father.

For Sickles to be found in his tent resting at that time of the morning, his troops still mostly in their overnight areas, does not reflect well on the general. However, there is perhaps an element of truth in his uncertainty over where Geary had been positioned, as that division had moved off very early from its bivouac area for Culp's Hill and had never really adopted a defensive line along Cemetery Ridge that included Little Round Top.

Within half an hour Captain Meade was back, this time to repeat to Sickles that his corps was to form on the left of Hancock's II Corps and occupy the position formerly held by Geary's Division of XII Corps. Sickles explained to Captain Meade that his troops were on the move but it was by no means clear what line he was to take up as Geary's position had been largely a camping area – which was true. Before Captain Meade left he was asked by Randolph to relay a request for Brigadier-General Hunt to come to check on III Corps' artillery positions.

When Sickles rode forward to check on his command he found that Birney had dispersed his division quite widely. Two regiments, the 63rd Pennsylvania (Graham's Brigade) and the 4th Maine (Ward's Brigade) had been spread out along or close to the Emmitsburg Road and had been reinforced by mid-morning by the 3rd Maine and 99th Pennsylvania (both Ward's Brigade – a very large formation with six regiments plus two more of sharpshooters). Captain Randolph had posted two batteries (Captain Judson Clark's and Lieutenant Francis W. Seeley's) in the open ground southwest of the Trostle Farm.

Sickles was becoming increasingly concerned over his situation and the suitability of the line on Cemetery Ridge he had been told to occupy. His worry was centered on the fact that the Emmitsburg Road climbed rising ground from where it crossed Rose's Run 300 yards south of the Peach Orchard crossroads to as far north as the Codori Farm. Although not high in relative terms, it dominated the northern part of the Plum Run valley where his command was then situated. At 590 feet above sea level the Peach Orchard was the highest point and dominated the Plum Run by 70 feet. Confederate guns in the Peach Orchard area was not a proposition Sickles liked to contemplate – it reminded him of Hazel Grove

(Chancellorsville), where enemy guns on a similar piece of ground had caused him considerable grief. He believed that his position there in the lower ground was definitely untenable – but he was well forward of the ground that Meade had earmarked for him. He had to move, but his inclination was to go forward onto the Emmitsburg Road rather than to pull back. This was because the ground carrying that section of the road was slightly higher than the southern end of Cemetery Ridge (20–30 feet higher). He had details out in the fields demolishing fences running north–south – hardly sensible if you intended to defend Cemetery Ridge.

Sometime late morning, Buford's cavalry division began withdrawing from its screening positions to the west of the Emmitsburg Road. Pleasonton had pleaded exhaustion (true – Buford's horsemen had been in the saddle and fighting continuously since Brandy Station on June 9, so men and most horses were completely worn out) and heavy casualties (untrue – they had only 127 casualties on July 1). He was given permission to pull out by Meade, who assured Sickles the cavalry would be replaced. Pleasonton sent Buford and his men all the way back to Westminster but neglected to replace them. Meade was furious when he learned there was no mounted screen in front of the position and had Butterfield send dispatches (one at 12:50 p.m. and another five minutes later) telling Pleasonton that cavalry must patrol the Emmitsburg Road. Pleasonton told Brigadier-General David McM. Gregg to sent a regiment – it never came.

At around 11:00 a.m. Sickles, still reluctant to move back onto Cemetery Ridge, arrived at Meade's headquarters to explain his doubts. Meade was becoming exasperated with his subordinate's persistent inability to understand where he was to deploy, and it is likely that it was on this occasion that Meade took Sickles outside the Leister House and actually pointed out Little Round Top as the place his left flank should rest. Sickles appeared to understand, but asked if he could post his corps as he saw fit. Meade agreed provided he kept within the limits of the general instructions just given him. Sickles then asked for Brigadier-General Warren, Meade's chief engineer, to return with him to examine the position. Warren was absent so Sickles asked for Hunt, the chief of artillery, instead, as he claimed his position was unsuitable for the deployment of guns. Meade agreed, so Hunt and Sickles rode off together sometime after eleven o'clock.

Meade's Signal to Halleck, 3:00 p.m., July 2

The signal given below shows how puzzled Meade was that by this time the Rebels had yet to launch any attack, and how anxious he still was that Lee might try to interpose his army between him and Washington – the very move Longstreet was so keen to advocate.

> I have concentrated my army at this place to-day. The Sixth Corps is just coming in, very much worn out having been marching since 9 p.m. last night. The army is fatigued. I have to-day, up to this hour, awaited the attack of the enemy, I having a strong position for defensive. I am not determined, as yet, on attacking him till his position is more developed . . . Expecting a battle, I have ordered all my trains to the rear. If not attacked, and I can get any positive information of the position of the enemy which will justify me in doing so, I shall attack. If I find it hazardous to do so, or am satisfied the enemy is endeavoring to move to my rear and interpose between me and Washington, I shall fall back to my supplies at Westminster . . .

Instead of riding down Cemetery Ridge, Sickles led down the Emmitsburg Road to the Peach Orchard area, where he forcefully put forward his arguments that this was a better place to deploy than back on Cemetery Ridge. It would provide a good platform for his guns; it would prevent the Rebels using it for the same purpose; the high ground dominated the Cemetery Ridge position and it would provide a good jump-off point for any Union offensive in the area. Hunt was only half convinced. He saw the obvious drawbacks – the position would create a salient that would be vulnerable to attack and enfilade artillery fire from two sides; and the distance to be covered was considerably more than on Cemetery Ridge, so Sickles would need reinforcing if he was to hold it – and it would clearly not be in accordance with the army commander's wishes. There was also the question of whether the enemy was already behind the Pitzer's Wood only 300 yards west of the Peach Orchard and stretching north to Spangler Woods, which was plainly in Rebel hands as their skirmishers were in front of it. Sickles agreed a reconnaissance was needed, but when he asked for Hunt's authority to move forward the chief of artillery replied, "Not on my authority. I will report to General Meade for his instructions." It must have been about noon that Hunt departed.

Birney was told to go ahead with checking Pitzer's Wood shortly after Hunt's departure. He sent four companies of Colonel Hiram Berdan's 1st U.S. Sharpshooter Regiment (only about 100 strong) under Lieutenant-Colonel Casper Trepp, supported by the 200 men of Colonel Moses B. Lakeman's 3rd Maine, then posted on the Emmitsburg Road. The advance of this force led to a sharp clash with Brigadier-General Cadmus M. Wilcox's Brigade in Pitzer's Wood and the Yankees were forced to retire. Berdan's report reinforced Sickles' increasing concern that the Rebels were likely to attack and take the ground he wanted to occupy or move round his left flank. Having heard nothing from Meade as a result of Hunt's tour of the area, Sickles decided he could wait no longer and on his own initiative ordered his corps forward to hold the Peach Orchard–Emmitsburg Road position. He considered the situation sufficiently threatening to justify ignoring Meade's repeated instructions – not that Sickles, in the eight or nine hours since dawn, had made any attempt to occupy Cemetery Ridge.

At around 2:00 p.m. the soldiers of II Corps back on Cemetery Ridge watched the move forward by III Corps with amazement. Humphreys' Division advanced in grand style for a full threequarters of a mile to the Emmitsburg Road. Major-General Gibbon later wrote, "We could not conceive what it meant as we had heard of no orders for an advance and did not understand the meaning of this break in our line." Meade had summoned a corps commanders meeting at 3:00 p.m. An hour earlier the station on Little Round Top had signaled seeing a large column of Rebel infantry moving to the right along the Chambersburg Pike toward Herr's Tavern – probably part of Longstreet's column countermarching on its approach march to the Union left (see page 404 and Map 45).

Previously Meade had been alerted to a substantial Confederate presence in and around Pitzer's Wood by Berdan's fight in that area. He had been agreeably surprised that no Rebel assault had materialized during the morning as expected, but now he was unsure where it would fall. At 3:00 p.m. Meade had reported to Halleck in Washington that the enemy was moving on both of his flanks and that he found it "difficult to tell exactly his movements."

Shortly before Sickles' arrival at the Leister House, Brigadier-General Warren pointed out to the army commander that all was still not well on III Corps' front as the troops were not in the correct position – indeed they were mostly well out in front of Cemetery Ridge. Sickles had a frosty reception when he arrived. Meade told him he need not bother to dismount. According to Captain Paine, "I never saw General Meade so angry if I may so call it." He then "ordered General Sickles to retire his line to the position he had been instructed to take. This was done in a few sharp words." Within minutes of Sickles' departure Meade followed in a hurry, accompanied by Warren and followed by numerous staff officers, to see the situation on the left for himself. Meade was dismayed by the gap now opened up in his line and the exposed position adopted by III Corps. When he joined Sickles east of the Peach Orchard he was in no mood to listen to his corps commander's justification of his actions. Sickles' attempt to explain that he needed to occupy the high ground at the Peach Orchard for his artillery was shot down with the comment, "General Sickles, this is neutral ground, our guns command it, as well as the enemy's. The very reason you cannot hold it applies to them." Sickles offered to withdraw but at almost the same moment the Confederate artillery opened fire – it was too late: the fighting on July 2 was about to begin in earnest. Meade rode off to hurry forward reinforcements. The battle was not beginning as he had intended nor to his liking. But neither was it for the Rebels, as the presence of a heavily defended Peach Orchard area came as an unwelcome shock.

Comments

It is hard to tell whether Sickles was just being deliberately difficult or whether he genuinely did not understand where his corps should be deployed. He certainly felt strongly that his left was vulnerable, his artillery ammunition train was expected up the Emmitsburg Road and that he needed to occupy the higher ground along the road to prevent its falling into Rebel hands. However, he had neglected the obvious: that he would have to create a dangerous salient by bending back his line to the Devil's Den area and that he had insufficient troops to man this extended line – all of which is immaterial really, as he disobeyed or ignored his army commander's orders. Sickles never occupied the line he was instructed to, despite being told no fewer than four times. Meade told him in the early hours of the morning; then he was instructed via Captain Meade around 9:00 a.m; by Captain Meade again half an hour later; and finally he had the position actually pointed out by Meade shortly after 11:00 a.m. Three hours later he began to move forward even further. This disobedience was to cause considerable confusion, as reinforcements had to be rushed to the salient in a piecemeal fashion with no single directing person, and even they were insufficient to prevent eventual retreat. The Union's fight for "Sickles' salient," during which Sickles paid for his stubbornness with the loss of a leg, was the only defensive action in the battle where the defenders lost more than the attackers.

Longstreet's Corps Moves South and Stuart Arrives on the Scene (Map 45)

At about 11:00 a.m., while waiting for Law's Brigade to arrive, Longstreet summoned Colonel E. Porter Alexander and told him to take command of the corps artillery for the forthcoming attack and to find a suitable route for the guns that was concealed from the enemy's view. Only the Washington Artillery Battalion under Major Eshleman was to remain at the rear. Alexander led his battalion of twenty-four guns (a very mixed bag of four 24-pounder and four 12-pounder howitzers, six Napoleons, seven 3-inch ordnance rifles, two 20-pounder and one 10-pounder Parrotts) and associated caissons and wagons (the battalions of Colonel Henry C. Cabell and Major Mathias W. Henry moved with their divisions, McLaws' and Hood's respectively). Alexander started out around 11:00 a.m., leading his battalion along the same route that was taken about an hour later by Longstreet, until he reached the Black Horse Tavern where the road was visible from the Union signal station on Little Round Top. At that point Alexander turned off the road to the right and moved across the fields until he could rejoin the tracks that led to the Pitzer's Schoolhouse area alongside the Willoughby Run without being seen. The precise route is uncertain but could have been one of the three shown on Map 45, with no. 1 the most likely. There he parked his guns and waited for the infantry. After some time they had not appeared, so, leaving the guns under command of Major Frank Huger, Alexander rode back to find out what had happened.

Notes

- This flank march was intended to strike the left flank of the enemy, supposedly on the Emmitsburg Road. Lee had noticed that the Union signal station on Little Round Top was clearly visible from his place of observation at the Lutheran Seminary and so had stressed that Longstreet's Corps should take a concealed route to its jump-off position.
- The order of march for Longstreet's two divisions was Col. Porter Alexander's artillery battalion (it started out well before the infantry), McLaws' Division led by Kershaw's Brigade, Hood's Division with Law's Brigade at the rear. Maj. Benjamin F. Eshleman's artillery battalion was left behind. The column totaled around 14,500 men and 35 guns with their associated limbers, caissons and wagons. Alexander's 24 guns had preceded the main column.
- The march developed into one in excess of 6 miles, with a starting point on Herr's Ridge near the Chambersburg Pike (**A**) and finishing on Warfield Ridge opposite the Peach Orchard (**C**). Each division with its accompanying guns would occupy at least 1.5 miles of road. As shown, when the leading elements of the column halted just south of the Black Horse Tavern, Law's Brigade would probably not yet have started marching.
- The leading troops of Kershaw's Brigade came into view from the signal station on Little Round Top as it crested the rise south of the Black Horse Tavern and the whole column was turned back to try to avoid discovery (**B**). Alexander's artillery, however, had found an alternative route forward that was not in view of the signalers by moving across fields to the south and turning east to reach the Pitzer Schoolhouse road where he waited for the infantry.
- Not long after noon, Capts. Norton and Taylor, Union signal officers on Little Round Top, reported considerable wagon and troop movement on the Chambersburg Pike near Abraham Spangler's house and Herr's Ridge. This was surely the march getting under way. At 1:30 p.m. Captain Hall, then in command of the station, signaled, "A heavy column of enemy's infantry, about ten thousand, is moving from opposite our extreme left toward our right." Later he clarified this by saying the troops were probably on the road between Dr. Hall's house and the Black Horse Tavern. This was, almost certainly, part of the column doubling back on itself and had the effect of confusing Meade as to the destination of these troops.
- The march ended on Warfield Ridge for the leading brigade at around 4:00 p.m. after 3.5–4 hours on the road – perhaps an average speed of 1.5 miles in the hour.

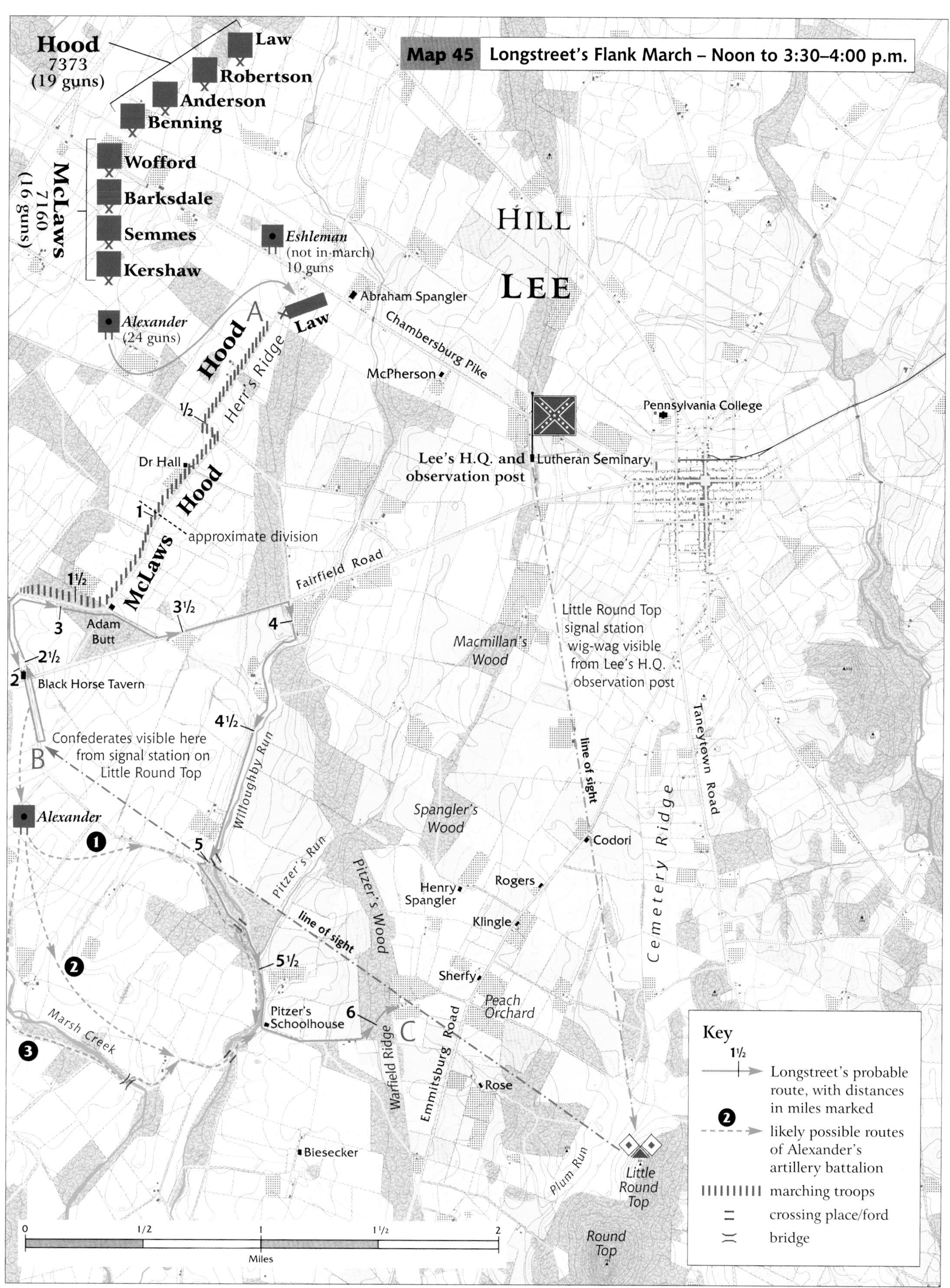
Map 45 Longstreet's Flank March – Noon to 3:30–4:00 p.m.
Hood
7373
(19 guns)
Law
Robertson
Anderson
Benning
McLaws
7160
(16 guns)
Wofford
Barksdale
Semmes
Kershaw
Eshleman
(not in march)
10 guns
Alexander
(24 guns)
HILL
LEE
Abraham Spangler
Chambersburg Pike
McPherson
Herr's Ridge
Law
Hood
Dr Hall
approximate division
Pennsylvania College
Lee's H.Q. and observation post
Lutheran Seminary
Fairfield Road
Adam Butt
Black Horse Tavern
Little Round Top signal station wig-wag visible from Lee's H.Q. observation post
Macmillan's Wood
Confederates visible here from signal station on Little Round Top
Willoughby Run
line of sight
Taneytown Road
Cemetery Ridge
Alexander
Spangler's Wood
Codori
Pitzer's Run
Pitzer's Wood
Henry Spangler
Rogers
Klingle
Sherfy
Peach Orchard
Pitzer's Schoolhouse
Marsh Creek
Warfield Ridge
Emmitsburg Road
Rose
Biesecker
Plum Run
Little Round Top
Round Top
Miles
Key
Longstreet's probable route, with distances in miles marked
likely possible routes of Alexander's artillery battalion
marching troops
crossing place/ford
bridge

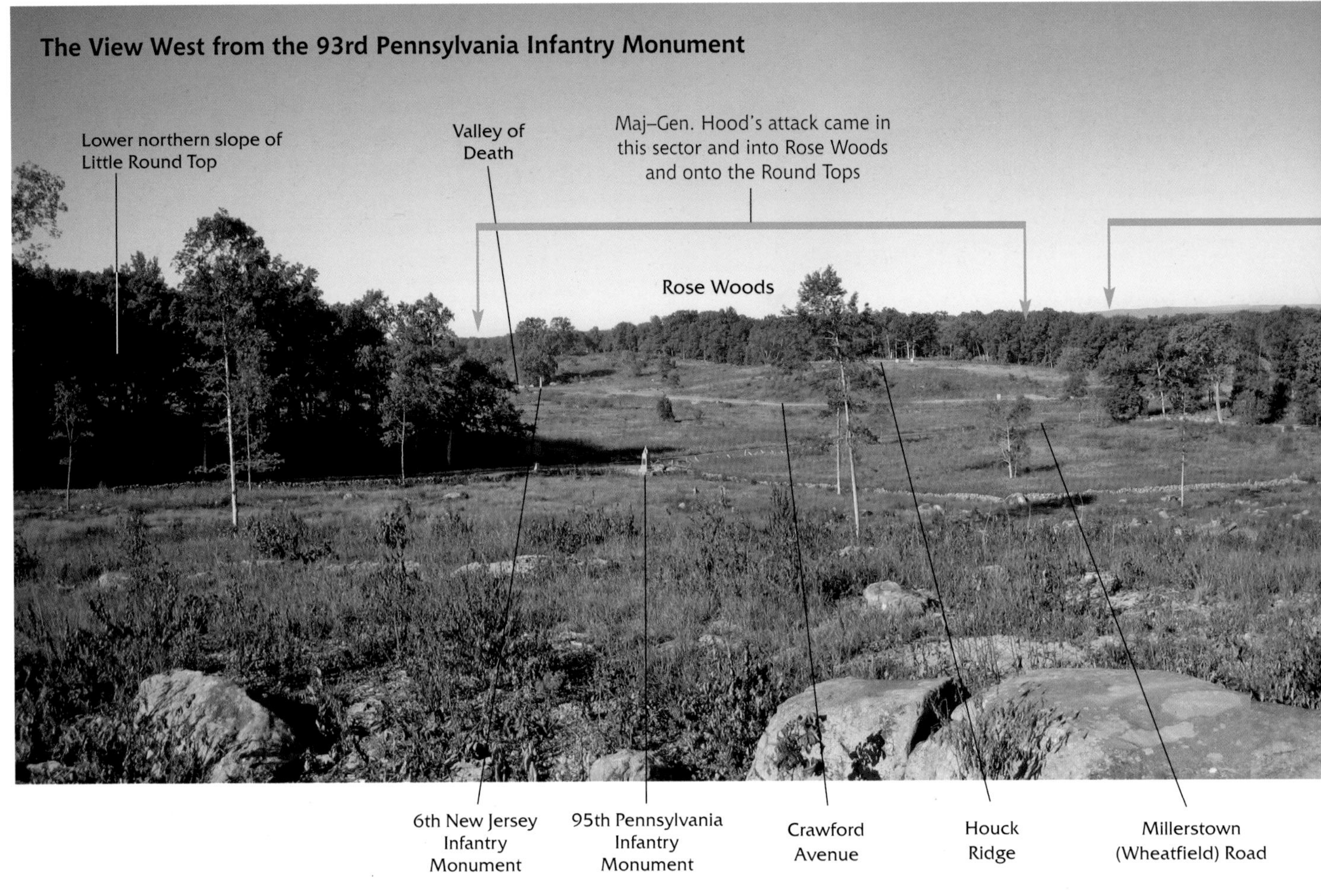

At about noon, just as Longstreet's long-delayed flank march was getting under way, the long-lost Stuart arrived at Lee's headquarters. He had left his column on the Carlisle Road and ridden ahead to report in person. There is no record of their meeting, but subsequent rumors described it as less than cordial. According to Colonel Alexander in his later writings, Lee said, "Well, General, you are here at last." His manner implied a rebuke, and Stuart realized as much. Lee instructed him to group his horsemen on the army's left and support Ewell.

Longstreet was still disgruntled and annoyed when his corps finally began its march, with Kershaw's Brigade of McLaws' Division in the lead. The effect of his attitude on the march and subsequent operations is discussed in detail below under "Controversies," page 452. Sufficient to say that he considered the responsibility for the march had been given by Lee to Captain Johnston, who, according to that officer, had merely been attached to Longstreet's headquarters to advise on the route as necessary. Longstreet deliberately decided to ride with Hood's Division, following McLaws. The two divisions had a combined strength of some 14,500 men, more or less equally divided between them. This meant a division, marching four abreast with its artillery battalion, would occupy at least 1.5 miles of road. After marching just under 2.5 miles and about to crest the rise at Black Horse Tavern, it was realized that the column would be visible from the signal station on Little Round Top. Knowing that to continue would jeopardize security, McLaws called a halt while he and Johnston rode off to look for an alternative route. While they were away, Alexander arrived and pointed out the track he had followed, which must have been fairly obvious as so many guns had crossed the fields. However, with the divisional commander away no one wanted the responsibility of changing the course, so Alexander left to return to his guns. At this stage the corps column would have stretched back to Herr's Ridge and, as noted earlier, it is possible that the last brigade, Law, had yet to start. However, the halt and then countermarching back caused some doubling up of the line, confusion and delay as Hood's Division tried to continue its march.

McLaws returned from his search for an alternative route swearing profusely and in a foul mood. It was then that Longstreet appeared to investigate the delay and both he and McLaws rode to the top of the rise. After seeing the problem Longstreet declared, "Why, this won't do. Is there no way to avoid it?" There was – but for some unknown reason neither took it. Not only had Alexander pointed out his route to several unknown officers, but also the evidence of his passage across the fields must have been plainly visible. Either it was overlooked or deemed unsuitable for some inexplicable reason, because McLaws stated the column must double back on itself and take a route he had found earlier. Longstreet accepted this. There was further delay while the column untangled itself and first countermarched, then took a 2.5-mile circuitous route along Fairfield Road before turning south along the Willoughby Run to the point where the Black Horse Tavern Road joined it (see Map 45). It had added about an hour and a half to the march.

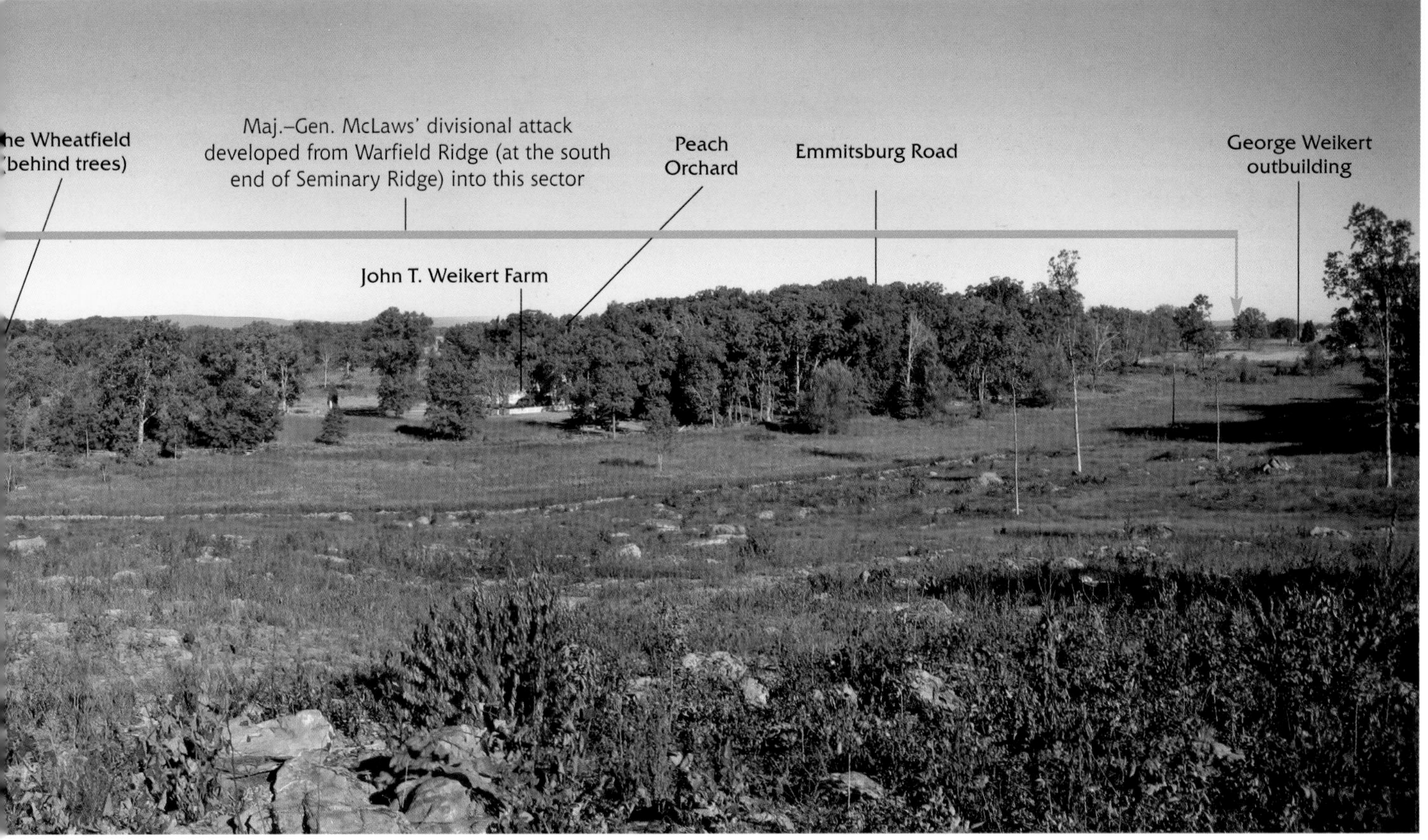

This photograph shows the view west from the southern end of Cemetery Ridge, from on what is now called Munshower Hill. The Union defenders of the left wing of Sickles' salient were initially deployed on Houck Ridge and at the Peach Orchard, as well as along the Emmitsburg Road against the advance of Longstreet's Corps. See Maps 46 and 47.

With Kershaw's Brigade still leading, the column turned left at Pitzer's Schoolhouse and started to climb the western slope of Seminary Ridge. At this point Longstreet joined McLaws to ask, "How are you going in?" To which McLaws responded, "That will be determined when I can see what is in my front." Longstreet observed, "There is nothing in your front; you will be entirely on the flank of the enemy." "Then I will continue my march in column of companies, and after arriving on the flank as far as is necessary will face to the left and march on the enemy." Longstreet rode off with the words, "That suits me."

As Kershaw's Brigade broke through the treeline on Seminary Ridge opposite the Peach Orchard, Union guns opened up on the emerging Rebel infantry. The Peach Orchard and line of the Emmitsburg Road were swarming with Yankees and guns. A few days later, writing to his wife, McLaws said, "The view presented astonished me as the enemy was massed in my front, and extended to my right and left as far as I could see." He deployed his division and then informed his corps commander of the situation, suggesting he come to see for himself. This further delay infuriated Longstreet who sent no fewer than three couriers to demand why the attack had not yet started. On receipt of the third – which was a direct order to attack immediately – McLaws replied that he would do so in five minutes. However, before he could advance, another courier galloped up, this time to stop the attack – Hood's Division was moving round behind McLaws to the right flank. Soon after this Longstreet at last appeared in person.

AN OVERVIEW (Map 46)

The second day at Gettysburg was probably the most critical. It was the day that saw the most intense, sustained Rebel assaults on both ends of the Yankee line, as well as considerable pressure being applied to their center. Little Round Top, Devil's Den, Houck Ridge, Rose Woods, the Peach Orchard, the Wheatfield, Culp's and East Cemetery Hills were the scenes of desperate attacks and counterattacks, with the protagonists fighting at close range and often hand to hand. While July 3 is famous for Lee's final fling – Pickett's charge – which lasted less than an hour (excluding the artillery bombardment), the action on July 2 flared up along most of the Union line at intervals from around 4:30 p.m. to 9:00 p.m.

Upon arriving opposite the Peach Orchard, McLaws' Division of Longstreet's Corps found not the exposed flank of the enemy but a strong position supported by artillery batteries. Hood's Division moved to his right and faced the Rose Woods–Devil's Den–Round Tops features. Preceded by a bombardment from Longstreet's massed artillery, Hood's Division attacked first at about 4:30 p.m., advancing into what was to become the hell of Devil's Den and the Slaughter Pen (the Plum Run valley between Little Round Top and the eastern edge of Rose Woods). Here there was considerable close-quarter combat. Several regiments swept past this rocky eminence to challenge the Yankees, who only minutes before had occupied Little Round Top. Here the 20th Maine withstood several charges by Hood's men and then counterattacked just as the Rebels were withdrawing, tumbling

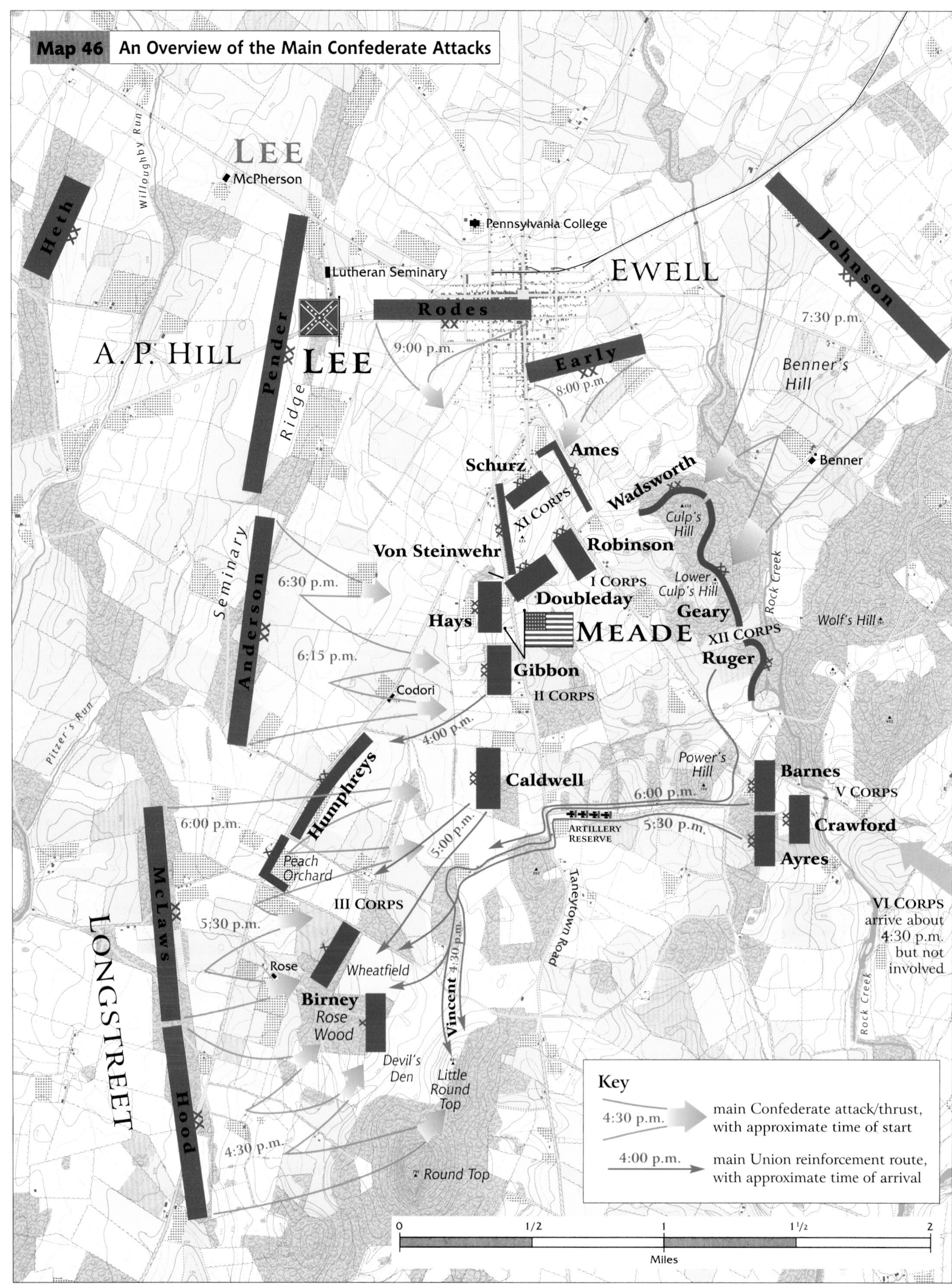
Map 46 An Overview of the Main Confederate Attacks
LEE
McPherson
Willoughby Run
Heth
Pennsylvania College
Lutheran Seminary
EWELL
Johnson
Rodes
Pender
A. P. HILL
LEE
9:00 p.m.
Early
8:00 p.m.
7:30 p.m.
Benner's Hill
Benner
Ridge
Seminary
Ames
Schurz
XI CORPS
Wadsworth
Culp's Hill
Von Steinwehr
Robinson
Anderson
6:30 p.m.
I CORPS
Doubleday
Lower Culp's Hill
Rock Creek
Hays
Geary
MEADE
XII CORPS
Wolf's Hill
6:15 p.m.
Gibbon
Ruger
Codori
II CORPS
Pitzer's Run
4:00 p.m.
Humphreys
Caldwell
Power's Hill
Barnes
V CORPS
6:00 p.m.
6:00 p.m.
ARTILLERY RESERVE
5:30 p.m.
Crawford
5:00 p.m.
Peach Orchard
Ayres
Taneytown Road
McLaws
III CORPS
LONGSTREET
5:30 p.m.
VI CORPS arrive about 4:30 p.m. but not involved
4:30 p.m.
Rose
Wheatfield
Birney
Rose Wood
Vincent
Rock Creek
Hood
Devil's Den
Little Round Top
Key
4:30 p.m.
main Confederate attack/thrust, with approximate time of start
4:00 p.m.
main Union reinforcement route, with approximate time of arrival
4:30 p.m.
Round Top
0
1/2
1
1 1/2
2
Miles

them off the hill. The Confederates fell back to Devil's Den where they were still in musketry range of Little Round Top and from there they exchanged fire with the Yankees across the Plum Run. Despite reinforcements from II and V Corps and several gallant counterattacks by Union regiments, Houck Ridge was eventually lost to the combined efforts of Robertson's and Benning's Brigades of Hood's Division.

At this time, around 5:30 p.m., McLaws' Division attacked and overran the Union positions in the Peach Orchard, pushing on into the adjacent Wheatfield where the fighting was again hand-to-hand and with the field changing hands several times. Eventually McLaws' men and several of Hood's regiments had the better of the struggle, although their losses were so severe that their advance stalled along the banks of the Plum Run when they ran into a reorganized Union line on Cemetery Ridge.

Then Anderson's Division joined the battle. Hancock, who had control of the Union center, had weakened this part of the line to support Sickles and toward that weakened center Anderson's three brigades advanced between about 6:15 and 6:30 p.m. Elements of one brigade (Wright) reached the crest of Cemetery Ridge. The Union 1st Minnesota counterattacked Wilcox's Brigade and, although losing 68 percent of its strength, succeeded in slowing the attack long enough for Hancock to establish a new defensive line. The new line held and Anderson began the long retreat back across the valley.

On the other end of the long curving line of battle Ewell had waited all day, until around 7:30 p.m., to deliver his demonstration, which had been supposed to start when he heard Longstreet's guns – they had opened fire well over three hours earlier. One division (Johnson) assaulted Culp's Hill and another (Early) East Cemetery Hill half an hour later. Both attacks met with initial success. It looked for a moment as if the opportunity Lee sought might have arisen. Early's Division actually pierced the Union line when several Rebel regiments charged up East Cemetery Hill in the growing gloom. However, they were unsupported and, faced with Union counterattacks, were forced to withdraw.

July 2 had been a bloody day for both sides, with losses probably amounting to 10,000 each.

Notes

• This map shows the Confederate attacks on July 2 and the principal Union responses in rushing reserves to threatened areas. It was a classic exterior lines versus interior lines situation, with Lee trying to crush his enemy with assaults or demonstrations on both flanks and in the center, thus preventing Meade from using his interior lines position to switch reserves quickly. The distance from Johnson's left to Hood's right through Gettysburg and down Seminary Ridge was 5.5 miles, whereas from XII Corps' right to the Union left was not much over 2 miles.

• Although the Rebels eventually crushed Sickles' salient, their attacks were poorly coordinated, with the initial assault by Hood starting around 4:30 p.m. and the final half-hearted advance by Rodes at 9:00 p.m. As is clear from the timings, the main attacks were staggered and in echelon from the right. The demonstration by Ewell that was supposed to start when Longstreet's guns opened fire did not begin until some three hours later. This was a serious flaw in the execution of the Confederate plan, as it allowed Union reinforcements to be moved from quiet sectors of the line to threatened ones.

• At the end of the day Sickles had been driven out of his salient at very considerable cost in casualties, but the Union line on Cemetery Ridge was intact and VI Corps had arrived. After some really intense fighting around the Peach Orchard, Devil's Den, the Wheatfield and Little Round Top by Longstreet's divisions, some remarkable advances by brigades from Anderson's Division in Hill's Corps, and a desperate, but largely unsuccessful, struggle by Johnson's Division to take Culp's Hill, Lee's line still faced the unbroken Union "fishhook" from Culp's Hill to Little Round Top.

• A comparison of losses (killed, wounded, and missing) for the day is difficult, but a rough guide of those suffered by both sides in the fighting along Cemetery Ridge to Little Round Top and in crushing or defending Sickles' salient are shown below:

Longstreet – 4,400
Hill – 1,600
Total – 6,000

II Corps – 2,800
III Corps – 4,200
V Corps – 2,000
Total – 9,000

One of the few instances in any major offensive where the defenders have lost considerably more than their attackers.

HOOD'S DIVISIONAL ATTACK, 4:30 P.M.

Hood Advances (Map 47)

By 4:00 p.m. Longstreet was belatedly running out of patience at the delay in launching the attack on the Union flank. Although it had been his continual foot-dragging that had prevented his corps getting into position earlier, he now realized that time was fast running out. He had been forced into an attack he did not agree with and with only two of his three divisions present (Pickett had yet to arrive). As Longstreet himself was fond of saying, "I never like to go into action with one boot off." Now, as McLaws and Hood were confronted by the unexpected strength of the enemy positions only a few hundred yards away, it was realized that Lee's plan of striking a vulnerable flank and attacking up the Emmitsburg Road was in ruins. The intended flank attack was now likely to be a costly frontal one.

Hood had moved his division behind McLaws to deploy on the extreme right of the line at the southern end of Seminary Ridge. Opposite him, half a mile away, was the tree-covered, steep-sided, conical hill now known as Round Top (or Big Round Top); to its left was the smaller, lower hill with an open western slope later referred to as Little Round Top. In front of Little Round Top were the lower, wood-covered Houck Ridge and a tangle of fields criss-crossed with stone walls and fences. While his troops were getting into position, Hood sent out some Texas scouts to reconnoiter. They returned to say that the Union left was still open and vulnerable to an attack over and round the Round Tops. When informed of this Longstreet would have none of it. Already pressed for time, still smarting from Lee's rebukes, his response was, in effect, "General Lee's orders are to attack up the Emmitsburg Road." Hood was dismayed and twice more protested, but was twice more given the same implacable response. Just before the advance started Longstreet rode up to the front and Hood went to plead for a final time for a change of plan. The corps commander's response was, "We must obey the orders of General Lee."

While Hood was desperately trying to get Longstreet to use his discretion and change the plan, and while his troops were shaking out into attack formation, the Rebel artillery under Alexander (the batteries of Captains Reilly and Latham) had started pounding the enemy positions. This bombardment brought a fierce response from the Union guns. It is an unnerving experience for troops to have to endure shelling as they await the order to advance. As a Captain Barziza in the 4th Texas reflected:

> The enemy's shells screamed and bursted around us, inflicting considerable damage. It is very trying among men to remain still and in ranks under a severe cannonading. One has time to reflect upon the danger and there being no wild excitement as in a charge, he is more reminded of the utter helplessness of his present condition. The men are all flat on the ground, keeping their places in ranks, and as a shell is heard, generally try to bury themselves into the earth.

Hood had deployed his four brigades, some 7,000 men, in two lines. Leading the advance would be Brigadier-General Evander Law's five Alabama regiments on the right, with Brigadier-General Jerome Robertson's three Texan and one Arkansas regiment on the left. The second supporting line had Brigadier-General Henry Benning's four Georgian regiments behind Law and four more Georgian regiments under Brigadier-General George Anderson behind Robertson. The British observer Fremantle described the Texans, Alabamians and Arkansans on the march as being "queer to look at. They carry less than other troops; many of them have only got an old piece of carpet or rug as baggage; all are ragged and dirty, but full of good humor and confidence in themselves and in their general, Hood."

Whatever Lee's original plan, no matter how often Longstreet insisted Lee's orders must be obeyed, there was no attack up the Emmitsburg Road. Hood's Division would not wheel north but would advance to its front into what became several hours of bloody fighting amongst the massive boulders of Devil's Den, on the rocky slopes of Little Round Top, through Rose Woods and amongst the trees on Houck Ridge. Whether this change of direction was sanctioned by Longstreet or made deliberately and defiantly by Hood is unclear, as the regimental commanders later stated that they were uncertain about their objectives. Lieutenant-Colonel William Oates, commanding the 15th Alabama, claimed, "No communication as to what was intended to be done was made to the regimental commanders, until after the advance began." At the very last moment Hood, standing up in his stirrups at the front of his Texans, shouted, "Fix bayonets, my brave Texans; forward and take those heights!" Regimental commanders took up the cry. Lieutenant-Colonel Phillip A. Work, commanding the 1st Texas, yelled, "Follow the Lone Star flag to the top of the mountain." The distinctive shape of the Round Tops would guide the leading brigades forward.

The first to move out were the skirmishers, three companies from the 47th and two from the 48th Alabama in front of Law's Brigade, soon to be followed by the double-ranked lines of the regiments marching with shoulders almost touching, the Confederate flag held proudly aloft in the center of each regiment. It was some 750 yards from Law's start line to the Plum Run and a tendency for regiments to hurry had to be checked, as it was difficult enough keeping formation across the fields and over walls and fences. Of particular concern was the accurate fire directed at them by Captain James E. Smith's guns on Houck Ridge. As Law's Brigade approached the Plum Run, Law decided he must deal with Smith's battery directly. While allowing his three center regiments to continue toward the Round Tops, he pulled the 44th and 48th

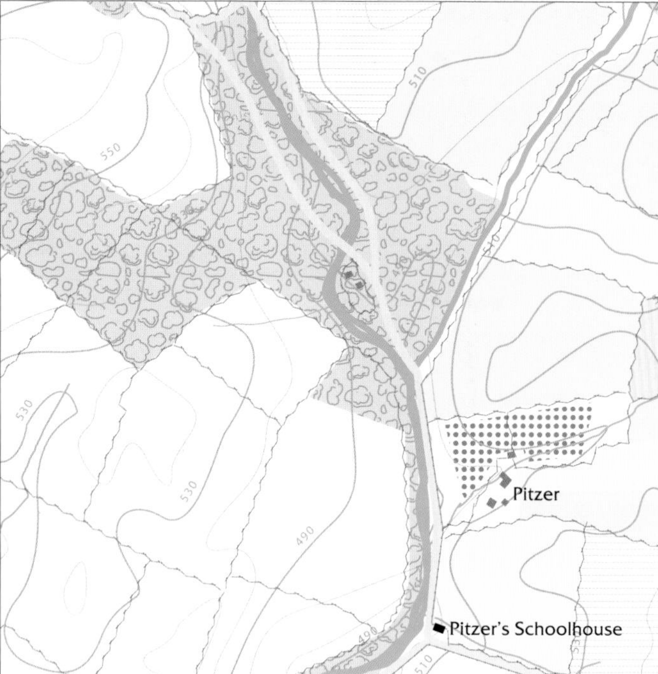

Notes

- The nine regiments of the leading two brigades (Law and Robertson) stepped off around 4:30 p.m. after the completion of the preparatory bombardment. Their combined strength was around 3,650 muskets. The regiments were deployed in double-rank lines, with the soldiers shoulder to shoulder, covering almost 800 yards of frontage. The regiments attacking Little Round Top had almost a mile to go, including a very steep climb up the slopes of Round Top. Those advancing to Devil's Den and the Rose Woods had over 1,000 yards to their objective.
- Within half an hour the supporting brigades (Benning and Anderson) advanced to the attack – another 3,300 muskets. Benning bore left, heading toward Houck Ridge, while Anderson on the left went for Rose Woods. About 7,000 Rebels were committed to the assault on the Union left flank.
- Initially Little Round Top was unoccupied except for the Union signal station. However, by the time Law's Alabamians began their assault, Col. Strong Vincent's four regiments, totaling some 1,330 men, were defending the hill. At the start Houck Ridge was held by Brig.-Gen. Hobart Ward's Brigade (Birney's Division, III Corps) with just under 1,500 soldiers.
- The numerical odds were stacked in favor of Hood as his two leading brigades outnumbered their Yankee opponents two to one. When the supporting brigades joined the fight the theoretical odds rose to four to one. However, Meade was able to hold the line through several hours of bitter, close-quarter fighting on Little Round Top, Devil's Den, the Rose Woods and the Wheatfield by the piecemeal dispatch of large numbers of reinforcements. In all, over a period of more than an hour, Meade sent nine brigades to support III Corps and the troops on Little Round Top. After Vincent occupied Little Round Top he was later reinforced by Brig.-Gen. Stephen H. Weed's Brigade, while the others arrived in succession into the maelstrom of savage fighting that was the Wheatfield and Rose Woods. The result was that Hood failed to take Little Round Top but succeeded, with the assistance of McLaws' Division (see Map 48), in securing Houck Ridge, Rose Woods and the Wheatfield. Sickles' left flank collapsed and retreated to Cemetery Ridge.

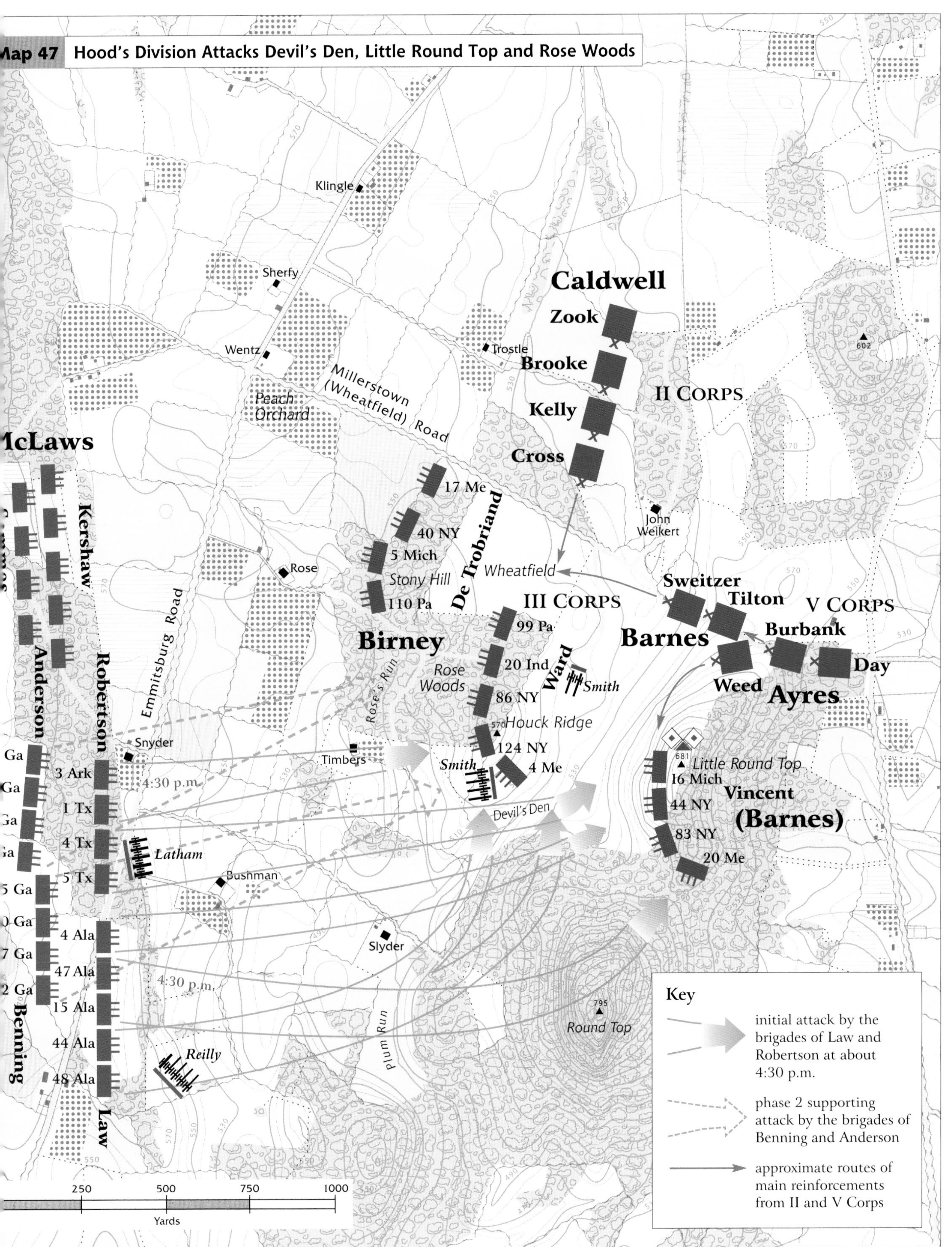
Map 47 Hood's Division Attacks Devil's Den, Little Round Top and Rose Woods
Klingle
Sherfy
Wentz
Trostle
Peach Orchard
Millerstown (Wheatfield) Road
Caldwell
Zook
Brooke
Kelly
Cross
II CORPS
McLaws
Kershaw
Anderson
Robertson
17 Me
40 NY
5 Mich
Stony Hill
110 Pa
De Trobriand
Wheatfield
John Weikert
Rose
Emmitsburg Road
Birney
III CORPS
99 Pa
20 Ind
86 NY
Ward
Smith
Rose Woods
Rose's Run
Houck Ridge
124 NY
4 Me
Sweitzer
Tilton
Barnes
V CORPS
Burbank
Day
Weed
Ayres
Little Round Top
16 Mich
44 NY
83 NY
20 Me
Vincent
(Barnes)
Snyder
Timbers
3 Ark
1 Tx
4 Tx
5 Tx
4:30 p.m.
Latham
Devil's Den
Bushman
Slyder
4 Ala
47 Ala
15 Ala
44 Ala
48 Ala
Law
Benning
Reilly
Plum Run
Round Top
Key
initial attack by the brigades of Law and Robertson at about 4:30 p.m.
phase 2 supporting attack by the brigades of Benning and Anderson
approximate routes of main reinforcements from II and V Corps
Yards

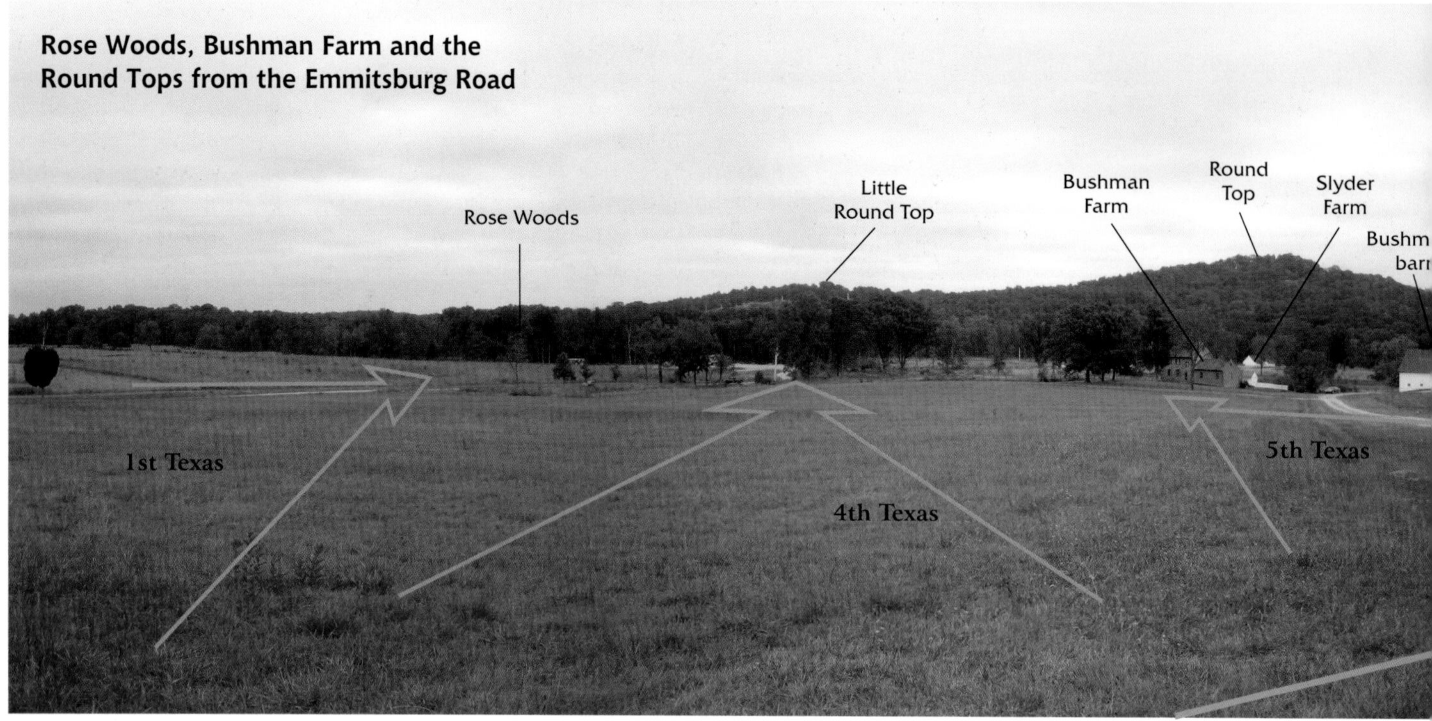

This photograph, taken from near the Texas Brigade monument, looking east, shows the line of advance of Robertson's regiments and of the 4th Alabama of Law's Brigade on the right. At this stage the Union defenders consisted of Ward's Brigade positioned on Stony Hill, hidden by the trees of Rose Woods. At about this time the advance was seen by Gen. Warren on Little Round Top, resulting in Vincent's Brigade occupying the hill just before it was attacked. See Map 47.

Alabama from the right and swung them behind the others to advance northward directly into the Devil's Den area at the southern end of Houck Ridge and the troublesome guns. Having given these instructions Law rode forward to speak to Oates, whose 15th Alabama now formed the extreme right of the attackers' line. Oates later recalled that finally he was given definite orders as to his objective. Law told him "to hug the base of Great Round Top and go up the valley between the two mountains, until I found the left of the Union line, to turn it and do all the damage I could." He would be supported on his left by the 47th Alabama. Oates was unable to communicate this change in direction to the five companies of skirmishers ahead; they continued eastward and ended up skirting round to the south of Round Top, meeting no opposition and being lost to the main battle. As it transpired, Oates did not wheel to the northeast at the base of Round Top either. Union sharpshooters had been a considerable nuisance during the advance and as the Rebels came on they fell back, some up Round Top. Oates felt a left wheel would further expose his right flank to their damaging fire and opted to continue east up the slopes of Round Top. After a brief rest to catch their breath after the steep climb to the summit, Captain Leigh R. Terrell from Law's staff appeared to inform Oates that Hood was down and Law now commanded the division, and that he, Oates, was to attack Little Round Top (see also page 413).

Within twenty minutes of the advance starting Hood had been hit in the arm by a shell fragment and seriously wounded. He was taken from the field in an ambulance and command devolved onto Law. It was a major blow to the division's attack, as Hood was widely recognized as a capable, forceful and dynamic commander. Law was by no means his equal. Meanwhile, on the division's left Robertson's Texas Brigade had stepped off briskly behind a skirmisher screen, crossed the Emmitsburg Road and headed down the slope into the small valley of Rose's Run (the western branch of Plum Run). It very soon became clear to Robertson that he could not comply with his original instructions to maintain contact with Law's left and at the same time keep in contact with the Emmitsburg Road. With Law heading east this was impossible and Robertson elected to forget the road and try to keep contact with Law. The brigade, under fire from Union guns at the Peach Orchard, Smith's Battery on Houck Ridge and enemy skirmishers in Rose Woods, advanced through Rose Woods to confront Ward's Brigade defending Houck Ridge.

In accordance with his instructions, Benning advanced when Law had got about 400 yards ahead, but on the left "Tige" Anderson's Georgians did not move until a little later when he received an appeal from Robertson for assistance. Worryingly, McLaws on the division's left had not advanced.

The Struggle for Devil's Den and Houck Ridge (Map 48)

The Confederate batteries ceased firing as the long lines of gray-clad infantry of Law and Robertson passed through them. The Union artillery commander, Hunt, was watching from Smith's gun position above Devil's Den and, realizing that the position on Houck Ridge would soon be outflanked, rode off to find reinforcements. During his ride Hunt had a disconcerting encounter with a stampeding herd of cows that had been driven crazy by shellfire (see box, page 155). He left the defense of Houck Ridge to just under 1,500 men in five regiments commanded by Brigadier-General Hobart Ward, plus the three (the fourth had been disabled by Rebel gunfire) 10-pounder Parrotts of Smith's Battery – there

Latham's 3 Napoleons, 6-pounder and howitzer positioned near here

was no room for the other two, which were in position some 200 yards to the rear on a small spur overlooking the Plum Run.

On the right Law's Brigade's advance became divided, and its strength thus dissipated, when the two regiments on the extreme right (44th and 48th Alabama) swung north to become entangled in Devil's Den and the fight for the southern end of Houck Ridge and Smith's guns. This left only three regiments (4th, 15th and 47th Alabama) to tackle Little Round Top, which had been occupied just minutes before they came within attacking distance by Vincent's Union Brigade. The fight for Little Round Top is described in detail on pages 413–21. On the left, in Robertson's Brigade, the 1st Texas and 3rd Arkansas had the shortest distance to go and thus were the first to give the Rebel yell as they advanced through Rose Woods and assaulted Houck Ridge. As the 900 Rebels climbed through the trees they were met by a blast of fire from the 900 rifle-muskets of three Yankee regiments (20th Indiana, 86th and 124th New York). This clash developed into a bitter stand-up fight at close quarters, with the 1st Texas and 124th New York struggling in and around a triangle of stone walls on the southwestern slope of Houck Ridge.

In Devil's Den and the Plum Run valley the confrontation among the rocks was between Law's 44th and 48th Alabama and Ward's 4th Maine and 99th Pennsylvania, the latter having been rushed from the far right of the line to the left. Along Houck Ridge and in Devil's Den something of a bloody stalemate had developed, with a gap opening up between Law's two regiments on the right in Devil's Den and the Plum Run valley and Robertson's two on the left. Just as the Rebels had been brought to a standstill and were on the verge of wavering, Hood's (now Law's) second line appeared through the smoke and confusion. Benning brought his four regiments (2nd, 15th, 17th and 20th Georgia) into the gap at "the Triangle" and forced back the 124th New York. At about this time Birney, the divisional commander, desperate to save his left brigade, sent the 40th New York (known as the "Mozart Regiment" from its link with New York's Mozart Hall political machine) from De Trobriand's Brigade to charge into that part of the Plum Run valley that became known as the "Slaughter Pen." The fighting in Devil's Den and the Slaughter Pen was, according to a Texas participant, "one of the wildest, fiercest struggles of the war," ending with the Rebels occupying the rocks and establishing a presence on the southern end of Houck Ridge and Captain Smith having to abandon his three workable guns.

"Friendly Fire"

So called "friendly fire" incidents have occurred on battlefields since man went to war, and unfortunately are still happening today as, despite huge advances in technology, people do make mistakes, especially when frightened and confused. At Gettysburg there were at least fifteen instances of friendly fire by both artillery and infantry units, including the following two on July 2.

In the late afternoon the 4th and 5th Texas Regiments from Robertson's Brigade were involved in the fight to take Little Round Top. After several charges had failed, a final effort was ordered which was regarded with horror by many of the Texans, even when assured that their guns would soften up the enemy first. Private William Fletcher of the 5th Texas wrote:

> I tried to force manhood to the front, but fright would drive it back with a shudder. [When the Rebel's own artillery opened fire] The guns were not elevated enough and were doing fine work on our position. The bursting and flying pieces of shell and rock put us in a panic condition – we could not drop to the front and protect ourselves, for we would be exposed to the enemy. All was confusion . . .

Officers had to gallop back to the guns to stop the firing.

In the second incident, after helping to drive the Yankees out of Devil's Den, the 2nd Georgia Regiment took shelter among the boulders and commenced firing up at their enemy on Little Round Top. Among them was John Bowden, who thought he had found a good spot and began firing. After his sixth shot he was concerned that he appeared to be drawing fire from three different directions. He scrabbled into what he thought a less vulnerable position and opened fire again. He later recounted what happened:

> My attention was attracted by a piece of bullet fired from the rear, which had split against the rock and struck my thigh. Upon investigation I found to my surprise that many of our men had selected hiding places along our route of charge from fifty to a hundred yards in the rear of our front rank, thus placing us between two fires. The smoke was so dense that evidently they thought they were in the front rank.

Map 48 The Struggle for Devil's Den and Houck Ridge

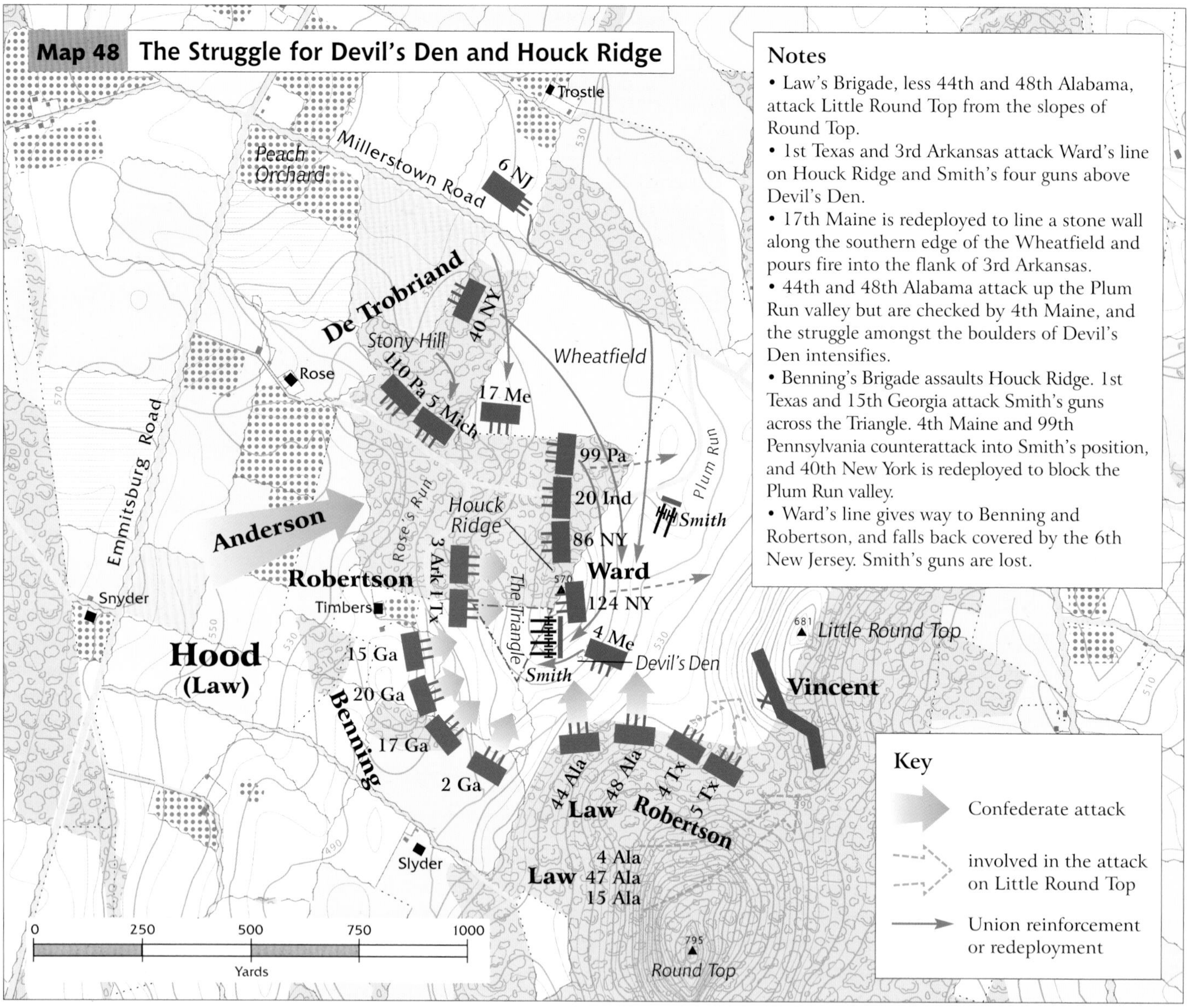

Notes

- Law's Brigade, less 44th and 48th Alabama, attack Little Round Top from the slopes of Round Top.
- 1st Texas and 3rd Arkansas attack Ward's line on Houck Ridge and Smith's four guns above Devil's Den.
- 17th Maine is redeployed to line a stone wall along the southern edge of the Wheatfield and pours fire into the flank of 3rd Arkansas.
- 44th and 48th Alabama attack up the Plum Run valley but are checked by 4th Maine, and the struggle amongst the boulders of Devil's Den intensifies.
- Benning's Brigade assaults Houck Ridge. 1st Texas and 15th Georgia attack Smith's guns across the Triangle. 4th Maine and 99th Pennsylvania counterattack into Smith's position, and 40th New York is redeployed to block the Plum Run valley.
- Ward's line gives way to Benning and Robertson, and falls back covered by the 6th New Jersey. Smith's guns are lost.

Key

Confederate attack

involved in the attack on Little Round Top

Union reinforcement or redeployment

Trostle
Peach Orchard
Millerstown Road
6 NJ
De Trobriand
40 NY
Stony Hill
110 Pa
5 Mich
17 Me
Wheatfield
Rose
Emmitsburg Road
Anderson
99 Pa
20 Ind
86 NY
Plum Run
Smith
Houck Ridge
Rose's Run
3 Ark
1 Tx
Robertson
Ward
124 NY
Snyder
Timbers
The Triangle
4 Me
Devil's Den
Smith
Little Round Top
Hood (Law)
15 Ga
20 Ga
17 Ga
2 Ga
Benning
Vincent
44 Ala
48 Ala
4 Tx
5 Tx
Law
Robertson
Slyder
Law
4 Ala
47 Ala
15 Ala
Round Top

0 250 500 750 1000
Yards

Little Round Top, from the "Valley of Death"

The northern part of Little Round Top, looking east from the 6th New Jersey Infantry Monument on Crawford Avenue. This is the section of the Plum Run valley known as the "Valley of Death." The 6th New Jersey was rushed from behind the Peach Orchard to cover the withdrawal of Ward's Brigade from Houck Ridge (behind the camera) as the Rebels attacked up the valley from the right.

Meanwhile, an equally intense combat was taking place on Ward's right in the Rose Woods and along the northern part of Houck Ridge, where, weakened by the removal of the 99th Pennsylvania, the Yankees were being pushed back. Also by this stage Anderson's Brigade had entered Rose Woods and threatened De Trobriand's left. The 17th Maine, lining a stone wall running along the southern edge of the Wheatfield, bitterly contested its possession with the 11th Georgia (Anderson's Brigade). Eventually the Yankees had the better of it and Anderson was forced to recoil and regroup; while doing so he was hit in the right leg and carried from the field. Nevertheless, this temporary success was not sufficient to prevent Ward initiating a withdrawal, covered by the 6th New Jersey, which had been sent from Burling's Brigade (Humphreys' Division).

At around 5:30 p.m. back on Warfield Ridge, Longstreet launched the second phase of his echeloned attack: he ordered forward part of McLaws' Division to coincide with Anderson's renewed advance – another monumental clash was about to occur, this time for the possession of the Wheatfield (see pages 423–28).

Confederate dead at the edge of Rose Woods.

Highlight: The Attack and Defense of Little Round Top (Maps 49–51)

More visitors stand beside the statue of Brigadier-General Gouverneur K. Warren atop Little Round Top to gaze out over a vista of much of the southern half of the battlefield than at any other spot. The attack and defense of this hill has gone into the folklore of American history, and its successful defense, primarily by Union troops of Colonel Strong Vincent's Brigade, is certainly one of the highlights of the fighting on July 2, although whether the holding or taking of Little Round Top would have dramatically altered the overall result of the battle is, and continues to be, debatable. The 20th Maine Volunteer Infantry Regiment, commanded by Colonel Joshua L. Chamberlain, fought its famous engagement on the extreme left flank of Meade's entire army. It culminated in a downhill charge that chased the 15th Alabama Infantry off the southern slope of the hill, becoming one of the most well-known actions of the battle, perhaps even of the Civil War. That said, the hill was not held, indeed could never have been held, by the 20th Maine alone. Some equally intense fighting took place along the whole brigade line. Had it not been for the timely arrival of the 140th New York Volunteer Infantry under Colonel Patrick O'Rorke on the right of the brigade line at the height of the battle, Vincent's Brigade might have lost Little Round Top.

As we have seen, "Little Round Top" was not identified by this name in July 1863. Its adjoining and higher neighbor was known locally as Round Top, Round Top Mountain or Round Hill – it is now usually referred to as "Big Round Top," although this *Companion* has retained the name "Round Top." Accounts written in 1863 referred to the smaller hill by such names as "Rock Hill," "Sugar Loaf Hill," "Broad Top Summit" and "High Knob."

The ground (Map 49)

Little Round Top was located some 3.5 miles south of the town square in Gettysburg at the southern end of Cemetery Ridge, Meade's main line of defense at the battle. It rose about 170 feet above the Plum Run to the west and formed the eastern side of the valley of that stream, the other side being Houck Ridge. On account of the intensity of the fighting and density of the bodies strewn over the ground after the battle, this valley became known as the "Valley of Death." Viewed from this valley, Little Round Top appeared as a shallow inverted V with a more gradual slope at the northern end than in the west. Here the slope was steep but largely open and covered with large numbers of granite rocks of varying sizes, "from the size of a wash pot to that of a wagon bed," some of which seemed to form irregular terraces across the slope. The rocks here were not the enormous boulders found piled up in the Devil's Den, but nevertheless some provided good cover for soldiers defending the hill or trying to crawl up its slope. This slope had a few isolated trees and patches of scrub. The eastern side of the hill was steep but not as steep as the west. However, this side was entirely covered in trees, among which were more scattered rocks making access to the summit extremely difficult for artillery or other wheeled vehicles. The Taneytown Road was only 300 yards east of the summit. In the south and inside the woods Little Round Top had a small spur, later known as "Vincent's Spur," which pointed to and sloped down to the saddle of high ground that joined the hill to its larger and higher neighbor, Round Top.

Round Top was over 100 feet higher than Little Round Top, and their summits were separated by 400 yards; thus Round Top dominated and overlooked its smaller companion. However, Round Top, whose sides near the top were almost sheer in both the east and west, was entirely covered in woods and scattered rocks. This made it virtually inaccessible to all but the most determined infantry and provided limited fields of observation in all directions.

From the point of view of the Union defenders of Little Round Top, the hill provided high ground and with it good observation to the north along Cemetery Ridge and in other directions, except to the east and south where the trees and Round Top blocked the line of sight. The Union signal station near the summit of Little Round Top was not only able to communicate by wigwag to army and corps headquarters but also report Confederate movements on Herr's Ridge, the Chambersburg Pike, near Black Horse Tavern and in the woods on Warfield Ridge as Longstreet's Corps assembled prior to its advance on July 2. As the enemy was in the west, so the virtually clear western slope, with its rock terraces and walls, allowed for good fields of fire for infantry and a fairly stiff, if short, climb for attackers. The rocks could provide some shelter

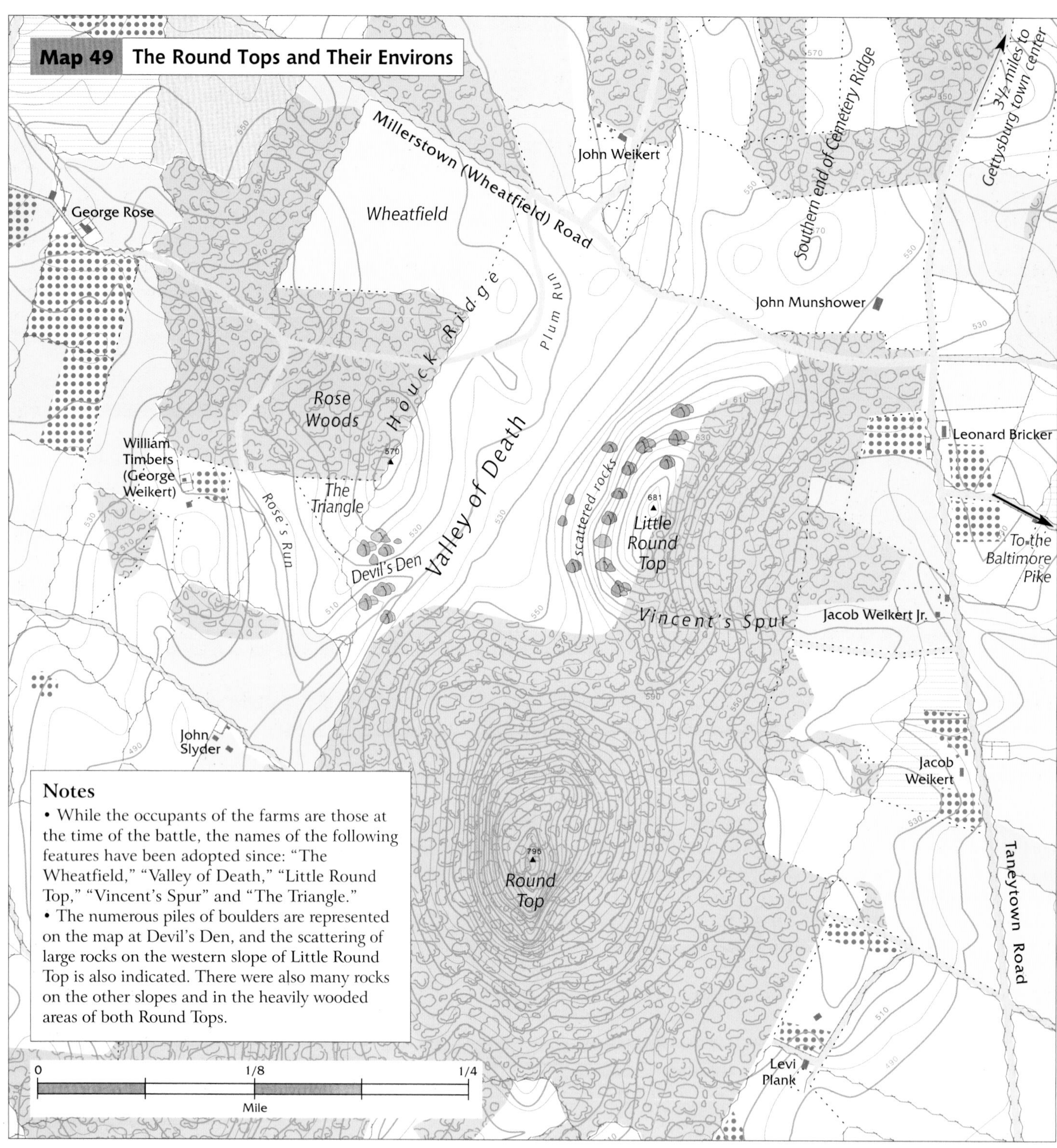

for a lying or crouching man from musket fire but not much from shells. While the eastern, or reverse, slope provided a secure covered approach to the western side, wagons could not be dragged up so ammunition supply would rely on the slow and laborious humping of boxes by soldiers. The other problem for the Yankees was the saddle between Little Round Top and Round Top. It was only some 50 yards long and covered in trees. Although the trees were not dense and there was little undergrowth, the saddle was a potential covered approach for the Rebels. Climbing through the trees on the northern slopes of Round Top, enemy infantry could be on the saddle before the defenders were aware of the danger.

From the attackers' point of view, assaulting the open western side of Little Round Top was not an attractive option, although artillery fire onto the slope would make things easier. As will be seen, the advancing Confederates had hoped to find Little Round Top unoccupied except for a signal station. Had this been so the ground would not have been a factor in their seizing the hill, but when confronted with serious resistance the ground dictated that their only realistic approach was along the saddle and from the trees on the lower slopes of Round Top. The subsequent naming of the Plum Run valley was proof of the folly of trying to assault Little Round Top from that direction.

Union breastworks on Round Top.

Tactical significance

The tactical significance of Little Round Top arose from its being dominating high ground on the extreme left of the Union defensive line. It was an anchor with which Meade could secure that flank. He recognized this soon after his arrival on the field in the early hours of July 2, which is why he wanted Sickles to occupy it. That Sickles failed to do so resulted in the hill's being occupied by only a signal station until late afternoon.

There is some conflict of opinion as to the value of Little Round Top as an artillery position. During the battle the six 10-pounder Parrott rifles of Captain Charles F. Hazlett's Battery D, 5th U.S. Artillery were eventually dragged with considerable difficulty up the eastern slope. There was certainly no room on the top for more, but, although dangerously exposed and not able to depress their guns low enough to hit close targets, they could fire effectively across the Plum Run, and their presence was of considerable value to the morale of the defending infantry. On July 3 these guns were able to take Pickett's Division in enfilade fire as it advanced across the fields west of Codori Farm. The other problem was the time and labor needed to keep the guns supplied with ammunition when every round had to be manhandled up the eastern slope.

Part of the hill's tactical significance to the Confederates rested with the fact that, if captured, they could dominate most of Cemetery Ridge as it ran north. Its whole length was visible up to and including Meade's headquarters in Leister House. However, as already noted, not more than six guns could be brought to the summit area and they themselves presented an obvious target for incoming fire. Nevertheless, a Rebel battery on Little Round Top enfilading much of the Union line would have been an unacceptable thorn in Meade's side. With this hill in enemy possession, the Yankee line would be outflanked. It opened up the possibility of infantry attacks rolling up the line from the south or getting troops onto the Taneytown Road and thus behind the Union line. Such an event would probably have forced a hasty, indeed precipitate, Yankee withdrawal. Meade had strong reserves to hand (VI Corps) to counter this threat, but Lee, Longstreet and Hood could not know this, and if the Rebel attacks all along the line had been simultaneous these reserves might have been committed elsewhere with not enough nearby to cope. Had Little Round Top not been occupied at the last moment by Vincent's Brigade these tactical possibilities would have been opened up to the Confederates at little cost. There was even a track (marked "To the Baltimore Pike" on Map 49) that led from the bottom of the eastern slope of Little Round Top directly to the Pike, the Union Army's lifeline, only 2 miles away. The possession of Little Round Top had significant tactical importance to both sides.

Force comparison

When the two leading brigades of Hood's Division, Law's on the right and Robertson's on the left, advanced just before 4:30 p.m. they were intended to find and strike the left flank of the Union line. Apart from the signalers, Little Round Top was thought to be unoccupied. These two brigades mustered some 3,600 men in nine regiments – a very substantial force. However, due to enemy resistance and control problems (see "Command and control," page 417), the force that became involved in the assaults on Little Round Top was reduced to five regiments, two from Robertson's Brigade (the 4th and 5th Texas under Colonels John C. G. Key and Robert M. Powell respectively) and three from Law's Brigade (4th, 15th and 47th Alabama, the 4th commanded by Lieutenant-Colonel Lawrence H. Scruggs and the 15th and 47th by Colonels William C. Oates and, initially, Colonel James W. Jackson). When the first attack on the hill was made these five regiments were divided into two separate forces, one composed of the 4th and 5th Texas and 4th Alabama and the other of the 47th and 15th Alabama, which attacked at a different time.

On the Union side, at the outset, the defenders of Little Round Top had the four regiments of Colonel Strong Vincent's Brigade in position to meet the Rebels' first assault – about 1,330 men with each regiment from a different state. They were the 16th Michigan (Lieutenant-Colonel Norval E. Welch), 44th New York (Colonel James C. Rice), 83rd Pennsylvania (Captain Orpheus S. Woodward) and the 20th Maine (Colonel Joshua L. Chamberlain).

When the five Rebel regiments stepped off from Warfield Ridge, their strength was approximately as shown in the table below, which also gives Vincent's regimental strengths.

Confederate (Robertson and Law)		**Union (Vincent)**	
4th Texas	415	16th Michigan	263
5th Texas	409	44th New York	391
4th Alabama	346	83rd Pennsylvania	295
47th Alabama	347	20th Maine	386
15th Alabama	499		
Artillery – none		Bat. D, 5th U.S. Artillery 6 x 10-pounder Parrotts	
Total	**2,016**	**Total**	**1,335**

During the later stages of the fight both sides received support as follows:

48th Alabama	374	140th New York	453

- The strength of the five Southern regiments that attacked Little Round Top had been substantially reduced by the time the first attack, or rather two attacks, went in. First, they suffered casualties from the 2nd U.S. Union Sharpshooters under Major Homer R. Stoughton in their approach to the Plum Run and lower slopes of Round Top. When Oates reached the top of that hill, the 15th and 47th Alabama had between them lost at least forty men through heat exhaustion on the stiff climb and the twenty-two men Oates sent to fill canteens had not returned. Then, just before attacking the hill Oates sent Company A off to try to capture several Union wagons spotted near the eastern base of Little Round Top – another fifty or sixty men. The 47th had, according to Colonel Jackson, over forty deserters, and three companies (A, D and F) under Captain H. C. Lindsey had been sent ahead as skirmishers, ending up on the north side of Round Top without encountering any enemy, and were thus absent from the fight for Little Round Top. That these companies listed their losses as just two missing supports the contention that they missed the fight. These figures, added to casualties in the approach due to the heat and enemy action,

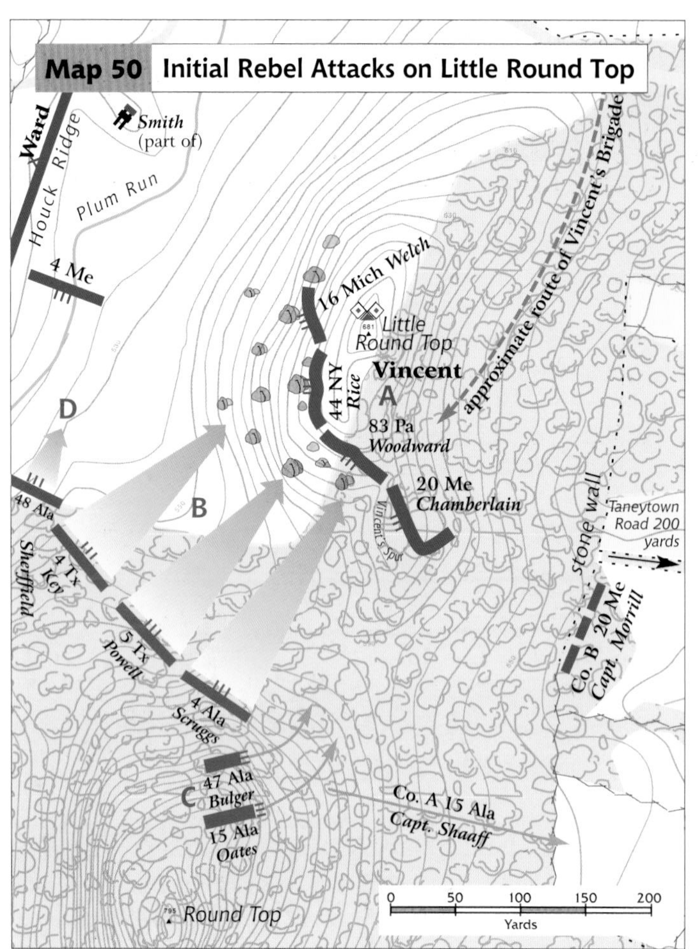

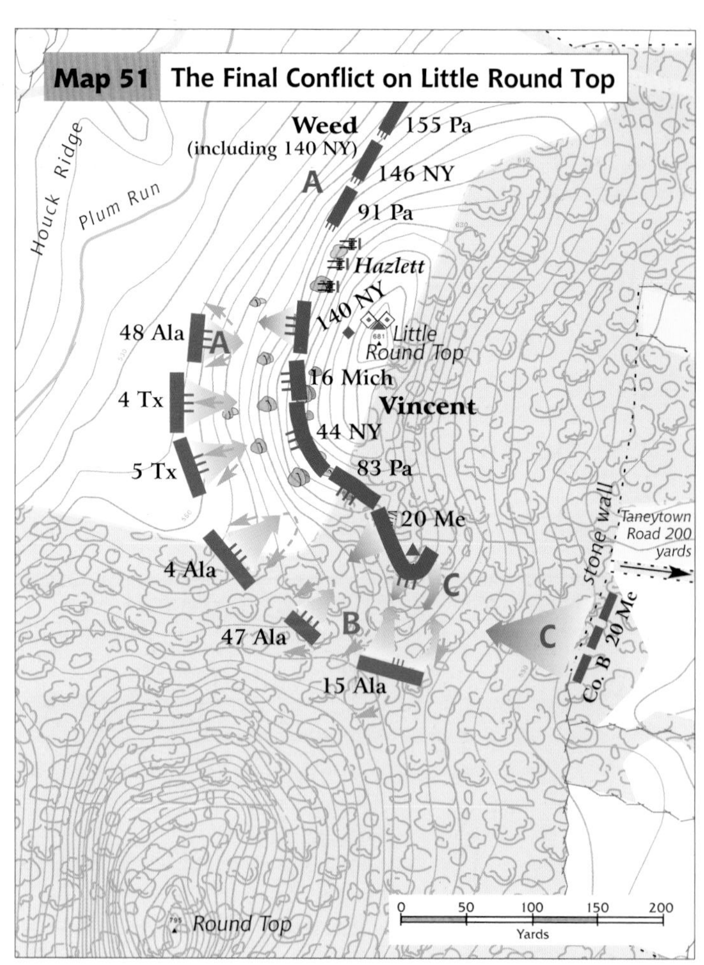

Notes

A Vincent's Brigade deploy on the southern and western slopes just in time to meet and repel the initial Rebel attacks (**B**).

C Both the 47th and 15th Alabama pause to rest near the summit of Round Top before being ordered into the attack. The map shows them moving down the slope onto the saddle prior to attacking 20th Maine on Vincent's Spur. En route Oates detaches Co. A to try to capture Union wagons. As the attacks develop and threaten 20th Maine's left flank, it is beaten back (refused) to meet the danger.

D Simultaneously the remainder of Law's Brigade (44th and 48th Alabama) tries to attack up the Plum Run valley.

Key

Confederate attack

Confederate advance

Confederate retreat

Union counterattack

scattered rocks

O'Rorke killed near here

Vincent mortally wounded near here

Notes

AA The 48th Alabama joins the attacks, threatening to outflank the 16th Michigan, but the 140th New York under Col. O'Rorke arrives in time to drive them back. The remainder of Weed's Brigade arrive but the Rebels are withdrawing.

B The 47th Alabama breaks and the 15th Alabama makes a final attack and tries to outflank the 20th Maine. Col. Oates's men are utterly exhausted and he orders a retreat.

C Col. Chamberlain, with the 20th Maine virtually out of ammunition, orders a charge which coincides with the Rebels retreating. This counterattack is joined by Co. B and the Rebels run for their lives with a number being captured.

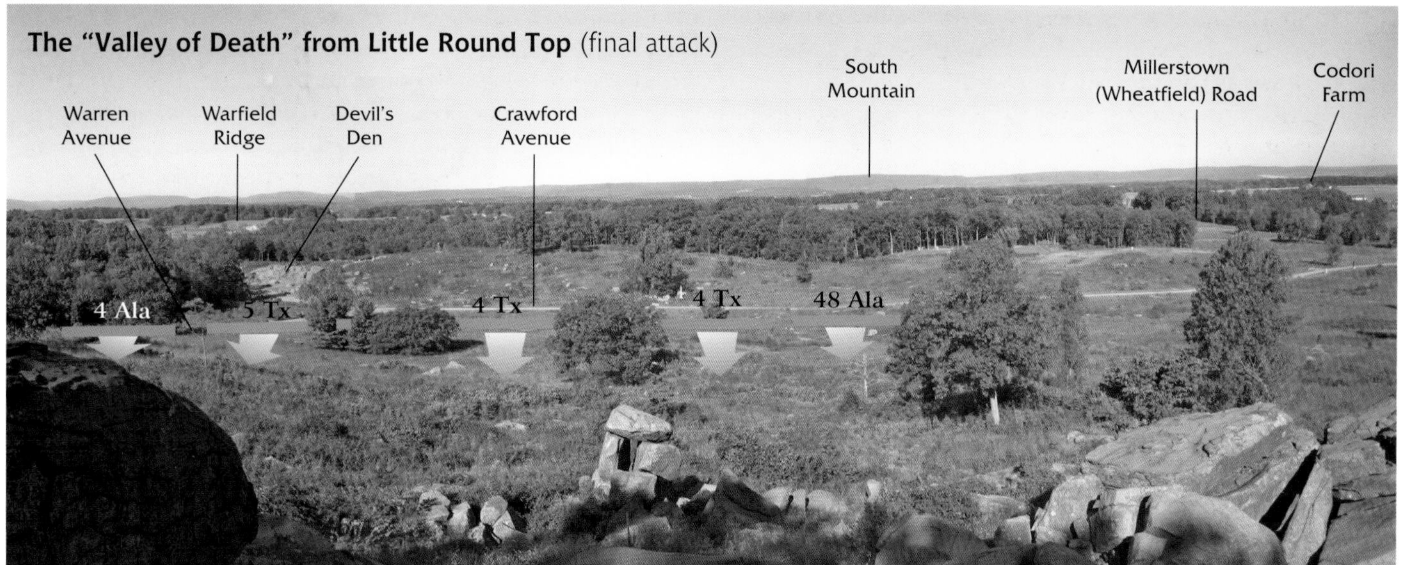

Looking west from the area of General Warren's statue on Little Round Top into the "Valley of Death." This view shows the approximate line of the final assaults by regiments of Law's and Robertson's Brigades in the early evening of July 2. All these attacks were driven off and Little Round Top secured for the Yankees for the rest of the battle. See Map 51.

meant that the 47th Alabama probably had around 175 men available to attack (Tom Desjardin, who analyzed the strengths and losses carefully in his book *Stand Firm, Ye Boys From Maine*, puts the 47th strength at 154). In all, perhaps 300 men were missing, mostly from Oates's two regiments, when the attack started. Thus a total of 1,600–1,700 Rebels launched the initial attacks on just over 1,330 defending Yankees. The odds on success were, in numerical terms, not good for the aggressors.

- The injection of the 450 fresh men of the 140th New York under Colonel Patrick O'Rorke (Brigadier-General Stephen H. Weed's Brigade) at a critical moment later in the struggle proved too much for the Rebels, and was not compensated for by the support of the weakened and exhausted 48th Alabama for the final attempts to take the hill.
- Weed's remaining three regiments of over 1,000 men (146th New York, 91st and 155th Pennsylvania) arrived in the final moments and contributed little to the repulse of the Rebels.

Command and control

In general terms, the command and control of Hood's right flank disintegrated as the advance and attacks progressed. First to go was Hood, who was wounded in the arm early in the action. The senior brigade commander was Law, who had by then advanced with his brigade, so there was some delay in informing him of his new responsibilities. The senior regimental commander in Law's Brigade was Colonel James L. Sheffield of the 48th Alabama. This regiment was soon to be hotly engaged and Sheffield fully committed to controlling it. There is no evidence that Law specifically informed Sheffield of his new duties and none that he was ever able to exercise them during the fighting. Only afterward, in the report of Major James M. Campbell, then commanding the 47th Alabama, was Sheffield mentioned as the brigade commander. Campbell wrote, "After the firing ceased, in obedience to orders from Colonel Sheffield, commanding the brigade, I threw my regiment out as skirmishers on the right . . ."

The other command problem was Colonel James W. Jackson commanding the 47th Alabama. There is little doubt he, and possibly his adjutant, was not present during the fight for Little Round Top and that the command was assumed by Lieutenant-Colonel Michael J. Bulger (an elderly gentleman of over sixty). When he was wounded, Major Campbell took over. In his report Campbell did not mince his words:

> There was some confusion in these companies [the seven involved in the fighting], owing to the fact that in the charge the lieutenant-colonel expected the colonel to give all the necessary commands, and the colonel remained so far behind that his presence on the field was but a trammel on the lieutenant-colonel . . .

According to Jackson, he was in the thick of the fight, but this is highly unlikely. He resigned from the army shortly aftwards and died, aged thirty-five, on July 1, 1865 – so it is possible that ill-health was the cause of his poor performance at Gettysburg.

There was more confusion and disruption of the Rebel command set-up before the real assaults began. This resulted from Law switching the two right-hand regiments (44th and 48th Alabama) across to the left, where they merged into the two right-hand regiments of Robertson's Brigade line (4th and 5th Texas). Thus the initial attack on Little Round Top consisted of five regiments, three from Law (Sheffield) and two from Robertson, with no coordination at brigade level. The attack was further divided when Colonel Oates, with the 47th and his own 15th Alabama, climbed to the summit of Round Top while the other three on his left remained on the lower slopes and attacked first. The overall effect was that the attacks on Little Round Top were the result of the initiatives of the various regimental commanders from two brigades conducted without co-ordination at higher level.

Colonel William C. Oates. Oates commanded the 15th Alabama and, because of his seniority in rank, became responsible for the control of the 47th Alabama, the other regiment that climbed

Round Top prior to the assault on Little Round Top, although in the event there is little evidence that he exercised much control over the 47th's activities.

Oates was twenty-nine at Gettysburg, having been born in Pike County, Alabama, on November 30, 1833. He had a wild and violent youth, ending with his having to leave the county at seventeen for Florida with what he thought was an arrest warrant for murder hanging over his head. In fact the man he had seriously injured in a fight did not die, but Oates was unaware of this. For several years he wandered around the southwest getting into a variety of scrapes, womanizing and brawling. He himself later agreed he also became "much addicted to gaming at cards." He always managed to keep one step ahead of the law, moving smartly out of town when things became too hot. He undoubtedly had a vicious temper and his first reaction to anyone who annoyed him (not hard to do) was to swing his fists. A particularly unsavory tactic when engaged in a fight, and one that invariably incapacitated his opponent, was to press his thumbs into his adversary's eyes. Eventually, his younger brother, John, was sent to bring him back to Alabama – although not to Pike County. Surprisingly, Oates gave up his wild ways, studied law and by the late 1850s had become a respectable attorney and pillar of the community.

In the spring of 1861 he raised a company of volunteers called the Henry Pioneers and was elected its captain. The company was later incorporated into the newly formed 15th Alabama as Company G. Oates served in Jackson's Shenandoah Valley campaign of 1862, first seeing action at the Battle of Cross Keys. He was with the regiment at Gaines' Mill, Cedar Mountain, Second Manassas, Chantilly and Fredericksburg. In early 1863 his regiment was transferred to Longstreet's Corps and thus missed Chancellorsville. Oates was a tough disciplinarian but well respected by his men for his courage, aggressiveness and leading from the front – although some claimed he was too foolhardy at times. He assumed command of the 15th Alabama in the spring of 1863 but was technically never promoted colonel, although his commission as such was received by Lee. For some unknown reason, the Confederate Congress never confirmed the promotion. Nevertheless, he claimed the rank for the rest of his service.

At Gettysburg Oates had yet to experience a battle as a regimental commander. He led his men forward and soon became engaged with enemy sharpshooters. Before reaching the Plum Run he received an order from Law to wheel left after crossing the stream, but he failed to do so and kept advancing up the slope of Round Top, with the 47th following on his left. As the Union sharpshooters were pushed back they split into two groups, one going north, the other south onto Oates's right – a move that caused him to send Company A after them; it rejoined the regiment near the summit of Round Top. It was a long and exhausting struggle to reach the top of the hill in the intense heat. Oates and a number of officers who were normally mounted were unfit and by that stage on the point of collapse – there is evidence he had to be helped up the hill. A number of men succumbed to heat exhaustion and Oates wisely ordered a halt on the top to recover, although recovery was not helped by the fact that the twenty-two men sent to fill the men's canteens had not returned. While on the summit Captain Leigh R. Terrell, from Law's staff, rode up – he had seemingly found a track up the southeast slope – and told Oates to continue and turn the Union left by attacking Little Round Top. This was not to his liking. Oates wanted to remain on the summit and defend it, bring up artillery (an impossibility, and they could not fire through the trees) and, in his own words, written much later, "convert it into a Gibraltar." This was errant nonsense and he was told to get on and obey his instructions. Reluctantly, Oates did so.

As the regiment descended the northern slope of the hill toward the saddle connecting it to Little Round Top, some enemy wagons were spotted at its base on the eastern side, prompting Oates to dispatch Company A again to try to capture them. They did not return for the main fight. For the next hour the 15th Alabama and the 47th on its left were involved in a series of desperate and gallant attacks primarily against the 83rd Pennsylvania and 20th Maine deployed behind the rocks on the southern end of Little Round Top and Vincent's Spur. It was brutal, close-quarter fighting, sometimes at a distance of only a few paces. During the action Oates's brother, Lieutenant John A. Oates, was killed – a tragedy William never got over, as although John was ill with a fever and suffering from rheumatism he had refused the chance not to go into action.

Oates attempted to outflank the left of the 20th Maine, but the Yankees had refused their flank so that the men were almost fighting back to back and the Rebels were again repulsed. When it was reported to Oates that there were enemy on his exposed right, this, coupled with the heavy losses and exhaustion, prompted him to order a withdrawal. At the same moment Chamberlain ordered the 20th Maine to charge. The result was anything but an orderly withdrawal. "When the signal was given we ran like a herd of wild cattle" – including Oates. In his report dated August 8, 1863, he had this to say of the final moments of the action:

> Finally, I discovered that the enemy had me on the right [correct], and two regiments were moving rapidly upon my rear [it was one company of sharpshooters] and not 200 yards distant, when to save my regiment from capture or destruction, I ordered a retreat . . . Having become exhausted from fatigue and the excessive heat of the day, I turned the command of the regiment over to Captain B. A. Hill, and instructed him to take the men off the field, and reform the regiment and report to the brigade.

Oates must have been really pleased to be reunited with his horse.

Oates continued to serve as a regimental commander until he lost an arm, his fifth and most debilitating wound, in August 1864. After the war he resumed his law practice, was elected to the House of Representatives and later served for a short period as Governor of Alabama. He married a beautiful woman half his age and was promoted brigadier-general in 1898, aged sixty-five, during the Spanish-American War. He never saw action but quipped, "I am now a Yankee General, formerly a Rebel Colonel, and right each time!" He died on September 9, 1910, and was buried with full military honors.

Command and control of the Union defense of Little Round Top was disjointed and theoretically rested with the most senior officer on the hill. However, Brigadier-General Warren left the position during the fight, Colonel Vincent was mortally wounded and the defenders on the northwestern slopes could not see what was happening on the southern ones due to the summit intervening. This meant that control of the defense largely rested with regimental commanders for much of the action. This was particularly so in the south on Vincent's Spur, where Colonel Chamberlain conducted a prolonged and bitter fight by his 20th Maine to safeguard the Union extreme left flank.

Possibly the most important aspect of Union leadership in this area was who was responsible for ensuring Little Round Top was occupied and defended at all. As we have seen, this hill was of major importance to Meade's defensive line and yet until after 4:00 that afternoon only a handful of signalers occupied it – the reason being that Sickles had disobeyed his instructions to include it in III Corps' line. That it was occupied in the nick of time was due to the initiative of two senior officers – Brigadier-General Warren and Colonel Vincent – with the help of one junior officer, Lieutenant Ranald S. McKenzie. Warren, with his escort and three aides, arrived on the hill around 3:30 p.m. to discover only Captains Hall and Taylor with their signalers on the summit. They pointed out to him the obvious enemy activity in the woods opposite along Seminary Ridge. Warren quickly realized the danger to the Union left and the importance of holding Little Round Top. He sent two aides spurring away for reinforcements – Lieutenant Chauncey B. Reese to Meade and McKenzie to Sickles. Meade sent instructions that Humphreys' Division (III Corps) should go. However, Humphreys had already moved forward to comply with Sickles' move to the Peach Orchard and sent the aide back to Meade saying that a move to Little Round Top would create a huge gap in III Corps' line. Meade cancelled his order and instructed that V Corps provide the reinforcements instead.

Meanwhile, McKenzie found Sickles near the Trostle Farm and stated Warren's request for a brigade. Sickles, rightly at the time, as he was then fully committed to defending his salient, flatly refused. On his way back McKenzie found Major-General Sykes leading V Corps and on his own initiative asked him for a brigade. Sykes agreed and sent a message to Brigadier-General James Barnes commanding his 1st Division to provide it. When Sykes' aide rode up to Barnes's leading brigade (commanded by Colonel Vincent) asking for the divisional commander, the following exchange took place:

"Captain, what are your orders?" The aide replied, "Where is General Barnes?" Vincent then pressed him further. "What are your orders? Give me your order." The captain replied, "General Sykes told me to direct General Barnes to send one of his brigades to occupy that hill yonder," pointing to Little Round Top. Vincent immediately said, "I will take the responsibility of taking my brigade there."

Having said that, he personally rode off with his flag-bearer, Private Oliver W. Norton, to Little Round Top to reconnoiter a position for his troops, at the same time instructing the senior colonel, James C. Rice, commanding the 44th New York, to bring up the brigade. It was Vincent who hastily deployed his four regiments along the rocky ledges below the crest on the western and southern slopes of the hill just minutes before the Rebels attacked.

Brigadier-General Gouveneur K. Warren. Warren was born on January 8, 1830, in Cold Spring, New York. He entered West Point at sixteen, graduated second in his class in 1850 and was assigned to the Army Corps of Topographical Engineers. He served on several important survey expeditions on the Mississippi River and examining the best route for a transcontinental railroad. He was chief topographical engineer during the expedition against the Sioux Indians in southern Nebraska Territory in 1855. Further survey missions followed, including along the Missouri River and up the Yellowstone. He produced a map of the United States from the Mississippi to the Pacific Ocean and then spent three years (1859–61) as an assistant mathematics professor at West Point. When war broke out Warren was a highly regarded technical officer but had no experience of command. In early summer 1861 he was promoted lieutenant-colonel of volunteers in the 5th New York Volunteer Infantry. By October he was a full colonel in command. He led his regiment at the siege of Yorktown before getting a brigade. He was lightly wounded at Gaines' Mill in 1862, and at Malvern Hill his brigade repulsed a Rebel division. His brigade fought well at Second Manassas but suffered heavy losses. At Antietam and Fredericksburg his command was kept in reserve. On September 26, 1862, Warren was promoted to brigadier-general of volunteers. He had by then proved himself a competent commander of troops. In February 1863 Warren was made chief topographical engineer of the Army of the Potomac and in May appointed chief engineer. It was in this capacity that he was serving on Meade's staff at Gettysburg.

Warren had married two weeks prior to the battle and on Meade's appointment had turned down the offer to take over as chief of staff from Butterfield. He did not arrive on the battlefield until about mid-morning on July 2 and Meade used him as an adviser throughout the day. First, after visiting the Culp's Hill area, he advised that the terrain was unsuitable for offensive operations and Meade accepted this. Warren accompanied Meade on his tour of the left of the line that afternoon and, according to one of his aides, Lieutenant Washington A. Roebling, went to Little Round Top when directed by Meade to "ride over and if anything serious was going on . . . attend to it." Something serious *was* about to happen and Warren attended to it. He stayed on the hill and met Lieutenant Hazlett when, on his own initiative, he arrived on the summit looking for a suitable place for his six guns to support V Corps. He did not see Vincent's arrival, later writing, "I did not see Vincent's brigade come up, but I suppose it was about this time they did, and coming up behind me through the woods and taking post to the left (their proper place) I did not see them . . ." Warren remained after the attacks and later received a slight neck wound from a musket ball but was able to stay in the field. As the fighting progressed he became concerned that more troops were needed and rode off to find them. As he came down the slope toward the Millerstown (Wheatfield) Road he found the 140th New York led by Colonel Patrick O'Rorke at the head of Brigadier-General Stephen H. Weed's Brigade (a formation he himself had previously commanded), leading Brigadier-General Ayres Division of V Corps to support Sickles. According to Captain Joseph Leeper (one of O'Rorke's staff), Warren shouted out as he approached, "Paddy give me a regiment." O'Rorke explained that his brigade commander, Weed, was away, but Warren responded, "Never mind that, bring your regiment up here and I will take the responsibility." O'Rorke did not hesitate, pulled his regiment out of the column and led it up the slope, where it arrived just in time to steady the line of the 16th Michigan and defeat another Rebel assault. Warren then rode off to report to Meade.

By March 1864 Warren had command of V Corps in time for General Grant's Wilderness campaign but was wrongly blamed for a failed attack on Petersburg. Almost a year later he was relieved of his command (with the agreement of Grant) by General Sheridan for delays in reinforcing Sheridan at the Battle of Five Forks at the end of March 1865. He resigned his volunteer commission a few days later and reverted to his regular army rank of major. After the war he continued with his survey and mapping work (one of the reference maps of the Gettysburg battlefield used for this book was prepared under his direction). Later he worked on bridge-building and harbor-improvement projects and was eventually promoted to lieutenant-colonel. He died aged fifty-two in 1882, supposedly of liver failure related to diabetes, without ever knowing his name was to be cleared by a court of inquiry held that year. At his own request he was buried in civilian clothes without military honors.

Colonel Strong Vincent. The importance of Colonel Vincent's role in the defense of Little Round Top has been overshadowed by that of Colonel Chamberlain commanding the 20th Maine. This is probably due to the fact that Vincent was mortally wounded on the hill, while Chamberlain survived and was eventually awarded the Medal of Honor for his gallant actions commanding his regiment on the extreme left of the line and his ordering a charge of the 20th as the final effort that drove Oates's Rebels down the hill. Nevertheless, if Vincent had not demanded to know Warren's aide's orders and then, entirely on his own authority, immediately ordered his brigade to the hill, it would not have been defended at all. Had he waited to seek the views of his divisional (Barnes) or corps (Sykes) commander, the Rebels would have won the race to Little Round Top, with huge potential consequences for the conduct of the remainder of the battle.

Vincent was twenty-six years old at Gettysburg. He had qualified as a lawyer after graduating from Harvard. At the outbreak of the conflict he served as a lieutenant in a militia regiment (he got married on the same day he enlisted) for a few months before becoming the lieutenant-colonel of the 83rd Pennsylvania Infantry. His name, "Strong," was unusual but apt, as he was a big, barrel-chested man, very athletic and looked very much the tough military leader. When the commander of the 83rd was killed in June 1862 Vincent was promoted into his place, but malaria (caught in the Peninsula) put him out of action until Fredericksburg in December that year. He was offered the appointment of judge advocate for the army but rejected it on the grounds that he had come to fight.

It was Vincent who positioned the brigade on Little Round Top and in particular appreciated the importance of holding the southern spur, which was defended by the 20th Maine and which afterward bore Vincent's name. At the height of the action he spent much of the time on the right of the line encouraging the 16th Michigan. It was while doing so that a Minie ball struck him in the thigh and groin, breaking the thigh bone and lodging in his body. It was an agonizing and mortal wound. He was carried to a farm where he died a lingering death five days later, the seriousness of his wound meaning he was unable to be taken home as he so desperately wanted. His promotion to brigadier-general was approved and dated July 3, 1863, but it is not known if Vincent knew of this before he died. His wife gave birth to a daughter two months later, but the baby died within a year and was buried alongside her father.

Plans and orders

The Confederate plan for Longstreet's Corps to attack the Union left at the Peach Orchard could not be implemented as the Yankees were not where they were supposed to be. Nevertheless, Longstreet overrode Hood, who protested three times, insisting, "General Lee's orders are to attack up the Emmitsburg Road." But that is not what happened. Both of Longstreet's divisions were deployed south of the Peach Orchard, with the Emmitsburg Road actually angled through Hood's Division (see Map 47). To attack up that road would mean the corps advancing across it then doing a massive left wheel. If this was the intention, then the enemy positions prevented it. The advance started as a frontal one in echelon from the right and immediately came up against the enemy in strength in Rose Woods and Houck Ridge. Further right, Law's Brigade clashed with U.S. Sharpshooters. Law, who had personally objected to Hood over the "attack up the Emmitsburg Road" plan, afterward considered his task was to take Round Top as the key to the position – there is no mention of wheeling left up the Emmitsburg Road in Law's account, entitled *The Struggle for "Round Top"*. It seems none of the regimental commanders of Hood's Division were given any orders as to their objectives. Their reports make no mention of a left wheel and all, it seemed, were content to advance forward until the enemy was struck. Oates later stated, "No communication as to what was intended to be done was made to the regimental commanders until after the advance began" – although this was far from unusual.

As the advance pressed forward, Smith's guns on the southern end of Houck Ridge proved extremely damaging and Law ordered his two right-hand regiments (44th and 48th Alabama) to wheel half-left to help deal with them. The remainder of the brigade continued east toward the Round Tops. According to Oates, writing many years after the war, it was about this time that he received the first of two specific orders. "Before we reached the Plum Run, General Law ordered me to keep my right close to the base of Round Top, penetrate the valley between the mountains." Oates did not comply, as he was concerned about the Yankee sharpshooters on his right, and instead pressed on up the slopes of Round Top. His second order arrived as he and his men rested to catch their breath on the summit. Law's aide, Captain Terrell, told him that Law was now the divisional commander, Hood having been injured, and Oates was to "press on, turn the Union left, capture Little Round Top, if possible, and to lose no time."

Thus we see that the assaults on Little Round Top were not preplanned or ordered; on the contrary, they were the result of changed circumstances as the advance developed into a stiff fight for ground that the Rebel commanders had originally thought unoccupied.

Meade, however, had always intended Little Round Top to be occupied and defended, and he had given instructions to that effect to Sickles. Due to that officer's disobedience the hill was unoccupied until after 4:00 p.m. Fresh orders to occupy it were the result of the initiative General Warren and Colonel Vincent were given at the last minute after Longstreet's advance was under way.

Outline of events

See Maps 50 and 51.

Casualties

Bearing in mind that the Rebels had up to 300 men who missed the fighting for Little Round Top for various reasons, and that none of these regiments had much to do on July 3, the estimated total losses are shown below.

Confederate		**Union**	
Staff	4	Staff	1
4th Alabama	92	20th Maine	125
15th Alabama	178	16th Michigan	60
47th Alabama	69	44th New York	111
48th Alabama	106	83rd Pennsylvania	55
Total (Law's Brigade)	**449**	**Total (Vincent's Brigade)**	**352**
4th Texas	112	140th New York	133
5th Texas	211	146th New York	28
Total (Robertson's Brigade)	**323**	91st Pennsylvania	19
		155th Pennsylvania	19
		Total (Weed's Brigade)	**199**
		Hazlett's battery	13
Total Confederate losses	**772**	**Total Union losses**	**564**

Discounting the three regiments in Weed's Brigade that arrived when the serious fighting was over, the Union forces lost about 42 percent of the 1,330 engaged. The losses were far from equally spread amongst the regiments, with the last regiment to arrive losing the most – 133 men. Considering the length and severity of the fighting, the 16th Michigan and 83rd Pennsylvania got off comparatively lightly with 60 and 55 respectively. The Confederates lost 47 percent overall, assuming around 1,650 took part in the attacks. This was severe, with the 15th Alabama's total of 178 representing 44 percent. However, it was the 5th Texas that suffered the most with a loss of 211, or 52 percent.

The Confederates did not lose a brigade commander, whereas the Union lost two – Weed killed and Vincent mortally wounded. With regimental commanders, the Confederates lost five (Lieutenant-Colonel Carter, 4th Texas, killed; Lieutenant-Colonel Bulger, 47th Alabama, wounded and captured; Colonel Key (4th Texas), Colonel Powell and Lieutenant-Colonel King (both 5th Texas) wounded. The Union had one killed, O'Rorke (140th New York), and one wounded, Colonel Chamberlain (20th Maine).

Comments

- It bears repeating that, had the struggle for Little Round Top gone the other way and the Rebels reinforced their success, the course of the battle would have been very different. It is quite possible that Meade would have withdrawn to the Pipe Creek line had his rear and the link with his base been seriously threatened on July 2. That night, when Meade had repelled all Rebel attacks, he called a conference to seek the opinions of his corps commanders on whether to stay and fight the next day. Had he lost Little Round Top that evening there might not have been any need of a conference. Longstreet's third division, under Major-General George Pickett, had arrived near the field by mid-afternoon after a long, exhausting march, but with a little rest might have exploited success on the right. Also, had Ewell been moved to the center as Lee had wanted earlier, there would have been plenty of reserves to hand.
- It was only through the initiative of, first, Warren that little Round Top was defended at all. But if Vincent had not insisted on diverting his brigade immediately instead of waiting for higher approval, the defenders would probably have arrived too late.
- There is little doubt that Hood advanced reluctantly, having three times voiced his doubts and sought a better plan as a result of his scouts finding the Round Tops area unoccupied. Then he was wounded, and from that point on there was little co-ordination or control on the Rebel right. The attacks on Little Round Top lacked a senior commander in overall control and were conducted by five regiments from two different brigades, the decisions being made at regimental level with these officers unable to exert any influence beyond their own command. Even the initial attack was made by only three of the five regiments, as the two on the right were either resting on the summit of Round Top or still moving down its northern slopes.
- Oates's leadership up to the actual start of his attacks was anything but inspiring. He was personally extremely unfit: in one account he had to be helped up the hill, then he wanted to rest and sit on the summit of Round Top to defend it rather than continuing the advance – indeed he had to be ordered to get moving. Then, on the way down toward the saddle, he sent Company A on a wagon-hunting expedition, thus depriving himself of fifty or sixty men from his already depleted command. Once the fighting started, Oates showed much more spirit, although he was unable to coordinate his actions with the tiny 47th Alabama on his left, theoretically under his orders. At the end of it all he was physically a spent force and temporarily handed over command to a captain!
- The Confederate soldiers fought hard and well, at times getting to within a few paces of the defenders, and but for the timely arrival of the 140th New York might well have secured the hill. However, they were fighting under several disadvantages. First, their numbers only exceeded the enemy's by the equivalent of one regiment at most – when the 450 men of the 140th New York appeared the Rebels were outnumbered. There was little or no supporting gunfire to soften up the defenders, who were well posted behind rocks and could only be reached after a stiff climb.
- The Union defense was well conducted all along the line, with resistance being fierce. On the left the 20th Maine fought splendidly under Colonel Chamberlain, who was able to adjust his line and refuse his left at an acute angle to see off the danger from flanking attacks – he was defending the left flank of the entire army.

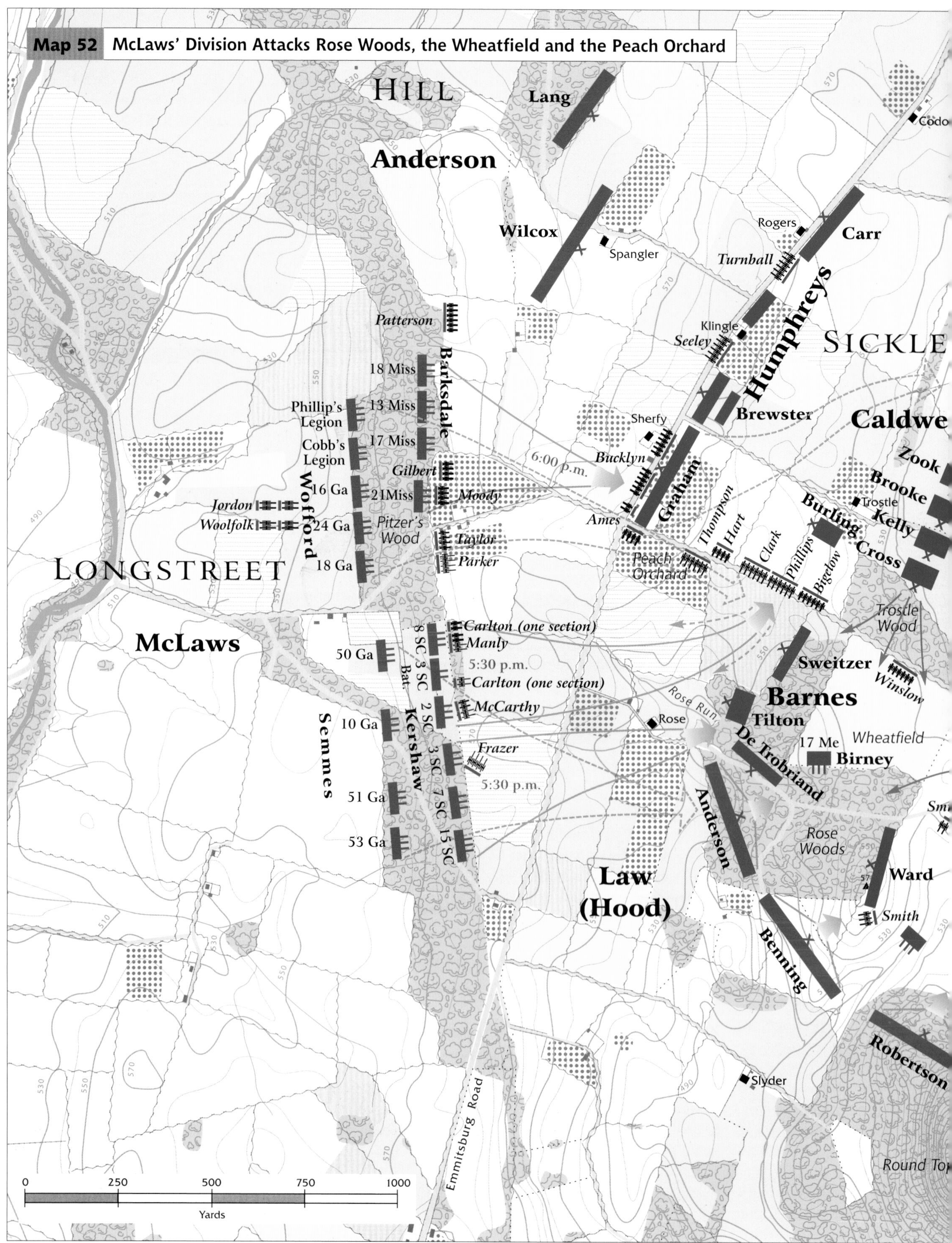

Map 52 McLaws' Division Attacks Rose Woods, the Wheatfield and the Peach Orchard
HILL
Lang
Anderson
Wilcox
Spangler
Rogers
Carr
Turnball
Humphreys
SICKLE
Klingle
Seeley
Patterson
18 Miss
Barksdale
Phillip's Legion
13 Miss
Brewster
Caldwe
Sherfy
Cobb's Legion
17 Miss
Zook
Gilbert
6:00 p.m.
Bucklyn
Graham
Brooke
Trostle
16 Ga
21Miss
Moody
Wofford
Thompson
Burling
Kelly
Jordon
Woolfolk
24 Ga
Pitzer's Wood
Ames
Hart
Cross
Taylor
Parker
Clark
Phillips
LONGSTREET
18 Ga
Peach Orchard
Bigelow
Trostle Wood
Carlton (one section)
Manly
McLaws
50 Ga
8 SC
3 SC Bat.
5:30 p.m.
Sweitzer
Winslow
Carlton (one section)
Barnes
Rose Run
2 SC
McCarthy
Rose
Tilton
Semmes
10 Ga
Kershaw
De Trobriand
Wheatfield
17 Me
Birney
Frazer
3 SC
5:30 p.m.
51 Ga
7 SC
Anderson
Rose Woods
53 Ga
15 SC
Law (Hood)
Ward
Smith
Benning
Robertson
Slyder
Emmitsburg Road
Round To
0 250 500 750 1000
Yards

Notes

• McLaws' Division advanced about an hour after Hood's on its right and this enabled Meade to switch his reserves very effectively from quiet sectors to threatened points, although this was done in a piecemeal fashion from different corps and resulted in a confused chain of command, particularly in the Rose Woods–Wheatfield area.

• By the time Kershaw, followed by Semmes, attacked, the defense of Rose Woods and Stony Hill had been bolstered by the brigades of Tilton and Sweitzer from Barnes's Division in V Corps. Despite this, after some vicious and protracted fighting, the Rebels were able to secure Rose Woods, Stony Hill and the Wheatfield. However, this success was quickly reversed by a strong counterattack by Caldwell's Division from II Corps which drove the Confederates back to the Rose Farm area.

• McLaws' other two brigades were not allowed to advance until half an hour after Kershaw. Barksdale charged the Peach Orchard and Wofford, veering right, attacked astride the Millerstown Road. This assault, combined with renewed attacks by Kershaw, Semmes and Anderson's Brigades, was too much for the left side of III Corps' salient and the Union forces scrambled back to Cemetery Ridge in some disorder, having lost more men than their attackers.

• The final collapse came immediately with the advance of Anderson's Division across the Emmitsburg Road to the north – see page 435 and Map 54.

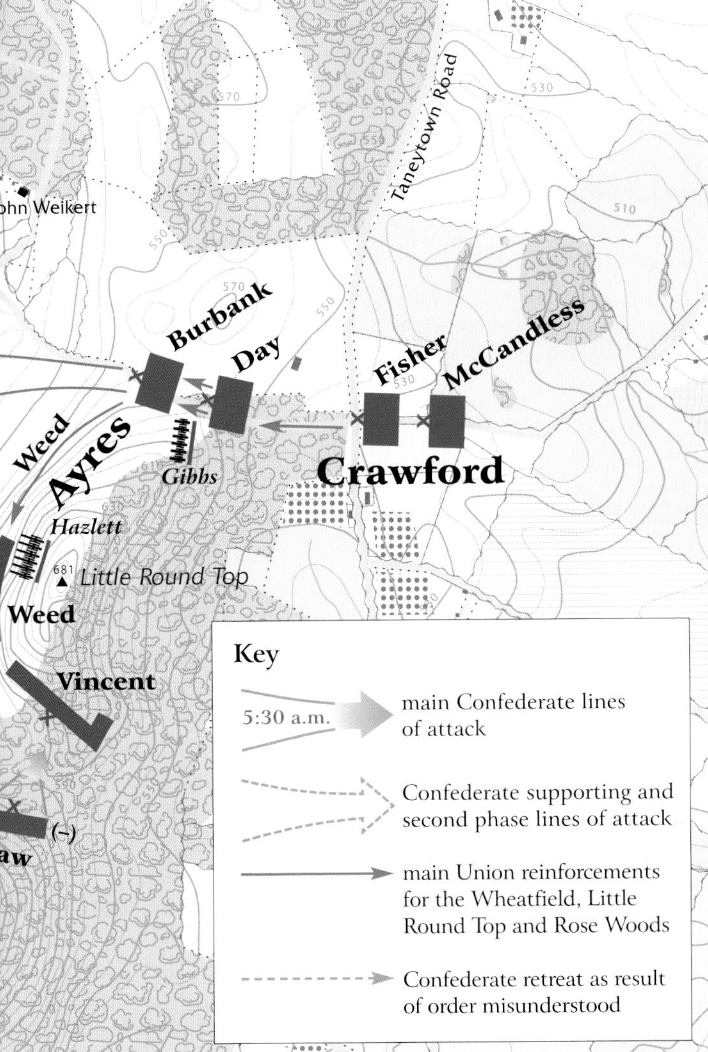

MCLAWS' DIVISIONAL ATTACK, 5:30 P.M.

McLaws Advances (Map 52)

The next phase of the echeloned assault was the advance of McLaws' Division on Rose Woods and the Peach Orchard. As Colonel Alexander was later to write, the delay of as much as an hour after Hood's men went forward before McLaws stepped off was not thought sensible. To make matters worse, McLaws' two left brigades under Barksdale and Wofford – nine regiments – did not advance for about another thirty minutes. Alexander put his opinion forcefully:

> During all this time McLaws was standing idle, though Barksdale was begging to be allowed to charge, and McLaws was awaiting Longstreet's order. Even when prolonged by Anderson's Georgians, the Texans' line was still so overlapped by the Federals that it could not advance. Law, placing his two brigades on the defensive on the captured hill, now came to the left and made a strong appeal to Kershaw for help. This was referred to McLaws and probably to Longstreet, for now the order was given for the advance of Kershaw supported by Semmes. But, by some unaccountable lack of appreciation of the situation, Barksdale, Wofford, and all the brigades of Anderson's division are still left idle spectators of the combat while Hood's division is wearing itself out against superior numbers in a strong position . . . [the delay] was especially unfortunate in this case, because advancing Kershaw without advancing Barksdale would expose Kershaw to enfilade by the troops whom Barksdale would easily drive off. Few battlefields can furnish examples of worse tactics.

As we will see, this half-hour delay, combined with a misunderstood order, resulted in Kershaw's three left-hand regiments being forced to recoil from the Union guns along the Millerstown (Wheatfield) Road.

Cabell's guns ceased firing. Then three shots in rapid succession signaled Kershaw's advance. Kershaw described that moment:

> The brigade moved off at the word with great steadiness and precision, followed by Semmes with equal promptness. Longstreet accompanied me in this advance on foot as far as the Emmitsburg road. All the field and staff officers were dismounted on account of the many obstacles in the way.
>
> When we were about the Emmitsburg road I heard Barksdale's drums beat the assembly and knew then I should have no immediate support on my left about to be squarely presented to the heavy force of infantry and artillery at and in rear of the Peach Orchard.

Kershaw, with his front covered by a skirmish screen provided by the 2nd South Carolina, was headed for a quarter of a mile of open fields and passed Rose Farm before he reached Rose Woods. The brigade consisted of five South Carolina regiments and one battalion in line – over 2,000 men covering a 400-yard frontage. The Yankee defenders of Rose Woods, which covered Stony Hill and fringed the Wheatfield, were the much reduced De Trobriand's Brigade, which had just been reinforced by two brigades (Tilton and Sweitzer) from Barnes's 1st Division from V Corps. Hunt had

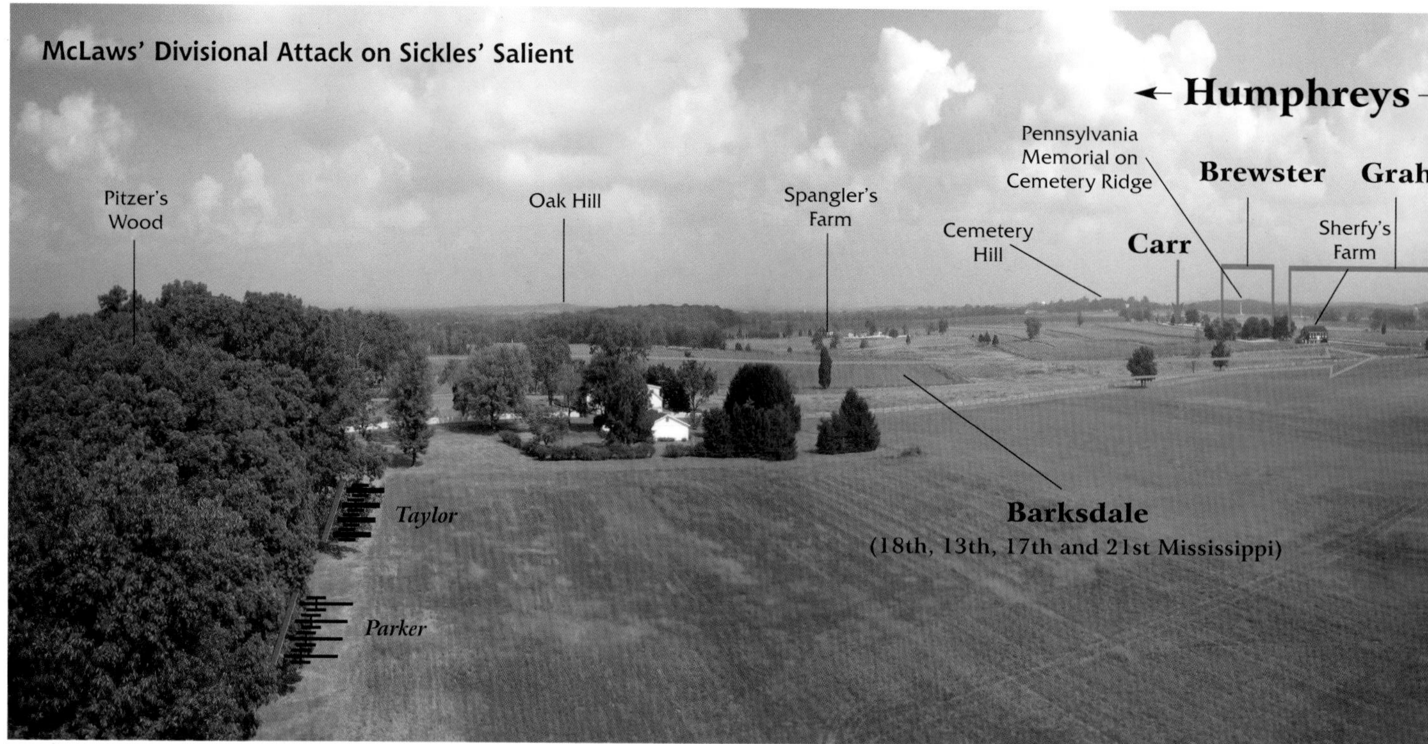

This panorama shows the general direction of the main thrusts by the leading brigades of McLaws' Division in its attack on Sickles' salient. Kershaw's Brigade advanced past Rose Farm and into the woods at about 5:30 p.m. It was followed about half an hour later by Barksdale's Brigade, attacking the Peach Orchard and along the Emmitsburg Road up to Sherfy's Farm. See Map 52.

also brought up five additional artillery batteries (twenty-eight guns under Captains Ames, Bigelow, Hart, Phillips and Thompson) from the Artillery Reserve to bolster the line defending Sickles' salient. They were positioned along the Millerstown Road to fire south, and together with the twelve guns of Captains Clark and Winslow made a formidable gun line capable of producing a potentially devastating weight of fire. Unfortunately for Kershaw, his advance would take him across the front of most of these guns. The Rebel infantry's open left flank would present the gunners with an ideal target. Kershaw's right was far less exposed as his advance coincided with the renewed attack of Anderson's Brigade.

Under heavy fire and losing men at every step, Kershaw's regiments clambered over the two fences bordering the Emmitsburg Road and advanced across more open fields. It was then that the two left-hand regiments and the battalion felt the full effect of the massed batteries along the Millerstown Road. These regiments were ordered to wheel left and charge the guns. The three regiments on the right pushed on past Rose Farm and into the woods.

The Struggle for the Wheatfield and Peach Orchard
(Map 52)

The Rebel line charging the Yankee guns along the Millerstown Road had, allowing for casualties already received, around 850 men in it. On the left was the 8th South Carolina, in the center the 3rd South Carolina Battalion and on the right the 2nd South Carolina. Over twenty guns were firing at them at a rapidly diminishing range, but they still came on. With the Rebel bayonets not much over 100 yards away, the gunners, lacking close infantry support, began to prepare to pull back and firing slackened. Then, just as it looked as though the infantry would punch a huge hole in Sickles' line, the Union gunners watched incredulously as the enemy line ceased its charge and wheeled to the right. Seeing this amazing maneuver, the gunners continued pounding the now recoiling Rebels. What had happened suddenly to snatch defeat from the jaws of a likely victory? According to Private John Coxe, 2nd South Carolina, "But just then – and, ah me! To think of it makes my blood curdle even now, nearly fifty years afterward – the insane order was given to 'right flank.'" Kershaw was to say, "Hundreds of the bravest and best men of Carolina fell, victims of this fatal blunder." The officer who gave the order has never been identified, but the mistake may have resulted from Kershaw's shouting to the 7th South Carolina to move to the right to straighten out the line over on the right as it crossed the boggy Rose's Run valley for its assault on Rose Woods and Stony Hill.

Kershaw's three right-hand regiments – from the right the 15th, 7th and 3rd South Carolina – surged forward and up the slope against Tilton's and Sweitzer's men, who met them with a blaze of musket fire. To Kershaw's right Anderson renewed his assault on De Trobriand. The Union line held and the Rebels were checked. Then it was the Yankees' turn to blunder at the moment of success. Brigadier-General James Barnes, commanding the 1st Division of V Corps, without consulting or informing anyone, ordered both Tilton and Sweitzer to fall back to the Millerstown Road. To De Trobriand it was unbelievable. He later wrote, "I saw these troops rise up and fall back hurriedly at the command of their officers." Frantic enquiries by De Trobriand of the nearest officers produced no answer that made sense, but with these two brigades retiring he had no choice but to follow – the Wheatfield was abandoned to the now advancing Rebels and Captain Winslow was forced to withdraw his guns from the northern edge of the field. The Rebels now held Devil's Den, Rose Woods, Stony Hill and the Wheatfield

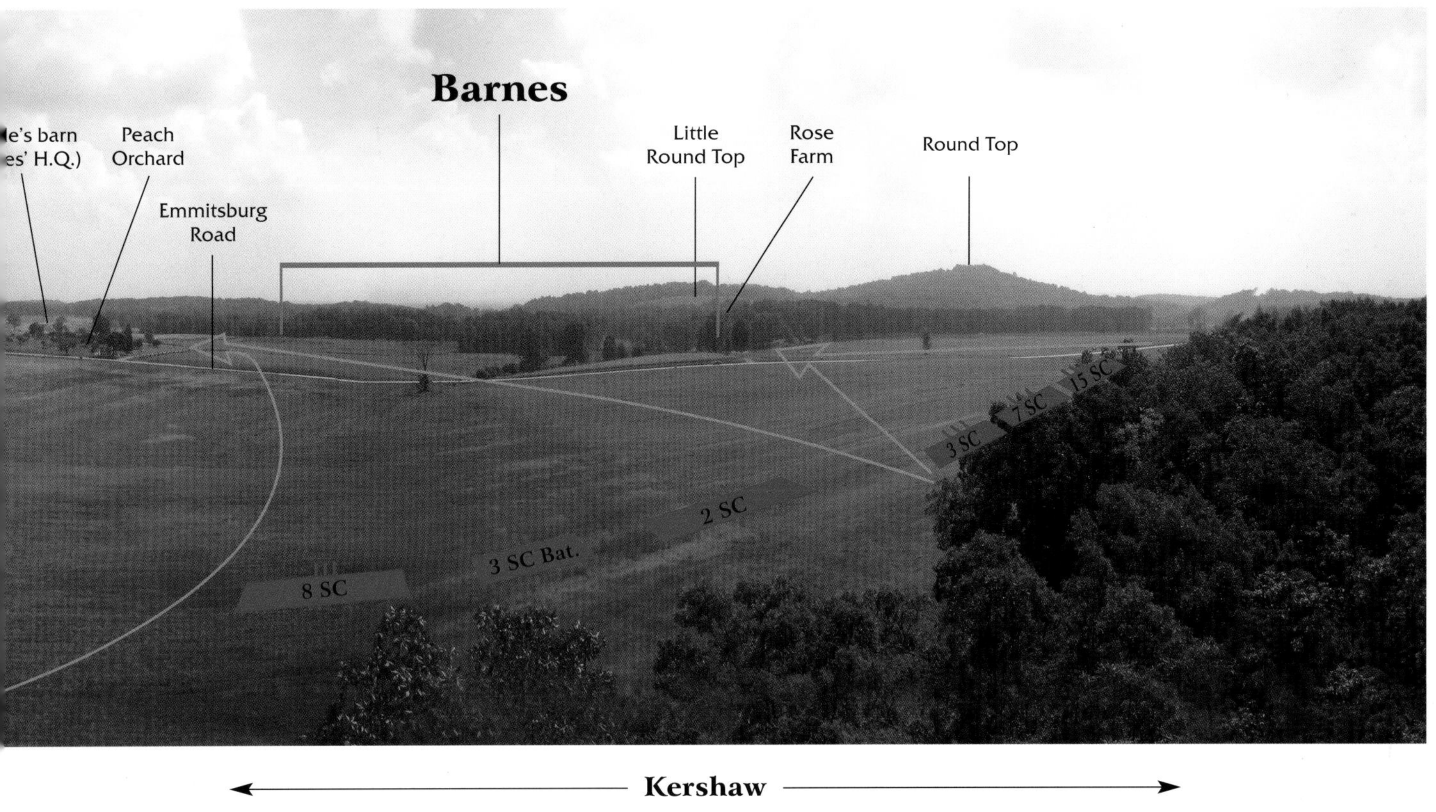

– the left side of Sickles' salient had been stove in and both III and V Corps were perilously near defeat.

It was the Yankees that rushed reinforcements to the critical area first. The Union II Corps division arriving was commanded by Brigadier-General John C. Caldwell. It had been sent to reinforce Sickles earlier but had fallen back on finding Barnes's Division already there. Within an hour Meade had told Hancock to send him back. The division was rushed south "in brigade column of regiments, closed en mass." Leading the division was Colonel Edward Cross's 1st Brigade, followed in turn by Colonel Patrick Kelly's 2nd or Irish Brigade, Colonel John Brooke's 4th and at the rear Brigadier-General Samuel Zook's 3rd – in all some 3,300 men. During the approach one of Sickles' aides, unbeknown to Caldwell, plucked Zook's Brigade from the back of the column and deployed it independently of the rest of the division. As Cross reached the Millerstown Road he deployed into line and charged into the Wheatfield, followed on his right by the Irish Brigade, with Brooke holding back as a reserve. Zook was committed on the extreme right. Kelly and Zook advanced into the northern and central part of the Wheatfield before wheeling to their right to attack toward Stony Hill. They gradually pushed Kershaw back off the hill to the area of Rose Farm. Meanwhile Cross, assisted by Brooke, drove

In the Wheatfield

Corporal Henry Meyer's regiment, the 148th Pennsylvania Infantry in Cross's Brigade, was rushed along with the Irish Brigade to help check the Rebel breakthrough at the Wheatfield. Meyer described what he saw:

> We had read in the papers of McClellan's soldiers, in the series of battle on the Peninsula, lying down alongside of batteries and going to sleep while the roar of battle went on; this seemed incredible, but such a possibility was verified that day at Gettysburg. While lying in the hot sun in line of battle, some of the boys slept, though shells and solid shot came crashing into our midst . . .
>
> The Irish Brigade, which belonged to the Division, was the first assembled in solid mass and their Chaplain, or Priest, performed some religious ceremony of a few minutes duration, while the men stood undisturbed by bursting shells, with bowed heads in reverent silence. The whole Division was marched off at a "double quick" across fields and through patches of woods in the direction of the conflict . . . We were the first troops to cross the field, and the yellow grain was still standing. I noticed how the ears of wheat flew in the air all over the field as they were cut off by the enemy's bullets . . .
>
> Men in battle will act very differently; some become greatly excited, others remain perfectly cool. One of the boys in my rear was sitting flat on the ground and discharging his piece in the air at an angle of forty-five degrees, as fast as he could load. "Why do you shoot in the air?" I asked. "to scare 'em," he replied.
>
> He was a pious young man, and the true reason he did not shoot at the enemy direct, was because of his conscientious scruples on the subject. What struck me as being peculiar was that some of the boys swore energetically, who never before were heard to utter an oath.

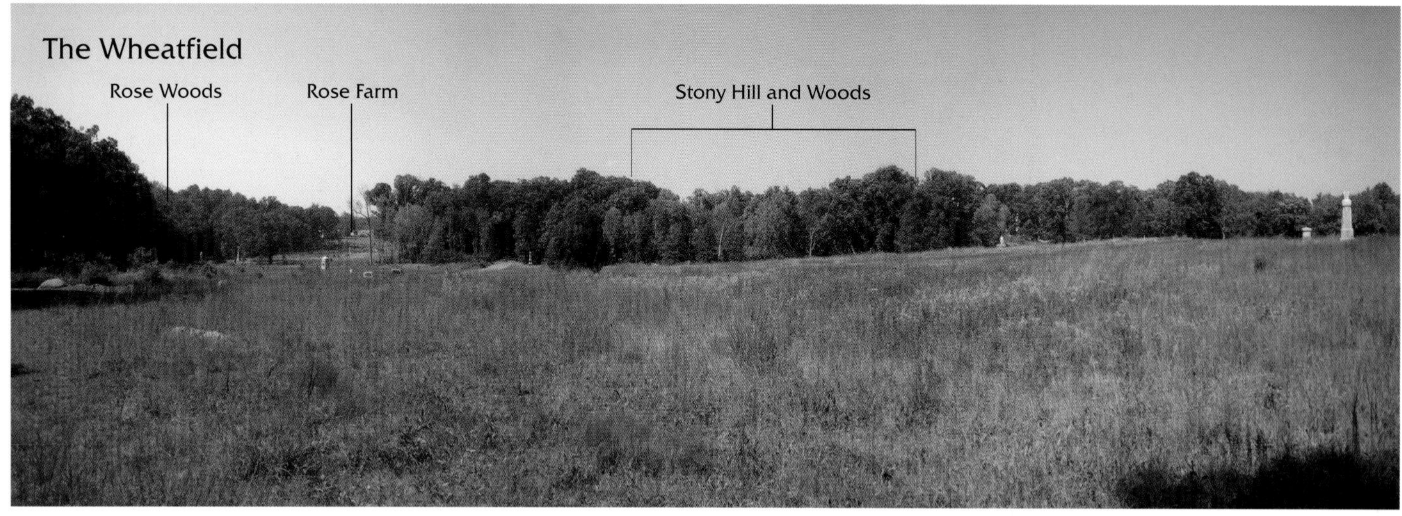

The view from near the 148th Pennsylvania Infantry monument on the southern corner of the Wheatfield, looking west. The Rebels of McLaws' Division attacked from the west, eventually taking Stony Hill from De Trobriand's Brigade. The Wheatfield was the scene of some of the most desperate fighting of the battle, with numerous attacks and counterattacks across the field. It was ultimately taken by the Rebels as Sickles' salient collapsed in the early evening of July 2.

Anderson's men out of Rose Woods. The fight was bitterly contested with soldiers on both sides falling fast. On Stony Hill Major St. Clair Mulholland of the 11th Pennsylvania in the Irish Brigade, whose muskets were loaded with buck and ball, described suddenly meeting the Rebels in the trees:

> No orders were given but in an instant every musket on the line was at its deadly work. A blind man could not have missed the mark. In charging we literally ran right in among them. Firing instantly ceased, and we found there were as many of the enemy as there were of ourselves . . . [we] looked for a time at each other utterly bewildered; the fighting had stopped, yet the Confederate soldiers stood there facing us, still retaining their arms and showed no disposition to surrender.

Mulholland was the first to react. He yelled, "Confederate troops lay down your arms and go to the rear." A substantial number complied, while the rest disappeared through the trees. Caldwell's counterattack had regained the Wheatfield and much of Rose Woods. It was to be a temporary triumph.

Within minutes of Caldwell's success, his brigades were under pressure as Longstreet, who had waited for about half an hour, committed Brigadier-General William Barksdale's Mississippians, followed by Brigadier-General William Wofford's Georgians, to the fray. The seesaw struggle for the Wheatfield was far from over.

The Yankees Lose the Peach Orchard

Captain Francis E. Moran of the 73rd New York (Zouaves) vividly described the loss of the Peach Orchard:

> showers of branches fell from the peach trees . . . in the leaden hurricane that swept it from two sides. Couriers and aides dashed right and left with orders, officers bandished [sic] swords and pistols, and shouted commands which could not be heard 20 feet away . . . The rebel infantry entered the orchard and we received their fire almost in our very backs . . . A glance to the left at that moment revealed a thrilling battle picture. The shattered line was retreating in separated streams artillerists heroically clinging to their still smoking guns, and brave little infantry squads assisting them with their endangered cannon over the soft ground. The position of these batteries showed broken carriages, caissons and wheels, while scores of slain horses and men lay across each other in mangled and ghastly heaps.

Moran was knocked unconscious by a shellburst and when he recovered found himself a prisoner, partially blinded and wounded in the ankle. The condition of the injured horses saddened him: "The poor horses had fared badly, and as we passed scores of these ungazetted heroes stood upon their maimed limbs regarding us with a silent look of reproach that was almost human in expression."

Barksdale's men, deployed right behind the Rebel guns in Pitzer's Wood, had had to endure sustained and prolonged artillery fire while waiting to advance. Alexander's batteries had been engaged at ranges of about 400 yards with the Union guns along the Emmitsburg Road and in the Peach Orchard. It was this orchard that Barksdale's 1,600 men had as their first objective. The Peach Orchard fronting the Emmitsburg Road was defended by Brigadier-General Charles K. Graham's Pennsylvanians. He started the battle with six regiments totaling about 1,500 men but at that moment only 1,000 faced the Mississippians, as the 141st was posted along the Millerstown Road and the 63rd, which had used up all its ammunition skirmishing, was, strangely, sent to the rear. Interspersed along the road supporting the Yankee infantry were Lieutenant John K. Bucklyn's six Napoleons of Battery E, 1st Rhode Island Light Artillery, and on the left at the crossroads two 3-inch ordnance rifles from Captain James Thompson's battery from the Artillery Reserve.

Bucklyn had his guns in the Sherfy Farm with a section in the flower garden. He had a rough afternoon with heavy losses, as he later recorded:

> I fire slow and carefully. Men and horses fall around me. The rebel infantry advance to within 40 yards of me and give me a volley . . . I limber up and move slowly to

Saving Regimental Colors

Color Sergeant Jacob B. Funk of the 62nd Pennsylvania Infantry, 1s Division, V Corps, carried his regiment's state color during the desperate fighting for possession of the Wheatfield. Outflanked to the south and under attack from the front, the regiment was eventually forced to retire with heavy loss. Sergeant Funk left the following account of his part in the struggle:

> Just then I came up to where some Prisoners were that had been taken a short time before. The bullets were falling like hail & the Guard that had the prisoners ran and left the Prisoners go when they immediately picked up Guns and began to shoot our men. I saw [one] pick up a Gun and looking round he spied me with the Colors of the Old Keystone state immediately he leveled his Gun and ordered me to surrender my Colors or he would shoot me but I thought that was rather a saucy demand & I could not see the point. I took Leg Bail for security and increased the distance between him and me very fast I had to jump a stone fence and came very near losing my balance but managed to get over. I then went straight ahead when directly I heard the report of a Gun just behind me. I just concluded that was for me, and sure enough the Ball struck my arm four or five inches from the shoulder passing under the Bone and coming out in the chest near the arm pit. I called out for some one to take the Colors and one of the men ran out & took them & I then made tracks to get out of farther danger . . . after leaving the battlefield I went about 2 miles and then got my wound dressed.

Funk recovered and was discharged in December 1863, but re-enlisted as a veteran volunteer. On May 24, 1864, he was mortally wounded at the Battle of Laurel Hill, Virginia.

> the rear . . . I have a case shot through my left shoulder and feel faint. My battery is torn and shattered and my brave boys have gone, never to return. Curse the rebels.

Barksdale's Brigade had deployed in line with, from the right, the 21st, 17th, 13th and 18th Mississippi Regiments. Following immediately behind were Wofford's five regiments with about another 1,600 men. Instead of following exactly behind Barksdale, Wofford veered slightly right and attacked astride the Millerstown Road. As the brigade moved forward through the Rebel gun line they were given a rousing cheer and Captain Parker saluted the bald-headed Wofford as he passed, later writing, "Oh he was a grand sight, and my heart is full now while I write of it . . ." The Mississippian's charge on the Peach Orchard and Emmitsburg Road was unstoppable. During a furious exchange of musketry, the 68th Pennsylvania lost half of its men and the Union line collapsed and fell back. Once the infantry along the Emmitsburg Road gave way, then the artillery batteries along the Millerstown Road were exposed to attack from the rear and were forced to limber up and retire in haste. The Peach Orchard fell. Graham's Brigade retreated in confusion back to Cemetery Ridge, its commander seriously wounded and shortly afterward captured. Meanwhile, Barksdale swung toward his left, threatening to get behind Brewster's Brigade holding the center of Sickles' line along the Emmitsburg Road. On the right Wofford had joined forces with Kershaw's regrouped brigade, driving Caldwell's brigades from the Rose Woods and the Wheatfield by the combined assault of Anderson, Semmes and Wofford. The left flank of Sickles' salient was collapsing. The final disintegration under the combined attack of Anderson's Division and Barksdale's Brigade, culminating in the Rebel advance to the Plum Run, and in one instance to Cemetery Ridge itself, are described below with Anderson's divisional attack (page 435).

Under Fire in the Peach Orchard

Lieutenant Adolfo Cavada was on the staff of Brigadier-General Andrew A. Humphreys and watched the collapse of Sickles' salient at the Peach Orchard and the retreat of the "red legs" (Zouaves) of 114th Pennsylvania, of which his brother, Frederick, was the commander.

> A copious shower of shell and canister from the enemy was followed up by a diabolical cheer and yell and "here they come" rang along our line. At this moment my horse was shot in the leg and pranced around frantically. Our batteries opened, our troops rose to their feet, the crash of Artillery and the tearing rattle of our musketry was staggering and added to the noise on our side. The advancing roar and cheer of the enemy masses, coming on like devils incarnate. But our fire had not checked them and our line showed signs of breaking. The battery enfilading us redoubled its fire, portions of Birney's command were moving to the rear broken and disordered. Our left regiments took the contagion and fled, leaving a wide gap through which the enemy poured in upon us. In vain did staff officers draw their swords to check the flying soldiers and endeavor to inspire them with confidence.
>
> For a moment the rout was complete. Finding myself precisely at the point where the enemy pierced us, I endeavored to make towards our right Brigade which by Genl. Humphreys orders had changed front in order to meet the enemy's charge, but my horse could scarcely stand and moved so slowly that I was enveloped by our retreating soldiers borne down the hill. On reaching the hollow [Plum Run] I tried together with several other officers, to stop our men, and partially succeeded. Three rebel battle flags were now within a few yards of me. Squads of our men dropping behind rocks and fallen trees kept up a spirited fire and just as I saw the head of the column of rebels hesitate . . . my poor Brickbat [horse] received his death wound and fell, holding me down to the ground by the weight of his body on my leg. After struggling for a few seconds I disengaged myself from my horse and taking my brandy flask and pistol off the saddle stumbled on as fast as my weary legs would carry me.

Cavada's elder brother was captured during this time, but both survived the war. However, both succumbed during the Cuban independence war, Adolfo of disease while the Spanish authorities executed Frederick.

Comments

- When McLaws' Division finally arrived opposite the Peach Orchard on July 2 things were not as expected. Lee's plan to attack the open left flank of the Union line and roll it up along the Emmitsburg Road was seen to be based on outdated intelligence. Where no enemy was anticipated was found be swarming with Yankees. The plan for McLaws to attack supported by Hood was changed to the Rebel line being extended with Hood on the right and his division being the first to attack. Meade's plan to act on the defensive along Cemetery Ridge had to be abandoned at the last moment when it was realized III Corps' unauthorized advance of threequarters of a mile could not be withdrawn before it came under attack.
- Longstreet finally started to take an interest in the proceedings but refused to entertain Hood's repeated suggestion of trying to outflank the Union left as his scouts had reported the Round Tops unoccupied. This idea had always been Longstreet's favored option, but at a strategic rather than tactical level. In refusing to contemplate Hood's pleas, he was probably influenced by the lateness of the hour (after 4:00 p.m.) and the need to get an attack under way quickly – exploring the possibility of an outflanking move would take time. Also, shifting Hood further right would dangerously extend the Confederate line, which was already spread around an arc some 5 miles long. In the event Hood interpreted his orders fairly loosely and did make an attempt to outflank the Union line by his right-flank regiments attacking Little Round Top via Round Top. It very nearly succeeded, as Little Round Top's defenders consisted only of a signal station until shortly before the Rebels attacked.
- Longstreet's attack was not only late starting, but developed into a series of echeloned assaults from the right. It may have been what was originally intended, but it proved a serious tactical error. Not only were all the attacks that day to be launched at different times, but also even within Longstreet's Corps itself they were staggered. Hood's Division advanced around 4:30 p.m., McLaws not until about an hour later and even then Barksdale's Brigade moved off half an hour after Kershaw's on its right. Colonel Alexander's comment on these staggered attacks bears repeating: "Few battlefields can furnish examples of worse tactics." Apologists for this argue that the first assault is intended to draw off the enemy reserves and, once they are committed, the next attack goes in. For an army operating on exterior lines this theory seldom works and certainly did not at Gettysburg. To have the best chance of winning, history demonstrates that an army on tactical exterior lines should launch its attacks, advances or demonstrations simultaneously, and that requires careful coordination. In these circumstances the advantages given to the defender on interior lines of being given the time to switch reserves over comparatively short distances can often be negated. July 2 at Gettysburg is a classic example of the truth of this tactical lesson. If Hood, McLaws, Anderson, Early, Rodes and Johnson had all advanced at more or less the same time, the chances of a Confederate success would surely have been substantially enhanced.
- Meade reacted to the emergency situation that afternoon with considerable dispatch, although it was the initiative of several of his subordinate commanders, especially regarding the occupation of Little Round Top, that ensured the timely implementation of the army commander's decisions. Reinforcements (first Vincent's and then Weed's Brigades) were rushed to Little Round Top just in time to prevent its falling, as were the two brigades of Tilton and Sweitzer to Stony Hill and Rose Woods. Then, after Union setbacks, the four brigades of Caldwell's Division arrived to throw the Rebels, albeit temporarily, out of the Wheatfield. Eventually Sickles' left flank gave way and then the whole edifice disintegrated, but it was not the debacle it might have been had there been attacks in the north and center of Meade's line at the same time. Hard fighting by the Yankees ensured that the retreat was only as far as Cemetery Ridge, by which time the Rebel assaults were running out of steam.

Highlight: The 9th Massachusetts Battery at the Millerstown Road and Trostle Farm

This highlight was in fact two separate actions. The first took place between about 4:30 p.m. and 6:00 p.m. when the six 12-pounder Napoleons of Captain John Bigelow's 9th Massachusetts Battery took part first in an artillery duel, followed by the defense of the Millerstown Road gun line plugging the gap in the left flank of Sickles' salient. The second was a much shorter action that involved the battery being the last to withdraw from the Millerstown Road, by prolonge to the corner of a field adjacent to the Trostle Farm. There it carried out a final stand to cover the formation of another gun line east of the Plum Run in front of Cemetery Ridge. The battery was eventually overrun, losing four pieces.

The ground (Maps 52 and 53)

On the Millerstown Road the battery formed the left of the gun line overlooking an open field that ran gradually down to the Rose Run about 400 yards to its front. To its half left was the wood-covered Stony Hill, defended by troops of Brigadier-General James Barnes (V Corps). The view was good. To their right front the gunners were able to see as far as the long sweep of woods cresting the southern part of Seminary Ridge which were the jump-off point for Longstreet's advance, and in front of which the Rebels' batteries were deployed. However, the position was exposed and equally visible to the enemy gunners, so Bigelow's Battery tended to receive as good as it gave.

At the Trostle Farm things were completely different. Here the battery was formed in a tight semicircle with its back to the corner of the field fronting Trostle's house. The field corner was defined by stone walls (not as on the battlefield maps, where worm fences are shown). There was only one exit gate through the walls through which the other batteries had withdrawn after their retreat from the Millerstown Road. According to Bigelow, "the position was an impossible one for artillery." It appeared to trap the battery and block its line of retreat, especially if they had to get out in a hurry. Bigelow said that the ground "was broken by boulders . . . neither was there room enough to work six guns at their usual intervals." The position was certainly extremely cramped, with around sixty men, six guns, six limbers and the horse teams combining to make the area a difficult target to miss.

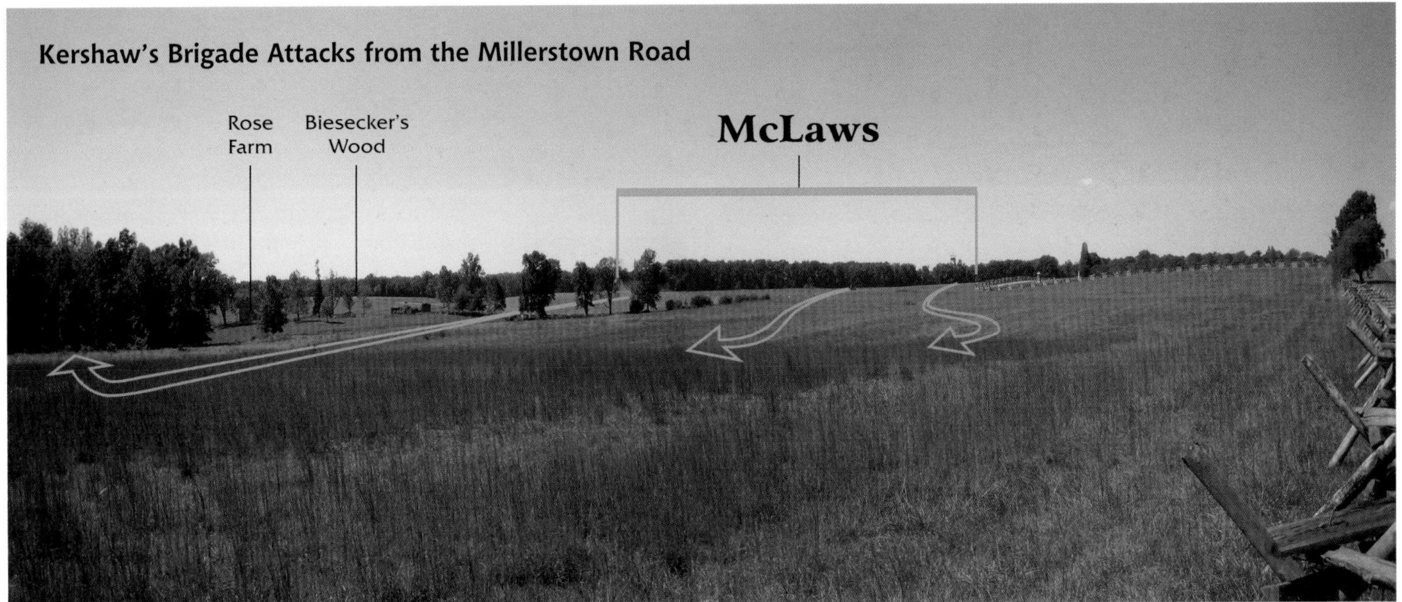

This photograph is taken from Capt. Bigelow's battery position on the Millerstown (Wheatfield) Road, looking southwest toward Seminary Ridge and the jump-off area of McLaws' divisional attack on the afternoon of July 2. It shows the approximate route of the three regiments of Kershaw's Brigade as they wheeled left to attack the Union gun line along the road and then, at the last moment, due to a misunderstood order, wheeled to their right. This allowed the Union gunners to return to their pieces and resume firing – the South Carolinians staggered back. See Map 52.

To the left was the Trostle Wood, which, once abandoned by Tilton's Brigade, provided excellent cover for Rebel skirmishers to approach close and get easy shots at men and horses while sheltering behind the stone wall that was its western boundary. But probably the worst feature was the restricted vision of the gunners caused by rising ground immediately to their front. As Bigelow later explained, "When we reached the angle of the stone wall at Trostle's House, a swell of ground, 50 yards to our right front, covered us from Barksdale's approaching line . . ." It also prevented the battery being able to fire directly at the enemy until they were extremely close. This, coupled with the clouds of smoke over the position as firing became continuous, meant the gunners were often firing blind. In summary, the Trostle Farm position was a bad one for three reasons. There was an extremely restricted field of fire, it was much too cramped and there was no easy line of retreat.

Tactical significance

The tactical importance of the gun line along the Millerstown Road, of which Bigelow's Battery was but one of six (from right to left: Captains Ames, Thompson, Hart, Clark, Phillips and Bigelow), was that it filled an enormous 500-yard gap in the southern flank of Sickles' salient. There were infantry in the Peach Orchard and on Stony Hill but none in the gap between. Lieutenant-Colonel Freeman McGilvery's artillery battalion of four batteries had been ordered forward from the Artillery Reserve to reinforce the III Corps' guns.

The significance of the Trostle Farm position was that it represented a desperate but successful attempt to cover the withdrawal of the other batteries long enough for them to be used, by McGilvery, to form yet another line on rising ground east of the Plum Rum to plug yet another gap, this time in the Cemetery Ridge defenses. Once again there was no infantry immediately available, the enemy advance was closing in and artillery was used to check them. Without the heroic defense of the Trostle Farm position and the sacrifice of four guns, the chances are that the Rebels might have gained a foothold on Cemetery Ridge.

Force comparison

When the 9th Massachusetts were sent forward to the Millerstown Road they had an estimated strength of four officers, eight sergeants, ninety-two enlisted men and eighty-eight horses, with six 12-pounder Napoleons and their associated limbers and caissons. The senior ranks included:

Battery Commander	Capt. John Bigelow (w)
1st Bugler	Pte. Charles W. Reed
2nd Bugler	Pte. William B. Pearce
Guidon	Pte. Thomas Fisher (w)
Right Section Detachment nos. 1 and 2	
	Senior 1st Lt. Christopher Erickson (k)
Gun no. 1	Sgt. George Murray (w)
Gun no. 2	Sgt. Charles Dodge (k)
Center Section	Junior 2nd Lt. Richard S. Milton
Gun no. 3	Sgt. A. N. Other
Gun no. 4	Sgt. John L. Fenton (mw)
Left Section	Junior 1st Lt. Alexander H. Whitaker (mw)
Gun no. 5	Sgt. Joseph Hirst (w)
Gun no. 6	Sgt. Levi W. Baker (w), then Stable Sgt. Nelson Lovell
Line of Caissons	Q.M. Sgt. James W. Reed Jr. (w)

A number of casualties occurred, including the serious wounding of Lieutenant Erickson and Sergeant Baker, during its time on the Millerstown Road and its retreat to the Trostle Farm. This final position was, according to Bigelow, held by around sixty men, although it may have been slightly more.

Captain Bigelow's 9th Massachusetts Battery Deployed along the Millerstown Road

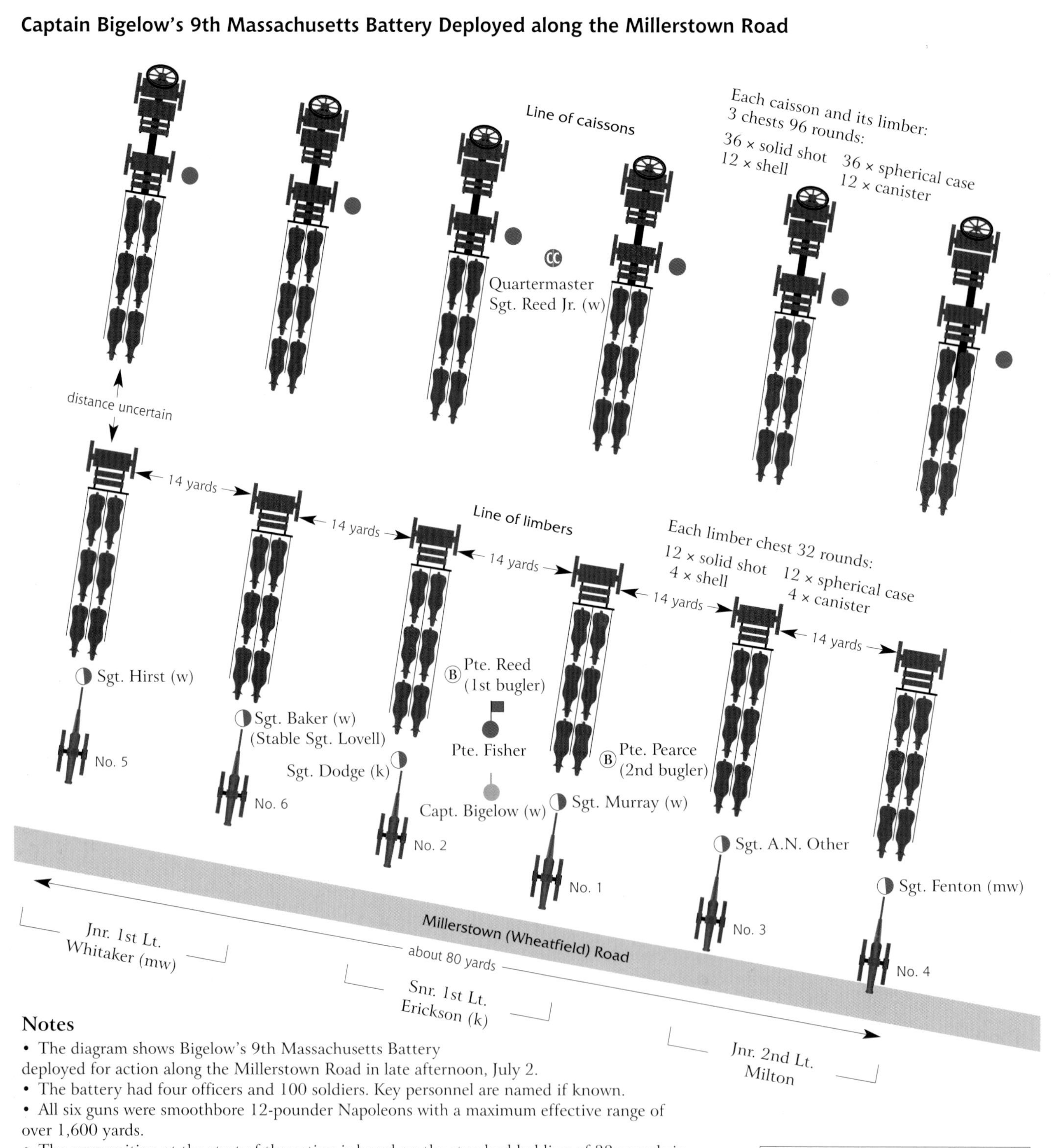

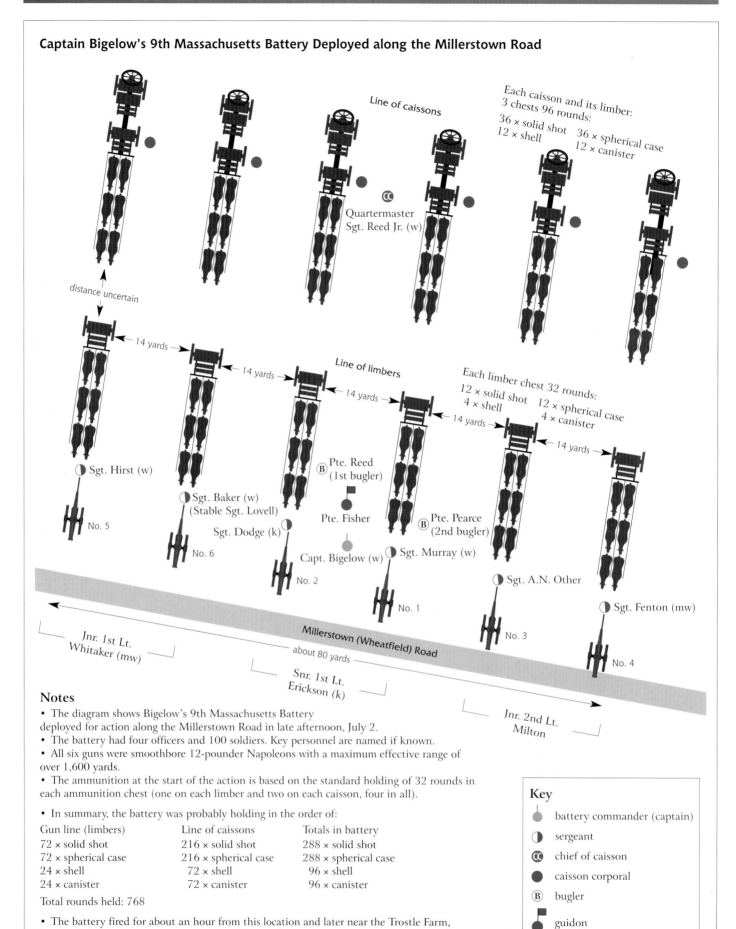

Notes

• The diagram shows Bigelow's 9th Massachusetts Battery deployed for action along the Millerstown Road in late afternoon, July 2.

• The battery had four officers and 100 soldiers. Key personnel are named if known.

• All six guns were smoothbore 12-pounder Napoleons with a maximum effective range of over 1,600 yards.

• The ammunition at the start of the action is based on the standard holding of 32 rounds in each ammunition chest (one on each limber and two on each caisson, four in all).

• In summary, the battery was probably holding in the order of:

Gun line (limbers)	Line of caissons	Totals in battery
72 × solid shot	216 × solid shot	288 × solid shot
72 × spherical case	216 × spherical case	288 × spherical case
24 × shell	72 × shell	96 × shell
24 × canister	72 × canister	96 × canister

Total rounds held: 768

• The battery fired for about an hour from this location and later near the Trostle Farm, by which time most guns were out, or nearly out, of ammunition.

Key

- battery commander (captain)
- sergeant
- chief of caisson
- caisson corporal
- bugler
- guidon

The Confederates attacking at Trostle Farm consisted of up to 100 skirmishers from Kershaw's Brigade, and the 21st Mississippi, which started the battle with well over 400 but by this time was down to perhaps 325. So between sixty and seventy Union gunners with all six guns still firing faced in excess of 400 attacking infantry. These odds, particularly as the infantry were able to approach to within 50–60 yards of the guns before being subject to direct fire, could have only one result.

Command and control

Colonel Benjamin Grubb Humphreys. The 21st Mississippi was commanded by Humphreys – he was also to command the brigade the next day after Barksdale was mortally wounded that evening. He was, at fifty-five, a somewhat elderly colonel at Gettysburg, but one who had seen plenty of active service. Born in 1808, he had served in the Mississippi State Legislature in 1837 and two years later in the Mississippi Senate. He took command of the 21st Mississippi after it mustered in September 1861 and thereafter fought with the regiment at Antietam, Maryland Heights, Fredericksburg and Chancellorsville (at Fredericksburg). At Gettysburg he led his regiment forward on the right wing of Barksdale's advance. The 21st swept all opposition before it, overcame Bigelow's battery in hand-to-hand fighting and pushed on to be the only regiment of the brigade to cross the Plum Run.

Promoted to brigade command after Gettysburg, Humphreys fought at Chickamauga, Chattanooga, the Wilderness, Knoxville, Cold Harbor and the Siege of Petersburg. However he was badly wounded and disabled in the summer of 1864 while campaigning near Winchester. After the war he became Governor of Mississippi (1865–68) until being physically ejected from office by armed force on the orders of the military commander in Mississippi. He died in 1882.

Lieutenant-Colonel Freeman McGilvery. Born in Maine in 1823, McGilvery was a sailor and ship's master before he became a soldier. On the outbreak of war he was in Rio de Janeiro, Brazil, but immediately sailed home and raised the 6th Maine Battery, which first saw action at Cedar Mountain. At Antietam his battery supported the attack of XII Corps. In early 1863 he was promoted to major and given command of the 1st Volunteer Artillery Brigade in the Army of the Potomac, which he commanded during the Chancellorsville campaign.

McGilvery had been a lieutenant-colonel for less than two weeks at Gettysburg. It was he who selected the battery positions, including Bigelow's, along the Millerstown Road, but it was his later initiative that was probably instrumental in preventing the Rebels gaining a hold on Cemetery Ridge on July 2. He ordered Bigelow to check the enemy advance at the Trostle Farm at all costs while he grabbed every available nearby artillery unit to form what became known as "the Plum Run line" – a line of guns that filled a vital gap in the Cemetery Ridge defenses until the arrival of Union infantry. It was a superb and timely intervention by a comparatively junior officer who acted urgently without reference to any senior commander. The next day it was his line of guns that inflicted considerable damage on the attack known as Pickett's charge, in particular halting the supporting brigades of Cadmus Wilcox and David Lang (see Section Eleven).

Promoted colonel two months later, he continued to command his reserve artillery brigade until May 1864 when he replaced Robert O. Tyler in command of the army's Artillery Reserve. In August 1864 he was promoted chief of artillery of X Corps, in command of fifteen batteries. A week later he was wounded in a finger but the injury refused to heal properly and it was amputated. During the operation McGilvery died of an overdose of chloroform.

Bugler Charles Reed Saves Captain Bigelow's Life

When Bigelow was hit he soon slumped to the ground from his horse. Reed and his orderly, Private John H. Kelly, lifted him and tried to get him back on his horse. At this moment Lieutenant Whitaker rode up and offered Bigelow "the benefit of his whiskey flask." The captain "took three small swallows (all that I had in the service), which strengthened me very much." It gave him enough strength with the help of Reed and Kelly to haul himself back into his saddle. Incredibly, with the Rebels swarming into the battery position only yards away, Reed was able to lead Bigelow's mount at a walk back toward McGilvery's new gun line east of the Plum Run. This sanctuary was almost 400 yards away and they had to cross the intervening ground exposed to the fire of both sides. When about halfway back, an officer from Lieutenant Edwin B. Dow's 6th Maine Battery galloped up, explaining that they were directly in his guns' (four Napoleons) line of fire and to hurry up. The hurrying up was impossible, but Bigelow told the officer the battery should open fire anyway. Dow did so and Bigelow later praised Reed, saying, "Bugler Reed did not flinch; but steadily supported me; kept the horses at a walk although between the two fires and guided them, so we entered the Battery between two of the guns that were firing heavily . . ." With Bigelow slumped in the saddle and Reed on foot supporting him with one arm and leading the two horses with his other hand, the two succeeded in reaching safety unscathed.

For his gallantry, Reed was awarded the Medal of Honor in 1895.

Captain John Bigelow. Bigelow was born in 1841 and graduated from Harvard at the age of twenty. He immediately enlisted as a private in the 2nd Battery, Massachusetts Light Artillery, but was soon promoted to second lieutenant. In December he was appointed adjutant of the 1st Maryland Battalion of Artillery and served with it during the Peninsular campaign. At Malvern Hill in July 1862 he was seriously wounded in the left forearm and was away from duty until the fall of that year. He fought at Fredericksburg, but shortly afterward contracted malaria, resigned and went home to Boston. However, within a few months he "was annoyed so much at the comments of the papers and people on the conduct of the war, that he went to Gov. [John Albion] and tendered his services again . . ." His appointment was as captain and battery commander of the 9th Massachusetts Light Artillery, then based in the Washington defenses where the men were suffering from poor morale and feeling disgruntled at the dull routine and lack of action.

Bigelow, with his bushy black sideburns that merged with his mustache, looked much older than his twenty-two years; according to one of his soldiers, David Brett, Bigelow was "30 or 35 years old." Nevertheless, he had two years' field experience and his strict enforcement of discipline and rigorous training regime was not initially appreciated. Charles Reed, who was years later to receive the Medal of Honor for saving his captain's life at Gettysburg, wrote home that his new commander "is a regular aristocrat . . . he is worse than any regular that ever breathed." It was not long before Reed was to change his tune, writing that Bigelow "understands his business, lately he has relaxed his strictness . . . I think the strictness was to make the men know what he is." And Brett was to state "on the whole our capt does very well."

At Gettysburg his leadership of the 9th Massachusetts was exemplary in what was one of the battle's most famous artillery exploits, and one that was certainly a major factor in the successful Union defense of Cemetery Ridge on July 2. During the battery's final stand at the Trostle Farm, Bigelow was struck twice by bullets in his side and hand. It was the gallantry of his first bugler, Charles Reed, that saved his life (see box, page 431).

The wounds were extremely painful but not as severe as first thought and Bigelow was able to return to duty on August 16. His battery saw action in the Mine Run campaign at the end of the year and in the Wilderness, at Spotsylvania, North Anna, Bethesda Church and Cold Harbor. He then succumbed to another bout of malaria, which lasted throughout the summer and fall of 1864. He was in action once more at Petersburg, after which, at last, he was promoted brevet major. However, his bouts of malaria had weakened him and he was honorably discharged on December 31, 1864. He returned to Boston, married, and died in 1917 aged seventy-six.

Plans and orders

As far as the Confederates were concerned, their actions were a small part of the general plan to attack the left of the Union line. The attacks on the 9th Massachusetts Battery by Kershaw's and Barksdale's Brigades were part of the general Rebel advance and not planned specifically.

With the Union forces, both the Millerstown Road and Trostle Farm actions were the result of urgent decisions and specific orders. Levi W. Baker, in his *History of the Ninth Mass. Battery*, published in 1888, wrote of the first order to move:

> A little after 4 P.M. an aide-de-camp rode up to the wall near the left piece of our battery, and enquired for Col. McGilvery, commanding the brigade, and said, "Capt. Randolph, chief of artillery of the 3rd Corps, sends his compliments and wishes you to send him two batteries of light twelves." Col. McGilvery turned around and said: "Capt. [Patrick] Hart and Capt. Bigelow, take your batteries and report to Capt. Randolph."

At about the same time Hunt told Tyler [commanding the Artillery Reserve] to send "two batteries, one of light twelves and one of rifles." Within minutes of Hart's and Bigelow's departure they were followed by Captain Charles Phillips' (5th Massachusetts) and Captain James Thompson's (C and F, Pennsylvania Light) Batteries. This was the emergency plan to fill the gap in Sickles' hugely overextended left flank.

Later, when Bigelow arrived in the field opposite the Trostle Farm after his fighting retreat from the Millerstown Road, he was expecting to continue the withdrawal to Cemetery Ridge, but his expectation was quickly dashed when his battalion commander galloped up. Bigelow's Battery was about to be offered as a sacrifice for the better good of the army – there was another gap to be plugged. McGilvery's order was:

> Captain Bigelow, there is not an infantryman back of you along the whole line which Sickles moved out; you must remain where you are and hold your position at all hazards, and sacrifice your battery, if need be, until at least I can find some batteries to put in position and cover you.

Outline of events

Sergeant Baker later described the first move forward to the Millerstown Road through the field they would later defend so desperately:

> Soon the order was "Forward," and we filed into a lane by Trostle's house, then turned to the left through a gateway. Before the left piece was through, the order rang out: "Forward into line, left oblique. Trot!" and before the left piece was in the line, "Action front!"

The battery crossed the field at a gallop – it was surely a thrilling experience for the gunners going into action for the first time. After deploying along the road, they had their first casualty. Bigelow later described this sobering event:

> they opened and I saw Fen[n] stretched on the ground[,] they asked me, seemingly regardless of the shells exploding about themselves, if they could take him to the rear. The poor fellow, however, was unconscious and dying; I saw there was no hope and answered them "No! But back to your guns and give them as good as you have received." They did so, but horrified at my heartlessness, but before the day ended the men had been initiated thoroughly in the horrors of war.

The battery was initially engaged with Rebel guns until such time as McGilvery pointed out the Rebels of Kershaw's infantry advancing. The battery instantly switched targets and opened up with canister – Kershaw later wrote, "I remember well the clatter of the . . . [canister] against the stone wall and houses [of the Rose buildings]." When Kershaw's men swung to the right as a result of a misunderstood shouted order, Bigelow described how "the battery immediately enfiladed them with a rapid fire of canister, which tore through their ranks and sprinkled the field with their dead and wounded, until they disappeared in the woods on our left [Rose Woods], apparently a mob."

Despite this success, the fall of the Peach Orchard on the battery's right meant it, along with all the batteries along the Millerstown Road, was outflanked and retreat became inevitable. Thus, after at least an hour in that position, the battery conducted its famous fighting retreat by prolonge across the field to Trostle Farm. There the gunners faced the enemy skirmishers in Trostle Wood on the left and the sweeping advance of Barksdale's Brigade mainly on their right. The problems of the position have been described above, but Bigelow's account of the guns opening fire as the enemy began to appear over the rising ground to their front bears quoting:

> Waiting until they were breast high, my battery was discharged at them every gun loaded . . . with double shotted canister and solid shot, after which through the smoke [we] caught a glimpse of the enemy, they were torn and broken, but still advancing, again gun after gun was fired as fast as possible and enfilading their line when it could.

Map 53 The Final Stand of Captain Bigelow's 9th Massachusetts Battery at Trostle Farm

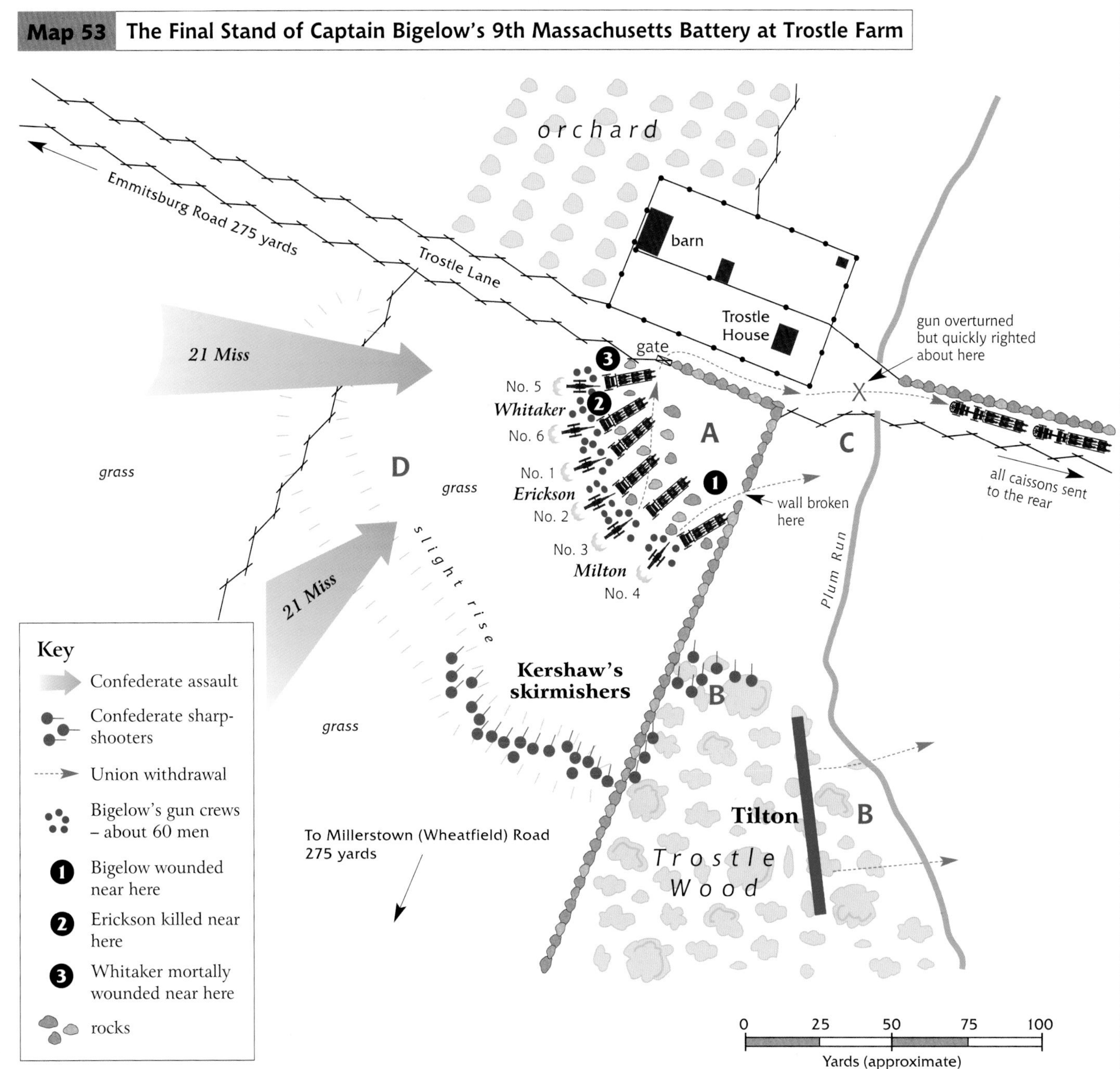

Notes

• This map shows the cramped position of the final stand of Captain Bigelow's 9th Massachusetts Battery at Trostle Farm early in the evening of July 2. To reach this position the battery had withdrawn by prolonge, firing and retiring across a rough field from the Millerstown Road. The position at A was extremely crowded with six guns, limbers, horse teams and around 60 men. Although the map shows an orchard in the area in which the battery deployed, there is no contemporary account that mentions one and contemporary photographs show the ground to be open fields.

• The retreat of Tilton's Brigade B allowed Kershaw's skirmishers into Trostle Wood B and they were able to bring a galling, close-range fire onto the gunners.

• The gunners' view was very limited due to rising ground less than 100 yards to their front and initially ball was fired to ricochet over the rise to hit the Rebels beyond. Bigelow had sent the caissons to the rear and ordered all ammunition chests taken from the limbers and placed near the guns. The main enemy assault came from the right as well over 300 men (allowing for losses) topped the rise and charged home.

• As the battery fired canister and double-shotted case and ball in a desperate effort to keep the Rebels at bay, there was no time to realign the guns after each shot, so the recoils slowly drove the pieces into an ever-tighter, more cramped area opposite the Trostle House. Milton's guns were driven back into rocks and up against a stone wall, so Bigelow ordered them to retire C. One gun went through and over the wall and the other through the gate into the lane, where it overturned but was quickly righted and withdrawn. While supervising the breaking down of the wall, Bigelow was seriously wounded. Erickson, already wounded, was shot in the head and killed and Whitaker was hit in the knee, from which he was later to die.

• There was no stopping the Rebels D and the position was overrun, with the four remaining guns being captured, although most of the unwounded gunners escaped back to Cemetery Ridge. The battery lost 8 killed, 17 wounded and 2 missing, as well as a large number of horses.

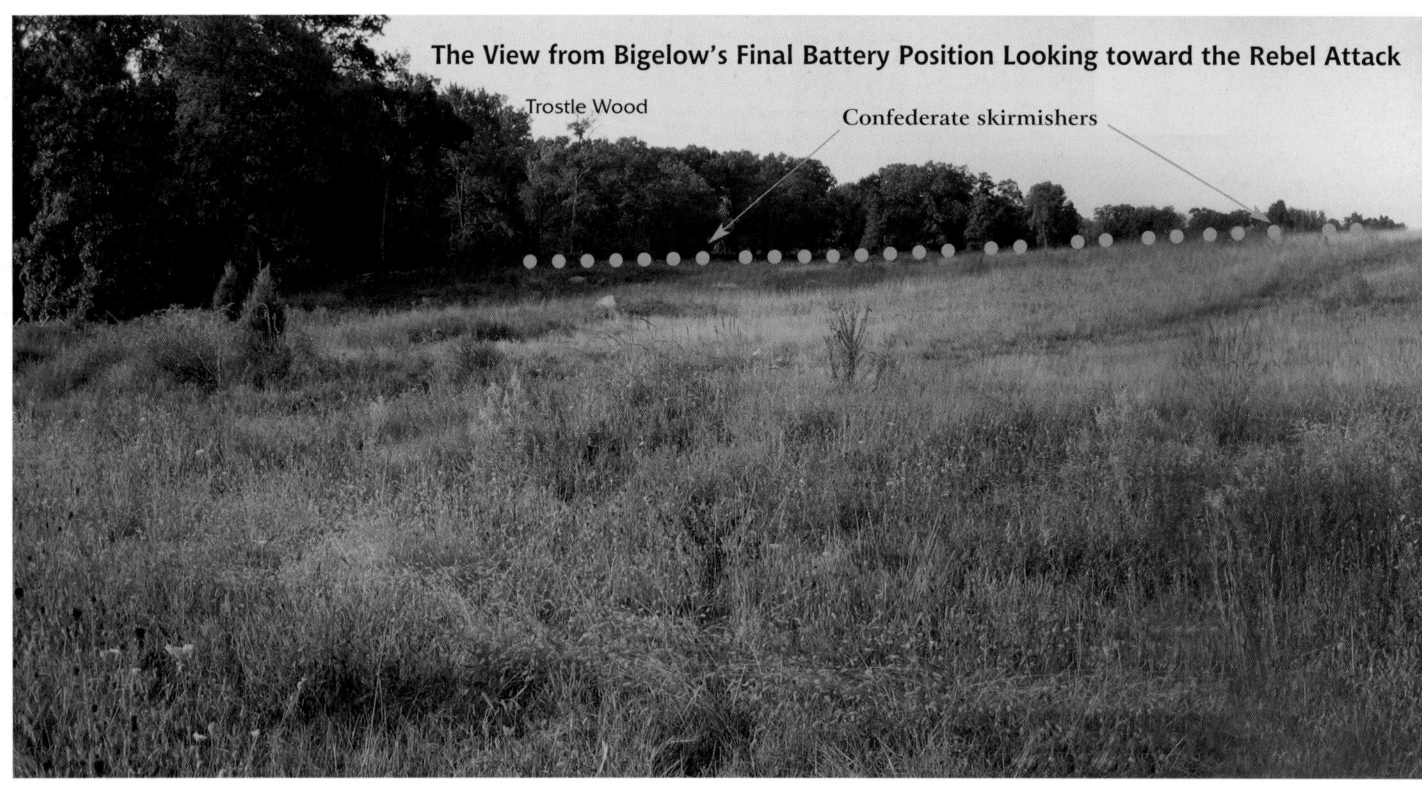

The View from Bigelow's Final Battery Position Looking toward the Rebel Attack

With the enemy pressing hard, casualties mounting (particularly among the sergeants), ammunition running low and the guns and horses being driven into an ever-diminishing area by the recoils, Bigelow gave orders for the left-hand pieces (nos. 3 and 4) under Milton to retire. They got out with great difficulty. Many horses were down and had to be cut from their harnesses, the first gun overturned in the lane causing delay and forcing the gunners with the second one to start frantically taking stones off the wall to make a gap. In desperation, the gun was "driven right over the stone wall." Amazingly, with the horses dragging and men heaving and pushing, the limber and then the gun crashed over to the other side.

These were the only guns to escape the inevitable overrunning of the position after about half an hour's action, much of it at close quarters with rammer and handspike versus bayonet and clubbed musket.

Casualties

The casualties among the 21st Mississippi amounted to 139 killed, wounded and missing out of an engaged strength of 424, or 33 percent. Virtually all of these occurred on July 2, as it was not engaged on the other two days. However, it is impossible to attribute a specific number to its attack on Bigelow's Battery. An approximate estimate might be between sixty and seventy.

By 7:00 p.m. the 9th Massachusetts Battery was crippled. Three of the four officers were down, one dead (Erickson), one mortally wounded (Whitaker) and one wounded (Bigelow). Six of the eight sergeants had been hit, Dodge killed, Fenton mortally wounded and Reed, Hirst, Murray and Baker wounded. Of the ninety-two enlisted men, nineteen were casualties. The total out of action was twenty-eight, or 27 percent of those engaged. This was perhaps not as high a number as might be expected from the severity of the fighting and the fact that the position was overrun. However, four

Lieutenant Christopher Erickson

Erickson commanded nos. 1 and 2 guns in Captain Bigelow's 9th Massachusetts Battery on July 2. His gallantry and devotion to his duty, even when mortally wounded and in great pain, was exceptional. He was hit in the chest by a piece of spherical case while the battery was defending the corner of the field opposite the Trostle Farm "at all hazards." When first hit, Bigelow recalled that Erickson had ridden up to him "with his hand pressing his breast and reported that he was wounded." Bigelow sent him to the rear but he soon returned, either unable to find a field hospital or determined to see out his first action. His battery commander was glad to have him back and supposed the wound to be less serious than at first thought. However, the shrapnel had penetrated his lungs and his mouth was full of bloody froth, so he could not speak except in a whisper. He asked Private Willis for a drink of water and nearly emptied the canteen. He was soon afterward hit again and killed. In the mad scramble to get the guns through the one gate, Private John K. Norwood described what happened: "Blaisdell and I were trying to limber up the gun when Lieut. Erickson rode up and asked if he could help us. Just then a bullet crashed through his head, and he fell dead, his horse going into the lines of Barksdale's men." According to Bigelow, Erickson was "riddled with bullets, his wrist shattered, one in his body [,] one in his hip, his leg broken about his ankle . . ." As the Rebels charged home, both Erickson's guns were lost (but later retrieved). When Erickson's body was recovered it had been stripped of everything except his underclothes.

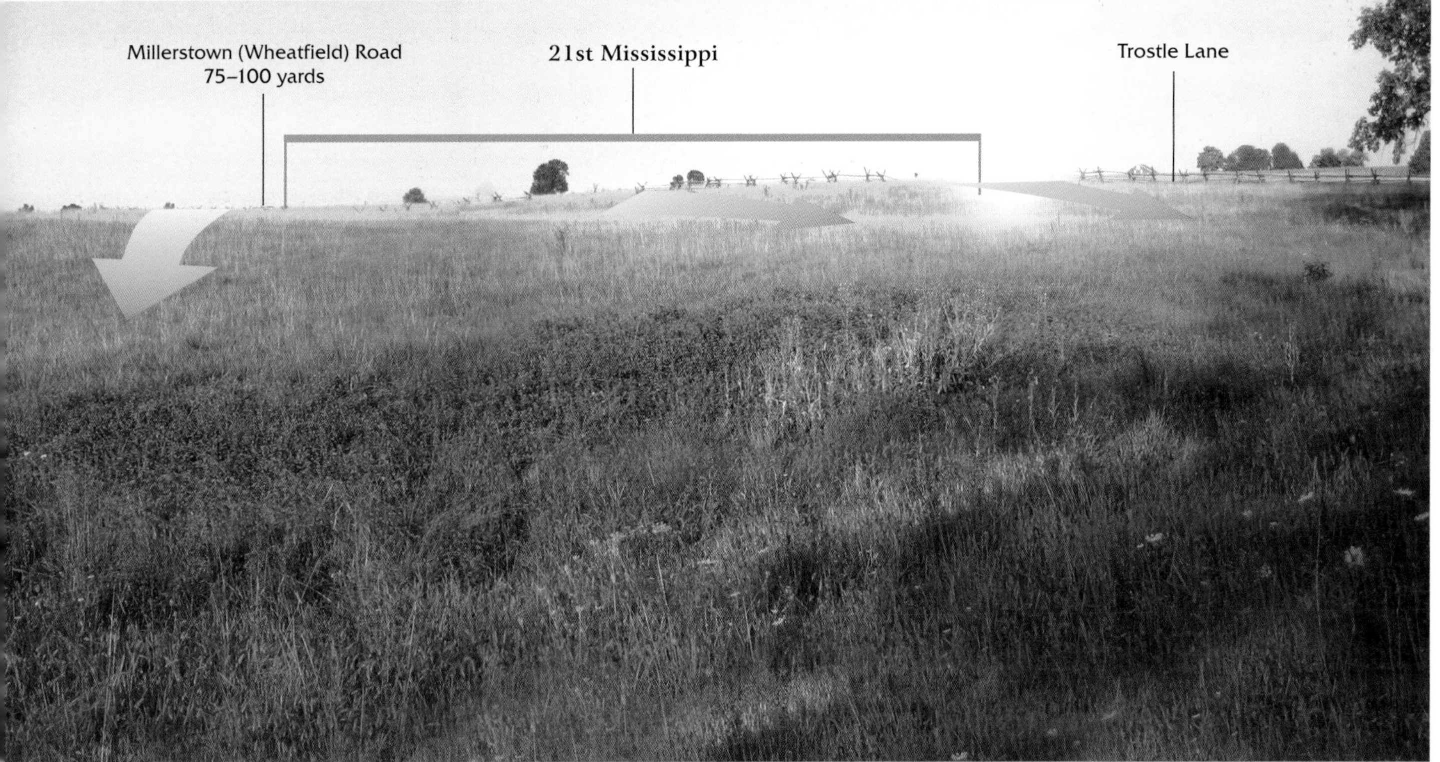

This view is taken from the final position of Bigelow's Battery after it had retired by prolonge from the Millerstown Road. It clearly shows how the guns deployed around the area of the camera had their view obscured by the slight ridge in front. They fired ball and shell, the former ricocheting over the ridge into the dead ground beyond the rise. Only when the Rebel infantry appeared over the crest were the gunners able to fire directly – even then the smoke from continuous firing meant many shots were fired blind. Note how Trostle Wood, once it had been abandoned by Tilton's Brigade, gave good cover for enemy skirmishers to fire directly, at close range, at the gunners and horses. Four guns out of the battery's six had to be abandoned on the position as the infantry charged home. See Map 53.

guns were abandoned out of six, which for one battery was a devastating loss. Another factor was that only a handful of horses were unscathed: around forty-five battery horses were killed or injured. A glance at the photograph on page 328 showing piles of horses' bodies in front of the Trostle house bears witness to the severity of the loss of animals. Without horses the battery was immobilized and virtually useless as a fighting unit. The uninjured officer, Milton, did remarkably well in parading with a complete section the following day. He was assigned to the Zeigler's Grove area after Pickett's attack had been repulsed. It was ten months before the 9th Massachusetts Battery was able to field six guns again.

The Trostle Farm action was one example from several of how a potentially disastrous situation – the Rebels securing a foothold on Cemetery Ridge – can be countered by the initiative of a single comparatively junior officer (McGilvery). It illustrates how artillery could in an emergency be used without close infantry support to hold a line, and how it is sometimes necessary to sacrifice one unit for the greater good of the whole.

On the technical level it showed how guns in combat could be manhandled by prolonge, firing and retiring by this method over a distance of more than 200 yards (Lieutenant John G. Turnbull's F and K Battery, 3rd U.S. Artillery, did the same that afternoon). The battery personnel fought a brilliant and courageous action, and resorted to firing at such a rate that the recoil of the guns was ignored in the reloading and aiming process – this being necessary because the enemy was so close. As far as the attacking infantry was concerned, Kershaw's men who approached to within 100 yards through Trostle Wood demonstrated the value of skirmishers being able to get close to a battery and therefore being able to inflict considerable damage on men and horses. The 21st Mississippi was fortunate that the swell in the ground enabled it to get to within less than 100 yards of the guns before being subject to direct fire.

ANDERSON'S DIVISIONAL ATTACK, 6:15 P.M. (Map 54)

Richard "Dick" Anderson was a forty-two-year-old West Pointer at Gettysburg and a South Carolinian of some distinction. He looked every bit the Southern gentleman with his neatly trimmed, iron-gray beard. He had a kindly, easygoing nature with no apparent wish to advertise himself. Nevertheless, he had proved a competent battlefield commander, having led a brigade under Longstreet in early 1862 and fought at Williamsburg, Seven Pines, and in the Seven Days Battles. He was promoted major-general in July of that year, commanded a division at Second Manassas, was wounded at Antietam, was back on duty for Fredericksburg and Chancellorsville, where he did exceptionally well against Hooker's left. By June 1862 Anderson was earmarked for promotion. His performance at Gettysburg, however, was decidedly mediocre.

Anderson had a very powerful division of over 7,000 men who had not been engaged the previous day. These troops were distributed among twenty regiments in five brigades from five different states. When the division lined up in one continuous line along the

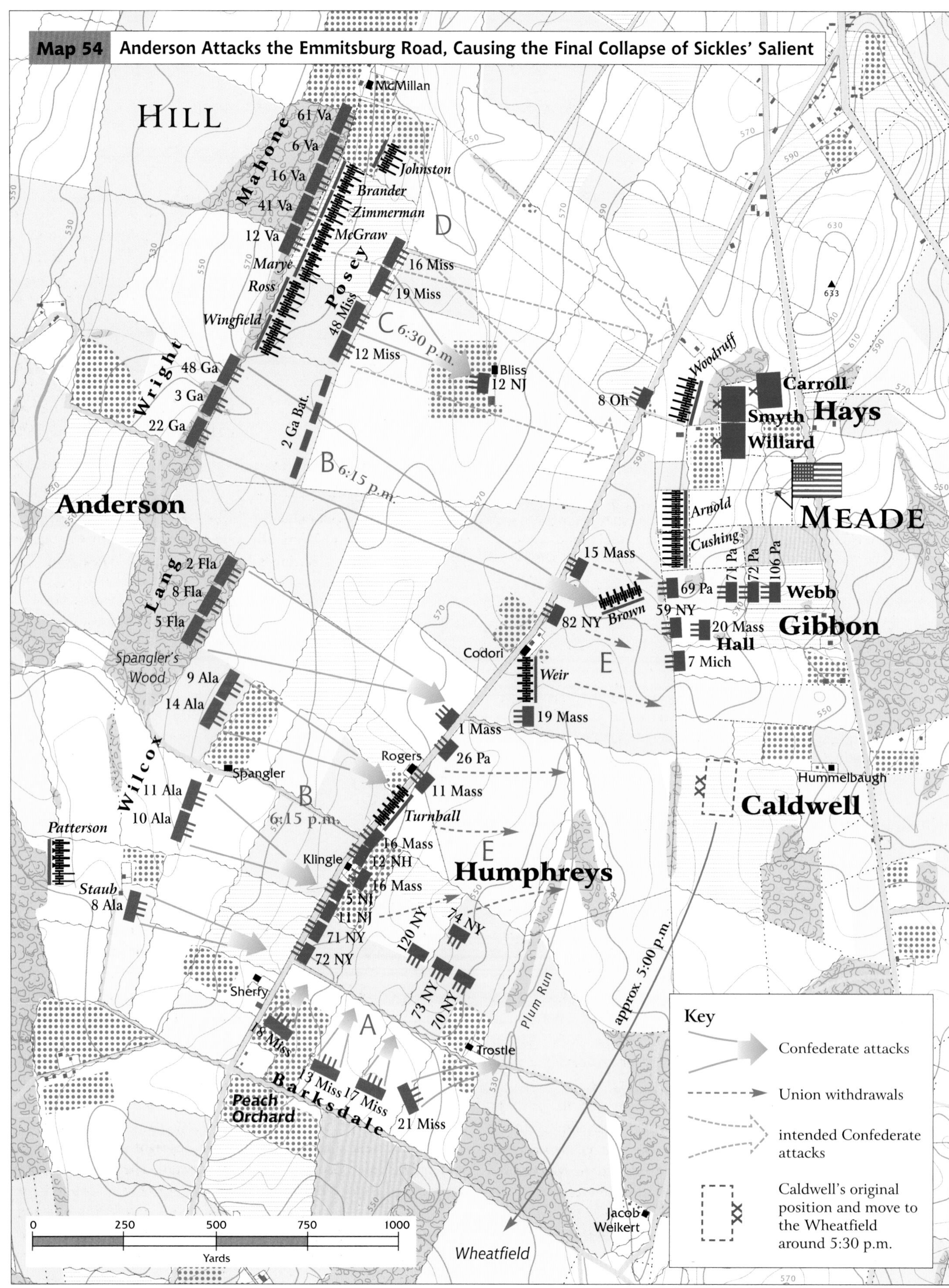
Map 54 Anderson Attacks the Emmitsburg Road, Causing the Final Collapse of Sickles' Salient
HILL
McMillan
Mahone
61 Va
6 Va
16 Va
41 Va
12 Va
Johnston
Brander
Zimmerman
McGraw
Marye
Ross
Wingfield
Posey
16 Miss
19 Miss
48 Miss
12 Miss
D
C 6:30 p.m.
Bliss
12 NJ
Wright
48 Ga
3 Ga
22 Ga
2 Ga Bat.
B 6:15 p.m.
Anderson
Lang
2 Fla
8 Fla
5 Fla
Spangler's Wood
9 Ala
14 Ala
Wilcox
11 Ala
10 Ala
Spangler
B 6:15 p.m.
Patterson
Staub
8 Ala
Codori
Weir
19 Mass
1 Mass
26 Pa
Rogers
11 Mass
Turnball
16 Mass
12 NH
16 Mass
Klingle
5 NJ
11 NJ
71 NY
72 NY
120 NY
74 NY
73 NY
70 NY
E
Humphreys
Sherfy
18 Miss
A
13 Miss
17 Miss
Barksdale
21 Miss
Peach Orchard
Trostle
Plum Run
approx. 5:00 p.m.
Jacob Weikert
Wheatfield
8 Oh
Woodruff
Carroll
Smyth
Hays
Willard
MEADE
Arnold
Cushing
15 Mass
69 Pa
71 Pa
72 Pa
106 Pa
Webb
Brown
59 NY
82 NY
20 Mass
Gibbon
Hall
7 Mich
E
Hummelbaugh
Caldwell
633
Key
Confederate attacks
Union withdrawals
intended Confederate attacks
Caldwell's original position and move to the Wheatfield around 5:30 p.m.
0
250
500
750
1000
Yards

Notes

• Anderson's Division was tasked with attacking the center of the Union position along the Emmitsburg Road – the western edge of Sickles' salient. Longstreet's Corps was pushing the southern flank of the salient out of the Rose Woods, the Devil's Den, Stony Hill and the Wheatfield, and a bitter struggle for Little Round Top had developed.

• Anderson's Division was a strong one, with well over 7,000 men in five brigades and 20 regiments. It had the direct support of eight batteries of artillery – a mixture of rifles, howitzers and Napoleons. By the time the advance started at around 6:15 p.m. Barksdale's Brigade (McLaws' Division) had secured the Peach Orchard and was threatening the Union line's left flank (**A**).

• At about this time the brigades of Wilcox, Lang and Wright began to advance directly on the Emmitsburg Road (**B**), following a prolonged and damaging artillery duel. The division was supposed to advance simultaneously but the distances each brigade had to march varied considerably, so the attack would be en echelon from the right. Wilcox on the right had a mere 500 yards to cover, while Wright had 900 and Mahone 1,000.

• Further north, Wright's Brigade, after a long advance, smashed through the two enemy regiments on the Emmitsburg Road just north of the Codori Farm. However, this brigade was not supported on the left, as Posey's men had mostly got bogged down scrapping for the Bliss buildings and only a small number of the 48th Mississippi from that brigade advanced further with Wright (**C**). Things were even worse on the extreme left of the advance as Mahone, with the second largest brigade in the division, refused to budge (**D**). He disobeyed Anderson's aide, who told him to attack, claiming he was sticking to a previous order unless told otherwise personally by the general. The Bliss Farm sideshow and Mahone's intransigence cost the divisional assault some 2,800 men, or 39 percent of its strength.

• Behind the center of the Union line there was no immediate reserve as Caldwell's Division had been sent south to support Barnes's Division contesting the Wheatfield. As the attack developed in the south there was no stopping the Rebels from Alabama. Their determined advance, supported by the tiny Florida Brigade, coupled with the thrust of Barksdale to their left rear, forced the Yankees, infantry and guns, to retire in haste and some confusion to the Cemetery Ridge (**E**).

edge of the woods on Seminary Ridge, it extended for well over a mile. The whole division was deployed in the front line, with no supporting line or reserves. The right of the line was only 500 yards from the enemy, while the extreme left had double that to reach the Emmitsburg Road. On the right was Brigadier-General Cadmus M. Wilcox with over 1,700 Alabamians; on his left the smallest brigade in the army under Colonel David Lang with some 740 men from Florida; next left were the 1,400 Georgians under Brigadier-General Ambrose R. Wright; to his left Brigadier-General Carnot Posey with 1,300 Mississippians; and finally, on the extreme left, the 1,540 Virginians under Brigadier-General William Mahone. Under Anderson's command was an artillery battalion under Major John Lane with three batteries under Captains Hugh M. Ross, George M. Patterson and John T. Wingfield. Also in direct support was Major William J. Pegram's artillery battalion from the Corps Reserve. These five batteries were commanded by Captains Thomas A. Brander, Joseph McGraw and Edward A. Marye, and Lieutenants Andrew Johnston and William E. Zimmerman. These thirty-six guns (one of Zimmerman's had been put out of action the previous day), along with another nine rifled pieces from Lieutenant-Colonel John Garnett's Battalion (off map), deployed north of the McMillan house, were engaged in pounding the Union line for nearly two hours prior to the attack – a bombardment that attracted a lively response from the Yankee guns.

According to Lee's report, Hill's Corps was to "threaten the enemy's center, to prevent re-enforcements being drawn to either wing, and to co-operate with his right division [Anderson] in Longstreet's attack." In the event, only three of Anderson's five brigades cooperated with Longstreet's attack, and his division did not prevent reinforcements moving from the center (Caldwell, see above) or the right (Williams, see below) to other parts of the line to meet critical situations. Anderson wrote that he was "ordered to put the troops of my division into action by brigades, as soon as those of General Longstreet's corps had progressed so far in their assault as to be connected with my right." It was little short of two hours after Hood advanced that Anderson deemed that situation had arrived and ordered Wilcox forward at about 6:15 p.m.

The main weight of the attack on the right by Wilcox and Lang would fall on Humphreys' Division of the Union III Corps. Humphreys started the battle with almost 5,000 men, but his line along the Emmitsburg Road had barely half that. Colonel George C. Burling's New Jersey Brigade was missing. It had been broken up into regimental pieces and rushed hither and thither to bolster other formations. The 2nd New Hampshire and 7th New Jersey had gone to the Peach Orchard area, the 5th New Jersey was now under Graham's command providing skirmishers, the 6th New Jersey went south to Ward's Brigade and then the 8th New Jersey disappeared without Burling's knowledge to the Wheatfield. The brigade commander was left with one very weak regiment, the 115th Pennsylvania. As Burling wrote in his report, "my command being now all taken from me and separated, no two regiments being together, and being under the command of the different brigade commanders to whom they reported, I with my staff, reported to General Humphreys for instructions . . ." The 150 men of his remaining regiment ended up in the Wheatfield area.

The 750 yards of the Emmitsburg Road line from the Trostle Lane to 200 yards north of Rogers' house was defended by the six regiments of Brigadier-General Joseph B. Carr's Brigade – around 1,700 men. On the left of this brigade were two regiments (71st and 72nd New York) belonging to Colonel William R. Brewster and the 5th New Jersey, mostly on picket duty – a grand total of some 2,470 infantrymen. By an extraordinary quirk of statistics, and discounting casualties on both sides, the Rebels advancing against this part of the line under Wilcox and Lang amounted to virtually precisely the same number. However, it was not the frontal assault that forced Humphreys back, but rather its combination with the collapse of the line on his left rear before the sweeping advance of Barksdale. Humphreys was told of Sickles' departure from the field with a smashed leg and that Birney now commanded III Corps, and that he was to pull back his left and try to form a new line. As this was being implemented, a second order arrived to retire to Cemetery Ridge. The division scrambled back as best it could under huge pressure and with heavy losses. Those regiments facing Barksdale's forceful thrust fared the worst.

About fifteen minutes after Lang on his right advanced, Wright ordered his three Georgian regiments forward. They had a long way to go, over 1,000 yards, and across much the same ground over which Pickett would make his famous charge the next day. En route these 1,200 men were to pick up their 2nd Georgia Battalion, which had already been deployed forward as skirmishers. This comparatively small force was to achieve a remarkable success

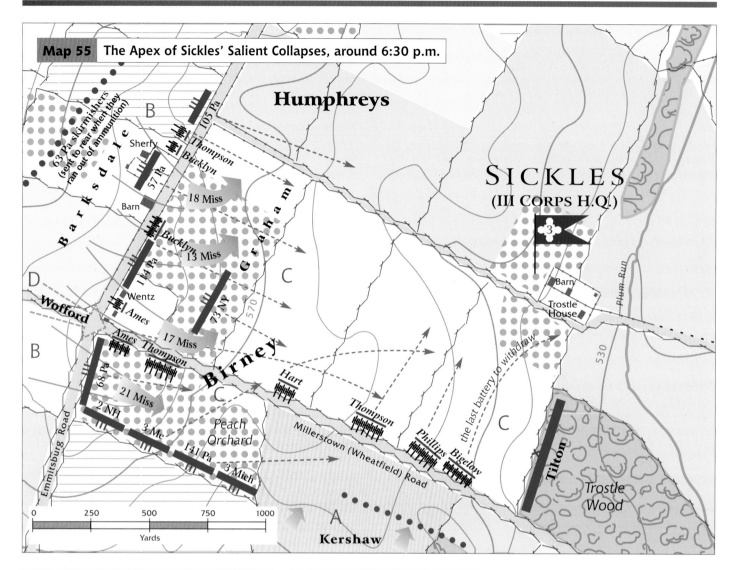

Map 55 The Apex of Sickles' Salient Collapses, around 6:30 p.m.

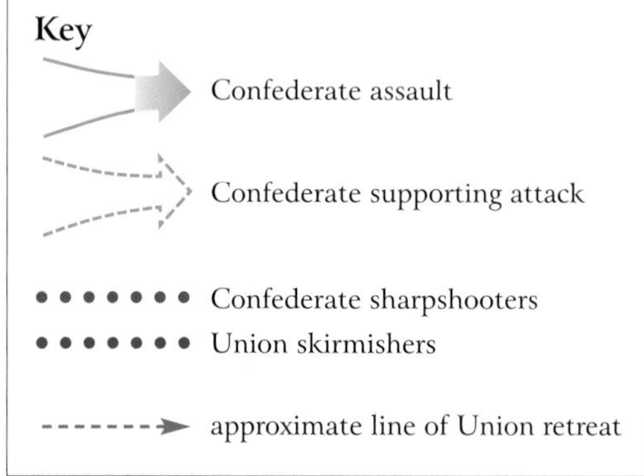

Notes

A Kershaw's Brigade attack with three regiments is initially checked by the guns along the Millerstown Road and because of a misunderstood order.

B Barksdale's Brigade storms the Peach Orchard and the line of the Emmitsburg Road to the north. Heavily outnumbered, the Union line is outflanked and forced to retreat in haste. Barksdale's three left-hand regiments wheel north to take Humphreys' line further north along the road in flank.

C All Union units, including the guns along the Emmitsburg and Millerstown Roads, retreat with the infantry. The last battery to withdraw under heavy pressure is Capt. Bigelow's 9th Massachusetts.

D Wofford's Brigade follows Barksdale and thrusts with his right-hand regiments down the line of the Millerstown Road.

before finally being forced to retire – it secured a toehold on Cemetery Ridge. The brigade was aiming for the "Copse of Trees" that marked the center of the Union position. The only units deployed forward in their path along the Emmitsburg Road were the 82nd New York and 15th Massachusetts – about 570 men from Brigadier-General William Harrow's Brigade in Gibbon's 2nd Division of II Corps. They were supported by Lieutenant T. Fred Brown's battery of six Napoleons in their rear. These two Union regiments had erected some flimsy breastworks along the fence line but these were quickly smashed by Rebel gunfire. Their exposed predicament was not improved when some of the artillery fire from Union guns in their rear caused casualties in their ranks – one of several incidents of "friendly fire" during the battle (see also box, page 411). Both Yankee regiments were driven back by Wright's attack, losing a number of prisoners in what one soldier described as a "stampede." Weir's Battery to the south of the Codori Farm was overrun and Brown lost two of his guns. It was a splendid advance that continued up onto Cemetery Ridge, where it was confronted by Colonel Norman Hall's Brigade (Gibbon's Division).

It was now Wright's turn to be isolated. On his left Posey's Brigade had failed to advance much beyond the Bliss Farm – apart from some of the 48th Mississippi, who joined Wright's

Brigade. Wright had sent an aide galloping to find Anderson to report the fact that his left was becoming dangerously exposed. He returned to say that Posey had been ordered forward and that Anderson would repeat it, but that in the meantime he, Wright, should press on. He did so, but of Posey's support there was still no sign. Posey later claimed his orders were to "advance two of my regiments, and deploy them closely as skirmishers." The 19th and 48th Mississippi went forward to contest Bliss Farm, followed by the 16th and later the 12th Mississippi.

While some of Posey's men did get beyond the Bliss Farm, none of Mahone's Brigade moved from its position on Seminary Ridge. Posey had asked for his assistance, but Mahone had declined to move. Anderson sent an aide, Lieutenant Samuel D. Shannon, with orders for Mahone to advance his brigade but Mahone still refused, claiming that Anderson had told him "to remain in position." He would not budge unless ordered by Anderson in person. Later, in his report on Gettysburg, Mahone wrote, "The brigade took no special or active part in that battle beyond that which fell to the lot of its line of skirmishers." Its total loss of 102 for the battle was the lowest of any Confederate Brigade and was mostly the result of enemy artillery fire.

Anderson Retires (Map 56)

Three brigades of Anderson's Division (Wilcox, Lang and Wright), together with Barksdale's Brigade from McLaws' Division, almost succeeded in breaching the Union center by 7:00 p.m. Wright's Brigade's advance was to be the high water mark of Rebel progress that day. Nevertheless, like a wave surging up a beach, the attack had lost much of its power by the time it reached the Plum Run and the lower slopes of Cemetery Ridge. Much of the attack's impetus had been expended in crushing Sickles' salient, and by evening heavy losses, fatigue and lack of support on the left made the whole divisional attack highly vulnerable to counterattacks. And that is what the Yankees produced with fresh troops. A series of local counterattacks spread over a mile of Cemetery Ridge, coupled with a determined resistance by Union regiments in the line, including artillery batteries, drove Anderson's men and Barksdale back to where they started west of the Emmitsburg Road.

After Bigelow's sacrifice at the Trostle Farm, Lieutenant-Colonel McGilvery cobbled together a line of guns from any battery he could find and deployed it in a line below the crest of Cemetery Ridge and just east of the Plum Run. He certainly had seventeen guns, only four of them Napoleons, in this "grand battery," and possibly a few more. On the left was Watson's Battery, then Lieutenant Edwin Dow's, next three guns of Phillips, then two of Thompson's and on the right Captain James McKay Rorty's four. With these guns the gap in the line was held until infantry arrived. They did so in the form of Colonel George L. Willard's Brigade – 1,500 New Yorkers in four regiments led into position personally by Major-General Hancock. These regiments, particularly the 126th New York, had marched to Gettysburg with their reputation still under a cloud from when they cut and ran at Harper's Ferry back in September 1862. Hancock pointed out the advancing Rebel line and the brigade charged to the cry of, "Remember Harper's Ferry!" It was too much for the exhausted and depleted Mississippians, who fell back despite Barksdale's efforts to check the retreat. His attempt was rewarded with a mortal wound. On the extreme left, somewhat separated from the other regiments and east of the Plum Run, the 39th New York was able to drive away the 21st Mississippi, who had given Bigelow such a rough time, and recapture the guns of Watson's Battery which the Rebels had just taken.

Also arriving to bolster McGilvery's makeshift Plum Run line was the leading brigade of Brigadier-General Thomas H. Ruger's Division from XII Corps (Brigadier-General Alpheus S. Williams was acting corps commander, as Slocum still regarded himself as the right-wing commander). At the head of the column were the three regiments of Brigadier-General Henry H. Lockwood with around 1,800 men. By the time they arrived there was little fighting left to do, although the brigade advanced to the Trostle Farm area and recaptured Bigelow's four guns.

Brigadier-General William Barksdale

A former lawyer who had fought in the Mexican War, the forty-two-year-old Barksdale had acquired a reputation as what in modern terminology would be described as a "gung-ho" leader: fiery, always craving action, and always leading from the front. Large and heavy, he did not sit elegantly on a horse, but as one of his men said, "he is very much attached to the boys, as the boys are to him." At Gettysburg, while waiting with unconcealed impatience to attack toward the Emmitsburg Road late in the afternoon of July 2, Barksdale accosted Longstreet as he passed nearby to plead to be allowed to attack immediately. He was told to wait. Moments before he was given the order to advance, he told his officers that only he and his staff were to remain mounted. Not until around 6:00 p.m. was he able to shout "Attention, Mississippians! Battalions, forward!" to start the brigade's advance on the Sherfy Orchard.

According to one Rebel who watched, it "was the most magnificent charge I witnessed during the war." A Yankee colonel agreed, saying, "It was the grandest charge ever made by mortal man." As recounted in the main text, the charge swept through the Union position on the Emmitsburg Road, the 21st Mississippi overran Bigelow's Battery and the brigade was only checked at the Plum Run. When finally driven back by Willard's men, Barksdale was not with them. He had been badly wounded but nobody had noticed his fall, although a soldier of the 13th Mississippi claimed to have given him a drink of water from his canteen. He was eventually carried to a Union field hospital on the Taneytown Road, where he was placed, unrecognized, on blankets in the yard. When it was discovered who he was, a surgeon examined his wounds and found he had been hit at least three times – one large chest wound and two others in his leg. There was little that could be done apart from giving morphine, and Barksdale soon lost consciousness and died during the night. A Union officer who had known him before the war saw him the next morning, "with open unblinking eyes . . . uncovered in the sunshine. There he lay alone, without a comrade to brush the flies from his corpse." He was later buried near the Jacob Hummelbaugh house, but eventually his remains were returned to his beloved Mississippi.

After deploying Willard's Brigade, Hancock rode back north up the ridge to discover that the Rebels under Wilcox were still treading on the heels of Humphreys' disorganized and retreating command, and that the six Napoleons of Lieutenant Thomas were all that lay between them and a foothold on Cemetery Ridge. Under fire that wounded his aide, Hancock galloped up, casting around desperately for infantry. Nearby was a single regiment, the 1st Minnesota under Colonel William Colvill. Hancock demanded to know the name of the regiment and, on being told, pointed through the swirling smoke in the direction of the rapidly approaching enemy line and shouted, "Advance, Colonel, and take those colors!" The 300 or so Minnesotans charged immediately with fixed bayonets, catching the Alabamians by surprise and pushing them back. However, Wilcox rallied his regiments sufficiently to return a devastating fire into the Yankees as they scrambled for cover along the Plum Run. Nevertheless, this charge tipped the balance and convinced Wilcox that, with troops on his right pulling back, it was time to withdraw. In about fifteen minutes of intense action the 1st Minnesota had lost most of the 224 casualties it suffered during the battle – 67 percent of its engaged strength of 335. Hancock later wrote, "I cannot speak too highly of this regiment and its commander in its attack . . ."

Meanwhile, the center of the ridge by the Copse of Trees was still under attack by Wright's three Georgian regiments. The 69th Pennsylvania were behind a stone wall, and their historian would write of the Rebel advance: "still came on the mad Georgians until they reached point-blank range of our rifles. We met their charge with such a destroying fire that they were forced back in confusion." Despite his urgent requests sent back to Anderson earlier, Wright remained isolated with both flanks exposed. The regiment on his right, the 22nd Georgia, had actually clambered over the wall on the crest of the ridge before being hit by yet another Yankee regiment plucked from the seemingly inexhaustible reservoir of reserves behind the ridge. This time it was the inexperienced 13th Vermont from I Corps under Colonel Francis Randall, a "nine-month wonder" regiment of volunteers, part of Brigadier-General George Stannard's Brigade straight from the Washington defenses. Hancock asked the colonel if he thought he could recapture a battery (Weir's) that was then barely visible through the smoke. Randall responded that he would try. The regiment deployed into line, its commander in front on his horse, and advanced down the slope into the smoke. Almost at once Randall's horse was hit and in falling trapped its rider underneath. Randall yelled at his men, "Go on boys, go on. I'll be at your head as soon as I can get out of this damn saddle." His regiment swept on, followed by its now dismounted colonel. The charge caught the 22nd Georgia by surprise in the right flank and threw it back. The boys from Vermont pressed on and retook Weir's guns, with the whole Rebel line now receding as a wave that has lost its impetus recedes on a beach.

On the Confederate left, the 106th Pennsylvania advanced through Cushing's guns, fired several volleys and charged. Wright's Brigade's resistance collapsed – a full-scale retreat was now in progress. Wright was, naturally, somewhat bitter and defensive in his later account of what happened:

> My advanced position and the unprotected condition of my flanks invited an attack . . . We were now in a critical condition. The enemy's converging line was rapidly closing upon my rear; a few moments more, and we would be completely surrounded, and with painful hearts we abandoned our captured guns, and prepared to cut our way through the closing lines in our rear. This was affected in tolerable order, but with immense loss.

Anderson's Division had suffered heavily, although overall the attacking Rebels inflicted more losses than they received. The three brigades of Wilcox, Lang and Wright, whose regiments reached the Plum Run and beyond, started with about 3,880 men. At the end of the battle these brigades' total losses amounted to 1,929 or 50 percent, although not all were sustained on July 2, as both Wilcox and Lang went forward again the next day on the right of Pickett's Division. Among the regiments, the most severely hit was the 8th Florida with losses of 61 percent, the 48th Georgia with 57 percent and the 8th Alabama with 56 percent. In comparison with Posey's Brigade's losses of 112 or 8.5 percent, or Mahone's 102 or 6.6 percent, these figures were devastatingly high.

Notes

• This map shows the high water mark of Anderson's divisional attack on the evening of July 2. Sickles' salient had been crushed and the Rebels had pushed up to the Plum Run in the south, while in the center Wright's Brigade had reached the forward slope of Cemetery Ridge with the 22nd Georgia crossing the wall and gaining a toehold on the ridge itself. In the north it was a different story, with the majority of Posey's Brigade not getting much beyond the Bliss Farm and Mahone still sitting on his hands back at the jump-off point.

• At this point, when the Yankee defenses looked as though they might be breached, the hasty, in several instances desperate, use of reserves checked the enemy and a series of local counterattacks drove the Rebels back. The important events were:

A McGilvery established an ad hoc gun line on the forward slope of Cemetery Ridge northeast of the George Weikert Farm. This effectively plugged a dangerous hole in the line until infantry arrived.

B Guided by Maj.-Gen. Hancock in person, Col. George L. Willard's Brigade of 1,500 men from Brig.-Gen. Alexander Hays's Division was rushed south over a considerable distance to back up McGilvery's guns.

C Willard's Brigade drove Barksdale's back over the Emmitsburg Road. The 39th New York recaptured Watson's Battery from the 21st Mississippi.

D The charge of the 1st Minnesota checked Wilcox. The advance of Willard and the fire from Thomas's guns forced Wilcox to retire.

E Strong resistance and the withdrawal of Lang forced the small Florida Brigade to fall back as well.

F The right wing of Wright's Brigade succeeded in reaching the crest of Cemetery Ridge. However, it was exposed and isolated and a charge by the 13th Vermont on its right and the 106th Pennsylvania on its left drove the survivors back. Wright was totally unsupported and, with both flanks under attack, the brigade retreated in some disorder with heavy losses, many of them prisoners.

G Posey's Brigade, except for the 48th Mississippi, some of whom made it to the Emmitsburg Road, failed to get much beyond Bliss Farm. Mahone's Brigade never left its start line.

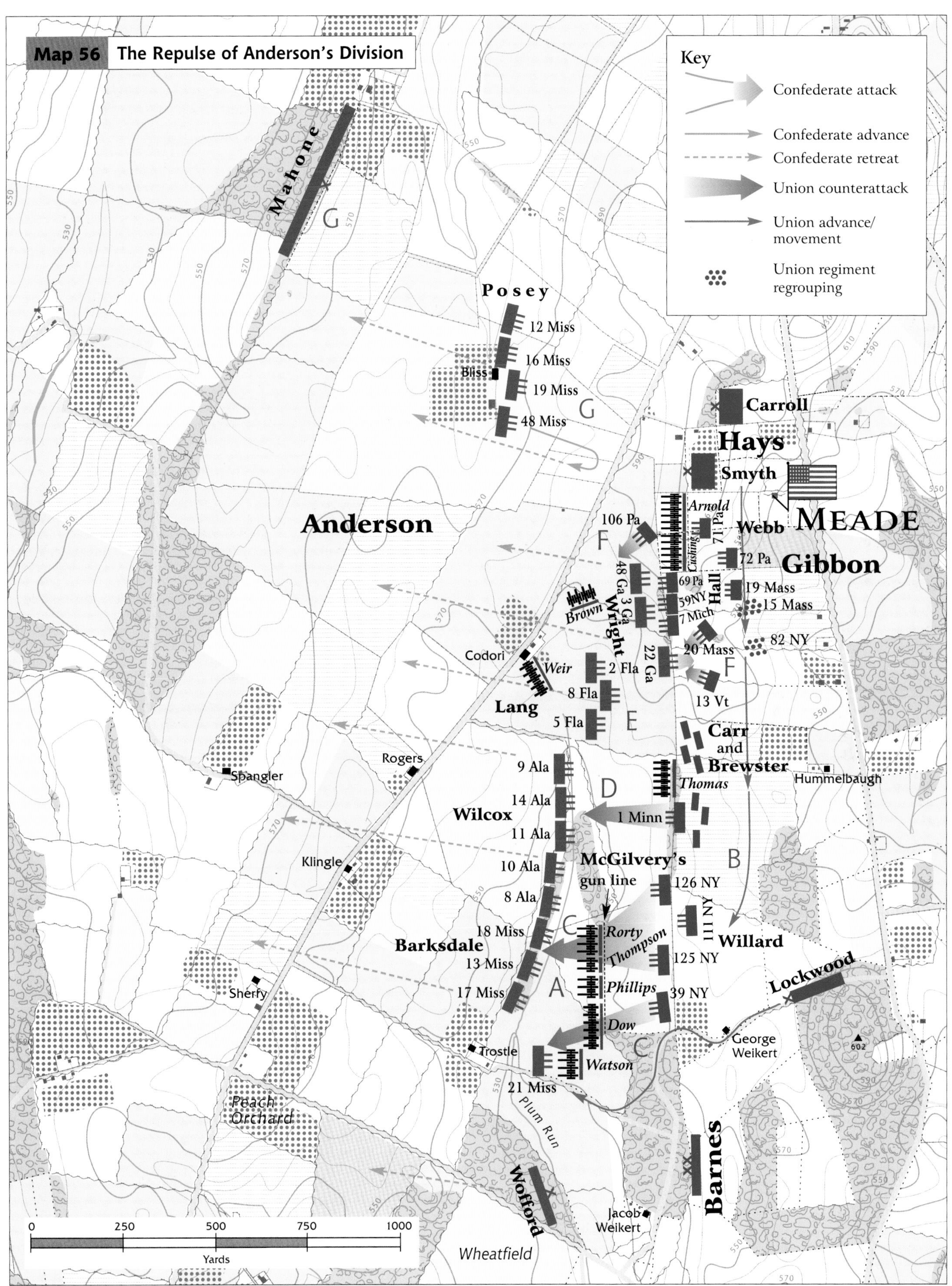

Map 56 The Repulse of Anderson's Division
Key
Confederate attack
Confederate advance
Confederate retreat
Union counterattack
Union advance/ movement
Union regiment regrouping
Mahone
Posey
12 Miss
16 Miss
19 Miss
48 Miss
Bliss
Anderson
Carroll
Hays
Smyth
MEADE
Webb
Gibbon
Arnold
Cushing
71 Pa
72 Pa
106 Pa
69 Pa
59NY
7 Mich
Hall
19 Mass
15 Mass
82 NY
20 Mass
13 Vt
48 Ga
3 Ga
Wright
22 Ga
Brown
Codori
Weir
2 Fla
8 Fla
Lang
5 Fla
Carr and Brewster
Thomas
Hummelbaugh
Rogers
Spangler
9 Ala
14 Ala
Wilcox
11 Ala
1 Minn
McGilvery's gun line
Klingle
10 Ala
8 Ala
126 NY
111 NY
Willard
18 Miss
Barksdale
13 Miss
Rorty
Thompson
125 NY
Phillips
39 NY
17 Miss
Sherfy
Lockwood
Dow
George Weikert
Trostle
Watson
21 Miss
Peach Orchard
Plum Run
Barnes
Wofford
Jacob Weikert
Wheatfield
0 250 500 750 1000
Yards

Comments

Including Anderson's attack, a total of eleven Rebel brigades had attempted to get the better of twenty-two Yankee brigades, discounting those in I, VI or XII Corps whose contribution was comparatively minor. Of these Union brigades, only six belonged to III Corps. This reveals just how much the defense of Sickles' salient depended on reinforcements from outside his corps, and how much he had isolated his command by moving forward threequarters of a mile contrary to orders. These figures are also a graphic illustration of just how Meade, Hancock and other senior Union commanders made use of their interior-lines position to rush reserves to threatened areas. This, combined with the determination and hard fighting that included several spirited counterattacks by the Union soldiers, had eventually been able to turn a potential disaster into a successful defense all along Cemetery Ridge.

The Confederate brigade and regimental leadership had, with just a few exceptions, proved first class. This, coupled with the great gallantry of the majority of the Rebel troops, had been sufficient to smash Sickles' salient despite all the reserves thrown in to save it, and to roll the Union line back beyond the Plum Run to Cemetery Ridge. It was a remarkable achievement in which they inflicted more losses on their enemy than they themselves sustained – a difficult thing for any attacker to achieve.

It was surely at the higher level of command that the Confederates were found wanting on July 2.

- Lee continued with his reluctance to supervise or interfere with his corps commanders once he had given them their instructions – in one instance direct to a divisional commander (McLaws). Such delegation failed him again on this second day of battle. He did nothing to hasten Longstreet's movement or attack, despite knowing Longstreet was decidedly less than enthusiastic about the plan. Neither did he move to his right to check personally on the changed situation on that flank and if necessary to revise his original plan to meet altered circumstances. Similarly, despite being close to Hill, he allowed that officer's seeming lack of control of events within his command to go unchecked. Then there is the question of whether Lee should have insisted that Pender's Division – of which one brigade, Thomas's, had not been involved the previous day – be used to bolster the attack of Anderson's Division. Brigadier-General James Lane, who took over command when Pender was wounded that afternoon, later reported that he was to "advance, if I saw a good opportunity for doing so." Neither Lee nor Hill thought to ensure this division went forward with Anderson, although Pender might have done so had he not been wounded. Had this division advanced, the chances of overall Confederate success would surely have been substantially increased. Then there was Pickett's Division, which had arrived down the Chambersburg Pike to within 2 miles of the field by mid-afternoon – that is just before Hood's Division started its advance. These troops had just completed an exhausting 25-mile march and Lee was content to let them rest, although there is evidence that, with the thunderous roar of battle so close, they expected, indeed wanted, to be involved. However, in the circumstances at the time, Lee was probably right in keeping them out of the fray.
- Hill played no part in the tactical coordination of the attack of Anderson's Division. He made no effort to intervene when he saw that the half-hearted advance of Posey and lack of movement by Mahone were jeopardizing the divisional attack. Accounts of the action make virtually no mention of Hill acting the part of corps commander. It was almost as if he was not present. Perhaps his illness was affecting him more severely than usual that day, or he considered his close proximity to Lee absolved him of taking decisive action.
- Hood was wounded quite early on and McLaws did his best, although far from happy with the insistence of his corps commander that Lee's plan be implemented despite the radically changed circumstances at the Peach Orchard and along the Emmitsburg Road at 4:00 p.m. Anderson, however, put in a decidedly poor performance as a divisional commander. After launching three of his brigades he seemed to lose interest in events. After the war Wilcox alleged that one of his staff officers found Anderson well to the rear, "lying on the ground with all his staff as though nothing was going on." True or not, a decisive commander would have ensured both Posey and Mahone participated in the attack, particularly when it became obvious that Wright's Brigade's left flank was becoming exposed by their lack of action. If Mahone had refused to budge he should have been relieved of his command immediately. After the battle, Anderson claimed in Southern newspapers that after receiving Wilcox's urgent request for support he could not find Hill to get authority to send Posey and Mahone into the attack. They were Anderson's brigades, he was their divisional commander – would he expect to be asked for permission for the use of a regiment by one of his brigade commanders?
- The failure of Posey and Mahone, for whatever reason, to attack that afternoon undoubtedly meant Anderson's assault was doomed to fail. The division was compelled to form up in a thin line covering over 2,000 yards with (unlike Hood and McLaws) no supporting line or reserves of any sort. In those circumstances, two brigades failing to advance gave the defenders a huge advantage in dealing with a frontal attack. Had both kept up with Wright's outstanding achievement in getting troops onto Cemetery Ridge, the day might have ended differently. Although Mahone deserved severe censure for insubordination, he received none. He was not courtmartialed, perhaps because of Anderson's and Hill's poor showing; indeed the following May he was given command of a division, which he led competently until the end of the war.

Culp's Hill and Cemetery Hill – July 2 (Map 57)

These two hills were the northern anchor of the Union line, just as the Round Tops were the southern anchor. Cemetery Hill had been the rallying point for Union forces the previous day and the main bastion of the Union line thereafter, and as such was of greater importance than Culp's Hill. Three hours after Longstreet launched his infantry in the south, Ewell launched his in the north. By this time it was dusk and the southern attacks had finally been halted or repulsed. Ewell's task was to provide a demonstration in the north with the proviso to develop it into a full-scale attack if the opportunity presented itself. On the evening of July 1 Ewell had baulked at attacking what he and Early considered difficult terrain; now he was to attack that same terrain, which had been substantially reinforced with guns and infantry, while over 1,000 yards of barricades had been erected across Culp's and Lower Culp's Hills.

Meade had given the defense of Cemetery Hill to the somewhat battered and demoralized XI Corps under Howard. While their infantry's numbers had shrunk as a result of the first day's fighting, the number of guns on Cemetery and East Cemetery Hill had been increased to fourteen batteries or sixty-three pieces of ordnance. Of these, Major Thomas W. Osborn, chief of artillery of XI Corps, commanded the thirty-eight on Cemetery Hill, while Colonel Charles S. Wainwright, chief of artillery of I Corps, commanded the twenty-five on East Cemetery Hill. Of these latter, the six Napoleons under Lieutenant James Stevens posted on the knoll (which now bears his name) between Cemetery Hill and Culp's Hill were particularly well positioned to fire across the entire front of the Union defenders along Brickyard Lane – the main defensive line of East Cemetery Hill.

Culp's Hill had been given to I Corps, now seriously depleted as a result of the prolonged struggle west of Gettysburg the previous day. Meade had more than doubled the numbers on the hill by sending the two divisions of Slocum's XII Corps to strengthen what he regarded as a key position. However, the chain of command in that corps had become complicated. Slocum had been temporarily given command of the right wing of the army (XII and V Corps) during the advance north and when a move to the Pipe Creek was contemplated, but now, on the battlefield, he still considered this was his role and that Brigadier Alpheus S. Williams was XII Corps commander. This meant that Brigadier-General Thomas H. Ruger acted as commander of the 1st Division and his 3rd Brigade was taken over by Colonel Silas Colgrove of the 27th Indiana. Meade appeared unaware of this unnecessary arrangement. An added complication was the arrival of Brigadier-General Henry H. Lockwood with two large brigades (the third arrived the next day). He was inexperienced but senior to Ruger, whose 1st Division had only two brigades whereas Geary's had three. Williams avoided the problem by keeping Lockwood's Brigade outside the divisional structure – in effect regarding it as an independent formation within the corps.

As noted before, from late afternoon Meade had been heavily reinforcing his left as the pressure on Sickles' salient increased, first with V Corps and then with units from II Corps. As the defense of the salient began to falter, VI Corps, just arriving, was summoned to assist, as was XII Corps, until then constructing barricades on Culp's Hill. However, there is confusion over how much of XII Corps was supposed to abandon its defenses and march south. Slocum later claimed it was the entire corps. Meade never clarified the issue, although a biographer stated it was only one division. Williams later wrote that he was told to "detach all I could spare – at least one Divn to support our left." Slocum and Williams seemingly agreed that one division needed to remain on Culp's Hill and Ruger's Division, along with Lockwood's Brigade, was ordered south at around 6:00 p.m. At the same time Slocum sent an aide to Meade to say that one division was all he could safely spare. The aide, Lieutenant-Colonel Hiram C. Rodgers, returned to say that Meade considered the situation on the left critical and that Slocum should retain only a brigade on the right – seeming to indicate that Meade originally wanted the whole of XII Corps. Slocum dispatched two brigades of Brigadier-General John W. Geary's Division (Colonel Charles Candy's 1st Brigade and Colonel George A. Cobham's 2nd Brigade). They started out about half an hour after Ruger. Thus a total of around 7,750 men had been taken from the Culp's Hill defenses. Only the sixty-two-year-old Brigadier-General George "Old Pap" Greene with his 1,400 men in the 3rd Brigade had been left to defend the long line of abandoned barricades. Lockwood led the march south, followed by Ruger's Division, turning right off the Baltimore Pike at Power's Hill onto the Granite Schoolhouse Lane, but by the time they arrived there was little for them to do as the Rebels were withdrawing. Geary, however, who had just been told to follow Ruger, had no clear idea of where he was supposed to go. Ruger had disappeared, so Geary went barreling on down the Baltimore Pike as far as the bridge over Rock Creek, where he was told (by whom is not clear) to "hold the position down to the creek at all hazards." It was growing dark – Geary deployed and waited.

Johnson's Division Attacks Culp's Hill, 7:30 p.m.

Ewell's Corps had done little all day, while above them on the hills the Yankees were consolidating their defenses. As Lieutenant Randolph McKim on the staff of Brigadier-General George H. Steuart's Brigade put it, "Greatly did officers and men marvel as morning, noon and afternoon passed in inaction – on our part, not on the enemy's, for, as we well knew, he was plying axe and pick and shovel . . ." At Greene's instigation and insistence, a concerted effort had been made to construct strong barricades of logs, rocks and earth, some with head logs so that firers were almost completely protected. This line of breastworks wriggled its way through the woods for 1,000 yards, from the saddle connecting Culp's Hill to Cemetery Hill in the north to close to Spangler's Spring in the south. It, combined with the woods and steepness of the slopes, was to prove a battle-winning feature in the coming clash. In addition, a "traverse" of obstacles was built out at right angles of the main line about 100 yards north of the Pardee Field on Lower Culp's Hill.

At around 4:00 p.m. Ewell's demonstration started. Shortly after Longstreet's distant guns were heard, Ewell's artillery opened fire. On Benner's Hill the nineteen-year-old "Boy Major" Joseph Latimer had a hard time, as over thirty Union guns were able to bring fire to bear on his exposed position. After two hours of dueling with the Yankee guns, firing over 1,000 rounds and with ten men dead and

In the Union Battery on Culp's Hill

Eventually five Union guns were dragged to the summit of Culp's Hill to duel with the Rebel artillery 800 yards away across Rock Creek on the bare, open slope of Benner's Hill. Three 10-pounder Parrotts were under the command of Lieutenant Edward R. Geary, the son of Brigadier-General Geary. In a letter to his mother, Lieutenant Geary later described in a somewhat graphic manner the circumstances of the wounding of three of his men:

> One had a piece of his head knocked off, all the flesh between his shoulder and neck taken away, and his right hand almost knocked off, he was still living when we left Gettysburg. He was a terrible sight when first struck, and when I had him carried to the rear, it almost turned my stomach, which is something that, as yet, has never been done. The other two were not so severely wounded. I made one very narrow escape from a shell. One of the gunners, who saw the flash of one of the rebel guns, hallowed to me to "look out, one's coming," and I just had time to get behind a tree before the shell exploded within a foot of where I had been standing.

Artillery Key

Confederate

Batteries	
Raine, Dement, Carpenter, Brown	12 pieces firing on Culp's Hill and Cemetery Hill
Graham, Smith, Cunningham, Johnson, Hurt, Wallace, Maurin, Moore, Lewis, Grady, Brander, McGraw, Zimmerman, Johnson, Marye	41 pieces firing at Cemetery Hill • Rice's battery in Mcintosh's Bat. was kept in reserve • Only the 9 rifled pieces from Garnett's Bat. were used at this time

• Also, 12 pieces of Dance's Battalion (off map) positioned north of the Fairfield Road were able to fire on Cemetery Hill

Union

Batteries	
Stevens	6 pieces (Wainwright)
Norton, Taft	12 pieces (Osborn)
Reynolds (Breck), Rickets, Wiedrich (4 pieces), Stewart	19 pieces (Wainwright)
Dilger, Wilkeson (Bancroft), Eakin, Wheeler, Hill, Wiedrich (2 pieces), Hall	26 pieces (Osborn)
Geary & Reed	5 pieces

• Col. Charles S. Wainwright, Chief of Artillery, I Corps, commanded the guns east of the Baltimore Pike

• Maj. Thomas W. Osborn, Chief of Artillery, XI Corps, commanded the guns west of the Pike

Notes

• Ewell's Corps' attack on Culp's and Cemetery Hills was the last of the Rebel assaults to go in on July 2. At around 4:00 p.m. Ewell's artillery opened fire. He had about 65 pieces available, deployed in an arc from Benner's Hill in the east round to the north of Gettysburg to Seminary Ridge in the west. The Union defenders mustered virtually the same number, 68, but the advantage overall was with the Rebels, as their fire converged onto Cemetery Hill in particular – although the Confederate guns on Benner's Hill were very exposed.

• At about 6:00 p.m. Ruger's (Williams') Division was ordered south to bolster the Union left, under extreme pressure, and half an hour later Geary was told to follow (**A** and **A**). Some 7,750 men had been pulled out of the Culp's Hill defenses, leaving only Greene's Brigade of 1,400 to man the barricades south from Culp's Hill down to Lower Culp's Hill.

• At about 7:30 p.m. three of Johnson's Brigades advanced across Rock Creek and assaulted Culp's Hill (**B**). The steepness of the hill, the gathering gloom in the woods and above all the strongly made line of breastworks among the trees and rocks were too much for the Rebels to overcome, despite some of the most vicious and confused fighting of the entire battle. Only on the Confederate left, where Steuart's left was able to outflank the 137th New York, were the Rebels able to seize the barricades and force the 137th back behind the "traverse" (**B1**).

• Meanwhile, Greene's calls for assistance had been met by Howard, who sent four regiments (1,000 men), Wadsworth who sent three (600 men) and Hancock who sent two (380 men) (**C**). These, coupled with the strong defenses and confusion among the attackers in the darkness, were sufficient to drive the Rebels back. Only on the left were some of Steuart's men able to remain on Lower Culp's Hill.

• Only two of Early's four brigades attacked East Cemetery Hill, starting around 8:00 p.m. (**D**). It was a long advance, involving a huge right wheel by six of the eight attacking regiments. As they advanced on the defenders of the Brickyard Lane, they were subjected to devastating artillery fire, with Stevens' Battery catching them in enfilade. Despite this, the Union line along the lane was pierced in several places and some Rebels became involved in hand-to-hand fighting among the gun crews at the top of the slope. Nevertheless, they could not sustain their position unsupported and the division was forced to retire.

• On the Rebel right Rodes' Division never got in on the action due to miscalculation of the time required to form up his brigades. Rodes handed over command to Ramseur, but it was dark by the time the division had formed along Long Lane (**E**). By then the attacks by Early and Johnson were receding and, although Ramseur advanced toward the Emmitsburg Road, he decided against attacking.

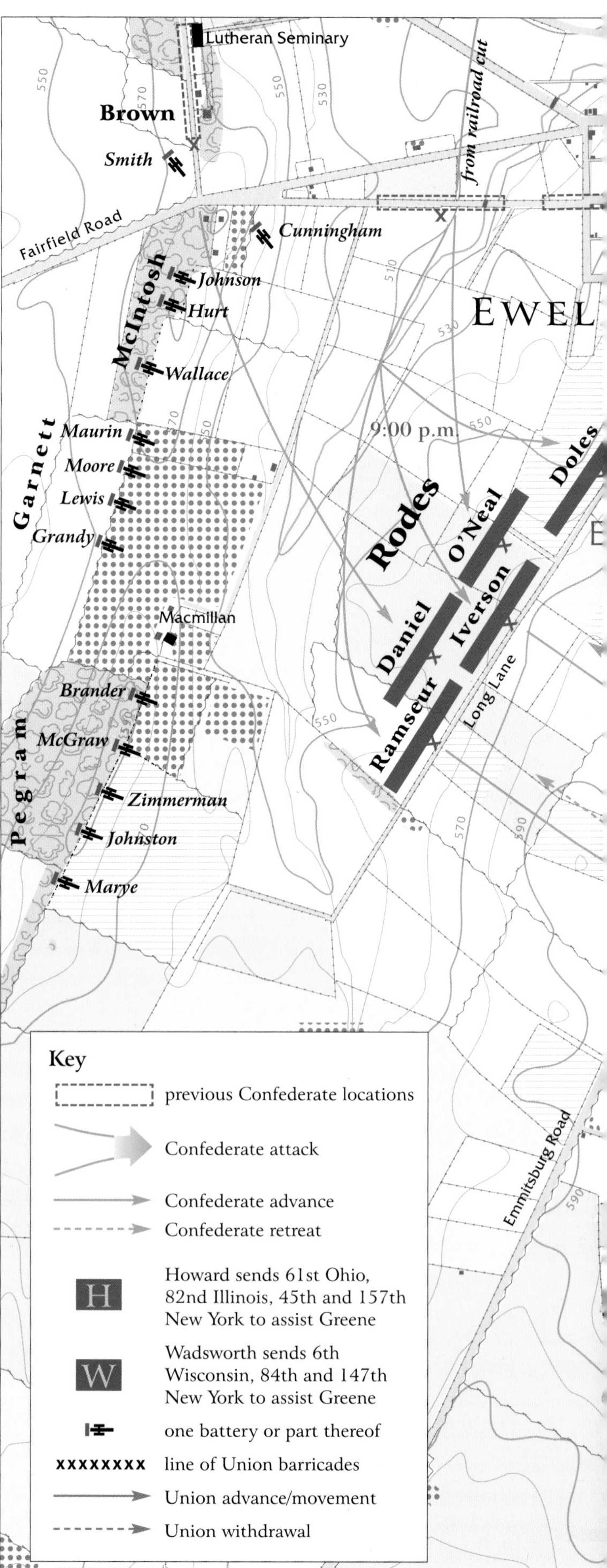

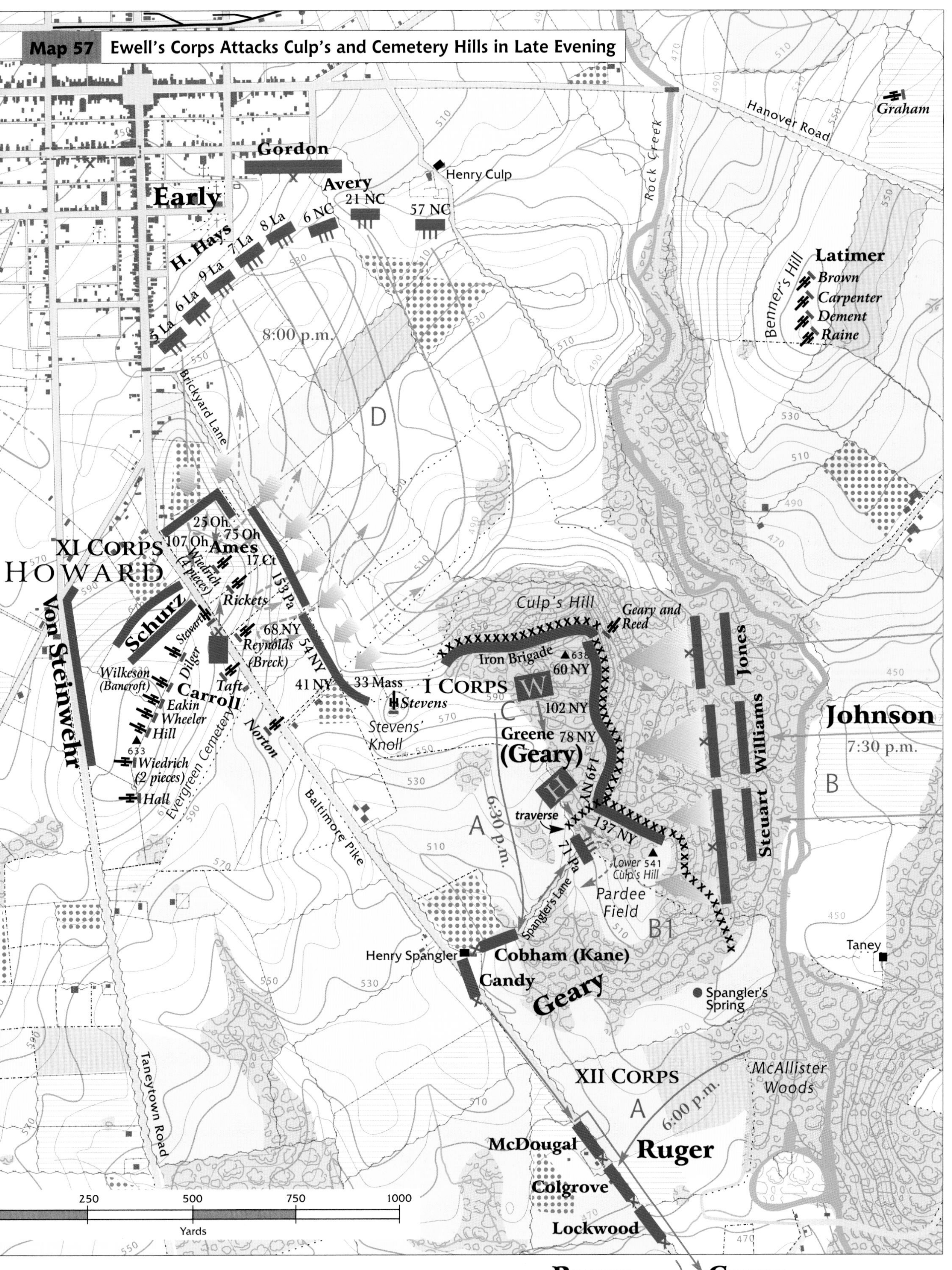
Map 57 Ewell's Corps Attacks Culp's and Cemetery Hills in Late Evening
Gordon
Early
Avery
21 NC
57 NC
Henry Culp
H. Hays
5 La
6 La
9 La
7 La
8 La
6 NC
8:00 p.m.
Brickyard Lane
D
Hanover Road
Rock Creek
Graham
Benner's Hill
Latimer
Brown
Carpenter
Dement
Raine
25 Oh
75 Oh
107 Oh
Ames
17 Ct
XI Corps
HOWARD
Wiedrich (4 pieces)
Rickets
153 Pa
Von Steinwehr
Schurz
Stewart
68 NY
Reynolds (Breck)
54 NY
Dilger
Wilkeson (Bancroft)
Carroll
Taft
41 NY
33 Mass
Eakin
Wheeler
Hill
Wiedrich (2 pieces)
Hall
Evergreen Cemetery
Norton
Stevens
Stevens' Knoll
Culp's Hill
Geary and Reed
Iron Brigade
60 NY
I Corps
W
102 NY
C
Greene (Geary)
78 NY
149 NY
H
traverse
137 NY
71 Pa
Jones
Williams
Steuart
Johnson
7:30 p.m.
B
A
6:30 p.m.
Baltimore Pike
Lower Culp's Hill
Pardee Field
B1
Spangler's Lane
Henry Spangler
Cobham (Kane)
Candy
Geary
Spangler's Spring
Taney
XII Corps
McAllister Woods
A
6:00 p.m.
McDougal
Ruger
Colgrove
Lockwood
Taneytown Road
250 500 750 1000
Yards
Ruger
Geary

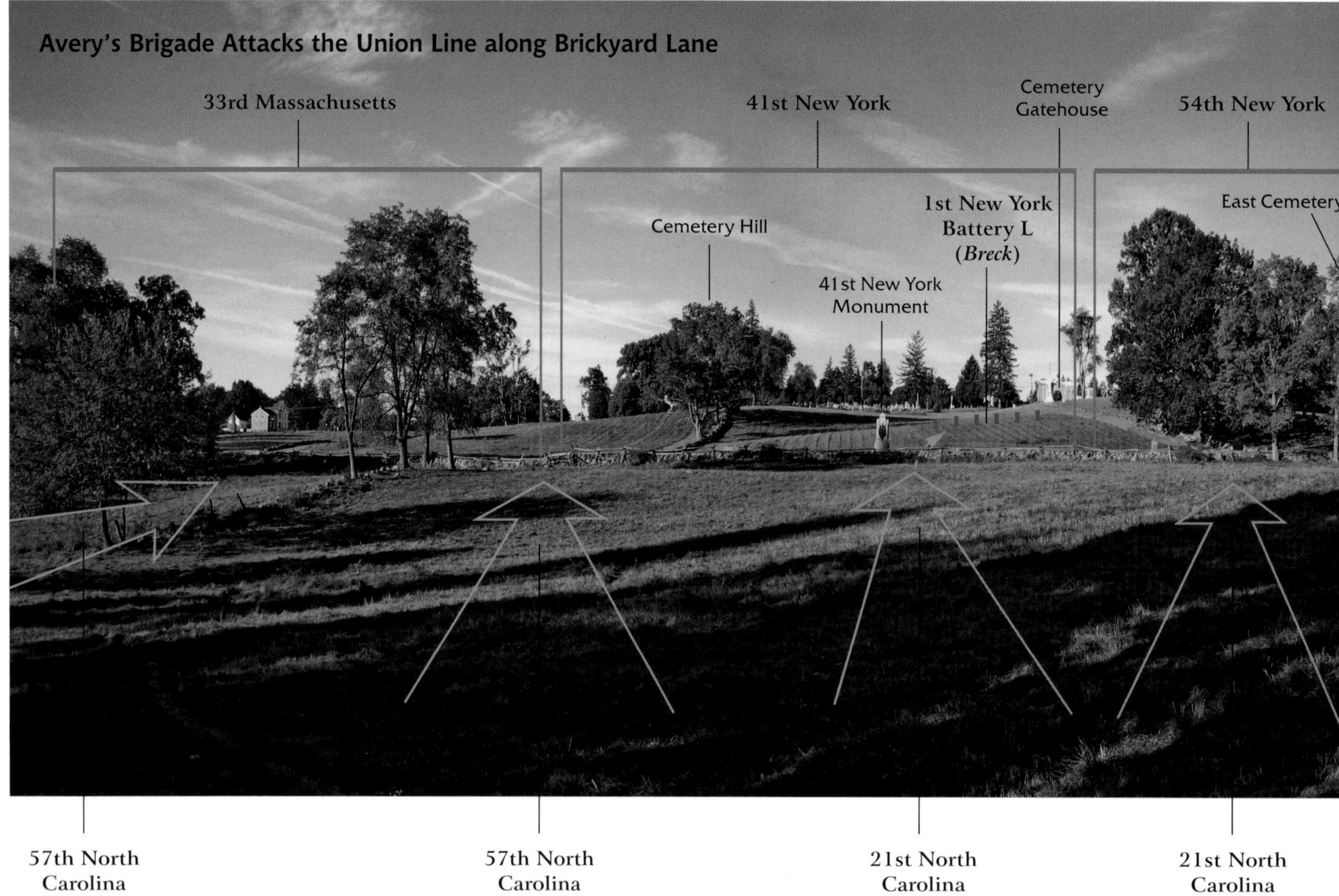

This photograph is taken from about 150 yards east of the 41st New York monument, looking west toward Cemetery and East Cemetery Hills. It shows the line of the Union defenses along Brickyard Lane at its southern end, which was attacked by Brig.-Gen. Avery's three regiments. The approximate locations of the Union regiments defending the stone wall are indicated, along with the main thrust lines of the Rebel attackers. The photograph was taken in bright sunlight, but the Confederate attack took place at about 8:00 p.m. in gathering darkness. The dotted red lines indicate the general direction of the Rebels, who broke through the defenses here and temporarily drove back the Yankees in some areas to attack Lt. Breck's Battery. All these penetrations were repelled. See Map 57.

forty wounded, Latimer requested he be allowed to withdraw. Except for four guns this was allowed, but while directing their fire the young major was mortally wounded. It was not until 7:30 p.m. that Johnson's infantry advanced.

The timing of Johnson's attack was, purely by accident, perfect. The only defenders left along the eastern face of Culp's Hill were Greene's 1,400 men, now spread very thinly along the barricades with the southern part down the slope toward Spangler's Spring unmanned. Advancing across Rock Creek were all three of Johnson's brigades, some 4,700 men. Because the frontage of the attack was so narrow (about 650–700 yards), once the creek was crossed the divisional formation was in two lines (one witness thought three). On the right was Jones's Brigade, then Williams, with Steuart on the left. Jones's Virginians had the steepest slope to climb through the trees, scrub and rocks, and with the sun going down in the west there was little light once into the woods west of Rock Creek. It rapidly developed into a night attack with all that that meant in terms of loss of control. A soldier of the 44th Virginia claimed "all was confusion and disorder." But what really stopped the assault in its tracks was the barricade. The sheets of flame from the leveled muskets firing from behind this protection came as a deadly shock to the attackers. The Rebels were unable to cope with the close-range volleys, the darkness, the smoke, the chaos and the loss of so many men. The attack was halted.

In the center Williams' attack was similarly checked, with the defending 78th and 102nd New York suffering negligible loss in comparison to the Louisianans. During this time the defenders had been reinforced in response to an urgent request by Greene. Howard sent four regiments (61st Ohio, 82nd Illinois and the 45th and 157th New York), about 1,000 men, which were later followed by three (6th Wisconsin and the 84th and 147th New York) from Wadsworth. Howard also dispatched the 71st and 106th Pennsylvania. Of these last two, the 71st was positioned on the right to support the 137th New York, but after receiving a smattering of shots the commanding officer, Colonel Richard Smith, turned his men around and retired from the fight. When his action was questioned he replied that he would not have his men murdered and insisted he had orders to return to his corps – seemingly a deliberate lie.

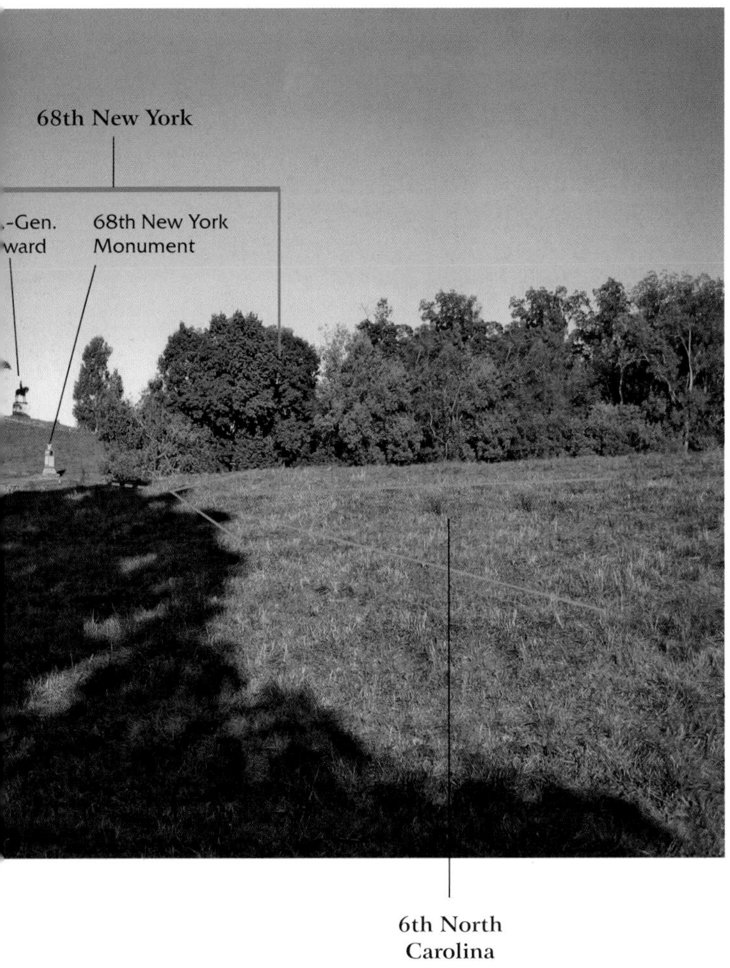

On the extreme Confederate left – the 10th Virginia under Colonel Edward T. H. Warren – the attackers' line overlapped the right of the defending 137th New York, enabling the Rebels to fire into the rear of the Yankees and force them back behind the traverse, then occupy the vacated positions. It was the high water mark of the Rebel success on Culp's Hill. Although most of Johnson's Division was forced back, Steuart was able to hold his ground at the barricades on Lower Culp's Hill throughout the night. This was despite the return of the five missing brigades from XII Corps, whose presence had achieved nothing in the south and who in the dark considered it impractical to attempt to retake their former positions until daylight.

Early's Division Attacks East Cemetery Hill, 8:00 p.m.

Cemetery Hill, with its adjoining East Cemetery Hill, formed the apex or top of the Union fishhook defense line at Gettysburg. As such it was probably the most crucial terrain of the entire position, dominating the ground in every direction. The problem from a defensive point of view was that in the current situation it formed a salient and could thus be attacked from two opposite directions simultaneously, and enemy artillery fire could be easily concentrated on it from the west through the north to the east. Its defense on July 2 was the responsibility of the considerably weakened XI Corps, which had been chased through the town the previous evening. Howard understood the problems and had based his defense on artillery, with about half his guns facing northeast and the other half northwest. On East Cemetery Hill the artillery was supported by Ames's (Barlow's) Division, mostly lining the fences along Brickyard Lane with the guns behind them up the slope, some protected by lunettes, able to fire over the infantry. It was this line that Early was about to attack. On the other side, on Cemetery Hill itself, the infantry defense was in the hands of Schurz's and Von Steinwehr's Divisions.

Early began his advance just before dark, at about 8:00 p.m. However, only about half of his command was committed to the attack. Smith's small brigade was still out on the York Pike and Gordon's Brigade was kept back behind the jump-off point as a reserve. This meant the actual attack, with Hays on the right and Avery on the left, consisted only of about 2,500 men at most. Although they did not face such a steep climb or barricades as on Culp's Hill, their objective was going to be a tough position to take. The defending infantry were well posted on a fairly gentle slope overlooking the open fields over which an attack must advance, and they were partially protected by the fences and stone walls along Brickyard Lane. But it was the artillery that posed the biggest potential threat to the attackers as they closed on the Union line. Not only were at least four batteries ranged on the slope above the infantry, able to bring fire to bear at some point, but Stevens' Battery was able to enfilade much of the Rebel front from its position on the knoll. However, the gathering gloom coupled with the smoke of firing did, at least partially, assist the Rebels – as brigade commander Hays explained, "owing to the darkness of the evening, now verging into night, and the deep obscurity afforded by the smoke of the firing, our exact locality could not be discovered by the enemy's gunners, and we thus escaped what in the full light of day could have been nothing else than horrific slaughter."

Adding to the Rebels' difficulties was the fact that six of Early's eight regiments would have to perform a right wheel of varying degrees of acuteness in the failing light, and possibly under artillery fire, in order to face their enemy for a frontal attack. Avery's three regiments on the left had over 1,000 yards to cover, while Hays's two right regiments were only 350 yards from their nearest enemy, so it would be hard to ensure the assault was simultaneous.

Light was failing fast as the assault went in. Stevens' guns "enfiladed their lines, at a distance of 800 yards [the entire frontage of the defended part of Brickyard Lane], with spherical case and shell, and later with solid shot and canister." Despite this, Colonel Andrew Harris, commanding the 2nd Brigade in Ames's Division, was impressed with what he saw: "But on, still on they came, moving steadily to the assault, soon the [Union] infantry opened fire, but they never faltered. They moved forward as steadily, amid this hail of shot shell and minie ball, as though they were on parade . . ." On the left of the Union line the charging Louisiana Tigers drove the 107th and 25th Ohio from their wall and back up the slope. The Rebels rushed on into the guns of Wiedrich's Battery, where a savage brawl developed with the gunners. One officer described how:

> the officers and men instantly began to fight to save their guns, using everything they could lay their hands upon. They could no longer fire their guns as the enemy was in the battery. They seized the rammers, handspikes, fence rails, threw shot . . . and the officers used their sabers and pistols with remarkable activity and energy.

The Ohio infantry rallied around the guns and, with the arrival of two more regiments sent at the double-quick by Schurz from

Cemetery Hill, the Confederates were finally driven back off the hill.

On the left of the Rebel advance Avery had elected to lead his three regiments mounted and from the front. This made him an obvious target, and before halfway across the fields he was struck in the neck and fell from his horse mortally wounded. Knowing death was near, he scribbled a note for his second-in-command, Colonel Archibald C. Godwin: "Tell my father I died with my face to the enemy." As the North Carolinians neared the Brickyard Lane on the Union right, Colonel Adin B. Underwood, commanding the 33rd Massachusetts, saw how:

> The gaps close bravely up and still they advance. Canister cannot check them . . . My regiment opened a severe musketry fire on them, which caused gaps in their line and made it stagger back a little. It soon rallied and bravely came within a few feet of our wall . . . their colors nearly within reach [when their line] was broken and finally driven back, leaving great heaps of dead and wounded just in front of us.

In the center things had not gone so well for the defenders. Here the 54th and 68th New York and several companies of the 41st New York were driven from their wall, although the 17th Connecticut and 153rd Pennsylvania held their positions. This breakthrough resulted in another wild fight amongst Captain R. Bruce Ricketts' guns. In his report afterward Ricketts was scathing in his comments on the performance of the infantry at the wall:

> As soon as the charge commenced, they, although they had a stone-wall in their front, commenced running in the greatest confusion to the rear, hardly a shot was fired, certainly not a volley, and so panic stricken were they that several ran into the canister fire of my guns and were knocked over.

In fairness, the historian of the 153rd Pennsylvania claimed that his regiment fought desperately at the wall with "clubs, knives, stones, fists – anything calculated to inflict death or pain was resorted to." Both no doubt very subjective opinions, with the truth probably lying somewhere between. The fight among Ricketts' Battery was so chaotic, with bayonets, rammers and clubbed muskets, that with the light now gone Lieutenant Joseph Jackson of the 8th Louisiana later claimed no one could tell "whether we were shooting our own men or not."

Meanwhile, the balance was about to be tipped by the intervention of General Hancock, who "directed General Gibbon of II Corps to send a brigade instantly to Genl. Howard's assistance." It came in the form of Colonel Samuel S. Carroll's three regiments (14th Indiana, 4th Ohio and 7th West Virginia – the 8th Ohio was posted on the Emmitsburg Road): some 700 men. Led by the 14th Indiana, the brigade crossed the Baltimore Pike; swept through Ricketts' gun line and chased the Rebels back down the hill. By this time it was completely dark and the Confederate attack had ebbed all along the line.

As the Rebels tried to regroup at the foot of East Cemetery Hill just east of the Brickyard Lane wall, Hays went back to summon support. He found Gordon's Brigade "occupying the precise position in the field occupied by me when I received the order to charge the enemy on Cemetery Hill, and not advancing." Early had decided not to reinforce failure.

Rodes' Division

There is no doubt Rodes failed to play any effective part in the Rebel attack on Cemetery Hill, but it had nothing to do with lack of resolution or disobedience to orders. It was more to do with failing to anticipate the time it would take him to assemble his somewhat scattered brigades. In his after-battle report, Rodes wrote that he was required "to co-operate with the attacking force as soon as any opportunity of doing so with effect was offered." It had been agreed that Rodes would attack in conjunction with Ewell's other two divisions. Johnson would go first against Culp's Hill, then Early followed by Rodes against East Cemetery Hill and Cemetery Hill respectively. Johnson advanced at around 7:30 p.m. when the sun was getting low. Early followed half an hour later, but it was not until 9:00 p.m. that Rodes had finally assembled his command along Long Lane and was ready to advance. Then for some unknown reason, possibly illness, he gave command of the actual attack to Ramseur. A considerable amount of movement, some in the approaching darkness, had been required to get three brigades from West Middle Street, one from the area of the railroad cut (O'Neal) and the other from near the Lutheran Seminary (Daniel). By the time all was ready, both Johnson and Early were being forced back.

Nevertheless, although it was dark by the time the division was positioned along Long Lane, Ramseur, after cautioning his men to leave haversacks and canteens behind to minimize noise, and ordering no firing at skirmishers, signaled the advance. At that moment Private Hufham in the 30th North Carolina recalled he felt his "heart rise in my throat, for I didn't like the idea of getting my life snatched out there in the dark." The other two brigades on the left moved off at the same time in order to keep in touch with Ramseur. When about 200 yards from the enemy, Ramseur got his men to lie down. According to one participant, the "rattle of musketry and the flash of artillery was terrible" as the struggle for East Cemetery Hill and Culp's Hill was not yet finished. Colonel Tyler Bennett of the 14th North Carolina stated: "so near were we that we could almost hear the movements of the enemy's men as they moved about with as little noise as possible." Ramseur went forward to reconnoiter. He did not like what he could make out in the darkness – several batteries and two lines of infantry behind walls. After speaking to Doles, Ramseur sent back for orders. The response from Rodes was to withdraw to Long Lane and await daylight.

Comments

- Ewell had been told to demonstrate (and develop an attack if circumstances were favorable) when he heard Longstreet's guns. Those guns fired around 4:00 p.m. but Ewell's demonstration was confined to artillery action for the next three and a half hours before Johnson's Division advanced. As the afternoon wore on with no infantry movement, Meade was able to assume that gunfire was all he had to worry about on his right and accordingly he moved troops from Culp's Hill to the left and center. The prolonged firing of guns did not constitute a believable demonstration. When Ewell finally advanced, it was intended as a full-scale attack. By pure good fortune, it was at the moment that the enemy facing Johnson were at their weakest. Despite the difficulties, some of Johnson's troops breached the enemy line and temporarily secured a foothold on East Cemetery Hill. This was the moment when support was desperately needed by both sides. It was immediately available to the Yankees but not to the Rebels. Had Gordon's Brigade been following in close support, had Rodes' Division been attacking Cemetery Hill, the outcome of the struggle could have been quite different. If Cemetery Hill had fallen, then the Battle of Gettysburg would probably have had a very different ending.

- A factor that negated Ewell's advantage on Culp's Hill, created when Meade removed some 7,750 men from the defenses, was that his attack was not as strong numerically as it might have been. The attack was piecemeal and uncoordinated. Johnson's Division was missing some 1,300 men under Brigadier-General James Walker (the Stonewall Brigade), which spent the day on the Brinkerhoff Ridge, 2 miles down the Hanover Road, confronting Union cavalry. Early was without Brigadier-General William Smith's 800 men, who were chasing rumors of enemy appearances on the York Pike. Then Early declined to use Gordon's 1,300 at the height of the attack because he could see no sign of Rodes attacking on the right. Rodes' absence deprived the attack of at least 5,000 men. For a variety of reasons, including losses the previous day, only some 7,000 men out of a corps that started the battle over 20,000 strong actually attacked the Union positions – it was far too few against such well-prepared defenses. In his report, Early put the blame squarely on Rodes: "No attack was made on the immediate right, as was expected, and not meeting with support from that quarter, these brigades [H. Hayes and Avery] could not hold the position they had attained" – no mention of his not using Gordon's Brigade!

- Lack of coordination by Ewell was a factor related to lack of numbers. Ewell had all day to plan and organize his demonstration-cum-attack. However, the end result was that only six brigades out of the eleven available got much beyond their jump-off points. This was partly due to Rodes' casual attitude to the time factor involved in moving his scattered brigades – some did not start until around 8:00 p.m.; but with all afternoon to ensure his divisions were being positioned, Ewell, as the corps commander, was surely primarily responsible.

- Yet again the folly of not mounting simultaneous attacks was demonstrated as another echeloned advance by troops operating on exterior lines failed against a defense based on interior ones. Unknown to Ewell, Meade had removed an entire corps except for one brigade from Culp's Hill shortly before Johnson attacked. Had Johnson, Early and Rodes advanced together, pressing the Union defenses on all sides at the same time, the chances of a Rebel success on this key position would surely have been doubled at least.

- The wisdom of timing the attack to start at sunset (sunset was officially 7:33 p.m. on July 2) is debatable. It meant that much of the fighting would be during darkness, which inevitably brings a host of problems, particularly for the attacker. Coordinating movement, direction finding, lack of visibility, together with the confusion and chaos once firing starts, add immensely to the difficulties of command and control for commanders and staff officers trying to locate, maneuver and lead units. For the defenders the problems are less acute and numerous, largely because they do not have to move about so much. They know their position; they know where their comrades and units are on either side. All they have to do on most occasions is stay put and keep firing. So it was for the Union regiments on the front line on Culp's and Cemetery Hills.

- The value of barricades by the defense was literally underlined in red. The defenders on Culp's Hill had twenty-four hours in which to prepare their defenses. On the insistence of "Old Pap" Greene, they were well constructed and extensive, covering the whole length of the Union line on the hill. They were also well sited and included a traverse so that the line could be shortened and the right flank protected should the need arise – which it did. These barricades were decisive in enabling a comparatively small force to see off superior numbers of attackers.

- Meade's competence as an army commander in a crisis became clear on July 2. He started in the early hours of the morning with his moonlight reconnaissance of the entire position when he evaluated the ground and allocated positions for each corps to the extent of having a map drawn and distributed to his corps commanders. He had expected an attack early on July 2, but when it did not materialize he made maximum use of the time donated by his opponent. By mid-morning all except VI Corps were in the field. It must be acknowledged that Meade was well served (with one notable exception) by his senior commanders and staff, and his confidence in delegating responsibilities on the battlefield was seldom misplaced. The exception was, of course, Sickles' III Corps. Its advance in disobedience to orders just as the battle was beginning in earnest brought about a major crisis for Meade. He handled it with coolness and skill. For over three hours he maneuvered his troops, sending formations from V, II, VI and XII Corps rushing around plugging gaps and supporting threatened points. In this he was ably supported

The Fight at Brinkerhoff Ridge

Brinkerhoff Ridge crossed the Hanover Road about 4 miles east of Gettysburg town square. It was there during the afternoon of July 2 that Confederates skirmished with Union infantry units until the arrival of the Union 2nd Cavalry Division (minus its 2nd Brigade at Westminster) under Brigadier-General David McM. Gregg. These Union forces were threatening the extreme left of the Confederates in Gettysburg, the security of which was supposed to be the responsibility of Brigadier-General Albert Jenkins' Brigade. However, Jenkins had been badly wounded near Blocher's Knoll by a chance long-range artillery shot and, due to poor staff work, his subordinates seemed unaware of the brigade's proper role. This led to Johnson having to deploy his Stonewall Brigade under Brigadier-General James D. Walker with over 1,300 men to block the threat. This meant that Johnson's divisional attack on Culp's Hill was substantially weaker than it should have been. Had this brigade been available to support his attack, it is conceivable that Culp's Hill might have fallen – another speculative "what if" of the battle.

by the initiative and leadership of a number of subordinates, but the overall credit for saving the fishhook must belong to Meade himself, backed by the stubborn fighting qualities of his Yankee soldiers.

- Finally, a tiny touch of hindsight. Lee had surely been right in thinking Ewell's Corps could have been put to better use if it had been deployed on Seminary Ridge.

MEADE'S "COUNCIL OF WAR"

Meade held two conferences with his corps commanders, the first at 3:00 p.m. just prior to discovering the full extent of Sickles' blunder, and the second at around 11:00 p.m. that night. In connection with the latter it is worth repeating part of his 8:00 p.m. message to Halleck in Washington: "I shall remain in my present position tomorrow, but I am not prepared to say, until better advised of the condition of the army, whether my operations will be of an offensive or defensive character." As a first step in the decision-making progress, he summoned Colonel Sharpe of the Bureau of Military Information to his headquarters.

When Sharpe arrived at the Leister house Generals Hancock and Slocum were present as well as Meade. Meade had already received a report from Babcock, who was responsible for prisoner interrogations. It read:

> Prisoners have been taken today and last evening from every brigade in Lee's army excepting the four brigades of Pickett's Division [Pickett actually brought three, as he had been compelled to leave two in North Carolina; see page 291]. Every division has been represented except Pickett's from which we have not had a prisoner. They are from nearly one hundred different regiments.

Sharpe went on to explain "Pickett's division has come up and is now in bivouac, and will be ready to go into action fresh tomorrow." This was indeed good news. VI Corps, Meade's largest with 14,000 men, had recently arrived under Major-General John "Uncle John" Sedgwick, more than compensating for Lee's additional division. This news, and the knowledge that his army had defeated every Rebel assault that day, must have given Meade considerable confidence for the morrow. Nevertheless, he needed to know the condition of his corps and the opinions of their commanders, so late that night he called his second conference, a meeting that historians have somewhat erroneously called a "Council of War."

The eleven men present in addition to Meade were Newton, acting commander of I Corps; Hancock, left-wing commander; Gibbon, II Corps; Birney, III Corps (Sickles having been wounded); Sykes, V Corps; Sedgwick, VI Corps; Howard, XI Corps; Williams, XII Corps; Slocum in his supposed role as right-wing commander; Chief of Staff Butterfield and Chief Engineer Warren – who apparently slept throughout the proceedings. According to Gibbon, the meeting was informal, the room small, lit by a single candle and thick with cigar smoke. The corps commanders reported on the situation within their commands. Newton was worried that Lee would not attack again frontally against a position proved to be strong, but might instead move around the army's left. Hancock voiced doubts about the practicality of withdrawing. There was also some discussion about the shortage of rations, with most corps down to a day's supply or less.

At the end of the discussions Butterfield posed three questions:

- Under existing circumstances, is it advisable for this army to remain in its present position or to retire to another nearer its base of supplies?
- It being determined to remain in present position, should the army attack or await the attack of the enemy?
- If we wait attack, how long?

The nine senior commanders gave their response in reverse order of seniority, starting with Gibbon. Gibbon and Newton voted to "Correct position of the army but would not retreat," with which Hancock agreed; Birney, Howard, Sedgwick, Sykes and Williams voted "Stay"; Slocum said, "Stay and fight it out." It was unanimous to remain and fight. On the second question all favored awaiting attack. As to how long to wait, opinion was varied due to the supply situation from one day to "until Lee moved." The meeting had no doubts as to the wisdom of staying to continue to fight a defensive battle in the present position. According to Gibbon's account, Meade concluded the meeting with the phrase, "Such then is the decision." As the meeting broke up Meade said to Gibbon, whose II Corps was in the center of the line on Cemetery Ridge, "If Lee attacks tomorrow, it will be in your front." When Gibbon asked why, he replied, "Because he has made attacks on both our flanks and failed and if he concludes to try it again, it will be on our center." An exact forecast of events.

CONTROVERSIES

Captain Johnston's Reconnaissance

It is difficult to overemphasize the importance of Captain Johnston's reconnaissance on Lee's plan for operations on July 2. When Johnston confirmed to Lee between 8:00 and 8:30 that morning that he had seen no enemy on their left flank in the area of Round Top, it was a crucial piece of information that Lee needed in order to confirm in his own mind that Meade's left was open to attack. The controversy rests in how Johnston could have given such a categorical statement when we know, with hindsight, there was considerable troop movement, overnight bivouac areas and forward picket lines in that area early that morning? Johnston has been accused of deliberately lying to disguise the fact that he got lost; of not going where he was supposed to go; or of being generally negligent and unobservant – or of any combination of these things. Equally puzzling – and there has never been an answer to this – was why Major John J. Clarke, an engineer officer on Longstreet's staff who accompanied Johnston, never spoke or wrote of the matter during the years of debate after the battle?

Critics of Johnston maintain that if he was on Little Round Top some time between 5:00 and 6:00 a.m., the chance of his not seeing or hearing considerable enemy activity in the vicinity was next to impossible, inexplicable. The present writer believes that Johnston gave an accurate report but that he saw no evidence of large bodies of enemy nearby because he was on Round Top, not Little Round Top, and anyway the time that he was on the hill coincided with the time during which Union forces had either already moved from, or not yet arrived into, the vicinity. When Johnston reported to Lee he gave a true account of the situation as he had seen it. If blame is to be attributed, then it lies more with the execution of a plan that took so long to implement that the battlefield and the tactical intelligence on which the plan was based was at least eight hours old when the attacking troops arrived at their jump-off points. The tactical situation at 4:00 p.m. was never likely to be the same as at 5:00 a.m. or 6:00 a.m. This famous, or infamous, reconnaissance bears a closer look under four headings: the naming of Little and Big Round Tops; Johnston and his instructions; his route and timings; and Union troops locations.

The naming of "Little" and "Big" Round Tops

At the time of the battle these hills had no such names. As far as the Confederates were concerned, they were unnamed and both hills were joined together, the larger dominating the smaller, and from many places on the battlefield it was only the larger that could be seen clearly. Thus the term "Round Top" was commonly used after the battle to identify both hills. Careful research by Bill Hyde for his article in *The Gettysburg Magazine*, issue 29, published in late 2003, clearly shows that of the four letters Johnston wrote concerning his reconnaissance, the first three refer to his getting to "Round Top." In Lee's final report on the battle he refers to both hills as a single elevation called "Round Top" and the accompanying map indicates a single hill with no particular name. Bill Hyde also points out that Union after-action reports show that out of eighty-one references identifying both hills, seventy-six use the term "Round Top." There is, apparently, evidence that even these terms were possibly inserted in the *Official Records* at later dates. There can surely be little doubt that when Lee, surprised that his engineer had got so far, asked Johnston, "Did you get there?" he was pointing or referring on his map to the unnamed feature later to be known as Round Top. Johnston assured him he did.

Johnston and his instructions

Johnston was trusted by Lee to carry out this important reconnaissance as he was an experienced engineer who had, before joining Lee's staff, been similarly employed at Jeb Stuart's headquarters. A key role of engineer officers in both armies was reconnaissance and Johnston himself described his job as "Reconnoitering Officer." Reports by Lee, Longstreet, Heth and Anderson had all, in the past, cited Johnston for his ability to locate enemy positions. At Chancellorsville Johnston had climbed a tree and watched enemy activity near Chancellor House through his telescope. There can be no doubt he knew his duties well.

Johnston stated his orders three times in various letters written during the years following the battle. To Fitzhugh Lee he wrote that they were to "make a reconnaissance of the enemy's left;" to Lafayette McLaws "to reconnoiter along the enemy's left;" and to Bishop George Petterkin "to make [a] reconnaissance as far as practical on our right." An officer of his ability and experience would not need to be told more, although it should be noted he was not specifically told where to go or actually to locate the enemy's left.

Johnston's route and timings

It is known that Captain Johnston did not have a watch, but it is generally accepted that he started around 4:00 a.m. or shortly afterward. On July 2, 1863, twilight was at 4:04 a.m. and sunrise 4:36 a.m. – so he started out just as it was getting light. The distance he would cover (along his probable route) onto either Little or Big Round Top would be about 4.5 miles each way – 9 miles in total. His party of himself, Clarke and two or three escorts were all mounted, so along parts of the route they would be able to trot, whereas at other points a walk or even a halt would be necessary – as it was on his return when he had to avoid Union cavalrymen on the Emmitsburg Road. An average speed of 3 miles in the hour would put Johnston on Round Top (Big or Little) around 5:30–5.45 a.m. He would have spent up to half an hour on the hill exploring and observing, so probably started his return journey between 6:00 and 6:15 a.m., arriving back with Lee about 8:00 a.m. or a little later, as he spent some time locating him. By 8:30 a.m. we can be fairly sure he had reported to Lee, having been away three and a half to four hours – certainly not less.

The most detailed description of his route occurs in his letter to McLaws, dated June 27, 1892:

> My general route was about the same that General Longstreet took when he made his march. I crossed the creek on the same bridge that he did and turned to the left at once and got on the ridge where you subsequently formed your line, following along that ridge in the direction of round top [note the terminology, and that he was using this highest hill as a general direction marker] across the Emmetsburg [*sic*] road and got up on the slopes of round top, where I had a commanding view, then rode along the base of round top to beyond the ground that was occupied by General Hood, and where there was later on a cavalry fight. When I thought I had gone far enough I turned back, and when I again got sight of the Emmetsburg road I saw three or four troopers moving slowly and very cautiously in the direction of Gettysburg. I had to let them out of my sight before crossing the road, as to see and not be seen was required of a reconnoitering officer . . . They might have seen me, but I do not think they did. I recrossed the bridge and took the most direct route regardless of fences, to where I had left General Lee. There was the usual delay in finding headquarters.

Map 41 shows the likely route out and some possibilities of the first part of his return route. It is clear that he arrived on the Warfield Ridge opposite the Peach Orchard ("where you subsequently formed your line"). He then turned right and followed the ridge south, probably just inside the woods for much of the time, using, as he said, the obvious hill, Round Top, as his guide. Just south of the Snyder Farm he would have crossed the Emmitsburg Road and found the lane leading past Slyder's Farm that pointed directly at Round Top. Nothing seen so far of the enemy; all was quiet. He then climbed the steep slope of Round Top and spent a while confirming no enemy was on the hill or in its vicinity. He may have climbed a tree or found a gap that gave him his "commanding view," then returned round the base of Round Top and Black Cat Knob until, on approaching the Emmitsburg Road, he spotted the enemy cavalrymen – the first sign of Union troops he had encountered or seen. The map shows the likely area of road where they were seen and several possible crossing places for Johnston when they had gone. His route back after that is unimportant. We know he went as quickly as possible.

Enemy locations
Knowing where Union troops were located or what they were doing in the vicinity of both Round Tops between 5:30 a.m. and 6:15 a.m. holds the key to where Johnston was at that time and what he could, or could not, see. Geary's Division with two brigades (Cobham's Brigade had spent the night 2 miles south of Gettysburg beside the Baltimore Pike) had bivouacked just 200 yards north of the Millerstown (Wheatfield) Road and a similar distance northwest of the summit of Munshower Hill. They had initially sent two regiments (5th Ohio and 147th Pennsylvania) onto Little Round Top, but later both had come off the hill to go forward on picket duty. The troops were roused at dawn and, having recalled the pickets, were on the move at or before 5:00 a.m. to their new position on Culp's Hill. At the same time the Union signal station on Little Round Top departed to join Geary. If Johnston had been on Little Round Top at 5:30 a.m. he might conceivably have seen the tail end of Geary's Division on the Taneytown Road – but he did not.

The only other Union formations nearby were the two brigades of Birney's Division of III Corps. They were encamped about 200 yards north of where Geary had been and were ordered to take over his part of the line after he had vacated it. Like most units of the Army of the Potomac that morning, they were aroused at dawn – around 4:30 a.m. If Johnston had been on Little Round Top with his "commanding view" any time between 5:00 a.m. and 6:00 a.m. it is almost inconceivable that he could not have seen Birney's men, their coffee fires and general bustle of movement, as well as heard the noises associated with it. At most Johnston and his telescope would have been 750 yards away with an uninterrupted view. But he saw nothing because he was on Round Top, almost a mile from Birney's men – and anyway troops that far away were not of his concern: he was exploring ground on the far left of any Union line, and there was no enemy to be seen. From Round Top he could also see there were no Yankees on Little Round Top.

Another enemy formation that is sometimes mentioned as being close is II Corps, which had spent the night several miles to the south on the Taneytown Road. It was under orders to march on Gettysburg early that morning. However, the leading elements did not appear on the road southeast of Round Top until between 6:30 a.m. and 7:00 a.m., by which time Johnston had departed.

The final point remains a puzzle. Why did Johnston not encounter or see any of Buford's cavalry apart from three or four horsemen plodding slowly along the Emmitsburg Road on his return journey? Cavalry pickets were supposedly guarding Meade's left and had patrols out as far as the Fairfield Road. They must certainly have been spread very wide as Johnston was able, either by good fortune or because there were none near the route he chose, to avoid them with ease.

Conclusion
Johnston almost certainly went to Round Top, not Little Round Top; he saw nothing of the enemy because there was none around at the time he was on the hill, so his report to Lee was basically correct – but its validity was later outdated.

Longstreet – Attitude, Actions and Consequences on July 2
Lee had made up his mind to renew the attack on July 2 but he had not decided where and how to do so until around 8:30 a.m. after receiving Captain Johnston's report. Lee was uncertain exactly what proportion of Meade's army was facing him that morning and he wanted confirmation of the precise whereabouts of the Union left flank. Stuart's continued absence prevented a proper reconnaissance of the enemy's position and the movement of his formations toward Gettysburg. Nevertheless, Lee clearly understood the need to mount his assault as soon as possible. The longer he waited, the more Meade was likely to receive reinforcements and the more time he would have to strengthen his position. From 8:30 to 9:30 a.m. Longstreet's two divisions (McLaws and Hood), with the exception of Law's Brigade (Hood's Division), were assembling in the fields on either side of the Chambersburg Pike in the Herr's Ridge area, mostly suffering various degrees of exhaustion. Longstreet, then McLaws followed by Hood, had arrived at his headquarters near the Lutheran Seminary in advance of their troops. At around 8:30 a.m. Lee gave out his orders for Longstreet's Corps to attack the Union left, which he thought rested on the Emmitsburg Road just north of the Peach Orchard, and to make the approach without being seen.

Longstreet, as we know, was strongly opposed to an attack and had tried to convince Lee that a strategic move around the Union left and then adopting a defensive position on suitable ground to await attack was the best way of defeating Meade. He was convinced, wrongly, in his own mind that Lee had agreed this strategy at the outset of the campaign. Porter Alexander, his artillery chief at the battle, normally an apologist for Longstreet, later commented, "The long & the short of the matter seems to me as follows. Longstreet did not wish to take the offensive. His objection to it was not based at all upon the peculiar strength of the enemy's position for that was not yet recognized, but solely on general principles." Longstreet was a confirmed sulker of long standing if denied his way and was also known for his slowness, one officer referring to him in his diary as "Old Snail," as if that was a common nickname.

There was no early Confederate offensive on July 2. The attack was launched on the Rebel right by Hood's Division at around 4:30 p.m., eight hours after Lee had first issued the necessary orders. The controversy that arose was over the extent to which Longstreet's behavior that day contributed to the delay. The case against him rests upon the following:

- He did not want to attack; he had no faith in the plan.
- He therefore adopted a surly and uncooperative attitude that resulted in his making the minimum effort in implementing the plan.
- Knowing the need for speed, he made no attempt to hasten the departure of his corps and insisted on waiting for the arrival of Law's Brigade before making preparations for the approach march, although this was not necessary as Law would have joined the corps on its start line in time for the attack. Thus Longstreet was allegedly culpable for the lateness of the attack, a factor in its eventual repulse.
- He absolved himself of responsibility for the route taken and general direction of the march by accompanying Hood's Division and regarding Captain Johnston (riding with

McLaws' Division, which was leading the march) as responsible for the movement of the corps.

- Despite the dramatically changed situation when the corps arrived opposite the Peach Orchard, and despite several pleas by Hood to change the plan, he insisted on implementing Lee's plan of attack without any modification and thus needlessly wasted lives.

Comments

There is little doubt Longstreet was angry that his proposals had been rejected and that an attack he disapproved of was to be made by his corps. His disgruntled attitude was made worse by Lee's issuing orders directly to his subordinate, McLaws, while Longstreet was pacing around nearby. Longstreet tried to change Lee's orders to McLaws by pointing to a jump-off point for the attack perpendicular to the one Lee had just indicated on the map. This drew the emphatic response from Lee, "No, General, I wish it placed just the opposite." When McLaws asked to go on a reconnaissance with Captain Johnston (not understanding that Johnston had just finished one), Longstreet snapped, "No, sir, I do not wish you to leave your division."

Certainly Longstreet was in a foul mood from early that morning as he had been put down in front of his divisional commander and Lee was determined he, Longstreet, should implement a plan in which he had no confidence.

Apart from Law's Brigade, seven of Longstreet's eight brigades were available around Herr's Ridge by 9:30–10:00 a.m. If the march had started at 10:00 a.m., and assuming it took the same time as it actually did (four hours), then Longstreet could have attacked around 2:00–2:30 p.m., just as Sickles was in the middle of moving his corps forward – although even then Meade would have had his entire army on the field except for VI Corps. However, Longstreet obviously never contemplated such an early start to the march. Strangely, Lee, knowing the urgency, seemingly gave no instructions for the march to begin at around 10:00 a.m. before riding over to the left to consult with Ewell.

On Lee's return at around 11:00 a.m. he gave Longstreet instructions to move, but raised no objections and did not overrule Longstreet when he insisted he must wait for Law's Brigade to catch up before starting to make preparations. As Longstreet later wrote, "I delayed until General Law's brigade joined its division." Even then he was not ready, having "after his arrival to make our preparations." All this resulted in another hour lost.

However, that the march did not begin until at least noon was not all Longstreet's fault. His sluggish movement could have been overruled by Lee if he was determined to mount the attack as early as possible. He could, indeed should, have told Longstreet to start moving before he left to see Ewell. There was a seeming lack of urgency and not much in the way of "battle procedure" – that is, concurrent activity.

It is relevant to note that nothing had been done during the night in the way of preparations for the next day's maneuvers, as Lee was still mulling over what to do and had allowed himself to be persuaded, twice, by Ewell that his corps should remain where it was out on the far left flank – arguably one of his most serious errors at Gettysburg.

Longstreet's attitude – developed during the long years of his inaccurate ramblings and vilification of his former subordinates after the war – that Lee, in making the obvious decision that Johnston should accompany his corps on the approach march, had somehow given the captain control over his corps during the move, was ludicrous. Writing in 1878, Longstreet claimed:

> A delay of several hours occurred in the march of the troops. The cause of this delay was that we had been ordered by General Lee to proceed cautiously upon the forward movement, so as to avoid being seen by the enemy. General Lee ordered Colonel [he was subsequently promoted] Johnston, of his engineer corps, to lead and conduct the head of the column. My troops, therefore, moved forward under guidance of a special officer of General Lee, and with instructions to follow his directions.

Seemingly Longstreet, out of pique, decided to ride at least 1.5 miles behind the leading troops with Hood, content to hand his responsibility for the direction of the corps to Johnston. Johnston emphatically contradicted this misrepresentation. In fact, he had no idea at the time that the corps commander regarded him as in charge of the march. Johnston wrote:

> The corps was not put under my charges from either Gen'l Lee or Gen'l Longstreet as to where the latter was to go. I was ordered by Gen'l Lee to "ride with Gen'l Longstreet." I had no

Longstreet's Letter to His Uncle, July 24, 1863

In the late afternoon of July 2, after he had joined Lee, Longstreet claimed he was surprised that Lee was considering attacking Meade the next day and suggested moving round his left flank to seek a defensive battle as had been the agreed plan of campaign. According to Longstreet, Lee replied, "If the enemy is here tomorrow we must attack him." Longstreet responded, "If he is there, it will be because he is anxious that we should attack him – a good reason in my judgment for not doing so."

Within three weeks of the battle Longstreet, while encamped at Culpeper Court House, could not refrain from criticizing Lee's handling of the army and making it plain that his proposals quoted above had been right from the start.

> My dear Uncle: . . . As to our late battle, I cannot say much. I have no right to say anything, in fact, but will venture a little to you alone. If it goes to aunt and cousins, it must be under promise that it will go no further. The battle was not made as I would have made it. My idea was to throw ourselves between the enemy and Washington, select a strong position and force the enemy to attack us. So far as is given to man the ability to judge, we may say with confidence that we should have destroyed the Federal army, marched into Washington, and dictated dour terms, or, at least, held Washington and marched over as much of Pennsylvania as we cared to, had we drawn the enemy into attack upon our carefully chosen position in his rear. General Lee chose the plans adopted; and he is the person appointed to choose and order. I consider it a part of my duty to express my views to the commanding-general. If he approves and adopts them, it is well; if not, it is my duty to adopt his views, and to execute his orders as faithfully as if they were my own.

Whether the last sentence reflects his attitude on July 2 is open to question.

> idea where he was going, except what I did infer from the movement having been ordered soon after I made my report. I suppose that Gen'l Lee's object in sending me with Gen'l Longstreet was that I should give him the benefit of information that I had obtained by reconnaissance I had made of the country and position of the enemy.

This latter Johnston was unable to do, as he was at the head of the column and Longstreet 1.5 miles behind, although whether this caused appreciable delay is debatable.

As noted above, Colonel Alexander had been sent ahead about an hour earlier with his artillery battalion and had found a route to the Willoughby Run that avoided the Black Horse Tavern ridge, which was visible to the Union signalers on Little Round Top. The main column consisted of some 14,500 men with thirty-five guns and their associated limbers and wagons. Each division would take up at least 1.5 miles of road marching four abreast. This meant that when a halt was called near the Black Horse Tavern the leading troops had covered just 2.5 miles (see Map 45), so the tail of the column had probably not yet started – a point overlooked in most accounts.

There was considerable delay when the column reached the Black Horse Tavern, as a decision had to be taken on a route that was concealed from the enemy signal station. Longstreet came forward and, for some unknown reason, the route taken by Alexander and his guns, which meant turning off across the fields on the right, was not taken despite the crushed crops being obvious and Alexander having pointed out the way to some officers shortly before (see page 404). The result was an about-turn, much doubling up, bunching, confusion and the march being about 2 miles more (at least an hour's marching) than it need have been, although it is not entirely clear that the blame for this lies solely with Longstreet.

An interesting point, seldom mentioned, is where was Major Clarke, Longstreet's staff officer who had accompanied Johnston on his earlier reconnaissance? Presumably he was riding with Longstreet. That being so, he would have been able to advise his commander on the best route, but there is no evidence he did so, or that Longstreet consulted him.

Kershaw's Brigade, the leading troops of the column, arrived on Warfield Ridge opposite the Peach Orchard at about 4:00 p.m. to discover the Yankees in strength in the orchard and along the Emmitsburg Road. This was not what was expected and negated Lee's plan to form south of the Peach Orchard and attack up the Emmitsburg Road. McLaws was to lead this attack with Hood following in support. This is probably the principle reason Longstreet sent Hood marching behind and to the right of McLaws to form on the extreme right of the line. As he did so, Hood sent his scouts forward. According to Hood, "They soon reported to me that it [the enemy's left flank] rested upon Round Top Mountain; that the country was open, and that I could march through an open woodland pasture around Round Top and assault the enemy in flank and rear . . ." This report led to his appeals to Longstreet to change Lee's plan, all of which his corps commander rejected. These refusals were probably due to a combination of sulky stubbornness and a realization that time was now pressing and an attack must be launched immediately, and a further move to the right would stretch his line to breaking point and beyond. In the two last reasons he was probably correct.

The Peach Orchard provided sparse cover for attacking troops.

Where was Lee during all these four hours of marching, countermarching and delays? It was his plan, he knew the need for haste, but when the situation on the flank was found to be entirely different to that on which his plan was based, Lee was nowhere around to make decisions. The reason probably lies in the fact that of the three corps commanders Longstreet was the only experienced one and Lee considered he should be allowed to get on with executing the plan delegated to him. In the event this was a mistake, and his presence close to Hill failed to galvanize that officer into doing anything worthwhile when problems arose with the execution of his corps' role in the plan. July 2 underlined that Lee's method of mission command was not working with the Army of Northern Virginia at Gettysburg.

A final point. If Lee had really been determined to mount an early attack that morning, then the only rested, unused division available was Anderson's.

Conclusion

A strong case can be made that the Confederates could – indeed should – have made an earlier attack on July 2. Alexander later stated, "There seems no doubt that had Longstreet's attack . . . been made materially sooner, we would have gained a decisive victory" – undoubtedly an exaggeration, but an earlier attack might have caught Sickles in the process of moving his corps forward. It is true that Longstreet was dragging his feet and could have energized his corps and need not have waited for Law's Brigade. However, as the commander-in-chief, the majority of the blame for the late start must surely rest with Lee. He could have ordered Longstreet to march as soon as possible after giving him (actually McLaws) his orders following Johnston's return. And he certainly allowed at least two hours (10:00 a.m.–noon) to be frittered away with nothing happening by going to see Ewell and not telling Longstreet to start moving. He then compounded the problem by allowing Longstreet to wait for Law.

SECTION ELEVEN

The Battle– Day Three

FRIDAY, JULY 3

PROBLEMS AND PLANS

Lee

Before midnight on July 2 Lee had resolved to continue his offensive the next day. Once again he had the theoretical choice of withdrawing, remaining on the defensive and inviting attack, attempting to outflank Meade round his left, or renewing the assault. There is no evidence that he seriously considered any of the first three. Lee still had huge faith in the ability, courage and morale of his infantry. He could take encouragement from the fact that he had defeated I and XI Corps on the first day, then smashed III Corps' salient on the second, while at the same time inflicting substantial losses on II and V Corps. That meant five out of seven Union infantry corps had been mauled – he must surely have assumed VI Corps had by now joined Meade. On his left Johnson had secured a foothold on Lower Culp's Hill. However, these successes had come at a heavy cost, although he now had a fresh division to hand – Pickett's – together with at least three brigades, Posey, Mahone and Thomas, that had been only lightly engaged (in total about 8,000 men). And he now, at long last, had Stuart's Division, hopefully in a position to influence events in Meade's rear. Then, the facts that some of Wright's Brigade had actually reached the crest of Cemetery Ridge and Barksdale's men had swept through to the Plum Run must have been at the forefront of Lee's mind when he determined that one more heave could throw Meade off his ridge. Above all, he had kept the initiative for two days; he was not about to surrender it on the third.

Not all accounts of the third day's action make it clear that Lee had two plans for July 3 – the so-called Pickett's charge being a second alternative. His first plan was really a continuation of the second day's fighting. In his report he made this abundantly clear:

> The result of this day's [July 2] operations induced the belief that, with proper concert of action, and with the increased support that the positions gained on the right [the Peach Orchard and up to the Plum Run] would enable to artillery to render the assaulting columns, we should ultimately succeed, and it was accordingly determined to continue the attack. The general plan was unchanged. Longstreet, re-enforced by Pickett's three brigades, which arrived near the battlefield during the afternoon of the 2d, was ordered to attack the next morning, and General Ewell was directed to assail the enemy's right at the same time. The latter, during the night, re-enforced General Johnson with two brigades from Rodes [Daniel and O'Neal] and one from Early's division [Smith].

Lee wanted an early-morning and simultaneous assault on both Union flanks, hoping to take advantage of the partial success he had had there on July 2. Stuart was to threaten Meade's rear and Longstreet was to use Pickett's fresh division to spearhead the attack on the right. All corps commanders were informed, but again Lee neglected to summon them all to a meeting to ensure that each understood his role or could voice problems; he was content to send verbal messages to Ewell.

Strangely, Longstreet gave no instructions (and Lee did not check) to Pickett to bring his troops forward and to the right of the line during the night. To mount a dawn or an early attack, the units attacking must move to their jump-off positions during darkness. To have Pickett on his start line by dawn or even by 8:00 a.m., Longstreet (or Lee) should have issued orders to this effect well before midnight. None was forthcoming. Reveille did not sound in Pickett's bivouac area along the Chambersburg Pike until after 3:00 a.m. Following a quick breakfast the division moved off – but not for long, as heavy firing erupted on Culp's Hill and the column was halted behind Seminary Ridge; it would remain there until around 10:00 a.m.

While Pickett's men were being wakened, others had already been preparing for the renewal of the assault. Colonel Porter Alexander, the officer Longstreet had put in charge of his corps artillery instead of Colonel James Walton, later recorded, "At three, I began to put the batteries in position again . . ." On the other flank was Ewell, who in his report stated, "I was ordered to renew my attack at daylight Friday morning [July 3] . . . as Johnson's position was the only one affording hopes of doing this to advantage, he was re-enforced." These reinforcements consisted of the brigades of Daniel, O'Neal and Smith to his left – they arrived to support the attack on Culp's Hill by 4:00 a.m. or shortly afterward. Hill received no specific orders for July 3, or if he did they were to hold his position.

Lee glossed politely over Longstreet's failure in his report by saying, "General Longstreet's dispositions were not completed as early as was expected, but before notice could be sent to General Ewell [to delay his attack], General Johnson had already become engaged, and it was too late to recall him." There would be no simultaneous early-morning attack on both enemy flanks – Geary had pre-empted Lee's plan by attacking first to try to recover the barricades on Culp's Hill lost to the Rebels the previous night. Lee's answer to this problem was his second plan for the day, what popular history now knows as Pickett's charge – although this is a misleading name as Pickett provided well under half the troops involved.

The fundamental difficulty in devising a new plan was that Lee's need to ensure a "proper concert of action" was now compromised by the enemy having attacked first, long before Longstreet was ready to resume serious offensive operations. It had been underlined to Lee the previous day that attacks from exterior lines must be coordinated so that they occurr at more or less the same time, and that promising assaults require swift follow-up support and secure flanks. Lee's decision was that Meade's center should be subjected to a two-phase assault, the first being a massive artillery bombardment of the point of attack, and the second an equally powerful infantry assault.

Lee's objective was now to break the Union line in the center in the vicinity of the Copse of Trees and threaten the enemy line from the rear with Stuart's cavalry, cutting off or harassing withdrawing Union forces east of Rock Creek. The main plan, under the direct command of Longstreet, was in three phases.

Phase 1. The positioning of massed Confederate batteries in front of the Rebel line, tasked with the silencing of the Union guns capable of firing on the infantry attackers, and at the same time causing considerable destruction in the area being assaulted.

Phase 2. A frontal infantry attack using the Copse of Trees as a landmark to guide the direction of the nine advancing infantry brigades. The leading wave would consist of Pickett's three brigades on the right and Pettigrew's four on the left (Brigadier-General James J. Pettigrew had been appointed to command Heth's Division after the latter was wounded on July 1). The immediate follow-up and direct support of the leading wave would be by two brigades under Major-General Isaac R. Trimble, who had assumed command of Pender's Division, Pender having been mortally wounded the previous day. Designated gun batteries would move forward behind the advancing infantry to provide close artillery support.

Phase 3. This was intended to merge into Phase 2 as it made progress, and involved the advance of Wilcox's and Lang's Brigades from Anderson's Division in direct support of Pickett, who would make the decision when they would go in, probably to guard the otherwise exposed right flank of the advance. The reserve was Anderson's other three brigades (Wright, Posey and Mahone) under his direct command. According to Hill's report, "Anderson had been directed to hold his division ready to take advantage of any success which might be gained by the assaulting column, or to support it if necessary." Anderson confirmed this in his report when he wrote, "I received orders to hold my division in readiness to move up in support [of the main attack], if it should become necessary." Thus Anderson had no specific objective: his action – direct reinforcement of the attacking line or protection of the flanks – would depend on the circumstances.

Comments

- This was a plan put together as an alternative to Lee's original intentions, which events had disrupted. As such, it could not take place early in the day – indeed a morning attack was virtually impossible. After the battle, and in the subsequent years of acrimonious correspondence, Longstreet gave five separate versions of his role in the planning and execution of Pickett's charge. In his first official report, written three weeks after the battle, he continued to harp on his preferred option of attacking around the enemy's left.

  > On the following morning arrangements were made for renewing the attack by my right, with a view to pass around the hill occupied by the enemy on his left, and to gain it by flank and reverse attack. This would have been a slow process, probably, but I think not very difficult. A few moments after my orders for the execution of this plan were given, the commanding general joined me, and ordered a column of attack to be formed of Pickett's, Heth's and part of Pender's divisions, the assault to be made directly at the enemy's main position, the Cemetery Hill.

  In the letter to his uncle dated July 24 (see box, page 453), Longstreet wrote the much-quoted conversation he supposedly had with Lee that morning.

  > "General, I have had my scouts out all night, and I find that you have an excellent opportunity to go around to the right of Meade's army and maneuver him into attacking us" [seemingly a strategic rather than a tactical move]. He replied, pointing with his fist at Cemetery Hill: "He is there, and I am going to strike him." I then felt that it was my duty to express my convictions; I said: "General, I have been a soldier all my life . . . and should know as well as any one what soldiers can do. It is my opinion that no 15,000 men ever arrayed for battle can take that position," pointing to Cemetery Hill.

- The attack was frontal and its phasing meant that there could be no element of surprise. Inevitably Meade would see it coming long before any Rebels began their advance.
- Considerable reliance was to be placed on the ability of the artillery to soften up the Union line in the area being assaulted, and particularly to knock out Union batteries that would otherwise inflict heavy losses on the attacking brigades.
- A key element, and one not often stressed, was the need for a reserve force able to be deployed quickly to reinforce success, exploit an opportunity or deal with an unexpected threat, particularly on the flanks.
- The plan was workable, but only with good cooperation and coordination by commanders and staff at every level down to brigade. Much hinged on the effectiveness of the preliminary artillery cannonade.

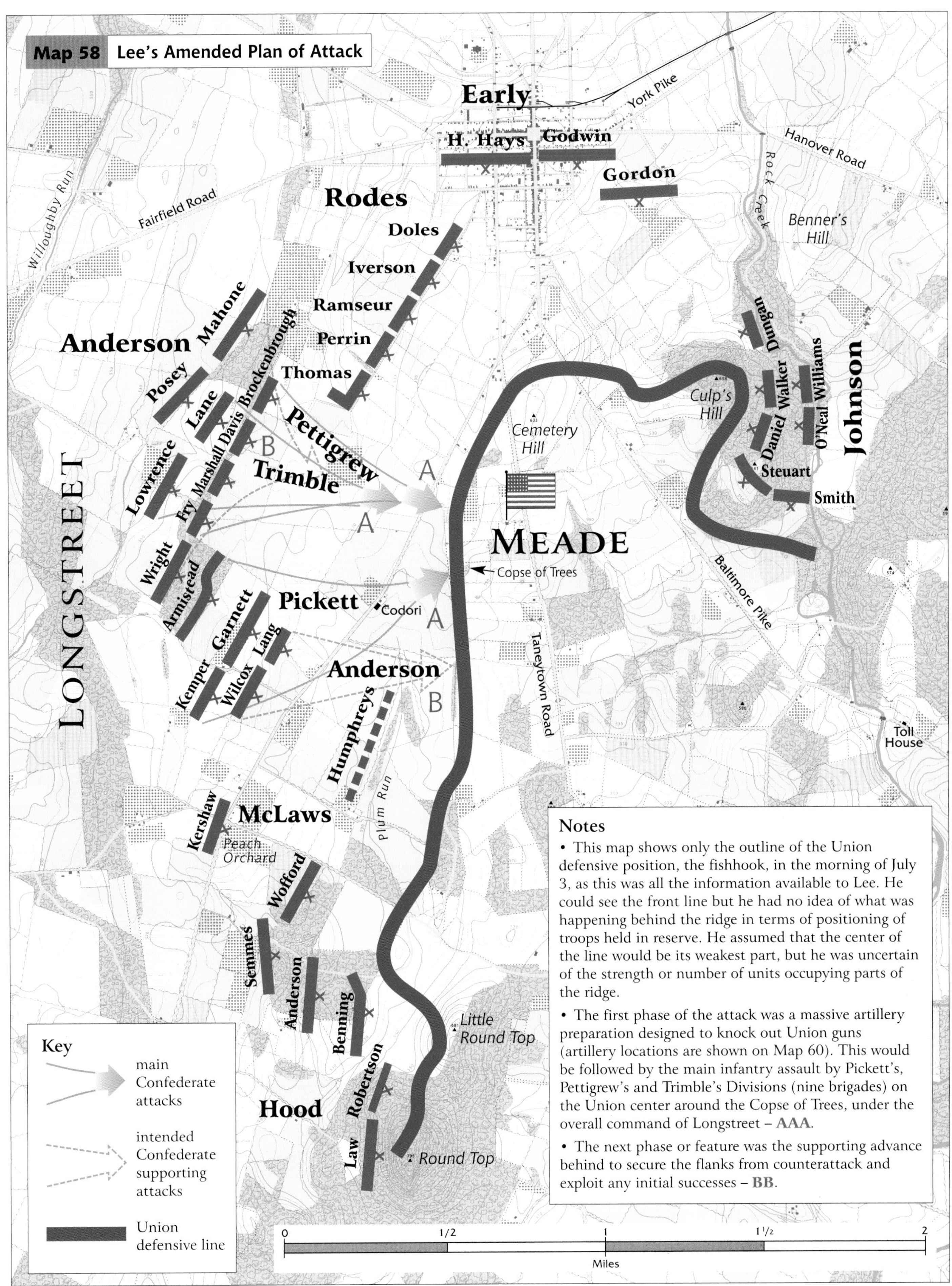

Notes

- This map shows only the outline of the Union defensive position, the fishhook, in the morning of July 3, as this was all the information available to Lee. He could see the front line but he had no idea of what was happening behind the ridge in terms of positioning of troops held in reserve. He assumed that the center of the line would be its weakest part, but he was uncertain of the strength or number of units occupying parts of the ridge.
- The first phase of the attack was a massive artillery preparation designed to knock out Union guns (artillery locations are shown on Map 60). This would be followed by the main infantry assault by Pickett's, Pettigrew's and Trimble's Divisions (nine brigades) on the Union center around the Copse of Trees, under the overall command of Longstreet – **AAA**.
- The next phase or feature was the supporting advance behind to secure the flanks from counterattack and exploit any initial successes – **BB**.

Meade

Meade had made the decision to stay and fight in his present strong position at the conference he held late on July 2 (see page 450), which broke up around midnight. His problems that morning were therefore straightforward tactical ones: ensuring that his senior commanders knew their role, his men were properly prepared, ammunition was replenished, his guns well sited, and above all that his reserves (infantry and artillery) were well placed to deal with developing threats. Despite his telling Gibbon that he thought the attack would come on his front, Meade still harbored worries about his left.

After a few hours' rest, Meade rose at around the time that fighting was renewed on Culp's Hill. He made that his first destination on his ride around the position, while at the same time sending Hunt to check the artillery deployment. A courier was sent to tell Pleasonton to bring the cavalry up on the right via the Hanover Road – a move that ended in the Union horsemen blocking Stuart's approach and the cavalry action at Rummel Farm (East Cavalry Field; see page 499). While watching the conflagration on Culp's Hill, Meade instructed Sedgwick's VI Corps to send a brigade to strengthen Williams' defense, which resulted in Brigadier-General Alexander Shaler's 1,800 men hurrying north. VI Corps, so far unbloodied and with some 14,000 men, was the strongest corps in the army and was Meade's main reserve force; coupled with the large Artillery Reserve, it made up the ace in his hand for that day. At 8:00 a.m. Butterfield issued Sedgwick the following order:

> The general directs me to say, that from information received from General Warren and General Howard of the movements of the enemy, it is their intention to make an attempt to pierce our center. He desires that, if any portion of your force is available and can be spared, they be massed in a central position near where they can support Howard or be thrown to right or left, as required. He is under the impression that you have three brigades in reserve, and thinks perhaps two of them might be disposed as above.

One consequence of this was that Brigadier-General Albion P. Howe's Division was split between opposite ends of the Union line as flank guards – one brigade (Brigadier-General Thomas H. Neill) on the right, just north of the Toll House on the Baltimore Pike east of Rock Creek; the other (Colonel Lewis A. Grant) at the Taneytown Road crossroads, just southeast of Round Top.

Meade, accompanied by Hancock, inspected the entire line, including Little Round Top, where he discussed the implications of the large-scale movement and positioning of Rebel guns. Orders were sent to every corps to keep men under arms and ready to move at a moment's notice. He sent a dispatch to General Couch at Harrisburg to advance when he heard the guns, as "by prompt cooperation we might destroy him." If Meade were forced to withdraw, Couch was to defend Harrisburg and the line of the Susquehanna. If Lee withdrew, General French at Frederick was told to "re-occupy Harper's Ferry and annoy and harass his retreat." If Lee were victorious, French was to hasten to the defense of Washington. During the morning Meade had several conversations with his artillery chief, Hunt, about the beset tactical use of the guns to defeat the impending attack; the details are discussed on page 469.

JULY 3 – OUTLINE OF EVENTS

The final day of the battle turned out to be extremely hot, both in terms of the temperature, which rose to the high 80s, and in terms of the intensity and variety of the fighting. It was a day that witnessed infantry assaulting and defending breastworks; the heaviest battlefield artillery bombardment of the Civil War; an infantry assault that was to enter the folklore of American history; and, finally, three cavalry actions, one involving the long-lost Stuart and his exhausted horsemen. For the sake of clarity, these events are described and discussed under separate headings:

The Struggle for Culp's Hill, 4:30–11:00 a.m.

Pickett's Charge:
the artillery duel, 1:00 p.m.–about 3:00 p.m.
the infantry assault, about 3:00–3:45 p.m.

Cavalry Actions
the clash at East Cavalry Field (Rummel Farm)
Farnsworth's charge against the Rebel right at Gettysburg (South Cavalry Field).
the cavalry fight at Fairfield.

THE STRUGGLE FOR CULP'S HILL (Map 59)

It was the Union offensive on Culp's Hill that pre-empted Lee's first plan for the day, forcing Johnson to respond long before Longstreet was ready to do anything useful on the Rebel right. The fighting for this hill started at first light and lasted until late morning. The Union objective was to recapture fortifications on Lower Culp's Hill that they had lost to Steuart the previous night. At 4:30 a.m. five batteries of Yankee guns opened up on the breastworks now occupied by Steuart's Brigade, the plan being to follow up with an attack by two brigades (Candy and Cobham – Kane was still incapacitated – who had returned from their wanderings down the Baltimore Pike) from Geary's Division. To be on the receiving end of this gunfire was a shattering experience. Major William C. Goldsborough, commanding the 1st Maryland, found "the fire was awful, the whole hillside seemed enveloped in a blaze." Canister and shell fragments "could be heard to strike the breastworks like hailstones upon the roof tops." To the fury of the 46th Pennsylvania, one or two rounds fell short and landed in amongst their ranks, causing several casualties. Another example of "friendly fire," this was halted when Colonel James Selfridge appeared in the gun line waving his pistol and threatening to shoot the battery commander if it happened again.

Although Geary's brigades were ready to attack as the guns ceased firing, the Rebels beat them to it. They had been heavily reinforced during the night by the brigades of Daniel, O'Neal and Smith, and the Yankee guns had goaded them into action. Johnson now had over 9,000 men but little or no supporting artillery. They were faced by at least an equal number of Union troops made up of XII Corps' two divisions (Geary and Ruger), Shaler's Brigade from the 3rd Division of VI Corps and Brigadier-General Lysander Cutler's 2nd Brigade of Wadsworth's 1st Division, I Corps. All these formations were either on or reinforced Culp's Hill.

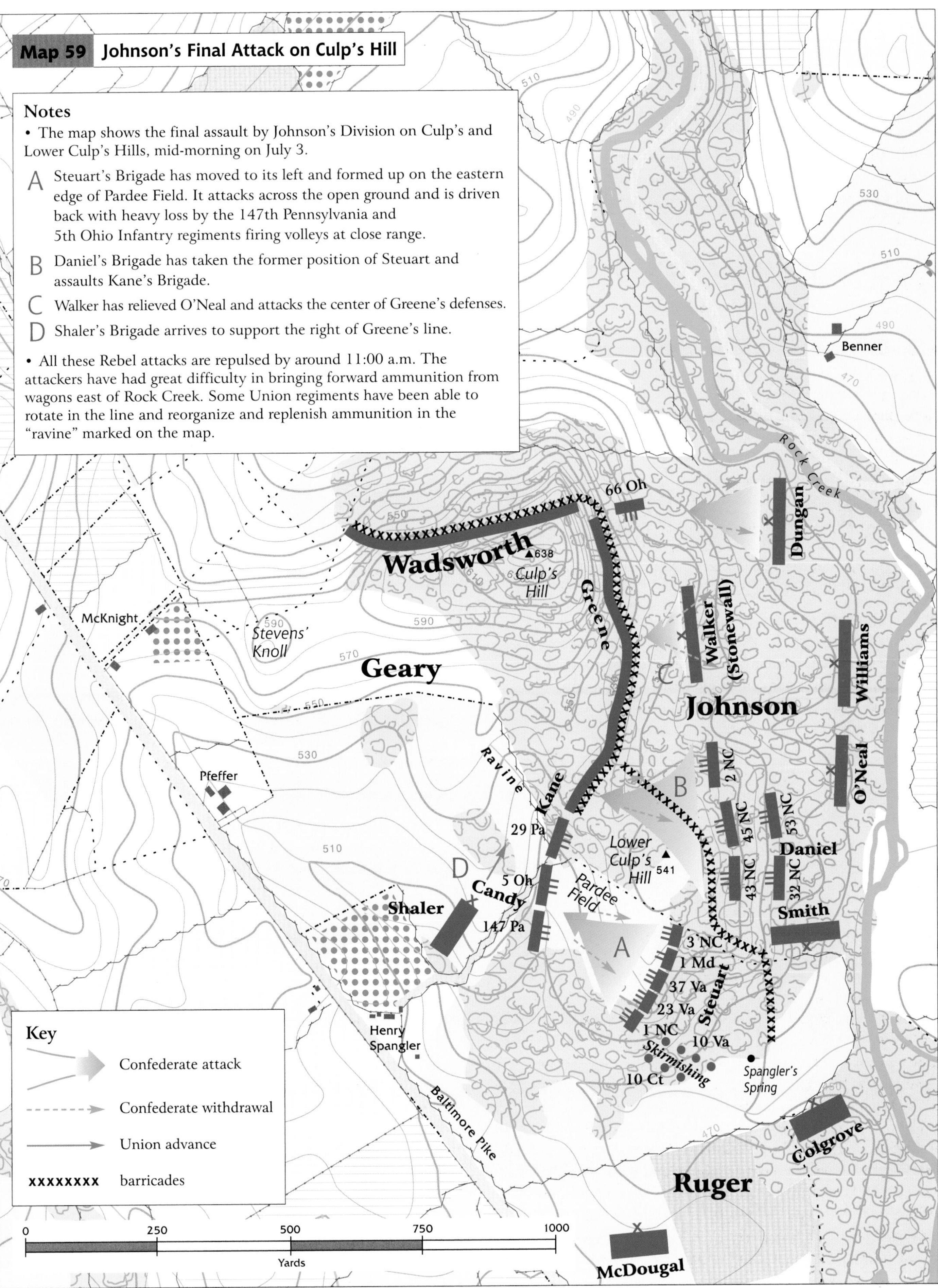
Map 59 Johnson's Final Attack on Culp's Hill
Notes
• The map shows the final assault by Johnson's Division on Culp's and Lower Culp's Hills, mid-morning on July 3.
A Steuart's Brigade has moved to its left and formed up on the eastern edge of Pardee Field. It attacks across the open ground and is driven back with heavy loss by the 147th Pennsylvania and 5th Ohio Infantry regiments firing volleys at close range.
B Daniel's Brigade has taken the former position of Steuart and assaults Kane's Brigade.
C Walker has relieved O'Neal and attacks the center of Greene's defenses.
D Shaler's Brigade arrives to support the right of Greene's line.
• All these Rebel attacks are repulsed by around 11:00 a.m. The attackers have had great difficulty in bringing forward ammunition from wagons east of Rock Creek. Some Union regiments have been able to rotate in the line and reorganize and replenish ammunition in the "ravine" marked on the map.
Key
Confederate attack
Confederate withdrawal
Union advance
xxxxxxxx barricades
0 250 500 750 1000
Yards
Wadsworth
Culp's Hill
638
Greene
66 Oh
Dungan
Rock Creek
Benner
Walker (Stonewall)
Williams
Johnson
O'Neal
McKnight
Stevens' Knoll
Geary
Ravine
Kane
29 Pa
5 Oh
Candy
147 Pa
Pardee Field
Lower Culp's Hill
541
2 NC
45 NC
53 NC
43 NC
32 NC
Daniel
Smith
3 NC
1 Md
37 Va
23 Va
1 NC
10 Va
Steuart
Skirmishing
10 Ct
Spangler's Spring
Shaler
Pfeffer
Henry Spangler
Baltimore Pike
Colgrove
Ruger
McDougal
510
490
530
470
550
590
570

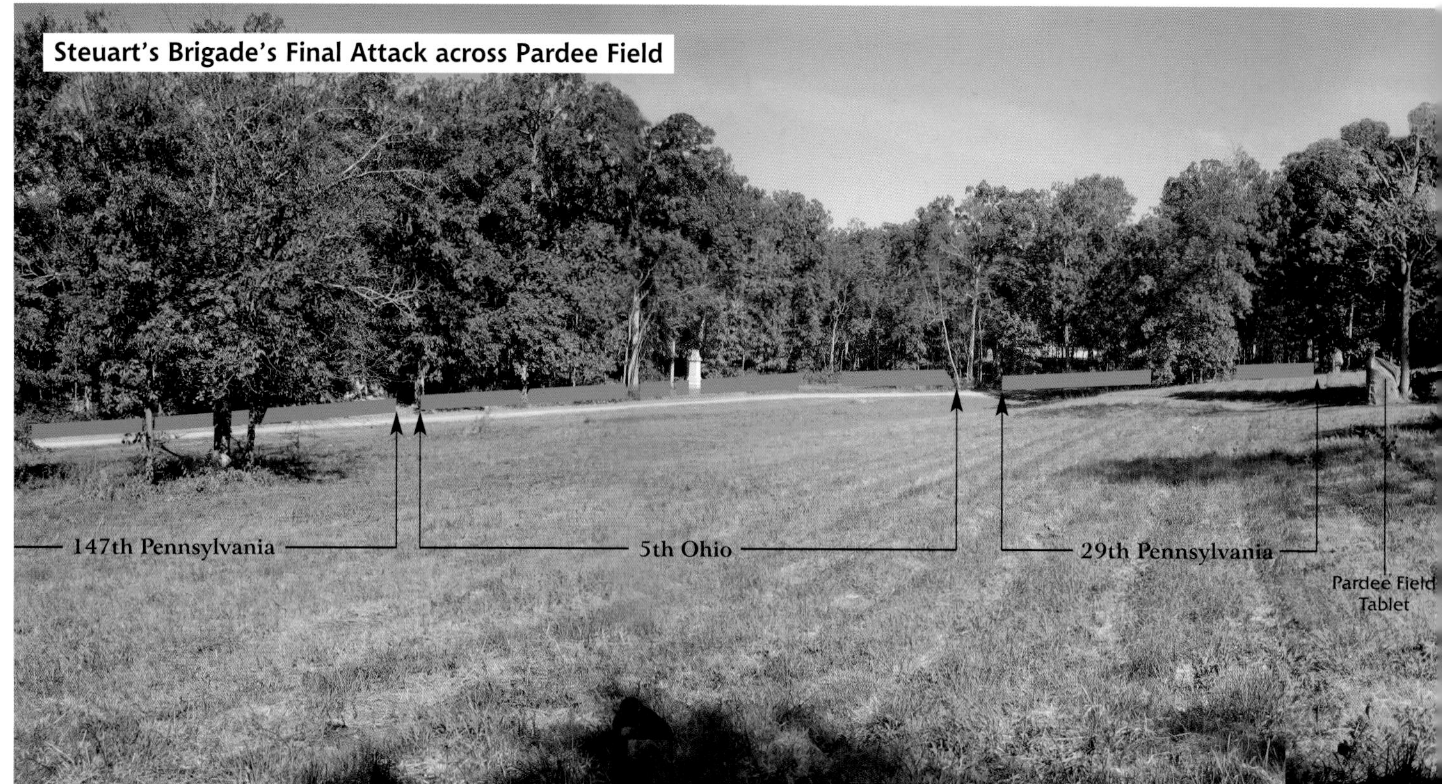

Looking north from near the southern edge of Pardee Field (named after the commander of 147th Pennsylvania). Another graphic demonstration of defending Union infantry regiments withholding their fire until the attackers were only 100 yards away (as indicated roughly by the red arrows). The whole line was staggered by the weight of fire. According to a soldier in the 147th Pennsylvania, "There was no retreat for the poor fellows in the front ranks who . . . came up to be mowed down by companies. Almost 900 men firing Springfields and Enfields at that range could not miss. Scores of Steuart's men collapsed dead or injured, some halted and tried to fire back, others lay on the ground and refused their officers' pleas to advance, many tried to retreat and a few surrendered. It was a Rebel disaster. Steuart, who had advanced behind his own 1st Maryland Battalion, was later seen with tears streaming down his cheeks crying, 'My poor boys!, My poor boys!'"

According to Private Mouat, in the trees just north of the field the 29th Pennsylvania held their fire until the 3rd North Carolina were only 50 yards away. The result was equally horrific. Union fire control had been superb. As an officer in the 147th Pennsylvania said of his regiment, "[It] poured a deliberate and most deadly fire into their ranks. It was done with cool and well-aimed precision . . ." See Map 59.

Caught in the Firing Line at Culp's Hill

Private David R. Howard, 1st Maryland Battalion, took part in Steuart's Brigade's attack across the Pardee Field on Culp's Hill early on July 3. In it he was badly wounded and later described in detail what it was like to lie exposed on the battlefield as a helpless target:

> We pressed on until near their breastworks, when, turning my head to the right, I saw a sight which was fearful to behold. It appeared to me as if the whole of my company was being swept away . . . Not wishing to surrender, I turned to go back, not expecting to reach my command alive . . . Catching my gun by the muzzle, I attempted to get a cartridge out of my box to reload, but before I could do so I felt a burning, stinging sensation in my thigh, and as if all the blood in my body was rushing to one spot. Finding I was falling on my back which brought me to a sitting position, facing the Federals, with my broken leg doubled up over the other. Taking it up tenderly, I put it in its natural position; then tied my handkerchief above the wound, took the bayonet off the gun and made a tourniquet with it; then took my knapsack off and put it under my head for a pillow . . .
>
> The firing was kept up after our men had gone back out of reach. It is a hard thing to say, but I am convinced the Federals deliberately shot at us while we lay there helpless on the field. Sergt. Thomas of my company, received two additional wounds; Nash of Co. C, was struck; a soldier at my left was shot and after writhing in agony for a few minutes, turned over and died. I was also struck in the hip, the ball striking a camp knife in my pocket breaking it up and cutting me in three places, but only deep enough to draw a little blood. You could tell by the sound when a ball hit a soldier, or went into the ground . . .
>
> I don't know how long I lay there . . . The Federals ran out and caught me under the arms, raising me just high enough from the ground to let my feet drag, and in this manner ran back with me to their lines, my broken leg swaying from side to side every step they took . . .

Howard recovered from his wound and was later exchanged. However, he was once again hit in the leg at the Weldon Railroad action in August 1864; this time his wound necessitated amputation.

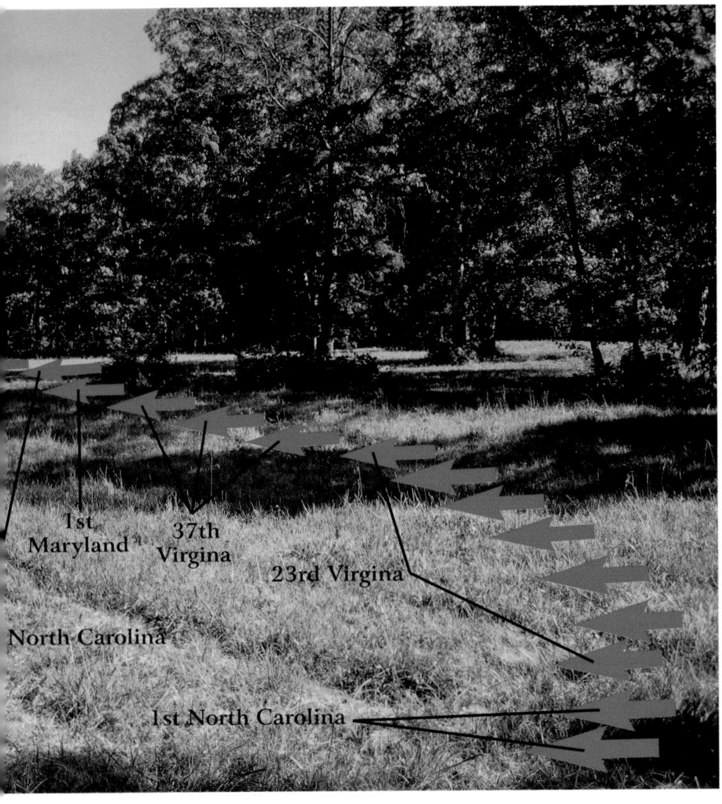

The Rebels launched at least three distinct attacks against the eastern slopes of Culp's Hill and across the open slope of Lower Culp's Hill, known as Pardee Field. Williams, the Union XII Corps commander on the hill, was able to rotate his defenders behind the breastworks by withdrawing them to a ravine in their rear to rest and replenish ammunition while replacing them with regiments from the reinforcements. The Rebels had no such respite, and ammunition supply from across Rock Creek became very problematic, with staff resorting to carrying it forward in blankets slung from poles. All Confederate assaults were pressed home with great gallantry, and the close combat struggle in the woods and at the barricades was grim and bloody. The sheer volume of the cannon and musketry fire stripped the leaves from the trees, and one Virginian soldier thought "it was the hardest battle we ever had." Geary reported that his division expended 277,000 rounds of rifle-musket fire. Steuart's assault across Pardee Field was particularly devastating for the Rebels: caught in the open at close range by a hurricane of fire, they were cut down in swathes, reducing Steuart to tears (see photograph above).

This bitterly contested fight continued until around 11:00 a.m., when the Rebels finally accepted that they could not take the hill. The struggle had cost Johnson's Division at least 2,000 men, with about another 700–800 losses across the brigades of Daniel, O'Neal and "Extra Billy" Smith. The Union corps commander, Williams, expressed the view of many when he wrote, "The wonder is that the rebels persisted so long in an attempt that the first half hour must have told them was useless." Johnson put it simply and accurately when he wrote, "The enemy were too securely entrenched and in too great numbers to be dislodged by the force at my command." Most of the Confederates fell back to Rock Creek, leaving hundreds of dead and wounded strewn amongst the trees and rocks.

PICKETT'S CHARGE

The High Tide at Gettysburg

A thousand fell where Kemper led;
A thousand died where Garnett bled:
In blinding flame and strangling smoke
The remnant through the batteries broke
And crossed the works with Armistead.
Will Henry Thompson

The Pickett–Pettigrew–Trimble charge was Lee's final fling of the dice at Gettysburg. This renowned and oft-recounted event falls neatly into two parts – the preliminary Rebel bombardment and Yankee response, and the infantry assault. The latter will be treated as a "highlight" (see page 476).

THE ARTILLERY DUEL

The Confederate Plan

Objective

Lee, and indeed all his senior commanders, were well aware that a major factor in the success of the intended infantry assault on Meade's center was the ability of Confederate guns to neutralize the Union guns on Cemetery Hill and Ridge. Lee later made this abundantly clear when he wrote:

> A careful examination was made of the ground secured by Longstreet [on July 2], and his batteries placed in positions, which, it was believed, would enable them to silence those of the enemy. Hill's artillery and part of Ewell's was ordered to open simultaneously, and the assaulting column was to advance under cover of the combined fire of the three.

Lee's emphasis on the infantry advance being made under cover of the guns is very significant and meant that the artillery plan envisaged both overhead fire and guns accompanying the attackers. This would be crucial, as the infantry must advance across three-quarters of a mile of open fields, with only a few swales or folds in the ground to give temporary protection. With large numbers of enemy guns able to fire continuously during the advance, and with the use of canister against the infantry as they reached the Emmitsburg Road, the Rebel attack could well be crippled.

A secondary objective was to give close artillery support to the infantry as they advanced, including some overhead fire. This would also entail batteries moving forward ahead of, and to the flanks of, the infantry, preferably to canister range (about 350 yards or less, and in this case to the Emmitsburg Road), deploying and shooting in support of the attackers until such time as they obscured their line of fire. This was a difficult tactic to get right, but could make all the difference by softening up the enemy position in the last few minutes before the final assault. If this tactic were not employed, it would mean that any enemy batteries not silenced by the preliminary bombardment would have a largely undisturbed shoot with canister at a very vulnerable soft target for about 5–8 minutes (the average time it would take to cross the ground between the Emmitsburg Road and the Yankee line). There can be little doubt that every Rebel artillery officer knew what was required – the problems arose, as with every plan, with the implementation.

Map 60 Artillery Deployment Around Noon, Indicating Confederate Cannonade

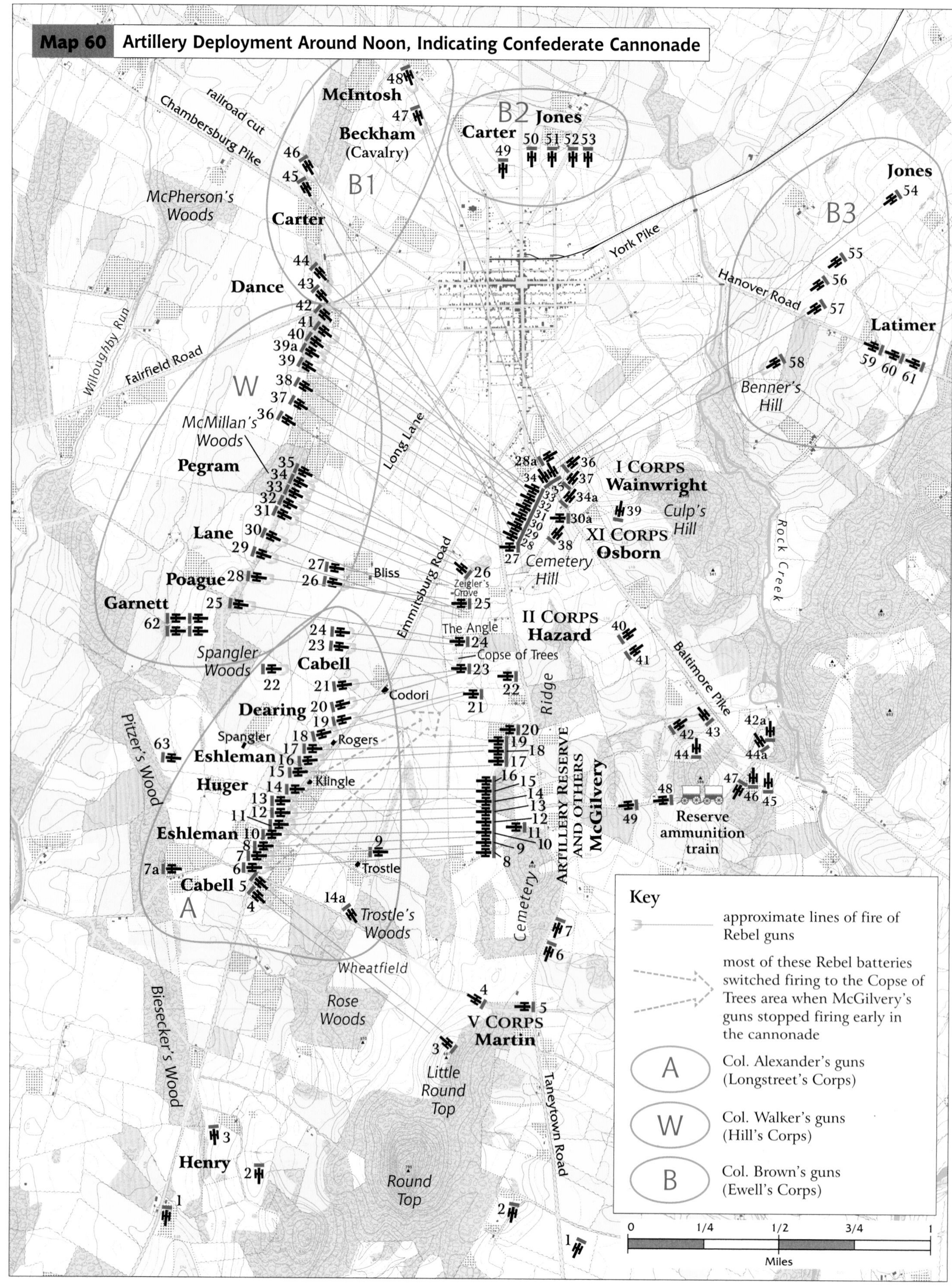
McIntosh
Beckham (Cavalry)
B1
Carter
Dance
B2
Carter
Jones
B3
Jones
Latimer
Benner's Hill
W
Pegram
Lane
Poague
Garnett
A
Cabell
Dearing
Eshleman
Huger
Eshleman
Cabell
Henry
I CORPS Wainwright
XI CORPS Osborn
II CORPS Hazard
ARTILLERY RESERVE AND OTHERS McGilvery
V CORPS Martin
Reserve ammunition train
railroad cut
Chambersburg Pike
McPherson's Woods
Willoughby Run
Fairfield Road
McMillan's Woods
Long Lane
York Pike
Hanover Road
Culp's Hill
Rock Creek
Cemetery Hill
Emmitsburg Road
Bliss
Zeigler's Grove
The Angle
Copse of Trees
Spangler Woods
Codori
Cemetery Ridge
Baltimore Pike
Pitzer's Wood
Spangler
Rogers
Klingle
Trostle
Trostle's Woods
Wheatfield
Rose Woods
Biesecker's Wood
Little Round Top
Round Top
Taneytown Road
Key
approximate lines of fire of Rebel guns
most of these Rebel batteries switched firing to the Copse of Trees area when McGilvery's guns stopped firing early in the cannonade
A Col. Alexander's guns (Longstreet's Corps)
W Col. Walker's guns (Hill's Corps)
B Col. Brown's guns (Ewell's Corps)
0 1/4 1/2 3/4 1
Miles

Confederate

Number on Map	Artillery Commander	Battery Commander	Ordnance	Fired	Not Fired
1.	Beckham	Hart	3 BR	–	3 BR
2.	Henry	Reilly	2N, 2P(10), 2OR	–	2N, 2P(10), 2OR
3.		Bachman	4N	–	4N
4.		Latham	3N, 1 6pdr, 1H(12)	3N, 1 6pdr, 1H(12)	–
5.		Garden	2N, 2P(10)	2N, 2P(10)	–
6.	Cabell	McCarthy	2OR	2OR	–
7.		Manley	2P(10)	2P(10)	–
7a		Manley	2H(12)	–	2H(12)
8.		Fraser	2OR, 2P(10)	2OR, 2P(10)	–
9.	Eshleman	Squires	1N	1N	–
10.	Huger*	Jordan	4OR	4OR	–
11.		Moody	4H(24)	4H(24)	–
12.		Parker	3OR, 1P(10)	3OR, 1P(10)	–
13.		Gilbert	4H(12)	4H(12)	–
14.		Taylor	3N	3N	–
14a		Taylor	1N	1N	–
15.	Eshleman	Miller	3N	3N	–
16.		Norcum	2N, 1H(12)	2N	1H(12)
17.		Richardson	2N, 1H(12)	2N	1H(12)
18.	Dearing	Stribling	4N, 2P(20)	4N, 2P(20)	–
19.		Macon	2N, 2P(10)	2N, 2P(10)	–
20.		Caskie	2N, 1OR, 1P(10)	2N, 1OR, 1P(10)	–
21.		Blount	4N	4N	–
22.	Huger	Woolfolk	2N, 2P(20)	2N, 2P(20)	–
23.	Cabell	Carlton	2P(10), 2H(12)	2P(10)	2H(12)
24.		McCarthy	2N	2N	–
25.	Poague	Wyatt	2OR, 1P(10), 1H(12)	2OR, 1P(10)	1H(12)
26.		Ward	3N, 1H(12)	3N	1H(12)
27.		Brooke	2N, 2H(12)	2N	2H(12)
28.		Graham	2N, 2H(12)	2N	2H(12)
29.	Lane	Wingfield	3Ny, 2P(10)	3Ny, 2P(10)	–
30.		Ross	3P(10), 1N, 1Ny, 1H(12)	3P(10), 1N, 1Ny	1H(12)
31.	Pegram	Marye	2N, 3OR	2N, 3OR	–
32.		Johnston	2N, 2H(12)	2N, 2H(12)	–
33.		Zimmerman	4OR	4OR	–
34.		McGraw	4N	4N	–
35.		Brander	2N, 2P(10)	2N, 2P(10)	–
36.	Dance	Griffin	2N, 2OR	2OR	2N
37.		Smith	4OR	4OR	–
38.		Watson	4P(10)	4P(10)	–
39.	McIntosh	Wallace	2N, 2OR	2OR	2N
39a		Rice	4N	4N	–
40.		Hurt	2OR	2OR	–
41.		Johnson	4OR	4OR	–
42.	Beckham	Griffin	2P(10)	2P(10)	–
43.	Dance	Cunningham	4OR	4OR	–
44.	T. Carter	Reese	4OR	4OR	–
45.		Fry	2OR, 2P(10)	2OR, 2P(10)	–
46.		W. Carter	2P(10)	2P(10)	–
47.	Beckham	Griffin	2P(10)	2P(10)	–
48.	McIntosh	Hurt	2W	2W	–
49.	T. Carter	Page	6N	–	6N
50.	Jones	Garber	4N	–	4N
51.		Green	2OR, 2P(10)	–	2OR, 2P(10)
52.		Carrington	4N	–	4N
53.		Tanner	4OR	–	4OR
54.	Dance	Graham	4P(20)	4P(20)	–
55.	Nelson	Massie	3N, 1OR	–	3N, 1OR
56.		Kirkpatrick	3N, 1OR	–	3N, 1OR
57.		Millege	2OR, 1P(10)	2OR, 1P(10)	–
58.	Latimer	Raine	2P(20), 1P(10), 1OR	2P(20)	1OR, 1P(10)
59.		Brown	4P(10)	–	4P(10)
60.		Carpenter	2N, 2OR	–	2N, 2OR
61.		Dement	4N	–	4N
62.	Garnett	Maurin	2OR, 1P(10)	–	2OR, 1P(10)
		Moore	2N, 1OR, 1P(10)	–	2N, 1OR, 1P(10)
		Lewis	2N, 2OR	–	2N, 2OR
		Grandy	2OR, 2H(12)	–	2OR, 2H(12)
63.	Lane	Patterson	2N, 2H(12)	–	2N, 2H(12)

* Maj. Huger commanded Col. Alexander's Battalion as Alexander was temporarily in command of Longstreet's Corps artillery for the cannonade.

Union

Number on Map	Artillery Commander	Battery Commander	Ordnance	Notes
1.	Martin	Barnes	4OR	
2.		Walcott	4N	
3.		Rittenhouse	6P(10)	
4.		Gibbs	6N	
5.	Tompkins	Adams	6P(10)	
6.		Williston	6N	
7.		McCartney	6N	
8.	Tyler*	Ames	6N	Battery fought under McGilvery on July 3
9.		Dow	4N	ditto
10		Sterling	4JR	ditto
11.	Randolph	Clark	6P(10)	
12.	Wainwright	Cooper	4OR	Battery fought under McGilvery on July 3
13.	Cavalry Corps	Rank	2OR	ditto
14.	Tyler	Hart	4N	ditto
15.		Phillips	6OR	ditto
16.		Thompson	6OR	ditto
17.		Thomas	6N	
18.	Cavalry Corps	Daniels	6OR	
19.	Tyler	Fitzhugh	6OR	
20.		Weir	6N	
21.	Hazard	Rorty	4P(10)	
22.		Brown	4N	
23.	Tompkins	Cowan	6OR	
24.	Hazard	Cushing	6OR	
25.		Arnold	6OR	
26.		Woodruff	6N	
27.	Wainwright	Hall	6OR	
28.	Osborn	Wiedrich	2OR	
28a		Wiedrich	2OR	
29.	Tyler	Hill	4P(10)	
30, 30a	Osborn	Wheeler	4OR	
31.	Tyler	Eakin	6N	
32.	Osborn	Bancroft	6N	
33.		Dilger	6N	
34.	Tyler	Taft	4P(10)	
34a		Taft	2P(10)	
35.	Wainwright	Stuart	6N	
36.	Tyler	Ricketts	6OR	
37.	Wainwright	Breck	6OR	
38.	Tyler	Norton	6OR	
39.	Wainwright	Stevens	6N	
40.	Muhlenberg	Rugg	6N	
41.		Kinzie	4N	
42, 42a		Winegar	4P(10)	
43.	Tyler	Rigby	6OR	
44.	Muhlenberg	Atwell	4P(10)	
44a		Atwell	2P(10)	
45.	Tompkins	Waterman	6OR	
46.		Harn	6P(10)	
47.		Butler	6N	
48.	Robertson(CAV)	Heaton	6OR	
49.		Martin	6OR	

* Tyler commanded the five artillery brigades of the Artillery Reserve.

Abbreviations

BR	Blakely rifle
N	12-pounder Napoleon
OR	3-inch Ordnance rifle
P(10)	10-pounder Parrott
P(20)	20-pounder Parrott
H(12)	12-pounder howitzer
H(24)	24-pounder howitzer
Ny	Navy rifle
JR	James rifle
W	Whitworth

Notes

- This map shows where the Confederate batteries were deployed shortly before they started their 90-minute preparatory bombardment of the Union line on Cemetery Hill and Ridge. Researchers are by no means unanimous as to which guns did or did not fire in the cannonade. The author has relied on the Desjardin map for July 3 and George Large's book, *Battle of Gettysburg, The Official History*, which lists the artillery unit memorial tablets, their inscriptions and locations for both armies. Not all Union batteries are marked, as the position of some deployed behind the line in reserve is uncertain and by no means all Union batteries were involved in firing, although some batteries shown as in reserve did deploy forward and fired on the Rebel attack.
- Lee had 255 guns on the battlefield, of which an estimated 161 took part in the cannonade prior to Pickett's charge, which means that 94 guns (37%) did not, the reasons for which are discussed in the text.
- From the map, which shows the lines of fire of the Confederate guns, it is clear that Lee's gunners had the potential to bring enfilade fire to bear from the northwest round to the northeast, with Cemetery Hill particularly vulnerable to fire from east and west. All guns firing were within range of their target, although some Napoleons were nearing the limit of their effective range. Union firing in response is not shown, although a fierce artillery duel developed until the Union gunners were ordered to cease firing to conserve ammunition for the infantry assault.

Gunnery planning factors

The technical planning of the Rebel bombardment had to be at two levels – higher and lower. The higher level involved the decisions made and leadership displayed by Lee, his chief of artillery, his corps commanders and artillery battalion commanders. These included the allocation of resources; their deployment to ensure maximum concentration and effectiveness; the achievement of cooperation and coordination; allocating target priorities; timings and overall ammunition-supply arrangements. The lower-level planning by battery commanders involved target identification, judging ranges, selection of ammunition type, type of fuse, type of fire and rate of fire to ensure accuracy.

Allocation of resources

Brigadier-General William N. Pendleton, Lee's chief of artillery, stated in his report that, "By direction of the commanding general the artillery along our entire line was to be prepared for opening as early as possible on the morning of the 3rd."

There were some 255 Confederate pieces of artillery on the field that morning, but in the event a maximum of 161 (almost exactly a third being smoothbore Napoleons) took part, at least to some extent, in the bombardment, meaning that for a variety of reasons 94 (37 percent) did not. To have well over a third of guns left out of the most crucial cannonade of the battle requires some explanation.

After Lee had given his instructions for the attack, the coordination of the artillery effort was the responsibility of Pendleton. It was his task to ensure that best use was made of the resources within each of the three corps. Each infantry division had its artillery battalion of four batteries (though Anderson's Division had three) and each corps had a reserve of two battalions, making fourteen battalions per corps – an impressive number, capable, in theory anyway, of producing a massive concentration of firepower. However, there was no army artillery reserve, so Pendleton had no guns under his direct control to use quickly as he saw fit. Nevertheless, it was his job to ensure the maximum number of guns from each corps was deployed in positions from which they could hit Cemetery Hill and Ridge, particularly the center of the line, which was the Rebel infantry's objective. He was the only artillery officer able to visit all parts of the Rebel line and give overall direction to the artillery effort. In the event, the Confederates had all morning on July 3 to get their guns positioned, stocked with ammunition, targets identified, ranges assessed and guns aligned. So why, when the cannonade opened at 1:00 p.m., were over a third of the guns not firing? Had Pendleton failed to ensure the maximum use of resources?

A number of factors prevented all 255 guns taking part in the cannonade, some unavoidable, others not:

- There was a need to give the extreme right flank of the Rebel line some artillery support – a task given to two batteries from Henry's Battalion (Hood's Division) and the three Blakely rifles of Captain Hart's Battery (Stuart's Cavalry Division). These amounted to thirteen pieces.
- There was a problem with the use of the howitzers in the bombardment due to their limited effective range. Of the twenty-eight howitzers on the field, only nine participated, these being the four 24-pounders in Moody's Battery; Gilbert's two 12-pounders in Huger's (Alexander's) Battalion on the Emmitsburg Road, from where they were just able to reach McGilvery's guns; Lieutenant Johnston's two 12-pounders on the eastern edge of Pegram's Woods; and the 12-pounder in Latham's Battery on the extreme right of the gun line. All four batteries that fired howitzers did so at the gun's maximum range. Of the seventeen that did not fire, Colonel Alexander had this to say:

> As I rode with him [Pendleton] & talked over matters he told me that Col. R. L. Walker, A. P. Hill's chief of arty., had nine 12 pr. Howitzers for which he had no special use as their range was too short. Gen. Pendleton asked me if I could make use of them. I jumped at the idea & thanked him & said, "Yes, I have the very place for them." And I rode on with him immediately, and had them turned over to me, under the command of a Maj. Richardson [serving in Garnett's artillery battalion].

Alexander continued, "I accepted them, intending to take them into the charge with Pickett; so I put them in a hollow behind a bit of wood, with no orders but to wait there until I sent for them." Unfortunately, this hollow has never been satisfactorily identified.

- There was justification for extracting the flank guard and howitzers from the total (thirty-two pieces) available, which left over sixty Napoleons and rifled cannon of various types that theoretically could have added their fire to the cannonade. That they did not was largely because both Hill and Ewell kept substantial reserves out of the firing line and Pendleton seemingly accepted this. Alexander, with the exception of the two batteries of Henry's battalion on the right flank and six howitzers, put every piece forward in his gun line. Hill, however, kept back all four batteries of Lieutenant-Colonel Garnett's Battalion. This amounted to thirteen pieces (nine rifles and four Napoleons). Ewell, whose corps was spread out from southwest of Gettysburg, through the town and to Culp's Hill to the southeast, retained the great majority of his guns in reserve or uncommitted to the bombardment. With the exception of Captain Raine's two 20-pounders and Captain Millege's two 3-inch ordnance rifles and 10-pounder Parrott on Benner's Hill, and Captain Carter's and Fry's four 10-pounder Parrotts and two 3-inch ordnance rifles north and south of the railway cut, Hill's artillery contributed little. As many as forty-four guns from the battalions of Jones, Latimer, Nelson and Carter played no part. While much of the terrain and the town were far from ideal for gun positions, and Napoleons had a range problem, no fewer than eighteen rifled cannons were unused. Of this Alexander was to say:

> The artillery of Ewell's corps, however, took only a small part, I believe, in this [the bombardment], as they were too far away around the town. Some of them [the rifled guns] might have done good service from positions between Hill and Ewell, enfilading the batteries fighting us. The opportunity to do that was the single advantage, in our having the exterior line, to compensate for all its disadvantages.

With regard to the allocation of ammunition resources for the cannonade, it is assumed that part of the preparation included the replenishing of the first-line ammunition so that all guns had the four chests on the limbers and caissons full. The details of Rebel artillery ammunition holdings are discussed on pages 167–69, but for the present calculation the estimated average holding per piece of 120 rounds is used. Assuming 160 guns participated, then the total ammunition available within easy reach of the gunners at the start was around 19,000 rounds. Of these, almost 80 percent was probably shell or spherical case, with about 10 percent each for solid shot and canister. This would mean some 15,000 rounds of shell and case, and 2,000 each of solid shot and canister. At least forty (mostly mixed) batteries or their equivalent fired at least some shots, so an approximate average holding per battery at the start of the cannonade would have been about 475 rounds.

Deployment (Map 60)

Colonel Porter Alexander, responsible for placing the guns of Longstreet's Corps, was up early that morning.

> About one o'clock [a.m.] I made a little bed of fence rails, as preferable to the trampled ground, in the Peach Orchard, and got two hours' sleep. At three I began to put the batteries in position again [to support the continuation of the previous day's attack] and was joined by the Washington Artillery [Eshleman's Battalion], which had been in reserve the day before. As daylight came, I found I had placed about twenty guns so that the enemy's batteries on Cemetery Hill enfiladed the line, and I had a panic, almost, for fear the enemy would discover the error and open before I could rectify it.
>
> Early in the morning [possibly around 8:30 a.m.] General Lee came round, and I was then told we were to assault Cemetery Hill, which lay rather to our left. This necessitated a good many changes of position which the enemy did not altogether approve of, and they took occasional shots at us . . . by ten o'clock, Dearing having come up, we had seventy-five [possibly 76] guns in what was practically one battery . . .

From this number, six 12-pounder howitzers would not fire, so Alexander's gun line had about seventy guns that actually participated. It was while deploying that Pendleton offered Alexander the additional nine howitzers from Hill's Corps, noted above, which he placed in reserve to follow up and support the infantry attack. These seventy Napoleons and rifled cannon were spread over just short of a mile, mostly along the Emmitsburg Road (nos. 4–24 on Map 60). They were deployed on the rising ground from the Peach Orchard along the road to about 400 yards south of the Codori Farm, where this slight ridge sloped very gently north. These batteries had a clear view across the Plum Run valley to Cemetery Ridge or the Copse of Trees area. At least one author has suggested that the Union guns under McGilvery were not observed by the Confederates and were therefore not shelled. While Lee may not have seen them, it is a myth that they went unobserved; Alexander's and McGilvery's gunners were visible to each other at a range of about 1,000 yards and the former's batteries opened up on the latter at the start of the cannonade; but, as we shall see, McGilvery deliberately stopped firing and Alexander switched to firing onto the Copse of Trees area, as shown on the map. Alexander had been compelled to deploy forward onto the Emmitsburg Road, or close to it, and to occupy the rising ground he considered as being "very unfavorable as regards shelter" in order that all his guns were within effective range of the enemy and had a clear view of the target area.

To Alexander's immediate north were the guns of Colonel R. Lindsay Walker, Hill's artillery chief. His gun line was spread over a mile in length, from the northern edge of Spangler Woods to the Fairfield Road, mostly deployed on the edge of the woods, with both Cemetery Hill and the ridge to the south considerably less than a mile away – comfortably in range of all guns except the howitzers. As noted above, nine howitzers were given to Alexander. It seems the two 12-pounder howitzers in Lieutenant Johnston's battery (no. 32 on Map 60) did fire – the distance from their position to Cemetery Hill was about 1,000 yards and thus just within effective range. The fifteen guns of Lieutenant-Colonel Garnett's Battalion were held back in reserve and positioned to the rear (west) of Spangler Woods. Apart from the two howitzers in Captain Grandy's Battery, nine of the remaining pieces were rifled cannon whose presence on the gun line would have added substantially to the weight of fire delivered.

The number of guns, excluding Garnett's, amounted to seventy-six, of which sixty-five participated in the bombardment. The combined "grand battery" of Alexander's and Walker's amounted to some 135 guns deployed over a distance of 2 miles. This equated to one gun every 26 yards, all primarily targeted on the threequarters of a mile that encompassed Cemetery Hill, the Copse of Trees area and the ground to its immediate south along Cemetery Ridge. With the exception of Garnett's guns and a handful of howitzers, every available gun from both Longstreet's and Hill's Corps was committed to the cannonade. The same could not be said for Ewell's Corps artillery.

Ewell's artillery, with battalions under Lieutenant-Colonels Carter, Jones and Nelson, Major Latimer and Captain Dance, was all under the overall charge of Colonel J. Thompson Brown. In all, the corps had seventy-one guns, none of which were howitzers. They were deployed in three separate groups (B1, B2 and B3 on Map 60). However, the participation of Brown's guns in the cannonade was poor in comparison with the other corps (only twenty-seven fired), although some guns, notably those firing from near the railroad cut and Benner's Hill, were very effective. Part of the problem was the extremely scattered nature of their deployment. Overall, Brown had guns spread in an arc over 5 miles in length, from Seminary Ridge in the west to Oak Hill in the north and thence to Benner's Hill in the east. Of greater significance was the range to the target, Cemetery Hill – well over a mile, although still in effective range, for those in group B1 by the railway cut, Griffin's section of 10-pounder Parrotts from the cavalry on the southern end of Oak Ridge. For the two Whitworths, the artillery's snipers from Hunt's Battery (Hill's Corps), the distance was 2 miles but well within their range. All the guns in this group of eighteen fired.

In stark contrast, not a single gun in the B2 group did so. It consisted of twenty-two guns, fourteen Napoleons (two from Carter's Battery) under Captain Page and eight rifled cannon. They were positioned just north of Gettysburg and in effect were just a reserve force with no particular mission. While the range to Cemetery Hill was just over a mile, which probably precluded the Napoleons from doing anything useful from their position, this was not true of the rifles. The reason they did not fire was almost certainly due to lack of initiative on the part of Pendleton or Brown, or indeed Ewell himself. While the town undoubtedly obscured much of the target from their deployment positions, no effort appears to have been made to find better ones, perhaps on the low ridge that carried the York Pike into Gettysburg just east of Rock Creek. Alexander felt they had been wasted and could have found positions northwest of the town. Had they done so, they would have added very considerably to the damaging enfilade fire that raked Cemetery Hill.

The third grouping, B3 on the map, consisted of thirty-one pieces, of which, seemingly, only nine fired. These were Captain Graham's four 20-pounder Parrotts, 1.5 miles northeast of their target, Cemetery Hill; Captain Millege's two ordnance rifles and one 10-pounder Parrott on the northern extension of Benner's Hill; and Captain Raine's two 20-pounder Parrotts on Benner's Hill itself. Lack of space may have precluded more guns on Benner's Hill, but it is difficult to understand why the hill was not occupied by some Napoleons, as Cemetery Hill was within their range, and their positions further back were not taken by rifled cannon. Major Latimer's Battalion of fourteen guns, with the exception of Raine's two large Parrotts, was kept in reserve near the Hanover Road behind Benner's Hill.

The Cannonade

Confederate

Apart from the major struggle for Culp's Hill, which had subsided by 11:00 a.m., there was also activity west of Cemetery Ridge that morning before the Rebel's massive bombardment opened. From first light, the skirmishers along the front of both armies had been active, with the rattle and pop of musketry at times intense, at times dying away. The infantry struggle for the Bliss Farm, the barn of which was built like a small fort, developed into something more than a skirmish. Rebels had ensconced themselves in the buildings after the heavy fighting of July 2, and from a range of about quarter of a mile they made themselves a nuisance to the Yankees on Cemetery Ridge. Several sallies by Union regiments pushed their enemy out, only to find they quickly infiltrated back. Finally, Brigadier-General Hays sent a strong force with orders to eject the Rebels and torch the buildings. This was carried out successfully by the 14th Connecticut. Private Henry Stevens stated, "This affair of the Bliss buildings was one of the most thrilling and perilous of the experiences of the Fourteenth."

As early as 7:00 a.m. some Confederate batteries on Seminary Ridge began shelling the area of Zeigler's Grove, drawing a response from Woodruff's Battery (no. 26 on Map 60). After this duel died down there was a pause of about an hour before yet again some Southern gunners opened up, this time at Cushing's and Arnold's Batteries (nos. 24 and 25 respectively). A shell hit Cushing's no. 2 limber, exploding two ammunition chests and terrifying the horses of no. 1 limber into bolting over the stone wall in front of them and galloping madly into the Rebel lines. Colonel Alexander, in his *Military Memoirs of a Confederate*, calls these exchanges of fire "most unwise, as it consumed uselessly a large amount of his [Hill's] ammunition, the lack of which was much felt in the subsequent fighting. Not a single gun of our Corps fired a shot, nor did the enemy in our front."

By 11:00 a.m. virtually all firing had ceased, but the blazing sun and lack of breeze saw the temperature rising rapidly (it was to hit 90 degrees), as was the stench from the rotting bodies of men and horses killed the previous day. Shortly before 1:00 p.m. a courier from Longstreet found Colonel Walton (although Alexander had charge of positioning Longstreet's guns, Walton remained the substantive artillery commander) near the Peach Orchard and handed him the following message:

> Colonel:- Let the batteries open; order great care and precision in firing. If the batteries at the peach orchard cannot be used against the point we intend attacking, let them open on the rocky hill.
>
> Most respectfully,
> J. Longstreet
> Lieut.Gen. Commanding
>
> To Col. Walton, Chief of Artillery

Union Pickets Are Relieved Under Fire

Private Henry Stevens, 14th Connecticut (3rd Division, II Corps) left an interesting personal account of pickets being relieved under fire near the Bliss Farm during the morning of July 3:

> Then Companies A and F were relieved from picket duty by Companies B and D. The work of these men on the picket line and the relief of the details was quite interesting and exciting to the observers in the rear and looked like a very pretty game – but to the participants it was not pretty. Our picket reserve station was in the Emmitsburg road in front of the regiment. The road was sunken there nearly two feet, affording some protection at the fence. The picket line was at a fence about two hundred yards in advance of the reserve, and the line of rebel pickets about the same distance further on, some of it by the trees of the Bliss orchard. Our men lay flat upon the ground by the fence, hidden and somewhat protected by the posts and lowest rails. Nothing was visible, usually to fire at, yet when any movement was apparent a shot or two would follow from vigilant watchers; then the rising riflesmoke would attract retaliating shots. When the reliefs went to their places there was excitement. The relieving squad would leave the reserve rendezvous moving in any way possible to avoid the observation of the enemy, but when a place was reached where exposure was unavoidable each would take a running at highest speed, and upon reaching the fence would throw himself at once upon the ground . . .
>
> The start of the pickets from either side, to or from their places was a signal for a lively popping all along the line of their opponents as long as a man was in sight. Not many of the runners were struck, for to hit such a rapidly moving object is a difficult feat; but the pop! pop! crack! crack! would go on all the same; and the eagerness to hit would make some shooters careless, so furnishing themselves targets for some hidden watchers.

This order was passed to Captain "Buck" Miller, commanding the three Napoleons of the 3rd Company, Washington Artillery (no. 15 on Map 60). He was to fire the two shots to signal for the great cannonade to start. The sharp crack of the first was heard over the entire battlefield. However, the second did not follow immediately. When the lanyard was pulled nothing happened, as the friction primer had failed. It was replaced, and just a few moments late the second shot rang out – the biggest bombardment of the war was under way.

A solid line of flame, smoke and noise stretched for well over 2 miles from the Peach Orchard to the railroad cut. On Oak Hill the two Whitworths joined in, then the batteries on or near Benner's Hill – 160 projectiles within a matter of perhaps thirty seconds.

How long did the cannonade last? In his book *Into the Fight – Pickett's Charge at Gettysburg*, John Michael Priest researched no fewer than forty-six Union and thirty-three Confederate first-hand sources who recorded their opinions on this question. The results vary from forty-five minutes to over two hours. Some 64 percent of the Southerners thought it lasted from under one hour to one hour and forty-five minutes and 45 percent of the Northerners agreed; 39 percent of the Confederates thought about two hours. It is impossible to be dogmatic about this, but if the time also includes the firing by some Rebel batteries over the heads of advancing infantry, then from one and a half to two hours seems a reasonable estimate.

Firing was initially at a brisk rate of about three shots per gun per minute, which for 160 guns would require 480 rounds. For this rate to continue for an hour would require 28,800 rounds, which was just not possible for a number of reasons besides ammunition expenditure. The gunners had been told to hit a specific target accurately with direct, concentrated fire; this required careful aiming and judging of range, neither of which could be done in a hurry, especially as dense clouds of smoke obscured the target for much of the time. Then there was the physical effort needed to fire at a rapid rate – to do so for even thirty minutes in the broiling sun was asking the near impossible. The Rebels' rate of fire soon slowed to one or two rounds a minute. If the guns averaged three rounds a minute for the first half hour, some 14,400 rounds would have been fired, which would almost have emptied every battery of its first-line holdings of suitable ammunition (canister being of no use). It is likely the rate slowed sharply as caissons went back to refill. Another sixty minutes at one round per gun per minute would have expended another 9,600 rounds. These estimates are very approximate, and do not cater for guns that stopped firing for various reasons during this time, but they do illustrate how quickly ammunition supplies could dwindle. Toward the end of the bombardment numerous batteries were very low on ammunition and some had none; also, the reserve train had been moved further back and its location was unknown to the caisson drivers. When it is considered that the total available to the Army of Northern Virginia was perhaps 50,000 rounds at the start of the battle, or even less if the figures of *The Report of Ordnance Stores on Hand* are accepted (see Section Three: Artillery, pages 167–69), then the above estimated expenditure for the bombardment is too high.

There is considerable difference of opinion among the Confederate batteries over the rate of fire used, and the truth is probably that it varied from battery to battery according to the orders given by their commanders. Major Eshleman claimed his guns fired steadily and judiciously. Major Dearing reported that his "commenced firing slowly and deliberately. To ensure more accuracy and to guard against the waste of ammunition, I fired by battery." Captain Manly confirmed his guns fired "slowly and with deliberation." However, Alexander expected his batteries to fire fast, at least to begin with. Private Felix Galloway (Ross's Battery, Lane's Battalion) claimed his battery was ordered to fire 100 rounds per gun and then let the infantry advance, and that forty rounds were expended before the enemy returned fire, which indicates some rapid firing of at least two rounds per gun per minute. At the receiving end, McGilvery recorded: "this fire was very rapid and inaccurate," while Captain Phillips (Battery E, Massachusetts Light Artillery) stated: "About one o'clock the enemy opened a heavy fire from a long line of batteries, which was kept up for an hour . . ." Using the estimated ammunition expenditure noted above, the number of projectiles fired during the bombardment proper was perhaps 15,000–20,000 rounds.

The Confederate gunners were endeavoring to concentrate their fire on the Union guns in the region of the Copse of Trees and Zeigler's Grove, Cemetery Hill to the north and Cemetery Ridge to the immediate south – a 700-yard stretch of the enemy line. But they were also to hit Union

Waiting for Battle

Most soldiers going into action would agree that it is the waiting that is the worst: once the fighting starts and given something to do, the adrenalin flows and the mind has less time to dwell upon the potential horrors ahead. Colonel Joseph C. Mayo, commanding the 3rd Virginia in Kemper's Brigade, noticed how his men appeared unusually subdued as they awaited the onset of the artillery cannonade:

> but one thing was especially noticeable, from being unusually merry and hilarious they on a sudden had become as still and thoughtful as Quakers at a love feast. Walking up the line to where Colonel Patton was standing in front of the Seventh [Virginia], I said to him, "This news has brought an awful seriousness with our fellows, Taz." "Yes," he replied, "and well may they be serious if they really know what's in store for them. I have been up yonder where Dearing is, and looked across at the Yankees."

The Confederate Cannonade Begins

Adjutant James Crocker of the 9th Virginia, in Armistead's Brigade, described the moment the Rebel guns opened fire:

> At last, in our immediate front, at 1 P.M., there suddenly leapt from one of our cannons a single sharp far-reaching sound, breaking the long-continued silence and echoing along the extended lines of battle and far beyond the far-off heights. All were now at strained attention. Then quickly followed another gun. Friend and foe at once recognized that these were signal guns. Then hundreds of cannon opened upon each other from the confronting heights. What a roar – how incessant! The earth trembled under the mighty resound of cannon. The air is darkened with sulphurous clouds. The whole valley is enveloped. The sun, lately so glaring, is itself obscured. Nothing can be seen but the flashing light leaping from the cannon's mouth amidst the surrounding smoke. The air which was so silent and serene is now full of exploding and screaming shells and shot . . . The storm of battle rages. It is appalling, terrific, yet grandly exciting.

guns on the flanks that could enfilade the attacking infantry. In particular this meant the ad hoc grouping of some thirty-six guns under Lieutenant-Colonel McGilvery (nos. 8–16 on Map 60). As mentioned above, it has been suggested by at least one author that McGilvery's guns were not observed by the Rebels on July 3 and were therefore not shelled, which left this powerful battery intact to smash Kemper's Brigade when it advanced on Pickett's right. These guns were sited just below the crest or on the forward slope of Cemetery Ridge and were clearly visible to all Alexander's gunners deployed along the slightly rising ground that carried the Emmitsburg Road north from the Peach Orchard to the Codori Farm. At most they were only 1,200 yards apart. The Confederates did shell them, as indicated on Map 60, but other than a few rounds McGilvery did not let his guns respond, and after a while Alexander's batteries switched to the main target area from which enemy guns were still firing.

How effective was the cannonade? As the first missiles screamed in there were yells of "Down! Down!" all along the Union line. Men flattened themselves behind walls, buildings, and piles of fence rails or knapsacks filled with dirt as the awful roar of exploding shells assailed their senses. Lieutenant Frank Haskell on the staff of Brigadier-General John Gibbon wrote:

> the projectiles shriek long and sharp, they hiss they scream, they growl, they splutter . . . The percussion shells would strike and thunder, and scatter the earth, and their whistling fragments, the hexagonal Whitworth bolts, would pound ricochet and bowl far away spluttering with the sound of a mass of hot iron plunged into water, and the great solid shot would smite the unresisting earth with a resounding "thud" . . .

Major Osborn used some purple prose to describe the Whitworth projectiles, claiming "their fiendish wailings sounding like the predatory howls of demons in search of prey." Gibbon himself wrote:

> The larger round shells could be seen plainly as in their nearly completed course they curved in their fall towards the Taneytown road, but the long rifled shells came with a rush and a scream and could only be seen in their rapid flight when they "upset" and went tumbling through the air, creating the uncomfortable impression that, no matter whether you were in front of the gun from which they came or not, you were liable to be hit.

One effect of firing at the crest of the ridge was that there were hundreds of "overs" as missiles cleared the crest and exploded above or hit the reverse slope, where numerous administrative soldiers or non-combatants were located. This area behind the center of the Union line was soon cleared as a throng of ambulance drivers, teamsters, servants, orderlies, camp followers, walking wounded, field hospitals and "a few brave soldiers with cowardly legs" all scrambled back to safer areas. The Baltimore Pike was briefly blocked by this rapidly retreating mob. Lieutenant-Colonel Morgan on the staff of II Corps described what he saw happening on the reverse slope of Cemetery Ridge:

> shells commenced falling about us and in our middle as though every gun was trained on us. The ambulance horses took fright and circled wildly about, a shell killed the driver, a faithful old soldier of Gibbon's battery, and horses and ambulance were all overturned in a heap. The officers sprang to secure their horses, which all appeared seized with unusual terror, and in less time than it has taken to tell it, the road [Taneytown Road] was cleared of every living thing. What took place in this little group was seen repeated at every point of the field in rear of the line. A mighty hurricane could not sooner have swept it clean and bare . . . Had their practice been good it is possible they might have stampeded the men [infantry] and forced them from the ground.

When the cannonade was at its height, Brigadier-General Tyler ordered the Reserve Artillery and its train to withdraw about half a mile to a safer location but left behind orderlies to deliver orders for ammunition. However, the most significant person to be driven from this area was the army commander himself, along with all his staff except for one signals officer. Widow Leister's house, at the very vortex of the deluge of missiles, forced Meade to move south to a barn several hundred yards down the Taneytown Road. This also proved unhealthy, so he established a temporary headquarters on Power's Hill alongside Major-General Slocum. Several senior officers were wounded, including Meade's chief of staff, Butterfield, as well as Doubleday, Barnes and brigade commander Smyth.

According to Major Osborn, who faced a storm of accurate and effective fire from two directions (Benner's Hill in the east and Oak Hill, the railroad cut area and Seminary Ridge south of the Lutheran Seminary in the west) onto his exposed positions on Cemetery Hill:

> We were in plain view of the batteries of the enemy on at least a mile and a half of his line. The slope of the hill in our rear was too steep to use as cover for the guns or even the caissons. The distance of the enemy's guns from us was from three-fourths of a mile to a mile and a half. An excellent range, the country all open, no woods . . . We made the best target for artillery practice the enemy had during the war . . .
>
> Nothing which can be written will convey to the non-military man the slightest idea of the fire concentrated on Cemetery Hill during the hour and a half it continued. The shells must have reached us at a rate of one hundred and upwards a minute at the least . . . The enemy turned their attention exclusively to the batteries on the crest of the hill . . . The officers, men and horses were killed or

The Hell of the Cannonade

The horror, noise and smoke of the bombardment as the 9th Virginia (Armistead's Brigade) awaited the order to advance were years later recalled by Lieutenant John H. Lewis of Company G:

> Man seldom sees or hears the like of this but once in a lifetime; and those that saw and heard this infernal crash and witnessed the havoc made by the shrieking, howling missiles of death as they plowed the earth and tore the trees will never forget it. It seemed that death was in every foot of space, and safety was only in flight; but none of the men did that. To know the tension of mind under fire like that, it must be experienced; it cannot be told in words . . . For two long hours this pandemonium was kept up, and then, as suddenly as it commenced, it ceased.

The view from just west of the Leister House, looking southwest. The defending Union regiments were deployed in line just out of sight over the crest. The area shown was subjected to a hail of shot and shell from the Confederate cannonade prior to Pickett's charge, forcing Meade to abandon the Leister House, and clearing the area of numerous administrative troops.

> wounded rapidly [his own artillery brigade of five batteries took sixty-nine casualties or 10 percent of its strength]. A caisson was blown up every few minutes, and now and then an artillery carriage was struck and knocked to pieces.

Major-General Howard recalled the start of the cannonade:

> The signal gun was fired by the enemy, and from the southwest, west, north and northeast, his batteries opened, hurling into the Cemetery grounds, missiles of every description. Shells burst in the air, on the ground at our right and left, and in front, killing men and horses, exploding caissons, over turning tombstones and smashing fences.

Colonel Wainwright, also on Cemetery Hill, stated he had never known the enemy "so lavish with ammunition" and that Lee "must have given special orders, and placed much reliance on this fire" – the latter part being an accurate assessment.

There is no doubt that the Rebel bombardment seemed both overwhelming and neverending to the Yankee infantry soldiers cowering under it – but its effectiveness in destroying men or guns could best be described as moderate. In Wainwright's judgment the cannonade was "by no means as effective as it should have been, nine-tenths [surely an exaggeration] of their shot passing over our men." It is certainly true that during this time the casualties were mostly borne by the artillerymen, who had to man their guns out in the open, whereas their infantry comrades lay down behind some sort of cover. The situation in Lieutenant Woodruff's Battery at Zeigler's Grove became so dire that he had to call for volunteers from the 108th New York to help man his guns. Similarly, Lieutenant Cushing at the Angle had a grim time, losing three caissons in one huge explosion, having four of his guns rendered unserviceable and being compelled to get infantrymen to replace lost gunners. Cushing was later killed, and his battery, the 4th U.S. Artillery, II Corps, suffered the highest losses (thirty-eight or 30 percent) of any Union battery at the battle. Thus most damage was inflicted on artillerymen, horses, caissons and limbers rather than on the infantry. Although Brigadier-General Webb, whose brigade (2nd Division, II Corps) was posted by the Angle and Copse of Trees, lost fifty men, it has been estimated that overall not more than 200 infantrymen were killed during this time. The Rebel bombardment was more successful, however, that many historians have made it out to be and this is best summarized in the Union chief of artillery's report:

> The destruction of the material was large. The enemy's cannonade, in which he must have almost exhausted his ammunition, was well sustained, and cost us a great many horses and the explosion of an unusually large number of caissons and limbers.

The author Richard Rollins has calculated that thirty-four Union guns failed to fire on the infantry assault, twenty-seven of them in the area of the Copse of Trees and the Angle. Of these, twelve were disabled by enemy fire, two had burst barrels and twenty were withdrawn as they were low on, or out of, ammunition. Good though this may have been, it was more than compensated for by the ability of the Union commanders to bring up replacement batteries when the cannonade ceased.

Union

Brigadier-General Henry J. Hunt, Meade's chief of artillery, fought Gettysburg with several significant advantages over his opposite number, Pendleton. They included having eighty-five more guns; having batteries of six pieces of the same type rather than mostly four mixed guns; having more plentiful ammunition of a higher quality (reliability); and having a powerful Army Artillery Reserve, which included additional ammunition above the normal holding. Hunt's after-action report clearly explains his plan for dealing with the Rebel attack he was certain would be made that morning, and is worth quoting at length:

> At 10 a.m. I made an inspection of the whole line, ascertaining that all the batteries – only those on our right serving with Twelfth Corps being engaged at the time – were in good condition and well supplied with ammunition. As the enemy was evidently increasing his artillery force in front of our left, I gave instructions to the batteries and to the chiefs of artillery not to fire at small bodies, nor to allow their fire to be drawn without promise of adequate results; to watch the enemy closely, and when he opened to concentrate the fire of their guns on one battery at a time until it was silenced; under all circumstances to fire deliberately, and to husband their ammunition as much as possible.
>
> I had just finished my inspection, and was with Lieutenant Rittenhouse on the top of [Little] Round Top, when the enemy opened at about 1 p.m., along his whole right, a furious cannonade on the left of our line. I estimated the number of his guns bearing on our west front from one hundred to one hundred and twenty [in a later letter he said 150, which was a more accurate estimate] . . . To oppose these we could not, from our restricted position, bring more than eighty to reply effectively. Our fire was well withheld until the first burst was over [about 15 minutes], excepting from the extreme right and left of our positions. It was then opened deliberately and with excellent effect. As soon as the nature of the enemy's attack was made clear, and I could form an opinion as to the number of his guns, for which my position afforded great facility, I went to the park of the Artillery Reserve, and ordered all the batteries to be ready to move at a moments notice, and hastened to report to the commanding general, but found he had left his headquarters. I then proceeded along the line, to observe the effects of the cannonade and to replace such batteries as should become disabled.

Hunt considered he had about eighty guns able to fire to the west, although he appears not to have included the Cemetery Hill or Little Round Top batteries, which would bring the total to approximately 130. He explained these tactics to artillery commanders along the line.

Hunt noted in his report that his guns initially refrained from firing except on the right and left flanks, omitting to mention that some centrally placed guns also fired. These flank batteries belonged to Osborn and McGilvery respectively. On Cemetery Hill, Osborn's gunners responded to the rain of Rebel shells by firing back as fast as they could load, sending off shots at the rate of at least three a minute in response to the guns on Benner's and Oak Hills and near the railroad cut, shots from which were raking his position. The reason for a number of batteries immediately returning fire was that Major-General Hancock, the corps commander, was busy countermanding Hunt's instructions. Hancock insisted that Union batteries should reply if only for the morale of his infantry, who he claimed would become demoralized lying under heavy enemy fire while their own gunners did nothing. When he tackled his own corps' artillery commander, Captain John C. Hazard, as to why he was not firing, the reply that it was on Hunt's orders infuriated the quick-tempered Hancock – who always swore at everybody, particularly on a battlefield. Hazard was told forcefully and colorfully that he was to do as his corps commander required: open fire. Cushing's Battery joined in. Similarly, on the left Hancock ordered McGilvery's guns to open up. Captain Charles A. Phillips, commanding the 5th Massachusetts Battery in McGilvery's line, had this to say about the effectiveness of the Confederate fire on his part of the line:

> As artillery ammunition was rather short, we had been ordered not to reply to their batteries, and so we could lie still and enjoy it. My men were entirely sheltered by our parapet [thrown up on McGilvery's orders during the morning], and about the only damage done was to kill 8 or 10 horses.
>
> Viewed as a display of fireworks, the rebel practice was entirely successful, but as a military demonstration it was the biggest humbug of the season: . . . about half past one, Gen. Hancock ordered us to reply, thereby showing how little an infantry officer knows about artillery. The rebels were doing us no harm . . . however we obeyed orders. Fortunately, Maj. [Lt.-Col.] McGilvery came up and stopped us before we had fired a great while.

It was this cessation that convinced the Southern batteries of Alexander's line to switch their fire to the Copse of Trees area – the result being that McGilvery's guns suffered the least from the enemy cannonade and had plenty of ammunition to expend on the advancing Rebel infantry. Nevertheless, dense clouds of white smoke soon enveloped both Seminary and Cemetery Ridges as the artillery duel got under way. A Union captain declared that

A Union Colonel Chases a Frightened Flag-bearer

Captain Abner Small, 16th Maine, later recounted an incident that occurred at the height of the Confederate cannonade near Meade's headquarters:

> Colonel [Richard] Coulter [then commanding Paul's Brigade of the 2nd Division, I Corps], tearing up and down the line to work off his impatience, all of a sudden drew rein and shouted: "Where in hell is my flag? Where do you think that cowardly son of a bitch has skeddadled to? Adjutant, you hunt him up and bring him to the front!"
>
> Away I went, hunting for the missing flag and man and finding them nowhere; and returned in time to see the colonel snake the offender from out from behind a stone wall, where he had lain down with the flag folded up to avoid attracting attention. Colonel Coulter shook out the folds, put the staff in the hands of the trembling man, and double quicked him to the front. A shell exploded close by, killing a horse, and sending a blinding shower of gravel and dirt broadcast. The colonel snatched up the flag again, planted the end of the staff where the shell had burst, and shouted:
>
> "There, Orderly; hold it! If I can't get you killed in ten minutes, by God, I'll post you right up among the batteries!" Turning to ride away he grinned broadly and yelled to me: "The poor devil couldn't be safer; two shells don't often hit the same place. If he obeys he'll be all right and I'll know where my headquarters are."

"objects could not be seen [at] a distance of 4 rods [22 yards]," while the smoke meant Cushing was reduced to firing more or less blind. Twelve hundred yards away across the valley, Lieutenant James F. Crocker in the 9th Virginia Infantry (Armistead's Brigade), watching from the edge of Spangler Woods, could see only the muzzle flashes of his own guns through the haze hiding the Emmitsburg Road.

Despite Hunt's having twenty rounds of extra ammunition in the reserve train, a number of Union batteries, particularly those in II Corps, ran short. Major Osborn wrote:

> Our fire to the front and on the flank rapidly used up the ammunition, and I ordered the ammunition chests to be refilled from the army ordnance train while the fighting was in full progress. This was done by sending one, two or more caissons at a time to have the caissons filled . . . While fire on Cemetery Hill was at its height, General Meade rode up into the batteries at great speed . . . as he came within hearing he shouted, "Where is Major Osborn?" As he came near me, I answered him. He then shouted, apparently greatly excited, "What are you drawing ammunition from the train for?" I said that some of the ammunition chests were giving out. He then said, "Don't you know that it is a violation of general orders and the army regulations to use up all your ammunition in a battle?" I replied that I had given that no thought and that General Hunt had directed me to draw what I might require from the ordnance train.

Hancock's after-action report confirmed that II Corps ran out of long-range ammunition:

> The artillery of the corps, imperfectly supplied with ammunition, replied to the enemy most gallantly . . . Brown's battery (B, First Rhode Island), which had suffered severely on the 2d, and expended all its canister on that day, retired before the cannonading ceased, not being effective for further service. The remaining batteries continued their fire until only canister remained to them, and then ceased . . .

While some batteries ceased firing due to ammunition shortages, and McGilvery's due to his repeated order to stop once Hancock had left the vicinity, when the general ceasefire took place it was primarily due to Hunt's desire, backed by Meade, that this would be the best way of convincing the enemy that they had won the artillery duel and it was therefore time to launch the infantry across the valley. It was always intended to lure the Rebels into the open and then hit them hard with artillery restocked with ammunition. After the cannonading had been going on for some time and ammunition was becoming a problem, Hunt determined to stop all Union guns firing, otherwise he worried that his plan would be thwarted. He sought out Meade for the authority. However, he was unable to locate him and instead conferred with Major-General Howard, who was, according to Major Osborn, himself on Cemetery Hill. Hunt suggested, with Howard's concurrence, that all the guns be ordered to cease fire (Osborn later insisted he originated the suggestion). Hunt then returned to Cemetery Ridge and rode down the line giving the order. In doing so he met Captain Henry Bingham, an aide on Hancock's staff, who told him that Meade's aides were looking for him with orders to stop the artillery fire. It appears that Brigadier-General Warren on Little Round Top had come to the same conclusion and sent an aide to Meade with the proposal. His message read:

> July 3, 1863/2 pm from Round Top sig sta
> To Gen Meade
>
> It would be better if all our guns ceased firing. The enemy do no damage, and are trying to get up a smoke to cover their infantry. When they advance I will open on them from this bat [Lt Rittenhouse].
>
> G. K. Warren

Meade had agreed. Thus it would seem that Hunt, Howard, Osborn, Warren and Meade made the decision almost simultaneously. It was the right decision. Afterward Meade claimed the overall credit when he recalled:

> After I became fully satisfied of the object of the enemy fire, I directed my artillery to cease fire in order to save their ammunition, and also with a view of making the enemy believe that they had silenced their [our] guns, and thus bring on the assault sooner. It resulted as I desired. As soon as we ceased firing the enemy ceased firing, and shortly afterwards they made their assault.

Confederate Problems

There is little doubt that the Confederates planned the cannonade in considerable detail and that the orders for it were specific with regard to the target, rate of fire and ammunition expenditure. Alexander later wrote:

> among the very unjust &, indeed absurd criticisms which poor Gen. Longstreet's detractors have brought against him, in connection with this battle, is one to the effect that Gen. Lee's orders were disobeyed & neglected the handling of our artillery in Pickett's Charge. Now the orders which I received, both from Longstreet and Pendleton were quite specific, & were carried out to the letter . . .

Despite the difficulties enumerated below, the Rebel bombardment did inflict serious losses on the enemy artillery in the area attacked by infantry (particularly the batteries of Cushing, Brown, Rorty and Thomas). In this central area, some thirty-four guns had been silenced by the time the Rebel infantry started their advance. Twelve had been disabled by gunfire, two had burst barrels and twenty had been withdrawn to avoid enemy fire or due to lack of ammunition. Nevertheless, the primary objective of the Confederate cannonade, that of so damaging the Union artillery that it was unable to bring substantial fire onto Pickett's assault, was not achieved. Apart from their not employing over a third of their guns, the reasons for which have been discussed above (page 465) and some poor coordination by the Rebel chief of artillery, Pendleton, there were a number of other problems. In combination, these helped to ensure less effective results than had been anticipated from such a spectacular pounding by so many guns for so long. They were:

1. Technical and tactical difficulties
2. The Union artillery response
3. Ammunition supply

Technical and tactical difficulties

Many of the Rebel projectiles were fired with the wrong elevation of the barrels; it was often set too high, with the result that the shots passed over the Union gun line and fell or burst in the rear of the Union positions on Cemetery Ridge. One Confederate reported that they cut their fuses for 1.25 miles, which, if correct, was far too long a range. This firing high was commented on by Hunt, Meade's chief of artillery, who said, "Most of the enemy's projectiles passed overhead [crucially, from the Confederates' point of view, these shots missed the Union guns], the effect being to sweep all the open ground in our rear, which was little benefit to the Confederates – a mere waste of ammunition." McGilvery commented that the enemy's fire was "very rapid and inaccurate, most of the projectiles passing from 20 to 100 feet above our lines." This view was endorsed by Osborn, who reported:

> As a rule, the fire of the enemy on all our front against Cemetery Hill was a little high. Their range or direction was perfect, but the elevation carried a very large proportion of their shells about twenty feet above our heads. The air just above us was full of shells and fragments of shells. Indeed if the enemy had been as successful in securing our elevation as they did the range there would have been not a living thing on the hill fifteen minutes after they opened fire. The batteries on our right flank [Nelson's guns on Benner's Hill] did secure both range and elevation perfectly, but in a few minutes we so demoralized them that they lost the elevation but not the direction, and they too fired high. As it was we suffered severely.

For maximum effect on the enemy's batteries, the Rebel gunners had to hit, or get shells to burst over, a very narrow, linear target stretched along the crest, or just on the forward slope, of Cemetery Ridge or Hill. This entailed accurate estimates of the range, the length of fuse needed and the correct elevation of the barrel from gunners who had little or no practice and had been unable to fire ranging shots. Although elevation tables (see page 163) were pasted inside the lids of ammunition boxes, to hit a strip of land up to a mile long but only 100 yards deep at a range of 1,200 yards was no easy task. As noted above by Osborn, even with the correct elevation, when the gunners came under fire themselves they became flustered, if not frightened, with detrimental effects on accuracy.

The unreliability of ammunition and fuses, which have been discussed in detail in Section Three: Artillery (pages 162–65), certainly played a major part in reducing the effectiveness of the cannonade. As Alexander put it, "its imperfections affected the fire . . . of the guns." Shells failed to explode, or did so too early or too late due to faulty or inappropriately cut fuses. It is worth remembering that it was the unreliability of fuses in shells that caused Dance's batteries to be ordered to fire only solid shot during the cannonade, as they were firing over the heads of Rodes' troops deployed along Long Lane (see also Section Three: Artillery, page 165). It is impossible to know what proportion of Rebel shells failed to explode or failed to do so when they should have done due to faulty fuses or fuses cut wrongly. Alexander estimated the number at 80 percent, a figure that, if even nearly true, would have had a very significant and detrimental effect. Unexploded ordnance was the source of ready cash to a number of small boys in the weeks after the battle (see box). This problem was compounded by so many Rebel batteries having mixed pieces, with the consequent difficulties in supplying them with the correct type and caliber of ammunition. It was just too easy for ordnance staff in a hurry, or short of the right caliber, to issue 3-inch ordnance rifle or "Navy" Parrott rounds for a 2.9-inch 10-pounder Parrott, leading to rounds getting lodged in the barrel or, worse, a burst barrel. Captain Green, in Jones's Battalion, told of one of his guns being put out of action:

> I had four guns in the engagement (two 10-pounder Parrott Rifles and two 3-inch Yankee rifles). Early in the action, one of the Parrotts was disabled by a shot too large lodging half way down the bore, which we found impossible to force home, and had to retire the piece.

Add the fact that with constant use barrels became overheated, sometimes red-hot, forcing firing to cease so the barrel could be cooled with water (if available); Captain Wallace stopped firing a number of times for this reason.

The obscuring of the target by smoke from guns of both sides undoubtedly affected the accuracy of a proportion of the Rebels' firing. Not only did it make estimating the range difficult, but it also often obscured the strike of the shot. With so many shells landing or bursting in the area, it was virtually impossible to judge which shell came from which battery, so that adjustment became impossible or merely guesswork.

The Confederates did not have a high enough proportion of the longer-range rifled cannon to achieve maximum effect in the bombardment. Lee was attacking, which meant that, generally speaking, he needed longer-range guns, whereas Meade on the defensive needed shorter-range Napoleons. The Rebels were unable to make use of their canister ammunition on July 3, as they could not get their guns far enough forward to make its use appropriate. They also had thirty howitzers, short-range indirect-fire weapons, most of which were kept back for the hoped-for artillery advance. However, a serious tactical error – and this was

Scavenging

After the armies had marched away from Gettysburg they left behind not only thousands of dead and injured men and horses, but also millions of bullets and thousands of unexploded shells – sources of lead for which the government would pay 13 cents a pound. When the inhabitants of Gettysburg found this out, scavenging for bullets lodged in walls and fences became a favorite activity for numerous young boys.

It was soon discovered that unexploded artillery shells contained scores of small lead balls and so the dangerous business of opening the shells and scooping out the lead balls became a common activity. A fourteen-year-old lad called Albertus McCreary and his friends spent days searching for these rich sources of lead. A common way of opening the shells was to pile some up and set them alight then scamper away to a safe distance and await the explosion. According to McCreary's diary, "It made a racket that put the Fourth of July in the shade" – although it must have made finding the lead balls much more difficult.

One of McCreary's friends unscrewed the cap of a shell and, before he could be warned to put water in it, banged it on a rock. The resultant explosion mortally wounded the boy. Similar accidents occurred in the town, with one man losing a leg and both hands.

Unexploded Confederate ordnance has been found recently on the site of the new Visitor Center at the Gettysburg National Military Park.

certainly down to Pendleton and the artillery commanders in Hill's and Ewell's Corps – was the failure to make use of the maximum number of long-range rifled cannon that they did have. Excluding those on the extreme Rebel right, no fewer than twenty-seven (27 percent of those available) out of 119 such cannon were not employed in the cannonade – mainly those in Garnett's, Latimer's and Jones's Battalions.

The Union artillery response

Although some accounts of the battle on July 3 barely mention it in such terms, there was a lengthy artillery duel prior to the main Rebel infantry attack. Most Union batteries on Cemetery Ridge and Hill engaged in counterbattery fire, even if they did not fire for long as it was against Hunt's orders. The facts that some guns ran short of long-range ammunition and that casualties were inflicted on the Confederates are proof that the Union artillery response was fierce and sustained. This undoubtedly affected the accuracy of the Rebel cannonade, not only by inflicting casualties on men and horses but also by unnerving the gunners, making them flustered and frightened and so leading to mistakes being made. There is considerable evidence that, like the Rebel gunners, the Yankees also tended to fire high, with many projectiles overshooting their primary target, the gun line. Confederate overs tended to hit the soon to be emptied reverse slope of Cemetery Ridge, while Union overs hit the waiting infantry regiments. It is probably true to say that, on balance, the artillery duel caused more damage to the Union batteries than to the infantry line, whereas for the Confederates the opposite was the case.

Interestingly, it was the Rebel artillery opposite McGilvery's batteries that suffered the most, even though his guns did not fire for as long as most of the others. One Confederate battery that was virtually crippled by this fire was the howitzer battery under Lieutenant Stephen C. Gilbert (Alexander's Battalion), which lost thirty-six men killed and wounded out of seventy-one engaged, twenty-five horses, two caissons, and two out of four howitzers disabled. Close by, the heavy howitzers of Captain George V. Moody (also Alexander) were almost equally badly hit, although not in percentage terms, losing thirty-three men out of 135. But also under Alexander's command, though not facing McGilvery, were Major Dearing's four batteries, where out of 420 men only twenty-four became casualties. Examples of damage to guns include a broken axle on a 3-inch ordnance rifle (Richardson) and another on a Napoleon (Norcom). Another of Norcom's Napoleons could not be loaded as the barrel was dented and a 3-inch rifle had a wheel shot away (McCarthy).

Some of the heaviest incoming fire was directed at the Rebel batteries under Alexander deployed along or close to the Emmitsburg Road. Two hundred yards behind the guns in the swale, 1,600 men of Brigadier-General James L. Kemper (Pickett's Division) were lying down in the broiling sun. Major Walter G. Harrison, on Pickett's staff, later recorded what he saw:

> The enemy had the exact range of our lines of battle, and just overshooting the artillery opposed to them, as usual, their shot and shell told with effect on the infantry, exposed as they were without cover of any sort . . . Many of the men, and several valuable officers were killed or disabled long before a movement was ordered; but the line remained steadily fixed . . .

Kemper was amazed to see his corps commander riding calmly along the line amid the hail of shot and shell. "I expected to see him fall every instant. Still he moved on, slowly and majestically, with an inspiring confidence, composure, self-possession . . ." Colonel Joseph C. Mayo, commanding the 3rd Virginia, left a grim account of how the infantry were suffering:

> The first shot or two flew harmlessly over our heads; but soon they began to get the range, and then came "pandemonium." First there was an explosion in the top of our friendly tree, sending showers of limbs upon us. In a second there was another, followed by a piercing shriek, which caused Patton [Colonel Waller T. Patton, commanding the 7th Virginia] to spring up and run to see what was the matter. Two killed and three frightfully wounded, he said on his return. Immediately after a like cry came from another apple tree close by in the midst of the Third [Virginia]. Company F has suffered terribly; First Lieutenant A. P. Gomer, legs shattered below the knee; one of the Arthur brothers, second and third lieutenants, one killed the other badly hit; Orderly Sergeant Murray mortally wounded, and of the privates, one killed and three wounded. Then for more than an hour it went on. Nearly every minute the cry of mortal agony was heard above the roar and rumble of the guns.

Garnett's Brigade on Kemper's left fared almost as badly, with the 8th Virginia having five killed by enemy gunfire. Private Randolph Shotwell of Company H described what he saw:

> The cannoneers opened their ammunition chests; the caison [*sic*] drivers crouch in shallow trenches they have scooped out for their protection . . . [With the cannonade underway] The earth quivered under the incessant concussion . . . I watched the struggles of wounded artillery horse, when a shell whizzed over my head and struck behind me . . . I also glanced around, and saw a most shocking spectacle. The heavy missile had descended six feet behind me, and plowed through the bodies of Morris and Jackson of my company . . .
>
> This was within the first ten minutes. Presently the air seemed full of flying lead and iron . . . Fortunately the Federal gunners began to aim higher, supposing the woods to our rear to be full of troops [this was Spangler Woods, with Armistead's Brigade lining the edge], and sending most of the missiles screaming beyond us.

In general it is true that the Union gunners gave almost as good as they received. They had the advantage of being able to bring forward reserve batteries to replace those unable to fire for any reason. The artillerymen of both sides were mostly in the open, visible and therefore very vulnerable, yet almost without exception they stood their ground, manned their guns and took their punishment. According to Alexander, writing later, the losses during the artillery duel "including the infantry that volunteered to help serve the guns, were 144 men and 116 horses, nearly all by artillery fire."

Ammunition supply

Colonel Alexander had originally planned for a brief but intense bombardment of the Union line, lasting fifteen to twenty minutes. This would be sufficient, so he thought, to suppress the enemy guns. Longstreet had given him the responsibility for deciding when the Yankee artillery had been sufficiently neutralized and the moment had arrived to order the infantry forward. Alexander soon realized that twenty minutes was not going to be anywhere near long enough.

> Before the cannonade opened I had made up my mind to give Pickett the order to advance within fifteen or twenty minutes after it began. But when I looked at the full development of the enemies batteries, and knew that his infantry was generally protected from our fire by stone walls and swells of the ground, I could not bring myself to give the word. It seemed madness to launch infantry into that fire, with three quarters of a mile to go in the midday July sun. I let the fifteen minutes pass, and twenty and twenty-five, hoping vainly for something to turn up.

Alexander's timings as to the length of the bombardment are suspect, as it has been established that the cannonade lasted for much longer than twenty-five minutes; but the above quote shows clearly how Alexander, knowing the limited ammunition supply available, wanted a furious fifteen minutes of fire concentrated on the enemy guns, as this would leave enough ammunition in the limbers and caissons for his guns to follow up the infantry and give them close support. A lengthy initial bombardment could jeopardize the whole plan. In the event, the Rebel guns had to keep firing for up to two hours, with numerous batteries running short of, or out of, ammunition. This would have a hugely significant effect on the ability of the Confederate artillery to assist the infantry during its long, exposed advance toward Cemetery Ridge. The seriousness of the situation is shown by the following four quotes

Colonel R. Lindsay Walker, commanding Hill's artillery:

> The artillery was retained in the same position on the 3d, and kept up an incessant fire from about 1 p.m. to the time of the advance of the infantry. This fire having been continued so long and with such rapidity, the ammunition was almost exhausted.

Captain Robert M. Stribling, commanding the Fanquier Artillery Battery (Dearing's Battalion):

> One-half hour before Pickett's division was put in motion, almost all the artillery ammunition was exhausted along the line, and none could be obtained from the ordnance train in time to be of service.

Major James Dearing, commanding Pickett's artillery battalion:

> About this time [when most Union guns ceased firing] my ammunition became completely exhausted, excepting a few rounds in my rifled guns . . . I had sent back my caissons an hour and a half before for a fresh supply, but they could not get it.

Colonel Eppa Hunton, commanding the 8th Virginia Infantry, saw Dearing galloping to the rear with his caissons just before the infantry advanced, and heard him shouting:

> For God's sake, wait till I get some ammunition and I will drive every Yankee from the heights.

So what had gone wrong? Three factors combined to produce an ammunition crisis. First, the Confederates' ammunition holdings, even at the start of the campaign, were far from generous and resupply by wagon train from Staunton was always going to be slow; second, the cannonade went on much longer than was intended, as the Union guns could not be suppressed quickly; third, the batteries could not restock from the reserve ammunition train as it had been moved further back, and battery commanders and caisson drivers could not find it.

According to Captain Robert Bright, an officer on Pickett's staff, an order was received in the early hours of July 3 that stated, "Col. E. P. Alexander will command the entire [corps] artillery in action today, and Brigadier-General Pendleton will have charge of the reserve artillery ammunition of the army." After Pickett's assault had gone in, and as his right flank was seen to be under threat by a Union force, Bright rode up to Dearing's gun line to get the batteries to fire on the Yankee troops. The first officer he met was a Captain William C. Marshall, to whom Bright gave the order. According to Bright, Marshall's response was, "The battalion has no ammunition. I have only three solid shot." When asked why this was so, Marshall replied, "The caissons had been away nearly three quarters of an hour there was a rumor that General Pendleton had sent the reserve artillery ammunition more than a mile in rear of the field."

Comments

- The artillery plan was detailed and considered comprehensive. In the event the Confederates had all morning to prepare, consult and issue orders. Ammunition chests were full, battery commanders knew their targets, ranges could be judged and fuses cut accordingly. There had been, unintentionally perhaps, plenty of time to get organized. Yet the artillery plan did not deliver the success needed.

- The reason for this failure, or more accurately partial failure, was a combination of problems compounded by an effective enemy response. Despite having the time, the Confederate leadership, with the exception of Alexander, failed to employ the maximum number of guns and in particular left out a substantial number of rifled cannon from the cannonade. Insufficient use was made of their advantage of exterior lines, which gave the opportunity of bringing enfilade fire onto Cemetery Hill and Ridge, and there was a serious underestimation of the time it would take to suppress the enemy's guns. This meant the bombardment was extended for up to two hours, consequently emptying many ammunition caissons that could not replenish because the reserve train could not be found. It was this ammunition shortage, plus the fact that nine howitzers held in reserve had also disappeared (see page 476), that meant that few guns were available to follow up the infantry attack. To these command errors must be added the technical problems of an overall shortage of long-range guns, a high proportion of faulty ammunition, incorrectly cut fuses and misjudged elevation of some barrels, leading to the failure of many projectiles to explode at all or to explode at the correct time, and too many shots going high and missing their intended target.

- Of equal importance to all the above was the reaction of the Union artillery. They had the advantage of good-quality ammunition; had reserve batteries able to replace disabled ones; and were able to inflict appreciable losses on the Rebel batteries and waiting infantry. The Union artillery leadership was excellent and their plan to cease fire to encourage the Rebel infantry to advance worked perfectly, with numerous batteries able to spring to life again as the Rebel regiments began their long walk in the sun.

PICKETT GETS HIS ORDER TO ADVANCE

Under Lee, Longstreet was the officer placed in overall charge of the Rebel attack on the Union center on July 3, yet he seemed reluctant to exercise that responsibility when it came to actually giving the order personally to Pickett, who was the divisional commander of the three brigades on the right of the advance. Longstreet's preferred method was to have Alexander tell Pickett when he thought the Rebel artillery had sufficiently neutralized the enemy guns. It was putting a huge responsibility on the artillery colonel and appeared to reflect Longstreet's general opposition to the attack. He certainly gave the impression that he wanted to pass this particular buck to his juniors when he sent the following message to Alexander that morning:

> Colonel: If the artillery fire does not have the effect to drive off the enemy or greatly demoralize him, so as to make our efforts pretty certain, I would prefer you not to advise Pickett to make the charge. I shall rely greatly on your judgment to determine the matter and shall expect you to let Gen. Pickett know when the moment offers.

None too happy at being given this responsibility, Alexander responded:

> General: I will only be able to judge of the effects of our fire on the enemy by his return fire, as his infantry is but little exposed to view and the smoke will obscure the whole field. If, as I infer from your note, there is an alternative to this attack, it should be carefully considered before opening our fire, for it will take all the artillery ammunition we have left to test this one, and if the result is unfavorable we will have none left for another effort. And even if this is entirely successful, it can only be so at a very bloody cost.

The exchange continued with Longstreet's reply:

> Colonel: The intention is to advance the infantry if the artillery has the desired effect of driving the enemy's off, or having other effect such as to warrant us in making the attack. When that moment arrives advise Gen. Pickett and of course advance such artillery as you can in aiding the attack.

Twice Longstreet had told his artillery chief that the decision to launch the attack was to be his. Alexander was obliged to accept this unwanted task. He replied, "General: when our fire is doing its best, I will advise General Pickett to advance."

As noted above, Alexander had wanted a short but intense, concentrated cannonade to conserve ammunition and quickly overwhelm the opposition's guns. It did not happen that way, and the artillery duel was sustained and fierce along the entire line. Alexander had seriously underestimated the time and weight of fire required. After a far longer bombardment than he anticipated, with no appreciable diminution of the enemy's fire, and with ammunition dwindling, Alexander reluctantly sent Pickett the order to advance:

> General: If you are to advance at all, you must come at once or we will not be able to support you [during the advance] as we ought. But the enemy's fire has not slackened materially and there are still 18 guns firing from the cemetery.

It was at about this time that the deceptive lull in Union artillery fire occurred. Batteries were being ordered to cease fire, coupled with the withdrawal and replacement of some batteries. There was a distinct slackening of fire – not a complete cessation, but a very substantial reduction. Alexander waited a few minutes before sending another note to Pickett: "For God's sake come quick. The 18 guns have gone. Come quick or my ammunition will not let me support you properly."

When Alexander wrote his *Military Memoirs* he gave in considerable detail the moment when the order to advance was confirmed, with, according to Alexander, considerable doubt and reluctance. Referring to this last note, he wrote:

> This was followed by two verbal messages to the same effect from an officer and sergeant from the nearest guns. The 18 guns had occupied the point at which our charge was to be directed I had been incorrectly told it was the cemetery. Soon only a few scattered federal guns were in action, and still Pickett's line had not come forward, though scarcely 300 yards behind my guns.
>
> I afterward learned what had followed the sending of my first note ["If you are to advance at all, you must come at once"]. It reached Pickett in Longstreet's presence. He read it and handed it to Longstreet. Longstreet read and stood silent. Pickett said, "General, shall I advance?" [passing the buck back to where it really belonged]. Longstreet knew it must be done, but was unwilling to speak the words. He turned in his saddle and looked away. Pickett saluted and said, "I am going to move forward, sir" and galloped off.
>
> Longstreet, leaving his staff, rode out alone and joined me on the left flank of the guns. It was doubtless 1.50 or later [it was later], but I did not look at my watch again. I had grown very impatient to see Pickett, fearing ammunition would run short [it already had], when Longstreet joined me. I explained the situation. He spoke sharply, – "Go and stop Pickett where he is and replenish your ammunition." I answered: "We can't do that, sir. The train has but little. It would take an hour to distribute it, and meanwhile the enemy would improve the time."
>
> Longstreet seemed to stand irresolute (we were both dismounted) and then spoke slowly and with great emotion: "I do not want to make this charge. I do not see how it can succeed. I would not make it now but that Gen. Lee has ordered it" . . . The suspense was brief and was ended by the emergence from the wood [actually an orchard] behind us of Garnett . . . I mounted and rode with him while his brigade swept through our guns. Then I rode down the line of guns, asking what each gun had left. Many had canister only. These and all having but a few shell were ordered to stand fast. Those with a moderate amount of ammunition were ordered to limber up and advance.

An important element of the plan was for as many guns as were able to fire over the heads of the advancing infantry wherever possible and for as long as possible, and at the same time for batteries to move forward to go into action just out of effective musket range to give close supporting fire. Part of this support was to be provided by the nine howitzers under Major Richardson that Alexander had been loaned by Pendleton prior to the start of the cannonade. The problem was they could not be found. Alexander stated that Pendleton had taken back four, while the other five had been moved to a more secure place out of the range of Union shells. Whatever the truth, as far as Alexander was concerned they had disappeared and could not be used when the attack got under way. Instead of numerous batteries moving forward, Alexander later said:

> I got, I think, fifteen or eighteen in all in a little while and went with them. Meanwhile the infantry had no sooner debouched on the plain than all the enemy's line, which had been nearly silent, broke out again with all its batteries. The eighteen guns were back in the cemetery and a storm of shell began bursting over and among our infantry. All of our guns, silent as the infantry passed between them, reopened when the lines had got a couple of hundred yards away, but the enemy's artillery let us alone and fired only at the infantry.

Union Skirmishers Suffer Under the Sun

Captain Silas Adams, 19th Maine (2nd Division, II Corps), described the effect of lying for hours in the open on picket duty under a blistering sun.

> To say that these companies had a severe and terrible day out there would be putting it very mildly, for no man could raise his head without receiving a compliment from the enemy's skirmish line, and I dare say we made it fully as uncomfortable for them. The heat in the glaring sun was intolerable, and we had been without food and water since the morning before, and our stomachs were getting to be a little shaky.

Adams recalled what happened as the Rebel advance approached:

> The thought came to me if we were able to get back, having lain there from sunrise to three P.M. on our faces in the burning sun, we were pretty well cooked through. When the enemy came near us we arose and started for the rear, and I can speak only from my own experience in describing my attempt to walk. I found I had no use of my legs, having lain so long that they had become numb or paralyzed, but in a few moments they got into working order so I could trudge slowly to the rear.

Highlight: The Confederate Infantry Assault

The leading five Confederate infantry brigades stepped off on what was to become America's most famous Civil War assault at around 3:00 p.m. Within less than five minutes the second wave of four brigades followed them. In under an hour the remnants had come streaming back, leaving behind thousands of dead, wounded and prisoners. Lee's final fling at Gettysburg had failed, and his only realistic option was to withdraw his army and retreat south down the Shenandoah Valley, his invasion of the North at an end. This Rebel charge was called by some the "high water mark of the Confederacy"; indeed there is a High Water Mark Memorial near the furthest spot on Cemetery Ridge reached by a handful of Southerners, as some believed – almost certainly erroneously – that had it succeeded the Confederacy might have survived.

The ground (Maps 61 and 62)

In general terms, the ground to be crossed by the attacking brigades was an open plain between the Seminary_and Cemetery Ridges, some 1,450 yards across at its widest point – the strip of woods opposite the Copse of Trees and the copse itself. This was approximately the distance that Pettigrew's men, the first to move off, would have to cover to reach their objective. With no impediments to movement and over a good surface, moving at quick-time (officially 82 yards a minute) but keeping formation in line, 1,450 yards might be covered in eighteen minutes. But that was not the situation for the Rebels that blisteringly hot afternoon. The ground was uneven, there were fences to cross, including the double fence along the Emmitsburg Road, large orchards near the Bliss and Codori Farms and a slope to climb up to the crest of Cemetery Hill. Add in the heat, the constant need to keep up proper alignment, and above all the fact that they were under fire and losing men for much of the way, to cover the distance in twenty to twenty-five minutes would be a very reasonable achievement.

The High Water Mark Memorial, commemorating the climax of Pickett's charge, with the Copse of Trees behind.

The present writer watched and timed a re-enactment group of the 26th North Carolina Infantry walk the ground that regiment covered in the charge, from the North Carolina State Memorial to the Angle – a distance of 1,400 yards. They started at 9:55 a.m. and charged home at 10:13 a.m., having indeed taken eighteen minutes. They had paused briefly to re-form after crossing the first fence line, and again for slightly longer after the Emmitsburg Road fences; otherwise their walk had been at a steady pace, covering about 78 yards a minute – slightly faster than the "common-time" march rate of 1863. From these estimates, and taking into account the battlefield situation at the time, it is likely that those members of Pettigrew's brigades that reached the enemy line took around twenty to twenty-five minutes to get there. There would not have been many of the 26th North Carolina among them, as it suffered the highest number of losses, 687, or 82 percent, of any regiment in either army during the battle – virtually all sustained during Pickett's charge. Captain Louis G. Young, one of Pettigrew's aides, commented on the ground over which Marshall's Brigade advanced:

> The ground over which we had to pass was perfectly open, numerous fences, some parallel and some oblique, to our lines of battle, were formidable impediments in our way.

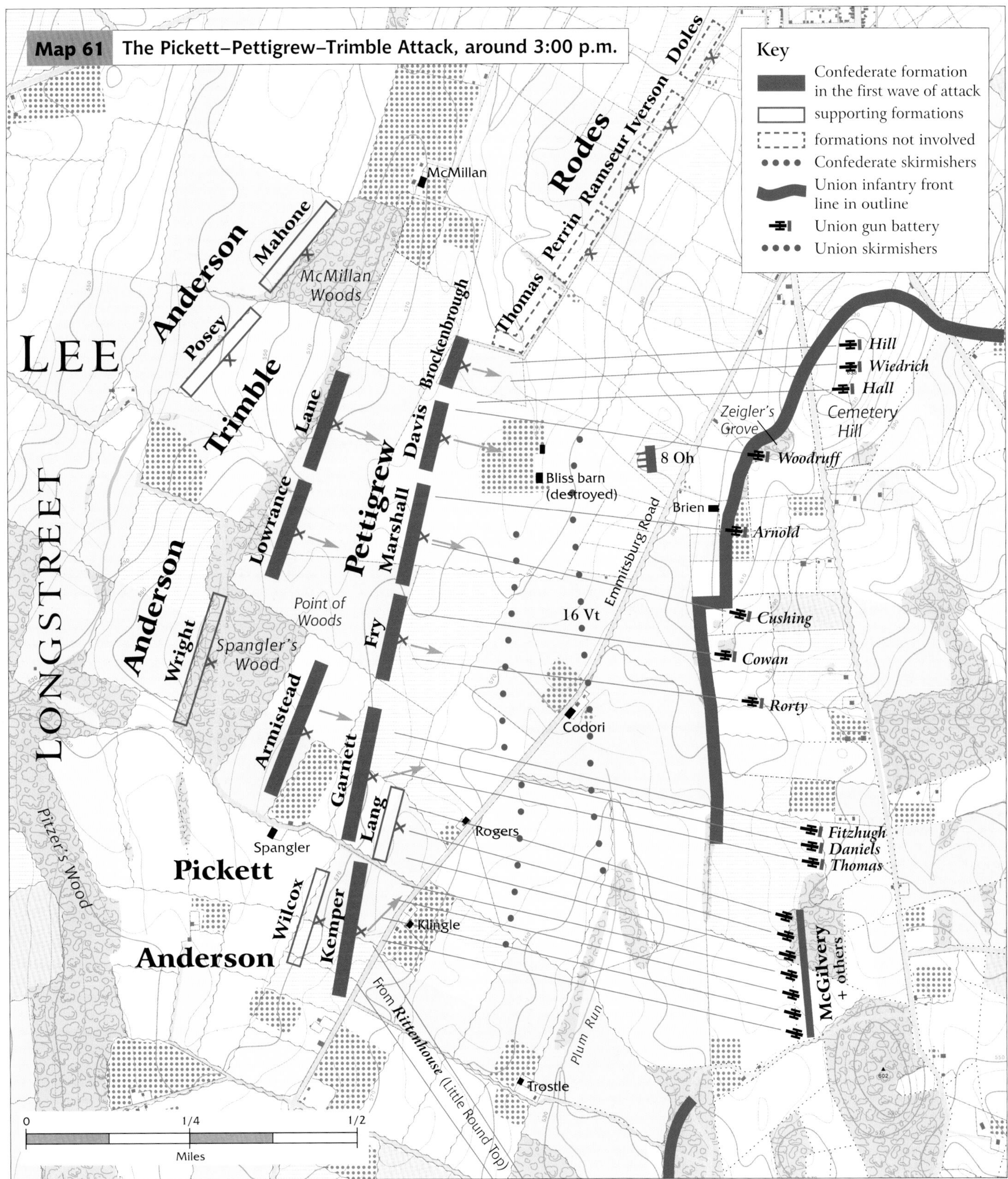

Notes

• This map shows the start of the Pickett–Pettigrew–Trimble attack. It does not depict the Confederate artillery lines and only the Union infantry in outline. Most Union gun batteries had six pieces and those shown firing were the principal ones in action against the infantry at this stage. At least 100 guns were involved, with the heaviest fire hitting Kemper and Garnett, and, from Cemetery Hill, Brockenbrough.

• There were six brigades in the leading line of the attack, with three more following in the second – in total nearly 12,000 men. At this stage Pettigrew's and Trimble's brigades had passed through the Rebel gun line but Pickett's had yet to do so. Kemper and Garnett were starting their left incline to close on Pettigrew's right flank. Apart from the skirmishers, there was no musketry fire at this time.

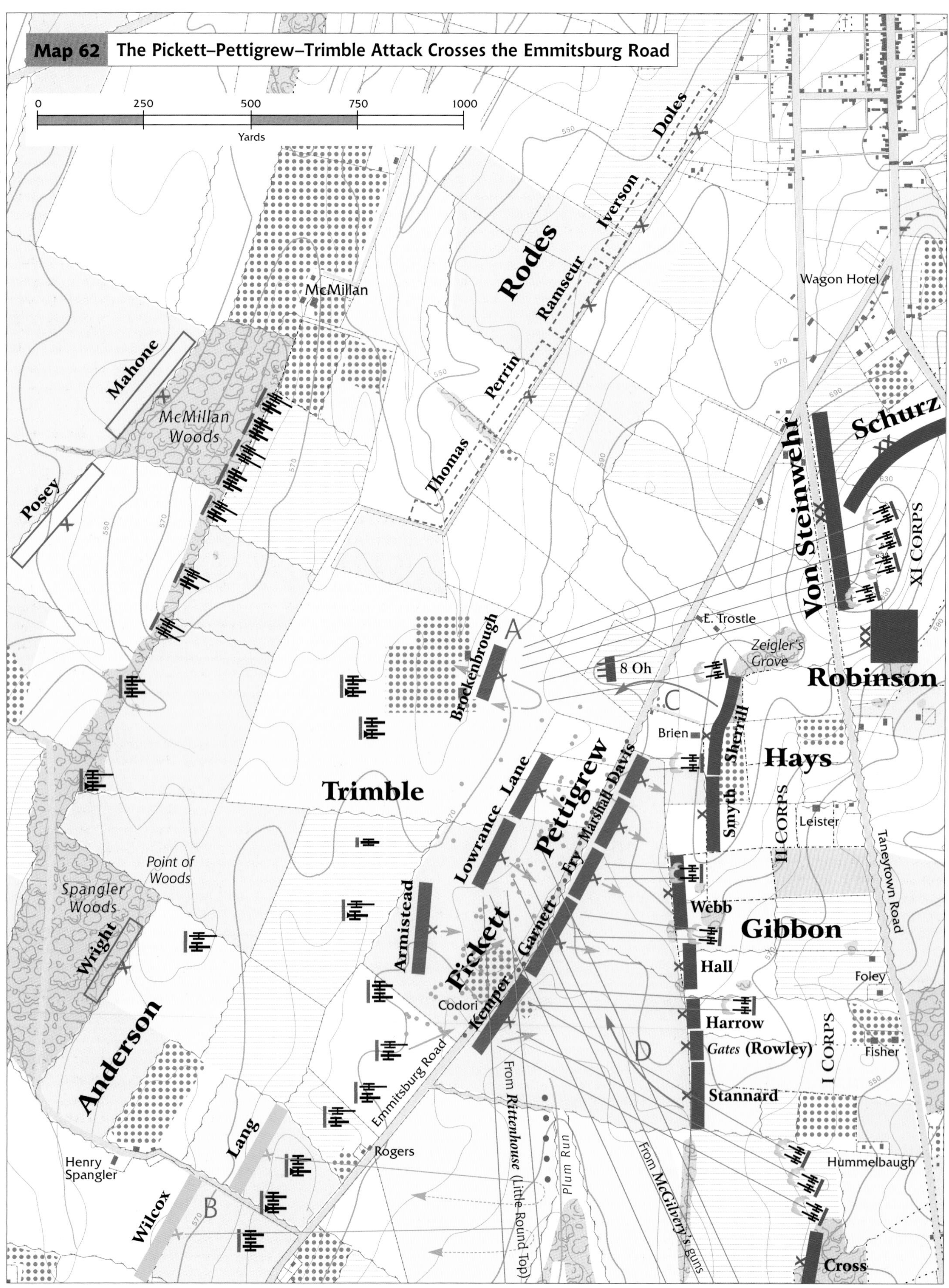
Map 62 The Pickett–Pettigrew–Trimble Attack Crosses the Emmitsburg Road
0
250
500
750
1000
Yards
Doles
Iverson
Rodes
Ramseur
Perrin
Thomas
McMillan
Mahone
McMillan Woods
Posey
Wagon Hotel
Schurz
Von Steinwehr
XI CORPS
E. Trostle
Zeigler's Grove
Robinson
A
Brockenbrough
8 Oh
C
Brien
Sherrill
Hays
Smyth
II CORPS
Leister
Trimble
Lane
Lowrance
Pettigrew
Davis
Marshall
Fry
Taneytown Road
Point of Woods
Spangler Woods
Wright
Armistead
Pickett
Garnett
Webb
Gibbon
Hall
Foley
Codori
Kemper
Harrow
Anderson
Emmitsburg Road
From Rittenhouse (Little Round Top)
D
Gates (Rowley)
I CORPS
Fisher
Stannard
Plum Run
From McGilvery's guns
Rogers
Lang
Henry Spangler
Hummelbaugh
Wilcox
B
Cross

> The position of the enemy was all he could desire. From the crest upon which he was entrenched the hill sloped gradually forming a natural glacis and the configuration of the ground was such that when the left of our line approached his works, it must come within the arc of a circle from which a direct, oblique enfilade fire could be, and was concentrated upon it.

This was certainly the case when the 8th Ohio and the other regiments enveloped Pettigrew's left flank. Young went on to say, "Under this fire from artillery [McCrea, 1st U.S. Artillery] and musketry the Brigade on our left [Davis's], reduced almost to skirmishers, gave way."

Notes

• This map depicts the approximate situation as the leading line of Pickett's and Pettigrew's Divisions crossed the Emmitsburg Road. The double line of fences bordering the road, and the slightly sunken nature of the road itself, acted as a check on the advance, as soldiers tended to halt and take cover. Regiments had already suffered severely from the Union artillery fire and officers endeavored to regroup and realign their commands. The Union gunners used the road as a marker to open fire with canister and the Union infantry, particularly in the north, to start firing their rifle-muskets. The intensity of this fire acted as a powerful deterrent to climbing the fences and continuing the attack. Many men remained in the road as their comrades braved the storm of firing and pushed ahead.
• Note the Confederate guns had largely ceased firing at this stage, either due to lack of ammunition or their own troops obscuring their line of fire. It is uncertain precisely which guns attempted to move forward with, or immediately behind, the infantry, but there were only a few and they had little chance of delivering effective supporting fire.
• On the left flank Brockenbrough's small brigade had suffered heavily from the concentrated fire from the guns on Cemetery Hill and were then hit in the flank by the rifle fire from the 8th Ohio – **A**. It proved more than they could stand and the brigade was halted and driven back, thus exposing Pettigrew's left flank. On the other flank – **B** – the brigades of Wilcox and Lang, whose task it was to support and secure the right flank, did not advance until later when the main assault had faltered and only reached the Plum Run line, by which time it was realized that to continue would be pointless.
• Of the reserve brigades of Anderson's Division (Wright, Posey and Mahone), totaling over 3,500 men, only Wright's and Posey's were put in motion, but on Longstreet's order pulled back. Mahone remained stationary.

Key

Confederate formation involved in main attack
Confederate reserve/supporting formation
Confederate supporting formation that advanced too late
Confederate formation not involved in attack
Confederate skirmishers
Confederates no longer advancing
Confederate direction of advance
Confederate withdrawal
main lines of fire of Union guns
C&D Union outflanking moves made as Rebel assault continues

All three advancing divisions used the obvious landmark of the Copse of Trees (it was larger than the copse today) to guide them in their march forward. There is no evidence that the main objective was Zeigler's Grove and thence Cemetery Hill, as has been mooted in several accounts of the charge. Colonel Birkett D. Fry's Brigade, in the center of the leading line, was selected as the unit of direction and formed up almost exactly opposite the Copse of Trees, which marked the salient of the enemy's position.

The other feature affecting all brigades was the Emmitsburg Road – it had to be crossed. On balance, it favored the defenders rather than the Rebels. For the Union infantry and artillery it provided a convenient marker to their front – the range to which they knew – which would delay the attackers as they climbed both fences and paused to adjust their alignment. As such it told the gunners it was time to switch to canister and the infantry that it was the moment to open fire with rifle-muskets. For the Confederates it provided a convenient place to check alignment but the slightly sunken nature of the road and the fence rails, combined with the increased tempo of the firing hitting them, quickly persuaded many Southerners to stay lying in this meager shelter and let their braver comrades press on without them.

Pickett's Division had a much shorter distance to cover to the Union line directly opposite it than Pettigrew (see Map 61). However, in order to assault the area of the Copse of Trees, the whole division would have to shift to its left during the advance and would therefore ultimately cover much the same distance as Pettigrew's men. This left oblique was particularly acute for Kemper's Brigade on the right, as it had some troops starting from south of the Klingle Farm. These men would have to cover some 150–200 yards more than regiments in Fry's Brigade and at the same time carry out the left oblique maneuver under fire. Pickett's Division would also have much further to go than their

Colonel Fry Gets His Orders

Colonel Birkett D. Fry had originally commanded the 13th Alabama (Heth's Division), but with the capture of Archer on Day One he had temporary command of the brigade. Positioned in the center of the leading line of the entire infantry attack, flanking units would align on him, making his position one of considerable importance. While waiting in his assembly area he was given his orders by Pettigrew:

> General Pettigrew rode up and informed me that after a heavy cannonade we would assault the position in our front, and added: "They will of course return the fire with all the guns they have; we must shelter the men as best we can, and make them lie down." At the same time he directed me to see General Pickett at once and have an understanding as to the dress [alignment] in the advance. I rode to General Pickett . . . he expressed great confidence in the ability of our troops to drive the enemy after they had been "demoralized by our artillery." General Garnett, who commanded his left brigade, having joined us, it was agreed he would dress on my command. I immediately returned and informed General Pettigrew of this agreement. It was then understood that my command should be considered the center, and that in the assault both divisions should align themselves by it. Soon after the two divisions moved forward about a hundred paces, and the men lay down behind our line of batteries.

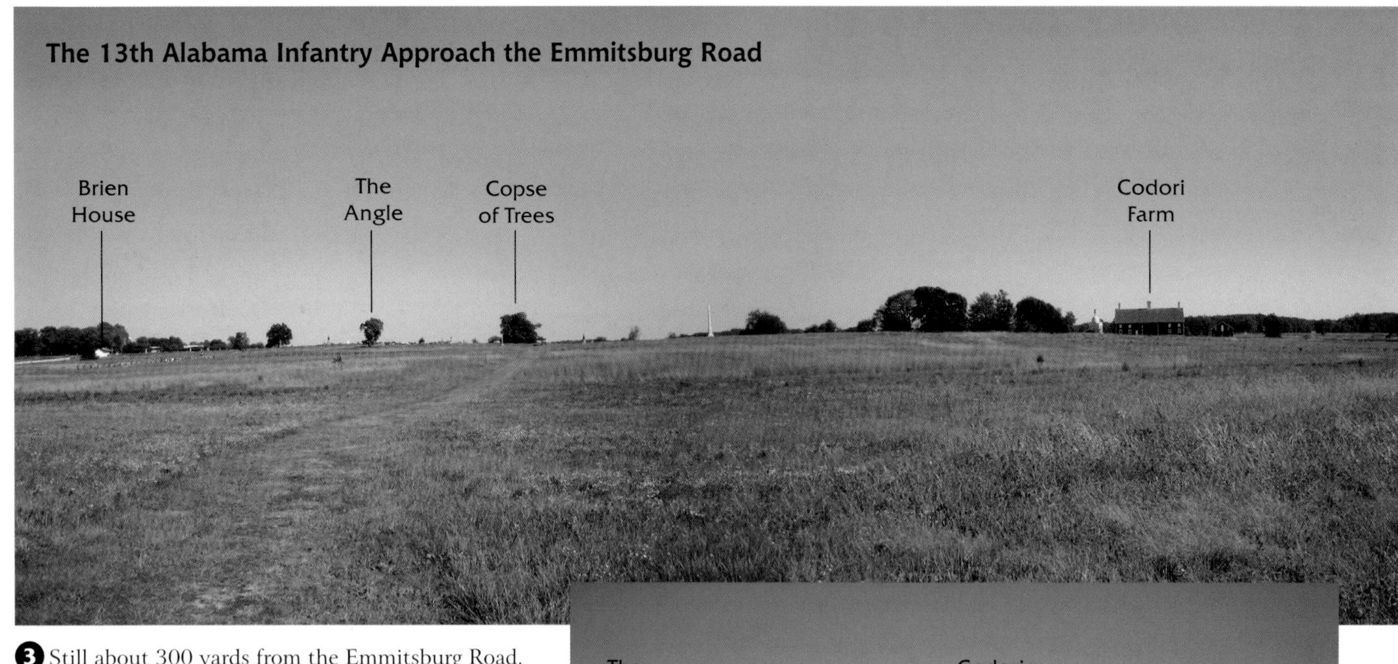

❸ Still about 300 yards from the Emmitsburg Road. The 13th Alabama would pass to the left of Codori Farm, now fully visible. The regiment is now exposed to artillery fire, particularly from Cemetery Hill and the Brien House area, but the range is too great and visibility too poor for rifle-muskets due to smoke from the Union guns. Note how the Copse of Trees provides a good marker throughout the advance.

The Angle
Codori Farm
Copse of Trees

❷ From about halfway between the Point of Woods and the Emmitsburg Road, all of the Codori building is not yet visible. Union infantry at the Copse of Trees and the Angle would still probably not be able to see the Rebels.

The Angle
Copse of Trees
Codori chimney

Note

These photographs trace the approximate route of the 13th Alabama Infantry, which formed on the right of Fry's Brigade, marching from just north of the Point of Woods toward the Copse of Trees. They clearly show the gentle rise up to the line of the Emmitsburg Road, running past (west of) the Codori Farm.

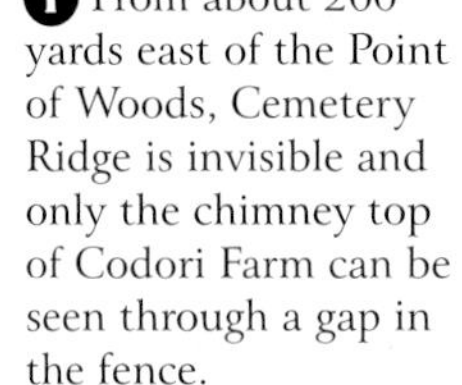

❶ From about 200 yards east of the Point of Woods, Cemetery Ridge is invisible and only the chimney top of Codori Farm can be seen through a gap in the fence.

more northerly comrades once the Emmitsburg Road was crossed, as it ran from northeast to southwest.

Finally, and importantly as regards the ground, there was the question of swales, or dips in the ground between the jump-off points and the objective. Reasonably deep dips provided a walking man with potentially life-saving protection from direct artillery fire at the longer distances. If a regiment suddenly disappeared from view for a while, not only could the gunners no longer usefully fire at it but they might be tempted to turn their attention to other visible targets.

For this final Rebel attack over apparently open ground it is best to consider the advance in two parts – the northern attack by Pettigrew's and Trimble's Divisions and the southern one by Pickett. As soon as Pettigrew's three leading brigades stepped off, they were visible to Union batteries as they moved down the gentle slope toward the Bliss Farm ruins, and its orchard, at the bottom of the dip. They were especially exposed to the Yankee guns on Cemetery Hill, which quickly troubled Brockenbrough's Brigade. Using the 26th North Carolina re-enactment group as an example, the regiment started at 9:55 a.m. and was clearly visible as it came down the slope for seven minutes before disappearing into a slight swale for three minutes. They reached the Emmitsburg Road in another three minutes, climbed the fences, and continued the attack, at all times in view from the Angle. So while they had a brief respite from the guns directly ahead (probably Weir and Cushing), Osborn's Cemetery Hill batteries could still hit them. Nevertheless, they were largely untouched by McGilvery's guns, which had other, easier targets, and by the Little Round Top battery for the same reason as well as the excessive range.

In the south Pickett's regiments faced a different situation. They had formed up on the reverse slope of the Emmitsburg Road ridge and behind Alexander's gun line. Here they were in a swale and concealed from both view and fire from McGilvery's large battery – although they suffered from "overs" aimed at the Rebel guns. As soon as they topped the rise as they approached the road they became visible and were hit by McGilvery's guns until they deliberately ceased fire, and by Rittenhouse's Battery on Little Round Top. However, they were screened from guns to their north until they reached and crossed the Emmitsburg Road.

Four Types of Rebel Casualty

Lieutenant John Dooley, 1st Virginia Infantry (Kemper's Brigade), described the moment his men received the order to advance.

> We rise to our feet, but not all. There is a line of men still on the ground with their faces turned, men affected in 4 different ways. There are the gallant dead who will never charge again; the helpless wounded, many of whom desire to share the fortunes of this charge; the men who have charged on many a battlefield but who are now helpless from the heat of the sun; and the men in whom there is not sufficient courage to enable them to rise . . .
>
> Some are actually fainting from the heat and dread. They have fallen to the ground overpowered by the suffocating heat and the terrors of that hour.

Tactical significance

Pickett's charge was the culmination for Lee of three days spent attacking. He had gained some successes on both previous days, but Meade remained in possession of the vital ground – Cemetery Hill and Ridge. Unless he could knock the Yankees off this ground, the best he could hope for at Gettysburg was a stalemate. He had rejected any idea of strategically maneuvering his enemy off the ground, so his only option was to drive him off tactically. Pickett's charge was his last attempt to do so. For Meade it was equally important to hold his ground. Upon the result of this assault would rest the outcome of the Battle of Gettysburg. When the Rebel regiments came tumbling back at around 4:00 p.m. that afternoon it spelled the end of Lee's hopes of winning a decisive battle, and indeed the end of the invasion of the North. He had no realistic option but to retreat (see Section Twelve: The Aftermath).

Force comparison (Map 63)

The nine Rebel brigades of Pickett, Pettigrew and Trimble carried out the assault proper (Perrin's and Thomas's Brigades from Trimble's Division did not take part). This infantry attack, as discussed above, did not have the close artillery support intended. The attackers ended up charging a line on Cemetery Ridge some 500–600 yards in length, centered on the Angle–Copse of Trees area. This length of the line was defended primarily by five brigades from Hays's and Gibbon's Divisions of II Corps (apart from the 8th Ohio, Carroll's Brigade was deployed as skirmishers at the foot of Cemetery Hill). They formed the front line of the defense and in the event were joined by two regiments from Rowley's Brigade and two from Stannard's (3rd Division, I Corps). Additionally, they had the support of an assortment of thirteen regiments from five corps (I, II, III, XI and XII), which were rushed to the threatened area during the attack, although most were not engaged. The Rebel infantry force stepped off some 11,800 strong to face about 6,350 Yankees in the front line of the defense, but who would have the support of another 2,570 if required. For details of the regiments included in this comparison, see Map 63.

The figures below are estimates; there is no way of compiling exact numbers for either side. For example, various accounts put the number of Confederates involved between 10,000–15,000. In researching the figures given here, account has been taken of the losses sustained by the units engaged on both sides during the fighting on the first two days, as well as those during the preliminary artillery duel. The results can only be approximate, but are sufficiently realistic to give the reader a fair idea of the relative strengths and the odds of success or failure in numerical terms. As the struggle was almost entirely between the attacking units and the front line of the defenders, those are the figures given in the main part of the comparison below.

Confederate Infantry Brigades

Commander	**Estimated strength**
Pickett's Division	
Brig.-Gen. Kemper	1,634
Brig.-Gen. Garnett	1,459
Brig.-Gen. Armistead	1,950
Total*	**5,043**
Pettigrew's Division	
Col. Fry	900
Col. Marshall	1,500
Brig.-Gen. Davis	1,400
Col. Brockenbrough	770
Total	**4,570**
Trimble's Division	
Col. Lowrance	500
Brig.-Gen. Lane	1,700
Total	**2,200**
Total starting the attack	**11,813 (say 11,800)**

*Not previously in action and shown at engaged strength for the battle.

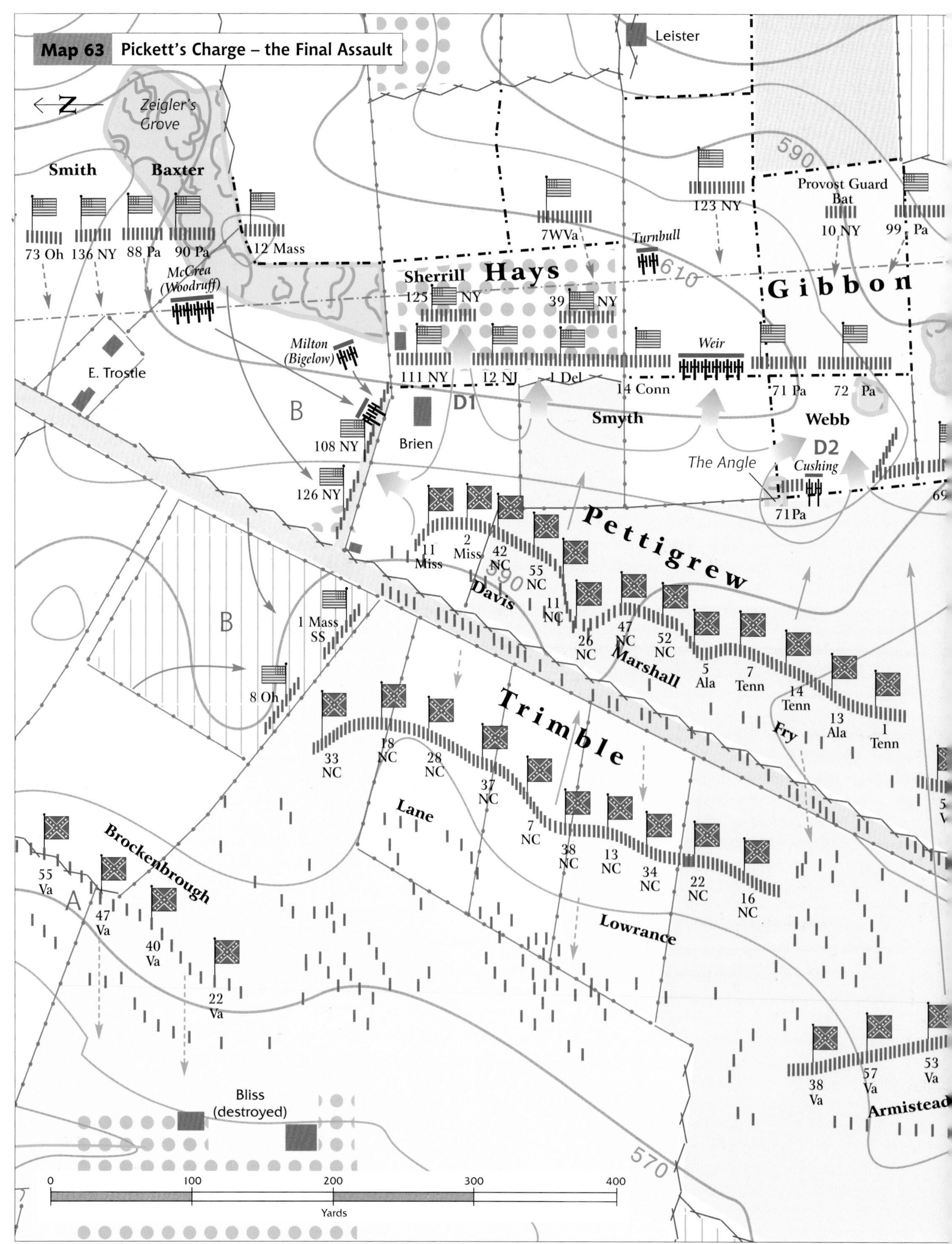
Map 63
Pickett's Charge – the Final Assault
Zeigler's Grove
Leister
Smith
Baxter
73 Oh
136 NY
88 Pa
90 Pa
12 Mass
McCrea (Woodruff)
E. Trostle
Milton (Bigelow)
B
108 NY
126 NY
Brien
Sherrill
Hays
125 NY
39 NY
7WVa
123 NY
Turnbull
610
590
Provost Guard Bat
10 NY
99 Pa
Gibbon
111 NY
12 NJ
1 Del
14 Conn
Weir
71 Pa
72 Pa
D1
Smyth
Webb
D2
The Angle
Cushing
71Pa
69
Pettigrew
11 Miss
2 Miss
42 NC
55 NC
Davis
11 NC
26 NC
47 NC
52 NC
Marshall
5 Ala
7 Tenn
14 Tenn
13 Ala
1 Tenn
Fry
1 Mass SS
8 Oh
Trimble
33 NC
18 NC
28 NC
37 NC
7 NC
38 NC
13 NC
34 NC
22 NC
16 NC
Lane
Lowrance
Brockenbrough
55 Va
47 Va
40 Va
22 Va
A
Bliss (destroyed)
570
38 Va
57 Va
53 Va
Armistead
0
100
200
300
400
Yards

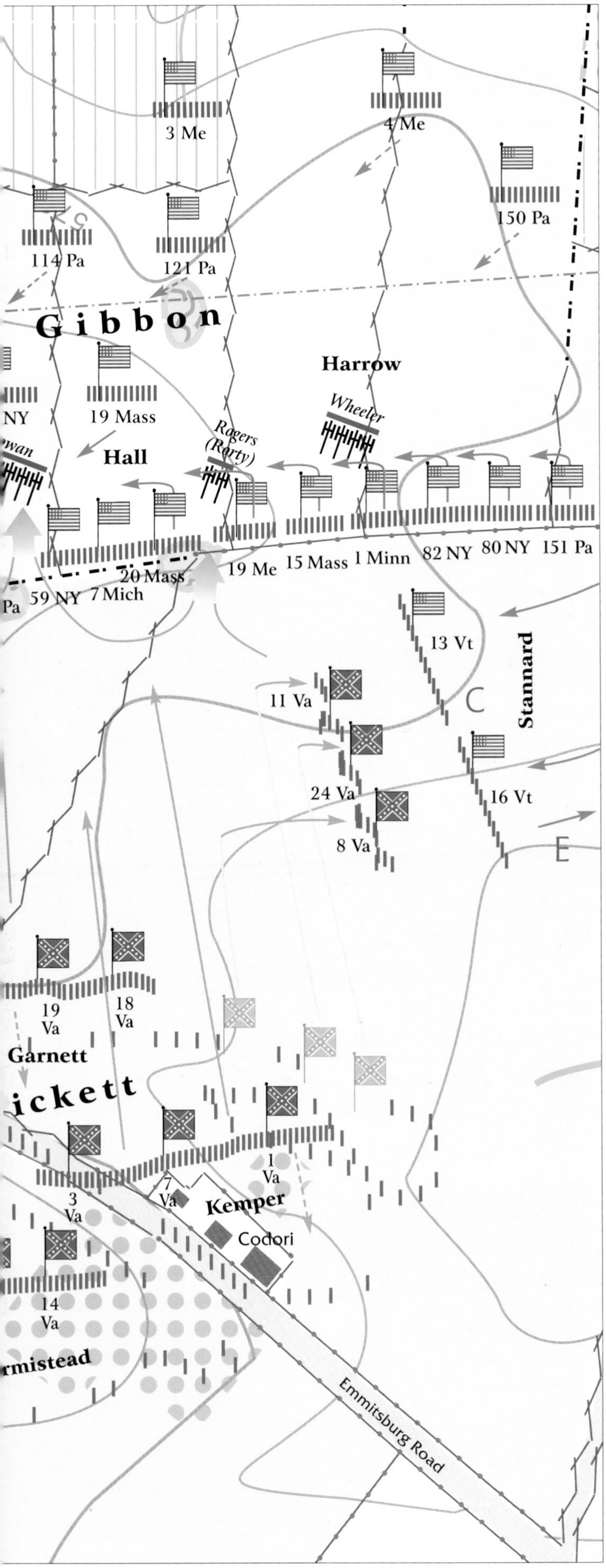

Notes

• This map shows Pickett's charge crossing the Emmitsburg Road, where many men decided to remain, and moving into the final assault. Throughout the final 200–300 yards they were subjected to the most intense rifle-musket and canister fire from the Union guns, some of which were double- or even triple-shotted. As shown, many men had fallen and many others were drifting back the way they had come. The Rebel regiments had shrunk considerably and were merging into smaller groups centered on their colors as they pressed forward.

• Meanwhile, Brockenbrough's Brigade had been crippled by gunfire from Cemetery Hill and musketry from the 8th Ohio, and after passing the Bliss Farm ruins halted and turned back – **A**.

• As the Rebels advanced both flanks became exposed – a weakness quickly exploited by the Yankees. On the Confederate left the 8th Ohio wheeled to fire into the advancing brigades of Davis and Lane. They were supported by the 1st Massachusetts Sharpshooters and the 108th and 126th New York, the former from Sherrill's Brigade, the latter from Smyth's (**B**). On the right the 13th and 16th Vermont advanced to take Garnett and Kemper in flank as they neared Hall and Harrow, forcing the 8th, 11th and 24th Virginia to turn to try, unsuccessfully, to check them and compelling the Virginians to drop out of the assault (**C**).

• The courageous remnants of numerous Rebel regiments, now inextricably mixed, hit the defenders, mostly protected by stone walls, on about a 500-yard front running from the Brien house southward. This line was the scene of desperate hand-to-hand fighting along and just over the wall. There were three distinct crossing places where Rebels penetrated into the Union positions. On the left the 11th Mississippi, close to Brien's house (**D1**); in the center, at the Angle, Armistead was mortally wounded, leading a crowd of mostly Virginians that overran two of Cushing's guns (**D2**); and to the right more Virginians closed with Cowan's Battery, forcing it to withdraw by prolonge as its ammunition was exhausted (**D3**).

• Note how about 20 Union regiments were moved forward to support the front line. In particular there was a rush to contain the central penetration that had driven back elements of the 71st Pennsylvania and forced the 69th Pennsylvania to refuse its right flank. The regiments from Hall's and Harrow's Brigades arrived at the threatened point through the Copse of Trees and were considerably disorganized and mixed up in the process.

• The assaulting regiments had lost huge numbers during the advance from both artillery and rifle-musket fire; many men had dropped out of the advance; both flanks were attacked; and those Rebels who reached and crossed the wall were met by a well-organized and mostly solid defense. There was no support forthcoming at the crucial moment, so Pickett's charge had reached its high water mark and, like the tide, began to recede rapidly. On the extreme right (**E**) the 16th Vermont was able to turn about and help the 14th Vermont check the belated advance of Lang's and Wilcox's Brigades further south.

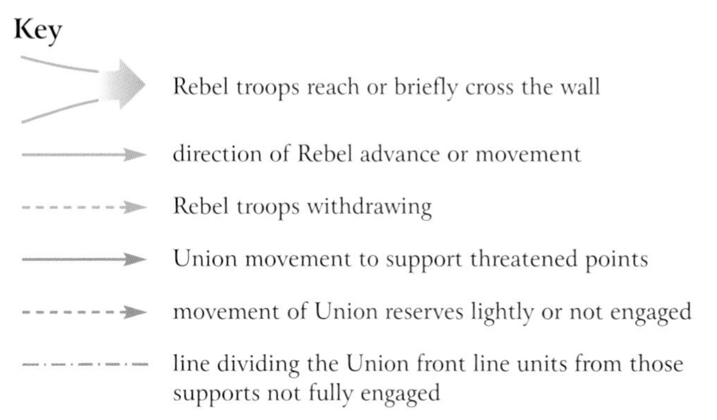

Confederate Artillery

While there was initially some overhead Rebel fire to support the advancing infantry, this was not prolonged. Although Alexander claims to have ordered forward about eighteen guns with some ammunition still in the caissons to accompany, or immediately follow, the infantry, it is difficult to be certain which they were. There is little evidence to indicate that these guns did much damage to the Union defenders. Nevertheless, those listed below have been tentatively identified after careful research by Richard Rollins in his article "The Failure of Pickett's Charge," which appeared in the *North & South* magazine, volume 3, no. 4.

Battery	Commander	12N	20P	10P	OR	12H	Total
Troup County (Ga)	Capt. Carlton					2	2
1st Co. Washington Art.	Capt. Squires	1					1
4th Co. Washington Art.	Lt. Woolfolk	4					4
Richmond (Va) Bat.	Capt. Parker				1	3	4
Bedford (Va) Art.	Capt. Jordan					4	4
Bath (Va) Bat.	Capt. Taylor	4					4
Totals		**9**		**1**	**7**	**2**	**19**

Union Infantry Brigades (front line)

Commander	Estimated strength
Hays's Division	
Col. Sherrill	1,100
Col. Smyth	700
Lt.-Col. Sawyer (Col. Carroll): 8th Ohio	200
Total	**2,000**
Gibbon's Division	
Brig-Gen Webb	950
Col. Hall	900
Brig.-Gen. Harrow	575
Total	**2,425**
Doubleday's Division	
Brig.-Gen. Stannard: 2 rgts.	1,300
Col. Gates: 2 rgts.	420
Total	**1,720**
Humphreys' Division	
Lt.-Col. Baldwin: 1st Mass S.S.	200
Total defending the front line	**6,345**
	(say 6,350)

Union Artillery

The guns shown below are those indicated on Map 63 as having played a significant part in inflicting casualties on the advancing Rebels. It was the batteries in this central area of the Union line that incurred most damage during the Confederate cannonade, in particular the batteries of Rorty, Brown, Cushing, Arnold and Woodruff. Arnold withdrew due to shortage of ammunition and was replaced by Weir, and Perrin was replaced by Cowan just before the charge began, while Cushing, Rogers (Rorty) and Woodruff ended up with only two serviceable pieces each. Wheeler was also brought forward as a reinforcement at the last moment.

Battery	Commander	12N	10P	OR	Total
1st U.S. Art., Bat. I	Lt. McCrea (Woodruff)	2			2
9th Mass Lgt. 2	Lt. Milton (Bigelow)	2			2
3rd U.S. Art., Bat. F&K	Lt. Turnbull	2			2
4th U.S. Art., Bat. A	Capt. Cushing			2	2
1st New York Ind. Bat.	Lt. Cowan			6	6
1st New York Lgt., Bat. B	Lt. Rogers (Rorty)		2		2
13th New York Ind. Bat.	Lt. Wheeler			4	4
Totals		**6**	**2**	**12**	**18**

Union Formations Moved to the Threatened Area

Brigade commander	Parent formation	Strength
Baxter: 3 regts.	2nd Div., I Corps	420
Smith: 2 regts.	2nd Div., XI Corps	670
McDougall: 123rd NY	1st Div., XII Corp	480
Carroll: 7th WVa	3rd Div., II Corps	200
Hopper: 10th NY Prov. Gd.	3rd Div., II Corps	76
Berdan: 3 regts.	1st Div., III Corps	400
Graham: 114th Pa	1st Div., III Corps	100
Rowley: 121st Pa	3rd Div., I Corps	120
Dana: 150th Pa	3rd Div., I Corps	100
Total		**2,566**
		(say 2,570)

Comments on force comparisons must be made with the benefit of hindsight. It was impossible for Lee to know the numbers that would oppose him, so he had no way of assessing the odds of success or failure in numerical terms. Once the advance started, Meade and his commanders could actually see what was coming at them, so he had twenty minutes or so to adjust the odds at the threatened area in his favor. Several aspects of the numbers' game are worthy of mention.

- Approximately 11,800 Rebels advanced on about 6,350 Yankees defending their front line. Put another way, forty-two regiments of attackers were advancing on twenty-six regiments. Conventional military doctrine was that, other things being equal, odds of 3:1 in favor of the attackers would give them a reasonable chance of success. Here the odds were just 1.85:1. If the reserves that became available to the defenders (another thirteen regiments) are included, then with 8,900 Union men, the revised odds of 1.3:1 make it theoretically – the emphasis being on theoretically – almost impossible for the Confederates to achieve victory. Add to this the fact that the defending infantry had largely avoided much of the bombardment, were protected by walls and fence rails piled up in front of them, and had a clear field of fire at a dense target for the final 300 yards, then the chances of them driving off an assault are boosted enormously.

- No comparison of numbers is complete without a look at the quality and status of the troops involved. As an extreme example, throwing exhausted, inexperienced troops with suspect morale, even in greatly superior numbers, against well-positioned and experienced veterans would not be conducive to success. In this instance, Pickett's Division, which provided less than half the assault force on the right flank of the attack, was composed entirely of Virginians who were comparatively fresh and so far unbloodied as they had not been on the battlefield during the first two days. However, the division had been compelled to leave two of its brigades at Richmond, and it was some time since the three present had seen action, as it had been only marginally engaged at Fredericksburg and had missed Chancellorsville. Nevertheless, morale was high and collectively the division was determined to get at the Yankees.

  On the left flank things were not so satisfactory. Pettigrew's Division had been severely mauled on July 1, losing about 40 percent of its strength and having to spend the next day tending wounded, burying dead and trying to reorganize. Fry had lost a quarter of his men and the brigade commander (Archer); Marshall and Davis had over 1,000 casualties each, while Brockenbrough's tiny brigade had performed poorly on the first day and shrunk by nearly half. In addition, Marshall and Davis commanded brigades that had little operational experience, having been sent from the backwater of North Carolina to join the army after its restructuring. Fry, however, had regiments that had done well at Fredericksburg and Chancellorsville. Trimble's two brigades were far from being raw troops, as Lane's men had fought as part of the famous Light Division and participated in every battle of the Army of Northern Virginia from Seven Days to Gettysburg, though they had not so far been in action at Gettysburg. Similarly, Lowrance commanded veteran troops, although they had suffered heavily on July 1.

  In the Union front line, Gibbon's three brigades were veteran troops, as the division had fought in most battles from the Peninsula to Chancellorsville, in which they were fortunately only lightly engaged. However, on July 2 Webb's Brigade and the 15th Massachusetts and 82nd New York from Harrow's Brigade had been badly cut up in repelling Wright's Brigade's attack. The division facing Pickett was between 900–1,000 men down on its original engaged strength. Of the two brigades of Hays's Division involved, one was a successful veteran formation, the other not. Smyth's men had fought at Antietam, Fredericksburg and Chancellorsville. At Fredericksburg the brigade had had a disastrous day, losing over 1,100 men attempting to storm Marye's Heights, to be followed by another 700 at Chancellorsville. It began July 3 at Gettysburg with not many more than 1,000 men, having lost some more during continuous bickering with the Rebels over the possession of Bliss Farm. Sherrill's Brigade was much stronger, but its likely performance was somewhat suspect as it had acquired the nicknames of the "Harper's Ferry Brigade" and the "Bandbox Soldiers," the former for its surrender at that place less than a year before and the latter for ever since stagnating in the Washington defenses. The 8th Ohio of Carroll's Brigade, which was to play such a prominent part in repelling the attackers' left wing, was down to about 200 men. Finally, there were the recently joined nine-month men of the two brigades of Doubleday's Division, each of which had two regiments involved in Pickett's repulse. Of these, Gates's troops had suffered heavily under Biddle on the first day, but Stannard, with some 650 men in each regiment (13th and 16th Vermont), had yet to see much action.

- The eight Union brigades that were deployed behind the front as reserves came from no fewer than five different corps, illustrating again how Meade split up his formations and sent them in various directions piecemeal to deal with threats as they arose. It was a policy that played havoc with some divisional commanders' control but was effective in achieving its purpose.

- The Pickett–Pettigrew–Trimble charge was very much a Virginia and North Carolina affair, with nineteen of the former and sixteen of the latter regiments taking part. Thirty-five regiments out of forty-two make 83 percent. Pickett's entire division was Virginian, as was Brockenbrough's Brigade. On the left wing, Trimble's two brigades consisted of North Carolina regiments, as did Marshall's Brigade in Pettigrew's command. The only other states represented were Tennessee (three regiments), and Alabama and Mississippi (two regiments each). On the Union side it was entirely different, with no fewer than ten states represented in either the front line or in immediate support.

- Including Union regiments in the supporting line, forty-two Rebel regiments averaging 281 men were launched against thirty-nine Yankee regiments at an average strength of 228 men.

Command and control

Confederate

Lee was responsible for launching Pickett's charge. He decided the plan and the troops that would take part, two aspects of which have yet to be mentioned, both reflecting on Lee's judgment or the inefficiency of his staff. The first concerns his selection of the divisions to carry it out. While Pickett's Division was an obvious choice as it had not yet been in action, the same was not true of Pettigrew's (Heth's) or Trimble's (Pender's) in Hill's Corps. It appears Lee either ignored or was not informed of the extent of the losses suffered by these commands. Pettigrew's brigades had been badly mauled, as had Lowrence's, now under Trimble. The reason usually given for Anderson's Division, which was in better shape numerically and under all its substantive brigade commanders, not being used is that Pettigrew's men were already in the right position and so no shifting around was required. Be that as it may, the weaker formation was given a major role. The second issue was that Lee seemed uninformed about the general shortage of artillery ammunition and the effect this might have on the execution of his plan.

The extreme reluctance of Longstreet to make the attack, his delegation of the authority for ordering Pickett to advance to his artillery chief, Alexander, and his last-minute attempt to halt the operation have been discussed above (page 475), so this section will be concerned with the command and control of the actual advance and important decisions made during it.

Once the attack got under way, Lee, who had had an active morning, positioned himself near the Point of Woods to watch events. Longstreet, who had also been well forward and under fire during the cannonade, did not advance with the attackers. As the corps commander, his key tasks were now to assess overall progress and make decisions concerning the use of the reserves, not to lead the troops himself – this was in the hands of Pickett, Pettigrew, Trimble, and the brigade and regimental commanders.

Pickett Is Not Amused

Pickett's long curls were the subject of much humor, which he did not enjoy. Lieutenant Francis W. Dawson, an officer on Longstreet's staff, was present in Hagerstown, on the road to Gettysburg, when Lee was introduced to a welcoming group of young ladies from the town. He recounted how one of them asked the general for a lock of his hair. Lee replied that he had none to spare but that surely General Pickett would be delighted to give her one of his many ringlets. Pickett was not amused and made no offer; the young lady did not press the matter.

Major-General George Edward Pickett. Pickett, who was a personal friend of Longstreet, had a reputation as something of a dandy who was not overendowed with intellect. The former was on account of his appearance, which he was at pains to cultivate. He had a neat, slim figure clad in a close-fitting, perfectly tailored uniform with burnished buttons, highly polished boots and gold spurs; he wore a small blue kepi on his head and carried a riding crop. However, it was his hair that usually drew most attention. Like Custer in the opposite camp, Pickett grew his hair long, wore ringlets that hung down to his shoulders and were perfumed, while "his beard likewise was curling and giving out the scent of Araby." This obsession with his locks made him the butt of much ribald comment (see box). His lack of academic attainment was evidenced by his graduating last at West Point in the Class of 1846. Major Moxley Sorrel, on Longstreet's staff, commented how when "taking Longstreet's orders in emergencies, I could always see how he looked after Pickett, and made us give him things very fully; indeed, sometimes stay with him to make sure he did not get astray."

Despite all this, Pickett was a popular, energetic commander whose military career thus far had been about average. He had seen service in the Mexican War, where he had led the party that stormed Chapultepec Castle, snatching a color from a wounded James Longstreet and unfurling it over the castle. Twelve years later, during a dispute with the British at Puget Sound (on the Pacific coast), Captain Pickett, while in command of sixty-eight men, won government approval for successfully facing down a force of several warships and 1,000 troops. While in the same area he learned the local Indian dialect (proving his intellect was perhaps better than many thought) and translated the Lord's Prayer and several hymns, thus gaining the title "Great Chief."

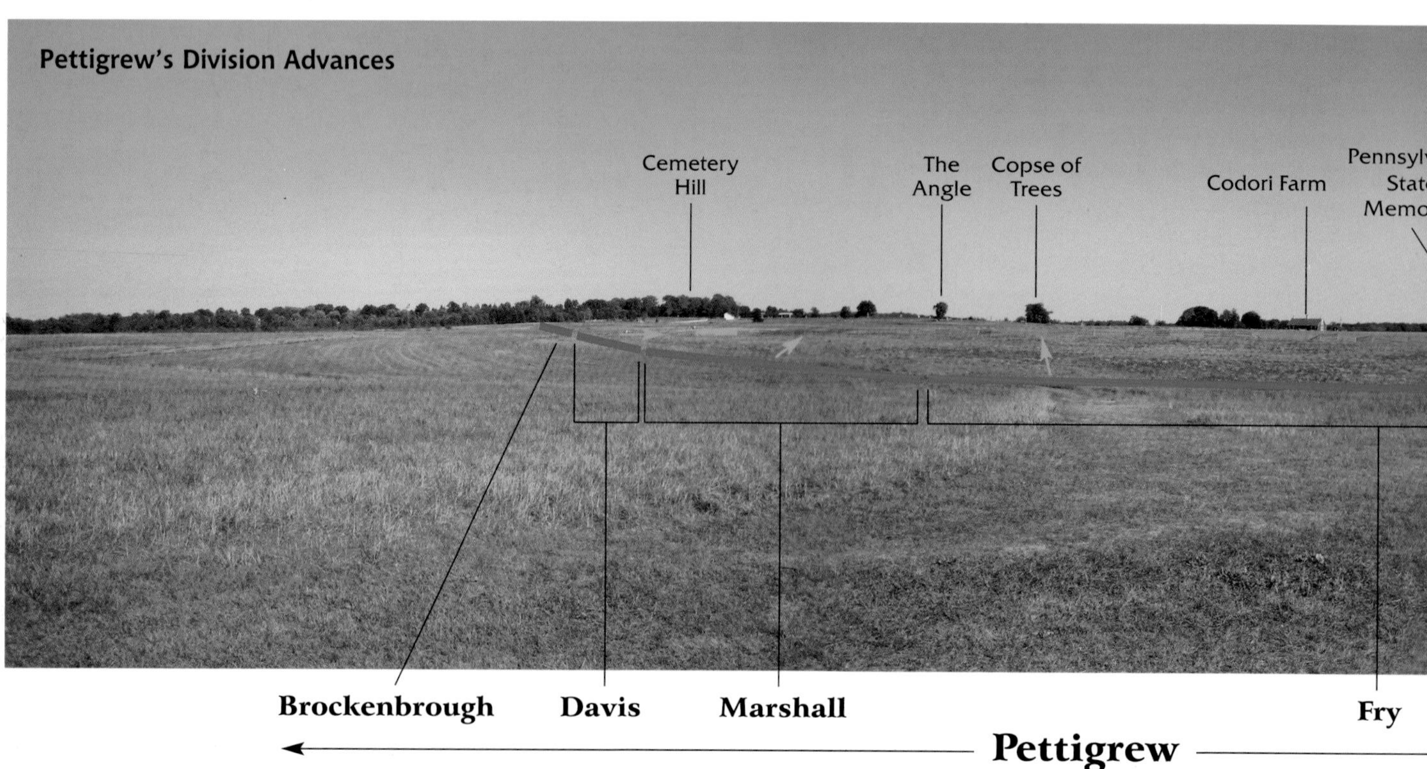

Lee watched the Confederate infantry attack from near the Point of Woods, from where this photograph was taken. Pettigrew's Division had moved through the Rebel gun line and were approaching the crest of the first swale (dip), where they came under intense long-range fire from the Union batteries on Cemetery Ridge, and particularly those on Cemetery Hill, which also took Brockenbrough and Davis in their

Made colonel shortly after the outbreak of war, Pickett missed First Manassas but his efforts defending the lower Rappahannock in September 1861 earned him promotion to brigadier-general in February the following year. He led his brigade successfully in the Peninsular campaign, where it earned the nickname the "Gamecock Brigade." Pickett was hit in the shoulder at Gaines' Mill, where his reputation also took a bit of a hit as he was discovered by a staff officer lying in a hollow "bewailing himself" and demanding attention as if mortally wounded. The officer found the wound to be less than mortal and rode off, declaring Pickett was "perfectly able to take care of himself." After three months' recuperation Pickett returned to duty and promotion to major-general – probably due to the influence of a Major-General Longstreet. Pickett had his division, but he had not been tested at this level of command until Gettysburg. As noted above, his division had been only lightly engaged at Fredericksburg (it suffered just one fatality) and had missed Chancellorsville altogether.

In addition to his own division, Pickett had the direct support of both Wilcox's and Wright's Brigades, which were under his command for this attack. At around 3:00 p.m. on July 3, starting on the left with Garnett and proceeding on to Kemper, Pickett rode along the lines telling them to prepare to advance. The colonel of the 7th Virginia (Kemper) recalled him shouting, "Charge the enemy, and remember old Virginia!" Not all brigades were ordered forward by Pickett personally, as this was not possible; he made use of his staff officers, who were dispersed to the various brigade commands. According to Captain Robert Bright on Pickett's staff, when he received the final order to advance:

> [Pickett] ordered his staff officers, four in number (Maj. Charles Pickett, Captain Baird, Captain Symington and myself), to Generals Armistead, Garnett and Kemper and to Dearing's Artillery Battalion . . . Orders to other staff officers I did not hear. But I was sent to General Kemper with this order: "You and your staff and field officers to go in dismounted; dress on Garnett and take the red barn [Codori] for your objective point" [from Kemper's position the Copse of Trees was directly behind the Codori barn].

Armistead Orders His Brigade to Advance

Lieutenant John H. Lewis, 9th Virginia, remembered the moment when Brigadier-General Lewis Armistead ordered his men forward at the start of Pickett's charge:

> The command "attention" was heard, and the men rose from the ground, where they had been lying during the fire of artillery.
>
> If I should live for a hundred years I shall never forget that moment or the command as given by General Louis [Lewis] A. Armistead on that day. He was an old army officer, and was possessed of a very loud voice, which could be heard by the whole brigade, being near my regiment. He gave the command, in words, as follows – "Attention, second battalion! Battalion of direction forward; guides center; march!" I shall never see at any time a battalion of soldiers but what it recalls those words. He turned, placed himself about twenty paces in front of his brigade, and took the lead. His place was in the rear, properly. After moving he placed his hat on the point of his sword, and held it above his head, in front of him.

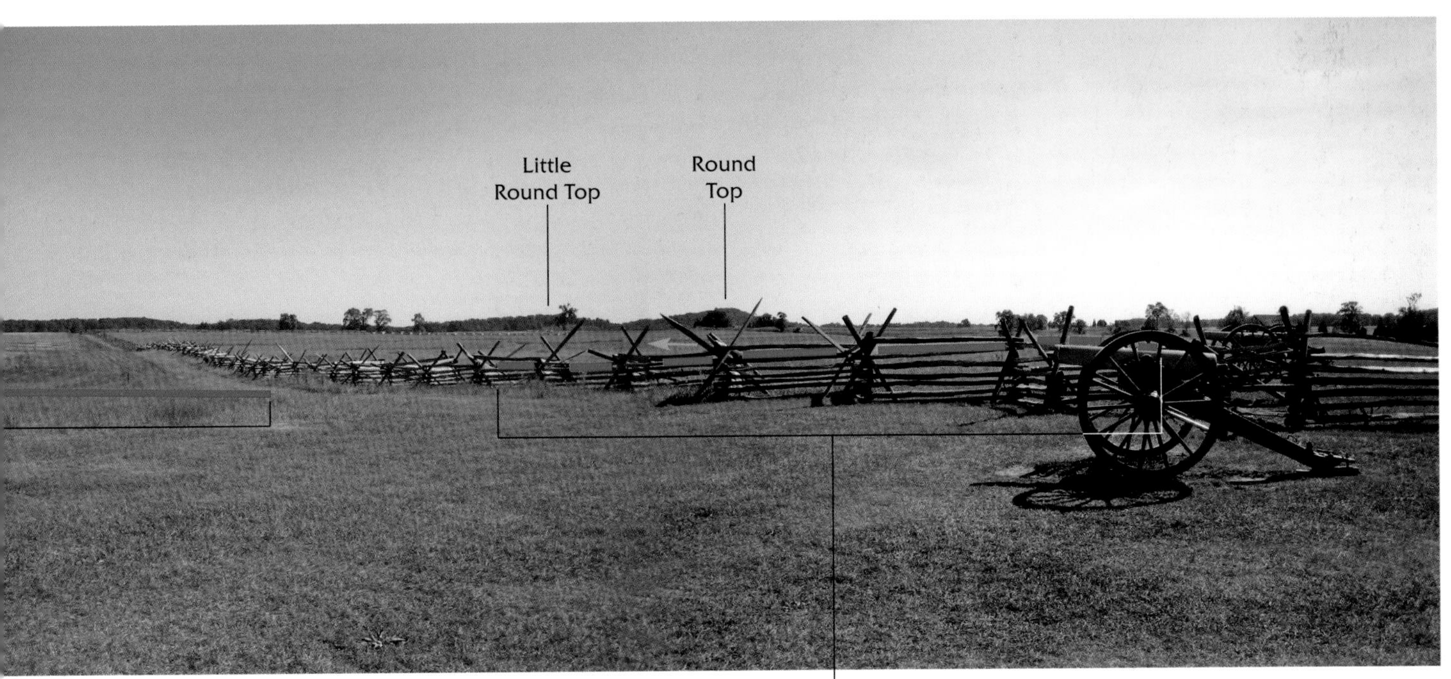

flank. On the right, Garnett and Kemper were hit by McGilvery's batteries straight ahead of them and by Rittenhouse's Battery on Little Round Top. Pettigrew's regiments could see the Copse of Trees clearly ahead of them, but Pickett's initially used the Codori Farm as a marker as they began their left oblique march to converge on their objective. See Map 61.

Apart from Pickett himself, there were some fifteen riders who remained mounted during the assault – two brigade commanders (Kemper and Garnett), eight staff officers, three couriers and two regimental commanders

Pickett followed his division as far as the Emmitsburg Road and probably remained in the vicinity of the Codori buildings as the final charge went in – it was a reasonable place from which to assess what was happening and from which to issue orders, and it was certainly not his duty to lead from the front at this stage. As the division approached the road, the order was given to "Left oblique" – a 45-degree turn to the left to close on Pettigrew's command prior to the final push on the Copse of Trees area after a pause for realignment.

It was time for Pickett to make a decision – he needed to summon the brigades of Wilcox and Lang whose task was to support his division and the right flank of the attack. As his leading brigades shifted left and prepared to cross the road to continue the attack, their right would became even more vulnerably exposed. As we know, this weakness was dramatically and effectively exploited by Stannard's regiments moving out to attack the divisional right, clinching the defeat of an already much depleted formation. Pickett sent Captain Bright to find Longstreet and get his authority, but this took some time and before Bright's return (when he was also sent to Wilcox) Pickett, in some desperation, summoned Wilcox and Lang with no fewer than three staff officers in quick succession. Captain Bright, the last to arrive in front of Wilcox, recorded that the brigade commander lifted his arms and exclaimed, "I know, I know." Wilcox and Lang advanced straight ahead and ran into one of the strongest parts of the

Colonel David Lang Orders a Retreat

Lang's and Wilcox's Brigades were eventually ordered forward to support Pickett's right flank, but it came too late to achieve that result and they were attacked on both flanks. Lang recalled:

> The noise of artillery and small-arms was so deafening that it was impossible to make the voice heard above the din, and the men were by this time so badly scattered in the bushes and among the rocks that it was impossible to make any movement to meet or check the enemy's advance [14th and 16th Vermont from Stannard's Brigade on the left]. To remain in this position unsupported by either infantry or artillery, with infantry on both flanks and in front and artillery [McGilvery] playing upon us with grape and canister, was certain annihilation. To advance was only to hasten that result, and, therefore, I ordered a retreat, which, however, was not in time to save a large number of the Second Florida Infantry, together with their colors, from being cut off and captured by the flanking force on the left. Owing to the noise and [the] scattered condition of the men, it was impossible to have the order to retreat properly extended and I am afraid that many men, while firing from behind rocks and trees, did not hear the order, and remained there until captured.

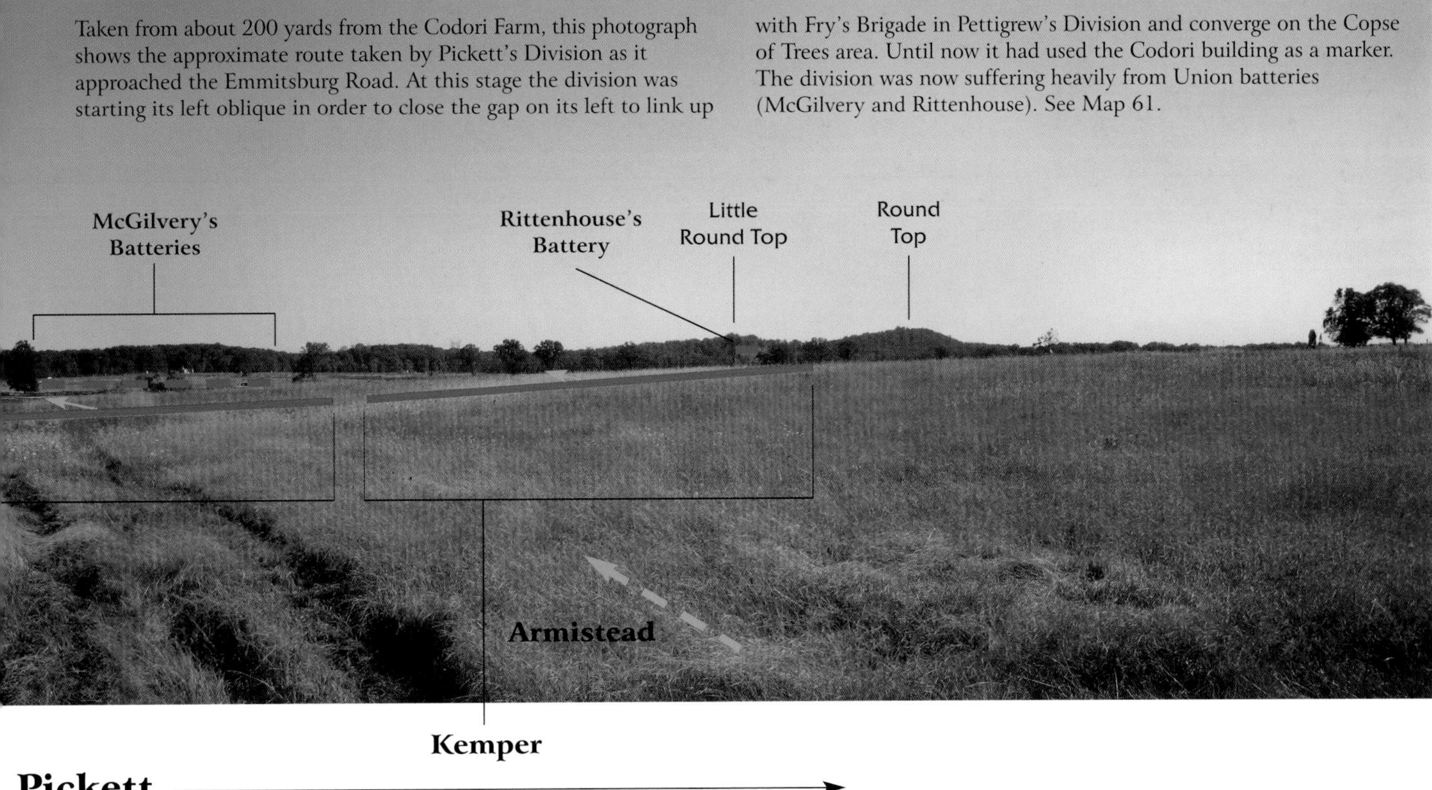

Taken from about 200 yards from the Codori Farm, this photograph shows the approximate route taken by Pickett's Division as it approached the Emmitsburg Road. At this stage the division was starting its left oblique in order to close the gap on its left to link up with Fry's Brigade in Pettigrew's Division and converge on the Copse of Trees area. Until now it had used the Codori building as a marker. The division was now suffering heavily from Union batteries (McGilvery and Rittenhouse). See Map 61.

Union line, including McGilvery's guns, with no support and both flanks exposed. It was too late and in the wrong place. By this time the main charge was over and the survivors were recoiling – Wilcox and Lang followed suit.

Brigadier-General James Johnston Pettigrew. Pettigrew was almost the exact opposite to Pickett in appearance and intellect. He was handsome, with carefully groomed hair and mustache and high forehead, which supposedly signified superior intelligence. Seemingly this was so, as he had the best grades ever recorded at the University of North Carolina, where he excelled at mathematics and classical languages as well as being a skilled fencer and boxer. He later studied law, first in Baltimore and later in Germany. During the course of extensive travel in Europe he became proficient in German, French, Italian and Spanish, with a working knowledge of Hebrew, Greek and Arabic. On his return, he practiced law in Charleston, entered the state legislature in 1856 and was appointed colonel of the 1st Regiment of Rifles, a militia unit. This regiment was disbanded at the outbreak of war and Pettigrew, after a short spell as a private in Hampton's Legion, was elected colonel of the 12th, later redesignated 22nd, North Carolina Regiment.

Appointed brigadier-general in February 1862, Pettigrew was severely wounded in the throat, the ball cutting an artery. He was hit again in the arm, bayoneted in the right leg and left for dead. Although in danger of bleeding to death, he miraculously recovered consciousness to find himself a prisoner. He survived and was later exchanged and given a brigade that saw little action until, along with Davis's Brigade, it was transferred to Lee's command in the Army of Northern Virginia on May 30, 1863. Although his experience as a commander was limited, Pettigrew was generally acknowledged as a courageous and competent officer. One comrade described him as "quick in his movements and quick in his deception and in his decision."

On the first day at Gettysburg, Pettigrew's Brigade suffered near crippling losses in the struggle to get the Iron Brigade off McPherson's Ridge. Among the wounded was Heth, which meant that Pettigrew, as the next senior, though least experienced, officer was now acting as divisional commander. The command setup within his division was not reassuring, with his former brigade now under Colonel Marshall, Archer's under Colonel Fry and the weakest in numbers and morale under Brockenbrough.

Pettigrew's most obvious leadership error was in placing this last brigade on his extreme left flank – the most important position of his division. It made little progress beyond the Bliss Farm and Pettigrew was unable to call on any other support. He rode at the head of his troops, an obvious target as the distance to the objective closed. First his horse was hit, then about 100 yards from the wall a piece of canister shell smashed his right hand. He remained in command, however, attempting to encourage and rally his remaining men in the desperate struggle to get over the wall. It was in vain and the survivors, including Pettigrew, were driven back.

Pettigrew had survived the bitter fighting on July 1 unscathed and had come back from Pickett's charge with a comparatively minor wound, only to succumb eleven days later at Falling Waters as the army retreated across the Potomac. A Union cavalryman's pistol ball hit him in the side just above his hip and came out through his back. He died a lingering and agonizing death a few days later.

Major-General Isaac Ridgeway Trimble. At sixty-one Trimble was very much an elderly, if ambitious, commander who had gained a ferocious reputation on most of the battlefields of the previous year under Stonewall Jackson. He was a West Point graduate who had spent ten years in the artillery before shedding his uniform for the lucrative and rapidly expanding railroad industry. At the outbreak of the war he moved from Maryland to Virginia to enlist in the Engineers in May 1861. By August he was a brigadier-general and by November he had his brigade.

He quickly made a name for himself as an aggressive battlefield commander in Jackson's Shenandoah Valley campaign of 1862. He fought at Winchester and Cross Keys, where his brigade destroyed a Union assault by close-range musket fire and his follow-up of the enemy placed his troops far in advance of the rest of the division. At this point, Trimble insisted on attacking, a request refused by his divisional commander, Ewell. However, Ewell was later to admit that "Trimble won the fight . . . if I had followed his views we would have destroyed Fremont's army." A characteristic recalled by his men at Cross Keys was the loudness of his commands – "Trimble gave the loudest command I ever heard, to 'Forward, guide center, march!' I could hear the echo . . . for miles." He became one of Jackson's favorite generals, displaying an insatiable eagerness to get at the enemy during the Seven Days Battles of Gaines' Mill and the last clash at Malvern Hill, where Trimble begged in vain to be allowed to launch a night attack. He performed well during the Second Manassas campaign, capturing Union guns at Manassas Junction after a crippling forced march. However, Trimble's luck ran out at the Battle of Second Manassas when he was struck in the left leg by an explosive bullet. His wound took a long time to heal, but despite this he achieved his long-held ambition of promotion to major-general's rank, on Jackson's strong recommendation, in January 1863. However, his wound forced him to relinquish his command in April and accept a dull, backwater post commanding the Shenandoah Valley District.

The prospect of missing Lee's invasion of Maryland and Pennsylvania was too much for Trimble, who attached himself to Lee's headquarters as an individual and supernumerary major-general. As such he was a nuisance, with his forthright opinions, strong views and no responsibility. On June 28, Lee was probably pleased when Trimble joined his old commander, Ewell, in Carlisle – although his appearance there and the consequent flow of opinions and unsolicited advice from this fractious and frustrated commander can hardly have been a welcome addition to the corps headquarters. It all came to a head on the evening of July 1 when Ewell was debating whether to attack Cemetery Hill after receiving Lee's "if practicable" instructions. Trimble was adamant that Culp's Hill could and should be taken. According to one witness the exchange went as follows: "Give me a division," said Trimble, "and I will engage to take that hill." When Ewell refused he said, "Give me a brigade and I will do it." Again a rejection, which prompted an exasperated and angry Trimble to snap, "Give me a regiment and I will engage to take that hill." Ewell had had enough and pulled rank: "When I need advice from a junior officer I generally ask for it." Trimble allegedly turned on his heel and stormed off.

On July 2 Major-General Pender (Hill's Corps) had been forced to hand command of his division to Brigadier-General James Lane after receiving a severe wound to his thigh, which would eventually kill him. The following morning Lane deployed his two brigades to support Pettigrew's Division for the main attack. Then, just before the advance, Trimble arrived to assume command and Lane reverted to his own brigade. Lee had finally found a job for his spare major-general. Trimble made no attempt to change the deployment of his understrength brigades, despite their being too far to the right to offer support to the extended left flank of Pettigrew's Division in front of him. Trimble's presence was in fact of little consequence, as by the time he was approaching the Emmitsburg Road Pettigrew was in serious difficulties ahead and on his left, while Trimble was hit in the ankle and his horse also wounded. Lane was told he was back in command. Trimble had commanded his division for perhaps half an hour. His wound necessitated the amputation of the lower part his leg. Told that any move would cause infection to set in, Trimble agreed to be left behind when Lee withdrew his army and thus became a prisoner. He was not exchanged until February 1865, not long before Lee's final surrender at Appomattox on April 9. The loss of a leg and a year and a half in captivity was rather a high price to pay for half an hour commanding a division in Pickett's charge.

Union

Meade did not have a lot to do in terms of control of the Union defense on July 3. He had resolved to stay and fight late the previous night; he occupied a sound, indeed good, defensive position; and he had positioned his reserves of infantry and artillery to make the most use of his interior lines' advantage. In particular, he gave careful instructions via Butterfield to Sedgwick, commanding VI Corps, his main, virtually untouched, reserve of around 14,000 men (see page 458). There was considerable reshuffling of other divisions and brigades, as well as gun batteries, to ensure all was ready to support any threat to the line, particularly the center. During the actual assault, Meade remained in the rear as control rested with Hancock and his divisional commanders, particularly Gibbon and Hays, whose troops manned the front line. Meade arrived on Cemetery Ridge just as the Rebels started to fall back.

Brigadier-General John Gibbon. By Gettysburg, Gibbon had gained a reputation as one of the most competent divisional commanders in the Army of the Potomac. To Colonel Theodore Lyman on Meade's staff, Gibbon was calmness personified when under fire. Lyman described him as "a tower of strength, cool as a steel knife, always, and unmoved by anything and everything." He was a professional soldier who had graduated from West Point in 1847 – a year late, as he had been put back a year for failing to know the date of American independence! This was the same year as A. P. Hill and Heth, a great friend, graduated, both of whom would be on the opposing side at Gettysburg. Gibbon served in the Mexican and Seminole Wars and against the Indians on the frontier plains before becoming an artillery instructor and quartermaster at West Point. There he wrote *The Artillerist's Manual* – used by both sides during the Civil War as the gunner's technical bible.

Gibbon was born in Philadelphia but raised in North Carolina, and at the outbreak of the war he was expected to offer his sword to the South. That he did not do so, despite having three brothers all in the Confederate camp (one was the brigade surgeon in Lane's Brigade at Gettysburg), led to his being disowned as a traitor. With promotion notoriously slow in the artillery, he transferred into the infantry in early 1862 and, as a brigadier-general, was given a brigade in the Army of the Potomac. Although a regular officer and inclined to be a disciplinarian, Gibbon's brigade consisted of volunteers and he soon appreciated they responded far better to positive leadership than to endless punishments. His men became known as the "Black Hat Brigade" on account of their black Hardee hats. He led them in some hard fighting at Brawner's Farm on August 28, 1862 and shortly afterward at South Mountain, followed by the Maryland campaign and at Antietam. After the carnage on this battlefield he wrote to his wife, "I am as tired of this terrible war as you are, and would be perfectly willing never to see another battlefield." Nevertheless, his leadership was rewarded with promotion and he was appointed to command the 2nd Division, II Corps. He was wounded in the wrist at Fredericksburg but recovered in time to serve at Chancellorsville, although his division was held in reserve.

At Gettysburg, the fact that Gibbon was held in high regard was evidenced by his twice being elevated to temporary corps command in preference to his senior, Brigadier-General John Caldwell. The first time was on July 1 when Meade sent Hancock ahead to take charge on the battlefield, and the second the following day when Sickles' wounding led Meade to extend Hancock's authority to include III Corps and part of I Corps, leaving Gibbon with the II Corps. During the Rebel assault on July 3, Gibbon had deployed all three of his brigades in the front line. Then he had little to do but sit out the bombardment and encourage his men to stand firm against the infantry advance. At the height of the Rebel charge, Gibbon was struck by a ball that entered his arm close to the shoulder and passed through his body, fracturing his shoulder blade. He retired from the field and command passed to Brigadier-General William Harrow.

Gibbon took some time to recover, but was able to resume command of his division for Ulysses S. Grant's Overland campaign of 1864. June of that year saw him promoted to corps command in the Army of the James in the final months of the war, and he was one of the surrender commissioners at Appomattox. After the war he dropped rank to colonel and was stationed on the frontier, fighting Indians for most of the rest of his service. It was Gibbon's column that marched to the relief of Custer at the Little Big Horn in 1876 and buried the massacre victims. He retired in 1891 and died five years later of pneumonia, aged sixty-three.

Brigadier-General Alexander Hays. Hays was a forty-four-year-old, popular, hard-fighting, hard-drinking professional soldier, commanding the 3rd Division in Hancock's II Corps at Gettysburg. One of his men described him as "a princely soldier; brave as a lion . . . one of those dashing, reckless, enthusiastic generals . . . His old brigade, the Third of his division, idolized him, and we would have followed him to the death."

Graduating from West Point in 1844, Hays spent two years on the frontier before getting married. Service in the Mexican War followed before he left the army to join an iron business, which failed. An attempt to recoup his losses in the California Gold Rush did little to improve his finances, so he took work in the engineering and construction industry in his home town of Pittsburgh. At the start of the war he moved quickly from captain to colonel, to raise and command the 63rd Pennsylvania Volunteers. He led his regiment at Yorktown, Fair Oaks, Peach Orchard (Savage's Station), Glendale and Malvern Hill in the Peninsular campaign. Both his brigade and divisional commanders praised him for what was termed his "heroic action." At Second Manassas, Hays was in the forefront of a divisional attack against Stonewall Jackson's men lining the railroad cut when he was struck in the leg by a bullet, which shattered the bone and put him out of action for several months. While on sick leave he was promoted to brigadier-general. When he was fit again in the spring of 1863, Hays commanded a reserve brigade in Washington before getting command of the 3rd Division, II Corps – by virtue of his seniority – for Gettysburg. He was new to this level of command, his previous battle experience having been as a regimental commander, and he was unfamiliar with two of his three brigades.

His division was positioned on Cemetery Ridge on July 2 and saw mostly skirmishing to its front until, during the afternoon, Colonel Willard's Brigade was dispatched to the south to bolster Sickles' crumbling salient. The next day, during the Rebel cannonade, Hays displayed his coolness under fire by walking round his front-line position getting his men to collect abandoned rifle-muskets, clean them, load them and keep them ready for the inevitable infantry attack. As the Rebels approached, Hays appeared to be enjoying himself as he rode up and down the line shouting, "Now, boys, you will see some fun!" and later, as the enemy crossed the Emmitsburg Road and the order was given to open fire, "Hurrah, boys, we are giving them hell." Then to clinch the matter, Hays ordered forward two regiments from his right to support the 8th Ohio in firing into the exposed left flank of the attackers. Although the 11th Mississippi briefly penetrated his line near the Brien barn, this outflanking move was decisive and the charge melted away. Hays, who had two horses shot under him, was ecstatic. He grabbed a captured battle flag and rode up and down the line dragging the flag along the ground, yelling at his men to cheer. Hancock was to praise Hays, saying his actions were "all that could be desired in a divisional commander."

In May 1864 a bullet through his brain killed Hays outright on the first day of the Wilderness battle.

Plans and orders

In outline Lee intended to breach the Union defenses on Cemetery Hill in the area of the Copse of Trees. The plan, as we have seen, was in two phases, the first to neutralize the Union artillery in order to protect the infantry during their assault in the second phase. About 160 guns were assembled for this task. Gun positions stretched from the Peach Orchard in the south to Oak Hill in the north, with more batteries on Benner's Hill. For the infantry, the intention was to use the two divisions of Pickett and Pettigrew in the leading wave of the assault – around 9,200 men. Following immediately behind were two more brigades under Trimble with another 2,550 men as close support. Pickett's Division and the right flank was to be supported by the brigades of Wilcox and Lang with another 1,500 men, who were to advance on Pickett's orders after Pickett had moved ahead and when he considered it the right moment. The reserve was Anderson's three remaining brigades of Wright, Posey and Mahone, with over 3,500 men. This meant a grand total of some 16,750 troops had a role in the plan. Of these, 11,800 would be the initial assault force led by Pickett, with Lee giving the less than enthusiastic Longstreet overall responsibility for the entire operation.

A long-distance view from Little Round Top of some of the ground covered by Pickett's charge.

Outline of events

See Maps 61–63, and their notes.

Several hundred Rebels reached the wall on Cemetery Ridge and clambered over at three or four places. Although they had lost large numbers of men, particularly after the Emmitsburg Road had been crossed and their flanks attacked, it is arguable that at least a substantial foothold could have been secured on Cemetery Ridge if the attack had been closely supported on the flanks and a reserve had been following in the rear of the center. That none was available was down to Confederate leadership, especially Lee and Longstreet. As usual, once the attack, indeed the cannonade, got under way, Lee was seemingly content to sit and watch, as was his style of command – he was always reluctant to intervene over the heads of his corps commanders once a battle was joined. In this case he sat on his horse near the Point of Woods and made no attempt to tell Longstreet to order forward Anderson's brigades.

There is some uncertainty regarding the command setup of the brigades of Wilcox and Lang – posted well forward on the right of the line and close to the Emmitsburg Road. Both belonged to Anderson but were under Pickett's immediate control for this attack. The uncertainty arises over who would decide when they were to advance and give the necessary order. Was it Wilcox, Pickett or Longstreet? Their role was to support the right flank of the attack and they were to advance after Pickett's Division, but precisely when was the critical judgment. In the event it was Pickett who sent a messenger to Longstreet asking for Wilcox to advance – according to this aide, Captain Bright, before his men had reached the Emmitsburg Road. When these brigades did eventually advance, more than twenty minutes had elapsed and this delay was compounded by their marching straight forward, allowing the wide gap between Lane's left and Kemper's right to open up further – a situation Stannard's Brigade was already exploiting.

On the left it was a combination of faulty initial deployment, weak leadership and a well-organized and aggressive enemy that brought defeat to Pettigrew's and Trimble's efforts. Brockenbrough's Brigade was the smallest in Lee's army, and its somewhat shaky morale was unlikely to improve much under its uninspiring colonel. Its performance on July 1 had been mediocre and it had shrunk to about 770 men – not as low as some accounts suggest. It was this brigade that was given the left of Pettigrew's line – the extreme left of the entire attack. To compound the problem, Trimble placed his two supporting brigades well to the right, nearly behind the center of the line, which meant that Brockenbrough was on his own, out on a limb with no troops behind to back him up. It was not a sensible deployment for Pettigrew to have made. Trimble arrived to take charge of his two brigades only a matter of minutes before the advance began, when it was far too late to make or suggest deployment changes. For some strange reason Brockenbrough had divided his tiny command into two wings. The 47th and 55th Virginia were to advance under the orders of Colonel Robert Mayo (47th), while Brockenbrough retained command of the 22nd and 40th Virginia. When the rest of the division moved off, Mayo could not be found and Colonel Christian of the 55th Virginia, who had been told not to move until Mayo gave the order, remained in position while the two regiments on the right marched forward. Only after some delay and hurried consultations, Mayo or no Mayo, did Christian give the order to follow. The result was a frantic dash to catch up with Brockenbrough. They did so, but, battered by the enemy guns on Cemetery Hill and fire from the 8th Ohio, Pettigrew's left wing collapsed shortly after passing the ruins of the Bliss Farm. Brockenbrough was later relieved of his command and replaced by a much junior officer (Henry H. Walker), to the fury of his men, who demanded their commander remain in post. They went to the extent of petitioning Lee on July 19, stating "they cannot be silent spectators to the direct insult and gross injustice done to Colonel Brockenbrough . . ." It was to no avail.

All of Hill's three divisions (Pettigrew, Trimble and Anderson) were earmarked for the attack or as reserves, but their corps commander seemingly played little or no part in events. In terms of numbers, Hill's troops assigned to the assault, as support (Wilcox and Lang) or as reserves (Wright, Posey and Mahone) far outnumbered those of Longstreet, so theoretically Hill should have overseen the entire attack. Lee, however, gave the task to Longstreet. Almost certainly the army commander did not consider Hill up to the task, perhaps because of his sickness or his showing on the previous two days, which had proved decidedly lackluster – it was likely the former caused the latter. The British observer, Fremantle, thought Hill looked "very delicate."

Early on Pickett knew he needed reinforcements, particularly on his right. His error was perhaps in not ordering Wilcox forward within five or ten minutes of the advance starting; instead he waited and then tried to get Longstreet to make the decision – an action that delayed matters irretrievably. According to Captain Bright, he found Longstreet well to the rear, sitting alone on a fence, and the corps commander was of the opinion that the attack had already failed as, although he could not see Pickett's line from his position, he could see streams of stragglers and wounded coming back. Bright was to return to tell Pickett so. However, as Bright rode off Longstreet shouted after him to tell "Pickett that Wilcox's Brigade is in that Peach Orchard [probably indicating the Klingle orchard], and he can order him to his assistance." Whether this meant reinforce him in the assault or cover a withdrawal is not clear, but more likely the latter, knowing Longstreet's lack of faith in the attack. All this took time, and when Bright returned Pickett had, in some desperation, already sent aides to order Wilcox to "come in." According to Major Charles Pickett (Pickett's brother and assistant adjutant general), he too was sent for reinforcements. He later wrote:

> Genl. Pickett turned to me, the only staff officer who had not been sent off – and directed me to find Genl. Longstreet as quickly as I could and urge upon him vigorous and immediate support. The point at which this order was given was beyond where we had passed two fences and near a road which I take to be the Emmitsburg Road . . . I fortunately got safely back to the position in which I had last seen Genl. Longstreet but could not find him and I was directed by some officer whom I did not know, to Hood's Head Quarters, and did not find Longstreet there. By this time the charge was ended and the few men left were in full retreat.

In any attack the judicious and timely use of the main reserve is often the key to success or failure. In this instance this reserve consisted of the brigades of Wright, Posey and Mahone under Anderson. The first had suffered severely the previous day, but the other two were composed of fresh troops. In total they constituted a strong force of at least 3,500 men – but they were not used. Again it was Longstreet who prevented this. Although Lee, Hill or Anderson could have sent them forward, all three awaited Longstreet's order. In his after-action report, dated July 27, 1863, Longstreet had this to say on his critical decision: "Major-General Anderson's division [only three brigades of it] was ordered forward to support and assist the wavering columns of Pettigrew and Trimble." Within a few minutes of giving this order Longstreet saw the left flank start to falter and fall back, so his report continued:

> This [the Union flank attack] gave the enemy time to throw his entire force upon Pickett, with a strong prospect of being able to break up his lines or destroy him before Anderson's division could reach him, which would, in its turn, have greatly exposed Anderson. He was, therefore, ordered to halt.

Whether Longstreet deliberately delayed sending Anderson forward earlier is speculation, but there is little doubt that when the order was given it was too late. Anderson's brigades were almost a mile from the Copse of Trees, so it would take them at least twenty minutes to arrive in an area where their presence might be decisive, by which time the whole attack would have collapsed. On August 7 Anderson wrote:

> Wilcox's and Perry's [Lang's] brigades had been moved forward, so as to be in position to render assistance, or take advantage of any success gained by the assaulting column, and, at what I supposed to be the proper time, I was about to move forward Wright's and Posey's brigades, when Lieutenant-General Longstreet directed me to stop the movement, adding that it was useless, and would only involve unnecessary loss, the assault having failed.

Inexplicably, Anderson intended to leave Mahone's Brigade behind. With 1,500 men who had yet to see action and deployed on the vital, exposed left flank, had Anderson been sent forward at the right time this decision would surely have proved a serious mistake. In the event, Mahone moved forward later to cover the retreat against any counterattack.

Casualties

Pickett's charge was a bloodbath. However, as with all casualty figures, those given below for the enlisted men are what the present author deems the best estimates, taken after consulting the results of research by several historians.

The Confederate leadership suffered horrendous losses. Pickett's three brigade commanders and all fifteen of his regimental commanders were casualties. Garnett was killed, Armistead mortally wounded and captured, and Kemper wounded and captured. No fewer than five regiments (1st, 7th, 11th, 24th and 9th Virginia) ended the day commanded by captains, while the 8th Virginia could only muster a lieutenant. At Gettysburg this division's contribution to the fight came only on the third day, so all its losses were inflicted on that day. In total they amounted to 2,762 all ranks, including Major Dearing's artillery battalion. Busey and Martin, in *Regimental Strengths and Losses at Gettysburg*, break this number down into 626 killed, 1,296 wounded and 840 missing/captured, or 50.5 percent.

In Pettigrew's Division, Pettigrew himself was wounded, as were the brigade commanders Marshall and Fry. Brockenbrough and Davis escaped unscathed. Because Pettigrew's Division had suffered heavily on the first day, estimates of its losses in this charge are difficult to assess; however, it is probable they amounted to between 1,200 and 1,500.

Pickett, Pettigrew and Trimble Cross the Emmitsburg Road to Charge the Copse of Trees and the Angle

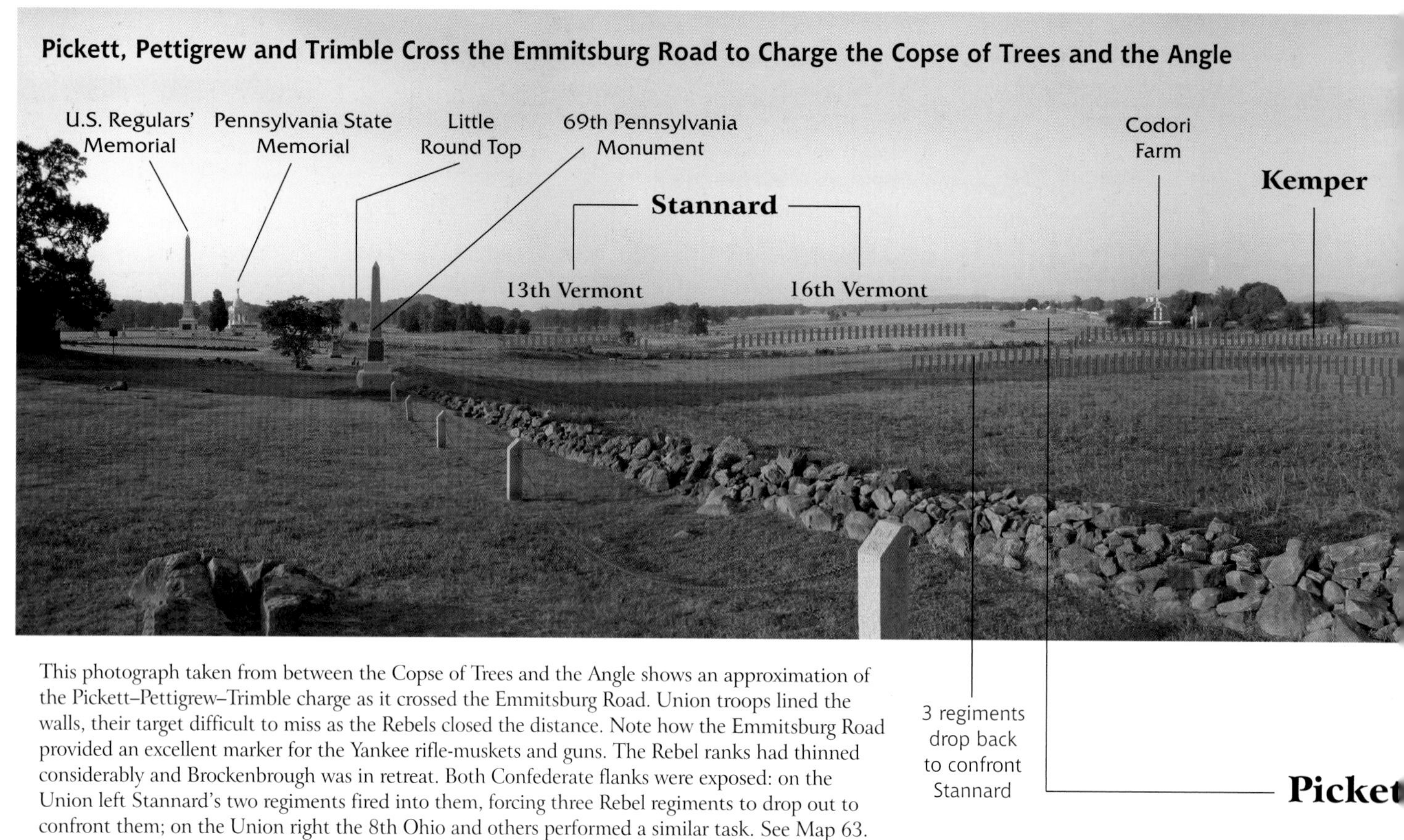

This photograph taken from between the Copse of Trees and the Angle shows an approximation of the Pickett–Pettigrew–Trimble charge as it crossed the Emmitsburg Road. Union troops lined the walls, their target difficult to miss as the Rebels closed the distance. Note how the Emmitsburg Road provided an excellent marker for the Yankee rifle-muskets and guns. The Rebel ranks had thinned considerably and Brockenbrough was in retreat. Both Confederate flanks were exposed: on the Union left Stannard's two regiments fired into them, forcing three Rebel regiments to drop out to confront them; on the Union right the 8th Ohio and others performed a similar task. See Map 63.

Armistead Is Hit

Sergeant Denis B. Easley, 14th Virginia, was a very old soldier when he penned a letter dated July 24, 1913. The letter is now held among the Easley papers in the U.S. Military History Institute in Carlisle barracks and, although Easley may, like most old soldiers, "talk up" his military adventures, it is certainly worth quoting here for the realism it gives to what it was like during those few brief moments over the wall at the Angle.

> There were others to my right and left. I took in all this at a glance and then saw Armistead. We went up to the second line of guns [Cushing's] almost as close as if we had been marching in the ranks. He fell to the left of our gun and I stepped in to the right. I might say here that our line was crossing the wall when I looked back; possibly half of them over. They went back to a man. The squad that killed Armistead was just about where the monument of the 71st Penn. is located . . . I dropped in behind the gun and commenced firing back at the squad that killed him using the gun as a rest. I fired several shots and then they paid their respects to me pouring back a volley similar to the one that killed Armistead. I was behind the gun between it and the wheels but something seemed to strike me all over. They must have fired too low and knocked gravels against me. I felt myself and when I found I was not hurt I grabbed for my ramrod to return their compliment and found it was shot off just where it enters the stock . . . [I went] back to the wall, looking for a gun. One of our men gave me his gun saying "He was wounded." I rammed a ball about half way down when it hung, and I began driving the rammer against the stone fence when he turned over and said "don't load it: it's loaded" I went off the handle and said "Where are you wounded anyhow; I don't see anything the matter with you." He turned over and groaned and made no answer . . . I grabbed another gun with the bayonet twisted like a cork screw, and blew through it. I expected if I fired it the bullet would have hit the bayonet, but just as I got it loaded three bayonets came against me and they hauled me in . . . I forgot to say that Armistead did not groan or move while I fired several shots near him, and I thought him dead, but he was an old man 63 [actually 46] and was probably exhausted . . .

Armistead was wounded in the upper right arm and above the left knee. It was not thought life-threatening, but he was indeed exhausted, both physically and mentally. He died in the temporary Union field hospital at Spangler's Farm at 9 a.m. on July 5 and was buried there shortly afterward. He was later reburied at St Paul's Cemetery, Baltimore, beside his uncle, George Armistead, the defender of the original "Star Spangled Banner" at Fort McHenry.

Another witness to Armistead's wounding was Lieutenant George W. Finley, Company K, 56th Virginia Infantry, Garnett's Brigade, who left this brief account:

> Gen. Armistead, on foot, strode over the stone fence, his hat on his sword and calling upon his men to charge. A few of us followed him until, just as he put his hand upon one of the abandoned guns, he was shot down. Seeing that most of the men still remained at the stone wall I returned, and was one of the very few who got back unhurt.

Trimble was wounded, as was his brigade commander Lowrance, but Lane was untouched. Overall losses for his division are put at around 1,000 men.

These figures give an estimated total loss for the main attacking force of 4,962–5,262 (say 5,000–5,250). On the assumption that around 11,800 men took part, then the losses amounted to 42–44 percent. The somewhat late and forlorn attack of Wilcox and Lang, which was not part of the main assault, produced about another 430 casualties. If these are added to the main attack losses, the grand total is between 5,430 and 5,680.

The Union losses to the front-line defenders are usually considered to be about 1,500. This represents around 24 percent of the 6,350 involved in repelling the charge. Put another way, the Rebels lost, to all causes, some 3.5 men to every Yankee.

There were numerous reasons why the defenders suffered so much less, among the most obvious being that their targets were exposed in the open while they crouched behind stone walls piled up with fence rails. One reason less often mentioned is that the defenders were stationary and had nothing to do but load and fire, many having several pre-loaded pieces to hand, while the men advancing had to stop to fire, then either continue with an unloaded musket or remain stationary while reloading. The obvious priority was to press on as fast as possible, so probably most of those Rebels that reached the wall had fired only once as they double-quicked the last 200 yards, while their opponents would have fired at least five or six times from when the Rebels crossed the Emmitsburg Road. This road crossing was also the marker for the Union guns to change to canister. The great majority of losses to the attackers occurred on that deadly stretch of grass between the Emmitsburg Road and the Angle–Copse of Trees. The carnage in this area was appalling. Captain Benjamin Thompson of the 111th New York, positioned near the Brien barn, has described what he saw that evening:

> No words can depict the ghastly picture. The track of the great charge was marked by bodies of men in all possible positions, wounded, bleeding, dying and dead. Near the line where the final struggle occurred, the men lay in heaps, the wounded wriggling and groaning under the weight of the dead among whom they were entangled. In my weak and exhausted condition I could not long endure the gory, ghastly spectacle. I found my head reeling, the tears flowing and my stomach sick at the sight. For months the specter haunted my dreams, and even after forty-seven years it comes back as the most horrible vision I have ever conceived.

Scott Hartwig, the Supervisory Historian at the Gettysburg National Military Park, had this to say in his article "It Struck Horror to Us All" in the *Gettysburg Magazine*, issue 4:

> The slaughter had been horrifying. General Webb counted 42 dead Confederates within the angle area. Many more lay along the stone wall and in the field beyond. John Buckley of Co. K wrote that "the slaughter was terrible, to which fact the ground [was] literally covered with the enemy's dead" . . . A member of the 13th Vermont, who looked upon this area, deemed it "the great slaughter pen on the field of Gettysburg" . . . Five hundred and twenty-two dead Confederates would be buried in a mass grave in the field that extended from the angle area to the Emmitsburg Road; a ghastly and tragic confirmation to the Vermont soldier's statements.

A word is needed on the relative importance of artillery or musketry fire in causing casualties. Obviously at the longer ranges – that is before the attackers reached the Emmitsburg Road – all losses were due to artillery firing long-range ammunition. In Hancock's report he stated: "No attempt was made to check the advance of the enemy until the first line had arrived within about 700 yards of our position when a feeble fire was opened upon it, but with no material effect, and without delaying for a moment its determined advance." The problem was that the Rebel cannonade had done the most damage to Union guns in the center of the line, the Angle–Copse of Trees area, and guns still firing were low or even out of long-range ammunition. It was the Union guns on the flanks that did the most damage to the advancing Confederates – those of McGilvery's batteries, and fire from Osborn on Cemetery Hill and Rittenhouse on Little Round Top. Nevertheless, the losses from gunfire sustained by the Southerners before the Emmitsburg Road was reached were comparatively small. Some men had collapsed with sunstroke, some were shirkers and dropped out quickly, some more were hit by artillery fire, and Brokenbrough's Brigade of about 800 was halted soon after passing the Bliss Farm. But of the 11,800 who participated, surely 9,000 reached the Emmitsburg Road. Here many more were hit as the Yankee infantry and artillery opened up with canister, and here many unwounded men decided they would go no further. Large numbers of Trimble's command did not get beyond the road, with more men deciding now was the time to take cover and do some shooting rather than charging. Perhaps 6,000 men pushed forward from the road into a hurricane of rifle-musket fire from the front and then from the flanks. As noted above, this was where the bodies of the dead and wounded lay so thickly on the ground. Perhaps 2,000 reached the wall or very close to it and several hundred clambered over while others sought shelter behind it.

We "literally mowed them down"

Captain Edward R. Bowen, whose regiment (114th Pennsylvania, 1st Division, III Corps) was moved into a reserve position, watched the Rebel assault hit by a storm of cannon fire followed by a blast of musketry.

> At a double quick we moved to the position assigned to us in the second line . . . Here we waited the coming assault of Pickett's brave men. For a brief space there was an ominous pause of the artillery fire of both sides, General Hunt, chief of the artillery of the Army of the Potomac, having ordered it to cease on our side in order that the guns might have an opportunity to cool and the ammunition to be economized for the assault he knew was about to be made . . . The enemy [infantry] rapidly crossed the intervening space. Our batteries, loaded with grape and canister, were trained upon them at point blank range and opened again upon them with deadly effect. Still they closed up the gaps and pressed on. Our men reserved their fire and allowed them to come so far as in their judgment was far enough and blazed upon them such a withering musketry fire as literally mowed them down.

CONTROVERSY

Should Pickett's Charge Have Been Made and Could It Have Succeeded?

There has been an acrimonious debate over this issue since July 3, 1863, not only among participants but also between historians and authors. The arguments will no doubt continue for as long as people maintain an interest in the greatest battle ever fought on American soil. The present writer will attempt to summarize the case for and against Pickett's charge being made, and its chances of success, and then comment on why it failed and what might have been the consequences of success.

Making the charge was a mistake and it could never have succeeded

The charge was heroic but foolish. On July 3 Lee knew that he faced the entire Army of the Potomac and that he was therefore outnumbered. Once his plan for a diversionary and simultaneous attack by Ewell was compromised by the early-morning Union attack at Culp's Hill, Lee should have known this reduced his chances of succeeding in a single frontal attack. He had seen how effective and how stubborn the Yankee defenses had been on the previous two days, and also the cost that partial victory had inflicted on his troops. He should have realized that the spectacular victory he needed for the campaign to be worthwhile in the wider arena of the war was now unattainable at Gettysburg. Lee was well aware that morning that the man he intended to command this final fling, Longstreet, had spoken out against it and was decidedly unenthusiastic – some would say a deliberate foot-dragger.

Dead Confederates lying as they fell near the center of the battlefield.

Not only had Lee lost the chance of early-morning coordinated attacks at both ends of the enemy's position, but he had also lost any prospect of surprise. He devised an alternative plan that would take time (in the event all morning) to prepare and had become blindingly obvious to the Union Army three-quarters of a mile away on Cemetery Ridge. Rebel preparations were thorough, but without the element of surprise the opposition could anticipate what was to happen and adjust their dispositions and defenses accordingly.

The Confederates were to launch a purely frontal attack, with the aim of punching a hole in a well-prepared defensive line and then exploit it with supporting troops. The attack would take place over about threequarters of a mile of largely open ground, with the attackers comparatively easy targets for most of the way, and certainly over the final 300 yards. Lee should have known that the chances of success were small and that even partial success would come at too high a price in terms of men lost. He was asking too much of his troops, most of whom had fought hard on the previous two days and suffered very heavily in the process. In brief, he was overestimating the capabilities of his own men and underestimating those of his enemy.

Lee Takes the Blame

Colonel Alexander, who had watched Pickett's charge from the Rebel gun line, described in his *Military Memoirs* how Lee visited him just as Wilcox's Brigade was making its forlorn attack on the right:

> While Wilcox's brigade was making its charge, Gen. Lee rode up and joined me. He was entirely alone, which could scarcely have happened except by design on his part. We were not firing, but holding position to prevent pursuit by the enemy. I have no doubt Lee was apprehensive of this, and had come to the front to help rally the fugitives if that happened. He remained with us perhaps an hour and spoke to nearly every man that passed, using expressions such as: "Don't be discouraged." "It was my fault this time." "Form your ranks again when you get under cover." "All good men must hold together now."

Lee should have given serious consideration to alternatives to an attack once his original plan of an early, coordinated continuation of the previous assaults on either flank became impossible. While the chances of a successful flank move, tactical or strategic, around the enemy's left (or right) was certainly impractical at this stage, was there not a strong case for either withdrawing to the South Mountain passes and awaiting attack or remaining at Gettysburg and inviting Meade to attack him there?

Making the charge was a viable option and could have succeeded

Lee was right to feel that his partial successes on the first two days should be exploited. He had fresh troops in the form of Pickett's Division, who were eager for the fight. He had retained the initiative as the attacker thus far in the battle and would be foolish now to hand it to his enemy. Lee was primarily an attacking general and it was, in his view, only by a successful attack at Gettysburg that he could obtain worthwhile strategic results from the campaign.

The prospect of going on the defensive at Gettysburg or further west would surrender the initiative and there was no guarantee Meade would immediately attack – although we now know he would almost certainly have been compelled to do so by Washington if he had seemed hesitant.

Lee's alternative plan for July 3 did have the ingredients of success. He understood that the basic requirement for this outcome was to get the maximum number of infantry across the long stretch of open ground with the minimum of losses and the maximum speed. He knew that for most of the advance his men could only be hit by artillery fire and so this had to be suppressed or neutralized before the infantry attack. If he could do that and at the same time bring up as many as possible of his own guns with or behind his infantry to give them supporting fire over the final quarter of a mile, when the enemy infantry would be more exposed, then sufficient numbers of his troops would reach their objective to take it. If his infantry was supported on each flank and by the follow-up of substantial reserves to exploit success, then victory was achievable. The preliminary artillery bombardment had to be massive, concentrated and, if necessary, prolonged until seen to be successful. It had to be well planned and coordinated, with all gunners clear of their tasks and targets. The infantry phase had to be equally well thought out, with the best troops selected for the assault and the follow-up reserves earmarked. All commanders had to understand their roles and the chain of command. Only thorough preparation, overwhelming firepower from the artillery followed by a massive infantry assault could negate the numerous difficulties. Lee's plan envisaged all these ingredients. The ultimate test would be in their implementation.

Comments

As we have seen, in the vast majority of military plans the unexpected happens, difficulties arise, delays occur, there are command errors, equipment fails and the plan does not produce the hoped-for results. This is what happened with Pickett's charge. It failed not so much because it was a bad idea, impossible to achieve, but due to faulty execution and the resilience, determination and sound leadership of the enemy. Longstreet, Pickett and the other commanders had not been given an impossible task. A breach in the Union defenses around the Copse of Trees was momentarily achieved. A hole was made in the defenses and the 71st and 69th Pennsylvania were pushed back; there was a hurried scramble by the defenders to plug the hole. The gallantry of the few hundred Rebels who crossed the wall was doomed because there were too few of them. Had the plan gone as intended, this might not have been the case.

The reasons the plan did not go as intended are fairly obvious from the account of the day's events given above, but as there are a considerable number, and as it was their cumulative effect that ruined the plan, it may be helpful to summarize them here.

The artillery cannonade

- Too many of the available guns were not employed, and insufficient use was made of possible enfilade gun positions. The chief responsibility for this lies with Pendleton, who permitted the corps artillery chiefs to work independently.
- Technical problems with ammunition led to a high percentage of shots not exploding or doing so too early or too late.
- Ammunition shortages, compounded by the move of the army reserve train to the rear, meant that many batteries ran short or out at the critical time when guns were needed to move forward to support the infantry advance. The length of

the cannonade had to be extended from an anticipated twenty minutes to up to two hours, which caused ammunition stocks to be seriously depleted.

- Hill and Walker, his artillery chief, exacerbated the potential ammunition shortage by wasting rounds on the morning artillery duel over Bliss Farm. Alexander later wrote of this, "I would not [have] let one of my guns fire a shot."
- The above resulted in only a handful of guns with a few rounds of ammunition advancing; thus their support was minimal just when the infantry needed it most. Neither Lee (he admitted in his report that shortages "were unknown to me") nor Longstreet appears to have taken any interest or made any enquiries about artillery ammunition availability or expenditure, crucial though these were to the plan.
- The difficulties of accurately firing at a linear target that was largely obscured by smoke ensured too many rounds went high and missed their primary target – the enemy guns – falling instead on the reverse slope, which was soon vacated by the administrative elements occupying it.
- Although Alexander carefully deployed all the guns of his corps (Longstreet's), those of Hill and Ewell were less well placed with too many left in reserve. This was largely a failure of Pendleton, along with the two corps commanders.
- The Union artillery was particularly well handled and reserves were available to replace batteries badly damaged or short of ammunition.
- The decision to order Union guns to cease fire to deceive the Confederates into believing that they had been put out of action worked well and the Rebels, who by then were chronically short of ammunition, began their advance when their guns had in fact failed to achieve their objective.

The infantry attack

- The fact that their artillery bombardment had failed to suppress or destroy sufficient enemy batteries cost the advancing infantry too much damage at long range (particularly from the flanks), to which they had no means of replying.
- Lee's selection of Longstreet, who thought the whole operation a mistake, was unfortunate but probably unavoidable, as Hill, who had the majority of the troops taking part, was sick and had performed poorly so far in the battle, while Ewell and his troops were too far away to be directly involved.
- The selection of the troops to participate could have been better, in that too many from Hill's Corps had been badly battered on either the first or second day, while brigades such as Posey's and Mahone's, which had suffered little, remained spectators. It seems likely that Lee had not been informed of which brigades had suffered badly during the earlier heavy fighting.

Three Rebel prisoners await the long march to jail.

Out of Ammunition

Brigadier-General Ambrose watched Pickett's charge from Seminary Ridge.

> On the men swept. Our Brigade being held in reserve, enabled us to take a position where we had a fair view of the whole field, and I am sure that I have never seen troops start better than this storming party did. Pickett pushed firmly and steadily forward, going over the ground our Brigade had passed the day before. Pettigrew followed in fine order. Our artillery now ceased firing, and upon inquiry, I learned they had exhausted their ammunition! And at such a time! There is Pickett and Pettigrew half across the valley; the enemy have run up new guns and are pouring deadly fire into their ranks. – The enemy infantry have opened upon them – they fall on every side . . . My God! All is as silent as death with our line of artillery [a slight exaggeration]; one hundred and twenty pieces of cannon standing mute and dumb while the very flower of the Confederate army is grappling on unequal terms in a struggle of life and death with an enemy strongly posted . . .

The actual deployment for the advance was poor on the left flank, where Brockenbrough's Brigade, the weakest and most suspect, was placed without any immediate support, as Trimble's brigades were behind and too far to the right (south).

There was a substantial gap at the outset of the advance between Pettigrew's right (Fry) and Pickett's left (Garnett), with Pickett having to make an awkward left incline in order to close the gap and move on his objective, the Copse of Trees, which was to his northeast at the start rather than straight ahead.

It was a long way for the infantry to march, with a number of obstacles (fences) to cross, under increasingly severe fire from guns and then massed rifle-musket fire, without them being able to respond. The Emmitsburg Road was more of a hindrance than a help, in that it was an obstacle and the meager protection it offered persuaded many men to stay there instead of pushing on, just at the time when enemy fire was intensifying dramatically as the Yankee infantry joined in with their guns firing canister.

One crucial failure was the lack of effective support on both flanks. On the right, Wilcox and Lang were launched too late to stop Stannard's regiments attacking that flank; and due to being unable to see Pickett's men, they advanced pointlessly straight ahead into McGilvery's guns. On the left, Brockenbrough's advance petered out well before the Emmitsburg Road and thus exposed Davis's Brigade to the envelopment of his flank by the 8th Ohio and other regiments.

Of equal significance was the halting of the advance of Anderson's three reserve brigades by Longstreet. The main attack had no reserve moving up behind. Only when it was seen to be failing did Anderson start to move. He had almost a mile to go, so by then it was far too late to influence events. For a commander determined to make his attack succeed, it was not the way to handle reserves – but then Longstreet never wanted to make the attack at all. It was this lack of support as the charging Rebels reached or clambered over the wall that was later most vehemently condemned by surviving Southern commanders.

The Yankee defenders had most of the advantages as far as the infantry were concerned. They were well led, determined, had not suffered excessively during the cannonade and were at least partially sheltered by walls and fence rails. Add to this their stockpiling of loaded rifles, their having time to fire five, six or more times to their enemy's once or twice, and the odds swung heavily in their favor. The Union troops could take good aim while resting their weapons on walls or fences, while their attackers could only get off a hasty, poorly aimed shot and then either stop to reload or press on with an unloaded weapon.

Meade had far more and better placed reserves, particularly VI Corps, available to counter any local enemy success. Mostly, they were not required.

Summary

While it should be acknowledged that the Confederates almost succeeded in securing a foothold on Cemetery Ridge, and given adequate and timely support might, just might, have held on, particularly if coupled with a general advance by Rodes on the left and McLaws on the right, it must be asked whether a victory at Gettysburg on Day Three would have achieved much. It would have been bought at a devastatingly high price. Lee would have had an exhausted army, crippled by losses, with thousands of wounded to be cared for and artillery that had virtually no ammunition until the ordnance train arrived from the south. Also, he needed to keep foraging to supply his army, which would have required the use of many men, including much of the cavalry. Almost certainly Meade would have pulled back, more or less intact, probably to the Pipe Creek line, keeping between Lee and Washington, from whence would come supplies and reinforcements. Lee would have won a victory that was not decisive, not spectacular enough to make an enduring strategic or political impact of sufficient force to affect favorably the survival of the Confederacy. To do this he had to win, and win well on Day One. It is doubtful if a successful Pickett's charge would have brought Lee more than a respite before a withdrawal back to Virginia became inevitable.

CAVALRY ACTIONS

EAST CAVALRY FIELD (RUMMEL FARM) (Map 64)

The largest cavalry action of the Battle of Gettysburg took place a few miles east of the town in the fields to the south of Rummel Farm. Jeb Stuart was now commanding a division of four brigades under Brigadier-Generals Wade Hampton and Fitzhugh Lee and Colonels John R. Chambliss and Milton Ferguson (he had replaced the wounded Jenkins, whose brigade had been absorbed into Stuart's command from Ewell's Corps). Stuart had a combined strength of around 5,500 men – fewer than when he started the campaign, due to casualties and men and horses dropping out through exhaustion during the final days of his march. He also had a mixed bag of fourteen guns (eight ordnance rifles, and two each of Napoleons, 10-pounder Parrotts and 12-pounder howitzers). Stuart complained in his report that "My command was increased by the addition of Jenkins' [Ferguson's] brigade, who here in the presence of the enemy allowed themselves to be supplied with but 10 rounds of ammunition . . . However, this was apparently rectified during the fighting by Lieutenant-Colonel Whitcher, 34th Virginia Battalion, obtaining replenishment."

Stuart's precise orders for July 3 are uncertain, but this is not surprising as Lee was not, and in this case could not be, specific in his orders to subordinates. Stuart only said, "I moved forward to a position to the left of General Ewell's left and in advance of it," which is not very informative. However, clearly Lee wanted Stuart to get into the rear of Meade's position, threaten his lines of communication (principally the Baltimore Pike) and at the same time be able to cut off and disrupt any retreating Yankees should his attack at Gettysburg succeed. It would be ideal if Stuart's presence in Meade's rear were felt as Lee launched his main assault. Undoubtedly it was with these thoughts in his mind that Stuart set off early on July 3, moving east along the York Pike. After about 2.5 miles he turned right and headed southeast across the fields to the Lower Dutch Road, which led to the Hanover Road directly east of Gettysburg town. Shortly before 11:00 a.m. Stuart, leading the brigades of Chambliss and Ferguson, arrived on Cress Ridge and moved forward some dismounted troops into the Rummel Farm area to act as skirmishers. He then awaited his remaining brigades, Hampton and F. Lee. At about 11:00 a.m., before these formations arrived, Stuart ordered a gun to fire four shots, one to each point of the compass. Why he did this remains something of a puzzle, as it merely alerted the enemy to his whereabouts. The most likely explanation was that it was a signal to Lee that he was in position in Meade's rear.

The Union forces in the area under Brigadier-General David Gregg were alerted. Gregg commanded about 4,000 men in three brigades under Colonels John B. McIntosh and David Gregg's cousin J. Irvin Gregg, and Brigadier-General George A. Custer, this last hastily borrowed from Kilpatrick's Division. His supporting artillery consisted of ten ordnance rifles, four with the 1st U.S. Artillery, Battery E and G, under Captain Alanson M. Randol, and another six in the 2nd U.S. Artillery, Battery M, under Lieutenant Alexander C. M. Pennington. David Gregg had already heard that Rebel cavalry were in the vicinity and might pose a threat, so he had persuaded Custer to remain with him instead of moving off to the west. It was Custer's regiments that first arrived south of Rummel Farm and deployed skirmishers to confront those of the enemy. Gregg moved up with McIntosh's Brigade, keeping that of his cousin in reserve, to begin the action with an artillery duel. The battle at East Cavalry Field had begun.

According to Stuart his plan had been to "engage the enemy in front with sharpshooters, and move a command of cavalry upon their left flank . . . ," but the Union skirmish line pushed back tenaciously, with the troopers of the 5th Michigan Cavalry armed

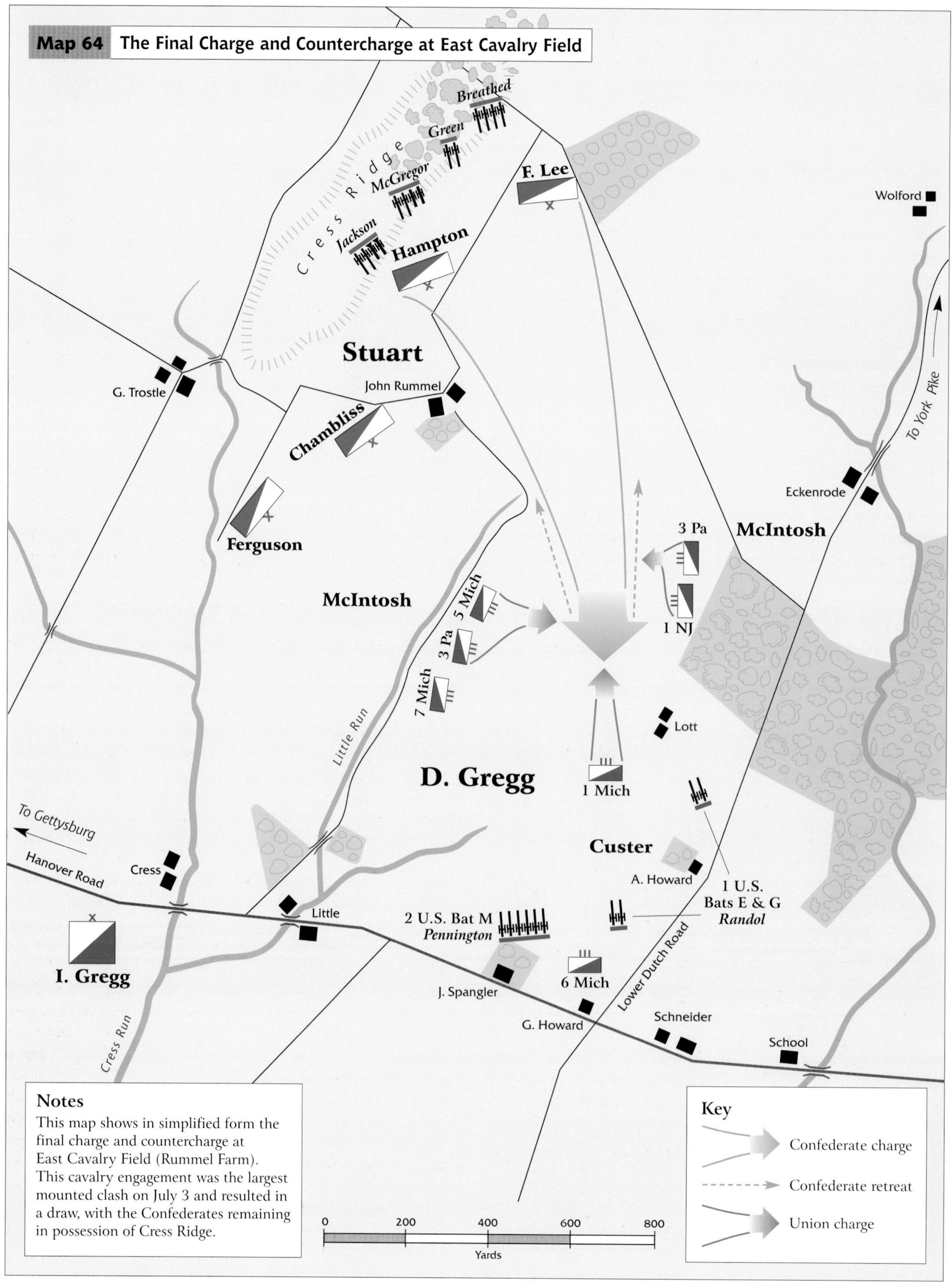

Notes

This map shows in simplified form the final charge and countercharge at East Cavalry Field (Rummel Farm). This cavalry engagement was the largest mounted clash on July 3 and resulted in a draw, with the Confederates remaining in possession of Cress Ridge.

with Spencer repeating carbines, multiplying their firepower considerably. Stuart decided on a direct cavalry charge to break their resistance. He ordered an assault by the 1st Virginia Cavalry, his own former regiment, now in Fitz Lee's Brigade. The battle started in earnest at around 1 p.m., at the same time that Lee's cannonade began pounding Cemetery Ridge at Gettysburg. Fitz Lee's troopers came pouring through the farm, scattering the Union skirmish line. Gregg ordered Custer to counterattack with the 7th Michigan. Custer personally led the regiment, shouting, "Come on you wolverines!" Waves of horsemen collided in furious fighting along the fence lines near the farm. Seven hundred men fought at point-blank range across the fences with carbines, pistols and sabers. Custer's horse was shot under him, forcing him to commandeer a bugler's horse, but eventually his men broke through the fence and forced the Virginians to fall back.

Stuart sent in reinforcements from all three of his brigades: the 9th and 13th Virginia (Chambliss's Brigade), the 1st North Carolina and the Jeff Davis Legion (Hampton's) and squadrons from the 2nd Virginia (F. Lee's). Custer's pursuit was broken and the 7th Michigan retired in some disorder.

The finale, launched at about the same time as Pickett's charge, was when Stuart tried for a decisive breakthrough by sending the bulk of Hampton's and Fitz Lee's men at a gallop, with sabers drawn in traditional cavalry style, down the slope into the midst of the Yankee position. Once again the first to confront the attack was Custer, this time at the head of Colonel Charles H. Town's 1st Michigan. A Union trooper described the clash: "As the two columns approached each other the pace of each increased, when suddenly a crash, like the falling of timber, betokened the crisis. So sudden and violent was the collision that many of the horses were turned end over end and crushed their riders beneath them."

A Union horse artilery battery assembled for maneuver.

However, as this desperate melee was taking place in the center, McIntosh led his brigade into Hampton's right flank and the 3rd Pennsylvania and 1st New Jersey hit the Rebels on their left. Hampton received a serious head wound and Custer lost his second horse. Assaulted on three sides, the Confederates withdrew to Cress Ridge. Their pursuers went no further than Rummel Farm – the battle had ended in a tactical draw. However, strategically Stuart had lost in that he had not achieved anything worthwhile, while Gregg had prevented it. The casualties, as with many cavalry-versus-cavalry engagements, were far from excessive. Stuart lost 181 and Gregg 254 – well over 200 of them in Custer's Brigade.

FARNSWORTH'S CHARGE AGAINST THE REBEL RIGHT (SOUTH CAVALRY FIELD) (Map 65)

On the morning of July 3 the Union Cavalry Corps commander sent two of his brigades to the left, or southern, flank of the Union Army. One was Brigadier-General Wesley Merritt's Reserve Brigade, which moved north from Emmitsburg, and the other that of Brigadier-General Elon J. Farnsworth (Custer's Brigade, as we have seen, was detained with David Gregg at East Cavalry Field). Both would be under the divisional command of Brigadier-General Judson Kilpatrick. He would have some 3,000 horsemen and two horse artillery batteries: Battery K of the 1st U.S. Artillery under Captain William M. Graham, with six ordnance rifles, and Battery E of the 4th U.S. Artillery under Lieutenant Samuel S. Elder, with three serviceable ordnance rifles – a total of nine guns.

Farnsworth reached the area south of Bushman's Hill at about the time the great artillery duel was starting across the main battlefield. Joined by Kilpatrick, they awaited Merritt's arrival, which occurred at around 3:00 p.m., just as the Pickett–Pettigrew–Trimble charge got under way. Kilpatrick's orders as to what he was to do when in position on Lee's flank were not clear. He had been told vaguely to press the enemy and "strike at the first opportunity." Conditions, however, were against him. The horsemen had to operate over ground covered with fences, boulders, steep slopes and large areas of woods while the Rebel infantry sheltered behind stone walls topped with fence rails. In other words, it was infantry country and for cavalry to have a chance they would need to fight dismounted. As a member of the 1st Texas commented, it was "simply a picnic to fight cavalry under such conditions."

Blocking Kilpatrick's progress was Brigadier-General George Anderson's Georgian Brigade, which had reinforced the 1st Texas from Robertson's Brigade, and the 1st South Carolina Cavalry regiment under Colonel John Black from Hampton's Brigade in Stuart's Division. Artillery support consisted of the Washington (South Carolina) Battery under Captain James F. Hart, with three Blakely Rifles; the Rowan (North Carolina) Artillery Battery under Captain James Reilly, with two Napoleons, two 10-pounder Parrotts and two ordnance rifles; and the Charleston (South Carolina) "German" Artillery Battery commanded by Captain William K. Bachman, with four Napoleons: a total of thirteen guns. The overall Rebel defense of their southern flank was in the hands of Brigadier-General Evander Law, who had assumed command of Hood's Division after his wounding the previous day. This force was deployed astride the Emmitsburg Road.

Kilpatrick, a "Boy General" at twenty-five, was about to earn, or justify, his nickname of "Killcavalry." His first error was to attack piecemeal. He launched Merritt's Brigade up and to the left (west) of the Emmitsburg Road. Much of the attack was by dismounted troopers, but it soon petered out, the assault being driven off with ease by Anderson's Georgians and Hart's Battery. What happened next has become the main controversy generated by Farnsworth's charge and death. Three accounts of the incident were written by Captain Henry C. Parsons, 1st Vermont Cavalry. According to his first unedited version, at about 4:00 p.m. an aide from Pleasonton (who was at Meade's headquarters) galloped up to Kilpatrick. Parsons claimed to have seen and overheard the following:

> In a moment an aide came down [from Pleasonton] and Kilpatrick sprang into his saddle and rode toward him. The verbal order I heard delivered was: "Hood is turning or pressing our left; play all your guns; charge in their rear; create a strong [diversion]. In a moment Farnsworth rode up. Kilpatrick impetuously repeated the order.

The ground to be covered was utterly unsuited to a cavalry action and Farnsworth, according to Parsons, made this view plain. There was allegedly a serious clash of personalities and disagreement over the wisdom of this charge, but in the end Farnsworth accepted the order (but see box, page 504).

Not only was the whole concept of a cavalry charge in the circumstances flawed, but also it was again delivered piecemeal. Farnsworth sent in the 1st West Virginia on its own without any artillery support. Private Thomas McCarty of the 1st Texas in the skirmish line stated, "They went through us cutting right and left, the firing for a few minutes was front, rear and toward the flanks. In a few minutes great numbers of riderless horses were galloping about, & others with riders were trying to surrender." Some Yankee horsemen went careering to behind the Rebel line and disappeared.

The 1st Vermont was the next to dash forward, but on this occasion Farnsworth had split the regiment into two groups or battalions. He accompanied the one commanded by Major William Wells, which was supported by the second under Captain Parsons. They burst through the thin skirmish line ahead of them and then veered right toward the lower western slope of Round Top. Sheffield's Alabamians were posted a little way up the slope and heard the crashing and yelling behind them. First the 4th Alabama, then the 15th, turned around and came dashing down the slope. The 4th were too late to catch the Wells/Farnsworth group but were crashed into by Captain Parsons (who was wounded) and his survivors trying to retreat in considerable disorder. The Wells/Farnsworth group had progressed north and then across the Plum Run behind the John Slyder Farm before they realized it was time to retrace their steps. It was a long way and many Rebels were between them and safety. Wells (and Parsons) succeeded, but Farnsworth was finally hit in the body by four bullets fired by the 15th Alabama as he tried to run the gauntlet through the trees on the lower slope of Round Top. Afterward it was alleged that he had taken his own life to avoid capture, but this was fiction – it would have been an impossibility after being hit by so many bullets.

It was a flawed attack and any threat to Lee's right never developed. Not far away, Longstreet warmly congratulated Law "on the manner in which the situation had been handled."

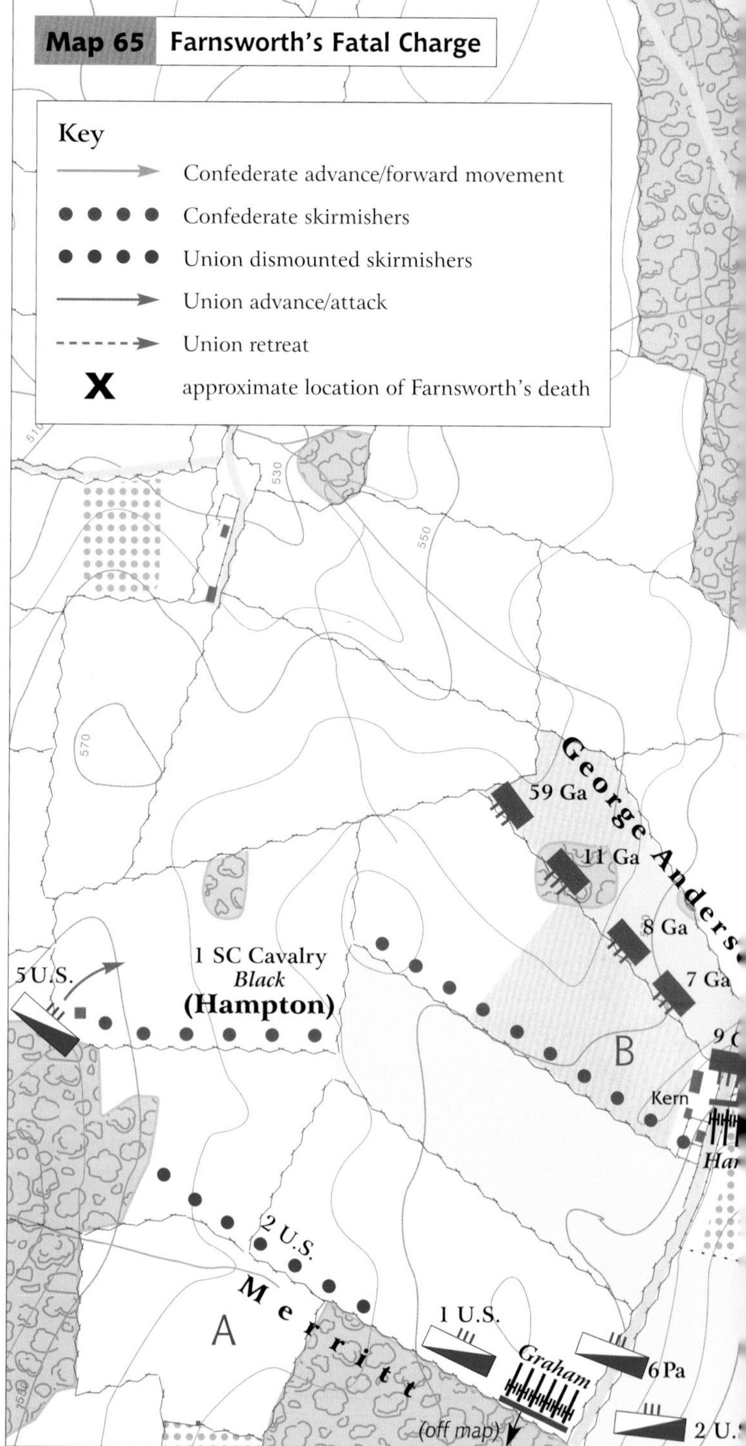

Notes

• This map shows the events on the Union left during the afternoon of July 3, the finale of which was Farnsworth's fatal charge, which took place after Pickett's endeavors had been repulsed on the main battlefield. Brig.-Gen. Judson Kilpatrick – commonly known by his nickname of "Killcavalry" – commanding the Union cavalry force, was keen to make an impressive impact on the Rebel right. The defense of the Confederate right was entrusted to Brig.-Gen. Evander Law, who had replaced Hood as divisional commander after the latter's wounding. Law had placed Brig.-Gen. George Anderson's Brigade, reinforced by the 1st Texas from Robertson's Brigade and Colonel John Black's 1st South Carolina Cavalry from Hampton's Brigade in Stuart's Division, in a blocking position astride the

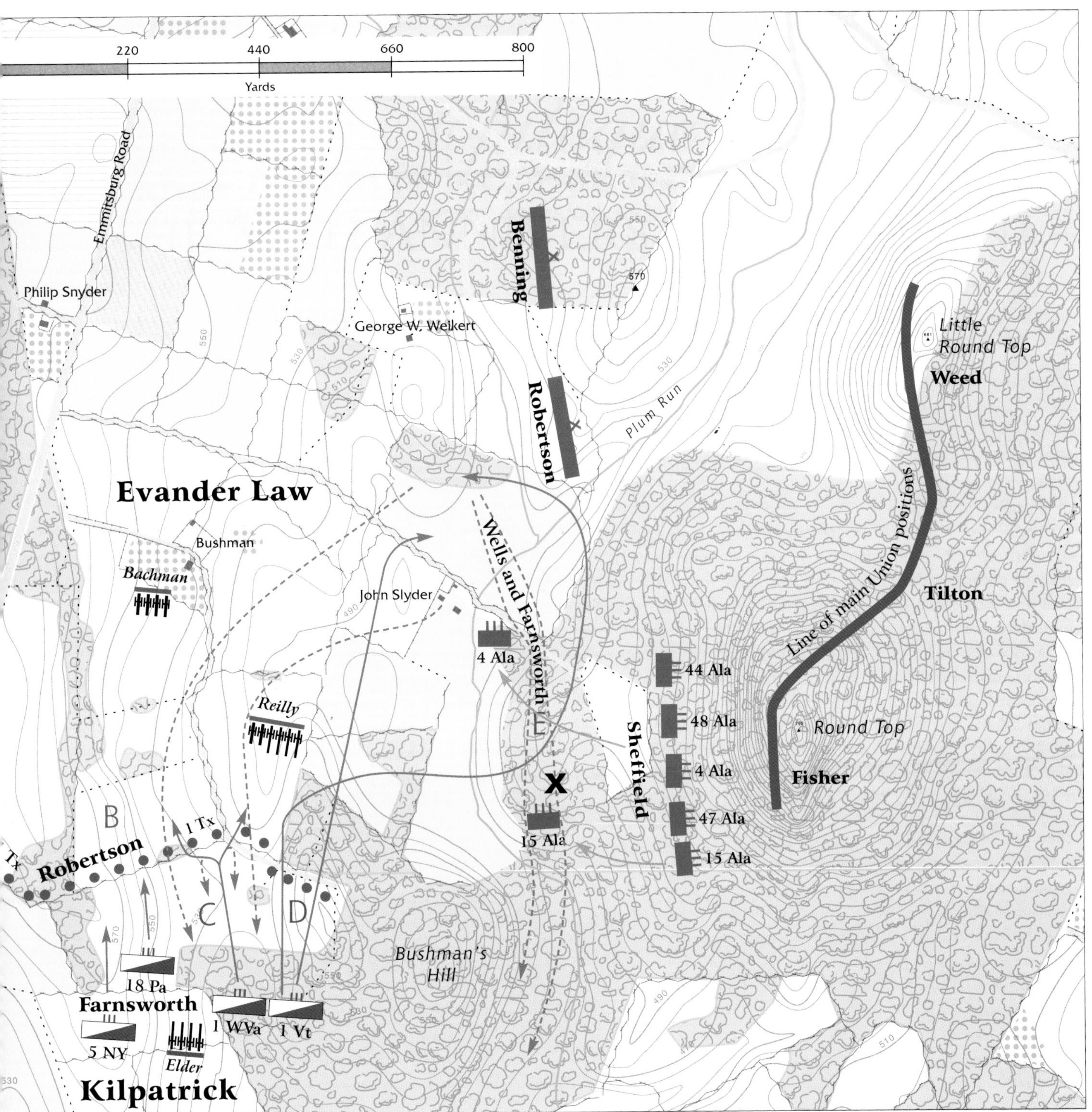

Emmitsburg Road. The remainder of Law's command occupied defensive positions facing the main Union line on the Round Tops.

• Kilpatrick's attacks were uncoordinated, with Merritt's Reserve Brigade (Custer's Brigade was detached and fighting around Rummel Farm at this time) advancing on the left, first with his largely dismounted attack petering out around position **A**. By this time Anderson had his line extended approximately as shown at **B** with the 1st Texas and 1st South Carolina acting as skirmishers behind fences and stone walls. Then Kilpatrick told Farnsworth to charge with his brigade, an order that Farnsworth objected to but then agreed to carry out after some argument. He first launched the 1st West Virginia (**C**). Many of this regiment were killed or forced to retire by the heavy fire from the 1st Texas. Some rode around the flanks of the strongest resistance and disappeared northward. Next, Farnsworth personally led forward the 1st Vermont (**D**). They crashed through the Rebel skirmishers, losing a number of men in the process, and then became separated into smaller, uncontrolled groups as they careered over fences and walls and through the woods. By the time Farnsworth's group had begun its retreat, the 4th and 15th Alabama had turned about and rushed into blocking positions. From these, effectively ambush, positions they were able to inflict serious losses on the Yankee horsemen as they tried to scramble back to safety (**E**). Farnsworth was shot and killed by the 15th Alabama in approximately the area marked **X** on the map.

• The whole episode was a minor disaster that illustrated the futility of mounted horsemen charging well-placed infantry over ground totally unsuited to such tactics.

The Kilpatrick–Farnsworth Argument

Captain Henry C. Parsons, 1st Vermont Cavalry, originated the account of the heated argument between Kilpatrick and Farnsworth over the feasibility of a cavalry charge in South Cavalry Field. Parsons made it clear that the order to charge came from Pleasonton, not Kilpatrick, who merely passed it on more or less verbatim to an incredulous Farnsworth. Parsons' first, unedited, account was:

> Kilpatrick impetuously repeated the order. Farnsworth, who is a tall man with military bearing, received the order in silence. It was repeated. Farnsworth spoke, with emotion, "General, do you mean it? Shall I throw my handful of men, over rough ground, through timber, against a brigade of infantry?" Kilpatrick said, "A handful! You have the four best regiments in the army!" Farnsworth answered: "You forget, the 1st Michigan is detached, the 5th New York you have sent beyond call, and I have nothing left but the 1st Vermont and the 1st West Virginia, regiments fought half to pieces. They are too good men to kill." Kilpatrick turned, greatly excited and said, "Do you refuse to obey my orders? If you are afraid to lead this charge, I will lead it." Farnsworth rose in his stirrups, with his saber half-drawn, he looked magnificent in his passion – and cried, "Take that back!" Kilpatrick rose defiantly, but repentingly said, "I did not mean it, forget it." For a moment nothing was said, then Farnsworth spoke calmly, "General, if you order the charge I will lead it, but you must take the awful responsibility" . . . as Farnsworth turned away, he said, "I will obey your order." Kilpatrick said earnestly: "I take the responsibility." They shook hands and parted in silence.

Extracts of this account have been used by numerous authors and historians, and became more or less accepted as an accurate part of the Gettysburg story – until research by Andie Custer, published in *The Gettysburg Magazine*, issue 28. She makes a strong case that the argument was not as Parsons described it, for the following reasons:

• Parsons' original version was supposedly confined to what he himself saw or heard, whereas in subsequent edited accounts he used considerable hearsay and second-hand accounts, though his acknowledgment that they were just that was edited out before publication. Thus the reader is led to believe that Parsons witnessed all he wrote.

• In the original version it is clear the order to charge came from Pleasonton, not initially from Kilpatrick.

• Even in Parsons' first version he makes several factual errors that he should have known to be wrong. The 1st Michigan was attached to Custer's Brigade, not Farnsworth's; the 5th New York was not beyond recall but close by, supporting Elder's guns; and the 1st Vermont and 1st West Virginia were far from battered, as they had until now had a comparatively easy campaign in terms of losses.

• His description of Farnsworth rising in his stirrups, his saber half-drawn, and then Kilpatrick apologizing and the two shaking hands does not ring true if Farnsworth was as furious, and had been accused of cowardice, as Parsons suggests.

• Then, to clinch the matter, Andie Custer quotes two Union officers who refute Parsons' version. The first, Major John W. Bennett, 1st Vermont, who was called to report to his general, later wrote:

> Generals Kilpatrick and Farnsworth, both dismounted, were engaged in conversation as I approached. General Farnsworth addressing me, said in substance: "General Kilpatrick thinks there is a fair chance to make a successful charge. You have been up in front all day, what do you think?" Before I could speak General Kilpatrick broke in saying, "The whole Rebel army is in full retreat. I have just heard from the right and our cavalry there is gobbling them up by the thousands. All we have to do is charge and the enemy will throw down their arms and surrender." This remark was addressed to me. I replied, "Sir, I don't know about the situation on the right, but the enemy on our front are not broken or retreating . . . in my opinion, no successful charge can be made against the enemy in my front." General Kilpatrick was evidently annoyed, not to say angered, at my remarks . . . yet he failed to challenge the accuracy of any part of my statement of fact [Bennett had stressed the difficulties of attacking infantry in those circumstances]. General Farnsworth was a listener during this conversation . . .

Kilpatrick then told Farnsworth to go and study the terrain personally. Bennett accompanied Farnsworth and later wrote:

> [As] we were returning to Kilpatrick's headquarters, he [Farnsworth] turned to me and said, "Major, I do not see the slightest chance of a successful charge." I fully acquiesced in his conclusion. Kilpatrick arose as we came up, and General Farnsworth . . . expressed his conclusions . . . General Kilpatrick replied: "General Farnsworth, well somebody can charge." He did not say that he would lead a charge; did not indicate he would do so while I was present. General Farnsworth's set lips turned white, as the sting of the insult seemed to burn into his very soul. There was a short pause [then he] replied, "General Kilpatrick, if anybody can charge, we can, sir." Only three persons were present during this interview, and I made the third.

• A second important eyewitness was Kilpatrick's staff officer, Lieutenant Eli Holden, 1st Vermont Cavalry. In 1892, long after Kilpatrick had died, he wrote:

> I was in the presence of the two generals . . . and believe I heard all the conversation between them in regard to the [charge].
>
> The ground to our front had been well examined by both Generals . . . and was as well known to one as the other. Some time during the afternoon General Kilpatrick . . . asked General Farnsworth what he thought of a charge. Farnsworth thought, from the nature of the ground and the disparity of the forces, a charge would be injudicious. The discussion was continued amicably at intervals for more than an hour. General Kilpatrick did not claim it would result in any success, only as being the only method left to execute his orders [from Pleasonton]. General Farnsworth said, "I am willing to make the charge, but you must order it." Some time passed before Kilpatrick said, "There is no other way Farnsworth, I order the charge made."

Although statements written many years after the event – often to defend a particular individual's reputation – cannot always be accepted at face value and will contain contradictions, it seems on balance that the order to attack originated from Pleasonton and not from Kilpatrick. It also seems that the difficulties of the ground were known to all involved, as were the slim chances of a charge succeeding. However, Kilpatrick ended by ordering Farnsworth to make a charge; Farnsworth did so reluctantly and probably with bad grace, but without the highly charged confrontation so often put forward as entirely factual.

THE CAVALRY FIGHT AT FAIRFIELD (Maps 66 and 67)

The cavalry fight just north of Fairfield was a minor affair, with a single Union regiment attacked and defeated by a Confederate cavalry brigade of three regiments and a battery of horse artillery. It had no effect on the outcome of the final stages of the main battle that were taking place concurrently about 8 miles to the northeast. Nevertheless, the Rebel success at Fairfield secured the important Hagerstown Road through the Monterey Pass (Fairfield Gap) in South Mountain that Lee would use on July 5 as a vital route for his withdrawal. Of course, neither Brigadier-General William E. "Grumble" Jones commanding the Confederate brigade, nor Major Samuel H. Starr commanding the 6th U.S. Cavalry had the slightest inkling that the result of their fight would have considerable strategic implications.

The 6th U.S. Cavalry was around 450 strong and had been sent from Brigadier-General Wesley Merritt's Brigade to attack or capture a Rebel wagon train in the Fairfield area that had been reported to Merritt by a civilian. Major Starr had been assigned a risky mission. He had to take his regiment well behind enemy lines to find wagons that could easily have moved by the time he got to Fairfield, and knowing that he could not expect any support if he ran into difficulties.

The early morning of July 3 had found the two Confederate cavalry brigades of Robertson and Jones breakfasting at Cashtown. They had been bringing up the rear of the Army of Northern Virginia and had so far seen no action. While at Cashtown a courier arrived from Lee requesting "a force of cavalry to be sent at once to the vicinity of Fairfield to the right of and rear of our line of battle." At around 1:00 p.m. Jones's Laurel Brigade began its march south, with Robertson's set to follow. In the lead was Lieutenant-Colonel Thomas Marshall's 7th Virginia Cavalry, followed at an interval by Major Campbell E. Flournoy with the 6th Virginia Cavalry, then Ashby's (Virginian) Battery of horse artillery under Captain Robert Chew with three ordnance rifles and a 12-pounder howitzer. Bringing up the rear was the 11th Virginia Cavalry commanded by Colonel Lunsford L. Lomax. In total, almost 1,600 men were on a collision course with Starr's 450, with the likely meeting point Fairfield or its vicinity.

Once in Fairfield, Starr learned that some wagons had recently left the town, heading north up the Cashtown Road. Captain Cram's squadron was detached to move up the nearby railroad while the remainder kept to the road. About 2 miles

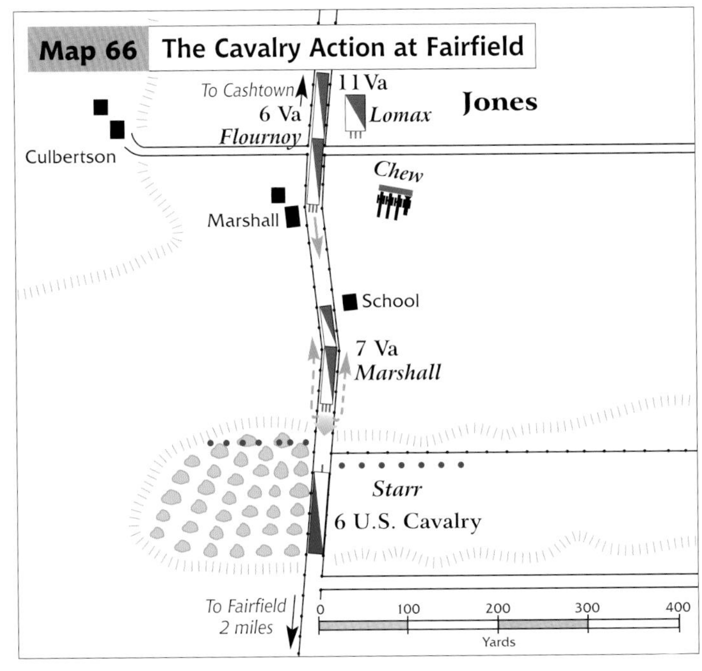

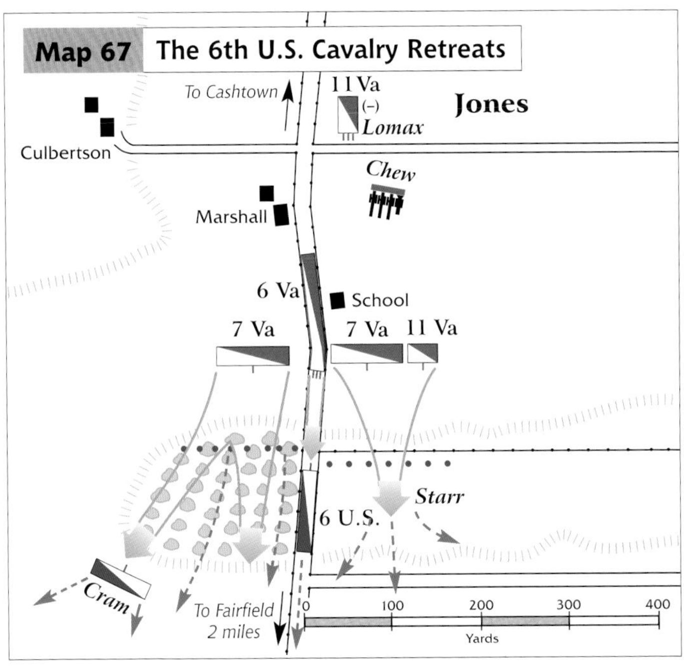

Notes

- 6th U.S. Cavalry, about 450 strong, under Maj. Samuel H. Starr, intent on capturing Rebel wagons, meets Brig.-Gen. William "Grumble" Jones's Brigade, over 1,500 strong, on the Cashtown Road 2 miles north of Fairfield.
- Starr deploys the equivalent of a squadron either side of the road, dismounted behind the fence and in the orchard. A squadron remains mounted on the road.
- The 7th Virginia charges down the road but cannot deploy into the fields due to the strong fences lining the road. The charge is easily defeated by the fire from each flank.

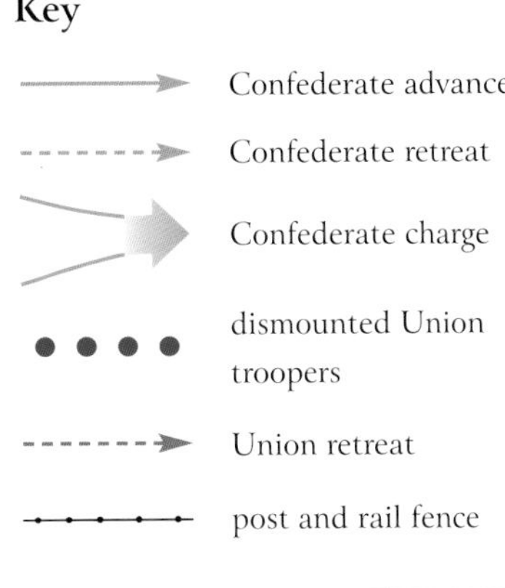

Notes

- Some Confederate gunfire is followed by a concerted charge by the whole brigade, except for three squadrons of the 11th Virginia that remain in reserve.
- The charge down the road and on both sides by such large numbers smashes into the Union defenders, who, despite a stiff resistance, are overwhelmed and turn to flee in all directions.
- The squadron under Captain Cram that has been moving along a nearby railroad arrives just as the retreat begins and is also forced to flee.
- The victory for the Rebels is total, with the 6th U.S. Cavalry being decimated and many prisoners taken.

north of the town the leading elements of the 6th U.S. Cavalry and the 7th Virginia spotted each other virtually simultaneously. Starr came forward to assess the situation and decided to make a fight of it by deploying his three squadrons (Cram was still absent), with one on either side of the road where it crossed a low ridge. These men dismounted and took up positions in the orchard to the left of the road and behind a stout post and rail fence on the right. The third remained mounted on the road.

Neither of the opposing commanders was sure at this stage exactly how strong an enemy he faced. Jones, hoping that aggression coupled with speed was the answer, ordered the 7th Virginia to charge. This proved a poor tactic. The 7th had no time to deploy and were hurled down a narrow road enclosed on either side by a strong fence for over 300 yards before they could reach the Yankees (Map 66). In doing so they provided a near-perfect target for the men armed with Sharps carbines on the ridge ahead. The result was predictable. A Captain McDonald, writing years later, said, "The failure of the Seventh . . . was clearly due to the fire from the mounted [dismounted] men on the flanks, who, being unmolested, shot with deadly effect into the charging column." The defeat and retreat of the 7th Virginia was decisive. Their hasty withdrawal was witnessed by the 6th Virginia, which was just arriving on the scene followed by the rest of the brigade.

Undeterred, Jones determined to try again as quickly as possible. Chew deployed to the left of the road, opposite James A. Marshall's farm, and opened fire. Meanwhile, Jones organized his regiments for a stronger and more coordinated assault (Map 67). Keeping the 11th Virginia, less three squadrons, in reserve, the 7th were positioned on either side of the road with a squadron of the 11th also on the left, while the 6th remained on the road. In total over 1,000 horsemen spurred forward on the hugely outnumbered 6th U.S. The carbine fire could not stop the Rebels and once the fighting began at close quarters, it was numbers that counted. Many of the dismounted Yankees on the right of the road were caught as they tried to mount, and suffered in consequence. There was much hacking and slashing with sabers and banging of revolvers, and very little control. Private John Opie of the 6th Virginia recalled "sabering right and left as they went . . . A great many of the enemy were knocked from their horses with the saber, but succeeded in escaping through the tall wheat, which had not yet been harvested." Major Starr went down with a pistol ball through his arm and a saber cut to the head. The melee quickly developed into a desperate flight by the Yankees, who disappeared in all directions, closely pursued by whooping Rebels. Captain Cram arrived just in time for his squadron to be caught up and swamped by the victorious Confederates as he tried to mount a countercharge.

The 6th U.S Cavalry had received a severe drubbing. Private Samuel Crockett, 1st U.S. Cavalry, wrote in his diary after seeing those who eventually returned to the brigade, "The 6th U.S. is cut to pieces, there are less than a hundred of them left." Among the officers Lieutenant Balder was killed; Major Starr had his arm amputated; Captain Cram and Lieutenants Tucker, Wood and Chafee were wounded, while Lieutenants Bould and Paulding were captured, as were surgeons Forwood and Notson. The tally among the men was 232 killed, wounded or captured – mostly the latter. Jones's command had come off lightly, with only fifty-eight casualties of any sort reported – twenty-eight from the 6th, thirty from the 7th, and none at all from the rest.

The Fairfield Medal of Honor

Thirty-two years after the fight at Fairfield, Private George C. Platt, Troop H of the 6th U.S. Cavalry was awarded the Medal of Honor for his gallantry in the melee on the ridge just north of the town. His citation reads:

RANK AND ORGANIZATION: Private, Troop "H," 6th United States Cavalry.
PLACE AND DATE: Fairfield, Pennsylvania, 3 July 1863.
ENTERED SERVICE AT: 6 Aug 1861, Philadelphia, Pennsylvania.
BIRTH: 17 Feb 1842, Londonderry, Ireland.
DATE OF ISSUE: 12 July 1895.
CITATION: Seized the regimental flag upon the death of the standard bearer in a hand-to-hand fight and prevented it from falling into the hands of the enemy.
SERVICE AT GETTYSBURG: On July 3 the 6th U.S. Cavalry rode to Fairfield, Pennsylvania, to investigate the report of an unescorted rebel wagon train. North of Fairfield, the Union troopers became engaged with the 7th Virginia Cavalry. The Virginians were easily repulsed. A second Confederate assault by General William "Grumble" Jones' Cavalry Brigade (including the regrouped 7th Va.) overwhelmed the 6th U.S. and soon the fight degenerated into isolated clusters of men in hand-to-hand combat. During this, the color-bearer of the 6th U.S. was shot down. Private Platt appeared and rescued the flag. Platt " . . . tore the color from the staff, placed it in his bosom, and rammed the staff through the first enemy that came before him, and then cut his way through the ranks of the enemy." The 6th U.S. Cavalry was defeated and suffered 242 casualties, but Private Platt and the unit's flag survived.
OTHER SERVICE: Served a 3-year enlistment, promoted to sergeant, participated in 49 battles.
DEATH: 20 June 1912.
PLACE OF BURIAL: Holycross Cemetery, Yeadon, Pennsylvania.

When Platt was discharged on August 6, 1864, his injuries included a saber wound to the head, a ventral hernia and gunshot wounds to the groin.

SECTION TWELVE

The Aftermath

This section covers the three major and immediate aspects of the aftermath of the battle as a whole. They were the casualties; the problems facing both army commanders on the night of July 3/4; and Lee's retreat, coupled with Meade's pursuit, until the Confederates crossed the Potomac back into Virginia on July 14.

CASUALTIES

Full details of all casualties down to regimental and battery level, including officers, can be found in Section One: The Orders of Battle, but for the reader's convenience army, corps and divisional losses are summarized below, with the commanders in post at the end of the battle named.

Confederate Statistics

Formation	Engaged strength	Losses	% loss
Army H.Q.	108	5	4.6
Longstreet's Corps			
Staff	16	–	–
E. M. Law's Division	7,373	2,407	32.6
McLaws' Division	7,160	2,327	32.5
Pickett's Division	5,474	2,762	50.4
Artillery (Walton)	918	169	18.4
Corps total	**20,941**	**7,665**	**36.6**
Ewell's Corps			
Staff	142	7	4.9
Johnson's Division	6,366	2,005	31.5
Early's Division	5,460	1,530	28.0
Rodes' Division	7,981	3,111	39.0
Artillery ((Brown)	648	33	5.1
Corps total	**20,597**	**6,686**	**32.5**
A. P. Hill's Corps			
Staff	15	–	–
Heth's Division*	7,458	3,765	50.5
Lane's Division	6,603	2,446	37.0
Anderson's Division	7,136	2,185	30.6
Artillery (Walker)	736	99	13.4
Corps total	**21,948**	**8,495**	**38.7**
Cavalry Division (Stuart)	**8,105**	**380**	**4.7**
Army totals	**71,699**	**23,231****	**32.4**

* Heth resumed command of his division after Pettigrew's wounding on July 3.
** This represents 4,708 killed, 12,693 wounded and 5,830 missing and captured.

As accurate an estimate as is possible of how these losses were divided between the corps and cavalry has been given by Busey and Martin in their *Regimental Strengths and Losses at Gettysburg*. These figures are:

Formation	Killed	Wounded	Missing/ captured
Army H.Q.	–	2	–
Longstreet's Corps	1,617	4,205	1,843
Ewell's Corps	1,301	3,629	1,756
Hill's Corps	1,724	4,683	2,088
Cavalry (Stuart)	66	174	140
Totals	**4,708**	**12,693**	**5,830**
	Army total 23,231		

Comments

Lee lost almost exactly a third of his army at Gettysburg between those killed, wounded, captured and missing. They were mostly veteran troops that could not be replaced. The Army of Northern Virginia would never be the same again in terms of strength, morale and fighting power. The Confederacy could not afford such losses, and, coupled with the 31,000 who surrendered at Vicksburg on July 4, it meant a manpower crisis from which the South never fully recovered. Inevitably, it was the infantry that was crippled. Of the total casualties at Gettysburg, 22,550 were infantrymen; this means that 36.8 percent of infantrymen were lost and it equates to 97 percent of all losses. A mere 380 cavalrymen and 301 artillerymen were lost during those three days. The cavalry and artillery provided 10,407 men to Lee's army at the battle and their losses amounted to 6.5 percent of that total. These figures underline in a dramatic way how big battles were infantry battles, and how the price paid by Lee's infantry for a defeat at Gettysburg was so devastating. Lee admitted, "I am gradually losing my best men" – something of an understatement with regard to Gettysburg.

Included in the above figures, but hidden by them, is the crippling damage Gettysburg did to the Confederate officer corps. The figures below refer to all infantry and cavalry senior commanders down to regimental level, including officers who temporarily acted up due to battle losses and who themselves became casualties while in command. The Army of Northern Virginia lost four divisional commanders out of the ten present (Heth, Pender, Hood and Trimble), all of whom were wounded, with Trimble being captured as well. At brigade level, eighteen were lost (43 percent), including seven killed or wounded and captured. No fewer than 136 regimental commanders became casualties, fifty-nine of whom were either killed, mortally wounded or lost permanently due to capture. Pickett's Division suffered the worst during its one assault on the last day. All three brigade commanders were lost (Kemper wounded and captured, Armistead mortally wounded and captured, and Garnett killed). Fifteen regiments attacked on July 3, and at the end of the day twenty-six regimental commanders had fallen, twelve of whom were permanently lost to the army in one way or another. These twenty-six included three captains who became casualties while in command of their regiments, or what was left of them (Captains Thomas Davis, 1st Virginia; James R. Hutter, 11th Virginia; and William N. Bentley, 24th Virginia – all in Kemper's Brigade).

These figures also show how the Confederate losses were fairly evenly spread throughout the army. Each of the three corps lost at least a third of its engaged strength, as did the army as a whole with a 32.4 percent loss. This indicates that the fighting – in general terms, as there were some exceptions – was equally spread. Hill's Corps suffered the most of the three with 8,495 casualties or 38.7 percent, while Ewell's with 6,686 (32.5 percent) was the lowest.

At divisional level there was more variation, the lowest loss in percentage terms being Early's with 28 percent and the highest being Pickett and Heth, both with just over 50 percent. Looking at the actual numbers, then Heth's Division, with 3,765 casualties, headed the divisional list, some 650 more than Rodes. Only one division, Early, had fewer than 2,000 losses. Although only a small division, losing just 1,530 men was ironic as it was the only division that was engaged on all three days of the battle (Smith's Brigade was involved in the early hours of July 3 in a clash with the Union regiments on the extreme left of the Rebel line east of Culp's Hill).

At brigade level, nine of the forty-two brigades (including cavalry) lost 50 percent or more of their strength. They were, with the highest first, Iverson, Garnett, Pettigrew, Lang, Archer, Armistead, Davis, Scales and Barksdale. Iverson lost 65.2 percent, almost entirely due to being ambushed so effectively on Oak Ridge on July 1. The lowest losses occurred in the two brigades that saw virtually no fighting throughout the battle, Posey with 8.5 percent (112 men) and Mahone with 6.6 percent (102 men).

For regiments, some of the figures are even more devastating. The worst ten were:

Regiment	% loss	Brigade commander
8th Virginia	92.2 (178)	Garnett
23rd North Carolina	89.2 (282)	Iverson
2nd North Carolina Battalion	82.9 (199)	Daniel
26th North Carolina	81.9 (687)	Pettigrew
18th Virginia	78.5 (245)	Garnett
13th North Carolina	77.2 (179)	Scales
13th Alabama	69.5 (214)	Archer
9th Virginia	68.9 (177)	Armistead
28th North Carolina	68.5 (237)	Lane
20th North Carolina	68.0 (253)	Iverson

Four regiments lost over 80 percent of their men, the 8th Virginia an astounding 92.2. This regiment was destroyed during Pickett's charge when it was on the right flank of Garnett's Brigade and had to try to cope with the flank attack by Stannard's regiments. Almost a quarter of Lee's infantry regiments suffered a 50 percent loss or more. The 26th North Carolina had the highest number of casualties, 687, of any regiment in either army. Its losses were more than the engaged strength of any other regiment at Gettysburg – a truly awful statistic obtained by their involvement in assaulting McPherson's Ridge on the first day and in Pickett's charge on the third.

Discounting cavalry, the five Rebel regiments with the lowest casualty rates were:

Regiment	% loss	Brigade commander
3rd Georgia Battalion S.S.	5.6 (13)	Wofford
7th Georgia	5.6 (21)	G. Anderson
12th Mississippi	4.3 (13)	Posey
6th Virginia	3.8 (11)	Mahone
1st South Carolina Rifles	1.9 (7)	Perrin

The only infantry unit to suffer no losses was the 94-strong 1st North Carolina Battalion serving as provost guard in Ewell's Corps.

Of the twelve states represented, the two that contributed the most men and suffered the highest losses in terms of numbers were North Carolina and Virginia. North Carolina lost 6,582 men (46.4 percent) and Virginia 4,800 (23.1 percent). North Carolina provided 14,182 soldiers at Gettysburg, whereas Virginia fielded 20,776: in total these two states together supplied almost exactly 49 percent of the manpower of Lee's army and suffered 49 percent of its total loss. However, the state with the highest percentage loss was Tennessee (56.1 percent), as 421 of its tiny contingent of 750 became casualties.

For the corps artillery brigades, Longstreet's 18.4 percentage loss was the largest, with virtually all the 169 casualties occurring during the afternoon of July 3 when they were deployed in an exposed position near the Emmitsburg Road during the two-hour artillery duel. The highest percentage loss (10.8), and also highest in terms of numbers (44), within the cavalry was suffered by the 1st North Carolina Cavalry in Hampton's Brigade. Most of these were sustained in the mounted melees on East Cavalry Field.

Hood's Divisional Hospital

This was located in the John E. Plank Farm some 2 miles west of the Emmitsburg Road, close to the Willoughby Run. Later Elizabeth Plank wrote:

> an ambulance arrived at the farm house and without any ceremony forced open the front door and carried in a wounded officer and placed him in the guest room and the best bed in the house . . . all over the floors in the halls on the porches in the out buildings, on the barn floor and every place were wounded men . . . many limbs and arms and their wounds dressed while the battle raged. These wounded soldiers were left at this hospital five or six weeks after the fight. Every morning they buried their dead in shallow graves in the orchards . . .

The Confederate surgeon left behind in charge of over 500 wounded (out of 2,407 casualties in Hood's Division) was Dr. Thomas A. Means, 11th Georgia. One of those wounded lying in an apple orchard was Private William C. Ward, 4th Alabama Infantry, who had been brought to the farm on July 2 and was still there on the 7th. One of his worst memories was the maggots, "Great green flies in swarms of millions gathered, grown unnaturally large, fattened on human blood. Fever-smitten, pain-racked, there came to us another terror; we were to be devoured while living by maggots – creeping, doubling, crawling in among the nerves and devouring the soldiers . . ."

Union Statistics

As with the Confederates, Union losses are summarized below with the name of the commander at the end of the battle in parenthesis.

Formation	Engaged strength	Losses	% loss
Army H.Q.	1,529	4	–
I Corps (Newton)			
Staff, escort/provost	71	5	14.3
1st Division (Wadsworth)	3,857	2,155	55.9
2nd Division (Robinson)	2,995	1,690	56.4
3rd Division (Doubleday)	4,701	2,103	44.7
Artillery (Wainwright)	596	106	17.8
Corps total	**12,220**	**6,059**	**49.6**
II Corps (Hays)			
Staff, escort/provost	70	7	50.0
1st Division (Caldwell)	3,320	1,275	38.4
2nd Division (Harrow)	3,588	1,647	45.9
3rd Division (Hays)	3,643	1,291	35.4
Artillery (Hazard)	605	149	24.6
Corps total	**11,226**	**4,369**	**38.9**
III Corps (Birney)			
Staff, escort/provost	60	2	22.2
1st Division (Ward)	5,094	2,011	39.4
2nd Division (Humphreys)	4,924	2,092	42.5
Artillery (Clark)	596	106	17.8
Corps total	**10,674**	**4,211**	**39.4**
V Corps (Sykes)			
Staff, escort/provost	187	–	–
1st Division (Barnes)	3,418	904	26.4
2nd Division (Ayres)	4,020	1,029	25.6
3rd Division (Crawford)	2,862	210	7.3
Artillery (Martin)	432	43	9.9
Corps total	**10,926**	**2,186**	**20.0**
VI Corps (Sedgwick)			
Staff, escort/provost	99	–	–
1st Division (Wright)	4,378	18	0.4
2nd Division (Howe)	3,731	16	0.4
3rd Division (Wheaton)	4,929	196	3.9
Artillery (Tompkins)	937	12	1.3
Corps total	**14,074**	**242**	**1.7**
XI Corps (Howard)			
Staff, escort/provost	137	4	9.1
1st Division (Ames)	2,481	1,306	52.6
2nd Division (Von Steinwehr)	2,903	952	32.8
3rd Division (Schurz)	3,117	1,476	47.3
Artillery (Osborn)	604	69	11.4
Corps total	**9,242**	**3,807**	**41.2**
XII Corps (Slocum)			
Staff, escort/provost	177	–	–
1st Division ((Williams)	5,256	533	10.1
2nd Division (Geary)	3,964	540	13.6
Artillery (Muhlenberg)	391	9	2.3
Corps total	**9,788**	**1,082**	**11.0**
Artillery Reserve (Tyler)	**2,376**	**242**	**10.1**
Cavalry Corps (Pleasonton)			
Staff	27	–	–
1st Division (Buford) (excluding 6th U.S. Cavalry)	4,069	418	10.2
2nd Division (D. McM. Gregg)	2,614	56	2.1
3rd Division (Kilpatrick)	3,852	355	9.2
Horse Artillery			
1st Horse Artillery (Robertson)	493	8	1.6
2nd Horse Artillery (Tidball)	276	15	5.4
Total cavalry (incl. Horse Artillery)	**11,331**	**852**	**7.5**
Army total	**93,386**	**23,054***	**24.7**

*This represents 3,155 killed, 14,530 wounded and 5,369 missing and captured.

Casualties were divided between the corps as below:

Formation	Killed	Wounded	Missing/ captured
Army H.Q.	–	4	–
I Corps	666	3,231	2,162
II Corps	797	3,194	378
III Corps	593	3,029	589
V Corps	364	1,611	211
VI Corps	27	185	30
XI Corps	369	1,924	1,514
XII Corps	205	811	66
Cavalry Corps	91	354	407
Artillery Reserve	43	187	12
Totals	**3,155**	**14,530**	**5,369**

Comments

Meade fared considerably better in terms of percentage loss than Lee, in that he lost almost exactly a quarter of his strength whereas Lee lost a third. In terms of numbers, however, casualties were virtually the same at just over 23,000 each. This was a rare event in military history – the defenders losing the same number as the attackers. One reason for this was the 10,000 losses – many of them taken prisoner – suffered by I Corps and XI Corps on the first day. To these must be added the heavy losses on July 2 by III Corps in Sickles' exposed salient. The cavalry, including the horse artillery, lost 852 all ranks (7.5 percent) – well above the Rebels' 380 (4.7 percent), due to Buford's prolonged dismounted action on July 1 and Kilpatrick's foolish attempts to attack infantry on July 3. These figures look a lot worse if the 242 men lost by the 6th U.S. Cavalry at Fairfield are added – the overall loss rises to 9.3 percent.

As regards senior officers down to regimental commanders and, as with the Confederates, including those temporarily in command during the battle, Meade suffered far more severely with his corps commanders, losing three out of eight (Reynolds killed, and Hancock and Sickles wounded). To these should be added Butterfield, who was wounded while chief of staff at Meade's headquarters. At divisional level the score was much more in favor of the Union, with only two, Gibbon and Barlow, being wounded out of twenty-two. Of the fifty-eight brigades in the army, nineteen commanders became casualties, almost a third, with eight of these being permanent losses. Worst hit was Paul's Brigade in Robinson's Division of I Corps, which had no fewer than four brigade commanders become casualties, one of whom (Colonel Adrian R. Root)

Sallie Myers

Elizabeth Salome "Sallie" Myers was a twenty-one-year-old teacher in Gettysburg who was involved in caring for the dying and wounded of both sides in the aftermath of the fighting. In her sixties she wrote an account of her experiences, *How a Gettysburg Schoolteacher Spent Her Vacation in 1863*, from which the following two extracts are taken.

> The Catholic and Presbyterian churches, a few doors east of my father's home were taken possession of as hospitals. Dr. James Fulton (143rd Pennsylvania Volunteers) did splendid work getting things into shape . . . "Girls," Dr. Fulton said, "you must come up to the churches and help us – the boys are suffering terribly!" . . . I went to the Catholic church. On pews and floors men lay, the groans of the suffering and dying were heartrending. I knelt beside the first man near the door and asked what I could do. "Nothing," he replied, "I am going to die." I went outside the church and cried. I returned and spoke to the man – he was wounded in the lungs and spine, there was not the slightest hope for him. The man was Sergeant Alexander Stewart of the 149th Pennsylvania Volunteers. I read a chapter of the Bible to him, it was the last chapter his father had read before he left home. The wounded man died on Monday, July 6 . . .
>
> I went daily to the hospitals with my writing materials, reading and answering letters. This work enlisted all my sympathies, and I received many kind and appreciative letters from those [friends and relatives] who could not come. Besides caring for the wounded, we did all we could for the comfort of friends who came to look after their loved ones. Many pleasant and enduring friendships were the result of this part of my work. It is a great pleasure to remember that during that long, trying summer, I was treated with the greatest courtesy and kindness by the soldiers, not one, in either army, ever addressing me except in the most respectful manner. They were men. They bore their suffering in the hospitals with the same matchless courage and fortitude with which they met the dangers and endured the hardships of army life. Their patience was marvelous. I never heard a murmur. Truly, we shall not look upon their like again.

was wounded and captured. A total of ninety-eight regimental commanders became casualties, twenty-eight of them either killed, mortally wounded or captured. At this level, because Union commanders were defending and not obliged to place themselves in front of their regiments in the open, their losses were substantially lower than the Confederates' 136. The division that lost the most regimental commanders was Gibbon's, with thirteen out of nineteen, or 68 percent, most of whom were lost in the desperate fighting along the Emmitsburg Road on July 2 when the division sought to defend Sickles' salient. Four divisions had no command casualties at all, at any level (Wright's and Howe's in VI Corps, Von Steinwehr's in XI Corps and Gregg's in the Cavalry Corps).

The fighting, and therefore the casualties, were much more unevenly spread amongst the Union corps and divisions than in those of the Confederates. I Corps lost over 6,000 men or almost 50 percent of its strength, while II, III and XI Corps each suffered around 40 percent. More modest were the losses in V and XII Corps with 20 and 11 percent respectively, while the Cavalry Corps lost only 7.5 percent. By a strange quirk of fate, VI Corps, the strongest in the army with over 14,000 men, had barely any casualties at all – only 242 or 1.7 percent – as it missed the first day's fighting and thereafter was Meade's main reserve force.

Among the divisions, the 2nd Division, I Corps (Robinson), with over 56 percent, had the highest loss, closely followed by the 1st Division (Wadsworth) with almost 56 percent. At the other extreme, the 1st and 2nd Divisions of VI Corps had a combined strength of over 8,000 men and a combined casualty count of thirty-four, or 0.4 percent.

Four brigades lost over 60 percent (Paul, Rowley, Stone and Meredith), all in I Corps, but only six of the fifty-eight brigades had 50 percent losses or more, compared to nine out of forty-two Confederate. Numerically, the Iron Brigade suffered the most with 1,153 casualties. Three brigades lost fewer than ten – Bartlett five, Russell two and Grant just one. As far as individual regiments are concerned, the losses of the ten worst hit exceeded those suffered by the Confederates, whose ten highest losses were 68 percent or higher. These ten Union regiments were:

Regiment	% loss	Brigade commander
25th Ohio	83.6 (184)	Ames
154th New York	83.3 (200)	Coster
147th New York	77.9 (296)	Cutler
16th Maine	77.9 (232)	Paul
2nd Wisconsin	77.2 (233)	Meredith
157th New York	75.1 (307)	Schimmelfennig
149th Pennsylvania	74.7 (336)	Stone
24th Michigan	73.2 (363)	Meredith
151st Pennsylvania	72.2 (337)	Rowley
141st Pennsylvania	71.3 (149)	Graham

Top of the percentage table, the 25th Ohio ranked only 35th out of the 247 regiments in terms of numbers lost. However, it started the battle with only 220, but like the 154th New York suffered heavily, particularly with missing and prisoners when XI Corps retreated through Gettysburg on the first day.

Taking the total number of men lost by the ten worst hit regiments of both armies, the figures are virtually identical, with the Rebels losing 2,651 and the Yankees 2,637, making an average percentage loss of 76.9 and 76.6 respectively. No fewer than thirty (12 percent) Union regiments (discounting headquarters and provost guards) had five or fewer casualties; fourteen of them had none at all. In the cavalry, the regiment that suffered the most in both armies was the 6th U.S. Cavalry. It lost 242 men, or 51 percent of its strength, when it was defeated at Fairfield.

Some states bore a much higher burden of the fighting than others. In terms of numbers, the biggest contributors, Pennsylvania with an engaged strength of just over 24,000 and New York with over 23,000, provided almost 50 percent of the army and between them accounted for nearly 55 percent of the losses – New York lost 6,752 and Pennsylvania 5,891. However, it was Minnesota with 59 percent losses that fared worst in those terms, although her total casualties were only 224, putting her 14th out of nineteen states. The state with the lowest percentage loss was Maryland with just over 7 percent, and in numbers West Virginia with sixty-seven.

Battlefield Reality

If the statistics of the battle were appalling, the reality on the battlefield was far more so. There were, in round numbers, 7,850 dead, 27,200 wounded (almost 4,000 of whom were to die of the wounds they received at Gettysburg) and 11,200 missing (mostly prisoners, but some deserters and stragglers) to be dealt with, as well as thousands of dead horses and many mules. These victims of the battle required burial, evacuation and treatment, or guarding – all matters that posed virtually insurmountable problems for both armies.

However, with Lee's mind set on the crucial requirement to quit the field and organize the retreat to Virginia, the burden of tackling nine-tenths of the problems left on the battlefield would rest with Meade. While many Confederate dead were buried in shallow graves by their comrades, most were left where they lay in the sun or the drenching rain that fell after the battle. Because the great majority of Rebels fell in the open, or in the woods between or close to the enemy lines, neither their dead bodies nor their wounded could be recovered. They had to be abandoned to the mercies of the Yankees, whose understandable priorities would be their own men. While Lee left some surgeons and medical staff behind when he marched away, he had to keep most with him to tend the wounded from his field hospitals who were declared fit to move and were carried in ambulances or other wagons. There was also the need for medical personnel to deal with further casualties that would surely occur as a result of future fighting. Full details of how the wounded were attended to and the system of field hospitals has been covered in Section Five: Other Arms and Services, so the notes that follow are primarily concerned with burials and the handling of prisoners, stragglers and deserters.

Burials

By late afternoon on July 4 rain was falling on the battlefield as the Rebels shouldered their packs and marched away. As Yankee troops cautiously moved forward to scout the field, many were unable to stop gagging at the sights and stench that confronted them. Sergeant Thomas Myer of the 148th Pennsylvania wrote that the overwhelming smell:

> would come up in waves and when at its worst the breath would stop in the throat; the lungs could not take it in, and a sense of suffocation would be experienced. We would cover our faces with our hands and turn the back toward the breeze and retch and gasp for breath.

The Soldiers' National Cemetery (now called the Gettysburg National Cemetery)

Some 3,200 Union soldiers were killed during the battle and most were given hasty, shallow graves in the days immediately following the fighting. Only crude wooden markers made from hardtack boxes or fence rails identified many graves, as fields, orchards, woods and farmyards became vast cemeteries. However, the heavy rains soon washed away the light soil covering many bodies and it became obvious that they would have to be disinterred and buried in a proper cemetery. With the backing of Pennsylvania Governor Andrew Curtin, a site was purchased on Cemetery Hill for the reburial of the Union dead – Confederate dead were to be left in their makeshift graves on the battlefield as they had been the enemy of the Union. However, there is one plot in the cemetery known to contain a Confederate. In it lie the remains of Lieutenant Sydney Carter, 14th South Carolina Infantry, who was severely wounded on July 1 and died a week later and whose body was mistaken for that of a Union soldier. He lies in the Connecticut plot, Row A, #5.

William Saunders, a highly respected landscape architect, was hired to design the layout of the cemetery. Local contracts were advertised for disinterring, removing the bodies to the Soldiers' Cemetery, digging the graves and burying the dead 3 feet deep. The contractor disinterring the bodies had to make sure they were Union dead and was not allowed to transport more than 100 bodies a day. When these tasks were put out to tender, the bids ranged from $1.59 to $8.00 per body. The cheapest bidder, Frank W. Biesecker, got the job and he hired a local man named Samuel Weaver to remove the dead to the new site for reburial. Weaver insisted on being present at the opening of every grave and the searching of the remains of each corpse. In his report in 1864 he stated that he saw:

> Every body taken out of its temporary resting place, and all pockets carefully searched; and where the grave was not marked, I examined all the clothing and everything about the body to find the name. I then saw the body, with all the hair and all the particles of bone, carefully placed in the coffin.

In the center of the Soldiers' Cemetery stands the Soldiers' National Monument, with the graves arranged in a series of semicircles around it. The graves are grouped by states, with two sections for the unknown and one for the Regular Army. Additional graves were added outside the original section for some of the dead of the Spanish–American War and World War I. The cemetery was dedicated on November 19, 1863 (before it was finished); this was the occasion of President Lincoln's famous Gettysburg Address (see Appendix 1). The burials at the cemetery were finally completed in March 1864 when the last of the 3,512 bodies was reburied. However, it was 1869 before the Soldiers' Monument was erected and 1872 before the project was finally completed.

It was not until 1871 that Confederate bodies began to be disinterred and brought south. This project was instituted by the efforts of the Ladies' Memorial Associations of Richmond, Raleigh, Savannah and Charleston. The work was supervised by Dr. Rufus B. Weaver (born in Gettysburg) and completed in October 1873 when the last of the 3,320 bodies arrived at Richmond. Of these, 2,935 were buried in Richmond's Hollywood Cemetery and the rest were buried in their home cemeteries. About forty dead were left, buried in Sherfy's orchard at Gettysburg, while many more could not be found.

Confederate dead gathered for burial.

On July 6 a writer for a Philadelphia newspaper described what he saw on the slope of Cemetery Hill:

> Here many of the rebel dead yet lie unburied, every one of their pockets turned inside out. Many rebel wounded lie in the wood adjacent, and the air is polluted with a heavy sickening, disgusting stench. Thanks for the heavy rain we have had, carrying off much of the blood, otherwise I do not see how people could live here. As it is, it is the most disgusting atmosphere I ever breathed, or thought it possible human beings could live in.

In Devil's Den scarcely any graves were dug. Confederate bodies were often dragged to the nearest crevice and thrown in with a few stones placed on top of them.

The two days immediately following the cessation of fighting saw burial parties organized by Meade's command. Union troops, pioneers, townsfolk from Gettysburg and other civilians were detailed for the massive task. Sergeant Thomas Meyer was in charge of a burial detail and left an illuminating account of how he went about his gruesome task:

> First we collected the men into rows, as usual laying one against another, heads all one way, Union and Confederate in separate rows . . . Some of the men buried the dead thus laid in rows; a shallow grave about a foot deep, [was dug] against the first man in a row and he was then laid down into it; a similar grave was dug where he had lain. The ground thus dug up served to cover the first man, and the second was laid in a trench, and so on, so the ground was handled only once. This was the regular form of burial on our battlefields. It is the most rapid, and is known as trench burial and is employed when time for work is limited . . .
>
> These burial trenches were dug here, there and everywhere over the field and contained three or four or fifty as the number of dead near required. Few of these men had anything about them by which they could be identified, and were buried as "unknown."

Meyer also described how the corpses had invariably been looted: "[The pockets] were cut open and rifled through the incision. The battlefield robbers were well known by the large amounts of money they had, and the watches, pocketbooks, pocket knives and other valuable trinkets they had for sale after the battle. All regiments had them." Corpses were also often stripped for articles of clothing, better weapons, ammunition and various pieces of useful equipment. Shoes were in great demand, as evidenced by the number of photographs showing shoeless bodies. *Harper's Weekly* of January 16, 1864 contained an article by an unknown soldier of the 6th New Jersey Infantry who described his ghastly experience when out on a burial detail on the night of July 4. He had stumbled in the darkness and put out his hand to break his fall.

> My feet rested on another body, and my lantern was out. I felt for a match. I had none. But presently some of the men came up; the lantern was relighted, and the glare revealed a sight which I pray God my eyes may never look upon again. The body upon which my hand had fallen was that of a corporal; both legs were blown completely off. That over which I had stumbled was the body of a private with one arm severed, not entirely off, at the shoulder . . . Within a circle of twenty feet . . . I counted seventeen bodies, all, alas! with blue jackets on. I had hoped among so many to find some gray-backed ones.
>
> How we buried these seventeen bodies you would not care to know.

While some attempt was made to mark the graves of those who died in the field hospitals, thousands were interred hastily in shallow trenches as described above and with little or no attempt to identify them. Sometimes larger, slightly deeper pits were dug, and after separating the Rebels from the Yankees, bodies were just laid together in a mass grave. Lieutenant Thomas Galwey, 8th Ohio, later recalled burials close to the Emmitsburg Road on July 5:

> [The bodies were] brought into rows and counted, the Confederates and Federals being separated into different rows. At the feet of each row of fifty or a hundred dead, a trench is dug about seven or eight feet wide and about three feet deep – for there is not time for normal grave depth. Then the bodies, which are black as ink and bloated from exposure to the sun, are placed in the shallow ditch and quickly covered with dirt.

Prisoners, stragglers and deserters

The Army of the Potomac marched away from Gettysburg in pursuit of Lee on July 6 and 7, leaving the huge task of continuing to clear the battlefield of wounded, dead, and arms and equipment to Meade's chief quartermaster, Brigadier-General Rufus Ingalls. He had detailed a Captain William C. Rankin from his staff to oversee the practical aspects of this monumental operation. It was not a good choice. Rankin was not up to the task and chaos resulted, possibly due to Rankin's fondness for the bottle – he was later courtmartialed for drunkenness. The manpower for the job consisted of the cavalrymen of the 2nd Pennsylvania from the provost guard and about 100 infantrymen from various regiments – in total around 650 men. The cavalry were mostly used for escorting prisoners to Westminster and patroling the battlefield, while the infantrymen provided sentries at the field hospitals. On July 7 Captains William W. Smith, an aide on Halleck's staff, and Henry B. Blood of the U.S. Quartermaster's Department arrived to sort out the mess. Gradually they began to bring some sort of order to burying the dead, collecting arms, arresting civilians for looting government property and overseeing the erection of hospital tents at what became known as Camp Letterman.

Gettysburg's Last Surviving Soldier

According to Professor Jay S. Hoar of the University of Maine at Farmington, the acknowledged expert on the last survivors of the Civil War, Gettysburg's last survivor was James Marion Lurvey – born December 2, 1847, died September 17, 1950, aged 102 years, nine months and fifteen days.

Lurvey enlisted when just fourteen years and seven months old as a drummer boy in Company A, 4th Massachusetts Infantry. Lurvey's granddaughter, Mrs. Norma Kwist of Bellevue, Nebraska, supplied Professor Hoar with the following information, later published in 1996 in the *Gettysburg Magazine*, issue 16. According to Mrs Kwist, when speaking of Gettysburg her grandfather said:

> At Gettysburg I was still a drummer boy. During much of that battle I served in the Medical Corps. Shot and shell and the screams of dying men and boys filled the humid air. A noncom told me to put away my drum. He tied a red rag around my left arm and told me I was now in the Medical Corps. I told him I was not big enough to lift my end of a stretcher, so he assigned me to a surgical field tent. It was stifling inside. I thought I'd keel over when they told me my assignment – (wisht then I could've hefted a stretcher) – I was to stand by and carry out the soldiers arms and legs as the doctors amputated them. I guess that was the day (July 3rd–4th) I grew up and left boyhood for ever. And I wasn't yet sixteen.

In a letter written in 1971, Lurvey's daughter, Mrs Cora L. Smith (who lived to be 100), remembered her father talking about his experiences in the war:

> I recall his saying that one hot day he crawled into a pup tent in the shade and went to sleep. Soon after, someone pulled him out by the feet and told him that a soldier had just died of smallpox in that tent. That was at Gettysburg. Luckily he didn't contract it. He said many times when crossing a river or pond, some big soldier would take him across on his back. Many times water to drink was scarce, and after rain the men were glad to drink from pools made by cavalry horses hoofs. They were not allowed to pick fruit from the trees, but some of the men would throw their boots up to the limbs and catch the fruit.

When he died, James Lurvey was buried with full military honors in Londonderry's Pleasant View Cemetery, survived by four children, eight grandchildren and eleven great-grandchildren.

Although the numbers of unwounded prisoners taken by both sides was roughly equal – the Confederates having taken about 5,200 Yankees while losing some 5,150 – they presented more difficulties to Lee than to Meade. Lee had not only to find troops to guard and escort them during the retreat, but they also consumed scarce rations. The choices confronting Lee were to keep them, parole them or exchange them, with this last being the preferred option. With this in mind, early on July 4 Lee sent an officer under a flag of truce to Meade proposing an exchange be "made at once to promote the comfort and convenience of the officers and men captured by the opposing armies in the recent engagement." Meade responded that "it is not in my power to accede to the proposed arrangement." Although paroles or exchanges were not forbidden, they had to be carefully controlled, and exchanges could take place only at certain locations. Meade perhaps also bore in mind Lincoln's directive that paroles should not take place "for the convenience of the captor," which in this case would certainly be Lee. This was undoubtedly the immediate reason for rejection, as Meade would much prefer his adversary to be burdened with thousands of prisoners than be reinforced by thousands of freed ones.

Despite the likelihood that Meade would not sanction parolees, up to 1,500 Yankees accepted the parole offered by Lee. They had the risk explained to them that once released on parole they would be liable to be sent straight back to their Union regiments, thus breaking the rule that such persons had promised "not to bear arms against the Confederate government until they had been honorably released from the obligation" – that is, unless properly exchanged. If caught under arms again by the South they would be certain of a long spell in a military prison. Those Union soldiers who took parole were marched north to Carlisle and

The Transportation of the Wounded after the Battle

Union Medical Inspector Edward P. Vollum arrived at Gettysburg to assess the situation with regard to the wounded and report back to Washington. His report, dated July 25, 1863, was as follows:

> The following are the numbers and destinations of Union and Confederate wounded sent from Gettysburg up to the 23d. The first one thousand four hundred and sixty-two had left before my arrival.
>
> Wounded sent from Gettysburg to 22d instant:
> Union: 7,608
> Confederate: 3,817
> Total: 11,425
> Union wounded sent to Baltimore, in addition to above:
> From Westminster: 2,000
> From Littleton: 2,000
> Total sent off: 15,425
> Deduct Confederate wounded: 3,817
> Total Union wounded sent off: 11,608
> Union wounded remaining on 22d instant: 1,995
> Total Union wounded: 13,503
> Confederate wounded remaining on 22d instant: 2,922
> Total Confederate wounded: 6,739
> Grand total in our hands: 20,342

Vollum goes on to list all the vital medical supplies that were so desperately needed:

> I endeavored to make up the deficiencies in medical supplies at Gettysburg by telegraphing Surgeon Simpson, U.S.A. at Baltimore. In reply, he ordered liberal supplies of alcohol, solution chloride of soda, tincture of iron, creasote [*sic*], nitric acid, permanganate of potassa, buckets, tin cups, stretchers, bed sacks and stationery of all kinds for ten thousand men in the field hospitals. On the day after my arrival, the demand for stationery, disinfectant, iodine, tincture of iron and some other articles was so great and immediate that I purchased them in Gettysburg, and sent the bills to the quartermaster there for payment.

thence to a special camp. The 5,000 Rebels in Union hands were marched to Westminster, then transported by train to prison camps to the south, the largest of which was Fort Delaware.

The 3,500 captured Yankees not paroled were initially the responsibility of Pickett's Division before he handed them over to Brigadier-General Imboden on July 6 for the long journey to Richmond. Like their prisoner comrades to the north, these unfortunates faced lengthy spells in Confederate prisons, with officers going to the notorious Libby Prison situated in a warehouse on the bank of the James River at Richmond. Many of the enlisted men ended up at Belle Isle (also on the James River at Richmond), which by the end of 1863 housed some 10,000 prisoners. Early in 1864 all prisoners at Richmond were transferred to Andersonville Prison in Georgia.

A substantial number of Rebel stragglers and deserters wandered the byways after the battle, intent on avoiding any further service – a few even went north. Harriet Bayley, who lived north of Gettysburg, had one young Rebel deserter knocking on her door while the battle was still in progress. She later referred to him as "a woebegone little 'Reb'." She took him in and years later wrote, "He was given a suit of citizen's clothes and remained with the family until the battle was over. He is now living on a farm near the battlefield and the size of his family indicates that he has been more successful in peaceful pursuits than those of war."

Straggling and desertion was not confined to the Confederates. An article for the *Lancaster Daily Express*, written on July 10, highlighted the Union problem:

> Several thousand men [Yankees] are counted among the missing but they are not prisoners – they are on a grand straggle, and the country from Frederick to Westminster, to Hanover, to Gettysburg, and back again to Frederick, swarms with loose men away from their commands – luxuriating among the farm houses as long as their money lasts, and safe from the gobble of provost guards, of which, by the way nobody has seen lately.

It was the job of Meade's provost marshal, Brigadier-General Marsena Patrick, to round these characters up. That he made efforts to do so, and the size of the problem, is evident from some of his diary entries for July:

> *July 3* I never saw such artillery fire . . . It was terrific & I had my hands full with those who broke to the rear, but we succeeded in checking the disorder & organized a guard of Stragglers to keep nearly 2000 Prisoners all safe.
> *July 4* Busy gathering men from their places of retreat & straggling . . .
> *July 7* It was a very hard march of 30 miles & I had a rough time in driving up Stragglers, Officers & Men . . .
> *July 13* The day has been rainy & . . . we have had a great deal to do with prisoners & all that kind of work . . .
> *July 21* our Army is in no condition to fight another battle – The discipline is horrible. There is no responsibility any where, & Commanders of every rank, cover up the rascality of their Troops – There is a vast deal of Stealing of Horses, & debradations [*sic*] of all kinds.
> *July 23* Officers & men are turned thieves and robbers – The whole country is full of stragglers & the officers all permit it and say nothing –

PROBLEMS AND PLANS

July 3 and 4 – Lee

There is little or no evidence that Lee ever contemplated doing anything other than retreating to Virginia after the collapse of Pickett's charge. His army was by no means totally demoralized, and in theory he could have waited along Seminary Ridge for a Union assault and hopefully driven it off with maximum losses to his enemy. He could possibly have withdrawn to the South Mountain passes to the west and chosen a good defensive position there, again to await attack. He did neither of these things, although he certainly thought Meade would counterattack during July 4. Lee made his decision to retreat on the evening of July 3 and thus set in motion one of the most difficult and dangerous operations of war – a withdrawal while in contact with the enemy. The object is to make a clean break, a task that involves deception, use of natural features to facilitate security and the most careful planning and coordination by commanders and staff.

Lee had four basic problems: how to prepare for, and repulse, an expected counterattack on July 4; how to get his enormous wagon trains with their subsistence, stores and ambulances (of which there was a chronic shortage) away safely; how to deal with the thousands of wounded; and finally how to get his troops away without being involved in a running fight with an aggressive enemy. In brief, he needed to get his wagons and troops over the Potomac into Virginia without losing the loot he had acquired or many more troops in the process.

The first step was to reposition his army to be better placed to repel any attacks and gain time for the wagons to get away. This entailed withdrawing Longstreet's Corps on the right back to Seminary Ridge, and refusing his right flank to guard against any attack from the south. Longstreet was the first to move, starting to pull back around 7:00 p.m. on July 3. Once in their new positions the troops were put to work constructing barricades. Ewell's Corps on the left had the furthest to move to its new position with its right (Rodes) resting on the Fairfield Road and its left (Johnson) on Oak Hill. This withdrawal took place during darkness, between 10:00 p.m. on July 3 and 3:00 the next morning. Like Longstreet's, Ewell's men busied themselves building barricades on arrival. Hill's Corps in the center of Seminary Ridge did not have to move. To the north and south Stuart's cavalry provided flank protection. The new line extended for 4 miles north–south, directly covering at right angles the two withdrawal routes to the west that the army would use.

As with his original advance, so with his withdrawal: Lee made skillful use of the natural features or obstacles on his route. As is clear from Map 68, the main obstacle behind him was the South Mountain and the passes or gaps through it. Control the gaps, or get through them before the enemy, and South Mountain became an aiding, transverse obstacle for Lee and a hindering one for Meade if he pursued directly. The two key gaps were those at Cashtown and Monterey Pass or Fairfield. Use them both and it would dramatically speed up the process of retreat. Once through them, a comparatively small force could delay a much larger one. Thus the first phase of the actual withdrawal would be getting his wagon trains and army safely through those gaps and at the same time securing the difficult but passable Raven's Rock Pass 10 miles south of the Fairfield Gap. This would need to be held, as would the Turner's and Crampton Gaps still further south, to protect

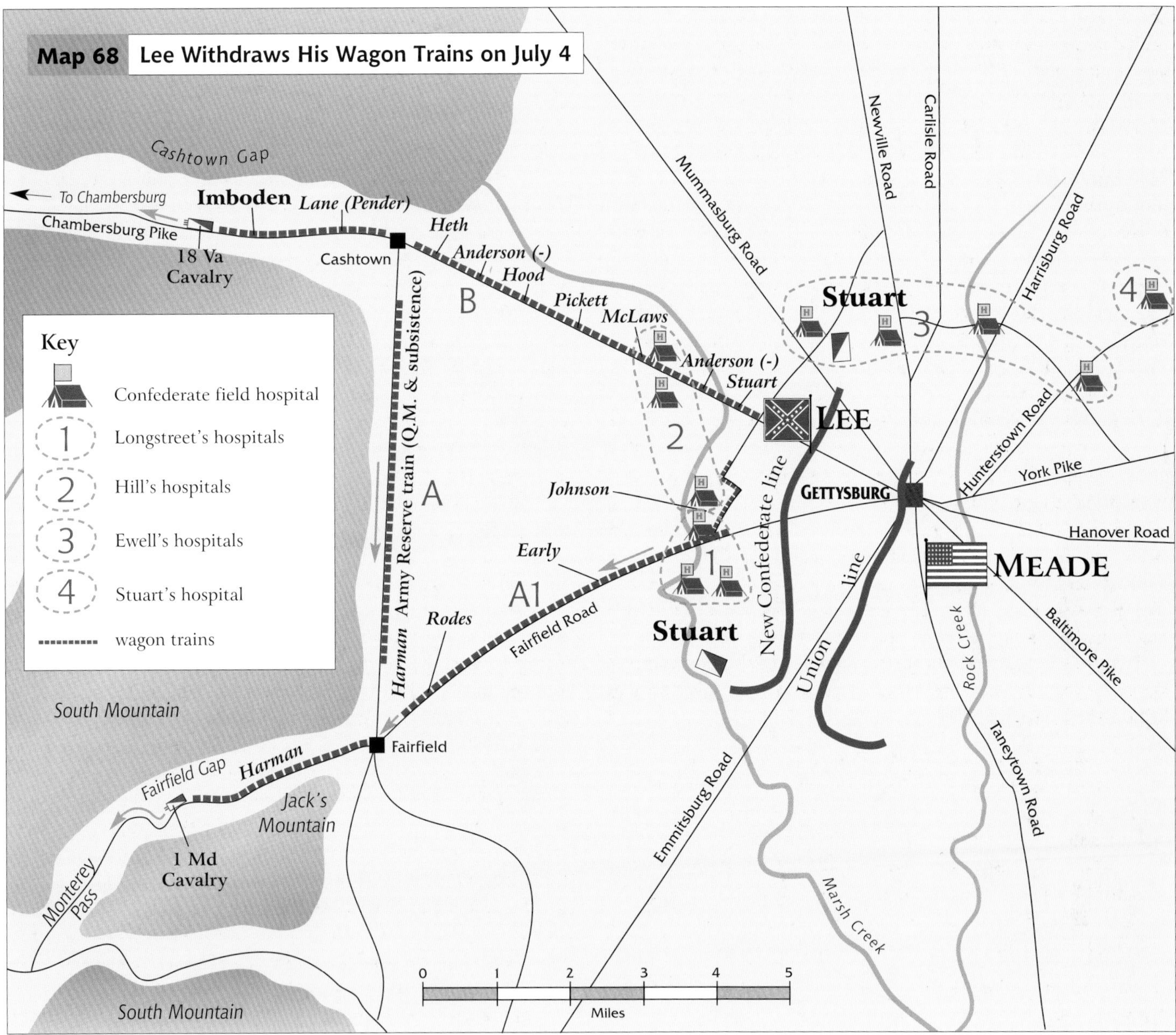

Notes

• Having decided to withdraw, Lee's first problem was to attend to the wounded and get his wagon trains away down the Cumberland Valley and across the Potomac into Virginia. There was a simple system of triage for the wounded. They were either walking wounded who could march back alongside the ambulance wagons; wounded who could not walk but were considered strong enough to travel, who were loaded onto wagons of various types; or wounded too serious to be moved who were left behind at the field hospitals to become prisoners. A number of surgeons and other medical staff remained behind to tend them. The map shows the main Confederate field hospitals at which these seriously wounded were left. These hospitals were mostly located with the divisional wagon trains, something that greatly facilitated the organization of the withdrawal.

• Lee withdrew his army to positions along Seminary Ridge to a line that extended north as far as Oak Hill, with cavalry on either flank. Its task was to construct breastworks and prepare to meet an expected Union counterattack on July 4 and gain time for the huge wagon trains to get away.

• The key to a successful withdrawal lay in getting through the two passes/gaps in South Mountain – the Cashtown Gap and the Monterey Pass/Fairfield Gap – and then south down the Cumberland Valley to the crossings over the Potomac at Williamsport and Falling Waters. Lee divided his wagons into two enormous trains.

• Maj. John Harman, as chief quartermaster of Ewell's Corps, commanded the largest train. He had been in charge of the Army Reserve quartermaster and subsistence trains located north of Fairfield, along with at least 5,000 cattle, a similar number of sheep and hundreds of hogs. To these would be added the divisional trains of Ewell's Corps – that is, all the wagons except those essential to accompany the marching troops. Together these stretched for up to 40 miles along the roads. As the Army Reserve train was close to Fairfield, Harman's train would be the first away (**A**). As the tail passed Fairfield it would be joined by Ewell's trains (**A1**). At 3:00 a.m. on July 4 Harman ordered his train to start. He was making for the Fairfield Gap.

• Brig.-Gen. John Imboden commanded the second train. It was to be called the "wagon train of misery," as it carried the bulk of the wounded whom it was thought might survive the journey; many did not. It was composed of the trains of Imboden's own brigade and the six divisions of Hill's and Longstreet's Corps, plus Stuart's Division (**B**). This train was some 20 miles in length and started its march at around 5:00 p.m. on July 4. It was headed for the Cashtown Gap.

Lee's army as it moved toward the Potomac crossings from being cut off from them or attacked in flank. The final obstacle – and this could prove a considerable hindrance to Lee until he was across – was the Potomac River. He intended to use the ford at Williamsport and the pontoon bridge at Falling Waters built by his own pontoon train engineers about 3 miles downstream from Williamsport. What Lee did not know on July 4 was that, on that very day, his lightly guarded bridge was being destroyed in a raid by 300 Union cavalry from Major-General William H. French's command headquartered at Frederick under the command of a Major Shadrack Foley. With the heavy rains falling, there was every likelihood that the Potomac would be swollen and, with no bridge, crossing might be impossible.

The problem of the wounded was an immediate and pressing one. There was a desperate shortage of proper ambulances, so every division was combed for empty wagons of any description and these were assembled near the field hospitals to load on those wounded deemed fit to travel. It would be a dreadful, agonizing journey, jolted and jarred in unsprung, unsuitable vehicles. Lightly wounded men were returned to their regiments; more serious walking wounded would march alongside the ambulance trains; and those unfit to move would remain behind at the field hospitals to become prisoners, although a number of Rebel surgeons, assistant surgeons and medical staff would stay with them.

Lee's plan once his army had withdrawn to the Seminary Ridge line was in two phases.

Phase 1 (Map 68)

This was the withdrawal of all wagon trains except the bare minimum that must accompany the marching troops. To get them away as quickly as possible, they were divided into two huge trains under the command of Major John Harman, Ewell's chief quartermaster, and Brigadier-General John Imboden. Harman's was by far the largest, consisting of the Army Reserve quartermaster and subsistence trains together with all the thousands of cattle, sheep and hogs that had been collected, plus the trains of Ewell's three divisions. Once on the move these combined trains would occupy up to 40 miles of road space. The Army Reserve train and animal herds were located between Fairfield and Cashtown, having been brought forward from Chambersburg (escorted by Imboden's mounted infantry brigade), and thus they would be the first to move, heading for the Fairfield/Monterey Pass. Ewell's trains would assemble on either side of the Fairfield Road and would join the column in the order of Rodes, Early and Johnson as the last of the Army Reserve wagons cleared Fairfield. Lee issued his orders for this move on July 3 and Harman was able to have the vast train assembled during the night of July 3/4, with the order to march being given around 3:00 a.m. on the 4th – a remarkable effort. It was about 35 miles to Williamsport via Waynesborough, Leitersburg and Hagerstown. The only troops that could be spared to escort this column were the 1st Maryland Cavalry Battalion of about 300 troopers under Major Harry W. Gilmor (originally from Fitzhugh Lee's Brigade) and a battery of four 3-inch ordnance rifles under Captain William A. Tanner. These two units formed the advance guard.

Imboden's train was a little less than half the length of Harman's, but he had been given the difficult and thankless task of transporting the bulk of the wounded who were fit to travel but could not walk, estimated at about 5,000, as well as the animals collected by Ewell's foragers. Imboden's train would consist of his own brigade's wagons, Lane's (Pender's) divisional train, followed by those of Anderson and Heth of Hill's Corps, then Hood's, Pickett's (then, in the event, part of Anderson's), McLaws' of Longstreet's Corps and Stuart's. This train would take the more northerly route to the Potomac via the Cashtown Gap, Marion and Greencastle. It, and its cavalry escort, would be the only Rebel troops to take this route, which at a distance of 45 miles was 10 miles longer than through the Monterey/Fairfield Gap.

Because it would be isolated from the rest of the army for much of the time, Imboden's train was given a much stronger

Major John A. Harman's Wagon Train

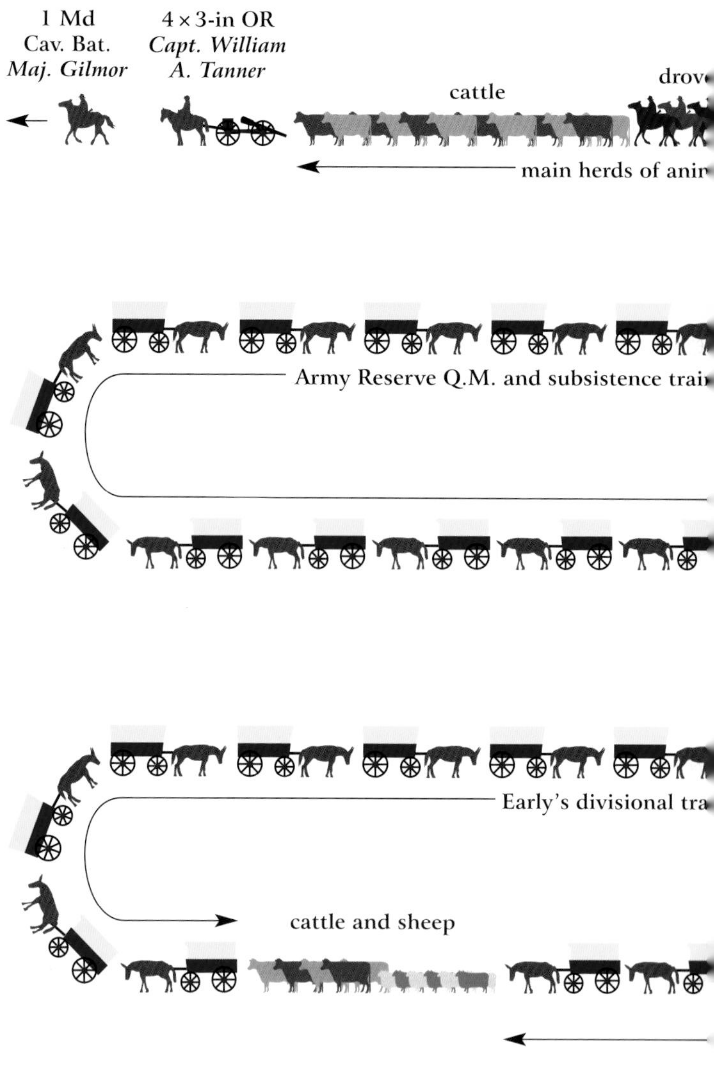

Notes

• Although Imboden's train with the majority of the wounded has had the most space in histories of the campaign, it was slightly less than half the size of Maj. John Harman's. This train was composed of the Army Reserve quartermaster and subsistence trains, some 5,000 cattle, a similar number of sheep, hundreds of hogs, either tied to the wagons or inside them, and Ewell's three divisional trains. As chief quartermaster of Ewell's Corps, it was Harman's task to get this enormous train from Fairfield to the Potomac crossing at Williamsport via the Monterey Pass, Waynesborough, Leitersburg and Hagerstown.

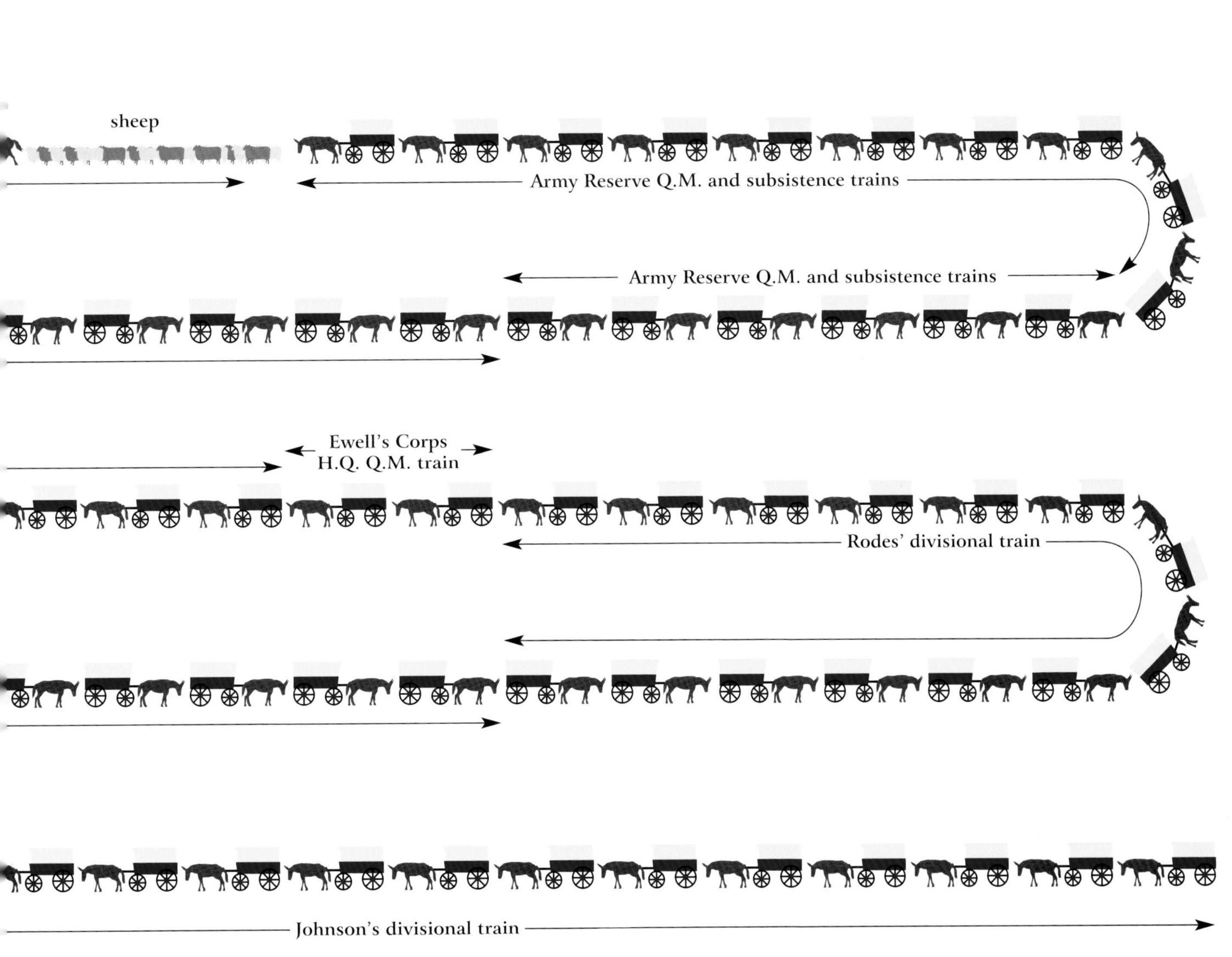

Once on the road, this train stretched for almost 40 miles, 20 of which 'ere taken up by the Army Reserve train that had most of the cattle and ıeep herds driven along by mounted drovers at the head of the column. : was an impossibility to escort and guard such an extensive column roperly and only the 300 or so troopers of the 1st Maryland Cavalry attalion (Fitzhugh Lee's Brigade) under Maj. Harry W. Gilmor, which ad been attached to Ewell's Corps from the outset of the campaign, ɔgether with the four 3-in ordnance rifles of Capt. William A. Tanner's ;ourtney Virginia Battery (Jones's Brigade), led and escorted the train. ee relied on getting this train away quickly and in darkness to provide sufficient security. Harman started to assemble the various trains late on July 3 and gave the order to march at 3:00 the next morning.

• It took some 10 hours just to get the Army Reserve train on the road, but when Kilpatrick's Yankee cavalry first attacked it in the Monterey Pass it was Rodes' train that was caught, as the head of the Army Reserve was already approaching Hagerstown. These night attacks, which had started 21 hours after leading elements of the entire train had begun their march, continued until around 3:00 a.m. on July 5. Lee's sending his largest, and in terms of subsistence and quartermaster's stores most valuable, train away first while his army was still deployed on the battlefield had succeeded.

escort. The advance guard was the 18th Virginia Cavalry, about 900 men, under Colonel George W. Imboden (the brigade commander's brother), with the six 12-pounder Napoleons of Captain John H. McClanahan's Staunton Horse Artillery Battery. Interspersed at intervals along the column were the squadrons of the 62nd Mounted Infantry under Colonel George H. Smith (a cousin of the brigade commander). Additional artillery in the form of six Napoleons and two 12-pounder howitzers from Major Benjamin F. Eshleman's Battalion was also split up along the column. Imboden was also allocated the batteries of Captain Joseph D. Moore (two Napoleons, three ordnance rifles and one 10-pounder Parrott) and Lieutenant R. Prosper Landry (three ordnance rifles and one 10-pounder Parrott), both under the command of Major Charles Richardson. At the rear was Captain William B. Hurt's battery of three Blakely rifles – a total of twenty-five artillery pieces. The rearguard consisted of the two cavalry brigades of Fitzhugh Lee and Baker (Hampton's) from Stuart's Division.

To allow for the collection of additional wagons for the wounded and their loading, and to allow Harman's train to get clear, Imboden was not scheduled to leave until around 5:00 p.m. on July 4 after a day spent assembling west of Gettysburg on either side of the Chambersburg Pike.

Typical Order of March of a Confederate Divisional Wagon Train

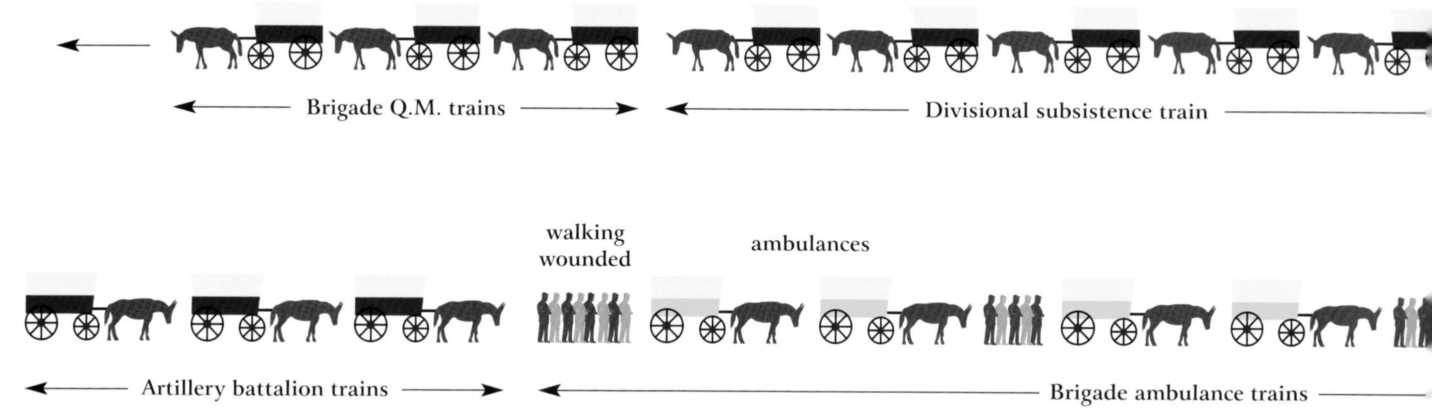

Notes

• The order of march could vary, but this is a typical one that might have been used by one of Ewell's divisional trains on its retreat from Gettysburg as part of Maj. Harman's train. It would have been at least 6 miles in length – probably a lot more, as the subsistence train and Q.M. trains were laden with a huge variety of produce and goods taken by foraging and requisitioning. It was important that these wagons reached Virginia as a visible sign that something of value had been achieved in the campaign.

• The herd of cattle and sheep, etc., added to the length of the train. They are shown as one group above but it is quite possible there were several herds interspersed along the column.

• Note the ambulance train is a long one and that numerous walking wounded accompanied the wagons – which were an odd assortment of wagons, carts and carriages, as indeed were the vehicles in all Rebel trains. Some were pulled by horses, but the majority would be drawn by mules in teams of four or, less often, six.

Phase 2

This involved the withdrawal of the troops from their position on Seminary Ridge. The three corps would all take the southern route via Fairfield and the Monterey Pass. Lee's written order for this phase is given below:

General ORDERS, No. 74
HDQRS. ARMY OF NORTHERN VIRGINIA
July 4, 1863

> The army will vacate its position this evening. General A.P. Hill's corps will commence the movement, withdrawing from its position after dark, and proceed on the Fairfield road to the pass in the mountains [Monterey], which it will occupy, selecting the strongest ground for defense toward the east; General Longstreet's corps will follow, and General Ewell's corps bring up the rear. These two latter corps will proceed through and go into camp. General Longstreet's corps will be charged with the escort of the prisoners, and will habitually occupy the center of the line of march. General Ewell's and General Hill's corps will alternately take the front and rear of the march.

In effect the entire army would provide the rearguard for Harman's train, as Hill's leading division was to follow the last of Ewell's wagons. Hill was to halt in the Monterey Pass area and take up a position to defend it while the rest of the army passed through. As Longstreet's and Ewell's troops cleared the pass they were to halt and "go into camp" to wait until the army was clear of the pass. At that stage the march would resume with Ewell's Corps in the lead and Hill's bringing up the rear (although in the event this did not happen). Longstreet's Corps would remain in the middle guarding the 3,500 prisoners – in practice a task given to Pickett's Division. Once through the Monterey Pass the army would head for Hagerstown and the Potomac crossings.

Stuart's cavalry would play a vital role in the withdrawal from the Gettysburg area and the retreat to the Potomac. As with an advance, so with a retreat: it was the cavalry's job to scout ahead and to the flanks, escort and protect the marching columns of infantry, as well as obtaining information on the enemy's movements. Many of these duties would involve holding open vital routes, bottlenecks, passes or crossing places, and often fighting dismounted. Cavalry had to be at the front, on the flanks and at the rear of the marching columns and wagon trains.

Lee gave his orders for the withdrawal during the night of July 3, but for some reason Stuart did not receive them and it was only after being informed on the morning of July 4 that Ewell had pulled back, and that Union troops were coming back into the town, that Stuart rode to Lee's headquarters to find out what was happening. Lee's plan for his cavalry was as given in the written order quoted below.

> General Stuart will designate a cavalry command, not exceeding two squadrons, to precede and follow the army in its line of march, the commander of the advance reporting to the leading corps, the commander of the rear to the commander of the rear corps. He will

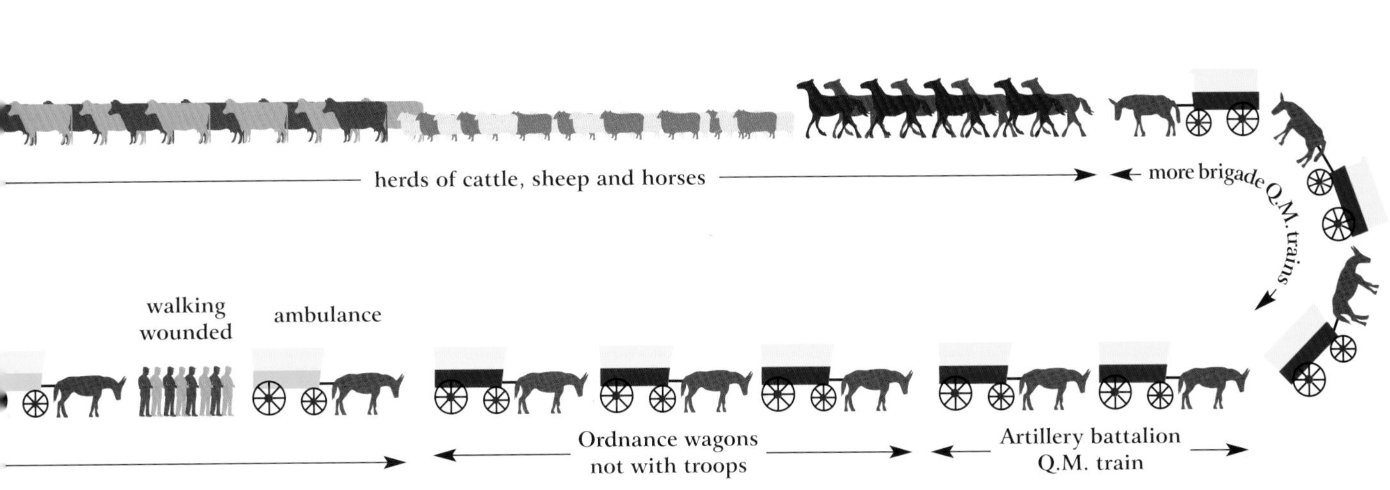

Frank Moore, a Northern newspaper reporter, recorded in the *Rebellion Record* the sort of items carried in Ewell's train:

"It is impossible to tell the number of vehicles of all descriptions; there were [wagons] filled with delicacies from stores in Pennsylvania; four and six mule and horse teams; some filled with barrels of molasses, others with flour, hams, meal, clothing, ladies' and children's shoes and underclothing – mainly obtained from the frightened inhabitants of Pennsylvania; wagons stolen from Pennsylvania and loyal Maryland farmers; wagons made for the Confederate government (a poor imitation of our own); wagons from North Carolina and wagons from Tennessee – a mongrel train – all stolen, or what is still worse – paid for in Confederate notes, made payable six months after the recognition of the southern Confederacy by the United States Government – or in other words – never."

> direct one or two brigades, as he may think proper, to proceed to Cashtown this afternoon, and hold that place until the rear of the army has passed Fairfield, and occupy the gorge in the mountains; after crossing which, to proceed in the direction of Greencastle, guarding the right and rear of the army on its march to Hagerstown and Williamsport. General Stuart, with the rest of the cavalry, will this evening [July 4] take the route to Emmitsburg, and proceed thence toward Cavetown and Boonsborough, guarding the left and rear of the army.

Stuart divided and tasked his division in accordance with these orders as follows:

- Fitzhugh Lee's and Lawrence Baker's Brigades to Cashtown to guard the trains of Longstreet and Hill and the right flank of the army during its retreat.
- The brigades of Robertson and Jones, along with the batteries of Captain Roger P. Chew (three ordnance rifles and one 12-pounder howitzer) and Captain Marcellus N. Moorman (two ordnance rifles, one Napoleon and one 12-pounder howitzer), already near Fairfield, were to proceed to Jack's Mountain and hold open the two roads round it to the Monterey Pass.
- Stuart would personally lead the brigades of Chambliss and Ferguson via Emmitsburg to cross the South Mountain by the Raven's Rock Pass and protect the left of the army.

Thus the cavalry's first task in the retreat was to secure the three passes through the South Mountain closest to Gettysburg – Cashtown, Monterey and Raven's Rock. The first would be used by Imboden's train; the second by the Army Reserve and Ewell's Corps trains under Harman, followed by the main body of the army; the third was a possible enemy cavalry route to be used in an attempt to cut off or attack the army as it moved southwest toward the Potomac. It had all the makings of a race to secure the passes.

July 4 and 5 – Meade

For the Yankee infantry and gunners, July 4 was mostly a day spent resting, recovering, starting to tackle some of the mountainous medical problems and trying to find something to eat. According to Provost Marshal Patrick, "Everybody was without anything to eat & waiting for subsistence." Patrick neglected to mention that the same was true of the thousands of horses and mules. By 2:00 p.m., with the battlefield covered with dead and dying men and animals, surgeons overwhelmed with casualties, soldiers exhausted and hungry, it started raining heavily. By 9:00 p.m. it was pelting down. Everybody was soaked and miserable.

Meade's immediate problem, aside from these administrative difficulties, was to ascertain his enemy's intentions and decide whether and how he was to follow up his advantage. Should he assume the offensive? If Lee retreated, in which direction would he move? Would he await attack in his present location, withdraw to the South Mountain passes and make a stand there, or head for Virginia as quickly as possible? At 7:00 that morning Meade sent the following message to Halleck in Washington:

> This morning the enemy has withdrawn his pickets from the positions of yesterday. My own pickets are moving out to ascertain the nature and extent of the enemy's movement. My information is not sufficient for me to decide its character yet – whether a retreat or maneuver for other purposes.

At noon Meade followed up the above message with another that was received in Washington more than three hours before the first:

> The position of affairs is not materially changed from my last dispatch, 7 a.m. The enemy apparently has thrown back his left [Early had withdrawn], and placed guns and troops in position in rear of Gettysburg, which we now hold. The enemy has abandoned large numbers of his killed and wounded on the field. I shall require some time to get up supplies, ammunition, &cm, rest the army, worn out by long marches and three days hard fighting. I shall probably be able to give you a return of our captures and losses before night, and return of the enemy's killed and wounded in our hands.

July 4, then, was a day spent resting, burying the dead, caring for wounded and watching the enemy seeking answers to Meade's questions. As early as 6:45 a.m. the signal station on Little Round Top under Lieutenants John C. Wiggins and Henry N. Camp reported, "The wagon trains of the enemy are moving toward Millerstown on the road leading from Gettysburg to the Fairfield Road." Early's Division had pulled out of the town back to Seminary Ridge, thus allowing Captains Hall and Taylor of the Signal Corps to move into the Gettysburg Court House and later up into the cupola of the Pennsylvania College. From the former at 5:15 p.m. Taylor sent the following signal to Meade, who had by then moved his headquarters from the Leister House to a strip of wood alongside the Taneytown Road:

> General Meade
> Three regiments of cavalry and four wagons passed along our front, 2 ½ miles out from town, halted on the hills northwest from the college building, and were joined by two more regiments, a battery of artillery, and two ambulances coming from behind the hills. The column is now moving toward the Chambersburg road.
> Dense smokes have been seen all day behind the hills in the direction of Cashtown.
>
> P.A. Taylor
> First Lieutenant, Acting Signal Officer

Two hours later another signal stated:

> General Meade
>
> A train of thirty-three wagons just passed from near Herr's tavern toward the Fairfield road. Several smaller trains have been seen during the day in the same direction.
> The column of cavalry reported this p.m. moving toward Chambersburg pike, halted behind the woods north of the seminary, head of column resting on the Tapeworm road. It is still there this hour; horses grazing.
>
> P.A. Taylor
> First Lieutenant, Acting Signal Officer

That Lee was on the move was reported from other signal stations, and in particular that wagons, ambulances and cavalry were heading west along the Fairfield Road. This last signal, received after dark from the station on Little Round Top, stated:

> All quiet in front. Enemy just relieved their outer pickets. There has been passing for the last twenty-five minutes (and is still passing), along what is called the Fairfield road, a steady stream of heavy wagons, ambulances, cavalry, and what seems to be artillery or else flying artillery and no cavalry. They move slowly and to our left.

By nightfall of that Saturday (July 4), Independence Day, indications were strong that the Army of Northern Virginia's wagon trains, escorted by cavalry, were moving westward – but could Meade be sure that Lee was about to withdraw his entire army, and if so in what direction?

Meade had reacted to the reports of enemy wagons on the march by sending cavalry in several directions to pursue, harass and if possible intercept them. Colonel J. Irvin Gregg's Brigade (David McM. Gregg's Division) was ordered north and west after the wagons moving toward Cashtown. Colonels Gamble and Devin (Buford's Division), located at Westminster, were sent to Frederick to join up with Merritt's Reserve Brigade; the division was then to head for the Cumberland Valley via Turner's Gap. Kilpatrick's Division was directed to link up with Colonel Pennock Huey's Brigade (not at Gettysburg, but part of David Gregg's Division) and then harass Lee's trains, reportedly routed through the Monterey Pass. Meade had sent his cavalry in three directions to probe three likely routes the Rebels would use if retreating, but not the Raven's Rock Pass, regarded as too difficult for an army and its wagons.

On July 4, anticipating a Rebel retreat, Meade signaled to Major-General William H. French commanding an infantry division at Frederick. He was to seize the South Mountain passes, harass Lee's lines of communication and re-occupy the Maryland Heights (overlooking Harper's Ferry). French sent a brigade to hold Turner's and Crampton Gaps. However, Meade was reluctant to make a decision affecting his entire army without more information, as at this stage he could still envisage Lee having several alternatives:

- To resume the offensive.
- To await a Union attack on Seminary Ridge.
- To withdraw west to the South Mountain pass at Cashtown and await attack there.
- To retreat as quickly and directly as possible to Virginia via the Fairfield Gap through the South Mountain into the Cumberland Valley and thence to the crossing points over the Potomac at Williamsport and Shepherdstown.

While the first of these was probably the least and the fourth the most likely, until Meade was certain he refused to commit himself to aggressive action other than sending out cavalry probes and instructions to French at Frederick. During the day he wrote to his wife explaining his predicament. "For my part as I have to follow and fight him I would rather do it at once & in Maryland than to follow him into Virginia . . . The most difficult part of my task is acting without correct information on which to predicate action." With the object of answering this question, Meade called another of his commanders' conferences on the evening of July 4 to elicit opinions and suggestions. As he later said, he "desired the earnest assistance and advice of every corps commander."

The nine generals attending were Newton (I Corps, replacing Reynolds), Hays (II Corps, replacing Hancock), Birney (III Corps, replacing Sickles), Sykes (V Corps), Sedgwick (VI Corps), Howard (XI Corps), Slocum (XII Corps), Pleasonton (Cavalry Corps) and Warren (Chief Engineer). The commanders gave Meade a report on the state of their corps, which they estimated totaling around 55,000 infantrymen who were fit and available to march and fight. Reinforcements were anticipated from Washington, French had a division at Frederick, and Major-General Darius N. Couch had been ordered by Halleck to advance the 9,000 militia under Brigadier-General William F. Smith south from Carlisle. Smith also had a small force of 2,000 infantry and cavalry west of McConnellsburg under a Colonel Lewis B. Pierce. According to President Lincoln, Smith's militiamen "will in my unprofessional opinion, be quite as likely to capture the Man-in-the-Moon, as any part of Lee's Army." Having heard the reports, Meade posed four questions to his generals:

1. "Shall this army remain here?" The response, a typical committee decision, was represented by Warren's answer that the army should stay where it was "until we see what they are doing."

2. "If we remain here, shall we assume the offensive?" To which Meade got a unanimous no.

3. "Do you deem it expedient to move toward Williamsport, through Emmitsburg?" The answer to this was yes, as it threatened to cut off Lee's withdrawal and at the same time keep the army between Lee and Washington.

4. "Shall we pursue the enemy if he is retreating on his direct line of retreat?" Howard thought yes, but only with a show of force; some thought cavalry only would be sufficient; while Birney considered no pursuit be made on the enemy's direct line of retreat. The majority supported Howard.

Meade's 10:00 p.m. dispatch to Halleck read: "I make a reconnaissance tomorrow [July 5] to ascertain what the intention of the enemy is. My cavalry is now moving toward South Mountain pass, and, should the enemy retreat, I shall pursue him on his flanks."

In summary, Meade's plan was to send his cavalry to harass Lee's trains, secure passes through the South Mountain and supply information and, largely following Howard's advice, probe the Rebel line early on July 5 with a strong force (VI Corps was given this task). Otherwise he would await confirmation of Lee's retreat. Once that was confirmed, his pursuit would initially be east of the South Mountain, thus still keeping his army between the enemy and Washington.

Outline of Important Events, July 3–14 (Map 69)

The key events that had a bearing on Lee's retreat and Meade's pursuit are summarized below. As with most timings, they are approximate or estimated.

July 3

- Early evening Lee ordered Longstreet's and Ewell's Corps to pull back to the Seminary Ridge–Oak Hill line and in the night gave instructions for the general retreat, using the Monterey Pass for Harman's train, to be followed by the bulk of the army.
- Colonel Pierce (12th Pennsylvania Cavalry), with his mixed force of Union cavalry, infantry and guns – mostly troops that had escaped from Winchester on June 14 – moved toward the Cumberland Valley from Bloody Run (off the map west of McConnellsburg).
- That evening Couch at Harrisburg was ordered by Halleck to send Major-General William F. Smith's Division of militia at Carlisle to advance south into the Cumberland Valley.

July 4

- At 1:00 a.m. Imboden received his orders from Lee to take Longstreet's and Hill's Corps trains and the bulk of the army's wounded fit to move back to the Potomac via the Cashtown Gap.
- At around 3:00 a.m. Harman's Army Reserve train started its march to the Potomac via the Monterey Gap, to be followed by the army headquarters train and the three divisional trains of Ewell's Corps.
- Before dawn the Army of Northern Virginia had occupied its new line and troops of the Union XI Corps had occupied Gettysburg, but unbeknown to Lee his pontoon bridge at Falling Waters had been destroyed in a Union cavalry raid from Frederick.
- Early in the morning Meade instructed French at Frederick to secure the passes through South Mountain, harass the enemy and re-occupy Maryland Heights – French sent a brigade of around 4,000 men to Turner's and Crampton Gaps.
- At about 6:30 a.m. Lee sent a message to Meade requesting an exchange of prisoners. It was rejected.
- All day Rebel wounded were loaded into wagons while Imboden's train assembled along the Chambersburg Pike. Meade received messages from his signal stations that Lee's wagons were on the move. He sent his cavalry to harass enemy trains at the Cashtown Gap, Monterey Pass and to secure Turner's Gap.
- By 1:00 p.m. Harman's train had cleared Fairfield and Ewell's trains were on the move behind him. At 4:00 p.m. Imboden's train began its march from Cashtown.
- After dark Hill's Corps started to withdraw along the Fairfield Road, followed around 11:00 p.m. by Longstreet.
- At about 9:00 p.m. the Union cavalry under Kilpatrick attacked Rodes' wagon train in the dark and rain as it negotiated the Monterey Pass. Fighting continued until 3:00 a.m. and a significant number of Rebel wagons were captured.
- That night Meade held his corps commanders' conference to get their views on what action to take. He remained uncertain if Lee was retreating and telegraphed Halleck that he intended to probe the Rebel line early the next day.
- Around midnight the head of Harman's train reached Williamsport, with the tail stretching back over 20 miles, to find only one or two flat-bottomed rafts of Lemen's Ferry working. These could take only two wagons at a time and had to be poled across the river.

Map 69 An Outline of Lee's Retreat and Meade's Pursuit after Gettysburg

Key

- A — Imboden's wagon train, followed by Fitz Lee's and Baker's Brigades
- B — Confederate cavalry under Stuart
- C — Harman's wagon train followed by main Confederate Army
- Confederate defensive line, July 11, 12 and 13
- D — Rebels cross Potomac at Williamsport and Falling Waters, July 13/14
- A — Union cavalry route – Gregg's Division
- B — Union cavalry route – Kilpatrick's Division
- C — Union cavalry route – Buford's Division
- D — routes of Union infantry corps

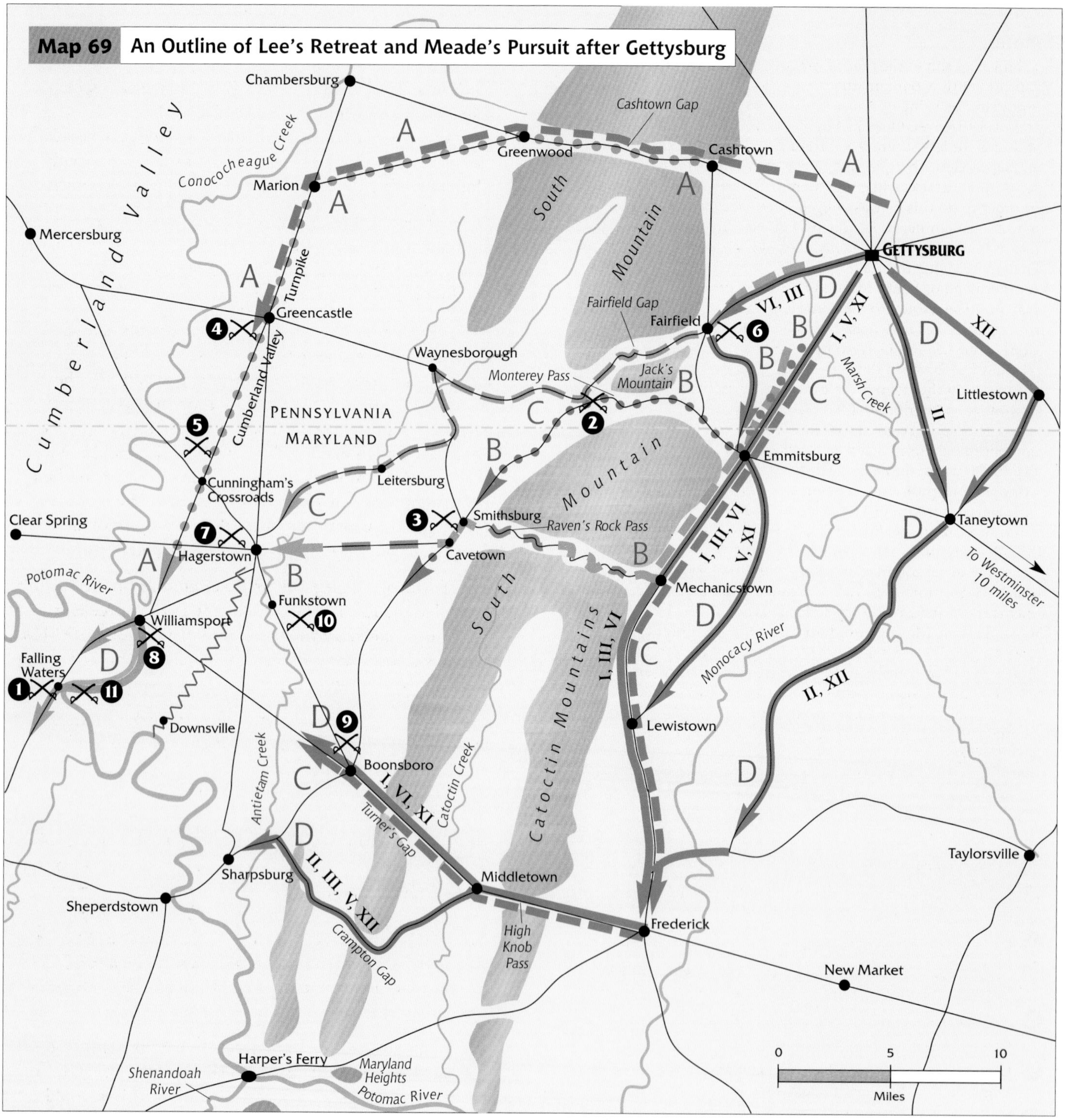

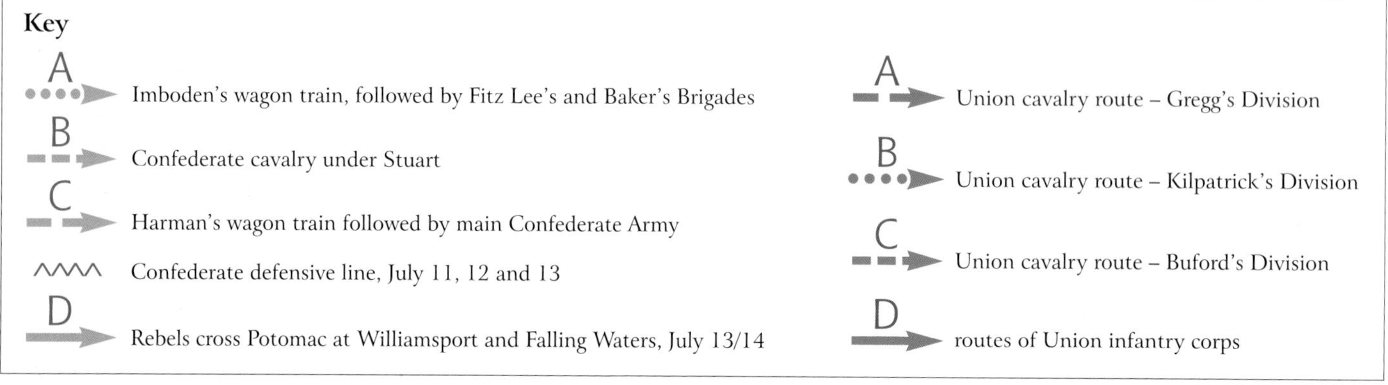

Notes

• This map shows the crucial importance to both sides of the gaps in South Mountain and the crossing places over the Potomac. Lee's line of retreat was down the Cumberland Valley and over the river. Once in Virginia he was in friendly territory and more or less secure. For Meade to reap the fruits of his victory at Gettysburg he had to cut off the Rebel retreat and press home attacks while they were still north of the Potomac. In order to do this he was obliged to move southeast of the mountains in order to keep between Lee and Washington. This meant he could only pursue by adopting a long left hook via Frederick, Middletown and Turner's and Crampton Gaps at the southern end of South Mountain. This in turn meant long marches (Gettysburg to Williamsport was 55 miles by this route), as he was now operating on exterior lines – along two sides of the triangle Gettysburg–Frederick–Williamsport, whereas Lee marched down one side. This was the reverse of the situation throughout the campaign so far, when the advantage of interior lines had been Meade's.

• In the event, Lee got his wagons away quickly on July 4 in two enormous trains, each on a separate route, and, making maximum use of darkness, had the last elements of his army away from its positions on Seminary Ridge by evening on July 5. Meade, uncertain of Lee's true intentions until late afternoon on July 6, did not finally order his army south to Middletown until then. He had sent his cavalry to harass and delay the Rebel columns on July 4, but although they captured some wagons from both Rebel columns, Stuart was able to keep them at bay and from doing serious harm.

• By the time Meade moved forward from the Boonsboro area on July 10, Lee's defensive line guarding the crossing was in place, and over the next few days was further reinforced by entrenchments and gun emplacements. Probably wisely at this stage, Meade declined to attack and the Army of Northern Virginia escaped over the Potomac at Williamsport and Falling Waters.

Site of clashes mentioned in text

1. Confederate pontoon bridge destroyed by Union cavalry raid, July 4.
2. Kilpatrick attacks Rodes' wagon train around 9:00 p.m., July 4.
3. Stuart (with Chambliss's and Ferguson's Brigades) attacks Kilpatrick at Smithstown and drives him toward Boonsboro.
4. A minor attack on Imboden's train by Capt. Dahlgren on July 5 is driven off.
5. Union cavalry from Col. Pierce's command capture about 130 wagons at Cunningham's Crossroads.
6. Early's rearguard clashes briefly with VI Corps.
7. At 1:00 p.m. on July 6 Stuart again engages Kilpatrick, who withdraws toward Williamsport.
8. Imboden successfully defends Williamsport against Buford in the "Wagoners' Fight" until supported by Fitzhugh Lee.
9. Stuart advancing from Funkstown clashes with Buford and then Kilpatrick on July 8.
10. July 10: day-long action between Buford, with VI Corps, and Stuart and then artillery and infantry from Longstreet's Corps. Union advance checked.
11. On July 14 Heth's rearguard defends the pontoon crossing at Falling Waters against Kilpatrick's cavalry. Pettigrew is mortally wounded.

July 5

- At 2:00 a.m. Ewell began to withdraw from Seminary Ridge.
- During the morning Sedgwick's VI Corps probed Seminary Ridge and found the enemy had gone. Meade issued orders for the army to march south to Middletown. However, because he was still uncertain if Lee would make a stand in the South Mountain passes, Meade cancelled the order around noon.
- At about 5:00 p.m. Stuart, with the brigades of Chambliss and Ferguson, which had crossed the South Mountain through the Raven's Rock Pass, attacked Kilpatrick's command at Smithsburg and drove him south toward Boonsboro.
- In the evening VI Corps encountered Lee's rearguard, a brigade of Early's Division, east of Fairfield and a brief, indecisive clash occurred. At about the same time the head of Imboden's trains arrived at Williamsport, having successfully driven off a minor attack on part of the train just south of Greencastle by troopers under Captain Ulric Dahlgren (see box, page 281). More serious was the capture of more than 130 wagons just 7 miles north of Williamsport at Cunningham's Crossroads by cavalry sent from Colonel Pierce's command under a Captain Abram Jones.
- That day Sedgwick reported that Lee appeared to be making a stand at the Fairfield Gap–Monterey Pass. Warren and Pleasonton temporarily replaced the wounded Butterfield as Meade's chief of staff, with the former being sent to VI Corps to assess the situation.
- The Army of Northern Virginia spent the night of July 5/6 in the area between Fairfield and the Monterey Pass.

July 6

- Early a.m. Longstreet's Corps, followed by Hill's, resumed the march. Because of the length of the column, Ewell was not able to start following Hill until mid-afternoon. It was not therefore until late afternoon that Meade was finally convinced that Lee was retreating. He then reissued the order for the army to march on Middletown with the aim of then turning west through Turner's and Crampton Gaps to prevent Lee crossing the Potomac without a fight.
- Lee, realizing he would probably have to fight to get across the Potomac, sent Colonel Alexander and engineer staff to make a reconnaissance of a position from which he could defend the crossing places.
- All day frustratingly slow ferrying operations continued over the swollen river at Williamsport as the trains of Harman and Imboden arrived – the former by the Cumberland Valley turnpike and the latter along the road from Hagerstown. Thousands of animals were driven across by mounted drovers.
- At around 1:00 p.m. a two-hour fight for Hagerstown took place between Stuart and Kilpatrick, which resulted in Kilpatrick withdrawing south toward Williamsport.
- In the late afternoon Imboden was attacked at Williamsport by Buford's Division. His improvised defense – sometimes called the "Wagoners' Fight," as every possible man was armed and

The "Vast Procession of Misery" — Brigadier-General John D. Imboden's Wagon Train*

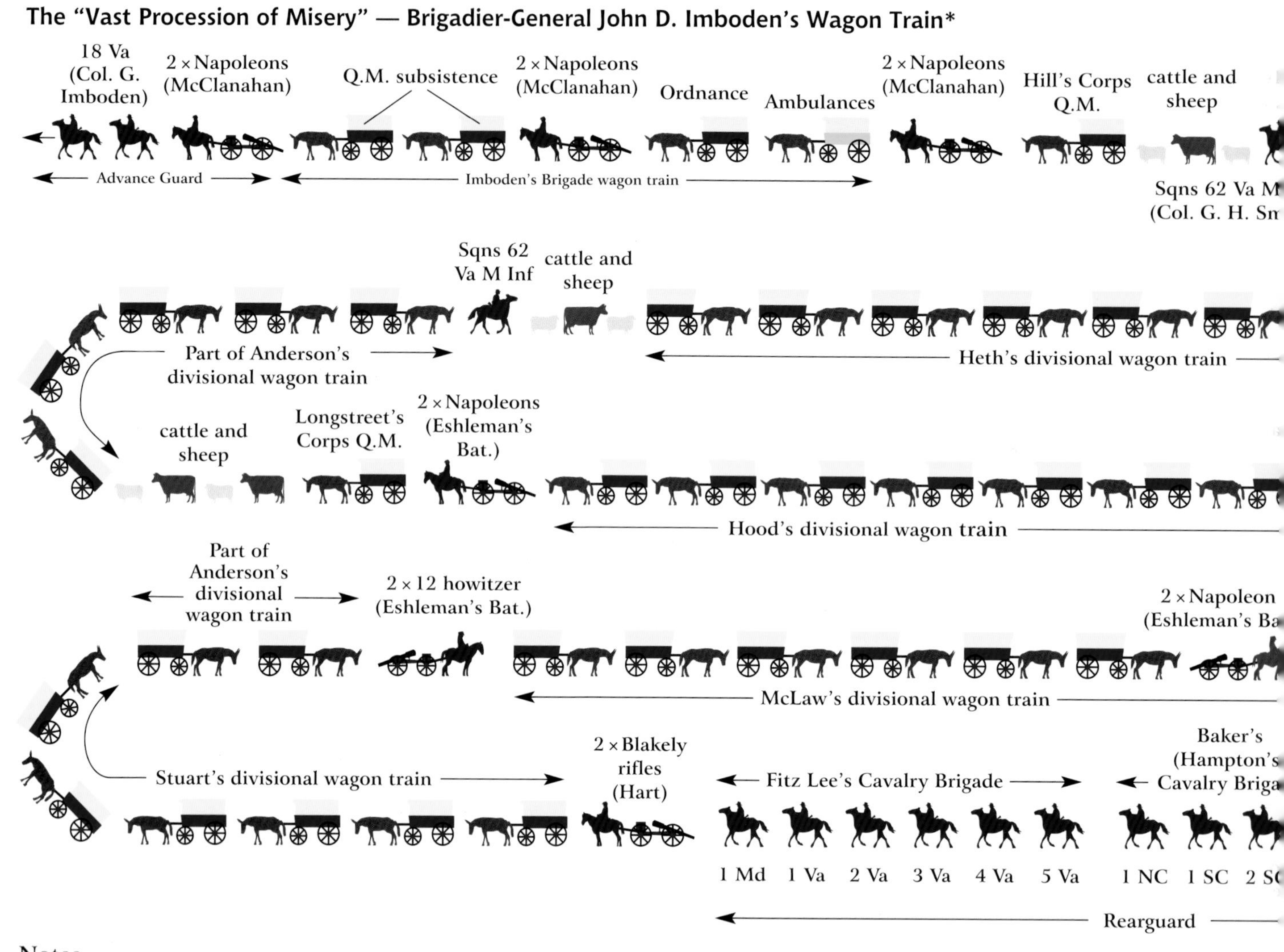

Notes

• Around 11:00 p.m. on July 3 Brig.-Gen. John Imboden was given orders by Lee for the next day: to take all the ordnance, quartermaster, subsistence, and ambulance trains (with wounded deemed fit to travel and walking wounded stumbling alongside the wagons) of Longstreet's and Hill's Corps and Stuart's Division, as well as his own, to the Potomac crossing at Williamsport.

• In addition to his own battery of six 12-pounder Napoleons under Capt. John H. McClanahan, Pendleton gave him a further 17 guns. From Garnett's Artillery Battalion (Hill) and under Major Charles Richardson, three 3-in ordnance rifles and two 10-pounder Parrotts, plus one Whitworth rifle from Capt. Hurt's Battery in McIntosh's Battalion (Hill). From Eshleman's Artillery Battalion (Longstreet), six Napoleons and two 12-pounder howitzers. In addition, Capt. Hart's (Stuart) three Blakely rifles were available, as they accompanied the rearguard composed of the cavalry brigades of Col. Lawrence S. Baker (Hampton) and Fitzhugh Lee. Imbode distributed these 23 guns by sections at intervals along the huge train.

• Acting as advance guard was the 18th Virginia Cavalry under Col. George W. Imboden. Leading the order of march was Imboden's Brigade wagon train, then Hill's quartermaster's train, Pender's divisional train, Heth's, par of Anderson's, Longstreet's quartermaster's train, then Hood's, Pickett's, McLaws', the remainder of Anderson's and Stuart's trains. At the rear came Baker's and Fitz Lee's cavalry brigades. Interspersed along the train were Imboden's 62nd Virginia Mounted Infantry under Col. George H. Smith.

Imboden's Report on the Retreat from Gettysburg

Imboden's report illustrates the horrors of the journey made by his column of wagons and animals from Cashtown to Williamsport.

> Shortly after noon of the 4th the very windows of heaven seemed to have opened. The rain fell in blinding sheets; the meadows were soon overflowed, and fences gave way before the raging streams. During the storm, wagons, ambulances and artillery carriages by hundreds by thousands were assembling in the fields along the road from Gettysburg to Cashtown, in one confused [and] apparently inextricable mass. As the afternoon wore on there was no abatement in the storm. Canvas was no protection against its fury, and the wounded men lying upon the naked boards of the wagonbodies were drenched. Horses and mules were blinded and maddened by the wind and water, and became almost unmanageable. The deafening roar of the mingled sounds of heaven and earth all around us made it almost impossible to communicate orders, and equally difficult to execute them . . .
>
> The column moved rapidly, considering the rough roads and the darkness, and from almost every wagon for many miles issued heartrending wails of agony . . . Many of the wounded in the wagons had been without food for thirty-six hours. Their torn and bloody clothing, matted and hardened, was rasping the tender and still

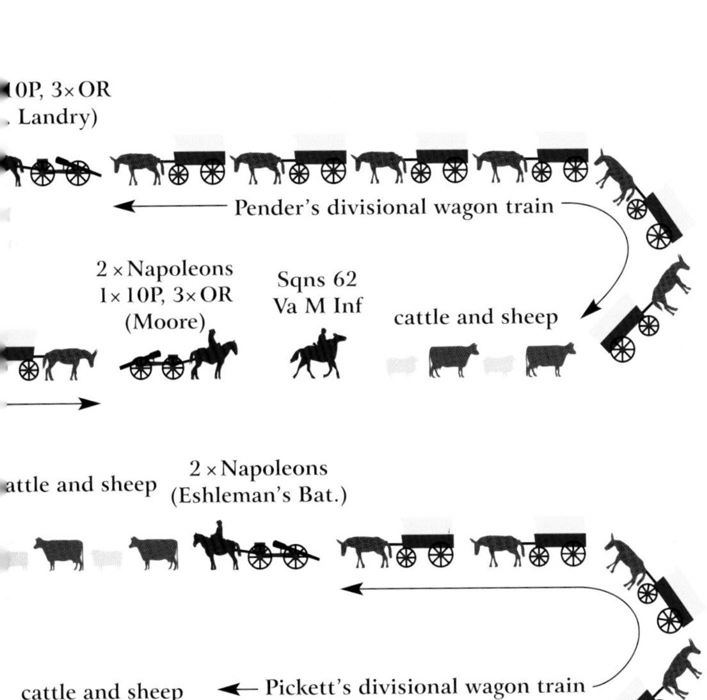

*This diagram gives an approximation of Imboden's train when it set off for the Cashtown Gap on July 4. The order of march shown is correct, but the exact location of the escorting squadrons of the 62nd Virginia Mounted Infantry, the artillery sections, and cattle herds is uncertain, other than that they were dispersed along the column. The 2,500 Yankee prisoners were initially escorted by Pickett's Division before being handed over to Imboden on July 6.

- The length of the train was 17–20 miles, carrying about 5,000 casualties, and along with it came some 6,000 animals (cattle, horses, sheep and hogs) in several herds. Escorting it and about 2,500 Yankee prisoners were over 5,000 horsemen in Imboden's, Fitz Lee's and Baker's Brigades.
- The train assembled in the Cashtown area and in the fields along the Chambersburg Pike throughout the morning and early afternoon of July 4. Imboden's route to Williamsport was via the Cashtown Gap, Greenwood, Marion and Greencastle, a distance of around 40 miles. By the time the leading elements started at 4:00 p.m. on July 4, the rain was cascading down. The rear of the train did not start moving until thirteen hours later, after daybreak the next morning.

oozing wounds. Very few of the wagons had even a layer of straw in them, and all were without springs. From nearly every wagon . . . came such cries and shrieks as these: "Oh God! Why can't I die? My God! Will no one have mercy and kill me. Stop! Oh! For God's sake, stop just for one minute; take me out and leave me to die on the roadside" . . .

Some were simply moaning; some were praying and others uttered the most fearful oaths and execrations that despair and agony could ring from them . . . while a majority . . . endured without complaint unspeakable tortures, and even spoke with cheer and [comfort] to their unhappy comrades of less will . . . Occasionally a wagon would be passed from which only low, deep moans could be heard.

took part – succeeded in holding out until Buford gave up as Rebel reinforcements in the form of Fitzhugh Lee's Brigade began to arrive. It was the highlight of Imboden's career and saved Lee 4,000 wagons and many thousands of animals.

- Buford and Kilpatrick regrouped around Boonsboro.
- Lee's long-awaited ordnance train arrived at Williamsport from the south. Lee was certainly in dire need of artillery ammunition. It has been estimated that during the three days' fighting at Gettysburg 566 tons of ammunition were expended, amounting to about 24 pounds for each casualty on both sides.

July 7

- A day of drenching rain, with mud stopping movement for both armies off the pikes and raising the water levels in the rivers even further. Lee's army reached the Hagerstown area and rested while the quartermasters and commissaries impressed supplies and many troops went on individual foraging expeditions. Meade's army was marching toward Middletown and making fair progress on the good roads. By 11:00 p.m. all of Meade's army except II and XII Corps had reached positions on either side of the Catoctin Mountains between Middletown and Mechanicsville, with Meade now intent on swinging west. Meanwhile, Smith's Division of raw Yankee militia struggled south from Waynesborough.
- The streets and environs of Williamsport were jammed solid with the 4,000–5,000 wagons and ambulances of Harman's and Imboden's trains and the 20,000 or more horses and mules pulling them – all waiting their turn to cross the river. This was the day when upward of 1,000 animals were swept downriver by the swirling, fast-flowing water.
- French, who replaced Birney in command of III Corps, had the railroad bridge at Harper's Ferry destroyed and sent a brigade to re-occupy Maryland Heights.

July 8

- With the swollen river, the huge build-up of wagons waiting to cross and the loss of the pontoon bridge at Falling Waters, Lee realized that Meade would catch up with him before he could get all his army across the Potomac. He therefore spent the day with his corps commanders and engineer staff reconnoitering a defensive line facing east from Hagerstown to Falling Waters. This line would be about 9 miles in length, but would cover the approaches to both Falling Waters and the crossing at Williamsport.
- Meade, screened by Buford's and Kilpatrick's horsemen, was approaching both Turner's and Crampton Gaps (the former only 12 miles by direct road from Williamsport), having made remarkably good progress considering the appalling weather conditions. Most of his men were still ravenously hungry and up to half were shoeless.
- Stuart advanced from Funkstown to check the Union advance from the passes and clashed with Buford and then Kilpatrick near Boonsboro. After dark Stuart withdrew about 2 miles up the Funkstown road.

July 9

- There was little movement by either army. Most of the Union forces were assembled in the Boonsboro area, where efforts were made to secure supplies for hungry men and animals. There was some intermittent skirmishing between the cavalry, with Stuart screening the Army of Northern Virginia as efforts continued to shift the enormous backlog of wagons trying to get across the river. Hospitals were opened in Williamsport and the Union prisoners were ferried across the river to be escorted to Staunton by the 62nd Virginia Mounted Infantry (Imboden).
- Lee again spent the day with his corps commanders and engineering staff planning the defensive line along an assortment of low ridges, known as Salisbury Ridge, running north–south from Hagerstown to Williamsport. This ridge overlooked the Antietam Creek in the north and the smaller Marsh Creek in the south. Much of this low ground was flooded and marshy due to the recent rain.
- Elsewhere, the Maryland Heights were reinforced and some 6,500 troops under Brigadier-General Henry Naglee from XIII Corps were deployed there.

July 10

- At around 5:00 a.m. Captain Summerfield Smith, commanding the engineer battalion encamped near Hagerstown, was ordered south to start building a bridge at Williamsport.
- A hot, humid day that saw Meade moving forward cautiously and a day-long clash just east of Funkstown, initially between Buford's and Sedgwick's VI Corps and Stuart's dismounted horsemen. Eventually Stuart was supported by artillery and infantry from Longstreet's Corps and was able to check the Union advance.
- During the afternoon and through until the early hours of July 11, Lee's army occupied its defensive line west of Funkstown and began, with the aid of laborers and under the direction of engineers, to fortify its positions with two lines of trenches and earthworks – the rearmost being the strongest.

Lee's Order of the Day on July 11

As his army moved to occupy Salisbury Ridge and take up positions in what the soldiers called the "Downsville Line," Lee issued an Order of the Day to be read out to every regiment.

> You have penetrated to the country of our enemies, and recalled to the defense of their own soil those who were engaged in the invasion of ours. Once more you are called upon to meet the enemy from whom you won, on so many fields, names that will never die. Let every soldier remember that on his courage and fidelity depend all that makes life worth having, the freedom of his country, the honor of his people, and the security of his home. Soldiers, your old enemy is before you. Win from him honor worthy of our right cause, worthy of your comrades dead on so many illustrious fields.

Both Lee and his soldiers were ready, eager to throw back the expected Yankee assault that never came.

Notes

- This map clearly shows the problem facing Meade once the Rebels had occupied the 9 miles of strongly entrenched positions along Salisbury Ridge. With his right resting on the Potomac and his left protected by cavalry, it is not surprising that Lee wanted Meade to attack. If he had done so, the odds were weighted heavily against his succeeding.
- **A** indicates the Confederate wagon trains that were continuously ferried slowly across by Lemen's Ferry after Harman's leading wagons arrived at Williamsport at about midnight on July 4. **A1** shows the arrival of the long-awaited Confederate ordnance train on July 6. **B** indicates the movement of wagons along the canal towpath from Williamsburg to Falling Waters once the new pontoon bridge was complete on July 12.
- The withdrawal took place during the night of July 13/14. Thousands of campfires were left burning to deceive the enemy. The first corps to move was Ewell's (**C1**), which began to march the 6 miles to Williamsport after dark on July 13. The soldiers would have to wade across, as would any of the wagons accompanying the troops that could not be accommodated on the ferry. The cavalry would eventually follow Ewell. Longstreet would pull out next (**C2**) in the early hours of July 14, using the Falling Waters rebuilt pontoon bridge. Last would come Hill's Corps (**C3**), also crossing at Falling Waters, with Heth's Division acting as rearguard. By then the rain was sheeting down and it was pitch black, making the march a real nightmare. Heth's divisions first moved south before being diverted west toward Williamsport and then turning southeast to join the Falling Waters Road. Heth's Division defended the pontoon crossing at around noon on July 14 from an attack by Kilpatrick's 6th Michigan Cavalry. It was during this action that Maj.-Gen. Pettigrew was mortally wounded; he died three days later.
- There was no serious attempt by Meade to disrupt the crossing and by early afternoon it was complete. The pontoon was dismantled by engineers and put onto wagons for future use. The Army of Northern Virginia marched south through friendly territory – the Gettysburg campaign was at an end.

The line of defenses was to be 9 miles long, extending from immediately west of Hagerstown southward to the tiny village of Downsville close to the Potomac. It was a formidable position to attack, made more difficult by the flooding of the Marsh Creek valley across which attackers would have to advance. Such an attack was precisely what Lee wanted, as he was confident it would be beaten back with heavy loss.

- Meade telegraphed Washington that he intended to "advance cautiously on the same line tomorrow until I can develop more fully the enemy's force and position, upon which my future operations will depend."

July 11

- Lee awaited an attack that Meade declined to make. Work on improving the defenses continued. This included engineers and pioneers from every division assembling the pontoon bridge for Falling Waters, with the energetic and resourceful Major Harman now in charge. While this construction was proceeding, wagons and ambulances continued to be ferried across on the two flats, with the return journey bringing ammunition from the ordnance train parked south of the river.
- The river level was starting to fall – good news for Lee, as he wanted some of his troops to be able to wade across if necessary.

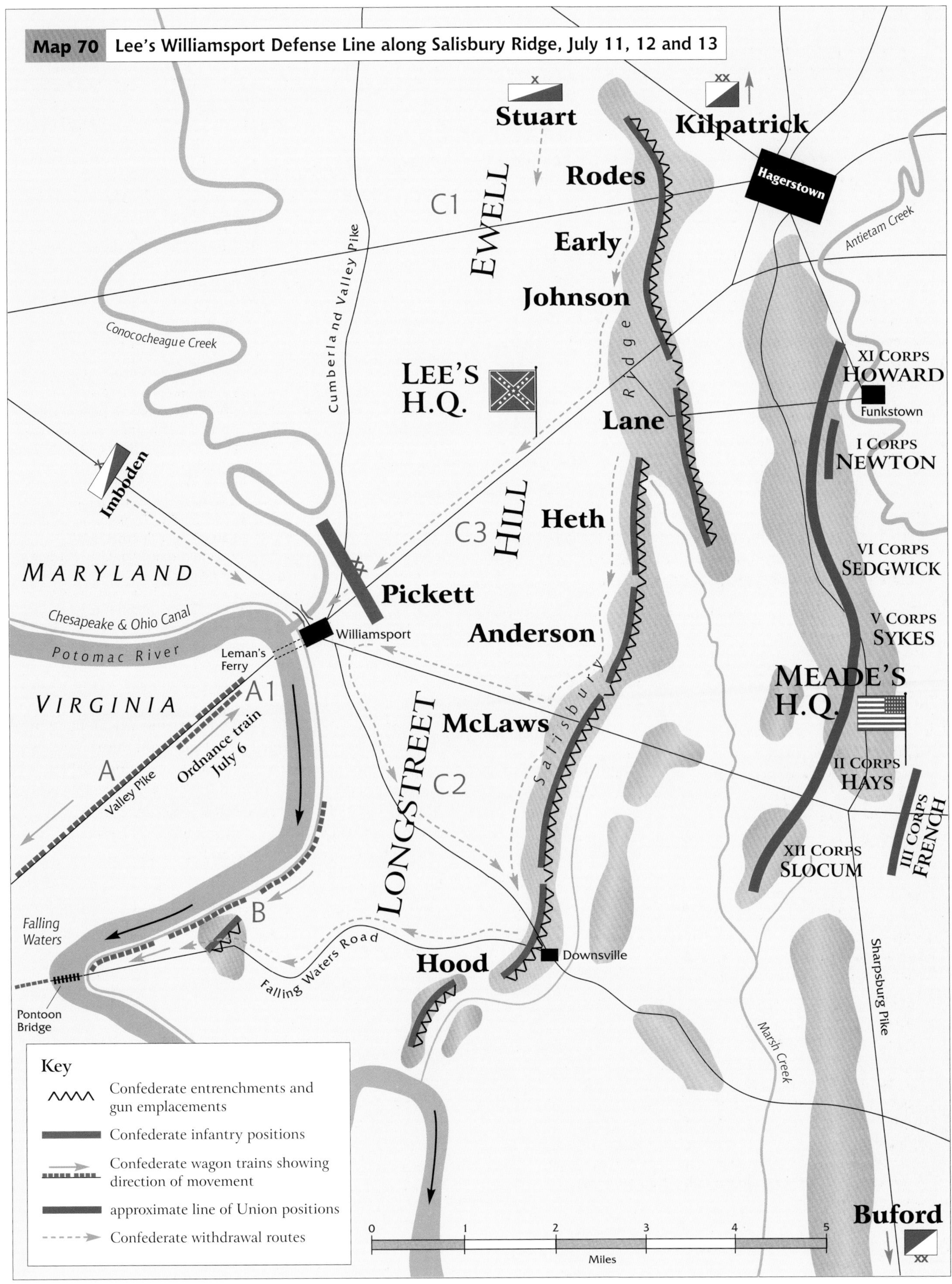
Map 70
Lee's Williamsport Defense Line along Salisbury Ridge, July 11, 12 and 13
Stuart
Kilpatrick
Rodes
Hagerstown
EWELL
C1
Early
Johnson
Antietam Creek
Cumberland and Valley Pike
Conococheague Creek
Ridge
LEE'S H.Q.
XI CORPS HOWARD
Funkstown
Lane
I CORPS NEWTON
Imboden
HILL
C3
Heth
VI CORPS SEDGWICK
MARYLAND
Pickett
Chesapeake & Ohio Canal
Williamsport
Anderson
V CORPS SYKES
Potomac River
Leman's Ferry
MEADE'S H.Q.
VIRGINIA
A1
Ordnance train July 6
LONGSTREET
McLaws
Salisbury
A
Valley Pike
C2
II CORPS HAYS
III CORPS FRENCH
XII CORPS SLOCUM
B
Falling Waters
Falling Waters Road
Hood
Downsville
Pontoon Bridge
Sharpsburg Pike
Marsh Creek
Key
Confederate entrenchments and gun emplacements
Confederate infantry positions
Confederate wagon trains showing direction of movement
approximate line of Union positions
Confederate withdrawal routes
0
1
2
3
4
5
Miles
Buford

July 12

- The stand-off continued on a foggy day. Lee's new pontoon was floated downstream to Falling Waters during the morning. He ordered all wagons and ambulances still waiting at Williamsport to move down to Falling Waters along the canal towpath and to cross the river there. The brigades of "Grumble" Jones and Imboden were sent south of the river to guard the trains as they moved south toward Winchester.
- As the last Rebel troops pulled back from Hagerstown it was occupied by Smith's troops.
- Meade telegraphed Halleck that he intended to attack the following day – but in reality he was still doubtful whether this was a prudent option.
- That evening Meade, still in two minds whether to attack, called the third of his corps commanders' meetings to gather opinions on what to do. Seemingly Meade favored an attack but, as he later explained, "I left it to their judgment, and would not do it unless it met with their approval." However, he had no plan of attack to suggest, although he claimed to favor one in principal. What did his generals think? Only Howard and Pleasonton were in favor; the others were emphatically opposed. According to Warren, "I did not think I ever saw the principal corps commanders so unanimous in favor of not attacking as on that occasion."

July 13

- Apart from light skirmishing there was little activity during the day, save for the endless columns of wagons rumbling across the pontoon bridge at Falling Waters .
- The withdrawal of the troops of the Army of Northern Virginia was successfully carried out during the night of July 13/14, starting on the left with Ewell's Corps. His divisions moved out after dark in pouring rain, leaving behind (with difficulty) burning campfires, hopefully to deceive the enemy about what was happening. They marched to Williamsport, where the troops waded across with water up to their armpits. The next across, but at Falling Waters over the bridge, was Longstreet, followed finally by Hill.
- Meade ordered a reconnaissance in force by four of his corps (II, V, VI and XII) to start at 7:00 a.m. the next day. That evening Halleck telegraphed: "You are strong enough to attack and defeat the enemy before he can affect a crossing. Act on your own judgment and make your generals execute your orders. Call no council of war. It is proverbial that councils of war never fight."
- By the time Meade received this he had done just that the previous evening. The decision had been as Halleck predicted.
- By dawn it was obvious to Meade that Lee had escaped. Despite this the Union Army would not cross for another three days.
- Heth's Division provided the rearguard at Falling Waters and there was a sharp, but brief, clash with Kilpatrick's advancing cavalry shortly before noon, during which Pettigrew was mortally wounded.
- By nightfall the Gettysburg campaign was, to all intents and purposes, at an end.

Rodes' Division Crosses the Potomac at Williamsport

In his report on the retreat, Rodes described how his division crossed the river:

> My division waded the river just above the aqueduct over the mouth of the Conococheague; the operation was a perilous one. It was very dark, raining, and excessively muddy. The men had to wade through the aqueduct, down the steep bank of soft and slippery mud, in which numbers lost their shoes and down which many fell. The water was cold, deep, and rising; the lights on either side of the river were dim, just affording enough light to mark the places of entrance and exit; the cartridge boxes of the men had to be placed around their necks; some small men had to be carried over by their comrades; the water was up to the armpits of a full-sized man. All the circumstances attending this crossing combined to make it an affair not only involving great hardship, but one of great danger to the men and company officers [field officers were mounted]; but be it said to the everlasting honor of these brave fellows, they encountered it not only promptly. But actually with cheers and laughter.
>
> We crossed without the loss of a single man, but I regret to say with the loss of some 25,000 or 30,000 rounds of ammunition, which was unavoidably wetted and spoiled.

Comments – Confederate

If Lee's handling of the battle had been less than masterful, his conduct of the retreat was masterly. His army had been defeated, it had lost a third of its strength, it was short of ammunition and he had to get it, with all its vast supply trains and ambulances, over a river some 40 miles in his rear without the enemy stopping him. Within ten days he had done so with minimal loss of men, wagons and animals. It was a brilliant success, achieved despite the appalling weather, mud, a swollen river, the loss of the pontoon bridge on July 4 at Falling Waters, and an active enemy cavalry. It was a combination of difficulties that would have overwhelmed many generals. In effect, the campaign had ended as a successful, gigantic foraging expedition, with thousands of horses, mules, cattle, sheep and hogs surviving the dreadful journey back, and with many wagons carrying thousands of tons of grain and fodder, along with flour and large quantities of equipment and stores.

Lee displayed firm and decisive leadership, giving orders to commanders and staff that displayed clear thinking. The Confederate staff at Gettysburg has sometimes been criticized as being weak, inexperienced and disorganized. These were not failings that could be leveled at them for their work during those ten days in July. This was especially so with Lee's quartermaster, commissary, medical and ordnance staff under the directions of Lieutenant-Colonel Corley (chief quartermaster), Lieutenant-Colonel Cole (chief commissary), Dr. Guild (medical director) and Lieutenant-Colonel Baldwin (chief of ordnance). That they were able to untangle the wagon and ambulance trains, the herds of animals, load up the thousands of wounded and get two vast trains moving out on July 4, with much of the time spent in darkness and drenching rain, is little short of miraculous. The situation had the makings of a monumental disaster.

Confederate Morale after the Campaign

There was no escaping the fact that the Army of Northern Virginia had been defeated at a terrible cost in lives. During June there had been men who were intent on deserting at the first opportunity – some losses from this cause were an integral part of army life – but once Lee brought his army back to their camps around Orange Court House, Virginia, after Gettysburg, unauthorized absence became something of an epidemic. Major William W. Goldsborough, 1st Maryland Infantry Battalion, described the situation as he saw it:

> But here [Orange Court House] . . . a new danger threatened the Confederate army, and one that never menaced it before. The army was threatened with disintegration. With its return to Virginia thousands of letters had been received from every part of the South from wives who made heart-rending appeals to their husbands to return home, even if for but a few days. Gaunt famine had so soon laid its cold hand upon these poor wives and their helpless children, and to whom were they to appeal but to their husbands . . . Furloughs were out of the question. Already the Federal army . . . was assembling but a few miles away, and if the appeals of these frantic men were heeded there would be few left to oppose the enemy. Was it a wonder, then, that they began to leave without authority? At first it was by twos and threes, and then, emboldened, in larger numbers. It is doubtful if during the whole campaign General Lee was more exercised than then, as he was powerless to resist them, and unable to prevent the exodus without resorting to extreme measures . . .

These measures included execution, a punishment Lee was normally reluctant to enforce. Major Goldsborough recounted an example of absence that led to murder. Ten men of the 3rd North Carolina Infantry left camp to visit their desperate families, without permission and carrying their weapons, as they intended to return. On this being discovered, Lieutenant Richardson Mallett Jr., the adjutant of the 47th North Carolina, was sent to bring them back. When he caught up with them they resisted arrest and killed the unfortunate lieutenant. Despite this, the men returned voluntarily and were arrested. Their court martial sentenced them to be shot – a punishment Lee approved. They were executed in front of their regiment by a firing party made up of their own comrades.

While all commanders and staff worked desperately hard as a team to make the withdrawal a success, three officers deserve particular mention – the first two being Major Harman and Brigadier-General Imboden. Harman had responsibility for the Army Reserve trains as well as for the majority of the herds of animals and the trains of Ewell's Corps, a column that took up to 40 miles of road. He was a dynamo of energy and initiative (and profanity). The leading wagons of his column started to move at 3:00 a.m. on July 4 and had reached Williamsport by the evening of July 5, when limited ferrying operations began immediately. Then, six days later, it was Harman who was put in charge of the construction of the pontoons at Williamsport and floating them down to Falling Waters the following day. That a new bridge, without which the whole withdrawal would have stalled, was opened so quickly was primarily down to Harman's efforts.

Imboden had the onerous task of transporting the majority of some 5,000 wounded and the trains of Longstreet and Hill – a 20-mile-long column – by the longest route, much of it in the dark and driving rain. The condition of the wounded was appalling in the mostly unsprung vehicles (see box, page 524), with many dying en route. Imboden successfully navigated this train to Williamsport and then, finding the crossing place about to be attacked, he scraped together every soldier, driver and wagoner he could find and organized a successful defense until reinforcements arrived. It was a sterling effort.

The third officer is Major-General Stuart. Engagements during the retreat were mostly cavalry affairs. It was the job of Rebel horsemen to screen and protect the trains and the army throughout the withdrawal, just as it was the task of the Yankee horsemen to harass, attack and delay the moving enemy columns. On balance, Stuart's men got much the better of their opponents (largely Buford and Kilpatrick). Union successes were the destruction of the pontoon bridge at Falling Waters on July 4; the attack on Rodes' train at the Monterey Pass that night; and the seizure of 130 wagons from Imboden's train north of Williamsport on July 5. Nevertheless, Stuart was able to delay and check the Union cavalry and thus protect the entire operation at Smithstown, north of Boonsboro, and Funkstown (assisted by infantry). But perhaps his greatest contribution was the screening of the army between July 10 and 14, giving it the vital time needed to construct the defensive works along Salisbury Ridge, build a new pontoon bridge and then cross the Potomac. Although helped by a cautious enemy, Stuart's energy and skill during the retreat perhaps made up, at least to some extent, for his failings during the advance.

Despite the successful withdrawal, the defeat at Gettysburg in the East, followed the next day by the fall of Vicksburg in the West, were major blows to the entire Confederacy – blows from which it never really recovered. Lee accepted the blame for Gettysburg, exclaiming "It's all my fault." Once back in Virginia he offered to resign. His letter of August 8 to President Davis reads as follows:

> The general remedy for the want of success in a military commander is his removal . . .
>
> I have been prompted by these reflections more than once since my return from Pennsylvania to propose to your Excellency the propriety of selecting another commander for this army. I do this with the more earnestness, because no one is more aware than myself of my inability for the duties of my position . . . [after explaining his physical difficulties he continued] I urge the matter upon your Excellency from my belief that a younger and abler man than myself can readily be obtained.

Davis would, unsurprisingly, have none of it. There was no one of Lee's stature to replace him. As Davis wrote:

> Where am I to find that new commander who is to possess the greater ability which you believe to be required? . . . To ask me to substitute you by some one in my judgment more fit to command, or who would possess more of the confidence of the army, or of the reflecting men of the country, is to demand an impossibility.

Comments – Union

Comments on Meade's performance inevitably revolve around whether or not he should, or could, have trapped Lee north of the Potomac and thus extracted the strategic fruits of his tactical victory at Gettysburg. Lee had lost a third of his army, but it was still very much intact as a fighting force and had escaped with most of its loot into Virginia. Was Meade too timid, too slow to pursue more aggressively on July 4 and 5, or was it impractical and imprudent to do so in the circumstances at the time? As early as July 6 Brigadier-General Herman Haupt, the energetic railroad transportation chief responsible for opening up the railroad to Gettysburg, was warning Halleck, "I fear that while Meade rests to refresh his men and collect supplies Lee will be off so far that he [Meade] cannot intercept him . . ."

Meade had proved himself a competent commander in demanding circumstances. He had been pitched into an encounter with the South's most illustrious general within three days of assuming command, and had won a great battle. Nevertheless, his inclination was to command by committee when really crucial decisions were needed – on three such occasions within ten days Meade made up his mind, or had his views confirmed or changed (as at Williamsport), by a vote among his corps commanders. This was not the way of great generals, and Meade's perceived tardiness in pursuit soon tarnished the reputation he had gained at Gettysburg. But was such criticism justified? Was the case against Meade merely what we would today call a "knee-jerk reaction" to the realization that Lee had slipped away with his army after what seemed a decisive defeat? Had the one chance to crush the Army of Northern Virginia and possibly end the rebellion been missed due to Meade's hesitation? A considerable number of people, including President Lincoln, took this view.

The dispatches that flew between Meade and Halleck in the period July 4–14 throw considerable light on how the situation developed during those crucial ten days, as they were not written with the benefit of hindsight. Relevant telegraphs, or extracts from them, are given below – they make illuminating reading.

Meade to Halleck, *July 5 at 6:00 p.m. (received 11:30 p.m.)*

My army is all in motion. I shall be in Frederick tomorrow night. I desire the forces mentioned in your dispatch to Major-General French to be thrown to Harper's Ferry by rail as soon as possible. I shall so instruct Major-General French. It is of importance to get possession of South Mountain passes and Maryland Heights.

> **Comment:** In fact Meade had cancelled his initial order to march south and the implication that all his corps were moving south by the evening of July 5 is inaccurate – they were not doing so until the following day.

Halleck to Meade, *July 5*

Your movements are perfectly satisfactory. Your call for reinforcements to Frederick has been anticipated. Call to you[rself] all of Couch's force.

Meade to Halleck, *July 7 at Frederick at 3:10 p.m. (received 4:45 p.m.)*

General Buford reports that he attacked Williamsport yesterday, but found it guarded by a large force of infantry and artillery [this was Imboden's "Wagoners' Fight"] . . . My army will be assembling today and tomorrow at Middletown. I will immediately move on Williamsport. Should the enemy succeed in crossing the river before I reach him, I should like to have your views of subsequent operations – whether to follow up the army in the Valley, or cross below or nearer Washington.

[P.S.] An officer of cavalry . . . reports the enemy's army as occupying Hagerstown and Williamsport, and guarding their artillery and trains, which they cannot cross. So soon as my command is supplied and their trains up, I shall move.

> **Comment:** Meade foresees the possibility of not catching Lee. It would be exactly a week later that he actually moved to attack and found the bird had flown. Here, within minutes, he changes his mind from "I will immediately move on Williamsport" to moving when he was supplied.

Halleck to Meade, *July 7 at 8:45 p.m.*

You have given the enemy a stunning blow at Gettysburg. Follow it up, and give him another before he can reach the Potomac. When he crosses, circumstances will determine whether it will be best to pursue him by the Shenandoah Valley or this side of Blue Ridge. There is strong evidence that he is short of artillery ammunition, and, if vigorously pressed, he must suffer.

> **Comment:** Halleck is now beginning to lose patience and prod Meade into more aggressive and speedy action.

Meade to Halleck, *July 8 at 2:00 p.m. (received 2:45 p.m.)*

The train at Williamsport is crossing very slowly . . . From all I can gather, the enemy extends from Hagerstown to Williamsport, covering the march of their train . . . We hold Boonsborough . . . My army is assembling slowly. The rains of yesterday and last night have made all roads but pikes almost impassable. Artillery and wagons are stalled; it will take time to collect them together. A large proportion of the men are barefooted. Shoes will arrive at Frederick today, and will be issued as soon as possible. The spirit of the army is high; the men are ready and willing to make every exertion to push forward. The very first moment I can get the different commands, the artillery and cavalry properly supplied and in hand, I will move forward . . . I expect to find the enemy in a strong position, well covered with artillery, and I do not desire to imitate his example at Gettysburg, and assault a position where the chances were so greatly against success. I wish in advance to moderate the expectations of those, who in ignorance of the difficulties to be encountered, may expect too much . . .

> **Comment:** Meade is now making the most of his problems in moving forward more quickly to deflect later accusations of tardiness (particularly from Washington), as he knows he may not be able to catch Lee north of the river.

Halleck to Meade, *July 8*

There is reliable information that the enemy is crossing at Williamsport [incorrect as regards troops as distinct from wagons]. The opportunity to attack his divided forces should not be lost. The President is urgent and anxious that your army should move against him by forced marches.

> **Comment:** Meade is now under pressure from a highly impatient and increasingly frustrated President.

Meade to Halleck, *July 8 at 3:00 p.m.*

My information as to the crossing of the enemy does not agree with that just received in your dispatch. His whole force is in position between Funkstown and Williamsport . . . My army is and has been making forced marches, short of rations and barefooted. One corps marched yesterday and last night over 30 miles. I take occasion to repeat that I will use my utmost efforts to push forward this army.

> **Comment:** Meade is now clearly angry that a deskbound Halleck and civilian politicians are criticizing the performance

of his army. On receipt of the above dispatch Halleck immediately backed down to some extent, but was still unclear about where the Rebels were or what they were doing. If they were half across the river, he stressed, "the importance of attacking the part on this side is incalculable." If they were not, then Meade was to "concentrate your forces." With the reinforcements he was sending, Halleck told Meade, "You will have forces to render your victory certain. My only fear now is that the enemy may escape by crossing the river."

Halleck to Meade, *July 10 at 9:30 p.m.*
I think it will be best for you to postpone till you can concentrate all your forces and get up your reserves and re-enforcements . . . Beware of partial combats. Bring up and hurl upon the enemy all your forces, good and bad.

> **Comment:** Another change of tune. Now Halleck is all in favor of concentration followed by a full-scale assault – no mention of enemy escaping, as he now understood that both armies were massing opposite each other.

Meade to Halleck, *July 12 at 4:30 p.m. (received 8:00 p.m.)*
Their position runs along high ground from Downsville to near Hagerstown. This position they are entrenching . . . It is my intention to attack them tomorrow, unless something intervenes to prevent it . . .

> **Comment:** Meade was careful to include a proviso to his offensive intentions. He knew when sending this dispatch that he was about to call a meeting of his corps commanders for their advice.

Meade to Halleck, *July 13 at 5:00 p.m. (received 6:40 p.m.)*
In my dispatch of yesterday I stated that it was my intention to attack the enemy today, unless something intervened to prevent it. Upon calling my corps commanders together and submitting the question to them, five out of six were unqualifiedly opposed to it. Under these circumstances, in view of the momentous consequences upon a failure to succeed, I did not feel myself authorized to attack until after I had made more careful examination of the enemy's position, strength and defensive works. These examinations are now being made. So far as completed, they show the enemy to be strongly entrenched on a ridge running from the rear of Hagerstown past Downsville to the Potomac. I shall continue these reconnaissances with the expectation of finding some weak point, upon which if I succeed, I shall hazard an attack . . .

> **Comment:** This dispatch caused uproar in Washington. Both the President and Halleck were convinced that Meade was being far too timid and dithering, so much so that he was running his army by a corps commanders' committee. Lee was going to escape. And the one chance of winning the war in the East, following on so soon after the Confederate surrender of Vicksburg in the West on July 4, would be lost because of Meade's excessive caution. The consternation in Washington triggered the scathing dispatch quoted above, but worth repeating here.

Halleck to Meade, *July 13 at 9:30 p.m.*
Yours of 5 p.m. is received. You are strong enough to attack and defeat the enemy before he can affect a crossing. Act upon your own judgment and make your generals execute your orders. Call no council of war. It is proverbial that councils of war never fight. Re-enforcements are pushed on as rapidly as possible. Do not let the enemy escape.

> **Comment:** Escaping was exactly what Lee was doing that same night – something that Meade was forced to concede the next morning

Meade to Halleck, *July 14 at 11:00 a.m. (received 12:10 p.m.)*
On advancing my army this morning, with a view to ascertaining the exact position of the enemy and attacking him if the result of the examination should justify me, I found, on reaching his lines, that they were evacuated. I immediately put my army in pursuit, the cavalry in advance . . . Your instructions as to further movements, in case the enemy are entirely across the river, are desired.

Halleck to Meade, *July 14 at 1:00 p.m.*
I need hardly say to you that the escape of Lee's army without another battle has created great dissatisfaction in the mind of the President, and it will require an active and energetic pursuit on your part to remove the impression that it has not been sufficiently active heretofore.

Meade to Halleck, *July 14 at 2:30 p.m.*
Having performed conscientiously and to the best of my ability, the censure of the President conveyed in your dispatch of 1 p.m. this day, is, in my judgment, so undeserved that I feel compelled most respectfully to ask to be immediately relieved from the command of this army.

> **Comment:** Meade's resignation, like that of Lee's, was not accepted and he remained commander of the Army of the Potomac until the end of the war, although Lieutenant-General Ulysses S. Grant, the newly appointed General-in-Chief of the Armies of the United States, accompanied Meade and gave him directions.

Meade was not only heavily condemned by the President and Halleck but also by some of his generals, by a number of the rank and file in his army, and by the newspapers. The opinions of two of his soldiers illustrate the feelings of a proportion of the rank and file. On July 17, Henry Clare, 83rd New York, wrote to his brother:

> Our army is greatly incensed at the bad generalship displayed by General Meade, in not attacking Lee . . . as it is positively known that his army was Decidedly crippled, out of ammunition, greatly discouraged & did not number more than 70,000 . . . We consider the golden opportunity was allowed to pass . . .

Sergeant Charles Bowen, 12th U.S. Infantry, wrote: "Great dissatisfaction exists among the troops at the escape of Lee . . . but the army has got used to bungles that it seems almost a matter of course." Although some soldiers held these simplified and inaccurate views, they could in no way understand the complexity of the difficulties faced by the army commander.

In addition, Meade was later forced to appear before the Committee on the Conduct of the War that sat during the early months of 1864. Leading Republicans on the committee became convinced that Meade was lukewarm in his loyalty to the Union cause. This was nonsense, but a number of his generals spoke against him, notably Howard, Sickles, Butterfield, Doubleday, Howe and Birney – some of whom went to the President to demand Meade be replaced by Hooker. Lincoln was not convinced. His earlier comment to Navy Secretary Gideon Welles was still valid:

The Letter Lincoln Never Sent to Meade

This letter from Lincoln to Meade was written on July 14, just after the President received the news that Lee's army had escaped across the Potomac without a fight. In it Lincoln reveals the depth of his disappointment and frustration with his general. However, on rereading it even he thought it too forthright to send and it was filed away.

Executive Mansion
Washington July 14, 1863.

Major-General Meade
I have just seen your dispatch to Gen. Halleck, asking to be relieved of your command, because of the supposed censure of mine. I am very – very – grateful to you for the magnificent success you gave the cause of the country at Gettysburg; and I am sorry now to be the author of the slightest pain to you. But I was in such deep distress myself that I could not restrain from some expression of it. I had been oppressed nearly ever since the battles at Gettysburg, by what appeared to be evidences that yourself, and Gen. Couch, and Gen. Smith, were not seeking a collision with the enemy, but were trying to get him across the river without another battle. What these evidences were, if you please, I hope to tell you at some time, when we shall both feel better. The case summarily stated is this. You fought and beat the enemy at Gettysburg; and, of course, to say the least, his loss was as great as yours. He retreated; and you did not, as it seemed to me, pressingly pursue him; but a flood in the river detrained him, till, by slow degrees, you were again upon him. You had at least twenty thousand veteran troops directly with you, and as many more raw ones within supporting distance, all in addition to those who fought with you at Gettysburg; while it is not possible that he had received a single recruit; and yet you stood and let the flood run down, bridges be built, and the enemy move away at his leisure, without attacking him. And Couch and Smith! The latter left Carlisle in time, upon ordinary calculation, to have aided you in the last battle at Gettysburg; but he did not arrive. At the end of more than ten days, I believe twelve, under constant urging, he reached Hagerstown from Carlisle, which is not an inch over fifty-five miles, if so much. And Couch's movement was very little different.

Again, my dear general, I do not believe you appreciate the magnitude of the misfortune involved in Lee's escape. He was within easy grasp, and to have closed upon him, in connection with our other late successes [the fall of Vicksburg being the major one], could have ended the war. As it is, the war will be prolonged indefinitely. If you could not safely attack Lee last Monday, how can you possibly do so south of the river, when you take with you very few more than two thirds of the force you then had in hand? It would be unreasonable to expect, and I do not expect you can now effect much. Your golden opportunity is gone, and I am distressed immeasurably because of it.

I beg you will not consider this a prosecution, or persecution of yourself as you have learned that I was dissatisfied, I have thought it best to kindly tell you why.

Abraham Lincoln

> What can I do with such generals as we have? Who among them is any better than Meade? To sweep away the whole of them from the chief command and substitute a new man would cause a shock, and be likely to lead to combinations and troubles greater than we now have.

In mid-July Lincoln's feelings of disappointment and frustration were indeed raw, and he expressed them in very forthright terms in a letter he wrote to Meade on July 14 – but which he never sent (see box above). However, a few days later he seemed more reconciled to the situation. Speaking to his secretary, John Hay, Lincoln said, "Still, I'm very grateful to Meade for the great service he did at Gettysburg."

As with so many critics, Meade's detractors had the benefit of hindsight when launching their attacks. How many in Meade's shoes at the time would have done differently? A great general perhaps would have anticipated Lee's direction of retreat and intentions earlier and thus inspired an immediate march south, but Meade was competent rather than great. He had just won a costly victory, losing 25 percent of his army in the process. His men were without supplies, hungry and exhausted, and thousands of wounded littered the battlefield, literally crying out for immediate attention. But Meade's real dilemma was his not knowing Lee's intentions and his instructions never to expose Washington. On July 4 some of his enemy's wagons were seen to be on the move, but not his army. Lee had merely pulled back his flanks to Seminary Ridge. Not until July 6 was Meade certain that Lee was in full retreat to the Potomac, rather than just pulling back to the gaps in the South Mountain a few miles to the west. Until he knew this, it would have taken a braver general than Meade (or any of his corps commanders) to rush south with the possibility that Lee intended to stay north.

When the Army of the Potomac did march south, it had perforce to follow a longer route than the Army of Northern Virginia and the weather was atrocious for much of the time, but despite this there was considerable forced marching by hungry troops, with thousands hobbling along barefoot. Perhaps Meade had a brief window of opportunity on July 9, although his men were still exhausted; but once Lee occupied the Salisbury Ridge position an attack became very problematic. Meade had seen the slaughter of Union troops at Fredericksburg and had just witnessed the Confederates suffer the same in an uncoordinated frontal attack on a well-defended position – the last thing he wanted the campaign to finish on was a Yankee version of Pickett's charge. However, his inclination was to attack if possible, if conditions were right, if he had located all the enemy positions – but when he tentatively broached the idea to his corps commanders a large majority advised strongly against it. He had lost Hancock and Reynolds, and those now in command were either men temporarily promoted to replace losses or mediocre men whose natural inclination was to be cautious. With reluctant corps commanders, Meade was surely right not to risk a hasty frontal attack across boggy ground against formidably entrenched positions on dominating hills and ridges. General Warren was later to agree that such an assault would have been unwise. In this opinion he was supported by artillerists Hunt and Wainwright, the latter writing of the Salisbury Ridge defenses, "These were by far the strongest I have seen yet; evidently laid out by engineers and built as if they meant to stand a month's siege." And a repulse at Williamsport would certainly have undone all that had been gained at Gettysburg.

Epilogue

THE 50TH ANNIVERSARY REUNION

The largest combined reunion of Civil War veterans ever held took place at Gettysburg in 1913. The Commonwealth of Pennsylvania hosted the event and extended invitations to every surviving, honorably discharged Union or Confederate veteran in the nation. It was scheduled to be a unique encampment, a combined reunion of members of the Grand Army of the Republic and the United Confederate Veterans (both national veterans' organizations). The response was overwhelming and, despite efforts to limit the numbers attending, over 50,000 veterans came to Gettysburg and settled into the great camp situated on the former battlefield. Former foes walked together over the old terrain, reliving the terrible days when so many of their comrades had lost their lives. Not only were there veterans of Gettysburg, but men who had fought under McClellan at Antietam, Jackson in the Shenandoah Valley, Sherman in Georgia, Bragg in Kentucky, Hood at Atlanta and Ord at Appomattox. This was the largest ever gathering of former soldiers who had changed the face of a nation, torn it apart, and now delighted in its reunification.

Pennsylvania Governor John K. Tener insisted from the beginning that the state be the sole host of the reunion, and provide funds for free rail transportation to all Pennsylvania's veterans. The governor urged other states to provide equal donations for their veterans. Though his request did not fall on deaf ears, the expense of sending hundreds of old soldiers from as far away as California was overwhelming, and many states could not provide cash donations. A handful of northern states were successful in passing legislation to assist their veterans, while others depended on personal contributions to help get the old men to Pennsylvania. The Virginia chapter of the United Daughters of the Confederacy (an organization formed in 1894 to honor the memory of all those who died for or served the Confederacy during the war) took an active role, supplying United Confederate Veterans' uniforms for those in the state who needed them.

Despite Pennsylvania's good intentions for hosting the reunion, Governor Tener was soon faced with a growing financial and political dilemma. The projected cost of the reunion rose as plans changed, and with it grew opposition in the legislature as more state money was appropriated. Tener finally approached the Federal government, which agreed to step in and provide funds to feed and house the veterans during the encampment. Additionally, U.S. Army personnel would support the event with cooks, bakers, quartermaster's staff and troops to help with crowd control. Emergency Federal money would also pay the bills until the states could appropriate some back payments. With this assurance of aid, the Pennsylvania legislature approved half a million dollars to cover the cost of the reunion.

Confederate veterans of Pickett's charge advance again on the Copse of Trees.

Enemies reconciled: veterans shake hands at the reunion.

Plans to establish a camp large enough to accommodate the numbers of guests and military support personnel were considered two years before the event. The number of tents required to house everyone would quickly deplete the state's supply, and again the Federal government stepped in to provide the additional tents and equipment necessary to complete the camp. Personnel from the United States Army Quartermaster Corps and Engineer Corps arrived at Gettysburg National Park in 1912 to coordinate military and civilian support for the encampment. The engineers surveyed the field adjacent to the fields of Pickett's charge, where they laid out the arrangement for the "Great Camp," divided into separate areas for Union and Confederate veterans. Soldiers installed utility systems, erected hundreds of tents, built picnic tables. The Great Camp occupied 280 acres, included 47.5 miles of avenues and company streets, was lit by 500 electric arc lights, and contained 32 bubbling iced-water fountains. Over 2,000 army cooks and bakers manned 173 field kitchens, ready to provide three hot meals a day for veterans and military personnel alike.

Two battalions of the 5th U.S. Infantry guarded the camp and supply depots, and provided security along with the 15th U.S. Cavalry. Pennsylvania also sent medical staff and a detachment of the Pennsylvania State Police and Pennsylvania National Guard to support the reunion activities. Several hundred members of the Boy Scouts of America served as escorts to the veterans and acted as aids and messengers in the army hospitals, as well as working as couriers for various officials. The American Red Cross and the U.S. Army Medical Corps gave medical care.

The first veterans arrived on June 25 and within days the Great Camp swelled to overflowing. Every veteran was provided with a cot and bedding in a tent that would hold eight men. Meals were served from a kitchen at the end of each company street, and varied from fried chicken suppers to roast pork sandwiches, with ice cream for dessert. By the end of the reunion the army kitchens had supplied over 688,000 meals. Invariably the days were hot, with the thermometer topping 100 degrees on July 2. Heat exhaustion and fatigue resulted in the hospitalization of several hundred veterans. Over 9,980 patients were treated by medical personnel, but remarkably only nine veterans died during the week-long event.

Despite the heat and dust, nothing could keep the old men in camp. Hundreds wandered the battlefield, visiting the sites where they or their comrades had fought fifty years before. Confederate veterans were especially pleased to find old cannon mounted on metal carriages to mark the locations where their batteries had been. Invariably, the sight of khaki-clad U.S. Army soldiers caused a lot of interest. These soldiers were there to guard the camp supplies, give demonstrations, and provide services to the veterans, who delighted themselves in discussing modern weapons of war. Many an aged veteran was eager to explain how much things had changed in fifty years to any modern soldier who was willing to listen, and old soldiers entertained army personnel at every turn.

The youngest veteran present was sixty-one years old; the oldest claimed to be 112. In spite of their advanced years, the old soldiers walked miles through the battlefield and packed into the Great Tent erected on the field of Pickett's charge for daily meetings and ceremonies. Every day there were programs, with speeches by dignitaries and several state governors. President Woodrow Wilson came on July 4 to address the veterans, saying:

> These venerable men crowding here to this famous field have set us a great example of devotion and utter sacrifice. They were willing to die that the people might live. But their task is done. Their day is turned into evening. They look to us to perfect what they have established. Their work is handed unto us, to be done in another way but not in another spirit. Our day is not over, it is upon us in full tide.

A highlight was the meeting of Pickett's Division Association and the Philadelphia Brigade Association near the High Water Mark on July 3. Despite the torrid heat, the veterans made speeches, traded ceremonial flags and shook hands over the stone wall that outlines the Angle, where fifty years before the two groups had met in mortal combat. The *Washington Post* summed up the event:

> Nothing could possibly be more impressive or more inspiring to the younger generation than this gathering. They feel the thrill of bygone days, without a knowledge of its bitterness, which, thank God, has passed us all. But even more touching must be the emotions of these time-worn veterans, as they assemble on an occasion that in itself constitutes a greater victory than that of half a century ago, and one too, in which every section of a united country has common part.

For a while it appeared that the Great Reunion was to be the last dual gathering of the Grand Army of the Republic and the United Confederate Veterans. The goodwill expressed at Gettysburg faded as the nation was plunged into World War I, raced through the "roaring twenties" and was traumatized by the Great Depression. By the 1930s a new generation of veterans of World War I vastly outnumbered the old veterans of the past, largely forgotten as their numbers dwindled. A more radical and less forgiving leadership altered the United Confederate Veterans, and with time the goodwill expressed in 1913 was just a memory. As the 75th anniversary approached, it appeared that another reunion at Gettysburg was out of the question. Had it not been for the persistent efforts of Gettysburg native Paul Roy it might never have happened. Roy spent five years pursuing the leadership of both organizations and finally convinced them to have one last meeting on the old battleground. Approximately 1,800 veterans from across the country came for a final great reunion in 1938, but it was a far cry from the great gathering of old soldiers twenty-five years earlier.

The above account is based on an article written by John Heiser of the Gettysburg National Park Service in 1998.

Appendix 1

LINCOLN'S GETTYSBURG ADDRESS

President Abraham Lincoln gave his famous address on Cemetery Hill on the occasion of the opening of the Soldiers' National Cemetery on November 19, 1863, only four and a half months after the last shot of the battle was fired and seventeen months before his assassination. The speech put the country and the conflict on a world scale, for Lincoln saw the Civil War as a test of democracy.

Four score and seven years ago our fathers brought forth on this continent, a new nation, conceived in Liberty, and dedicated to the proposition that all men are created equal.

Now we are engaged in a great civil war, testing whether that nation, or any nation so conceived and so dedicated, can long endure. We are met on a great battlefield of that war. We have come to dedicate a portion of that field, as a final resting place for those who gave their lives that that nation might live. It is altogether fitting and proper that we should do this.

But, in a larger sense, we can not dedicate – we can not consecrate – we can not hallow – this ground. The brave men, living and dead, who struggled here, have consecrated it, far above our poor power to add or detract. The world will little note, nor long remember what we say here, but it can never forget what they did here. It is for us the living, rather, to be dedicated here to the unfinished work which they who fought here have thus far so nobly advanced. It is rather for us to be here dedicated to the great task remaining before us – that from these honored dead we take increased devotion to that cause for which they gave the last full measure of devotion – that we here highly resolve that these dead shall not have died in vain – that this nation, under God, shall have a new birth of freedom – and that government of the people, by the people, for the people, shall not perish from the earth.

Appendix 2

THE CONGRESSIONAL MEDAL OF HONOR

The first decoration formally authorized by the American government was the Medal of Honor created by Act of Congress in December, 1861. General Order No. 91 dated July 29, 1862 contained the following resolution:

1. Public Resolution

No. 43 – A RESOLUTION to provide for the presentation of medals of honor to the enlisted men of the army and volunteer forces who have distinguished or may distinguish themselves in battle during the present rebellion.

Resolved by the Senate and House of Representatives of the United States of America, in Congress assembled, That the president of the United States be, and he is hereby, authorized to cause two thousand medals of honor to be prepared, with suitable emblematic devises, and to direct that the same be presented, in the name of Congress, to such non-commissioned officers and privates as shall most distinguish themselves by their gallantry in action, and other soldierlike qualities, during the present insurrection. And that the sum of ten thousand dollars be, and the same is hereby, appropriated out of any money in the Treasury not otherwise appropriated, for the purpose of carrying this resolution into effect.

Approved July 12, 1862.
By order of the Secretary of War;
E. D. TOWNSEND,
Assistant Adjutant-General

This resolution was to make army enlisted personnel eligible as, strangely, they had not been included with the navy and marine personnel authorized by the previous Act of Congress of March 3, 1861. Not until March 3, 1863, did Congress extend eligibility for the award to commissioned army officers. Only in 1915 was a Medal of Honor authorized for navy and marine officers.

As there was no other medal, and due to the rather loose wording of the Act, the award was made somewhat liberally with around 1,200 medals being presented for gallantry during the Civil War. In 1916 Congress tightened the rules for eligibility, requiring men actually to be involved in combat with an enemy and to perform gallantly at the risk of life and beyond the call of duty. Congress appointed a board of five retired generals to review all previous awards. They found that some 911 veterans, mostly of the Civil War, did not meet the new standards and struck them from the list – surely a decision that caused considerable, and justifiable, anger.

For gallantry at Gettysburg, the following sixty-one Union officers and soldiers were awarded the Medal of Honor:

Allen, Nathaniel M. Corporal, 1st Massachusetts Infantry. July 3 – Saving the regimental flag and the national flag.

Bacon, Elijah W. Private, 14th Connecticut Infantry. July 3 – Capture of flag of 16th North Carolina Regiment (C.S.A.).

Benedict, George G. Second Lieutenant, 12th Vermont Infantry. July 3 – Passed through a murderous fire of grape and canister in delivering orders and re-formed the crowded lines.

Brown, Morris Jr. Captain, 126th New York Infantry. July 3 – Capture of flag.

Carey, Hugh Sergeant, 82nd New York Infantry. July 2 – Although wounded twice, capturing the flag of 7th Virginia Infantry (C.S.A.).

Carlisle, Casper R. Private, Independent Pennsylvania Light Artillery. July 2 – Saved a gun under heavy musketry fire.

Chamberlain, Joshua L. Colonel, 20th Maine Infantry. July 2 – Daring heroism and great gallantry in holding his position on Little Round Top.

Clark, Harrison Corporal, 125th New York Infantry. July 2 – Seized the colors and advanced with them after color-bearer shot.

Clopp, John E. Private, 71st Pennsylvania Infantry. July 3 – Capture of flag of 9th Virginia Infantry (C.S.A.).

Coates, Jefferson Sergeant, 7th Wisconsin Infantry. July 1 – Unsurpassed courage in battle in which he had both eyes shot out.

De Castro, Joseph H. Corporal, 19th Massachusetts Infantry. July 3 – Capture of flag of 19th Virginia Infantry (C.S.A.).

Dore, George H. Sergeant,126th New York Infantry. July 3 – The colors being struck down by a shell as the enemy were charging, this soldier rushed out and seized the flag, exposing himself to the fire of both sides.

Enderlin, Richard Musician, 73rd Ohio Infantry. During July 1–2 – Voluntarily served with a rifle in the ranks and went into enemy lines at night to rescue a wounded comrade.

Falls, Benjamin F. Color Sergeant, 19th Massachusetts Infantry. July 3 – Capture of flag.

Fassett, John B. Captain, 23rd Pennsylvania Infantry. July 2 – While acting as an aide, voluntarily led a regiment to the relief of a battery and captured its guns.

Flynn, Christopher Corporal, 14th Connecticut Infantry. July 3 – Capture of flag of 52nd North Carolina Infantry (C.S.A.).

Fuger, Frederick Sergeant, 4th U.S. Artillery. July 3 – All the officers of his battery having been killed or wounded and five of its guns disabled in Pickett's assault, he succeeded to the command and fought the remaining gun with most distinguished gallantry until the battery was ordered withdrawn.

Furman, Chester S. Corporal, 6th Pennsylvania Reserves. July 2 – One of six volunteers who charged a log house near Devil's Den where a squad of enemy sharpshooters were sheltered, and compelled their surrender.

Gilligan, Edward L. First Sergeant, 88th Pennsylvania Infantry. July 1 – Assisted in the capture of a Confederate flag by knocking down the color sergeant.

Hart, John W. Sergeant, 6th Pennsylvania Reserves. July 2 – One of six volunteers who charged a log house near Devil's Den where a squad of enemy sharpshooters were sheltered, and compelled their surrender.

Hinks, William B. Sergeant-Major, 14th Connecticut Infantry. July 3 – During Pickett's charge the colors of the 14th Tennessee Infantry (C.S.A.) were planted 50 yards in front of his regiment. On a call for volunteers to capture the flag, Hicks and two others leapt the wall and ran forward. One of the soldiers was shot and Hicks outran the other. Under a storm of fire he seized the flag and returned to his lines.

Horan, Thomas Sergeant, 72nd New York Infantry. July 2 – Captured the flag of 8th Florida Infantry (C.S.A.).

Huidekoper, Henry S. Lieutenant-Colonel, 150th Pennsylvania Infantry. July 1 – When engaged in repelling an enemy attack was severely wounded in the right arm but continued to remain in front of the regiment.

Irsch, Francis Captain, 45th New York Infantry. July 1 – Gallantry in flanking the enemy and capturing a number of prisoners and in holding the town against heavy odds while the army was rallying on Cemetery Hill.

Jellison, Benjamin H. Sergeant, 6th Pennsylvania Reserves. July 3 – Capture of flag of 57th Virginia Infantry (C.S.A.).

Johnson, Wallace W. Sergeant, 6th Pennsylvania Reserves. July 2 – With five other volunteers gallantly charged a number of enemy sharpshooters concealed in a log house and captured them.

Knox, Edward M. Second Lieutenant, 15th New York Battery. July 2 – Held his ground with the battery after other batteries had fallen back until compelled to withdraw his piece by hand; he was severely wounded.
Lonergan, John Captain, 13th Vermont Infantry. July 2 – Gallantry in the capture of four guns and the capture of two additional guns from the enemy; also the capture of a number of prisoners.
Mayberry, John B. Private, 1st Delaware Infantry. July 3 – Capture of flag.
McCarren, Bernard Private, 1st Delaware Infantry. July 3 – Capture of flag.
Mears, George W. Sergeant, 6th Pennsylvania Reserves. July 2 – With five other volunteers he gallantly charged a number of enemy sharpshooters concealed in a log house and captured them.
Miller, John Captain, 3rd Pennsylvania Cavalry. July 3 – Without orders, led a charge of his squadron upon the flank of the enemy, checked his attack, and cut off and dispersed the rear of his column.
Miller, William E. Captain, 3rd Pennsylvania Cavalry. July 2 – Without orders, led a charge of his squadron upon the flank of the enemy, checked his attack, and cut off and dispersed the rear of his column.
Munsell, Harvey M. Sergeant, 99th Pennsylvania Infantry. July 1–3 – Gallant and courageous conduct as color-bearer. (This N.C.O. carried his regimental colors through thirteen engagements.)
O'Brien, Henry D. Corporal, 1st Minnesota Infantry. July 3 – Taking up the colors where they had fallen, he rushed ahead of his regiment, close to the muzzles of the enemy's guns, and engaged in the desperate struggle in which the enemy was defeated, and though severely wounded, held the colors until wounded a second time.
Pipes, James Captain, 140th Pennsylvania Infantry. July 2 – While a sergeant and while retiring before the rapid advance of the enemy, he and a companion stopped to carry a wounded comrade to safety; in this act both he and his companion were severely wounded.
Postles, James P. Captain, 1st Delaware Infantry. July 2 – Voluntarily carried an order in the face of heavy enemy fire.
Purman, James J. Lieutenant, 140th Pennsylvania Infantry. July 2 – Voluntarily assisted a wounded comrade to a place of apparent safety while the enemy were in close proximity; he received the fire of the enemy and a wound which resulted in the amputation of his left leg.
Raymond, William H. Corporal, 108th New York Infantry. July 3 – Voluntarily, and under severe fire, brought a box of ammunition to his comrades on the skirmish line.
Reed, Charles Bugler, Massachusetts Light Artillery. July 2 – Rescued his wounded captain from between the lines.
Reisinger J. Monroe Corporal,150th Pennsylvania Infantry. July 1 – Specially brave and meritorious conduct in the face of the enemy. Awarded under Act of Congress, January 25, 1907.
Rice, Edmond Major, 19th Massachusetts Infantry. July 3 – Conspicuous bravery on the counter charge against Pickett's Division where he fell severely wounded within the enemy's lines.
Richmond, James Private, 8th Ohio Infantry. July 3 – Capture of flag.
Robinson, John H. Private, 19th Massachusetts Infantry. July 3 – Capture of flag of 57th Virginia Infantry (C.S.A.).
Rood, Oliver P. Private, 20th Indiana Infantry. July 3 – Capture of flag of 21st North Carolina Infantry (C.S.A.).
Roosevelt, George W. First Sergeant, 26th Pennsylvania Infantry. July 2 – At Bull Run, Virginia, recaptured the colors that had been seized by the enemy. At Gettysburg he captured a Confederate color and color-bearer, during which effort he was severely wounded.
Roush, J. Levi Corporal, 6th Pennsylvania Reserves. July 2 – One of six volunteers who charged a log house near Devil's Den where a squad of enemy sharpshooters were sheltering, and compelled their surrender.
Rutter, James M. Sergeant, 143rd Pennsylvania Infantry. July 1 – At great risk of his life went to the assistance of a wounded comrade, and while under fire removed him to a place of safety.
Sellers, Alfred J. Major, 90th Pennsylvania Infantry. July 1 – Voluntarily led the regiment under withering fire to a position from which the enemy was repulsed.
Sherman, Marshall Private, 1st Minnesota Infantry. July 3 – Capture of flag of 28th Virginia Infantry (C.S.A.).
Sickles, Daniel E. Major-General, U.S. Volunteers. July 2 – Displayed most conspicuous gallantry on the field, vigorously contesting the advance of the enemy and continuing to encourage his troops after being severely wounded.
Smith, Thaddeus S. Corporal, 6th Pennsylvania Reserve Infantry. July 2 – One of six volunteers who charged a log house near Devil's Den where a squad of enemy sharpshooters were sheltered, and compelled their surrender.
Stacey, Charles Private, 55th Ohio Infantry. July 2 – Voluntarily took up an advanced position on the skirmish line for the purpose of ascertaining the location of Confederate sharpshooters, and under heavy fire held the position until his company withdrew to the main line.
Thompson, James B. Sergeant, 1st Pennsylvania Rifles. July 3 – Capture of flag of 15th Georgia Infantry (C.S.A.).
Tozier, Andrew J. Sergeant, 20th Maine Infantry. July 2 – At the crisis of this engagement, this soldier, a color-bearer, stood alone in an advanced position, the regiment having been borne back, and defended his colors with musket and ammunition picked up at his feet.
Veazey, Wheelock G. Colonel, 16th Vermont. July 3 – Rapidly assembled his regiment and charged the enemy's flank; changed front under heavy fire, and charged and destroyed a Confederate brigade, all this with new troops in their first battle.
Wall, Jerry Private, 126th New York Infantry. July 3 – Capture of flag.
Waller, Francis Corporal, 6th Wisconsin Infantry, July 1 – Capture of flag of 2nd Mississippi Infantry (C.S.A.).
Webb, Alexander Brigadier-General, U.S. Volunteers. July 3 – Distinguished personal gallantry in leading his men forward at a critical period in the battle.
Wells, William Major, 1st Vermont Cavalry. July 3 – Led the second battalion of his regiment in a daring charge.
Wiley, James Sergeant, 59th New York Infantry. July 3 – Capture of flag of a Georgia regiment.

Of the above awards, nine were for gallantry displayed on July 1, twenty-three on July 2 and twenty-nine on July 3, many for the capture of colors at the height of Pickett's charge. Four went to artillery soldiers, three to the cavalry and the remainder to the infantry. Two general officers received the award (Sickles and Webb), sixteen went to other officers and forty-three to enlisted men.

The Confederate Medal of Honor

Details of the Union Congressional Medal of Honor are given above, but it is not always realized that there was a Confederate Medal of Honor awarded posthumously for gallantry displayed during the Civil War by Southern soldiers and sailors. In 1977 the first man to be named by the committee established to decide who should receive it was Private Samuel Davis of Coleman's Scouts. The committee went on to award forty-eight medals – nine to Confederate States Navy personnel, thirty-seven to Confederate States Army soldiers (one of whom was a chaplain) and one to a nurse, Juliet Opie Hopkins, for services at Seven Pines, Virginia.

The five awarded for bravery at Gettysburg were:

- Private William J. Barbee, 1st Texas Infantry
- Colonel Henry K. Burgwyn, Jr., 26th North Carolina Infantry
- Brigadier-General Richard B. Garnett
- Brigadier-General Wade Hampton
- 1st Lieutenant William A. McQueen, Garden's Battery, Palmetto Light Artillery

In addition, Private Benjamin Welch Owens, 1st Maryland Infantry Battalion, was given the award for gallantry at Stephenson's Depot on June 15, 1863.

Appendix 3

THE NEW MUSEUM AND VISITOR CENTER AT GETTYSBURG NATIONAL MILITARY PARK

The new Museum and Visitor Center at Gettysburg National Military Park opened in April 2008. It serves as the gateway to Gettysburg, telling the story of the Battle of Gettysburg and its significance to America's history, within the context of the causes and consequences of the Civil War. The $103 million facility, adjacent to the battlefield, displays an extensive collection of artifacts and archival materials, and provides visitors with a distinctive perspective of the Civil War through the words of its participants and spectators, including Presidents Lincoln and Davis, Major-General Meade and General Lee, soldiers, correspondents and civilians. Through a variety of interactive exhibits and displays, cinematic productions and a host of research resources, the new museum offers the best Civil War experience available.

The 24,000 square feet of exhibition space includes:

- A rotunda setting the stage for the museum exhibits.
- Twelve galleries, eleven of which are based on phrases from Lincoln's Gettysburg Address and are organized to help visitors understand and appreciate the museum's major themes, including the Gettysburg campaign, the Civil War as a whole, its causes and consequences. Among more than 300,000 objects and artifacts, and 700,000 items of archive material, are: a portable wooden field desk believed to have been used at Gettysburg by Lee; a crutch made from a sapling branch pulled from the ground of the Peach Orchard by George Kistler of the 140th Pennsylvania Infantry after he was wounded during the fighting on the second day of the battle; the journal of Adams County physician Dr. John O'Neal, in which he identified and listed the location of several thousand Confederate dead and which he used after the war to help families from the South trace their loved ones and return them home.
- Interactive stations throughout the museum. Five of the galleries include short video presentations on the causes of the war, the three days of the battle and the results of the war. The two Voices theaters feature readings from battle participants.
- The twelfth gallery focuses on Special Exhibits, in the form of temporary and traveling exhibits to broaden the range of topics covered in the museum itself and displays items on loan from the Gilder Lehrman Institute of American History.
- The Cyclorama Gallery displays the cyclorama painting *The Battle of Gettysburg*, newly conserved and featuring the re-created skyline, canopy and three-dimensional diorama that have been missing for more than forty years. Further exhibits describe the painting and its conservation, the history of cyclorama paintings and their display.
- The Ford Motor Company Fund Education Center multi-purpose educational facilities provide dedicated space for workshops, classroom use and distance learning.
- Civil War era foods are served in the refreshment saloon, where visitors can learn about recipes of the time and about the vital role played by the volunteers who supplemented government-issue rations.
- The bookstore includes an extensive selection of titles on Gettysburg, the Civil War and Abraham Lincoln, as well as a variety of memorabilia.

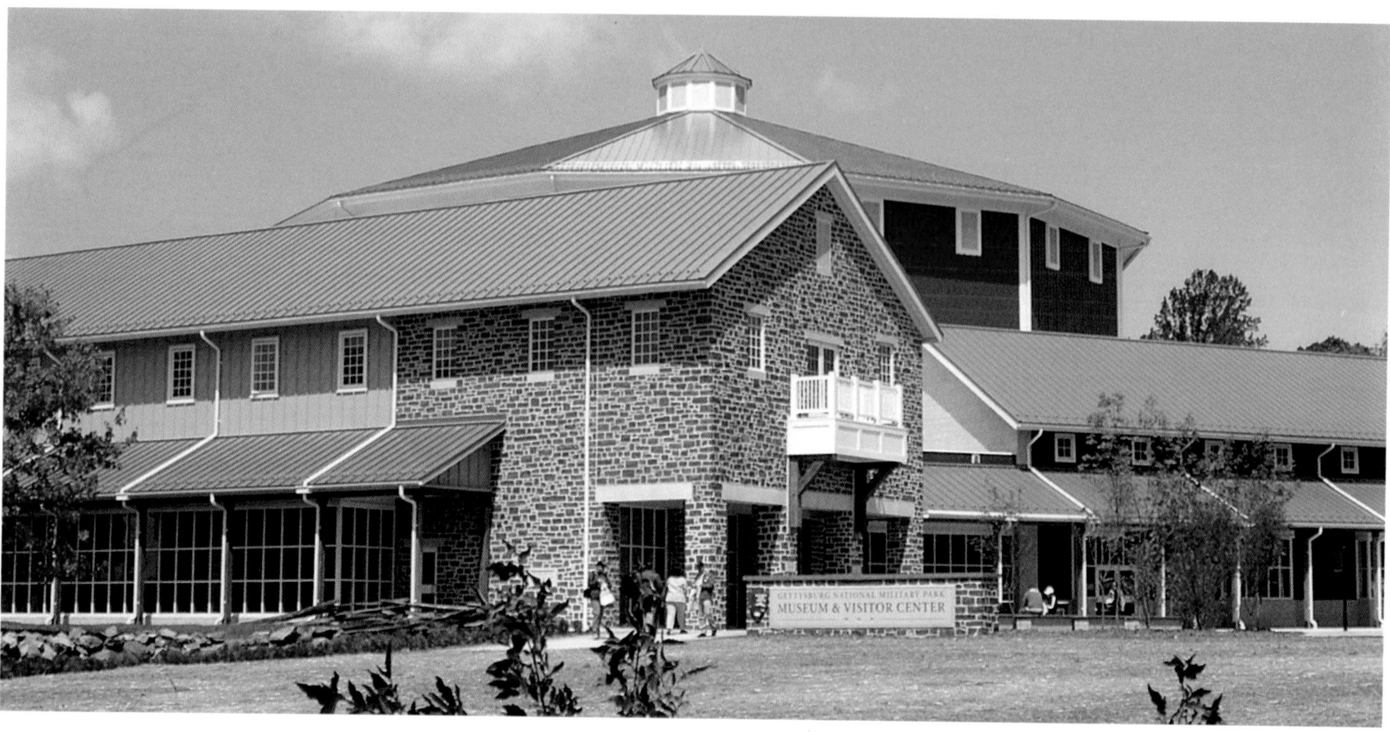

BIBLIOGRAPHY

Alexander, General E. P., *Military Memoirs of a Confederate*, Charles Scribner's Sons, New York, 1907

Alexander, General E. P., *The American Civil War*, Siegle, Hill & Co., London, 1908

Alexander, General, E. P., *Fighting for the Confederacy: The Personal Recollections of General Edward Porter Alexander*, Gary Gallager (ed.), University of North Carolina Press, Chapel Hill, 1989

Alexander, General E. P., *Confederate Artillery Service*, Southern Historical Society Papers, Richmond, Virginia, 1880s–1900s; Vol. 11, pp. 98–113

Arnold, James, and Wiener, Roberta, *Order of Battle, July 1, July 2 and July 3 Union: Army of the Potomac and Confederate: Army of Northern Virginia*, Osprey Publishing, Oxford, England, 1998

Baker, Levi W., *History of the Ninth Massachusetts Battery*, republished by VanBerg Publishing, Lancaster, Ohio, 1996

Barnes, Surgeon-General U.S.A. Joseph K. (ed.), *The Medical and Surgical History of the War of Rebellion*, Government Printing Office, Washington D.C., 1870

Bartholomees, J. Boone, *Buff Facings and Gilt Buttons*, University of South Carolina Press, Columbia, 1998

Bicheno, Hugh, *Gettysburg*, Cassell & Co., London, 2001

Bigelow, Major John, *The Peach Orchard, Gettysburg*, Kimball-Storer Co., Minneapolis, 1910

Billings, John D., *Hardtack and Coffee*, Corner House Publishers, Williamstown, Massachusetts, 1984

Boatner, Mark M., *Biographical Dictionary of the American Civil War*, Cassell & Company Ltd., London, 1959

Boritt, Gabor S. (ed.), *The Gettysburg Nobody Knows*, Oxford University Press, New York, 1997

Brown, J. Willard, *The Signal Corps in the War of Rebellion*, U.S. Veteran Corps Signal Association, Boston, Massachusetts, 1896

Brown, Kent Masterton, *Retreat from Gettysburg*, University of North Carolina Press, Chapel Hill and London, 2005

Busey, John W., and Martin, David G., *Regimental Strengths and Losses at Gettysburg*, 4th edn., Longstreet House, New York, 2005

Campbell, Eric A., *We Saved the Line from Being Broken*, Gettysburg National Military Park, Gettysburg, 1996

Campbell, Eric A. (ed.), *A Grand Terrible Drama, From Gettysburg to Petersburg: The Civil War Letters of Charles Wellington Reed*, Fordham University Press, New York, 2000

Clark, Champ, *The Civil War, Gettysburg*, Time-Life Books Inc., Alexandria, Virginia, 1985

Coco, Gregory A., *On the Bloodstained Field*, Thomas Publications, Gettysburg, 1987

Coco Gregory A., *On the Bloodstained Field II*, Thomas Publications, Gettysburg, 1989

Coco, Gregory A., *A Strange and Blighted Land*. Thomas Publications, Gettysburg, 1995

Coco, Gregory A., *A Concise Guide to the Artillery at Gettysburg*, Thomas Publications, Gettysburg, 1998

Coddington, Edwin B., *The Gettysburg Campaign*, Simon & Schuster, New York, 1979

Coggins, Jack, *Arms and Equipment of the Civil War*, Dover Publications, New York, 1990

Confederate Signals Corps, Southern Historical Society Papers, Vol. XVI, Richmond, Virginia, 1888

Cook, Brigadier-General Phillip St. G., *Cavalry Tactics, Regulations for the Instruction, Formations and Movements of the Cavalry*, J. B. Lippincott & Co., Philadelphia, 1862

Davis, William C. (photography Muench, David), *Gettysburg, The Story Behind the Scenery*, KC Publications, Las Vegas, 2003

Dowdey, Clifford, *Lee & His Men at Gettysburg*, University of Nebraska Press, Lincoln and London, 1999

Fiebeger, Colonel G. J., *The Campaign and Battle of Gettysburg*, Bloodstone Press, New Oxford, Pennsylvania, 1984

Field Artillery Tactics 1864, New Market Battlefield Military Museum, New Market, Virginia, 1994

Frassanito, William A., *Gettysburg Then and Now*, Thomas Publications, Gettysburg, 1996

Freeman, Douglas S., *Lee's Lieutenants*, Charles Scribner's Sons 1944; Vols. I, II and III

Gallagher, Gary W. (ed.), *Three Days at Gettysburg*, Kent State University Press, Kent, Ohio, 1999

Gettysburg Magazine, issues 1, 7, 8, 11, 13, 16, 17, 18, 19, 20, 21, 22, 23, 24, 25, 26, 27, 29, 31, and 32; 1989–2005

Guild, Surgeon C.S.A. Lafayette, *Report on The Gettysburg Campaign*, O.R. Series 1, 1863; Vol. XXVII/2 [S# 44]

Gottfried, Bradley M., *Roads to Gettysburg*, White Mane Books, Shippensburg, Pennsylvania, 2001

Gottfried, Bradley M., *Brigades of Gettysburg*, Da Capo Press, Cambridge, Massachusetts, 2002

Griffith, Paddy, *Battle in the Civil War*, Fieldbooks, Mansfield, England, 1986

Grimsley, Mark, and Simpson, Brooks D., *Gettysburg, A Battlefield Guide*, University of Nebraska Press, Lincoln and London, 1999

Hall, Jeffrey C., *The Stand of the U.S. Army at Gettysburg*, Indiana University Press, Bloomington, 2003

Harrison, Kathy, G., *Nothing But Glory*, Thomas Publications, Gettysburg, 2001

Hawthorne, Frederick W., *Gettysburg: Stories of Men and Monuments*, The Association of Licensed Battlefield Guides, Gettysburg, 1998

Henderson, Lieutenant-Colonel G. F. B., *Stonewall Jackson*, Longmans, Green and Co., London, 1908; Vol. II

Hoke, Jacob, *The Great Invasion*, Thomas Yoseloff, New York, 1959

Hubbell, John T. (ed.), *Battles Lost and Won*, Greenwood Press, Westport, Connecticut, 1975

Imboden, Brigadier-General C.S.A. John D., "The Confederate Retreat from Gettysburg," *Battles and Leaders of the Civil War*, The Century Co., New York, 1884

Iverson, Brigadier-General C.S.A. Alfred, *Report of, on The Gettysburg Campaign*, July 17, 1863; O.R. Series 1, Vol. XXVII/2 [S# 44]

Krick, Robert K., *The Smoothbore Volley That Doomed the Confederacy*, Louisiana State University Press, Baton Rouge, 2002

Large, George R., *Battle of Gettysburg, The Official History*, Burd Street Press, Shippensburg, Pennsylvania, 1999

Lee, General Robert E., *Report of, on The Gettysburg Campaign*, July 31, 1863; O.R. Series 1, Vol. XXVII/2 [S# 44]

Letterman, Dr. Jonathan A., *Report on Medical Operations at Gettysburg*, October 3, 1863; O.R. Series 1, Vol. XXVII/I [S# 43]

Longacre, Edward G., *The Cavalry at Gettysburg*, University of Nebraska Press, Lincoln and London, 1896

Longstreet, Lieutenant-General C.S.A. James, *From Manassas to Appomattox: A Memoir of the Civil War in America*, J. B. Lippincott, Philadelphia, 1896

Maine at Gettysburg – Report of the Maine Commissioners, 1898; reprinted by Stan Clark Military Books, Gettysburg, 1994

Martin, David G., *Gettysburg July 1*, Combined Books, Conshohocken, Pennsylvania, 1995

McGuire, Dr. Hunter (Medical Director of Jackson's Corps), *Death of Stonewall Jackson*, Southern Historical Society Papers, Richmond, Virginia, 1863; Vol. XIV

McKeever, General C. M., *Civil War Battle Flags of the Union Army and Order of Battle*, Knickerbocker Press, New York, 1997

McManus, Stephen, Thompson, Donald, and Churchill, Thomas, *Civil War Research Guide*, Stackpole Books, Mechanicsville, Pennsylvania, 2003

Meade, Major-General George G., *Report of, on The Battle of Gettysburg*, October 1, 1863

North & South Magazine Vol. 2, nos. 6 and 7; Vol. 3, nos. 1, 2, 5 and 7; Vol. 4, nos. 3, 5 and 6; Vol. 5, no. 6; Vol. 6, no. 5; Vol. 7, nos. 5, 7; Vol. 8, no. 1; 1999–2004

Norton, Captain Lemuel B. (Chief Signal Officer), *Report to Headquarters Army of the Potomac*, September 18, 1863; O.R. Series 1 Volume XXVII/I [S# 43]

Oeffinger, John C. (ed.), *A Soldier's General – The Civil War Letters of Major-General Lafayette McLaws*, University of North Carolina Press, Chapel Hill, 2002

Pfanz, Harry W., *Gettysburg The First Day*, University of North Carolina Press, Chapel Hill, 2001

Pfanz, Harry W., *Gettysburg The Second Day*, University of North Carolina Press, Chapel Hill, 1987

Pfanz, Harry W., *Culp's Hill and Cemetery Hill*, University of North Carolina Press, Chapel Hill, 1993

Priest, John M., *Into the Fight, Pickett's Charge at Gettysburg*, White Mane Books, Shippensburg, Pennsylvania, 1998

Return of Casualties in 20th Maine Volunteers at Gettysburg July 2nd & 3rd, Maine State Archives, Augusta, Maine

Revised Regulations for the Army of the United States 1861 – Table of Pay, Subsistence, Forage, &c.

Rogers, Colonel H. C. B., *The Confederates and Federals at War*, Ian Alan, London, 1973

Rollins, Richard, *Pickett's Charge!* Rank and File Publications, Redondo Beach, California, 1994

Rummel III, George A., *Gettysburg Cavalrymen*, White Mane Publishing Co., Bridgeport, West Virginia, 1999

Schultz, David, *Double Canister at Ten Yards*, Rank and File Publications, Redondo Beach, California, 1995

Sears, Stephen W., *Gettysburg*, Houghton Mifflin Company, New York, 2004

Shannon, Fred A., *Organization of the Union Army*, The Arthur H. Clark Company, Cleveland, Ohio, 1928

Smith M. D., Beverly C., *The Last Illness and Death of General Thomas Jonathon (Stonewall) Jackson*, Virginia Military Institute Alumni Review Article, Lexington, Virginia, 1975

Stackpole, Edward J., *They Met at Gettysburg*, Bonanza Books, New York, 1956

Stewart, George R., *Pickett's Charge*, Morningside Bookshop, Dayton, Ohio, 1980
Symonds, Craig L., *A Battlefield Atlas of the Civil War*, The Nautical and Aviation Publishing Company of America, Annapolis, Maryland, 1983
Tagg, Larry, *The Generals of Gettysburg*, Da Capo Press, Cambridge, Massachusetts, 1998
Thomas, James E., *The First Day at Gettysburg – A Walking Tour*, Thomas Publications, Gettysburg, 2005
Time-Life Books (ed.), *Voices of the Civil War*, Alexandria, Virginia, 1995
Trudeau, Noah A., *Gettysburg, A Testing of Courage*, HarperCollins, New York, 2002
Tucker, Glenn, *High Tide at Gettysburg*, Morningside House Inc., Dayton, Ohio, 1983
U.S. Infantry Tactics, Authorized and adopted by The Secretary of War, May 1, 1861, Naval and Military Press, Uckfield, England
Vandiver, Frank E., *Rebel Brass – The Confederate Command System*, Louisiana State University Press, Baton Rouge,1956
Voices of Battle, National Park Service, Gettysburg National Military Park, Gettysburg, 1998
Welcher, Frank J., *The Union Army 1861–1865 Vol I: The Eastern Theater*, Indiana University Press, Bloomington,1989
Wise, Jennings C., *The Long Arm of Lee*, University of Nebraska Press, Lincoln, New England, 1991
Wittenburg, Eric J., *Gettysburg's Forgotten Cavalry Actions*, Thomas Publications, Gettysburg, 1998
Wittenburg, Eric J., *The Battles for Brinkerhoff's Ridge and East Cavalry Field*, Ironclad Publishing, Celina, Ohio, 2002
Woodworth, Steven E. (ed.), *Civil War Generals in Defeat*, University Press of Kansas, Lawrence, Kansas, 1999

INDEX

Page numbers in *italic* refer to subjects in boxes, those in **bold** refer to illustrations.